Nissan X-Trail, Dualis, Qashqai Automotive Repair Manual

by Geoff Wilson and John H Haynes
Member of the Guild of Motoring Writers

Models covered:

X-Trail T31 and T32 – 2007 - 2018

Dualis J10 – 2007 - 2014

Qashqai J11 – 2014 - 2018

Two and four-wheel drive models

ABCDE
FGHIJ
KLMNO
PQRST

Haynes Australia Pty Limited
8/17 Willfox Street
Condell Park NSW 2200 Australia

Haynes Publishing Group
Sparkford Nr Yeovil
Somerset BA22 7JJ England

Haynes North America, Inc
859 Lawrence Drive
Newbury Park
California 91320 USA

Acknowledgements

Wiring diagrams provided by Rellim Publications.

© **Haynes Australia Pty Limited 2018**

With permission from J.H. Haynes & Co. Ltd.

A book in the Haynes Automotive Repair Manual Series

Printed in Malaysia

All rights reserved. No part of this book may be reproduced or transmitted in any form or by any means, electronic or mechanical, including photocopying, recording or by any information storage or retrieval system, without permission in writing from the copyright holder.

ISBN-13: 978-1-62092-300-9

ISBN-10: 1-62092-300-9

While every attempt is made to ensure that the information in this manual is correct, no liability can be accepted by the authors or publishers for loss, damage or injury caused by any errors in, or omissions from, the information given.

Contents

Introductory pages

About this manual	0-5
Introduction to the vehicles covered in this manual	0-5
Vehicle identification numbers	0-6
Buying parts	0-7
Maintenance techniques, tools and working facilities	0-7
Booster battery (jump) starting	0-14
Jacking and towing	0-15
Automotive chemicals and lubricants	0-16
Safety first!	0-17
Troubleshooting	0-18

Chapter 1
Tune-up and routine maintenance — 1-1

Chapter 2 Part A
2.5 litre petrol engine — 2A-1

Chapter 2 Part B
2.0 litre petrol engine — 2B-1

Chapter 2 Part C
2.0 litre diesel engine — 2C-1

Chapter 2 Part D
General engine overhaul procedures — 2D-1

Chapter 3
Cooling, heating and air conditioning systems — 3-1

Chapter 4 Part A
Fuel and exhaust systems - petrol engines — 4A-1

Chapter 4 Part B
Fuel and exhaust systems - diesel engine — 4B-1

Chapter 5
Engine electrical systems — 5-1

Chapter 6
Emissions and engine control systems — 6-1

Chapter 7 Part A
Manual transaxle — 7A-1

Chapter 7 Part B
Automatic transaxle — 7B-1

Chapter 7 Part C
Transfer case — 7C-1

Chapter 8
Clutch and driveline — 8-1

Chapter 9
Brakes — 9-1

Chapter 10
Suspension and steering systems — 10-1

Chapter 11
Body — 11-1

Chapter 12
Chassis electrical systems — 12-1

Wiring diagrams — 12-34

Index — IND-1

T31 X-Trail

T32 X-Trail

J10 Dualis

J11 Qashqai

About this manual

Its purpose

The purpose of this manual is to help you get the best value from your vehicle. It can do so in several ways. It can help you decide what work must be done, even if you choose to have it done by a dealer service department or a repair shop; it provides information and procedures for routine maintenance and servicing; and it offers diagnostic and repair procedures to follow when trouble occurs.

We hope you use the manual to tackle the work yourself. For many simpler jobs, doing it yourself may be quicker than arranging an appointment to get the vehicle into a shop and making the trips to leave it and pick it up. More importantly, a lot of money can be saved by avoiding the expense the shop must pass on to you to cover its labour and overhead costs. An added benefit is the sense of satisfaction and accomplishment that you feel after doing the job yourself.

Using the manual

The manual is divided into Chapters. Each Chapter is divided into numbered Sections, which are headed in bold type between horizontal lines. Each Section consists of consecutively numbered paragraphs.

At the beginning of each numbered Section you will be referred to any illustrations which apply to the procedures in that Section. The reference numbers used in illustration captions pinpoint the pertinent Section and the Step within that Section. That is, illustration 3.2 means the illustration refers to Section 3 and Step (or paragraph) 2 within that Section.

Procedures, once described in the text, are not normally repeated. When it's necessary to refer to another Chapter, the reference will be given as Chapter and Section number. Cross references given without use of the word "Chapter" apply to Sections and/or paragraphs in the same Chapter. For example, "see Section 8" means in the same Chapter.

References to the left or right side of the vehicle assume you are sitting in the driver's seat, facing forward.

Even though we have prepared this manual with extreme care, neither the publisher nor the author can accept responsibility for any errors in, or omissions from, the information given.

NOTE

A **Note** provides information necessary to properly complete a procedure or information which will make the procedure easier to understand.

CAUTION

A **Caution** provides a special procedure or special steps which must be taken while completing the procedure where the Caution is found. Not heeding a Caution can result in damage to the assembly being worked on.

WARNING

A **Warning** provides a special procedure or special steps which must be taken while completing the procedure where the Warning is found. Not heeding a Warning can result in personal injury.

Introduction to the vehicles covered in this manual

The Nissan X-Trail is a four door wagon available in two and all-wheel-drive. The T31 model was released in October 2007. In 2014, the T32 model was released. This change saw a new body and interior.

The Nissan Dualis was also released in October 2007. It continued until the release of the Nissan Qashqai in June 2014.

X-Trail models are available with a 2.5 litre petrol engine (QR25DE) or a 2.0 litre diesel engine (M9R). There is also a 2.0 litre petrol engine – T31 models are fitted with the MR20DE engine, while T32 models have the MR20DD direct injection engine.

Dualis models are equipped with the 2.0 litre (MR20DE) engine. Qashqai models have the 2.0 litre petrol (MR20DD) direct injection engine.

All models have a transversely mounted engine with either a continuously variable transaxle (CVT), 6-speed automatic transaxle or a 6-speed manual transaxle. Drive is transmitted to the front wheels via independent driveshafts with constant velocity joints. On AWD models, the rear wheels are also propelled by way of a transfer case, driveshaft, rear differential and two rear driveshafts.

All models have a steel uni-body structure and four-wheel independent suspension. The rack-and-pinion steering unit is mounted behind the engine. A small electric motor and control unit (EPS) is mounted to the steering column to provide power assistance.

All models are equipped with power assisted front and rear disc brakes, and an anti-lock braking system.

Vehicle identification numbers

Modifications are a continuing and unpublicised process in vehicle manufacturing. Since spare parts manuals and lists are compiled on a numerical basis, the individual vehicle numbers are essential to correctly identify the component required.

Vehicle Identification Number (VIN)

The Vehicle Identification Number (VIN), which appears on the vehicle registration papers, is embossed on a plate and viewed after removing the grille from the cowl cover or, on later models, through the lower passenger side of the windscreen. It is also on the compliance plate in the engine compartment **(see illustrations)** and on the ID stickers on the B pillars **(see illustrations)**. The VIN tells you when and where a vehicle was manufactured, its country of origin, make, type, passenger safety system, line, series, body style, engine and assembly plant.

Engine number

The engine number is stamped on the front of the engine block, forward of the flywheel/driveplate **(see illustration)**.

Transaxle number

The transaxle identification number is stamped into the top of the transaxle case **(see illustration)**.

3.2a The Vehicle Identification Number (VIN) is visible after removing the grille from the cowl cover

3.2b The VIN on early models with the grille removed from the cowl cover

3.2c On late models, the VIN is visible through the passenger side of the windshield

3.2d The vehicle compliance plate is near the RHF suspension tower - T31 X-Trail shown, other models similar

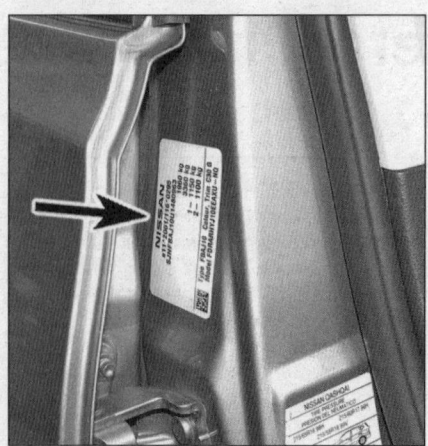

3.2e The vehicle ID sticker is usually on the RH B-pillar

3.3 Engine number location on a 2.5 litre petrol engine

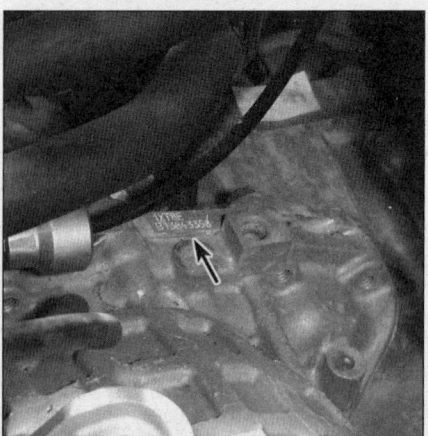

3.4 The CVT transaxle ID number is located on top of the transaxle housing

Buying parts

Replacement parts are available from many sources. Our advice concerning them is as follows:

Retail auto parts stores

Good auto parts stores will stock frequently needed components which wear out relatively fast, such as clutch components, exhaust systems, brake parts, tune-up parts, etc. These stores often supply new or reconditioned parts on an exchange basis, which can save a considerable amount of money. Discount auto parts stores are often very good places to buy materials and parts needed for general vehicle maintenance such as oil, grease, filters, spark plugs, belts, touch-up paint, bulbs, etc. They also usually sell tools and general accessories, have convenient hours, charge lower prices and can give you knowledgeable answers to your questions. To be sure of obtaining the correct parts, have engine and chassis numbers available and, if possible, take the old parts along for positive identification.

Authorized dealer parts department

This is the best source for parts which are unique to the vehicle and not generally available elsewhere. Prices for most parts tend to be higher than at retail auto parts stores.

Auto recyclers or salvage yards

Auto recyclers and salvage yards are good sources for components that are specific to the vehicle and not subject to wear, such as mudguards, bumpers, trim pieces, etc. You can expect substantial savings by going this route, and self-service salvage yards offer still more savings if you're willing to bring your own tools and pull the part(s) yourself.

Warranty information

If the vehicle is still covered under warranty, be sure that any replacement parts purchased - regardless of the source - do not invalidate the warranty! In most cases, replacement parts, even from aftermarket suppliers, are designed to meet manufacturer specifications. If in doubt, check with the parts supplier.

Maintenance techniques, tools and working facilities

Maintenance techniques

There are a number of techniques involved in maintenance and repair that will be referred to throughout this manual. Application of these techniques will enable the home mechanic to be more efficient, better organized and capable of performing the various tasks properly, which will ensure that the repair job is thorough and complete.

Fasteners

Fasteners are nuts, bolts, studs and screws used to hold two or more parts together. There are a few things to keep in mind when working with fasteners. Almost all of them use a locking device of some type, either a lockwasher, locknut, locking tab or thread adhesive. All threaded fasteners should be clean and straight, with undamaged threads and undamaged corners on the hex head where the wrench fits. Develop the habit of replacing all damaged nuts and bolts with new ones. Special locknuts with nylon or fiber inserts can only be used once. If they are removed, they lose their locking ability and must be replaced with new ones.

Rusted nuts and bolts should be treated with a penetrating fluid to ease removal and prevent breakage. Some mechanics use turpentine in a spout-type oil can, which works quite well. After applying the rust penetrant, let it work for a few minutes before trying to loosen the nut or bolt. Badly rusted fasteners may have to be chiselled or sawed off or removed with a special nut breaker, available at tool stores.

If a bolt or stud breaks off in an assembly, it can be drilled and removed with a special tool commonly available for this purpose. Most automotive machine shops can perform this task, as well as other repair procedures, such as the repair of threaded holes that have been stripped out.

Flat washers and lockwashers, when removed from an assembly, should always be replaced exactly as removed. Replace any damaged washers with new ones. Never use a lockwasher on any soft metal surface (such as aluminium), thin sheet metal or plastic.

Fastener sizes

For a number of reasons, automobile manufacturers are making wider and wider use of metric fasteners. Therefore, it is important to be able to tell the difference between standard (sometimes called U.S. or SAE) and metric hardware, since they cannot be interchanged.

All bolts, whether standard or metric, are sized according to diameter, thread pitch and length. For example, a standard 1/2 - 13 x 1 bolt is 1/2 inch in diameter, has 13 threads per inch and is 1 inch long. An M12 - 1.75 x 25 metric bolt is 12 mm in diameter, has a thread pitch of 1.75 mm (the distance between threads) and is 25 mm long. The two bolts are nearly identical, and easily confused, but they are not interchangeable.

In addition to the differences in diameter, thread pitch and length, metric and standard bolts can also be distinguished by examining the bolt heads. To begin with, the distance across the flats on a standard bolt head is measured in inches, while the same dimension on a metric bolt is sized in millimetres (the same is true for nuts). As a result, a standard wrench should not be used on a metric bolt and a metric wrench should not be used on a standard bolt. Also, most standard bolts have slashes radiating out from the centre of the head to denote the grade or strength of the bolt, which is an indication of the amount of torque that can be applied to it. The greater the number of slashes, the greater the strength of the bolt. Grades 0 through 5 are commonly used on automobiles. Metric bolts have a property class (grade) number, rather than a slash, moulded into their heads to indicate bolt strength. In this case, the higher the number, the stronger the bolt. Property class numbers 8.8, 9.8 and 10.9 are commonly used on automobiles.

Strength markings can also be used to distinguish standard hex nuts from metric hex nuts. Many standard nuts have dots stamped into one side, while metric nuts are marked with a number. The greater the number of dots, or the higher the number, the greater the strength of the nut.

Metric studs are also marked on their ends according to property class (grade). Larger studs are numbered (the same as metric bolts), while smaller studs carry a geometric code to denote grade.

It should be noted that many fasteners, especially Grades 0 through 2, have no distinguishing marks on them. When such is the case, the only way to determine whether it is standard or metric is to measure the thread pitch or compare it to a known fastener of the same size.

Standard fasteners are often referred to as SAE, as opposed to metric. However, it should be noted that SAE technically refers to a non-metric fine thread fastener only. Coarse thread non-metric fasteners are referred to as USS sizes.

Since fasteners of the same size (both standard and metric) may have different strength ratings, be sure to reinstall any bolts, studs or nuts removed from your vehicle in their original locations. Also, when replacing a fastener with a new one, make sure that the new one has a strength rating equal to or greater than the original.

Tightening sequences and procedures

Most threaded fasteners should be tightened to a specific torque value (torque is the twisting force applied to a threaded component such as a nut or bolt). Overtightening the fastener can weaken it and cause it to break, while undertightening can cause it to eventually come loose. Bolts, screws and studs, depending on the material they are made of and their thread diameters, have specific torque values, many of which are noted in the Specifications at the beginning of each Chapter. Be sure to follow the torque recommendations closely. For fasteners not assigned a specific torque, a general torque value chart is presented here as a guide. These torque values are for dry (unlubricated) fasteners threaded into steel or cast iron (not aluminium). As was previously mentioned, the size and grade of a fastener determine the amount of torque that can safely be applied to it. The figures listed here are approximate for Grade 2 and Grade 3 fasteners. Higher grades can tolerate higher torque values.

Fasteners laid out in a pattern, such as cylinder head bolts, oil pan bolts, differential cover bolts, etc., must be loosened or tightened in sequence to avoid warping the component. This sequence will normally be shown in the appropriate Chapter. If a specific pattern is not given, the following procedures can be used to prevent warping.

Initially, the bolts or nuts should be assembled finger-tight only. Next, they should be tightened one full turn each, in a crisscross or diagonal pattern. After each one has been tightened one full turn, return to the first one and tighten them all one-half turn, following the same pattern. Finally, tighten each of them one-quarter turn at a time until each fastener has been tightened to the proper torque. To loosen and remove the fasteners, the procedure would be reversed.

Component disassembly

Component disassembly should be done with care and purpose to help ensure that the parts go back together properly. Always keep track of the sequence in which parts are removed. Make note of special characteristics or marks on parts that can be installed more than one way, such as a grooved thrust washer on a shaft. It is a good idea to lay the disassembled parts out on a clean surface in

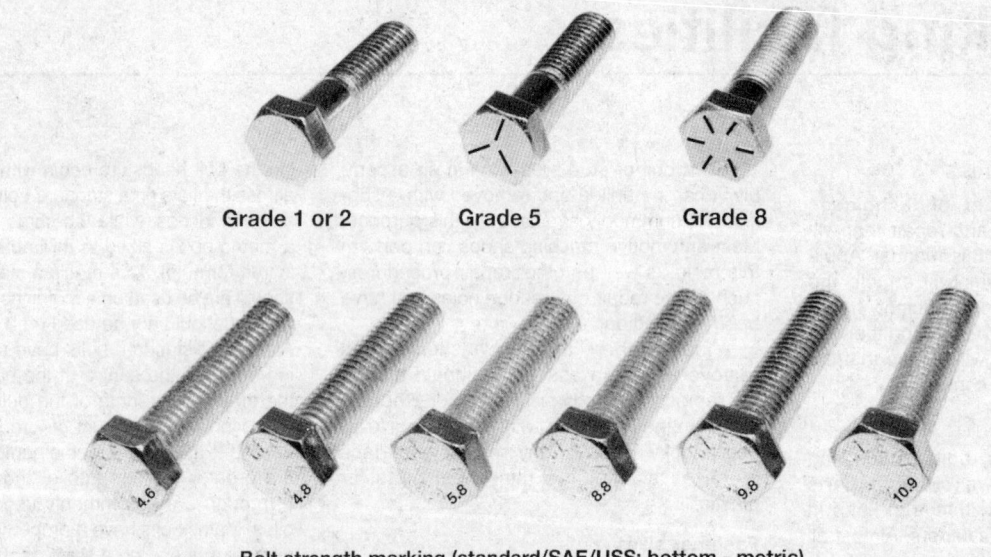

Bolt strength marking (standard/SAE/USS; bottom - metric)

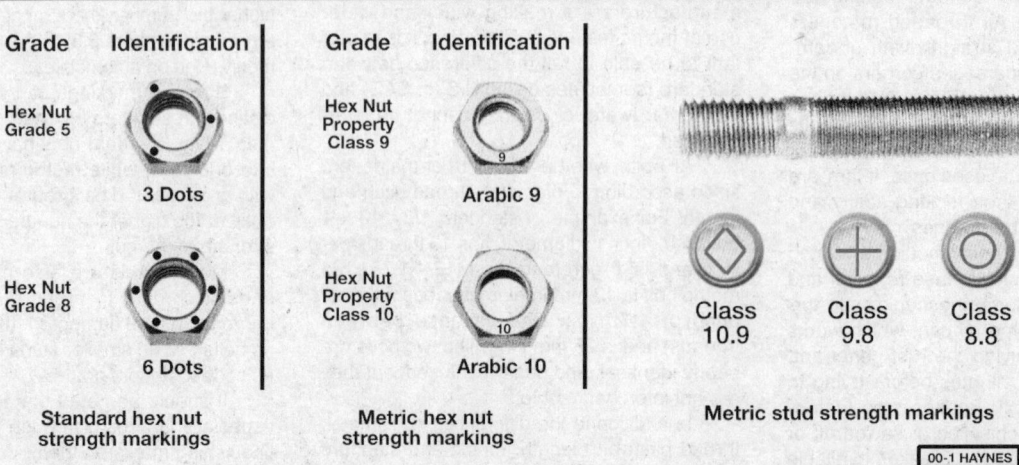

Standard hex nut strength markings

Metric hex nut strength markings

Metric stud strength markings

Maintenance techniques, tools and working facilities

the order that they were removed. It may also be helpful to make sketches or take instant photos of components before removal.

When removing fasteners from a component, keep track of their locations. Sometimes threading a bolt back in a part, or putting the washers and nut back on a stud, can prevent mix-ups later. If nuts and bolts cannot be returned to their original locations, they should be kept in a compartmented box or a series of small boxes. A cupcake or muffin tin is ideal for this purpose, since each cavity can hold the bolts and nuts from a particular area (i.e. oil pan bolts, valve cover bolts, engine mount bolts, etc.). A pan of this type is especially helpful when working on assemblies with very small parts, such as the alternator, valve train or interior dash and trim pieces. The cavities can be marked with paint or tape to identify the contents.

Whenever wiring looms, harnesses or connectors are separated, it is a good idea to identify the two halves with numbered pieces of masking tape so they can be easily reconnected.

Gasket sealing surfaces

Throughout any vehicle, gaskets are used to seal the mating surfaces between two parts and keep lubricants, fluids, vacuum or pressure contained in an assembly.

Many times these gaskets are coated with a liquid or paste-type gasket sealing

	Ft-lbs	Nm
Metric thread sizes		
M-6	6 to 9	9 to 12
M-8	14 to 21	19 to 28
M-10	28 to 40	38 to 54
M-12	50 to 71	68 to 96
M-14	80 to 140	109 to 154
Pipe thread sizes		
1/8	5 to 8	7 to 10
1/4	12 to 18	17 to 24
3/8	22 to 33	30 to 44
1/2	25 to 35	34 to 47
U.S. thread sizes		
1/4 - 20	6 to 9	9 to 12
5/16 - 18	12 to 18	17 to 24
5/16 - 24	14 to 20	19 to 27
3/8 - 16	22 to 32	30 to 43
3/8 - 24	27 to 38	37 to 51
7/16 - 14	40 to 55	55 to 74
7/16 - 20	40 to 60	55 to 81
1/2 - 13	55 to 80	75 to 108

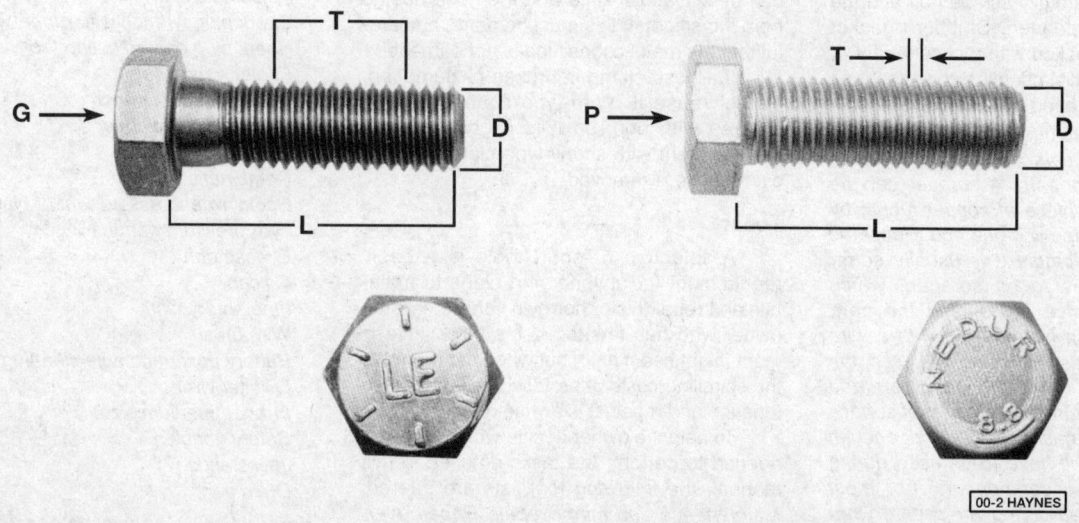

Standard (SAE and USS) bolt dimensions/grade marks

- G Grade marks (bolt strength)
- L Length (in inches)
- T Thread pitch (number of threads per inch)
- D Nominal diameter (in inches)

Metric bolt dimensions/grade marks

- P Property class (bolt strength)
- L Length (in millimeters)
- T Thread pitch (distance between threads in millimeters)
- D Diameter

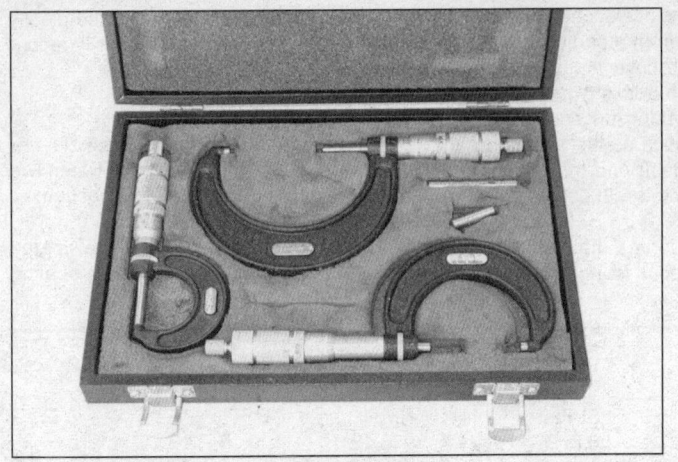

Micrometer set

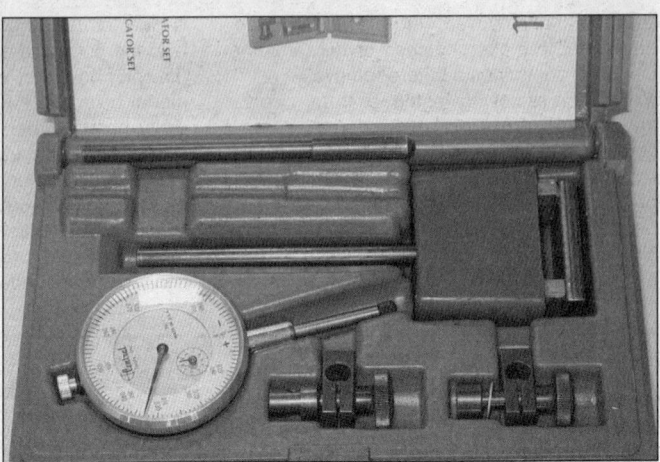

Dial indicator set

compound before assembly. Age, heat and pressure can sometimes cause the two parts to stick together so tightly that they are very difficult to separate. Often, the assembly can be loosened by striking it with a soft-face hammer near the mating surfaces. A regular hammer can be used if a block of wood is placed between the hammer and the part. Do not hammer on cast parts or parts that could be easily damaged. With any particularly stubborn part, always recheck to make sure that every fastener has been removed.

Avoid using a screwdriver or bar to pry apart an assembly, as they can easily mar the gasket sealing surfaces of the parts, which must remain smooth. If prying is absolutely necessary, use an old broom handle, but keep in mind that extra clean up will be necessary if the wood splinters.

After the parts are separated, the old gasket must be carefully scraped off and the gasket surfaces cleaned. Stubborn gasket material can be soaked with rust penetrant or treated with a special chemical to soften it so it can be easily scraped off.

Caution: *Never use gasket removal solutions or caustic chemicals on plastic or other composite components. A scraper can be fashioned from a piece of copper tubing by flattening and sharpening one end. Copper is recommended because it is usually softer than the surfaces to be scraped, which reduces the chance of gouging the part. Some gaskets can be removed with a wire brush, but regardless of the method used, the mating surfaces must be left clean and smooth. If for some reason the gasket surface is gouged, then a gasket sealer thick enough to fill scratches will have to be used during reassembly of the components. For most applications, a non-drying (or semi-drying) gasket sealer should be used.*

Hose removal tips

Warning: *If the vehicle is equipped with air conditioning, do not disconnect any of the A/C hoses without first having the system depressurized by a dealer service department or a service station.*

Hose removal precautions closely parallel gasket removal precautions. Avoid scratching or gouging the surface that the hose mates against or the connection may leak. This is especially true for radiator hoses. Because of various chemical reactions, the rubber in hoses can bond itself to the metal spigot that the hose fits over. To remove a hose, first loosen the hose clamps that secure it to the spigot. Then, with slip-joint pliers, grab the hose at the clamp and rotate it around the spigot. Work it back and forth until it is completely free, then pull it off. Silicone or other lubricants will ease removal if they can be applied between the hose and the outside of the spigot. Apply the same lubricant to the inside of the hose and the outside of the spigot to simplify installation.

As a last resort (and if the hose is to be replaced with a new one anyway), the rubber can be slit with a knife and the hose peeled from the spigot. If this must be done, be careful that the metal connection is not damaged.

If a hose clamp is broken or damaged, do not reuse it. Wire-type clamps usually weaken with age, so it is a good idea to replace them with screw-type clamps whenever a hose is removed.

Tools

A selection of good tools is a basic requirement for anyone who plans to maintain and repair his or her own vehicle. For the owner who has few tools, the initial investment might seem high, but when compared to the spiralling costs of professional auto maintenance and repair, it is a wise one.

To help the owner decide which tools are needed to perform the tasks detailed in this manual, the following tool lists are offered: *Maintenance and minor repair*, *Repair/overhaul* and *Special*.

The newcomer to practical mechanics should start off with the *maintenance and minor repair* tool kit, which is adequate for the simpler jobs performed on a vehicle. Then, as confidence and experience grow, the owner can tackle more difficult tasks, buying additional tools as they are needed. Eventually the basic kit will be expanded into the *repair and overhaul* tool set. Over a period of time, the experienced do-it-yourselfer will assemble a tool set complete enough for most repair and overhaul procedures and will add tools from the special category when it is felt that the expense is justified by the frequency of use.

Maintenance and minor repair tool kit

The tools in this list should be considered the minimum required for performance of routine maintenance, servicing and minor repair work. We recommend the purchase of combination spanners (box-end and open-end combined in one spanner). While more expensive than open end spanners, they offer the advantages of both types of spanner.

Combination spanner set (6 mm to 19 mm)
Adjustable spanner
Spark plug wrench with rubber insert
Spark plug gap adjusting tool
Feeler gauge set
Brake bleeder wrench
Standard screwdriver
Phillips screwdriver
Combination pliers
Hacksaw and assortment of blades
Tyre pressure gauge
Grease gun
Oil can
Fine emery cloth
Wire brush
Battery post and cable cleaning tool
Oil filter wrench
Funnel (medium size)
Safety goggles
Jackstands (2)
Drain pan

Note: *If basic tune-ups are going to be part of routine maintenance, it will be necessary to purchase a good quality stroboscopic timing light and combination tachometer/dwell meter. Although they are included in the list of special tools, it is mentioned here because they are absolutely necessary for tuning most vehicles properly.*

Maintenance techniques, tools and working facilities

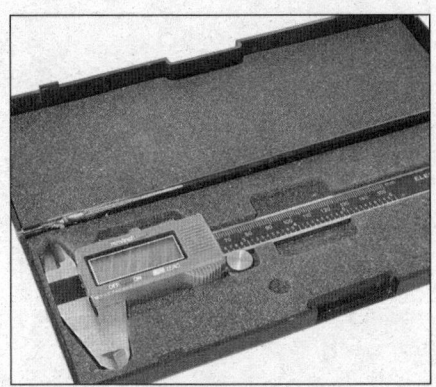
Vernier caliper

Hand-operated vacuum pump

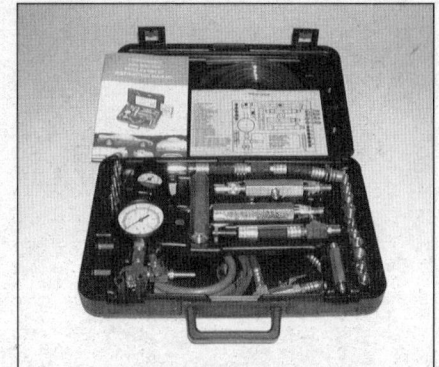
Fuel pressure gauge set

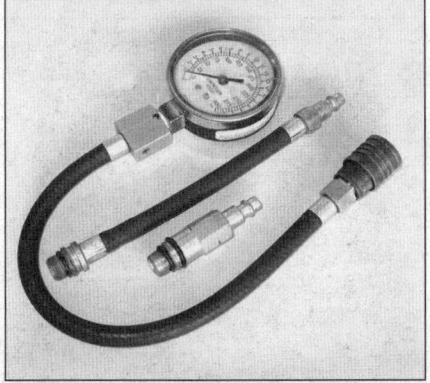
Compression gauge with spark plug hole adapter

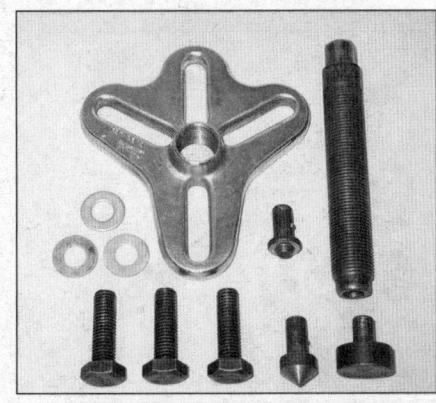
Damper/steering wheel puller

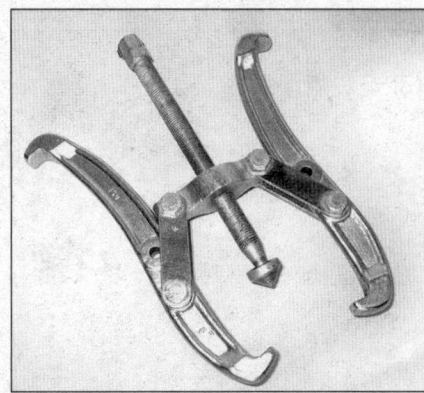
General purpose puller

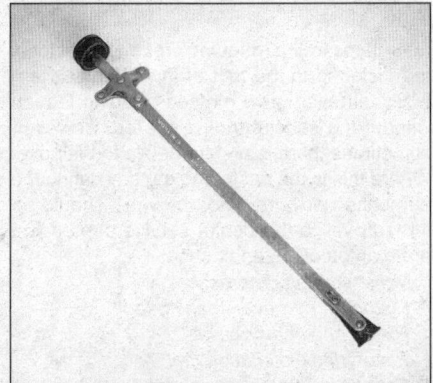
Hydraulic lifter removal tool

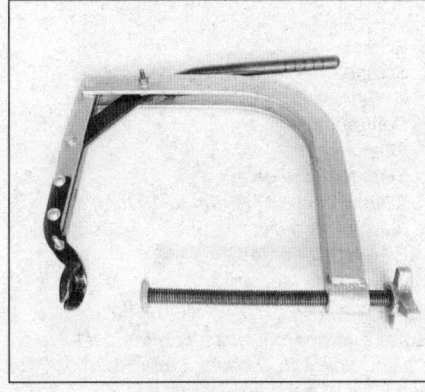
Valve spring compressor

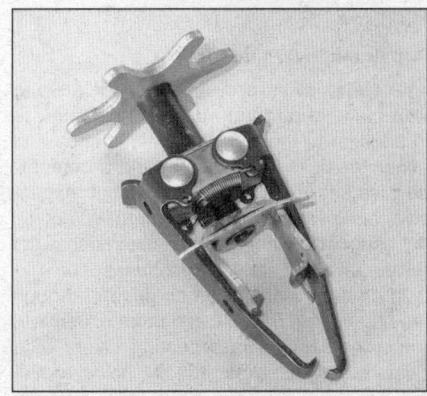
Valve spring compressor

Ridge reamer

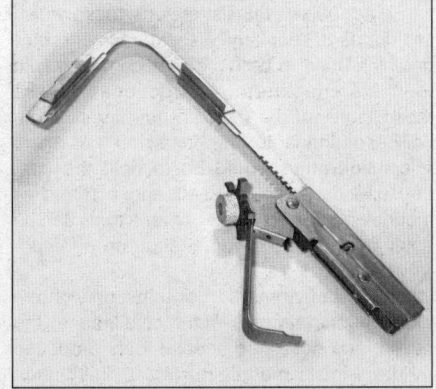
Piston ring groove cleaning tool

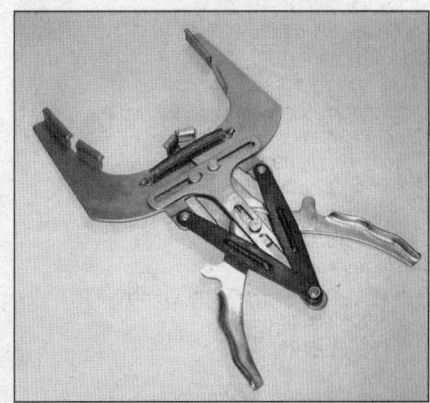
Ring removal/installation tool

Ring compressor

Cylinder hone

Brake hold-down spring tool

Torque angle gauge

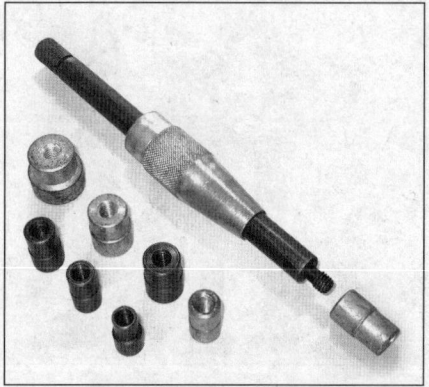
Clutch plate alignment tool

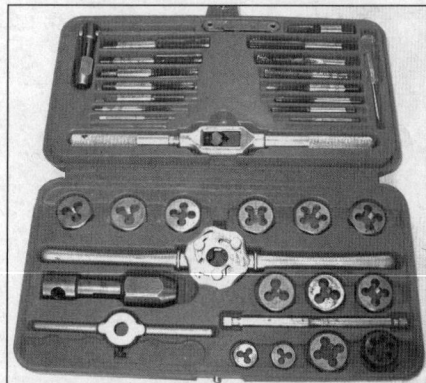
Tap and die set

Repair and overhaul tool set

These tools are essential for anyone who plans to perform major repairs and are in addition to those in the maintenance and minor repair tool kit. Included is a comprehensive set of sockets which, though expensive, are invaluable because of their versatility, especially when various extensions and drives are available. We recommend the 1/2-inch drive over the 3/8-inch drive. Although the larger drive is bulky and more expensive, it has the capacity of accepting a very wide range of large sockets. Ideally, however, the mechanic should have a 3/8-inch drive set and a 1/2-inch drive set.

Socket set(s)
Reversible ratchet
Extension
Universal joint
Torque wrench (same size drive as sockets)
Ball peen hammer
Soft-face hammer (plastic/rubber)
Standard screwdriver
Standard screwdriver (stubby)
Phillips screwdriver
Phillips screwdriver (stubby - No. 2)
Pliers - vice grip
Pliers - lineman's
Pliers - needle nose
Pliers - snap-ring (internal and external)
Cold chisel
Scribe
Scraper (made from flattened copper tubing)
Centrepunch
Pin punches
Steel rule/straightedge
Allen wrench set (4 mm to 10 mm)
A selection of files
Wire brush (large)
Jackstands (second set)
Jack (scissor or hydraulic type)

Note: *Another tool which is often useful is an electric drill with a chuck capacity of 10 mm and a set of good quality drill bits.*

Special tools

The tools in this list include those which are not used regularly, are expensive to buy, or which need to be used in accordance with their manufacturer's instructions. Unless these tools will be used frequently, it is not very economical to purchase many of them. A consideration would be to split the cost and use between yourself and a friend or friends. In addition, most of these tools can be obtained from a tool rental shop on a temporary basis.

This list primarily contains only those tools and instruments widely available to the public, and not those special tools produced by the vehicle manufacturer for distribution to dealer service departments. Occasionally, references to the manufacturer's special tools are included in the text of this manual. Generally, an alternative method of doing the job without the special tool is offered. However, sometimes there is no alternative to their use. Where this is the case, and the tool cannot be purchased or borrowed, the work should be turned over to the dealer service department or an automotive repair shop.

Valve spring compressor
Piston ring groove cleaning tool
Piston ring compressor
Piston ring installation tool
Cylinder compression gauge
Cylinder ridge reamer
Cylinder surfacing hone
Cylinder bore gauge
Micrometers and/or dial calipers
Hydraulic lifter removal tool
Balljoint separator
Universal-type puller
Impact screwdriver
Dial indicator set
Stroboscopic timing light (inductive pick-up)
Hand operated vacuum/pressure pump
Tachometer/dwell meter
Universal electrical multimeter
Cable hoist
Brake spring removal and installation tools
Floor jack

Maintenance techniques, tools and working facilities

Buying tools

For the do-it-yourselfer who is just starting to get involved in vehicle maintenance and repair, there are a number of options available when purchasing tools. If maintenance and minor repair is the extent of the work to be done, the purchase of individual tools is satisfactory. If, on the other hand, extensive work is planned, it would be a good idea to purchase a modest tool set from one of the large retail chain stores. A set can usually be bought at a substantial savings over the individual tool prices, and they often come with a tool box. As additional tools are needed, add-on sets, individual tools and a larger tool box can be purchased to expand the tool selection. Building a tool set gradually allows the cost of the tools to be spread over a longer period of time and gives the mechanic the freedom to choose only those tools that will actually be used.

Tool stores will often be the only source of some of the special tools that are needed, but regardless of where tools are bought, try to avoid cheap ones, especially when buying screwdrivers and sockets, because they won't last very long. The expense involved in replacing cheap tools will eventually be greater than the initial cost of quality tools.

Care and maintenance of tools

Good tools are expensive, so it makes sense to treat them with respect. Keep them clean and in usable condition and store them properly when not in use. Always wipe off any dirt, grease or metal chips before putting them away. Never leave tools lying around in the work area. Upon completion of a job, always check closely under the bonnet for tools that may have been left there so they won't get lost during a test drive.

Some tools, such as screwdrivers, pliers, wrenches and sockets, can be hung on a panel mounted on the garage or workshop wall, while others should be kept in a tool box or tray. Measuring instruments, gauges, meters, etc. must be carefully stored where they cannot be damaged by weather or impact from other tools.

When tools are used with care and stored properly, they will last a very long time. Even with the best of care, though, tools will wear out if used frequently. When a tool is damaged or worn out, replace it. Subsequent jobs will be safer and more enjoyable if you do.

How to repair damaged threads

Sometimes, the internal threads of a nut or bolt hole can become stripped, usually from overtightening. Stripping threads is an all-too-common occurrence, especially when working with aluminium parts, because aluminium is so soft that it easily strips out.

Usually, external or internal threads are only partially stripped. After they've been cleaned up with a tap or die, they'll still work. Sometimes, however, threads are badly damaged. When this happens, you've got three choices:

1. Drill and tap the hole to the next suitable oversize and install a larger diameter bolt, screw or stud.
2. Drill and tap the hole to accept a threaded plug, then drill and tap the plug to the original screw size. You can also buy a plug already threaded to the original size. Then you simply drill a hole to the specified size, then run the threaded plug into the hole with a bolt and jam nut. Once the plug is fully seated, remove the jam nut and bolt.
3. The third method uses a patented thread repair kit like Heli-Coil or Slimsert. These easy-to-use kits are designed to repair damaged threads in straight-through holes and blind holes. Both are available as kits which can handle a variety of sizes and thread patterns. Drill the hole, then tap it with the special included tap. Install the Heli-Coil and the hole is back to its original diameter and thread pitch.

Regardless of which method you use, be sure to proceed calmly and carefully. A little impatience or carelessness during one of these relatively simple procedures can ruin your whole day's work and cost you a bundle if you wreck an expensive part.

Working facilities

Not to be overlooked when discussing tools is the workshop. If anything more than routine maintenance is to be carried out, some sort of suitable work area is essential.

It is understood, and appreciated, that many home mechanics do not have a good workshop or garage available, and end up removing an engine or doing major repairs outside. It is recommended, however, that the overhaul or repair be completed under the cover of a roof.

A clean, flat workbench or table of comfortable working height is an absolute necessity. The workbench should be equipped with a vise that has a jaw opening of at least 100 mm.

As mentioned previously, some clean, dry storage space is also required for tools, as well as the lubricants, fluids, cleaning solvents, etc. which soon become necessary.

Sometimes waste oil and fluids, drained from the engine or cooling system during normal maintenance or repairs, present a disposal problem. To avoid pouring them on the ground or into a sewage system, pour the used fluids into large containers, seal them with caps and take them to an authorized disposal site or recycling centre. Plastic jugs, such as old antifreeze containers, are ideal for this purpose.

Always keep a supply of old newspapers and clean rags available. Old towels are excellent for mopping up spills. Many mechanics use rolls of paper towels for most work because they are readily available and disposable. To help keep the area under the vehicle clean, a large cardboard box can be cut open and flattened to protect the garage or shop floor.

Whenever working over a painted surface, such as when leaning over a mudguard to service something under the bonnet, always cover it with an old blanket or bedspread to protect the finish. Vinyl covered pads, made especially for this purpose, are available at auto parts stores.

Booster battery (jump) starting

1 Jump starting a vehicle can be dangerous if the procedure described below is not performed correctly. If any doubt exists, it is recommended that the services of a competent mechanic be obtained.
2 The range of vehicles covered by this manual are equipped with complex electronic circuitry which can be damaged by voltage surges. These voltage surges can be generated when jump starting or being jump started by another vehicle.
3 If available, use jumper leads equipped with a surge protection device and follow the lead manufacturer's instructions carefully, particularly regarding the connection and disconnection of the leads.
4 Ensure that the booster battery is 12 volts and the negative terminal is earthed.
5 Ensure that the vehicles are not touching and that the ignition and all accessories on both vehicles are switched Off.
6 Ensure that the transaxles on both vehicles are in Park or Neutral and the handbrakes are firmly applied.
7 Remove the vent caps from the battery and check the electrolyte level. Replenish with distilled water as necessary.
8 Place the vent caps loosely over the cell apertures.
9 Connect one end of the red jumper lead to the positive (+) battery terminal of the booster battery (connection 1) and the other end of the red lead to the positive (+) battery terminal of the discharged battery (connection 2).

Warning: *The battery emits hydrogen gas which is explosive. Do not expose the battery to naked flames or sparks. Do not lean over the battery when connecting the jumper leads. Do not allow the ends of the jumper leads to touch one another or any part of the vehicle.*

10 Connect one end of the black jumper lead to the negative (–) battery terminal of the booster battery (connection 3) and the other end of the black lead to a good earthing point on the engine of the vehicle with the discharged battery (connection 4).

Note: *Do not connect the jumper lead directly to the negative (–) battery terminal of the discharged battery.*

11 Start the engine on the vehicle with the booster battery and run the engine at a moderate speed for a few minutes.
12 Start the engine on the vehicle with the discharged battery.
13 Leave the engines of both vehicles running for at least 10 minutes. This will partially charge the discharged battery and reduce the risk of damage to electronic circuitry from voltage surges.
14 Switch the engines of both vehicles Off and disconnect the jumper leads in the reverse order of the connecting sequence.
15 Attempt to start the engine of the vehicle with the discharged battery.
16 If the battery has not charged sufficiently to start the engine, reconnect the jumper leads as previously described and start the engines of both vehicles.
17 Switch On the headlamps of the vehicle with the discharged battery.
18 Disconnect the jumper leads in the reverse order of the connecting sequence. Switch the headlamps Off.

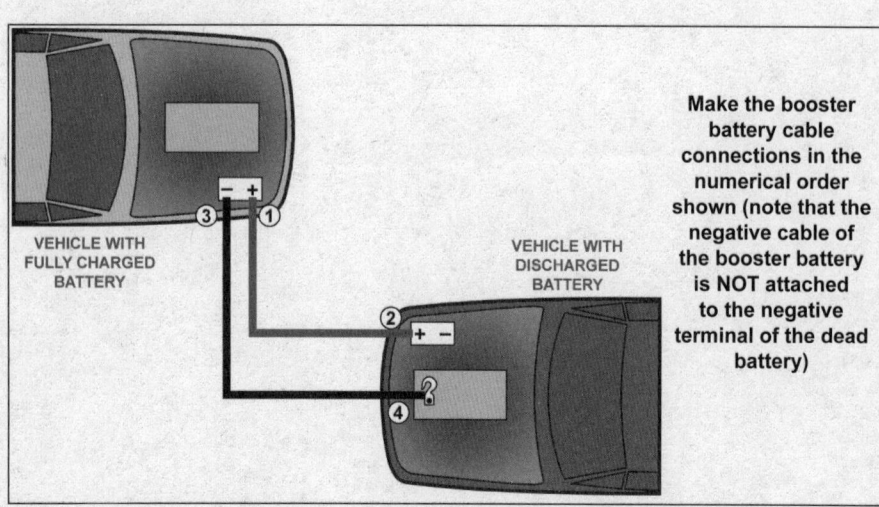

Make the booster battery cable connections in the numerical order shown (note that the negative cable of the booster battery is NOT attached to the negative terminal of the dead battery)

Jacking and towing

Jacking

Warning: *The jack supplied with the vehicle should only be used for changing a tyre or placing jackstands under the frame. Never work under the vehicle or start The engine while this jack is being used as the only means of support.*

1 The vehicle should be on level ground. Place the shift lever in Park, if you have an automatic, or Reverse if you have a manual transaxle. Block the wheel diagonally opposite the wheel being changed. Set the parking brake.

2 Remove the spare tyre and jack from stowage. Remove the wheel cover and trim ring (if so equipped) with the tapered end of the lug nut wrench by inserting and twisting the handle and then prying against the back of the wheel cover. Loosen the wheel nuts about 1/4 to 1/2 turn each.

3 Place the scissors-type jack under the side of the vehicle and adjust the jack height until it fits between the notches in the vertical rocker panel flange nearest the wheel to be changed. There is a front and rear jacking point on each side of the vehicle **(see illustration)**.

4 Turn the jack handle clockwise until the tyre clears the ground. Remove the wheel nuts and pull the wheel off. Replace it with the spare.

5 Install the wheel nuts with the beveled edges facing in. Tighten them snugly. Don't attempt to tighten them completely until the vehicle is lowered or it could slip off the jack. Turn the jack handle counterclockwise to lower the vehicle. Remove the jack and tighten the wheel nuts in a diagonal pattern.

6 Install the cover (and trim ring, if used) and be sure it's snapped into place all the way around.

7 Stow the tyre, jack and wrench. Unblock the wheels.

Towing

8 As a general rule, the vehicle should be towed with all wheels off the ground. If they can't be raised, place them on a dolly. The intelligent key must be in its slot in the instrument panel and the starter button display must be in the ACC position to unlock the steering column lock.

9 Equipment specifically designed for towing should be used. It should be attached to the main structural members of the vehicle, not the bumpers or brackets.

10 Safety is a major consideration when towing and all applicable state and local laws must be obeyed. A safety chain system must be used at all times.

7.3 The jack fits over the rocker panel flange (there are two jacking points on each side of the vehicle, indicated by notches in the rocker panel flange)

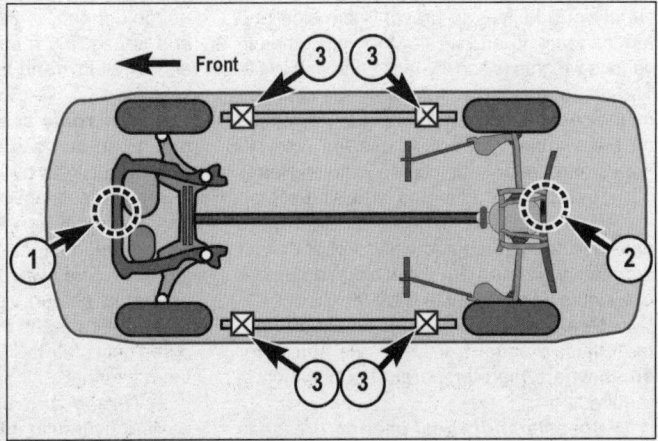

7.7 Jacking points

1 *Front floor jack jacking point*
2 *Rear floor jack jacking point*
3 *Chassis stand locations along the sill panels - the same spot as the vehicle jack jacking point*

Automotive chemicals and lubricants

A number of automotive chemicals and lubricants are available for use during vehicle maintenance and repair. They include a wide variety of products ranging from cleaning solvents and degreasers to lubricants and protective sprays for rubber, plastic and vinyl.

Cleaners

Carburettor cleaner and choke cleaner is a strong solvent for gum, varnish and carbon. Most carburettor cleaners leave a dry-type lubricant film which will not harden or gum up. Because of this film it is not recommended for use on electrical components.

Brake system cleaner is used to remove brake dust, grease and brake fluid from the brake system, where clean surfaces are absolutely necessary. It leaves no residue and often eliminates brake squeal caused by contaminants.

Electrical cleaner removes oxidation, corrosion and carbon deposits from electrical contacts, restoring full current flow. It can also be used to clean spark plugs, carburettor jets, voltage regulators and other parts where an oil-free surface is desired.

Demoisturants remove water and moisture from electrical components such as alternators, voltage regulators, electrical connectors and fuse blocks. They are non-conductive and non-corrosive.

Degreasers are heavy-duty solvents used to remove grease from the outside of the engine and from chassis components. They can be sprayed or brushed on and, depending on the type, are rinsed off either with water or solvent.

Lubricants

Motor oil is the lubricant formulated for use in engines. It normally contains a wide variety of additives to prevent corrosion and reduce foaming and wear. Motor oil comes in various weights (viscosity ratings) from 0 to 50. The recommended weight of the oil depends on the season, temperature and the demands on the engine. Light oil is used in cold climates and under light load conditions. Heavy oil is used in hot climates and where high loads are encountered. Multi-viscosity oils are designed to have characteristics of both light and heavy oils and are available in a number of weights from 0W-20 to 20W-50.

Gear oil is designed to be used in differentials, manual transmissions and other areas where high-temperature lubrication is required.

Chassis and wheel bearing grease is a heavy grease used where increased loads and friction are encountered, such as for wheel bearings, balljoints, tie-rod ends and universal joints.

High-temperature wheel bearing grease is designed to withstand the extreme temperatures encountered by wheel bearings in disc brake equipped vehicles. It usually contains molybdenum disulfide (moly), which is a dry-type lubricant.

White grease is a heavy grease for metal-to-metal applications where water is a problem. White grease stays soft under both low and high temperatures (usually from -100 to +190-degrees F), and will not wash off or dilute in the presence of water.

Assembly lube is a special extreme pressure lubricant, usually containing moly, used to lubricate high-load parts (such as main and rod bearings and cam lobes) for initial start-up of a new engine. The assembly lube lubricates the parts without being squeezed out or washed away until the engine oiling system begins to function.

Silicone lubricants are used to protect rubber, plastic, vinyl and nylon parts.

Graphite lubricants are used where oils cannot be used due to contamination problems, such as in locks. The dry graphite will lubricate metal parts while remaining uncontaminated by dirt, water, oil or acids. It is electrically conductive and will not foul electrical contacts in locks such as the ignition switch.

Moly penetrants loosen and lubricate frozen, rusted and corroded fasteners and prevent future rusting or freezing.

Heat-sink grease is a special electrically non-conductive grease that is used for mounting electronic ignition modules where it is essential that heat is transferred away from the module.

Sealants

RTV sealant is one of the most widely used gasket compounds. Made from silicone, RTV is air curing, it seals, bonds, waterproofs, fills surface irregularities, remains flexible, doesn't shrink, is relatively easy to remove, and is used as a supplementary sealer with almost all low and medium temperature gaskets.

Anaerobic sealant is much like RTV in that it can be used either to seal gaskets or to form gaskets by itself. It remains flexible, is solvent resistant and fills surface imperfections. The difference between an anaerobic sealant and an RTV-type sealant is in the curing. RTV cures when exposed to air, while an anaerobic sealant cures only in the absence of air. This means that an anaerobic sealant cures only after the assembly of parts, sealing them together.

Thread and pipe sealant is used for sealing hydraulic and pneumatic fittings and vacuum lines. It is usually made from a Teflon compound, and comes in a spray, a paint-on liquid and as a wrap-around tape.

Chemicals

Anti-seize compound prevents seizing, galling, cold welding, rust and corrosion in fasteners. High-temperature ant-seize, usually made with copper and graphite lubricants, is used for exhaust system and exhaust manifold bolts.

Anaerobic locking compounds are used to keep fasteners from vibrating or working loose and cure only after installation, in the absence of air. Medium strength locking compound is used for small nuts, bolts and screws that may be removed later. High-strength locking compound is for large nuts, bolts and studs which aren't removed on a regular basis.

Oil additives range from viscosity index improvers to chemical treatments that claim to reduce internal engine friction. It should be noted that most oil manufacturers caution against using additives with their oils.

Gas additives perform several functions, depending on their chemical makeup. They usually contain solvents that help dissolve gum and varnish that build up on carburettor, fuel injection and intake parts. They also serve to break down carbon deposits that form on the inside surfaces of the combustion chambers. Some additives contain upper cylinder lubricants for valves and piston rings, and others contain chemicals to remove condensation from the gas tank.

Miscellaneous

Brake fluid is specially formulated hydraulic fluid that can withstand the heat and pressure encountered in brake systems. Care must be taken so this fluid does not come in contact with painted surfaces or plastics. An opened container should always be resealed to prevent contamination by water or dirt.

Weatherstrip adhesive is used to bond weatherstripping around doors, windows and luggage compartment lids. It is sometimes used to attach trim pieces.

Undercoating is a petroleum-based, tar-like substance that is designed to protect metal surfaces on the underside of the vehicle from corrosion. It also acts as a sound-deadening agent by insulating the bottom of the vehicle.

Waxes and polishes are used to help protect painted and plated surfaces from the weather. Different types of paint may require the use of different types of wax and polish. Some polishes utilize a chemical or abrasive cleaner to help remove the top layer of oxidized (dull) paint on older vehicles. In recent years many non-wax polishes that contain a wide variety of chemicals such as polymers and silicones have been introduced. These non-wax polishes are usually easier to apply and last longer than conventional waxes and polishes.

Safety first!

Regardless of how enthusiastic you may be about getting on with the job at hand, take the time to ensure that your safety is not jeopardized. A moment's lack of attention can result in an accident, as can failure to observe certain simple safety precautions. The possibility of an accident will always exist, and the following points should not be considered a comprehensive list of all dangers. Rather, they are intended to make you aware of the risks and to encourage a safety conscious approach to all work you carry out on your vehicle.

Essential DOs and DON'Ts

DON'T rely on a jack when working under the vehicle. Always use approved jackstands to support the weight of the vehicle and place them under the recommended lift or support points.

DON'T attempt to loosen extremely tight fasteners (i.e. wheel nuts) while the vehicle is on a jack - it may fall.

DON'T start the engine without first making sure that the transmission is in Neutral (or Park where applicable) and the parking brake is set.

DON'T remove the radiator cap from a hot cooling system - let it cool or cover it with a cloth and release the pressure gradually.

DON'T attempt to drain the engine oil until you are sure it has cooled to the point that it will not burn you.

DON'T touch any part of the engine or exhaust system until it has cooled sufficiently to avoid burns.

DON'T siphon toxic liquids such as gasoline, antifreeze and brake fluid by mouth, or allow them to remain on your skin.

DON'T inhale brake lining dust - it is potentially hazardous (see *Asbestos* below).

DON'T allow spilled oil or grease to remain on the floor - wipe it up before someone slips on it.

DON'T use loose fitting wrenches or other tools which may slip and cause injury.

DON'T push on wrenches when loosening or tightening nuts or bolts. Always try to pull the wrench toward you. If the situation calls for pushing the wrench away, push with an open hand to avoid scraped knuckles if the wrench should slip.

DON'T attempt to lift a heavy component alone - get someone to help you.

DON'T rush or take unsafe shortcuts to finish a job.

DON'T allow children or animals in or around the vehicle while you are working on it.

DO wear eye protection when using power tools and when working under a vehicle.

DO keep loose clothing and long hair well out of the way of moving parts.

DO make sure that any hoist used has a safe working load rating adequate for the job.

DO get someone to check on you periodically when working alone on a vehicle.

DO carry out work in a logical sequence and make sure that everything is correctly assembled and tightened.

DO keep chemicals and fluids tightly capped and out of the reach of children and pets.

DO remember that your vehicle's safety affects that of yourself and others. If in doubt on any point, get professional advice.

Steering, suspension and brakes

These systems are essential to driving safety, so make sure you have a qualified shop or individual check your work. Also, compressed suspension springs can cause injury if released suddenly - be sure to use a spring compressor.

Airbags

Airbags are explosive devices that can **CAUSE** injury if they deploy while you're working on the vehicle. Follow the manufacturer's instructions to disable the airbag whenever you're working in the vicinity of airbag components.

Asbestos

Certain friction, insulating, sealing, and other products - such as brake linings, brake bands, clutch linings, torque converters, gaskets, etc. - may contain asbestos or other hazardous friction material. Extreme care must be taken to avoid inhalation of dust from such products, since it is hazardous to health. If in doubt, assume that they do contain asbestos.

Fire

Remember at all times that gasoline is highly flammable. Never smoke or have any kind of open flame around when working on a vehicle. But the risk does not end there. A spark caused by an electrical short circuit, by two metal surfaces contacting each other, or even by static electricity built up in your body under certain conditions, can ignite gasoline vapours, which in a confined space are highly explosive. Do not, under any circumstances, use gasoline for cleaning parts. Use an approved safety solvent.

Always disconnect the battery ground (-) cable at the battery before working on any part of the fuel system or electrical system. Never risk spilling fuel on a hot engine or exhaust component. It is strongly recommended that a fire extinguisher suitable for use on fuel and electrical fires be kept handy in the garage or workshop at all times. Never try to extinguish a fuel or electrical fire with water.

Fumes

Certain fumes are highly toxic and can quickly cause unconsciousness and even death if inhaled to any extent. Gasoline vapour falls into this category, as do the vapours from some cleaning solvents. Any draining or pouring of such volatile fluids should be done in a well ventilated area.

When using cleaning fluids and solvents, read the instructions on the container carefully. Never use materials from unmarked containers.

Never run the engine in an enclosed space, such as a garage. Exhaust fumes contain carbon monoxide, which is extremely poisonous. If you need to run the engine, always do so in the open air, or at least have the rear of the vehicle outside the work area.

The battery

Never create a spark or allow a bare light bulb near a battery. They normally give off a certain amount of hydrogen gas, which is highly explosive.

Always disconnect the battery ground (-) cable at the battery before working on the fuel or electrical systems.

If possible, loosen the filler caps or cover when charging the battery from an external source (this does not apply to sealed or maintenance-free batteries). Do not charge at an excessive rate or the battery may burst.

Take care when adding water to a non maintenance-free battery and when carrying a battery. The electrolyte, even when diluted, is very corrosive and should not be allowed to contact clothing or skin.

Always wear eye protection when cleaning the battery to prevent the caustic deposits from entering your eyes.

Household current

When using an electric power tool, inspection light, etc., which operates on household current, always make sure that the tool is correctly connected to its plug and that, where necessary, it is properly grounded. Do not use such items in damp conditions and, again, do not create a spark or apply excessive heat in the vicinity of fuel or fuel vapour.

Secondary ignition system voltage

A severe electric shock can result from touching certain parts of the ignition system (such as the spark plug wires) when the engine is running or being cranked, particularly if components are damp or the insulation is defective. In the case of an electronic ignition system, the secondary system voltage is much higher and could prove fatal.

Hydrofluoric acid

This extremely corrosive acid is formed when certain types of synthetic rubber, found in some O-rings, oil seals, fuel hoses, etc. are exposed to temperatures above 400-degrees C. The rubber changes into a charred or sticky substance containing the acid. *Once formed, the acid remains dangerous for years. If it gets onto the skin, it may be necessary to amputate the limb concerned.*

When dealing with a vehicle which has suffered a fire, or with components salvaged from such a vehicle, wear protective gloves and discard them after use.

Troubleshooting

Contents

Symptom	Section
Engine	
Engine will not rotate when attempting to start	1
Engine rotates but will not start	2
Engine hard to start when cold	3
Engine hard to start when hot	4
Starter motor noisy or excessively rough in engagement	5
Engine starts but stops immediately	6
Oil puddle under engine	7
Engine lopes while idling or idles erratically	8
Engine misses at idle speed	9
Engine misses throughout driving speed range	10
Engine stumbles on acceleration	11
Engine surges while holding accelerator steady	12
Engine stalls	13
Engine lacks power	14
Engine backfires	15
Pinging or knocking engine sounds during acceleration or uphill	16
Engine runs with oil pressure light on	17
Engine continues to run after switching off	18
Engine electrical system	
Battery will not hold a charge	19
Alternator light fails to go out	20
Alternator light fails to come on when key is turned on	21
Fuel system	
Excessive fuel consumption	22
Fuel leakage and/or fuel odour	23
Cooling system	
Overheating	24
Overcooling	25
External coolant leakage	26
Internal coolant leakage	27
Coolant loss	28
Poor coolant circulation	29
Automatic transaxle	
Fluid leakage	30
Transaxle fluid brown or has a burned smell	31
General shift mechanism problems	32
Transaxle will not downshift with accelerator pedal pressed to the floor	33
Engine will start in gears other than Park or Neutral	34
Transaxle slips, is noisy or has no drive in forward or reverse gears	35

Symptom	Section
Driveshafts	
Clicking noise in turns	36
Shudder or vibration during acceleration	37
Vibration at highway speeds	38
Brakes	
Vehicle pulls to one side during braking	39
Noise (high-pitched squeal when the brakes are applied)	40
Brake roughness or chatter (pedal pulsates)	41
Excessive brake pedal effort required to stop vehicle	42
Excessive brake pedal travel	43
Dragging brakes	49
Grabbing or uneven braking action	50
Brake pedal feels spongy when depressed	51
Brake pedal travels to the floor with little resistance	52
Parking brake does not hold	53
Suspension and steering systems	
Vehicle pulls to one side	54
Abnormal or excessive tyre wear	55
Wheel makes a thumping noise	56
Shimmy, shake or vibration	57
Hard steering	58
Poor returnability of steering to centre	59
Abnormal noise at the front end	60
Wander or poor steering stability	61
Erratic steering when braking	62
Excessive pitching and/or rolling around corners or during braking	63
Suspension bottoms	64
Cupped tyres	65
Excessive tyre wear on outside edge	66
Excessive tyre wear on inside edge	67
Tyre tread worn in one place	68
Excessive play or looseness in steering system	69
Rattling or clicking noise in steering gear	70

1 This Section provides an easy reference guide to the more common problems which may occur during the operation of your vehicle. These problems and their possible causes are grouped under headings denoting various components or systems, such as Engine, Cooling system, etc. They also refer you to the Chapter and/or Section which deals with the problem.

2 Remember that successful troubleshooting is not a mysterious black art practiced only by professional mechanics. It is simply the result of the right knowledge combined with an intelligent, systematic approach to the problem. Always work by a process of elimination, starting with the simplest solution and working through to the most complex - and never overlook the obvious. Anyone can run the gas tank dry or leave the lights on overnight, so don't assume that you are exempt from such oversights.

3 Finally, always establish a clear idea of why a problem has occurred and take steps to ensure that it doesn't happen again. If the electrical system fails because of a poor connection, check the other connections in the system to make sure that they don't fail as well. If a particular fuse continues to blow, find out why - don't just replace one fuse after another. Remember, failure of a small component can often be indicative of potential failure or incorrect functioning of a more important component or system.

Troubleshooting

Engine

1 Engine will not rotate when attempting to start

1 Battery terminal connections loose or corroded (see Chapter 1 Section 11).
2 Battery discharged or faulty (see Chapter 1 Section 11).
3 Automatic transaxle not completely engaged in Park (see Chapter 7B Section 5).
4 Broken, loose or disconnected wiring in the starting circuit (see Chapter 5 Section 12).
5 Starter motor pinion jammed in flywheel ring gear (see Chapter 5 Section 12).
6 Starter solenoid faulty (see Chapter 5 Section 12).
7 Starter motor faulty (see Chapter 5 Section 12).
8 Ignition switch faulty (see Chapter 12A Section 4).
9 Starter pinion or flywheel teeth worn or broken (see Chapter 5 Section 12).
10 Faulty Body Control Module (BCM) or Intelligent Power Distribution Module (IPDM) (see Chapter 12A Section 3).

2 Engine rotates but will not start

1 Fuel tank empty.
2 Battery discharged (engine rotates slowly) (see Chapter 1 Section 11).
3 Battery terminal connections loose or corroded (see Chapter 1 Section 11).
4 Leaking fuel injector(s), faulty fuel pump, pressure regulator, etc. (see Chapter 4A or Chapter 4B).
5 Broken timing chain (see Chapter 2A Section 8, Chapter 2B Section 9 or Chapter 2C Section 10).
6 Ignition system problem (see Chapter 5 Section 7).
7 Air in the fuel system (see Chapter 4B Section 3) - diesel models.
8 Glow plugs defective (see Chapter 5 Section 8) - diesel models.
9 Worn, faulty or incorrectly gapped spark plugs (see Chapter 1 Section 26).
10 Broken, loose or disconnected wiring in the starting circuit (see Chapter 5 Section 12).
11 Defective MAF sensor (see Chapter 6 Section 9).

3 Engine hard to start when cold

1 Battery discharged or low (see Chapter 1 Section 11).
2 Malfunctioning fuel system (see Chapter 4A, or Chapter 4B).
3 Faulty coolant temperature sensor or intake air temperature sensor (see Chapter 6).
4 Injector(s) leaking (see Chapter 4A or Chapter 4B).
5 Faulty ignition system (see Chapter 5).
6 Defective MAF sensor (see Chapter 6).
7 Glow plugs defective (see Chapter 5 Section 8) - diesel models.

4 Engine hard to start when hot

1 Air filter clogged (Chapter 1).
2 Fuel not reaching the fuel injection system (see Chapter 4A or Chapter 4B).
3 Corroded battery connections, especially ground (see Chapter 1).
4 Faulty coolant temperature sensor or intake air temperature sensor (see Chapter 6).

5 Starter motor noisy or excessively rough in engagement

1 Pinion or flywheel gear teeth worn or broken (see Chapter 2A Section 13, Chapter 2B Section 15 or Chapter 2C Section 18).
2 Starter motor mounting bolts loose or missing (see Chapter 5 Section 12).

6 Engine starts but stops immediately

1 Insufficient fuel reaching the fuel injector(s) (see Chapter 4A or Chapter 4B).
2 Vacuum leak at the gasket between the intake manifold/plenum and throttle body (see Chapter 4A Section 10 or Chapter 4B Section 7).

7 Oil puddle under engine

1 Oil pan gasket and/or oil pan drain bolt washer leaking (see Chapter 2A Section 11, Chapter 2B Section 12 or Chapter 2C Section 14).
2 Oil pressure sending unit leaking (see Chapter 2D Section 2).
3 Valve cover leaking (see Chapter 2A Section 4, or Chapter 2C Section 12).
4 Engine oil seals leaking (see Chapter 2A Section 14, Chapter 2B Section 14 or Chapter 2C Section 19).

8 Engine lopes while idling or idles erratically

1 Vacuum leakage (see Chapter 1 Section 13).
2 Air filter clogged (see Chapter 1 Section 21).
3 Fuel pump not delivering sufficient fuel to the fuel injection system (see Chapter 4A or Chapter 4B Section 3).
4 Leaking head gasket (see Chapter 2A Section 10, Chapter 2B Section 11 or Chapter 2C Section 13).
5 Timing chain and/or sprockets worn (see Chapter 2A Section 8, Chapter 2B Section 9 or Chapter 2C Section 10).
6 Camshaft lobes worn (see Chapter 2A Section 9, Chapter 2B Section 10 or Chapter 2C Section 12).

9 Engine misses at idle speed

1 Spark plugs worn or not gapped properly (Chapter 1 Section 26).
2 Vacuum leaks (see Chapter 1 Section 13).
3 Uneven or low compression (see Chapter 2D Section 3).
4 Problem with the fuel injection system (see Chapter 4A or Chapter 4B).
5 Faulty ignition coil(s) (see Chapter 5 Section 7).

10 Engine misses throughout driving speed range

1 Fuel filter clogged (see Chapter 4A Section 7 or Chapter 1 Section 6).
Note: *On petrol models, the filter isn't replaceable; the fuel pump module must be replaced.*
2 Low fuel output at the fuel injector(s) (Chapter 4A).
3 Faulty or incorrectly gapped spark plugs (Chapter 1 Section 26).
4 Faulty ignition coils (Chapter 5 Section 7).
5 Faulty emission system components (see Chapter 6 Section 19).
6 Low or uneven cylinder compression pressures (see Chapter 2D Section 3).
7 Vacuum leak in fuel injection system, throttle body, intake manifold, IAC/AAC valve or vacuum hoses (see Chapter 4A or Chapter 4B).

11 Engine stumbles on acceleration

1 Spark plugs fouled (Chapter 1 Section 26).
2 Problem with fuel injection system (see Chapter 4A or Chapter 4B).
3 Fuel filter clogged (see Chapter 4A Section 7) or (see Chapter 1 Section 6).
Note: *On petrol models, the filter isn't replaceable; the fuel pump module must be replaced.*
4 Intake manifold air leak (see Chapter 2A Section 5, Chapter 2B Section 5 or Chapter 2C Section 5).

Troubleshooting

12 Engine surges while holding accelerator steady

1 Intake air leak (see Chapter 2A Section 5, Chapter 2B Section 5 or Chapter 2C Section 5).
2 Fuel pump or fuel pressure regulator faulty (see Chapter 4A or Chapter 4B).
3 Problem with fuel injection system (see Chapter 4A or Chapter 4B).
4 Problem with the emissions control system (see Chapter 6).

13 Engine stalls

1 Fuel filter clogged (see Chapter 4A Section 7 or Chapter 1 Section 6).
Note: *On petrol models, the filter isn't replaceable; the fuel pump module must be replaced.*
2 Faulty emissions system components (see Chapter 6).
3 Faulty or incorrectly gapped spark plugs (see Chapter 1 Section 26).
4 Vacuum leak in the fuel injection system, intake manifold or vacuum hoses (see Chapter 2A Section 5, Chapter 2B Section 5 or Chapter 2C Section 5).
5 Valve clearances incorrectly set (see Chapter 1 Section 34).

14 Engine lacks power

1 Faulty or incorrectly gapped spark plugs (see Chapter 1 Section 26).
2 Problem with the fuel injection system (see Chapter 4A or Chapter 4B).
3 Plugged air filter (see Chapter 1 Section 21).
4 Brakes binding (see Chapter 1 Section 19).
5 Automatic transaxle fluid level incorrect (see Chapter 1 Section 8).
6 Clutch slipping (see Chapter 8 Section 5).
7 Fuel filter clogged (see Chapter 4A Section 7 or Chapter 1 Section 6).
Note: *On petrol models, the filter isn't replaceable; the fuel pump module must be replaced.*
8 Emission control system not functioning properly (see Chapter 6).
9 Low or uneven cylinder compression pressures (see Chapter 2D Section 3).
10 Obstructed exhaust system (see Chapter 4A Section 11 or Chapter 4B Section 11).

15 Engine backfires

1 Emission control system not functioning properly (see Chapter 6).
2 Problem with the fuel injection system (see Chapter 4A or Chapter 4B).
3 Vacuum leak at fuel injector(s), intake manifold or vacuum hoses (see Chapter 2A Section 5, Chapter 2B Section 5 or Chapter 2C Section 5).
4 Valve clearances incorrectly set and/or valves sticking (see Chapter 1 Section 34).

16 Pinging or knocking engine sounds during acceleration or uphill

1 Incorrect grade of fuel.
2 Fuel injection system faulty (see Chapter 4A or Chapter 4B).
3 Improper or damaged spark plugs (see Chapter 1 Section 26).
4 Malfunctioning knock sensor (see Chapter 6 Section 10).
5 Vacuum leak (see Chapter 2A, Chapter 2B or Chapter 4A).

17 Engine runs with oil pressure light on

1 Low oil level (see Chapter 1 Section 4).
2 Short in wiring circuit (see Chapter 12A Section 2).
3 Faulty oil pressure sender (see Chapter 2D Section 2).
4 Worn engine bearings and/or oil pump (see Chapter 2A, Chapter 2B, Chapter 2C or Chapter 2D)

18 Engine continues to run after switching off

Faulty ignition switch (see Chapter 12A Section 4), Powertrain Control Module (PCM) (see Chapter 6 Section 15), or Body Control Module (BCM).

Engine electrical system

19 Battery will not hold a charge

1 Alternator drivebelt defective or not adjusted properly (see Chapter 1 Section 12).
2 Battery electrolyte level low (see Chapter 1 Section 11).
3 Battery terminals loose or corroded (see Chapter 1 Section 11).
4 Alternator not charging properly (see Chapter 5 Section 2).
5 Loose, broken or faulty wiring in the charging circuit (Chapter 12A Section 2).
6 Defective battery (see Chapter 1 Section 11, Chapter 5 Section 5).

20 Alternator light fails to go out

1 Faulty alternator or charging circuit (see Chapter 5 Section 2).
2 Alternator drivebelt defective or out of adjustment (see Chapter 1 Section 12).
3 Alternator voltage regulator inoperative (see Chapter 5 Section 11).

21 Alternator light fails to come on when key is turned on

Fault in the instrument cluster, dash wiring or bulb holder (see Chapter 12A Section 9).

Fuel system

22 Excessive fuel consumption

1 Dirty or clogged air filter element (see Chapter 1 Section 21).
2 Emissions/engine control system not functioning properly (see Chapter 6 Section 1).
3 Fuel injection system not functioning properly (see Chapter 4A or Chapter 4B).
4 Low tyre pressure or incorrect tyre size (see Chapter 1 Section 7).

23 Fuel leakage and/or fuel odor

1 Leaking fuel feed or return line (see Chapter 1 Section 13 or Chapter 4A Section 5).
2 Tank overfilled.
3 Problem with fuel injection system (see Chapter 4A or Chapter 4B).

Cooling system

24 Overheating

1 Insufficient coolant in system (see Chapter 1 Section 4).
2 Drivebelt defective or out of adjustment (see Chapter 1 Section 12).
3 Radiator core blocked or grille restricted (see Chapter 3 Section 6).
4 Thermostat or water control valve faulty (see Chapter 3 Section 4).
5 Electric coolant fan inoperative or blades broken (see Chapter 3 Section 5).
6 Radiator cap not maintaining proper pressure (see Chapter 3 Section 2).

25 Overcooling

Faulty thermostat or water control valve (see Chapter 3 Section 4).

26 External coolant leakage

1 Deteriorated/damaged hoses; loose clamps (see Chapter 1 Section 13 and 14 or Chapter 3).

Troubleshooting 0-21

2 Water pump defective (see Chapter 3 Section 7).
3 Leakage from radiator core or coolant reservoir bottle (see Chapter 3 Section 6).
4 Engine drain or water jacket welch plugs leaking (see Chapter 3 Section 12).

27 Internal coolant leakage

1 Leaking cylinder head gasket (see Chapter 2A Section 10, Chapter 2B Section 11 or Chapter 2C Section 13).
2 Cracked cylinder bore or cylinder head (see Chapter 2A Section 10, Chapter 2B Section 11 or Chapter 2C Section 13).

28 Coolant loss

1 Too much coolant in system (see Chapter 1 Section 4).
2 Coolant boiling away because of overheating (see Chapter 3 Section 2).
3 Internal or external leakage (see Chapter 3 Section 2).
4 Faulty radiator cap (see Chapter 3 Section 2).

29 Poor coolant circulation

1 Inoperative water pump (see Chapter 3 Section 7).
2 Restriction in cooling system (see Chapter 3 Section 2).
3 Water pump drivebelt defective/out of adjustment (see Chapter 1 Section 12).
4 Thermostat or water control valve sticking (see Chapter 3 Section 4).

Automatic transaxle

30 Fluid leakage

1 On most models, automatic transaxle fluid is a deep red color. On CVT models it is a light green color. Fluid leaks should not be confused with engine oil, which can easily be blown onto the transaxle by air flow.
2 To pinpoint a leak, first remove all built-up dirt and grime from the transaxle housing with degreasing agents and/or steam cleaning. Then drive the vehicle at low speeds so air flow will not blow the leak far from its source. Raise the vehicle and determine where the leak is coming from. Common areas of leakage are:
  a Pan
  b Dipstick tube
  c Transaxle oil lines
  d Driveshaft oil seals (see Chapter 8 Section 7)

31 Transaxle fluid brown or has a burned smell

Transaxle fluid overheated (see Chapter 1 Section 8).

32 General shift mechanism problems

1 Chapter 7B deals with checking and adjusting the shift cable on automatic transaxles. Common problems which may be attributed to a poorly adjusted cable are:
  a Engine starting in gears other than Park or Neutral
  b Indicator on shifter pointing to a gear other than the one actually being used
  c Vehicle moves when in Park
2 Refer to Chapter 7B for the shift cable adjustment procedure.

33 Transaxle will not downshift with accelerator pedal pressed to the floor

The transaxle is electronically controlled. This type of problem - which is caused by a malfunction in the control unit, a sensor or solenoid, or the circuit itself - is beyond the scope of this book. Take the vehicle to a dealer service department or a competent automatic transmission shop.

34 Engine will start in gears other than Park or Neutral

Neutral start switch out of adjustment or malfunctioning (see Chapter 6 Section 13).

35 Transaxle slips, is noisy or has no drive in forward or reverse gears

There are many probable causes for the above problems, but the home mechanic should be concerned with only one possibility - fluid level. Before taking the vehicle to a repair shop, check the level and condition of the fluid as described in Chapter 1. Correct the fluid level as necessary or change the fluid if needed. If the problem persists, have a professional diagnose the cause.

Driveshafts

36 Clicking noise in turns

Worn or damaged outboard CV joint (see Chapter 8 Section 7).

37 Shudder or vibration during acceleration

1 Excessive toe-in (see Chapter 10 Section 20).
2 Worn or damaged inboard or outboard CV joints (see Chapter 8 Section 7).
3 Sticking inboard CV joint assembly (see Chapter 8 Section 7).

38 Vibration at highway speeds

1 Out of balance front wheels and/or tyres.
2 Out of round front tyres.
3 Worn CV joint(s) (Chapter).

Brakes

39 Vehicle pulls to one side during braking

1 Incorrect tyre pressures (see Chapter 1 Section 7).
2 Front end out of alignment (have the front end aligned).
3 Front, or rear, tyre sizes not matched to one another.
4 Restricted brake lines or hoses (see Chapter 9 Section 10).
5 Malfunctioning caliper assembly (see Chapter 9 Section 7 - front, or Chapter 9 Section 8 - rear).
6 Loose suspension parts (Chapter 1 Section 23).
7 Excessive wear of brake pad material or disc on one side.

40 Noise (high-pitched squeal when the brakes are applied)

Front and/or rear disc brake pads/rear shoes worn out. Replace pads or shoes with new ones immediately (see Chapter 9 Section 3 - front, or Chapter 9 Section 4 - rear).

41 Brake roughness or chatter (pedal pulsates)

1 Excessive lateral runout (see Section).
2 Uneven pad wear (see Section).
3 Defective brake disc (see Chapter 9 Section 5).

42 Excessive brake pedal effort required to stop vehicle

1 Malfunctioning power brake booster (see Chapter 9 Section 12).
2 Partial system failure (see Section).
3 Excessively worn pads (see Chapter 9 Section 3 or Chapter 9 Section 4).

4 Piston in caliper stuck or sluggish (see Chapter 9 Section 7 or Chapter 9 Section 8).
5 Brake pads contaminated with brake fluid, oil or grease (see Section).
6 Brake disc or drum grooved and/or glazed (see Chapter 9 Section 5).
7 New pads installed and not yet seated. It will take a while for the new material to seat against the disc.

43 Excessive brake pedal travel

1 Partial brake system failure (see Section).
2 Insufficient fluid in master cylinder (see Chapter 1 Section 4).
3 Air trapped in system. Bleed the brakes (see Chapter 9 Section 11).

49 Dragging brakes

1 Caliper pistons not returning correctly (see Chapter 9 Section 7 or Chapter 9 Section 8).
2 Restricted brakes lines or hoses (see Chapter 9 Section 10).
3 Incorrect parking brake adjustment (see Chapter 9 Section 13).

50 Grabbing or uneven braking action

Contaminated brake linings (see Section).

51 Brake pedal feels spongy when depressed

1 Air in hydraulic lines. Bleed the system (Chapter 9 Section 11).
2 Master cylinder defective (see Chapter 9 Section 9).

52 Brake pedal travels to the floor with little resistance

1 Leak in the brake system (see Section).
2 Loose or damaged brake lines (see Chapter 9 Section 10).

53 Parking brake does not hold

Parking brake improperly adjusted (see Chapter 9 Section 13).

Suspension and steering systems

54 Vehicle pulls to one side

1 Mismatched or uneven tyres.
2 Broken or sagging springs (see Chapter 10 Section 10).
3 Wheel alignment out of specifications (see Chapter 10 Section 20).
4 Front brake dragging (see Section).

55 Abnormal or excessive tyre wear

1 Wheel alignment out of specifications (see Chapter 10 Section 20).
2 Sagging or broken springs (see Chapter 10 Section 3 or Chapter 10 Section 10).
3 Tyre out of balance.
4 Worn strut damper (see Chapter 10 Section 3).
5 Overloaded vehicle.
6 Tyres not rotated regularly.

56 Wheel makes a thumping noise

1 Blister or bump on tyre.
2 Improper strut damper action (see Chapter 10 Section 3).

57 Shimmy, shake or vibration

1 Tyre or wheel out of balance or out of round.
2 Worn wheel bearings (see Chapter 10 Section 8)
3 Worn tie-rod ends (see Chapter 10 Section 15).
4 Worn balljoints (see Chapter 10 Section 6).
5 Excessive wheel runout.
6 Blister or bump on tyre.

58 Hard steering

1 Lack of lubrication at balljoints or tie-rod ends (see Chapter 10 Section 6 or Chapter 10 Section 15).
2 Front wheel alignment out of specifications (see Chapter 10 Section 20).
3 Low tyre pressure(s) (see Chapter 1 Section 7).

59 Poor returnability of steering to centre

1 Worn balljoints or tie-rod ends (see Chapter 10 Section 6 or Chapter 10 Section 15).

2 Binding in balljoints (see Chapter 10 Section 6).
3 Binding in steering column (see Chapter 10 Section 13).
4 Worn steering gear assembly (see Chapter 10 Section 17).
5 Front wheel alignment out of specifications (see Chapter 10 Section 20).

60 Abnormal noise at the front end

1 Worn balljoints or tie-rod ends (see Chapter 10 Section 6 or Chapter 10 Section 15).
2 Damaged strut mounting (see Chapter 10 Section 3).
3 Worn control arm bushings or tie-rod ends (see Chapter 10 Section 5 or Chapter 10 Section 15).
4 Loose stabiliser bar (see Chapter 10 Section 4).
5 Loose wheel nuts.
6 Loose suspension bolts (see Chapter 10).

61 Wander or poor steering stability

1 Mismatched or uneven tyres.
2 Worn balljoints or tie-rod ends (see Chapter 10 Section 6 or Chapter 10 Section 15).
3 Worn strut assemblies (see Chapter 10 Section 2 or Chapter 10 Section 9).
4 Loose stabiliser bar (see Chapter 10 Section 4).
5 Broken or sagging springs (see Chapter 10 Section 10).
6 Wheels out of alignment (see Chapter 10 Section 20).

62 Erratic steering when braking

1 Wheel bearings worn (see Chapter 10 Section 8).
2 Broken or sagging springs (see Chapter 10).
3 Leaking caliper (see Chapter 9 Section 7).
4 Warped brake discs (see Chapter 9).

63 Excessive pitching and/or rolling around corners or during braking

1 Loose stabiliser bar (see Chapter 10 Section 4).
2 Worn strut dampers or mountings (see Chapter 10).
3 Broken or sagging springs (see Chapter 10).
4 Overloaded vehicle.

Troubleshooting

64 Suspension bottoms

1 Overloaded vehicle.
2 Worn strut dampers or springs (see Chapter 10).

65 Cupped tyres

1 Front wheel or rear wheel alignment out of specifications.
2 Worn strut dampers (see Chapter 10 Section 3).
3 Wheel bearings worn (see Chapter 10 Section 8).
4 Excessive tyre or wheel runout.
5 Worn balljoints (see Chapter 10 Section 6).

66 Excessive tyre wear on outside edge

1 Inflation pressures incorrect (see Chapter 1 Section 7).
2 Excessive speed in turns.
3 Front end alignment incorrect (excessive toe-in). Have professionally aligned.
4 Suspension arm bent (see Chapter 10 Section 5).

67 Excessive tyre wear on inside edge

1 Inflation pressures incorrect (see Chapter 1 Section 7).
2 Front end alignment incorrect (toe-out). Have professionally aligned.
3 Loose or damaged steering components (see Chapter 10).

68 Tyre tread worn in one place

1 Tyres out of balance.
2 Damaged wheel.
3 Defective tyre (see Chapter 10 Section 19).

69 Excessive play or looseness in steering system

1 Wheel bearing(s) worn (see Chapter 10).
2 Tie-rod end loose (see Chapter 10 Section 15).
3 Steering gear loose (see Chapter 10 Section 17).
4 Worn or loose steering intermediate shaft (see Chapter 10 Section 17).

70 Rattling or clicking noise in steering gear

1 Steering gear loose (see Chapter 10 Section 17).
2 Steering gear defective.

Notes

Chapter 1
Tune-up and routine maintenance

Contents

	Section		Section
Air filter check and replacement	21	Fuel filter water draining - diesel models	5
Automatic and continuously variable transaxle (CVT) fluid change	30	Fuel system check	22
		Introduction	2
Automatic transaxle fluid level check	8	Maintenance schedule	1
Battery check, maintenance and charging	11	Manual transaxle lubricant change	29
Brake check	19	Manual transaxle lubricant level check	17
Cabin air filter replacement	20	Positive Crankcase Ventilation (PCV) valve check and replacement	31
Cooling system check	14		
Cooling system servicing (draining, flushing and refilling)	27	Spark plug check and replacement	26
Differential lubricant change (AWD models)	32	Steering and suspension check	23
Differential lubricant level check (AWD models)	16	Transfer case lubricant change (AWD models)	33
Drivebelt check and replacement	12	Transfer case lubricant level check (AWD models)	18
Driveshaft boot check	25	Tune-up general information	3
Engine oil and oil filter change	9	Tyre and tyre pressure checks	7
Evaporative emissions control system check	28	Tyre rotation	15
Exhaust system check	24	Underbonnet hose check and replacement	13
Fluid level checks (every 400 km or weekly)	4	Valve clearance check and adjustment	34
Fuel filter replacement - diesel models	6	Windshield wiper blade inspection and replacement	10

Specifications

Recommended lubricants and fluids

Note: *Listed here are manufacturer recommendations at the time this manual was written. Manufacturers occasionally upgrade their fluid and lubricant specifications, so check with your local auto parts store for current recommendations.*

Engine oil
    X-Trail
        T31 models
            Petrol engine
                Type .... API grade SL/SM or ILSAC GF-4
                Viscosity 5W-30
            Diesel engine
                Type .... ACEA Grade C3
                Viscosity 5W-30
        T32 models
            Petrol engine
                Type .... API grade SM/SN or ILSAC GF-4/GF-5
                Viscosity 5W-30
    Dualis
        Type .... API grade SL/SM or ILSAC GF-3/GF-4
        Viscosity 5W-30
    Qashqai
        Type .... ACEA A3/B4
        Viscosity 5W-30

Chapter 1 Tune-up and routine maintenance

Automatic transaxle fluid
   With continuously variable transaxle (CVT)
      X-Trail
         T31 petrol models.. Nissan CVT fluid NS-2
         T32 models.. Nissan CVT fluid NS-3
      Dualis.. Nissan CVT fluid NS-2 or NS-3
      Qashqai... Nissan CVT fluid NS-3
   With 6 speed automatic transaxle
      X-Trail T31 diesel models .... Nissan Matic J ATF
Manual transaxle fluid
   X-Trail
      T31 models
         2.0 petrol engine.. Nissan manual transaxle fluid (MTF) (XT4447M+) 75W-80 API GL4
         2.5 litre petrol & diesel engine .... Nissan manual transaxle fluid (MTF) HQ Multi 75W-85 or
            API GL-4,Viscosity SAE 75W-85
         Diesel engine... Nissan manual transaxle fluid (MTF) HQ multi 75W-85
      T32 models
         2.0 litre petrol engine.. Nissan manual transaxle fluid (MTF) (ETL8997B) 75W-80
            or SAE 75W-80 GL4
   Dualis
      2WD models .... Nissan MT-XZ gear oil TL/JR type or SAE 75W-80 GL4
      AWD models .... Nissan MT-XZ gear oil Sports + off-road vehicles or SAE 75W-85 GL4
   Qashqai .... Nissan MT-XZ gear oil TL/JR type or SAE 75W-80 GL4
Rear differential (AWD models)... API GL-5 80W-90 hypoid gear oil
Transfer case (AWD models) .... API GL-5 80W-90 hypoid gear oil
Brake and clutch fluid
   T31 X-Trail, Dualis .... DOT 3 brake fluid
   T32 X-Trail, Qashqai .... DOT 4 brake fluid
Engine coolant
   X-Trail
      T31 models .... Nissan Long Life antifreeze/coolant
      T32 models .... Nissan Long Life antifreeze/coolant (blue)
   Dualis... Nissan engine coolant
   Qashqai .... Nissan engine coolant

Capacities*

Engine oil (including filter)
   X-Trail models
      2.0 litre petrol
         T31 .... 4.4 litres
         T32 .... 3.8 litres
      2.5 litre petrol .... 4.6 litres
      Diesel .... 7.4 litres
   Dualis... 4.4 litres
   Qashqai .... 3.8 litres
Coolant (including reservoir tank)
   T31 X-Trail models
      2.0 litre petrol
         Manual transaxle .... 7.1 litres
         CVT .... 7.4 litres
      2.5 litre petrol
         Manual transaxle .... 6.8 litres
         CVT .... 7.1 litres
      2.0 litre diesel
         Manual transaxle .... 8.4 litres
         CVT .... 8.9 litres
   T32 X-Trail models
      2.0 litre petrol
         Manual transaxle .... 8.5 litres
         CVT .... 8.7 litres
      2.5 litre petrol .... 8.2 litres
   Dualis models
      Manual transaxle .... 7.0 litres
      CVT .... 7.4 litres
   Qaushqai models
      Manual transaxle .... 7.1 litres
      CVT .... 7.4 litres
Automatic transaxle .... 7.5 litres

Chapter 1 Tune-up and routine maintenance

CVT
  T31 X-Trail models
    Two-wheel drive models .... 8.3 litres
    Four-wheel drive models .... 9.5 litres
  T32 X-Trail models .... 7.9 litres
Manual transaxle .... 2.0 litres
Rear differential (AWD models) .... 0.55 litres
Transfer case (AWD models) .... 0.38 litres

Note: *All capacities approximate. Add as necessary to bring up to appropriate level.*

Tune-up information

Spark plugs
  Type
    X-Trail
      T31 models
        2.0 litre engine .... NGK LZKAR6AP-11
        2.5 litre engine .... NGK DILKAR6A-11
      T32 models
        2.0 litre engine .... NGK DILKAR7D11H
        2.5 litre engine .... NGK DENSO FXE20HE11C
    Dualis .... NGK PLZKAR6A-11
    Qashqai .... NGK PLZKAR6A-11
  Gap .... 1.1 mm
Firing order 1-3-4-2

Cylinder locations

Idle speed
  X-Trail
    T31 models
      Petrol
        2.0 litre petrol .... 675 to 725 rpm
        2.5 litre petrol .... 650 to 700 rpm
      Diesel .... 750 rpm
    T32 models
      Petrol
        Manual transaxle .... 650 to 700 rpm
        CVT .... 600 to 700 rpm
      Diesel .... 750 rpm
  Dualis .... 650 to 750 rpm
  Qashqai
    Manual transaxle .... 550 to 650 rpm
    CVT .... 600 to 700 rpm
Valve clearance (engine cold)
  2.5 litre petrol engine
    Intake valves .... 0.24 to 0.32 mm
    Exhaust valves .... 0.26 to 0.34 mm
  2.0 litre petrol engine
    MR20DE
      Intake valves .... 0.26 to 0.34 mm
      Exhaust valves .... 0.29 to 0.37 mm
    MR20DD
      Intake valves .... 0.24 to 0.32 mm
      Exhaust valves .... 0.26 to 0.34 mm
  Diesel engine
    Intake valves .... 0.015 to 0.048 mm
    Exhaust valves .... 0.030 to 0.063 mm

Brakes

Disc brake lining thickness (minimum)
  Front pad .... 2.0 mm
  Rear pad .... 1.5 mm
Brake pedal adjustment .... See Chapter 9
Parking brake adjustment .... See Chapter 9

Suspension and steering

Steering wheel freeplay limit .... 0 to 35 mm
Balljoint allowable movement .... 0 mm

Chapter 1 Tune-up and routine maintenance

Torque specifications — Nm

Automatic transaxle - diesel models
- Drain plug 7
- Level tube 8

CVT drain plug - petrol models 34
Differential drain/fill plugs 35
Drivebelt tensioner bolt(s)
- Petrol engines
  - 2.0 litre 40
  - 2.5 litre 30
- Diesel engine 25

Engine oil drain plug
- Petrol engines 35
- Diesel engine 45

Engine oil filter cap - diesel models 25
Manual transaxle filler and drain plugs
- Two-wheel-drive models
  - Drain plug 23
  - Filler/level check plug .... Finger tight
- Four-wheel-drive models 35

Spark plugs 20
Transfer case drain/fill plugs 35
Wheel nuts 113

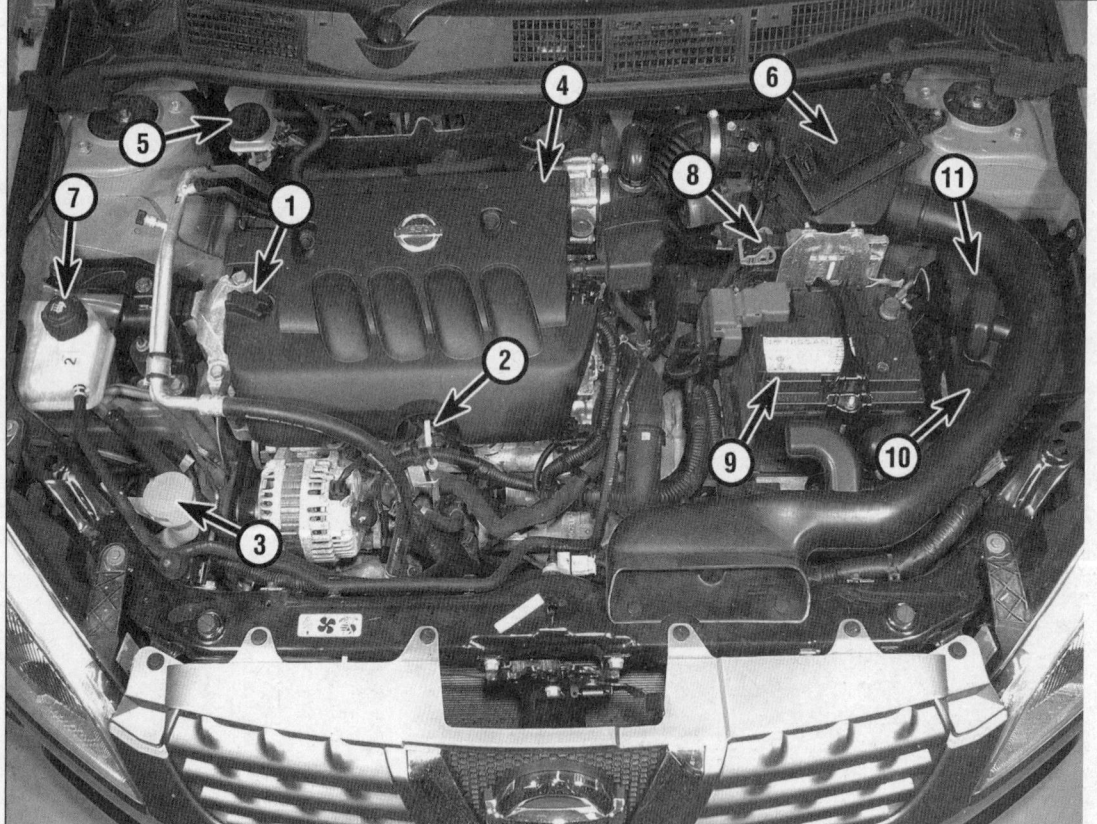

1 Engine oil filler cap
2 Engine oil dipstick
3 Windshield washer fluid reservoir
4 EGR valve
5 Brake/clutch fluid reservoir
6 Air filter element
7 Coolant expansion tank
8 Engine management control module (ECM)
9 Battery
10 Relay/fusebox
11 Intelligent Power Distribution Module (IPDM)

2.2a Dualis 2.0L petrol engine compartment components

Chapter 1 Tune-up and routine maintenance

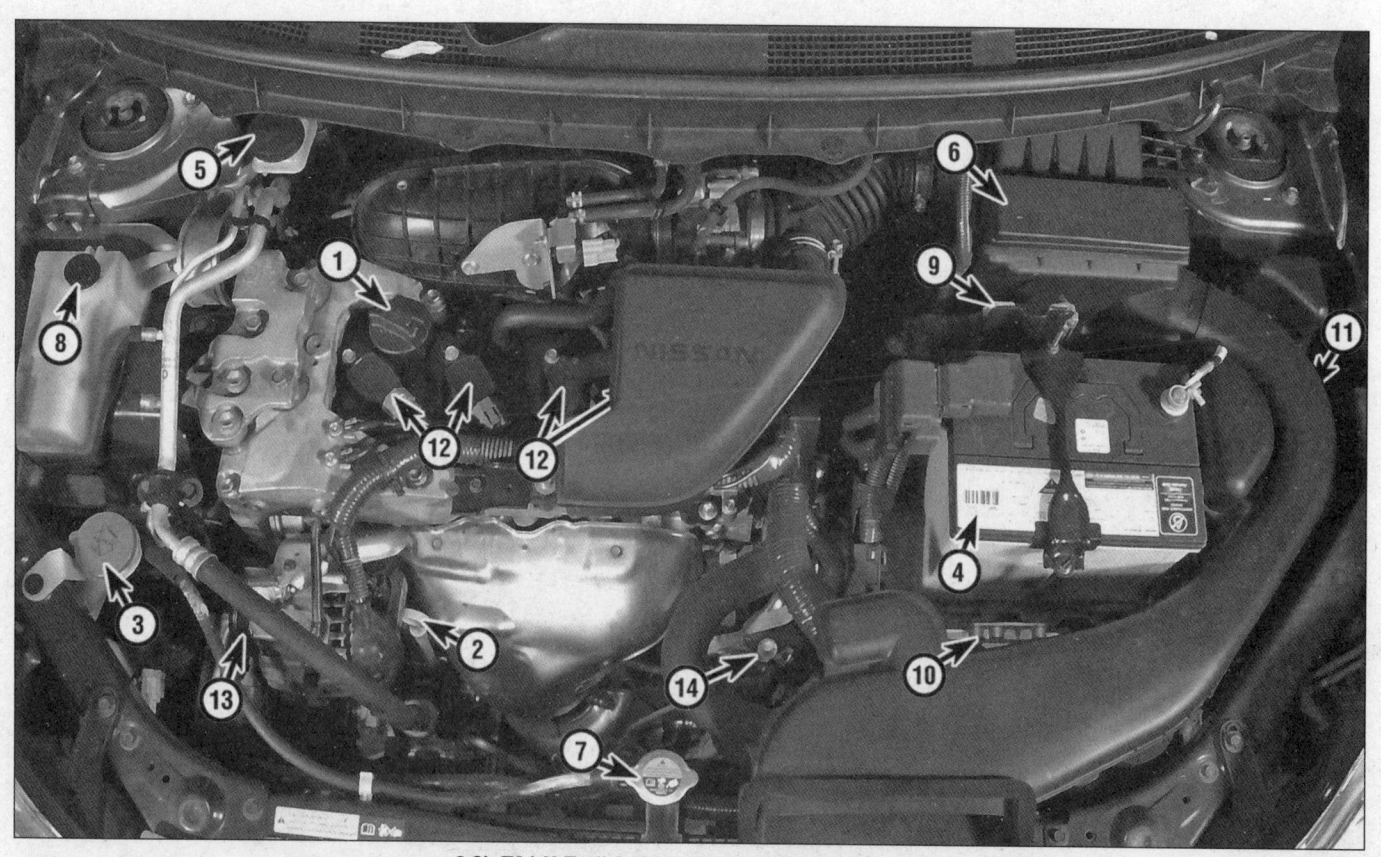

2.2b T31 X-Trail 2.5L petrol engine compartment

1. Engine oil filler cap
2. Engine oil dipstick
3. Windshield washer fluid reservoir
4. Battery
5. Brake/clutch fluid reservoir
6. Air filter element
7. Radiator pressure cap
8. Coolant expansion tank
9. Engine control module (ECM)
10. Transaxle control module (TCM)
11. Engine compartment fuse and relay boxes
12. Ignition coils
13. Drive belt
14. Continuously variable transaxle (CVT) dipstick

2.2c T32 X-Trail 2.5L petrol engine compartment

1 Engine oil filler cap
2 Engine oil dipstick
3 Windshield washer fluid reservoir
4 Battery
5 Brake/clutch fluid reservoir
6 Air filter element
7 Radiator pressure cap
8 Coolant expansion tank
9 Engine control module (ECM)
10 Transaxle control module (TCM)
11 Engine compartment fuse and relay box No.1
12 Engine compartment fuse and relay box No.2
13 Engine compartment fuse and relay box No.3
14 Continuously variable transaxle (CVT) dipstick
15 Drivebelt

Chapter 1 Tune-up and routine maintenance

2.2d J11 Qashqai engine compartment

1 Engine oil filler cap and dipstick
2 Engine oil dipstick
3 Windshield washer fluid reservoir
4 Battery
5 Brake/clutch fluid reservoir
6 Air filter element
7 Coolant expansion tank
8 Engine control module (ECM)
9 Transaxle control module (TCM)
10 Continuously variable transaxle (CVT) dipstick
11 Drivebelt

Chapter 1 Tune-up and routine maintenance

2.2e T31 X-Trail 2.0L diesel engine compartment

1. Engine oil filler cap and dipstick
2. Radiator pressure cap
3. Radiator expansion tank
4. Windshield washer fluid reservoir
5. Brake/clutch master cylinder reservoir
6. Battery
7. Air filter element
8. Fuel filter
9. Fuel filter prime pump
10. Engine compartment fuse and relay box
11. Engine control module (ECM)

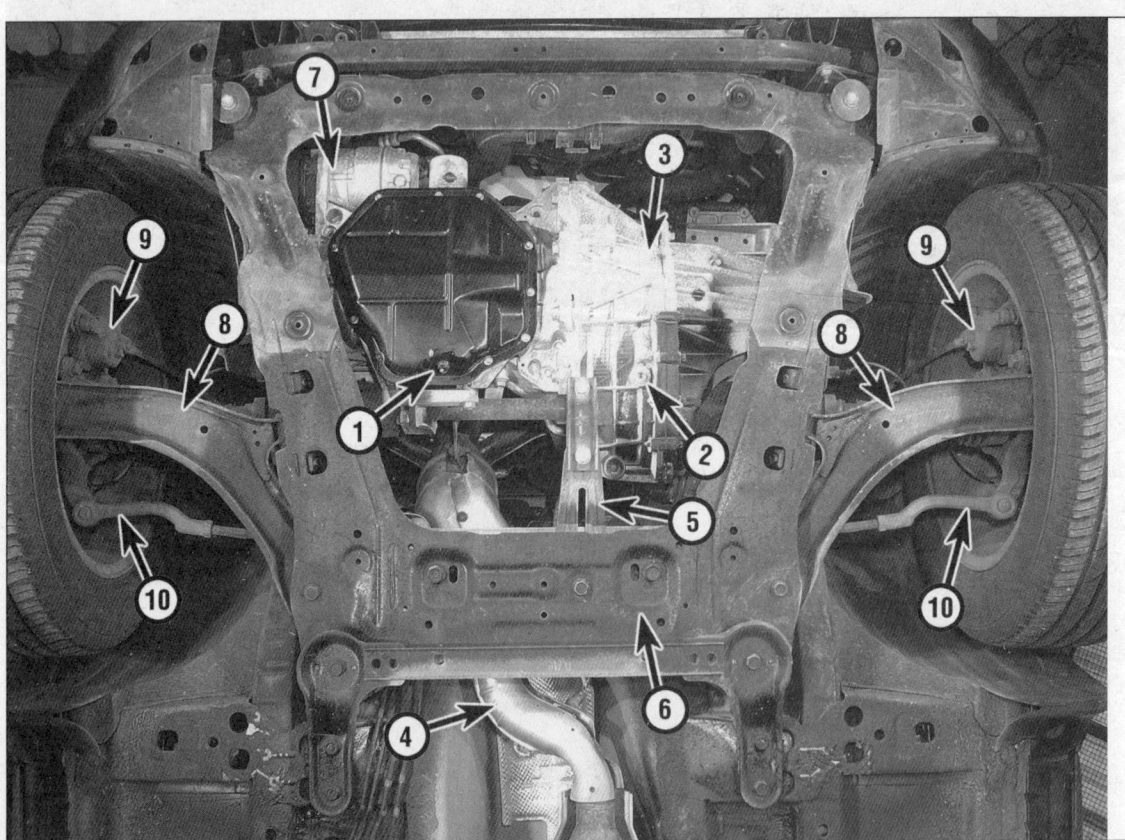

2.2f Typical engine compartment underside components

1. Engine oil drain plug
2. Transaxle drain plug
3. Transaxle
4. Exhaust front pipe
5. Rear engine steady bar
6. Subframe
7. A/C compressor
8. Lower control arm
9. Brake calipers
10. Tie rod ends

Chapter 1 Tune-up and routine maintenance

2.2g Typical rear underside components

1 Fuel tank
2 Handbrake cables
3 Rear axle assembly
4 Coil springs
5 Exhaust rear muffler and tailpipe
6 Stabiliser bar
7 Shock absorbers
8 Lower suspension arms
9 Rear trailing arms

1 Maintenance schedule

The maintenance intervals in this manual are provided with the assumption that you, not the dealer, will be doing the work. These are the minimum maintenance intervals recommended by the factory for vehicles that are driven daily. If you wish to keep your vehicle in peak condition at all times, you may wish to perform some of these procedures even more often. Because frequent maintenance enhances the efficiency, performance and resale value of your car, we encourage you to do so. If you drive in dusty areas, tow a trailer, idle or drive at low speeds for extended periods or drive for short distances (less than 10 kilometres) in below freezing temperatures, shorter intervals are also recommended.

When your vehicle is new, it should be serviced by a factory authorized dealer service department to protect the factory warranty. In many cases, the initial maintenance check is done at no cost to the owner.

Every 400 km or weekly, whichever comes first

Check the engine oil level (Section 4)
Check the engine coolant level (Section 4)
Check the windshield washer fluid level (Section 4)
Check the battery electrolyte (Section 4)
Check the brake fluid level (Section 4)
Check the clutch fluid level - M/T models (Section 4)
Check the tyres and tyre pressures (Section 7)

Every 5,000 km or 3 months, whichever comes first

Note: *All items above plus:*
Change the engine oil and oil filter (diesel models) (Section 9)
Inspect the air filter element (diesel models) (Section 21); if lightly dusty, the filter can be cleaned with compressed air or if heavily contaminated, replace the filter

Every 10,000 km or 6 months, whichever comes first

Note: *All items above plus:*
Change the engine oil and oil filter (petrol models) (Section 9)
Check the automatic transaxle fluid level (Section 8)
Inspect the air filter element (petrol models) (Section 21); if lightly dusty, the filter can be cleaned with compressed air or if heavily contaminated, replace the filter
Inspect the windshield wiper blades (Section 10)
Check and service the battery (Section 11)
Check the engine drivebelt (Section 12)
Inspect all under bonnet hoses (Section 13)
Check the cooling system (Section 14)
Inspect the brake system (Section 19)*
Inspect the exhaust system (Section 24)
Inspect the rear differential oil (AWD models) (Section 16)
Inspect the transfer case oil level (AWD models) (see Section 18)
Inspect the suspension and steering components (Section 23)
Rotate the tyres (Section 15)

Every 20,000 km or 12 months, whichever comes first

Note: *All items listed above plus:*
Check the manual transaxle oil level (Section 17)*
Replace the cabin air filter (Section 20)
Inspect the fuel system (Section 22)
Drain water from the fuel filter assembly (diesel models) (Section 5)
  - replace fuel filter if necessary (Section 6)
Check the driveshaft boots (Section 25)
Check the seat mounting fasteners for security and check the condition and operation of the seat belts

Every 40,000 km or 24 months, whichever comes first

Note: *All items listed above plus:*
Replace the air filter (Section 21)
Replace the fuel filter (diesel models) (Section 6)
Inspect the evaporative emissions control system (Section 28)
Replace the PCV filter (Section 31)
Replace the brake fluid every two years, regardless of distance, (Chapter 9 Section 11)
Change the automatic transaxle fluid (Section 30)**
Replace the rear differential oil (AWD models) (Section 32)

Every 80,000 km or 48 months, whichever comes first

Replace the coolant, initially at 160,000 km then every 80,000 km (Section 27)

Every 100,000 km or 60 months, whichever comes first

Replace the spark plugs (Section 26)

* If your vehicle is operated under "severe" conditions, perform all maintenance indicated with an asterisk (*) at half the indicated intervals. Severe conditions are indicated if you mainly operate your vehicle under one or more of the following conditions:

Operating in dusty areas
Towing a trailer
Idling for extended periods and/or low speed operation
Operating when outside temperatures remain below freezing and when most trips are less than 10 km

** If operated under one or more of the following conditions, change the manual or automatic transaxle fluid and differential lubricant every 50,000km

In heavy city traffic where the outside temperature regularly reaches 32-degrees C or higher
In hilly or mountainous terrain
Frequent trailer pulling

Chapter 1 Tune-up and routine maintenance 1-11

4.2 Engine oil dipstick location - petrol models

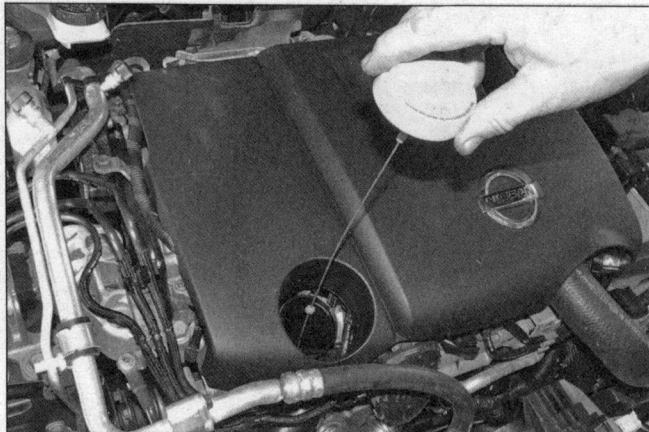

4.3 On diesel engines, the dipstick is inside the oil filler cap

2 Introduction

This Chapter is designed to help the home mechanic maintain their Nissan for peak performance, economy, safety and long life.

Included in this Chapter is a master maintenance schedule, followed by Sections dealing specifically with each item on the schedule. Visual checks, adjustments, component replacement and other helpful items are included. Refer to the accompanying illustrations of the engine compartment and the underside of the vehicle for the location of various components.

Servicing your Nissan in accordance with the maintenance schedule and following Sections will provide a planned maintenance program that should result in a long and reliable service life. This is a comprehensive plan, so maintaining some items but not others at the specified service intervals will not produce the same results.

As you service your vehicle you will discover that many of the procedures can, and should, be grouped together because of the nature of the particular procedure and the proximity of two otherwise unrelated components.

For example, if the vehicle is raised for any reason, you should inspect the exhaust, suspension, steering and fuel systems while you're under the vehicle. When you're rotating the tyres, it makes good sense to check the brakes and wheel bearings since the wheels are already removed.

Finally, let's suppose you have to borrow or rent a torque wrench. Even if you only need to tighten the spark plugs, you might as well check the torque of as many critical fasteners as time allows.

The first step of this maintenance program is to prepare yourself before the actual work begins. Read through all Sections pertinent to the procedures you're planning to do, then make a list of and gather together all the parts and tools you will need to do the job. If it looks as if you might run into problems during a particular segment of some procedure, seek advice from your local auto parts store.

3 Tune-up general information

The term tune-up is used in this manual to represent a combination of individual operations rather than one specific procedure.

If, from the time the vehicle is new, the routine maintenance schedule is followed closely and frequent checks are made of fluid levels and high wear items, as suggested throughout this manual, the engine will be kept in relatively good running condition and the need for additional work will be minimized.

More likely than not, however, there will be times when the engine is running poorly due to lack of regular maintenance. This is even more likely if a used vehicle, which has not received regular and frequent maintenance checks, is purchased. In such cases, an engine tune-up will be needed outside of the regular routine maintenance intervals.

The first step in any tune-up or engine diagnosis to help correct a poor running engine would be a cylinder compression check. A check of the cylinder compression (see Chapter 2D Section 3) will give valuable information regarding the overall performance of many internal components and should be used as a basis for tune-up and repair procedures. If, for instance, a compression check indicates serious internal engine wear, a conventional tune-up will not help the running condition of the engine and would be a waste of time and money.

The following series of operations are those most often needed to bring a generally poor running engine back into a proper state of tune.

Minor tune-up

a Check all engine related fluids (Section 4)
b Clean, inspect and test the battery (Section 11)
c Check the drivebelt (Section 12)
d Check all under bonnet hoses (Section 13)
e Check the cooling system (Section 14)
f Check the air filter (Section 21)
g Drain any water from the fuel filter (Section 22)

Major tune-up

Note: *All items listed under Minor tune-up, plus. . .*

a Replace the air filter (Section 21)
b Check the fuel system (Section 22)
c Replace the fuel filter - diesel models (Section 6)
d Replace the spark plugs (Section 26)
e Check the charging system (Chapter 5 Section 2)
f Check the ignition system (Chapter 5 Section 2)

4 Fluid level checks (every 400 km or weekly)

1 Fluids are an essential part of the lubrication, cooling, brake, clutch and other systems. Because these fluids gradually become depleted and/or contaminated during normal operation of the vehicle, they must be periodically replenished. See this Chapter's Specifications before adding fluid to any of the following components.

Note: *The vehicle must be on level ground before fluid levels can be checked.*

Engine oil

2 The engine oil level is checked with a dipstick located at the front of the engine **(see illustration)**.
3 On diesel models, the dipstick is inside the oil filler cap **(see illustration)**.
4 The oil level should be checked before the vehicle has been driven, or about 5 min-

Chapter 1 Tune-up and routine maintenance

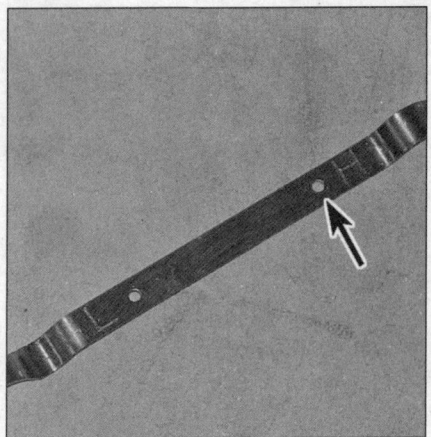

4.5 The oil level should be at or near the H mark - if it isn't, add enough oil to bring the level to near the H mark

4.7 Oil filler cap location

4.9a Location of the coolant reservoir; arrows indicate the Min and Max marks - T32 X-Trail shown, other models similar

utes after the engine has been shut off. If the oil is checked immediately after driving the vehicle, some of the oil will remain in the upper engine components, producing an inaccurate reading on the dipstick.

5 Pull the dipstick out and wipe all the oil from the end with a clean rag or paper towel. Insert the clean dipstick all the way back in and pull it out again. Observe the oil at the end of the dipstick; the level should be between the L and H marks **(see illustration)**.

6 It takes about one-half a litre of oil to raise the level from the L mark to the H mark on the dipstick. Do not allow the level to drop below the L mark or oil starvation may cause engine damage. Conversely, overfilling the engine (adding oil above the H mark) may cause oil fouled spark plugs, oil leaks or oil seal failures.

7 Wipe the area around the filler cap, then remove the cap from the valve cover to add oil **(see illustration)**. Use a funnel to prevent spills. After adding the oil, install the filler cap hand tight. Start the engine and look carefully for any small leaks around the oil filter or drain plug. Stop the engine and check the oil level again after it has had sufficient time to drain

from the upper block and cylinder head galleys.

8 Checking the oil level is an important preventive maintenance step. A continually dropping oil level indicates oil leakage through damaged seals, from loose connections, or past worn rings or valve guides. If the oil looks milky in color or has water droplets in it, a cylinder head gasket may be leaking. The cylinder head should be checked immediately. The condition of the oil should also be checked. Each time you check the oil level, slide your thumb and index finger up the dipstick before wiping off the oil. If you see small dirt or metal particles clinging to the dipstick, the oil should be changed (see Section 9).

Engine coolant

Warning: *Do not allow antifreeze to come in contact with your skin or painted surfaces of the vehicle. Flush contaminated areas immediately with plenty of water. Don't store new coolant or leave old coolant lying around where it's accessible to children or pets - they're attracted by its sweet smell and may drink it. Ingestion of even a small amount of coolant can be fatal! Wipe up garage floor and drip pan spills immediately. Keep antifreeze containers covered and repair cooling system leaks as soon as they're noticed.*

9 All vehicles covered by this manual are equipped with a pressurized coolant recovery system. A coolant reservoir located in the front of the engine compartment is connected by a hose to the base of the radiator cap **(see illustrations)**. If the coolant gets too hot during engine operation, coolant can escape through the relief valve in the radiator cap, then through a connecting hose into the reservoir. As the engine cools, the coolant is automatically drawn back into the cooling system to maintain the correct level.

10 The coolant level should be checked regularly. It must be between the Max and Min lines on the tank **(see illustration)**. The level will vary with the temperature of the engine. When the engine is cold, the coolant level should be at or slightly above the Min mark

on the tank. Once the engine has warmed up, the level should be at or near the Max mark. If it isn't, allow the fluid in the tank to cool, then remove the cap from the reservoir and add coolant to bring the level up to the Max line. Use only the specified type of coolant recommended by your owner's manual or in this Chapter's Specifications. Do not use supplemental inhibitor additives. If only a small amount of coolant is required to bring the system up to the proper level, water can be used. However, repeated additions of water will dilute the recommended antifreeze and water solution. In order to maintain the proper ratio of antifreeze and water, it is advisable to top up the coolant level with the correct mixture. Refer to your owner's manual for the recommended ratio.

11 If the coolant level drops within a short time after replenishment, there may be a leak in the system. Inspect the radiator, hoses, radiator cap, drain plugs and water pump. If no leak is evident, have the radiator cap pressure tested by your dealer.

Warning: *To prevent scalding, use caution when releasing the radiator cap if the engine*

4.9b On diesel models, the coolant reservoir has a pressure cap fitted

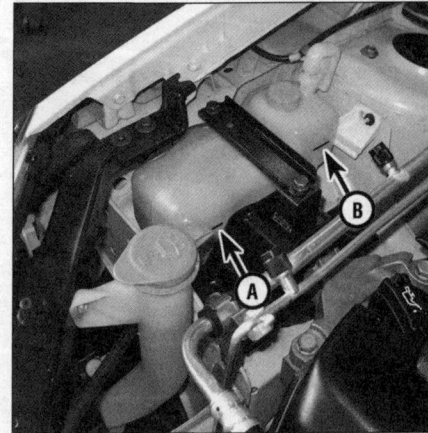

4.10 Coolant reservoir MIN (A) mark; add coolant to bring the level near the MAX (B) mark on the reservoir

Chapter 1 Tune-up and routine maintenance

4.15 Remove the cap to top up the windshield washer fluid reservoir

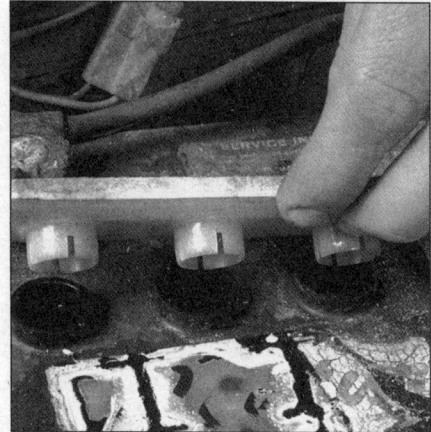

4.16 Remove the cell caps to check the water level in the battery - if the level is low, add distilled water only

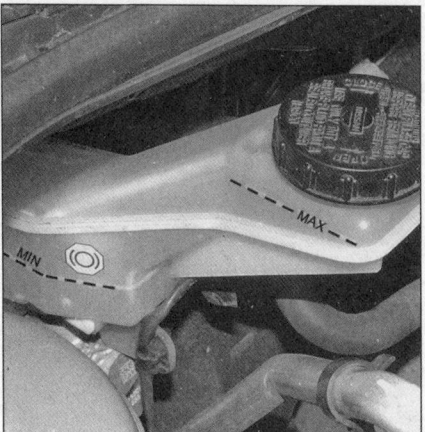

4.18a Ensure the fluid level is between the MAX and MIN marks on the reservoir - Dualis model shown

is warm. Squeeze the upper radiator hose. If resistance is felt, the system is pressurised and the cap should not be removed until the radiator hose can easily be squeezed together. Escaping steam and scalding liquid could cause serious injury.

Note: *If the engine has overheated allow, the engine to cool for at least 30 minutes and fill the system with coolant while the engine is running to avoid cracking the cylinder heads or block.*

12 If it is necessary to open the radiator cap, wait until the system has cooled completely, then wrap a thick cloth around the cap and slowly unscrew it. If any steam escapes, wait until the system has cooled further, then remove the cap.

13 When checking the coolant level, always note its condition. It should be relatively clear. If it is brown or rust colored, the system should be drained, flushed and refilled. Even if the coolant appears to be normal, the corrosion inhibitors wear out with use, so it must be replaced at the specified intervals.

14 Do not allow antifreeze to come in contact with your skin or painted surfaces of the vehicle. Flush contacted areas immediately with plenty of water.

Windshield washer fluid

15 Fluid for the windshield washer system is stored in a plastic reservoir which is located on the right side of the engine compartment just behind the headlight **(see illustration)**. In milder climates, plain water can be used to top up the reservoir, but the reservoir should be kept no more than two-thirds full to allow for expansion should the water freeze. In colder climates, the use of a specially designed windshield washer fluid, available at your dealer and any auto parts store, will help lower the freezing point of the fluid. Mix the solution with water in accordance with the manufacturer's directions on the container. Do not use regular antifreeze. It will damage the vehicle's paint.

Battery electrolyte

16 On models not equipped with a sealed battery, check the electrolyte level **(see illus-**

tration) of all six battery cells. It must be between the upper and lower levels. If the level is low, remove the filler/vent cap and add distilled water. Install and securely re-tighten the cap.

Caution: *Overfilling the cells may cause electrolyte to spill over during periods of heavy charging, causing corrosion or damage.*

Brake fluid

17 The brake master cylinder is mounted on the front of the brake booster unit in the engine compartment. On manual transaxle models, the brake master cylinder and clutch master cylinder share the fluid reservoir. A hose between the reservoir and the clutch master cylinder supplies fluid to the clutch system.

18 To check the fluid level of the brake master cylinder, simply look at the marks on the reservoir **(see illustrations)**. The level should be between the MIN and MAX marks.

19 If the level is low, wipe the top of the reservoir **(see illustration)** and the cap with

4.18b The brake fluid level should be kept between the MAX (1) and MIN (2) marks on the translucent plastic reservoir - T32 X-Trail model shown

4.19a Wipe the top of the reservoir and cap with a clean rag…

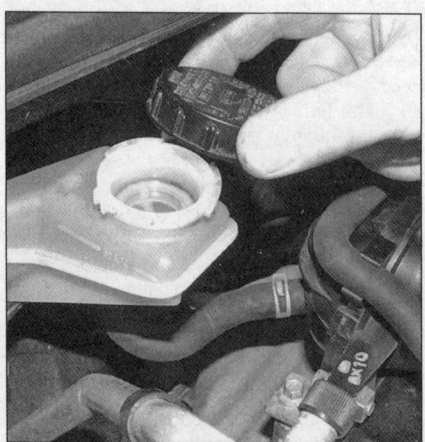

4.19b … before removing the cap

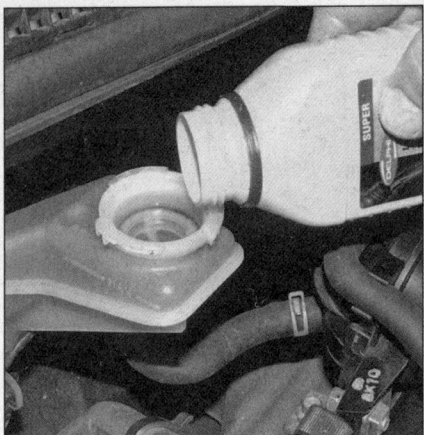

4.20 Topping up the brake fluid with new brake fluid

5.1 Water drain screw (arrow) fitted to base of filter

5.3 Hand priming pump location (arrow)

a clean rag to prevent contamination of the brake system before unscrewing the cover **(see illustration)**.

20 Add only the specified brake fluid to the brake reservoir (refer to Recommended lubricants and fluids in this Chapter's Specifications or your owner's manual) **(see illustration)**. Mixing different types of brake fluid can damage the system. Fill the brake master cylinder reservoir only to the MAX line.

Warning: *Use caution when filling the reservoir - brake fluid can harm your eyes and damage painted surfaces. Do not use brake fluid that is more than one year old or has been left open. Brake fluid absorbs moisture from the air. Excess moisture can cause a dangerous loss of braking.*

21 While the reservoir cap is removed, inspect the master cylinder reservoir for contamination. If deposits, dirt particles or water droplets are present, the system should be drained and refilled.

Note: *If the brake system is being flushed of old brake fluid, also flush the clutch system (Chapter 8 Section 2).*

22 After filling the reservoir to the proper level, make sure the cap is properly seated to prevent fluid leakage and/or system pressure loss.

23 The fluid in the brake master cylinder will drop slightly as the brake pads at each wheel wear down during normal operation. If the master cylinder requires repeated replenishing to keep it at the proper level, this is an indication of leakage in the brake system, which should be corrected immediately. If the brake system shows an indication of leakage, check all brake lines and connections, along with the calipers and booster (see Section 19 for more information).

24 If, upon checking the brake master cylinder fluid level, you discover the reservoir empty or nearly empty, the system should be bled. Check the brake and clutch system, on manual transaxle models, for the source of the fluid leakage.

5 Fuel filter water draining - diesel models

1 On most models a water drain screw is provided on the base of the fuel filter **(see illustration)**.

2 Place a suitable container beneath the drain screw. To make draining easier, a suitable length of tubing can be attached to the outlet pipe at the centre of the screw to direct the fuel flow – on some models a drain tube is provided as standard.

Note: *If desired, access can be improved by unscrewing the nuts securing the filter head bracket to the body and by raising the complete filter assembly to a more convenient position – if this is done, take care not to strain the fuel hoses and electrical wiring.*

3 Open the drain screw by turning it anticlockwise, operate the hand priming pump a couple of times to allow the fuel to flow through the filter **(see illustration)**.

4 Allow the entire contents of the filter to drain into the container, and then securely tighten the drain screw.

5 Prime and bleed the fuel system (see Chapter 4B Section 3).

6 Fuel filter replacement - diesel models

Caution: *Do not allow dirt to enter the fuel system during this procedure.*

1 The contents of the fuel filter can be drained (see Section 5). Place a piece of clean cloth around the fuel filter to soak up any spilt fuel, as the fuel lines are disconnected.

2 Where applicable, disconnect the fuel heater wiring connector from the top of the filter housing.

3 Release the retaining clips and disconnect the fuel lines from the priming bulb to the fuel filter housing **(see illustrations)**. Unclip

the priming bulb from the inner wing panel and move it to one side. Take care not to damage the fuel lines as they are removed; cover the ends of the fuel lines to prevent any dirt ingress.

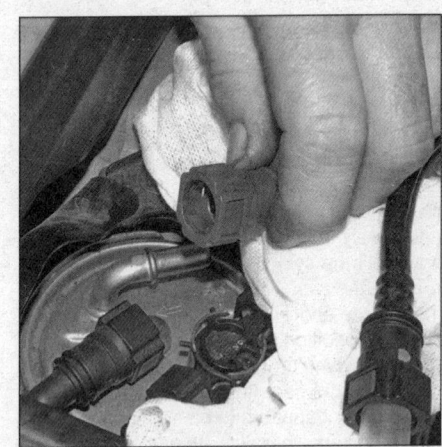

6.3a Disconnect the fuel lines...

6.3b ... plug the ends of the lines...

Chapter 1 Tune-up and routine maintenance

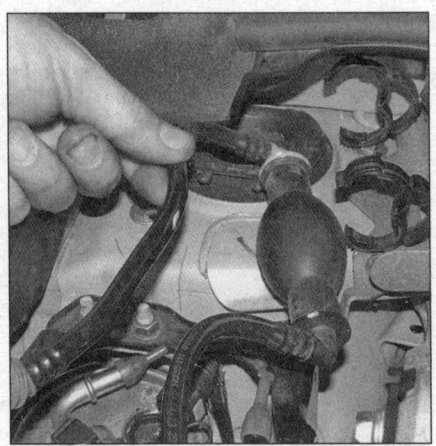

6.3c ... and remove the priming bulb with the fuel lines

6.4 Remove the filter housing bracket

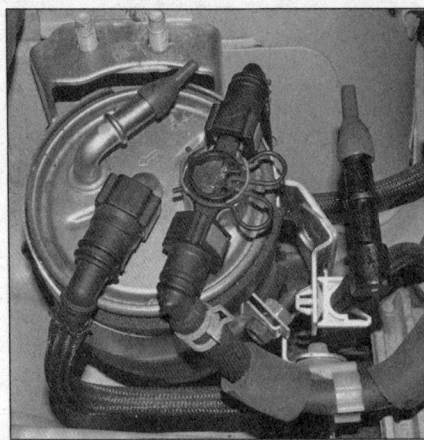

6.5 Note the fitted position of the fuel lines

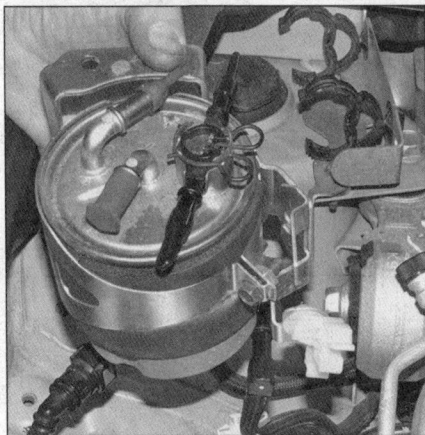

6.6 Withdraw the fuel filter from the engine compartment

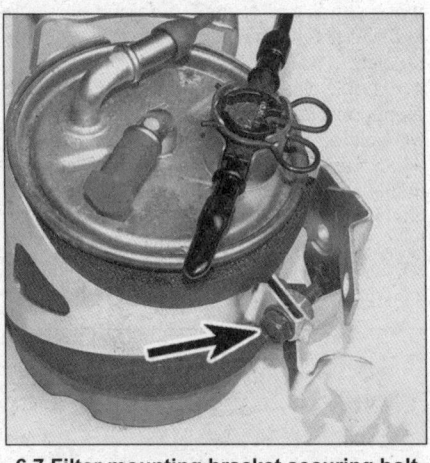

6.7 Filter mounting bracket securing bolt (arrowed)

the vehicle, slacken the mounting bracket securing bolt, and slide the fuel filter out from the bracket (see illustration).
8   Release the retaining clip on the top of the fuel filter, and then withdraw the fuel connector. Check the seal on the fuel connector is not damaged and renew seal if required.
9   Fit the new fuel filter into the mounting bracket and tighten the securing bolt. Refit the fuel connector to the top of the fuel filter, and secure it in position with the retaining clip.
10   Make sure the drain plug in the bottom of the fuel filter housing is tight.
11   Refit the filter and mounting bracket to the inner wing panel and reconnect the fuel lines to the top of the filter, taking care not to damage the pipes (see illustration).
12   Clip the fuel line back into the retaining clip on the side of the fuel filter bracket (see illustration).
13   Refit the fuel filter housing bracket to the inner wing panel and tighten the two retaining nuts (see illustration).
14   Refit the priming bulb fuel lines to the fuel filter, and then clip the priming bulb back in position.
15   Where applicable, reconnect the fuel heater wiring connector to the top of the filter housing.

4   Undo the two retaining nuts and remove the fuel filter housing bracket, from the inner wing panel (see illustration).
5   Note the fitted position of the fuel lines on top of the fuel filter, and then disconnect them. Take care not to damage the fuel lines as they are removed; cover the ends of the fuel lines to prevent any dirt ingress (see illustration).
6   Unclip the fuel line from the retaining clip on the fuel filter bracket and withdraw the fuel filter from the engine compartment (see illustration).
7   With the fuel filter housing removed from

6.11 Make sure that the fuel line securing clips are not damaged

6.12 Refit the fuel lines into the securing clips

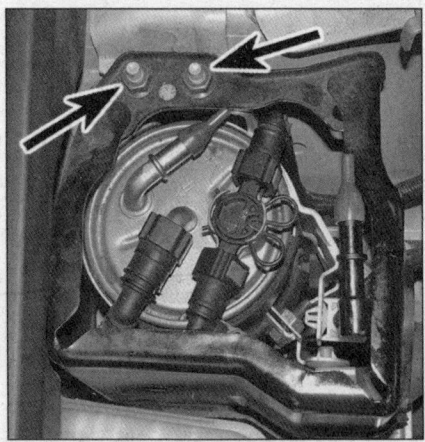

6.13 Tighten the bracket retaining nuts (arrowed)

1-16 Chapter 1 Tune-up and routine maintenance

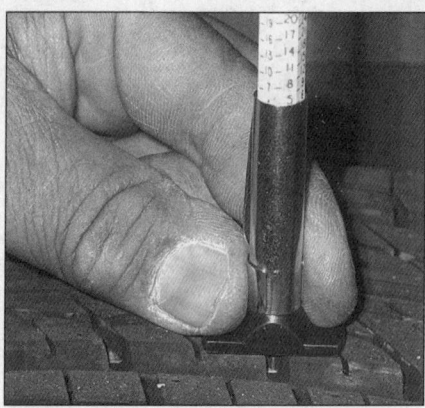

7.2 Use a tyre tread depth indicator to monitor tyre wear - they are available at auto parts stores and service stations and cost very little

7 Tyre and tyre pressure checks

1 Periodic inspection of the tyres may spare you from the inconvenience of being stranded with a flat tyre. It can also provide you with vital information regarding possible problems in the steering and suspension systems before major damage occurs.

2 Tyres have a 13 mm wide wear bands that will appear when tread depth reaches 1.5 mm, at which point the tyres can be considered worn out. Tread wear can be monitored with a simple, inexpensive device known as a tread depth indicator.

3 Note any abnormal tread wear (see illustration). Tread pattern irregularities such as cupping, flat spots and more wear on one side than the other are indications of front end alignment and/or balance problems. If any of these conditions are noted, take the vehicle to a tyre shop or service station to correct the problem.

4 Look closely for cuts, punctures and embedded nails or tacks. Sometimes a tyre will hold air pressure for a short time or leak down very slowly after a nail has embedded itself in the tread. If a slow leak persists, check the valve stem core to make sure it's tight (see illustration). Examine the tread for an object that may have embedded itself in the tyre or for a "plug" that may have begun to leak (radial tyre punctures are repaired with a plug that's installed in a puncture). If a puncture is suspected, it can be easily verified by spraying a solution of soapy water onto the puncture area (see illustration). The soapy solution will bubble if there's a leak. Unless the puncture is unusually large, a tyre shop or service station can usually repair the tyre.

5 Carefully inspect the inner sidewall of each tyre for evidence of brake fluid leakage.

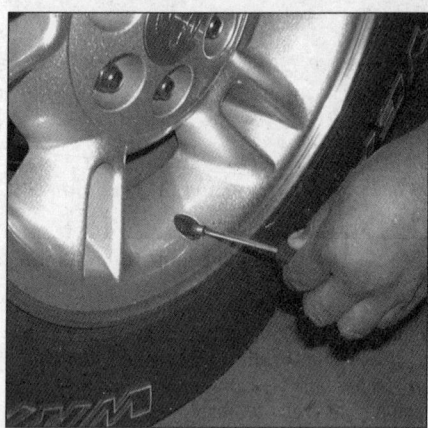

7.4a If a tyre loses air on a steady basis, check the valve stem core first to make sure it's snug (special inexpensive wrenches are commonly available at auto parts stores)

16 With all the fuel line connectors refitted, squeeze the priming bulb several times to pump the fuel back through the filter.

17 Turn the ignition key and crank the engine to start the engine. If required squeeze the priming bulb, to help the fuel flow through the system.

18 With engine running, check for leaks around the fuel filter and that the pipes are secure.

UNDERINFLATION

INCORRECT TOE-IN OR EXTREME CAMBER

CUPPING

Cupping may be caused by:
- Underinflation and/or mechanical irregularities such as out-of-balance condition of wheel and/or tire, and bent or damaged wheel.
- Loose or worn steering tie-rod or steering idler arm.
- Loose, damaged or worn front suspension parts.

OVERINFLATION

FEATHERING DUE TO MISALIGNMENT

7.3 This chart will help you determine the condition of the tyres and the probable cause(s) of abnormal wear

Chapter 1 Tune-up and routine maintenance

7.4b If the valve core is tight, raise the corner of the vehicle with the low tyre and spray a soapy water solution onto the tread as the tyre is turned slowly - slow leaks will cause small bubbles to appear

7.8 To extend the life of your tyres, check the air pressure at least once a week with an accurate gauge (don't forget the spare!)

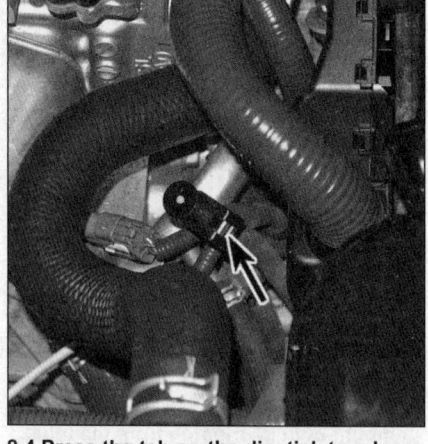

8.4 Press the tab on the dipstick to release the lock

If you see any, inspect the brakes immediately.

6 Correct air pressure adds many kilometres to the lifespan of the tyres, improves mileage and enhances overall ride quality. Tyre pressure cannot be accurately estimated by looking at a tyre, especially if it's a radial. A tyre pressure gauge is essential. Keep an accurate gauge in the vehicle. The pressure gauges attached to the nozzles of air hoses at gas stations are often inaccurate.

7 Always check tyre pressure when the tyres are cold. Cold, in this case, means the vehicle has not been driven more than two kilometres in the three hours preceding a tyre pressure check. A pressure rise of three to kPa is not uncommon once the tyres are warm.

8 Unscrew the valve cap protruding from the wheel or hubcap and push the gauge firmly onto the valve stem (see illustration). Note the reading on the gauge and compare the figure to the recommended tyre pressure shown on the placard on the driver's side door pillar. Be sure to reinstall the valve cap to keep dirt and moisture out of the valve stem mechanism. Check all four tyres and, if necessary, add enough air to bring them up to the recommended pressure.

9 Don't forget to keep the spare tyre inflated to the specified pressure (refer to your owner's manual or the tyre sidewall).

8 Automatic transaxle fluid level check

Models with continuously variable transaxle (CVT)

1 The level of the CVT fluid should be carefully maintained. Low fluid level can lead to slipping or loss of drive, while overfilling can cause foaming, loss of fluid and transaxle damage.

2 The transaxle fluid level should only be checked when the transaxle is hot (at its normal operating temperature). If the vehicle has just been driven for more than 10 minutes, and the fluid temperature is 50 to 80-degrees C, the transaxle is hot.

Caution: *If the vehicle has just been driven for a long time at high speed or in city traffic in hot weather, or if it has been pulling a trailer, an accurate fluid level reading cannot be obtained. Allow the fluid to cool down for about 30 minutes.*

3 If the vehicle has not been driven, park the vehicle on level ground, set the parking brake, then start the engine and bring it to operating temperature. While the engine is idling, depress the brake pedal and move the selector lever through all the gear ranges, beginning and ending in Park.

4 With the engine still idling, release and remove the dipstick from its tube (see illustration). Check the level of the fluid on the dipstick (see illustration 6.6) and note its condition.

5 Wipe the fluid from the dipstick with a clean rag and reinsert it back into the filler tube until the cap seats.

Note: *When inserting the dipstick, rotate it 1/2-turn so the tab on the cap doesn't lock into place when the dipstick is fully inserted.*

6 Pull the dipstick out again and note the fluid level (see illustration). If the level is at the low side of the range, add the specified automatic transaxle fluid through the dipstick tube with a funnel.

Caution: *This transaxle uses a special fluid designed specifically for Nissan CVTs. Don't use another fluid or damage may occur. See this Chapter's Specifications.*

7 Add just enough of the recommended fluid to fill the transaxle to the proper level. It takes about 0.5 litre to raise the level from the low mark to the high mark when the fluid is hot, so add the fluid a little at a time and keep checking the level until it is correct. Once the fluid level is correct, reinstall the dipstick with

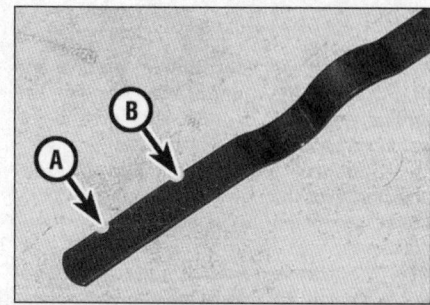

8.6 Check the CVT fluid with the engine idling at operating temperature and the gear selector in Park; if the fluid level is at the lower notch (A), add fluid to bring the level near the upper notch (B)

the locking tab or looped stopper oriented correctly, making sure it locks into place.

8 The condition of the fluid should also be checked along with the level. If the fluid at the end of the dipstick is black or a dark green color, or if it emits a burned smell, the fluid should be changed (see Section 30). If you are in doubt about the condition of the fluid, purchase some new fluid and compare the two for color and smell.

Models with automatic transaxle

Note: *The transaxle fluid temperature must be at 40 degrees C to achieve an accurate fluid level. A scan tool with data streaming is the best way to monitor the fluid temperature in the transaxle as the transaxle control module TCM is constantly monitoring the fluid temperature from signals it receives from the transaxle fluid temperature sensor. If a scan tool is not available, have the fluid level checked by someone that has one.*

Note: *Some transaxles do not have a fluid drain/level check plug; on these transaxles it will be necessary to have the fluid level check carried out by a Nissan dealer or transaxle specialist.*

1-18 Chapter 1 Tune-up and routine maintenance

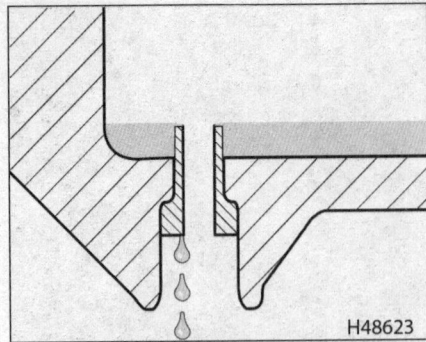

8.13 Automatic transaxle fluid level/drain hole; when the level tube plug beneath the drain plug is removed and there is a small amount of fluid dripping from the tube, the level is correct. Fluid pouring from the level tube indicates an overfilled transaxle while no signs of any fluid leaving the tube can indicate an under-filled transaxle

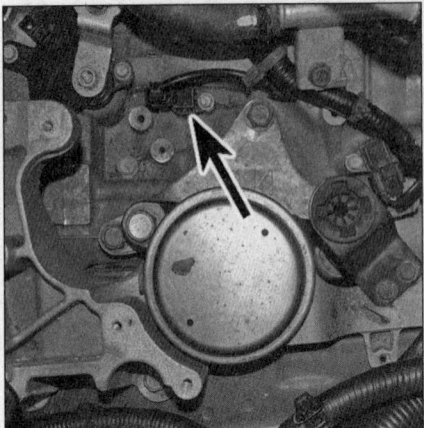

8.17 Battery and battery tray removed showing the turbine speed sensor (arrow)

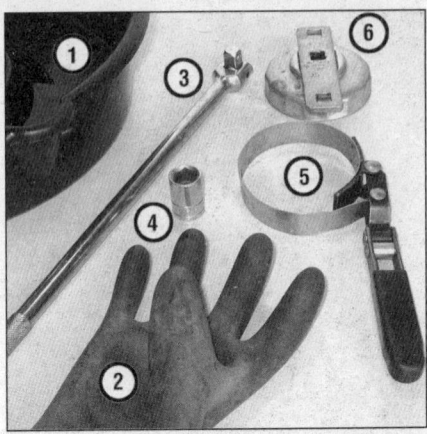

9.2 These tools are required when changing the engine oil and filter

1 Drain pan - It should be fairly shallow in depth, but wide in order to prevent spills
2 Rubber gloves - When removing the drain plug and filter, it is inevitable that you will get oil on your hands (the gloves will prevent burns)
3 Breaker bar - Sometimes the oil drain plug is pretty tight and a long breaker bar is needed to loosen it
4 Socket - To be used with the breaker bar or a ratchet (must be the correct size to fit the drain plug)
5 Filter wrench - This is a metal band-type wrench, which requires clearance around the filter to be effective
6 Filter wrench - This type fits on the top of the filter and can be turned with a ratchet or breaker bar (different size wrenches are available for different types of filters)

9 Park the vehicle on level ground and firmly apply the handbrake, remove the engine undershield and check around the transaxle casing for and fluid leaks.
10 Start the engine and move the gear selector lever through each of the gear positions, then place the selector lever in the P position.
11 The transaxle fluid needs to be at approximately 40ºC to be able to get the correct fluid level in the transaxle. The best way to know the transaxle fluid temperature is using a scan tool with a data stream capability. These tools will display the transaxle fluid temperature.

Note: *The fluid in the transaxle will reach approximately 40ºC, after ten minutes of the engine idling.*

12 Position a suitable container under the drain/level plug arrangement, situated on the base of the transaxle. Unscrew the inner plug (smaller one) and recover the sealing washer, a new one will be required for refitting.

Warning: *If the fluid is hot, take precautions against scalding.*

13 If the transaxle fluid overflows the level tube inside the drain hole and runs out into the container, the fluid level is correct **(see illustration)**.
14 If no transaxle fluid flows out of the drain hole, then the transaxle will need to be topped up as follows.
15 There is no filler plug on this transaxle, so the turbine speed sensor in the top of the transaxle housing has to be removed and the fluid is poured in through the sensor mounting hole.
16 The battery and battery tray have to be removed to allow access to the turbine speed sensor (Chapter 5 Section 5).
17 Locate the turbine speed sensor on top of the transaxle and wipe clean the area around the sensor **(see illustration)**. Disconnect the wiring connector, and then undo the retaining bolt and remove the sensor from the top of the transaxle housing. Nissan recommend that the O-ring be renewed when refitting.
18 Carefully add about 0.5 litres of specified fluid through the turbine speed sensor hole. More fluid can be added if a fluid line has been removed or the system has been drained.
19 Fit the new O-ring to the sensor. Lubricate the O-ring with the transaxle fluid being used to top up the transaxle and then refit the sensor to the top of the transaxle housing, tightening the bolt to the specified torque.
20 Refit the battery and battery tray (Chapter 5 Section 5).
21 Repeat steps 10 through 13 and check that the fluid level is correct. If no fluid flows from the overflow tube, add more fluid through the tubine speed sensor hole.
22 After topping-up, take the vehicle on a short run to distribute the fresh fluid, and then recheck the level again, topping-up if necessary.

9 Engine oil and oil filter change

1 Frequent oil changes are the best preventive maintenance the home mechanic can give the engine, because aging oil becomes diluted and contaminated, which leads to premature engine wear.
2 Make sure that you have all the necessary tools before you begin this procedure **(see illustration)**. You should also have plenty of rags or newspapers handy for mopping up any spills.
3 Park the vehicle on a level spot. Start the engine and allow it to reach its normal operating temperature (the needle on the temperature gauge should be at least above the bottom mark). Warm oil and contaminates will flow out more easily. Turn off the engine when it's warmed up. Remove the filler cap in the valve cover.
4 Raise the vehicle and support on jackstands (see Jacking and Towing).

Warning: *To avoid personal injury, never get beneath the vehicle when it is supported by only by a jack. The jack provided with your vehicle is designed solely for raising the vehicle to remove and replace the wheels. Always use jackstands to support the vehicle when it becomes necessary to place your body underneath the vehicle.*

5 Being careful not to touch the hot exhaust components, place the drain pan under the drain plug in the bottom of the pan and remove the plug **(see illustration)**. You may want to wear gloves while unscrewing the plug the final few turns if the engine is really hot.
6 Allow the old oil to drain into the pan. It may be necessary to move the pan farther under the engine as the oil flow slows to a trickle. Inspect the old oil for the presence of metal shavings and chips.
7 After all the oil has drained, wipe off the drain plug with a clean rag. Even minute metal particles clinging to the plug would immediately contaminate the new oil.
8 Clean the area around the drain plug opening, reinstall the plug and tighten it to the

Chapter 1 Tune-up and routine maintenance

9.5 Use a proper size ring spanner or socket to remove the oil drain plug and avoid rounding it off

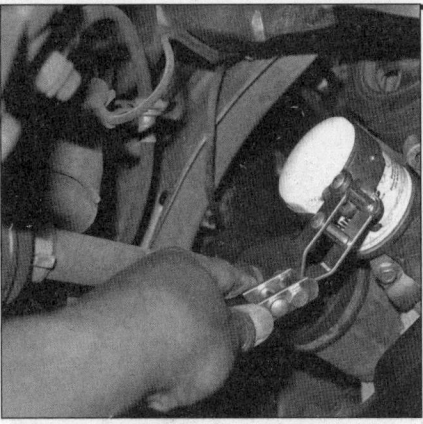

9.10a The oil filter is located on the right end of the engine. Use an oil filter wrench for removal; DO NOT use the wrench to tighten the new filter

9.10b Lubricate the oil filter gasket with clean engine oil before installing the filter on the engine

torque listed in this Chapter's Specifications.
9 Move the drain pan into position under the oil filter.
10 On petrol models, proceed as follows:
   a Loosen the oil filter by turning it anti-clockwise with the filter wrench **(see illustration)**. Any standard filter wrench should work. Once the filter is loose, use your hands to unscrew it from the block. Just as the filter is detached from the block, immediately tilt the open end up to prevent the oil inside the filter from spilling out.

   b With a clean rag, wipe off the oil filter mounting surface. Make sure that none of the old gasket remains stuck to the mounting surface. It can be removed with a scraper if necessary.
   c Compare the old filter with the new one to make sure they are the same type. Smear some engine oil on the rubber gasket of the new filter and screw it into place **(see illustration)**. Because over-tightening the filter will damage the gasket, do not use a filter wrench to tighten it. Tighten it by hand until the gasket contacts the seating surface, then seat the filter by giving it an additional 3/4-turn.
11 On diesel models, proceed as follows:
   a Using a suitably sized socket, unscrew the filter housing cap and withdraw the filter cartridge, draining the oil into the container.
   b Use a clean rag to remove any oil, dirt and sludge from inside the oil filter housing. Remove any old rubber seals from the oil filter housing and filter cap and fit the new seals, which should be supplied with the filter.

   c Apply a light coating of clean engine oil to the sealing rings **(see illustration)**, then insert the filter cartridge. Screw the filter cap into position on the engine. Tighten the filter cap firmly by hand at first, then use spanner to tighten securely.
12 Remove all tools, rags, etc. from under the vehicle, being careful not to spill the oil in the drain pan, then lower the vehicle.
13 Remove the filler cap and add new oil to the engine. Use a funnel to prevent oil from spilling onto the top of the engine. Pour five litres of fresh oil into the engine. Wait a few minutes to allow the oil to drain into the pan, then check the level on the oil dipstick (see Section 4 if necessary). If the oil level is at or near the H mark, install the filler cap hand tight, start the engine and allow the new oil to circulate.
14 Allow the engine to run for about a minute. While the engine is running, look under the vehicle and check for leaks at the oil pan drain plug and around the oil filter. If either is leaking, stop the engine and tighten the plug or filter slightly.
15 Wait a few minutes to allow the oil to trickle down into the pan, then recheck the level on the dipstick and, if necessary, add enough oil to bring the level to the H mark.

9.11a Oil filter location - diesel models

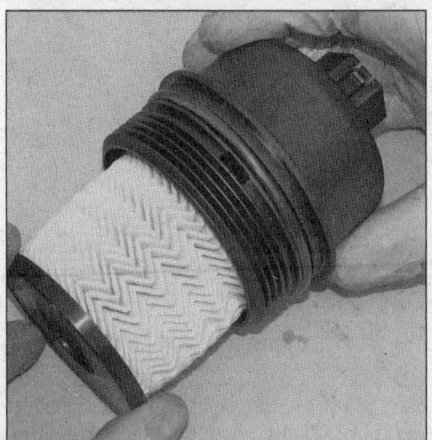

9.11b Removing the filter element from the filter cap

9.11c Install a new O-ring to the filter cap...

9.11d ... and then apply clean engine oil to the O-ring

Chapter 1 Tune-up and routine maintenance

10.3 Pry off the trim cap and check the tightness of the wiper arm retaining nut

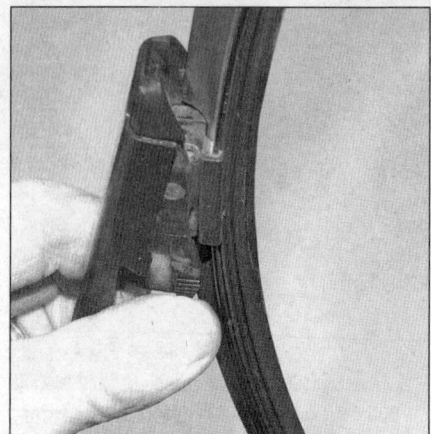

10.5a Press on the release tab and push the blade assembly down out of the hook in the arm

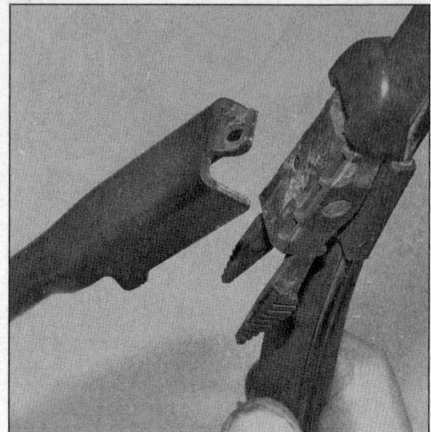

10.5b Slide the wiper blade assembly away from the arm...

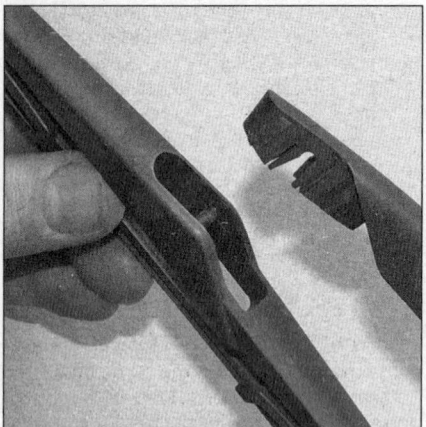

10.5c ... and separate the blade assembly from the wiper arm

16 During the first few trips after an oil change, make it a point to check frequently for leaks and proper oil level.
17 The old oil drained from the engine cannot be reused in its present state and should be disposed of. Check with your local auto parts store, disposal facility or environmental agency to see if they will accept the oil for recycling. After the oil has cooled it can be drained into a container (capped plastic jugs, topped bottles, milk cartons, etc.) for transport to one of these disposal sites. Don't dispose of the oil by pouring it on the ground or down a drain!

10 Windshield wiper blade inspection and replacement

1 The windshield wiper and blade assembly should be inspected periodically for damage, loose components and cracked or worn blade elements.
2 Road film can build up on the wiper blades and affect their efficiency, so they should be washed regularly with a mild detergent solution.
3 The action of the wiping mechanism can loosen the fasteners, so they should be checked and tightened, as necessary (see illustration), at the same time the wiper blades are checked.
4 If the wiper blade elements are cracked, worn or warped, or no longer clean adequately, they should be replaced with new ones.
5 Lift the arm assembly away from the glass for clearance, press on the release lever, then slide the wiper blade assembly out of the hook in the end of the arm (see illustrations).
6 Use needle-nose pliers to compress the blade element, then slide the element out of the frame and discard it (see illustrations).
7 Installation is the reverse of removal.

11 Battery check, maintenance and charging

Warning: *Certain precautions must be followed when checking and servicing the battery. Hydrogen gas, which is highly flammable, is always present in the battery cells, so keep lighted tobacco and all other open flames and sparks away from the battery. The electrolyte inside the battery is*

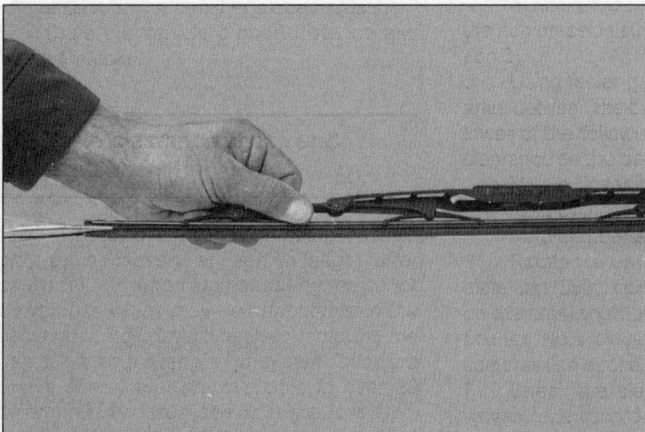

10.6a Use needle-nose pliers to compress the rubber element, then slide the element out - slide the new element in and lock the blade assembly retaining claw into the notches of the wiper rubber element

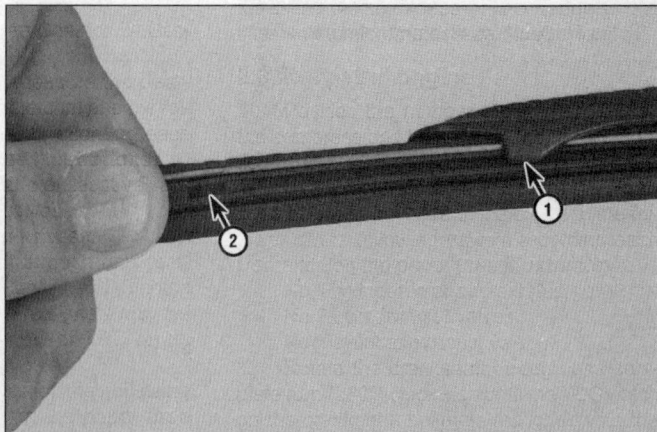

10.6b Slide the rubber back to release the retaining claw (1) from the locking groove in the rubber (2) and slide the rubber from the blade assembly

Chapter 1 Tune-up and routine maintenance   1-21

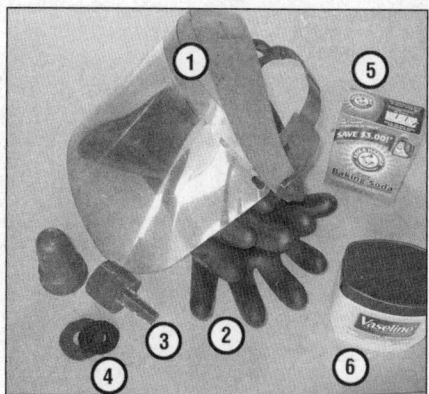

11.1 Tools and materials required for battery maintenance

1 *Face shield/safety goggles - When removing corrosion with a brush, the acidic particles can easily fly up into your eyes*
2 *Rubber gloves - Another safety item to consider when servicing the battery; remember that's acid inside the battery*
3 *Battery post/cable cleaner - This wire brush cleaning tool will remove all traces of corrosion from the battery posts and cable clamps*
4 *Treated felt washers - Placing one of these on each post, directly under the cable clamps, will help prevent corrosion*
5 *Baking soda - A solution of baking soda and water can be used to neutralize corrosion*
6 *Petroleum jelly - A layer of this on the battery posts will help prevent corrosion*

actually dilute sulphuric acid, which will cause injury if splashed on your skin or in your eyes. It will also ruin clothes and painted surfaces. When removing the battery cables, always detach the negative cable first and hook it up last!

11.6a Battery terminal corrosion usually appears as light, fluffy powder

1 A routine preventive maintenance program for the battery in your vehicle is the only way to ensure quick and reliable starts. But before performing any battery maintenance, make sure that you have the proper equipment necessary to work safely around the battery **(see illustration)**.
2 There are also several precautions that should be taken whenever battery maintenance is performed. Before servicing the battery, always turn the engine and all accessories off and disconnect the cable from the negative terminal of the battery.
3 The battery produces hydrogen gas, which is both flammable and explosive. Never create a spark, smoke or light a match around the battery. Always charge the battery in a ventilated area.
4 Electrolyte contains poisonous and corrosive sulphuric acid. Do not allow it to get in your eyes, on your skin or on your clothes. Never ingest it. Wear protective safety glasses when working near the battery. Keep children away from the battery.

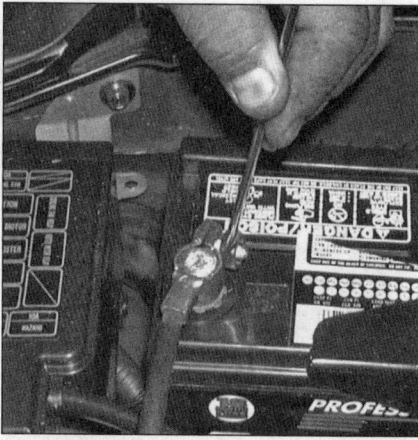

11.6b Removing a cable from the battery post with a spanner - sometimes special battery pliers are required for this procedure if corrosion has caused deterioration of the nut hex (always remove the ground cable first and hook it up last!)

5 Note the external condition of the battery. If the positive terminal and cable clamp on your vehicle's battery is equipped with a rubber protector, make sure it isn't torn or damaged. It should completely cover the terminal. Look for any corroded or loose connections, cracks in the case or cover or loose hold-down clamps. Also check the entire length of each cable for cracks and frayed conductors.
6 If corrosion, which looks like white, fluffy deposits **(see illustration)** is evident, particularly around the terminals, the battery should be removed for cleaning. Loosen the cable clamp bolts with a wrench, being careful to remove the ground cable first, and slide them off the terminals **(see illustration)**. Then disconnect the hold-down clamp bolt and nut, remove the clamp and lift the battery from the engine compartment.
7 Clean the cable clamps thoroughly with a battery brush or a terminal cleaner and a solution of warm water and baking soda **(see illustration)**. Wash the terminals and the top of the battery case with the same solution but make sure that the solution doesn't get into the battery. When cleaning the cables, terminals and battery top, wear safety goggles and rubber gloves to prevent any solution from coming in contact with your eyes or hands. Wear old clothes too - even diluted, sulphuric acid splashed onto clothes will burn holes in them. If the terminals have been extensively corroded, clean them up with a terminal cleaner **(see illustration)**. Thoroughly wash all cleaned areas with plain water.
8 Make sure the battery tray is in good condition and the hold-down clamp bolt or nut is tight. If the battery is removed from the tray, make sure no parts remain in the bottom of the tray when the battery is reinstalled. When reinstalling the hold-down clamp bolt or nut, do not over-tighten it.
9 Information on removing and installing the battery can be found in the Engine

11.7a When cleaning the cable clamps, all corrosion must be removed (the inside of the clamp is tapered to match the taper on the post, so don't remove too much material)

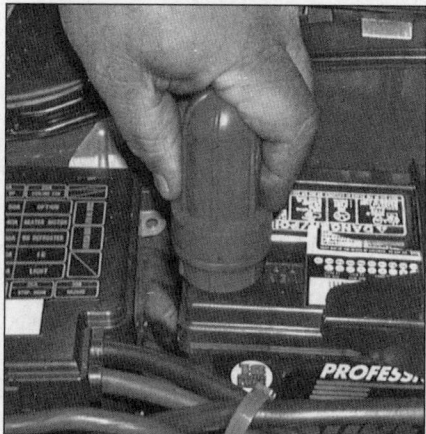

11.7b Regardless of the type of tool used to clean the battery posts, a clean, shiny surface should be the result

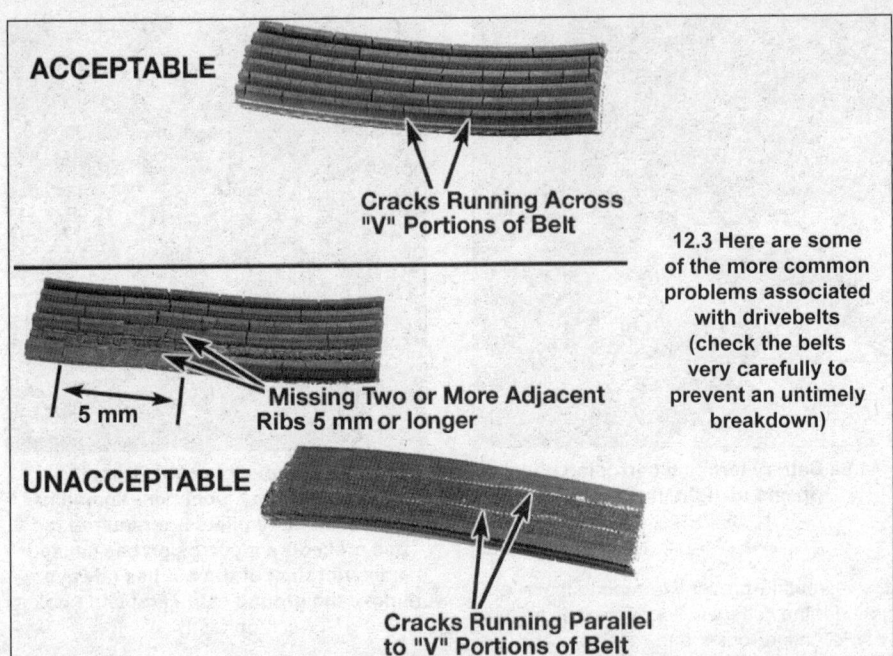

12.3 Here are some of the more common problems associated with drivebelts (check the belts very carefully to prevent an untimely breakdown)

12.4a Drivebelt indicator markings (viewed from between the alternator and the cylinder head); if the arrow is not within the range on the tensioner, the belt should be replaced - 2.0L MR20 engine

Electrical chapter (see Chapter 5 Section 5). Information on jump starting can be found at the front of this manual (see Chapter 0 Section 6).

Cleaning

10 Corrosion on the hold-down components, battery case and surrounding areas can be removed with a solution of water and baking soda. Thoroughly rinse all cleaned areas with plain water.
11 Any metal parts of the vehicle damaged by corrosion should be covered with a zinc-based primer, then painted.

Charging

Warning: *When batteries are being charged, hydrogen gas, which is very explosive and flammable, is produced. Do not smoke or allow open flames near a charging or a recently charged battery. Wear eye protection when near the battery during charging. Also, make sure the charger is unplugged before connecting or disconnecting the battery from the charger.*

12 Slow-rate charging is the best way to restore a battery that's discharged to the point where it will not start the engine. It's also a good way to maintain the battery charge in a vehicle that's only driven a few miles between starts. Maintaining the battery charge is particularly important in the winter when the battery must work harder to start the engine and electrical accessories that drain the battery are in greater use.
13 It's best to use a one or two-amp battery charger (sometimes called a "trickle" charger). They are the safest and put the least strain on the battery. They are also the least expensive. For a faster charge, you can use a higher amperage charger, but don't use one rated more than 1/10th the amp/hour rating of the battery. Rapid boost charges that claim to restore the power of the battery in one to two hours are hardest on the battery and can damage batteries not in good condition. This type of charging should only be used in emergency situations.
14 The average time necessary to charge a battery should be listed in the instructions that come with the charger. As a general rule, a trickle charger will charge a battery in 12 to 16 hours.

12 Drivebelt check and replacement

Check

1 These models use a serpentine drivebelt with an automatic adjuster tensioner. The good condition and proper tension of the belt is critical to the operation of the engine. Because of their composition and the high stresses to which they are subjected, drivebelts stretch and deteriorate as they get older. They must therefore be periodically inspected. The is no adjustment on these models.
2 The serpentine drivebelt transmits power to all the accessories.
3 With the engine off, open the bonnet and locate the drivebelt. With a flashlight, check each belt for separation of the adhesive rubber on both sides of the core, core separation from the belt side, a severed core, separation of the ribs from the adhesive rubber, cracking or separation of the ribs, and torn or worn ribs or cracks in the inner ridges of the ribs **(see illustration)**. Also check for fraying and glazing, which gives the belt a shiny appearance. Both sides of the belt should be inspected, which means you will have to twist the belt to check the underside. Use your fingers to feel the belt where you can't see it. If any of the above conditions are evident, replace the belt (see Steps 5 through 10).
4 Check the drivebelt indicator for excessive belt stretch **(see illustration)**. If the drivebelt indicator is out of limit, replace the drivebelt (see Steps 5 through 10).

Drivebelt replacement

5 Disconnect the negative (-) battery terminal (see Chapter 5 Section 3).
6 Raise the front of the vehicle and support on jackstands (see Chapter 0 Section 7). Remove the RHF wheel and the inner guard liner.
7 Rotate the belt tensioner clockwise using a spanner or socket on the pulley bolt to release tension on the drivebelt. The tensioner can be locked in position by inserting a drill bit or other metal rod into the lock holes **(see illustrations)**.
Caution: *Do not loosen the drivebelt tensioner pulley bolt or it will be necessary to replace the entire tensioner with a new one.*

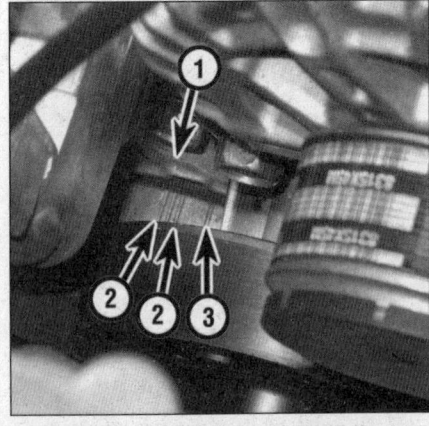

12.4b Drive belt tensioner wear indicators - 2.5L QR25DE petrol engine

1 Indicator window on tensioner body
2 Normal wear range
3 Belt worn indicator

Chapter 1 Tune-up and routine maintenance

12.7a Release the tension using a spanner…

12.7b … then insert an Allen key or drill bit into the hole to lock the tensioner in place - 2.0L MR20 petrol engine

12.7c Drive belt tensioner with an Allen key locking it in the retracted position - 2.5L QR25DE petrol engine

12.8 Removing the drivebelt from the pulleys

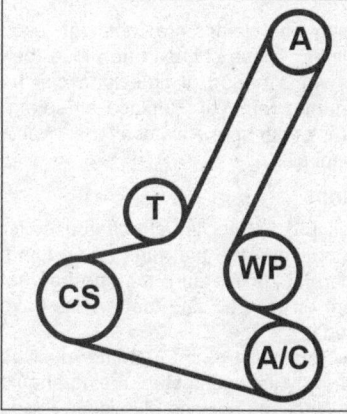

12.9a Drivebelt routing 2.0L MR20 petrol engine

- I   Idler pulley
- WP Water pump pulley
- A   Alternator
- A/C Air conditioning compressor
- CS Crankshaft pulley
- T   Automatic tensioner pulley

8 Remove the drivebelt from the tensioner and all accessories.

9 Install the new drivebelt, making sure that it's properly routed (see illustrations).

10 Reconnect the battery and perform the system initialisation procedure (see Chapter 5 Section 4)

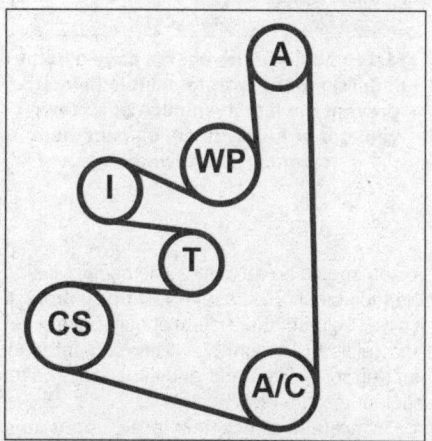

12.9b Drivebelt routing 2.5L QR25DE petrol engine - T31 X-Trail models

- I   Idler pulley
- WP Water pump pulley
- A   Alternator
- A/C Air conditioning compressor
- CS Crankshaft pulley
- T   Automatic tensioner pulley

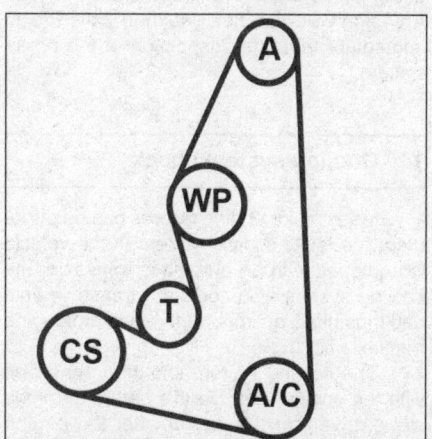

12.9c Drivebelt routing 2.5L QR25DE petrol engine - T32 X-Trail models

- I   Idler pulley
- WP Water pump pulley
- A   Alternator
- A/C Air conditioning compressor
- CS Crankshaft pulley
- T   Automatic tensioner pulley

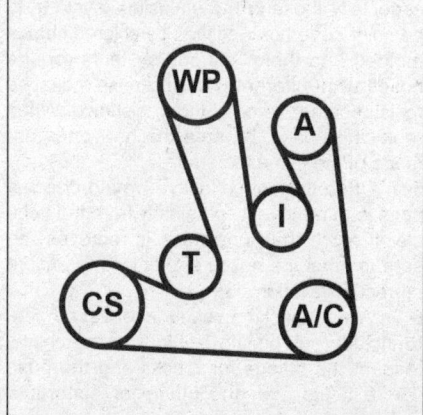

12.9d Drivebelt routing 2.0L M9R diesel engine

- I   Idler pulley
- WP Water pump pulley
- A   Alternator
- A/C Air conditioning compressor
- CS Crankshaft pulley
- T   Automatic tensioner pulley

1-24 Chapter 1 Tune-up and routine maintenance

Automatic tensioner replacement

11 Remove the drivebelt (see Steps 5 through 8).
12 Remove the drivebelt tensioner mounting bolts and remove the tensioner.
13 Installation is the reverse of removal. Tighten the tensioner mounting fasteners to the torque listed in this Chapter's Specifications.

13 Under bonnet hose check and replacement

Caution: *Replacement of air conditioning hoses must be left to a dealer service department or air conditioning shop that has the equipment to depressurize the system safely. Never remove air conditioning components or hoses until the system has been depressurized.*

General

1 High temperatures in the engine compartment can cause the deterioration of the rubber and plastic hoses used for engine, accessory and emission systems operation. Periodic inspection should be made for cracks, loose clamps, material hardening and leaks.
2 Information specific to the cooling system hoses can be found in Section 14.
3 Some, but not all, hoses are secured to the fittings with clamps. Where clamps are used, check to be sure they haven't lost their tension, allowing the hose to leak. If clamps aren't used, make sure the hose has not expanded and/or hardened where it slips over the fitting, allowing it to leak.

Vacuum hoses

4 It's quite common for vacuum hoses, especially those in the emissions system, to be color coded or identified by colored stripes molded into them. Various systems require hoses with different wall thickness, collapse resistance and temperature resistance. When replacing hoses, be sure the new ones are made of the same material.
5 Often the only effective way to check a hose is to remove it completely from the vehicle. If more than one hose is removed, be sure to label the hoses and fittings to ensure correct installation.
6 When checking vacuum hoses, be sure to include any plastic T-fittings in the check. Inspect the fittings for cracks and the hose where it fits over the fitting for distortion, which could cause leakage.
7 A small piece of vacuum hose (1/4-inch inside diameter) can be used as a stethoscope to detect vacuum leaks. Hold one end of the hose to your ear and probe around vacuum hoses and fittings, listening for the hissing sound characteristic of a vacuum leak.
Warning: *When probing with the vacuum hose stethoscope, be very careful not to come into contact with moving engine components such as the drivebelts, cooling fan, etc.*

Fuel hose

Warning: *There are certain precautions which must be taken when inspecting or servicing fuel system components. Work in a well ventilated area and do not allow open flames (cigarettes, appliance pilot lights, etc.) or bare light bulbs near the work area. Mop up any spills immediately and do not store fuel-soaked rags where they could ignite.*
8 Check all rubber fuel lines for deterioration and chafing. Check especially for cracks in areas where the hose bends and just before fittings, such as where a hose attaches to the fuel filter.
9 High quality fuel line, meeting the manufacturer's original specifications, should be used for fuel line replacement. Never, under any circumstances, use unreinforced vacuum line, clear plastic tubing or water hose for fuel lines.
10 Spring-type clamps are commonly used on fuel lines. These clamps often lose their tension over a period of time, and can be sprung during removal. Replace all spring-type clamps with screw clamps whenever a hose is replaced.

Metal lines

11 Sections of metal line are often used for fuel line between the fuel tank and engine. Check carefully to be sure the line has not been bent or crimped and that cracks have not started in the line.
12 If a Section of metal fuel line must be replaced, only seamless steel tubing should be used, since copper and aluminium tubing don't have the strength necessary to withstand normal engine vibration.
13 Check the metal brake lines where they enter the master cylinder and ABS unit (if used) for cracks in the lines or loose fittings. Any sign of brake fluid leakage calls for an immediate thorough inspection of the brake system.

14 Cooling system check

1 Many major engine failures can be attributed to a faulty cooling system. If the vehicle is equipped with an automatic transaxle, the cooling system also cools the transaxle fluid and thus plays an important role in prolonging transaxle life.
2 The cooling system should be checked with the engine cold. Do this before the vehicle is driven for the day or after the engine has been shut off for at least three hours.
3 Remove the radiator cap by turning it to the left until it reaches a stop. If you hear a hissing sound (indicating there is still pressure in the system), wait until it stops. Now press down on the cap with the palm of your hand and continue turning to the left until the cap can be removed. Thoroughly clean the cap, inside and out, with clean water. Also clean the filler neck on the radiator. All traces of corrosion should be removed. The coolant inside the radiator should be relatively transparent. If it's rust colored, the system should be drained and refilled (Section 27). If the coolant level isn't up to the top, add additional antifreeze/coolant mixture (see Section 4).
4 Carefully check the large upper and lower radiator hoses along with the smaller diameter heater hoses which run from the engine to the firewall. Inspect each hose along its entire length, replacing any hose which is cracked, swollen or shows signs of deterioration. Cracks may become more apparent if the hose is squeezed (see illustration). Regardless of condition, it's a good idea to replace hoses with new ones every several years.

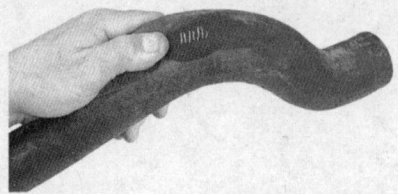
Check for a chafed area that could fail prematurely.

Check for a soft area indicating the hose has deteriorated inside.

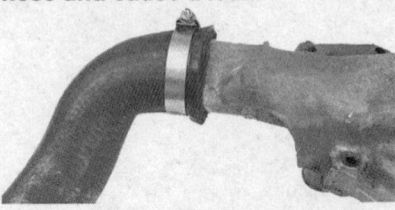
Overtightening the clamp on a hardened hose will damage the hose and cause a leak.

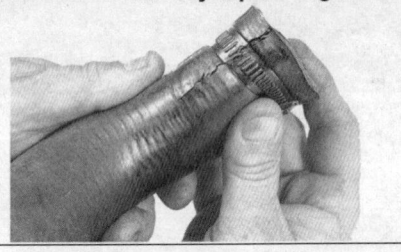
Check each hose for swelling and oil-soaked ends. Cracks and breaks can be located by squeezing the hose

14.4 Hoses, like drivebelts, have a habit of failing at the worst possible time - to prevent the inconvenience of a blown radiator or heater hose, inspect them carefully as shown here

Chapter 1 Tune-up and routine maintenance

1•25

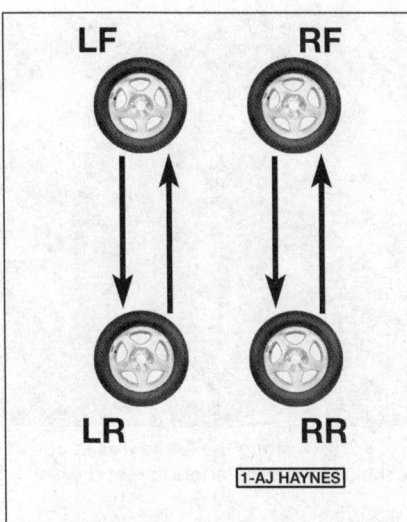

15.2 The recommended tyre rotation pattern for these vehicles

16.2 Remove the filler plug from the rear cover

17.2 Transaxle oil filler/level plug (arrowed)

5 Make sure that all hose connections are tight. A leak in the cooling system will usually show up as white or rust colored deposits on the areas adjoining the leak. If wire-type clamps are used at the ends of the hoses, it may be a good idea to replace them with more secure screw-type clamps.

6 Use compressed air or a soft brush to remove bugs, leaves, etc. from the front of the radiator or air conditioning condenser. Be careful not to damage the delicate cooling fins or cut yourself on them.

7 Every other inspection, or at the first indication of cooling system problems, have the cap and system pressure tested. If you don't have a pressure tester, most gas stations and repair shops will do this for a minimal charge.

15 Tyre rotation

1 The tyres should be rotated at the specified intervals and whenever uneven wear is noticed. Since the vehicle will be raised and the tyres removed anyway, check the brakes (see Section 19) at this time.

2 Radial tyres must be rotated in a specific pattern **(see illustration)**.

3 Refer to Chapter 0, Section 7 for the proper procedures to follow when raising the vehicle and changing a tyre. If the brakes are to be checked, do not apply the parking brake as stated.

4 Preferably, the entire vehicle should be raised at the same time. This can be done on a hoist or by jacking up each corner and then lowering the vehicle onto jackstands placed under the frame rails. Always use four jackstands and make sure the vehicle is firmly supported.

5 After rotation, check and adjust the tyre pressures as necessary and be sure to check the wheel nut tightness.

6 For further information on the wheels and tyres refer to Chapter 10 Section 19.

16 Differential lubricant level check (AWD models)

1 Raise the vehicle and support on jackstands (see Chapter 0 Section 7).

2 Remove the plug from the filler hole **(see illustration)** in the differential.

3 The lubricant should be up to the bottom of the filler hole. If not, use a pump or squeeze bottle to add the specified lubricant until it just starts to run out of the hole.

4 Place a new sealing washer on the filler plug. Install the plug in the filler hole and tighten it to the specified torque (see Specifications).

17 Manual transaxle lubricant level check

1 Park the car on a level surface. The oil level must be checked before the car is driven, or at least 5 minutes after the engine has been switched off. If the oil is checked immediately after driving the car, some of the oil will remain distributed around the transaxle components, resulting in an inaccurate level reading. To improve access, position the car over an inspection pit, or raise the front and rear of the vehicle and support on jackstands (see Chapter 0 Section 7) making sure the vehicle remains level to the ground.

2 Wipe clean the area around the filler/level plug, and unscrew it from the casing on the left-hand rear of the transaxle unit, behind the driveshaft **(see illustration)**.

3 The oil level should reach the lower edge of the filler/level hole. A certain amount of oil will have gathered behind the filler/level plug and will trickle out when it is removed; this does not necessarily indicate that the level is correct. To ensure that a true level is established, wait until the initial trickle has stopped, then add oil as necessary until a trickle of new oil can be seen emerging. The level will be correct when the flow ceases; use only good-quality oil of the specified type.

4 Remove the left-hand front road wheel for better access to the filler/level plug. Use a length of hose and a funnel to make topping up easier **(see illustrations)**.

17.4a Using a funnel and hose ...

17.4b ... to fill up the transaxle

18.2 Transfer case filler plug location (just to the rear of the right driveshaft intermediate shaft) - TY30A transfer case shown, TY21C similar

19.6 You will find an inspection hole like this in each caliper - placing a ruler across the hole should enable you to determine the thickness of remaining pad material

19.11 Check along the brake hoses and at each fitting for deterioration and cracks

5   Refilling the transaxle is an extremely awkward operation; above all, allow plenty of time for the oil level to settle properly before checking it. If a large amount had to be added to the transaxle and a large amount flows out on checking the level, refit the filler/level plug, and take the vehicle on a short journey. This will allow the new oil to be distributed fully around the transaxle components. On returning, recheck the level when the oil has settled again.

6   If the transaxle has been overfilled so that oil flows out as soon as the filler/level plug is removed, check that the car is completely level (front-to-rear and side-to-side). If necessary, allow the surplus to drain off into a suitable container.

7   When the level is correct, refit the filler/level plug, tightening it to the specified torque and wash off any spilt oil.

18 Transfer case lubricant level check (AWD models)

1   Raise the vehicle and support it securely on jackstands (see Chapter 0 Section 7). The vehicle should be as level as possible to ensure an accurate check.

2   Remove the plug from the filler hole in the transfer case **(see illustration)**.

3   The lubricant should be up to the bottom of the filler hole. If not, use a pump or squeeze bottle to add the specified lubricant until it just starts to run out of the hole.

4   Place a new sealing washer on the filler plug. Install the plug in the filler hole and tighten it to the specified torque (see Specifications).

19 Brake check

Warning: *The dust created by the brake system is harmful to your health. Never blow it out with compressed air and don't inhale any of it. An approved filtering mask should be worn when working on the brakes. Do not, under any circumstances, use petroleum-based solvents to clean brake parts. Use brake system cleaner only! Try to use non-asbestos replacement parts whenever possible.*

Note: *For detailed photographs of the brake system, refer to Chapter 9.*

1   In addition to the specified intervals, the brakes should be inspected every time the wheels are removed or whenever a defect is suspected. Any of the following symptoms could indicate a potential brake system defect:

  a The vehicle pulls to one side when the brake pedal is depressed;
  b the brakes make squealing or dragging noises when applied;
  c brake pedal travel is excessive;
  d the pedal pulsates;
  e brake fluid leaks, usually onto the inside of the tyre or wheel.

2   The disc brake pads have built-in wear indicators which should make a high pitched squealing or scraping noise when they are worn to the replacement point. When you hear this noise, replace the pads immediately or expensive damage to the discs can result.

3   Loosen the wheel nuts.

4   Raise the vehicle and support on jackstands (see Chapter 0 Section 7).

5   Remove the wheels.

Disc brakes

6   There are two pads (an outer and an inner) in each caliper. The pads are visible through inspection holes in each caliper **(see illustration)**, as well as from the top and bottom of each pad.

7   Check the pad thickness by looking at each end of the caliper and through the inspection hole in the caliper body. If the lining material is less than the thickness listed in this Chapter's Specifications, replace the pads.

Note: *Keep in mind that the lining material is bonded to a metal backing plate and the metal portion is not included in this measurement.*

8   If it is difficult to determine the exact thickness of the remaining pad material by the above method, or if you are at all concerned about the condition of the pads, remove the caliper(s), then remove the pads from the calipers for further inspection (see Chapter 9 Section 3).

9   Once the pads are removed from the calipers, clean them with brake cleaner and re-measure them with a ruler or a vernier caliper.

10 Measure the disc thickness with a micrometer to make sure that it still has service life remaining. If any disc is thinner than the specified minimum thickness, replace it (see Chapter 9 Section 5). Even if the disc has service life remaining, check its condition. Look for scoring, gouging and burned spots. If these conditions exist, remove the disc and have it resurfaced (see Chapter 9 Section 5, 6).

11 Before installing the wheels, check all brake lines and hoses for damage, wear, deformation, cracks, corrosion, leakage, bends and twists, particularly in the vicinity of the rubber hoses at the calipers **(see illustration)**. Check the clamps for tightness and the connections for leakage. Make sure that all hoses and lines are clear of sharp edges, moving parts and the exhaust system. If any of the above conditions are noted, repair, reroute or replace the lines and/or hoses as necessary (see Chapter 9 Section 10).

Brake booster check

12 Sit in the driver's seat and perform the following sequence of tests.

13 With the brake fully depressed, start the engine - the pedal should move down a little when the engine starts.

14 With the engine running, depress the brake pedal several times - the travel distance should not change.

15 Depress the brake, stop the engine and hold the pedal in for about 30 seconds - the pedal should neither sink nor rise.

Chapter 1 Tune-up and routine maintenance

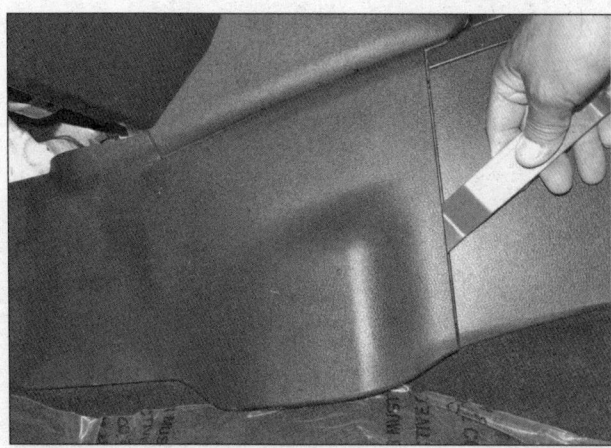

20.2 Carefully pry off this trim panel for access to the cabin air filter

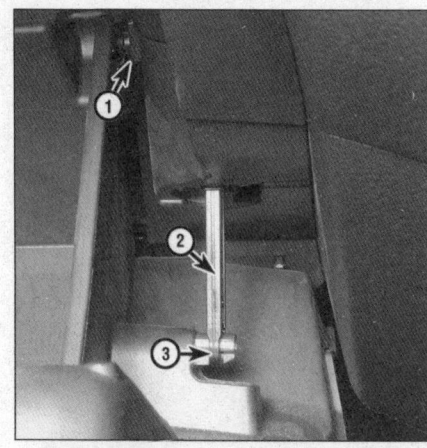

20.3a One of the glove box lock stops (1). Disengage the damping strut (2) by levering it in the direction of the arrow (3) at the glove box

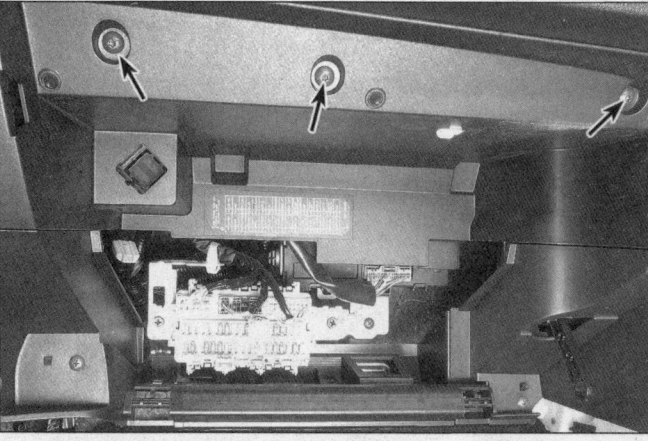

20.3b Glove box removed showing the upper surround panel screws that need to be removed

16 Restart the engine, run it for about a minute and turn it off. Then firmly depress the brake several times - the pedal travel should decrease with each application.

17 If your brakes do not operate as described above when the preceding tests are performed, the brake booster is either in need of repair or has failed. Refer to for the removal procedure.

Parking brake

18 Actuate the parking brake with a normal amount of force and count the number of clicks. The adjustment should be within the range listed in the Chapter 9 Specifications. If you hear more or fewer clicks, adjust the parking brake (see Chapter 9 Section 13).

19 An alternative method of checking the parking brake is to park the vehicle on a steep hill with the parking brake set and the transaxle in Neutral (be sure to stay in the vehicle during this check!). If the parking brake cannot prevent the vehicle from rolling, it is in need of adjustment (see Chapter 9 Section 13).

20 Cabin air filter replacement

1 The cabin air filter is fitted to the LH side of the A/C box and is accessed after removing the from LH panel from the console on T31 X-Trail and Dualis models, or after removing the glove compartment and upper surround panel on T32 X-Trail and Qashqai models.

2 On T31 X-Trail and Dualis models, remove the left instrument panel lower cover, forward of the console (see illustration).

3 On T32 X-Trail and Qashqai models, proceed as follows:
Open the glove box and squeeze the sides together until the glove box can be lowered past the locking stops.
Disengage the damping strut from the RH side of the glove box (see illustration) and remove the glove box from the vehicle.
Remove the screws retaining the upper glove box surround to the dashboard (see illustrations) and manoeuvre the surround from the dashboard.

4 Remove the cover from the side of the HVAC housing (see illustration).

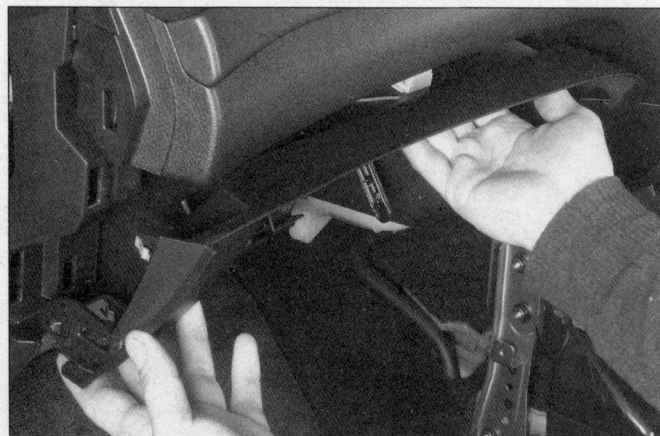

20.3c Partially remove the upper surround panel and then...

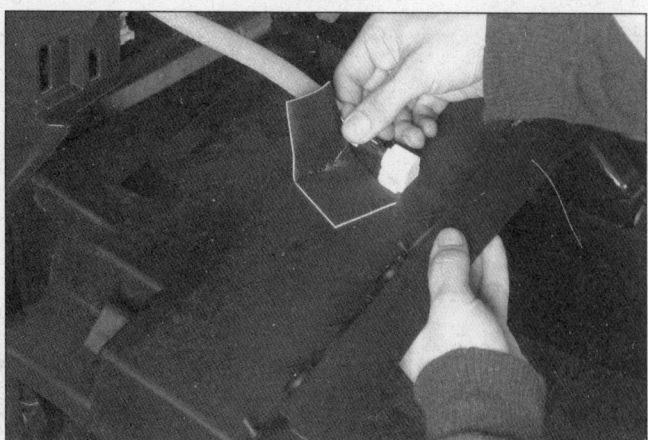

20.3d ... disconnect the wiring from the top of the panel

1-28 Chapter 1 Tune-up and routine maintenance

20.4a Unclip the bottom of the filter cover, swing it out and unhook the top - T31 X-Trail and Dualis models

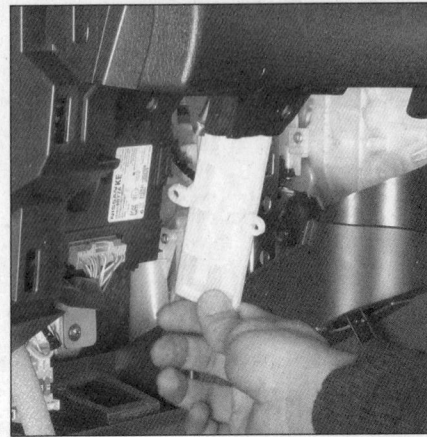

20.4b Reach in through the glove box opening and open the filter cover - T32 X-Trail shown, Qashqai similar

20.5a Removing the filter from the housing - T31 X-Trail and Dualis models

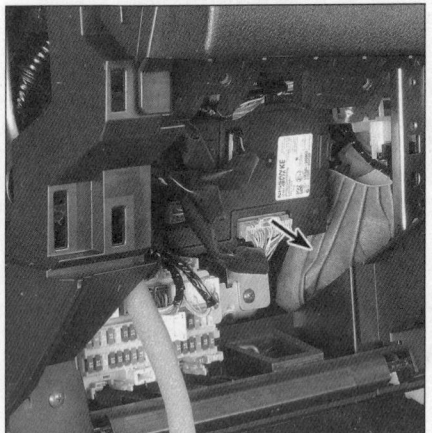

20.5b Filter partially removed - T32 X-Trail shown, Qashqai similar

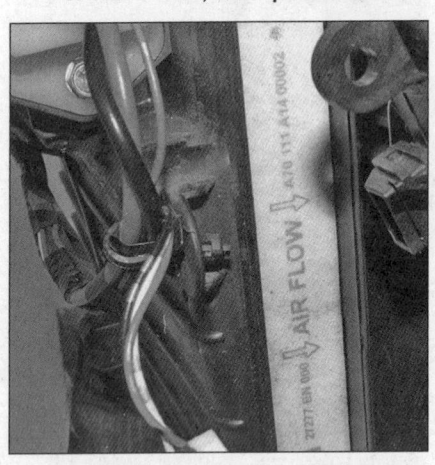

20.7 The air flow arrow should point toward the HVAC box

21.2a Release the clips and...

5 Pull the cabin air filter out of the housing (**see illustrations**).
6 Installation is the reverse of removal.
7 Make sure the arrow on the filter is pointing to the rear of the vehicle when installed (**see illustration**).

21 Air filter check and replacement

1 The air filter is located inside the air filter housing at the left hand side of the engine compartment.

Early type

2 Release the two locking tabs at the sides of the top cover, then pull the air filter out of the housing (**see illustrations**).

Note: *On some models, the filter element might be contained in a filter element holder. If so, separate the element from the holder, install the new element into the holder, then install the holder and element assembly into the air filter housing.*

21.2b... remove the cover...

21.2c... and pull out the filter element

21.2d Where fitted, separate the filter from the element holder

Chapter 1 Tune-up and routine maintenance

21.3 Releasing one of the locking clips

21.4 Move the outer housing duct away from the filter

21.5 Removing the filter from the filter housing

Late type
3 Release the two locking clips on the sides of the housing (see illustration).
4 Lift the housing and the housing duct assembly (see illustration) outwards until the both halves of the case can be separated.
5 Remove the filter from the case (see illustration).

All models
6 Inspect the outer surface of the filter element. If it is dirty, replace it. If it is only moderately dusty, it can be reused by blowing it clean from the back to the front surface with compressed air. Because it is a pleated paper type filter, it cannot be washed or oiled. If it cannot be cleaned satisfactorily with compressed air, discard and replace it. While the cover is off, be careful not to drop anything down into the housing.

Caution: *Never drive the vehicle with the air filter removed. Excessive engine wear could result and backfiring could even cause a fire under the bonnet.*

7 Wipe out the inside of the air filter housing.
8 Place the new filter into the holder or housing, making sure it seats properly.
9 On the early type housings, slide the filter cover onto the housing until the tabs snap into place.
10 On the later type housings, place the housing assembly back into place and snap the clips into place to lock the housing assembly together.

22 Fuel system check

Warning: *Petrol and diesel are extremely flammable, so take extra precautions when you work on any part of the fuel system. Don't smoke or allow open flames or bare light bulbs near the work area, and don't work in a garage where a gas-type appliance (such as a water heater or clothes dryer) is present. Since petrol is carcinogenic, wear fuel-resistant gloves when there's a possibility of being exposed to fuel, and, if you spill any fuel on your skin, rinse it off immediately with soap and water. Mop up any spills immediately and do not store fuel-soaked rags where they could ignite. The fuel system is under constant pressure, so, if any fuel lines are to be disconnected, the fuel pressure in the system must be relieved first (see Chapter 4A for more information). When you perform any kind of work on the fuel system, wear safety glasses and have a Class B type fire extinguisher on hand.*

1 If you smell fuel while driving or after the vehicle has been sitting in the sun, inspect the fuel system immediately.
2 Remove the fuel tank cap and inspect it for damage and corrosion. The gasket should have an unbroken sealing imprint. If the gasket is damaged or corroded, remove it and install a new one.
3 Inspect the fuel feed and return lines for cracks. Make sure the threaded flare nut type connectors (which secure the metal fuel lines to the fuel injection system) and the clamps (which secure the hoses to the in-line fuel filter) are tight.

22.5 Inspect the fuel filler hoses for cracks and make sure the clamps are tight

4 Since some components of the fuel system - the fuel tank and part of the fuel feed and return lines, for example - are underneath the vehicle, they can be inspected more easily with the vehicle raised on a hoist. If that's not possible, raise the vehicle and support it securely on jackstands.
5 With the vehicle raised and safely supported, inspect the fuel tank and filler neck for punctures, cracks and other damage. The connection between the filler neck and the tank is particularly critical. Sometimes a rubber filler neck will leak because of loose clamps or deteriorated rubber (see illustration). These are problems a home mechanic can usually rectify.
6 Carefully check all rubber hoses and metal lines leading away from the fuel tank. Check for loose connections, deteriorated hoses, crimped lines and other damage. Carefully inspect the lines from the tank to the fuel injection system. Repair or replace damaged sections as necessary (see Chapter 4A).

23 Steering and suspension check

Note: *For detailed illustrations of the steering and suspension components, refer to Chapter 10*

With the wheels on the ground
1 With the vehicle stopped and the front wheels pointed straight ahead, rock the steering wheel gently back and forth. If freeplay (see illustration) is excessive, a front wheel bearing, main shaft yoke, intermediate shaft yoke, control arm balljoint or steering system joint is worn or the steering gear is worn. Refer to Chapter 10 for the appropriate repair procedure.
2 Other symptoms, such as excessive vehicle body movement over rough roads, swaying (leaning) around corners and binding as the steering wheel is turned, may indicate faulty steering and/or suspension components.

23.1 Steering wheel freeplay is the amount of travel between an initial steering input and the point at which the front wheels begin to turn (indicated by a slight resistance)

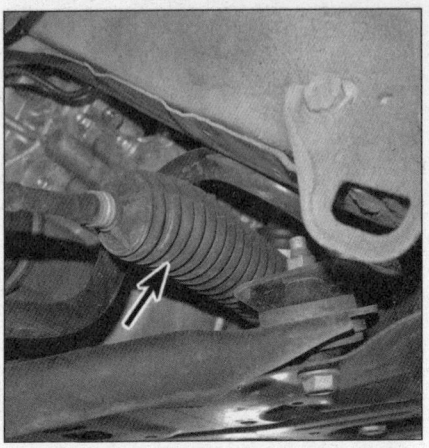

23.6a Check the steering gear boots for cracks or tears

23.6b Check the stabiliser bar bushings for deterioration at the front and the rear of the vehicle

3 Check the shock absorbers by pushing down and releasing the vehicle several times at each corner. If the vehicle does not come back to a level position within one or two bounces, the shocks/struts are worn and must be replaced. When bouncing the vehicle up and down, listen for squeaks and noises from the suspension components.

Under the vehicle

4 Raise the vehicle with a floor jack and support it securely on jackstands (see Chapter 0 Section 7).
5 Check the tyres for irregular wear patterns and proper inflation. See Section 7 for information regarding tyre wear.
6 Inspect the universal joint between the steering shaft and the steering gear housing. Check the steering gear housing for grease leakage. Make sure that the boots are not damaged and that the boot clamps are not loose **(see illustration)**. Check the steering linkage for looseness or damage. Check the tie-rod ends for excessive play. Look for loose bolts, broken or disconnected parts and deteriorated rubber bushings on all suspension and steering components **(see illustration)**. While an assistant turns the steering wheel from side to side, check the steering components for free movement, chafing and binding. If the steering components do not seem to be reacting with the movement of the steering wheel, try to determine where the slack is located.
7 Check the balljoints by moving each control arm up and down with a prybar to ensure that its balljoint has no play. If any balljoint does have play, replace it. See Chapter 10 Section 6 for the front balljoint replacement procedure.
8 Inspect the balljoint boots for damage and leaking grease. Replace the balljoints with new ones if they are damaged (see Chapter 10 Section 6).

24 Exhaust system check

1 Raise the vehicle with a floor jack and support it securely on jackstands (see Chapter 0 Section 7).
2 With the engine cold (at least three hours after the vehicle has been driven), check the complete exhaust system from its starting point at the engine to the end of the tailpipe.
3 Check the pipes and connections for evidence of leaks **(see illustration)**, severe corrosion or damage. Make sure that all brackets and hangers are in good condition and tight.
4 At the same time, inspect the underside of the body for holes, corrosion, open seams, etc. which may allow exhaust gases to enter the passenger compartment. Seal all body openings with silicone or body putty.
5 Rattles and other noises can often be traced to the exhaust system, especially the mounts and hangers **(see illustration)**. Try to move the pipes, muffler and catalytic converter. If the components can come in contact with the body or suspension parts, secure the exhaust system with new mounts.
6 Check the running condition of the engine by inspecting inside the end of the tailpipe. The exhaust deposits here are an indication of engine state-of-tune. If the pipe is black and sooty or coated with white deposits, the engine is in need of a tune-up, including a thorough engine management and fuel system inspection.

25 Driveshaft boot check

1 The driveshaft boots are very important because they prevent dirt, water and foreign material from entering and damaging the constant velocity (CV) joints.

24.3 Check the flange connections for exhaust leaks - also check that the retaining bolts or nuts are securely tightened

24.5 Check the exhaust system hangers for damage and cracks

Chapter 1 Tune-up and routine maintenance

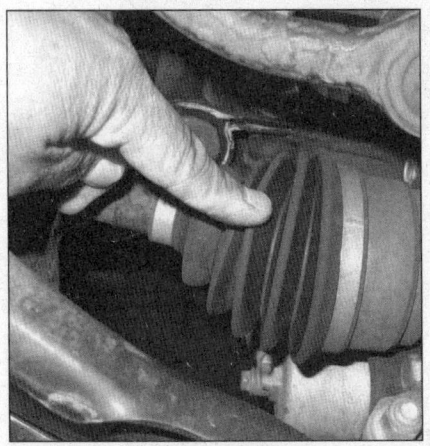

25.2 Check the driveshaft boot for cracks or leaking grease

2   Inspect the boots for tears and cracks as well as loose clamps (see illustration). If there is any evidence of cracks or leaking lubricant, they must be replaced (see Chapter 8 Section 7).

26 Spark plug check and replacement

1   Spark plug replacement requires a spark plug socket and extension which fits onto a ratchet. This socket is lined with a rubber grommet to protect the porcelain insulator of the spark plug and to hold the plug while you remove it. You will also need a wire-type feeler gauge to check and adjust the spark plug gap and a torque wrench to tighten the new plugs to the specified torque (see illustration).
2   Inspect each of the new plugs for defects. If there are any signs of cracks in the porcelain insulator of a plug, don't use it.
3   Check the electrode gaps of the new plugs. Check the gap by inserting the wire gauge of the proper thickness between the

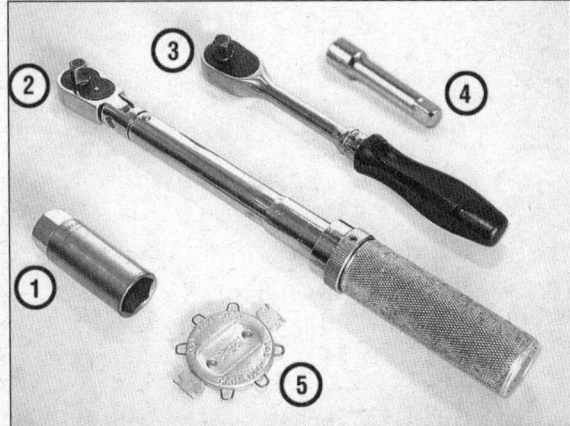

26.1 Tools required for changing spark plugs

1 *Spark plug socket - This will have special padding inside to protect the spark plug porcelain insulator*
2 *Torque wrench - Although not mandatory, use of this tool is the best way to ensure that the plugs are tightened properly*
3 *Ratchet - Standard hand tool to fit the plug socket*
4 *Extension - Depending on model and accessories, you may need special extensions and universal joints to reach one or more of the plugs*
5 *Spark plug gap gauge - This gauge for checking the gap comes in a variety of styles. Make sure the gap for your engine is included*

electrodes at the tip of the plug (see illustration). The gap between the electrodes should be identical to that listed in this Chapter's Specifications. If the gap is incorrect, the spark plug must be replaced.
Caution: *The gap can only be checked. Do not adjust the gap, the spark plug must be replaced if the gap is incorrect.*
4   If the side electrode is not exactly over the centre electrode, the spark plug should be replaced.
Caution: *These spark plug tips are covered in iridium or platinum; do not use a wire brush or wheel to clean them.*

Removal

5   Remove the ignition coils (see Chapter 5 Section 7).
6   If compressed air is available, blow any dirt or foreign material away from the spark plug area before proceeding (a common bicycle pump will also work).
7   Remove the spark plugs (see illustration).
8   Whether you are replacing the plugs at this time or intend to reuse the old plugs, compare each old spark plug with the chart to determine the overall running condition of the engine.

Installation

9   Prior to installation, apply a coat of anti-seize compound to the plug threads (see illustration). It's often difficult to insert spark plugs into their holes without cross-threading them. To avoid this possibility, fit a short piece of snug-fitting rubber hose over the end of the spark plug (see illustration). The flexible hose acts as a universal joint to help align the

26.3 Spark plug manufacturers recommend using a wire-type gauge when checking the gap - if the wire does not slide between the electrodes with a slight drag, the spark plug will need to be replaced

26.7 Use a spark plug socket with a ratchet and an extension to remove the spark plugs

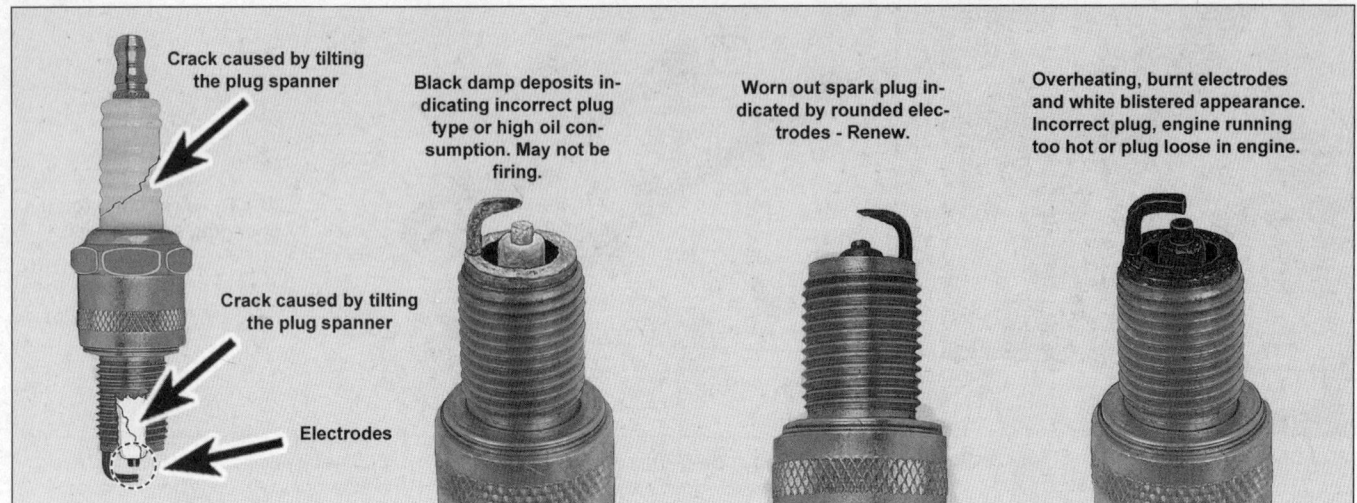

26.8 Compare the spark plugs from the engine to determine the overall operating condition of each cylinder

plug with the plug hole. Should the plug begin to cross-thread, the hose will slip on the spark plug, preventing thread damage. Tighten the plug to the torque listed in this Chapter's Specifications.

10 Follow the above procedure for the remaining spark plugs.

11 After replacing all the plugs, install the ignition coils (see Chapter 5 Section 7)

27 Cooling system servicing (draining, flushing and refilling)

Warning: *Do not allow engine coolant (antifreeze) to come in contact with your skin or painted surfaces of the vehicle. Rinse off spills immediately with plenty of water. Antifreeze is highly toxic if ingested. Never leave antifreeze laying around in an open container or in puddles on the floor; children and pets are attracted by it's sweet smell and may drink it. Check with local authorities about disposing of used antifreeze. Many communities have collection centres which will see that antifreeze is disposed of safely.*

Warning: *The engine must be completely cool before beginning this procedure.*

1 Periodically, the cooling system should be drained, flushed and refilled to replenish the antifreeze mixture and prevent formation of rust and corrosion, which can impair the performance of the cooling system and cause engine damage. When the cooling system is serviced, all hoses and the radiator cap should be checked and replaced if necessary.

Draining

2 Apply the parking brake and block the wheels. If the vehicle has just been driven, wait several hours to allow the engine to cool down before beginning this procedure.

3 Raise the front of the vehicle and support it securely on jackstands (see Chapter 0 Section 7). Remove the splash shield between the bumper cover and the subframe.

4 Remove the radiator cap. Move a large container under the radiator drain to catch the coolant. Using a large screwdriver, open the radiator drain plug and direct the coolant into the container **(see illustration)**.

5 After the coolant stops flowing out of the radiator, move the container under the engine block drain plug **(see illustration)**. Remove the plug and allow the coolant in the block to drain.

Note: *The engine block drain plug is located on the right end of the engine, on the firewall side.*

6 While the coolant is draining, check the condition of the radiator hoses, heater hoses and clamps (refer to Section 13 if necessary).

7 Replace any damaged clamps or hoses (see Section 13).

Flushing

8 Once the system is completely drained, flush the radiator with fresh water from a garden hose until water runs clear at the drain. The flushing action of the water will remove sediments from the radiator but will not remove rust and scale from the engine and cooling tube surfaces.

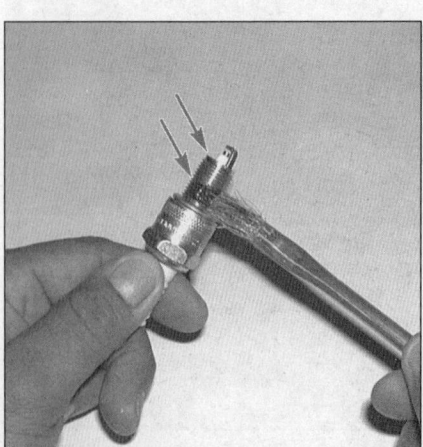

26.9a Apply a coat of anti-seize compound to the spark plug threads, being careful not to get any near the lower threads

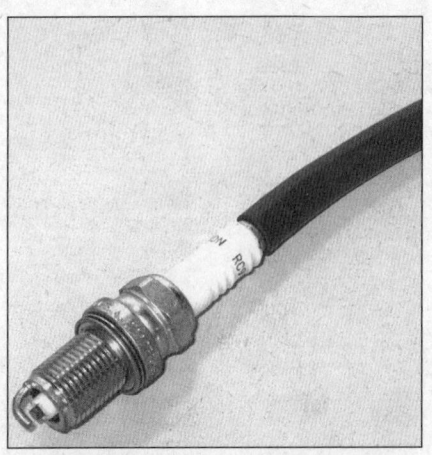

26.9b A length of snug-fitting rubber hose will save time and prevent damaged threads when installing the spark plugs

27.4 The radiator drain fitting is located at the bottom of the radiator

Chapter 1 Tune-up and routine maintenance

27.5 After draining the radiator, fully drain the cooling system by removing the engine block drain plug - 2.0L petrol shown, 2.5L petrol engine similar. Note, diesel engines do not have a cylinder block drain plug

27.8a Removing one of the heater hoses from the heater core for flushing

27.8b Remove the radiator hoses to flush the radiator

9   These deposits can be removed by the chemical action of a cleaner. Follow the procedure outlined in the manufacturer's instructions. If the radiator is severely corroded, damaged or leaking, it should be removed (see Chapter 3) and taken to a radiator repair shop.

10   Remove the overflow hose from the coolant recovery reservoir. Drain the reservoir and flush it with clean water, then reconnect the hose.

Refilling

11   Close and tighten the radiator drain. Install and tighten the engine block drain plug.

12   Make sure the heater temperature control is in the maximum heat position.

13   Slowly refill the radiator with the specified coolant until coolant reaches the lip on the radiator filler neck. Add coolant to the reservoir up to the lower mark.

14   Install the radiator cap and run the engine in a well-ventilated area until the thermostat opens (coolant will begin flowing through the radiator and the upper radiator hose will become hot).

15   Rev the engine to approximately 2500 rpm for ten seconds, then let it idle; do this a few times.

16   Turn the engine off and let it cool. Add more coolant mixture to bring the level back up to the lip on the radiator filler neck.

17   Squeeze the upper radiator hose to expel air, then add more coolant mixture if necessary. Replace the radiator cap.

18   Start the engine, allow it to reach normal operating temperature and check for leaks.

29.4 Oil filler/level plug (arrowed)

29.6 Oil drain plug (arrowed)

29.7 Drain the transaxle oil

28 Evaporative emissions control system check

1   The function of the evaporative emissions control system is to draw fuel vapors from the gas tank and fuel system, store them in a charcoal canister, then burn them during normal engine operation.

2   The most common symptom of a fault in the evaporative emissions system is a strong fuel odor. If a fuel odor is detected, inspect the charcoal canister, located beneath the RH front headlamp, on T32 X-Trail models and at the right rear corner of the vehicle, to the rear of the wheel. Check the canister and all hoses for damage and deterioration (see Chapter 6 Section 19).

29 Manual transaxle lubricant change

1   This operation is much quicker and more efficient if the car is first taken on a journey of sufficient length to warm the engine/transaxle up to normal operating temperature.

2   Park the car on level ground, switch off the ignition and apply the handbrake firmly. For improved access, jack up the front of the car and support it securely on axle stands (see Chapter 0 Section 7). Note that the car must be level to ensure accuracy when refilling and checking the oil level.

3   Undo the retaining bolts and remove the plastic undershield from below the engine/transaxle.

4   Wipe clean the area around the filler/level plug, which is screwed into the left-hand side of the transaxle, to the rear of the driveshaft **(see illustration)**.

5   Remove the oil filler/level plug, be prepared for some oil spillage as the plug is removed.

6   Position a suitable container under the drain plug, which is situated at the lower rear of the transaxle differential housing **(see illustrations)**.

7   Remove the drain plug and allow the oil to drain completely into the container **(see illustration)**. If the oil is hot, take precautions

Chapter 1 Tune-up and routine maintenance

29.8 Use a new sealing washer when refitting the drain plug

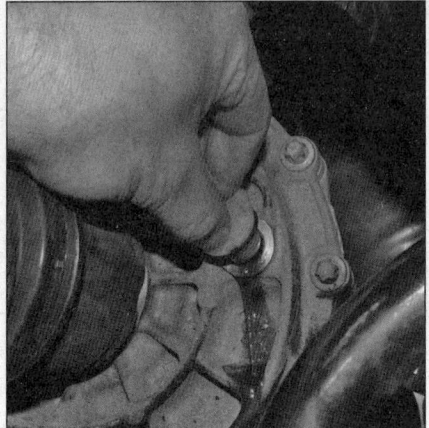

29.11 Refit the filler/level plug when fluid is correct

30.7a Automatic transaxle fluid drain plug - CVT on petrol model shown, diesel models similar

against scalding. Clean both the filler/level and the drain plug, discard the sealing washers, as new ones will be required on refitting.

8 When the oil has finished draining, clean the drain plug threads and those of the transaxle casing, then fit the new sealing washer and refit the drain plug **(see illustration)**, tightening it to the specified torque wrench setting. If the car was raised for the draining operation, lower it to the ground, to make sure it is level.

9 Refilling the transaxle is an awkward operation. Above all, allow plenty of time for the oil level to settle properly before checking it. Note that the car must be parked on flat level ground when checking the oil level.

10 Refill the transaxle with the exact amount of the specified type of oil, then check the oil level as described in this, ; if the correct amount was poured into the transaxle, and a large amount flows out on checking the level, refit the filler/level plug and take the car on a short journey so that the new oil is distributed fully around the transaxle components, then check the level again on your return.

11 When the level is correct, refit the filler/level plug **(see illustration)**. On two-wheel-drive models, tighten the plastic filler plug finger tight only. On all-wheel-drive models, tighten the filler plugto the specified torque. Wash off any spilt oil.

30 Automatic and continuously variable transaxle (CVT) fluid change

Note: *Failure to use the correct fluid will damage the transaxle and void the warranty.*

1 At the specified time intervals, the CVT fluid should be drained and replaced.
2 Before beginning work, purchase the specified transaxle fluid (see Specifications).
3 Other tools necessary for this job include jackstands to support the vehicle in a raised position, a wrench, a large drain pan, newspapers and clean rags.
4 The fluid should be drained after the vehicle has been driven and brought to operating temperature. Hot fluid is more effective than cold fluid at removing built up sediment.
Warning: *Fluid temperature can exceed 100-degrees C in a hot transaxle. Wear protective gloves.*
5 Raise the vehicle and support it securely on jackstands (see Chapter 0 Section 7). Put the transaxle in Park and turn off the engine.

Note: *Note that the car must be level to ensure accuracy when refilling and checking the fluid level.*

6 Move the necessary equipment under the vehicle, being careful not to touch any of the hot exhaust components.
7 Place the drain pan under the drain plug and remove the drain plug **(see illustration)**. Be sure the drain pan is in position, as fluid will come out with some force. Once the fluid is drained, reinstall the drain plug and tighten it to the torque listed in this Chapter's Specifications.

Note: *On diesel models, remove the level tube, which is the larger hex, to drain the fluid.*

8 Lower the vehicle.

Petrol models with CVT

9 With the engine off, add new fluid to the transaxle through the dipstick tube (see Section 8). Use a funnel to prevent spills. It is best to add a little fluid at a time, checking the level with the dipstick. Allow the fluid time to drain into the pan.
10 Start the engine and move the shift selector into all positions from Park through Low then shift into Park and apply the parking brake.
11 With the engine idling, check the fluid level. Add fluid, a little at a time, until it's up to the Cool level on the dipstick.

Note: *After the fluid has been changed, the CVT fluid deterioration date must be changed using a factory CONSULT scanner; see your dealer service department or other properly equipped repair shop for this procedure.*

Diesel models with an automatic transaxle

12 There is no filler plug on this transaxle, so the turbine speed sensor in the top of the transaxle housing has to be removed and the

30.11 Arrow indicates the clip retaining the top of the dipstick to the dipstick tube

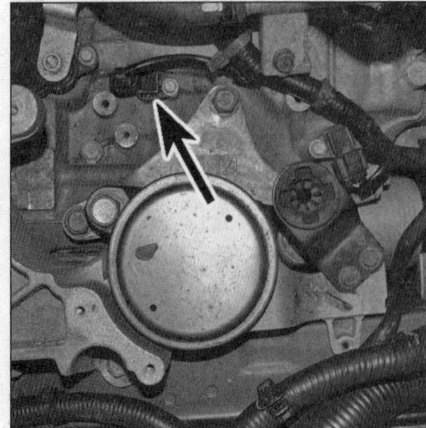

30.14 Battery and battery tray removed showing the turbine speed sensor (arrow)

Chapter 1 Tune-up and routine maintenance   1-35

31.1 PCV valve location

31.2a Using a pair of pliers, disconnect the clamp and pull the hose off the valve

31.2b Always replace the O-ring when the PCV valve is removed

fluid is poured in through the sensor mounting hole.

13 The battery and battery tray have to be removed to allow access to the turbine speed sensor (see Chapter 5 Section 5).

14 Locate the turbine speed sensor on top of the transaxle and wipe clean the area around the sensor (see illustration). Disconnect the wiring connector, and then undo the retaining bolt and remove the sensor from the top of the transaxle housing. Nissan recommend that the O-ring be renewed when refitting.

15 Calculate how much fluid was removed from the transaxle and pour the same quantity plus approximately 0.5 litres through the turbine speed sensor hole.

Note: *Adding the extra 0.5 litres will hopefully eliminate the need to remove the battery again to access the turbine speed sensor for further top-ups.*

16 Install the turbine speed sensor and then the battery and battery tray (see Chapter 5 Section 5).

17 Check the transaxle fluid level (see Section 8).

31 Positive Crankcase Ventilation (PCV) valve check and replacement

1 Locate the PCV valve on the valve cover (see illustration).

2 Disconnect the hose, then remove the PCV valve (see illustrations).

3 Reconnect the hose to the valve. With the engine idling at normal operating temperature, place your finger over the end of the valve. If there's no vacuum at the valve, check for a plugged hose or valve. Replace any plugged or deteriorated hoses.

4 When purchasing a replacement PCV valve, make sure it's for your particular vehicle and engine size. Compare the old valve with the new one to make sure they're the same.

5 Installation is the reverse of removal.

32 Differential lubricant change (AWD models)

1 This procedure should be performed after the vehicle has been driven so the lubricant will be warm and therefore will flow out of the differential easily.

2 Raise the vehicle and support it securely on jackstands. Place a drain pan under the differential.

3 Remove the fill plug, then remove the drain plug (see illustration) and allow the lubricant to drain into the pan. Clean and reinstall the drain plug, using a new sealing washer. Tighten the plug to the torque listed in this Chapter's Specifications.

4 Using a hand pump, syringe or squeeze bottle, fill the differential housing with the specified lubricant until it's level with the bottom of the fill plug hole.

5 Clean and reinstall the fill plug, using a new sealing washer. Tighten the plug to the torque listed in this Chapter's Specifications.

6 Drive the vehicle a short distance and check for leaks.

33 Transfer case lubricant change (AWD models)

1 This procedure should be performed after the vehicle has been driven so the lubricant will be warm and therefore will flow out of the transfer case easily.

2 Raise the vehicle and support it securely on jackstands. Position a drain pan, rags under the transaxle (the transfer case is the rear portion of the transaxle).

3 Remove the fill plug (see illustration 18.2), then remove the drain plug (see illustration) and allow the lubricant to drain into the pan. Clean and reinstall the drain plug, using a new sealing washer. Tighten the plug to the torque listed in this Chapter's Specifications.

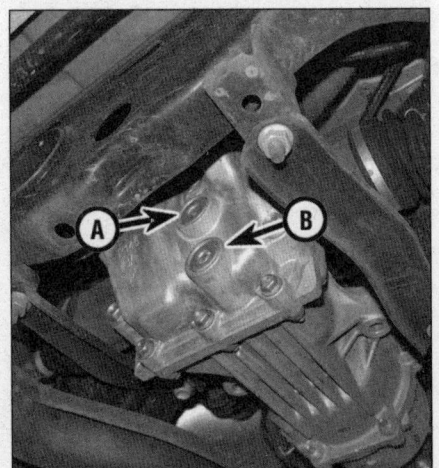

32.3 Remove the fill plug (A) and the drain plug (B) and allow the lubricant to drain

33.3 Transfer case details

1 Transfer case drain plug (TY30A transfer case shown, TY21C transfer case similar)
2 Tooth contact test plug (TY30A transfer case only) - Do Not Remove

Chapter 1 Tune-up and routine maintenance

34.5a When the No.1 piston is at TDC on the compression stroke, the valve clearance for the No.1 and No.3 cylinder exhaust valves and the No.1 and No.2 cylinder intake valves can be measured

34.5b You will feel drag as you pull the feeler gauge if the adjustment is correct

34.7 When the No.4 piston is at TDC on the compression stroke, the valve clearances for the No.2 and No.4 cylinder exhaust valves and the No.3 and No.4 cylinder intake valves can be measured

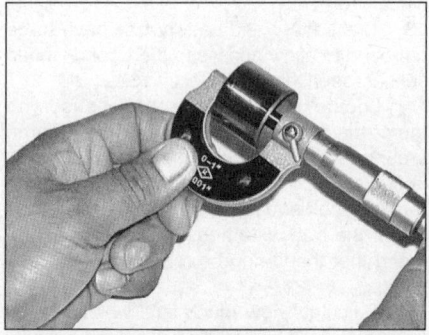

34.9 Measure the lifter thickness with a micrometer

Warning: *Never remove the tooth contact test plug - severe damage may occur.*

4   Using a hand pump, syringe or squeeze bottle, fill the transfer case with the specified lubricant until it's level with the bottom of the fill plug hole.

5   Clean and reinstall the fill plug, using a new sealing washer. Tighten the plug to the torque listed in this Chapter's Specifications.

6   Drive the vehicle a short distance and check for leaks.

34 Valve clearance check and adjustment

Note: *This is not a routine operation. It should only be necessary at high mileage, after overhaul, or when investigating noise or power loss which may be attributable to the valve gear. Adjustment involves removing the camshafts and changing the cam followers (valve lifters) that are available in over 20 different thicknesses (see Specifications 1).*

Note: *Diesel models have hydraulic lifters and require no valve clearance adjustment.*

1   Disconnect the negative (-) battery terminal (see Chapter 5 Section 3)

2   Remove the spark plugs (see Section 26).

3   Remove the valve cover (see Chapter 2A Section 4 - 2.5L petrol engines or see Chapter 2B Section 4 - 2.0L petrol engines).

2.5 litre petrol engines

4   Position the number 1 piston at TDC on the compression stroke (see Chapter 2A Section 3).

5   Using feeler gauges, measure the clearance between the base of the cam and the follower of the following valves, recording each clearance on the paper **(see illustrations)**.
   No.1 cylinder intake and exhaust valves.
   No.2 cylinder intake valves.
   No.3 cylinder exhaust valves.

6   Rotate the crankshaft through one complete turn (360°) clockwise until the TDC notch on the crankshaft pulley is realigned with the pointer. No.4 cylinder is now at TDC on its compression stroke.

7   Check the clearances of the following valves, and record them on the paper **(see illustration)**.
   No.2 cylinder exhaust valves.
   No.3 cylinder intake valves.
   No.4 cylinder intake and exhaust valves.

8   These engines don't use valve adjusting shims. If a clearance is out of specification, the lifter must be replaced with a new lifter that has a different thickness head to correct the clearance. Remove the camshafts to access the lifters (see Chapter 2A Section 9).

9   Mark the lifters that are to be replaced, and record which valve they came from. Measure the thickness of the centre of the lifter with a micrometer **(see illustration)**.

2.0 litre petrol engine

10 Position the number 1 piston at TDC on the compression stroke (see Chapter 2B Section 3).

11 Using feeler gauges, measure the clearance between the base of the cam and the follower of the following valves, recording each clearance on the paper **(see illustrations)**.
   No.1 cylinder inlet and exhaust valves.
   No.2 cylinder inlet valves.
   No.3 cylinder exhaust valves.

12 Rotate the crankshaft through one complete turn (360°) clockwise until the TDC notch on the crankshaft pulley is realigned with the pointer. No.4 cylinder is now at TDC on its compression stroke.

Chapter 1 Tune-up and routine maintenance

34.11a Check the clearances between the camshafts and the followers (arrowed)

34.11b Check clearances at the following valves

No.1 cylinder intake and exhaust valves
No.2 cylinder intake valves.
No.3 cylinder exhaust valves.

13 Check the clearances of the following valves, and record them on the paper (see illustration).
   No.2 cylinder exhaust valves.
   No.3 cylinder intake valves.
   No.4 cylinder intake and exhaust valves.

All models

Note: *A micrometer or dial gauge and probe will be required for this operation.*

14 To calculate the correct thickness of a replacement lifter that will place the valve clearance within the specified value, use the following formula:

15 Where a valve clearance differs from the specified value, then the cam follower (valve lifter) for that valve must be substituted with a thinner or thicker one accordingly. The cam followers have the thickness stamped on the bottom face of the follower; e.g. 324 indicates the follower is 3.24 mm thick at the top centre of the follower (see illustration).

16 If required use a micrometer or dial gauge to measure the true thickness of any follower removed, as it may have been reduced by wear.

Note: *Followers are available in various thicknesses increasing in increments of 0.02 mm.*

17 To access the cam followers (valve lifters), first remove the camshafts (see 2A Section 9 - 2.5L engines) or (see 2B Section 10 - 2.0L engines). Remove and refit each follower separately, to avoid any confusion.

18 To calculate the thickness of the replacement shim, use the following formula:
- $N = T + A - V$
- N = thickness of the new lifter
- T = thickness of the old lifter
- A = valve clearance measured
- V = desired valve clearance (see Specifications)

19 Select a lifter with a thickness as close as possible to the valve clearance calculated.

20 Mark the new lifters as to their destination, lubricate them with engine assembly lube and install them. After replacing the lifters, install the camshaft(s) (see 2A Section 9 - 2.5L engines) or (see 2B Section 10 - 2.0L engines).

21 The remainder of installation is the reverse of removal.

22 Reconnect the battery and perform the system initialisation procedure (see Chapter 5 Section 4).

34.13 Check clearances at the illustrated valves

34.15 Markings inside the follower for thickness

Notes

Chapter 2 Part A
2.5 litre petrol engine

Contents

	Section		Section
Camshafts and lifters - removal, inspection and installation	9	Intake manifold - removal and installation	5
Crankshaft front oil seal - replacement	7	Oil pans - removal and installation	11
Cylinder compression check	See Chapter 2D	Oil pressure check	See Chapter 2D
Cylinder head - removal and installation	10	Oil pump - removal, inspection and installation	12
Drivebelt check and replacement	See Chapter 1	Rear main oil seal - replacement	14
Driveplate - removal and installation	13	Repair operations possible with the engine in the vehicle	2
Engine - removal and installation	See Chapter 2D	Timing chain/oil pump drive chain or balance shaft chain and sprockets - removal, inspection and installation	8
Engine mounts - check and replacement	15		
Engine oil and oil filter change	See Chapter 1		
Exhaust manifold - removal and installation	6	Top Dead Centre (TDC) for number one piston - locating	3
General information	1	Valve cover - removal and installation	4

Specifications

General
Engine Designation	QR25DE
Capacity	2,488 cc
Bore	89.0
Stroke	100.0
Direction of crankshaft rotation	Clockwise (viewed from right hand side of engine)
Cylinder numbers (timing chain end-to-transaxle end)	1-2-3-4
Firing order	1-3-4-2
Valve clearances	See Chapter 1

Cylinder head
Warpage limits
Cylinder head-to-block surface
- Standard: Less than 0.03 mm
- Limit: 0.1 mm

Camshaft
Endplay	0.115 to 0.188 mm
Camshaft journal diameter	
No. 1	27.935 to 27.955 mm
No. 2 through 5	23.435 to 23.455 mm
Camshaft bearing inside diameter	
No. 1	28.000 to 28.021 mm
No. 2 through 5	23.500 to 23.521 mm
Bearing oil clearance	
Standard	0.045 to 0.086 mm
Service limit	0.15 mm
Camshaft runout	0.02 mm

Cylinder location: ① ② ③ ④ Front ↓

Chapter 2 Part A 2.5 litre petrol engine

Intake lobe height	
T31 models	44.815 to 45.005 mm
T32 models	45.865 to 46.055 mm
Exhaust lobe height	
T31 models	43.975 to 44.165 mm
T32 models	44.175 to 44.365 mm
Oil pump	
Body-to-outer rotor clearance	0.114 to 0.179 mm
Inner rotor-to-outer rotor tip clearance	0.170 to 0.220 mm
Inner rotor-to-cover clearance	0.030 to 0.070 mm
Outer rotor-to-cover clearance	0.060 to 0.110 mm
Inner rotor-to-body clearance	
T31 Models	0.045 to 0.091 mm
T32 models	0.035 to 0.070 mm

Torque specifications   Nm

Balance shaft assembly bolts [1, 2, 3]	
Step 1	
Bolts 1 through 5	42
Bolt 6	36
Step 2	
Bolts 1 through 5	Tighten an additional 120 degrees
Bolt 6	Tighten an additional 90 degrees
Step 3	Loosen all bolts completely in reverse sequence
Step 4	
Bolts 1 through 5	42
Bolt 6	36
Step 5	
Bolts 1 through 5	Tighten an additional 120 degrees
Bolt 6	Tighten an additional 90 degrees
Balance shaft drive sprocket bolt [1]	65
Camshaft bearing cap bolts (all bolts) [3]	
Step 1 (bolts 9 through 11)	2
Step 2 (bolts 1 through 8)	2
Step 3 (bolts 1 through 11)	6
Step 4 (bolts 1 through 11)	11
Camshaft signal plate fastener	55
Camshaft sprocket bolt [2]	
T31 model	
Intake sprocket assembly	103
Exhaust sprocket	142
T32 model	
Step 1	50
Step 2	Tighten an additional 45 degrees
Crankshaft pulley bolt [2]	
Step 1	42
Step 2	Tighten an additional 60 degrees
Cylinder head bolts [1, 2, 3]	
Step 1	50
Step 2	Tighten an additional 60 degrees
Step 3	Loosen all bolts completely in reverse sequence
Step 4	40
Step 5	Tighten an additional 75 degrees
Step 6	Tighten an additional 75 degrees
Driveplate/flywheel bolts	108
Engine mount bolts/nuts	
Upper (torque rod) mount bolts	
T31 model	120
T32 model	85
Right (timing chain end) mount bolts	
T31 model	55
T32 model	65
Right (timing chain end) mount bracket-to-engine bolts	
T31 model	55
T32 model	49
Left (transaxle) insulator-to-transaxle bolts	50
Left (transaxle) insulator bracket-to-body bolts	80
Left (transaxle) support bracket nuts/bolts	10
Rear (torque rod) mount bolts	110
Rear (torque rod) support bracket bolts	110

Chapter 2 Part A 2.5 litre petrol engine

Torque specifications (continued)	Nm
Exhaust manifold nuts	42
Intake manifold fasteners	
T31 models	20
T32 models	25
IVT cover bolts	13
IVT solenoid mounting bolts	7
Oil pump fasteners	7
Timing chain components	
Timing chain slack guide bolts	17
Timing chain tension guide bolts	17
Timing chain tensioner bolts	7
Oil pump drive chain tensioner bolts	7
Aluminium section-to-block [3]	22
Aluminium section-to-transaxle [3]	
Vertical bolts (2)	9
Horizontal bolts	
T31 model	43
T32 model	50
Steel pan to aluminium section [3]	7
Timing chain cover bolts [3]	
M8 bolts	13
M10 bolts	49
Valve cover bolts [3]	
Step 1	2
Step 2	9

[1] Fastener must be replaced with NEW ones
[2] Lubricate fastener threads and heads with clean engine oil prior to installation
[3] Tighten the fasteners in the correct sequence. See text for diagrams

1 General information

This Part of Chapter 2 is devoted to in-vehicle repair procedures for the 2.5L QR25DE petrol engine. All procedures concerning engine removal and refitting, and engine overhaul options can be found in Part 2D of this Chapter.

The following repair procedures are based on the assumption that the engine is installed in the vehicle. If the engine has been removed from the vehicle and mounted on a stand, many of the steps outlined in this Part of Chapter 2 will not apply.

Engine description

The engine is of the sixteen-valve, in-line four-cylinder, double overhead camshaft (DOHC) type, mounted transversely at the front of the car with the transmission attached to the left-hand end.

The crankshaft runs in five main bearings. Thrustwashers are fitted to No 3 main bearing (upper half) to control crankshaft endfloat.

The camshaft is driven by a timing chain, and operates the sixteen valves via bucket-type followers. The followers are situated directly below the camshafts. Valve clearances are adjusted by replacing the relevant follower with a different thickness. The camshafts rotate directly in the cylinder head.

Lubrication is by means of an oil pump, which is inside the timing chain cover and is driven off the crankshaft. The balance shaft has a sprocket on the end, which is driven by a chain from the right-hand end of the crankshaft. The oil pump draws oil through a strainer located in the oil pan, and then forces it through an externally mounted filter into galleries in the cylinder block/crankcase. From there, the oil is distributed to the crankshaft (main bearings) and camshaft. The big-end bearings are supplied with oil via internal drillings in the crankshaft, while the camshaft bearings also receive a pressurised supply. The camshaft lobes and valves are lubricated by splash, as are all other engine components.

2 Repair operations possible with the engine in the vehicle

Warning: *The models covered by this manual are equipped with a Supplemental Restraint System (SRS), more commonly known as airbags. Always disarm the airbag system before working in the vicinity of any airbag system component to avoid the possibility of accidental deployment of the airbag, which could cause personal injury (see Chapter 12A Section 20). Do not use a memory saving device to preserve the PCM's memory when working on or near airbag system components.*

Many major repair operations can be accomplished without removing the engine from the vehicle.

Clean the engine compartment and the exterior of the engine with some type of degreaser before any work is done. It will make the job easier and help keep dirt out of the internal areas of the engine.

Depending on the components involved, it may be helpful to remove the bonnet to improve access to the engine as repairs are performed (see Chapter 11 Section 9). Cover the mudguards to prevent damage to the paint. Special pads are available, but an old bedspread or blanket will also work.

If vacuum, exhaust, oil or coolant leaks develop, indicating a need for gasket or seal replacement, the repairs can generally be made with the engine in the vehicle. The intake and exhaust manifold gaskets, oil pan gasket, crankshaft oil seals and cylinder head gasket are all accessible with the engine in place.

Exterior engine components, such as the intake and exhaust manifolds, the oil pan, the oil pump, the water pump, the starter motor, the alternator, and the fuel system components can be removed for repair with the engine in place.

Since the cylinder head can be removed without pulling the engine, camshaft and valve component servicing can also be accomplished with the engine in the vehicle. Replacement of the timing chain and sprockets is also possible with the engine in the vehicle.

In extreme cases caused by a lack of necessary equipment, repair or replacement of piston rings, pistons, connecting rods and rod bearings is possible with the engine in the vehicle. However, this practice is not recommended because of the cleaning and preparation work that must be done to the components involved.

3.9 Compression gauge installed to No.1 cylinder spark plug hole

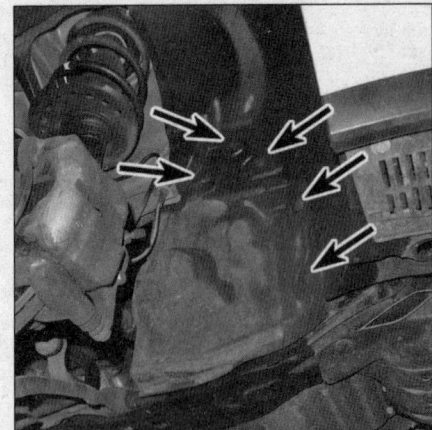

3.10 Remove the right inner guard liner retainers to access the crankshaft pulley

3.12 Top Dead Centre (TDC) details

1 Pointer on timing chain cover
2 TDC mark

3 Top Dead Centre (TDC) for number one piston - locating

1 Top Dead Centre (TDC) is the highest point in the cylinder that each piston reaches as it travels up-and-down when the crankshaft turns. Each piston reaches TDC on the compression stroke and again on the exhaust stroke, but TDC generally refers to piston position on the compression stroke.
2 Positioning the number one piston at TDC is an essential part of certain procedures, such as camshaft and timing chain/sprocket removal.
3 Disconnect the negative (-) battery terminal (see Chapter 5 Section 3).
4 Before beginning this procedure, place the transaxle in Park or Neutral and apply the parking brake or block the rear wheels.
5 Disconnect the negative (-) battery terminal (see Chapter 5 Section 3).
6 To access the crankshaft pulley, raise the front of the vehicle and support on jackstands (see Chapter 0 Section 7). Remove the RH front wheel.
7 In order to bring any piston to TDC, the crankshaft must be turned using a large breaker bar or ratchet and socket placed on the crankshaft pulley bolt. When looking at the RH side of the engine, normal crankshaft rotation is clockwise.
8 Remove the spark plugs (see Chapter 1 Section 26).
9 Install a compression gauge in the number one spark plug hole. It should be a gauge with a screw-in fitting and a hose at least 150 mm long **(see illustration)**.
10 Remove the inner guard liner **(see illustration)**. Rotate the crankshaft while observing for pressure on the compression gauge. The moment the gauge shows pressure indicates that the number one cylinder has begun the compression stroke.
11 Once the compression stroke has begun, TDC for the compression stroke is reached by bringing the piston to the top of the cylinder.
12 Continue turning the crankshaft until the TDC notch in the crankshaft damper is aligned with the pointer on the timing chain cover **(see illustration)**. At this point, the number one cylinder is at TDC on the compression stroke. If the marks are aligned but there was no compression, the piston was on the exhaust stroke. Continue rotating the crankshaft 360-degrees (1-turn).

Note: *If a compression gauge is not available, you can simply place a hand over the spark plug hole and listen for compression as the engine is rotated. Once compression at the*

No.1 spark plug hole is noted, the remainder of the Step is the same.

13 After the number one piston has been positioned at TDC on the compression stroke, TDC for any of the remaining cylinders can be located by turning the crankshaft 180-degrees and following the firing order (refer to Specifications). For example, rotating the engine 180-degrees past TDC for No.1 cylinder will put the engine at TDC compression for No.3 cylinder; rotating another 180-degrees puts No.4 cylinder at TDC compression and another 180-degrees puts No.2 cylinder at TDC compression.

4 Valve cover - removal and installation

Removal

1 Disconnect the negative (-) battery terminal (see Chapter 5 Section 3).
2 Remove the upper air intake resonator (see Chapter 4A).
3 Detach the fresh air hose from the left-rear corner of the cover.
4 Remove the ignition coils (see Chapter 5 Section 7) and spark plugs (see Chapter 1).
5 Remove the intake manifold (see Section 5).
6 Support the engine from below using a block of wood on a floor jack or from above using an engine support fixture. Remove the right upper engine mount and mount bracket (see Section 15).
7 Disconnect the PCV hose.
8 Remove the bolts in the reverse of the tightening sequence **(see illustration 4.13a or 4.13b)**. Loosen the bolts starting at the ends and work toward the centre. If the cover is stuck to the cylinder head, bump the end with a wood block and a hammer to jar it loose. If that doesn't work, try to slip a flexible putty knife between the cylinder head and cover to break the seal.

4.2 Upper air intake resonator on a T31 model

A Air duct clamp
B Crankcase ventilation hose clamp
C Mounting bolt

Chapter 2 Part A 2.5 litre petrol engine

2A-5

4.9 Remove the gasket from the cover

4.13a Valve cover bolt tightening sequence - Type 1 (used on 2011 and earlier models and some 2012 and 2013 models)

Caution: *Don't pry at the cover or housing-to-cylinder head joint or damage to the sealing surfaces may occur, leading to oil leaks after the cover is reinstalled.*

9 Remove the gasket from the valve cover **(see illustration).**

Installation

10 The mating surfaces of the valve cover and cylinder head must be clean when the cover is installed. Use a gasket scraper to remove all traces of sealant, then clean the mating surfaces with brake system cleaner. If there's residue or oil on the mating surfaces when the cover is installed, oil leaks may develop.

Caution: *Use care when scraping the soft aluminium of the cylinder head or the plastic valve cover. They are soft, and deep scratches may lead to oil leaks.*

11 Apply RTV sealant at the timing chain cover-to-cylinder head joints.
12 Install the valve cover and bolts.
13 Tighten the bolts in the indicated sequence **(see illustrations)** to the torque listed in Specifications.
14 The remainder of installation is the reverse of removal.

15 Reconnect the battery and perform the system initialisation procedure (see Chapter 5 Section 4).

5 Intake manifold - removal and installation

Warning: *The engine must be completely cool before beginning this procedure.*

Removal

1 Relieve the fuel system pressure (see Chapter 4A Section 3).
2 Remove the engine cover fasteners and remove the cover from the top of the engine, if equipped.
3 Remove the air filter housing, resonator and the air intake duct from between the front of the engine bay and the throttle body.
4 Remove the cowl top cover and the extension panel (see Chapter 11 Section 25).
5 Disconnect the negative (-) battery terminal (see Chapter 5 Section 3).
6 Label and detach the PCV hose, brake booster hose, throttle control actuator, EVAP hose and the purge control solenoid.

7 Remove the throttle body and gasket (see Chapter 4A) and position it aside.

Note: *Doing it this way allows for the coolant hoses to stay connected to the throttle body.*

8 With the throttle body removed, remove the intake manifold support bracket fasteners and remove the bracket, if equipped.
9 Disconnect the fuel line from the fuel rail (see Chapter 4A).

Note: *It may be necessary to remove the fuel injectors and fuel rail to gain access to the mounting bolts.*

10 On T32 models, disconnect the oil cooler hose clamps and the wiring harness clips from the bottom of the intake manifold and position clear of the work area.
11 Remove the intake manifold mounting nuts and bolts in the reverse of the tightening sequence **(see illustration 5.16a or 5.16b).**
12 Remove the intake manifold from the cylinder head.

Note: *Some T31 models may have an adapter plate between the head and the manifold. On these models, remove the adapter plate once the manifold is removed and then discard the gasket between adapter plate and cylinder head.*

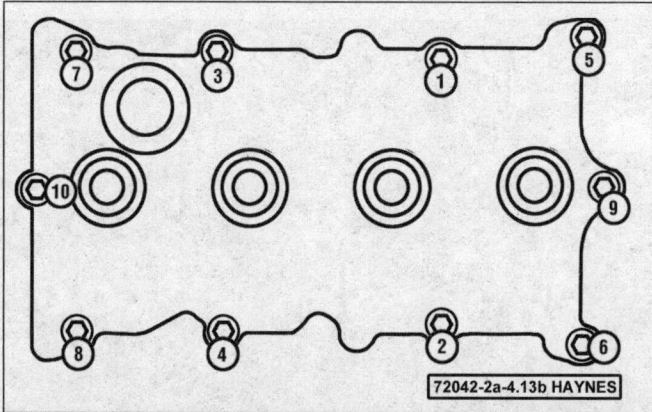

4.13b Valve cover bolt tightening sequence - Type 2 (used on some 2012 and 2013 models, and all 2014 and later models)

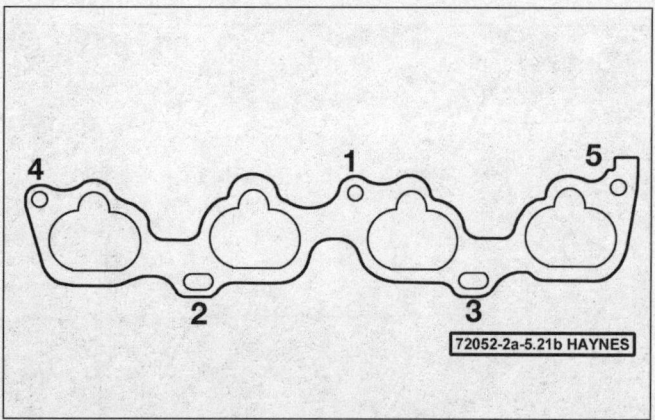

5.16a Intake manifold bolt tightening sequence - re-torque bolt 1 after finishing (T31 models)

2A-6 Chapter 2 Part A 2.5 litre petrol engine

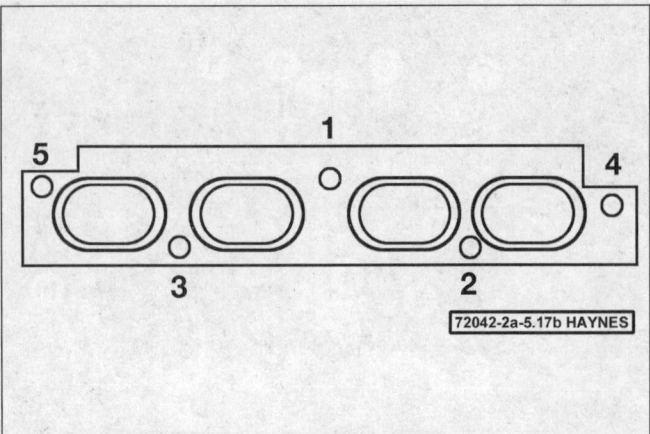

5.16b Intake manifold bolt tightening sequence - re-torque bolt 1 after finishing (T32 models)

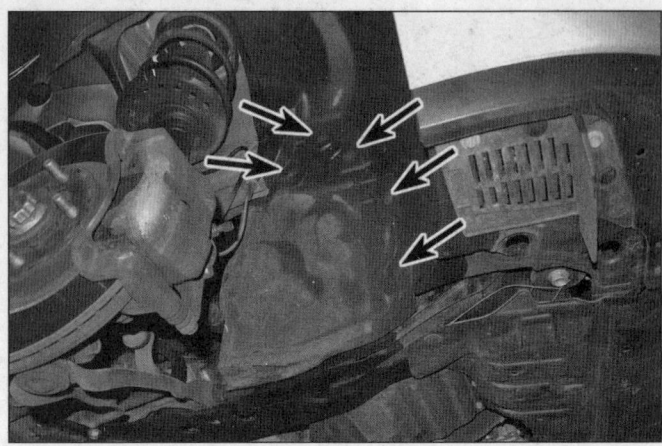

6.4 Remove the inner guard liner retaining clips (arrows)

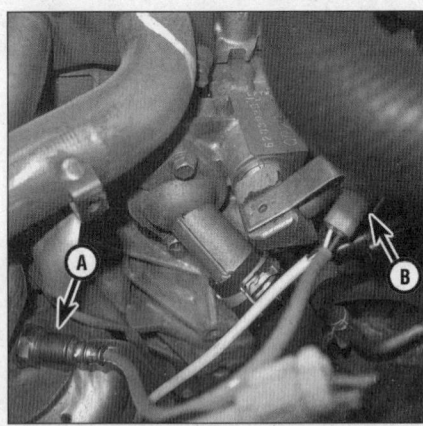

6.5 Front oxygen sensor (A) and wiring connector (B)

Installation

13 Use a scraper to remove all traces of old gasket material and sealant from the manifold and cylinder head, then clean the mating surfaces with brake system cleaner.

14 Where fitted, install a new gasket and position the intake manifold adapter on the cylinder head studs.

15 Install a new gasket, then position the intake manifold on the studs and install the nuts/bolts.

16 Tighten the nuts/bolts in sequence **(see illustrations)** to the torque listed in Specifications, then re-torque bolt number one.

17 The remainder of installation is the reverse of removal.

18 Reconnect the battery and perform the system initialisation procedure (see Chapter 5 Section 4).

6 Exhaust manifold - removal and installation

Warning: *The engine must be completely cool before beginning this procedure.*

Note: *The primary catalytic converter is integrated into the exhaust manifold and cannot be serviced separately.*

Removal

1 Disconnect the negative (-) battery terminal (see Chapter 5 Section 3).

2 Raise the front of the vehicle and support on jackstands (see Chapter 0 Section 7).

3 Remove the engine splash shields.

4 Remove the inner guard liner **(see illustration)**, then remove the drivebelt (see Chapter 1 Section 12).

5 Disconnect the electrical connector from the oxygen sensor **(see illustration)**.

6 Remove the heat shield from the exhaust manifold **(see illustration)**.

7 Disconnect the exhaust pipe from the catalytic converter.

Note: *Applying penetrating oil to the exhaust manifold fasteners may make removing the nuts/bolts easier.*

8 Unbolt the exhaust manifold brace.

9 Remove the exhaust manifold-to-cylinder head nuts, in the reverse order of the tightening sequence **(see illustration 6.13)**, and detach the manifold and gasket.

Installation

10 Use a scraper to remove all traces of old gasket material and carbon deposits from the exhaust manifold and cylinder head mating surfaces.

11 Position the new exhaust manifold gasket over the cylinder head studs.

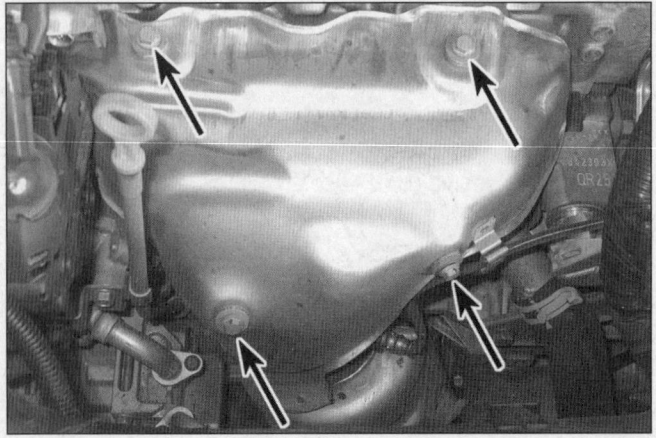

6.6 Remove the exhaust manifold heat shield bolts

6.13 Exhaust manifold nuts must be tightened twice in sequence

Chapter 2 Part A 2.5 litre petrol engine

7.4 Use a pin spanner to hold the pulley from turning, so the bolt can be loosened

7.5 Remove the pulley from the crankshaft using a puller

7.6 Use a seal puller, or screwdriver with the tip wrapped in tape, to pry the seal out of the timing chain cover

12 Install the manifold and thread the mounting nuts into place.
13 Working in the correct sequence **(see illustration)**, tighten the nuts to the torque listed in Specifications.
14 The remainder of installation is the reverse of removal. Use anti-seize lubricant on the exhaust pipe studs.
15 Reconnect the battery and perform the system initialisation procedure (see Chapter 5 Section 4).

7 Crankshaft front oil seal - replacement

1 Raise the front of the vehicle and support on jackstands (see Chapter 0 Section 7).
2 Remove the right inner guard liner **(see illustration 6.4)**.
3 Remove the drivebelt (see Chapter 1).
4 Using a pin spanner, hold the crankshaft pulley from turning and remove the crankshaft pulley bolt **(see illustration)**.
5 Use a puller to remove the pulley from the crankshaft **(see illustration)**.

Caution: *Use the proper adapter on the end of the crankshaft to prevent damage to the threads or end of the crankshaft. Also, the jaws of the puller must bolt to the hub of the pulley or grasp the hub of the pulley, not the outer diameter.*

6 Use a seal-puller tool, or wrap the tip of a screwdriver with tape, to pry out the seal, being careful not to damage the seal bore or scratch the surface of the crankshaft snout **(see illustration)**.
7 Clean the bore in the timing chain cover and coat the outer edge of the new seal with engine oil or multi-purpose grease. Also lubricate the seal lips.
8 Using a seal driver or a socket with an outside diameter slightly smaller than the outside diameter of the seal, carefully drive the new seal into place **(see illustration)**. Make sure it's installed squarely and driven in to the same depth as the original. Check the seal after installation to make sure the garter spring didn't pop out of place.

Caution: *The oil seal lip goes toward the engine, and the dust seal lip toward the pulley.*

9 Reinstall the crankshaft pulley **(see illustration)**. Tighten the crankshaft pulley bolt to the torque listed in Specifications.
10 The remainder of installation is the reverse of removal.
11 Run the engine and check for oil leaks.

8 Timing chain/oil pump drive chain or balance shaft chain and sprockets - removal, inspection and installation

Warning: *The engine must be completely cool before beginning this procedure.*

Caution: *The timing system is complex. Severe engine damage will occur if you make any mistakes. Do not attempt this procedure unless you are highly experienced with this type of repair. If you are at all unsure of your abilities, consult an expert. Double-check all your work and be sure everything is correct before you attempt to start the engine.*

Note: *On T32 models, the manufacturer recommends that the engine be removed for this procedure. This Section describes servicing the timing chain assembly with the engine in the vehicle, however it is usually easier to remove the engine first. See Chapter 2D Section 7 for more information on engine removal. If you choose to remove the engine for this procedure, ignore the steps which don't apply.*

Note: *These models use a balance shaft drive chain and balance shaft assembly. The balance shaft unit cannot be disassembled.*

Removal

1 Position the engine at TDC for cylinder number one (see Section 3).
2 Disconnect the negative (-) battery terminal (see Chapter 5 Section 3).
3 Raise the front of the vehicle and support on jackstands (see Chapter 0 Section 7).
4 Remove the inner guard liner **(see illustration 3.8)**.
5 Drain the engine oil (see Chapter 1 Section 9).

7.8 Drive the new seal squarely into the timing chain cover with a seal driver or a large socket

7.9 It's best to use a pulley installation tool to press the crankshaft pulley into place

Chapter 2 Part A 2.5 litre petrol engine

8.12 IVT solenoid wiring connector (1); retaining bolt (2) and the camshaft sprocket cover retaining bolts (3)

6 Remove the coolant reservoir (see Chapter 3 Section 6).
7 Remove the drive belt and the drivebelt tensioner (see Chapter 1 Section 12).
8 Remove the alternator and bracket (see Chapter 5 Section 11).
9 Remove the valve cover, including the right upper engine mount and mount bracket (see Section 4) and intake manifold (see Section 5).
10 Support the engine from above with an engine hoist or engine support fixture.
11 Remove the oil pans (see Section 11).
12 On T31 models, disconnect the electrical connector for the Intake Valve Timing (IVT) control solenoid, then remove the mounting bolt and control solenoid from the timing chain cover (see illustration).
13 On T32 models, disconnect the electrical connectors for the Intake Valve Timing (IVT) intermediate lock control solenoid valve, Intake Valve Timing control solenoid valve, Exhaust Valve Timing (EVT) control solenoid valve, then remove the mounting bolts and control solenoids from the timing chain cover.
14 Remove the bolts retaining the valve timing (VT) camshaft sprocket cover to the timing chain main cover. Remove the cover. Remove the bolts in the reverse of the tightening sequence (see illustration 8.11).

Note: *Use a sharp tool to cut the RTV sealant securing the cover.*

15 Remove the upper chain guide from between the two camshaft sprockets.
16 Check the positions of the camshaft sprockets. They should be aligned at No.1 cylinder TDC (see illustrations).
17 Remove the crankshaft pulley (see Section 7). Don't allow the crankshaft to turn while removing the bolt.
18 Remove the timing chain cover mounting bolts in the reverse of the tightening sequence (see illustration 8.33) and remove the cover.

Note: *Make notes on the timing chain cover bolt locations so they can be installed in their original locations.*

19 Using the tip of a screwdriver, push down on the tensioner plunger and insert a stopper pin of the correct diameter into the hole on the tensioner. Once the tensioner is locked in the retracted position, remove the bolts and the tensioner from the front of the engine.
20 Remove the timing chain.
21 Use an open-end wrench on the hex of the camshaft to hold it as you remove the camshaft sprocket bolts. If the chain is being removed only for removal of the camshafts or cylinder head, skip the remainder of this removal procedure.
22 Remove the balance shaft chain tensioner, locate the stop tab underneath the tensioner arm and press the stop tab away from the guide until a stopper pin of the correct diameter can be inserted into the hole on the tensioner. Once the tensioner is locked in the retracted position, the tensioner can be removed from the front of the engine.

Balance shaft chain and balance shaft assembly removal

23 Remove the balance shaft chain tensioner bolts, tensioner and tensioner guide.
24 Remove the balance shaft chain and crankshaft sprocket.
25 Remove the balance shaft unit mounting bolts following the reverse of the tightening sequence (see illustration 8.27).

Inspection

26 Inspect the camshaft, idler and crankshaft sprockets for wear of the teeth and keyways. Inspect the chains for cracks or excessive wear of the rollers. Inspect the facing of the chain guides for excessive wear.

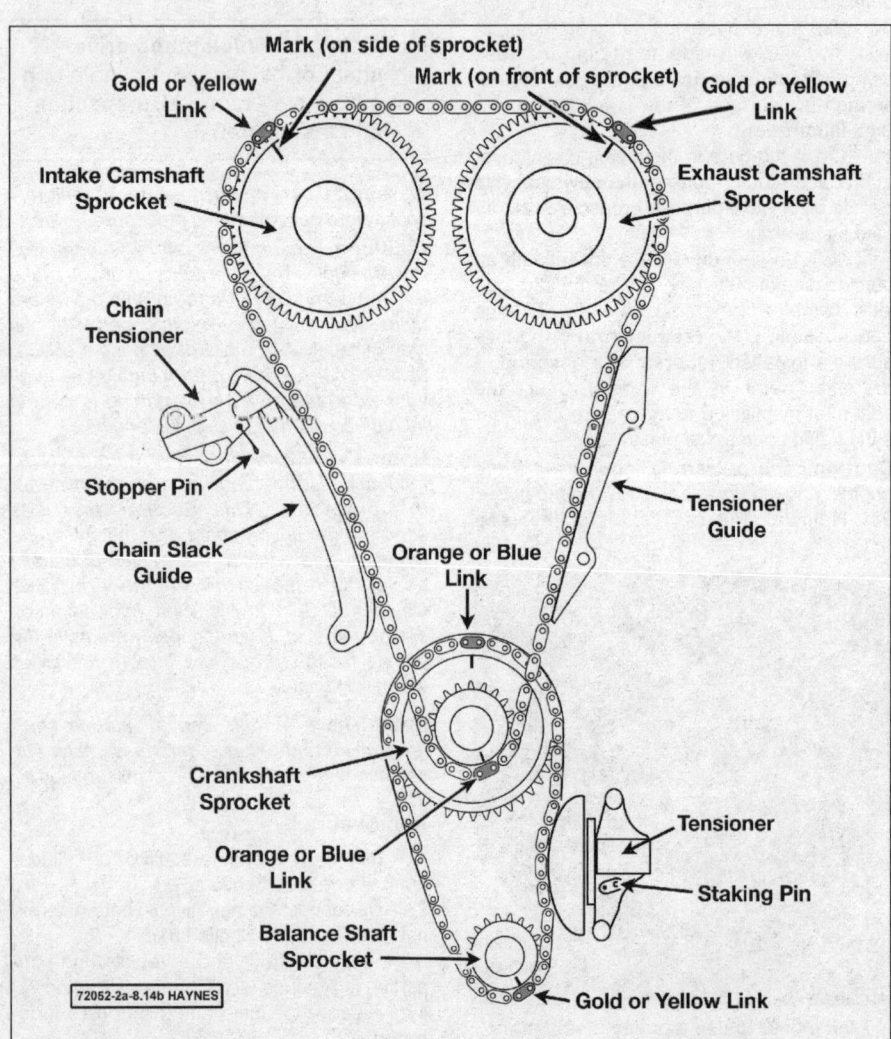

8.16a Timing chain details - with the engine set at No.1 cylinder TDC - T31 models

Chapter 2 Part A 2.5 litre petrol engine

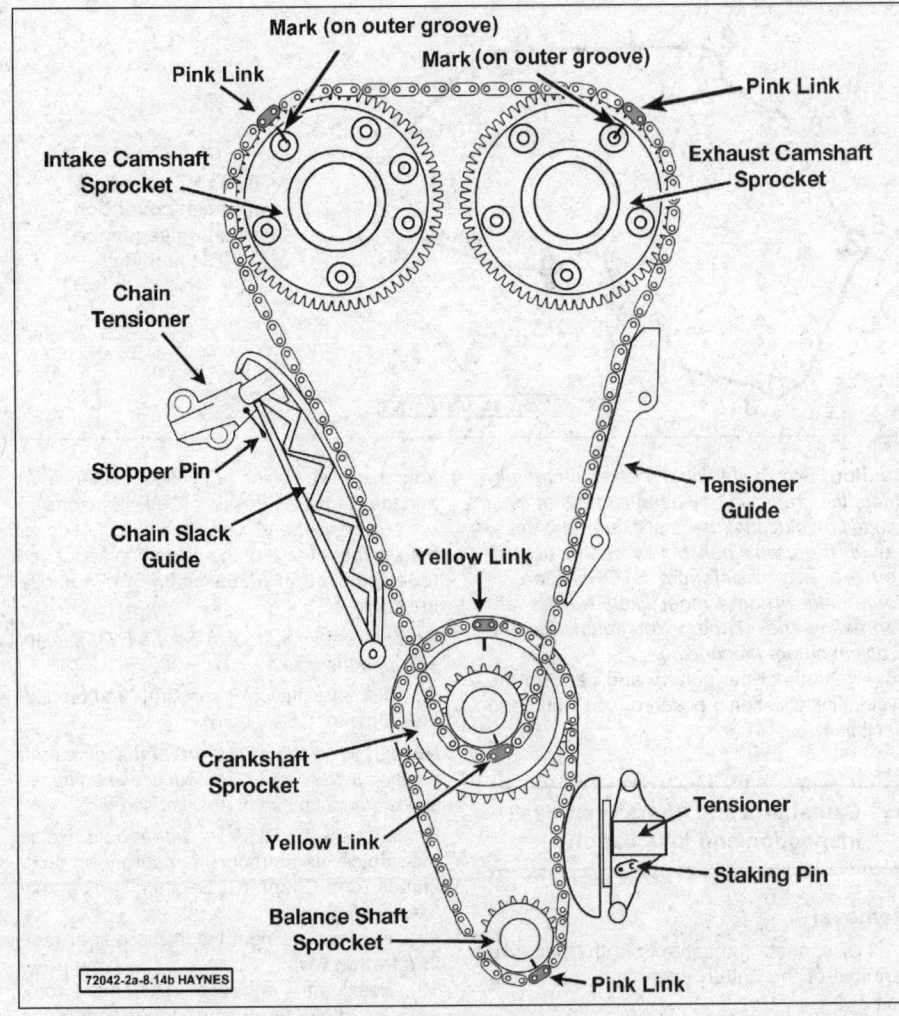

8.16b Timing chain details - with the engine set at No.1 cylinder TDC - T32 models

Installation

27 Install the balance shaft unit using new bolts; tighten the bolts, in sequence (see illustration), to the torque listed in Specifications.

28 Install the crankshaft sprocket and the oil pump/balance shaft drive chain. Make sure the coloured links on the oil pump or balance shaft chain align with the mating marks on the crankshaft sprocket and the oil pump or balance shaft sprocket (see illustration 8.16a or 8.16b).

29 Install the oil pump/balance shaft drive chain tensioner bolts and the tensioner. The bolt hole positions may have changed since the tensioner was removed. The chain guide and the tensioner move freely with the staking pin as the pivot. Align and tighten the two chain tensioner bolts, then move the tensioner to match the bolt holes.

30 Double-check the drive chain alignment marks. Repeat the procedure if the alignment marks are incorrect. Release the staking pin from the tensioner to apply tension to the drive chain.

31 Install the timing chain, aligning the coloured links with the mating marks on the camshaft and crankshaft sprockets (see illustration 8.16a or 8.16b).

32 Install the timing chain guide and chain slack guide. Tighten the bolts to the specified torque (see Specifications).

33 Install the timing chain tensioner and release the stopper pin. Double-check the timing chain alignment marks; if they are incorrect, repeat the procedure. Tighten the sprocket bolts to the specified torque (see Specifications).

34 Apply a bead of RTV sealant to the mating surfaces around the perimeter of the timing chain cover, as well as around the bolt hole in the centre (bolt No.11 in illustration 8.35a or illustration 8.35b).

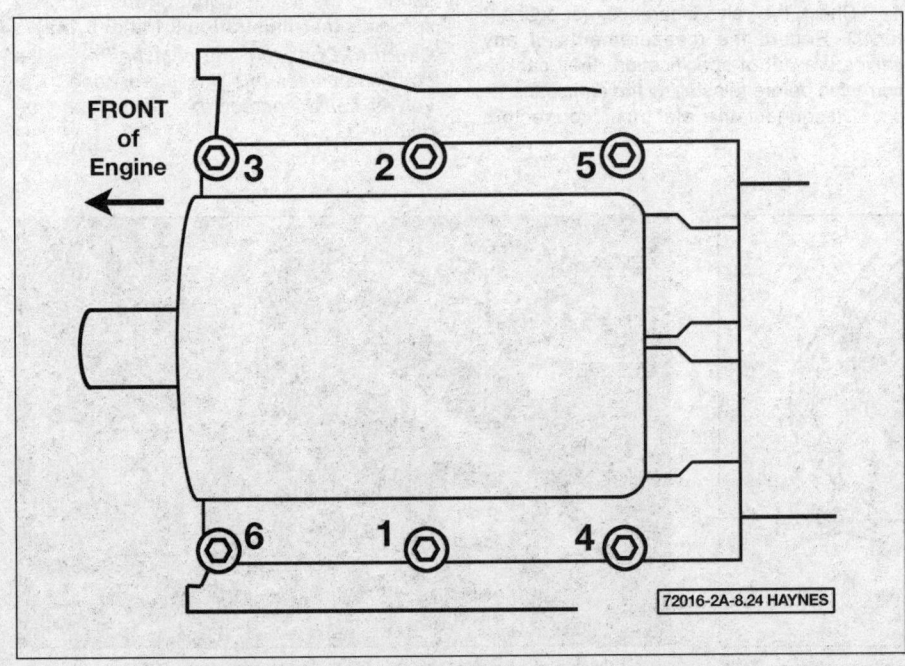

8.27 Balance shaft assembly bolt tightening sequence

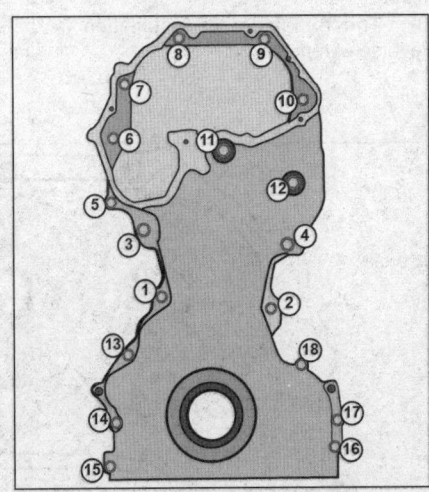

8.35a Timing chain main cover bolt tightening sequence - bolts of different diameters have different torque values, as noted in this Chapter's Specifications - T31 models shown

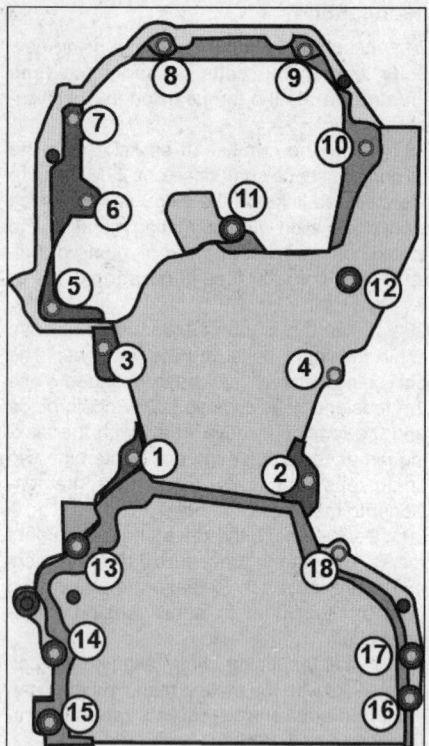

8.35b Timing chain main cover bolt tightening sequence - bolts of different diametres have different torque values, as noted in this Chapter's Specifications - T32 models shown

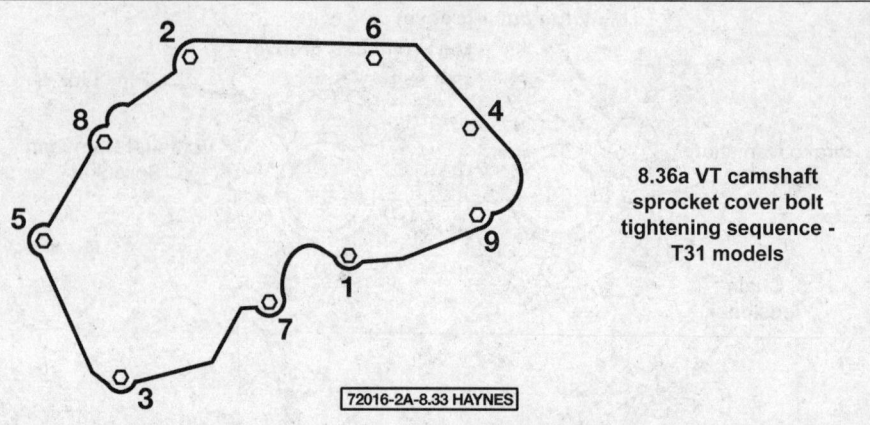

8.36a VT camshaft sprocket cover bolt tightening sequence - T31 models

35 Install the timing chain cover. Tighten the cover bolts in the correct sequence **(see illustrations)**, to the specified torque (see Specifications).

36 Apply a bead of RTV sealant to the mating surfaces around the perimeter of the (VT) camshaft sprocket cover. Install the cover and tighten the bolts, in the correct sequence **(see illustration)**, to the torque listed in Specifications.

37 The remainder of installation is the reverse of removal.

Caution: *Before starting the engine, carefully rotate the crankshaft by hand through at least two full revolutions (use a socket and breaker bar on the crankshaft pulley centre bolt). If you feel any resistance, STOP! There is something wrong - most likely valves are contacting the pistons. You must find the problem before proceeding.*

38 Reconnect the battery and perform the system initialisation procedure (see Chapter 5 Section 4).

9 Camshafts and lifters - removal, inspection and installation

Removal

1 Disconnect the cable from the negative terminal of the battery (see Chapter 5 Section 3).
2 Remove the valve cover (see Section 4).
3 Remove the intake manifold (see Section 5).
4 Check the valve clearances (see Chapter 1). Record the measurements; if any valves are out of specification, they can be corrected before reinstalling the camshafts.
5 Disconnect the electrical connectors from the Valve Timing (VT) control solenoid(s) and the Camshaft Position (CMP) sensor(s).
6 Remove the VT camshaft sprocket cover bolts in the reverse of the tightening sequence **(see illustration 8.36a or 8.36b)**. Remove the cover.

Note: *Use a sharp tool to cut the RTV sealant securing the cover.*

7 Remove the CMP sensor(s) and bracket (see Chapter 6 Section 5).

Note: *T31 models use an intake camshaft position sensor and T32 models use an intake and exhaust camshaft position sensor.*

8 Loosen the RH front wheel nuts. Raise the vehicle and support it securely on jackstands (see Chapter 0 Section 7). Remove the right front wheel.
9 Remove the right inner guard liner **(see illustration 6.4)**.
10 Position the engine at TDC on the compression stroke for number one cylinder (see Section 3). Using paint or an indelible marker, mark the links of the timing chain that correspond to the timing marks on the camshaft sprockets **(see illustration 8.14a or 8.14b)**.

Caution: *Don't turn the camshaft(s) or the crankshaft after this has been done. The valves could contact the pistons and be damaged.*

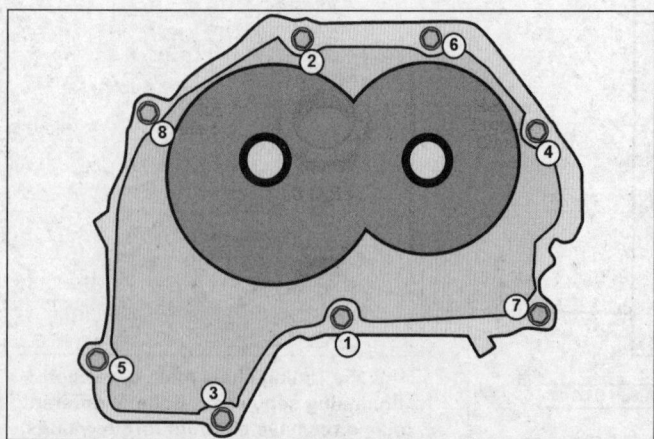

8.36b VT camshaft sprocket cover bolt tightening sequence - T32 models

9.14 With a dial indicator in place, pry the camshaft forward and back to check the camshaft endplay

Chapter 2 Part A 2.5 litre petrol engine

9.17a Pull the lifters straight up to remove them

9.17b The lifters can be stored in individually-marked plastic bags, or in a divided, marked box like this one

9.19 Measure the lobe heights - if any lobe height is less than the minimum listed in this Chapter's Specifications, replace the camshaft

11   Use a screwdriver to retract the plunger of the chain tensioner, then insert a drill bit or Allen wrench into the hole to secure the plunger in place. Remove the tensioner.
Note: *This procedure is done through the camshaft sprocket cover opening.*
12   Hold the hexagon part of the camshaft with a wrench, then remove the camshaft sprocket bolts. Remove the sprockets.
Note: *It isn't necessary to maintain tension on the timing chain; the timing chain won't separate from the crankshaft sprocket.*
13   Remove the upper timing chain guide through the timing chain cover.
14   Before removing the camshafts, use a dial indicator to check camshaft endplay **(see illustration)**. Mount the dial indicator so the gauge tip can be placed at the end of the camshaft. Move the camshaft all the way to the rear and zero the dial indicator. Next, use a screwdriver to pry it all the way forward. If the endplay (the total amount of movement) exceeds the limit listed in Specifications, replace the camshaft and/or cylinder head.
15   Loosen the camshaft bearing caps in the reverse of the tightening sequence **(see illustration 9.24b)**.
Caution: *Keep the caps in order. They must be installed in their original locations.*
16   Remove the bearing caps or bridge and lift the camshafts straight up and out.
17   Pull the lifters straight up and store them in numbered plastic bags or a marked box **(see illustrations)**.

Inspection

18   Visually examine the camshaft lobes, journals, bearing caps and lifters. Check for score marks, pitting and evidence of overheating (blue, discoloured areas). If wear is excessive or damage is evident, the component will have to be replaced.
19   Using a micrometer, measure camshaft journal diameter and lobe height **(see illustration)**, and compare your measurements to Specifications. If the lobe height is less than the minimum allowable, the camshaft is worn and must be replaced.
20   Check the oil clearance for each camshaft journal as follows:

a Clean the bearing caps and the camshaft journals with brake system cleaner.
b Carefully lay the camshafts in place in the cylinder head. DON'T use any lubrication.
c Lay a strip of Plastigage on each journal.
d Install the bearing caps with the arrows pointing toward the front (timing chain end) of the engine.
e Tighten the bolts in sequence **(see illustration 9.24b)**, to the torque listed in Specifications, in 1/4-turn increments.
Caution: *Don't turn the camshaft while the Plastigage is in place.*
f Remove the bolts, in the proper sequence, and detach the bearing caps.
g Compare the width of the crushed Plastigage (at its widest point) to the scale on the Plastigage envelope **(see illustrations)**.
h If the clearance is greater than specified, replace the camshaft and/or cylinder head.

21   Scrape off the Plastigage with your fingernail or the edge of a credit card - don't scratch or nick the journals or bearing caps.

9.20a Place a strip of Plastigage under each camshaft bearing cap and tighten the caps to Specifications

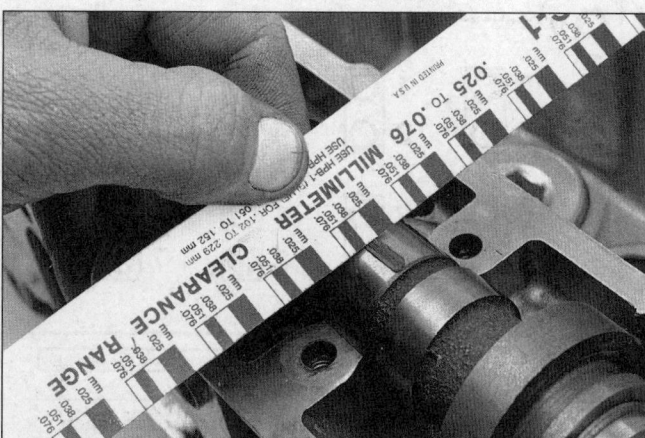

9.20b Compare the width of the crushed Plastigage to the scale on the envelope to determine the oil clearance

Chapter 2 Part A 2.5 litre petrol engine

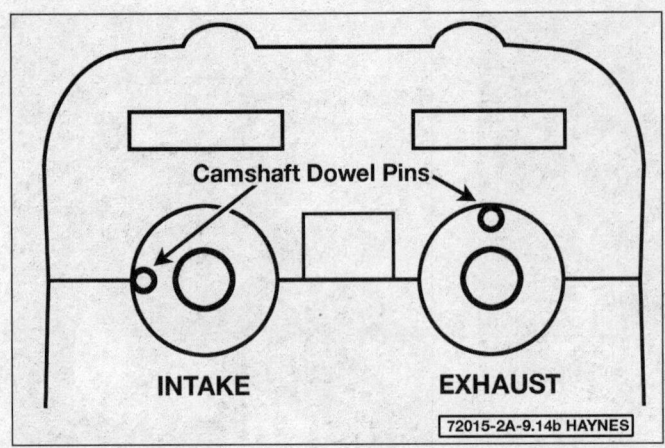

9.23 Correct positions of the dowel pins for camshaft installation

9.24a Camshaft bearing cap designations

Installation

22 Apply moly-based engine assembly lubricant to the camshaft lobes and journals.

23 Install the camshafts in their original positions at TDC. The camshaft dowel pins must face the 12 o'clock position (exhaust camshaft) and the 9 o'clock position (intake camshaft) **(see illustration)**.

24 Apply a 1/8-inch bead of RTV sealant to the mating surface of the timing chain cover. Install the bearing caps and bolts and tighten them in sequence **(see illustrations)** to the specified torque (see Specifications).

Note: *When installing the No.1 bearing cap (the one closest to the timing chain), be careful not to disturb the sealant while lowering it into place.*

25 Install the camshaft sprockets and timing chain (see Section 8). Align the marks on the timing chain (made in Step 10) with the timing marks on the camshaft sprockets

26 The remainder of installation is the reverse of removal. If any part of the valve train was replaced, check and adjust the valve clearance (see Chapter 1 Section 34).

27 Reconnect the battery and perform the system initialisation procedure (see Chapter 5 Section 4).

10 Cylinder head - removal and installation

Warning: *The engine must be completely cool before beginning this procedure.*

Removal

1 Relieve the fuel system pressure (see Chapter 4A Section 3).
2 Disconnect the negative (-) battery terminal (see Chapter 5 Section 3).
3 Position the engine at No.1 cylinder TDC compression (see Section 3)
4 Drain the coolant (see Chapter 1 Section 27).
5 Remove the timing chain (see Section 8).
6 Remove the camshafts (see Section 9).
7 Remove the exhaust manifold (see Section 6).
8 Remove the intake manifold (see Section 5).
9 Label and remove any remaining items attached to the cylinder head, such as coolant fittings, tubes, cables, hoses or wiring harnesses.
10 Using a breaker bar and the appropriate-sized hex bit, loosen the cylinder head bolts in 1/4-turn increments until they can be removed by hand. Loosen the bolts in reverse of the tightening sequence **(see illustration 10.21)** to avoid warping or cracking the cylinder head.
11 Lift the cylinder head off the engine block. If it's stuck, very carefully pry up at the transaxle end, beyond the gasket surface, at a casting protrusion **(see illustration)**.
12 Remove all external components from the cylinder head to allow for thorough cleaning and inspection.

Installation

13 The mating surfaces of the cylinder head and block must be perfectly clean when the cylinder head is installed.
14 Use a gasket scraper to remove all traces of carbon and old gasket material **(see illustration)**, then clean the mating surfaces with lacquer thinner or acetone. If there's oil on the mating surfaces when the cylinder head is installed, the gasket may not seal correctly and leaks could develop. When working on the block, stuff the cylinders with clean shop rags to keep out debris. Use a vacuum cleaner to remove material that falls into the cylinders.

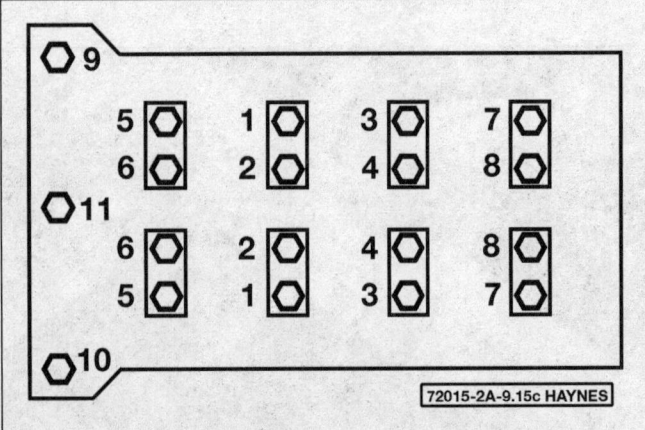

9.24b Camshaft bearing cap bolt tightening sequence

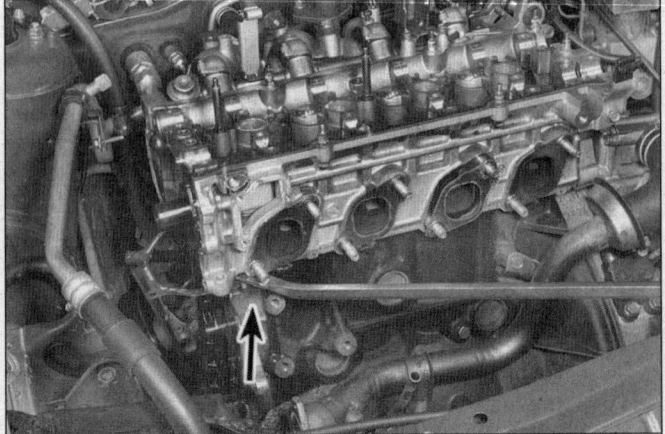

10.11 Pry under the cylinder head under casting protrusions only - do not pry between mating surfaces

10.14 Remove all traces of old gasket material - the cylinder head and block mating surfaces must be perfectly clean to ensure a good gasket seal

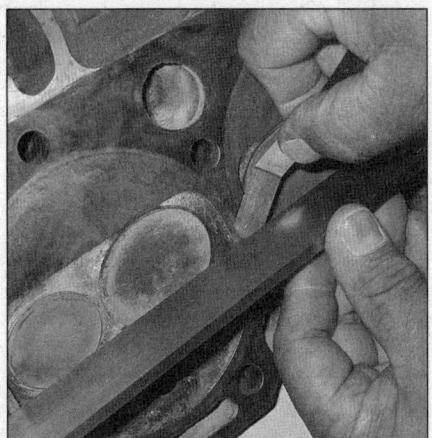

10.17 Check the cylinder head gasket surface for warpage by trying to insert a feeler gauge under the straightedge

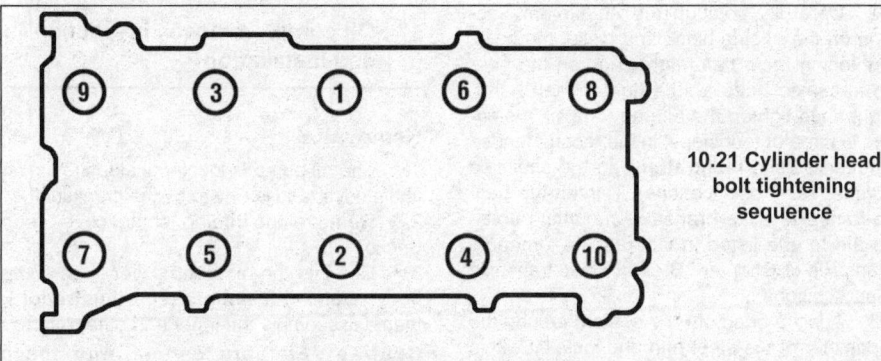

10.21 Cylinder head bolt tightening sequence

15 Check the block and cylinder head mating surfaces for nicks, deep scratches and other damage. If damage is slight, it can be removed with a fine file; if it's excessive, machining may be the only alternative.

16 Use a tap of the correct size to chase the threads in the cylinder head bolt holes, then clean the holes with compressed air - make sure that nothing remains in the holes.

Warning: *Wear eye protection when using compressed air!*

17 Once the cylinder head's gasket surface is clean, check the cylinder head for warpage **(see illustration)**. Check the cylinder head gasket, intake and exhaust manifold surfaces and compare with Specifications.

18 Install any components that were removed from the cylinder head.

19 Position the new cylinder head gasket over the dowel pins in the block and carefully set the cylinder head on the block without disturbing the gasket.

20 Before installing the new cylinder head bolts, apply a small amount of clean engine oil to the threads and hardened washers. The chamfered side of the washers must face the bolt heads, and the flat side of the washers must face the cylinder head.

21 Install the new cylinder head bolts and tighten them, following the recommended sequence **(see illustration)**, to the specified torque (see Specifications).

22 Install the lifters and camshafts (see Section 9).

23 Install the timing chain (see Section 8), then check the valve clearances (see Chapter 1 Section 34).

24 The remainder of installation is the reverse of removal.

25 Refill the cooling system (see Chapter 1 Section 27), install a new oil filter and add oil to the engine (see Chapter 1 Section 9).

26 Reconnect the battery and perform the system initialisation procedure (see Chapter 5 Section 4).

11 Oil pans - removal and installation

Note: *The following procedure describes removing the lower (steel) oil pan and the upper (aluminium) oil pan. If you're just removing the lower oil pan, many of the following steps are not necessary, as the pan is readily accessible.*

Removal

1 Disconnect the negative (-) battery terminal (see Chapter 5 Section 3).

2 Raise the front of the vehicle and support on jackstands (see Chapter 0 Section 7). Remove the right front wheel.

3 Drain the engine oil and remove the filter (see Chapter 1 Section 9).

4 Remove the engine oil dipstick tube fastener and remove the tube from the oil pan. Discard the O-ring and use a new one on installation.

5 Remove the front Section of the exhaust pipe.

6 Remove the drivebelt (see Chapter 1 Section 12).

7 Remove the right side driveshaft bearing bracket (see Chapter 8 Section 7).

8 Remove the air conditioning compressor (without disconnecting the lines) and secure it out of the way (see Chapter 3 Section 11).

9 Remove the lower torque rod (see Section 15).

10 On AWD models, remove the transfer case (see Chapter 7C Section 3).

11 Remove the stabiliser bar link (see Chapter 10 Section 4).

12 Remove the front subframe (see Chapter 10 Section 18).

13 The oil pan is a two-piece design. A steel pan is attached to an aluminium Section which is bolted to the engine block. Remove the oil pan bolts following the reverse of the recommended tightening sequence **(see illustrations 12.22a or 12.22b)**. Separate the steel pan by inserting a thin putty knife between the steel and aluminium sections.

Caution: *Do not pry with a screwdriver between the steel pan and the aluminium flange or damage to the sealing surface may result.*

Note: *Mark each bolt to ensure they are positioned in their original locations on reassembly.*

14 Remove the oil pump screen fasteners and remove the screen.

15 Remove the bolts attaching the aluminium section (upper oil pan) to the engine block, following the reverse of the tightening sequence **(see illustration 12.21)**.

16 The sealant used to seal the aluminium Section to the engine block can be very difficult to separate without damaging the aluminium section. Using a thin putty knife, work around the perimeter, cutting the pan free before prying the pan down at the transaxle end **(see illustration)**.

11.16 After cutting the pan seal with a putty knife, pry at the rear corners near the transaxle - do not pry in the gasket area

2A-14 Chapter 2 Part A 2.5 litre petrol engine

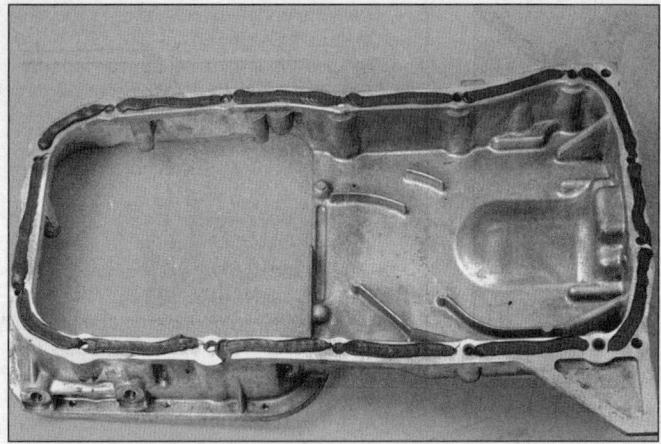

11.20 Apply a bead of RTV sealant around the perimeter of the aluminium Section of the pan - typical bead shown

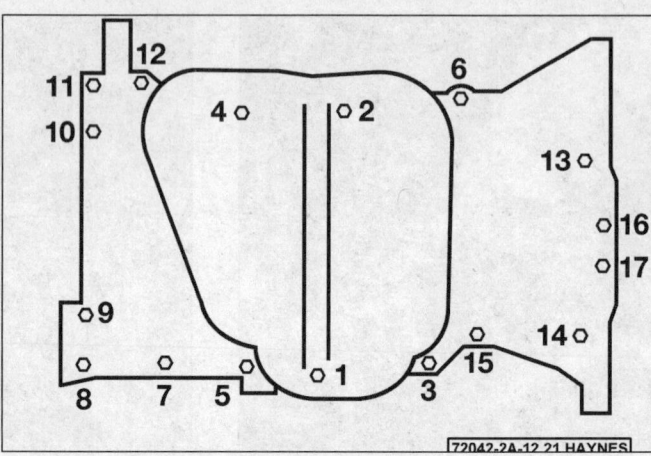

11.22 Bolt tightening sequence for the aluminium upper oil pan

Installation

17 Use a scraper to remove all traces of old gasket material and sealant from the block and oil pan. Clean the mating surfaces with brake system cleaner.

Caution: *Be careful not to scratch or gouge the gasket surface of the block or oil pan. A leak could develop after the repairs have been completed.*

18 Make sure the threaded bolt holes in the block are clean.

19 Check the steel pan flange for distortion, particularly around the bolt holes. If necessary, place the pan on a wood block and use a hammer to flatten and restore the gasket surface.

20 Apply a 3/16-inch wide bead of RTV sealant around the perimeter of the aluminium section (upper oil pan) **(see illustration)**.

Note: *The oil pan must be installed within 15 minutes once the sealant has been applied.*

21 Install new O-rings into the upper oil pan, if equipped.

22 Carefully position the aluminium Section on the engine block and install the bolts, tightening them hand-tight. Tighten the pan-to-transaxle bolts a little tighter than hand-tight, then tighten the oil pan-to-block fasteners in three or four steps, in the recommended sequence **(see illustration)**, to the specified torque (see Specifications). Tighten the pan-to-transaxle bolts (transaxle mounting bolts) to the torque listed in Chapter 7A - manual transaxle or Chapter 7B - automatic transaxle Specifications.

23 Apply a bead of RTV sealant around the perimeter of the steel pan and install it within 15 minutes of application. Tighten the bolts in sequence **(see illustrations)** to the torque listed in.

24 The remainder of installation is the reverse of removal. Install a new oil filter and wait at least thirty minutes for the RTV to set-up before adding oil.

25 Reconnect the battery and perform the system initialisation procedure (see Chapter 5 Section 4).

12 Oil pump - removal, inspection and installation

Removal

1 The oil pump is located inside the timing chain cover and is driven by the crankshaft.

2 Remove the timing chain cover (see Section 8).

3 Remove the oil pump cover-to-oil pump body retaining fasteners **(see illustration)**, then disassemble the inner and outer rotors.

Caution: *Be very careful with these components; the close tolerances are critical in creating the correct oil pressure. Any nicks or damage will require replacement of the complete pump/timing chain cover assembly.*

Inspection

4 Clean all the components, including the timing chain cover and engine block gasket surfaces, with solvent, then inspect all surfaces for excessive wear and/or damage.

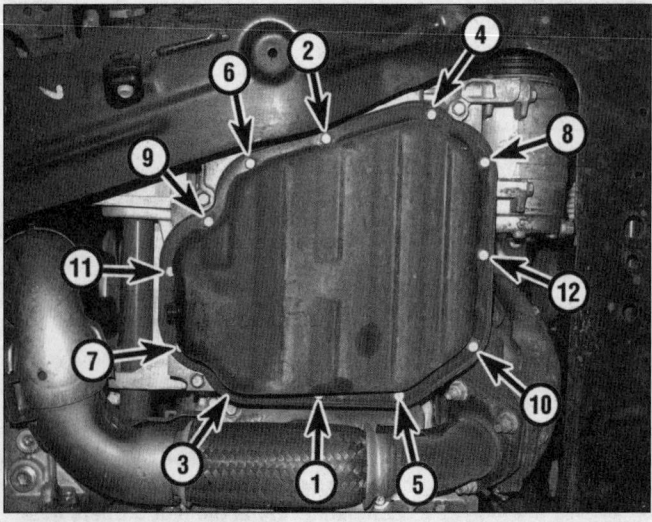

11.23a Bolt tightening sequence for the steel lower oil pan - T31 models

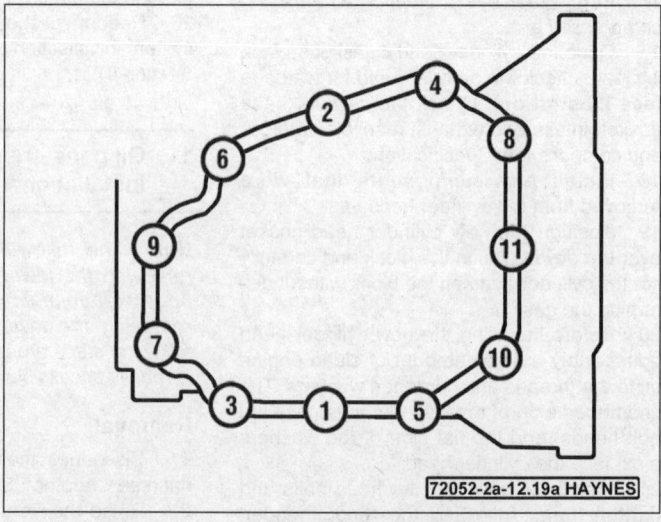

11.23b Bolt tightening sequence for the steel lower oil pan - T32 models

Chapter 2 Part A 2.5 litre petrol engine 2A-15

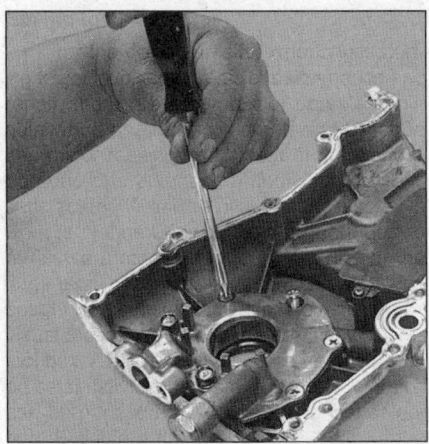

12.3 The oil pump is located inside the timing chain cover - remove the fasteners, then remove the oil pump cover

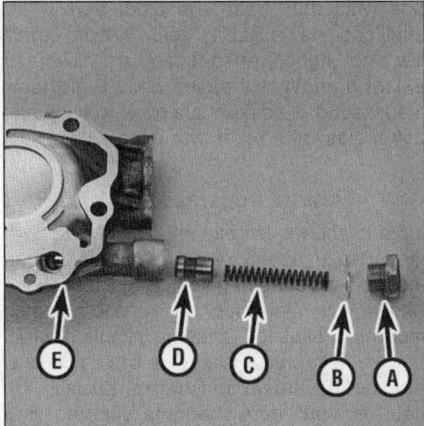

12.5 Remove the oil pump pressure regulator valve assembly for cleaning and inspection

A Cap
B Washer
C Spring
D Relief valve
E Oil pump cover

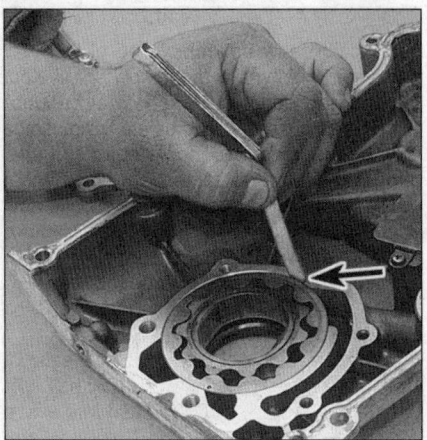

12.6a Check the outer rotor-to-body clearance with a feeler gauge as shown

12.6b Check the clearance between the inner and outer rotor tips

5   Disassemble the relief valve by removing the cap, washer, spring and regulator valve **(see illustration)**. Check the oil pressure regulator valve sliding surface and valve spring. The regulator, when clean and oiled, should slide easily in the valve bore. If either the spring or the valve is damaged, they must be replaced as a set. If no damage is found, reassemble the relief valve parts, coating the parts with clean engine oil, and reinstall it in the oil pump cover.
6   Check the oil pump component clearance with a feeler gauge **(see illustrations)** and compare the results to Specifications. If any of the measurements are out of specification, replace both the timing chain cover and the oil pump components.

Installation

7   Assemble the oil pump components. There is a punch mark on each rotor; these marks must face away from the timing chain cover and toward the engine. Pour a generous amount of clean engine oil into the pump cavity and around the rotors. Install the cover to the pump body and tighten the fasteners to the torque listed in Specifications.
8   Install the timing chain cover, using a bead of RTV sealant on the cover-to-block surface (see Section 8).

Note: *Align the flats on the inner oil pump rotor with the crankshaft when installing the timing chain cover.*

9   Install the cylinder head and other components (see Section 9 and Section 10).
10 Install the oil pan (see Section 11). Install a new oil filter and add engine oil to the crankcase (see Chapter 1 Section 9).
11 Start the engine and check for oil pressure and leaks.
12 Recheck the engine oil level.

13 Driveplate - removal and installation

Removal

1   Remove the engine/transaxle assembly (see Chapter 2D Section 7), then separate the transaxle from the engine (see Chapter 7A Section 5 - manual transaxle or Chapter 7B Section 11 - automatic transaxle).

12.6c With a precision straightedge placed over the pump body and rotors, check the clearance between the inner and outer rotors and the pump body cover

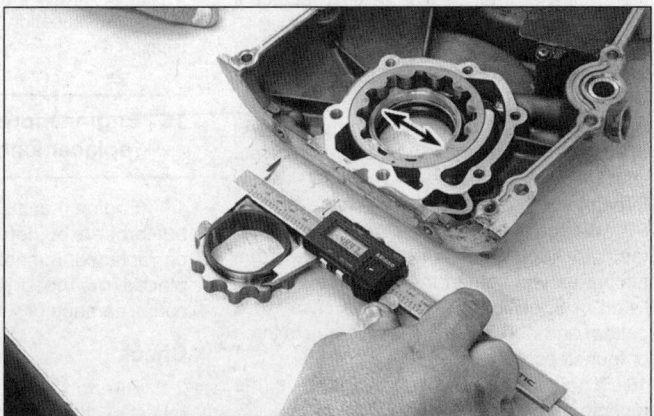

12.6d Measure the outer flanged surface of the inner rotor with a micrometer or precision calipers, then measure its bearing surface in the pump body - the difference is the inner rotor bearing clearance

Chapter 2 Part A 2.5 litre petrol engine

13.3 Mark the driveplate and the crankshaft so they can be reassembled in their original positions

15.6 A long prybar can be used to check for relative movement in the engine mounts

15.10 Upper torque rod mounting bolt locations

2 If equipped with a manual transaxle, remove the pressure plate and clutch disc (see Chapter 8 Section 5).
3 Use a centrepunch or paint to make alignment marks on the flywheel/driveplate and crankshaft to ensure correct alignment during installation **(see illustration)**.
4 Remove the bolts that secure the flywheel/driveplate to the crankshaft.
5 Remove the flywheel/driveplate from the crankshaft.
Warning: *Since the flywheel is fairly heavy, be sure to support it while removing the last bolt. Flywheel teeth can be sharp; wear gloves or use rags to hold the flywheel.*

Installation

6 If equipped with a manual transaxle, clean the flywheel to remove grease and oil. Inspect the surface for cracks, rivet grooves, burned areas and score marks. Light scoring can be removed with emery cloth. Check for cracked and broken ring-gear teeth. Lay the flywheel on a flat surface and use a straight-edge to check for warpage.
7 Clean and inspect the mating surfaces of the flywheel/driveplate and the crankshaft. If the crankshaft rear seal is leaking, replace it before reinstalling the flywheel/driveplate.
8 Position the flywheel/driveplate against the crankshaft. Install the spacer (if equipped) and align the marks made during removal. Some engines have an alignment dowel or staggered bolt holes to ensure correct installation. Before installing the bolts, apply thread-locking compound to the threads.
9 Wedge a screwdriver in the ring gear teeth to keep the flywheel/driveplate from turning as you tighten the bolts to the torque listed in Specifications. Follow a criss-cross pattern and work up to the final torque in three or four steps.
10 The remainder of installation is the reverse of removal.
11 Reconnect the battery and perform the necessary system initialisation procedure (see Chapter 5 Section 4).

14 Rear main oil seal - replacement

1 Remove the engine/transaxle assembly (see Chapter 2D Section 7), then separate the transaxle from the engine (see Chapter 7A Section 5 - manual transaxle or Chapter 7A Section 5 - automatic transaxle).
2 Remove the flywheel/driveplate (see Section 13).
3 Use a seal removal tool or a screwdriver wrapped with tape to pry out the seal, being careful not to gouge or nick the housing.
4 Lubricate the crankshaft seal journal and the lip of the new seal with multi-purpose grease.
5 Install the seal with the seal lip toward the engine and the dust seal toward the transaxle.
6 Tap the seal into place using a seal driver to make sure that it doesn't become tilted.
7 Install the seal so that its rear edge is flush with the face of the engine block, or up to 0.5 mm recessed.
8 The remainder of installation is the reverse of removal.
9 Reconnect the battery and perform the system initialisation procedure (see Chapter 5 Section 4).

15 Engine mounts - check and replacement

1 Engine mounts seldom require attention, but broken or deteriorated mounts should be replaced immediately or the added strain placed on the driveline components may cause damage or wear.

Check

2 During the check, the engine must be raised slightly to remove the weight from the mounts.
3 Raise the vehicle and support it securely on jackstands (see Chapter 0 Section 7). Remove the splash shields.
4 Position a jack under the engine oil pan. Place a large wood block between the jack head and the oil pan, then carefully raise the engine just enough to take the weight off the mounts. Do not place the wood block under the oil pan drain plug.
Warning: *DO NOT place any part of your body under the engine when it's supported only by a jack!*
5 Check the mounts to see if the rubber is cracked, hardened or separated from the metal plates. Sometimes the rubber will split right down the centre.
6 Check for relative movement between the mount plates and the engine or frame using a large screwdriver or prybar to attempt to move the mounts **(see illustration)**. If movement is noted, lower the engine and tighten the mount fasteners.
7 Rubber preservative should be applied to the mounts to slow deterioration.

Replacement

8 Disconnect the negative (-) battery terminal (see Chapter 5 Section 3).
9 Raise the vehicle and support on jackstands (see Chapter 0 Section 7). Support the engine as described in Step 4.
10 To remove the upper torque rod, remove the through-bolts and bracket bolts **(see illustration)**.
11 To remove the front engine mount, place a floor jack with a block of wood under the oil pan the remove the torque rod bracket, the engine mount to body bolts the engine mount-to-engine bolts and remove the mount **(see illustration)**.
12 To remove the lower torque rod, remove the through-bolts and bracket bolts **(see illustration)**.
13 To remove the left hand mount (transaxle end) remove the battery and battery tray (see Chapter 5 Section 5) and air filter housing (see Chapter 4A Section 9), then support the transaxle with a floor jack.
14 Remove the mount top bolts, then the side bolts **(see illustrations)** and remove the mount.

Chapter 2 Part A 2.5 litre petrol engine

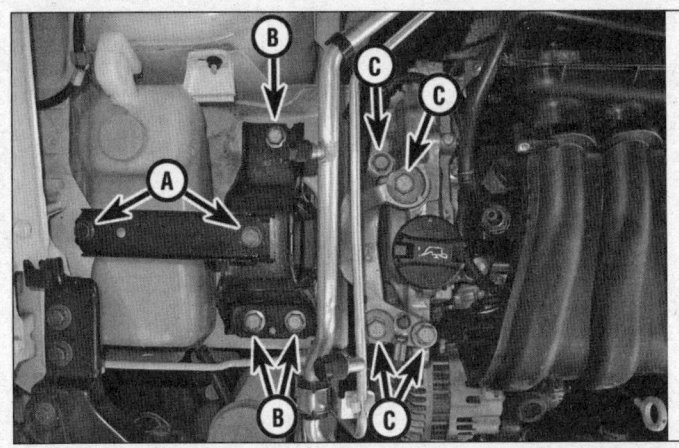

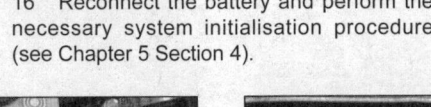

15.11 Front mount details T31 models, T32 models similar

- A Mount-to-body bolts
- B Mount-to-engine bolts
- C Bracket-to-engine bolts

15.12 Lower torque rod mounting bolt locations

15 Installation is the reverse of removal. Use thread-locking compound on the mount bolts/nuts and tighten them securely.

16 Reconnect the battery and perform the necessary system initialisation procedure (see Chapter 5 Section 4).

15.14a Remove the mount top bolts...

15.14b ... and the side bolts through the inner guard

Notes

Chapter 2 Part B
2.0 litre petrol engine

Contents

	Section		Section
Balance shaft, drive chain and sprockets – removal, inspection and refitting	16	General information	1
Camshafts and followers – removal, inspection and refitting	10	Intake manifold – removal and refitting	5
Crankshaft oil seals – renewal	14	Oil pans – removal and refitting	12
Crankshaft pulley – removal and refitting	7	Oil pressure check	See Chapter 2D
Cylinder compression check	See Chapter 2D	Oil pump – removal and refitting	13
Cylinder head – removal and refitting	11	Repair operations possible with the engine in the vehicle	2
Drivebelt check and replacement	See Chapter 1	Timing chain cover – removal and refitting	8
Engine - removal and installation	See Chapter 2D	Timing chain, tensioner, guides and sprockets – removal, inspection and refitting	9
Engine mounts – inspection and renewal	17	Top Dead Centre (TDC) for number one piston - locating	3
Engine oil and oil filter change	See Chapter 1	Valve cover – removal and refitting	4
Exhaust manifold – removal and refitting	6		
Flywheel/driveplate – removal, inspection and refitting	15		

Specifications

Engine (general)

Engine designations

X-trail	
T31 models	MR20DE
T32 Models	MR20DD
Dualis	MR20DE
Qashqai	MR20DD
Capacity	1,997 cc
Bore	84.0 mm
Stroke	90.1 mm
Direction of crankshaft rotation	Clockwise, viewed from timing chain end
Cylinder numbers (timing chain end to transaxle end)	1-2-3-4
Firing order	1-3-4-2
Valve clearances	See Chapter 1

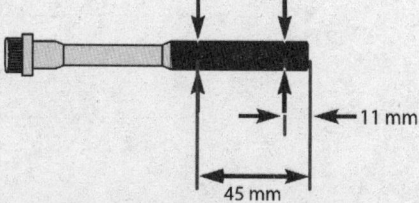

Measure the cylinder head bolt outer diameter at the illustrated points

Cylinder head

Warpage limit	0.01 mm
Cylinder head height - standard	130.9 mm
Cylinder head bolts outer diameter limit (see illustration)	0.15 mm

Chapter 2 Part B 2.0 litre petrol engine

Camshaft and followers

Drive	Chain
Number of bearings	5
Endfloat	0.075 to 0.153 mm

Camshaft lobe height:
- MR20DE
  - Intake
    - T31 X-Trail .... 44.605 to 44.795 mm
    - Dualis .... 45.265 to 45.455 mm
  - Exhaust
    - T31 X-Trail .... 43.175 to 43.365 mm
    - Dualis .... 43.775 to 43.965 mm
- MR20DD
  - Intake .... 45.265 to 45.455 mm
  - Exhaust .... 43.775 to 43.965 mm

Camshaft bearing journal outer diameter:
- No 1 bearing .... 27.935 to 27.955 mm
- Nos 2 to 5 bearings .... 24.950 to 24.970 mm

Camshaft cylinder head bearing journal internal diameter:
- No 1 bearing .... 28.000 to 28.021 mm
- Nos 2 to 5 bearings .... 25.000 to 25.021 mm

Camshaft journal-to-bearing clearance:
- No 1 bearing .... 0.045 to 0.086 mm
- Nos 2 to 5 bearings .... 0.030 to 0.071 mm

Camshaft run-out:
- Standard .... 0.02 mm
- Limit .... 0.05 mm

Camshaft sprocket run-out .... Less than 0.15 mm

Camshaft follower outer diameter:
- Intake .... 33.977 to 33.987 mm
- Exhaust .... 29.977 to 29.987 mm

Cylinder head hole diameter for follower:
- Intake .... 34.000 to 34.021 mm
- Exhaust .... 30.000 to 30.021 mm

Camshaft follower to cylinder head clearance .... 0.013 to 0.044 mm

Torque specifications   Nm

Balance shaft sprocket retaining bolt	55
Balance shaft chain tensioner bolts	10

Camshaft ladder bracket bolts (see text)
- Stage 1 2
- Stage 2 6
- Stage 3 10

Camshaft sensor retaining bolt 7
Camshaft signal plate retaining bolt (end of intake camshaft) 55

Camshaft sprocket retaining bolts
- MR20DE
  - Intake
    - Stage 1 35
    - Stage 2 .... Tighten an additional 67 degrees
  - Exhaust 88
- MR20DD
  - Stage 1 35
  - Stage 2 .... Tighten an additional 30 degrees

Crankshaft pulley bolt
- MR20DE
  - Stage 1 68
  - Stage 2 .... Fully slacken bolt
  - Stage 3 30
  - Stage 4 .... Tighten an additional 60 degrees
- MR20DD
  - Stage 1 30
  - Stage 2 .... Tighten an additional 60 degrees

Chapter 2 Part B 2.0 litre petrol engine

Cylinder head bolts [1]	
Stage 1	40
Stage 2	Tighten an additional 100 degrees
Stage 3	Fully slacken all the bolts
Stage 4	40
Stage 5	Tighten an additional 100 degrees
Stage 6	Tighten an additional 100 degrees
Drivebelt tensioner-to-timing chain cover	40
Driveplate (automatic transmission)	108
Engine mounts	
Left-hand transaxle mount	
Through-bolt/stud nut [2]	65
Through-bolt/stud-to-bracket	
MR20DE	65
MR20DD	95
Mounting-to-bracket nuts	105
Mounting bracket-to-inner guard bolts	80
Mounting-to-transmission bolts	
MR20DE	45
MR20DD	75
CVT	110
Rear engine/transmission torque/link arm mounting	
MR20DE	
Mounting-to-front subframe bolt	110
Mounting bracket-to-transmission bolt	110
MR20DD	
Mounting-to-front subframe bolt	
T32 X-Trail	125
Qashqai	210
Mounting bracket-to-transmission bolt	125
Right-hand engine mounting	
Bracket bolts to engine	55
Mounting bolts to inner guard	
MR20DE	55
MR20DD	65
Stay bracket to mounting bracket and inner guard bolts	19
Engine-to-transmission mounting bolts	62
Exhaust manifold	
Heat shield bolts	6
Oxygen sensor	50
Support bracket bolts	51
To cylinder head nuts	33
To cylinder head studs	12
To engine pipe	
T31 X-Trail and Dualis	49
T32 X-Trail and Qashqai	21
Flywheel (manual transmission)	108
Intake manifold	27
Oil drain plug	See Chapter 1
Oil pan lower bolts	10
Oil pan upper bolts to transmission	26
Oil pan upper casing bolts to cylinder block	25
Throttle body-to-intake manifold	See Chapter 4A
Timing chain	
Cover bolts	
M6 bolts	10
M8 bolts	25
M10 bolts	55
M12 bolts	75
Guide bolts	25
Tensioner bolts	10
VT camshaft sprocket cover - late models with the MR20DD engine	10
Valve cover bolts	
Stage 1	3
Stage 2	10

[1] *Lubricate fastener threads and heads with clean engine oil prior to installation*
[2] *Fastener must be replaced with NEW ones*

1 General information

This Part of Chapter 2 is devoted to in-vehicle repair procedures for the 2.0 litre MR20DE and MR20DD petrol engines. All procedures concerning engine removal and refitting, and engine overhaul options can be found in Part 2D of this Chapter.

The following repair procedures are based on the assumption that the engine is installed in the vehicle. If the engine has been removed from the vehicle and mounted on a stand, many of the steps outlined in this Part of Chapter 2 will not apply.

Engine description

The engine is of the sixteen-valve, in-line four-cylinder, double overhead camshaft (DOHC) type, mounted transversely at the front of the car with the transmission attached to the left-hand end.

The crankshaft runs in five main bearings. Thrustwashers are fitted to No 3 main bearing (upper half) to control crankshaft endfloat.

The connecting rods rotate on horizontally split bearing shells at their big ends. The pistons are attached to the connecting rods by gudgeon pins, which are a sliding fit in the connecting rod small-end eyes and retained in the pistons by circlips. The aluminium-alloy pistons are fitted with three piston rings – two compression rings and an oil control ring.

The cylinder block is made of aluminium alloy and the cylinder bores are an integral part of the block. On this type of engine the cylinder bores are sometimes referred to as having dry liners.

The intake and exhaust valves are each closed by coil springs, and operate in guides pressed into the cylinder head; the valve seat inserts are also pressed into the cylinder head, and can be renewed separately if worn. The intake camshaft has a variable valve sprocket to the end which is oil fed through a control solenoid valve.

The camshaft is driven by a timing chain, and operates the sixteen valves via bucket-type followers. The followers are situated directly below the camshafts. Valve clearances are adjusted by replacing the relevant follower with a different thickness. The camshafts rotate directly in the cylinder head.

Lubrication is by means of an oil pump, which is driven off the end of a balance shaft, which is positioned below the crankshaft in the upper alloy oil pan housing. The balance shaft has a sprocket on the end, which is driven by a chain from the right-hand end of the crankshaft. The oil pump draws oil through a strainer located in the oil pan, and then forces it through an externally mounted filter into galleries in the cylinder block/crankcase. From there, the oil is distributed to the crankshaft (main bearings) and camshaft. The big-end bearings are supplied with oil via internal drillings in the crankshaft, while the camshaft bearings also receive a pressurised supply. The camshaft lobes and valves are lubricated by splash, as are all other engine components.

2 Repair operations possible with the engine in the vehicle

Warning: *The models covered by this manual are equipped with a Supplemental Restraint System (SRS), more commonly known as airbags. Always disarm the airbag system before working in the vicinity of any airbag system component to avoid the possibility of accidental deployment of the airbag, which could cause personal injury (see Chapter 12A Section 20). Do not use a memory saving device to preserve the PCM's memory when working on or near airbag system components.*

1 Many major repair operations can be accomplished without removing the engine from the vehicle.

2 Clean the engine compartment and the exterior of the engine with some type of degreaser before any work is done. It will make the job easier and help keep dirt out of the internal areas of the engine.

3 Depending on the components involved, it may be helpful to remove the bonnet to improve access to the engine as repairs are performed (refer to Chapter 11 Section 9). Cover the mudguards to prevent damage to the paint. Special pads are available, but an old bedspread or blanket will also work.

4 If vacuum, exhaust, oil or coolant leaks develop, indicating a need for gasket or seal replacement, the repairs can generally be made with the engine in the vehicle. The intake and exhaust manifold gaskets, oil pan gasket, crankshaft oil seals and cylinder head gasket are all accessible with the engine in place.

5 Exterior engine components, such as the intake and exhaust manifolds, the oil pan, the oil pump, the water pump, the starter motor, the alternator, and the fuel system components can be removed for repair with the engine in place.

6 Since the cylinder head can be removed without pulling the engine, camshaft and valve component servicing can also be accomplished with the engine in the vehicle. Replacement of the timing chain and sprockets is also possible with the engine in the vehicle.

7 In extreme cases caused by a lack of necessary equipment, repair or replacement of piston rings, pistons, connecting rods and rod bearings is possible with the engine in the vehicle. However, this practice is not recommended because of the cleaning and preparation work that must be done to the components involved.

3 Top Dead Centre (TDC) for number one piston - locating

1 Top Dead Centre (TDC) is the highest point in the cylinder that each piston reaches as it travels up-and-down when the crankshaft turns. Each piston reaches TDC on the compression stroke and again on the exhaust stroke, but TDC generally refers to piston position on the compression stroke.

2 Positioning the number one piston at TDC is an essential part of certain procedures, such as camshaft and timing chain/sprocket removal.

3 Disconnect the negative (-) battery terminal (see Chapter 5 Section 3).

4 Before beginning this procedure, place the transaxle in Park or Neutral and apply the parking brake or block the rear wheels.

5 To access the crankshaft pulley, raise the front of the vehicle and support on jackstands (see Chapter 0 Section 7). Remove the RH front wheel.

6 In order to bring any piston to TDC, the crankshaft must be turned using a large breaker bar or ratchet and socket placed on the crankshaft pulley bolt. When looking at the RH side of the engine, normal crankshaft rotation is clockwise.

7 Remove the spark plugs (see Chapter 1 Section 26).

8 From underneath the front of the car, release the retaining clips and remove the inner guard liner to access the crankshaft pulley **(see illustrations)**. If necessary, also

3.8a Release the retaining clips ...

3.8b ... and remove the inner guard liner

3.9 Compression gauge installed to No.1 cylinder spark plug hole

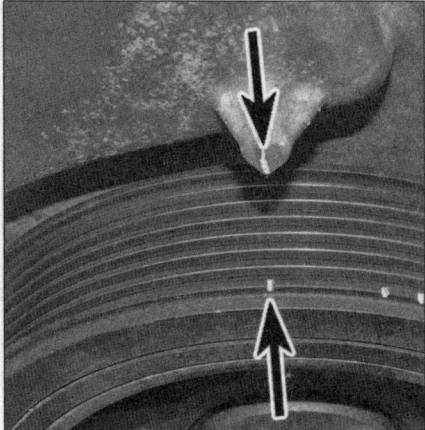

3.12 Align the TDC markings (arrowed)

4.3 Cover the intake ports using duct tape

undo the retaining bolts and remove the engine undershield to improve access.

9 Install a compression gauge in the number one spark plug hole. It should be a gauge with a screw-in fitting and a hose at least 150 mm long **(see illustration)**.

10 Rotate the crankshaft while observing for pressure on the compression gauge. The moment the gauge shows pressure indicates that the number one cylinder has begun the compression stroke.

11 The timing marks are in the form of notches on the crankshaft pulley which align with a pointer on the timing chain cover. The TDC mark is the notch on its own to the left of the two other notches in the pulley, as viewed from under the right-hand front wheel arch.

12 Continue turning the crankshaft until the TDC notch in the crankshaft damper is aligned with the pointer on the timing chain cover **(see illustration)**. At this point, the number one cylinder is at TDC on the compression stroke. If the marks are aligned but there was no compression, the piston was on the exhaust stroke. Continue rotating the crankshaft 360-degrees (1-turn).

Note: *If a compression gauge is not available, you can simply place a hand over the spark plug hole and listen for compression as the engine is rotated. Once compression at the No.1 spark plug hole is noted, the remainder of the Step is the same.*

13 After the number one piston has been positioned at TDC on the compression stroke, TDC for any of the remaining cylinders can be located by turning the crankshaft 180-degrees and following the firing order (refer to Specifications). For example, rotating the engine 180-degrees past TDC for No.1 cylinder will put the engine at TDC compression for No.3 cylinder; rotating another 180-degrees puts No.4 cylinder at TDC compression and another 180-degrees puts No.2 cylinder at TDC compression.

4 Valve cover – removal and refitting

Removal

1 Disconnect the negative (-) battery terminal (see Chapter 5 Section 3).

2 Remove the intake manifold (see Section 5).

3 To prevent anything dropping down into the intake ports in the cylinder head, use duct tape or similar to cover up the ports **(see illustration)**.

4 Disconnect the wiring connectors from the ignition coils, undo the retaining bolts and withdraw the ignition coils from the valve cover **(see illustration)**.

5 Release the retaining clips and disconnect the wiring loom from the front and the transmission end of the valve cover **(see illustration)**.

6 If not already disconnected, release the retaining clip and disconnect the PCV hose from the timing chain end of the valve cover.

7 Working in the reverse of the tightening sequence **(see illustration 4.13)**, slacken and remove the valve cover retaining bolts.

8 Lift off the valve cover, and disconnect the wiring loom securing clip from the timing chain end of the cover **(see illustrations)**. Recover the rubber seal, which goes around the outer edge of the cover, and also around each of the spark plug holes.

9 Inspect the cover seals for signs of damage and deterioration, and renew as necessary. Nissan recommends that the valve cover seal should always be renewed, if the cover is removed.

4.4 Remove the ignition coils

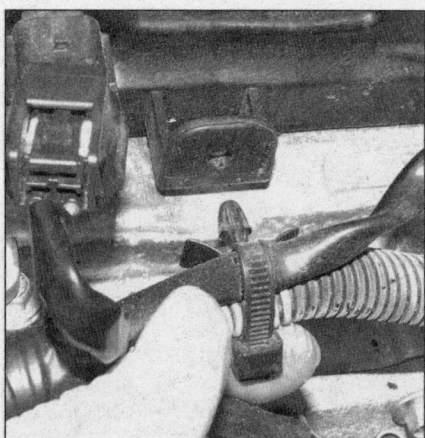

4.5 Unclip the wiring loom from the valve cover

4.8a Unclip the wiring loom connector ...

4.8b ... and remove the valve cover

4.11 Fit the new rubber gasket to the valve cover

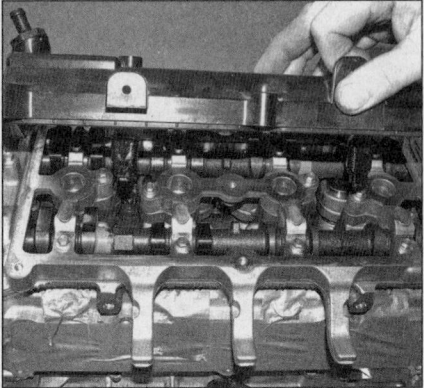

4.12 Refit the valve cover

4.13 Tighten the retaining bolts in the sequence shown

18 Reconnect the battery negative terminal (see Chapter 5 Section 3). Run the engine and check for any oil leaks around the engine valve cover.

5 Intake manifold – removal and refitting

Warning: *The engine must be completely cool before beginning this procedure.*

Removal

1 Where fitted, undo the retaining bolts and remove the plastic trim cover from the top of the engine (**see illustration**).
2 Remove the throttle body (see Chapter 4B Section 7).
3 Disconnect the breather (PCV) hose from the rear of the manifold and move it to one side (**see illustration**).
4 Slacken and remove the left-hand rear mounting bracket bolt from the manifold (**see illustrations**).
5 Slacken and remove the right-hand rear mounting bracket bolt from the manifold (**see illustration**).
6 Disconnect the brake vacuum hose from the right-hand rear of the manifold (**see illustration**).

Refitting

10 Carefully clean the cylinder head and cover mating surfaces, and remove all traces of oil.
11 Fit the rubber seal to the valve cover groove, ensuring that it is correctly located along its entire length, and around the four spark plug holes in the centre of the cover (**see illustration**).
12 Carefully lower the valve cover onto the cylinder head, taking great care not to displace any of the rubber seal (**see illustration**).
13 Make sure the cover is correctly seated, and then install the retaining bolts. Working in sequence, tighten all the cover screws to Specifications (**see illustration**).
14 Refit the wiring loom securing clips to the locating holes in the outer edge of the valve cover.
15 Refit the ignition coils and reconnect their wiring connectors.
16 Refit the PCV hose and secure in position with the retaining clip.
17 Remove the duct tape (where used) from the intake ports in the cylinder head, and clean the intake manifold mating surface. Refit the intake manifold (see Section 5)

5.1 Remove the engine trim cover

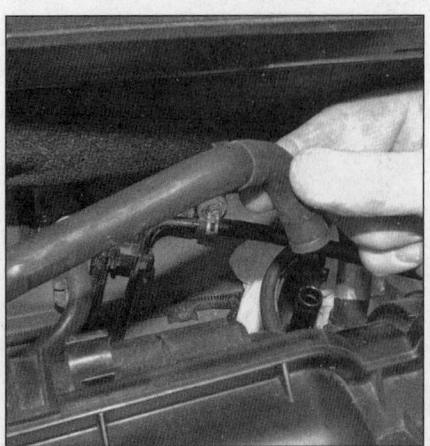

5.3 Remove the breather hose

5.4 Undo the manifold left-hand rear securing bolt (arrowed)

Chapter 2 Part B 2.0 litre petrol engine

5.5 Undo the manifold right-hand rear securing bolt

5.6 Disconnect the vacuum pipe from the rear of the manifold

5.7 EVAP canister purge solenoid valve

5.8 Unclip the wiring loom bracket

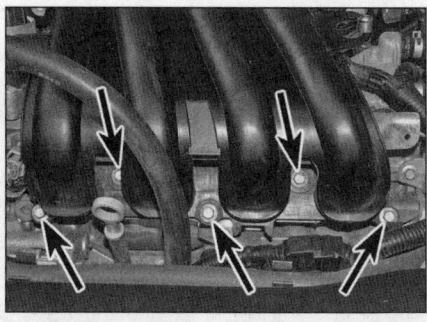

5.10 Undo the manifold securing bolts (arrowed)

5.11 Removing the intake manifold

7 Disconnect the vacuum hose and wiring connector from the EVAP canister purge solenoid valve, which is located on the left-hand side of the manifold (see illustration).
8 Unclip the wiring loom retaining clip from the transmission end of the manifold (see illustration).
9 Withdraw the oil level dipstick to make access to the manifold centre bolt easier.
10 Make a final check that all the necessary vacuum/breather hoses have been disconnected from the manifold then, working from the outside to the centre, slacken and remove the manifold retaining bolts (see illustration).
11 Manoeuvre the manifold away from the head (see illustrations), and out of the engine compartment. Remove the manifold rubber gasket and discard it, a new one will be required for refitting.

Refitting

12 Refitting is the reverse of the removal procedure, noting the following points:
13 Ensure that the manifold and cylinder head mating surfaces are clean and dry, and fit the new rubber gasket to the manifold (see illustration).
14 Refit the throttle body (see Chapter 4A Section 10), using a new O-ring seal/gasket (see illustration).
15 Install the manifold, and tighten its retaining bolts to the specified torque, starting at the centre and working outwards (see Specifications).
16 Ensure that all relevant hoses are reconnected to their original positions, and are securely held (where necessary) by their retaining clips.

6 Exhaust manifold – removal and refitting

Note: *The exhaust manifold and catalytic converter are a complete assembly, and cannot be renewed separately.*

Removal

1 Raise the front of the vehicle and support on jackstands (see Chapter 0 Section 7)
2 Trace the wiring back from the two oxygen sensors, to the wiring connectors, and disconnect them from the main wiring harness. The upper oxygen sensor connection is on the top left-hand side of the exhaust manifold and the lower oxygen sensor connection is under the vehicle on the rear of the front subframe (see illustrations).

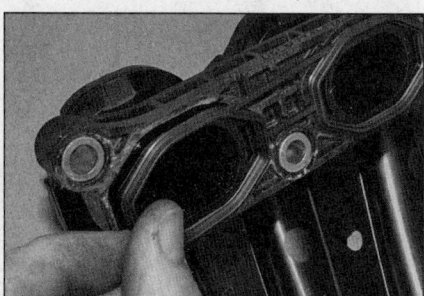

5.13 Ensure new gaskets are fitted to the manifold

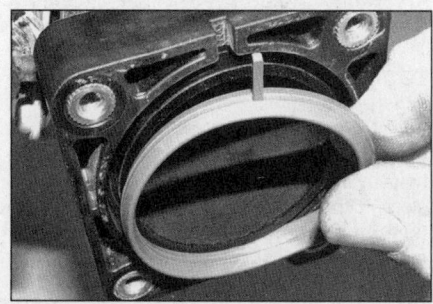

5.14 Also fit a new seal to the throttle body opening

6.2a Disconnect oxygen sensor upper (arrowed) ...

6.2b ... and lower wiring connectors

6.4 Undo the lower support bracket bolt (arrowed)

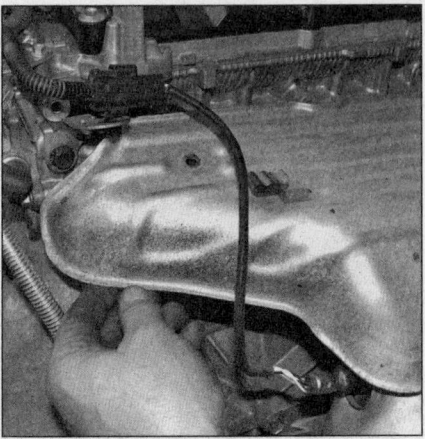

6.5 Remove the upper heatshield

6.6 Undo the manifold securing nuts

6.10 Always use a new manifold gasket

3 Remove the fasteners retaining the engine pipe to the bottom of the exhaust manifold.
4 Undo the retaining bolts and remove the mounting stay bracket from under the exhaust manifold **(see illustration)**.
5 Working from the top in the engine compartment, undo the retaining bolts, and remove the heat shield from above the exhaust manifold **(see illustration)**.
6 Make sure there is nothing still attached to the manifold, and then working from the outside to the centre, slacken and remove the manifold retaining nuts **(see illustration)**.
7 Manoeuvre the manifold out of the engine compartment, and discard the manifold gasket.

Refitting

8 Refitting is the reverse of the removal procedure, noting the following points:
9 Examine all the exhaust manifold studs and nuts for signs of damage and corrosion; remove all traces of corrosion, and repair or renew any damaged studs.

Note: *Nissan recommends that the nuts and studs should always be renewed if removed.*

10 Ensure that the manifold and cylinder head sealing faces are clean and flat, and fit the new manifold gasket **(see illustration)**.
11 Install the manifold, and tighten its retaining bolts to the specified torque (see Specifications), starting at the centre and working outwards.
12 Refit the engine pipe to the bottom of the exhaust manifold.

7 Crankshaft pulley – removal and refitting

Removal

1 Remove the drivebelt (see Chapter 1 Section 12).
2 If necessary, position No.1 cylinder at TDC on its compression stroke (see Section 3).
3 To prevent crankshaft rotation while the pulley bolt is unscrewed, the pulley should be held by a suitable tool which locates in the slots in the pulley to prevent it from turning **(see illustration)**. If this is not available, on manual transmission models, select top gear and have an assistant apply the brakes firmly. On automatic transmission models lock the flywheel; the starter motor may need to be removed to do this.
4 Unscrew the pulley bolt, along with its washer (where applicable), and remove the pulley from the crankshaft **(see illustration)**.
5 If the pulley is a tight fit on the end of the crankshaft, use a puller to withdraw the pulley from the end of the shaft. Refit the pulley bolt and screw it back into the end of the crankshaft, leaving it approx. 5mm out from the pulley face. Fit the puller (this can be a

7.3 Using a homemade tool to hold the pulley

Chapter 2 Part B 2.0 litre petrol engine

7.4 Remove the crankshaft pulley bolt

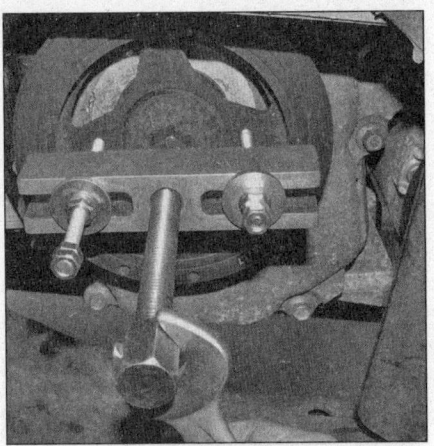

7.5a Remove the pulley using a suitable puller. If one is not available, you can manufacture one…

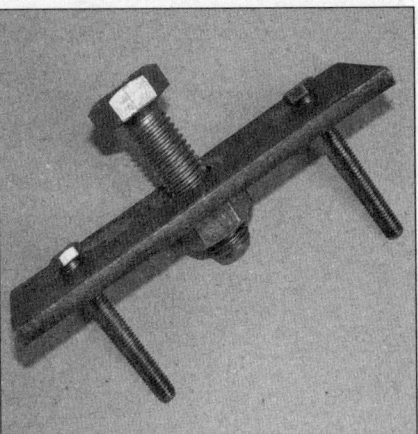

7.5b … using a piece of flat metal bar and some bolts

7.6 Make sure the woodruff key (arrowed) is located securely

7.8 Align the slot in the pulley centre hub with the Woodruff key

homemade puller, using a piece of flat bar and three bols/nuts) to the pulley and tighten the centre bolt to withdraw the pulley from the end of the crankshaft (see illustration).

6 If the pulley Woodruff key is a loose fit in the end of the crankshaft (see illustration), remove it and store it with the pulley for safekeeping.

Refitting

7 Refit the Woodruff key (where removed).
8 Align the crankshaft pulley groove with the key (see illustration), then slide the sprocket onto the crankshaft.
9 Lubricate under the head of the bolt, also the bolt threads with new engine oil (see illustration), and then refit the retaining bolt/washer.
10 Lock the crankshaft by the method used on removal, and tighten the pulley retaining bolt to the specified torque (see Specifications). The head of the bolt/washer has markings around its edge, dividing it into 60° segments. To carry out the final stage of the tightening procedure (angle tighten 60°), paint one of the marks on the bolt head, and also paint a mark on the pulley alongside the following 60° mark to the right of the first mark. As the bolt is tightened, when the two paint marks are aligned, the bolt has then been tightened through 60° (see illustrations).
11 Install the drivebelt (see Chapter 1 Section 12).

7.9 Apply a small amount of oil to the bolt

7.10a Make alignments marks at 60° on the pulley and bolt …

7.10b … and turn the bolt until the marks are aligned

8.3 Remove the inner wheel arch liner

8.7 Using a trolley jack to support the engine

8.8 Release the wiring loom clip from the cover

8.9a Undo the retaining bolt …

8.9b … and remove the intake valve timing control solenoid

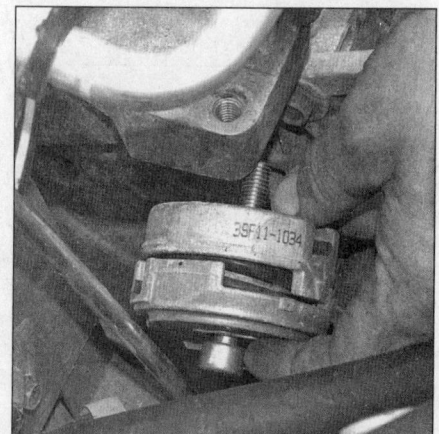

8.11 Remove the drive belt tensioner

8 Timing chain cover – removal and refitting

Removal

1 Disconnect the negative (-) battery terminal (see Chapter 5 Section 3).
2 Raise the front of the vehicle and support on jackstands (see Chapter 0 Section 7). Remove right-hand front wheel.
3 Undo the retaining bolts and remove the plastic inner wheel arch liner (see illustration), and guard liner from beneath the right-hand front guard and the engine.
4 Drain the engine oil, then clean and refit the engine oil drain plug using a new sealing washer, tightening it to the specified torque (see Chapter 1). It is recommended that the filter is also removed, and a new one fitted. After reassembly, the engine can then be refilled with fresh oil (see Chapter 1 Section 9).
5 Remove the valve cover (see Section 4).
6 Remove the crankshaft pulley (see Section 7).
7 Use a jack to support the engine (see illustration), and then remove the bolts retaining the right-hand engine mounting (see Section 17).
8 Disconnect the wiring connector from the intake valve timing control solenoid, and release the wiring loom securing clips from the timing chain cover (see illustration).
9 Undo the retaining bolt and withdraw the intake valve timing control solenoid from the timing chain cover (see illustrations). To make access easier, the engine can be lifted slightly using the jack supporting the engine.

Note: *As the control solenoid is withdrawn, there will be oil spillage. Renew the control solenoid O-ring on installation.*

10 On MR20DD engines, remove the bolts retaining the VT camshaft sprocket cover to the timing chain main cover in the reverse of the tightening sequence (see illustration 8.22).
11 Undo the retaining bolt and withdraw the drive belt tensioner from the timing chain cover (see illustration).
12 Working in the reverse of the tightening sequence (see illustrations 8.21a and 8.21b), progressively loosen and then remove the timing chain cover retaining bolts. Note the correct fitted location of each bolt, as some of the bolts are different lengths. Also there are three sizes (diameter) of bolts.
13 The timing chain cover has been fitted using a liquid gasket, and is bonded to the engine. Taking care not to damage the timing chain cover work your way around the outside of the cover to release it from the engine. There are three lever points to pry the cover away from the engine (see illustrations 8.21a and 8.21b). Also note at the lower end of the cover there are two steel dowels, which can become very tight in the alloy cover (see illustrations).

8.13a Two steel dowels are located in holes at each side of the cover (arrowed)

Chapter 2 Part B 2.0 litre petrol engine

8.13b Carefully work your way around the cover …

8.13c … to remove it from the engine

8.14 Retrieve the O-ring seal from the cylinder block

8.17 Fit a new O-ring seal to the cylinder block

8.18a Apply a bead of sealant around the outside of the cover …

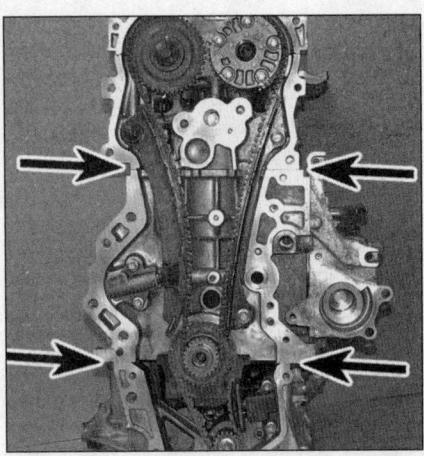

8.19 Apply sealant to the joints (arrowed) at both sides of the cylinder block

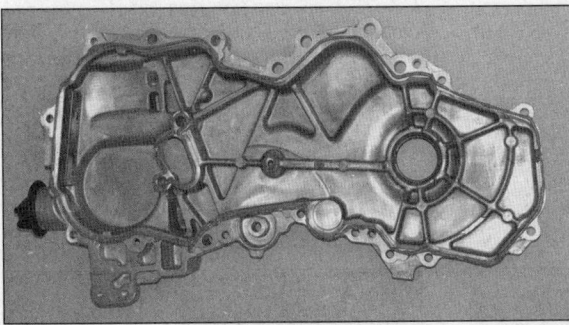

8.18b … and around the centre mountings as shown, on early models

14 There is an O-ring oil seal fitted to the cylinder block, to the front of the fixed timing chain guide (see illustration). Discard the O-ring oil seal, as a new one will be required on refitting.

Refitting

15 Prior to refitting the cover, it is recommended that a new crankshaft oil seal is used. Note the seals fitted position and the carefully lever the old seal out of the cover using a large flat-bladed screwdriver. Fit the new seal to the cover, making sure its sealing lip is facing inwards. Drive the seal into position until it seats squarely in the position noted on removal, for further information see Section 14 of this Chapter.

16 Ensure that the timing chain cover and engine cylinder block/cylinder head mating surfaces are clean/dry and free from any silicone sealer.

17 Fit a new O-ring oil seal to the cylinder block, use a small amount of grease to hold it in position (see illustration).

18 Apply a thin bead of suitable sealant (3 mm to 4 mm diameter) to the timing chain cover surface, not forgetting to apply sealant to the area around the three engine mounting bolt passages in the upper centre of the cover (see illustrations).

19 Also apply a small amount of sealant to where the cylinder block joins the cylinder

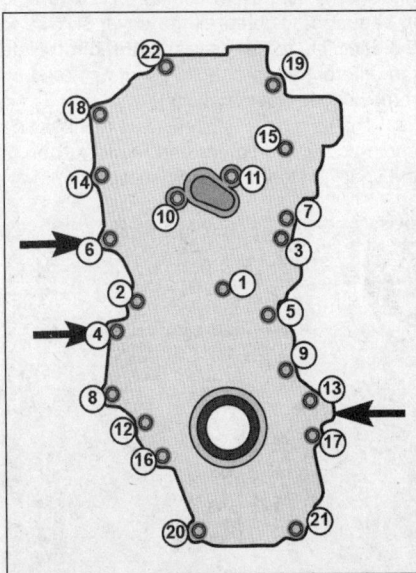

8.21a Tightening sequence for the timing chain cover on the MR20DE engines. The large black arrows are the levering points to pry the cover away from the engine on removal

Chapter 2 Part B 2.0 litre petrol engine

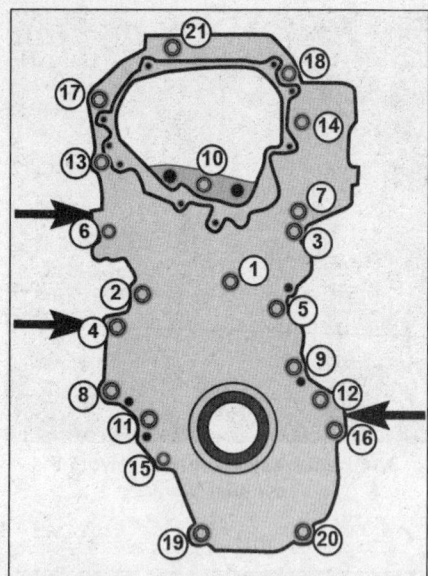

8.21b Tightening sequence for the timing chain cover on the MR20DD engines. The large black arrows are the levering points to pry the cover away from the engine on removal

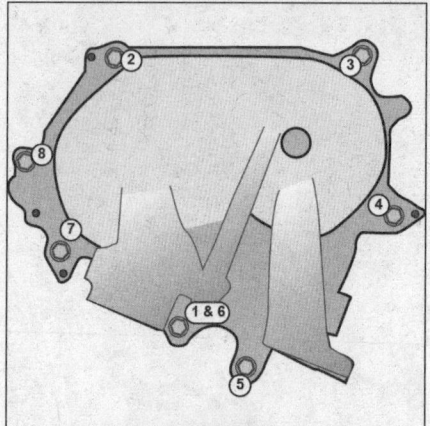

8.23 Tightening sequence for the VT camshaft sprocket cover on MR20DD engines

9.4a Align the markings on the camshaft sprockets (arrowed) ...

head, and where the cylinder block joins the upper oil pan housing **(see illustration)**.

20 For this procedure the help of an assistant would be advisable; lower the timing chain cover into position taking care not to wipe the sealer of the face off the cover or dislodge the O-ring seal on the cylinder block. With the assistant under the right-hand front wheel arch manoeuvre the cover into position over the end of the crankshaft, taking great care not to damage the oil seal lip.

21 Make sure the cover is correctly seated, and then install the retaining bolts. Working in sequence, tighten all the cover screws to the specified torque **(see illustrations)**. Note the different sizes of bolts used, as noted on removal (see Specifications).

22 Refit the drive belt tensioner to the timing chain cover and tighten the retaining bolt to the specified torque (see Specifcations).

23 On MR20DD engines, remove the old O-rings from the rear of the cover and install new ones. Apply a bead of RTV sealant to the mating surfaces around the perimeter of the VT camshaft sprocket cover. Install the cover and tighten the bolts, in the correct sequence **(see illustration)**, to the specified torque (see Specifications).

24 Use a new O-ring and install the valve timing control solenoid(s) to the timing chain cover and tighten the retaining bolt. Reconnect the wiring connector and clip the loom securing clips into the cover.

25 Refit the right-hand engine mounting as described in Section 17 of this Chapter. When the engine mounting is in place, remove the jack from under the engine.

26 Refit the crankshaft pulley (see Section 7 of this Chapter).

27 Refit the valve cover (see Section 4).

28 After reassembly, the engine can then be refilled with fresh oil and a new oil filter installed (see Chapter 1 Section 9).

29 Refit the plastic inner wheel arch liner and guard liner.

30 Install the front wheel and lower the vehicle to the ground. Tighten the wheel nuts to the specified torque (see Chapter 1).

9 Timing chain, tensioner, guides and sprockets – removal, inspection and refitting

Removal

1 Position No 1 cylinder at TDC on its compression stroke (see Section 3)

2 Remove the valve cover (see Section 4).

3 Remove the timing chain cover as described in Section 8.

4 With No 1 cylinder set at TDC, the markings on the camshaft sprockets should be in line. Apply paint marks to the timing chain links which are in line with the markings on the sprockets **(see illustrations)**.

Note: If the markings on the camshaft are not aligned, it may be that the engine is positioned at No.4 cylinder TDC on the compression stroke. Turn the crankshaft one complete turn clockwise to get it firing on number 1 cylinder. Note the cam lobes on number 1 cylinder, should be pointing upwards and towards each other when firing on this cylinder.

5 Check the crankshaft sprocket is positioned at TDC **(see illustration)**.

Note: The keyway will also be in the 12 o'clock position, as seen from the right-hand end of the engine.

6 Whilst holding the plunger back into the body of the tensioner, insert a small-diameter

9.4b ... in this position the cam lobes should be pointing as shown

9.5a Crankshaft alignment marks

9.6 Insert locking pin through tensioner body

Chapter 2 Part B 2.0 litre petrol engine

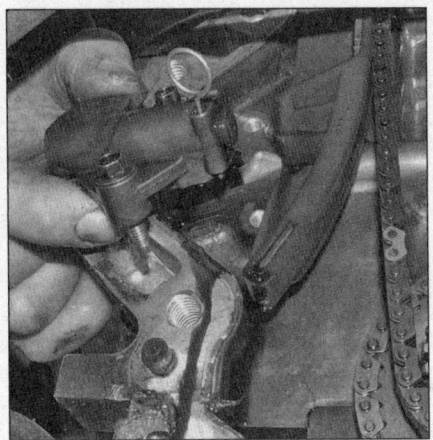

9.7 Undo the retaining bolts and remove the tensioner

9.8 Remove upper pivot bolt and withdraw the tensioner guide

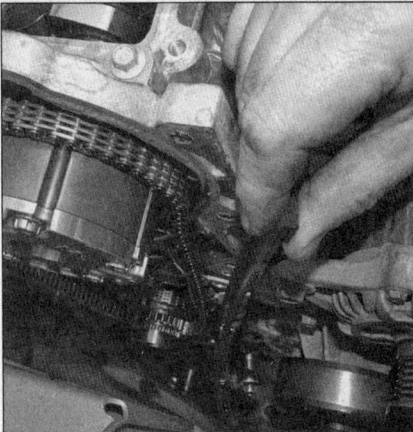

9.9 Removing the fixed chain guide

rod through the hole in the body to lock the plunger **(see illustration)**.

7   Undo the two retaining bolts, and remove the tensioner from the end of the cylinder block. Keep the rod inserted into the tensioner to prevent the plunger from springing out **(see illustration)**.

9.10 Disengage the timing chain from the crankshaft sprocket

8   Undo the chain tensioner guide upper pivot bolt, and remove it from the rear of the crankcase **(see illustration)**.
9   Unscrew the two mounting bolts, and remove the chain front guide from the crankcase **(see illustration)**.
10 Disengage the timing chain from the crankshaft sprocket, and manoeuvre it out from the engine **(see illustration)**.
Warning: *Do not turn the crankshaft or camshafts while the timing chain is removed, otherwise piston and valve contact may occur causing damage.*
11 Slacken the camshaft sprocket retaining bolts, whilst retaining the camshafts with a large open-ended spanner fitted to the hexagonal Section of each shaft. Remove the bolts along with its washers (where applicable), disengage the sprockets from the end of the camshafts **(see illustrations)**.
12 To remove the crankshaft sprocket from the end of the crankshaft requires removing the balance shaft drive chain (see Section 16).

Inspection

13 Examine the teeth on the camshaft and crankshaft sprockets for any sign of wear or damage such as chipped, hooked or missing teeth. If there is any sign of wear or damage on either sprockets or timing chain then they should be renewed as a set.
14 Inspect the links of the timing chain for signs of wear or damage on the rollers. The extent of wear can be judged by checking the amount by which the chain can be bent sideways; a new chain will have very little sideways movement. If there is an excessive amount of side play in either timing chain, it must be renewed.
15 Note that it is a sensible precaution to renew the timing chain, regardless of apparent condition, if the engine has covered a high mileage, or if it has been noted that the chain has sounded noisy when the engine running. Although not strictly necessary, it is always worth renewing the chain and sprockets as a matched set, since it is false economy to run a new chain on worn sprockets and vice versa. If there is any doubt about the condition of the timing chain and sprockets, seek the advice of a Nissan dealer service department, who will be able to advise you as to the best course of action.

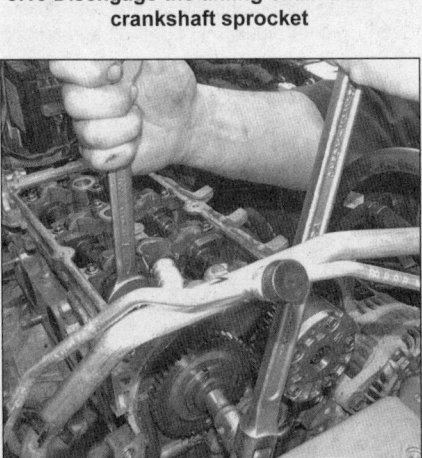

9.11a Undo the sprocket retaining bolts, while counter holding the camshaft ...

9.11b ... with an open-ended spanner on the hexagonal on the camshaft ...

9.11c ... then remove the camshaft sprockets

Chapter 2 Part B 2.0 litre petrol engine

9.18 Check the crankshaft is still at TDC

9.19a Align the locating peg on the end of the camshaft with the sprocket

9.19b Tighten the sprocket retaining bolt, while counter holding the camshaft

9.20a Align the slot in the sprocket with the locating peg in the camshaft

9.20b Tighten the sprocket retaining bolt, while counter holding the camshaft

16 Examine the chain guides for signs of wear or damage to their chain contact faces, renewing any which are badly marked.
17 Check the chain tensioner for signs of wear, and check that the plunger is free to slide freely in the tensioner body. The condition of the tensioner spring can only be judged in comparison to a new component. Renew the tensioner if it is worn or there is any doubt about the condition of its tensioning spring.

Refitting

18 Check the crankshaft is still positioned at TDC (see illustration), and that the timing marks on the balance shaft drive chain and sprockets have not been disturbed. See Section 16 for further information.
19 Refit the intake camshaft sprocket into position, ensuring that the locating peg is aligned (see illustrations). Tighten the camshaft bolt to the specified torque (see Specifications), whilst retaining the camshaft with a large open-ended spanner as used on removal.
20 Refit the exhaust camshaft sprocket into position, ensuring that the timing marks are facing the position noted on removal (see illustrations). Tighten the camshaft bolt to the specified torque (see Specifications), whilst retaining the camshaft with a large open-ended spanner as used on removal.
21 Manoeuvre the chain around the sprockets, making sure the coloured links on the chain align with the camshaft and crankshaft timing marks. The orange link aligns with the crankshaft sprocket timing mark and the two dark blue links align with the camshaft sprockets alignment marks (see illustrations).
22 Fit the timing chain front and rear guides to the cylinder block, and tighten the retaining

9.21a Align the coloured links with the camshaft sprockets (arrowed) ...

9.21b ... and the crankshaft markings (arrowed)

Chapter 2 Part B 2.0 litre petrol engine

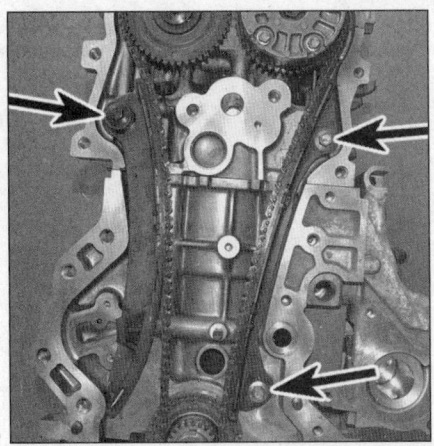

9.22 Fit the timing chain guides to the cylinder block

9.23a Refit the tensioner

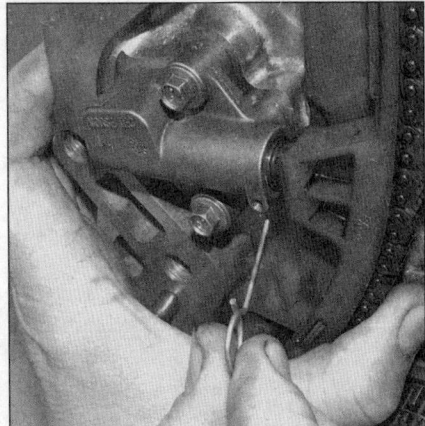

9.23b Hold pressure against the tensioner and remove the locking pin

10.4 Covering up the injector holes using duct tape

bolts to the specified torque (see Specifications) **(see illustration)**.

23 Fit the chain tensioner to the cylinder block, and tighten its retaining bolts to the specified torque (see Specifications). Whilst holding the guide against the tensioner plunger, withdraw the rod, and check that the tensioner plunger is forced out against the guide to take up the slack in the chain **(see illustrations)**.

24 Check that all the timing marks are still correctly aligned with the chain links. If all timing marks are aligned, fit the crankshaft pulley and turn the engine two complete turns, and check the timing marks on the sprockets are all re-aligned.

Note: *The coloured links on the chain will not be re-aligned with the marks on the sprockets. The coloured links are just for the initial set up, and will take many turns before they will line up again, with the marks on the sprockets.*

25 Remove the crankshaft pulley and refit the timing chain cover (see Section 8).
26 Refit the crankshaft pulley (see Section 7).
27 Refit the valve cover (see Section 4).

10 Camshafts and followers – removal, inspection and refitting

Removal

1 Remove the timing chain cover, as described in Section 8.

2 Remove the camshaft sprockets, as described in Section 9.
3 Remove the fuel rail from across the front of the cylinder head (see Chapter 4A Section 6). Plug all openings, to prevent loss of fuel and entry of dirt into the fuel system.
4 To prevent anything dropping down into the intake ports or injector holes in the cylinder head, use duct tape or similar to cover up the ports **(see illustration)**.
5 Release the wiring loom and hoses from the mounting brackets on the transmission end of the cylinder head, then undo the retaining bolts and remove the brackets **(see illustrations)**.
6 Undo the retaining bolt and remove the camshaft position sensor from the top of the camshaft ladder bracket **(see illustration)**.
7 Working in the reverse of the tightening sequence **(see illustration 10.23)**, evenly and progressively slacken the seventeen camshaft bearing ladder bracket retaining bolts by one turn at a time, to relieve the pressure of the valve springs on the bearing ladder gradually and evenly. Once the valve spring pressure has been relieved, the bolts can be fully unscrewed and removed.

10.5a Remove the bracket from the front left-hand corner of the cylinder head

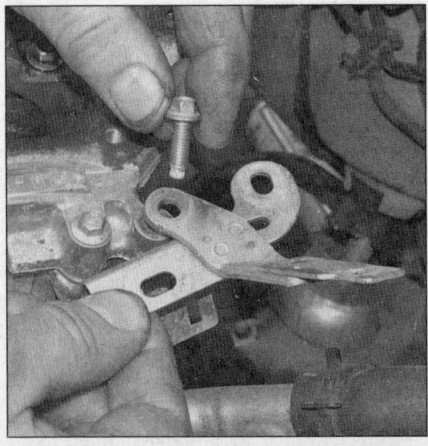

10.5b Remove the bracket from the rear left-hand corner of the cylinder head

10.6 Remove the camshaft position sensor

10.8a Carefully prise the camshaft ladder ...

10.8b ... noting the steel dowels at the rear ...

10.8c ... and front of the camshaft ladder

Note: *Bolts 13, 14 and 15 are longer than the other bolts.*

8 The camshaft ladder bracket has been fitted using a liquid gasket, and is bonded to the cylinder head. Taking care not to damage the ladder bracket or cylinder head work your way around the outside of the housing to release it from the cylinder head. Nissan show the starting point at the front left-hand corner, and the rear right-hand corner of the ladder bracket (as viewed from the front of the vehicle), where there is an area to start prying. Also note that at the rear left-hand corner, and front right-hand corner of the ladder bracket (as viewed from the front of the vehicle), there are two steel dowels, which can become very tight in the alloy ladder bracket **(see illustrations)**.

9 With the camshaft bearing ladder bracket removed the camshafts can now be simply lifted off the top of the cylinder head, noting their fitted position. Note the position of the dowel on the sprocket end of the camshafts, and the position of the cam lobes, so that they can be refitted in the correct position for TDC on No.1 cylinder **(see illustrations)**.

Caution: *Take care not to damage the signal plate for the camshaft position sensor on the end of the intake camshaft.*

10 Obtain sixteen small, clean plastic containers, and number them 1 to 16. Alternatively, divide a larger container into sixteen compartments. Using a rubber sucker, withdraw each follower (valve lifter) in turn, and place it in its respective container **(see illustration)**. Do not interchange the cam followers in the cylinder head, or the rate of wear will be increased.

Note: *The diameter of the intake cam followers is larger than the exhaust cam followers.*

Inspection

11 Inspect the cam bearing surfaces of the head and the bearing ladder bracket. Look for score marks and deep scratches. Check the camshaft lobes for heat discoloration (blue appearance), score marks, chipped areas or flat spots.

12 Camshaft run-out can be checked by supporting each end of the camshaft on V-blocks, and measuring any run-out at the centre of the shaft using a dial gauge. If the run-out exceeds the specified limit, a new camshaft will be required.

13 Measure the height of each lobe with a micrometer **(see illustration)**, and compare the results to the figures given in the Specifications. If damage is noted or wear is exces-

10.8d Remove the camshaft ladder from the top of the cylinder head

10.9a Lift the camshafts from the cylinder head ...

10.9b ... noting the intake camshaft has the target ring for the position sensor

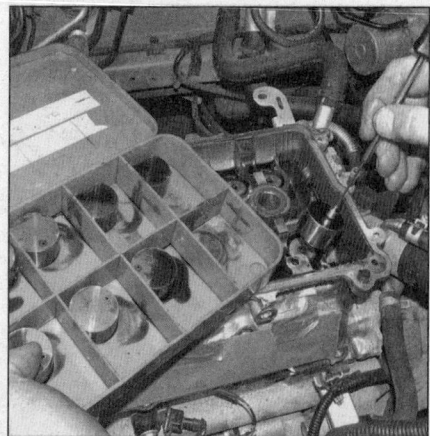
10.10 Remove the cam followers

Chapter 2 Part B 2.0 litre petrol engine

10.13 Checking the cam lobe height with a micrometer

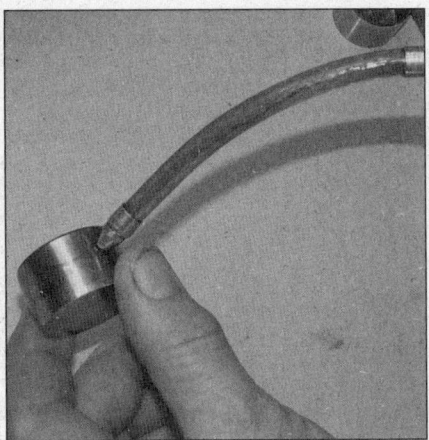

10.17a Lubricate the cam followers outer surface …

10.17b … and slide them back into place

10.17c Lubricate the camshaft bearing lower surfaces

10.18 Align the locating pegs on the end of the camshaft

damage. Clean the steel dowels on the cylinder head, and apply a small amount of oil to aid fitting.

Refitting

17 Liberally oil the cylinder head cam follower bores and the followers. Carefully refit the followers to the cylinder head; ensuring that each follower is refitted to its original bore **(see illustrations)**. Some care will be required to enter the followers squarely into their bores. Liberally oil the camshaft bearing and lobe contact surfaces.

18 Refit the camshafts to their correct locations in the cylinder head, as noted on removal **(see illustration)**.

19 Check that the crankshaft is still in the TDC position, as positioned on removal **(see illustration)**.

20 Liberally oil the camshaft bearing surfaces in the ladder bracket **(see illustration)**.

21 Ensure that the ladder bracket and head mating surfaces are completely clean, unmarked and free from oil. Apply a thin bead of suitable sealant (3.4 mm to 4.4 mm diameter) to the under side of the bearing ladder bracket surface, not forgetting to apply sealant to the area around the spark plug hole

sive, new camshaft(s) must be fitted.

14 The camshaft bearing oil clearance should now be checked.

15 Fit the bearing ladder bracket to the cylinder head, and tighten the retaining bolts to the specified torque in sequence **(see illustration 10.23)** (see Specifications). Measure the diameter of each bearing cap journal, and compare the measurements obtained with the results given in the Specifications at the start of this Chapter. If any journal is worn beyond the service limit, the cylinder head must be renewed. The camshaft bearing oil clearance can then calculated by subtracting the camshaft bearing journal diameter from the bearing cap journal diameter.

16 Check the cam follower and cylinder head bearing surfaces for signs of wear or

10.19 Check the crankshaft is still aligned

10.20 Lubricate the camshaft bearing upper surfaces

10.21a Apply a bead of sealant around the outside of the ladder …

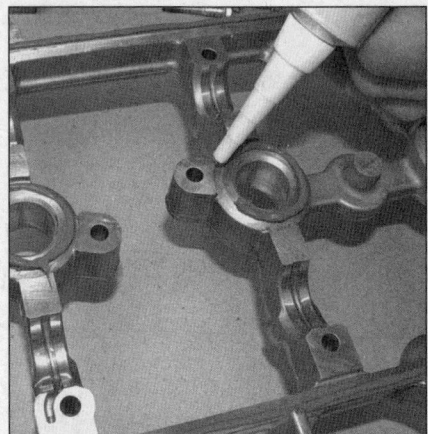

10.21b ... and around the centre mountings ...

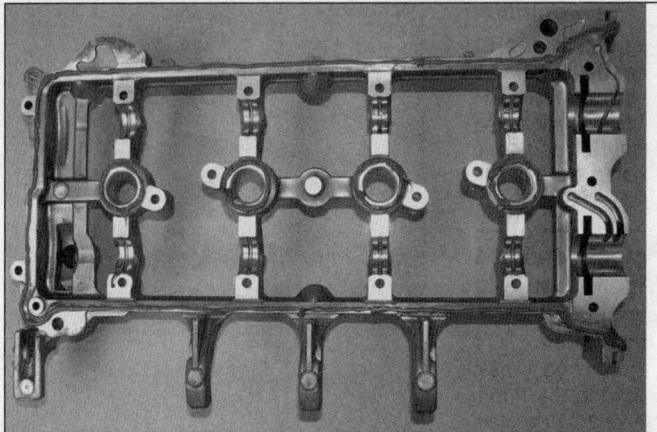

10.21c ... as shown

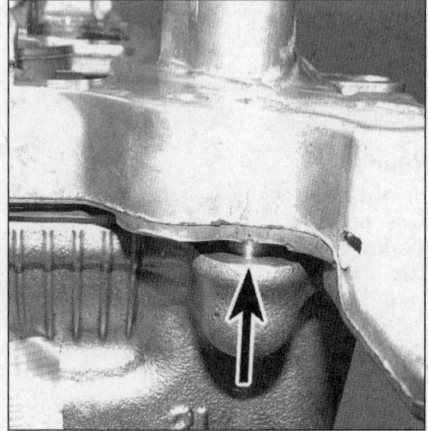

10.22 Align the dowels when fitting the ladder

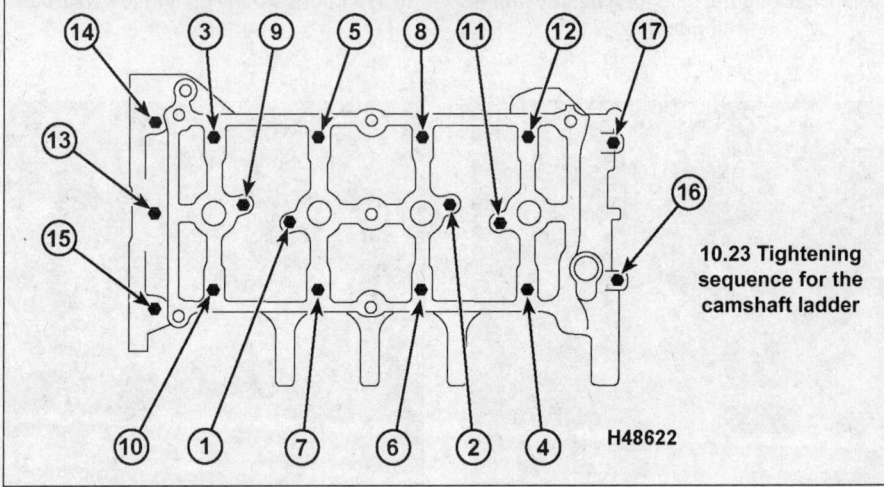

10.23 Tightening sequence for the camshaft ladder

recesses in the centre of the ladder bracket **(see illustrations)**.

22 Lower the bearing ladder bracket into position, taking care not to wipe the sealer of the face of the ladder bracket. Make sure the two locating dowels are aligned **(see illustration)**, before installing the bolts.

23 Working in sequence, evenly and progressively tighten the camshaft bearing ladder bracket bolts by one turn at a time until the ladder touches the cylinder head **(see illustration)**. Then go round again and tighten all the bolts to the specified torque (see Specifications). Work only as described, to impose the pressure of the valve springs gradually and evenly on the bearing ladder bracket.

24 Refit the camshaft position sensor to the top of the camshaft ladder bracket and tighten the retaining bolt.

25 Refit the mounting brackets to the transmission end of the cylinder head, and tighten the retaining bolts, clip the wiring loom and hoses back into the brackets.

26 Remove the duct tape (where used) from the intake ports in the cylinder head, and clean the intake manifold mating surface. Refit the fuel rail (see Chapter 4A Section 6).

27 Refit the camshaft sprockets and timing chain (see Section 9).

28 Refit the timing chain cover (see Section 8)

29 If the cylinder head/camshafts have been overhauled, check the valve clearances 'cold' prior to refitting the cylinder head cover (see Chapter 1 Section 34).

11 Cylinder head – removal and refitting

Removal

1 Depressurise the fuel system (see Chapter 4A Section 3)

2 Disconnect the negative (-) battery terminal (see Chapter 5 Section 3).

3 Remove the timing chain (see Section 9).

4 Remove the camshafts (see Section 10).

5 Remove the exhaust manifold (see Section 6).

11.6 Disconnect the temperature sensor wiring connector

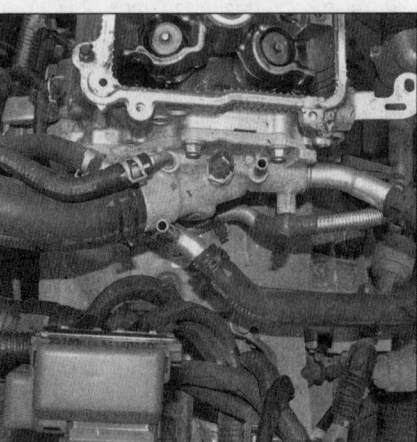

11.7a Note the fitted position of the hoses ...

Chapter 2 Part B 2.0 litre petrol engine

11.7b ... and disconnect them from the coolant housing

11.8 Unclip the wiring loom from the coolant housing

11.9a Undo the two retaining bolts ...

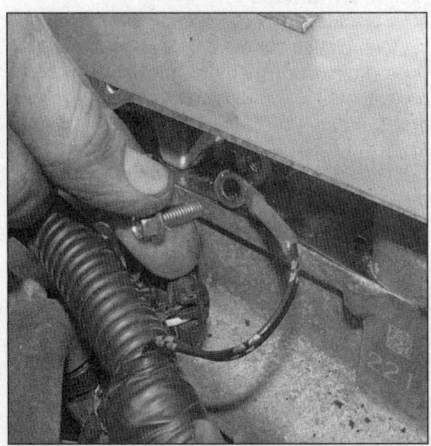

11.9b ... and remove the earth wires from the front of the cylinder head

11.11a Remove the cylinder head bolts ...

6 Disconnect the wiring connector from the temperature sensor (see illustration).
7 Noting their fitted position, slacken the retaining clips and disconnect the coolant hoses from the coolant housing on the transmission end of the cylinder head (see illustrations).
8 Unclip the wiring loom securing clip from the coolant housing (see illustration).
9 Undo the retaining bolts and disconnect the two earth cables from the front of the cylinder head (see illustrations).
10 Working in the reverse of the tightening sequence, progressively slacken the ten cylinder head bolts by half a turn at a time, until all bolts can be unscrewed by hand (see illustration 11.24).
11 Withdraw the cylinder head bolts and then lift the cylinder head away from the dowels on the cylinder block. If required, have an assistant to help removal, as it is a heavy assembly (see illustrations).
12 Remove the gasket from the top of the block, noting the two locating dowels fitted to the top of the cylinder block (see illustration). If they are a loose fit in the block, remove the locating dowels, noting which way round they are fitted, and store them with the head for safekeeping.

Preparation for refitting

13 Check the condition of the cylinder head bolts, and particularly their threads, whenever they are removed. Wash the bolts and wipe dry, then check each for any sign of visible wear or damage, renewing any bolt if necessary.

11.11b ... and remove the cylinder head

11.12 Remove the cylinder head gasket

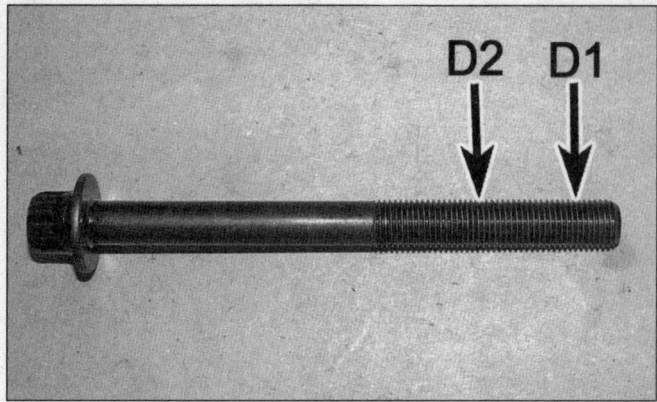

11.14 Check the cylinder head bolt for wear

11.18 Check the oil filter in the cylinder block

14 Check the cylinder head bolt (see illustration).
  a *Measure 11 mm up from the threaded end of the bolt and note the reading = D1.*
  b *Measure 45 mm up from the threaded end of the bolt and note the reading = D2*
  c *Take the second reading away from the first reading (D1 – D2), and it should be no more than 0.15 mm.*

15 Although the manufacturer does not specify renewing the cylinder head bolts, it is strongly recommended that the bolts should be renewed as a complete set whenever they are disturbed.

16 The mating faces of the cylinder head and cylinder block/crankcase must be perfectly clean before refitting the head. Use a hard plastic or wood scraper to remove all traces of gasket and carbon; also clean the piston crowns. Take particular care, as the surfaces are damaged easily. Also, make sure that the carbon is not allowed to enter the oil and water passages – this is particularly important for the lubrication system, as carbon could block the oil supply to any of the engine's components. Using adhesive tape and paper, seal the water, oil and bolt holes in the cylinder block/crankcase. To prevent carbon entering the gap between the pistons and bores, smear a little grease in the gap. After cleaning each piston, use a small brush to remove all traces of grease and carbon from the gap, and then wipe away the remainder with a clean rag. Clean all the pistons in the same way.

17 Check the mating surfaces of the cylinder block/crankcase and the cylinder head for nicks, deep scratches and other damage. If slight, they may be removed carefully with a file, but if excessive, machining may be the only alternative to renewal.

18 Remove the oil filter for the intake valve timing control, which is situated in the front right-hand corner of the cylinder block. Clean the oil filter and refit it to the cylinder block making sure it does not protrude above the surface of the cylinder block. If filter is damaged or blocked, a new one will be required (see illustration).

19 Once the cylinder head's gasket surface is clean, check the cylinder head for warpage (see illustration). Check the cylinder head gasket, intake and exhaust manifold surfaces and compare with Specifications.

Refitting

20 Wipe clean the mating surfaces of the cylinder head and cylinder block/crankcase. Check the locating dowels are in position at

11.19 Check the cylinder head gasket surface for warpage by trying to insert a feeler gauge under the straightedge

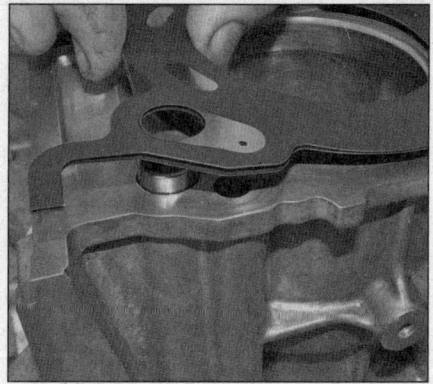

11.21 Align the new gasket with the locating dowels in the cylinder block

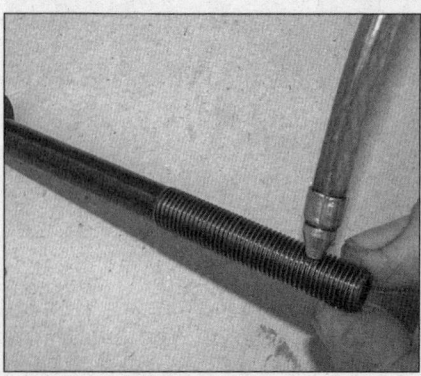

11.23 Lubricate the threads and underside of the head

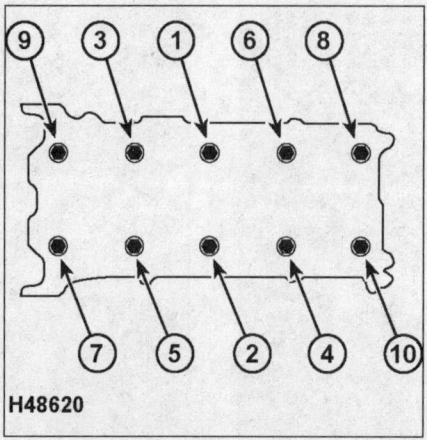

11.25 Tightening sequence for the cylinder head

11.26 Using an angle gauge to tighten bolts

Chapter 2 Part B 2.0 litre petrol engine

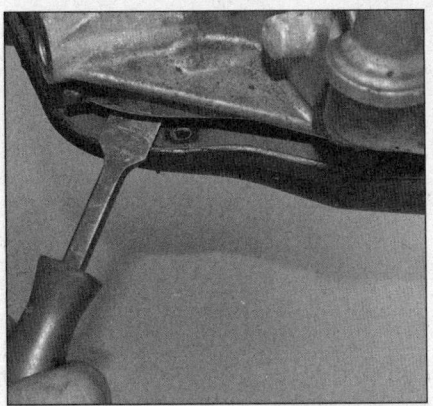

12.5 Using a flat ended scraper to prise the lower oil pan away

12.7a Apply a bead of sealant …

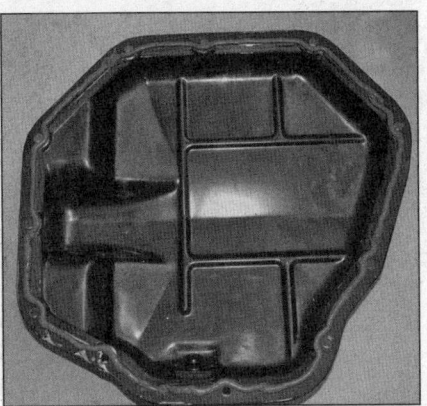

12.7b … around the outside of the oil pan, as shown

each end of the cylinder block/crankcase surface.
21 Fit a new gasket to the cylinder block/crankcase surface, aligning it with the locating dowels **(see illustration)**.
22 With the aid of an assistant, carefully refit the cylinder head assembly to the block, aligning it with the locating dowels.
23 Apply a smear of clean oil to the threads, and to the underside of the heads, of the ten cylinder head bolts **(see illustration)**.
24 Carefully enter each bolt into its relevant hole (do not drop them in) and screw in, by hand only, until finger-tight.
25 Working progressively and in sequence, tighten the cylinder head bolts to their Stage 1 specified torque, using a torque wrench and suitable socket **(see illustration)** (see Specifications).
26 Go around again in the specified sequence and tighten the head bolts through the specified Stage 2 angle setting **(see illustration)**.
27 For Stage 3, leave the bolts a minute then, working in the reverse of the specified sequence **(see illustration 11.24)**, progressively slacken the head bolts by half a turn at a time, until all bolts can be unscrewed by hand.
28 Tighten the head bolts again by hand, then go around again in the specified sequence and tighten them to the specified Stage 4 torque setting.
29 Go around again in the specified sequence and tighten the head bolts to the specified Stage 5 angle setting.
30 Finally, go around again in the specified sequence and tighten the head bolts through the specified Stage 6 angle setting.
31 Reconnect the coolant hoses to the coolant housing, on the transmission end of the cylinder head, and then securely tightening the retaining clips.
32 Reconnect the wiring connector to the temperature sensor and clip the wiring loom securing clip back into the coolant housing.
33 Refit the two earth cables to the front of the cylinder head and tighten retaining bolts.
34 Refit the exhaust manifold (see Section 6).
35 Refit the camshafts (see Section 10).

36 Refit the timing chain (see Section 9).
37 If the cylinder head has been overhauled, check the valve clearances 'cold' prior to refitting the cylinder head cover (see Chapter 1 Section 34).
38 Start the engine and warm it up to normal operating temperature, check for any leaks from the engine, cooling circuit and fuel system.
39 Reconnect the battery and perform the system initialisation procedure (see Chapter 5 Section 4).

12 Oil pans – removal and refitting

Note: *The oil pans are made up of two parts; an upper alloy part and a lower steel oil pan. The following procedure is for the lower oil pan part. To remove the upper alloy part, the engine will need to be removed and the upper oil pan then split from the cylinder block.*

Removal

1 Firmly apply the handbrake, and then jack up the front of the vehicle and support it securely on axle stands (see Chapter 0 Section 7).
2 Slacken and remove the retaining bolts and remove the plastic undershield from beneath the engine.
3 Drain the engine oil, then clean and refit the engine oil drain plug, fit a new sealing washer on refitting. And then tighten it to the specified torque. If the engine is nearing its service interval when the oil and filter are due for renewal, it is recommended that the filter is also removed, and a new one fitted (see Chapter 1 Section 9).
4 Progressively slacken and remove all of the steel oil pan retaining bolts.
5 The lower steel oil pan is sealed to the upper oil pan casing with strong liquid gasket sealer, which is very difficult to remove, however methodical use of a spatula or thin knife will release the oil pan **(see illustration)**. Take care not to distort or damage the mating surfaces of the lower oil pan and upper oil pan. Take adequate precautions to catch any oil remaining inside the oil pan as it is removed.

Refitting

6 Clean all traces of sealant from the mating surfaces of the upper and lower oil pans, then use a clean rag to wipe out the oil pan interior.
7 Ensure that the lower oil pan mating surfaces are clean and dry. Apply a continuous bead of suitable sealant to the mating surface of the lower oil pan. Apply a 4 mm to 5 mm diameter bead of sealant to the oil pan, going around the inner edge of each bolt hole **(see illustrations)**.

12.8a Align the bolts and refit the oil pan

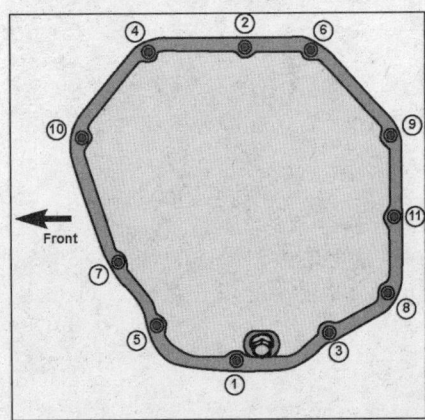

12.8b Lower oil pan bolt tightening sequence

14.2 Carefully prise out the oil seal

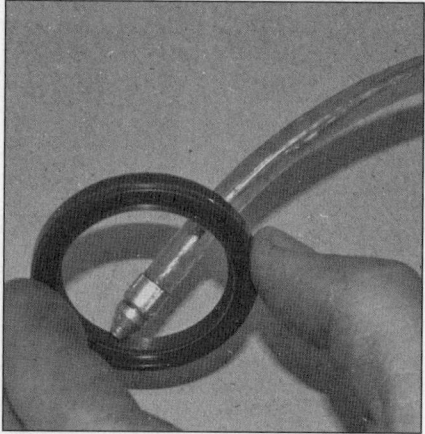

14.4a Lubricate the inner lip of the seal ...

14.4b ... press the seal into position ...

8 Offer up the lower oil pan, locating it in the correct position and then install the bolts. Tighten the bolts evenly and progressively to the specified torque (see Specifications) and in the correct sequence **(see illustration)**.
9 Refit the engine undershield and securely tighten the retaining bolts.
10 After reassembly, the engine can then be refilled with fresh oil and a new oil filter installed (see Chapter 1 Section 9).

13 Oil pump – removal and refitting

1 The oil pump is driven from the balance shaft assembly, which is located in the upper oil pan. At the time of writing there was no procedure for the removal and refitting of the oil pump.

14 Crankshaft oil seals – renewal

Front oil seal

1 Remove the crankshaft pulley as described in Section 7.
2 Carefully lever the oil seal out of position, using a large flat-bladed screwdriver, tak-

14.4c ... carefully fit the seal into the cover

ing care not to damage the end of the crankshaft or timing cover **(see illustration)**.
3 Clean the seal housing, and polish off any burrs or raised edges, which may have caused the seal to fail in the first place.
4 Lubricate the lips of the new seal with a smear of clean oil and offer up the seal; ensuring its sealing lip is facing inwards. Carefully ease the seal into position, taking care not to damage its sealing lip. Drive the seal into position until it seats flush with the

14.7a Carefully drill a hole in the seal ...

face of the timing chain cover **(see illustrations)**. Take care not to damage the seal lips during fitting.
5 Wash off any traces of oil, then refit the crankshaft pulley as described in Section 7.

Rear oil seal

6 Remove the flywheel or driveplate, as applicable, as described in Section 15.
7 Note the fitted position of the old seal, then prise it out of the engine using a screw-

14.7b ... insert a self tapping screw ...

14.7c ... and lever the seal out from the casing

14.8 Clean around the seal fitting surface area

Chapter 2 Part B 2.0 litre petrol engine

14.9a Using clean oil to lubricate the inner lip of the seal ...

14.9b ... press the seal into position ...

14.10a Apply some sealant around the outer edge of the seal ...

driver or suitable hooked instrument, taking care not to damage the surface of the crankshaft. Alternatively, the oil seal can be removed by drilling a hole in the seal, and then inserting a self-tapping screw. A pair of grips/pliers can then be used to pull out the oil seal **(see illustrations)**.

Note: *Take care when drilling the hole to not drill into anything other than the seal.*

8 Clean the seal housing, and polish off any burrs or raised edges, which may have caused the seal to fail in the first place **(see illustration)**.

9 Lubricate with clean oil the lips of the new seal and the crankshaft shoulder, then offer up the seal to the cylinder block/crankcase. Ease the sealing lip of the seal over the crankshaft shoulder by hand only, and press the seal evenly into its recess to make it square in the casing **(see illustrations)**.

10 With the seal still protruding out from the cylinder block, apply a coat of liquid gasket/sealant all the way around the outer edge of the seal. Carefully drive the seal into position until it seats flush with the face of the cylinder block, and then wipe off the excess liquid gasket/sealant from the casing **(see illustrations)**. Make sure the outer edge of the seal

is sitting flush with the cylinder block casing.
11 Wash off any traces of oil or sealant, then refit the flywheel/driveplate as described in Section 15.

15 Flywheel/driveplate – removal, inspection and refitting

Removal

1 Remove the transmission (see Chapter 7A Section 5 for manual transaxle models) or (see Chapter 7B Section 11 for automatic transaxle models). Ensure the engine is well supported during this and subsequent procedures in this Section.
2 On manual transmission, remove the clutch assembly (see Chapter 8 Section 5)
3 Prevent the flywheel/driveplate from turning by locking the ring gear teeth **(see illustration)**. Alternatively, bolt a strap between the flywheel/driveplate and the cylinder block.
4 Slacken and remove the retaining bolts **(see illustration)**, then remove the flywheel/driveplate from the end of the crankshaft. Do not drop it, as it is very heavy.

Inspection

5 On manual transmission models, if the flywheel's clutch mating surface is deeply scored, cracked or otherwise damaged, the flywheel must be renewed. Seek the advice of a Nissan dealer or engine reconditioning specialist.

14.10b ... press the seal fully into position ...

14.10c ... then clean off the excess sealant from around the casing

15.3 Using a tool to prevent the flywheel from turning ...

15.4 ... when slackening the flywheel bolts

Chapter 2 Part B 2.0 litre petrol engine

15.10 Checking the end thrust of the flywheel

15.11a Putting pressure clockwise make a mark on the flywheel ...

15.11b ... then put pressure on in anticlockwise direction and make another mark ...

6 If the ring gear is badly worn or has missing teeth, it must be renewed. This job is best left to a Nissan dealer or engine reconditioning specialist. The temperature to which the new ring gear must be heated for installation is critical and, if not done accurately, the hardness of the teeth will be destroyed.

Checking – Dual Mass

7 If not already done refit the flywheel back to the end of the crankshaft.
8 To inspect the dual mass flywheel a dial test indicator (DTI) gauge will be required, along with a spring balance to apply force on the flywheel.
9 The run-out (deflection) of the flywheel can be checked, by setting the dial gauge at 105 mm from the centre onto the flywheel surface. Rotate the crankshaft one complete turn and check the deflection reading on the gauge. This should be no more than 0.45 mm, if the measured value is more than 0.45 mm the flywheel will need to be renewed.
10 To measure the fore and aft (thrust) direction of the flywheel, set the dial gauge at 125 mm from the centre onto the flywheel surface. Then apply 10.2 kgm (100 N) of force to the flywheel at 125 mm from the centre of the flywheel and take a reading of the distance travelled (see illustration). This should be no more than 1.8 mm, if the measured value is more than 1.8 mm the flywheel will need to be renewed.
11 To check the radial direction of the flywheel, insert one of the clutch cover bolts to the flywheel and tighten.

 a Put a force of 1.0 Kgm (9.8 Nm) to the bolt in a clockwise direction and mark one of the flywheel teeth and the dual mass surface plate with a paint mark (see illustration).
 b Again putting a force of 1.0 Kgm (9.8 Nm) to the bolt, but this time in an anti-clockwise direction, make a paint mark on the flywheel tooth that is now inline with the mark you made originally on the dual mass surface plate (see illustration).
 c Measure the distance between the two paint marks on the teeth of the flywheel and it should be no more than 33.2 mm (see illustration). If the measured value is more than 33.2 mm the flywheel will need to be renewed.

Refitting

12 Clean the mating surfaces of the flywheel/driveplate and crankshaft.
13 Apply a smear of clean oil to the threads, and to the underside of the heads, of the flywheel bolts (see illustration).
14 Offer up the flywheel/driveplate, and refit the retaining bolts (see illustration).
15 Lock the ring gear using the method employed on dismantling, and tighten the retaining bolts to the specified torque (see Specifications).
16 On manual transmission models, refit the clutch (see Chapter 8 Section 5).
17 Remove the locking tool, and refit the transaxle (see Chapter 7A Section 5) or (see Chapter 7B Section 11).

16 Balance shaft, drive chain and sprockets – removal, inspection and refitting

Removal

1 Remove the timing chain (see Section 9)

15.11c ... then measure the distance between the marks

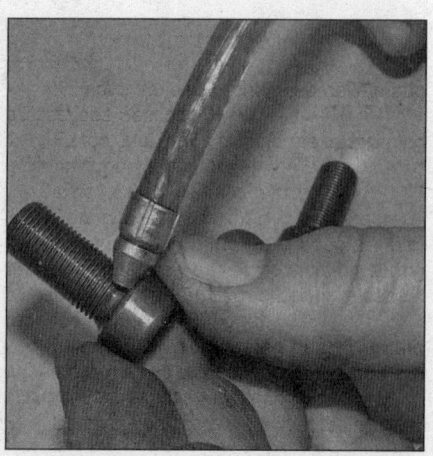

15.13 Lubricate the threads on the bolt

15.14 Fit the flywheel retaining bolts

16.3 Hold pressure against the tensioner and fit locking pin

16.4 Remove the tensioner from the cylinder block

16.5a Slacken the sprocket retaining bolt …

16.5b … whilst counter holding the shaft (arrowed) with an open-ended spanner

16.6a Remove the sprocket bolt …

2   Remove the lower oil pan (see Section 12)

3   Whilst holding the plunger back into the body of the tensioner, insert a small-diameter rod through the hole in the body to lock the plunger **(see illustration)**.

4   Undo the two retaining bolts, and remove the tensioner from the end of the upper oil pan housing. Keep the rod inserted into the tensioner to prevent the plunger from springing out **(see illustration)**.

Warning: *Do not turn the crankshaft or camshafts while the timing chain is removed, otherwise piston and valve contact may occur causing damage.*

5   Slacken the balancer shaft sprocket retaining bolt. Use a large open-ended spanner fitted to the flat Section on the shaft (accessed through the oil pan aperture), to retain the balance shaft whilst slackening the bolt **(see illustrations)**.

6   Remove the bolt, then disengage the balancer shaft sprocket and drive chain from the crankshaft sprocket **(see illustrations)**.

7   If required, slide the crankshaft sprocket of the end of the crankshaft, noting its fitted position **(see illustration)**.

Inspection

8   The balance shaft unit is bolted to the underside of the upper oil pan **(see illustration)**. The oil pump is also driven from the balance shaft assembly. At the time of writing there was no procedure for the removal and refitting of the balance shaft unit.

9   Clean the components and carefully examine the chain, sprockets and tensioner for any signs of excessive wear. If evident, it is recommended that all the components be renewed as a set.

10   Before refitting the balancer shaft drive chain and sprocket, refit the crankshaft sprocket and check it is positioned at TDC **(see illustration)**.

Note: *The keyway will also be in the 12 o'clock position, as seen from the right-hand end of the engine.*

16.6b … then remove the sprocket and chain from the balance shaft

16.7 Removing the crankshaft sprocket

16.8 Balance shaft unit retaining bolts

16.10 Crankshaft alignment marks (arrowed)

16.11 Align the coloured link with the mark on the crankshaft sprocket

16.12 Align the coloured link with the mark on the balance shaft sprocket

16.14 Check the timing marks (arrowed)

16.15 Refit the tensioner and remove the pin

17.6 Supporting the engine on a jack

Refitting

11 Fit the drive chain around the crankshaft sprocket, aligning the orange link on the chain with the balancer shaft timing mark on the crankshaft sprocket **(see illustration)**.

12 Fit the balancer shaft sprocket into the drive chain, aligning the dark blue link on the chain with the timing mark on the balancer shaft sprocket **(see illustration)**.

13 Apply a smear of clean oil to the threads, and to the underside of the head of the retaining bolt, and then run it by hand into the balancer shaft.

14 With the timing marks in position **(see illustration)**, tighten the balancer shaft sprocket retaining bolt to the specified torque (see Specifications), whilst retaining the shaft with a large open-ended spanner as used on removal.

15 Fit the chain tensioner to the upper oil pan, and tighten its retaining bolts to the specified torque (see Specifications). Whilst holding some pressure against the tensioner plunger, withdraw the rod, and check that the tensioner plunger is forced out to take up the slack in the chain **(see illustration)**.

16 Refit the lower oil pan (see Section 12).

17 Refit the timing chain (see Section 9).

17 Engine mounts – inspection and renewal

Inspection

1 Raise the front of the vehicle and support on jackstands (see Chapter 0 Section 7).

2 Check the mounting rubber to see if it is cracked, hardened or separated from the metal at any point; renew the mounting if any such damage or deterioration is evident.

3 Check that all the mounting's fasteners are securely tightened; use a torque wrench to check if possible.

4 Using a large screwdriver or a crowbar, check for wear in the mounting by carefully levering against it to check for free play. Where this is not possible, enlist the aid of an assistant to move the engine/transmission back-and-forth, or from side-to-side, while you watch the mounting. While some free play is to be expected even from new components, excessive wear should be obvious. If excessive free play is found, check first that the fasteners are correctly secured, and then renew any worn components as described below.

Renewal

Right-hand mounting

5 Disconnect the negative (-) battery terminal (see Chapter 5 Section 3).

6 Place a jack beneath the engine, with a block of wood on the jack head. Raise the jack until it is supporting the weight of the engine **(see illustration)**.

17.7 Undo the earth cable securing bolt

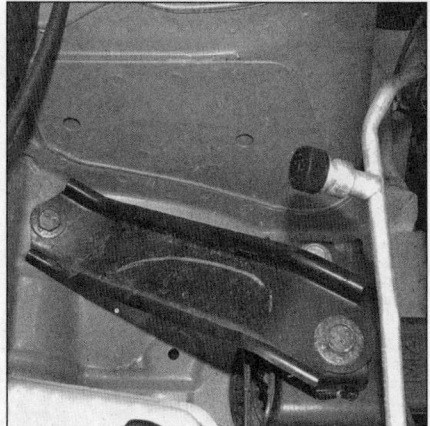

17.8a Undo the retaining bolts ...

17.8b ... and remove the support bracket

17.9a Undo the retaining nut ...

17.9b ... and remove the dynamic damper

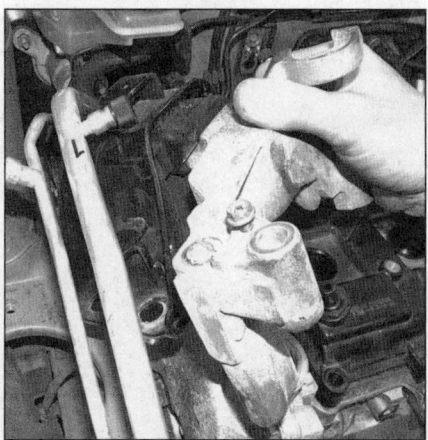

17.10 Undo the bolts and remove the mounting from the engine compartment

12 On refitting, fit the engine mounting and bracket to the inner wing panel and engine, and then securely tighten its retaining bolts to the specified torque (see Specifications).
13 Refit the stay bracket and dynamic damper bobbin, back to the engine mounting bracket.
14 With the engine mounting back in position, lower the jack and remove it from underneath the engine.
15 Reconnect the earth cable to the top of the engine mounting and then reconnect the battery negative terminal.

Left-hand mounting

16 Remove the battery and tray (see Chapter 5 Section 5)
17 Place a jack and block of wood beneath the transmission, and raise the jack to take the weight of the transmission (see illustration).
18 Slacken and remove the through-bolt/stud retaining nut from the centre of the mounting, and (where fitted) the vibration damper (see illustration).
19 Slacken and remove the two outer retaining nuts, and withdraw the mounting from the upper mounting bracket (see illustration).

7 Slacken the securing bolt and disconnect the earth wire from the top of the mounting bracket (see illustration).
8 Undo the retaining bolts and remove the stay bracket from the mounting bracket to the inner wing panel (see illustrations).
9 Undo the retaining nut and remove the dynamic damper bobbin from the front of the mounting bracket (see illustrations).

10 Slacken and remove the three retaining bolts from the inner wing panel, remove the three retaining bolts from the engine mounting bracket, and then withdraw the complete mounting from the engine compartment (see illustration).
11 Check carefully for signs of wear or damage on all components, and renew them where necessary.

17.17 Supporting the transmission on a trolley jack

17.18 Undo the centre retaining nut and remove vibration damper

17.19 Undo the two outer securing nuts and remove the mounting

17.21 Remove the mounting bracket from the transmission

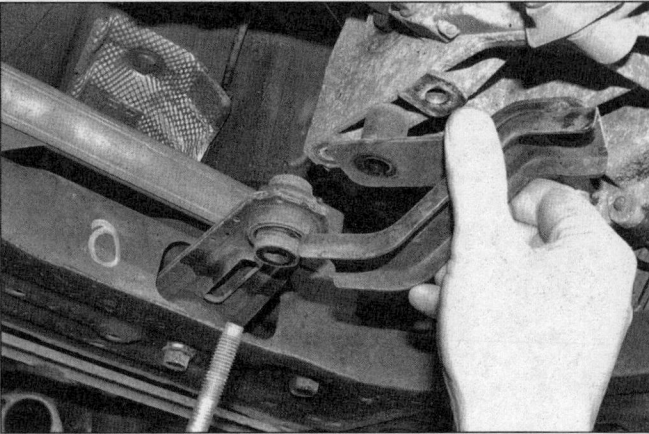

17.29 Remove the mounting bracket from the transmission

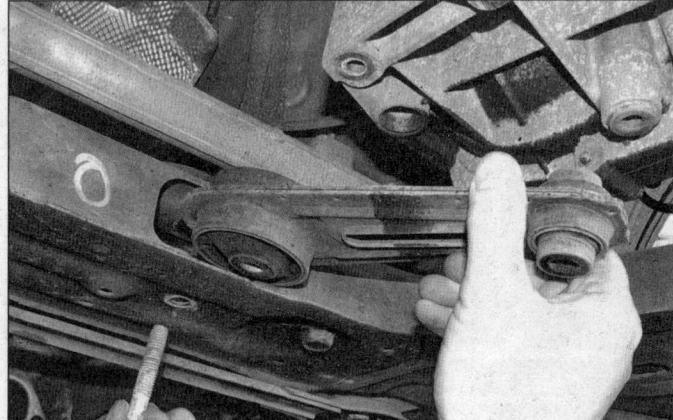

17.30 Remove the torque rod from the subframe

20 If required, undo the retaining bolts from the inner wing panel to remove the upper mounting bracket.

21 Also, if required, undo the retaining bolts from the transmission to remove the lower mounting bracket **(see illustration)**.

22 Check carefully for signs of wear or damage on all components, and renew them where necessary.

23 On refitting, fit the upper and lower mounting brackets (where removed) and securely tighten the retaining bolts.

24 Align the left-hand rubber mounting with the bolt/stud on the lower mounting bracket and tighten its nut to the specified torque (see Specifications).

25 Refit the two outer retaining nuts, and tighten to the specified torque (see Specifications).

26 With the transmission mounting back in position, lower the jack and remove it from underneath the transmission.

27 Refit the battery and battery tray (see Chapter 5 Section 5).

Rear lower mounting

28 If not already done, firmly apply the handbrake, and then jack up the front of the vehicle and support it securely on jack stands (see Chapter 0 Section 7).

29 Slacken and remove the bolts securing the rear mounting bracket to the transmission, and then withdraw the bracket from transmission **(see illustration)**.

30 Slacken and remove the bolt securing the rear mounting link to the subframe, and then withdraw the mounting link from subframe **(see illustration)**.

31 Check carefully for signs of wear or damage on all components, and renew them where necessary.

32 On reassembly, fit the rear mounting to the subframe, and tighten the retaining bolt to the specified torque (see Specifications).

33 Refit the mounting bracket to the lower part of the transmission and tighten its retaining bolts to the specified torque (see Specifications).

34 With the transmission rear mounting link arm back in position, lower the vehicle to the ground.

Chapter 2 Part C
2.0 litre diesel engine

Contents

Section		Section	
Balancer shaft unit – removal and refitting	17	Intercooler – removal and refitting	9
Camshafts – removal, inspection and refitting	12	Oil cooler – removal and refitting	21
Crankshaft oil seals – renewal	19	Oil level sensor – removal and refitting	23
Crankshaft pulley – removal and refitting	4	Oil pan – removal and refitting	14
Cylinder block baseplate – removal and refitting	16	Oil pressure check	See Chapter 2D
Cylinder compression check	See Chapter 2D	Oil pressure sensor – removal and refitting	22
Cylinder head – removal and refitting	13	Oil pump, drive chain and sprocket – removal, inspection and refitting	15
Drivebelt check and replacement	See Chapter 1	Repair operations possible with the engine in the vehicle	2
Engine - removal and installation	See Chapter 2D	Timing chain, sprockets and guides – removal, inspection and refitting	10
Engine oil and oil filter change	See Chapter 1	Timing gears – removal, inspection and refitting	11
Engine/transmission mountings – inspection and renewal	20	Top Dead Centre (TDC) for No 1 piston – locating	3
Exhaust manifold – removal and Installation	6	Turbocharger – description and precautions	7
Flywheel – removal, inspection and refitting	18	Turbocharger – removal and refitting	8
General Information	1	Vacuum pump – removal, refitting and testing	24
Intake manifold – removal and refitting	5		

Specifications

General

Engine designation	M9R
Capacity	1995 cc
Bore	84.0 mm
Stroke	90.0 mm
Direction of crankshaft rotation	Clockwise, viewed from timing chain end
Cylinder numbers	1-2-3-4 (timing chain end-to-transaxle end)
Firing order	1-3-4-2
Valve clearances	See Chapter 1

Cylinder head

Warpage limit - standard	0.05 mm
Cylinder head height - standard	133.6 mm
Cylinder head gasket thickness	1.116 to 1.184 mm

Camshafts

Drive	Chain
Number of bearings on each	6
Camshaft journal diameter	24.979 to 25.000 mm
Cylinder head housing and camshaft bracket inner diameter	25.040 to 25.061 mm
Camshaft journal oil clearance	0.040 to 0.082 mm

Manifolds

Warpage limits	
Intake manifold	0.05 mm
Exhaust manifold	0.7 mm

Torque specifications

	Nm
Camshaft bearing caps	10
Camshaft housing	
Stage 1	5
Stage 2	12
Crankshaft oil seal	
Timing end	47
Transmission end	
Stage 1	5
Stage 2	10
Crankshaft position ring to crankshaft	17
Crankshaft pulley bolt	
Stage 1	60
Stage 2	Tighten an additional 85 degrees
Cylinder block baseplate	25
Cylinder head bolts [1]	
Stage 1	5
Stage 2	30
Stage 3	Tighten an additional 300 degrees
EGR rigid pipe	
To cooler	35
To exhaust manifold	35
EGR rigid pipe on cylinder head	10
EGR rigid pipe heatshield	10
Exhaust manifold	
Studs	9
Mounting nuts	
Stage 1	18
Stage 2	30
Exhaust camshaft sprocket to timing gear	
Stage 1	10
Stage 2	Tighten an additional 40 degrees
Flywheel bolts[1]	
Stage 1	25
Stage 2	Tighten an additional 45 degrees
High-pressure pump drive gear to exhaust camshaft	
Stage 1	40
Stage 2	Tighten an additional 34 degrees
High-pressure pump sprocket	90
Intake manifold bolts	
Stage 1	15
Stage 2	25
Injector clamp bolts	35
Intake timing gear	
Stage 1	20
Stage 2	Tighten an additional 35 degrees
Left-hand transmission mounting	
Mounting-to-bracket bolts	110
Mounting bracket-to-inner wing panel bolts	80
Mounting bracket-to-transmission bolts	45
Main timing chain tensioner guide	25
Oil cooler/filter housing to block	
Stage 1	5
Stage 2	25
Oil level dipstick guide tube	10
Oil level sensor	25
Oil pressure sender unit	35
Oil pump strainer	10
Oil pump to cylinder block	
Stage 1	5
Stage 2	25
Oil pan	
Stage 1	5
Stage 2	16
Oil separator	
Stage 1	5
Stage 2	10
Oil splash plate to oil pump	10

Chapter 2 Part C 2.0 litre diesel engine

Torque specifications

	Nm
Rear lower engine torque/link arm mounting	
Torque link arm to front subframe bolt	110
Torque link arm to mounting bracket bolt	155
Mounting bracket-to-oil pan bolts	80
Right-hand engine mounting:	
Alloy mounting bracket to cylinder head mounting bracket	55
Mounting bracket bolts to inner wing	55
Torque arm mounting bolts	130
Static timing chain guide	
Stage 1	5
Stage 2	25
TDC setting pin hole plug	25
Timing chain hydraulic tensioner	10
Timing cover bolts	
Stage 1	5
Stage 2	
M8 bolt	18
M6 bolt	16
Turbocharger outlet air duct bolt on the intake manifold	8
Turbocharger pressure sensor nut on damper valve	8

[1] New bolt must be used

1 General Information

This Part of Chapter 2 is devoted to in-vehicle repair procedures for the 2.0 litre M9R diesel engine. All procedures concerning engine removal and refitting, and engine overhaul options can be found in Part 2D of this Chapter.

The following repair procedures are based on the assumption that the engine is installed in the vehicle. If the engine has been removed from the vehicle and mounted on a stand, many of the steps outlined in this Part of Chapter 2 will not apply.

Engine description

The engine is a four-cylinder overhead camshaft 16-valve design, mounted transversely at the front of the vehicle with the transmission bolted to the left-hand side. The power steering pump, coolant pump, alternator and air conditioning compressor are driven by the auxiliary drivebelt. The brake servo vacuum pump is driven directly by the exhaust camshaft at the flywheel end.

The crankshaft is supported in five shell-type main bearings. Thrustwashers are fitted one of the main bearings to control crankshaft endfloat. The connecting rods are attached to the crankshaft by horizontally split shell-type big-end bearings, and to the pistons by gudgeon pins. The gudgeon pins are a sliding fit in the connecting rods and are retained by cir-clips. The aluminium alloy pistons are of the slipper type, and are fitted with three piston rings – two compression rings and a scraper-type oil control ring.

The double overhead camshafts are mounted in the cylinder head, and are driven by a timing chain direct from the crankshaft to the exhaust camshaft sprocket. The intake camshaft is driven by gear direct from the exhaust camshaft at the timing end. The high-pressure fuel pump is gear-driven from the flywheel-end of the intake camshaft.

The camshaft operates the 16 valves, which are mounted in the cylinder head, through rocker arms situated directly above the camshaft. Automatic adjustment of the valve-to-rocker arm clearance is provided by hydraulic lifters located in the cylinder head.

A balancer shaft unit is bolted to the crankcase and driven by gear direct from the crankshaft. The unit incorporates two shafts with counter-weights that rotate in opposite directions in order to minimise vertical oscillation of the engine caused by the pistons and connecting rods.

A dual-mass flywheel acts as an acoustic filter to reduce boom at low engine speeds.

Engine lubrication is by pressure feed from a gear-type oil pump, chain-driven off the timing end of the crankshaft. Engine oil is fed through an externally mounted oil filter and oil cooler to the main oil gallery feeding the crankshaft and camshaft. The oil cooler helps keep the oil temperature constant under arduous operating conditions.

2 Repair operations possible with the engine in the vehicle

Warning: *The models covered by this manual are equipped with a Supplemental Restraint System (SRS), more commonly known as airbags. Always disarm the airbag system before working in the vicinity of any airbag system component to avoid the possibility of accidental deployment of the airbag, which could cause personal injury (see Chapter 12A Section 20). Do not use a memory saving device to preserve the PCM's memory when working on or near airbag system components.*

1 Many major repair operations can be accomplished without removing the engine from the vehicle.

2 Clean the engine compartment and the exterior of the engine with some type of degreaser before any work is done. It will make the job easier and help keep dirt out of the internal areas of the engine.

3 Depending on the components involved, it may be helpful to remove the bonnet to improve access to the engine as repairs are performed (refer to Chapter 11 Section 9). Cover the guards to prevent damage to the paint. Special pads are available, but an old bedspread or blanket will also work.

2C-4 Chapter 2 Part C 2.0 litre diesel engine

3.9a Unscrew the TDC plug...

3.9b... then insert the crankshaft TDC setting tool...

3.9c... and tighten securely

3 Top Dead Centre (TDC) for No 1 piston – locating

1 Top Dead Centre (TDC) is the highest point in the cylinder that each piston reaches as the crankshaft turns. Each piston reaches TDC at the end of the compression stroke and again at the end of the exhaust stroke. However, for the purpose of timing the engine, TDC refers to the position of No.1 piston at the end of its compression stroke. No.1 piston is at the flywheel end of the engine.
2 Positioning the No.1 piston at TDC is an essential part of certain procedures, such as camshaft and timing chain/sprocket removal.
3 Disconnect the negative (-) battery terminal (see Chapter 5 Section 3).
4 To access the crankshaft pulley, raise the front of the vehicle and support on jackstands (see Chapter 0 Section 7). Remove the RH front wheel.
5 Remove the engine undertray and the right-hand wheel arch liner in order to gain access to the crankshaft pulley bolt.
6 To facilitate turning the engine easily, remove the glow plugs (see Chapter 5 Section 9).

7 With the help of an assistant and using a socket on the crankshaft pulley bolt, turn the engine clockwise until pressure can be felt in the No.1 glow plug hole, indicating that the No.1 piston is rising on its compression stroke.
8 Continue to turn the crankshaft clockwise until the pressure in No.1 cylinder ceases, then turn the crankshaft an additional quarter turn so the piston is approximately midway down its bore.
9 Unscrew the TDC plug from the front of the cylinder block and insert Nissan TDC tool Mot 1766, tightening it securely **(see illustrations)**.
10 Turn the crankshaft anticlockwise until it just contacts the TDC tool.
11 The engine is now positioned with No.1 piston at TDC on its compression stroke. For further information on setting the timing up see timing chain removal and refitting in Section 10.

Caution: *Do not attempt to rotate the engine whilst the crankshaft and camshaft timing pins are in position. If the engine is to be left in this state for a long period of time, it is a good idea to place suitable warning notices inside the vehicle, and in the engine compartment. This will reduce the possibility of the engine being accidentally cranked on the starter motor, which would cause considerable damage.*

4 Crankshaft pulley – removal and refitting

Removal

1 Disconnect the negative (-) battery terminal (see Chapter 5 Section 3).
2 Raise the front of the vehicle and support on jackstands (see Chapter 0 Section 7). Remove the RH front wheel.
3 Unbolt and remove the plastic undertray from the beneath the engine/transmission and the liner from within the right-hand wheel arch.
4 Remove the drivebelt (see Chapter 1 Section 12).
5 Slacken the crankshaft pulley retaining bolt. To prevent crankshaft rotation whilst the retaining bolt is slackened, select 4th gear and have an assistant apply the brakes firmly. If this fails to prevent rotation, lock the flywheel ring gear; the starter motor may need to be removed to access the flywheel ring gear.
6 Do not be tempted to use the crankshaft timing pin to prevent the crankshaft from rotating (see Section 3).
7 Remove the retaining bolt, spacer and pulley from the end of the crankshaft **(see illustrations)**.

Refitting

8 Remove all traces of locking compound from the crankshaft threads.
9 Clean the threads of the crankshaft pulley retaining bolt and apply a few drops of thread locking compound.
10 Refit the pulley to the crankshaft followed by the spacer, then screw in the retaining bolt. Tighten the bolt first to the specified Stage 1 torque and then through the specified Stage 2 angle, using the method employed on removal to prevent rotation **(see illustration)**.

4.7a Unscrew and remove the crankshaft pulley bolt and spacer...

4.7b... then remove the pulley

Chapter 2 Part C 2.0 litre diesel engine

4.10 Angle-tightening the crankshaft pulley bolt

5.6a Remove the EGR cooler pipe ...

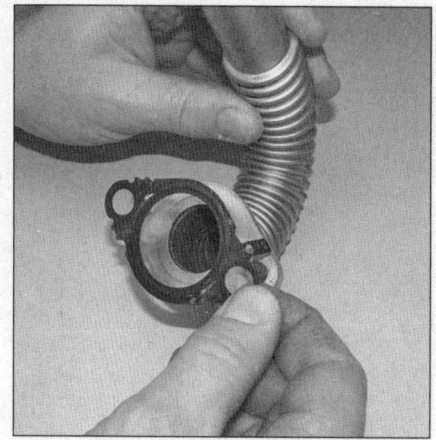

5.6b ... and gaskets

5.7a Remove the inlet manifold ...

7   Unscrew and remove the mounting bolts and withdraw the inlet manifold from the cylinder head. Recover the gasket and discard it as a new gasket must be used on refitting **(see illustrations)**. Also obtain new gaskets for the EGR cooler pipe.

8   Refitting is the reverse of removal using new gaskets, and tightening the manifold retaining bolts to the torque listed in Specifications.

6 Exhaust manifold – removal and Installation

Removal

1   The exhaust manifold is located on the rear of the cylinder head. Remove the engine top cover.

2   Disconnect the negative (-) battery terminal (see Chapter 5 Section 3).

3   Apply the handbrake, and then jack up the front of the vehicle and support it on axle stands (see Chapter 0 Section 7).

4   Disconnect the exhaust front pipe/ particle filter - where fitted (see Chapter 4B Section 11).

11 Install the drivebelt (see Chapter 1 Section 12).

12 Install the wheel arch liner and wheel before lowering the vehicle to the ground.

5 Intake manifold – removal and refitting

1   The intake manifold is located on the front of the cylinder head.

2   Remove the engine top cover.

3   Remove the battery and battery tray (see Chapter 5 Section 5).

4   Remove the intake air ducting and intercooler inlet pipe from the front of the engine.

5   Remove the throttle body (see Chapter 4B Section 7).

6   Unbolt the EGR cooler pipe from the inlet manifold and cooler and recover the gaskets **(see illustrations)**.

5.7b ... and recover the gasket

6.7a Unbolt the EGR rigid pipe from the exhaust manifold ...

Chapter 2 Part C 2.0 litre diesel engine

6.7b ... and recover the gasket

6.8a Unscrew the nuts and remove the spacers ...

6.8b ... remove the exhaust manifold ...

5 Remove the turbocharger (see Section 8). If the reason for removing the manifold is simply to renew the gasket, the turbocharger can remain attached to the manifold.
6 Unscrew the bolts securing the EGR rigid pipe to the exhaust manifold and cylinder head, then unbolt and remove the heat shield from the rigid pipe.
7 Unbolt the EGR rigid pipe from the EGR cooler and exhaust manifold, and recover the gaskets **(see illustrations)**.

8 Unscrew and remove the nuts and spacers and withdraw the exhaust manifold from the cylinder head. Recover the manifold gasket and discard it as a new gasket must be used on refitting **(see illustrations)**. Also obtain new EGR rigid pipe seals. Nissan state that the manifold nuts must also be renewed.
9 Check the condition of the exhaust manifold studs and renew them if necessary. Tighten into the cylinder head to the specified torque.

Refitting

10 Refitting is the reverse of removal using a new gasket and seals, and tightening the manifold retaining nuts to the specified torque. When positioning the gasket on the studs, the gasket end tab must be towards the flywheel end of the engine.

7 Turbocharger – description and precautions

1 A turbocharger increases engine efficiency by raising the pressure in the inlet manifold above atmospheric pressure. Instead of the air simply being sucked into the cylinders, it is forced in. Additional fuel is supplied in proportion to the increased air intake.
2 Energy for the operation of the turbocharger comes from the exhaust gas. The gas flows through a specially shaped housing (the turbine housing) and in so doing, spins the turbine wheel. The turbine wheel is attached to a shaft, at the end of which is another vaned wheel known as the compressor wheel. The compressor wheel spins in its own housing and compresses the inducted air on the way to the inlet manifold.
3 Between the turbocharger and the inlet manifold, the compressed air passes through an intercooler. This is an air-to-air heat exchanger, mounted behind the front bumper, in front of the air conditioning condenser and the coolant radiator. The purpose of the intercooler is to remove some of the heat gained in being compressed from the inducted air. Because cooler air is denser, removal of this heat further increases engine efficiency.
4 Boost pressure (the pressure in the inlet manifold) is limited by a wastegate, which diverts the exhaust gas away from the turbine wheel in response to a pressure-sensitive actuator. Turbocharging pressure is controlled by a pressure sensor located on the air intake **(see illustration)**.
5 The boost control solenoid valve is located at the left-hand rear of the engine compartment by the air filter housing **(see illustration)**.

6.8c ... and recover the gasket

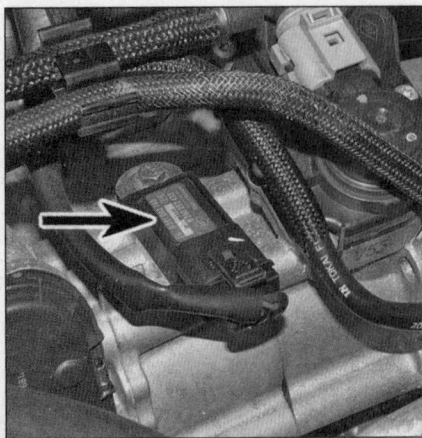

7.4 Turbo pressure sensor location (arrowed)

7.5 The boost control solenoid valve is adjacent to the air filter housing

Chapter 2 Part C 2.0 litre diesel engine

7.7a Electric coolant pump for turbocharger on subframe

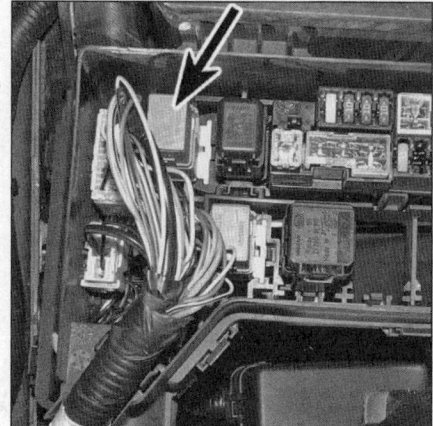

7.7b Relay for electric coolant pump (arrowed)

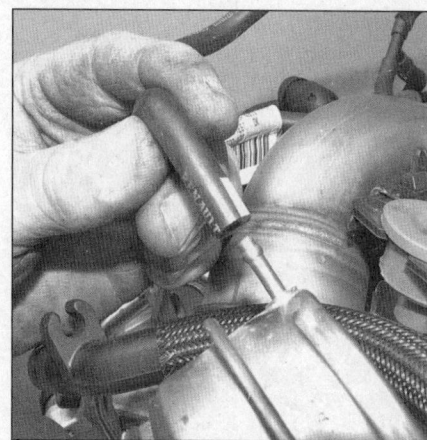

8.6 Disconnecting the vacuum pipe

6 The turbo shaft is pressure-lubricated by an oil feed pipe from the main oil gallery. The shaft 'floats' on a cushion of oil. A drain pipe returns the oil to the oil pan.

7 On some models, there is an electric coolant pump located on the rear of the subframe, below the transmission, to help cool the turbocharger. There is a relay in the engine compartment fusebox to operate this electric coolant pump **(see illustrations)**.

Precautions

- *The turbocharger operates at extremely high speeds and temperatures. Certain precautions must be observed to avoid premature failure of the turbo or injury to the operator.*
- *Do not race the engine immediately after start-up, especially if it is cold. Give the oil a few seconds to circulate.*
- *Always allow the engine to return to idle speed before switching it off – do not blip the throttle and switch off, as this will leave the turbo spinning without lubrication.*
- *Allow the engine to idle for several minutes before switching off after a high speed run.*

- *Observe the recommended intervals for oil and filter changing, and use a reputable oil of the specified quality. Neglect of oil changing, or use of inferior oil, can cause carbon formation on the turbo shaft and subsequent failure.*

Warning: *Do not operate the turbo with any parts exposed. Foreign objects falling onto the rotating vanes could cause damage and (if ejected) personal injury.*

8 Turbocharger – removal and refitting

Note: *New turbocharger-to-exhaust manifold nuts must be used on refitting.*

Note: *New oil supply pipe O-rings and copper washers must be used on refitting.*

1 Raise the front of the vehicle and support on jackstands (see Chapter 0 Section 7).
2 Disconnect the negative (-) battery terminal (see Chapter 5 Section 3).
3 Remove the engine top cover, and then remove the air cleaner housing (see Chapter 4B Section 6).

Removal

4 Remove the catalytic converter (see Chapter 4B Section 11).
5 Loosen the clips and remove the air duct from the air mass meter and turbocharger.
6 Disconnect the wiring and vacuum pipe **(see illustration)**.
7 Unscrew the union bolt and flange nuts and disconnect the oil supply and return pipes from the turbocharger. Unscrew the support bolt and remove the pipes from the cylinder block **(see illustration)**.
8 Unscrew the nuts/bolts and remove the turbocharger and mounting bracket from the exhaust manifold.
9 Remove the gasket noting that its end tab is facing the flywheel end of the engine.
10 Unbolt and remove the mounting bracket.

Refitting

11 Refitting is a reversal of removal, but renew any damaged hose clamps, and use new turbocharger-to-exhaust manifold nuts which should be tightened to the specified torque. Fit new oil supply pipe O-rings and copper seals, then apply Loctite (or similar

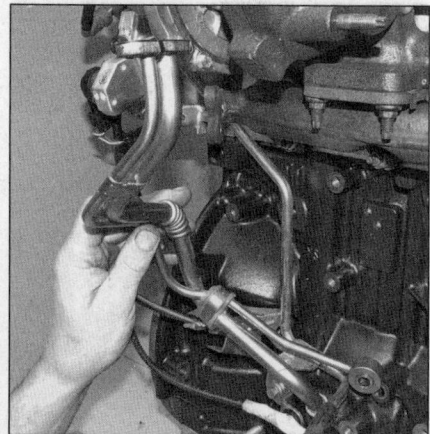

8.7 Removing the turbocharger oil supply and return pipes

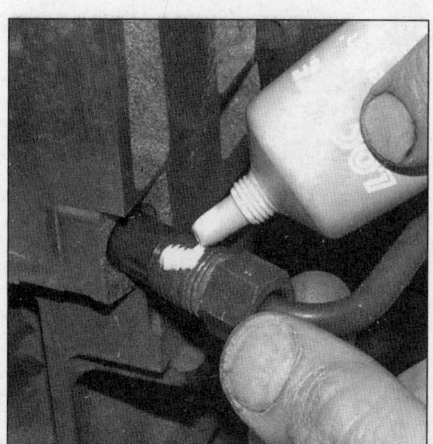

8.11a Applying sealant to the threads of the oil supply pipe union

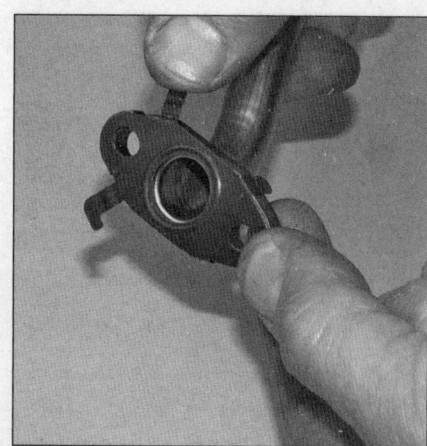

8.11b Fit a new gasket to the top of the oil return pipe. . .

Chapter 2 Part C 2.0 litre diesel engine

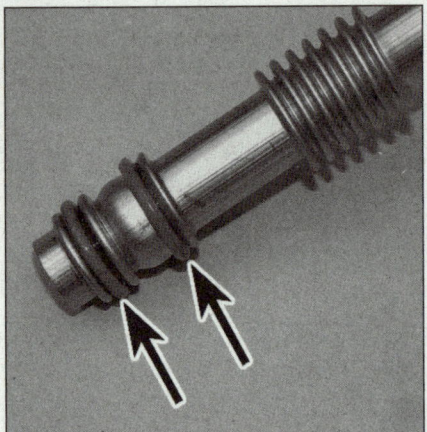

8.11c . . . and fit new O-ring seals to the grooves in the bottom of the pipe

9.3a Release the retaining clips …

9.3b … then remove the lower …

9.3c … and upper trim panels

sealant) to the union threads before refitting the pipe and tightening the union nuts to the specified torque. Fit a new gasket to the top of the oil return pipe, and new O-ring seals to the grooves in the bottom of the pipe (see illustrations). On completion, the following procedure must be observed before starting the engine in order to establish initial oil pressure in the turbocharger.

a Disconnect the wiring from the fuel injectors.
b Crank the engine on the starter motor until the instrument panel oil pressure warning light goes out (this may take several seconds).
c Reconnect the wiring to the injectors, then start the engine using the normal procedure.
d Run the engine at idle speed, and check the turbocharger oil unions for leakage.
e After the engine has been run, check the engine oil level, and top-up if necessary.

9 Intercooler – removal and refitting

Removal

1 The intercooler is located behind the front bumper, in front of the air conditioning condenser.
2 Remove the front bumper (see Chapter 11 Section 18).
3 Release the retaining clips and remove the plastic covers from each end of the condenser and intercooler (see illustrations).
4 Slacken the retaining clips and disconnect the air inlet and outlet hoses from each end of the intercooler (see illustrations).
5 Undo the intercooler mounting bolts (one at each end of the intercooler), then pull the intercooler upwards to release it from the lower rubber mountings, and remove it from the front of the vehicle (see illustrations).

Refitting

6 Refitting is a reversal of removal, making sure all the connections are securely fitted.

10 Timing chain, sprockets and guides – removal, inspection and refitting

Note: *Removal of the engine from the car is necessary in order to carry out the procedure in this Section. Also, special Nissan tool Mot. 1766 is required to set the engine to TDC, and tool Mot. 1769 to tighten the exhaust camshaft sprocket bolts. When renewing the timing chain, Nissan recommend renewal of the sprockets, guides and the hydraulic tensioner at the same time.*

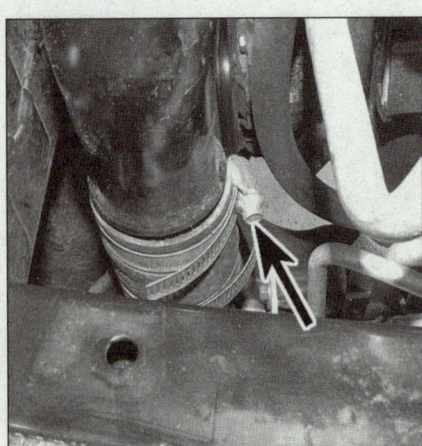

9.4a Disconnect the hoses (arrowed) …

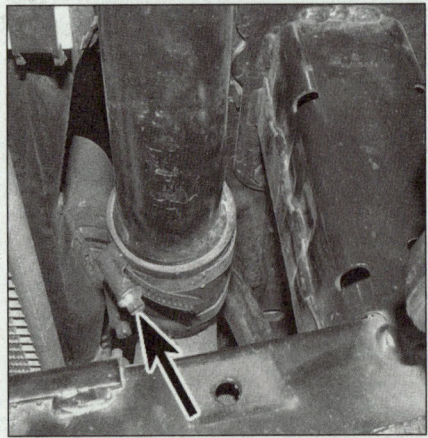

9.4b … at each end of the intercooler

9.5a Undo the intercooler mounting bolts …

Chapter 2 Part C 2.0 litre diesel engine

9.5b ... and lift it out from its rubber mountings

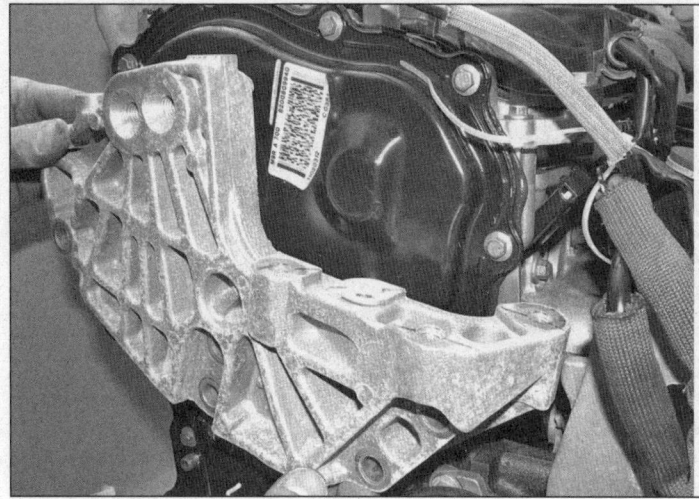

10.7 Right-hand engine mounting bracket

Removal

1 Remove the engine and gearbox assembly (see Chapter 2D Section 7) and place on a workbench. If not already done, drain the engine oil.

10.9 Removing the timing cover

2 Remove the drivebelt (see Chapter 1 Section 12).
3 Remove the water pump (see Chapter 3 Section 7).
4 Remove the crankshaft pulley (see Section 4).
5 A new crankshaft oil seal will be required for refitting, so it is recommended that the old one is removed from the timing cover (see Section 19)
6 From the right-hand top of the cylinder head, unbolt the engine mounting reinforcement bracket.
7 Unbolt the right-hand engine mounting bracket from the engine (see illustration).
8 Progressively unscrew the bolts securing the timing cover to the engine, including the bolt concealed in the hole where the engine mounting bracket was fitted. Note the location of the M8 bolt at the bottom of the engine.
9 Ease the timing cover away while cutting the silicone sealant/adhesive to release it (see illustration). This is a very difficult and time consuming job, however methodical use of a suitable spatula or thin knife will eventually release the cover.

10 If fitted, remove the crankshaft/flywheel locking device used in the crankshaft pulley removal procedure.
11 Using a spanner on the crankshaft nose flats, turn the crankshaft clockwise until the crankshaft groove is aligned with the bolt hole on the cylinder block (see illustration). This will position the pistons half way up the cylinder bores.
12 Unscrew the TDC plug/bolt from the front of the cylinder block and insert Nissan TDC tool Mot. 1766, tightening it securely.
13 Turn the crankshaft anticlockwise until it just contacts the TDC tool. The engine is now set with No 1 piston at TDC on its compression stroke
14 If the timing chain is to be re-used, mark it with a dab of paint to ensure it is refitted the same way round. Loosen only the three exhaust camshaft sprocket retaining bolts.
15 Compress the timing chain hydraulic tensioner piston by pressing the guide, then lock it by inserting a 3.0 mm diameter Allen key or pin in the hole provided (see illustration).
16 Unscrew the bolts and remove the tensioner (see illustration).

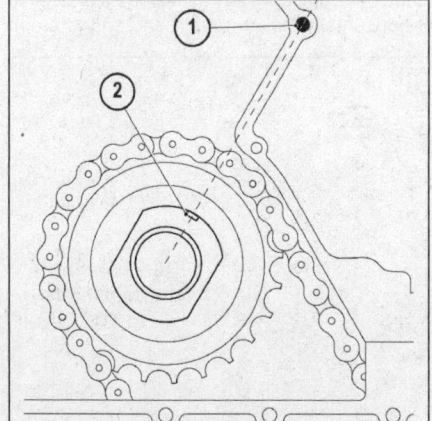

10.11 Align the groove (2) in the crankshaft nose with the bolt hole (1) on the cylinder block to position the pistons half way up the cylinder bores

10.15 Locking the hydraulic tensioner piston in its retracted position with a 3.0 mm rod

10.16 Removing the hydraulic tensioner

2C-10 Chapter 2 Part C 2.0 litre diesel engine

10.17a Unscrew the bolt. . .

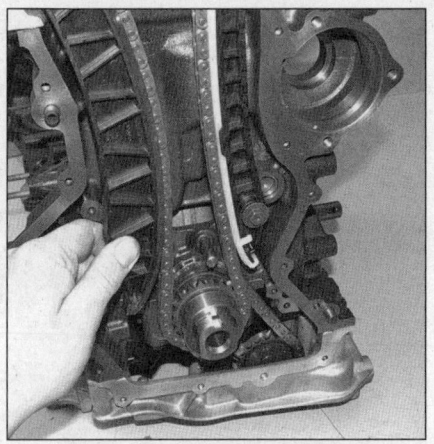

10.17b. . . and remove the dynamic tensioner guide

10.18a Remove the bolts. . .

10.18b. . . and special washer. . .

10.18c. . . and withdraw the sprocket and chain from the exhaust camshaft

10.19 Removing the timing chain sprocket from the nose of the crankshaft

17 Unscrew the single bolt and remove the dynamic tensioner guide **(see illustrations)**.
18 Completely remove the three exhaust camshaft sprocket bolts, remove the special washer and withdraw the sprocket and chain from the camshaft. If available, use the Nissan tool Mot. 1769 to hold the sprocket stationary. Release the timing chain from the camshaft and crankshaft sprockets **(see illustrations)**.
19 Withdraw the sprocket from the nose of the crankshaft **(see illustration)**.
20 Unbolt and remove the static timing chain guide **(see illustration)**.
21 Unscrew and remove the TDC tool from the front of the cylinder block.

Inspection

22 Thoroughly clean then visually inspect all parts for wear and damage. Check the timing chain for loose pins, cracks, worn rollers and side plates. Check the sprockets for hook-shaped, chipped and broken teeth. Also check the timing chain for wear by extending it horizontally, holding each end and attempt-

10.20 Removing the static timing chain guide

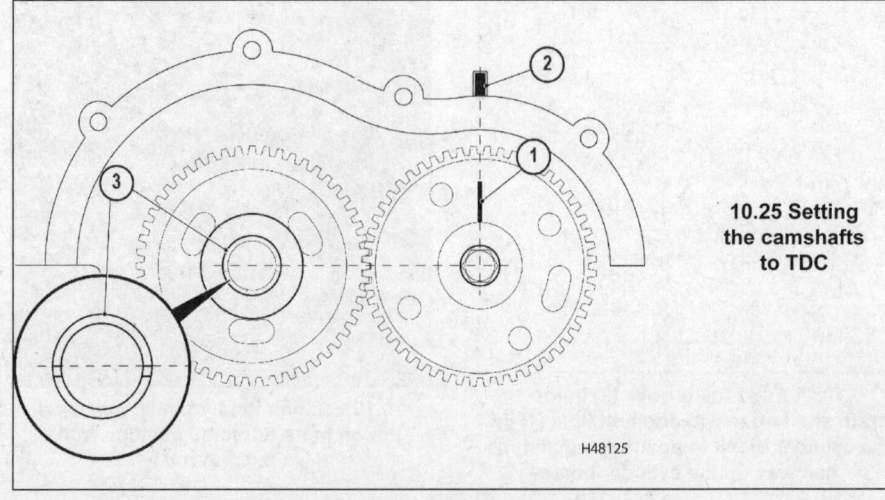

10.25 Setting the camshafts to TDC

Chapter 2 Part C 2.0 litre diesel engine

10.27a Align the copper link with the TDC mark on the crankshaft sprocket. . .

10.27b. . . then fit the exhaust camshaft sprocket with the copper link aligned with the TDC hole

10.34 Angle-tightening the exhaust camshaft sprocket bolts

10.35 Refitting the TDC hole plug

ing to flex the chain. Renew the timing chain and sprockets as a set if the engine has high mileage or fails inspection. Check the chain guides for excessive wear and scoring and renew them if necessary. Note that some scoring is normal but if they are deeply grooved they must be renewed.

Refitting

23 Carefully clean the surfaces of the timing cover, cylinder block and cylinder head, taking care not to damage the surfaces.
24 Check that the engine is still set to its TDC position as described in Section 3 using the TDC setting tool Mot 1766.
25 Position the timing mark on the inlet camshaft timing gear at 12 o'clock and align it with the boss on the camshaft housing. Make sure that the groove on the exhaust camshaft is horizontal with the larger offset uppermost **(see illustration)**.
26 Refit the static timing chain guide and tighten the bolts to the specified torque.
27 Locate the timing chain on the crankshaft sprocket so that the copper link is aligned with the timing mark, and then locate the sprocket on the nose of the crankshaft. Raise the chain to keep it engaged with the crankshaft sprocket while locating it onto the rigid

tensioner guide, and then locate the exhaust camshaft sprocket in the upper loop so that the copper link aligns with the TDC hole in the sprocket **(see illustrations)**.

Note: *A new timing chain may be fitted either way round, however a re-used chain should be fitted in its original position as noted during removal.*

28 Fit the exhaust camshaft sprocket onto its timing gear.
29 Locate the new special washer and bolts on the exhaust camshaft timing gear and finger-tighten the bolts at this stage. The sprocket must be free to rotate within the elongated holes
30 Locate the dynamic tensioner guide in position and tighten the single bolt.
31 Refit the hydraulic tensioner together with locking Allen key, insert the bolts and tighten to the specified torque. Make sure the tensioner is in contact with the cylinder block before tightening the bolts.
32 Remove the locking Allen key or pin to allow the tensioner piston to tension the timing chain.
33 At this stage Nissan tool Mot. 1769 is required to hold the gears and sprocket in position while the exhaust sprocket bolts are tightened. Engage the tool with the slot on the end of the exhaust camshaft then turn the tool until it is possible to locate the dowels in the inlet camshaft timing gear. Insert the bolt through the top of the tool and tighten into the hole in the camshaft housing.
34 Tighten the exhaust camshaft sprocket bolts in the two stages given in Specifications. The special tool has a hole for access to one of the bolts **(see illustration)**.
35 Remove tool Mot. 1769 and the TDC tool. Apply locking fluid to the threads of the TDC hole plug, then insert and tighten it to the specified torque **(see illustration)**.
36 Apply a bead of silicone adhesive/sealant to the timing cover contact face on the engine of the dimensions shown **(see illustrations)**.

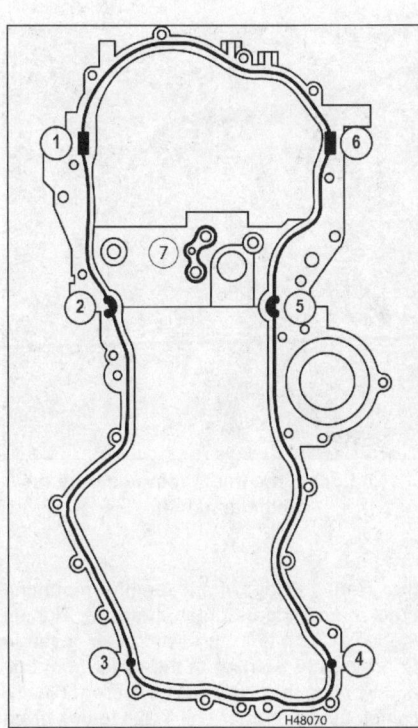

10.36a Sealant application for the timing cover

Bead diameter 5 ± 2 mm from points 1 to 6 passing around the lower part of the engine
Bead diameter 11 ± 2 mm for a length of 10 to 15 mm on points 1, 2, 3, 4, 5, 6
Bead diameter 3.5 ± 1 mm from points 6 to 1 passing around the upper part of the cylinder head
Bead diameter 3.5 ± 1 mm around the inner edge 7

37 Refit the timing cover and finger-tighten the bolts, then tighten them in the two stages given in Specifications starting at the bottom right M8 bolt and working in an anticlockwise direction so that the final bolt to tighten is the M6 bolt.

Chapter 2 Part C 2.0 litre diesel engine

10.36b Apply a bead of silicone adhesive/sealant to the timing cover contact face. . .

10.36c. . . including the central 'island'

11.7a Using the Nissan bench tool to set the wear compensator on the inlet timing gear

11.8 Locate the inlet timing gear on the inlet camshaft. . .

38 Refit the right-hand engine mounting bracket and finger-tighten the bolts. Tighten the lower 5 bolts in the two stages given in Specifications starting at the upper front bolt and working in a clockwise direction. Finally, tighten the upper rear bolt to the torque given in Specifications.

11.9. . . and fit the spacer and bolt

39 Refit the engine mounting reinforcement bracket and finger-tighten the bolts, then tighten them to the specified torque.
40 Fit a new crankshaft oil seal (see Section 19)
41 Refit the crankshaft pulley (see Section 4).
42 Refit the water pump (see Chapter 3 Section 7).
43 Refit the drivebelt (see Chapter 1 Section 12).
44 Refit the engine and transmission assembly (see Chapter 2D Section 7).
45 Refill the engine with oil (see Chapter 1 Section 9).

11 Timing gears – removal, inspection and refitting

Note: *Removal of the engine from the car is necessary in order to carry out the procedure in this Section. Also, special Nissan tool Mot. 1769 is required to lock the camshaft gears, and tool Mot. 1773 to set the inlet camshaft timing gear automatic play compensator. The gear is in two parts, which are spring-loaded to keep the gear teeth accurately engaged.*

Removal

1 Remove the timing chain, sprockets and guides (see Section 10)
2 Fit tool Mot. 1769 to hold the inlet timing gear stationary, then loosen the bolt securing the timing gear to the inlet camshaft.
3 Remove the tool, then insert a screwdriver in the inlet timing gear special hole, and compress the wear compensation spring by lifting the screwdriver in order to release it from the exhaust timing gear.
4 Slide the exhaust timing gear from the exhaust camshaft extension and release the screwdriver from the inlet timing gear.
5 Completely unscrew the inlet timing gear bolt and remove the spacer followed by the timing gear.

Inspection

6 Thoroughly clean then visually inspect the timing gears for wear and damage. Check for chipped and broken gear teeth and renew the gears if necessary.

Refitting

7 Before the inlet timing gear can be refitted, the wear compensation spring must be compressed and a 4.0 mm diameter pin inserted in the special hole to lock it. Moderate force is necessary to compress the spring and it is recommended that Nissan bench tool Mot. 1773 be used to carry out the work safely, however a similar home-made tool may be used. Clamp the baseplate of the tool in a vice and locate the inlet timing gear on it making sure that the key is engaged to lock it. Now locate the tool lever on its pivot and tighten the wing nut. Engage the lever teeth with the lower wear compensation teeth and turn the lever anticlockwise until the wear compensation teeth are aligned with the gear teeth. Lock the two gear sections in this position using a 4.0 mm diameter pin inserted in the special hole **(see illustration)**.

Note: *New inlet timing gears are supplied with a plastic locking pin already fitted.*

8 Remove the inlet timing gear from the tool and locate it on the inlet camshaft **(see illustration)**.
9 Refit the spacer and finger-tighten the bolt **(see illustration)**.
10 Position the timing mark on the inlet camshaft timing gear at 12 o'clock and align it with the boss on the camshaft housing. Make sure that the groove on the exhaust camshaft is horizontal with the larger offset uppermost.
11 Offer the exhaust camshaft timing gear onto the camshaft so that the mounting holes are central within the gear elongated slots, then engage the gear teeth with the inlet timing gear and press it fully into position **(see illustrations)**.
12 Check the alignment of the inlet timing gear with the boss, and the exhaust timing

Chapter 2 Part C 2.0 litre diesel engine

2C-13

11.11a Locate the exhaust timing gear on the exhaust camshaft...

11.11b... so that the mounting holes are central within the gear elongated slots

11.12 Removing the locking pin from the inlet timing gear

11.13a Hold the gear with the special Nissan tool, then tighten the bolt to the specified torque...

11.13b... and angle

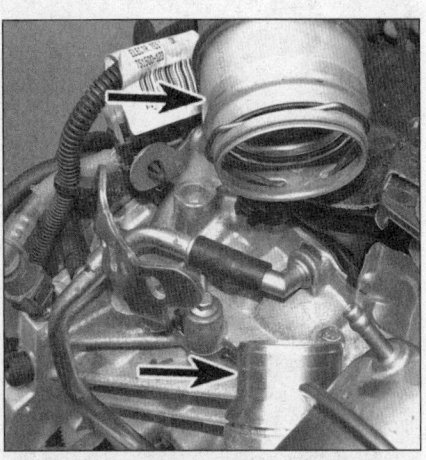

12.2a Disconnect the intercooler air inlet pipe end fittings...

gear with the camshaft slots, then remove the locking pin from the inlet timing gear **(see illustration)**.

13 The inlet timing gear bolt must now be tightened. Fit Nissan tool Mot. 1769 to hold the gear then tighten the bolt in the two stages given in Specifications. Remove the tool **(see illustrations)**.

14 Refit the timing chain, sprockets and guides (see Section 10).

12 Camshafts – removal, inspection and refitting

Note: *Removal of the engine from the car is necessary in order to carry out the procedure in this Section.*

Removal

1 Remove the timing chain, sprockets (see Section 10) and gears (see Section 11). This involves removal of the engine from the car.

2 Remove the intercooler air inlet pipe by disconnecting the end fittings and unscrewing the mounting bolts, then remove the protector seat **(see illustrations)**.

3 Remove the brake vacuum pump (see Section 24).

4 Remove the high-pressure pipe between the pump and fuel rail (see 4B Section 8).

5 Unbolt and remove the injector cover then the oil separator from the top of the engine **(see illustrations)**.

12.2b ... note the O-ring seals inside the pipe end fittings

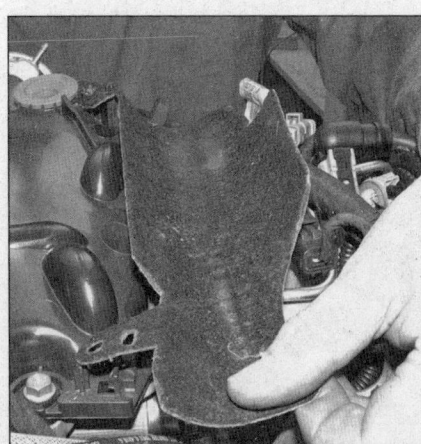

12.2c Removing the intercooler air inlet pipe protector seat

12.5a Removing the injector cover...

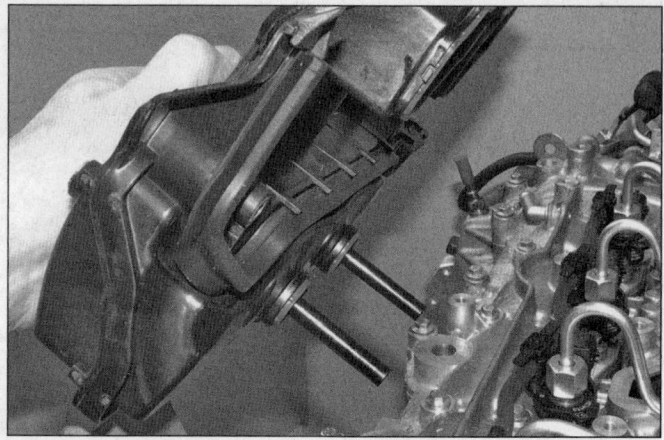

12.5b... and the oil separator from the top of the engine

12.9a Inlet camshaft bearing cap marking

12.9b Exhaust camshaft bearing cap marking

12.10a Removing the camshaft bearing caps

6 Remove the injector fuel return rail, the high-pressure pipes between the rail and injectors, then the injectors (see Chapter 4B Section 9).

7 Unscrew the bolts and remove the fuel collector outlet pipe from the rear of the cylinder head.

8 Progressively unscrew the camshaft housing retaining bolts then carefully remove the housing complete with camshafts from the top of the cylinder head. If necessary, use a screwdriver and block of wood to lever the housing but take care not to damage the joint faces of the housing and cylinder head. There is no need to remove the camshaft followers and hydraulic tappets from the cylinder head.

9 With the housing upside down on the workbench, note the location of the inlet and exhaust camshafts, and the marks on the bearing caps to identify their position. The caps are marked ADM1 and ADM2 for the inlet camshaft, and ECH1 and ECH2 for the exhaust camshaft (see illustrations).

10 Progressively unscrew the bolts, remove the bearing caps and lift the camshafts from the housing (see illustrations).

11 If the exhaust camshaft is to be renewed, remove the high-pressure pump drivegear from it as follows (see illustration). Grip the gear in a vice equipped with soft metal plates to protect the gear, then loosen the bolt, support the camshaft and fully unscrew the bolt.

Inspection

12 Thoroughly clean all components taking care to remove all traces of sealant from the joint faces.

13 Examine the camshaft bearing surfaces and cam lobes for signs of wear ridges and scoring. Renew the camshaft if any of these conditions are apparent. Examine the condition of the bearing surfaces, both on the camshaft journals and in the cylinder head/bearing caps/housing. If the bearing surfaces are worn excessively, the cylinder head, camshafts and housing will need to be renewed. Check the teeth of the high-pressure pump drivegear for wear and chipping, and if necessary renew the gear.

Refitting

14 If removed, refit the high-pressure pump drivegear by gripping it in the soft metal jawed vice, locating the camshaft from beneath, then screwing on the bolt. Tighten the bolt in the stages given in Specifications.

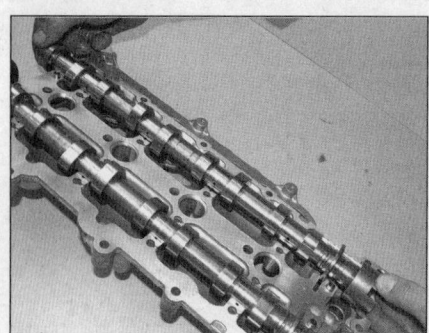

12.10b Removing the inlet camshaft...

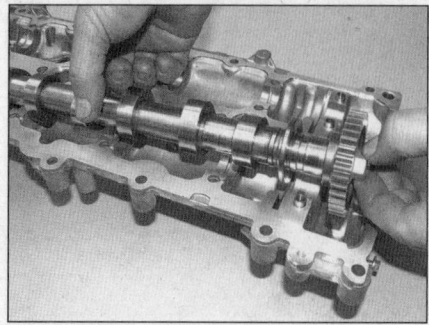

12.10c... and exhaust camshaft

12.11 High-pressure pump drivegear on the exhaust camshaft

Chapter 2 Part C 2.0 litre diesel engine

12.15 Oil the bearing surfaces before fitting the camshafts

12.17 Camshafts set to their TDC positions

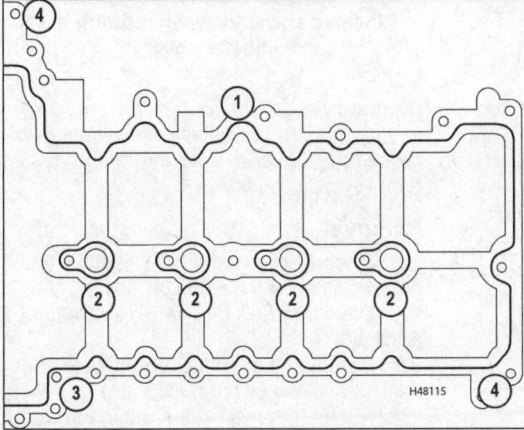

12.18a Silicone adhesive/sealant application to the cylinder head

1 Exhaust side bead
2 Central 'islands'
3 Inlet side bead
4 Locations for guide studs

12.18b Apply sealant to the edges. . .

15 Lubricate the bearing surfaces with clean engine oil then locate the camshafts in the housing in their previously-noted positions **(see illustration)**.

16 Refit the bearing caps, making sure they make contact with the housing before inserting the bolts finger-tight. Finally, tighten the bolts to their specified torque.

17 The camshafts must now be set to their TDC positions. Temporarily place the housing on the bench in its normal position with the camshafts facing downward. Turn the exhaust camshaft as necessary so that the timing end grooves are horizontal with the larger offset uppermost. Turn the inlet camshaft as necessary so that the timing mark is at 12 o'clock and aligned with the boss on the camshaft housing **(see illustration)**.

18 Ensure the contact faces are clean, then apply a bead of silicone 1.5 ± 1.0 mm in diameter around the edges and central 'islands' of the cylinder head upper face. Make sure the bead runs on the inner side of the outer bolt holes **(see illustrations)**.

19 To assist in locating the camshaft housing correctly on the cylinder head, temporarily screw two M6 studs, 60 mm long in the diagonally opposite holes **(see illustration)**.

20 Set the crankshaft in its TDC position with pistons 1 and 4 at the top of their cylinders.

21 Carefully locate the camshaft housing complete with camshafts onto the top of the cylinder head, making sure that the guide studs enter the correct holes before lowering it into position **(see illustration)**.

12.18c. . . and central 'islands' of the cylinder head upper face

12.19 Use two M6 studs as guides when refitting the camshaft housing

12.21 Locating the camshaft housing on the cylinder head

Chapter 2 Part C 2.0 litre diesel engine

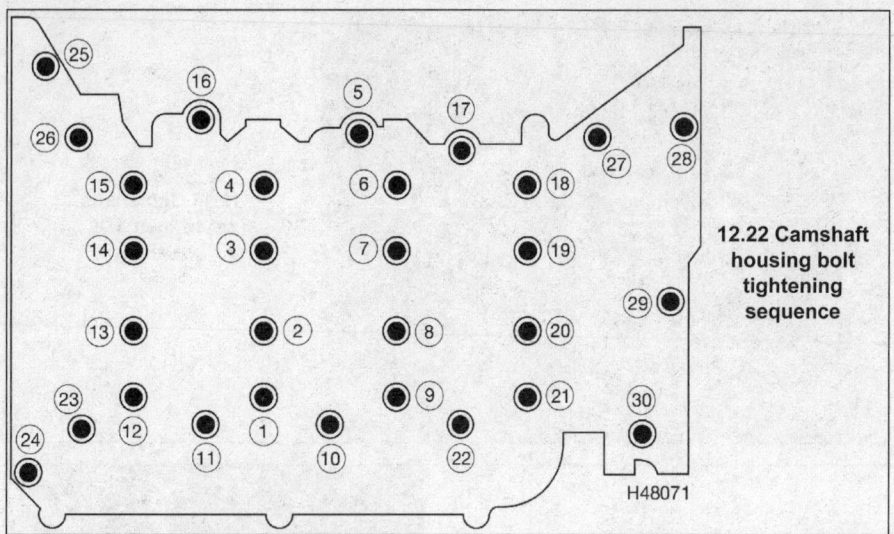

12.22 Camshaft housing bolt tightening sequence

12.27 Make sure the leak-off pipes are located correctly when refitting the injector cover

22 Referring to the diagram **(see illustration)** first insert then progressively tighten bolts 12, 15, 18 and 21 to the specified torque. Remove the two guide studs.
23 Insert the remaining retaining bolts and finger-tighten them at this stage.
24 Completely loosen bolts 12, 15, 18 and 21, then finger-tighten them.
25 Tighten the camshaft housing bolts to the specified torque in the sequence shown **(see illustration 12.22)**. Wipe away excess sealant from the outer joint face.
26 Refit the fuel collector outlet pipe and tighten the bolts.
27 Refit the injectors, high-pressure pipes and fuel return rail (see Chapter 4B Section 9), and then refit the injector cover to the top of the cylinder head, making sure that the leak-off pipes are correctly located **(see illustration)**.
28 Refit the oil separator together with a new gasket and new sealing rings **(see illustrations)**.
29 Refit the high-pressure pipe between the pump and common rail (see Chapter 4B Section 8).
30 Refit the brake vacuum pump (see Section 24).

31 Refit the camshaft gears (see Section 11), timing chain and sprockets (see Section 10).
32 On completion check the engine oil level (see Chapter 1 Section 4). Start the engine and check for any noises.

Note: *Do not run the engine at high speeds until the correct oil pressure has been reached.*

13 Cylinder head – removal and refitting

Note: *Removal of the engine is necessary in order to carry out the procedure in this Section. Also, special Nissan tools are required to lock the inlet and exhaust camshafts.*

Note: *New cylinder head bolts will be required on refitting.*

Note: *Before restarting the engine, it may be necessary to use a diagnostic tool to clear any faults that may be stored in the injection ECU.*

Caution: *Be careful not to allow dirt into the injection pump or injector pipes during this procedure. Cover or plug the open ends as they are disconnected.*

Removal

1 Disconnect the negative (-) battery terminal (see Chapter 5 Section 3).
2 Drain the cooling system (see Chapter 1 Section 27).
3 Remove the timing chain (see Section 10) and gears (see Section 11). This work involves the removal of the engine from the car.
4 Remove the camshaft housing (see Section 12).
5 Remove the throttle valve (also referred to as damper valve) (see Chapter 4B Section 7).
6 Remove the exhaust gas recirculation rigid pipes (see Chapter 6 Section 19).
7 According to version, remove the catalytic pre-converter or the catalytic converter from the turbocharger outlet (see Section 8). Remove the turbocharger oil feed and return pipes.
8 Remove the brake vacuum pump (see Section 24).

12.28a Fitting a new gasket...

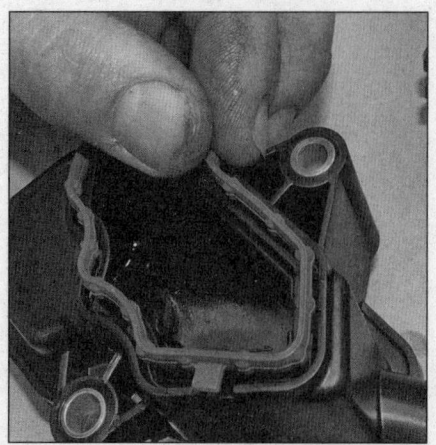

12.28b ...entry sealing ring...

12.28c ...and return sealing rings

Chapter 2 Part C 2.0 litre diesel engine   2C-17

13.15a Hydraulic tappet and follower assembly in position

13.15b Removing the hydraulic tappet and follower assemblies

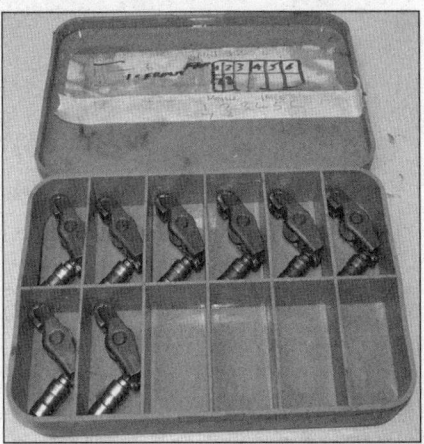

13.15c Keep the inlet and exhaust camshaft hydraulic tappet and follower assemblies identified for location and immersed in oil while removed from the cylinder head

9 Remove the oil level dipstick/filler cap then unbolt and remove the guide tube.
10 Remove the air pipe between the EGR cooler control solenoid valve and the EGR cooler.
11 Progressively slacken the cylinder head bolts by half a turn at a time until all bolts can be unscrewed by hand and removed.

13.18 Check the cylinder head for distortion with feeler blades

13.20 Head locating dowel in the cylinder block

12 Lift the cylinder head upwards and off the cylinder block. If it is stuck, tap it upwards using a hammer and block of wood. Do not try to rotate it (it is located by two dowels), nor attempt to prise it free using a screwdriver inserted between the block and head faces. If the locating dowels are a loose fit, remove them and store them with the head for safe-keeping. As the head is removed, check around the cylinder head to make sure everything has been disconnected.
13 Remove the cylinder head gasket. Note that new gaskets are supplied in two thicknesses according to engine code – the thickness is not measurable as it is defined as the 'crushed' thickness. Make sure the correct one is obtained for refitting.
14 Before removing the hydraulic tappets and rockers, have ready a container with 16 compartments and fill the container with engine oil to the depth of the tappets.

Note: The tappets must remain immersed in oil during the period they are removed from the cylinder head to prevent air entering them.

15 Remove each hydraulic tappet and follower assembly and place in the container so that they can each be identified for location in the cylinder head. It is important they are each refitted to their correct bore on reassembly **(see illustrations)**.

Inspection

16 The mating faces of the cylinder head and block must be perfectly clean before refitting the head. Use a scraper (taking care not to damage the surface of the head) to remove all traces of gasket and carbon, and also clean the tops of the pistons. Take particular care with the aluminium cylinder head, as the soft metal is damaged easily. Also, make sure that debris is not allowed to enter the oil and water channels – this is particularly important for the oil circuit, as carbon could block the oil supply to the camshaft or crankshaft bearings. Using adhesive tape and paper, seal the water, oil and bolt holes in the cylinder block. To prevent carbon entering the gap between the pistons and bores, smear a little grease in the gap. After cleaning the piston, rotate the crankshaft so that the piston moves down the bore, and then wipe out the grease and carbon with a cloth rag. Clean the piston crowns in the same way.
17 Check the block and head for nicks, deep scratches and other damage. If slight, they may be removed carefully with a file. More serious damage may be repaired by machining, but this is a specialist job.
18 If warpage of the cylinder head is suspected, use a straight-edge to check it for distortion **(see illustration)**.
19 Ensure that the cylinder head bolt holes in the block are clean and free of oil. Syringe or soak up any oil left in the bolt holes. This is most important in order that the correct bolt tightening torque can be applied and to prevent the possibility of the block being cracked by hydraulic pressure when the bolts are tightened.
20 Examine the cylinder head bolt threads in the cylinder block for damage. If necessary, use the correct-size tap to chase out the threads in the block, and use a die to clean the threads on the bolts. The cylinder head bolts must be discarded and renewed, regardless of their apparent condition. Also, check that the locating dowels are in good condition and correctly located in the cylinder block **(see illustration)**.

Refitting

21 Ensure that the mating faces of the cylinder block and head are spotlessly clean, that the retaining bolt threads are also clean and dry, and that they screw easily in and out of their locations.
22 Ensure that the locating dowels are correctly fitted to the block, and then apply 2 drops of silicone adhesive/sealant (5 to 7 mm diameter) to the surface of the two extremities at the timing end of the block **(see illustration)**.
23 Locate the new cylinder head gasket on

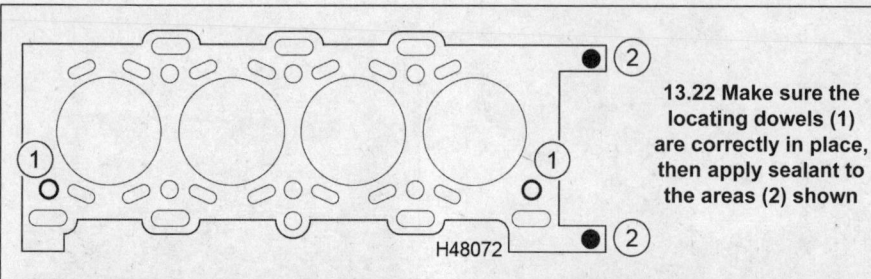

13.22 Make sure the locating dowels (1) are correctly in place, then apply sealant to the areas (2) shown

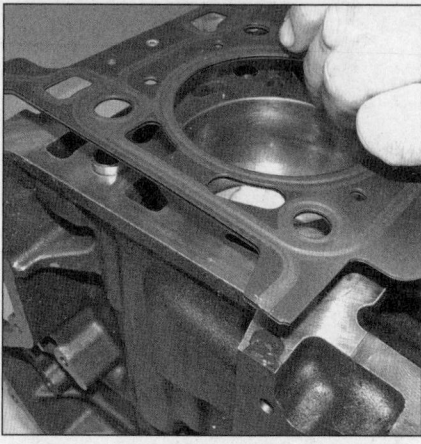

13.23a Locate the cylinder head gasket on the block...

13.23b... and apply silicone adhesive sealant to the timing end extremities

13.25a Lower the cylinder head onto the block...

the block; then again apply 2 drops of silicone adhesive/sealant (5 to 7 mm diameter) to the timing end extremities of the gasket **(see illustrations)**.

24 Using a spanner on the crankshaft nose flats; turn the crankshaft clockwise until the groove is aligned with the bolt hole on the cylinder block **(see illustration 10.11)**. This will position the pistons half way up the cylinder bores.

25 Carefully lower the cylinder head onto the block, engaging it over the dowels. Insert the cylinder head bolts and finger-tighten them at this stage **(see illustrations)**.

26 Working progressively, starting from the centre bolts and working outwards in a spiral motion, tighten the cylinder head bolts to their Stage 1 torque setting, using a torque wrench and suitable socket.

27 Using the same sequence, tighten the cylinder head bolts to their Stage 2 torque setting.

28 Once all bolts are tightened to the Stage 2 torque setting, using the same sequence, tighten each bolt through its specified final Stage 3 angle, using a socket and extension bar **(see illustration)**. It is recommended that an angle-measuring gauge be used during this stage of the tightening, to ensure accuracy.

29 Clean away any excess sealant from the timing end of the head gasket.

30 If the hydraulic tappets and rockers have remained immersed in oil, no air will have entered them, however if there is any doubt, compress the piston head of the tappet and check that it does not move. If it does, the tappet may be reprimed by immersing it in clean diesel fuel. Also, check that the rocker-to-tappet clips are correctly in place.

31 Lubricate the tappet bores in the cylinder head with engine oil, then refit each hydraulic tappet and rocker assembly to its previously-noted location making sure that the rockers are correctly positioned on the valves.

32 Refit the air pipe between the EGR cooler control solenoid valve and the EGR cooler, tightening the upper-outer mounting bolt first, the upper-inner bolt next, and the lower bolt last.

33 Refit the dipstick guide tube to the block together with a new seal, and tighten the mounting bolts. Do not rotate the tube as it is being refitted otherwise the seal may be displaced. Insert the oil level dipstick/filler cap.

34 Refit the brake vacuum pump (see Section 24).

35 Refit the turbocharger oil feed and return pipes.

36 According to version, refit the catalytic pre-converter or the catalytic converter to the turbocharger outlet.

37 Refit the exhaust gas recirculation rigid pipes.

38 Refit the throttle valve (see Chapter 4B Section 7).

39 Refit the camshaft housing (see Section 12).

40 Refit the timing chain (see Section 10).

41 Reconnect the battery negative terminal (see Chapter 5 Section 3).

42 Refill the cooling system (see Chapter 1 Section 27).

13.25b... and insert the retaining bolts

13.28 Angle-tightening the cylinder head bolts

Chapter 2 Part C 2.0 litre diesel engine

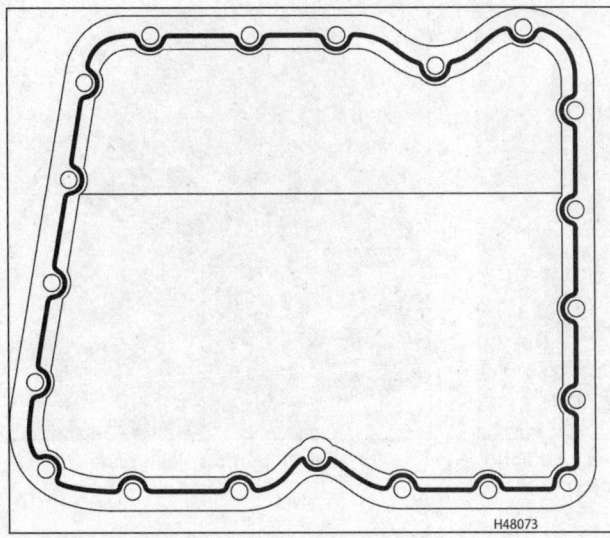

14.8a Apply silicone adhesive/sealant to the oil pan perimeter as shown

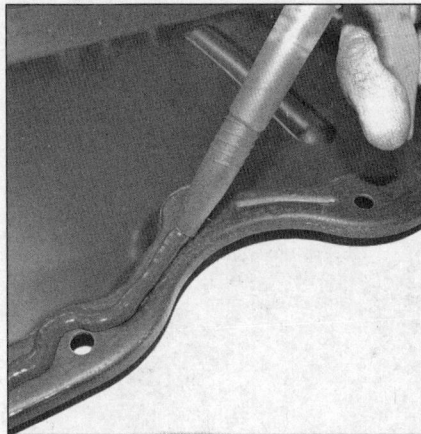

14.8b Applying silicone adhesive/sealant to the oil pan

14 Oil pan – removal and refitting

Removal

1 Raise the front of the vehicle and support on jackstands (see Chapter 0 Section 7). Undo the retaining screws and remove the plastic undertray from beneath the engine/transmission.
2 Drain the engine oil (see Chapter 1 Section 9) and then refit and tighten the drain plug, using a new sealing washer. Ensure all the oil is completely drained.

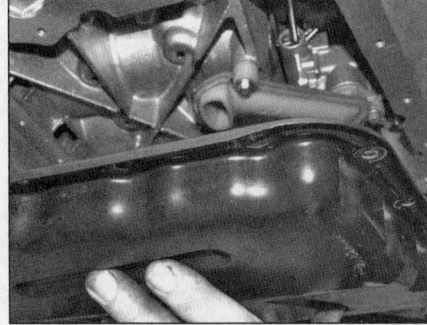

14.9 Lift the oil pan into position on the crankcase

3 Remove the engine oil level dipstick.
4 Unscrew and remove the bolts securing the oil pan to the cylinder block baseplate.
5 The oil pan is sealed to the cylinder block baseplate with strong silicone adhesive/sealant that is very difficult to cut, however methodical use of a suitable spatula or thin knife will release the oil pan.
6 Take care not to distort or damage the mating surfaces of the oil pan and baseplate, and take adequate precautions to catch any oil remaining in the oil pan.

Refitting

7 Thoroughly clean the mating surfaces of the oil pan and cylinder block baseplate, taking care not to damage their surfaces.
8 Apply a 5 ± 2 mm diameter bead of silicone adhesive/sealant to the oil pan as shown **(see illustrations)**.
9 Lift the oil pan into position making sure it is correctly aligned with the holes in the baseplate, then insert the bolts and finger-tighten them **(see illustration)**.
10 Tighten the oil pan bolts to the Stage 1 torque given in Specifications using the sequence shown **(see illustration)**.
11 Tighten the oil pan bolts to the Stage 2 torque using the same sequence.

12 Refit the undertray and lower the vehicle to the ground.
13 Fill the engine with fresh oil (see Chapter 1 Section 9).

15 Oil pump, drive chain and sprocket – removal, inspection and refitting

Note: *Drive chain removal is only possible after removal of the engine.*

Removal

Oil pump

1 Remove the oil pan (see Section 14).
2 Unscrew the two bolts and remove the oil pump strainer from the baseplate **(see illustration)**.
3 Unscrew the bolt securing the splash plate to the oil pump. The bolt goes through the oil pump housing to the splash plate located on the crankshaft side of the oil pump.
4 Unscrew the mounting bolts then release the drive sprocket from the drive chain and withdraw the oil pump **(see illustrations)**. If necessary, a length of bent wire may help to unhook the chain from the sprocket.

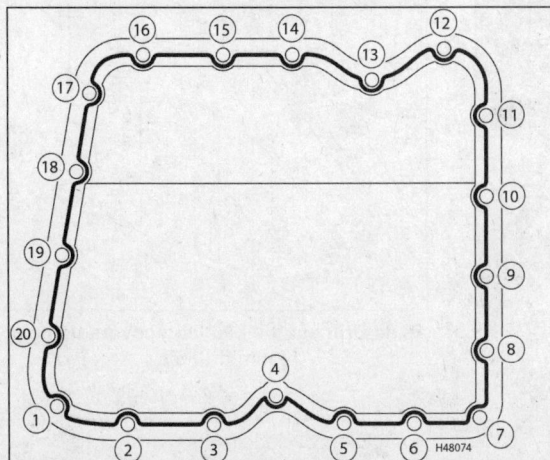

14.10 Tightening sequence for the oil pan bolts

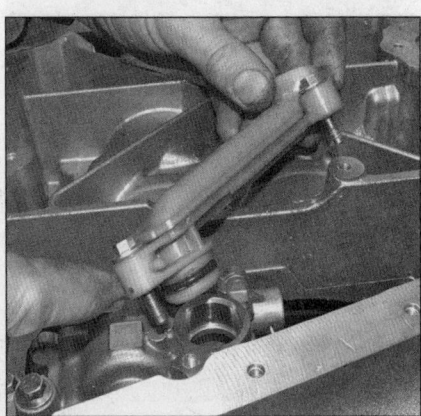

15.2 Removing the oil pump strainer

2C-20 Chapter 2 Part C 2.0 litre diesel engine

15.4a Unscrew the mounting bolts...

15.4b... then unhook the drive chain and remove the oil pump

15.5 Oil pump splash plate

5 If necessary, remove the splash plate through the access aperture – this is quite difficult as there is limited room **(see illustration)**.

Drive chain and sprocket

6 Remove the engine and transmission from the car (see Chapter 2D Section 6).
7 To remove the drive chain and sprocket first remove the oil pump as described in paragraphs 1 to 4.
8 Remove the timing chain and crankshaft sprocket (see Section 10).
9 Unhook the drive chain from the drive sprocket on the crankshaft and remove the chain **(see illustration)**.
10 Slide the drive sprocket from the nose of the crankshaft, while noting its fitted position **(see illustration)**.

Inspection

11 Clean the components and carefully examine the chain, sprockets and pump for any signs of excessive wear. If evident, it is recommended that all the components be renewed as a set.
12 Before refitting the oil pump, prime it by filling with clean engine oil whilst rotating the sprocket clockwise.

Refitting

Drive chain and sprocket

13 Wipe clean the oil pump and cylinder block mating surfaces.
14 Slide the drive sprocket fully onto the crankshaft as previously noted, then feed the chain through the baseplate aperture and onto the sprocket.
15 Refit the timing chain and crankshaft sprocket (see Section 10).
16 Refit the engine and transmission (see Chapter 2D Section 6).

Oil pump

17 Lift the oil pump into position on the cylinder block, then engage it with the drive chain.
18 Insert the oil pump mounting bolts and the splash plate-to-pump bolt finger-tight at this stage.
19 Tighten the oil pump mounting bolts in the two stages given in the Specifications.
20 Tighten the splash plate to pump bolt to the specified torque.
21 Refit the oil pump strainer together with a new seal and finger-tighten the bolts, then fully tighten the bolts to the specified torque.
22 Refit the oil pan (see Section 14).

16 Cylinder block baseplate – removal and refitting

Note: *Removal of the engine is not essential to carry out this procedure; however, removal of the timing cover with the engine in position is extremely difficult.*

Removal

1 Remove the timing cover with reference to Section 10, paragraphs 1 to 10.
2 Remove the transmission (see Chapter 7A Section 5 - manual transmission, or Chapter 7B Section 11 - automatic transmission). Ensure the engine is well supported during this and subsequent procedures in this Section.
3 On manual transmission, remove the clutch assembly (see Chapter 8 Section 5).
4 Remove the flywheel (see Section 18).
5 Remove the transmission end crankshaft oil seal housing (see Section 19).
6 Remove the oil pan (see Section 14).

15.9 Unhook the chain from the drive sprocket...

15.10... then slide the drive sprocket from the nose of the crankshaft

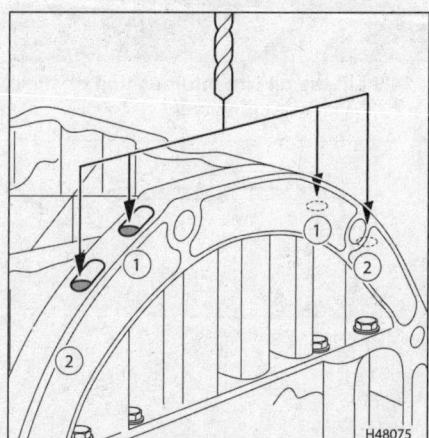

16.8a Drill out the blanking covers using a 13 mm drill bit...

1 Inner cover locations
2 Outer cover locations

Chapter 2 Part C 2.0 litre diesel engine

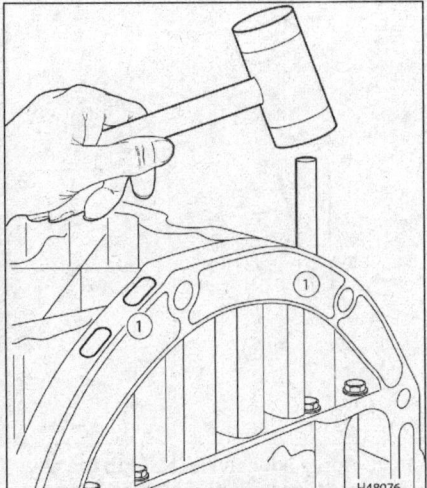

16.8b . . . then drive out the inner covers using a suitable tube or drift

1 Method of removing inner covers

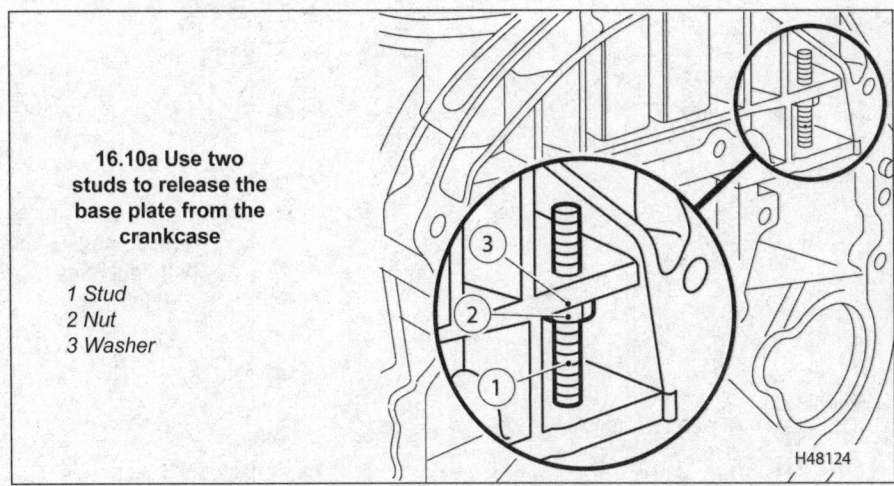

16.10a Use two studs to release the base plate from the crankcase

1 Stud
2 Nut
3 Washer

16.10b Removing the baseplate

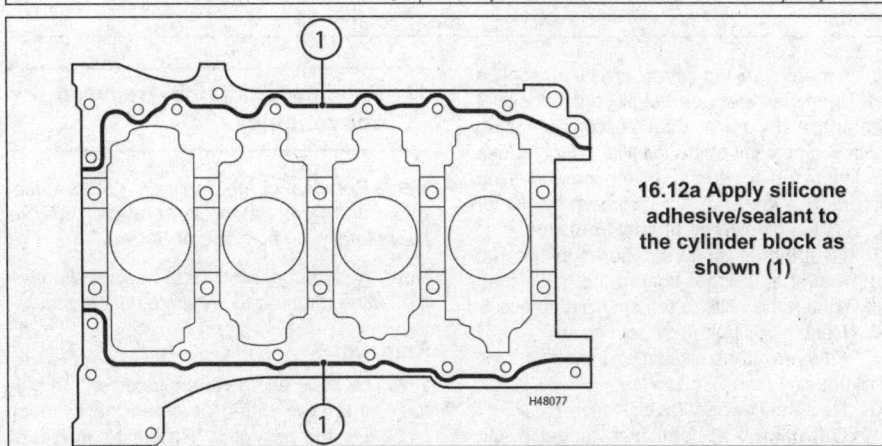

16.12a Apply silicone adhesive/sealant to the cylinder block as shown (1)

a 13 mm drill bit so that a socket can be inserted onto the bolts. The outer covers will have to be cut with a chisel, and the inner covers driven out using a suitable tube or drift **(see illustrations)**. Obtain new covers for refitting. Where blanking covers are not fitted, extra long bolts are used instead.

9 Progressively unscrew and remove the 16 baseplate bolts.

10 The baseplate is sealed to the crankcase with silicone adhesive/sealant and is likely to be difficult to remove. To help break the seal, insert two long studs into the outer bolt holes at the transmission end, and fit a nut and washer to each stud as shown. Progressively tighten the nuts to force the baseplate off of the crankcase **(see illustrations)**. On completion, remove the studs.

Refitting

11 Thoroughly clean the mating surfaces of the baseplate, crankcase and timing cover, taking care not to damage their surfaces.

12 Apply a 5 ± 2 mm diameter bead of silicone adhesive/sealant to the cylinder block as shown **(see illustrations)**.

13 If necessary, the studs used to separate the baseplate from the crankcase may be used without their nuts and washers as guides during refitting. Locate the baseplate on the crankcase making sure the bolt holes are correctly aligned, then insert the bolts and finger-tighten them **(see illustration)**.

14 Tighten the baseplate bolts to the specified torque, working in sequence from the timing end near the oil pump, then around the transmission end and returning to the timing end on the opposite side **(see illustration)**. Wipe away any excess sealant.

15 Remove the guide studs.

7 Unscrew the two bolts and remove the oil pump strainer from the baseplate. It is not necessary to remove the oil pump.

8 The baseplate bolt access holes at the transmission end may be fitted with blanking covers. If so, drill and cut them out using

16.12b Apply sealant to the cylinder block

16.13 Insert the baseplate retaining bolts

Chapter 2 Part C 2.0 litre diesel engine

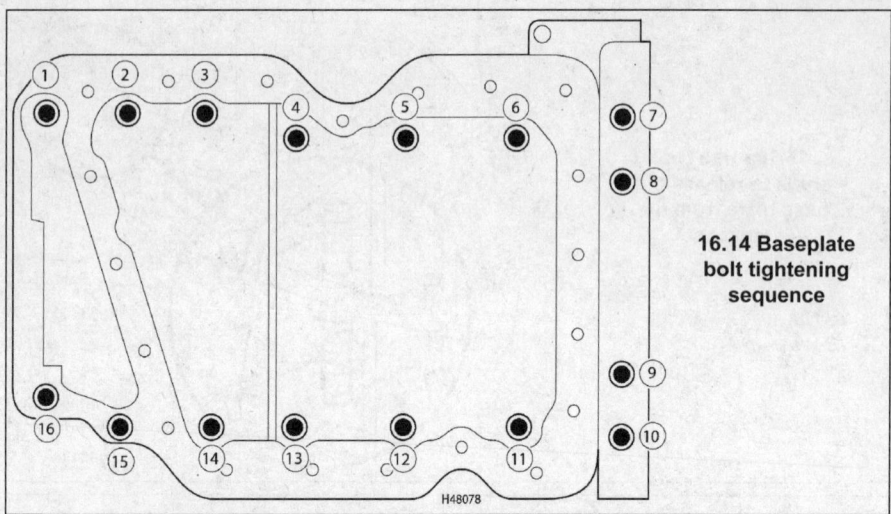

16.14 Baseplate bolt tightening sequence

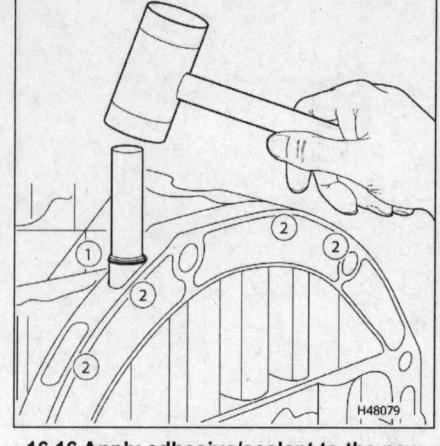

16.16 Apply adhesive/sealant to the new covers (1) before driving them into the holes (2)

16 Where blanking covers are fitted, apply a 5 ± 2 mm diameter bead of silicone adhesive/sealant to the new covers before pressing them into position by hand initially. Finally, use a suitable tube or drift to drive in new blanking covers to a depth of 3.0 mm from the lower edge of the holes **(see illustration)**.
17 Refit the oil pump strainer together with a new seal and finger-tighten the bolts, then fully-tighten the bolts to the specified torque.
18 Refit the oil pan (see Section 14).
19 Fit a new transmission end crankshaft oil seal housing (see Section 19).
20 Refit the flywheel (see Section 18).
21 On manual transmission models, refit the clutch (see Chapter 8 Section 5).
22 Refit the transmission (see Chapter 7A Section 5 - manual transmission, or Chapter 7B Section 11 - automatic transmission).
23 Refit the timing cover (see Section 10).

17 Balancer shaft unit – removal and refitting

Note: Removal of the engine is not essential to carry out this procedure, however refer to the note at the beginning of Section 16.

Note: Nissan tool Mot. 1802 or an alternative pin will be required to set the balancer shaft.

Removal

1 The M9R engine is equipped with a balancer shaft unit fitted between the cylinder block and the baseplate. The unit consists of two counter-rotating balance shafts driven by the crankshaft.
2 Remove the cylinder block baseplate (see Section 16).
3 Before removing the balancer shaft unit, first set the engine to its TDC position (see Section 3).
4 Insert a suitable close-fitting pin through the balance shaft extensions to lock them in their TDC position (Nissan technicians use tool Mot. 1802). The weights on both shafts must be facing away from the crankshaft **(see illustration)**.
5 Progressively unscrew the mounting bolts and lift the balancer shaft unit from the crankcase. Note the location of the adjustment shims then remove them. Discard the bolts and new ones must be used during refitting.
Caution: *The shims are very sharp. Protective gloves should be worn when handling them.*
6 Clean the balancer shaft unit, the shims and the drive ring on the crankshaft.

Refitting

7 To ensure the correct clearance between the balance shaft and crankshaft gears, the correct thickness shims must always be fitted. The thickness is indicated on the shims; therefore if new shims are fitted they must be of identical thickness to those removed.

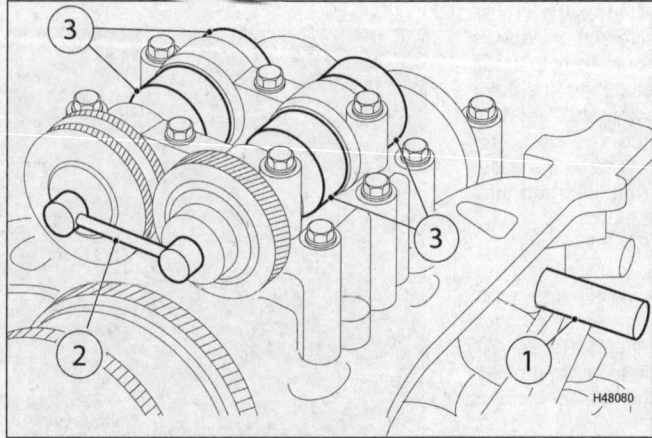

17.4 Balancer shaft unit removal
1 TDC setting tool for crankshaft
2 TDC setting tool for balancer shafts
3 The balance shaft weights must face away from the crankshaft

17.9 Balancer shaft unit bolt tightening sequence
A Shims

Chapter 2 Part C 2.0 litre diesel engine

18.3 Home-made tool for locking the flywheel

18.4a Unscrew and remove the bolts...

18.4b... and withdraw the flywheel from the crankshaft flange

Locate the shims on the crankcase (if necessary use grease to retain them while fitting the unit).

8 Check that the crankshaft and balancer shafts are set to their TDC positions, then locate the unit onto the shims and fit the new bolts finger-tight at this stage.

9 Ensure that the shims are correctly located by pressing them in against the bolts from the outside, and then tighten the bolts to the specified torque and angle given in the Specifications in the order shown **(see illustration)**.

10 Remove the TDC pin from the balance shaft extensions.

11 Refit the cylinder block baseplate (see Section 16).

18 Flywheel – removal, inspection and refitting

Removal

1 Remove the transmission (see Chapter 7A Section 5 - manual transmission models, or Chapter 7B Section 11 - automatic transmission models). Ensure the engine is well supported during this and subsequent procedures in this Section.

2 On manual transmission, remove the clutch assembly (see Chapter 8 Section 5).

3 Prevent the flywheel from turning by locking the ring gear teeth with a screwdriver or homemade tool **(see illustration)**. Make alignment marks between the flywheel and crankshaft using paint or a suitable marker pen.

4 Slacken and remove the retaining bolts and remove the flywheel from the crankshaft flange **(see illustrations)**. Do not drop it, as it is very heavy. If the locating dowel (where fitted) is a loose fit in the crankshaft end, remove and store it with the flywheel for safekeeping. Discard the bolts, as they should be renewed whenever they are disturbed.

Inspection

5 Examine the flywheel for scoring of the clutch face, and for wear or chipping of the ring gear teeth. If the clutch face is scored, the flywheel may be surface-ground, but renewal is preferable. Seek the advice of a Nissan dealer or engine-reconditioning specialist to see if machining is possible. If the ring gear is worn or damaged, the flywheel must be renewed, as it is not possible to renew the ring gear separately. Clean the bolt hole threads in the crankshaft – an old retaining bolt with three cuts on the threads is ideal for doing this **(see illustration)**.

Refitting

6 Clean the mating surfaces of the flywheel and crankshaft.

7 Ensure that the locating dowel is in position (where fitted) and offer up the flywheel, locating it on the dowel, and fit the new retaining bolts. If the original is being refitted, align the marks made prior to removal.

8 Lock the flywheel using the method employed on dismantling, and tighten the retaining bolts to the specified torque and angle. To ensure all the bolts are tightened to the correct angle, make marks on the bolts and flywheel bolt holes **(see illustration)**.

9 On manual transmission models, refit the clutch (see Chapter 8 Section 5).

10 Refit the transmission (see Chapter 7A Section 5 - manual transmission models, or Chapter 7B Section 11 - automatic transmissions models).

19 Crankshaft oil seals – renewal

Timing end oil seal

Note: *Unlike conventional oil seals, the timing end oil seal is screwed into the timing cover.*

1 Remove the crankshaft pulley (see Section 4).

2 A socket adapter is provided with the new crankshaft oil seal. Using the adapter, unscrew the old oil seal from the timing cover.

3 Clean the crankshaft and timing cover.

4 The new oil seal must not be lubricated during fitting. First, position the seal with its three raised segments aligned with the cutouts in the timing cover and push the seal into

18.5 Old flywheel bolt with three hacksaw cuts on the threads is ideal to clean the threads in the crankshaft

18.8 Mark the bolts and holes to ensure correct angle-tightening of the flywheel bolts

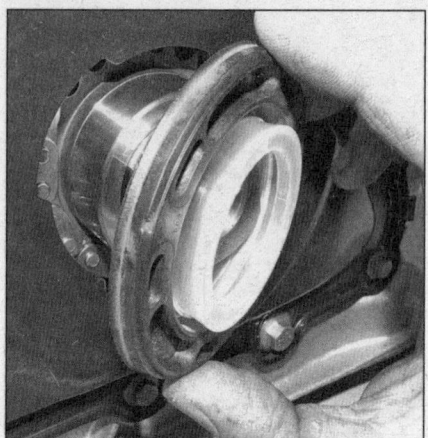

19.4 Locate the new oil seal on the timing cover with the raised segments aligned with the cut-outs

19.5a Fit the adapter. . .

19.5b. . . and tighten to the specified torque

19.8 Removing the transmission end oil seal housing

19.10 Use 3 bolts to act as guides when fitting the new oil seal housing

the cover using hand pressure only. This will force the plastic protector from the centre of the oil seal **(see illustration)**.

5 Using the adapter, tighten the oil seal to the specified torque given in the Specifications **(see illustrations)**.

6 Refit the crankshaft pulley (see Section 4).

Transmission end oil seal

Note: *The transmission end oil seal is supplied together with the oil seal housing and cannot be renewed separately.*

7 Remove the flywheel (see Section 18).
8 Unscrew the bolts and remove the oil seal housing from the cylinder block/baseplate **(see illustration)**.
9 Clean the contact faces of the cylinder block and baseplate. Do not remove the protector or touch the lip of the new oil seal during fitting as this will result in oil leakage.
10 Carefully locate the oil seal and housing onto the crankshaft and insert three 90 mm long M6 bolts loosely to act as guides **(see illustration)**. Do not press the housing into position at this stage.
11 Apply even pressure to the housing and press it into position until it contacts the cylinder block. Now remove the protector and the three guide bolts **(see illustration)**.
12 Insert the retaining bolts and finger-tighten, and then tighten them to the initial torque given in the Specifications in the sequence shown **(see illustration)**.
13 Tighten the bolts to their final torque using the same sequence.
14 Refit the flywheel (see Section 18).

19.11 Press the housing into position and remove the protector

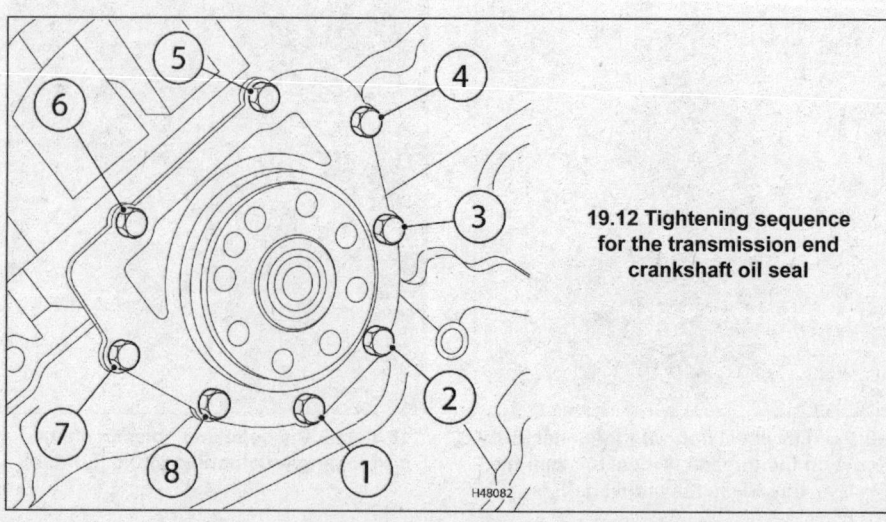

19.12 Tightening sequence for the transmission end crankshaft oil seal

Chapter 2 Part C 2.0 litre diesel engine

20.7 Remove the filter support bracket

20.8a Unclip the fuel lines ...

20.8b ... and unbolt the bracket from the mounting

20 Engine/transmission mountings – inspection and renewal

Inspection

1 Raise the front of the vehicle and support on jackstands (see Jacking and Towing 0 Section 7)
2 Check the mounting rubber to see if it is cracked, hardened or separated from the metal at any point; renew the mounting if any such damage or deterioration is evident.
3 Check that all the mounting's fasteners are securely tightened; use a torque wrench to check if possible.
4 Using a large screwdriver or a crowbar, check for wear in the mounting by carefully levering against it to check for free play. Where this is not possible, enlist the aid of an assistant to move the engine/transmission back-and-forth, or from side-to-side, while you watch the mounting. While some free play is to be expected, even from new components, excessive wear should be obvious. If excessive free play is found, check first that the fasteners are correctly secured, and then renew any worn components as described below.

Renewal

Right-hand mounting

5 Disconnect the negative (-) battery terminal (see Chapter 5 Section 3).
6 Place a jack beneath the engine, with a block of wood on the jack head. Raise the jack until it is supporting the weight of the engine.
7 To make access easier, remove the fuel filter and support bracket (see illustration) (see Chapter 1 Section 6).
8 Unclip the fuel lines then slacken the securing bolt and disconnect the earth wire and bracket from the top of the engine mounting bracket (see illustrations).
9 Slacken the retaining bolts and remove the torque link from the rear of the engine mounting (see illustration).
10 Slacken and remove the three retaining bolts from the inner wing panel, remove the three retaining bolts from the engine mounting bracket, and then withdraw the complete mounting from the engine compartment (see illustrations).
11 Check carefully for signs of wear or damage on all components, and renew them where necessary.

12 On refitting, fit the engine mounting and bracket to the inner wing panel and engine, and then securely tighten its retaining bolts to the specified torque setting.
13 Refit the torque link to the rear of the engine mounting and tighten the retaining bolts to the specified torque setting.
14 With the engine mounting back in position, refit the fuel filter and mounting bracket (see Chapter 1 Section 6).
15 Lower the jack and remove it from underneath the engine.
16 Reconnect the earth cable and bracket to the top of the engine mounting and secure the fuel lines back in the clips, and then reconnect the battery (see Chapter 5 Section 3).

Left-hand mounting

17 Remove the battery and tray (see Chapter 5 Section 3).
18 Place a jack and block of wood beneath the transmission, and raise the jack to take the weight of the transmission (see illustration).
19 Undo the retaining bolts and remove the air filter housing lower locating bracket from the top of the transmission mounting (see illustration).

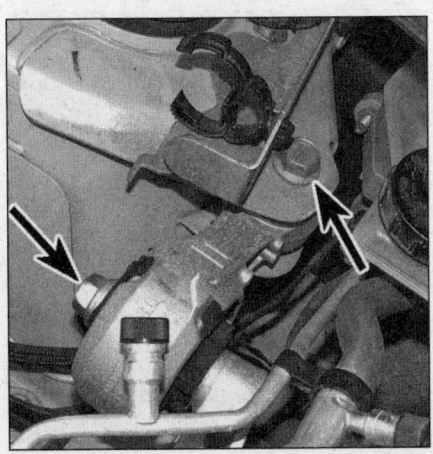

20.9 Unbolt the torque link (arrowed) from the rear of the bulkhead

20.10a Unbolt the inner wing panel bolts ...

20.10b ... and the engine mounting bolts

20.18 Support the transmission with a trolley jack

20.19 Unbolt the air filter housing lower mounting bracket (arrowed)

20.20 Undo the two outer securing bolts and remove the mounting

20 Slacken and remove the two outer retaining bolts, and withdraw the mounting from the upper mounting bracket (see illustration).
21 If required, undo the retaining bolts from the inner wing panel to remove the upper mounting bracket.
22 Also, if required, undo the retaining bolts from the transmission to remove the lower mounting bracket (see illustration).
23 Check carefully for signs of wear or damage on all components, and renew them where necessary.
24 On refitting, fit the upper and lower mounting brackets (where removed) and securely tighten the retaining bolts.
25 Align the left-hand rubber mounting with the bolt/stud on the lower mounting bracket and tighten its nut to the specified torque setting.
26 Refit the two outer retaining nuts, and tighten to the specified torque setting.
27 With the transmission mounting back in position, lower the jack and remove it from underneath the transmission.
28 Refit the battery and battery tray (see Chapter 5 Section 3).

Rear lower mounting

29 Raise the front of the vehicle and support on jackstands (see Chapter 0 Section 7). Remove engine undertray.
30 Slacken and remove the bolts securing the rear mounting link to the subframe and the mounting bracket, and then withdraw the mounting link from under the vehicle (see illustration).
31 If required, slacken and remove the three bolts securing the rear mounting bracket to the lower cylinder block base plate, and then withdraw the bracket from under the vehicle.
32 Check carefully for signs of wear or damage on all components, and renew them where necessary.
33 Refit the mounting bracket to the rear of the oil pan housing and tighten its retaining bolts to the specified torque.
34 Fit the rear mounting link to the mounting bracket and subframe, and then tighten the retaining bolts to the specified torque.
35 With the transmission rear mounting link arm back in position, lower the vehicle to the ground.

21 Oil cooler – removal and refitting

Note: The oil cooler is part of the oil filter housing; it would be good practice to renew the oil and oil filter whenever the oil cooler is removed.

Removal

1 Disconnect the negative (-) battery terminal (see Chapter 5 Section 3).
2 Raise the front of the vehicle and support on jackstands (see Chapter 0 Section 7).
3 Undo the retaining screws and remove the engine undertray to gain access to the oil cooler, which is part of the oil filter housing and is mounted on the front of the cylinder block. Also remove the engine upper covers for access to the top of the engine.
4 Drain the engine oil and remove the oil filter (see Chapter 1 Section 9), and then refit and tighten the drain plug.
5 Drain the cooling system (see Chapter 1 Section 27). Alternatively, clamp the oil cooler coolant hoses as close to the cooler as possible, and be prepared for some coolant loss as the hoses are disconnected.

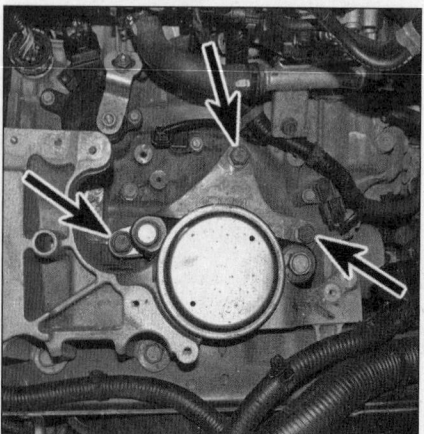

20.22 Mounting bracket-to-transmission retaining bolts (arrowed)

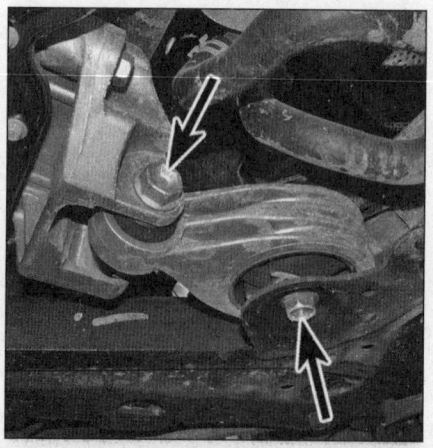

20.30 Remove the torque rod bolts

21.6a Remove the oil level dipstick/filler cap...

Chapter 2 Part C 2.0 litre diesel engine

21.6b... unscrew the mounting bolt...

21.6c... withdraw the guide tube from the cylinder block...

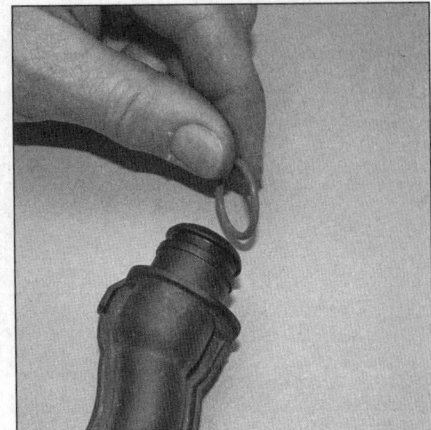

21.6d... and recover the O-ring seal

6 Withdraw the oil level dipstick/filler cap from the guide tube, then unscrew the upper mounting bolt and remove the guide tube from the engine. Discard the guide tube seal, as a new one must be used on refitting **(see illustrations)**.
7 Disconnect the wiring from the alternator and oil pressure sensor, and position to one side.
8 Where a coolant heating element unit is fitted to the bottom of the radiator, unscrew the mounting bolts from the bracket and position the unit to one side.
9 Unscrew the bolt securing the power steering high-pressure pipe to the engine and position the pipe to one side.
10 Release the clips and disconnect the coolant inlet (bottom) and outlet (top) hoses from the oil cooler/filter housing.
11 Unscrew the four mounting bolts and remove the oil cooler/filter housing from the front of the cylinder block. Discard the gasket, as a new one must be used on refitting **(see illustrations)**.

Refitting

12 Fit a new gasket to the oil cooler/filter housing, then offer the housing to the cylinder block. Ensure that the housing is correctly positioned then refit the mounting bolts and finger-tighten initially.
13 Tighten the bolts in diagonal sequence to the Stage 1 torque, and then tighten them to the Stage 2 torque using the same sequence.
14 Reconnect the inlet and outlet hoses and secure with the clips.
15 Refit the power steering high-pressure pipe to the engine and tighten the mounting bolt to the specified torque.
16 Where applicable, refit the coolant heating element to its mounting bracket and tighten the bolts securely.
17 Reconnect the wiring to the alternator and oil pressure sensor.
18 Fit a new seal to the dipstick guide tube and lubricate with engine oil, then refit the guide tube and tighten the mounting bolt to the specified torque. Check that the seal remains in position during fitting.
19 Insert the oil level dipstick/filler cap in the guide tube.
20 Reconnect the battery negative terminal (refer to Disconnecting the battery in the Reference Section of this manual).
21 Fit a new oil filter and refill the engine with oil (see Chapter 1 Section 9).

22 Refill or top-up the cooling system (see Chapter 1 Section 27). Start the engine, and check the oil cooler/filter housing for signs of leakage.
23 Refit the engine undertray and upper covers and lower the car to the ground.

22 Oil pressure sensor – removal and refitting

1 The oil pressure sensor gives a vital early warning of low oil pressure. The sensor operates the oil warning light on the instrument panel – the light should come on with the ignition, and go out almost immediately when the engine starts.
2 If the light does not come on, there could be a fault on the instrument panel, the switch wiring, or the switch itself. If the light does not go out, low oil level, worn oil pump (or oil pan pick-up blocked), blocked oil filter, or worn main bearings could be to blame – or again, the switch may be faulty.
3 If the light comes on while driving, the best advice is to turn the engine off immediately, and not to drive the car until the problem has been investigated – ignoring the light could mean expensive engine damage.

Removal

4 The oil pressure sensor is located on the front of the engine, in the top of the oil filter housing.
5 It may be easier to access the sensor from underneath the vehicle, raise the front of the vehicle and support on jackstands (see Chapter 0 Section 7). Undo the retaining bolts and remove the engine undertray.
6 Disconnect the wiring plug from the sensor.
7 Unscrew the sensor from the housing, and remove it together with its sealing washer. There should only be a very slight loss of oil when this is done.

21.11a Remove the oil cooler/filter housing...

21.11b... and recover the gasket

Chapter 2 Part C 2.0 litre diesel engine

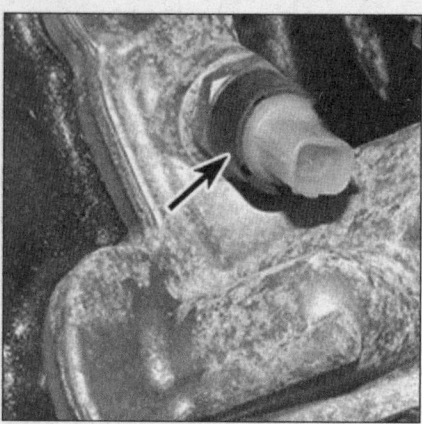

22.5 The oil pressure sensor is mounted to the top of the oil filter/oil cooler housing

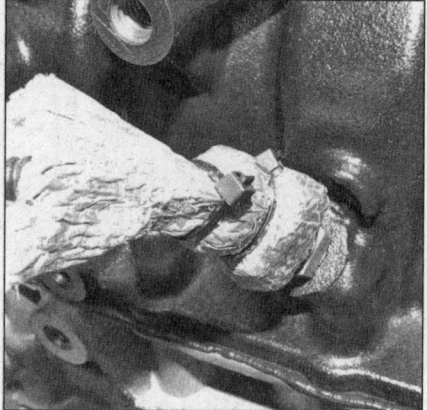

23.6 Heat-resisting insulation fitted to the oil level sensor

23.7a Disconnect the wiring. . .

Inspection

8 Examine the sensor for signs of cracking or splits. If the top part of the sensor is loose, this is an early indication of impending failure.
9 Check that the wiring connector terminals are good, then trace the wire from the switch connector until it enters the main loom – any wiring defects will give rise to apparent oil pressure problems.

Refitting

10 Refitting is the reverse of the removal procedure, noting the following points:
a Clean the sensor threads before fitting. Tighten the switch to the specified torque.
b Reconnect the sensor wiring, making sure it is routed away from any hot or moving parts.
c Lower the car to the ground, then check the engine oil level and top-up if necessary (see Chapter 1 Section 9).
d Check for signs of oil leaks once the engine has been restarted and warmed-up to normal operating temperature.

23 Oil level sensor – removal and refitting

Removal

1 The oil level sensor is located at the rear, right-hand side of the engine, above the right-hand driveshaft intermediate bearing.
2 Access to the sensor may be easiest from under the right-hand front wheel arch. First, jack up the front of the car, and support it on axle stands (see). Remove the front right-hand roadwheel.
3 Undo the fasteners and remove the wheel arch liner.
4 Remove the stabiliser bar-to-strut link arm (see Chapter 10 Section 4).
5 Unbolt and remove the short tie-bar between the front suspension subframe and underbody in order to gain access to the sensor.
6 The oil level sensor and wiring are fitted with heat-resisting insulating material (see illustration). Cut the clip and move the material to one side.
7 Disconnect the wiring plug, and then unscrew the oil level sensor from the cylinder block (see illustrations).

Refitting

8 Refitting is a reversal of removal. Tighten the sensor, tie-rod and link arm to their specified torques.

24 Vacuum pump – removal, refitting and testing

Note: *The vacuum pump is bolted to the transmission end of the cylinder head; a new gasket will be required before refitting.*

Removal

1 Where applicable, remove the plastic trim cover from the top of the engine (see illustration).
2 If required to give better access to the vacuum pump, remove the air intake hose and brackets.
3 Release the retaining clip and disconnect the vacuum hoses from the pump (see illustration).
4 Slacken and remove the mounting bolts securing the pump to the end of the cylinder head, then remove the pump (see illustrations). Recover the gasket and discard, as a new one will be required for refitting.

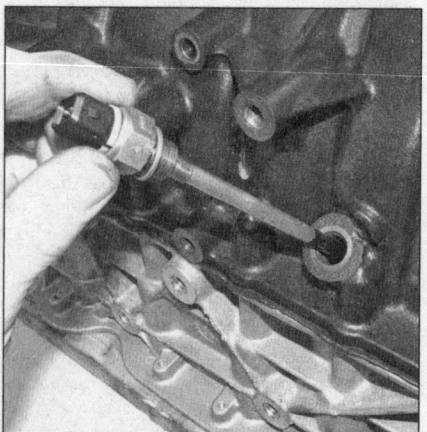

23.7b. . . then unscrew and remove the oil level sensor from the cylinder block

24.1 Remove the engine upper trim cover (where fitted)

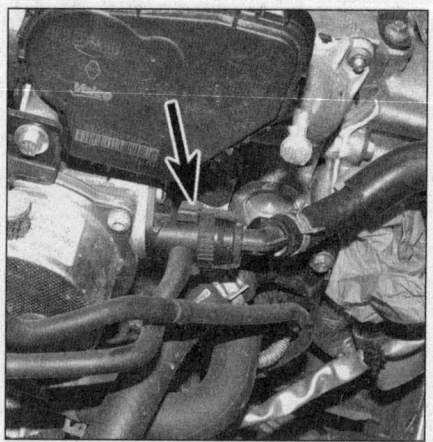

24.3 Disconnect the vacuum hose (arrowed)

Chapter 2 Part C 2.0 litre diesel engine

24.4a Undo the two retaining bolts (arrowed) – one out of view

24.4b Removing the vacuum pump

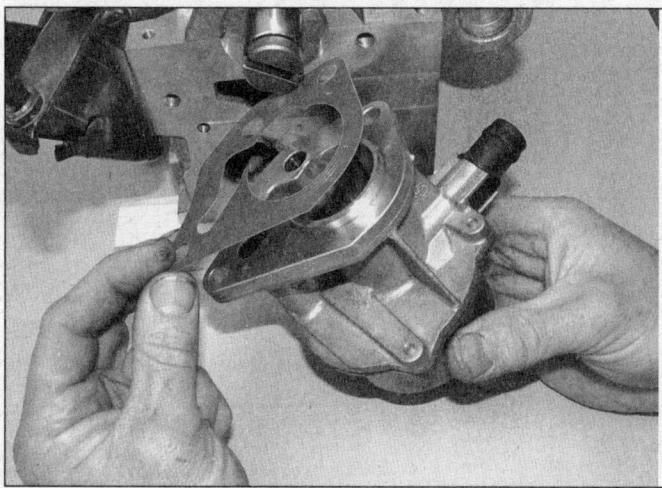

24.5 Fit a new gasket to the vacuum pump

Refitting

5 Ensure that the pump and cylinder head mating surfaces are clean and dry, and then fit the new gasket **(see illustration)**.

6 Manoeuvre the pump into position, aligning the drive gear with the slot in the end of the camshaft. Refit the pump mounting bolts and tighten securely.

7 Reconnect the vacuum hoses to the pump, making sure that the hoses are clipped into their relevant retaining clips.

8 If removed refit the air intake hoses and brackets (see Chapter 4B Section 7), then refit the engine trim cover.

9 On completion, test the operation of the brakes as follows.

Testing

10 The operation of the braking system can be checked using a vacuum gauge.

11 Disconnect the vacuum hoes from the pump and connect the gauge to the pump using a length of hose.

12 Start the engine and allow it to idle, and then measure the vacuum created by the pump. As a guide after one minute, a minimum of approx. 500 mm Hg should be recorded.

13 If the vacuum registered is significantly less than this, it is likely that the pump is faulty. However seek the advice of a specialist, before condemning the pump.

14 Overhaul of the vacuum pump may not be possible; check the availability of spares.

Notes

Chapter 2 Part D
General engine overhaul procedures

Contents

	Section		Section
Cylinder compression check..	3	General information - engine overhaul	1
Engine - removal and installation	7	Initial start-up and break-in after overhaul	9
Engine overhaul - disassembly sequence	8	Oil pressure check..	2
Engine rebuilding alternatives	5	Vacuum gauge diagnostic checks	4
Engine removal - methods and precautions..................	6		

Specifications

General

Engine designation
    2.0 litre petrol MR20DE
    2.0 litre petrol (direct injection) MR20DD
    2.5 litre petrol QR25DE
    2.0 litre diesel M9R

Capacity
    2.0 litre petrol .... 1,997 cc
    2.5 litre petrol .... 2,488 cc
    2.0 litre diesel .... 1,995 cc

Cylinder compression pressure
    2.0 litre (MR20DE) petrol
        Standard .... 1,390 kPa
        Minimum .... 1,140 kPa
    2.0 litre (MR20DD) petrol
        Standard .... 1,530 kPa
        Minimum .... 1,280 kPa
    2.5 litre petrol
        Standard .... 1.412 kPa
        Minimum .... 1.216 kPa
    2.0 litre diesel
        Standard .... 2,599 kPa
        Minimum .... 2,099 kPa

Maximum variation between cylinders
    Petrol models.. 100 kPa
    Diesel models .... 500 kPa

Oil pressure (minimum, warm engine)
  2.0 litre petrol
    Idle .... 80 kPa
    2000 rpm .... 450 kPa
  2.5 litre petrol
    Idle .... 98 kPa
    2000 rpm .... 294 kPa
  2.0 litre diesel
    Idle .... 88 kPa
    3000 rpm .... 402 kPa

Torque specifications Nm

Engine mounts
  2.0 litre petrol .... See Chapter 2B
  2.5 litre petrol .... See Chapter 2A
  2.0 litre diesel .... See Chapter 2C
  Spark plugs .... See Chapter 1
Glow plugs .... See Chapter 4B
Oil pressure sender unit
  Petrol engines 15
  Diesel engine 35

Refer to Chapters 2A, 2B and 2C for additional torque specifications.

1 General information - engine overhaul

Overhauling an engine is a difficult and time-consuming task. Special tools and knowledge are required. For these reasons, we recommend that engine overhaul is best left to a professional engine rebuilder. A competent engine rebuilder will handle the inspection of your old parts and offer advice concerning the reconditioning or replacement of the original engine.

Be aware that some engine builders can only rebuild the engine you bring them, which can take several weeks, while other rebuilders have rebuilt exchange engines in stock. If time is an issue, an exchange engine may be the best solution. If an exchange engine is fitted, check with your state registry authority as some insist the engine number on the new engine is included on your registration and insurance details.

An engine overhaul involves restoring the internal parts to the specifications of a new engine. During an overhaul, the piston rings are replaced and the cylinder walls are reconditioned (rebored and/or honed). If a rebore is done by an automotive machine shop, new oversize pistons will also be installed. The main bearings and connecting rod bearings are generally replaced with new ones and, if necessary, the crankshaft may be reground to restore the journals. Generally, the valves are serviced as well, since they're usually in less-than-perfect condition at this point. The end result should be a like-new engine that will give many trouble-free miles.

For those with engine overhaul experience and access to the necessary tools who wish to undertake the overhaul themselves, engine specifications have been included at the start of this chapter. Also included in this Chapter are general information and diagnostic testing procedures for determining the overall mechanical condition of your engine.

It is important to establish the condition of the cylinder block. Never purchase parts or have machine work done on other components until the block has been thoroughly inspected by a professional machine shop.

High mileage is not necessarily an indication that an overhaul is needed, while low mileage doesn't preclude the need for an overhaul. Frequency of servicing is probably the most important consideration. An engine that's had regular and frequent oil and filter changes, as well as other required maintenance, will most likely give many thousands of miles of reliable service. Conversely, a neglected engine may require an overhaul very early in its service life.

The following Sections have been written to help you determine whether your engine needs to be overhauled and how to remove and install it once you've determined it needs to be rebuilt. For information concerning in-vehicle engine repair, see Chapter 2A, Chapter 2B or Chapter 2C.

The Specifications included relate to engine overhaul. Refer to the previous Engine chapters for additional engine Specifications.

It's not always easy to determine when, or if, an engine should be completely overhauled, because a number of factors must be considered.

High mileage is not necessarily an indication that an overhaul is needed, while low mileage doesn't preclude the need for an overhaul. Frequency of servicing is probably the most important consideration. An engine that has had regular and frequent oil and filter changes, as well as other required maintenance, will most likely give many thousands of miles of reliable service. Conversely, a neglected engine may require an overhaul very early in its service life.

Excessive oil consumption is an indication that piston rings, valve seals and/or valve guides are in need of attention. Make sure that oil leaks aren't responsible before deciding that the rings and/or valve guides are bad. Perform a cylinder compression check to determine the extent of the work required (see Section 3).

Check the oil pressure with a gauge installed in place of the oil pressure sending unit and compare it to this chapter's Specifications (see Section 2). If it's extremely low, the bearings and/or oil pump are probably worn out.

Loss of power, rough running, knocking or metallic engine noises, excessive valve train noise and high fuel consumption rates may also point to the need for an overhaul, especially if they're all present at the same time. If a complete tune-up doesn't remedy the situation, major mechanical work is the only solution.

Note: *Critical cooling system components such as the hoses, drivebelts, thermostat and water pump should be replaced with new parts when an engine is overhauled. The radiator should be checked carefully to ensure that it isn't clogged or leaking (see Chapter 3 Section 6). If you purchase a rebuilt engine or short block, some rebuilders will not warranty their engines unless the radiator has been professionally flushed.*

2 Oil pressure check

1 Low engine oil pressure can be a sign of an engine in need of rebuilding. A low oil pressure indicator (often called an "idiot light") is not a test of the oiling system. Such indicators only come on when the oil pressure is dangerously low. Even a factory oil pressure gauge in the instrument panel is only a rela-

Chapter 2 Part D General engine overhaul procedures   2D-3

2.2a The oil pressure sensor is located on the firewall side of the engine, just behind the timing chain cover (as seen from the right side wheel well) on petrol models

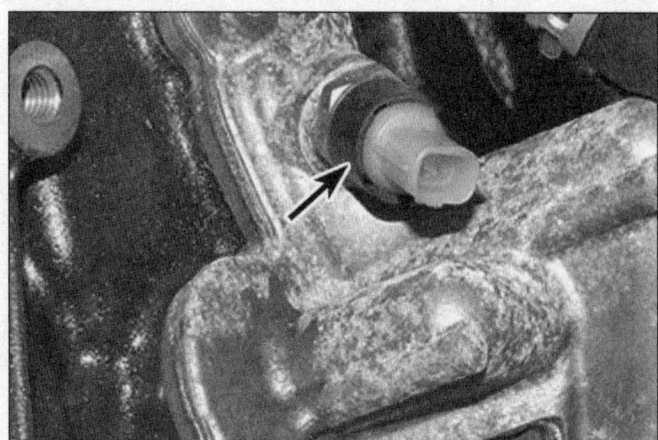

2.2b The oil pressure sensor is located on the front of the engine, in the top of the oil filter housing on diesel models

3.2a Use a compression gauge with a threaded fitting for the spark plug hole, not the type that requires hand pressure to maintain the seal

tive indication, although much better for driver information than a warning light. A better test is with a mechanical (not electrical) oil pressure gauge.

2   The oil pressure sending unit is threaded into an adapter on the right end of the engine, firewall side, just behind the timing chain cover **(see illustration)**.

3   Unscrew and remove the oil pressure sending unit and then screw in the hose for your oil pressure gauge. If necessary, install an adapter fitting. Use Teflon tape or thread sealant on the threads of the adapter and/or the fitting on the end of your gauge's hose.

4   Connect an accurate tachometer to the engine, according to the tachometer manufacturer's instructions.

5   Check the oil pressure with the engine running (normal operating temperature) at the specified engine speed, and compare it to Specifications. If it's extremely low, the bearings and/or oil pump are probably worn out.

3   Cylinder compression check

1   A compression check will tell you what mechanical condition the upper end of your engine (pistons, rings, valves, head gaskets) is in. Specifically, it can tell you if the compression is down due to leakage caused by worn piston rings, defective valves and seats or a blown head gasket.

Note: *The engine should be at normal operating temperature and the battery must be fully charged for this check.*

2   On petrol models, proceed as follows:
  a *Begin by cleaning the area around the spark plugs before you remove them (compressed air should be used, if available). The idea is to prevent dirt from getting into the cylinders as the compression check is being done.*
  b *Remove the ignition coil assemblies (see Chapter 5 Section 7). Also disable the fuel pump by removing the fuel pump fuse (see Chapter 4A Section 3).*
  c *Remove all of the spark plugs (see Chapter 1 Section 26).*
  d *Block the throttle wide open.*
  e *Install a compression gauge in the spark plug hole* **(see illustration)**.

3   On diesel models, proceed as follows:
  a *Begin by cleaning the area around the glow plugs before you remove them (compressed air should be used, if available). The idea is to prevent dirt from getting into the cylinders as the compression check is being done.*
  b *Disconnect the wiring from each fuel injector to isolate the fuel injection system.*
  c *Remove the glow plugs (see Chapter 5 Section 9).*

4   Crank the engine over at least seven compression strokes and watch the gauge. The compression should build up quickly in a healthy engine. Low compression on the first stroke, followed by gradually increasing pressure on successive strokes, indicates worn

3.4a Typical remote starter switch (A) and alligator clips (B)

Chapter 2 Part D General engine overhaul procedures

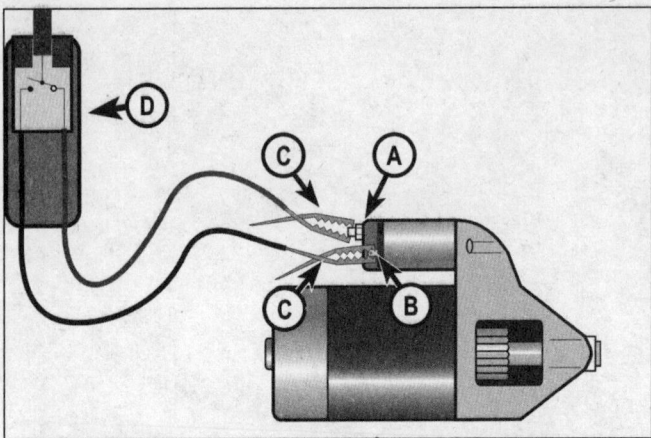

3.4b Illustration showing how to connect the remote starter switch. Connect one alligator clip to the large terminal on the starter motor that goes to the battery (A). Connect the second terminal to the solenoid terminal after disconnecting the wire from the solenoid (B). Ensure the alligator clips (C) are not touching. When the switch (D) is pressed, the starter motor will operate

3.4c Checking the engine compression using the remote starter to crank the engine

piston rings. A low compression reading on the first stroke, which doesn't build up during successive strokes, indicates leaking valves or a blown head gasket (a cracked head could also be the cause). Deposits on the undersides of the valve heads can also cause low compression. Record the highest gauge reading obtained.

5 Repeat the procedure for the remaining cylinders and compare the results to Specifications.

6 If the readings are below normal, add some engine oil (about three squirts from a plunger-type oil can) to each cylinder, through the spark plug hole, and repeat the test.

7 If the compression increases after the oil is added, the piston rings are definitely worn. If the compression doesn't increase significantly, the leakage is occurring at the valves or head gasket. Leakage past the valves may be caused by burned valve seats and/or faces or warped, cracked or bent valves.

8 If two adjacent cylinders have equally low compression, there's a strong possibility the head gasket between them is blown. The appearance of coolant in the combustion chambers or the crankcase would verify this condition.

9 If one cylinder is about 20-percent lower than the others, and the engine has a slightly rough idle, a worn exhaust lobe on the camshaft could be the cause.

10 If the compression is unusually high, the combustion chambers are probably coated with carbon deposits. If that's the case, the cylinder heads should be removed and decarbonised.

11 If compression is way down or varies greatly between cylinders, it would be a good idea to have a leak-down test performed by an automotive repair shop. This test will pinpoint exactly where the leakage is occurring and how severe it is.

4 Vacuum gauge diagnostic checks

Note: *These checks are applicable to petrol models.*

1 A vacuum gauge provides inexpensive but valuable information about what is going on in the engine. You can check for worn rings or cylinder walls, leaking head or intake manifold gaskets, incorrect carburetor adjustments, restricted exhaust, stuck or burned valves, weak valve springs, improper ignition or valve timing and ignition problems.

2 Unfortunately, vacuum gauge readings are easy to misinterpret, so they should be used in conjunction with other tests to confirm the diagnosis.

3 Both the absolute readings and the rate of needle movement are important for accurate interpretation. Most gauges measure vacuum in inches of mercury (in-Hg). The following references to vacuum assume the diagnosis is being performed at sea level. As elevation increases (or atmospheric pressure decreases), the reading will decrease. For every 300 metres increase in elevation above approximately 600 metres, the gauge readings will decrease about 25-mm of mercury.

4 Connect the vacuum gauge directly to the intake manifold vacuum, not to ported (throttle body) vacuum **(see illustration)**. Some models are equipped with a vacuum fitting built into the brake booster vacuum hose grommet at the brake booster. Other models are equipped with a vacuum hose fitting on the intake manifold. Use a T-fitting to access the vacuum signal. Be sure no hoses are left disconnected during the test or false readings will result.

5 Before you begin the test, allow the engine to warm up completely. Block the wheels and set the parking brake. With the transaxle in Park, start the engine and allow it to run at normal idle speed.

Warning: *Keep your hands and the vacuum gauge clear of the fans.*

6 Read the vacuum gauge; an average, healthy engine should normally produce about 432-559 mm-Hg with a fairly steady needle **(see illustration)**. Refer to the following vacuum gauge readings and what they indicate about the engine's condition:

7 A low, steady reading usually indicates a leaking gasket between the intake manifold and cylinder head(s) or throttle body, a leaky vacuum hose, late ignition timing or incorrect camshaft timing. Check ignition timing with a timing light and eliminate all other possible causes, utilizing the tests provided in this Chapter before you remove the timing chain cover to check the timing marks.

8 If the reading is three to eight inches below normal and it fluctuates at that low reading, suspect an intake manifold gasket leak at an intake port or a faulty fuel injector.

4.4 A simple vacuum gauge can be handy in diagnosing engine condition and performance - be sure to connect it to intake manifold vacuum (not ported vacuum)

Chapter 2 Part D General engine overhaul procedures

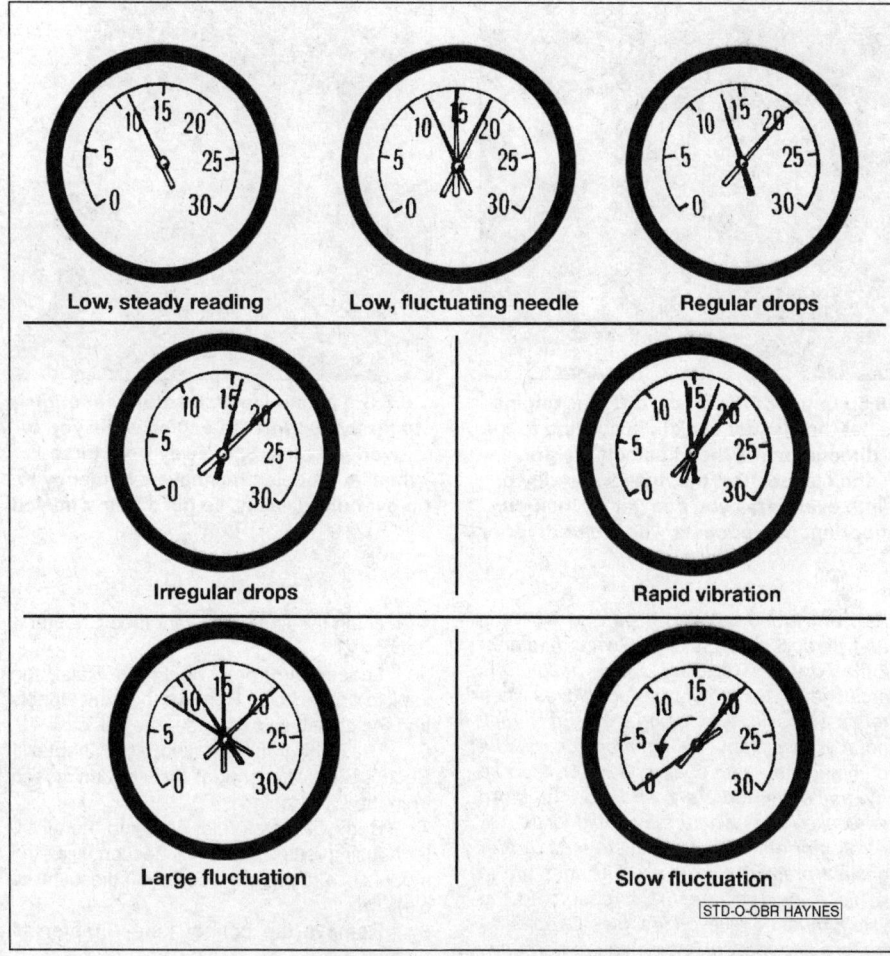

4.6 Typical vacuum gauge readings

9   If the needle has regular drops of about two-to-four inches at a steady rate, the valves are probably leaking. Perform a compression check or leak-down test to confirm this.

10   An irregular drop or down-flick of the needle can be caused by a sticking valve or an ignition misfire. Perform a compression check or leak-down test and read the spark plugs.

11   A rapid vibration of about four in-Hg vibration at idle combined with exhaust smoke indicates worn valve guides. Perform a leak-down test to confirm this. If the rapid vibration occurs with an increase in engine speed, check for a leaking intake manifold gasket or head gasket, weak valve springs, burned valves or ignition misfire.

12   A slight fluctuation, say one inch up and down, may mean ignition problems. Check all the usual tune-up items and, if necessary, run the engine on an ignition analyser.

13   If there is a large fluctuation, perform a compression or leak-down test to look for a weak or dead cylinder or a blown head gasket.

14   If the needle moves slowly through a wide range, check for a clogged PCV system, incorrect idle fuel mixture, throttle body or intake manifold gasket leaks.

15   Check for a slow return after revving the engine by quickly snapping the throttle open until the engine reaches about 2,500 rpm and let it shut. Normally the reading should drop to near zero, rise above normal idle reading (about 127 mm-Hg over) and then return to the previous idle reading. If the vacuum returns slowly and doesn't peak when the throttle is snapped shut, the rings may be worn. If there is a long delay, look for a restricted exhaust system (often the muffler or catalytic converter). An easy way to check this is to temporarily disconnect the exhaust ahead of the suspected part and redo the test.

5   Engine rebuilding alternatives

1   The do-it-yourselfer is faced with a number of options when purchasing a rebuilt engine. The major considerations are cost, warranty, parts availability and the time required for the rebuilder to complete the project. The decision to replace the engine block, piston/connecting rod assemblies and crankshaft depends on the final inspection results of your engine. Only then can you make a cost effective decision whether to have your engine overhauled or simply purchase an exchange engine for your vehicle.

2   Some of the rebuilding alternatives include:

3   Individual parts - If the inspection procedures reveal that the engine block and most engine components are in reusable condition, purchasing individual parts and having a rebuilder rebuild your engine may be the most economical alternative. The block, crankshaft and piston/connecting rod assemblies should all be inspected carefully by a machine shop first.

4   Short block - A short block consists of an engine block with a crankshaft and piston/connecting rod assemblies already installed. All new bearings are incorporated and all clearances will be correct. The existing camshafts, valve train components, cylinder head and external parts can be bolted to the short block with little or no machine shop work necessary.

5   Long block - A long block consists of a short block plus an oil pump, oil pan, cylinder head, valve cover, camshaft and valve train components, timing sprockets and chain or gears and timing cover. All components are installed with new bearings, seals and gaskets incorporated throughout. The installation of manifolds and external parts is all that's necessary.

6   Low mileage used engines - Some companies now offer low mileage used engines which is a very cost effective way to get your vehicle up and running again. These engines often come from vehicles which have been in totalled in accidents or come from other countries which have a higher vehicle turn over rate. A low mileage used engine also usually has a similar warranty like the newly remanufactured engines.

7   Give careful thought to which alternative is best for you and discuss the situation with local automotive machine shops, auto parts dealers and experienced rebuilders before ordering or purchasing replacement parts.

6   Engine removal - methods and precautions

1   If you've decided that an engine must be removed for overhaul or major repair work, several preliminary steps should be taken. Read all removal and installation procedures carefully prior to committing to this job.

2   Locating a suitable place to work is extremely important. Adequate work space, along with storage space for the vehicle, will be needed. If a shop or garage isn't available, at the very least a flat, level, clean work surface made of concrete or asphalt is required.

3   These engines are removed by lowering the engine to the floor, along with the transaxle, and then raising the vehicle sufficiently to slide the assembly out; this will require a vehicle hoist.

4   An engine hoist will also be necessary. Make sure the hoist is rated in excess of the

2D-6 Chapter 2 Part D General engine overhaul procedures

6.5a After tightly wrapping water-vulnerable components, use a spray cleaner on everything, with particular concentration on the greasiest areas, usually around the valve cover and lower edges of the block. If one Section dries out, apply more cleaner

6.5b Depending on how dirty the engine is, let the cleaner soak in according to the directions and then hose off the grime and cleaner. Get the rinse water down into every area you can get at; then dry important components with a hair dryer or paper towels

6.7 Get an engine stand sturdy enough to firmly support the engine while you're working on it. Stay away from three-wheeled models; they have a tendency to tip over more easily, so get a four-wheeled unit

combined weight of the engine and transaxle. Safety is of primary importance, considering the potential hazards involved in removing the engine from the vehicle.

5 Cleaning the engine compartment and engine before beginning the removal procedure will help keep tools clean and organized **(see illustrations)**.

6 If you're a novice at engine removal, get at least one helper. One person cannot easily do all the things you need to do to remove a big heavy engine and transaxle assembly from the engine compartment. Also helpful is to seek advice and assistance from someone who's experienced in engine removal.

7 Plan the operation ahead of time. Arrange for or obtain all of the tools and equipment you'll need prior to beginning the job **(see illustration)**. Some of the equipment necessary to perform engine removal and installation safely and with relative ease are (in addition to a vehicle hoist and an engine hoist) a heavy duty floor jack (preferably fitted with a transmission jack head adaptor), complete sets of wrenches and sockets as described in the front of this manual, wooden blocks, plenty of rags and cleaning solvent for mopping up spilled oil, coolant and gasoline.

8 Plan for the vehicle to be out of use for quite a while. A machine shop can do the work that is beyond the scope of the home mechanic. Machine shops often have a busy schedule, so before removing the engine, consult the shop for an estimate of how long it will take to rebuild or repair the components that may need work.

7 Engine - removal and installation

Warning: *Fuel is extremely flammable, so take extra precautions when you work on any part of the fuel system. Don't smoke or allow open flames or bare light bulbs near the work area, and don't work in a garage where a gas-type appliance (such as a water heater or clothes dryer) is present. Since gasoline is carcinogenic, wear fuel-resistant gloves when there's a possibility of being exposed to fuel, and, if you spill any fuel on your skin, rinse it off immediately with soap and water. Mop up any spills immediately and do not store fuel-soaked rags where they could ignite. On petrol models, the fuel system is under constant pressure, so, if any fuel lines are to be disconnected, the fuel pressure in the system must be relieved first (see Chapter 4A for more information). When you perform any kind of work on the fuel system, wear safety glasses and have a Class B type fire extinguisher on hand.*

Warning: *The engine must be completely cool before beginning this procedure.*

Note: *Engine removal on these vehicles is a difficult job, especially for a do-it-yourselfer working at home. The manufacturer states that the engine and transaxle have to be removed as a unit from the bottom of the vehicle, not the top. With a floor jack and jackstands, it can't be raised high enough or supported safely enough for the engine/transaxle to slide out from underneath. The manufacturer recommends that removal of the engine/transaxle only be performed with a frame-contact type hoist.*

Note: *During this procedure you'll have to adjust the height of the vehicle with the vehicle hoist to perform certain operations.*

Removal

1 Park the car on a vehicle hoist, then raise the hoist arms to contact the jacking points on each side of the vehicle, but don't raise the vehicle yet.

2 Remove the engine cover, if equipped.

3 Relieve the fuel system pressure (see Chapter 4A Section 3), then remove the battery and battery tray (see Chapter 5 Section 5).

4 Drain the engine coolant (see Chapter 1 Section 27).

5 Loosen the front wheel nuts. Raise the vehicle on the hoist. Remove the front wheels and the splash shields under the vehicle.

6 Drain the transaxle fluid (see Chapter 1 Section 30). Disconnect the coolant hoses from the CVT cooler.

7 Remove the air inlet duct and the air filter housing (see Chapter 4A Section 9 - petrol models or Chapter 4B Section 6 - diesel models).

8 Remove the bonnet (see Chapter 11 Section 9).

9 Remove the cowl cover and the lower cowl panel (see Chapter 11 Section 25).

10 Remove the inner splash shields from each front wheel arch.

11 Remove the driveshafts (see Chapter 8 Section 7).

12 Disconnect the heater and radiator hoses (see Chapter 3 Section 6).

13 Disconnect the fuel supply and, where fitted, return hoses (see Chapter 4A Section 5 - petrol engines, or Chapter 4B Section 8 - diesel engines).

7.10a Release the plastic securing clips ...

Chapter 2 Part D General engine overhaul procedures

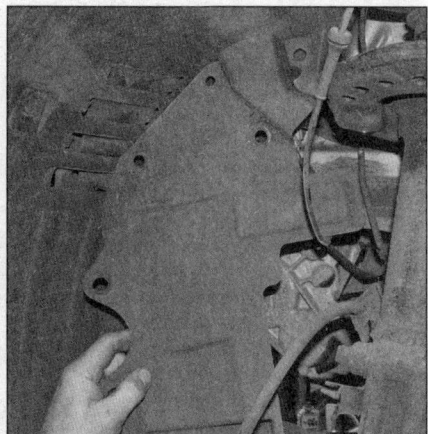

7.10b ... and remove the inner splash shield

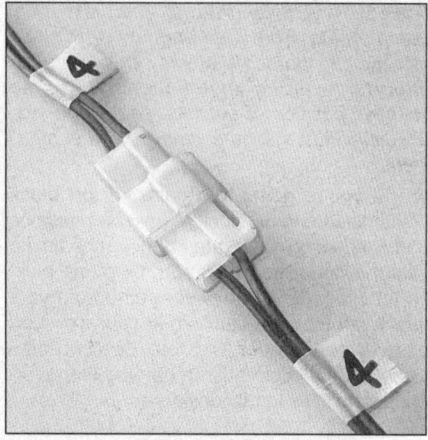

7.21 Label both ends of each wire or vacuum connection before disconnecting them

14 Disconnect the shift cable, wiring and any ground straps from the transaxle (see Chapter 7A Section 2 - manual transaxle, or Chapter 7B Section 5 - automatic transaxle).
15 Disconnect all vacuum hoses between the engine and chassis.
16 On petrol models, disconnect the EVAP hose from the purge control solenoid valve (see Chapter 6 Section 19).
17 Unbolt the air conditioning compressor (see Chapter 3 Section 11) and secure it out of the way without disconnecting the refrigerant lines.
18 Disconnect the ground straps from the engine, transaxle and alternator, if equipped.
19 Disconnect and remove the Intelligent Power Distribution Module (IPDM) (see Chapter 12A Section 3), and, on automatic transaxle models, the Transaxle Control Module (TCM) (see Chapter 7B Section 8). Also remove the mounting brackets.
20 Disconnect the wiring from the PCM (see Chapter 6 Section 15). Remove the PCM and the bracket.
21 Disconnect the engine harness wiring, then remove it along with its bracket. Label and disconnect all interfering wiring **(see illustration)**. Make sure that nothing will prevent the engine from being lowered.
22 Remove the front portion of the exhaust system.
23 Separate the steering shaft from the steering gear (see Chapter 10 Section 17).
24 Remove the drivebelt (see Chapter 1 Section 12).
25 Remove the alternator (see Chapter 5 Section 11).
26 Remove the starter (see Chapter 5 Section 12).
27 Remove the cooling fan assembly (see Chapter 3 Section 5).
28 Remove the rear (lower) torque rod (see Chapter 2A Section 15 - 2.5 litre petrol models, Chapter 2B Section 17 - 2.0 litre petrol models or Chapter 2C Section 20 - 2.0 litre diesel models).
29 On AWD models, remove the propeller shaft (see Chapter 8 Section 13).

30 Remove the transaxle joint bolts that penetrate the oil pan on the lower rear side of the engine.
31 Remove the torque converter nuts (see Chapter 7B Section 11).
32 Attach an engine hoist to the engine lifting brackets and raise it just enough to take weight off of the engine mounts. If no brackets are present, check with a Nissan dealer parts department to see if you can order them. Alternatively, attach the lifting chains or straps to substantial parts of the engine, such as threaded holes in the cylinder head and transaxle. Use washers under the bolt heads to prevent pull-through. The chains must be attached so they don't apply force to components that could be damaged.

Warning: *Don't put any part of your body under the engine or transaxle when it's supported only by a hoist or other lifting device.*

33 Take up the slack in the chain until there is slight tension on the hoist. Make sure it's connected so that the engine/transaxle is balanced.

Note: *The chain must be long enough to allow the hoist to lower the engine/transaxle assembly to the ground without letting the hoist arm contact the vehicle.*

34 Remove the front subframe **(see illustration)** (see Chapter 10 Section 18).
35 Remove the right-side torque rod and engine mount, and the transaxle mount (see Chapter 2A Section 15 - 2.5 litre petrol models, Chapter 2B Section 17 - 2.0 litre petrol models or Chapter 2C Section 20 - 2.0 litre diesel models).
36 Check that there is nothing connecting the engine/transaxle to the vehicle. Label and disconnect anything remaining.
37 Lower the engine/transaxle assembly slowly to the floor.
38 Disconnect the engine hoist after blocking the engine so it can't tip.
39 Raise the vehicle on the hoist.
40 Reconnect the chain of the engine hoist to the engine/transaxle to support it. The assembly can now be moved from under the vehicle to another work area.
41 Separate the transaxle from the engine. Be careful to support the engine and the transaxle securely so they can't fall.
42 Mount the engine on an engine stand using the hoist.

Installation

43 Installation is the reverse of removal noting these points:

a *Check the engine and transaxle mounts. If they're worn or damaged, replace them.*
b *Attach the transaxle to the engine (see Chapter 7A Section 5) - manual transaxle, or (see Chapter 7B Section 11) - automatic transaxle.*
c *Tighten the subframe mounting bolts to the torque listed in the Suspension and Steering Systems Chapter (see Chapter 10).*
d *Tighten the wheel nuts to the specified torque (see Chapter 1).*
e *Tighten the driveshaft/hub nut to the specified torque (see Chapter 8).*
f *Tighten the steering and suspension fasteners to the torque values listed in the Suspension and Steering Systems Chapter (see Chapter 10).*
g *Refill the engine coolant, oil, power steering fluid, clutch fluid and transaxle fluid (see Chapter 1).*
h *Recheck all fluid levels (see Chapter 1).*

7.34 Front subframe lowered from the vehicle

8 Engine overhaul - disassembly sequence

1 It's much easier to remove the external components if it's mounted on a portable engine stand. A stand can often be rented quite cheaply from an equipment rental yard. Before the engine is mounted on a stand, the flywheel/driveplate should be removed from the engine.
2 If a stand isn't available, it's possible to remove the external engine components with it blocked up on the floor. Be extra careful not to tip or drop the engine when working without a stand.
3 If you're going to obtain a rebuilt engine, all external components must come off first, to be transferred to the replacement engine. These components include:
- *Clutch system - manual transaxle models*
- *Flywheel/driveplate*
- *Ignition coils and wiring harnesses*
- *Emissions-related components*
- *Engine mounts and mount brackets*
- *Intake/exhaust manifolds*
- *Fuel injection components*
- *Oil filter and oil cooler*
- *Spark plugs*
- *Thermostat and housing assembly*
- *Glow plugs*
- *Water pump*

Note: *When removing the external components from the engine, pay close attention to details that may be helpful or important during installation. Note the installed position of gaskets, seals, spacers, pins, brackets, washers, bolts and other small items.*

4 If you're going to obtain a short block (assembled engine block, crankshaft, pistons and connecting rods), then remove the timing chain, cylinder head, oil pan, oil pump pick-up tube, oil pump and water pump from your engine so that you can turn in your old short block to the rebuilder as a core. See Section 5 for additional information regarding the different possibilities to be considered.

9 Initial start-up and break-in after overhaul

Warning: *Have a fire extinguisher handy when starting the engine for the first time.*
1 Once the engine has been installed in the vehicle, double-check the engine oil and coolant levels.
2 With the spark plugs or glow plugs out of the engine and the and the fuel pump disabled (see Chapter 4A, Section 3), crank the engine until oil pressure registers on the gauge or the light goes out.
3 Install the spark plugs and ignition coils or glow plugs. Reinstall the fuel pump fuse and if disconnected, reconnect the wiring to the fuel injectors.
4 Start the engine. It may take a few moments for the fuel system to build up pressure, but the engine should start without a great deal of effort.
5 After the engine starts, it should be allowed to warm up to normal operating temperature. While the engine is warming up, make a thorough check for fuel, oil and coolant leaks.
6 Shut the engine off and recheck the engine oil and coolant levels.
7 Drive the vehicle to an area with minimum traffic, accelerate from 40 to 80 Km/h, then allow the vehicle to slow to 20 km/h with the throttle closed. Repeat the procedure 10 or 12 times. This will load the piston rings and cause them to seat properly against the cylinder walls. Check again for oil and coolant leaks.
8 Drive the vehicle gently for the first 1,000 km (no sustained high speeds) and keep a constant check on the oil level. It is not unusual for an engine to use oil during the break-in period.
9 At approximately 1,000 km, change the oil and filter.
10 For the next few hundred kilometres, drive the vehicle normally. Do not pamper it or abuse it.
11 After 5,000 km, change the oil and filter again and consider the engine broken in.

Chapter 3
Cooling, heating and air conditioning systems

Contents

	Section		Section
Air conditioning and heating system - check and maintenance	3	Heater and air conditioning control assembly - removal and installation	9
Air conditioning compressor - removal and installation	11	Heater core - removal and installation	10
Blower motor and resistor - removal and installation	8	Radiator and coolant reservoir - removal and installation	6
Cooling system check	See Chapter 1	Thermostat and water control valve - replacement	4
Cooling system servicing	See Chapter 1	Troubleshooting	2
Drivebelt check and replacement	See Chapter 1	Water pump – removal, inspection and installation	7
Engine cooling fans and resistor - removal and installation	5	Welch plugs - replacement	12
General information	1		

Specifications

General

Radiator cap pressure rating	Refer to pressure specification on cap
Cooling system capacity	See Chapter 1
Refrigerant type	R-134a
Thermostat opening temperature	
Petrol engines	80.5 to 83.5 degrees C
Diesel engine	86 to 89 degrees C

Torque specifications

	Nm
Thermostat water inlet bolts	
2.0 litre petrol engine	17
2.5 litre petrol engine	22
Diesel model	11
Water outlet housing	25
Cooling fan shroud mounting bolts	5
Cooling fan blade assembly-to-motor shaft nut	4
Cooling fan motor-to-shroud mounting bolts	4
Water pump	
Mounting bolts	25
Pulley-to-water pump	
Qashqai	10
Diesel engine	21
Housing-to-block bolts - 2.5 litre petrol engine	22
Air conditioning compressor mounting bolts	
Except T32 X-Trail	25
T32 X-Trail	31

2.2 The cooling system pressure tester is connected in place of the pressure cap, then pumped up to pressurize the system

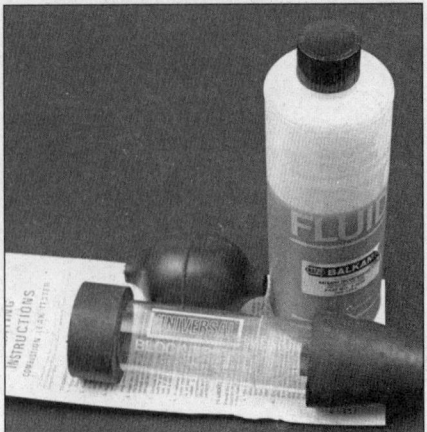

2.5a The combustion leak detector consists of a bulb, syringe and test fluid

2.5b Place the tester over the cooling system filler neck and use the bulb to draw a sample into the tester

1 General information

Warning: *Do not allow coolant to come in contact with your skin or painted surfaces of the vehicle. Rinse off spills immediately with plenty of water. Coolant is highly toxic if ingested. Never leave coolant lying around in an open container or in puddles on the floor; children and pets are attracted by it's sweet smell and may drink it. Check with local authorities about disposing of used coolant. Many communities have collection centres which will see that coolant is disposed of safely. Never dump used coolant on the ground or pour it into drains.*

Warning: *To prevent scalding, use caution when releasing the radiator cap if the engine is warm. Squeeze the upper radiator hose. If resistance is felt, the system is pressurised and the cap should not be removed until the radiator hose can easily be squeezed together. Escaping steam and scalding liquid could cause serious injury.*

Note: *If the engine has overheated allow, the engine to cool for at least 30 minutes and fill the system with coolant while the engine is running to avoid cracking the cylinder heads or block.*

Engine cooling system

1 All modern vehicles employ a pressurized engine cooling system with thermostatically controlled coolant circulation. The cooling system consists of a radiator, an expansion tank or coolant reservoir, a pressure cap (located on the expansion tank or radiator), a thermostat, a water control valve on some models, a cooling fan, and a water pump.

2 The water pump circulates coolant through the engine. The coolant flows around each cylinder and around the intake and exhaust ports, near the spark plug areas and in close proximity to the exhaust valve guides.

3 A thermostat controls engine coolant temperature. During warm up, the closed thermostat prevents coolant from circulating through the radiator. As the engine nears normal operating temperature, the thermostat opens and allows hot coolant to travel through the radiator, where it's cooled before returning to the engine.

Heating system

4 The heating system consists of a blower fan and heater core located in a housing under the dash, the hoses connecting the heater core to the engine cooling system and the heater/air conditioning control head on the dashboard. Hot engine coolant is circulated through the heater core. When the heater mode is activated, a flap door in the housing opens to expose the heater core to the passenger compartment through air ducts. A fan switch on the control head activates the blower motor, which forces air through the core, heating the air.

Air conditioning system

5 The air conditioning system consists of a condenser mounted in front of the radiator, an evaporator mounted adjacent to the heater core, a compressor mounted on the engine, a receiver-drier or accumulator and the plumbing connecting all of the above components.

6 A blower fan forces the warmer air of the passenger compartment through the evaporator core (sort of a radiator-in-reverse), transferring the heat from the air to the refrigerant. The liquid refrigerant boils off into low pressure vapour, taking the heat with it when it leaves the evaporator.

2 Troubleshooting

Coolant leaks

1 A coolant leak can develop anywhere in the cooling system, but the most common causes are:

- a A loose or weak hose clamp
- b A defective hose
- c A faulty pressure cap
- d A damaged radiator
- e A bad heater core
- f A faulty water pump
- g A leaking gasket at any joint that carries coolant

2 Coolant leaks aren't always easy to find. Sometimes they can only be detected when the cooling system is under pressure. Here's where a cooling system pressure tester comes in handy. After the engine has cooled completely, the tester is attached in place of the pressure cap, then pumped up to the pressure value equal to that of the pressure cap rating **(see illustration)**. Now, leaks that only exist when the engine is fully warmed up will become apparent. The tester can be left connected to locate a nagging slow leak.

Coolant level drops, but no external leaks

3 If you find it necessary to keep adding coolant, but there are no external leaks, the probable causes include:

- a A blown head gasket
- b A leaking intake manifold gasket (only on engines that have coolant passages in the manifold)
- c A cracked cylinder head or cylinder block

4 Any of the above problems will also usually result in contamination of the engine oil, which will cause it to take on a milkshake-like appearance. A bad head gasket or cracked head or block can also result in engine oil contaminating the cooling system.

5 Combustion leak detectors (also known as block testers) are available at most auto parts stores. These work by detecting exhaust gases in the cooling system, which indicates a compression leak from a cylinder into the coolant. The tester consists of a large bulb-type syringe and bottle of test fluid **(see illustration)**. A measured amount of the fluid is added to the syringe. The syringe is placed over the cooling system filler neck and, with the engine running, the bulb is squeezed and a sample of the gases present in the cooling

Chapter 3 Cooling, heating and air conditioning systems

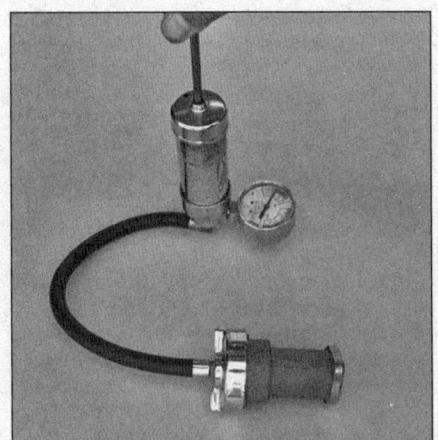

2.8 Checking the cooling system pressure cap with a cooling system pressure tester

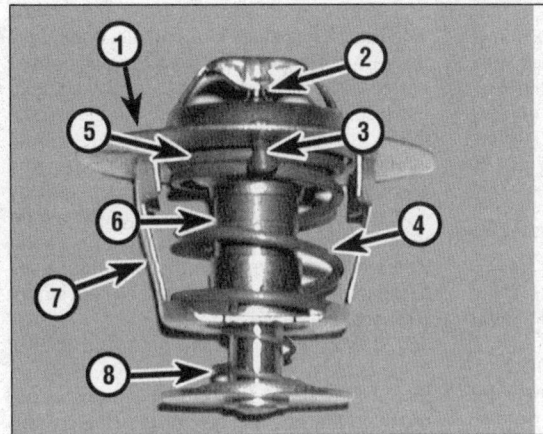

2.10 Typical thermostat:

1 Flange
2 Piston
3 Jiggle valve
4 Main coil spring
5 Valve seat
6 Valve
7 Frame
8 Secondary coil spring

system are drawn up through the test fluid **(see illustration)**. If any combustion gases are present in the sample taken, the test fluid will change colour.

6 If the test indicates combustion gas is present in the cooling system, you can be sure that the engine has a blown head gasket or a crack in the cylinder head or block, and will require disassembly to repair.

Pressure cap

Warning: *Wait until the engine is completely cool before beginning this check.*

7 The cooling system is sealed by a spring-loaded cap, which raises the boiling point of the coolant. If the cap's seal or spring are worn out, the coolant can boil and escape past the cap. With the engine completely cool, remove the cap and check the seal; if it's cracked, hardened or deteriorated in any way, replace it with a new one.

8 Even if the seal is good, the spring might not be; this can be checked with a cooling system pressure tester **(see illustration)**. If the cap can't hold a pressure within specified pressure (which is marked on the cap), replace it with a new one.

9 The cap is also equipped with a vacuum relief spring. When the engine cools off, a vacuum is created in the cooling system. The vacuum relief spring allows air back into the system, which will equalize the pressure and prevent damage to the radiator (the radiator tanks could collapse if the vacuum is great enough). If, after turning the engine off and allowing it to cool down you notice any of the cooling system hoses collapsing, replace the pressure cap with a new one.

Thermostat

10 Before assuming the thermostat or water control valve **(see illustration)** is responsible for a cooling system problem, check the coolant level (see Chapter 1 Section 4), drivebelt tension (see Chapter 1 Section 12) and temperature gauge (or light) operation.

11 If the engine takes a long time to warm up (as indicated by the temperature gauge or heater operation), the thermostat is probably stuck open. Replace the thermostat or water control valve with a new one.

12 If the engine runs hot or overheats, a thorough test of the thermostat should be performed.

13 Definitive testing of the thermostat or water control valve can only be made when it is removed from the vehicle. If the thermostat is stuck in the open position at room temperature, it is faulty and must be replaced.

Caution: *Do not drive the vehicle without a thermostat. The computer may stay in open loop and emissions and fuel economy will suffer.*

14 To test a thermostat, suspend the (closed) thermostat on a length of string or wire in a pot of cold water.

15 Heat the water on a stove while observing thermostat. The thermostat should fully open before the water boils.

16 If the thermostat doesn't open and close as specified, or sticks in any position, replace it.

Cooling fan

17 If the engine is overheating and the cooling fan is not coming on when the engine temperature rises to an excessive level, unplug the fan motor electrical connector(s) and connect the motor directly to the battery with fused jumper wires. If the fan motor doesn't come on, replace the motor.

18 If the radiator fan motor is okay, but it isn't coming on when the engine gets hot, the fan relay might be defective. A relay is used to control a circuit by turning it on and off in response to a control decision by the Powertrain Control Module (PCM). These control circuits are fairly complex, and checking them should be left to a qualified automotive technician. Sometimes, the control system can be fixed by simply identifying and replacing a bad relay.

19 Locate the fan relays in the engine compartment fuse/relay box.

20 Test the relay (see Chapter 12A Section 3).

21 If the relay is okay, check all wiring and connections to the fan motor. Refer to the wiring diagrams in Chapter 12A Section 22. If no obvious problems are found, the problem could be the Engine Coolant Temperature (ECT) sensor or the Powertrain Control Module (PCM). Have the cooling fan system and circuit diagnosed by a dealer service department or repair shop with the proper diagnostic equipment.

Note: *These models are equipped with a cooling fan motor resistor. Have the resistor checked if the fan motor does not respond to the speed variations signalled by the PCM.*

Water pump

22 A failure in the water pump can cause serious engine damage due to overheating.

Drivebelt-driven water pump

23 There are two ways to check the operation of the water pump while it's installed on the engine. If the pump is found to be defective, it should be replaced with a new or rebuilt unit.

24 Water pumps are equipped with weep (or vent) holes **(see illustration)**. If a failure occurs in the pump seal, coolant will leak from the hole.

2.24 The water pump weep hole is generally located on the underside of the pump

25 If the water pump shaft bearings fail, there may be a howling sound at the pump while it's running. Shaft wear can be felt with the drivebelt removed if the water pump pulley is rocked up and down (with the engine off). Don't mistake drivebelt slippage, which causes a squealing sound, for water pump bearing failure.

Timing chain or timing belt-driven water pump

26 Water pumps driven by the timing chain or timing belt are located underneath the timing chain or timing belt cover.

27 Checking the water pump is limited because of where it is located. However, some basic checks can be made before deciding to remove the water pump. If the pump is found to be defective, it should be replaced with a new or rebuilt unit.

28 One sign that the water pump may be failing is that the heater (climate control) may not work well. Warm the engine to normal operating temperature, confirm that the coolant level is correct, then run the heater and check for hot air coming from the ducts.

29 Check for noises coming from the water pump area. If the water pump impeller shaft or bearings are failing, there may be a howling sound at the pump while the engine is running.

Note: *Be careful not to mistake drivebelt noise (squealing) for water pump bearing or shaft failure.*

30 It you suspect water pump failure due to noise, wear can be confirmed by feeling for play at the pump shaft. This can be done by rocking the drive sprocket on the pump shaft up and down. To do this you will need to remove the tension on the timing chain or belt as well as access the water pump.

All water pumps

31 In rare cases or on high-mileage vehicles, another sign of water pump failure may be the presence of coolant in the engine oil. This condition will adversely affect the engine in varying degrees.

Note: *Finding coolant in the engine oil could indicate other serious issues besides a failed water pump, such as a blown head gasket or a cracked cylinder head or block.*

32 Even a pump that exhibits no outward signs of a problem, such as noise or leakage, can still be due for replacement. Removal for close examination is the only sure way to tell. Sometimes the fins on the back of the impeller can corrode to the point that cooling efficiency is diminished significantly.

Heater system

33 Little can go wrong with a heater. If the fan motor will run at all speeds, the electrical part of the system is okay. The three basic heater problems fall into the following general categories:
 a Not enough heat
 b Heat all the time
 c No heat

34 If there's not enough heat, the control valve or door is stuck in a partially open position, the coolant coming from the engine isn't hot enough, or the heater core is restricted. If the coolant isn't hot enough, the thermostat in the engine cooling system is stuck open, allowing coolant to pass through the engine so rapidly that it doesn't heat up quickly enough. If the vehicle is equipped with a temperature gauge instead of a warning light, watch to see if the engine temperature rises to the normal operating range after driving for a reasonable distance.

35 If there's heat all the time, the control valve or the door is stuck wide open.

36 If there's no heat, coolant is probably not reaching the heater core, or the heater core is plugged. The likely cause is a collapsed or plugged hose, core, or a frozen heater control valve. If the heater is the type that flows coolant all the time, the cause is a stuck door or a broken or kinked control cable.

Air conditioning system

37 If the cool air output is inadequate:
 a Inspect the condenser coils and fins to make sure they're clear
 b Check the compressor clutch for slippage
 c Check the blower motor for proper operation
 d Inspect the blower discharge passage for obstructions
 e Check the system air intake filter for clogging

38 If the system provides intermittent cooling air:
 a Check the circuit breaker, blower switch and blower motor for a malfunction
 b Make sure the compressor clutch isn't slipping
 c Inspect the plenum door to make sure it's operating properly
 d Inspect the evaporator to make sure it isn't clogged
 e If the unit is icing up, it may be caused by excessive moisture in the system, incorrect super heat switch adjustment or low thermostat adjustment

39 If the system provides no cooling air:
 a Inspect the compressor drivebelt; make sure it's not loose or broken
 b Make sure the compressor clutch engages; if it doesn't, check for a blown fuse
 c Inspect the wire harness for broken or disconnected wires
 d If the compressor clutch doesn't engage, bridge the terminals of the AC pressure switch(es) with a jumper wire; if the clutch now engages, and the system is properly charged, the pressure switch is bad
 e Make sure the blower motor is not disconnected or burned out
 f Make sure the compressor isn't partially or completely seized
 g Inspect the refrigerant lines for leaks
 Check the components for leaks
 h Inspect the receiver-drier/accumulator or expansion valve/tube for clogged screens

40 If the system is noisy:
 a Look for loose panels in the passenger compartment
 b Inspect the compressor drivebelt; it may be loose or worn
 c Check the compressor mounting bolts; they should be tight
 d Listen carefully to the compressor; it may be worn out
 e Listen to the idler pulley and bearing, and the clutch; either may be defective
 f The winding in the compressor clutch coil or solenoid may be defective
 g The compressor oil level may be low
 h The blower motor fan bushing or the motor itself may be worn out
 i If there is an excessive charge in the system, you'll hear a rumbling noise in the high pressure line, a thumping noise in the compressor, or see bubbles or cloudiness in the sight glass
 j If there's a low charge in the system, you might hear hissing in the evaporator case at the expansion valve, or see bubbles or cloudiness in the sight glass

3 Air conditioning and heating system - check and maintenance

Air conditioning system

Warning: *The air conditioning system is under high pressure. Do not loosen any hose fittings or remove any components until after the system has been discharged. Air conditioning refrigerant should be properly discharged at a dealer service department or an automotive air conditioning repair facility. Always wear eye protection when disconnecting air conditioning system fittings.*

1 The following maintenance checks should be performed on a regular basis to ensure that the air conditioning continues to operate at peak efficiency.
 a Inspect the condition of the compressor drivebelt. If it is worn or deteriorated, replace it (see Chapter 1 Section 12).
 b Check the drivebelt tension (see Chapter 1 Section 12).
 c Inspect the system hoses. Look for cracks, bubbles, hardening and deterioration. Inspect the hoses and all fittings for oil bubbles or seepage. If there is any evidence of wear, damage or leakage, replace the hose(s).
 d Inspect the condenser fins for leaves, bugs and any other foreign material that may have become embedded in the fins. Use a fin comb or compressed air to remove debris from the condenser.
 e Make sure the system has the correct refrigerant charge.

Chapter 3 Cooling, heating and air conditioning systems   3-5

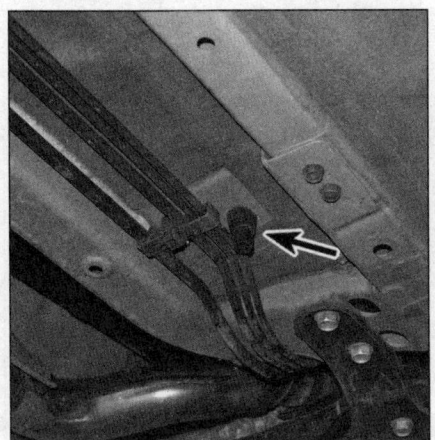

3.1a The evaporator drain hose extends through the floor to allow collected water to run out

f   If you hear water sloshing around in the dash area or have water dripping on the carpet, check the evaporator housing drain tube **(see illustration)** and insert a piece of wire into the opening to check for blockage.

2   It's a good idea to operate the system for about ten minutes at least once a month. This is particularly important during the winter months because long term non-use can cause hardening, and subsequent failure, of the seals. Note that using the Defrost function operates the compressor.

3   If the air conditioning system is not working properly, proceed to Step 6 and perform the general checks outlined below.

4   Because of the complexity of the air conditioning system and the special equipment necessary to service it, in-depth troubleshooting and repairs beyond checking the refrigerant charge and the compressor clutch operation are not included in this manual. However, simple checks and component replacement procedures are provided in this Chapter. For more complete information on the air conditioning system, refer to the Haynes Automotive Heating and Air Conditioning Manual.

5   The most common cause of poor cooling is simply a low system refrigerant charge. If a noticeable drop in system cooling ability occurs, one of the following quick checks will help you determine if the refrigerant level is low.

Heating systems

6   If the carpet under the heater core is damp, or if coolant vapour or steam is coming through the vents, the heater core is leaking. Remove it and install a new unit (see Section 10).

7   If the air coming out of the heater vents isn't hot, the problem could stem from any of the following causes:

a   *The thermostat is stuck open, preventing the engine coolant from warming up enough to carry heat to the heater core. Replace the thermostat (see Section 4).*

b   *There is a blockage in the system, preventing the flow of coolant through the heater core. Feel both heater hoses at the firewall. They should be hot. If one of them is cold, there is an obstruction in one of the hoses or in the heater core, or the heater control valve is shut. Detach the hoses and back flush the heater core with a water hose. If the heater core is clear but circulation is impeded, remove the two hoses and flush them out with a water hose.*

c   *If flushing fails to remove the blockage from the heater core, the core must be replaced (see Section 10).*

Eliminating air conditioning odours

8   Unpleasant odours that often develop in air conditioning systems are caused by the growth of a fungus, usually on the surface of the evaporator core. The warm, humid environment there is a perfect breeding ground for mildew to develop.

9   The evaporator core on most vehicles is difficult to access, and factory dealerships have a lengthy, expensive process for eliminating the fungus by opening up the evaporator case and using a powerful disinfectant and rinse on the core until the fungus is gone. You can service your own system at home, but it takes something much stronger than basic household germ-killers or deodorisers.

10   Aerosol disinfectants for automotive air conditioning systems are available in most auto parts stores, but remember when shopping for them that the most effective treatments are also the most expensive. The basic procedure for using these sprays is to start by running the system in the RECIRC mode for ten minutes with the blower on its highest speed. Use the highest heat mode to dry out the system and keep the compressor from engaging by disconnecting the wiring connector at the compressor.

11   The disinfectant can usually comes with a long spray hose. Insert the nozzle into an intake port inside the cabin, and spray according to the manufacturer's recommendations. Follow the manufacturer's recommendations for the length of spray and waiting time between applications.

12   Once the evaporator has been cleaned, the best way to prevent the mildew from coming back again is to make sure your evaporator housing drain tube is clear **(see illustration 3.1)**.

Automatic heating and air conditioning systems

13   Some vehicles are equipped with an optional automatic climate control system. This system has its own computer that receives inputs from various sensors in the heating and air conditioning system. This computer, like the PCM, has self-diagnostic capabilities to help pinpoint problems or faults within the system. Vehicles equipped with automatic heating and air conditioning systems are very complex and considered beyond the scope of the home mechanic. Vehicles equipped with automatic heating and air conditioning systems should be taken to dealer service department or other qualified facility for repair.

4   Thermostat and water control valve - replacement

Warning: *See the coolant Warnings in Section 1.*
Warning: *Wait until the engine is completely cool before beginning this procedure.*
Note: *These engines use a thermostat on the coolant inlet (located on the cylinder block), and a water control valve on the coolant outlet (at the driver's end of the cylinder head). Although they have different names, these devices perform similar functions and are very similar in appearance. If you are experiencing an overheating condition attributed to a faulty thermostat or water control valve, it is recommended that both of them be replaced at the same time.*

1   Raise the front of the vehicle and support on jackstands (see Chapter 0 Section 7). Remove the splash guard between the bumper cover and the subframe.

2   Drain the cooling system (see Chapter 1 Section 27). If the coolant is relatively new, or is in good condition save it and re-use it. After the coolant has drained, lower the vehicle.

Thermostat

3   Loosen the clamps and remove the lower radiator hose and transaxle fluid cooler hose (if equipped) from the thermostat water inlet housing. If the hose is stuck, grasp it near the end with a pair of large adjustable pliers and twist it to break the seal, then pull it off. If the hose is old or deteriorated, cut it off and install a new one.

4   Unscrew the water inlet mounting bolts and remove the water inlet **(see illustration)**. If the water inlet is stuck, tap it with a soft-face

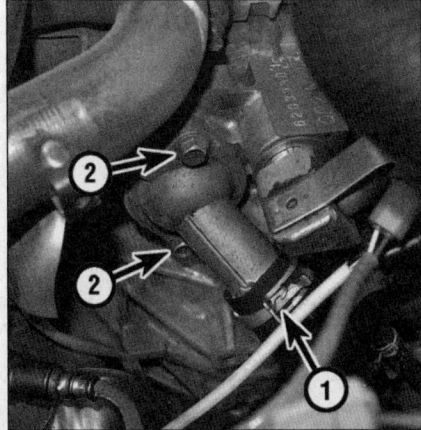

4.4 Water inlet housing location

1   *Lower radiator hose clamp*
2   *Water inlet housing mounting bolts*

Chapter 3 Cooling, heating and air conditioning systems

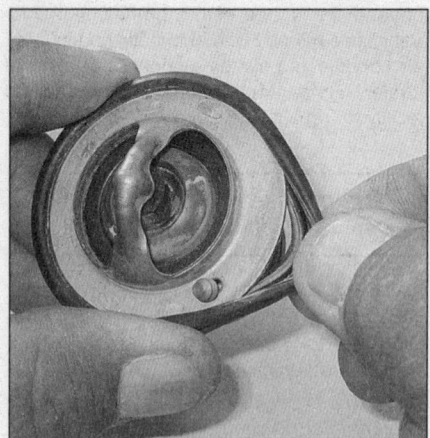

4.6 The thermostat (and water control valve earlier 2.5 litre engines) sealing ring fits around the edge of the flange

1 Radiator hose
2 Heater pipe bolt
3 Heater hose
4 Hose to transaxle fluid cooler
5 Heater hose
6 Throttle body hose
7 Oil cooler hose
8 Throttle body hose
9 Engine Coolant Temperature (ECT) sensor
10 Water control valve mounting fastener (others not visible in this photo)

4.13 Water control valve details (earlier models)

hammer to jar it loose. Be prepared for some coolant to spill as the gasket seal is broken.
5 Remove the thermostat. Clean the water inlet and engine block mating surfaces.
6 Install a new sealing ring onto the thermostat **(see illustration)**, then insert the thermostat into the housing. Make sure that the air bleed valve (jiggle valve) faces up, and the spring end of the valve is directed toward the engine.
7 The remainder of installation is the reverse of removal. Tighten the fasteners to the specified torque (see Specifications).
8 Refill the cooling system (see Chapter 1 Section 27).
9 Start the engine and allow it to reach normal operating temperature, then check for leaks and proper thermostat operation.

Coolant outlet housing and water control valve

Note: *Some models are equipped with a water control valve in the control valve housing.*

10 Remove the air inlet/resonator duct Chapter 4A Section 9 or Chapter 4B Section 6.
11 Disconnect the electrical connectors from the PCM Chapter 6 Section 15 and TCM Chapter 7B Section 8 and move the harness out of the way
12 Remove the battery and battery tray Chapter 5 Section 5.
13 Disconnect the hoses from the coolant outlet **(see illustration)**. If a hose is stuck, grasp it near the end with a pair of large adjustable pliers and twist it to break the seal, then pull it off. If the hose is old or deteriorated, cut it off and install a new one.
14 Detach the hoses from the heater pipe, then unscrew the fastener and remove the heater pipe from the engine. Install a new O-ring on the end of the heater pipe where it mates with the engine.
15 Remove the fasteners and detach the water control valve housing. If it is stuck, tap it

with a soft-face hammer to jar it loose. Be prepared for some coolant to spill as the gasket seal is broken.
16 Remove the water control valve, if equipped. Clean the mating surfaces of all gasket or sealant.
17 On models with a water control valve, install a new sealing ring onto the water control valve **(see illustration 4.6)**, then insert the valve into the housing. Make sure the air bleed valve (jiggle valve) faces up and the spring end of the valve is directed toward the housing.
18 Install the housing, with a new gasket and tighten the bolts evenly to the specified torque (see Specifications).
19 The remainder of installation is the reverse of removal.
20 Refill the cooling system (see Chapter 1 Section 27).
21 Start the engine and allow it to reach normal operating temperature, then check for leaks and proper thermostat/water valve operation.

5 Engine cooling fans and resistor - removal and installation

Warning: *The engine must be completely cool before beginning this procedure.*
Warning: *The models covered by this manual are equipped with a Supplemental Restraint System (SRS), more commonly known as airbags. Always disarm the airbag system before working in the vicinity of any airbag system component to avoid the possibility of accidental deployment of the airbag, which could cause personal injury Chapter 12A Section 20. Do not use a memory saving device to preserve the PCM's memory when working on or near airbag system components.*
Warning: *See the coolant Warning in Section 1.*

1 Remove the lower splashield to access the bottom of the radiator and the radiator drain plug (see Chapter 1 Section 27). Drain approximately two litres of coolant from the radiator.
2 Remove the fresh air intake duct from between the radiator support panel and the air filter housing (see Chapter 4A Section 9 - petrol models, or Chapter 4B Section 6 - diesel models).

T31 X-Trail models

3 Disconnect the wiring from the fan motors **(see illustration)**.
4 Disconnect the upper radiator hose from the radiator and bend it clear of the work area. Also disconnect the hose going from the radiator neck to the coolant reservoir and position clear of the work area.
5 Unclip the wiring harness from the cooling fan shroud.
6 Remove the bolts retaining the top of the cooling fan assembly to the radiator. Lift the cooling fan assembly up, disengaging the retaining clips on the bottom **(see illustration)** and manoeuvre it from the engine compartment.
7 Installation is a reversal of the removal procedure, with attention to the following points:
  a Use care not to damage the radiator core when installing the cooling fan assembly
  b Ensure the bottom clips engage before tightening the upper bolts.
  c Check the coolant level and top up as necessary.

Chapter 3 Cooling, heating and air conditioning systems

5.3 Cooling fan components - T31 X-Trail

1. Cooling fan shroud and fan assembly
2. Cooling fan motor wiring connectors
3. Upper radiator hose
4. Wiring harness
5. One of the upper retaining bolts; there are two

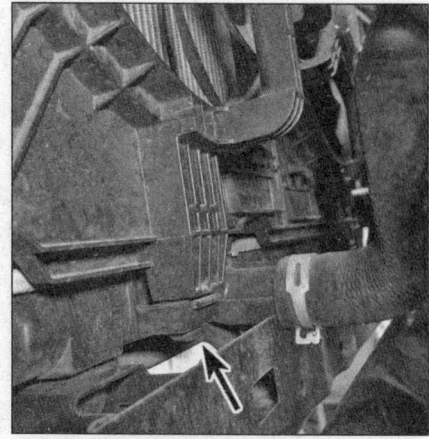

5.6 One of the retaining clips on the bottom of the cooling fan assembly

T32 X-Trail models

8 Remove the front bumper (see Chapter 11 Section 18).
9 Remove the headlights (see Chapter 12A Section 8).
10 Remove upper radiator support then remove upper guide bracket **(see illustrations)**.
11 Detach the upper radiator hose from the radiator and the coolant reservoir hose from the fan shroud.
12 Disconnect the electrical connectors from the fan motors **(see illustration)**.
13 Disconnect the upper radiator hose from the radiator and bend it clear of the work area. Also disconnect the hose going from the radiator neck to the coolant reservoir and position clear of the work area.
14 Unclip the wiring harness from the radiator assembly and position clear of the work area.

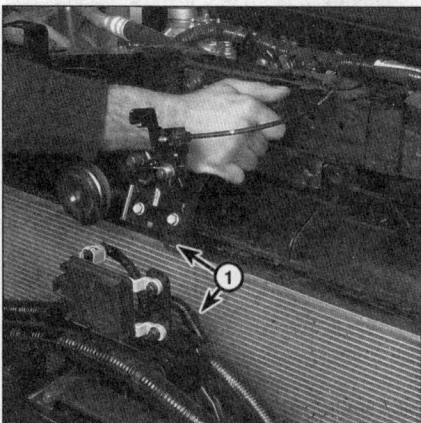

5.10a Partially removing the upper radiator support panel after disconnecting the impact sensor wiring harness from the bracket (1) and removing the retaining bolts (2) - there are three more bolts on the opposite side

d Run the engine and check that the cooling fans operate once the engine reaches operating temperature.

5.10b Remove the upper guide bracket bolts - there is another one on the opposite side and then…

15 Remove the bolts retaining the top of the cooling fan assembly to the radiator. Lift the cooling fan assembly up, disengaging the retaining clips on the bottom **(see illustration)** and manoeuvre it from the engine compartment.

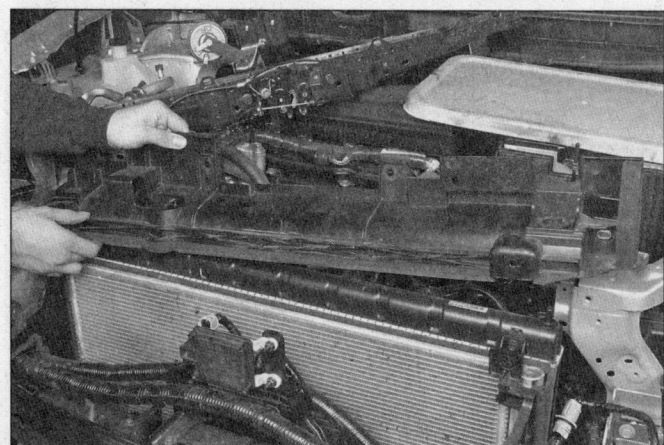

5.10c … remove the upper guide bracket from the vehicle

5.12 Cooling fan components - T32 X-Trail

1. Upper radiator hose
2. One of the cooling fan wiring connectors
3. One of the cooling fan assembly mounting bolts
4. Wiring harness clips

Chapter 3 Cooling, heating and air conditioning systems

5.18a Disconnecting the fan resistor wiring connector

5.18b Disconnecting one of the fan motor wiring connectors

5.19a Some models have clips retaining the upper part of the cooling fan assembly, push clip toward radiator to unclip

16 Installation is a reversal of the removal procedure, with attention to the following points:
   a Use care not to damage the radiator core when installing the cooling fan assembly

5.19b If clips aren't used to retain the upper part of the cooling fan assembly, remove the mounting bolts

   b Ensure the bottom clips engage before tightening the upper bolts.
   c Check the coolant level and top up as necessary.
   d Run the engine and check that the cooling fans operate once the engine reaches operating temperature.

Dualis and Qashqai models

17 On Qashqai models, remove the front bumper (see Chapter 11 Section 18).
18 Disconnect the electrical connectors from the fan motors (see illustration) and the fan resistor (see illustration). Also, detach the transaxle fluid cooler hoses from the fan shroud (where applicable).
19 Remove the cooling fan assembly-to-radiator fasteners on some models the fasteners are on the bottom and clips on the top (see illustration).
20 Remove the cooling fan assembly (see illustration).
21 Installation is a reversal of the removal procedure, with attention to the following points:
   a Use care not to damage the radiator core when installing the cooling fan assembly

   b Ensure the wiring is connected back onto the fan motors and the resistor.
   c Check the coolant level and top up as necessary.
   d Run the engine and check that the cooling fans operate once the engine reaches operating temperature.

All models

22 If necessary, remove the nuts for each fan blade assembly and remove them from their motor shafts.
23 Remove the fan motor-to-fan support retaining bolts, then remove the motor.
24 Installation is the reverse of removal.
25 Tighten all fasteners to the torque values

Cooling fan resistor

26 The cooling fan resistor is fitted to the top side of the fan shroud on some models.
27 Disconnect the fan resistor wiring connector (see illustration).
28 Undo the retaining bolt, release the locating clips and then slide the resistor out from the fan shroud (see illustrations).

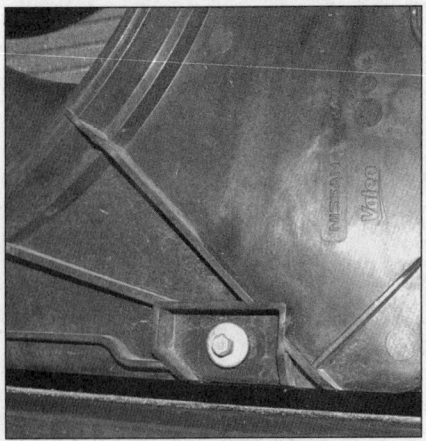

5.19c Some models have fasteners on the bottom of the shroud

5.20 Removing the cooling fan assembly from the vehicle

5.27 Disconnecting the fan resistor wiring connector

Chapter 3 Cooling, heating and air conditioning systems

5.28a Undo the retaining bolt (arrowed) …

5.28b … slide the resistor (arrowed) …

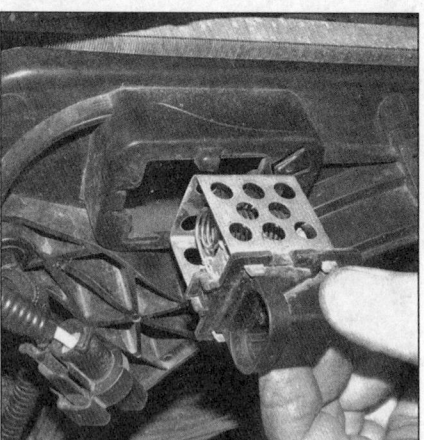

5.28c … and withdraw the resistor

29 Installation is a reversal of removal.

6 Radiator and coolant reservoir - removal and installation

Warning: *Wait until the engine is completely cool before beginning this procedure.*

Warning: *The models covered by this manual are equipped with a Supplemental Restraint System (SRS), more commonly known as airbags. Always disarm the airbag system before working in the vicinity of any airbag system component to avoid the possibility of accidental deployment of the airbag, which could cause personal injury (see Chapter 12A Section 20). Do not use a memory saving device to preserve the PCM's memory when working on or near airbag system components.*

Warning: *See the coolant Warning in Section 1.*

Radiator

1 Remove the lower splashield to access the bottom of the radiator and the radiator drain plug (see Chapter 1 Section 27). Drain the cooling system.

2 Remove the fresh air intake duct from between the radiator support panel and the air filter housing (see Chapter 4A Section 9 - petrol models, or Chapter 4B Section 6 - diesel models).
3 Disconnect the upper and lower radiator hoses from the radiator **(see illustration)** and also the overflow hose from the radiator filler neck. If a hose is stuck, grasp it near the end with a pair of large adjustable pliers and twist it to break the seal, then pull it off. If the hose is old or deteriorated, cut it off and install a new one.
4 Remove the cooling fan assembly from the vehicle (see Section 5).
5 On models with A/C, unscrew the bolts or unclip the condenser from the front of the radiator **(see illustration)**. Where fitted, unbolt the A/C receiver/drier from the radiator tank **(see illustration)**.
6 On models with clip-on upper retainers, pull the tabs on the radiator upper clips outwards then side the clips out and remove the rubber mounts from the mounting pins **(see illustration)**.
7 On models with bolt-on upper retainers, remove the bolt and slide the retainer out from beneath the radiator support panel **(see illustration)**.

6.3 Disconnect the upper and lower radiator hoses

8 Tilt the radiator assembly toward the rear of the vehicle, then lift up to remove it.

Caution: *Avoid damaging the radiator or A/C condenser fins and tanks during radiator removal.*

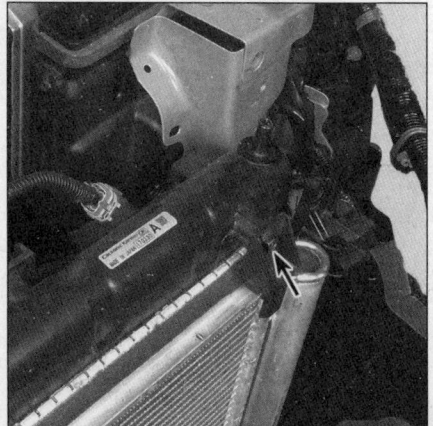

6.5a One of the condenser to radiator bolts - T32 X-Trail shown, other models similar

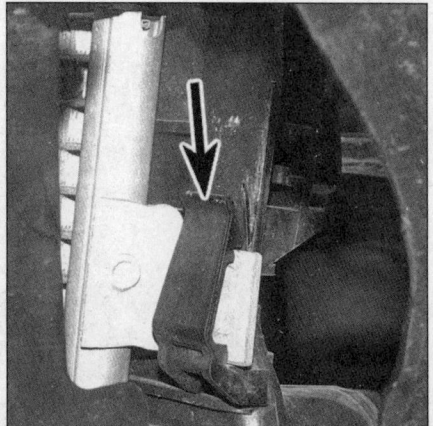

6.5b On some models, the A/C condenser is clipped to the radiator side tank

6.5c On some models, the A/C receiver/drier is mounted to the radiator side tank

Chapter 3 Cooling, heating and air conditioning systems

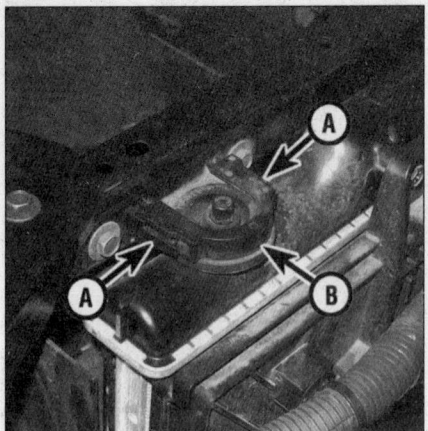

6.6 Pull the tabs on the radiator upper clips (A) outwards then side the clip (B) out from the radiator (left-side shown)

6.7 Removing one of the upper radiator support bolts

6.10a Bugs and organic matter commonly get caught between the front of the radiator and the A/C condenser. With the radiator removed,...

6.10b ... direct a stream of water from the engine side of the radiator to the outside to remove

6.10c Reverse flushing the radiator by inserting the hose in the radiator's lower hose fitting and forcing water out of the upper hose fitting until the water expelled from the radiator is clean

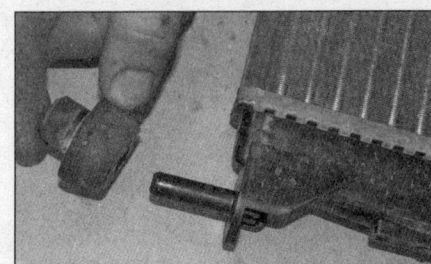

6.11 Installing the radiator mounting pads

All models

9 With the radiator removed, it can be inspected for leaks and damage. If it needs repair, have a radiator shop or dealer service department perform the work, as special techniques are required.

10 Bugs and dirt can be removed from the radiator with a soft brush, followed by forcing water from a garden hose through the core from the engine side. Don't bend the cooling fins as this is done.

Caution: *Avoid damaging the radiator or A/C condenser fins and tanks during radiator installation.*

11 Installation is the reverse of removal. Be sure the radiator mounting pads are seated properly at the base of the radiator **(see illustration)**.

12 Refill the cooling system (see Chapter 1 Section 27).

13 Reconnect the battery and perform the system initialisation procedure (see Chapter 5 Section 4).

14 Allow the engine to reach normal operating temperature, indicated by the upper radiator hose becoming hot. Recheck the coolant level and add more if required.

Coolant reservoir

15 Disconnect the overflow hose from the fitting by the radiator cap.

16 Remove the coolant reservoir mounting nut **(see illustration)**.

17 Pull the coolant reservoir upwards to disengage the stud from its grommet, then remove the coolant reservoir from the vehicle.

18 Pour the coolant into a container. Wash out the reservoir, using soapy water and a long brush to make the coolant level easier to read. Inspect the reservoir for cracks and chafing. Replace it if any damage is found.

19 Installation is the reverse of removal. Add coolant to the reservoir up to the Min mark.

7 Water pump – removal, inspection and installation

Note: *A new gasket will be required when refitting the coolant pump.*

Removal

1 Disconnect the battery negative terminal (see Chapter 5 Section 3).

2 Drain the cooling system (see Chapter 1 Section 27).

6.16 Coolant reservoir details

1 Coolant reservoir mounting fastener
2 Mounting stud (underneath, plugs into grommet)

Chapter 3 Cooling, heating and air conditioning systems   3-11

7.5a On Dualis and T31 X-Trail 2.0 litre petrol models, remove the two front coolant pump bolts (arrowed) …

7.5b … and the two bolts at the rear …

7.5c … then remove the pump and gasket

7.5d On all other models all of the bolts are accessed at the front of the water pump

7.7a Hold the pulley stationary using an oil filter removal strap, and undo the bolts

7.7b Removing the pulley

3 Remove the drivebelts and some models remove drive belt tensioner (see Chapter 1 Section 12).

Petrol engines

4 To make access easier remove the alternator (see Chapter 5 Section 11).

5 Unscrew the four retaining bolts, and remove the coolant pump from the housing. Note on some model two of the bolts are accessed from the front of the pump and two from the rear (see illustrations). Remove the gasket and discard, as a new one will be required for refitting.

Diesel engine

Note: *There is not sufficient room to remove the water pump with the engine in the vehicle. It is necessary to remove the front crossmember and lower the engine from the body.*

6 Remove the engine from the vehicle (see Chapter 2D Section 7).

7 Unscrew the three retaining bolts, and remove the pulley from the coolant pump (see illustrations). If required, counter hold the pulley in order to unscrew the bolts. This is most easily achieved by wrapping an old drivebelt tightly around the pulley to act in a similar manner to a strap wrench.

8 Unscrew the retaining bolts, and withdraw the coolant pump from the cylinder block (see illustrations). Prise out the O-ring seal from the groove in the pump body, discard, as a new one will be required for refitting.

Inspection

9 Check the pump body and impeller for signs of excessive corrosion. Turn the impeller, and check for stiffness due to corrosion, or roughness due to excessive endplay.

10 No spare parts are available for the pump, and if faulty, worn or corroded, a new pump should be fitted.

7.8a Unbolt and remove the coolant pump …

7.8b … then remove the O-ring seal

3-12 Chapter 3 Cooling, heating and air conditioning systems

7.12 Fit new gasket to the water pump

8.4 Disconnect the wiring connector and securing clip (arrowed)

8.5 Disconnect the wiring connector

Installation

11 Commence installation by thoroughly cleaning all traces of gasket/sealant from the mating faces of the pump and cylinder block.
12 Where applicable, fit new gasket/seal to the coolant pump **(see illustration)**.
13 Place the pump in position in the cylinder block, refit the bolts to their correct locations and tighten to the specified torque.
14 On diesel engines, refit the pump pulley and tighten to the specified torque. Counter hold the pulley using an old drivebelt as during removal.
15 Refit and tension the drivebelts and some models drive belt tensioner (see Chapter 1 Section 12).
16 Refill the cooling system (see Chapter 1 Section 27).
17 Reconnect the battery negative terminal (see Chapter 5 Section 3).

8 Blower motor and resistor - removal and installation

Warning: *The models covered by this manual are equipped with a Supplemental Restraint System (SRS), more commonly known as airbags. Always disarm the airbag system before working in the vicinity of any airbag system component to avoid the possibility of accidental deployment of the airbag, which could cause personal injury (see Chapter 12A Section 20). Do not use a memory saving device to preserve the PCM's memory when working on or near airbag system components.*

Note: *If the blower motor is found to be faulty, replace the entire blower motor and fan. The blower motor unit is balanced at the factory; individual components cannot be replaced.*

1 Disconnect the negative (-) battery terminal (see Chapter 5 Section 3).

Blower motor

2 On T-31 X-Trail and Dualis models, remove the glove compartment and glove compartment surround panel (see Chapter 11 Section 21). Reach inside the glove box opening and the blower motor is mounted to the passenger side of the heater housing.
3 On T-32 X-Trail and Qashqai models, remove the dashboard (see Chapter 11 Section 24).
4 On Dualis models to make removal of the motor easier, disconnect the wiring connector from the heater flap control motor and release the wiring loom securing clips and move it to one side **(see illustration)**.
5 Reaching up around the rear of the heater housing, disconnect the wiring connector from the top of the blower motor **(see illustration)**.
6 Undo the retaining screw, then turn the blower motor anticlockwise to withdraw it from the rear of the heater housing **(see illustrations)**.
7 Installation is the reverse of removal.
8 Reconnect the battery and perform the system initialisation procedure (see Chapter 5 Section 4).

Resistor

9 Remove the glove compartment and surround panel (see Chapter 11 Section 21).
10 The resistor is located below the blower motor, in the left-hand side of the heater housing **(see illustration)**.

8.6a Remove the retaining screw (arrowed)

8.6b Rotate the motor anticlockwise...

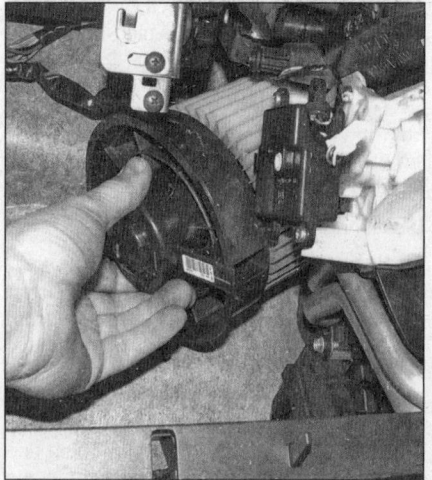
8.6c ... and remove it from the heater housing

Chapter 3 Cooling, heating and air conditioning systems

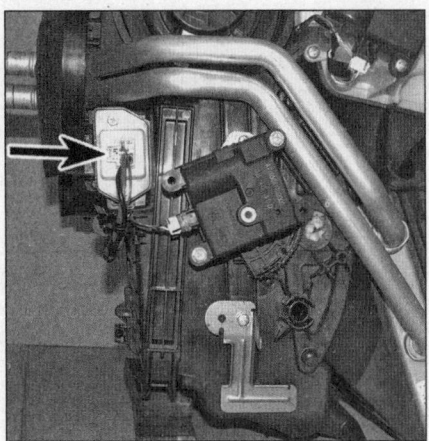

8.10 Location of heater blower resistor (arrowed)

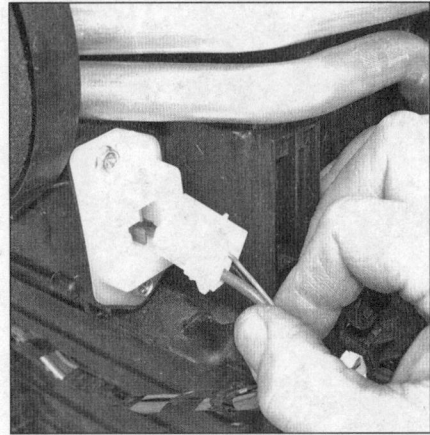

8.11 Disconnect the wiring connector

8.12a Remove the two retaining screws …

11 Disconnect the wiring connector from the blower motor resistor **(see illustration)**.
12 Undo the retaining screws and withdraw the resistor from the rear of the heater housing **(see illustrations)**.
13 Refitting is a reversal of removal.

9 Heater and air conditioning control assembly - removal and installation

Warning: *The models covered by this manual are equipped with a Supplemental Restraint System (SRS), more commonly known as airbags. Always disarm the airbag system before working in the vicinity of any airbag system component to avoid the possibility of accidental deployment of the airbag, which could cause personal injury (see Chapter 12A Section 20). Do not use a memory saving device to preserve the PCM's memory when working on or near airbag system components.*

1 Disconnect the negative (-) battery terminal (see Chapter 5 Section 3).

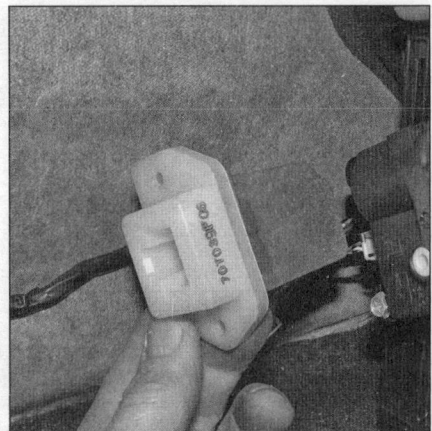

8.12b … and withdraw it from the heater housing

2 Use a plastic trim tool or a screwdriver wrapped with tape to carefully pry up the gear shift cover. Remove the cover **(see illustration)**.
3 Use a plastic trim tool or a screwdriver

9.2 Pry up and remove the gear shift cover - Dualis models

wrapped with tape to carefully pry out the heating and air conditioning control panel or centre panel to access the control panel. Pull out the assembly and disconnect the electrical connectors **(see illustrations)**.

9.3a Using a trim tool to pry out the centre panel from around the audio centre - T31 X-Trail

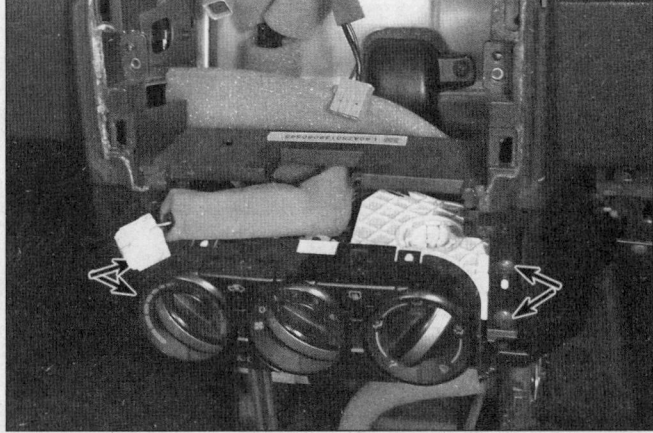

9.3b Centre trim panel removed revealing the heater and air conditioning control panel retaining screws - T31 X-Trail models

3-14 Chapter 3 Cooling, heating and air conditioning systems

9.3c On Dualis models, pry out and remove the heating and air conditioning control panel/cover assembly…

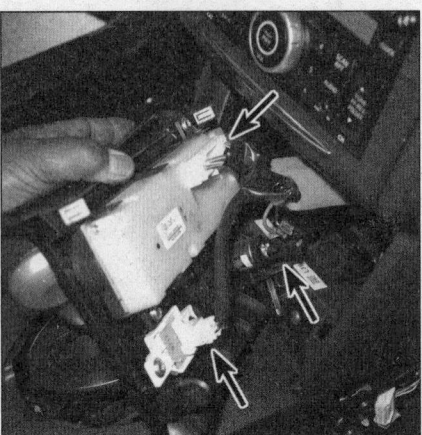

9.3d… then disconnect the electrical connectors from the assembly

9.3e With the heating and air conditioning control panel assembly partially removed…

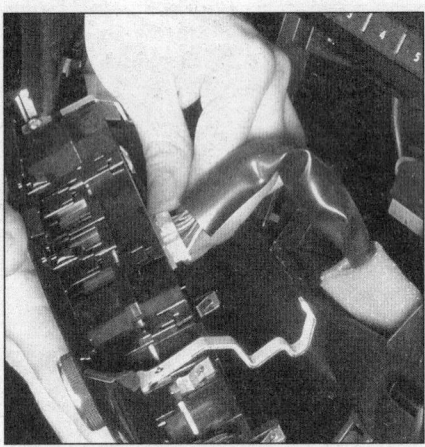

9.3f … reach behind the panel and disconnect the wiring from the rear - T32 X-Trail and Qashqai models

4 Remove the heater and air conditioning control assembly-to-cover screws **(see illustration)** and separate the cover from the assembly.

5 Installation is the reverse of removal.
6 Reconnect the battery and perform the system initialisation procedure (see Chapter 5 Section 4).

10 Heater core - removal and installation

Warning: *Wait until the engine is completely cool before beginning this procedure.*

Warning: *The models covered by this manual are equipped with a Supplemental Restraint System (SRS), more commonly known as airbags. Always disarm the airbag system before working in the vicinity of any airbag system component to avoid the possibility of accidental deployment of the airbag, which could cause personal injury (see Chapter 12A Section 20). Do not use a memory saving device to preserve the PCM's memory when working on or near airbag system components.*

Note: *Replacement of the heater core is a difficult procedure for the home mechanic,* *involving removal of the entire dashboard, console, and many wiring connectors. If you attempt it at home, keep track of the assemblies by taking notes and keeping screws and other hardware in small, marked plastic bags for reassembly.*

1 Have the air conditioning system evacuated by a properly equipped workshop.
2 Disconnect the negative (-) battery terminal (see Chapter 5 Section 3).
3 Drain the cooling system (see Chapter 1 Section 27). If the coolant is relatively new, or is in good condition, save it and re-use it.
4 Move aside the lower dash insulation to access the heater core pipes.
5 Disconnect the heater hoses from the pipes protruding through the firewall.
6 Disconnect the refrigerant lines from the evaporator.

Note: *Plug all open fittings of disconnected lines to prevent entry of dirt and moisture into the lines.*

7 Remove the steering column (see Chapter 10 Section 13).

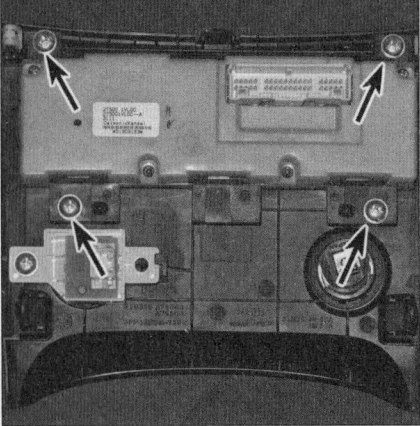

9.4 Remove the screws holding the cover to the heating and air conditioning control assembly - Dualis models

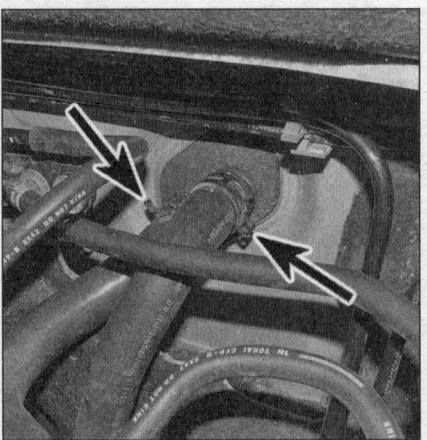

10.5a Location of the heater hoses at the firewall

10.5b Removing one of the heater hoses from the heater core

Chapter 3 Cooling, heating and air conditioning systems   3-15

10.6 Evaporator line fitting bolt at the firewall

10.9 Removing the crashbar from the vehicle

8   Remove the entire instrument panel assembly (see Chapter 11 Section 24).
9   Disconnect the connectors for the wiring that will interfere with removal of the crashbar. Remove the fasteners and remove the crashbar from the vehicle **(see illustration)**.
10 Disconnect the evaporator drain hose.
Caution: *Handle the heating and air conditioning unit carefully during removal to avoid accidental damage to the interior.*
11 Remove the heater core insulation to expose the heater core pipe bracket screws.
12 Remove the heater core pipe bracket screws and remove the bracket **(see illustrations)**, if equipped.
13 Slide out the heater core and remove it from the HVAC housing **(see illustration)**.
14 Installation is the reverse of removal, noting the following:
Note: *Do not use old O-rings for the refrigerant lines, replace with new ones and apply compressor oil to them before installation.*
15 Refill the cooling system (see Chapter 1 Section 27).
16 Reconnect the battery and perform the system initialisation procedure (see Chapter 5 Section 4).
17 Check for leaks and proper system operation.
18 Check the operation of all electrical components of the steering column and dash.
19 Have the air conditioning system re-gassed

11 Air conditioning compressor - removal and installation

Warning: *The air conditioning system is under high pressure. Do not loosen any fittings or remove any components until after the system has been discharged. Air conditioning refrigerant should be properly discharged at a dealer service department or an automotive air conditioning repair facility. Always wear eye protection when disconnecting air conditioning system fittings.*
Warning: *Wait until the engine is completely cool before beginning this procedure.*
1   Have the refrigerant discharged at a dealer service department or an automotive air conditioning repair facility.
Note: *If you are going to install a new compressor, inform the shop doing the work to record the amount of refrigerant oil recovered when the system is discharged (this measurement will be used when adding refrigerant oil to the system during installation).*
2   Disconnect the negative (-) battery terminal (see Chapter 5 Section 3).
3   Loosen the right front wheel nuts. Raise the vehicle and support it securely on jackstands (see Chapter 0 Section 7). Remove the wheel and the inner mudguard splash shield.
4   Remove the splash guard underneath the engine.
5   Remove the fresh air intake duct (see Chapter 4A Section 9 - petrol models, or Chapter 4B Section 6 - diesel models).
6   Remove the drivebelt (see Chapter 1 Section 12).
7   Disconnect the electrical connector from the air conditioning compressor.
8   Remove the fasteners and disconnect the refrigerant lines from the compressor **(see illustration)**.
Note: *Plug all open fittings to prevent entry of dirt and moisture into the lines.*
9   Remove the compressor mounting bolts and remove the compressor from the engine

10.12a Remove the heater core pipe bracket screws. . .

10.12b. . . and remove the heater core pipe bracket

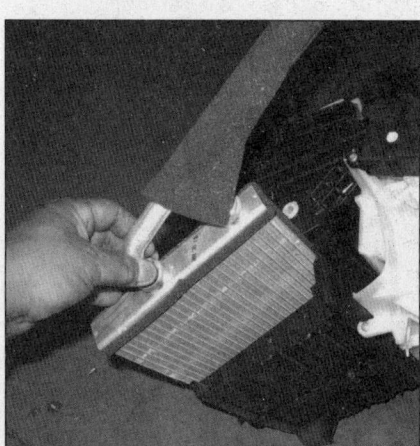

10.13 Slide out and remove the heater core

3-16 Chapter 3 Cooling, heating and air conditioning systems

11.7 Disconnecting the compressor wiring connector

11.8a Refrigerant line fitting fasteners

11.8b Use plastic caps to seal the refrigerant line openings to prevent contamination in the system

11.9a Remove the air conditioning compressor mounting bolts - early models

10 If a new compressor is being installed, follow the directions with the compressor regarding the measuring and adding of oil prior to installation. Add to that the amount of oil measured during recovering of the refrigerant.

11 Installation is the reverse of removal. Tighten the compressor mounting bolts to the torque value listed in this Chapter's Specifications.

Note: *Do not use old O-rings for the refrigerant lines; replace them with new ones and apply compressor oil to them before installation.*

12 Reconnect the battery and perform the system initialisation procedure (see Chapter 5 Section 4).

13 Have the system evacuated, charged and leak tested by the shop that discharged it.

12 Welch plugs - replacement

1 To facilitate the casting of the cylinder block and cylinder heads, a number of openings were made during manufacture. These openings are sealed with welch plugs.

2 The welch plugs will have to be renewed when cleaning the water jackets or when they become defective due to corrosion.

Note: *If a welch plug is found to be corroded, it is advisable to renew all the welch plugs.*

To renew

3 Drain the cooling system (see Chapter 1 Section 27).

4 Remove the necessary engine components or accessories to gain ample working space around the damaged plug.

Note: *To access the welch plugs in the rear of the cylinder head and the rear of the cylinder block, it will be necessary to remove the engine.*

5 Using a punch and hammer, tap the welch plug on its outer circumference into its opening **(see illustration)**.

6 Grasp the edge of the welch plug with a pair of multigrip pliers and using the shoulder of the pliers as a fulcrum, lever the plug out of its opening **(see illustration)**.

7 Thoroughly clean and dry the welch plug opening.

8 Lightly smear the edge of the new welch plug and the opening with a suitable jointing

compartment **(see illustrations)**.

Note: *If a new compressor is being installed, the clutch assembly may have to be transferred to the new compressor. The removal of the clutch assembly will require the use of several special tools; this procedure should be performed by an air conditioning shop or dealer service department.*

11.9b Remove the air conditioning compressor mounting bolts (lower bolt not shown) - late models

11.9c Removing the compressor from the engine

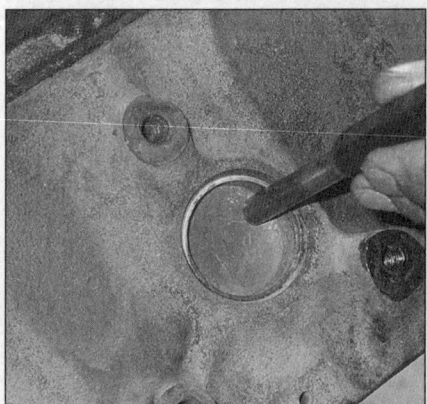

12.5 Tap the edge of the welch plug into the block...

compound, such as Loctite No 2.

9 Place the new welch plug onto the opening and using a large socket or piece of tubing fitting neatly inside the rim of the welch plug, tap the plug squarely into the opening **(see illustration)**.

Note: *The welch plug must be entered squarely into its opening or leakage may occur.*

10 Install the components which were removed to gain access to the welch plug.
11 Refill the cooling system (see Chapter 1 Section 27).
12 With the radiator cap installed, run the engine until it reaches normal operating temperature and check for coolant leaks. Rectify as necessary.

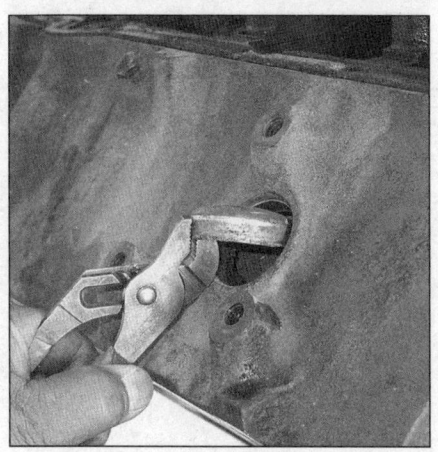

12.6 ... then, use multi-grip pliers to lever the old welch plug from the block

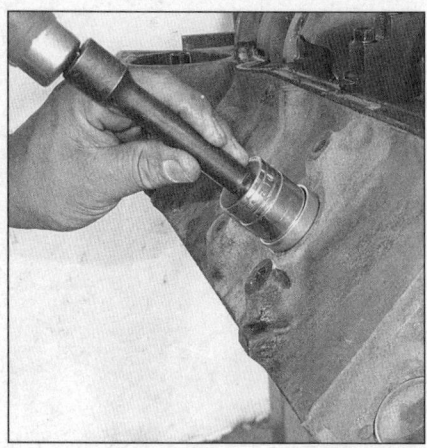

12.9 Use a socket that sits around the edge of the welch plug to tap it squarely into the block

Notes

Chapter 4 Part A
Fuel and exhaust systems - petrol engines

Contents

	Section
Accelerator Pedal Position (APP) sensor - replacement	See Chapter 6
Air filter housing - removal and installation	9
Exhaust system servicing - general information	11
Fuel lines and fittings - general information and disconnection	5
Fuel pressure - check	4
Fuel pressure relief procedure	3

	Section
Fuel pump/fuel level sensor module - removal and installation	7
Fuel rail and injectors - removal and installation	6
Fuel tank - removal and installation	8
General information	1
Injection system electronic components – removal and refitting	See Chapter 6
Throttle body - removal and installation	10
Troubleshooting	2

Specifications

Fuel system pressure
- T31 X-Trail, Dualis .... 350 kpa (at idle)
- Qashqai, T32 X-Trail .... 500 kPa (at idle)

Fuel injector resistance - at 10 to 60 degrees C
- T31 X-Trail, Dualis, T32 X-Trail (2.5 litre) .... 11.1 to 14.5 ohms
- T32 X-Trail (2.0 litre), Qashqai .... 1.44 to 1.73 ohms

Fuel pump resistance - at 25 degrees C .... 0.2 to 5.0 ohms

Torque specifications   Nm
- Fuel rail mounting bolts 25
- Throttle body mounting fasteners
  - T31 X-Trail
    - 2.0 litre 10
    - 2.5 litre 8
  - Dualis 10
  - T32 X-Trail 10
  - Qashqai 10
- Fuel tank
  - Shield nuts 5
  - Strap bolts
    - T31 X-Trail 31
    - Dualis 43
    - T32 X-Trail 40
    - Qashqai 40

Chapter 4 Part A Fuel and exhaust systems - petrol engines

2.2a The fuel pump fuse is located in the engine compartment on the Intelligent Power Distribution Module (IPDM) on Dualis models. The fuse is No.57

2.2b The fuel pump fuse is located in the engine compartment on the Intelligent Power Distribution Module (IPDM) on T31 X-Trail models (arrow)

1 General information

Fuel system warnings

1 Petrol is extremely flammable and repairing fuel system components can be dangerous. Consider your automotive repair knowledge and experience before attempting repairs which may be better suited for a professional mechanic.

  a Don't smoke or allow open flames or bare light bulbs near the work area
  b Don't work in a garage with a gas-type appliance (water heater, clothes dryer)
  c Use fuel-resistant gloves. If any fuel spills on your skin, wash it off immediately with soap and water
  d Clean up spills immediately
  e Do not store fuel-soaked rags where they could ignite
  f Prior to disconnecting any fuel line, you must relieve the fuel pressure (see Section 3)
  g Wear safety glasses
  h Have a proper fire extinguisher on hand

Fuel system

2 The fuel system consists of the fuel tank, electric fuel pump/fuel level sending unit (located in the fuel tank), fuel rail and fuel injectors. The fuel injection system is a multi-port system; multi-port fuel injection uses timed impulses to inject the fuel directly into the intake port of each cylinder. The Powertrain Control Module (PCM) controls the injectors. The PCM monitors various engine parameters and delivers the exact amount of fuel required into the intake ports.

3 Fuel is circulated from the fuel pump to the fuel rail through fuel lines running along the underside of the vehicle. Various sections of the fuel line are either rigid metal or nylon, or flexible fuel hose. The various sections of the fuel hose are connected either by quick-connect fittings or threaded metal fittings.

Exhaust system

4 The exhaust system consists of the exhaust manifold(s), catalytic converter(s), muffler(s), tailpipe and all connecting pipes, flanges and clamps. The catalytic converters are an emission control device added to the exhaust system to reduce pollutants.

2 Troubleshooting

Fuel pump

1 The fuel pump is located inside the fuel tank. Sit inside the vehicle with the windows closed, turn the ignition key to ON (not START) and listen for the sound of the fuel

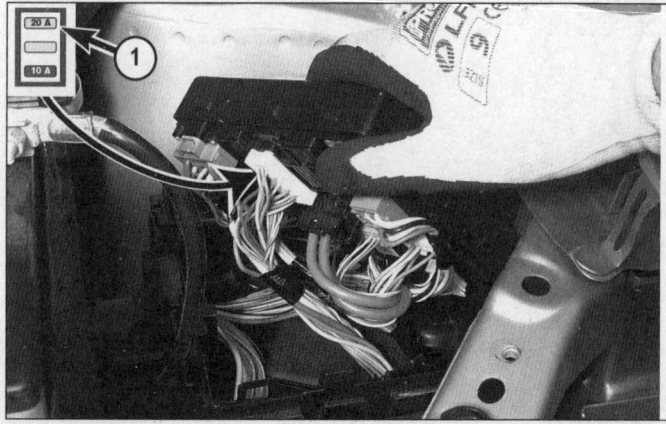

2.2c The fuel pump fuse is located in the engine compartment on the Intelligent Power Distribution Module (IPDM) on T32 X-Trail models (arrow)

pump as it's briefly activated. You will only hear the sound for a second or two, but that sound tells you that the pump is working. Alternatively, have an assistant listen at the fuel filler cap.

2 If the pump does not come on, check the fuel pump fuse (see illustrations). If the fuse is okay, check the wiring back to the fuel pump. If the fuse and wiring are okay, the pump might be defective. Other possibilities include a faulty fuel pump relay, which is also part of the Intelligent Power Distribution Module (which is part of the under bonnet fuse/relay box), or a faulty Powertrain Control Module (PCM).

Fuel injection system

Note: *The following procedure is based on the assumption that the fuel pump is working and the fuel pressure is adequate (see Section 4).*

3 Check all electrical connectors that are related to the system. Check the ground wire connections for tightness.
4 Verify that the battery is fully charged (see Chapter 1).
5 Inspect the air filter element (see Chapter 1).
6 Check all fuses related to the fuel system (see Chapter 12).
7 Check the air induction system between the throttle body and the intake manifold for air leaks. Also inspect the condition of all vacuum hoses connected to the intake manifold and to the throttle body.
8 Remove the air intake duct from the throttle body and look for dirt, carbon, varnish, or other residue in the throttle body, particularly around the throttle plate. If it's dirty, clean it with carb cleaner, a toothbrush and a clean shop towel.
9 With the engine running, place an automotive stethoscope against each injector, one at a time, and listen for a clicking sound that indicates operation (see illustration).
Warning: *Stay clear of the drivebelt and any rotating or hot components.*
10 If you can hear the injectors operating, but the engine is misfiring, the electrical circuits are functioning correctly, but the injectors might be dirty or clogged. Try a com-

Chapter 4 Part A Fuel and exhaust systems - petrol engines

2.9 An automotive stethoscope is used to listen to the fuel injectors in operation

4.1a Remove the safety cover from the quick disconnect fuel line connector

4.1b Insert the special fuel line disconnect tool into the fuel line

mercial injector cleaning product (available at auto parts stores). If cleaning the injectors doesn't help, replace the injectors.

11 If an injector is not operating (it makes no sound), disconnect the injector electrical connector and measure the resistance across the injector terminals with an ohmmeter. Compare this measurement to the other injectors. If the resistance of the non-operational injector is quite different from the other injectors, replace it.

12 If the injector is not operating, but the resistance reading is within the range of resistance of the other injectors, the PCM or the circuit between the PCM and the injector might be faulty.

3 Fuel pressure relief procedure

Warning: *Petrol is extremely flammable. See Fuel Systems Warnings in Section 1.*

Note: *After the fuel pressure has been relieved, it's a good idea to lay a shop towel over any fuel connection to be disassembled,* to absorb the residual fuel that may leak out when servicing the fuel system.

1 Remove the fuel pump fuse from the IPDM underbonnet fuse/relay box, located next to the battery **(see illustrations 2.2a to 2.2d)**.

2 Start the engine and allow it to run until it stops. This should take only a few seconds. Disconnect the cable from the negative terminal of the battery before working on the fuel system (see Chapter 5 Section 3).

3 The fuel system pressure is now relieved. It is a good idea to surround any fuel line that will be disconnected with a shop rag to catch fuel that might spill out.

4 When you're finished working on the fuel system, install the fuel pump fuse back into the fuse panel, connect the negative cable to the battery and perform the system initialisation procedure (see Chapter 5 Section 4).

4 Fuel pressure - check

Warning: *Petrol is extremely flammable. See Fuel system warnings in Section 1.*

Note: *To perform the fuel pressure test, you will need to obtain a special fuel pressure gauge and adapter set (fuel line fittings).*

1 Relieve the fuel pressure (see Section 3). Disconnect the quick-connect fuel supply line fitting at the fuel rail **(see illustrations)**. You must connect a special tee adapter in the line that incorporates a fuel pressure gauge. This special tee can be purchased or you can fabricate your own out of various fittings, hose and hose clamps **(see illustration)**.

2 With the gauge connected and leak-tested, start the engine and allow it to idle. Note the gauge reading as soon as it stabilizes and compare it with the pressure listed in this Chapter's Specifications.

3 If the fuel pressure is out of specification, check the following:

  a If the pressure is lower than specified, check for a restriction in the fuel system (kinked fuel line, plugged fuel pump inlet strainer or clogged fuel filter). If no restrictions are found, replace the fuel pump module (see Section 7).

4.1c Using upward pressure, push the tool into the fuel line to unlock the fuel line connector

4.1d Remove the fuel line from the fuel rail

4.1e Use a fuel pressure gauge with hoses and fittings suitable for tee-ing into the fuel line at the fuel rail

Disconnecting Fuel Line Fittings

Two-tab type fitting; depress both tabs with your fingers, then pull the fuel line and the fitting apart

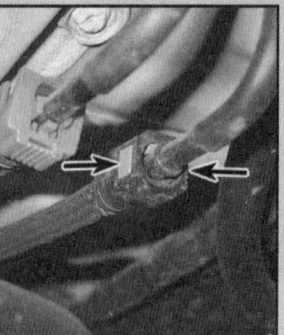

On this type of fitting, depress the two buttons on opposite sides of the fitting, then pull it off the fuel line

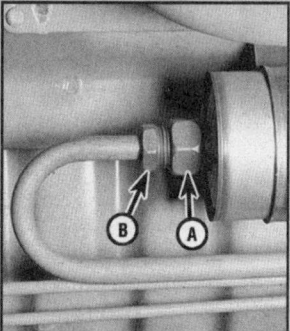

Threaded fuel line fitting; hold the stationary portion of the line or component (A) while loosening the tube nut (B) with a flare-nut wrench

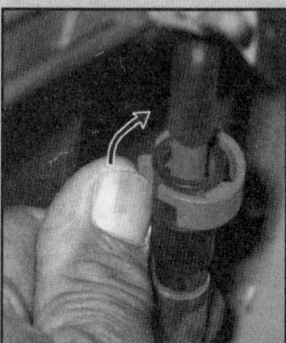

Plastic collar-type fitting; rotate the outer part of the fitting

Metal collar quick-connect fitting; pull the end of the retainer off the fuel line and disengage the other end from the female side of the fitting . . .

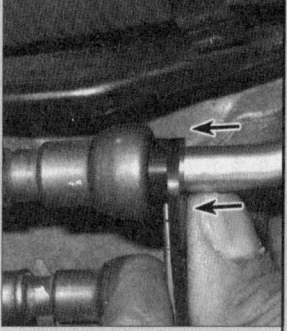

. . . insert a fuel line separator tool into the female side of the fitting, push it into the fitting and pull the fuel line off the pipe

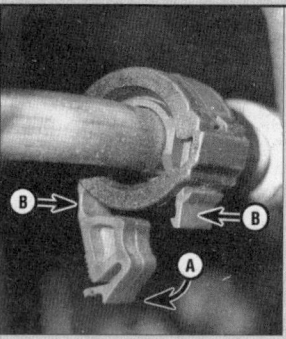

Some fittings are secured by lock tabs. Release the lock tab (A) and rotate it to the fully-opened position, squeeze the two smaller lock tabs (B) . . .

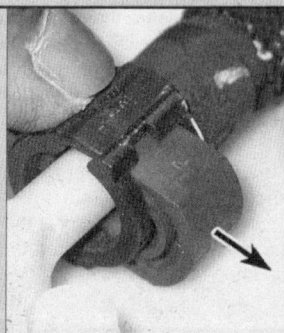

. . . then push the retainer out and pull the fuel line off the pipe

Spring-lock coupling; remove the safety cover, install a coupling release tool and close the tool around the coupling . . .

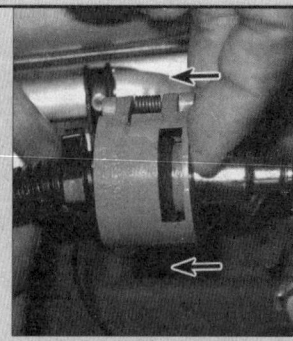

. . . push the tool into the fitting, then pull the two lines apart

Hairpin clip type fitting: push the legs of the retainer clip together, then push the clip down all the way until it stops and pull the fuel line off the pipe

Chapter 4 Part A Fuel and exhaust systems - petrol engines

5.10 Plastic plugs and caps in various sizes are available in packs from spare parts and accessory suppliers and are a great way to protect the components while you're working on them

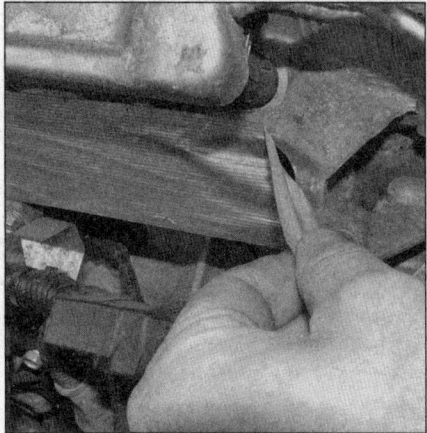

6.5 Cover the intake ports with duct tape to prevent anything falling into the cylinders

6.6 Disconnecting the injector wiring connectors

b If the fuel pressure is higher than specified, replace the fuel pump module (see Section 7).

4   Turn off the key. Fuel pressure should not fall significantly over a five minute period. If it does, the problem could be a leaky fuel injector, fuel line leak, or faulty fuel pump module.

5   Disconnect the fuel pressure gauge. Wipe up any spilled fuel.

5   Fuel lines and fittings - general information and disconnection

Warning: *Petrol is extremely flammable. See Fuel system warnings in Section 1.*

1   Relieve the fuel pressure before servicing fuel lines or fittings (see Section 3), then disconnect the negative (-) battery terminal (see Chapter 5 Section 3) before proceeding.

2   The fuel supply line connects the fuel pump in the fuel tank to the fuel rail on the engine. The Evaporative Emission (EVAP) system lines connect the fuel tank to the EVAP canister and connect the canister to the intake manifold.

3   Whenever you're working under the vehicle, be sure to inspect all fuel and evaporative emission lines for leaks, kinks, dents and other damage. Always replace a damaged fuel or EVAP line immediately.

4   If you find signs of dirt in the lines during disassembly, disconnect all lines and blow them out with compressed air. Inspect the fuel strainer on the fuel pump pick-up unit for damage and deterioration.

Steel tubing

5   It is critical that the fuel lines be replaced with lines of equivalent type and specification.

6   Some steel fuel lines have threaded fittings. When loosening these fittings, hold the stationary fitting with a wrench while turning the tube nut.

Plastic tubing

7   When replacing fuel system plastic tubing, use only original equipment replacement plastic tubing.

Caution: *When removing or installing plastic fuel line tubing, be careful not to bend or twist it too much, which can damage it. Also, plastic fuel tubing is NOT heat resistant, so keep it away from excessive heat.*

Flexible hoses

8   When replacing fuel system flexible hoses, use only original equipment replacements.

9   Don't route fuel hoses (or metal lines) within 100 mm of the exhaust system or within 250 mm of the catalytic converter. Make sure that no rubber hoses are installed directly against the vehicle, particularly in places where there is any vibration. If allowed to touch some vibrating part of the vehicle, a hose can easily become chafed and it might start leaking. A good rule of thumb is to maintain a minimum of 5 mm clearance around a hose (or metal line) to prevent contact with the vehicle underbody.

Disconnecting Fuel Line Fittings

10 After disconnecting any fuel pipes or components, the open union or orifice must be immediately sealed to prevent the entry of dirt or foreign material. Plastic plugs and caps in various sizes are available in packs from parts and accessory outlets, and are particularly suitable for this application **(see illustration).** Fingers cut from disposable rubber gloves should be used to protect components such as fuel pipes, fuel injectors and wiring connectors, and can be secured in place using elastic bands.

6   Fuel rail and injectors - removal and installation

Warning: *Petrol is extremely flammable. See Fuel system warnings in Section 1.*

1   Relieve the fuel system pressure (see Section 3).

2   Disconnect the negative (-) battery terminal (see Chapter 5 Section 3).

3   Disconnect the fuel supply line from the fuel rail (see Section 5).

4   Remove the intake manifold (see Chapter 2A Section 5 - 2.5 litre petrol engine, or Chapter 2B Section 5 - 2.0 litre petrol engine).

5   Using duct tape or similar, cover the intake ports in the cylinder head to prevent anything being dropped into the cylinders **(see illustration).**

6.7a On 2.0 litre models, remove the upper cover mounting bolts, then...

6.7b ... remove the lower mounting bolts before...

4A-6 Chapter 4 Part A Fuel and exhaust systems - petrol engines

6.7c ... removing the cover from the engine

6.8a Fuel rail mounting bolts - 2.5 litre models

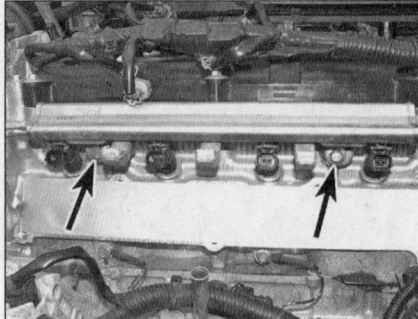

6.8b Fuel rail mounting bolts - 2.0 litre models

6.8c Removing the fuel rail and injectors from the engine

6.9 To free each injector from the fuel rail, pull off the retaining clip with a pair of pliers

6.10 Pull the injector straight out of its bore in the fuel rail

6 Disconnect the electrical connector from each fuel injector.
7 On 2.0 litre models, undo the fasteners for the fuel rail cover and remove the cover from the vehicle (see illustrations).
8 Remove the fuel rail mounting bolts (see illustration).
9 Remove the fuel injector retaining clips (see illustration).
10 Remove the injectors from the fuel rail (see illustration), then remove and discard the O-rings.
11 Replace both O-rings of each fuel injec-

tor and lubricate them with clean engine oil prior to installation (see illustration).
12 Install the injector retaining clips and insert each injector into its bore in the fuel rail until the retaining clip snaps into place (see illustration).
13 The remainder of installation is the reverse of removal.

a Reconnect the battery and perform the system initialisation procedure (see Chapter 5 Section 5).
b Run the engine and check for fuel leaks.

7 Fuel pump/fuel level sensor module - removal and installation

Warning: *Petrol is extremely flammable. See Fuel System Warnings in Section 1.*

Note: *On 4WD models, two fuel level sender units are used. The fuel pump/fuel level sensor module is on the right side of the fuel tank; the sub fuel level sensor module is on the left side of the tank.*

6.11a Whether you're installing new injectors or reusing the old ones, always remove the old O-rings and replace them with new ones

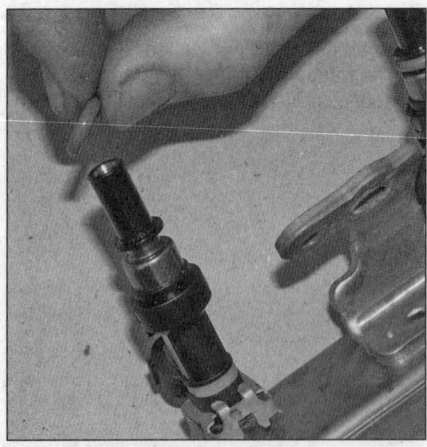

6.11b Installing a new injector to the bottom of the injector

6.11c Lubricate the O-rings with clean engine oil

Chapter 4 Part A Fuel and exhaust systems - petrol engines

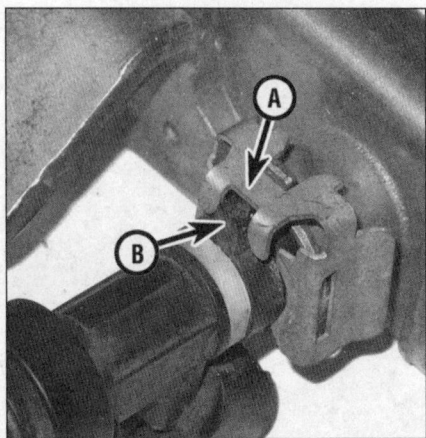

6.12 To install an injector, align the slot in the clip (A) with the tab (B) on the fuel rail, then push the injector firmly into place until the clip snaps onto the ridge of the fuel rail

7.4a Turn the fuel pump/fuel level sensor access cover fasteners 90 degrees to remove the cover

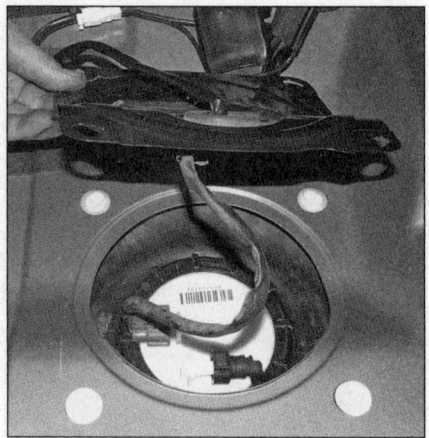

7.4b Remove the cover from the floor of the vehicle

2 Disconnect the negative (-) battery terminal (see Chapter 5 Section 3).
3 Remove the rear seat cushion (see Chapter 11 Section 26).
4 Remove the access cover for the fuel pump/fuel level sensor module (see illustration).
5 Disconnect the electrical connector from the fuel pump/fuel level sending unit (see illustration).
6 Make a mark across the top of the module, locking ring and the fuel tank (see illustration) to aid in correct alignment when the assembly is reinstalled.
7 Disconnect the fuel supply line from the fuel level sending unit/fuel pump assembly (see illustration).

Note: *To remove the quick connector, hold the sides of the connector, push in the tabs, and pull off the tube.*

8 Turn the fuel pump/fuel level sensor module lock ring counterclockwise (see illustrations), then remove it.

Caution: *The manufacturer recommends that the metal lock ring and the O-ring (on all models) be replaced with new ones.*

7.5 Depress the tab and disconnect the electrical connector, then detach the fuel feed hose

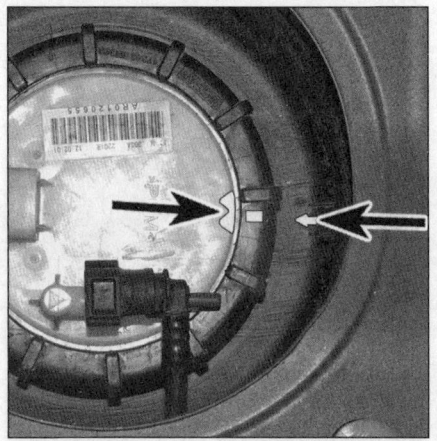

7.6a Make a set of matching marks for correct alignment of the locking ring on installation - plastic retaining ring

Fuel pump/fuel level sensor module

Removal

1 Relieve the fuel pressure (see Section 3).

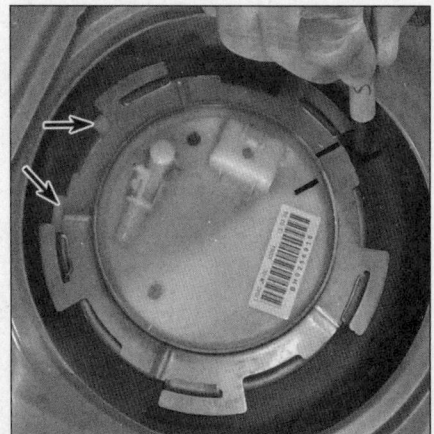

7.6b Making a set of matching marks for correct alignment of the locking ring on installation - metal locking ring. Note on installation the two tabs (arrows) must face toward the front of the vehicle

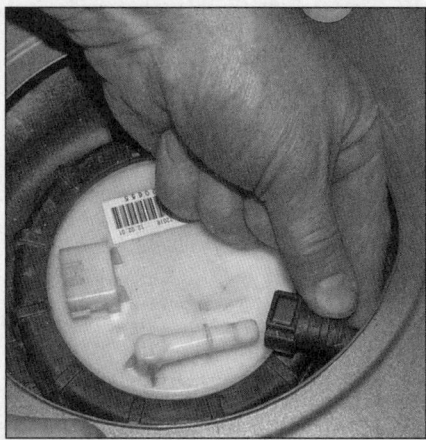

7.7 Depress the release button and disconnect the fuel pipe(s)

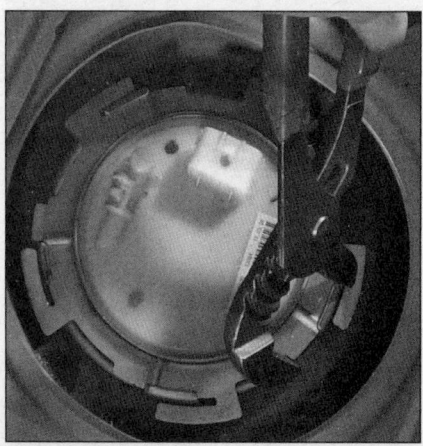

7.8a Some models have a metal lock ring; multigrip pliers can be used to turn it counterclockwise to remove it

Chapter 4 Part A Fuel and exhaust systems - petrol engines

7.8b On other models, the module is retained by a plastic lock ring; use a special lock ring removal tool (available at most auto parts stores) to unscrew it

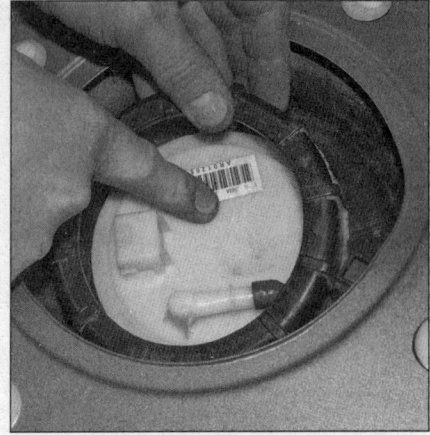

7.8c Removing the retaining ring

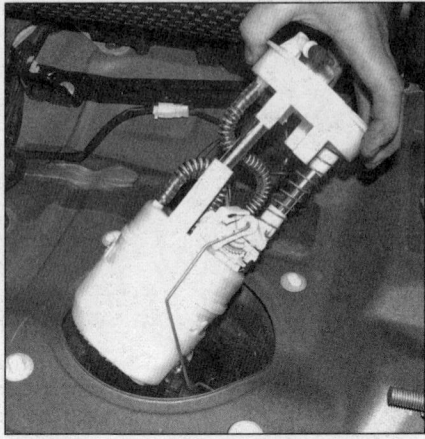

7.9 The fuel level float arm is easily bent, so proceed carefully when lifting the fuel pump module out

7.10 Removing the O-ring from the fuel tank

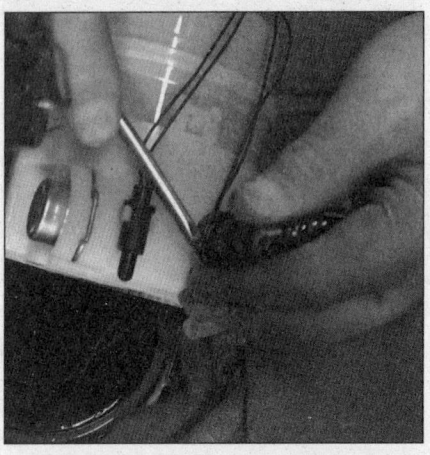

7.11 To remove the quick-connector, hold the sides of the connector, push in the tabs, and pull out the tube

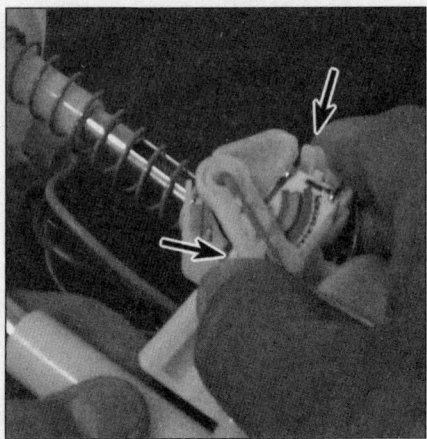

7.12 The fuel level sensor is secured with two retaining tangs; squeeze the tangs and slide the sensor off the module frame

9   Lift the fuel pump module from the fuel tank. Manipulate it as you lift so you don't bend the float arm **(see illustration)**.
10   Remove the O-ring from the top of the fuel tank **(see illustration)**.
11   If equipped, disconnect the fuel tube quick-connector at the bottom of the module **(see illustration)**, then remove the module.

Fuel level sensor replacement

12   Squeeze the retaining tangs and remove the fuel level sensor from the module frame (see illustration). To install, slide the sensor onto the frame until the tangs click into place.

Installation

13   Replace the O-ring seal **(see illustration)**.
14   Connect the fuel tube quick connector at the bottom of the module **(see illustration 7.11)**, and sub fuel level sensor module harness electrical connectors, if equipped.
15   Carefully lower the fuel pump module into the fuel tank.
16   Position the assembly so the two plastic tangs are facing the front of the vehicle **(see illustration 7.6b)**.
17   Install and tighten the lock ring.
18   Reconnect the hoses and electrical connector, then reinstall the access cover.
19   Reinstall the rear seat cushion (see Chapter 11 Section 26).
20   Reconnect the battery and perform the system initialisation procedure (see Chapter 5 Section 4).

Sub fuel level sensor module

Note: *A second "sub" fuel level sensor module, located on the left side of the fuel tank, is used on AWD models.*

Removal

21   Relieve the fuel pressure (see Section 3).
22   Disconnect the negative (-) battery terminal (see Chapter 5 Section 3).
23   Remove the rear seat cushion (see Chapter 5 Section 3).
24   Remove the fuel pump/fuel level sensor module and disconnect the wiring harness and fuel tube (see Steps 4 through 10). Connect a length of fuel-resistant wire or rope to the fuel tube and wiring harness (this will be used to pull the tube and harness back through the tank during installation).

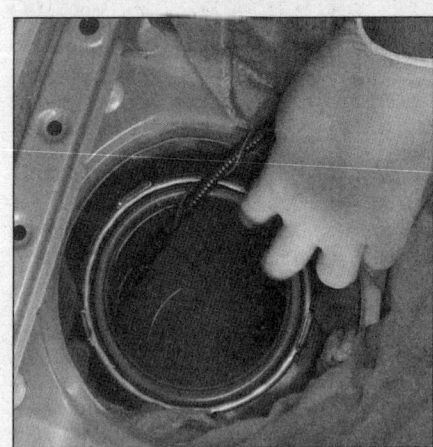

7.13 Install a new O-ring seal

Chapter 4 Part A Fuel and exhaust systems - petrol engines

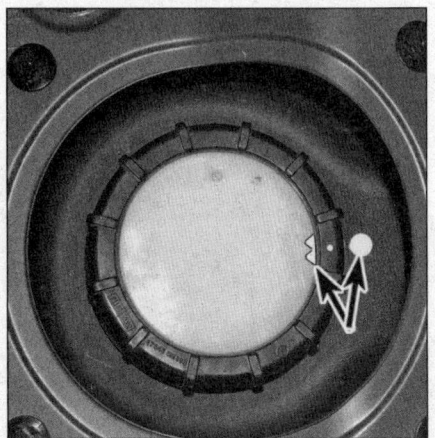

7.26 Mark the module, retaining ring and tank to aid installation

7.27 Loosening the locking ring

7.28 Removing the sub fuel level sensor module

25 Locate the inspection hole cover on the passenger side of the vehicle, then turn the cover fasteners 90 degrees and remove the access cover for the sub fuel level sensor assembly **(see illustration 7.4)**.
26 Make a mark across the top of the module, locking ring and the fuel tank **(see illustration)** to aid in correct alignment when the assembly is reinstalled.
27 Remove the lock ring **(see illustration)**.
Note: *The manufacturer recommends that where fitted, the metal lock ring and the O-ring be replaced with new ones.*
28 Lift the sub fuel level sensor module from the fuel tank **(see illustration)**. Manipulate it as you lift so you don't bend the float arm.
29 Remove the module until the wire or rope connected to the fuel tube is pulled out of the tank opening, then disconnect the wire or rope.
Caution: *The fuel tube is not removable from the sub fuel level sensor assembly, if the tube is damaged, the sub fuel level sensor assembly must be replaced.*

Installation

30 Replace the O-ring seal **(see illustration 7.13)**.
31 Tie the wire or rope to the fuel tube and wiring harness, then carefully lower the sub fuel level sensor module into the fuel tank while pulling the rope or wire until the fuel tube reaches the fuel pump/level sensor module opening on the right side of the tank.
32 Rotate the assembly until the tabs are facing the front of the vehicle **(see illustration 7.26)**.
33 Reconnect the fuel tube and electrical connector to the fuel pump/fuel level sensor module.
34 Install the lock ring.
35 Install the fuel pump/fuel level sensor module (see Steps 12 through 17).
36 Reinstall the access covers and the rear seat cushion (see Chapter 11 Section 26).
37 Reconnect the battery and perform the system initialisation procedure (see Chapter 5 Section 4).

8 Fuel tank - removal and installation

Warning: *Petrol is extremely flammable. See Fuel System Warnings in Section 1.*
Note: *The following procedure is much easier to perform if the fuel tank is empty. Drain the fuel into an approved fuel container using a commercially available siphoning kit (NEVER start the siphoning action by mouth) or wait until the fuel tank is nearly empty, if possible.*

1 Remove the fuel tank filler cap to relieve fuel tank pressure.
2 Relieve the fuel system pressure (see Section 1).
3 Disconnect the negative (-) battery terminal (see Chapter 5 Section 3).
4 Disconnect the lines and wiring from the fuel pump module at the top of the fuel tank. If desired, the fuel pump module can be removed at this time (see Section 7).
5 Raise the vehicle and support on jackstands (see Chapter 0 Section 7).
6 If there is still fuel in the tank, siphon it out from the fuel feed line. Remember - NEVER start the siphoning action by mouth! Use a siphoning kit, which can be purchased at most auto parts stores.
7 Remove the exhaust pipe and muffler assembly.
8 On AWD models, remove the rear propeller shaft (see Chapter 8 Section 13).
9 Remove the fuel tank heat shield mounting nuts and heat shield.
10 Disconnect the hose from the fuel pump/fuel level sensor module **(see illustration 7.5)**.
11 On AWD X-Trail models, it is necessary to lower the front of the rear differential to allow the fuel tank to clear the pinion. Loosen the rear mounting nut (do not remove) and remove the front mounting bolts (see Chapter 8 Section 9), lower the front of the differential and support with timber.
12 Disconnect the parking brake cables from their brackets. Move the cables aside and secure them in place with wire.
13 Loosen the fuel filler hose clamp and remove the fuel filler hose from the fuel tank **(see illustration)**. Also disconnect the vent and EVAP hoses.
14 Support the fuel tank with a floor jack. Position a wood plank between the jack head and the fuel tank to protect the tank.
15 Remove the fuel tank strap bolts **(see illustrations)**.
16 Remove the tank from the vehicle.

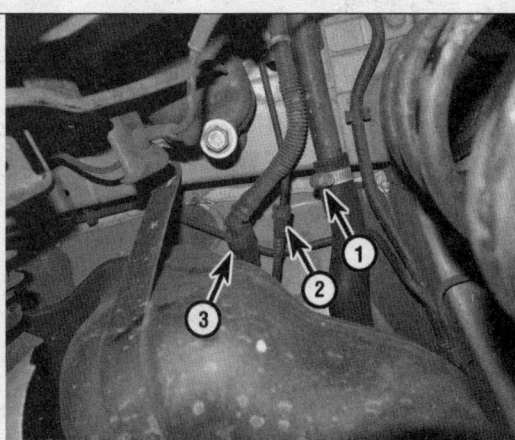

8.13 Disconnect the hoses near the right-rear corner of the fuel tank

1 Fuel tank filler hose
2 Fuel line
3 EVAP canister vent hose

4A-10　Chapter 4 Part A　Fuel and exhaust systems - petrol engines

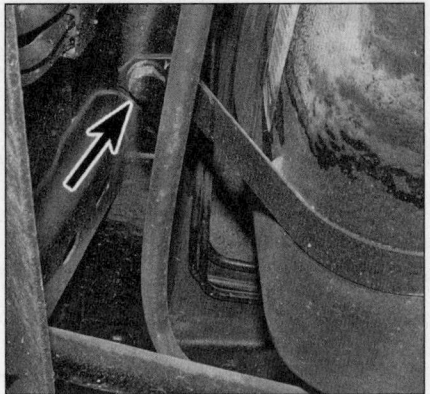

8.15a Front strap bolt

8.15b Rear strap bolt

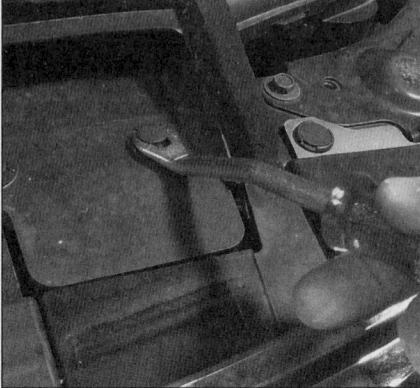

9.1a Remove the plastic fasteners at the front of the air inlet duct…

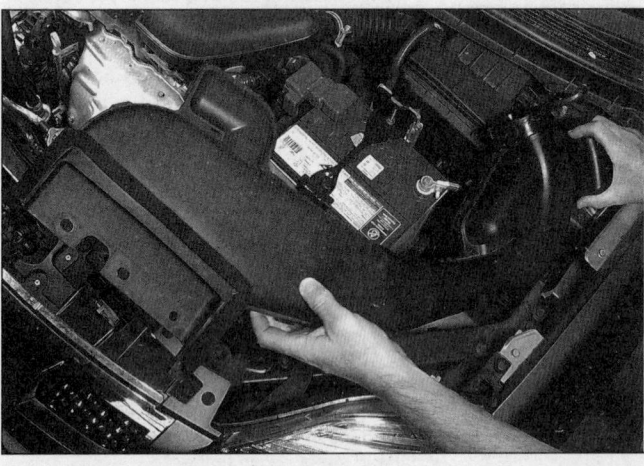

9.1b … then free the rear of the duct from the clips on the air filter housing

9.3a Disconnecting the MAF sensor connector

17　Installation is the reverse of removal.
18　Reconnect the battery and perform the system initialisation procedure (see Chapter 5 Section 4).

9　Air filter housing - removal and installation

Air filter housing

1　Remove the air inlet duct **(see illustration)**.

2　Remove the battery and battery tray (see Chapter 5 Section 5).
3　Disconnect the electrical connector from the MAF sensor **(see illustration)**, unclip the wiring harness from the air filter housing **(see illustration)**.
4　Loosen the hose clamp and remove the retaining bolt and partially remove the resonator from the valve cover. Disconnect the breather hose from the valve cover **(see illustration)**.
5　Loosen the hose clamp on the duct at the air filter housing and throttle body and remove the hose.

6　Remove the air filter housing fasteners **(see illustrations)**.
7　Installation is the reverse of removal.

Resonator

Upper resonator

8　Loosen the clamp connecting the resonator to the air duct between the throttle body and air filter housing **(see illustration)**.
9　Squeeze the hose clamp and slide it back on the crankcase ventilation hose, then disconnect the hose from the resonator.

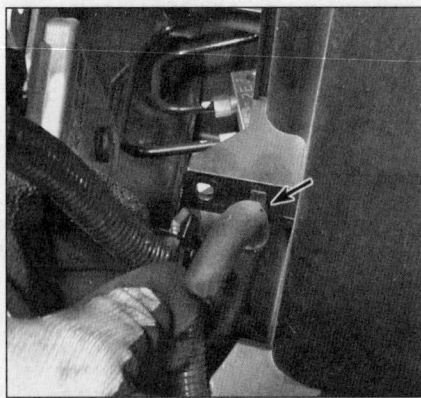

9.3b Unclip the diff breather (arrow) and the MAF sensor wiring from the air filter housing

9.4 Partially remove the resonator and unclip the breather hose from the valve cover

9.5 Air duct (1) and hose clamps (2)

Chapter 4 Part A Fuel and exhaust systems - petrol engines   4A-11

9.6a Arrows indicate the air filter housing fasteners, the lower fastener is accessed after removing the battery tray

9.6b Lift the housing off the stud on the strut tower and manoeuvre the housing out from under the cowl panel

9.8a Loosen the hose clamp at the air intake duct

9.8b Remove the mounting bolt from the front of the upper resonator

9.9 Partially remove the resonator and unclip the breather hose from the valve cover

9.13 Remove the air duct from the top of the resonator

10 Remove the resonator mounting bolt, then pull the resonator up and off of its grommet.
11 Installation is the reverse of removal.

Lower resonator

12 Remove the air inlet duct (see illustration 9.1a and 9.1b).
13 Remove the air duct from the top of the resonator (see illustration).
14 Remove the inner guard liner (see Chapter 11 Section 18).

15 Remove the resonator fasteners (see illustration), then remove the resonator through the wheel well opening.
16 Installation is the reverse of removal.

10 Throttle body - removal and installation

Caution: *The engine must be completely cool before beginning this procedure.*

1 Disconnect the negative (-) battery terminal (see Chapter 5 Section 3).
2 Remove the upper air intake resonator (see Section 9).
3 Remove the air duct between the throttle body and the air filter housing (see Section 9).
4 Clamp-off the coolant hoses to the throttle body, then disconnect them (see illustration).
5 Disconnect the electrical connector from the throttle body.

9.15 Location of the resonator mounting fasteners - bumper cover removed for clarity

10.4 Throttle body coolant hoses

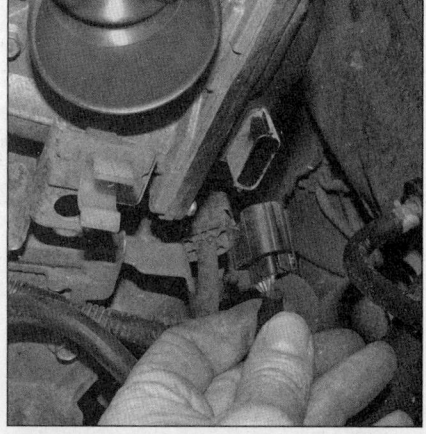

10.5 Disconnecting the throttle body wiring connector

Chapter 4 Part A Fuel and exhaust systems - petrol engines

10.6 Throttle body mounting fasteners

10.7 Removing the throttle body from the plenum

10.8 Throttle body O-ring location - use a new one on assembly if the old one looks distorted or damaged

11.1a Rear muffler assembly on a T31 X-Trail uses three rubber exhaust hangers for mounting

11.1b All other models have a rear muffler running across the rear of the vehicle - arrows indicate the rear hanger locations

11.2a Check that any heatshields are securely installed - this one reduces the amount of heat being transferred to the rear differential on AWD models

6 Loosen the throttle body mounting bolts a little at a time in a criss-cross pattern to prevent distortion.
7 Remove the throttle body.
8 Installation is the reverse of removal; use a new throttle body O-ring if the old one is not in perfect condition. Tighten the bolts a little at a time in a criss-cross pattern to the torque listed in this Chapter's Specifications.
9 Reconnect the battery and perform the system initialisation procedure (see Chapter 5 Section 4).

11 Exhaust system servicing - general information

Warning: *Allow exhaust system components to cool before inspection or repair. Also, when working under the vehicle, make sure it is securely supported on jackstands (see Chapter 0 Section 7).*
1 The exhaust system consists of the exhaust manifolds, catalytic converter, muffler, tailpipe and all connecting pipes, flanges and clamps. The exhaust system is isolated from the vehicle body and from chassis components by a series of rubber hangers. Periodically inspect these hangers for cracks or other signs of deterioration, replacing them as necessary.
2 Conduct regular inspections of the exhaust system to keep it safe and quiet. Look for any damaged or bent parts, open seams, holes, loose connections, excessive corrosion or other defects which could allow exhaust fumes to enter the vehicle. Do not repair deteriorated exhaust system components; replace them with new parts.
3 If the exhaust system components are extremely corroded, or rusted together, a cutting torch is the most convenient tool for removal. Consult a properly-equipped repair shop. If a cutting torch is not available, you can use a hacksaw, or if you have compressed air, there are special pneumatic cutting chisels that can also be used. Wear safety goggles to protect your eyes from metal chips and wear work gloves to protect your hands.
4 Here are some simple guidelines to follow when repairing the exhaust system:

a *Work from the back to the front when removing exhaust system components.*
b *Apply penetrating oil to the exhaust system component fasteners to make them easier to remove.*
c *Use new gaskets, hangers and clamps.*
d *Apply anti-seize compound to the threads of all exhaust system fasteners during reassembly.*
e *Allow sufficient clearance between newly installed parts and all points on the underbody to avoid overheating the floor pan and possibly damaging the interior carpet and insulation. Pay particularly close attention to the catalytic converter and heat shield.*

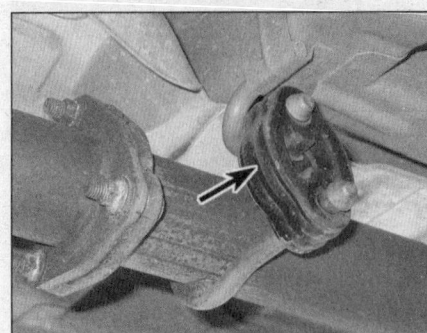

11.2b Check that the exhaust hangers are not torn or cracked - these can be easily replaced if necessary

11.2c Black soot between a joint as shown is an indication of a leaking joint

Chapter 4 Part B
Fuel and exhaust systems - diesel engine

Contents

	Section		Section
Accelerator Pedal Position (APP) sensor - replacement	See Chapter 6	General information and precautions	1
Air filter housing - removal and installation	6	High-pressure pump – removal and refitting	8
Exhaust system servicing - general information	11	Idle speed – general	2
Fuel injectors – testing, removal and refitting	9	Injection system electronic components – removal and refitting	See Chapter 6
Fuel pump and fuel gauge sender unit – removal and refitting	4	Injector rail (common rail) – removal and refitting	10
Fuel system – priming and bleeding	3	Throttle body - removal and installation	7
Fuel tank – removal and refitting	5		

Specifications

Fuel injectors
Fuel injector resistance... 178.2 to 181.8 ohms

Fuel pump
Fuel pump resistance .... 2 to 6 ohms

1 General information and precautions

General information

1 The fuel system consists of a rear-mounted fuel tank, a fuel filter, a high-pressure pump with common rail injection system, electronic injectors and associated components.

2 The main components of the system are as follows:
- Priming bulb on the low-pressure circuit.
- Fuel filter.
- High-pressure fuel pump.
- Injector rail.
- Pressure sensor located on the injector rail.
- Four electronic solenoid injectors.
- Fuel temperature sensor.
- Coolant temperature sensor.
- Air temperature sensor.
- Cylinder reference sensor.
- Engine speed sensor.
- Turbocharging pressure sensor.
- EGR solenoid valve.
- Accelerator pedal potentiometer.
- Atmospheric pressure sensor.
- Engine Control Module (ECM).

3 The common rail injection system operates as follows. Fuel is drawn from the fuel tank to the high-pressure pump by a low-pressure transfer pump integrated in the high-pressure pump. Before reaching the high-pressure pump, the fuel passes through a fuel filter, where foreign matter and water are removed. As the fuel passes through the filter, it is heated by an electric heater. On reaching the high-pressure pump, the fuel is pressurised according to demand, and accumulates in the injection common-rail. The pressure in the rail is accurately maintained using a pressure sensor in the rail and a pressure regulator under the control of the engine management ECM. This arrangement keeps heat generation to a minimum, and improves engine output. The rail pressure is also maintained by the injectors themselves; short electrical pulses which are not long enough to open the injector allow fuel into the return (leak-off) circuit, and also the normal pulses which open the injectors cause a reduction in pressure. The ECM determines the exact timing and duration of the injection period according to engine operating conditions.

4 The four fuel injectors inject a homogeneous spray of fuel into the combustion chambers located in the cylinder head. The injectors operate sequentially according to the firing order of the cylinders, and each injec-

1.8 Vehicle diagnostic connector (arrowed)

tor needle is lubricated by fuel, which accumulates in the spring chamber. Each injector has its own unique flow characteristics, which are used by the system ECM to calculate the exact quantity of fuel to inject.

5 In terms of the sensors used by the ECM to control a modern common-rail diesel system, these engines are very similar to their petrol equivalents. The ECM determines engine speed and position from a TDC sensor fitted to the transmission bellhousing, which detects a reference tooth on the flywheel ring gear, and signals the ECM. A similar sensor is fitted to monitor the camshaft, to give a reference for No 1 cylinder. Further sensors are used to monitor airflow into the engine, air temperature, and turbocharging pressure. On the fuel side, fuel pressure, temperature and flow rate are all monitored, according to model, via sensors on the high-pressure pump and/or the fuel rail. As with the petrol-engine models, an 'electronic' throttle is fitted, with an accelerator position sensor instead of the mechanical cable previously used.

6 Provided that the specified maintenance is carried out, the fuel injection equipment will give long and trouble-free service. The main potential cause of damage to the high-pressure pump and injectors is dirt or water in the fuel. It is highly recommended that a set of fuel line plugs is obtained – these are available from motor accessory shops and better motor factors.

7 Servicing of the high-pressure pump, injectors, and electronic equipment and sensors is very limited for the home mechanic, and any dismantling or adjustment other than that described in this Chapter must be entrusted to a Nissan dealer or a diesel fuel injection specialist.

8 If a fault appears in the injection system, first ensure that all the system wiring connectors are securely connected and free of corrosion. Should the fault persist, the vehicle should be taken to a Nissan dealer or specialist who can test the system on a diagnostic tester **(see illustration)**. The tester will locate the fault quickly and simply, alleviating the need to test all the system components individually, which is a time-consuming operation that carries a risk of damaging the ECM. It is advisable to have any faulty components renewed by the dealer as in many instances the tester is required to reprogram the ECM in the event of component or sensor renewal.

Precautions

Warning: *It is necessary to take certain precautions when working on the fuel system components, particularly the fuel injectors and high-pressure pump. Before carrying out any operations on the fuel system, refer to the precautions given in 'Safety first!' at the beginning of this manual, and to any additional warning notes at the start of the relevant Sections. Allow the engine to cool for 5 to 10 minutes to ensure the fuel pressure and temperatures are at a minimum.*

Warning: *Exercise extreme caution when working on the high-pressure fuel system. Do not attempt to test the fuel injectors or disconnect the high-pressure lines with the engine running. Never expose the hands or any part of the body to injector spray, as the high working pressure can cause the fuel to penetrate the skin, with possibly fatal results. You are strongly advised to have any work that involves testing the injectors under pressure carried out by a dealer or fuel injection specialist.*

2 Idle speed – general

1 The engine management ECM uses the following inputs to calculate the recommended idle speed according to the varying load on the engine by peripheral electrical or mechanical components.

- Engine coolant temperature.
- Battery voltage.
- The gear selected.
- Electrical consumers (heater fan, climate control system, etc).

2 At normal engine temperature with no electrical consumers switched on and neutral selected, the engine idle speed will be 700 to 800 rpm, depending on engine type.

3 If the accelerator pedal potentiometer internal tracks are faulty, the ECM will override the idle speed to approx. 1200 rpm, and the injection warning light will be illuminated on the instrument panel. If the brake pedal is depressed, the idle speed will revert to its normal level.

4 If there is an injector fault, the idle speed will be set to 1200 rpm and the warning light will be illuminated.

5 Should the idle speed be repeatedly incorrect, the car should be taken to a Nissan dealer who will have the necessary diagnostic equipment to pinpoint the faulty component responsible.

3 Fuel system – priming and bleeding

Warning: *Refer to the precautions in Section 1 before proceeding.*

1 Do not attempt to bleed the system by loosening any of the unions on the high-pressure circuit.

Note: *Priming of the fuel system after filter renewal will be improved if the filter is filled with clean diesel fuel before securing it to the filter head. To avoid spillages of fuel, keep the filter upright during refitting.*

2 After disconnecting part of the fuel supply system or running out of fuel, it is necessary to prime the system and bleed off any air that may have entered the system components.

3 There is a priming pump to enable the system to be bled; this consists of a hand-operated priming bulb located next to the filter assembly on the right-hand side rear of the inner wing panel **(see illustration)**.

4 Squeeze the priming bulb several times to purge the low-pressure circuit of air **(see illustration)**.

5 Attempt to start the engine normally, however, do not operate the starter motor for more than 5 seconds at a time. If necessary, operate the starter motor in 4 to 5 second

3.3 Diesel hand priming pump location

3.4 Squeeze the priming pump to purge the circuit

Chapter 4 Part B Fuel and exhaust systems - diesel engine

3.6 Fuel bleed point

3.7 Lift the cap (arrowed) to get rid of the air

6.3a Release the retaining clips …

6.3b … and remove the air intake ducting

6.4 Unclip the turbo boost valve

6 Air filter housing - removal and installation

Removal

1 To make removal of the air cleaner assembly easier, remove the battery (see Chapter 5 Section 5).

2 Remove the PCM (see Chapter 6 Section 15).

3 Remove the two retaining clips and release the air intake ducting from the front crossmember, and then withdraw it from the air cleaner housing (see illustrations).

4 Unclip the turbocharger boost control solenoid valve from the air filter mounting bracket, and move it to one side (see illustrations).

5 Disconnect the wiring connector from the mass airflow sensor (see illustrations); unclip the wiring from any retaining clips on the housing.

6 Slacken the retaining clip and disconnect the air intake hose from the air cleaner assembly (see illustration).

7 Undo the retaining nut that secures the air cleaner housing to the inner wing panel (see illustration).

8 Pull the air cleaner upwards, disengaging the locating pegs on the bottom of the air cleaner assembly, from the rubber mountings,

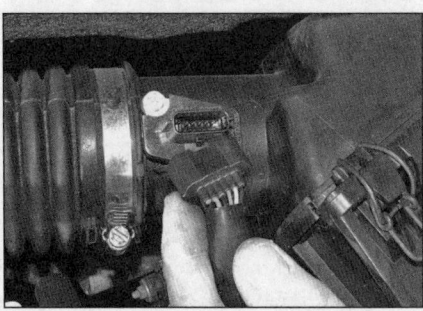

6.5a Disconnect the wiring connector …

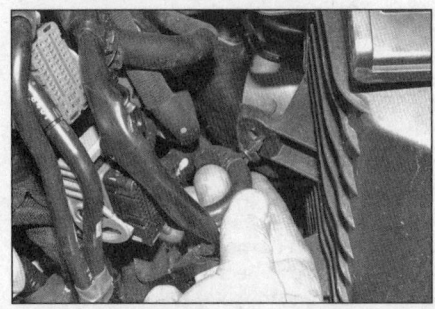

6.5b … and unclip the breather hose securing clip

bursts followed by pauses of 8 to 10 seconds. As soon as the engine starts, let it run at fast idle speed until a regular idle speed is reached.

6 If difficulty in purging the air from the system is experienced (engine may hunt), it is possible to bleed the system through the return pipe (see illustration).

7 Place some clean rags around the fuel pipe, and then using a flat bladed screwdriver, lift the cap on the fuel return pipe connection (see illustration), and crank the engine until the air is removed. When complete push the cap down to seal the return pipe and check for any leaks.

8 Start the engine, let it run at fast idle speed until a regular idle speed is reached, and then check for any fuel leaks.

4 Fuel pump and fuel gauge sender unit – removal and refitting

1 The diesel engine fuel pump/gauge sender unit has the same removal procedure as the petrol engines. Remove the fuel pump/gauge sender unit, as described in Part A of this Chapter (see Chapter 4A Section 7).

5 Fuel tank – removal and refitting

1 The diesel engine fuel tank has the same removal procedure as the petrol engines. Remove the fuel tank, as described in Part A of this Chapter (see Chapter 4A Section 8).

6.6 Slacken the hose retaining clip (arrowed)

4B-4 Chapter 4 Part B Fuel and exhaust systems - diesel engine

6.7 Undo the air filter housing securing nut (arrowed)

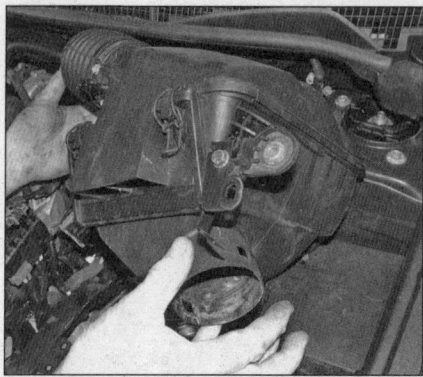

6.8a Remove the air cleaner housing

6.8b Withdrawing it from the lower mountings (arrowed)

7.2 Lifting the engine cover from the engine

7.4 Loosening the air intake hose clamp

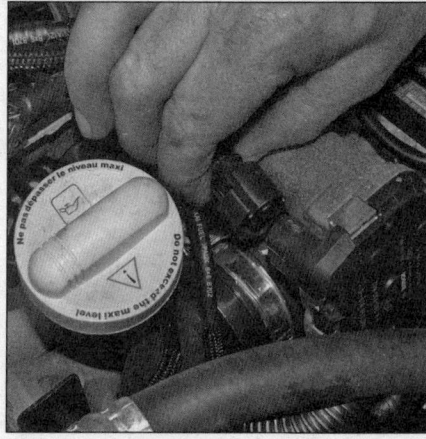

7.5 Disconnecting the throttle control motor wiring connector

and then remove it from the engine compartment **(see illustrations)**.

9 If required remove the air filter element (see Chapter 1 Section 21).

Refitting

10 Refitting is a reversal of the relevant removal procedure, ensuring that all hoses are properly reconnected, and that all ducts are correctly seated and securely held by their retaining clips.

7 Throttle body - removal and installation

Caution: *The engine must be completely cool before beginning this procedure.*

1 Disconnect the negative (-) battery terminal (see Chapter 5 Section 3).

2 Lift up and remove the engine cover from the top of the engine **(see illustration)**.

3 Disconnect the wiring connector from the turbocharger pressure sensor and the EGR solenoid valve.

4 Loosen the hose clamp and disconnect the air intake hose from the throttle body **(see illustration)** and then move the hose to one side.

5 Disconnect the wiring from the throttle body **(see illustration)**.

7 Remove and discard the gasket/seal **(see illustrations)**.

8 Refitting is a reversal of removal, using a new gasket/seal and tightening to the specified torque.

8 High-pressure pump – removal and refitting

Warning: *Refer to the warning note in Section 1 before proceeding.*

Caution: *Before starting work, allow the engine to cool for 5 to 10 minutes, to ensure the fuel pressure and temperature are at a minimum.*

Note: *Cleanliness is of critical importance when working on the fuel system of any modern diesel engine. The smallest speck of grit or dirt can cause extensive damage to the pump and injectors. Always clean thoroughly the pump and injector unions before*

7.7a Removing the throttle body from the intake manifold

7.7b Remove and discard the gasket from the throttle body - use a new one on installation

8.1 Disconnect the fuel pipe (arrowed) from the fuel rail

8.3 Remove the plastic cover (arrowed) from the fuel connection

8.4 Disconnect the fuel supply hose (arrowed)

8.5a Unscrew the mounting bolts …

8.5b …withdraw the pump from the cylinder head …

dismantling. Immediately plug and seal all pipes and components. Components that are removed from the engine should immediately be placed in clean plastic bags.

Removal

1 Remove the cylinder head cover, then unscrew the union nut and disconnect the high-pressure pipe from the fuel rail **(see illustration)**, refer to Section 10, to gain access to the fuel rail. As a precaution against remaining pressure in the pipes, first wrap them loosely in cloth/rag. Cap or plug the open connections to reduce fuel loss and prevent entry of dirt.

2 For improved access, remove the battery, as described in.

3 Unclip the plastic cover, then unscrew the union nut and disconnect the high-pressure pipe from the fuel pump **(see illustration)**. Cap or plug the open connections to reduce fuel loss and prevent entry of dirt.

4 Disconnect the quick-release fuel supply and return hoses from the high-pressure pump and plug the openings **(see illustration)**.

5 Progressively unscrew the mounting bolts then withdraw the high-pressure pump from the cylinder head. Remove the O-ring seal from the groove, a new one will be required for refitting **(see illustrations)**.

6 If necessary, the pinion may be removed from the high-pressure pump drive shaft **(see illustration)**. To do this, first lock the pinion in a soft-jawed vice and unscrew the retaining nut. A puller will now be required to remove the pinion from the drive shaft.

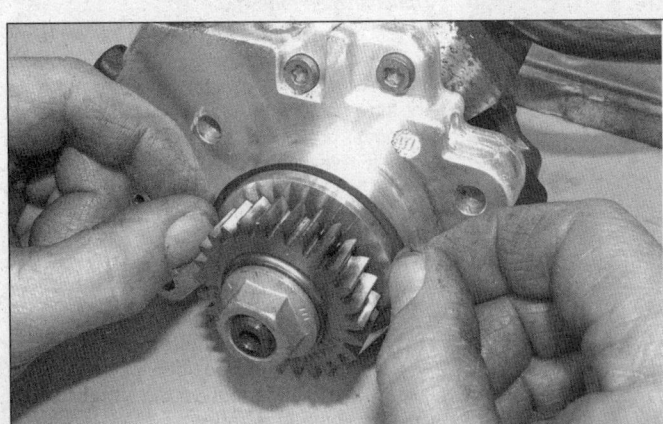
8.5c … and remove the O-ring seal

8.6 High-pressure pump pinion

4B-6 Chapter 4 Part B Fuel and exhaust systems - diesel engine

9.4 Remove the oil separator (arrowed)

9.6 Disconnect the injector wiring connectors

9.7 Removing the leak-off pipes from the injectors

Refitting

Note: *The manufacturers stipulate that the high-pressure pipe is renewed whenever it is removed.*

7   Refitting is a reversal of removal, but take care not to place the new high-pressure pipe under any stress. If fitting a new pump, it is highly recommended that the pump is primed with diesel on the bench before fitting.

8   Install a new O-ring seal to the pump and new retaining bolts.

9   New high-pressure pipes are supplied with a lubricant for the threads on the pipe. If no lubricant is supplied the pipes are self-lubricating and lubricant should not be applied.

10   Tighten all nuts and bolts to the specified torque and angle as applicable.

11   Prime and bleed the fuel system as described in.

12   Before restarting the engine, it may be necessary to use a diagnostic tool to clear any faults that may be stored in the engine control module (ECM).

9   Fuel injectors – testing, removal and refitting

Warning: *Exercise extreme caution when working on the high-pressure fuel system. Do not attempt to test the fuel injectors or disconnect the high-pressure lines with the engine running. Never expose the hands or any part of the body to injector spray, as the high working pressure can cause the fuel to penetrate the skin, with possibly fatal results. You are strongly advised to have any work that involves testing the injectors under pressure carried out by a dealer or fuel injection specialist. Refer to the precautions given in Section 1 of this Chapter before proceeding. After switching off the engine, allow the engine to cool for 5 to 10 minutes to allow the fuel pressure to drop before disconnecting any of the high-pressure fuel pipes.*

Note: *Each new injector is supplied with a unique code, which specifies its flow characteristics. This code must be programmed into the engine management PCM with a special diagnostic tool; therefore this work should be entrusted to a Nissan dealer or suitably equipped garage.*

Testing

1   It is not possible to test the fuel injectors without specialist equipment, therefore, if they are thought to be faulty, consult a Nissan dealer or diesel specialist.

Removal

Note: *Take care not to allow dirt into the injectors or fuel pipes during this procedure; clean around the area before commencing work. Note that all high-pressure pipes removed must be renewed as a matter of course. The injector flame shield washers must also be renewed.*

2   Disconnect the negative (-) battery terminal (see Chapter 5 Section 3).

3   Remove the injector cover from the top of the engine with reference to the camshaft removal procedure in Part C of the Engine chapter (see Chapter 2C Section 12).

4   Undo the retaining bolts and remove the oil separator from the top of the cylinder head **(see illustration)**.

5   Carefully clean around the fuel injectors and injector pipe union nuts.

6   Disconnect the wiring connectors from the fuel injectors **(see illustration)**.

7   Note the fitted position of the leak-off pipes, and then disconnect them from the fuel injectors **(see illustration)**.

9.8a Unscrew the union nuts ...

9.8c ... and disconnect the pipes from the injectors and fuel rail

9.8b ... where necessary undo the pipe support clamp bolts ...

Chapter 4 Part B Fuel and exhaust systems - diesel engine

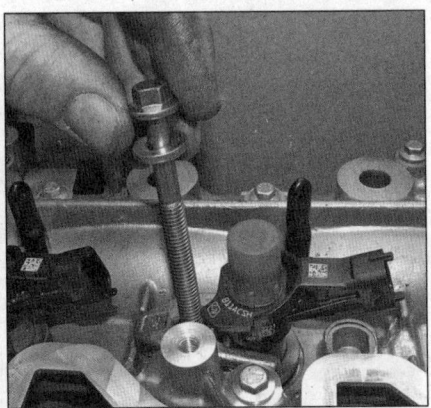
9.10a Unscrew the retaining bolts ...

9.10b ... remove the clamp plates ...

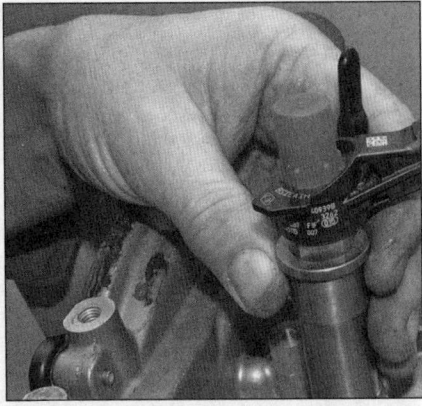
9.10c ... then withdraw the injector ...

8 Unscrew the union nuts securing the injector pipes to the fuel rail whilst being prepared for some fuel spillage, then unscrew the union nuts and disconnect the pipes from the injectors. Where necessary, undo the pipe support clamp bolts **(see illustrations)**. As a precaution against remaining pressure in the pipes, first wrap them loosely in cloth/rag. Plug all fuel apertures to prevent entry of dust and dirt.

9 Using a felt-tipped pen, mark each injector for its position (No 1 cylinder at the timing chain end). This is important because the engine management ECM recognises each injector by the cylinder it is located in. If new injectors are obtained, the code on each injector must be noted and programmed into the ECM.

10 Unscrew the bolt securing each injector clamp plate, lift off the clamp plates and withdraw the injectors. Recover the flame shield washer between the injectors and the cylinder head **(see illustrations)**.

Refitting

11 Take care not to drop the injectors or allow the needles at their tips to become damaged. The injectors are precision-made to fine limits and must not be handled roughly.

In particular, do not mount them in a bench vice. It is recommended that the injectors are stored vertically at all times.

12 Clean the cylinder head, taking care to prevent foreign matter entering the fuel apertures. The injectors can be cleaned with a lint-free cloth soaked in brake cleaning fluid or fresh diesel. Do not clean them with a wire brush or emery cloth.

13 Obtain new injector sealing washers and new fuel pipes for refitting.

14 Fit new sealing shims between the injectors and the cylinder head. Insert the injectors then fit the clamp plates. Tighten the clamp plate bolts to the specified torque.

15 Fit new injector pipes, and tighten the union nuts on the injectors and the fuel rail by hand at first. Make sure the pipe clamps are in their previously noted positions. Bearing in mind the high vibration levels with a diesel engine, if the clamps are wrongly positioned or missing, problems may be experienced with pipes breaking or splitting. With all the pipes in place tighten them to the specified torque setting.

16 Renew the injector leak-off pipes, and refit in the position noted on removal.

17 Reconnect the fuel injector wiring.

18 Refit the engine cylinder cover (see Chapter 2C Section 12).

19 Reconnect the negative battery terminal (see Chapter 5 Section 3).

20 If new injectors have been fitted, have the code programmed into the engine management PCM by a Nissan dealer.

21 Start the engine. If difficulty is experienced, bleed the fuel system (see Section 3).

10 Injector rail (common rail) – removal and refitting

Warning: *Refer to the warning note in Section 1 before proceeding. After switching off the engine, allow several minutes for the fuel pressure so subside before disconnecting any of the high-pressure fuel pipes.*

Note: *Take care not to allow dirt into the fuel pipes during this procedure, clean around the area before commencing work. Note that all high-pressure pipes removed must be renewed as a matter of course.*

Removal

1 Disconnect the negative (-) battery terminal (see Chapter 5 Section 3).

2 Remove the plastic engine cover (where fitted) from the top of the engine.

3 The fuel rail is located on the side of the camshaft housing, with the injector and pump connections emerging from inside the housing upper cavity. First, remove the injector cover from the top of the engine with reference to the camshaft removal procedure in Part C of the Engine chapter (see Chapter 2C Section 12).

4 Disconnect the wiring connectors from the fuel rail switches, at each end of the fuel rail **(see illustrations)**.

Note: *The one on the passenger side of the rail is the fuel rail pressure sensor, and the one on the driver side of the fuel rail is the fuel rail pressure control valve.*

5 Disconnect the fuel return hose from the right-hand end of the fuel rail **(see illustration)**.

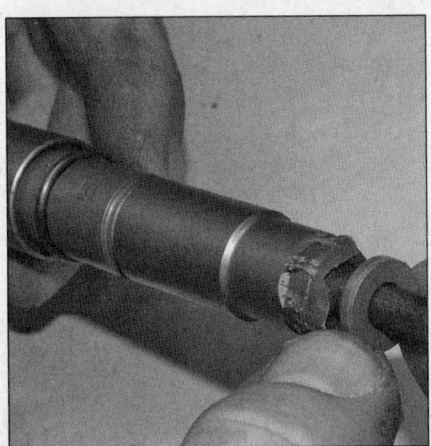
9.10d ... and recover the flame shield washer

10.4a Disconnect the pressure sensor wiring connector (arrowed)

Chapter 4 Part B Fuel and exhaust systems - diesel engine

10.4b Disconnect the pressure control valve wiring connector (arrowed)

10.5 Disconnect the fuel return hose (arrowed)

10.7 Undo the fuel pipe union nut and release the pipe retaining clamp bolt (arrowed)

10.8 Remove the four injector-to-fuel rail pipes

6 Unclip the plastic cover, then unscrew the union nut and disconnect the high-pressure pipe from the fuel pump, see Section 8. As a precaution against remaining pressure in the pipes, first wrap them loosely in cloth/rag.

7 Unscrew the union nut and disconnect the high-pressure pipe from the fuel rail, undo the pipe securing clamp bolt and remove the pipe from the engine (see illustrations). Discard the fuel pipes, as new ones will be required for refitting.

8 With reference to Section 9, unscrew the union nuts and disconnect the fuel supply pipes from the injectors and fuel rail, new ones will be required for refitting (see illustration). Release the fuel pipes and unclip from any retaining clips, note their position for refitting. Discard the fuel pipes, as new ones will be required for refitting.

9 Cover or plug all fuel apertures to prevent entry of dust and dirt into the fuel system.

10 Unbolt and remove the fuel rail from the front of the cylinder head (see illustrations).

Refitting

11 Refitting is a reversal of removal, but take care not to place the new high-pressure pipe under any stress. Before fitting the new pipe, lubricate the threads of the union nuts with oil from the sachet provided, and finger-tighten the nuts before tightening them to the specified torque. When tightening the pipe union nuts onto the injectors, counter-hold the injectors with a further spanner.

12 On completion, prime and bleed the fuel system as described in Section 3. Run the engine, and check for fuel leaks.

10.10a Undo the mounting bolts ...

10.10b ...and lower the fuel rail to withdraw

Chapter 4 Part B Fuel and exhaust systems - diesel engine

11.2 Front flexible exhaust pipe

11.3a Exhaust rubber mounting ...

11 Exhaust system servicing - general information

General information

1 The exhaust system consists of the exhaust manifold (see Chapter 2C Section 6), the turbocharger (see Chapter 2C Section 7), the catalytic converter, the front pipe/particle filter (depending on model) and the remaining exhaust section consisting of the intermediate pipe/tailpipe and silencer.
2 The front pipe is connected by a flexible length of pipe **(see illustration)**.
3 The system is suspended throughout its entire length by rubber mountings **(see illustrations)**, and all exhaust sections are joined by flanged joints, which are then secured together by nuts and/or bolts.
4 To remove the system or part of the system, firmly apply the handbrake, and then jack up the vehicle and support it securely on axle stands (see Chapter 0 Section 7). Alternatively, position the car over an inspection

11.3b ... some models have a mounting block on the front subframe

pit, or on car ramps. Where fitted, remove the engine compartment undertray.

Front pipe

5 Undo the nuts securing the front pipe to the catalytic converter **(see illustration)**. With the nuts removed retrieve the washers and springs, and then separate the front pipe from the catalytic converter/manifold.
6 Slacken and remove the two bolts securing the front pipe/silencer flange joint to the intermediate pipe. Withdraw the front pipe from underneath the vehicle, and recover the gasket from the joint **(see illustration)**.

11.5 Undo the front pipe-to-catalytic converter bolts/nuts

11.6 Undo the front pipe to intermediate pipe bolts

11.13a Undo the retaining clips ...

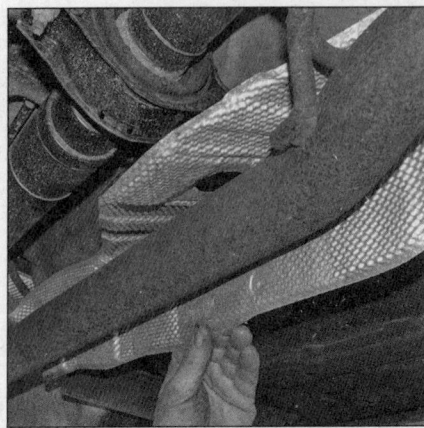
11.13b ... and remove the heat shield

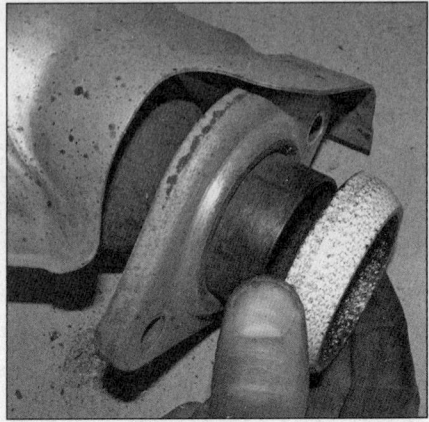
11.14a Fit new sealing rings to the silencer ...

11.14b ... and the exhaust front pipe

Intermediate pipe/silencer/tailpipe

7 Slacken and remove the two bolts securing the front pipe flange joint to the intermediate pipe and separate. Support the disconnected front pipe so as not to place undue strain on the front part of the exhaust system.

8 With the aid of an assistant, working along the underside of the vehicle, unhook the intermediate pipe/silencer/tailpipe from its mounting rubbers, and then manoeuvre the pipe out from underneath the vehicle.

Catalytic converter

9 Remove the exhaust front pipe as described previously in this Section.

10 Undo the retaining bolts and remove the heat shield from around the catalytic converter.

11 Undo the retaining bolts and remove the support bracket from the bottom of the catalytic converter.

12 Slacken the retaining nuts securing the catalytic converter to the turbocharger, and lower the catalytic converter from under the vehicle.

Heat shield(s)

13 The heat shields are secured in position by a mixture of fasteners. Some heat shields are fitted to the underside of the vehicle. And also some are fitted to parts of the exhaust system. When an exhaust section is renewed, transfer any relevant heat shields from the original over to the new section before installing the exhaust section on the vehicle (see illustrations).

Refitting

14 Each section is refitted by a reverse of the removal sequence, noting the following points:

a Ensure that all traces of corrosion have been removed from the flanges, and renew all necessary gaskets (see illustrations).

b Inspect the rubber mountings for signs of damage or deterioration, and renew as necessary.

c Prior to tightening the exhaust system fasteners, ensure that all rubber mountings are correctly located, and that there is adequate clearance between the exhaust system and vehicle underbody/suspension components, etc.

Chapter 5
Engine electrical systems

Contents

	Section		Section
Alternator – removal and installation	11	Glow plugs – removal, inspection and installation	9
Battery - disconnection and reconnection	3	Ignition coil(s) - replacement	7
Battery and battery tray - removal and installation	5	Pre-heating system – testing	8
Battery cables - replacement	6	Pre-heating system control unit – removal and installation	10
Booster battery (jump) starting	See Chapter 0	Starter motor – removal and installation	12
Drivebelt check and replacement	See Chapter 1	System initialisation	4
General information and precautions	1	Troubleshooting	2

Specifications

Charging voltage	14.1 to 14.7 Volts
Glow plug resistance at 20 degrees C	0.1 to 1.0 ohms

Torque specifications

	Nm
Alternator mounting bolts	
Petrol engines	
2.0 litre	25
2.5 litre	
T31 X-Trail	65
T32 X-Trail	25
Diesel engine	25
Glow plugs - diesel engine	17
Ignition coils	
2.0 litre engine	
2.5 litre engine	7
Starter motor mounting bolts	
Petrol engines	
2.0 litre	62
2.5 litre	
T31 X-Trail	112
T32 X-Trail	
Upper bolt	113
Lower bolt	47
Diesel engine	48

Chapter 5 Engine electrical systems

1 General information and precautions

General information

Ignition system - petrol engines

1 The electronic ignition system consists of the Crankshaft Position (CKP) sensor, the Camshaft Position (CMP) sensor, the Knock Sensor (KS), the Powertrain Control Module (PCM), the ignition switch, the battery, the individual ignition coils or a coil pack, and the spark plugs. For more information on the CKP, CMP and KS sensors, as well as the PCM (see Chapter 6).

Charging system

2 The charging system includes the alternator (with an integral voltage regulator), the Powertrain Control Module (PCM), the Body Control Module (BCM), a charge indicator light on the dash, the battery, a fuse or fusible link and the wiring connecting all of these components. The charging system supplies electrical power for the ignition system, the lights, the radio, etc. The alternator is driven by a drivebelt.

Starting system

3 The starting system consists of the battery, the ignition switch, the starter relay, the Powertrain Control Module (PCM), the Body Control Module (BCM), the Transmission Range (TR) switch, the starter motor and solenoid assembly, and the wiring connecting all of the components.

Preheating system - diesel engines

4 The preheating/post-heating system consists of glow plugs screwed into the combustion chambers, a control unit mounted next to the battery on the left-hand side of the engine compartment, and a coolant temperature sensor located on the thermostat housing. The control unit is itself activated by the engine management ECM.

5 The glow plugs are supplied with current from the control unit in several phases, namely variable preheating, fixed preheating, starting heating, and variable post-heating.

6 The variable preheating phase occurs when the ignition is switched on, and during this phase the preheating warning light is illuminated on the instrument panel. The period of preheating depends on the temperature of the coolant and battery voltage. The maximum period of 15 seconds occurs if the coolant temperature is low and the battery voltage is less than 9.3 volts. The period varies from 15 seconds to zero seconds according to the temperature of the coolant, and when the temperature reaches 80°C, no preheating occurs. With normal battery voltage the maximum period is 10 seconds.

7 The fixed preheating phase occurs straight after the variable phase finishes, after the warning light has extinguished, and lasts for up to 5 seconds. Normally, the driver will start the engine at some point during this phase.

8 During the period when the starter motor is in operation, the glow plugs are continuously supplied with current.

9 The variable post-heating phase occurs immediately after the engine has been started, and the period of post-heating depends on the temperature of the coolant. The maximum period of variable post-heating is 60 seconds, at which point the system is switched off. Variable post-heating will cease if the coolant temperature exceeds 80°C.

Precautions

10 Always observe the following precautions when working on the electrical system: Be extremely careful when servicing engine electrical components. They are easily damaged if checked, connected or handled improperly.

  a Never leave the ignition switched on for long periods of time when the engine is not running.
  b Never disconnect the battery cables while the engine is running.
  c Maintain correct polarity when connecting battery cables from another vehicle during jump starting (see Chapter 0 Section 6).
  d Always disconnect the cable from the negative battery terminal before working on the electrical system, but read the battery disconnection procedure first (see Section 3).

11 It's also a good idea to review the safety-related information regarding the engine electrical systems located in (see Chapter 0, Section 9) before beginning any operation included in this Chapter.

2 Troubleshooting

Ignition system

1 If a malfunction occurs in the ignition system, do not immediately assume that any particular part is causing the problem. First, check the following items:

  a Make sure that the cable clamps at the battery terminals are clean and tight.
  b Test the condition of the battery (see Steps 15 through 18). If it doesn't pass all the tests, replace it.
  c Check the ignition coil or coil pack connections.
  d Check any relevant fuses in the engine compartment fuse and relay box (see Chapter 12A Section 3). If they're burned, determine the cause and repair the circuit.

Check

Warning: *Because of the high voltage generated by the ignition system, use extreme care when performing a procedure involving ignition components.*

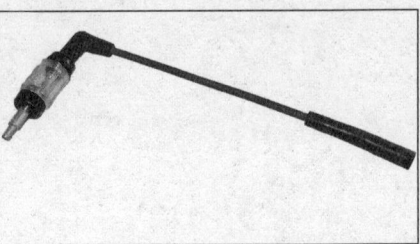

2.3 Spark tester

Note: *The ignition system components on these vehicles are difficult to diagnose. In the event of an ignition system failure that you can't diagnose, have the vehicle tested at a dealer service department or other qualified auto repair facility.*

Note: *You'll need a spark tester for the following test. Spark testers are available at most auto supply stores.*

2 If the engine turns over but won't start, verify that there is sufficient ignition voltage to fire the spark plugs as follows.

3 Remove a coil and install the tester between the boot at the lower end of the coil and the spark plug **(see illustration)**.

4 Crank the engine and note whether or not the tester flashes.

Caution: *Do NOT crank the engine or allow it to run for more than five seconds; running the engine for more than five seconds may set a Diagnostic Trouble Code (DTC) for a cylinder misfire.*

5 If the tester flashes during cranking, the coil is delivering sufficient voltage to the spark plug to fire it. Repeat this test for each cylinder to verify that the other coils are OK.

6 If the tester doesn't flash, remove a coil from another cylinder and swap it for the one being tested. If the tester now flashes, you know that the original coil is bad. If the tester still doesn't flash, the PCM or wiring harness is probably defective. Have the PCM checked out by a dealer service department or other qualified repair shop (testing the PCM is beyond the scope of the do-it-yourselfer because it requires expensive special tools).

7 If the tester flashes during cranking but a misfire code (related to the cylinder being tested) has been stored, the spark plug could be fouled or defective.

Charging system

8 If a malfunction occurs in the charging system, do not automatically assume the alternator is causing the problem. First check the following items:

  a Check the drivebelt tension and condition (see Chapter 1 Section 12). Replace it if it's worn or deteriorated.
  b Make sure the alternator mounting bolts are tight.
  c Inspect the alternator wiring harness and the connectors at the alternator and voltage regulator. They must be in good condition, tight and have no corrosion.

Chapter 5 Engine electrical systems

2.15 To test the open circuit voltage of the battery, touch the black probe of the voltmeter to the negative terminal and the red probe to the positive terminal of the battery; a fully charged battery should be at least 12.6 volts

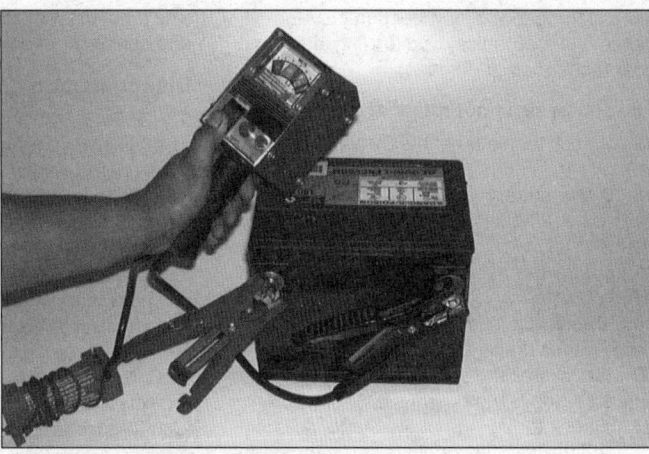

2.17 Connect a battery load tester to the battery and check the battery condition under load following the tool manufacturer's instructions

d Check the fusible link (if equipped) or main fuse in the engine compartment fuse/relay box. If it is burned, determine the cause, repair the circuit and replace the link or fuse (the vehicle will not start and/or the accessories will not work if the fusible link or main fuse is blown).
e Start the engine and check the alternator for abnormal noises (a shrieking or squealing sound indicates a bad bearing).
f Check the battery. Make sure it's fully charged and in good condition (one bad cell in a battery can cause overcharging by the alternator).
g Disconnect the battery cables (negative first, then positive). Inspect the battery posts and the cable clamps for corrosion. Clean them thoroughly if necessary (see Section 3). Reconnect the cables (positive first, negative last).

Alternator - check

9   Use a voltmeter to check the battery voltage with the engine off. It should be at least 12.6 volts (see illustration 2.15).
10 Start the engine and check the battery voltage again. It should now be approximately 13.5 to 15 volts.
11 If the voltage reading is more or less than the specified charging voltage, the voltage regulator is probably defective, which will require replacement of the alternator (the voltage regulator is not replaceable separately). Remove the alternator and have it bench tested (most auto electricians will do this for you).
12 The charging system (battery) light on the instrument cluster lights up when the ignition key is turned to ON, but it should go out when the engine starts.
13 If the charging system light stays on after the engine has been started, there is a problem with the charging system. Before replacing the alternator, check the battery condition, alternator belt tension and electrical cable connections.

14 If replacing the alternator doesn't restore voltage to the specified range, have the charging system tested by a dealer service department or other qualified repair shop.

Battery - check

Note: *The battery's surface charge must be removed before accurate voltage measurements can be made. Turn on the high beams for ten seconds, then turn them off and let the vehicle stand for two minutes.*

15 Check the battery state of charge. Visually inspect the indicator eye on the top of the battery (if equipped with one); if the indicator eye is black in colour, charge the battery. Next perform an open circuit voltage test using a digital voltmeter. With the engine and all accessories Off, touch the negative probe of the voltmeter to the negative terminal of the battery and the positive probe to the positive terminal of the battery (see illustration). The battery voltage should be 12.6 volts or slightly above. If the battery is less than the specified voltage, charge the battery before proceeding to the next test. Do not proceed with the battery load test unless the battery charge is correct.
16 Disconnect the negative battery cable, then the positive cable from the battery.
17 Perform a battery load test. An accurate check of the battery condition can only be performed with a load tester (see illustration). This test evaluates the ability of the battery to operate the starter and other accessories during periods of high current draw. Connect the load tester to the battery terminals. Load test the battery according to the tool manufacturer's instructions. This tool increases the load demand (current draw) on the battery.
18 Maintain the load on the battery for 15 seconds and observe that the battery voltage does not drop below 9.6 volts. If the battery condition is weak or defective, the tool will indicate this condition immediately.

Note: *Cold temperatures will cause the minimum voltage reading to drop slightly.*

Follow the chart given in the manufacturer's instructions to compensate for cold climates. Minimum load voltage for freezing temperatures (0 degrees Celsius) should be approximately 9.1 volts.

Starting system

The starter rotates, but the engine doesn't

19 Remove the starter. Check the overrunning clutch and bench test the starter to make sure the drive mechanism extends fully for proper engagement with the flywheel ring gear. If it doesn't, replace the starter.
20 Check the flywheel ring gear for missing teeth and other damage. With the ignition turned off, rotate the flywheel so you can check the entire ring gear.

The starter is noisy

21 If the solenoid is making a chattering noise, first check the battery (see Steps 15 through 18). If the battery is okay, check the cables and connections.
22 If you hear a grinding, crashing metallic sound when you turn the key to Start, check for loose starter mounting bolts. If they're tight, remove the starter and inspect the teeth on the starter pinion gear and flywheel ring gear. Look for missing or damaged teeth.
23 If the starter sounds fine when you first turn the key to Start, but then stops rotating the engine and emits a zinging sound, the problem is probably a defective starter drive that's not staying engaged with the ring gear. Replace the starter.

The starter rotates slowly

24 Check the battery (see Steps 15 through 18).
25 If the battery is okay, verify all connections (at the battery, the starter solenoid and motor) are clean, corrosion-free and tight. Make sure the cables aren't frayed or damaged.
26 Check that the starter mounting bolts are tight so it grounds properly. Also check

the pinion gear and flywheel ring gear for evidence of a mechanical bind (galling, deformed gear teeth or other damage).

The starter does not rotate at all

27 Check the battery (see Steps 15 through 18).
28 If the battery is okay, verify all connections (at the battery, the starter solenoid and motor) are clean, corrosion-free and tight. Make sure the cables aren't frayed or damaged.
29 Check all of the fuses in the engine compartment fuse/relay box.
30 Check that the starter mounting bolts are tight so it grounds properly.
31 Check for voltage at the starter solenoid "S" terminal when the ignition key is turned to the start position. If voltage is present, replace the starter/solenoid assembly. If no voltage is present, the problem could be the starter relay, the Transmission Range (TR) switch or clutch start switch, or with an electrical connector somewhere in the circuit (see the wiring diagrams Chapter 12A). Also, on many modern vehicles, the Powertrain Control Module (PCM) and the Body Control Module (BCM) control the voltage signal to the starter solenoid; on such vehicles a special scan tool is required for diagnosis.

3 Battery - disconnection and reconnection

Caution: *Always disconnect the negative (-) battery terminal FIRST and reconnect LAST or the battery may be shorted by the tool being used to loosen the cable clamps.*

1 Some systems on the vehicle require battery power to be available at all times, either to maintain continuous operation (alarm system, power door locks, etc.), or to maintain control unit memory (radio station presets, powertrain control module and other control units). When the battery is disconnected, the power that maintains these systems is cut. So, before you disconnect the battery, please note that on a vehicle with power door locks, it's a wise precaution to remove the key from the ignition and to keep it with you, so that it does not get locked inside if the power door locks should engage accidentally when the battery is reconnected!
2 Devices known as "memory-savers" are available to avoid some of these problems. However there is always a risk of shorting a circuit within the vehicle while carrying out any work - resulting in a very expensive repair bill if one of the control modules is damaged, or the Supplement Restraint System (SRS) or airbags are accidently deployed. It is for this reason that we do not recommend using any form of memory saving device.

Warning: *If you're going to work near any of the airbag system components, the battery MUST be disconnected and a memory saver must NOT be used. If a memory saver is used, power will be supplied to the airbag,* which means that it could accidentally deploy and cause serious personal injury.

Disconnection

3 Prior to disconnecting the battery, if possible, leave a window open and remove the key from the vehicle. On models with a power back door, ensure the door is closed.
4 Wait at least one minute between switching the ignition Off and disconnecting the battery to allow the multi-media receiver to store any necessary parameters.
5 To disconnect the battery for service procedures requiring power to be cut from the vehicle, loosen the negative battery terminal and disconnect the cable from the battery **(see illustrations)**.
Caution: *Isolate the cable end to prevent it from coming into accidental contact with the battery terminal.*
6 When reconnecting the battery terminal, ensure the inside of the cable end and the battery terminal are clean (see Chapter 1) before installing the terminal back onto the battery. Tighten the terminal bolt securely.
7 Perform the system initialisation procedure (see Section 4).

4 System initialisation

1 Initialise the following systems after reconnecting or replacing the battery, or after recharging a low battery.

Power windows

2 The power window system might not operate correctly, or at all, and the jam protection function will not operate correctly, after you reconnect or replace the battery or recharge a low battery. To initialise the system:
3 Switch ignition On.
4 Sit in the driver seat and close the door.
5 Open the driver door window completely and then release the switch.
6 Close the driver door window and hold the window switch up down for more than 3 seconds after the window has fully closed. Release the power window switch.
7 Open the driver door window and check that the Auto function now works. If not, repeat the procedure.

Sunroof system

Note: *Only perform the initialisation procedure below if the sunroof system switch LEDs are flashing or the sunroof is not operating correctly.*

8 The sunroof might not operate correctly, or at all, and the jam protection function will not operate correctly, after you reconnect or replace the battery or recharge a low battery. If this condition occurs, initialise the sunroof as follows:
9 Perform the following procedure if the sunroof closes and then opens slightly:
10 If the Close switch is released before the following procedure is complete, the procedure will need to be restarted from the beginning.
11 If open, close the sunroof and sunshade (where fitted). Release the switch
12 Press and hold the Close switch for approximately 10-seconds. The sunshade will reopen, the sunroof will tilt down; the sunroof will fully open; the sunroof will fully close and the sunshade will fully close.
13 Release the switch and after a pause check that the Auto close/open function now works. If it doesn't work, repeat the procedure.

Power back door system

Note: *This procedure is applicable to T32 X-Trail models only.*

14 The power back door system should only have to be reset if it is open when the battery is disconnected or goes flat. To initialise the power back door system, simply open the back door using the power back door function and then close the back door completely, by hand. If the power back door still doesn't operate correctly after closing it by hand, have the system checked. A scan tool with activation function is needed to check the system.

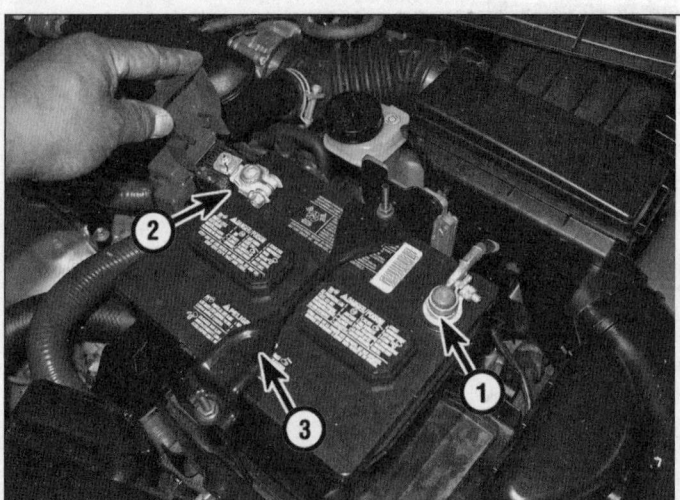

5.1 Battery details

1 *Negative battery cable*
2 *Positive battery cable*
3 *Hold-down bracket*

Chapter 5 Engine electrical systems

5.11 Battery tray mounting bolts

7.2a Disconnect the coil wiring connector – 2.0 litre engine

5 Battery and battery tray - removal and installation

Battery

1 Disconnect the negative battery cable, then the positive battery cable, from the battery **(see illustration)**.

Warning: *Always disconnect the negative cable first and hook it up last or the battery may be shorted by the tool being used to loosen the cable clamps.*

2 Remove the battery hold-down bracket on top of the battery.

3 Lift out the battery. Special battery removal and installation tools are available at auto parts stores; lifting and moving the battery is much easier if you use one.

4 Installation is the reverse of removal:

5 Connect the positive cable first, then the negative cable.

6 Perform the system initialisation procedure (see Section 4).

Battery tray

7 Remove the battery (see Steps 1 through 5).

8 Remove the inlet duct (see Chapter 4A Section 9 - petrol models or Chapter 4B Section 6 - diesel models).

9 Remove the battery tray liner.

10 Remove the fasteners and detach the PCM from the battery tray (see Chapter 6 Section 15). On A/T models, detach the TCM from the battery tray (see Chapter 7B Section 8).

11 Remove the battery tray mounting bolts **(see illustration)** and lift the tray out.

12 Installation is the reverse of removal:

13 Connect the positive cable first, then the negative cable.

14 Perform the system initialisation procedure (see Section 4).

6 Battery cables - replacement

1 When removing the cables, always disconnect the cable from the negative battery terminal first and hook it up last, or you might accidentally short out the battery with the tool you're using to loosen the cable clamps. Even if you're only replacing the cable for the positive terminal, be sure to disconnect the negative cable from the battery first.

2 Disconnect the old cables from the battery, then trace each of them to their opposite ends and disconnect them. Note the routing of each cable before disconnecting it to ensure correct installation.

3 If you are replacing any of the old cables, take them with you when buying new cables. It is vitally important that you replace the cables with identical parts.

4 Clean the threads of the solenoid or ground connection with a wire brush to remove rust and corrosion. Apply a light coat of battery terminal corrosion inhibitor or petroleum jelly to the threads to prevent future corrosion.

5 Attach the cable to the solenoid or ground connection and tighten the mounting nut/bolt securely.

6 Before connecting a new cable to the battery, make sure that it reaches the battery post without having to be stretched.

7 Connect the cable to the positive battery terminal first, then connect the ground cable to the negative battery terminal.

7 Ignition coil(s) - replacement

1 Remove the upper intake air resonator on 2.5 litre engine (see Chapter 4A Section 9) or remove intake manifold on 2.0 litre engines (see Chapter 2B Section 5).

2 Disconnect the electrical connector(s) from the coil(s) **(see illustration)**.

3 Remove the coil mounting bolt(s), then twist the coil slightly and pull it straight out.

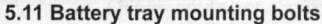

7.2b Coil electrical connectors (A) and mounting bolts (B) - 2.5 litre engine

7.3a Undo the retaining bolt …

7.3b ... and withdraw the ignition coil

8.6 Using an ohmmeter to check the resistance of a glow plug, compare the results with Specifications

9.4 Disconnect the wiring connector

4 Installation is the reverse of removal. Before installing the ignition coils, coat the interior of the boots with silicone dielectric compound.

8 Pre-heating system – testing

1 If the system malfunctions, testing is best carried out by a Nissan dealer or suitably equipped garage using dedicated test equipment, however, some preliminary checks may be made as follows.
2 Connect a voltmeter or 12 volt test lamp between the glow plug supply cable and earth (engine or vehicle metal). Make sure that the live connection is kept clear of the engine and bodywork.
3 Have an assistant switch on the ignition and check that voltage is applied to the glow plugs. Note the time for which the warning light is lit and the total time for which voltage is applied before the system cuts out Switch off the ignition and compare to the times given in the previous Section.
4 If there is no supply at all, the relay, control unit or associated wiring is at fault.
5 To locate a defective glow plug, disconnect the main supply cable and the interconnecting wire from the top of the glow plugs.
6 Use a continuity tester, or 12-volt test lamp connected to the battery positive terminal, to check for continuity between each glow plug terminal and earth. The resistance of a glow plug in good condition is very low (less than 1 ohm), so if the test lamp does not light or the continuity tester shows a high resistance, the glow plug is defective.
7 If an ammeter is available, the current draw of each glow plug can be checked. After an initial surge of around 15 to 20 amps, each plug should draw around 10 amps. Any plug that draws much more or less than 10 amps is probably defective.
8 As a final check, the glow plugs can be removed and inspected (see Section 9).
9 If the pre-heating system is faulty, first check the wiring to each individual component. If this does not locate the fault, ideally each component should be substituted with known good units until the fault is located. If this is not possible, take the vehicle to a diesel specialist who will have the diagnostic equipment necessary to pin point the fault quickly.

9 Glow plugs – removal, inspection and installation

Caution: *If the preheating system has just been energised, or if the engine has been running, the glow plugs may be very hot.*

Removal

1 Disconnect the negative (-) battery terminal (see Section 3).

2 Remove the plastic trim cover from the top of the engine.
3 Slacken the retaining clips and disconnect the intercooler pipe rubber hoses from across the top of the engine.
4 Pull the plastic leg to disconnect the wiring plugs from the glow plugs **(see illustration)**.
5 Clean the surrounding area, then unscrew and remove the glow plugs from the cylinder head **(see illustration)**.

Inspection

6 Inspect the glow plugs for physical damage. Burnt or eroded glow plug tips can be caused by a bad injector spray pattern. Have the injectors checked if this sort of damage is found.
7 If the glow plugs are in good physical condition, check them electrically using a 12-volt test lamp or continuity tester (see Section 8).
8 The glow plugs can be energised by applying 12-volts to them, this will verify that they heat up evenly and in the required time. Observe the following precautions:

   a Support the glow plug by clamping it carefully in a vice or self-locking pliers. Remember it will become red-hot.
   b Make sure that the power supply or test lead incorporates a fuse or overload trip to protect against damage from a short-circuit.
   c After testing, allow the glow plug to cool for several minutes before attempting to handle it.

9 A glow plug in good condition will start to glow red at the tip after drawing current for 5 seconds or so. Any plug that takes much longer to start glowing, or which starts glowing in the middle instead of at the tip, is defective.

Installation

10 Refit by reversing the removal operations. Apply a smear of copper based anti-seize compound to the plug threads and tighten the glow plugs to the specified torque **(see illustration)**. Do not overtighten, as this can damage the glow plug element.

9.5 Unscrew the glow plugs from the cylinder head

9.10 Tighten the glow plugs to the correct torque

Chapter 5 Engine electrical systems

10.1 Location of the pre-heating relay (arrowed)

10.2 Remove the air intake ducting

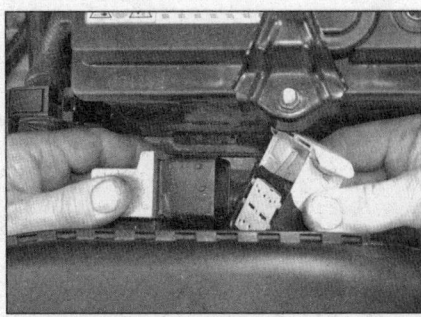

10.3 Release the wiring connector

10.4a Undo the mounting bolt – manual transmission models

10.4b Undo the mounting bolt – automatic transmission models

11.2 Remove the drivebelt from around the pulley

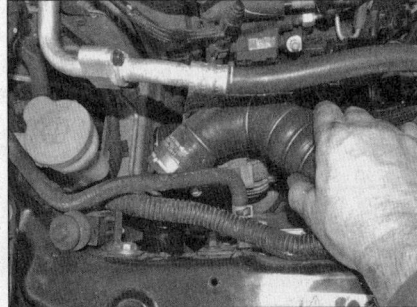

11.3 Remove the intercooler hose

10 Pre-heating system control unit – removal and installation

Removal

1 The pre-heating control unit is located on a bracket in front of the battery, on the left-hand side of the engine compartment (see illustrations). Before proceeding, make sure that the ignition is switched off.
2 To gain better access release the retaining clips, and then remove the air intake ducting from the front left-hand side of the engine compartment (see illustration).
3 Disconnect the wiring from the control unit (see illustration).
4 Unscrew the mounting nuts/bolts and remove the control unit from the mounting bracket (see illustrations).

Installation

5 Installation is a reversal of removal.

11 Alternator – removal and installation

Removal

1 Disconnect the battery negative terminal (see Section 3).
2 Slacken the drivebelt (see Chapter 1 Section 12), and then disengage it from the alternator pulley (see illustration).
3 Slacken the retaining clips and remove the intercooler air intake hose from above the alternator (see illustration).
Caution: *Cover the open ends of the intercooler and hoses to prevent anything being dropped inside them.*

4 Remove the rubber covers (where fitted) from the alternator terminals, then unscrew the retaining nut(s) and disconnect the wiring cable from the rear of the alternator (see illustrations).
5 Release the locking clip and disconnect the wiring plug connector from the rear of the alternator (see illustration).

11.4a Undo the retaining nut ...

11.4b ... and disconnect the alternator wiring cable

11.5 Disconnect the wiring plug connector

11.6a Undo the two alternator mounting bolts (arrowed) ...

11.6b ... and withdraw the alternator

11.7 Recess in bracket to allow removal (arrowed) – 2.0 litre petrol shown

12.3 On turbo models, remove the air intake hose

12.4 Unclip the wiring loom from the front of the transmission

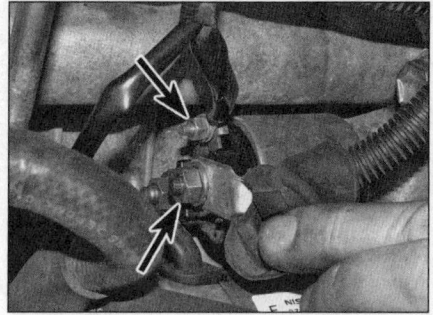

12.5a Undo the retaining nuts (arrowed) ...

6 Unscrew the alternator upper mounting bracket and lower mounting bolt and washers, and then manoeuvre the alternator away from its mounting brackets and out of position **(see illustrations)**.

7 On some models, the lower mounting bolt cannot be removed completely, as it contacts the body side member. On these models, the mounting bracket has a cut out to allow the alternator to be withdrawn with the bolt still in place **(see illustration)**.

Installation

8 Installation is a reversal of removal, tensioning the drivebelt (see Chapter 1 Section 12), ensuring that the alternator mountings are tightened to the specified torque.

12 Starter motor – removal and installation

Removal

1 Disconnect the battery negative terminal (see Section 3).
2 On 2.5 litre models, remove the battery and battery tray (see Section 5).
3 On diesel models, slacken the retaining clips and remove the intercooler air intake hose from above the starter motor **(see illustration)**.

Caution: *Cover the open ends of the intercooler and hoses to prevent anything being dropped inside them.*

4 Working down the front of the engine compartment, move the wiring loom and hoses to one side to access the starter motor **(see illustration)**, which is located at the front of the cylinder block, bolted to the transmission bell housing.

5 Pull back the rubber cover, and then slacken and remove the two retaining nuts. Disconnect the main battery cable, and the small solenoid wiring from the starter motor solenoid **(see illustrations)**.

6 Unscrew the starter motor mounting bolts **(see illustrations)**, supporting the motor as the bolts are withdrawn, and manoeuvre the starter motor out from its location.

Installation

7 Installation is a reversal of removal.

12.5b ... and disconnect the starter wiring cables

12.6a Undo the starter motor mounting bolts (arrowed) – 2.0 litre petrol

12.6b Remove the starter motor from the transmission housing

Chapter 6
Emissions and engine control systems

Contents

	Section
Accelerator Pedal Position (APP) sensor - replacement	4
Camshaft Position (CMP) sensor - replacement	5
Catalytic converter - replacement	18
Crankshaft Position (CKP) sensor - replacement	7
Engine Coolant Temperature (ECT) sensor - replacement	8
Engine Oil Temperature Sensor - replacement	12
Evaporative Emissions Control (EVAP) system - component replacement	19
General information	1
Intake Valve Timing (IVT) and Exhaust Valve Timing (EVT) control solenoid(s) - replacement	6
Knock sensor - replacement	10
Mass Air Flow/Intake Air Temperature (MAF/IAT) sensor - replacement	9
Obtaining and clearing Diagnostic Trouble Codes (DTCs)	3
On Board Diagnosis (OBD) system	2
Oxygen sensors - replacement	11
Positive Crankcase Ventilation (PCV) valve - replacement	16
Powertrain Control Module (PCM) - removal and installation	15
Throttle Position (TP) sensor - replacement	17
Transmission range switch - replacement and adjustment	13
Transmission speed sensors - replacement	14

Specifications

Sensor resistances

Air/fuel ratio sensor heater resistance - 2.5 litre petrol engine	2.0 to 2.7 ohms
Coolant temperature sensor resistances (terminals 1 and 2)	
At 20 degrees C - 2.0 litre models	2,100 to 2,900 ohms
At 20 degrees C - 2.5 litre and Qashqai models	2,370 to 2,630 ohms
At 50 degrees C	680 to 1,000 ohms
At 90 degrees C	236 to 260 ohms
Heated oxygen sensor resistance (between terminals 2 and 3)	
2.0 litre petrol engine	3.4 to 4.4 ohms
2.5 litre petrol engine	3.3 to 4.4 ohms
Intake air temperature sensor	
At 20 degrees C	1,800 to 2,200 ohms
At 80 degrees C	283 to 359
Engine oil temperature sensor resistance	
At 20 degrees C	2,370 to 2,630 ohms
At 50 degrees C	680 to 1,000 ohms
At 90 degrees C	236 to 260 ohms
At 110 degrees C	143 to 153 ohms
Exhaust gas temperature sensor resistance - diesel models	
At 250 degrees C	132,500 ohms
At 300 degrees C	44,300 to 63,500 ohms
At 500 degrees C	3,173 to 3,264 ohms
At 600 degrees C	1,378 ohms
At 800 degrees C	323 to 371 ohms

1 General information

To prevent pollution of the atmosphere from incompletely burned and evaporating gases, and to maintain good driveability and fuel economy, a number of emission control systems are incorporated. They include the:

Catalytic converter

A catalytic converter is an emission control device in the exhaust system that reduces certain pollutants in the exhaust gas stream. There are two types of converters: oxidation converters and reduction converters.

Oxidation converters contain a monolithic substrate (a ceramic honeycomb) coated with the semi-precious metals platinum and palladium. An oxidation catalyst reduces unburned hydrocarbons (HC) and carbon monoxide (CO) by adding oxygen to the exhaust stream as it passes through the substrate, which, in the presence of high temperature and the catalyst materials, converts the HC and CO to water vapor (H_2O) and carbon dioxide (CO_2).

Reduction converters contain a monolithic substrate coated with platinum and rhodium. A reduction catalyst reduces oxides of nitrogen (NOx) by removing oxygen, which in the presence of high temperature and the catalyst material produces nitrogen (N) and carbon dioxide (CO_2).

Catalytic converters that combine both types of catalysts in one assembly are known as "three-way catalysts" or TWCs. A TWC can reduce all three pollutants.

Evaporative Emissions Control (EVAP) system

The Evaporative Emissions Control (EVAP) system prevents fuel system vapors (which contain unburned hydrocarbons) from escaping into the atmosphere. On warm days, vapors trapped inside the fuel tank expand until the pressure reaches a certain threshold. Then the fuel vapors are routed from the fuel tank through the fuel vapor vent valve and the fuel vapor control valve to the EVAP canister, where they're stored temporarily until the next time the vehicle is operated. When the conditions are right (engine warmed up, vehicle up to speed, moderate or heavy load on the engine, etc.) the PCM opens the canister purge valve, which allows fuel vapors to be drawn from the canister into the intake manifold. Once in the intake manifold, the fuel vapors mix with incoming air before being drawn through the intake ports into the combustion chambers where they're burned up with the rest of the air/fuel mixture. The EVAP system is complex and virtually impossible to troubleshoot without the right tools and training.

Exhaust Gas Recirculation (EGR) system

The EGR system reduces oxides of nitrogen by recirculating exhaust gases from the exhaust manifold, through the EGR valve and intake manifold, then back to the combustion chambers, where it mixes with the incoming air/fuel mixture before being consumed. These recirculated exhaust gases dilute the incoming air/fuel mixture, which cools the combustion chambers, thereby reducing NOx emissions.

The EGR system consists of the Powertrain Control Module (PCM), the EGR valve, the EGR valve position sensor and various other information sensors that the PCM uses to determine when to open the EGR valve. The degree to which the EGR valve is opened is referred to as "EGR valve lift." The PCM is programmed to produce the ideal EGR valve lift for varying operating conditions. The EGR valve position sensor, which is an integral part of the EGR valve, detects the amount of EGR valve lift and sends this information to the PCM. The PCM then compares it with the appropriate EGR valve lift for the operating conditions. The PCM increases current flow to the EGR valve to increase valve lift and reduces the current to reduce the amount of lift. If EGR flow is inappropriate to the operating conditions (idle, cold engine, etc.) the PCM simply cuts the current to the EGR valve and the valve closes.

Secondary Air Injection (AIR) system

Some vehicles are equipped with a secondary air injection (AIR) system. The secondary air injection system is used to reduce tailpipe emissions on initial engine start-up. The system uses an electric motor/pump assembly, relay, vacuum valve/solenoid, air shut-off valve, check valves and tubing to inject fresh air directly into the exhaust manifolds. The fresh air (oxygen) reacts with the exhaust gas in the catalytic converter to reduce HC and CO levels. The air pump and solenoid are controlled by the PCM through the AIR relay. During initial start-up, the PCM energizes the AIR relay, the relay supplies battery voltage to the air pump and the vacuum valve/solenoid, engine vacuum is applied to the air shut-off valve which opens and allows air to flow through the tubing into the exhaust manifolds. The PCM will operate the air pump until closed loop operation is reached (approximately four minutes). During normal operation, the check valves prevent exhaust backflow into the system.

Powertrain Control Module (PCM)

The Powertrain Control Module (PCM) is the brain of the engine management system. It also controls a wide variety of other vehicle systems. In order to program the new PCM, the dealer needs the vehicle as well as the new PCM. If you're planning to replace the PCM with a new one, there is no point in trying to do so at home because you won't be able to program it yourself.

Positive Crankcase Ventilation (PCV) system

The Positive Crankcase Ventilation (PCV) system reduces hydrocarbon emissions by scavenging crankcase vapors, which are rich in unburned hydrocarbons. A PCV valve or orifice regulates the flow of gases into the intake manifold in proportion to the amount of intake vacuum available.

The PCV system generally consists of the fresh air inlet hose, the PCV valve or orifice and the crankcase ventilation hose (or PCV hose). The fresh air inlet hose connects the air intake duct to a pipe on the valve cover. The crankcase ventilation hose (or PCV hose) connects the PCV valve or orifice in the valve cover to the intake manifold.

2 On Board Diagnosis (OBD) system

General description

1 All models are equipped with the second generation OBD-II system. This system consists of an on-board computer known as the Powertrain Control Module (PCM), and information sensors, which monitor various functions of the engine and send data to the PCM. This system incorporates a series of diagnostic monitors that detect and identify fuel injection and emissions control system faults and store the information in the computer memory. This system also tests sensors and output actuators, diagnoses drive cycles, freezes data and clears codes.

2 The PCM is the brain of the electronically controlled fuel and emissions system. It receives data from a number of sensors and other electronic components (switches, relays, etc.). Based on the information it receives, the PCM generates output signals to control various relays, solenoids (fuel injectors) and other actuators. The PCM is specifically calibrated to optimize the emissions, fuel economy and driveability of the vehicle.

3 It isn't a good idea to attempt diagnosis or replacement of the PCM or emission control components at home while the vehicle is under warranty. Because of a federally-mandated warranty which covers the emissions system components and because any owner-induced damage to the PCM, the sensors and/or the control devices may void this warranty, take the vehicle to a dealer service department if the PCM or a system component malfunctions.

Scan tool information

4 Because extracting the Diagnostic Trouble Codes (DTCs) from an engine management system is now the first step in troubleshooting many computer-controlled systems and components, a code reader, at the very least, will be required (see illustration). More powerful scan tools can also perform many of the diagnostics once associated with expensive factory scan tools (see illustration). If you're planning to obtain a generic scan tool for your vehicle, make sure that it's compatible with OBD-II systems. If you don't plan to purchase a code reader or scan tool and don't

Chapter 6 Emissions and engine control systems

Information Sensors

Accelerator Pedal Position (APP) sensor - as you press the accelerator pedal, the APP sensor alters its voltage signal to the PCM in proportion to the angle of the pedal, and the PCM commands a motor inside the throttle body to open or close the throttle plate accordingly

Camshaft Position (CMP) sensor - produces a signal that the PCM uses to identify the number 1 cylinder and to time the firing sequence of the fuel injectors

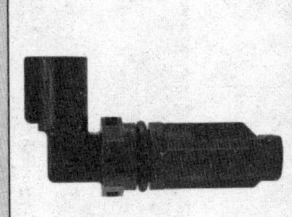

Crankshaft Position (CKP) sensor - produces a signal that the PCM uses to calculate engine speed and crankshaft position, which enables it to synchronize ignition timing with fuel injector timing, and to detect misfires

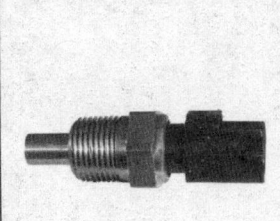

Engine Coolant Temperature (ECT) sensor - a thermistor (temperature-sensitive variable resistor) that sends a voltage signal to the PCM, which uses this data to determine the temperature of the engine coolant

Fuel tank pressure sensor - measures the fuel tank pressure and controls fuel tank pressure by signaling the EVAP system to purge the fuel tank vapors when the pressure becomes excessive

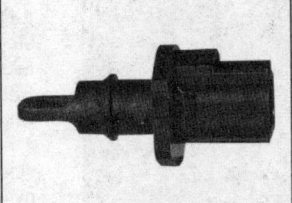

Intake Air Temperature (IAT) sensor - monitors the temperature of the air entering the engine and sends a signal to the PCM to determine injector pulse-width (the duration of each injector's on-time) and to adjust spark timing (to prevent spark knock)

Knock sensor - a piezoelectric crystal that oscillates in proportion to engine vibration which produces a voltage output that is monitored by the PCM. This retards the ignition timing when the oscillation exceeds a certain threshold

Manifold Absolute Pressure (MAP) sensor - monitors the pressure or vacuum inside the intake manifold. The PCM uses this data to determine engine load so that it can alter the ignition advance and fuel enrichment

Mass Air Flow (MAF) sensor - measures the amount of intake air drawn into the engine. It uses a hot-wire sensing element to measure the amount of air entering the engine

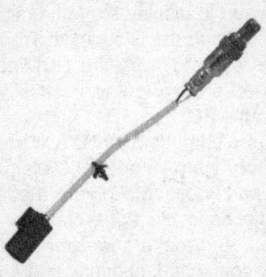

Oxygen sensors - generates a small variable voltage signal in proportion to the difference between the oxygen content in the exhaust stream and the oxygen content in the ambient air. The PCM uses this information to maintain the proper air/fuel ratio. A second oxygen sensor monitors the efficiency of the catalytic converter

Throttle Position (TP) sensor - a potentiometer that generates a voltage signal that varies in relation to the opening angle of the throttle plate inside the throttle body. Works with the PCM and other sensors to calculate injector pulse width (the duration of each injector's on-time)

Photos courtesy of Wells Manufacturing, except APP and MAF sensors.

Chapter 6 Emissions and engine control systems

2.4a Simple code readers are an economical way to extract trouble codes when the Check engine light comes on

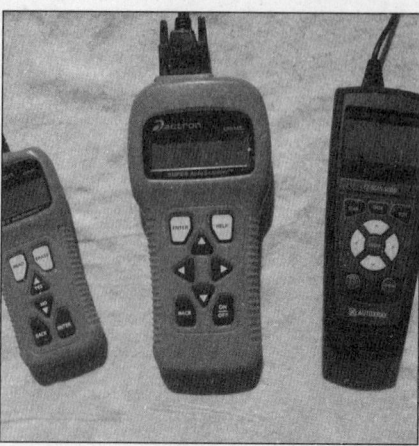

2.4b Hand-held scan tools like these can extract computer codes and also perform diagnostics

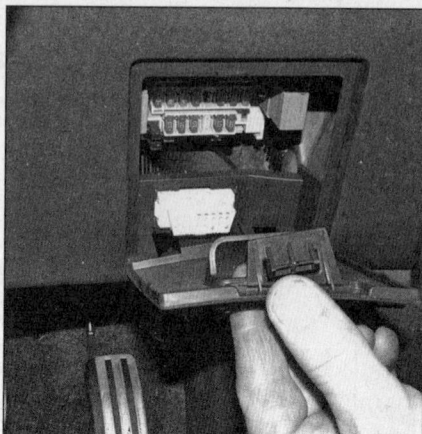

3.3a The OBD connector is located with the inside fuse box to the bottom right of steering wheel in some models

3.3b On other models the OBD connector is located under a cover just under the steering wheel, pull trim towards you

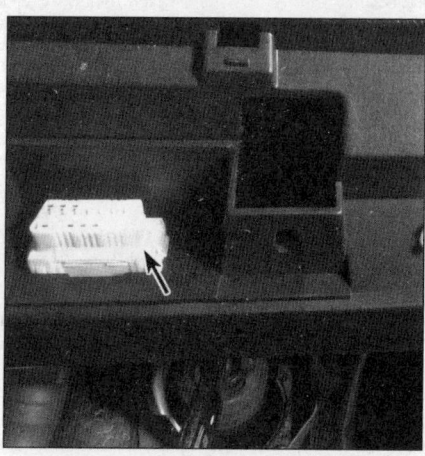

3.3c Cover removed revealing OBD connector

Accessing the DTCs

3   The Diagnostic Trouble Codes (DTCs) can only be accessed with a code reader or scan tool. Professional scan tools are expensive, but relatively inexpensive generic code readers or scan tools (see illustrations 2.4a and 2.4b) are available at most auto parts stores. Simply plug the connector of the scan tool into the diagnostic connector (see illustration). Then follow the instructions included with the scan tool to extract the DTCs.

4   Once you have outputted all of the stored DTCs, look them up on the accompanying DTC chart.

5   After troubleshooting the source of each DTC, make any necessary repairs or replace the defective component(s).

Clearing the DTCs

6   Clear the DTCs with the code reader or scan tool in accordance with the instructions provided by the tool's manufacturer.

Diagnostic Trouble Codes

7   The accompanying tables are a list of the Diagnostic Trouble Codes (DTCs) that can be accessed by a do-it-yourselfer working at home (there are many, many more DTCs available to professional mechanics with proprietary scan tools and software, but those codes cannot be accessed by a generic scan tool). If, after you have checked and repaired the connectors, wire harness and vacuum hoses (if applicable) for an emission-related system, component or circuit, the problem persists, have the vehicle checked by a dealer service department or other qualified repair shop.

3   Obtaining and clearing Diagnostic Trouble Codes (DTCs)

1   All models covered by this manual are equipped with on-board diagnostics. When the PCM recognizes a malfunction in a monitored emission or engine control system, component or circuit, it turns on the Malfunction Indicator Light (MIL) on the dash. The PCM will continue to display the MIL until the problem is fixed and the Diagnostic Trouble Code (DTC) is cleared from the PCM's memory. You'll need a scan tool to access any DTCs stored in the PCM.

2   Before outputting any DTCs stored in the PCM, thoroughly inspect ALL electrical connectors and hoses. Make sure that all electrical connections are tight, clean and free of corrosion. And make sure that all hoses are correctly connected, fit tightly and are in good condition (no cracks or tears).

have access to one, you can have the codes extracted by a dealer service department or an independent repair shop.

Note: *Some auto parts stores even provide this service.*

Chapter 6 Emissions and engine control systems

Code	Setting parameters
P0011	Intake valve timing control solenoid performance problem
P0014	Exhaust valve timing control solenoid performance problem
P0031	Upstream oxygen sensor heater control circuit low voltage signal
P0032	Upstream oxygen sensor heater control circuit high voltage signal
P0037	Downstream oxygen sensor heater control circuit low voltage signal
P0038	Downstream oxygen sensor heater control circuit high voltage signal
P0057	Downstream oxygen sensor heater control circuit low voltage signal (Bank 2)
P0058	Downstream oxygen sensor heater control circuit high voltage signal (Bank 2)
P0101	Mass Air Flow sensor circuit range or performance fault
P0102	Mass Air Flow sensor circuit low input
P0103	Mass Air Flow sensor circuit high input
P0111	Intake Air sensor sensor circuit range/performance problem
P0112	Intake Air Temperature sensor circuit low input
P0113	Intake Air Temperature sensor circuit high input
P0116	Engine coolant temperature circuit range/performance problem
P0117	Engine coolant temperature circuit, low input
P0118	Engine Coolant Temperature sensor circuit high input
P0122	Throttle Position Sensor circuit low input
P0123	Throttle Position Sensor circuit high input
P0125	Engine Coolant Temperature sensor or circuit fault
P0127	Intake Air Temperature too high
P0128	Thermostat function - engine coolant does not reach correct temperature after warm-up
P0130	Upstream oxygen sensor or circuit fault

Code	Setting parameters
P0131	Upstream oxygen sensor lean shift monitor fault
P0132	Upstream oxygen sensor rich shift monitor fault
P0137	Downstream oxygen sensor minimum voltage monitor fault
P0138	Downstream oxygen sensor maximum voltage monitor fault
P0139	Downstream oxygen sensor circuit slow response fault
P014C	Oxygen sensor 1 problem
P014D	Oxygen sensor 1 problem
P015A	Oxygen sensor 1 problem
P015B	Oxygen sensor 1 problem
P0171	Fuel injection system lean
P0172	Fuel injection system rich
P0174	System too lean
P0175	System too rich
P0181	Fuel Tank Temperature sensor circuit range or performance
P0182	Fuel Tank Temperature sensor circuit low input
P0183	Fuel Tank Temperature sensor circuit high input
P0196	Fuel rail pressure sensor circuit, range or performance problem
P0197	Fuel rail pressure sensor circuit, low input
P0198	Fuel rail pressure sensor circuit, high input
P0222	Throttle Position Sensor circuit low input
P0223	Throttle Position Sensor circuit high input
P0300	Multiple cylinder misfire detected
P0301	Cylinder no. 1 misfire detected
P0302	Cylinder no. 2 misfire detected
P0303	Cylinder no. 3 misfire detected
P0304	Cylinder no. 4 misfire detected
P0327	Knock Sensor circuit low input
P0328	Knock Sensor circuit high input
P0322	Crankshaft Position (CKP) sensor/engine speed (RPM) sensor - no signal

Code	Setting parameters
P0323	Crankshaft Position (CKP) sensor/engine speed (RPM) sensor - circuit intermittent
P0340	Camshaft Position sensor or circuit fault
P0345	Camshaft Position sensor or circuit fault (Bank 2)
P0420	Catalyst system defective (Bank 1)
P0441	EVAP control system incorrect purge flow
P0442	EVAP system small leak (negative pressure check)
P0443	EVAP canister purge control valve circuit fault
P0444	EVAP canister purge control valve circuit open
P0445	EVAP canister purge control valve circuit shorted
P0447	EVAP canister vent control valve circuit open
P0448	EVAP canister vent control valve remains closed under certain driving conditions
P0451	EVAP system pressure sensor or circuit fault
P0452	EVAP system pressure sensor low input voltage signal
P0453	EVAP system pressure sensor high input
P0455	EVAP system gross leak
P0456	EVAP system very small leak (negative pressure check)
P0460	Fuel level sensor or circuit fault
P0461	Fuel level sensor or circuit fault
P0462	Fuel level sensor circuit low input
P0463	Fuel level sensor circuit high input
P0500	Vehicle Speed Sensor or circuit fault
P0506	Idle Air Control system signal low
P0507	Idle Air Control system signal high
P050A	Cold start control problem
P050B	Cold start control problem
P050E	Cold start control problem
P0520	Engine Oil Pressure (EOP) switch circuit problem
P0524	Engine oil pressure too low
P0603	PCM back-up RAM does not function properly

6-6 Chapter 6 Emissions and engine control systems

Code	Setting parameters
P062F	Internal control module EEPROM error
P0604	Internal control module random access memory (RAM) error
P0605	PCM or EEPROM fault
P0606	Control Module processor problem
P0607	Control module performance
P060A	Internal control module monitoring processor performance problem
P060B	Internal control module monitoring A/D processing performance problem
P0643	PCM detects sensor power supply low or high voltage
P0850	Park/Neutral position switch circuit fault in Drive and Park
P1148	Closed loop control fault
P1211	Traction Control System (TCS), problem with ABS control unit
P1217	Engine overheating
P1225	Closed throttle position learning value low
P1226	Closed throttle position learning performance fault

Code	Setting parameters
P1550	Battery current sensor problem
P1551	Battery current sensor problem
P1552	Battery current sensor problem
P1553	Battery current sensor problem
P1554	Battery current sensor problem
P1564	ACSD steering switch problem
P1572	ASCD brake switch or circuit fault
P1574	ASCD speed sensor signal performance fault
P1700	Automatic transmission control system problem
P1715	Input speed sensor problem
P1720	Vehicle speed sensor problem
P1800	VIAS control solenoid valve circuit performance fault
P1805	Brake switch or circuit fault
P2A00	Oxygen sensor 1
P2A03	Oxygen sensor 1
P2004	Tumble control valve problem

Code	Setting parameters
P2014	Tumble control valve position sensor problem
P2100	Throttle Control motor voltage signal is open or low voltage
P2103	Throttle Control motor relay voltage signal is shorted (ON)
P2101	Electric throttle control function problem
P2118	Throttle Control motor performance fault in circuit and/or throttle control motor
P2119	Throttle Control motor defective or stuck in position
P2122	Accelerator Pedal Position sensor 1 circuit low
P2123	Accelerator Pedal Position sensor 1 circuit high
P2127	Accelerator Pedal Position sensor 2 circuit low
P2128	Accelerator Pedal Position sensor 2 circuit high
P2135	Throttle Position Sensor circuit range or performance
P2138	Accelerator Pedal Position sensor or circuit range or performance
P2423	HC absorption catalyst function

4 Accelerator Pedal Position (APP) sensor - replacement

1 Disconnect the cable from the negative terminal of the battery (see Chapter 5 Section 3).
2 Disconnect the wiring from the sensor/pedal assembly **(see illustration)**.
3 Remove the nuts and remove the pedal.
4 Installation is the reverse of removal.
5 Reconnect the battery and perform the system initialisation procedure (see Chapter 5 Section 4).

5 Camshaft Position (CMP) sensor - replacement

Petrol models

Note: *On earlier models a camshaft position (CMP) sensor is only used on the intake camshaft. On later models two CMP sensors are used (one for each camshaft).*

1 The CMP sensor(s) is mounted on the camshaft position sensor bracket at the passenger side of the cylinder head **(see illustration)**.
2 Remove the upper intake air resonator (see Chapter 4A Section 9).
3 Disconnect the electrical connector from the sensor.
4 Remove the mounting bolt and pull out the sensor.
5 Installation is the reverse of removal. Be sure to use a new O-ring.

4.2 Disconnect the electrical connector to the Accelerator Pedal Position (APP) sensor

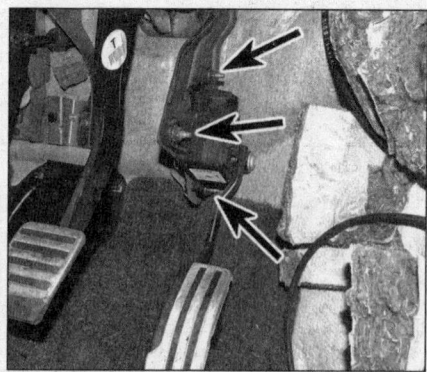

4.3 Remove the illustrated nuts

5.1 The Camshaft Position (CMP) sensor(s) is located at the passenger side of the engine (earlier model shown)

1. Camshaft position sensor (CMP)
2. Camshaft position sensor bracket

Chapter 6 Emissions and engine control systems

5.6 Camshaft sensor location - diesel engine

5.7a Remove the air intake pipe ...

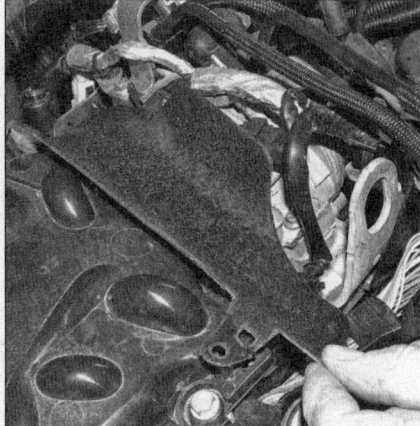

5.7b ... and heat protection shield

5.8 Disconnect the wiring connector

5.9 Undo the bolt and remove the sensor

from the cylinder head cover (see illustrations).

8 Disconnect the wiring connector from the camshaft position sensor (see illustration).
9 Undo the retaining bolt and withdraw the sensor from the cover (see illustration).
10 Discard the O-ring seal; a new one must be used on refitting.
11 Refitting is a reversal of the removal procedure, noting the following points:
12 Fit a new O-ring seal to the sensor.
13 Apply a smear of engine oil to the O-ring to aid installation, and then ease the sensor into position.

6 Intake Valve Timing (IVT) and Exhaust Valve Timing (EVT) control solenoid(s) - replacement

1 Earlier models use an intake valve timing (IVT) solenoid. Later models use an intake valve timing intermediate lock control solenoid, an intake valve timing (IVT) control solenoid valve and an exhaust valve timing (EVT) solenoid. All the solenoid(s) are located on the upper part of the timing chain cover on the control cover (bolted to the timing chain cover). The solenoid valves direct oil to the intake camshaft actuator or exhaust camshaft actuator to vary the intake or exhaust camshaft timing.
2 Remove the mounting bolt, then pull out the solenoid valve (see illustration).
3 Installation is the reverse of removal. Replace the O-ring with a new one, if necessary.

7 Crankshaft Position (CKP) sensor - replacement

1 The CKP sensor is mounted on the back side of the cylinder block near the transaxle end of the engine, just below the starter.
2 If equipped, remove the CKP sensor heat shield attaching bolt and remove the shield.
3 Disconnect the electrical connector from the CKP sensor.

6.2 The IVT control solenoid valve is located on the control cover, on the front of the timing chain cover (EVT control solenoid similar)

Diesel models

6 The camshaft position sensor is fitted to the transmission end of the cylinder head cover (see illustration).
7 Undo the retaining bolts and remove the air intake pipe from across the top of the cylinder head, then unclip the heat protector shield

7.4a CKP sensor mounting bolt - petrol models

7.4b Removing the CKP sensor on a diesel model

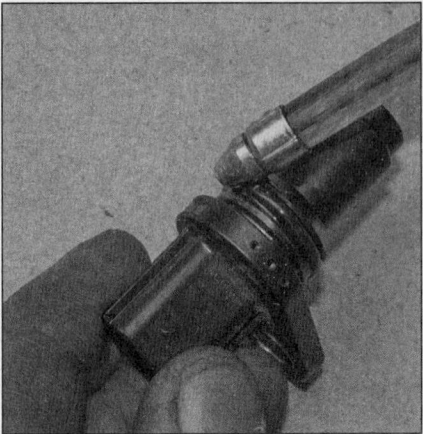

7.6 Lubricating the crankshaft position sensor O-ring

8.1 The Engine Coolant Temperature (ECT) sensor is located in the water outlet at the left (passenger) side of the engine.

4   Remove the mounting bolt from the CKP sensor and extract the sensor from the engine block **(see illustration)**.
5   Before installation, check the O-ring for cracks or tears and replace it if necessary.
6   Lubricate the O-ring with engine oil **(see illustration)** prior to installing the sensor.
7   Installation is the reverse of removal.

8 Engine Coolant Temperature (ECT) sensor - replacement

Warning: *Wait until the engine has completely cooled before beginning this procedure.*

Petrol models

1   The ECT sensor is mounted in the water outlet, where the upper radiator hoses is connected to the engine, at the passenger side of the engine **(see illustration)**.
2   Drain some engine coolant to minimize coolant spillage (see Chapter 1 Section 27).
3   Disconnect the electrical connector from the ECT sensor.
4   Unscrew the sensor from the engine and discard the sealing washer (a new one should be used).
5   Installation is the reverse of removal. Refill the cooling system (see Chapter 1 Section 27).

Diesel models

6   The ECT sensor is mounted to the thermostat housing on the LH side of the engine **(see illustration)**.
7   Drain some engine coolant to minimize coolant spillage (see Chapter 1 Section 27).
8   Disconnect the electrical connector from the ECT sensor.
9   The sensor is clipped in place. Prise out the sensor retaining circlip then remove the sensor and sealing ring from the housing **(see illustrations)**. If the system has not been drained, plug the sensor aperture to prevent further coolant loss.

10   Installation is the reverse of removal. Refill the cooling system (see Chapter 1 Section 27).

9 Mass Air Flow/Intake Air Temperature (MAF/IAT) sensor - replacement

Note: *Earlier models are equipped with a (MAF/IAT). Later models are equipped with (MAF) sensor.*

1   The MAF/IAT sensor is mounted on the air filter housing, near the air duct going to the throttle body **(see illustration)**.
2   Disconnect the electrical connector from the MAF/IAT sensor.
3   Remove the screws and remove the sensor from the air filter housing.
4   Installation is the reverse of removal.

10 Knock sensor - replacement

1   The knock sensor is mounted on the firewall side of the engine block on 2.5 litre engines, on 2.0 engines on the radiator side of engine **(see illustration)**.
2   Disconnect the electrical connector from the knock sensor.
3   Remove the sensor mounting bolt, then remove the sensor.
4   Installation is the reverse of removal.

11 Oxygen sensors - replacement

Note: *Because it is installed in the exhaust system, which contracts when cool, an oxygen sensor can be very difficult to loosen when the engine is cold. Rather than risking damage to the sensor or its mounting threads, run the engine for a minute or two, then shut it off. Be careful to avoid burns during this procedure.*

1   Be very careful when servicing an oxygen sensor:
   * *The oxygen sensor has a permanently attached pigtail and electrical connector which should not be removed from the sensor. Damage or removal of the pigtail or electrical connector can adversely affect operation of the sensor.*
   * *Grease, dirt and other contaminants should be kept away from the electrical connector and the louvered end of the sensor.*
   * *Do not use cleaning solvents of any kind on the oxygen sensor.*
   * *Do not drop or roughly handle the sensor.*
   * *The silicone boot must be installed in the correct position to prevent the boot from being melted and to allow the sensor to operate properly.*

Replacement

Upstream oxygen sensor

2   Locate the upstream oxygen sensor electrical connector and disconnect it **(see illustration)**. Detach the sensor wiring harness from any clips.
3   Unscrew the sensor with an oxygen sensor socket if one is available. You may have to raise the vehicle and support it securely on jackstands to reach it.
4   If you're going to install the old sensor, apply anti-seize compound to the threads to ease future removal. If you're installing a new sensor, the threads will already have anti-seize on them.
5   Installation is the reverse of removal. Tighten the sensor securely.

Downstream oxygen sensor

6   Raise the vehicle and support it securely on jackstands.
7   Disconnect the wiring harness from the pigtail of the sensor **(see illustration)**.

Note: *On later models the downstream oxygen sensor is located in the front exhaust pipe.*

Chapter 6 Emissions and engine control systems

8.9a Removing the retaining clip from the coolant temperature sensor

8.9b Discard the O-ring from the ECT sensor and use a new one on installation

9.1 The Mass Air Flow/Intake Air Temperature (MAF/IAT) sensor is installed in the air filter housing and is retained by two screws - later model shown all other models similar

10.1a The knock sensor is located on the back side of the engine block, below the intake manifold (2.5 litre engine shown)

10.1b The knock sensor is located on the front side of engine block, below the intake manifold (2.0 engine shown)

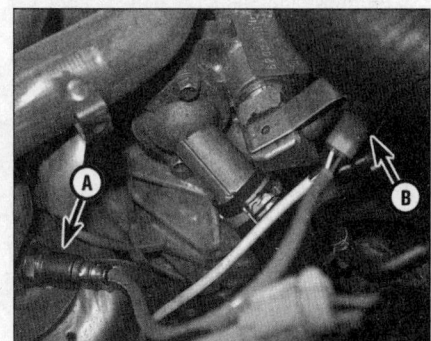

11.2 The upstream oxygen sensor (A), installed in the exhaust manifold just before the catalytic converter, and its electrical connector (B)

8 Unscrew the sensor using an oxygen sensor socket if one is available.
9 If you're going to install the old sensor, apply anti-seize compound to the threads to ease future removal. If you're installing a new sensor, the threads will already have anti-seize on them.
10 Installation is the reverse of removal. Tighten the sensor securely.

12 Engine Oil Temperature Sensor - replacement

Note: *Later petrol models are equipped with an engine oil temperature sensor.*

1 The engine oil temperature sensor is mounted on the firewall side of the engine block, near the oil cooler on 2.5 litre engine and on the radiator side of the block, near the knock sensor on 2.0 litre engine (**see illustration**).
2 Disconnect the electrical connector from the engine oil temperature sensor.
3 Unscrew the sensor from the engine block.
4 Installation is the reverse of removal.

13 Transmission range switch - replacement and adjustment

Replacement

1 The transmission range switch is mounted on the top of the transaxle (**see illustration**).

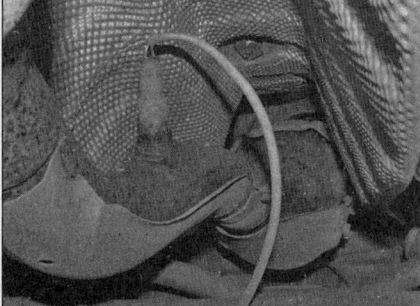

11.7 The downstream oxygen sensor is installed in the outlet side of the catalytic converter - Earlier models shown

12.1 The engine oil temperature sensor (1) is adjacent and below the oil pressure sensor (2) - (3) is the knock sensor wiring connector - Qashqai models

6-10 Chapter 6 Emissions and engine control systems

13.1 Transmission range switch location.

13.11 Transmission range switch mounting bolts

13.12 Insert a 4 mm drill bit through the hole in the manual lever and into the hole in the switch body to align it

2 Remove the battery and the battery tray (see Chapter 5 Section 5).
3 Remove the shift cable from the manual shaft.
4 Disconnect the electrical connector from the switch.
5 Unscrew the mounting bolts and remove the switch.
6 Installation is the reverse of removal. Adjust the switch.
7 Verify that the engine will start only in Park or Neutral. Verify that the back-up lights come on only in Reverse. Adjust the range switch as necessary to ensure that these conditions are met.

Adjustment

8 Set the parking brake.
9 Move the shifter to the "N" position.
10 Loosen the control cable-to-manual lever nut.
11 Loosen the range switch mounting bolts **(see illustration)**.
12 Rotate the switch and insert a drill bit (4 mm) into the adjusting holes **(see illustration)** on both the switch and manual lever.

13 Tighten the mounting bolts.
14 Tighten the control cable-to-manual lever nut.

14 Transmission speed sensors - replacement

Note: *On earlier models, the transaxle uses two speed sensors: primary and secondary.*

Note: *On later models, the transaxle uses three speed sensors: input speed, primary speed and output speed sensor.*

On earlier models

1 The primary sensor is located on the front side of the transaxle, facing the radiator. The secondary sensor is located on the left end of the transaxle case.
2 If you're replacing the primary speed sensor, remove the left inner mudguard splash shield. If you're removing the secondary speed sensor, remove the battery (see Chapter 5 Section 5) and the air filter housing

(see Chapter 4A Section 9 - petrol models or Chapter 4B Section 6 - diesel models).
3 Disconnect the electrical connector from the speed sensor **(see illustrations)**.
4 Remove the mounting bolt and remove the sensor. Discard the O-ring.
5 Apply some transmission fluid to the new O-ring and install it on the sensor.
6 Installation is the reverse of removal.

On later models

7 The input sensor is located on the front side of the transaxle facing the radiator. The primary speed sensor in located on the end of the transaxle facing the left wheel. The output speed sensor is located just above the left driveshaft.

Input speed sensor

8 Remove the battery and battery tray (see Chapter 5 Section 5).
9 Remove the starter motor (see Chapter 5 Section 12).
10 Disconnect the electrical connector from the speed sensor.
11 Remove the mounting bolt and remove the sensor. Discard the O-ring.
12 Apply some transmission fluid to the new O-ring and install it on the sensor.
13 Installation is the reverse of removal.

Primary speed sensor and output speed sensor

14 Loosen the left front wheel nuts, raise the vehicle and support it securely on jackstands (see Chapter 0 Section 7). Remove the left front wheel.
15 Remove the left inner mudguard splash shield.
16 Disconnect the electrical connector from the speed sensor.
17 Remove the mounting bolt and remove the sensor. Discard the O-ring.
18 Apply some transmission fluid to the new O-ring and install it on the sensor.
19 Installation is the reverse of removal.

14.3a Primary transmission speed sensor

14.3b Secondary transmission speed sensor

Chapter 6 Emissions and engine control systems

15.3 Unclip the vacuum pipes from the mounting bracket

15.4 Rotate the connector lock upward to disconnect the connector

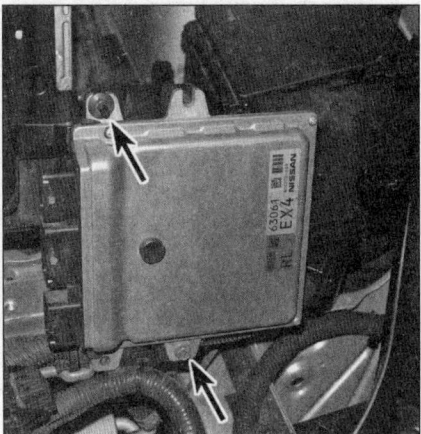

15.5 PCM mounting fasteners

15 Powertrain Control Module (PCM) - removal and installation

Note: *The Powertrain Control Module (PCM) cannot be replaced at home because the new unit must be programmed with the Vehicle Identification Number (VIN) and other data. Doing so is impossible without a factory scan tool. This Section only shows PCM removal to gain access to other components.*

1 The PCM is located on a bracket mounted to the battery tray.
2 On petrol models, remove the air inlet duct and the tube to the lower resonator.
3 On diesel models, unclip the vacuum pipes from across the top of the mounting bracket **(see illustration)**.
4 Starting with the top connector, push in on the tang in the centre of the PCM connector lock, then rotate the connector lock upward. Pull the connector away from the PCM to disconnect it. Repeat the procedure on the other two connectors **(see illustration)**.
5 On petrol models, remove the two mounting fasteners and remove the PCM **(see illustration)**.

6 On diesel models, proceed as follows:
  a Release the wiring loom retaining clips from the bottom of the mounting bracket **(see illustration)**.
  b Undo the retaining bolts and remove the mounting bracket, complete with control unit from the engine compartment **(see illustrations)**.
  c If required, undo the four retaining nuts and remove the ECM from the mounting bracket **(see illustration)**.
7 Installation is the reverse of removal.

16 Positive Crankcase Ventilation (PCV) valve - replacement

1 Refer to Chapter 1, Section 31 for information on the PCV system.

17 Throttle Position (TP) sensor - replacement

1 The throttle position sensor on these vehicles is an integral part of the throttle body and is not serviceable separately. Refer to the throttle body replacement procedure (see Chapter 4A Section 10 - petrol models or Chapter 4A Section 10 - diesel models).

15.6a Release the wiring loom retaining clips (arrowed)

15.6b Undo the retaining bolts ...

15.6c ... and remove the ECM with mounting plate

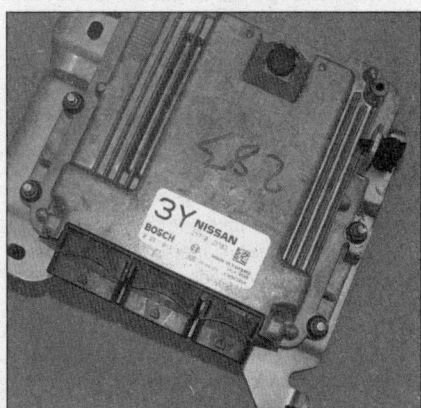

15.6d Undo the four retaining nuts to remove the ECM

18 Catalytic converter - replacement

General information

1 The catalytic converter reduces harmful exhaust emissions by chemically converting the more poisonous gases to ones that (in theory at least) are less harmful. The chemical reaction is known as an 'oxidising' reaction, or one where oxygen is 'added'.

2 Inside the converter is a honeycomb structure, made of ceramic material and coated with the precious metals palladium, platinum and rhodium (the 'catalyst' which promotes the chemical reaction). The chemical reaction generates heat, which itself promotes the reaction – therefore, once the car has been driven several miles, the body of the converter will be very hot.

3 The ceramic structure contained within the converter is understandably fragile, and will not withstand rough treatment. Since the converter runs at a high temperature, driving through deep standing water (in flood conditions, for example) is to be avoided, since the thermal stresses imposed when plunging the hot converter into cold water may well cause the ceramic internals to fracture, resulting in a 'blocked' converter – a common cause of failure. A catalytic converter that has been damaged in this way can be checked by shaking it, do not strike it – if a rattling noise is heard, this indicates probable failure.

Precautions

4 The catalytic converter is a reliable and simple device which needs no maintenance in itself, but there are some facts of which an owner should be aware if the converter is to function properly for its full service life.

Petrol models

a DO NOT use leaded petrol (or lead-replacement petrol, LRP) in a car equipped with a catalytic converter – the lead (or other additives) will coat the precious metals, reducing their converting efficiency and will eventually destroy the converter.

b Always keep the ignition and fuel systems well maintained in accordance with the manufacturer's schedule.

c If the engine develops a misfire, do not drive the car at all (or at least as little as possible) until the fault is cured.

d DO NOT push- or tow-start the car – this will soak the catalytic converter in unburned fuel, causing it to overheat when the engine does start.

e DO NOT switch off the ignition at high engine speeds.

f DO NOT use fuel or engine oil additives – these may contain substances harmful to the catalytic converter.

g DO NOT continue to use the car if the engine burns oil to the extent of leaving a visible trail of blue smoke.

h Remember that the catalytic converter operates at very high temperatures. DO NOT, therefore, park the car in dry undergrowth, over long grass or piles of dead leaves after a long run.

i Remember that the catalytic converter is FRAGILE – do not strike it with tools during servicing work.

j In some cases a sulphurous smell (like that of rotten eggs) may be noticed from the exhaust. This is common to many catalytic converter-equipped cars and once the car has covered a few thousand miles the problem should disappear.

k The catalytic converter, used on a well-maintained and well-driven car, should last at least 150,000 km. However, if the converter is no longer effective it must be renewed.

l If a substantial loss of power is experienced, remember that this could be due to the converter being blocked. This can occur simply as a result of high mileage, but may be due to the ceramic element having fractured and collapsed internally (see paragraph 3). A new converter is the only cure in this instance.

m As mentioned above, driving through deep water should be avoided if possible. The sudden cooling effect may fracture the ceramic honeycomb, damaging it beyond repair.

Diesel models

5 The catalytic converter fitted to diesel models is simpler than that fitted to petrol models, but it still needs to be treated with respect to avoid problems:

a DO NOT use fuel or engine oil additives – these may contain substances harmful to the catalytic converter.

b DO NOT continue to use the car if the engine burns (engine) oil to the extent of leaving a visible trail of blue smoke.

c Remember that the catalytic converter operates at very high temperatures. DO NOT, therefore, park the car in dry undergrowth, over long grass or piles of dead leaves after a long run.

d As mentioned above, driving through deep water should be avoided if possible. The sudden cooling effect will fracture the ceramic honeycomb, damaging it beyond repair.

e Remember that the catalytic converter is FRAGILE – do not strike it with tools during servicing work, and take care handling it when removing it from the car for any reason.

f If a substantial loss of power is experienced, remember that this could be due to the converter being blocked. This can occur simply as a result of high mileage, but may be due to the ceramic element having fractured and collapsed internally (see paragraph 3). A new converter is the only cure in this instance.

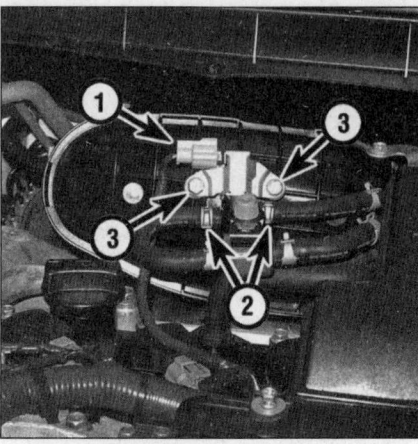

19.1 Canister purge control solenoid valve details - earlier model shown other models similar

1 Electrical connector
2 Hoses
3 Mounting bolts

g The catalytic converter, used on a well-maintained and well-driven car, should last at least 150,000 km. However, if the converter is no longer effective it must be renewed.

Primary catalytic converter

6 The primary catalytic converter is an integral part of the exhaust manifold (see Chapter 2A Section 6).

19 Evaporative Emissions Control (EVAP) system - component replacement

Petrol engine emission control systems – testing and component renewal

Purge control solenoid valve

1 Disconnect the hoses from the valve **(see illustration)**.
2 Disconnect the electrical connector from the valve.
3 Remove the mounting bolts and detach the valve from the intake manifold.
4 Installation is the reverse of removal.

EVAP canister

Note: *The EVAP canister is located at the front of the vehicle underneath the drivers side headlight.*

5 Raise the rear of the vehicle and support it securely on jackstands (see Chapter 0 Section 7).
6 Remove drivers side inner guard liner (see Chapter 11 Section 18).
7 Disconnect the canister purge hose from the canister.
8 Disconnect the fuel tank EVAP breather hose.

Chapter 6 Emissions and engine control systems

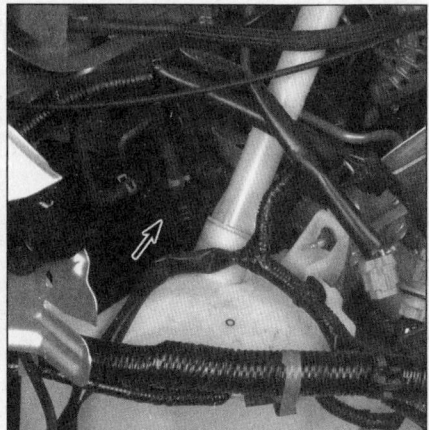

19.10 Canister location

19.21 Disconnect the EGR valve wiring connector

19.22 Undo the six EGR mounting screws

9 Disconnect the vent control valve hose.
10 Remove the canister by lifting it up **(see illustration)**.
11 Remove the EVAP canister.
12 Installation is the reverse of removal.

Diesel engine emission control systems – testing and component renewal

Crankcase emission control

13 The components of this system require no attention other than to check that the hose(s) are clear and undamaged at regular intervals.
14 If the system is thought to be faulty, first check that the hoses are unobstructed and not damaged.
15 On high-mileage cars, particularly when regularly used for short journeys, a sludge-like deposit may be evident inside the system hoses and oil separators. If excessive deposits are present, the relevant component(s) should be removed and cleaned.
16 Periodically inspect the system components for security and damage, and renew them as necessary.

Exhaust emission control

Testing

17 The performance of the catalytic converter can be checked by measuring the exhaust gases using an exhaust gas analyser, which is suitable for diesel engines.

Catalytic converter renewal

18 The catalytic converter, on diesel models, is installed between the turbo exhaust outlet and the exhaust pipe. For general information on exhaust component removal, see the Fuel and exhaust systems - Diesel engine chapter (see Chapter 4B Section 11).

Exhaust gas recirculation system

Testing

19 Testing of the system should be entrusted to a Nissan dealer, who will have the specialist diagnostic equipment to carry out any tests.

EGR valve renewal

20 The EGR solenoid valve is located on the front of the intake manifold on the front of the engine. First disconnect the wiring from the unit.
21 Remove the plastic engine cover and disconnect the wiring from the EGR solenoid valve **(see illustration)**.

22 Undo the screws and lift the solenoid valve from the throttle valve housing **(see illustration)**. Recover the gasket.
23 Refitting is a reversal of removal, using a new gasket and ensuring that the valve and housing surfaces are clean and the bolts are securely tightened.

EGR cooler renewal

24 The EGR cooler is located on the front of the engine, below the inlet manifold and throttle valve (damper) housing. First drain the cooling system (see Chapter 1 Section 27).
25 Remove the engine top cover, then remove the battery and battery tray (see Chapter 5 Section 5).
26 Remove the intake air ducting and intercooler inlet pipe from the front of the engine.
27 Remove the throttle valve housing (see Chapter 4B Section 7).
28 Unbolt the EGR cooler pipe from the inlet manifold and cooler and recover the gaskets **(see illustrations)**.
29 Unscrew the bolts and disconnect the EGR transfer pipe from the cooler.
30 Loosen the clips and disconnect the coolant hoses from the cooler **(see illustrations)**.
31 Unbolt the EGR cooler from the front of the cylinder block **(see illustration)**.

19.28a Unbolt and remove the EGR cooler pipe …

19.28b … and recover the gasket

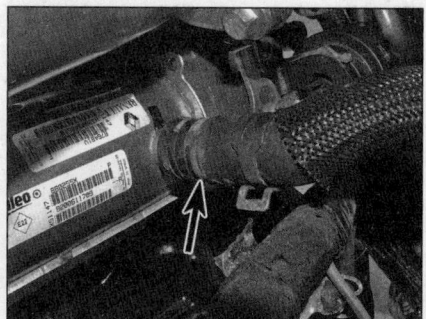

19.30a Disconnecting the inlet coolant hose (arrowed) …

Chapter 6 Emissions and engine control systems

19.30b ...and outlet coolant hose from the cooler

19.31 EGR cooler mounting bolts (arrowed)

32 Refitting is a reversal of removal, but tighten the bolts to the specified torque.

Particulate filter system

Particulate filter renewal

33 The particle filter is part of the exhaust front section. Remove the front pipe/particle filter (see Chapter 4B Section 11).

Temperature sensors renewal

34 The temperature sensors monitor the exhaust gas temperature both upstream and downstream of the particulate filter during regeneration **(see illustrations)**. To remove the sensors, disconnect the wiring at the connector, unbolt the wiring support and unscrew the sensor from the exhaust.

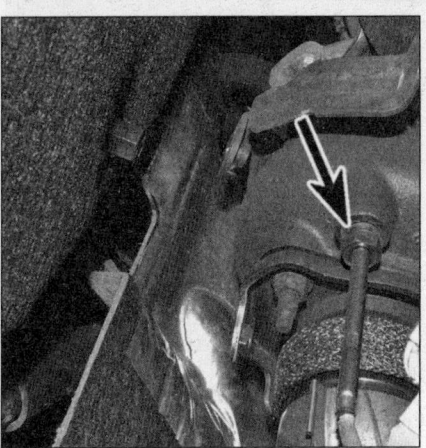

19.34a Particulate filter upper temperature sensor ...

19.34b ... and lower temperature sensor

Chapter 7 Part A
Manual transaxle

Contents

	Section		Section
General Information	1	Manual transaxle overhaul – general information	6
Manual transaxle – removal and installation	5	Oil seals – renewal	3
Manual transaxle lubricant change	See Chapter 1	Reversing light switch – testing, removal and installation	4
Manual transaxle lubricant level check	See Chapter 1	Shift cable – removal and installation	2

Specifications

General

Transaxle
Type.. 6-speed manual transaxle
Designation
  Petrol engines:
    2WD (two wheel drive)............................. RS6F94R
    4WD (four wheel drive)............................. RS6F52A
  2.0 litre diesel (2WD and 4WD)..................... RS6F52A

Gear ratio

	RS6F94R	RS6F52A	RS6F52A-diesel model
1st gear	3.7273	3.727	3.727
2nd gear	2.1053	2.043	2.043
3rd gear	1.5185	1.392	1.322
4th gear	1.1714	1.055	0.947
5th gear	0.9143	0.865	0.723
6th gear	0.7674	0.732	0.596
Reverse gear	3.6865	3.641	3.641

Lubrication
Lubricant type and capacity........................... see Chapter 1

Torque wrench settings   Nm
Transaxle-to-engine bolts
  2.0 litre petrol engines **(see illustration 11.35a)**............ 62
  2.5 litre X-Trail T31 model **(see illustration 11.35b)**
    Bolts 1... 35
    Bolts 2 and 5... 75
    Bolts 3 and 4... 43
    Bolts 6.. 50
  2.5 litre X-Trail T32 model **(see illustration 11.35b)**
    Bolt 1.. 35
    Bolts 2 and 5... 75
    Bolts 3 and 4... 43
    Bolts 6.. 48
  2.0 litre X-Trail T31 diesel **(see illustration 11.35c)**
    Bolt length 55 mm and nut..................... 48
    Bolt length 70 mm................................. 20
Oil drain plug.. see Chapter 1
Oil filler/level plug (plastic plug)..................... see Chapter 1
Reversing light switch.................................... 23

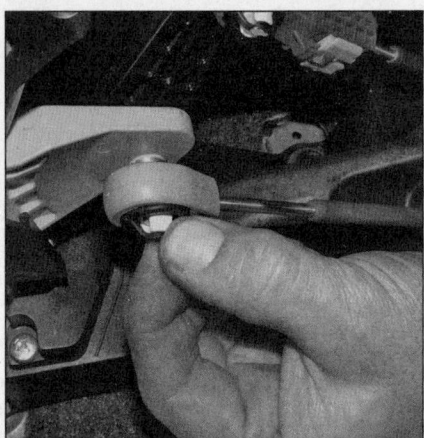
2.2a Release the locking clips …

2.2b … and disconnect the cables from the ball joint

2.3a Pull out the locating pins …

1 General Information

1 The transmission is contained in a cast-aluminium alloy casing bolted to the left-hand end of the engine, and consists of the gearbox and final drive differential, often called a transaxle.

2 Drive is transmitted from the crankshaft via the clutch to the input shaft, which has a splined extension to accept the clutch friction disc, and rotates in sealed ball-bearings. From the input shaft, drive is transmitted to the output shaft, which rotates in a roller bearing at its right-hand end, and a sealed ball-bearing at its left-hand end. From the output shaft, the drive is transmitted to the differential crownwheel, which rotates with the differential case and planetary gears, thus driving the sun gears and driveshafts. The rotation of the planetary gears on their shaft allows the inner roadwheel to rotate at a slower speed than the outer roadwheel when the car is cornering.

3 The input and output shafts are arranged side-by-side, parallel to the crankshaft and driveshafts, so that their gear pinion teeth are in constant mesh. In the neutral position, the output shaft gear pinions rotate freely, so that drive cannot be transmitted to the crownwheel.

4 Gear selection is via a floor-mounted lever and dual cable arrangement. The selector cables cause the appropriate selector fork to move its respective synchro-sleeve along the shaft, to lock the gear pinion to the synchro-hub. Since the synchro-hubs are splined to the output shaft, this locks the pinion to the shaft so that drive can be transmitted. To ensure that gearchanging can be made quickly and quietly, a synchromesh system is fitted to all forward gears, consisting of baulk rings and spring-loaded fingers, as well as the gear pinions and synchro-hubs; the synchromesh cones are formed on the mating faces of the baulk rings and gear pinions.

2 Shift cable – removal and installation

Removal

Shift lever assembly

1 Remove the centre console (see Chapter 11 Section 22).

2 Release the white securing clips and disconnect the two cables from the ball joints on the gear shift levers **(see illustrations)**.

3 Pull out the locating pin and withdraw the two outer cables from the gear change housing **(see illustrations)**.

4 With the cables disconnected, undo the four mounting bolts from the bottom of the shift lever housing **(see illustration)**, and manoeuvre the gear lever assembly out of position.

Gear change cables

5 Release the cables from the shift lever assembly, as described in paragraphs 1 to 3.

2.3b … and unclip the outer cables …

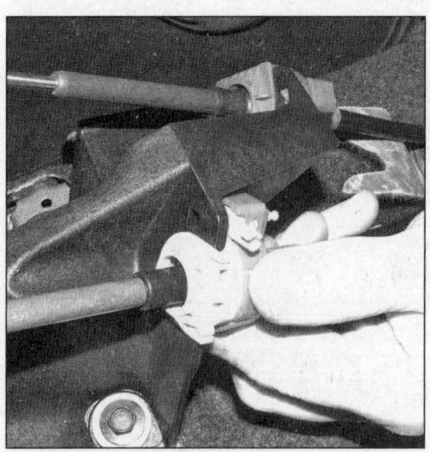
2.3c … from the gear lever bracket

2.4 Undo the gear change mounting bracket bolts (arrowed)

Chapter 7 Part A Manual transaxle   7A-3

2.8a Release the locking clips (arrowed) …

2.8b … and disconnect the cables from the ball joint

2.9a Pull out the locating pins …

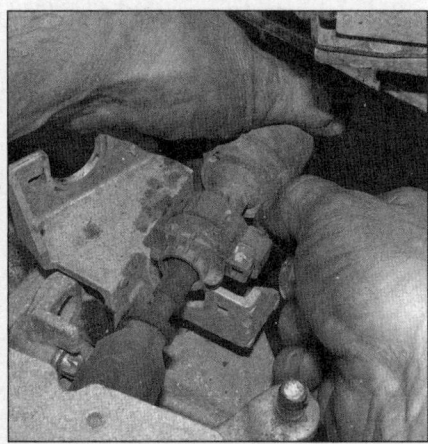

2.9b … and unclip the outer cables from the transaxle bracket

2.11a Undo the retaining clips …

the gear change selector levers (see illustrations).

9   Pull out the locating pin and withdraw the two outer cables from the transaxle mounting bracket (see illustrations).

10   Firmly apply the handbrake, and then raise the front of the vehicle and support it securely on jack stands (see Chapter 0 Section 7).

11   From underneath the vehicle, release the fasteners and remove the heat shield from under the centre tunnel of the vehicle (see illustrations). Note depending on model, it may be necessary to remove the exhaust front pipe or prop shaft (4WD models) to give better access to the heat shield.

12   Unclip the outer cables from the mounting bracket on the underside of the vehicle, and then release the rubber grommet from the floor panel and withdraw the cables from under the vehicle (see illustrations).

13   Inspect all the gear linkage components for signs of wear or damage, paying particular attention to the cables, renew worn components as necessary.

6   Remove the battery (see Chapter 5 Section 5).

7   Also to make access to the cables on top of the transaxle housing easier, remove the air cleaner housing (see Chapter 4A Section 9 or Chapter 4B Section 6).

8   Release the white securing clips and disconnect the two cables from the ball joints on

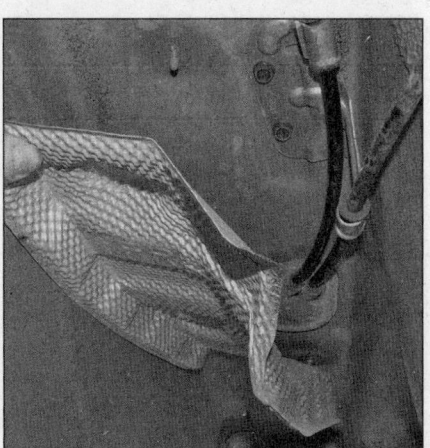

2.11b … and remove the heatshield

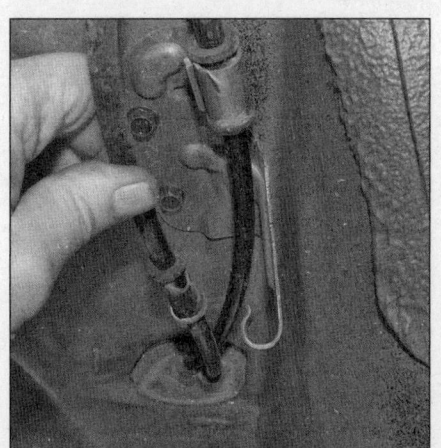

2.12a Release the cables from the retaining bracket …

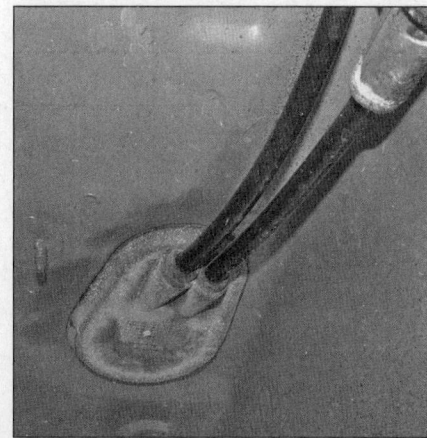

2.12b … and remove the rubber grommet from the floor panel

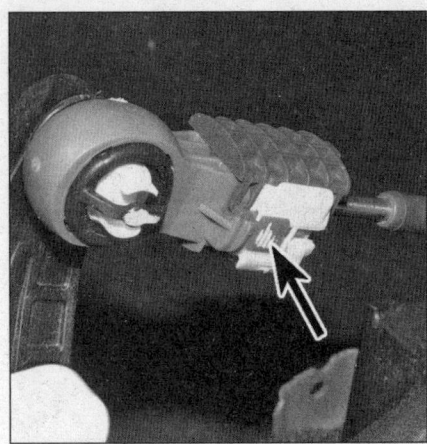

2.15 Release the locking clip (arrowed) to adjust the cable

2.18 Insert pin through slot in the gear lever (arrowed)

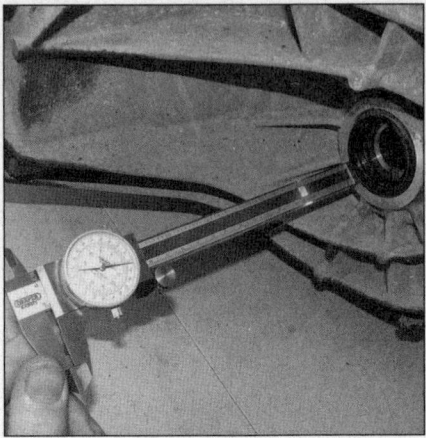

3.4a Using a vernier gauge to measure the seal depth

Refitting

14 Refitting is a reversal of the removal procedure, applying a smear of multipurpose grease to the gear lever pivot ball and bushes.

Adjustment

15 Adjustment is made from inside the vehicle, on the shift lever end of the left-hand selector cable (see illustration).
16 Remove the centre console.
17 Slide the centre clip and withdraw the locking clip from the end of the gear change cable; this will disengage the inner cable.
18 Position the shift lever so that the slot in the lever aligns with the hole in the gear lever housing (see illustration), and then insert a 3 mm locating pin (drill bit) to lock the gear lever in position.
19 With the gear lever in position, slide the centre locking clip back into position, securing the cable in position.
20 When completed remove the 3 mm locating pin and move the gear lever through all gears to check smooth operation.
21 Refitting is a reversal of the removal procedure.

3 Oil seals – renewal

Driveshaft oil seal

1 Firmly apply the handbrake, and raise the front of the vehicle and support it securely on jack stands (see Chapter 0 Section 7). Remove the appropriate front wheel.
2 Drain the transaxle oil (see Chapter 1 Section 29).
3 Remove the drive shaft from the transaxle (see Chapter 8 Section 7).
4 Before removing the seal, use a vernier gauge to check the seal depth in the transaxle casing (see illustration). This will give you the position of the seal in the transaxle casing for refitting, see following measurements:

a On 6-speed (RS6F94R) transaxles the left and right-hand side seals should be flush with casing. Left-hand side seal should be 1.2 to 1.8 mm. Right-hand side seal should be 2.7 to 3.3 mm

b On CVT (continuously variable-ratio transaxle): Left-hand side should be 1.8 to 1.9 mm from transaxle case; Right-hand side should be 2.2 to 2.3 mm from transaxle case.

c On automatic (RE6F01A) transaxles: Left-hand side seal should be 5.7 to 6.2 mm; Right-hand side seal should be 22.7 to 23.5 mm.

d On 4WD transaxles, the transfer case side seal should be set at 7.5 to 8.0 mm depth.

5 Carefully prise the oil seal out of the transaxle using a large flat-bladed screwdriver (see illustration). Take care not to damage the transaxle casing as the seal is removed.
6 Remove all traces of dirt from the area around the oil seal aperture, then apply a smear of oil to the lip of the new oil seal, and locate it in its aperture (see illustration).
7 Drive the seal squarely into position, using a suitable tubular drift (such as a socket), which bears only on the hard outer edge of the seal (see illustration). Drive the seal into position until it is at the depth noted on removal.

3.5 Use a large flat-bladed screwdriver to prise out the driveshaft oil seals

3.6 Fit the new seal squarely to the transaxle…

3.7 … and tap it into position using a tubular drift/socket

4.1 Location of reversing light switch

4.5 Disconnect the switch wiring connector

5.0a Label with transaxle model code

8 On 4WD models, transfer case seals are covered in the Transfer Case Chapter (see Chapter 7C Section 4).
9 Refit the driveshaft (see Chapter 8 Section 7).
10 Refill the transaxle with the specified type and quantity of oil (see Chapter 1 Section 29).

Input shaft oil seal

11 To renew the input shaft seal, the transaxle must be dismantled. This task should therefore be entrusted to a transmission specialist with the necessary tools.

4 Reversing light switch – testing, removal and installation

Testing

1 The reversing light circuit is controlled by a plunger-type switch that is screwed into the front of the transaxle housing (see illustration).
2 If a fault develops in the circuit, first ensure that the circuit fuse has not blown (see Chapter 12A Section 3).
3 To test the switch, disconnect the wiring connector, and use a multimeter (set to the resistance function) or a battery-and-bulb test circuit to check that there is continuity between the switch terminals only when reverse gear is selected. If this is not the case, and there are no obvious breaks or other damage to the wires, the switch is faulty and must be renewed.

Removal

4 Firmly apply the handbrake, and then raise the front of the vehicle and support it securely on jackstands (see Chapter 0 Section 7).
5 Disconnect the wiring connector from the reversing light switch (see illustration).
6 Unscrew the switch from the transaxle, and remove it. Plug the housing aperture to prevent dirt entry.

Refitting

7 Fit a new sealing washer to the switch, and then screw it back into the transaxle housing.
8 Tighten it securely, then reconnect the wiring connector.
9 Lower the vehicle to the ground and check the operation of the circuit.

5 Manual transaxle – removal and installation

Note: *This Section describes the removal of the transaxle leaving the engine in position in the car. Alternatively the engine and transaxle can be removed together, as described in Chapter 2D Section 7, and then separated on the bench.*

Note: *Transaxle model code number is on a label on the top of the transaxle housing (see illustration); see Specifications at the beginning of this Chapter.*

Removal

1 Firmly apply the handbrake, and then jack up the front of the vehicle and support it securely on axle stands (see Chapter 0 Section 7). Remove both front wheels. Undo the retaining screws, and remove the plastic undershields from beneath the engine/transaxle, and the covers from underneath both wheel arches (see illustration).
2 Drain the transaxle oil (see Chapter 1 Section 29), then refit the drain and filler/level plugs and tighten them to their specified torque settings.
3 Remove the battery (see Chapter 5 Section 3).
4 Remove the front subframe (see Chapter 10 Section 18).
5 Remove the starter motor (see Chapter 5 Section 12).
6 Remove the air filter housing (see Chapter 4A Section 9 or Chapter 4B Section 6).
7 Remove the exhaust system front pipe (see Chapter 4A Section 11 or Chapter 4B Section 11).
8 On 4WD models, remove the transfer case (see Chapter 7C Section 3).
9 Release the gearchange cables from the transaxle (see Section 2).
10 Remove the two front driveshafts from the transaxle (see Chapter 8 Section 7).

Note: *Note that there is no need to unscrew the driveshaft retaining nuts – each driveshaft*

5.1 Remove the inner trim panel

5.10 Using a dummy shaft in the differential

5.11 Undo the earth cable retaining bolt (arrowed)

5.13a Release the locking clip (arrowed) …

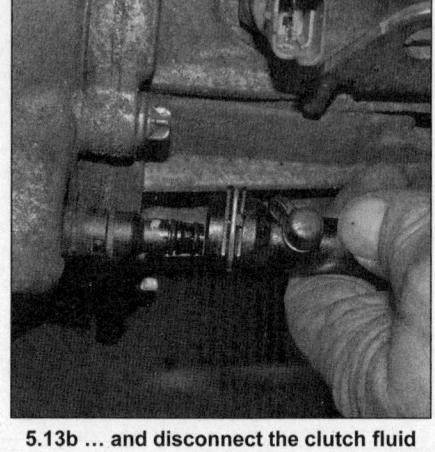

5.13b … and disconnect the clutch fluid hose

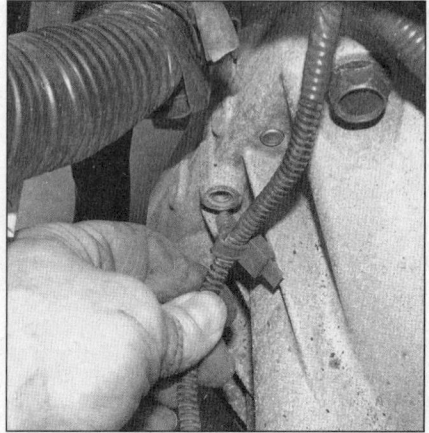

5.14a Release the wiring loom …

11   Undo the retaining bolt and disconnect the earth cable from the left-hand end of the transaxle **(see illustration)**.
12   Disconnect the wiring connector from the reversing light switch, (see Section 4) for reversing light switch location.
13   Be prepared for some fluid loss as the pipe is disconnected, place some cloth around the fitting. Release the retaining spring clip and disconnect the clutch fluid hose from the slave cylinder connector pipe **(see illustrations)**. Plug the ends of the slave cylinder pipe and clutch fluid hose to prevent fluid leakage and dirt ingress.
14   Work around the transaxle and free the wiring loom from any relevant retaining clips **(see illustrations)**, and position the wiring clear of the transaxle.
15   Make sure the breather pipe on top of the transaxle housing is not secured to any other components. This does not have to be completely removed and left across the top of the transaxle.
16   Place a jack with interposed block of wood beneath the engine, to take the weight of the engine **(see illustration)**. Alternatively, attach a hoist or support bar to the engine and take the weight of the engine.

17   Also place a jack and block of wood beneath the transaxle, and raise the jack to take the weight of the transaxle.
18   Slacken and remove the nut from the centre stud on the left-hand engine/transaxle mounting. Undo the two bolts securing the mounting to the bracket, and remove the rubber mounting **(see illustration)**. For further information on engine/transaxle mounting removal, see the relevant Engine Chapters (see Chapter 2A Section 15, Chapter 2B Section 17 or Chapter 2C Section 20).
19   Unclip the clutch fluid pipe from the clip on the mounting bracket, and then undo the three bolts and remove the mounting from the top of the transaxle **(see illustration)**.
20   With the jack positioned beneath the transaxle taking the weight, slacken and remove the remaining bolts securing the transaxle housing to the engine **(see illustrations)**. Note the correct fitted positions of each bolt (and the relevant brackets) as they are removed, to use as a reference on refitting – the bolts are of different lengths. Note that it may be necessary to raise the transaxle slightly to gain access to the lower bolts.
21   Make a final check that all necessary components have been disconnected, and

can be left secured to the hub. But take care and support the driveshafts, to avoid placing any strain on the driveshaft joints or gaiters. With the driveshafts out of the transaxle, insert a dummy shaft into differential recess **(see illustration)**.

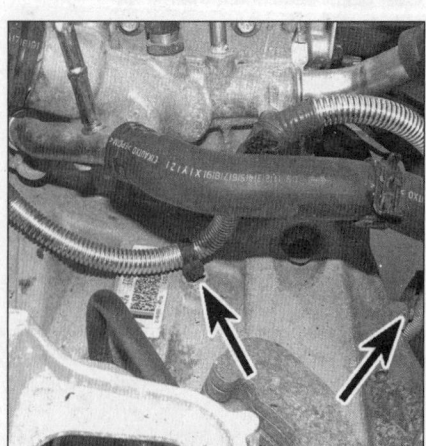

5.14b … retaining clips (arrowed) from the transaxle

5.16 Support the transaxle with a trolley jack

5.18 Remove the transaxle mounting

5.19 Undo the mounting bracket retaining bolts

5.20a Remove the upper mounting bolts ...

5.20b ... rear mounting bolts ...

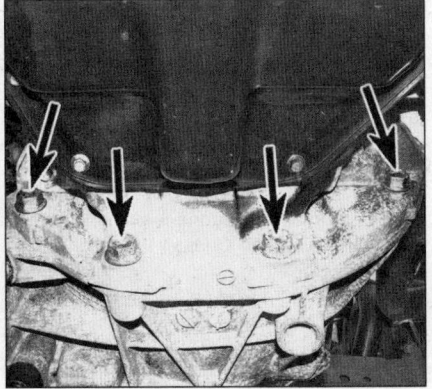
5.20c ... lower mounting bolts ...

5.20d ... and front mounting bolt

5.23 Lower the transaxle from under the vehicle

are positioned clear of the transaxle so that they will not hinder the removal procedure.
22 Move the trolley jack and transaxle to the left to free it from its locating dowels. Keep the transaxle fully supported until the input shaft is free of the engine.
23 Once the transaxle is free, lower the jack and manoeuvre the unit out from under the car (see illustration). If they are loose, remove the locating dowels from the transaxle or engine, and keep them in a safe place.

Refitting

24 The transaxle is refitted by a reversal of the removal procedure, bearing in mind the following points:

a Apply a little high melting-point grease to the splines of the transaxle input shaft. Do not apply too much; otherwise there is a possibility of the grease contaminating the clutch friction disc.

b Ensure that the locating dowels are correctly positioned prior to installation.
c Insert the transaxle-to-engine bolts into their original locations, as noted on removal (see illustrations). Tighten all nuts and bolts to the specified torque (where given).
d Refit the driveshafts (see Chapter 8 Section 7).
e Bleed the clutch system (see Chapter 8 Section 2).

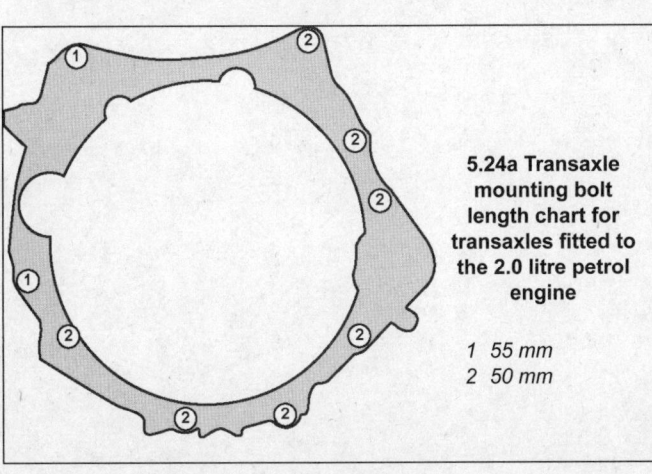

5.24a Transaxle mounting bolt length chart for transaxles fitted to the 2.0 litre petrol engine

1 55 mm
2 50 mm

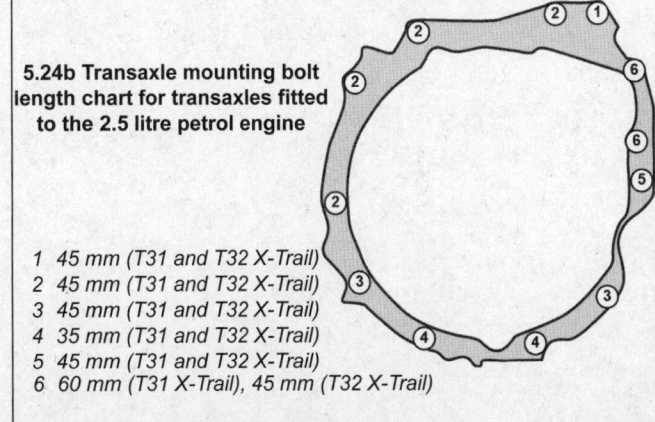

5.24b Transaxle mounting bolt length chart for transaxles fitted to the 2.5 litre petrol engine

1 45 mm (T31 and T32 X-Trail)
2 45 mm (T31 and T32 X-Trail)
3 45 mm (T31 and T32 X-Trail)
4 35 mm (T31 and T32 X-Trail)
5 45 mm (T31 and T32 X-Trail)
6 60 mm (T31 X-Trail), 45 mm (T32 X-Trail)

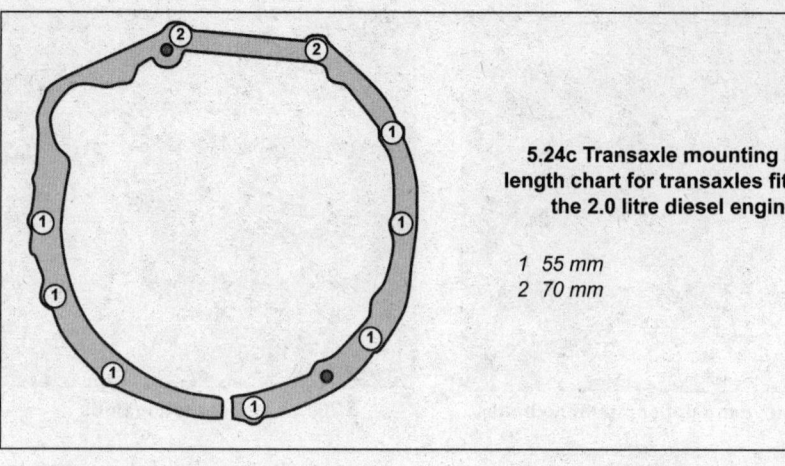

5.24c Transaxle mounting bolt length chart for transaxles fitted to the 2.0 litre diesel engine

1 55 mm
2 70 mm

f Refit the shift cables (see Section 2), and check operation.
g On completion, refill the transaxle with the specified type and quantity of lubricant (see Chapter 1 Section 29).

6 Manual transaxle overhaul – general information

1 Overhauling a manual transaxle is a difficult and involved job for the DIY home mechanic. In addition to dismantling and reassembling many small parts, clearances must be precisely measured and, if necessary, changed by selecting shims and spacers. Internal transaxle components are also often difficult to obtain, and in many instances, extremely expensive. Because of this, if the transaxle develops a fault or becomes noisy, the best course of action is to have the unit overhauled by a specialist repairer, or to obtain an exchange reconditioned unit.

2 Nevertheless, it is not impossible for the more experienced mechanic to overhaul the transaxle, if the special tools are available, and the job is done in a deliberate step-by-step manner so that nothing is overlooked.

3 The tools necessary for an overhaul include internal and external circlip pliers, bearing pullers, a slide hammer, a set of pin punches, a dial test indicator, and possibly a hydraulic press. In addition, a large, sturdy workbench and a vice will be required.

4 During dismantling of the transaxle, make careful notes of how each component is fitted, to make reassembly easier and accurate.

5 Before dismantling the transaxle, it will help if you have some idea which area is malfunctioning. Certain problems can be closely related to specific areas in the transaxle, which can make component examination and renewal easier (see Chapter 0 Section 10).

Chapter 7 Part B
Automatic transaxle

Contents

	Section		Section
Automatic CVT transaxle fluid change	see Chapter 1	Shift interlock cable - replacement and adjustment	9
Automatic transaxle - removal and installation	11	Shift knob - removal and installation	3
Automatic transaxle fluid level check	see Chapter 1	Shifter assembly - removal and installation	4
Diagnosis - general	2	Transmission Control Module (TCM) - removal and installation	8
General information	1		
Oil seal - replacement	10	Transmission range switch - replacement and adjustment	6
Shift cable - replacement and adjustment	5	Transmission speed sensors - replacement	7

Specifications

Model

T31 X-Trail petrol	RE0F10A
Model code number	
With 2.0 litre petrol engine	1XF0E
With 2.5 litre petrol engine	1XF6A
T31 X-Trail diesel	RE6F01A
Model code number	1XN0A
J10 Dualis	
Model code number	RE0F10D
Two-wheel-drive	1XF2B
Four-wheel-drive	1XF2D
T32 X-Trail, J11 Qashqai	RE0F10D

Torque specifications

	Nm
Driveplate-to-torque converter nuts	51
Shift cable nut at transaxle	13
Transaxle-to-engine mounting bolts	
2.0 litre petrol engines **(see illustration 11.35a)**	62
2.5 litre X-Trail T31 model **(see illustration 11.35b)**	
Bolts 1	35
Bolts 2 and 5	75
Bolts 3 and 4	43
Bolts 6	50
2.5 litre X-Trail T32 model **(see illustration 11.35b)**	
Bolt 1	35
Bolts 2 and 5	75
Bolts 3 and 4	43
Bolt 6	48
2.0 litre X-Trail T31 diesel **(see illustration 11.35c)**	
Bolt length 55 mm and nut	48
Bolt length 70 mm	20

1 General information

1 The vehicles covered by this manual are equipped with an automatic transaxle or a continuously variable-ratio transaxle (CVT).
2 Because of the complexity of the automatic transaxle and the specialized equipment needed to service it, this Chapter contains only those procedures related to general diagnosis, routine maintenance, adjustment, and removal and installation.
3 If the transaxle requires major repair work, it should be taken to a dealer service department or an automotive or transmission repair shop. You can, however, save money by removing and installing the transaxle yourself, even if the repair work is done by a shop.

2 Diagnosis - general

Note: *Automatic transaxle malfunctions may be caused by five general conditions: poor engine performance, improper adjustments, hydraulic malfunctions, mechanical malfunctions or malfunctions in the computer or its signal network. Diagnosis of these problems should always begin with a check of the easily repaired items: fluid level and condition (see Chapter 1 Section 8), shift cable adjustment and throttle linkage adjustment. Next, perform a road test to determine if the problem has been corrected or if more diagnosis is necessary. If the problem persists after the preliminary tests and corrections are completed, additional diagnosis should be done by a dealer service department or transmission repair shop (see Chapter 0, Section 10) for information on symptoms of transaxle problems.*

Preliminary checks

1 Drive the vehicle to warm the transaxle to normal operating temperature.
2 Check the fluid level (see Chapter 1 Section 4).
  a If the fluid level is unusually low, add enough fluid to bring the level within the designated area of the dipstick, then check for external leaks (see below).
  b If the fluid level is abnormally high, drain off the excess, then check the drained fluid for contamination by coolant. The presence of engine coolant in the automatic transmission fluid indicates that a failure has occurred in the internal radiator walls that separate the coolant from the transmission fluid (see Chapter 3 Section 6).
  c If the fluid is foaming, drain it and refill the transaxle, then check for coolant in the fluid, or a high fluid level.
3 Check for the presence of any stored diagnostic trouble codes (see Chapter 6 Section 2). There are many potential transaxle-specific trouble codes that could be set, but certain engine-related problems can also affect transaxle operation.
4 Inspect the shift cable (see Section 5). Make sure that it's properly adjusted and operates smoothly.

Fluid leak diagnosis

5 Most fluid leaks are easy to locate visually. Repair usually consists of replacing a seal or gasket. If a leak is difficult to find, the following procedure may help.
6 Identify the fluid. Make sure it's transmission fluid and not engine oil or brake fluid (the fluid used in CVT transaxles is a light green colour and a red colour for the automatic transaxle).
7 Try to pinpoint the source of the leak. Drive the vehicle several kilometres, then park it over a large sheet of cardboard. After a minute or two, you should be able to locate the leak by determining the source of the fluid dripping onto the cardboard.
8 Make a careful visual inspection of the suspected component and the area immediately around it. Pay particular attention to gasket mating surfaces. A mirror is often helpful for finding leaks in areas that are hard to see.
9 If the leak still cannot be found, clean the suspected area thoroughly with a degreaser or solvent, then dry it.
10 Drive the vehicle for several kilometres at normal operating temperature and varying speeds. After driving the vehicle, visually inspect the suspected component again.
11 Once the leak has been located, the cause must be determined before it can be properly repaired. If a gasket is replaced but the sealing flange is bent, the new gasket will not stop the leak. The bent flange must be straightened.
12 Before attempting to repair a leak, check to make sure that the following conditions are corrected or they may cause another leak.

Note: *Some of the following conditions cannot be fixed without highly specialized tools and expertise. Such problems must be referred to a transmission shop.*

Gasket leaks

13 Check the pan periodically. Make sure the bolts are tight, no bolts are missing, the gasket is in good condition and the pan is flat (dents in the pan may indicate damage to the valve body inside).
14 If the pan gasket is leaking, the fluid level or the fluid pressure may be too high, the vent may be plugged, the pan bolts may be too tight, the pan sealing flange may be warped, the sealing surface of the transaxle housing may be damaged, the gasket may be damaged or the transaxle casting may be cracked or porous. If sealant instead of gasket material has been used to form a seal between the pan and the transaxle housing, it may be the wrong sealant.

Seal leaks

15 If a transaxle seal is leaking, the fluid level or pressure may be too high, the vent may be plugged, the seal bore may be damaged, the seal itself may be damaged or improperly installed, the surface of the shaft protruding through the seal may be damaged or a loose bearing may be causing excessive shaft movement.
16 Make sure the dipstick tube seal is in good condition and the tube is properly seated. Periodically check the area around the speedometer gear or sensor for leakage. If transmission fluid is evident, check the O-ring for damage.

Case leaks

17 If the case itself appears to be leaking, the casting is porous and will have to be repaired or replaced.
18 Make sure the oil cooler hose fittings are tight and in good condition.

Fluid comes out vent pipe or fill tube

19 If this condition occurs, the transaxle is overfilled, there is coolant in the fluid, the case is porous, the dipstick is incorrect, the vent is plugged or the drain-back holes are plugged.

3 Shift knob - removal and installation

Warning: *The models covered by this manual are equipped with Supplemental Restraint Systems (SRS), more commonly known as airbags. Always disable the airbag system before working in the vicinity of any airbag system components to avoid the possibility of accidental deployment of the airbags, which could cause personal injury (see Chapter 12A Section 20).*

1 Move the shifter to the Neutral position. If necessary, push the shift interlock release with a screwdriver to allow shifting on some models you have to remove a small cover **(see illustrations)**.
2 Slide down the lower shift knob cover, on later models lift up selector indicator panel and remove cable tie.

3.1a Removal of small cover on some models

Chapter 7 Part B Automatic transaxle

3.1b Push down on the manual shift release on earlier models

3.1c Push down on the manual shift release using a small screwdriver on later models

3.2a Using a screwdriver to pry the shift knob cover - T31 X-Trail model and Dualis models

3.2b Lifting indicator panel on T32 X-Trail and Qashqai models

3.3 After sliding the cover down, pry out the spring clip

4.2 Disconnect the shifter electrical connector

3 Using a small screwdriver or similar tool, remove the spring clip at the front of the shift knob.
4 Remove the shift knob from the shifter.
5 Installation is reverse of removal.

4 Shifter assembly - removal and installation

Warning: *The models covered by this manual are equipped with Supplemental Restraint Systems (SRS), more commonly known as airbags. Always disable the airbag system before working in the vicinity of any airbag system components to avoid the possibility of accidental deployment of the airbags, which could cause personal injury (see Chapter 12A Section 20).*

1 Remove the centre console (see Chapter 11 Section 22).
2 Disconnect the shifter assembly wiring harness **(see illustration)**.
3 Disconnect the shift lock solenoid electrical connector **(see illustration)** then remove the solenoid by inserting a feeler gauge under the solenoid to release the locking tab and remove the solenoid.

4 Remove the shift interlock cable from the shifter assembly (see Section 9).
5 Remove the shift cable from the shifter assembly (see Section 5).
6 Remove the shifter assembly mounting bolts **(see illustration)** and remove the assembly.
7 Installation is the reverse of removal. Adjust the shift cable and the shift interlock cable (see Section 9).

4.3 Disconnect the shift lock solenoid electrical connector (A), then insert a feeler gauge under the solenoid (B) to release the locking tab

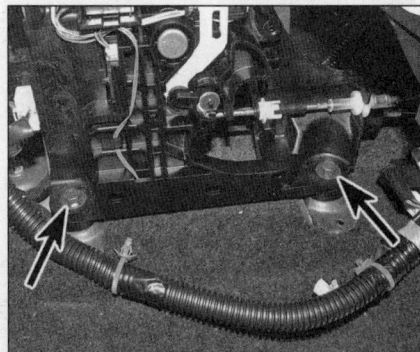

4.6 Remove the shifter assembly mounting bolts - Two of four bolts shown

Chapter 7 Part B Automatic transaxle

5.2a Pry the shifter cable from the pivot

5.2b Slide the cable up to disconnect it from the bracket

5.3 Remove the battery tray bracket fasteners

5.5 Shift cable details at the transaxle

1 Cable-to-manual lever locknut
2 Cable-to-bracket retaining clip

5 Shift cable - replacement and adjustment

Replacement

Warning: *The models covered by this manual are equipped with Supplemental Restraint Systems (SRS), more commonly known as airbags. Always disable the airbag system before working in the vicinity of any airbag system components to avoid the possibility of accidental deployment of the airbags, which could cause personal injury (see Chapter 12A Section 20).*

1 Place the shifter in Park.
2 Detach the shift cable from the shifter assembly **(see illustrations)**.
3 Remove the battery and battery tray (see Chapter 5 Section 5). Once the tray is removed, remove the bracket mounting bolts and bracket **(see illustration)**.
4 Remove the air filter housing (see Chapter 4A Section 9 or Chapter 4B Section 6).
5 Detach the cable from the shift lever and bracket on the transaxle **(see illustration)**.
6 Raise the vehicle and support it securely on jackstands.
7 Unbolt the cable support bracket from the floorpan.
8 Dislodge the grommet from the floorpan and remove the cable.
9 Installation is the reverse of removal, making sure the grommet seats properly in the floorpan. Adjust the cable (see Steps 10 through 15).

Adjustment

10 Remove the battery and battery tray (see Chapter 5 Section 5) and the air filter housing (see Chapter 4A Section 9 or Chapter 4B Section 6).
11 Place the shift lever in the "P" position.
12 Loosen the shift cable-to-manual lever locknut (see illustration 5.5) and place the transaxle manual shift lever fully in the Park position.
13 Holding the manual lever in position, tighten the locknut.
14 Move the shift lever from "P" to "1." Make sure that it moves smoothly and that the shift indicator on the cluster matches the actual positions of the shift lever.
15 Verify the engine can be started only in Park and Neutral.

6 Transmission range switch - replacement and adjustment

1 The transmission range switch replacement and adjustment procedure is covered in the Emissions and Engine Control Chapter (see Chapter 6 Section 13).

7 Transmission speed sensors - replacement

1 The transmission speed sensor replacement procedures are covered in the Emissions and Engine Control Chapter (see Chapter 6 Section 14).

8 Transmission Control Module (TCM) - removal and installation

Note: *The Transaxle Control Module (TCM) cannot be replaced at home because the new unit must be programmed with the Vehicle Identification Number (VIN) and other data. Doing so is impossible without a factory scan tool. This Section only shows TCM removal to gain access to other components.*

1 Disconnect the cable from the negative terminal of the battery Chapter 5 Section 3

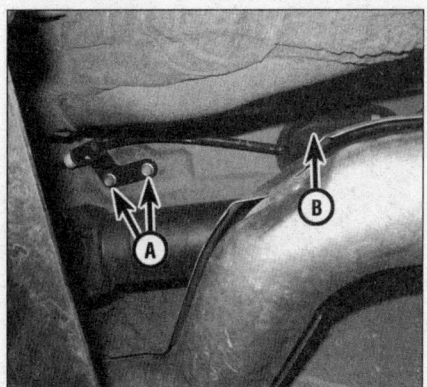

5.7 Shift cable support bracket bolts (A) and cable grommet (B)

8.3 Rotate the connector lock away from the TCM to disconnect the connector

Chapter 7 Part B Automatic transaxle

9.5 Shift interlock cable details

1 Casing cap
2 Slider
3 Slider tangs
4 Adjuster holder (lock)
5 Interlock rod

9.9 Remove the clip from the holder and remove the cable

1 Clip
2 Holder
3 Interlock cable

2 The TCM is mounted to a bracket on the battery tray.
3 Push in on the tang in the centre of the TCM connector lock, rotate the lock lever back, then unplug the connector **(see illustration)**.
4 Remove the TCM mounting nut and bolt and remove the TCM from the bracket.
5 Installation is the reverse of removal.

9 Shift interlock cable - replacement and adjustment

Replacement

1 Move the shift lever to the Neutral position.
2 Remove the shift knob (see Section 3).
3 Remove the centre console (see Chapter 11 Section 22).
4 Move the shift lever to the Park position.
5 Disconnect the shift interlock cable from the interlock rod by pressing in on the slider tangs **(see illustration)**, and sliding slider away from the adjuster holder.
6 Pry the shift interlock cable from the shifter assembly bracket.
7 Remove the lower steering column surround panel (see Chapter 10 Section 13).
8 Remove the steering column covers (see Chapter 10 Section 13).
9 On models with a key lock cylinder, remove the clip from the holder then remove the cable by pulling it from the lock cylinder **(see illustration)**.
10 Remove the cable from the vehicle.
11 Installation is the reverse of removal, noting the following:
 a Ensure the shift lever is in the Park position
 b Turn the ignition switch to ACC or ON when installing the lock plate and cable into the ignition switch. After installing, turn the ignition switch to LOCK.

Adjustment

12 Adjustment is not possible on the shift interlock cable. If the key cannot be removed when in Park, check the shift cable adjustment (see Section 5).

10 Oil seal - replacement

Drive shaft oil seals

1 The driveshaft oil seal replacement procedure is the same as for manual transaxle models. Refer to the procedure in the Manual Transaxle Chapter (see Chapter 7A Section 3).

11 Automatic transaxle - removal and installation

Warning: *Wait until the engine is completely cool before beginning this procedure.*

Removal

1 Drain the transaxle fluid (see Chapter 1 Section 30).

X-Trail T31 and Dualis

2 Remove the battery, battery tray (see Chapter 5 Section 5) and the battery tray bracket **(see illustration 5.3)**.
3 Remove the air inlet ducts and air filter housing (see Chapter 4A Section 9 or Chapter 4B Section 6).
4 Loosen the front wheel nuts and the driveshaft/hub nuts. Raise the vehicle and support it securely on jackstands (see Chapter 0 Section 7).
5 Remove the engine splash shield before draining the engine coolant (see Chapter 1 Section 27).
6 Remove the transaxle dipstick tube fastener and tube. Be sure to replace the O-ring on the tube.
7 On models equipped with a transaxle cooler, disconnect the lines and plug the lines and openings.
8 Disconnect the electrical connectors from the transaxle then release the harness retaining clips and place the harness out of the way.
9 Disconnect the coolant hoses from the transaxle.
10 Remove the front Section of the exhaust system (see Chapter 4A Section 11 - petrol models or Chapter 4B Section 11 - diesel models).
11 Remove the driveshafts (see Chapter 8 Section 7) and on AWD models remove the propeller shaft (see Chapter 8 Section 13)
12 Remove the shift cable (see Section 5).
13 Remove the starter motor (see Chapter 5 Section 12).
14 Remove the inspection cover fasteners and cover **(see illustration)**, then paint match marks on the torque converter and driveplate so they can be assembled in the same position, then remove the torque converter nuts through the starter opening **(see illustration)**.
15 Support the engine securely from above with a fixture that mounts between the mudguards. These can be rented at most equipment rental yards.
16 Remove the transaxle upper mounting bolts.
17 Make sure that the engine is solidly supported by the fixture. Remove the subframe (see Chapter 10 Section 18).
18 Put a transmission jack (or a floor jack with an appropriate saddle) under the transaxle. Safety chains will help steady the transaxle on the jack.

11.14a Remove the inspection cover fasteners

11.14b Mark the position of a torque converter stud to the driveplate, then remove the torque converter nuts by turning the crankshaft to bring each nut into the opening

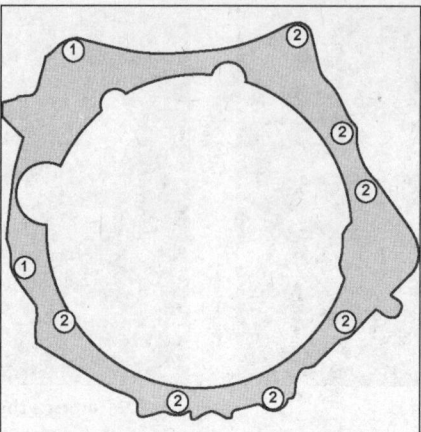

11.35a Transaxle mounting bolt length chart for transaxles fitted to the 2.0 litre petrol engine

1 55 mm   2 50 mm

19 Remove the remaining transaxle-to-engine bolts. Check to make certain that all connections between the transaxle and the vehicle are disconnected.
20 Move the transaxle to the rear to disengage it from the engine block dowel pins; make sure the torque converter is detached from the driveplate. Lower the transaxle with the jack. Clamp a pair of locking pliers on the bellhousing case. The pliers will prevent the torque converter from falling out while you're removing the transaxle.
21 Pull the transaxle out from beneath the vehicle, remove it from the jack and set it where it can't roll over and become damaged.

X-Trail T32 and Qashqai

22 Remove the engine and transaxle assembly from the vehicle (see Chapter 2D Section 7).
23 Disconnect the component connectors and any harness brackets and remove the wiring harness from the transaxle.
24 Remove the starter (if not already done).
25 Remove the inspection cover fasteners and cover **(see illustration 10.14a)**. Paint match marks on the torque converter and driveplate so they can be assembled in the same position, then remove the torque converter nuts through the starter opening **(see illustration 10.14b)**.
26 Support the transaxle with a floor jack (preferably equipped with a transmission adapter). Remove the engine-to-transaxle bolts. Keep them organized so they can be installed in the same positions.
27 Separate the transaxle from the engine and slide it away.

28 If necessary, remove any external transaxle components.
29 Seal any openings to prevent contamination while removed.

Installation

Caution: *Use new O-rings and copper washers during installation; DO NOT reuse any of these.*

30 Flush the transaxle cooler and the cooler hoses and lines with solvent whenever the transaxle is removed from the vehicle. Flush the lines and fluid cooler thoroughly and make sure no solvent remains in the lines or cooler after flushing. It's a good idea to repeat the flushing procedure with clean automatic transmission fluid to ensure that no solvent remains in the lines or cooler.
31 Prior to installation, make sure that the torque converter hub is securely engaged in the pump. The front face of the torque converter must be 1/2-inch or more behind the front edge of the transaxle housing to be fully seated. Use a straight-edge and ruler to measure this distance so as to not damage the transaxle after installation.
32 Manoeuvre the transaxle to the rear of the engine.
33 Turn the torque converter to line it up with the driveplate. The marks you made on the torque converter and the driveplate must line up.
34 Move the transaxle forward carefully until the dowel pins and the torque converter are engaged.
35 Install the transaxle mounting bolts. Make sure the bolts are installed in the proper locations **(see illustrations)**.
Caution: Don't use the bolts to force the transaxle and engine together. If the transaxle doesn't slide easily up against the engine, find out why before you tighten the bolts.
36 Tighten the bolts to the torque values listed in (see Specifications 7B).
37 Install the torque converter nuts and tighten them to the torque listed in (see Specifications 7B).
38 The remainder of installation is the reverse of removal.
39 Refill the cooling system (see Chapter 1 Section 27).
40 Refill the transaxle with fluid to the specified level (see Chapter 1 Section 8). Note that the transaxle may require more fluid than in a normal fluid and filter change, since the torque converter may be empty (the converter is not drained during a fluid change).
41 Start the engine, set the parking brake and shift the transaxle through all gears three times. Make sure the shift cable is working properly (see Section 5).
42 Allow the engine to reach its proper operating temperature with the transaxle in Park or Neutral, then turn it off and check the fluid level.
43 Road test the vehicle and check for fluid leaks.

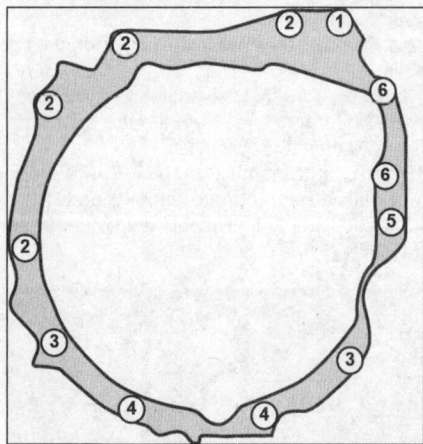

11.35b Transaxle mounting bolt length chart for transaxles fitted to the 2.5 litre petrol engine

1 45 mm (T31 and T32 X-Trail)
2 45 mm (T31 and T32 X-Trail)
3 45 mm (T31 and T32 X-Trail)
4 35 mm (T31 and T32 X-Trail)
5 45 mm (T31 and T32 X-Trail)
6 60 mm (T31 X-Trail),
   45 mm (T32 X-Trail)

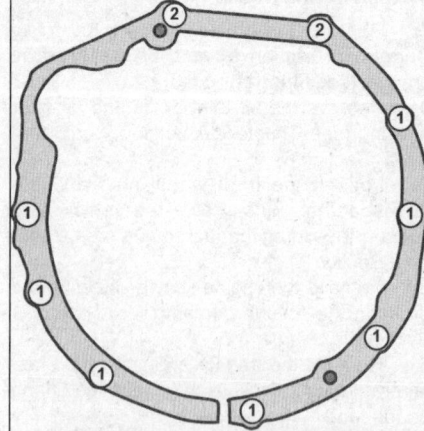

11.35c Transaxle mounting bolt length chart for transaxles fitted to the 2.0 litre diesel engine

1 55 mm
2 70 mm

Chapter 7 Part C
Transfer case

Contents

	Section		Section
Final drive electric controlled coupling – removal and refitting......		Transfer case – removal and installation..	3
Four wheel drive (4WD) control unit – removal and installation	6	Transfer case lubricant change .... See Chapter 1	
General Information..	1	Transfer case lubricant level check .... See Chapter 1	
Transfer case – draining and refilling	2	Transfer case oil seals – renewal	4
Transfer case – overhaul...	5		

Specifications

Models
- T31 X-Trail and Dualis TY30A
- T32 X-Trail and Qashqai TY21C

Gear ratio
- TY30A 0.656
- TY21C 0.404

Drive pinion (number of teeth)
- TY30A 32
- TY21C 17

Drive gear (number of teeth)
- TY30A 21
- TY21C 42

Flange runout limit
- TY30A .... 0.1 mm
- TY21C .... 0.15 mm

Backlash (ring gear to drive gear)
- TY30A .... 0.13 to 0.19 mm
- TY21C .... 0.16 to 0.21 mm

Drive pinion bearing preload
- TY30A .... 0.52 to 1.01 Nm
- TY21C .... 0.25 to 1.15 Nm

Total preload
- With all oil seals fitted
  - TY30A .... 0.76 to 0.96 Nm
  - TY21C .... 0.7 to 1.0 Nm
- Without adaptor case oil seal fitted
  - TY30A .... 0.55 to 0.75 Nm
  - TY21C .... 0.5 to 0.8 Nm

Torque specifications

	Nm
Four wheel drive actuator (part of rear differential)	16
Transfer case	
Bracket-to-transfer gearbox	48
Bracket-to-cylinder block	50
Filler and drain plug	Chapter 1
Mounting bracket to transaxle mounting bolts	44
Pinion retaining nut * (collapsible washer)	127 to 294

Note: *Use new fastener

1 General Information

The four-wheel drive (4WD) system controls the distribution of drive between the front and rear wheels, according to signals from various sensors. The 4WD control unit, which is located behind the glovebox or in the boot in later models, transmits and receives signals from the ABS, Engine Control Module and Steering angle sensors.

AUTO Mode

The electronic control module allows optimal distribution of torque to the front and rear wheels to match the road conditions. Four-wheel drive mode makes stable driving, with no wheel spin on slippery surfaces. On road surfaces that do not require 4WD, AUTO mode contributes to improve fuel economy by putting more drive power to the front wheels. The sensors detect tight cornering or heavy braking; this then puts more torque to the rear wheels.

LOCK Mode

In this mode the front and rear wheels are fixed, ensuring stable driving when climbing slopes. It will switch to AUTO mode if the vehicle speed increases. If the vehicle speed then decreases, the vehicle automatically returns to direct four-wheel drive. If there is a significant difference in tyre pressures, full vehicle speed will not be available. LOCK mode may also be prohibited, or speeds at which LOCK mode is enabled may be restricted.

2 Transfer case – draining and refilling

The transfer case lubricant change procedure is part of the Tune-up and Routine Maintenance chapter (see Chapter 1 Section 33).

3 Transfer case – removal and installation

Removal

1 Firmly apply the handbrake, and then jack up the front of the vehicle and support it securely on jackstands (see Chapter 0 Section 7).
2 Drain the transfer case oil (see Chapter 1 Section 33).
3 Remove the exhaust front pipe and exhaust manifold (see Chapter 4A Section 9 or Chapter 4B Section 6).
4 Make alignment marks on the propeller shaft and the flange, to make sure that it is fitted in the same position on refitting. Undo the four retaining bolts and disconnect the front of the propeller shaft from the flange on the rear of the transfer case **(see illustration)**. Discard the retaining bolts, as new ones will be required for refitting.
5 Remove the right-hand side driveshaft (see Chapter 8 Section 7). Then undo the retaining bolts and remove the driveshaft support mounting bracket form the rear of the cylinder block **(see illustration)**.

3.4 Undo the propeller shaft front flange bolts

6 On automatic transmission models, undo the retaining bolt and disconnect the hose mounting bracket from the transfer case mounting bracket **(see illustration)**.
7 On 2.0 litre diesel engines, undo the retaining bolts and remove the mounting bracket from the right-hand side of the transfer case **(see illustration)**.
8 To make access to the transfer case easier, undo the retaining bolts and remove the lower rear torque arm (mounting link arm), from the subframe **(see illustration)**. Insert a block of wood between the engine and the subframe, to make more room for removal of the transfer gearbox. Take care not to put any stress on any other components when doing this.

3.5 Driveshaft support mounting bracket

3.6 Undo the retaining bolts (arrowed)

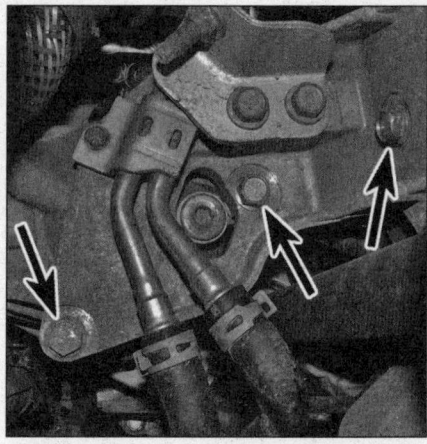

3.7 Undo the mounting bracket retaining bolts (arrowed)

Chapter 7 Part C Transfer case

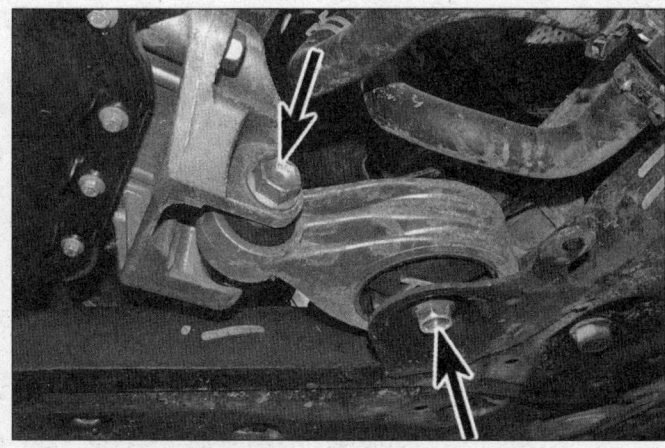

3.8 Remove the engine lower torque arm

6.2 Four-wheel drive ECU location (arrowed)

9 Undo the transfer case securing bolts and withdraw it from the right-hand side of the transmission. Note, there are five bolts securing the transfer case to the transmission; four are bolted from the transfer case side into the transmission casing and one is bolted from the transmission side into the transfer case.

10 Remove the O-ring seal from between the transfer case and the transmission and discard it, as a new one will be required for refitting.

Installation

11 Installation is a reversal of the removal procedure, noting the following points.
   a Make sure a new outer O-ring seal is fitted to the transfer case before installing.
   b Apply a small amount of multi-purpose grease, evenly to the seal before refitting to the transfer case.
   c Fit new retaining bolts to the propeller shaft and tighten to the specified torque setting.
   d Align the marks made on removal, when refitting the propeller shaft.
   e When completed, refill the transfer case oil (see Chapter 1 Section 33).

4 Transfer case oil seals – renewal

Note: *Although the seals in the adapter plate can be removed and refitted as described in this Section, Nissan recommend that the backlash, tooth contact, preload and flange runout should be checked if dismantled. Take the transfer case to a local specialist to have this checked before refitting.*

Note: *The only seal that can be renewed without any dismantling is the outer O-ring seal.*

1 Remove the transfer case (see Section 3).

Adapter case O-ring seals

2 Remove the outer O-ring seal from the transfer case and discard it, as a new one will be required for refitting.

3 Undo the five adapter plate securing bolts and withdraw it from the transfer case. This may be a tight fit on the dowels, lightly tap the adapter plate with a plastic hammer to remove.

4 With the adapter plate removed, remove the inner O-ring seal from the inside the transfer case and discard it, as a new one will be required for refitting.

5 Refitting is a reversal of the removal procedure, noting the following points. Make sure a new O-ring seals are fitted correctly to the transfer case. Apply a small amount of multi-purpose grease, evenly to the seals before refitting to the transfer case. When completed, refit the transfer case (see Section 3).

Adapter case oil seals

6 There are also, inner and outer seals fitted to the centre of the adapter plate.

7 If not already done undo the five retaining bolts and remove the adapter plate from the transfer case.

8 Note the fitted position of the seals, and then carefully lever them out from their position in the adapter plate. Use a large flat-bladed screwdriver, taking care not to damage the adapter plate.

9 Clean the seal housing in the adapter plate, and polish off any burrs or raised edges, which may have caused the seals to fail in the first place.

10 Apply a small amount of multi-purpose grease, evenly to the lips of the seals, and gear oil onto the outer circumference, before fitting them back to the adapter plate. Carefully ease the seals into position, taking care not to damage its sealing lip. Using a drift drive the seals into the adapter plate, in the position noted on removal. Take care not to damage the seal lips during fitting.

11 Refit the adapter plate and new O-ring seals, as described in paragraphs 2 to 5.

12 Refit the transfer case (see Section 3).

5 Transfer case – overhaul

1 Overhauling a transfer case is a difficult and involved job for the DIY home mechanic. In addition to dismantling and reassembling many small parts, clearances must be precisely measured and, if necessary, changed by selecting shims and spacers. Internal components are also often difficult to obtain, and in many instances, extremely expensive. Because of this, if the transfer case develops a fault or becomes noisy, the best course of action is to have the unit overhauled by a specialist repairer, or to obtain an exchange reconditioned unit.

2 Nevertheless, it is not impossible for the more experienced mechanic to overhaul the transfer case, if the special tools are available, and the job is done in a deliberate step-by-step manner so that nothing is overlooked.

3 The tools necessary for an overhaul include internal and external circlip pliers, bearing pullers, a slide hammer, a set of pin punches, a dial test indicator, and possibly a hydraulic press. In addition, a large, sturdy workbench and a vice will be required.

4 During dismantling of the transfer case, make careful notes of how each component is fitted, to make reassembly easier and accurate.

5 Before dismantling the transfer case, it will help if you have some idea which area is malfunctioning. Certain problems can be closely related to specific areas in the transmission, which can make component examination and renewal easier.

6 Four wheel drive (4WD) control unit – removal and installation

Removal

X-Trail T31 and Dualis

1 Remove the glovebox (see Chapter 11 Section 21).

2 The control unit is located on a bracket, screwed to the facia rear crossmember **(see illustration)**.

3 Disconnect the wiring connector from the control unit, undo the two retaining screws,

6.3 Disconnect the wiring connector and undo the two retaining screws

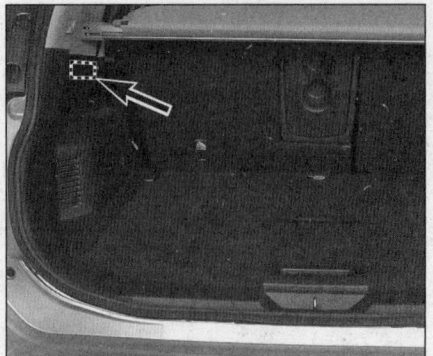

6.4 Remove the illustrated trim panel to reveal the control unit

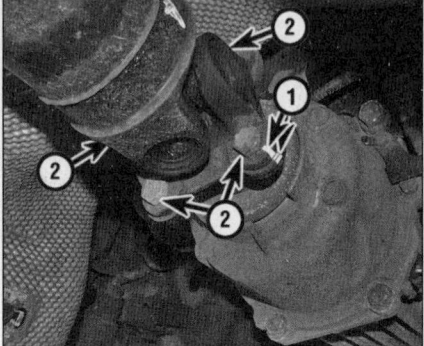

7.2 Place alignment marks between the propeller shaft and the flange (1) prior to removing the rear propeller shaft flange bolts (2)

and then remove the control unit from the mounting bracket **(see illustration)**.

X-Trail T32 and Qashqai

4 Remove lower left hand side boot trim **(see illustration)**.
5 The control unit is located on a bracket bolted to inside of the vehicle.
6 Disconnect the wiring connector from the control unit, undo the two retaining bolts, then remove the control unit.

Installation

7 Refitting is a reversal of the removal procedure, making sure the wiring connector is secure, and then refit the lower left hand side trim panel.

7 Final drive electric controlled coupling – removal and refitting

Removal

1 Raise the rear of the vehicle and support on jackstands (see Jacking and Towing 0 7).
2 Undo the four retaining bolts and disconnect the rear of the propeller shaft from the flange on the final drive flange **(see illustration)**. Make alignment marks on the propeller shaft and the flange to make sure that it is fitted in the same position on refitting.
3 Use a length of bar, bolted to two of the holes in the flange, hold the flange on the front of the final drive unit in place, and then undo the flange lock nut. Make alignment marks on the flange and the shaft to make sure that it is fitted in the same position on refitting. Discard the locknut, as a new one will be required on refitting.
4 Disconnect the wiring connector to the coupling, then undo the retaining bolt and move the wiring loom bracket to one side **(see illustration)**.
5 Disconnect the breather pipe from the right-hand side of the coupling and move it to one side **(see illustration)**.
6 Undo the six bolts from around the electric controlled coupling housing, then withdraw the housing, complete with electric coupling from the front of the final drive unit **(see illustration)**.

Installation

7 Renew the oil seal in the front of the electric controlled coupling housing (see Chapter 8 Section 10).
8 On refitting, fit the electric controlled coupling to the front of the final drive casing. Align the locating pin on the right-hand side of the coupling with the slot in the final drive casing. Also align the splines on the rear of the coupling with the final drive shaft, taking care not to damage the seal on the inside of the final drive unit.
9 Clean the contact face of the final drive casing and the coupling housing, then apply a bead of sealant around the coupling housing mating surface with a 3 mm bead of sealant.
10 Fit the coupling housing, making sure it is the correct way up (arrow facing up, at the bottom right-hand corner). As the housing is fitted over the electric coupling, make sure the wiring loom is located correctly in the housing to prevent it getting trapped.
11 Fit the housing bolts, starting with the ones at each side of the housing and carefully pull the housing into position over the electric controlled coupling. Tighten all the bolts evenly to their specified torque setting.
12 The remainder of the refitting procedure is the reversal of the removal procedure, noting the following points:

   a Align the marks made on removal, when refitting the flange to the shaft.
   b Fit a new locknut to the flange and tighten to the specified torque setting.
   c Align the marks made on removal, when refitting the propeller shaft.
   d When completed, refill the final drive unit, as described in Section 6.

7.4 Coupling wiring connector location

7.5 The breather hose is on the RH side of the coupling

7.6 Undo the six bolts from around the coupling housing

Chapter 8
Clutch and driveline

Contents

	Section		Section
Clutch assembly – removal, inspection and installation	5	Driveshaft boots - replacement	14
Clutch fluid type and level	See Chapter 1	Driveshaft - removal and installation	7
Clutch hydraulic system – bleeding	2	General Information	1
Clutch pedal – removal and installation	3	Master cylinder – removal and installation	4
Clutch release mechanism – removal, inspection and installation	6	Propeller shaft (AWD models) - removal and installation	13
Differential – overhaul	11	Rear differential – draining and refilling (AWD models)	8
Differential electric controlled coupling – removal and installation	12	Rear differential – removal and installation (AWD models)	9
Differential oil seals – renewal	10		

Specifications

Clutch

Type	Single dry plate
Operation	Hydraulic, self adjusting
Pressure plate spring	Diaphragm type
Driven plate	
Maximum run-out	1.0 mm
Wear limit	0.3 mm
Pressure plate	
Tolerance for diaphragm spring lever unevenness	
Petrol engines	0.7 mm or less
Diesel engines	0.8 mm or less
Maximum flywheel runout	0.45 mm or less
Clutch pedal	
Clearance between clutch pedal and ASCD clutch switch threaded end while clutch pedal is fully released	0.10 to 1.96 mm

Chapter 8 Clutch and driveline

Driveshafts

Front driveshafts

Front driveshafts boot and damper installation measurements (see illustration 14.22a)
- X-Trail T31
  - Two-wheel drive - 2.0 litre
    - Dimension A .... 269 to 273 mm
    - Dimension B .... 70 mm
    - Dimension C .... 133.5 mm
    - Dimension D .... 165.6 mm
  - Two-wheel drive - diesel engine
    - Dimension A .... 229 to 236 mm
    - Dimension B .... 70 mm
    - Dimension C .... 164 mm
    - Dimension D .... 173 mm
  - Four-wheel drive - 2.0 litre M/T
    - Dimension A .... 219 to 223 mm
    - Dimension B .... 70 mm
    - Dimension C .... 133.5 mm
    - Dimension D .... 165.6 mm
  - Four-wheel drive - 2.0 litre CVT
    - Dimension A .... 238 to 242 mm
    - Dimension B .... 70 mm
    - Dimension C .... 133.5 mm
    - Dimension D .... 165.6 mm
  - Four-wheel drive - 2.5 litre M/T
    - Dimension A .... 192.5 to 198.5 mm
    - Dimension B .... 70 mm
    - Dimension C .... 133.5 mm
    - Dimension D .... 161.1 mm
  - Four-wheel drive - 2.5 litre CVT
    - Dimension A .... 207 to 213 mm
    - Dimension B .... 70 mm
    - Dimension C .... 133.5 mm
    - Dimension D .... 165.6 mm
  - Four-wheel drive - Diesel M/T
    - Dimension A .... 194 to 200 mm
    - Dimension B .... 70 mm
    - Dimension C .... 164 mm
    - Dimension D .... 173 mm
  - Four-wheel drive - Diesel A/T
    - Dimension A .... 236.8 to 241.3 mm
    - Dimension B .... 70 mm
    - Dimension C .... 164 mm
    - Dimension D .... 173 mm
- X-Trail T32
  - Two-wheel drive - 2.0 litre M/T
    - Dimension A .... 273 to 279 mm
    - Dimension B .... 70 mm
    - Dimension C .... 141.5 mm
    - Dimension D .... 202.1 mm (LH); 188.9 mm (RH)
  - Two-wheel drive - 2.0 litre CVT
    - Dimension A .... 273 to 279 mm
    - Dimension B .... 70 mm
    - Dimension C .... 141.5 mm
    - Dimension D .... 196.9 mm (LH); 188.9 mm (RH)
  - Four-wheel drive - 2.0 litre
    - Dimension A .... 273 to 279 mm (LH); 243 to 249 mm (RH)
    - Dimension B .... 70 mm
    - Dimension C .... 141.5 mm
    - Dimension D .... 196.9 mm (LH); 188.9 mm (RH)
  - Four-wheel drive - 2.5 litre
    - Dimension A .... 240 to 246 mm
    - Dimension B .... 70 mm (LH); 50 mm (RH)
    - Dimension C .... 141.5 mm
    - Dimension D .... 196.9 mm (LH); 188.9 mm (RH)

Chapter 8 Clutch and driveline

Dualis
  Two-wheel drive - 2.0 litre M/T
    Dimension A .... 269 to 273 mm
    Dimension B .... 70 mm
    Dimension C .... 133.5 mm
    Dimension D .... 190.8 mm (LH); 177.6 (RH)
  Two-wheel drive - 2.0 litre CVT
    Dimension A .... 282 to 286 mm
    Dimension B .... 70 mm
    Dimension C .... 133.5 mm
    Dimension D .... 185.6 mm (LH); 177.6 mm (RH)
  Four-wheel drive - 2.0 litre M/T
    Dimension A .... 219 to 233 mm
    Dimension B .... 70 mm
    Dimension C .... 133.5 mm
    Dimension D .... 165.6 mm (LH); 177.6 mm (RH)
  Four-wheel drive - 2.0 litre CVT
    Dimension A .... 238 to 242 mm
    Dimension B .... 70 mm
    Dimension C .... 133.5 mm
    Dimension D .... 185.6 mm (LH): 177.6 mm (RH)
Qashqai
  Two-wheel drive - 2.0 litre M/T
    Dimension A .... 269 to 273 mm
    Dimension B .... 70 mm
    Dimension C .... 133.5 mm
    Dimension D .... 190.8 mm (LH); 177.6 mm (RH)
  Two-wheel drive - 2.0 litre CVT
    Dimension A .... 282 to 286 mm
    Dimension B .... 70 mm
    Dimension C .... 133.5 mm
    Dimension D .... 185.6 mm (LH); 177.6 mm (RH)
  Four-wheel drive - 2.0 litre M/T
    Dimension A .... 219 to 223 mm
    Dimension B .... 70 mm
    Dimension C .... 133.5 mm
    Dimension D .... 189.6 mm (LH); 177.6 mm (RH)
  Four-wheel drive - 2.0 litre CVT
    Dimension A .... 238 to 242 mm
    Dimension B .... 70 mm
    Dimension C .... 133.5 mm
    Dimension D .... 185.6 mm (LH); 177.6 mm (RH)

Rear driveshaft

Rear driveshaft boot installation measurements (see illustration 14.22b)

	Inner joint (Dimension A)	Outer joint (Dimension B)
X-Trail T31 and Dualis	125.8 to 127.8 mm	90.2 to 92.2 mm
X-Trail T32 and Qashqai	151.5 to 153.5 mm	90.2 to 92.2 mm

Differential

Model R145
Gear ratio 2.466
Drive pinion (number of teeth) 15
Drive gear (number of teeth) 37
Flange runout limit .... 0.13 mm
Drive gear (back face runout) .... 0.05 mm
Backlash (drive gear to drive pinion gear) .... 0.10 to 0.15 mm
Pre-load
  Pinion bearing .... 0.69 to 1.18 Nm
  Side bearing
    X-Trail T31, Dualis and Qashqai .... 0.64 to 0.98 Nm
    X-Trail T32 .... 0.66 to 1.00 Nm
  Side bearing to pinion bearing (total pre-load)
    X-Trail T31, Dualis and Qashqai .... 1.33 to 2.16 Nm
    X-Trail T32 .... 1.35 to 2.18 Nm
Drive pinion adjustment spacer type .... Collapsible

Torque specifications — Nm

Clutch
Clutch pedal bracket nuts	14
Concentric slave cylinder (CSC) retaining bolts	21
Transmission to engine	see Chapter 7A
Pressure plate to flywheel	
Petrol engines	
Stage 1	15
Stage 2	25
Diesel engine	25

Driveshafts
Driveshaft/hub nut	
Front	
X-Trail T31 and Dualis	125
X-Trail T32 and Qashqai	225
Rear	125
Driveshaft support bearing retainer plate bolts	26
Driveshaft support bearing bracket-to-engine block bolts	
X-Trail T31, Dualis and Qashqai	48
X-Trail T32	
2.0 litre	48
2.5 litre	
M10 bolts	48
M12 bolt	97

Propeller shaft
Centre bearing nuts*	45
Propeller shaft flange fasteners*	
X-Trail T31 and Dualis	50
X-Trail T32 Qasqhai	
Propeller shaft to transfer case	50
Propeller shaft to rear differential	65

Differential
Electric controlled coupling mounting bolts	16
Filler/level plug	see Chapter 1
Mounting bolts	
Front bolts	63
Rear nut	78
Front flange locknut *	
X-Trail T31 and Dualis	
2.0 litre	111
2.5 litre	
Manual transaxle	111
Continuously variable transaxle (CVT)	140
2.0 litre diesel and Qashqai	140

*Use new fastener

1 General Information

Clutch

The clutch consists of a friction disc, a pressure plate assembly, a release bearing and the release mechanism. All of these components are contained in the large cast-aluminium alloy bellhousing, and sandwiched between the engine and the transmission. The release mechanism is hydraulic, operated by a master cylinder and a slave cylinder, which is part of the release bearing. The hydraulic master cylinder is located in the pedal bracket on the firewall, and the clutch fluid reservoir is shared with the brake fluid reservoir on the top of the brake master cylinder. Inside the reservoir each circuit has its own compartment, so that in the event of fluid loss in the clutch circuit, the brake circuit remains fully operational.

The friction disc/plate is fitted between the engine flywheel and the clutch pressure plate, and is allowed to slide on the transmission input shaft splines. It consists of two circular facings of friction material to provide the clutch bearing surface, and a spring-cushioned hub to damp out transmission shocks.

The pressure plate assembly is bolted to the engine flywheel, and is located by dowel pins. When the engine is running, drive is transmitted from the crankshaft via the flywheel to the friction disc (these components being clamped securely together by the pressure plate assembly), and from the friction disc to the transmission input shaft.

To interrupt the drive, the spring pressure must be relaxed. This is achieved by a sealed release bearing fitted concentrically around the transmission input shaft; when the driver depresses the clutch pedal, the release bearing is pressed against the fingers at the centre of the diaphragm spring. The pressure at its centre causes the springs to deform, so

Chapter 8 Clutch and driveline

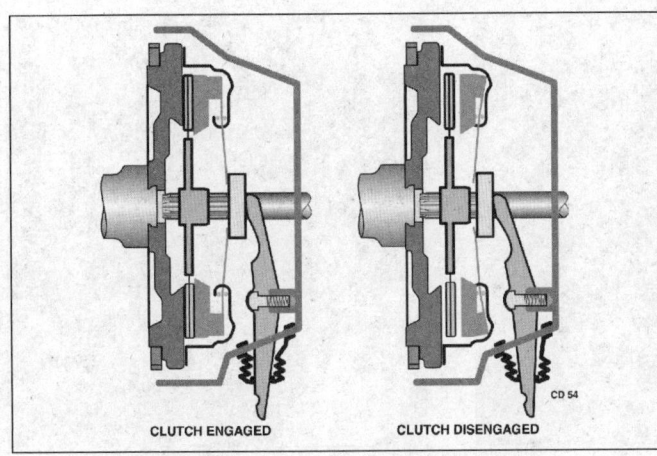

1.2 Illustration showing how a clutch operates

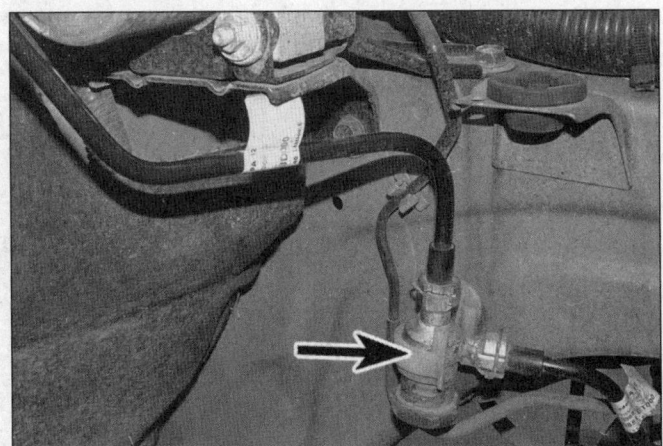

1.6 Pulsation damper location (arrowed)

that it flattens and thus releases the clamping force it exerts at its periphery on the pressure plate.

When the pedal is released, the diaphragm spring forces the pressure plate into contact with the friction linings on the friction plate. The disc is now firmly sandwiched between the pressure plate and the flywheel, thus transmitting engine power to the transmission.

Wear of the friction material on the friction plate is automatically compensated for by the operation of the hydraulic system. As the friction material on the friction plate wears, the pressure plate moves towards the flywheel causing the clutch diaphragm spring inner fingers to move outwards. When the clutch pedal is released, excess fluid is expelled through the master cylinder into the fluid reservoir. There is a pulsation damper fitted in the hydraulic hose from the master cylinder to the (concentric) slave cylinder. It is located in the left-hand rear corner of the engine compartment below the air cleaner assembly **(see illustration)**.

Warning: *Hydraulic fluid is poisonous, thoroughly wash off spills from bare skin without delay. Seek immediate medical advice if any fluid is swallowed or gets into the eyes. Certain types of hydraulic fluid are inflammable and may ignite when brought into contact with hot components. Hydraulic fluid is also an effective paint stripper. If spillage occurs onto painted bodywork or fittings, it should be washed off immediately, using copious quantities of cold water. It is also hygroscopic (i.e. it can absorb moisture from the air) which then renders it useless. Old fluid may have suffered contamination, and should never be re-used.*

Driveline

2WD models

Drive is transmitted from the differential to the front wheels by means of two solid steel driveshafts of unequal length.

Both driveshafts are splined at their outer ends, to accept the wheel hubs, and are threaded so that each hub can be fastened to the driveshaft by a large nut and locked in position with a split pin. The inner end of each driveshaft is splined, to accept the differential sun gear.

Constant velocity (CV) joints are fitted to each end of the driveshafts, to ensure the smooth and efficient transmission of power at all suspension and steering angles. The outer constant velocity joints are of the ball-and-cage type, and the inner joints are of the tripod type.

4WD models

The front wheels are driven the same as it is on 2-wheel drive models by means of two solid steel driveshafts of unequal length.

Drive is transmitted from the transfer gearbox to the rear final drive unit through a two-piece propeller shaft with three joints. The joints on each end are a flange type connecting to the transfer gearbox and final drive unit, and there is a CV joint at the centre.

The rear final drive unit then transmits the drive through two solid steel driveshafts of equal length to the both rear wheels. Both driveshafts are splined at their outer ends, to accept the wheel hubs, and are threaded so that each hub can be fastened to the drive-

2.5 Remove the dust cap from the bleed screw

shaft by a large nut and locked in position with a split pin. The inner end of each driveshaft is splined, to accept the gears in the final drive unit.

Constant velocity (CV) joints are fitted to each end of the driveshafts, to ensure the smooth and efficient transmission of power at all suspension and steering angles. The outer constant velocity joints are of the ball-and-cage type, and the inner joints are of the tripod type.

2 Clutch hydraulic system – bleeding

Note: *Refer to the warning at the beginning of Section 1, regarding the hazards of working with hydraulic fluid.*

1 If any part of the hydraulic system is dismantled, or if air has accidentally entered the system, the system will need to be bled. The presence of air is characterised by the pedal having a spongy feel and it results in difficulty in changing gear.

2 Obtain a clean container, a suitable length of rubber or clear plastic tubing that is a tight fit over the bleed screw on the clutch slave cylinder, and a container of the specified hydraulic fluid. The help of an assistant will also be required. If a one-man do-it-yourself bleeding kit for bleeding the brake hydraulic system is available, this can be used quite satisfactorily for the clutch also.

3 Remove the air cleaner inlet ducting from the front left-hand side of the engine compartment (see Chapter 4A Section 9 - petrol models or Chapter 4B Section 6 - diesel models) to access the clutch bleed screw.

4 Remove the filler cap from the brake master cylinder reservoir, and if necessary top-up the fluid. Keep the reservoir topped-up during subsequent operations.

5 Remove the dust cap from the bleed screw at the hydraulic connection, located on the lower front facing side of the transmission **(see illustration)**.

2.6 Air bleed bottle connected to bleed screw

2.7 Release the retaining clip (arrowed)

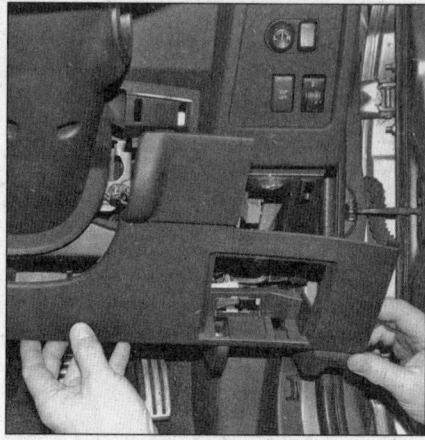

3.2 Unclip the trim panel from under the dashboard

6 Connect one end of the bleed tube to the bleed screw, and insert the other end of the tube in the container with sufficient clean hydraulic fluid to keep the end of the tube submerged **(see illustration)**.

7 With the tube on the bleed screw, press down on the hose retaining clip **(see illustration)**, and then carefully pull the clutch fluid hose outwards from the bell housing by 10 mm. Be careful not to pull the clutch fluid hose completely out from the connection.

8 Have your assistant depress the clutch pedal and then slowly release it. Continue this procedure until clean hydraulic fluid, free from air bubbles, emerges from the tube. At the end of a downstroke, push the clutch fluid hose back into position, making sure the retaining clip secures the hose in place.

9 Make sure that the brake master cylinder reservoir is checked frequently to ensure that the level does not drop too far, allowing air into the system.

10 Check the operation of the clutch pedal. After a few strokes it should feel normal. Any sponginess would indicate air still present in the system, if so; carry out the procedure once again.

11 On completion remove the bleed tube and refit the dust cover. Top-up the master cylinder reservoir if necessary and refit the cap. Fluid expelled from the hydraulic system should now be discarded, as it will be contaminated with moisture, air and dirt, making it unsuitable for further use.

3 Clutch pedal – removal and installation

Removal

1 Disconnect the negative (-) battery terminal (see Chapter 5 Section 3).

2 Working inside the vehicle in the driver's side footwell, unclip the dashboard lower trim panel **(see illustration)**.

3 On some models undo the plastic retaining nut and then unclip the kick panel from the driver's side front footwell. Release the retaining clip and remove the heater ducting from across the top of the drivers pedal assembly **(see illustrations)**.

4 Disconnect the wiring connector from the clutch pedal switch, and unclip the wiring loom securing clips from the pedal mounting bracket **(see illustrations)**.

5 Release the securing clips, and then using a flat bladed screwdriver, prise the master cylinder pushrod end from the pedal pin **(see illustration)**.

6 Hold the clutch pedal down and remove the return spring from the locating pegs on

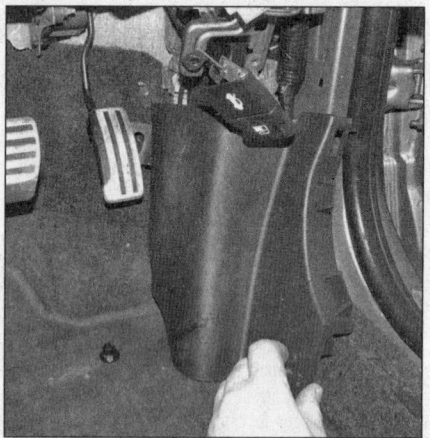

3.3a Unclip the kick panel ...

3.3b ... release the retaining clip ...

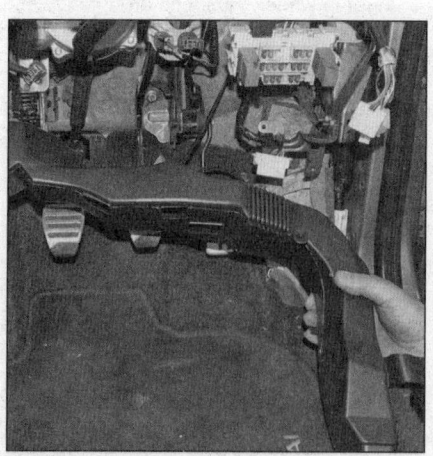

3.3c ... and withdraw the heater ducting

3.4a Disconnect the switch wiring connector ...

Chapter 8 Clutch and driveline   8-7

3.4b ... and unclip the wiring loom retaining clip (arrowed)

3.5 Release the end of the pushrod from the pedal

3.6 Unclip the return spring from the pedal and mounting bracket

the mounting bracket and pedal **(see illustration)**.

7 Slacken and remove the clutch pedal mounting bracket retaining nuts, then withdraw the pedal and mounting bracket out from under the dashboard **(see illustration)**.

8 Check the condition of the pedal, pivot bush and return spring assembly and renew any components as necessary.

Installation

9 Lubricate the pedal pivot bolt with multi-purpose grease, then manoeuvre and locate the pedal and mounting bracket on the firewall. Refit the retaining nuts and tighten securely.

10 Reconnect the return spring to the pedal and pedal bracket; making sure it locates correctly **(see illustration)**.

11 Reconnect the clutch master cylinder pushrod to the clutch pedal.

12 Depress the pedal two or three times and check the operation of the clutch release mechanism.

13 Reconnect the wiring connector to the clutch switch, and then secure the wiring loom back into position with the retaining clips on the pedal mounting bracket.

14 Refit the heater ducting back across the top of the pedal assembly and then refit the dashboard lower trim panels.

15 Reconnect the battery negative (see Chapter 5 Section 3).

4 Master cylinder – removal and installation

Note: *Refer to the warning at the beginning of Section 1 regarding the hazards of working with hydraulic fluid.*

Removal

1 Working inside the driver's footwell, release the securing clips, and then prise the master cylinder pushrod end from the pedal pin **(see illustration 3.5)**. Press on the securing clips to free the pushrod from the pedal.

2 To minimise hydraulic fluid loss, remove the brake master cylinder reservoir filler cap then tighten it down onto a piece of polythene to obtain an airtight seal.

3 Working inside the engine compartment, undo the fasteners and remove the sound proofing protector from down the back of the engine compartment **(see illustration)**.

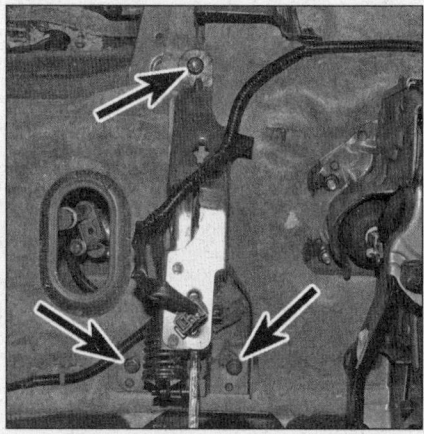

3.7 Clutch pedal mounting bracket nuts (arrowed)

4 Place absorbent rags under the clutch master cylinder pipe connections in the engine compartment and be prepared for some hydraulic fluid loss.

5 Clamp the upper hydraulic fluid supply hose leading from the brake fluid reservoir to the clutch master cylinder using a brake hose clamp **(see illustration)**.

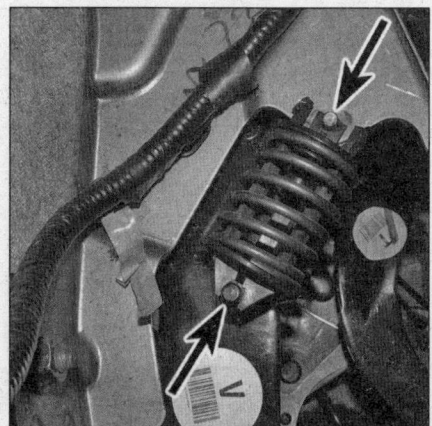

3.10 Make sure the return spring is located on the pegs correctly

4.3 Remove the firewall soundproofing

4.5 Clamp the fluid pipe from the reservoir

4.6 Disconnect the fluid pipes from the master cylinder

5.2 Mark the position of the pressure plate on the flywheel

5.3a Undo the pressure plate bolts (arrowed) ...

6 Release the master cylinder hydraulic pressure pipe from the retaining clip on the engine compartment firewall. Be prepared for some hydraulic fluid loss, then prise out the retaining wire clip and disconnect the pipe from the master cylinder (see illustration). Suitably plug or cap the pipe end to prevent further fluid loss and dirt entry.

7 Be prepared for some hydraulic fluid loss and disconnect the fluid supply hose from the top of the master cylinder. Suitably plug or cap the pipe end to prevent further fluid loss and dirt entry.

8 Rotate the master cylinder 45 degrees clockwise, and remove it from the firewall.

Installation

9 Refitting the master cylinder is the reverse sequence to removal, bearing in mind the following points.

  a Ensure that the pedal-to-master cylinder pushrod is correctly fitted.
  b Ensure all retaining clips are correctly refitted.
  c Remove the piece of polythene from the top of the reservoir.
  d On completion, bleed the clutch hydraulic system (see Section 2).

5 Clutch assembly – removal, inspection and installation

Warning: *Dust created by clutch wear and deposited on the clutch components may contain asbestos, which is a health hazard. DO NOT blow it out with compressed air, or inhale any of it. DO NOT use petrol or petroleum-based solvents to clean off the dust. Brake system cleaner or methylated spirit should be used to flush the dust into a suitable receptacle. After the clutch components are wiped clean with rags, dispose of the contaminated rags and cleaner in a sealed, marked container.*

Note: *Although some friction materials may no longer contain asbestos, it is safest to assume that they DO, and to take precautions accordingly.*

Removal

1 Unless the complete engine/transmission is to be removed from the car, and separated for major overhaul (see Chapter 2D Section 7), the clutch can be reached by removing the transmission (see Chapter 7A Section 5).

2 Before disturbing the clutch, use a dab of quick-drying paint or a marker pen to mark the relationship of the pressure plate assembly to the flywheel (see illustration).

3 Working in a diagonal sequence, slacken the pressure plate bolts by half a turn at a time, until the spring pressure is released and the bolts can be unscrewed by hand (see illustrations). If required lock the flywheel to prevent it from turning, by locking the ring gear teeth.

4 Prise the pressure plate assembly off its locating dowels, and collect the friction disc, noting which way round the friction disc is fitted (see illustration).

Inspection

Note: *Due to the amount of work necessary to remove and refit clutch components, it is usually considered good practice to renew the clutch friction disc, pressure plate assembly and release bearing as a matched set, even if only one of these is actually worn enough to require renewal. It is worth considering the renewal of the clutch components on a preventative basis if the engine and/or transmission have been removed for some other reason.*

5.3b ... using a homemade tool to prevent the flywheel from turning

5.4 Remove the pressure plate complete with friction disc

5.13 Markings on friction disc – P.P.SIDE (pressure plate side)

Chapter 8 Clutch and driveline

5.16a Using a special tool to centralise the friction disc ...

5.16b ... on the pressure plate

5.17a Align the pressure plate on the dowels on the flywheel

5 When cleaning clutch components, first read the warning at the beginning of this Section. Remove the dust only as described – working with dampened cloths will help to keep dust levels to a minimum. Wherever possible, work in a well-ventilated atmosphere.

6 Check the friction disc facings for signs of wear, damage or oil contamination. If the friction material is cracked, burnt, scored or damaged, or if it is contaminated with oil or grease (shown by shiny black patches), the friction disc must be renewed.

7 If the friction material is still serviceable, check that the centre boss splines are unworn, that the torsion springs are in good condition and securely fastened, and that all the rivets are tightly fastened. If excessive wear or damage is found, the friction disc must be renewed.

8 If the friction material is fouled with oil, this must be due to an oil leak from the crankshaft left-hand oil seal, from the oil pan-to-cylinder block joint, or from the transmission input shaft. Renew the seal or repair the joint, as appropriate, (see Chapter 2A Section 14, Chapter 2B Section 14, Chapter 2C Section 19 or Chapter 7A Section 3), before installing the new friction disc, or the new disc will quickly go the same way.

9 Check the pressure plate assembly for obvious signs of wear or damage; shake it to check for loose rivets, or worn or damaged fulcrum rings. Check that the drive straps securing the pressure plate to the cover do not show signs (such as a deep yellow or blue discoloration) of overheating. If the diaphragm spring is worn or damaged, or if its pressure is in any way suspect, the pressure plate assembly should be renewed.

10 Examine the machined bearing surfaces of the pressure plate and of the flywheel; they should be clean, completely flat, and free from scratches or scoring. If either is discoloured from excessive heat, or shows signs of cracks, it should be renewed; however, minor damage of this nature can sometimes be polished away using emery paper.

11 Check that the release bearing contact surface rotates smoothly and easily, with no sign of noise or roughness, and that the surface itself is smooth and unworn, with no signs of cracks, pitting or scoring. If there is any doubt about its condition, the bearing must be renewed.

Installation

12 On installation, ensure that the bearing surfaces of the flywheel and pressure plate are completely clean, smooth, and free from oil or grease. Use solvent to remove any protective grease from new components.

13 Fit the friction disc/plate so that its spring hub assembly faces away from the flywheel; there may also be a marking showing which way round the plate is to be refitted **(see illustration)**.

14 Refit the pressure plate assembly, aligning the marks made on dismantling (if the original pressure plate is re-used), and locating the pressure plate on its locating dowels. Fit the pressure plate bolts, but tighten them only finger-tight so that the friction disc can still be moved.

15 The friction disc must now be centralised, so that when the transmission is refitted, its input shaft will pass through the splines at the centre of the friction disc.

16 Centralisation can be achieved by passing a screwdriver or other long bar through the friction disc, and into the hole in the crankshaft. The friction disc can then be moved around until it is centred on the crankshaft hole. Alternatively, a clutch-aligning tool can be used to eliminate the guesswork; these can be obtained from most accessory shops **(see illustrations)**.

17 When the friction disc is centralised, tighten the pressure plate bolts evenly and in a diagonal sequence to the specified torque setting **(see illustrations)**. Lock the ring gear to prevent the flywheel from turning, using the method employed when dismantling.

18 Apply a thin smear of high melting-point grease to the splines of the friction disc and the transmission input shaft.

19 Refit the transmission (see Chapter 7A Section 5).

6 Clutch release mechanism – removal, inspection and installation

Note: *Refer to the warning concerning the dangers of asbestos dust at the beginning of (see Section 5).*

Removal

1 Unless the complete engine/transmission is to be removed from the car, and separated for major overhaul (see Chapter 2D Section 7), the clutch can be reached by removing the transmission (see Chapter 7A Section 5).

2 With the transmission removed, undo the two mounting bolts from inside the bellhousing **(see illustration)**.

3 Withdraw the concentric slave cylinder/release bearing by sliding it over the transmission input shaft. Withdraw it complete with plastic fluid pipe out from the bellhousing.

4 If required, withdraw the securing clip from the plastic fluid pipe **(see illustration)**, to disconnect it from the clutch slave cylinder/release bearing.

5.17b Tighten the bolts to the correct torque setting

Chapter 8 Clutch and driveline

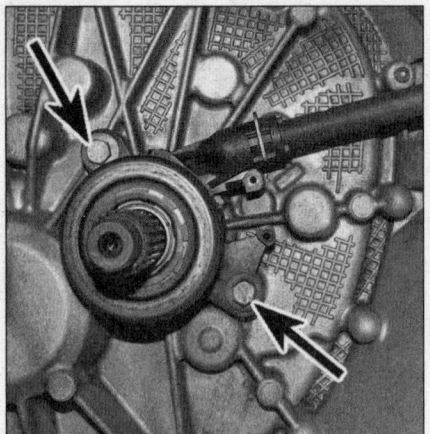

6.2 Undo the concentric slave cylinder (CSC) mounting bolts

6.4 Retaining clip (arrowed) securing plastic pipe to the slave cylinder

7.2 Place a prybar between two wheel studs while you loosen the driveshaft nut

Inspection

5 Check the release mechanism, renewing any component, which is worn or damaged. Carefully check all bearing surfaces and points of contact.

6 When checking the release bearing itself, note that it is often considered worthwhile to renew it as a matter of course, given that a significant amount of work is required to gain access to it. Check that the contact surface rotates smoothly and easily, with no sign of noise or roughness. Also check that the surface itself is smooth and unworn, with no signs of cracks, pitting or scoring. If there is any doubt about its condition, the bearing must be renewed.

Installation

7 Slide the concentric slave cylinder/ release bearing over the transmission input shaft and tighten the retaining bolts to the specified torque setting.

8 Refit the transmission (see Chapter 7A Section 5).

7 Driveshaft- removal and installation

Front

Removal

1 Loosen the front wheel nuts, raise the vehicle and support it securely on jackstands (see Chapter 0 Section 7). Remove the wheel.
Note: *As an alternative you can leave the vehicle on the ground, remove the hubcap or centre cap, remove the split pin and loosen the driveshaft nut.*

2 Remove the split pin and nut lock (if equipped) and unscrew the driveshaft/hub nut **(see illustration)**.

3 Remove the lock nut and washer from the end of the driveshaft.

4 Remove the ABS wheel speed sensor from the steering knuckle (see Chapter 9 Section 2).

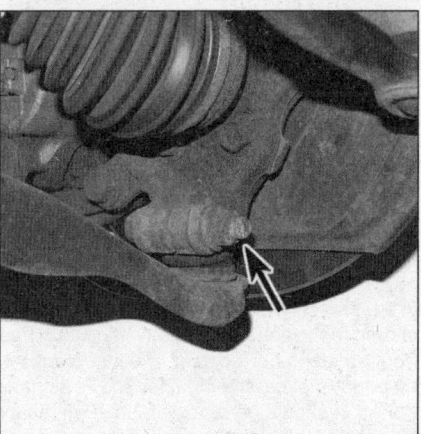

7.5 Remove the pinch-bolt

5 Remove the control arm balljoint-to-steering knuckle pinch bolt **(see illustration)**.

6 Pry downward on the control arm to separate the balljoint from the steering knuckle **(see illustration)**.

7 Push the driveshaft out of the hub while pulling outward on the steering knuckle and hub assembly. If the driveshaft splines are frozen, free them by tapping the end of the driveshaft with a soft-faced hammer or a hammer and a brass punch, or use a puller to push the driveshaft from the hub. Use a puller if necessary.

8 Place a drain pan underneath the transaxle to catch any lubricant that may spill out when the driveshaft are removed.

9 For the left driveshaft, use a prybar to carefully pry the inner CV joint out of the transaxle, and remove the driveshaft **(see illustration)**.

10 The inner CV joint housing on the right (passenger's side) driveshaft terminates at a support bracket. To detach the right driveshaft assembly from the bracket, remove the retainer-to-bracket bolts **(see illustration)**, mark the relationship of the bearing to the support bracket and pull out the driveshaft

7.6 Pry downward to remove the balljoint from the knuckle

assembly. Do not try to separate the bearing from the inner CV joint until you have the entire assembly on the bench.

11 Install a new driveshaft oil seal on the transfer case (see Chapter 7C Section 4).

7.9 If you're removing the left driveshaft, carefully pry the inner CV joint out of the transaxle

Chapter 8 Clutch and driveline

7.10 Remove the retainer plate-to-bracket bolts

7.13 Install a new retaining clip if reusing the old driveshaft

9.3 Undo the propeller shaft rear flange bolts

Installation

12 Installation is the reverse of removal, noting the following:
13 If reusing the old shaft, install a new retaining clip on the shaft end before installation **(see illustration)**.
14 When installing the right driveshaft, tighten the retainer plate-to-bracket bolts in two steps to the specified torque (see Specifications).
15 When installing the left driveshaft, push the driveshaft in sharply to seat the retaining ring on the inner CV joint into its groove in the differential side gear. To ease insertion and seating of the retaining ring, position the gap in the ring at the bottom.
16 Tighten the control arm balljoint-to-steering knuckle pinch bolt to the torque (see Chapter 10).
17 Tighten the driveshaft/hub nut to the specified torque (see Specifications), then install a new split pin.
18 Install the wheel and wheel nuts, lower the vehicle and tighten the wheel nuts to the specified torque (see Chapter 1).
19 Check the transaxle lubricant and add, if necessary, to bring it to the proper level (see Chapter 1 Section 8, or Section 17).

Rear

Removal

20 Loosen the rear wheel nuts, raise the vehicle and support it securely on jackstands (see Chapter 0 Section 7). Remove the wheel(s).

Note: *As an alternative you can leave the vehicle on the ground, remove the hubcap or centre cap, remove the split pin and loosen the driveshaft nut.*

21 Remove the split pin, then place a prybar between two wheel studs while you loosen the driveshaft nut **(see illustration 3.2)**. Unscrew the driveshaft/hub nut until it is flush with the end of the shaft.
22 To loosen the driveshaft from the hub splines, place a block of wood between the nut and driveshaft end and strike it with a hammer, or use a hammer and brass punch to tap the end of the driveshaft in. If the driveshaft is stuck in the hub splines and won't move, it may be necessary to push the driveshaft with a suitable puller.
23 Once the shaft is free, remove the nut from the end of the driveshaft.
24 Remove the wheel speed sensor from the trailing arm (see Chapter 9 Section 2).
25 Remove the rear brake disc (see Chapter 9 Section 6).
26 Unbolt the rear stabiliser bar link from the lower suspension arm (see Chapter 10 Section 12).
27 Place a floor jack under the coil spring pocket of the trailing arm and raise it slightly.
Warning: *The jack must stay in this position throughout the procedure.*
28 Unbolt the lower end of the shock absorber from the trailing arm (see Chapter 10 Section 9).
29 Unbolt the upper and lower control arms from the trailing arm (see Chapter 10 Section 11).
30 Push the driveshaft out of the hub while pulling outward on the trailing arm assembly. Adjust the height of the jack as necessary.
31 Place a drain pan underneath the differential to catch any lubricant that may spill out when the driveshafts are removed.
32 Use a prybar to carefully pry the inner CV joint out of the differential, and remove the driveshaft.
33 If necessary, install a new driveshaft oil seal on the differential housing

Installation

34 Installation is the reverse of removal, noting the following:
35 If reusing the old shaft, install a new retaining clip on the shaft end before installation.
36 When installing the right driveshaft, tighten the retainer-to-bracket bolts in two steps to the specified torque (see Specifications).
37 When installing the driveshaft, push the driveshaft in sharply to seat the retaining ring on the inner CV joint into its groove in the differential side gear. To ease insertion and seating of the retaining ring, position the gap in the ring at the bottom.
38 Tighten the control arms bolts to the specified torque (see Chapter 10)
39 Tighten the driveshaft/hub nut to the specified torque (see Specifications), then install a new split pin.
40 Install the wheel and wheel nuts, lower the vehicle and tighten the wheel nuts to the specified torque (see Chapter 1).
41 Check the differential lubricant and add, if necessary, to bring it to the proper level (see Chapter 1 Section 16).

8 Rear differential – draining and refilling (AWD models)

1 The procedure to inspect (see Chapter 1 Section 16), drain and refill the rear differential fluid is covered in the Tune-up and Routine Maintenance Chapter (see Chapter 1 Section 32).

9 Rear differential – removal and installation (AWD models)

Removal

1 Raise the vehicle and support on jackstands (see Jacking and Towing 0 Section 7).
2 Drain the differential (see Chapter 1 Section 32).
3 Undo the four retaining bolts and disconnect the rear of the propeller shaft from the flange on the differential flange **(see illustration)**. Make alignment marks on the propeller shaft and the flange to make sure that it is fitted in the same position on refitting. Discard the retaining bolts, as new ones will be required for refitting (see Section 13).

9.5 Disconnect the wiring connector (arrowed)

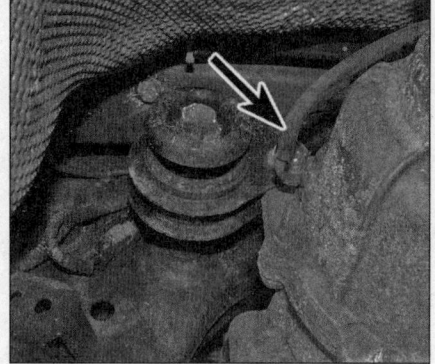

9.6 Disconnect the breather pipe (arrowed)

9.8a Undo the front mounting bolts (arrowed) …

4 Remove both driveshafts from the differential (see Section 7).
5 Disconnect the wiring connector to the coupling, then undo the retaining bolt and move the wiring loom bracket to one side (see illustration).
6 Disconnect the breather pipe from the right-hand side of the coupling and move it to one side (see illustration).
7 Place a jack with interposed block of wood beneath the rear differential, to take the weight.
8 Slacken and remove the two front upper mounting bolts, and then undo the rear mounting nut (see illustrations).
9 Support the differential on the trolley jack, and then lower it down and out from under the vehicle. As the differential is lowered, disconnect the breather hose from the top of the unit at the rear; note its fitted position for refitting.

Installation

10 Installation is a reversal of the removal procedure, noting the following points.
  a Make sure the electric coupling wiring connector is secure.
  b Make sure breather pipes are fitted correctly and not trapped.

9.8b … and the rear mounting nut (arrowed)

  c Fit new retaining bolts to the propeller shaft.
  d Tighten bolts to the specified torque setting, where given.
  e Align the marks made on removal, when refitting the propeller shaft.
  f When completed, refill the differential (see Chapter 1 Section 32).

10 Differential oil seals – renewal

Front (electric coupling) oil seal

1 Raise the vehicle and support on jackstands (see Chapter 0 Section 7).
2 Undo the four retaining bolts and disconnect the rear of the propeller shaft from the flange on the differential flange (see illustration 9.3). Make alignment marks on the propeller shaft and the flange to make sure that it is fitted in the same position on refitting.
3 Use a length of bar, bolted to two of the holes in the flange, hold the flange on the front of the differential in place, and then undo the flange lock nut. Make alignment marks on the flange and the shaft to make sure that it is fitted in the same position on refitting. Discard the locknut, as a new one will be required on refitting.
4 With the flange removed, note the fitted position of the seal, and then carefully lever it out from the front of the housing. Use a large flat-bladed screwdriver, taking care not to damage the casing.
5 Clean the seal housing in the front of the differential, and polish off any burrs or raised edges, which may have caused the seal to fail in the first place.
6 Apply a small amount of multi-purpose grease; evenly to the lips of the seal, and gear oil onto the outer circumference, before fitting the seal back to the housing. Making sure the seal is sitting square in the housing, carefully ease it into position, taking care not to damage its sealing lip. Using a drift drive the seal into the adapter plate, in the position noted on removal. Take care not to damage the seal lips during fitting.

7 Refitting is a reversal of the removal procedure, noting the following points.
  a Align the marks made on removal, when refitting the flange to the shaft.
  b Fit a new locknut to the flange and tighten to the specified torque (see Specifications).
  c Align the marks made on removal, when refitting the propeller shaft.
  d When completed, if required, check and top-up the differential lubricant (see Chapter 1 Section 16).

Side (driveshaft) oil seals

8 Raise the vehicle and support on jackstands (see Chapter 0 Section 7).
9 Drain the differential oil (see Chapter 1 Section 32).
10 Free the inner end of the driveshaft from the differential (see Section 7), and place it clear of the seal, noting that there is no need to completely remove the driveshaft; the driveshaft can be left secured to the outer hub. Support the driveshaft, to avoid placing any strain on the driveshaft joints.
11 Before removing the seal, use a vernier gauge to check the seal depth in the transmission casing. This will give you the position of the seal for refitting.
12 Carefully prise the oil seal out of the differential casing using a large flat-bladed screwdriver. Take care not to damage the casing as the seal is removed.
13 Remove all traces of dirt from the area around the oil seal aperture, then apply a small amount of multi-purpose grease; evenly to the lips of the new seal, and gear oil onto the outer circumference, and locate it in its aperture.
14 Drive the seal squarely into position, using a suitable tubular drift (such as a socket), which bears only on the hard outer edge of the seal. Drive the seal into position until it is at the depth noted on removal.
15 Refit the driveshaft (see Section 7).
16 Refill the differential with the specified quantity of oil (see Chapter 1 Section 32). Refer to the Tune-up and Routine Maintenance Chapter for the specified type and quantity of oil required (see Chapter 1).

Chapter 8 Clutch and driveline

12.6 Undo the six bolts from around the coupling housing

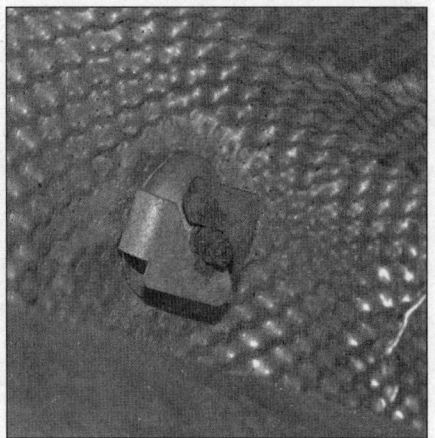

13.3a Undo the fasteners …

13.3b … and remove the heat shield

11 Differential – overhaul

1 Overhauling a differential is a difficult and involved job for the DIY home mechanic. In addition to dismantling and reassembling many small parts, clearances must be precisely measured and, if necessary, changed by selecting shims and spacers. Internal components are also often difficult to obtain, and in many instances, extremely expensive. Because of this, if the differential develops a fault or becomes noisy, the best course of action is to have the differential overhauled by a specialist repairer, or to obtain an exchange reconditioned differential.
2 Nevertheless, it is not impossible for the more experienced mechanic to overhaul differential, if the special tools are available, and the job is done in a deliberate step-by-step manner so that nothing is overlooked.
3 The tools necessary for an overhaul include internal and external circlip pliers, bearing pullers, a slide hammer, a set of pin punches, a dial test indicator, and possibly a hydraulic press. In addition, a large, sturdy workbench and a vice will be required.
4 During dismantling of the differential, make careful notes of how each component is fitted, to make reassembly easier and accurate.
5 Before dismantling the differential, it will help if you have some idea which area is malfunctioning. Certain problems can be closely related to specific areas in the differential, which can make component examination and renewal easier.

12 Differential electric controlled coupling – removal and installation

Removal

1 Raise the rear of the vehicle and support on jackstands (see Chapter 0 Section 7).
2 Undo the four retaining bolts and disconnect the rear of the propeller shaft from the flange on the differential flange (see illustration 9.3). Make alignment marks on the propeller shaft and the flange to make sure that it is fitted in the same position on refitting.
3 Use a length of bar, bolted to two of the holes in the flange, hold the flange on the front of the differential in place, and then undo the flange lock nut. Make alignment marks on the flange and the shaft to make sure that it is fitted in the same position on refitting. Discard the locknut, as a new one will be required on refitting.
4 Disconnect the wiring connector to the coupling, then undo the retaining bolt and move the wiring loom bracket to one side (see illustration 9.5).
5 Disconnect the breather pipe from the right-hand side of the coupling and move it to one side (see illustration 9.6).
6 Undo the six bolts from around the electric controlled coupling housing, then withdraw the housing, complete with electric coupling from the front of the differential (see illustration).

Installation

7 Renew the oil seal in the front of the electric controlled coupling housing (see Section 10).
8 On installation, fit the electric controlled coupling to the front of the differential casing. Align the locating pin on the right-hand side of the coupling with the slot in the differential casing. Also align the splines on the rear of the coupling with the differential shaft, taking care not to damage the seal on the inside of the differential.
9 Clean the contact face of the differential casing and the coupling housing, then apply a bead of sealant around the coupling housing mating surface approximately 3 mm diameter.
10 Fit the coupling housing, making sure it is the correct way up (arrow facing up, at the bottom right-hand corner). As the housing is fitted over the electric coupling, make sure the wiring loom is located correctly in the housing to prevent it getting trapped.
11 Fit the housing bolts, starting with the ones at each side of the housing and carefully pull the housing into position over the electric controlled coupling. Tighten all the bolts evenly to their specified torque setting.
12 The remainder of the installation procedure is the reversal of the removal procedure, noting the following points.
  a Align the marks made on removal, when refitting the flange to the shaft.
  b Fit a new locknut to the flange and tighten to the specified torque setting.
  c Align the marks made on removal, when refitting the propeller shaft.
  d When completed, refill the rear differential with lubricant (see Chapter 1 Section 32).

13 Propeller shaft (AWD models) - removal and installation

Note: *If you're concerned about a possibly bent propeller shaft causing a vibration, mount a dial indicator to the floor of the vehicle and check the propeller shaft runout in the middle of the front and rear sections.*

1 Raise the rear of the vehicle and support it securely on jackstands (see Chapter 0 Section 7). Block the front wheels to prevent the vehicle from rolling.
2 Turn the key On, then shift the transaxle into Neutral. Turn the key Off. Release the parking brake.
3 On models where the heatshield interferes with the propeller shaft removal, proceed as follows:
  a *Remove the exhaust front pipe (see Chapter 4A Section 11 - petrol models or Chapter 4B Section 11 - diesel models).*
  b *Make alignment marks on the propeller shaft and front and rear universal joint flanges, to make sure that it is fitted in the same position on refitting.*
  c *Release the retaining clips and remove the heat shield from the propeller shaft centre mounting (see illustrations).*

13.4 Mark the relationship of the propeller to the differential (shown) and transfer case flanges

13.5 Propeller shaft centre support bearing bracket nuts

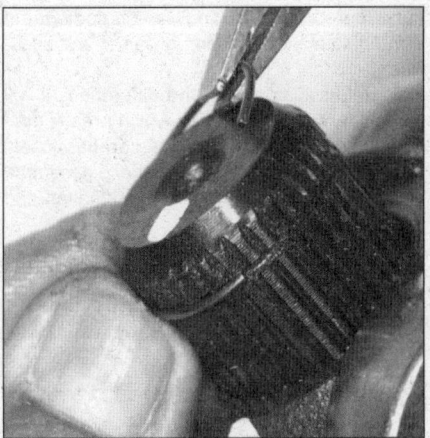

14.3 Cut off the boot clamps and discard them

d Note the fitted position of the upper and lower bracket, and then remove the two plastic locating clips, one each side of the mounting bracket.

4 Mark the relationship of the propeller shaft flanges to the differential and transfer case flanges **(see illustration)**.

5 Loosen (but don't remove) the nuts of the centre bearing brackets **(see illustration)**.

6 Remove the flange bolts from each end of the propeller shaft. You'll have to insert a tool into the u-joint to keep the propeller shaft from turning as you break the nuts and bolts loose.

7 Remove the centre support bearing nuts and remove the propeller shaft.

8 Remove the centre bearing bracket from the propeller shaft.

9 Installation is the reverse of removal. Attach the centre bearing bracket so that the arrow on it is facing forward. Align the match marks you made previously as you attach each end of the driveshaft. Tighten the nuts and bolts to the specified torque (see Specifications).

14 Driveshaft boots - replacement

Note: *If the CV joints are worn, indicating the need for an overhaul (usually due to torn boots), explore all options before beginning the job. Complete rebuilt driveshafts are available on an exchange basis, which eliminates much time and work.*

Note: *Some auto parts stores carry split type replacement boots, which can be installed without removing the driveshaft from the vehicle. This is a convenient alternative; however, the driveshaft should be removed and the CV joint disassembled and cleaned to ensure the joint is free from contaminants such as moisture and dirt which will accelerate CV joint wear.*

1 Remove the driveshaft (see Section 7).

2 Mount the driveshaft in a vise. The jaws of the vise should be lined with wood or rags to prevent damage to the driveshaft.

Removal

Inner CV joint and boot

3 Remove the boot clamps **(see illustration)**.

4 Pull the boot back from the inner CV joint and slide the joint housing off. Mark the relationship of the tripod to the outer race **(see illustration)**.

5 Mark the tripod and driveshaft to ensure that they are reassembled properly **(see illustration)**.

6 Spread the ends of the retainer clip and remove from the end of the driveshaft **(see illustration)**.

7 Use a hammer and a brass punch to drive the tripod joint from the driveshaft **(see illustration)**.

8 Remove the stop-ring from the driveshaft and discard it.

Inspection

9 Clean the old grease from the outer race and the tripod bearing assembly. Carefully disassemble each section of the tripod assembly, one at a time so as not to mix up

14.4 Mark the relationship of the tripod assembly to the outer race

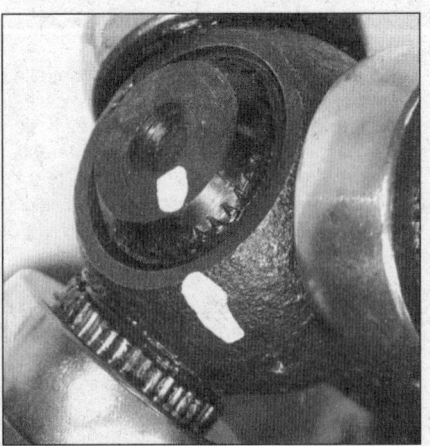

14.5 Make marks on the tripod and the driveshaft to ensure that they are properly reassembled

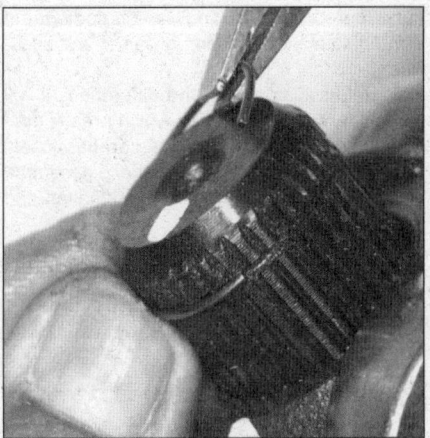

14.6 Spread the ends of the retainer clip and slide it from the shaft

Chapter 8 Clutch and driveline

14.7 Drive the tripod joint from the driveshaft with a brass punch and hammer - make sure you don't damage the bearing surfaces or the splines on the shaft

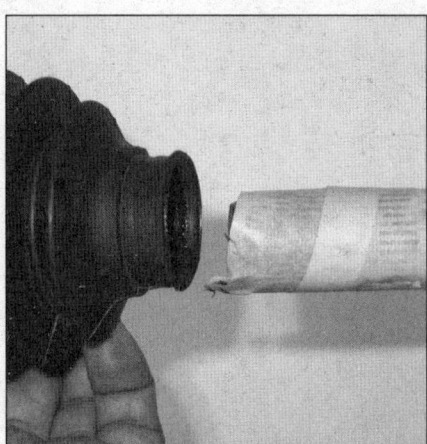

14.13 Wrap the splined area of the driveshaft with tape to prevent damage to the boot(s) when installing it

14.18 Pack the outer race with CV joint grease and slide it over the tripod assembly - make sure the match marks on the CV joint housing and tripod line up

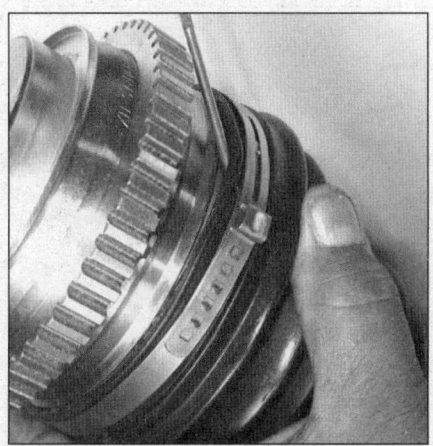

14.20 Equalize the pressure inside the boot by inserting a small, dull screwdriver between the boot and the outer race

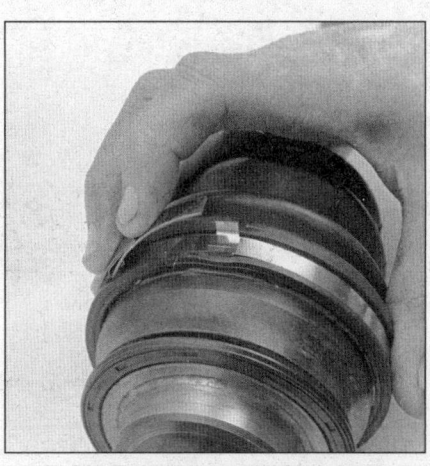

14.21a To install new fold-over type clamps, bend the tang down…

14.21b … and flatten the tabs to hold it in place

14.21c To install band-type clamps you'll need a special tool; install the band with its end pointing in the direction of axle rotation and tighten it securely. Pivot the tool up 90-degrees and tap the centre of the clip with a centre punch…

the parts. Clean the needle bearings with solvent.

10 Inspect the rollers, tripod, bearings and outer race for scoring, pitting or other signs of abnormal wear, which will warrant the replacement of the inner CV joint.

Outer CV joint and boot

11 If the outer driveshaft boot requires replacement, remove the boot clamps **(see illustration 14.3)**.

12 Slide the boot from the outer joint and along the shaft until it can be removed.

Reassembly

Outer CV joint and boot

13 Inspect the outer joint for lack of lubricant, entry of dirt or water or damage at the joint. If any there is any damage to the joint, the driveshaft must be renewed as an assembly. If not, add some CV joint grease to the outer joint and slide a new boot onto the shaft and over the outer joint. It's a good idea to wrap the driveshaft splines with tape to prevent damaging the boot **(see illustration)**.

14 Install new clamps and tighten securely.

Inner CV joint and boot

15 Slide the clamps and boot onto the driveshaft. It's a good idea to wrap the driveshaft splines with tape to prevent damaging the boot **(see illustration 14.13)**.

16 Install a new stop-ring on the driveshaft, but don't seat it in its groove; position it on the shaft past the groove.

17 Place the tripod on the shaft (making sure the marks are aligned) and install a new bearing retainer clip. Slide the tripod up against the retainer clip and seat the stop-ring in its groove.

18 Apply CV joint grease to the tripod assembly, the inside of the joint housing and the inside of the boot **(see illustration)**.

v19 Slide the boot into place.

20 Position the CV joint mid-way through its travel, then equalize the pressure in the boot **(see illustration)**.

21 Ensure that the inner end of the boot is positioned over the groove in the drive shaft before installing and tightening the inner boot clamp **(see illustrations)**.

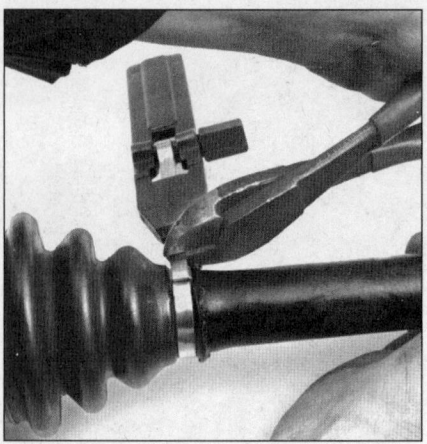

14.21d ... then bend the end of the clamp back over the clip and cut off the excess

14.21e If you're installing crimp-type boot clamps, you'll need a pair of special crimping pliers (available at most auto parts stores)

22 Measure the distance between the two ends of the boot as illustrated (see illustration). Move the outer end of the boot until the specified distance is obtained and then tighten the outer boot clamp (see illustrations 14.21a through 14.21e).

23 Install the driveshaft assembly (see Section 7).

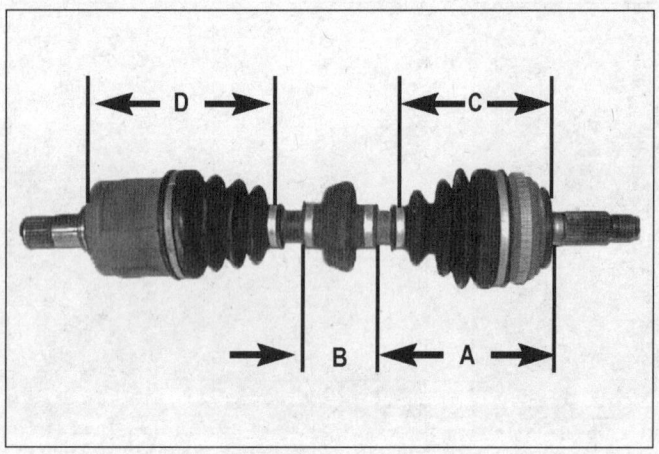

14.22a Front driveshaft boot and clamp and damper clamp measuring points; refer to Specifications

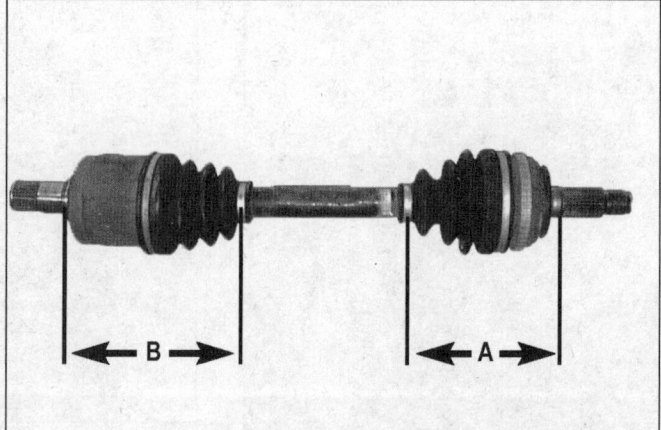

14.22b Rear driveshaft boot clamp measuring points; refer to Specifications

A Distance between face of outer joint and outer damper clamp
B Distance between damper clamps
C Distance between face of outer joint and inner clamp
D Distance between face of inner joint and inner joint clamp

A Distance between face of outer joint and inner clamp
B Distance between face of inner joint and inner clamp

Chapter 9
Brakes

Contents

	Section		Section
Anti-lock braking system (ABS) – general information and component renewal	2	Front brake disc – inspection, removal and refitting	5
Brake booster - check, replacement and adjustment	12	Front brake pads – replacement	3
Brake check	See Chapter 1	General information	1
Brake hoses and lines - inspection and replacement	10	Master cylinder – removal and refitting	9
Brake hydraulic system – bleeding and replacing brake fluid	11	Parking brake - check and adjustment	13
Brake light switch, cruise control cancel switch and brake pedal position sensor - adjustment and replacement	17	Parking brake cables – removal and Installation	14
Brake pedal - adjustment	16	Parking brake shoes - replacement	15
Front brake caliper – removal and refitting	7	Rear brake caliper – removal and refitting	8
		Rear brake disc – inspection, removal and refitting	6
		Rear brake pads – replacement	4

Specifications

General
Brake fluid type .... see Chapter 1

Disc brakes
Minimum pad thickness .... see Chapter 1
Brake disc minimum thickness .... Cast into disc
Maximum disc runout
   Front .... 0.035 mm
   Rear .... 0.070 mm
Maximum disc thickness variation
   Front .... 0.020 mm
   Rear .... 0.020 mm

Brake booster
Booster-to-clevis hole centre dimension
   X-Trail T31 and Dualis .... 124.5 to 125.5 mm
   X-Trail T32 .... 124.25 to 125.75 mm
   Qashqai .... 150.7 to 157.7 mm

Brake pedal
Pedal free play
   X-Trail models .... 3.0 to 11.0 mm
   Dualis and Qashqai .... Not specified
Clearance between switch plungers and pedal bracket
   X-Trail T31 and Dualis .... 0.7 to 2.0 mm
   X-Trail T32 and Qashqai .... 0.2 to 2.0 mm
Pedal height from floor to top of pedal
   X-Trail T31 and Dualis .... 130.2 to 140.2 mm
   X-Trail T32 .... 176.0 to 186.0 mm
   Qashqai .... 175.0 to 185.0 mm

Parking brake
Parking brake adjustment .... 7 to 8 clicks

Chapter 9 Brakes

Torque specifications — Nm

- ABS wheel speed sensor 10
- Brake booster mounting nuts 14
- Brake caliper
  - Caliper mounting bolts
    - Front 34
    - Rear
      - X-Trail T31 and Dualis 43
      - X-Trail T32 and Qashqai 34
  - Caliper mounting bracket bolts
    - Front
      - X-Trail T31, Dualis and Qashqai 152
      - X-Trail T32 165
    - Rear 84
- Brake hose-to-caliper banjo bolt 18
- Master cylinder-to-brake booster retaining nuts
  - X-Trail T31, Dualis and Qashqai 15
  - X-Trail T32 20
- Parking brake actuator to caliper bolts
  - Qashqai 18
- ABS wheel speed sensor 10

1 General information

Warning: *Note that the dust created by wear of the pads may contain asbestos, which is a health hazard. Never blow it out with compressed air, and don't inhale any of it. An approved filtering mask should be worn when working on the brakes. DO NOT use petrol or petroleum-based solvents to clean brake parts; use brake cleaner or methylated spirit only.*

General

1 The vehicles covered by this manual are equipped with hydraulically operated front and rear brake systems. The front and rear brakes are self-adjusting disc-type brakes.

Hydraulic system

2 The hydraulic system consists of two separate circuits. The master cylinder has separate reservoirs for the two circuits, and, in the event of a leak or failure in one hydraulic circuit, the other circuit will remain operative and a warning indicator will light up on the instrument panel when a substantial amount of brake fluid is lost, showing that a failure has occurred.

Brake booster

3 The brake booster uses engine manifold vacuum to provide assistance to the brakes. It is mounted on the firewall in the engine compartment, directly behind the master cylinder.

Parking brake

4 On models with a lever operated parking brake, a pair of parking brake shoes mounted inside a drum (hub) portion of each rear brake disc are expanded against the drum to prevent the rear wheels turning.

5 Some later models have an electronic parking brake system consisting of a switch on the centre console which, when activated, operates an electronic motor on the inside of each rear disc brake caliper. The motor winds a threaded rod on each caliper piston forcing the piston out of the caliper, compressing the brake pads against the brake disc.

Caution: *On models with an electronic handbrake you will need a scan tool to retract the brake pistons. Do not attempt to do this procedure unless you have a scan tool capable of performing this function.*

Service

6 After completing any operation involving disassembly of any part of the brake system, always test drive the vehicle to check for proper braking performance before resuming normal driving. When testing the brakes, perform the tests on a clean, dry, flat surface. Conditions other than these can lead to inaccurate test results.

7 Test the brakes at various speeds with both light and heavy pedal pressure. The vehicle should stop evenly without pulling to one side or the other. Under hard braking, the ABS system may engage, resulting in brake pedal pulsation. This is considered normal operation.

8 Tires, vehicle load and wheel alignment are factors which also affect braking performance.

Precautions

9 There are some general cautions and warnings involving the brake system on this vehicle:

  a Use only brake fluid conforming to DOT 3 or DOT4 specifications.
  b The brake pads and linings contain fibres which are hazardous to your health if inhaled. Whenever you work on brake system components, clean all parts with brake system cleaner. Do not allow the fine dust to become airborne. Also, wear an approved filtering mask.
  c Safety should be paramount whenever any servicing of the brake components is performed. Do not use parts or fasteners which are not in perfect condition, and be sure that all clearances and torque specifications are adhered to. If you are at all unsure about a certain procedure, seek professional advice. Upon completion of any brake system work, test the brakes carefully in a controlled area before putting the vehicle into normal service. If a problem is suspected in the brake system, don't drive the vehicle until it's fixed.
  d Used brake fluid is considered a hazardous waste and it must be disposed of in accordance with federal, state and local laws. DO NOT pour it down the sink, into septic tanks or storm drains, or on the ground.
  e Clean up any spilled brake fluid immediately and then wash the area with large amounts of water. This is especially true for any finished or painted surfaces.

2 Anti-lock braking system (ABS) – general information and component renewal

General information

1 Anti-lock braking is available as standard equipment on the models covered by this manual. The system is fail-safe, and is fitted

Chapter 9 Brakes

2.5a Location of front wheel speed sensor

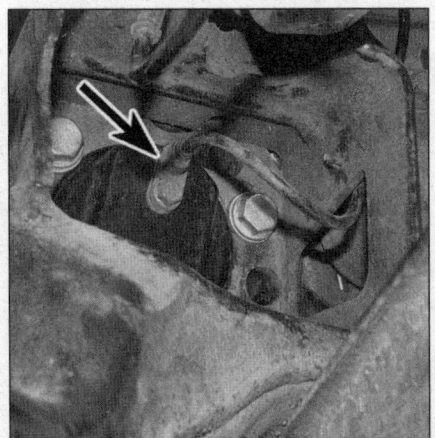

2.5b Location of rear wheel speed sensor (arrowed) - 2WD models

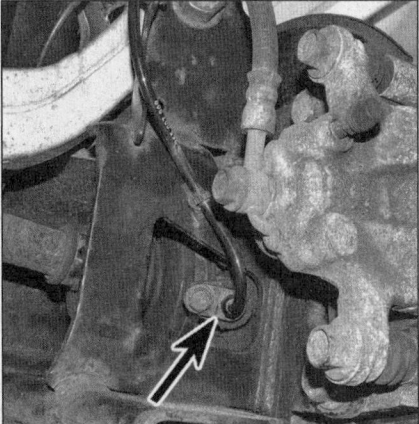

2.5c Location of rear wheel speed sensor (arrowed) – 4WD models

2.6 Remove the inner wing trim panel

2.7a Disconnect the front sensor wiring connector (arrowed) ...

can only be satisfactorily tested using specialist diagnostic equipment available to a Nissan dealer. For safety reasons, owners are strongly advised against attempting to diagnose complex problems with the ABS using standard workshop equipment.

Component renewal

Wheel speed sensors

4   Jack up the front or rear of the vehicle (as applicable), and support it securely using axle stands Chapter 0 Section 7. Remove the relevant road wheel.

5   The front speed sensors are located on the rear side of each wheel hub carrier, whilst the rear sensors are located on the inner face of the stub axle assembly on 2WD models and on the rear of the wheel hub carrier on 4WD models (see illustrations).

6   For access to the front wheel sensor connector, release the retaining clips and remove the plastic inner trim from inside the wheel arch (see illustration).

7   Trace the sensor wiring back to the connector, and separate the two halves of the wiring plug. Release the wiring from any retaining brackets/clips (see illustrations).

in addition to the conventional braking system, meaning that the vehicle retains conventional braking in the event of an ABS failure.

2   To prevent wheel locking, the system provides a means of modulating (varying) the hydraulic pressure in the braking circuits, to control the amount of braking effort at each wheel. To achieve this, sensors mounted at all four wheels monitor the rotational speeds of the wheels, and are thus able to detect when there is a risk of wheel locking (low rotational speed, relative to vehicle speed). Solenoid valves are positioned in the brake circuits to each wheel, and the solenoid valves are incorporated in a modulator assembly, which is controlled by an electronic control unit. The electronic control unit controls the braking effort applied to each wheel, according to the information supplied by the wheel sensors.

3   Should an ABS fault develop, the system

2.7b ... and release the wiring from the support bracket

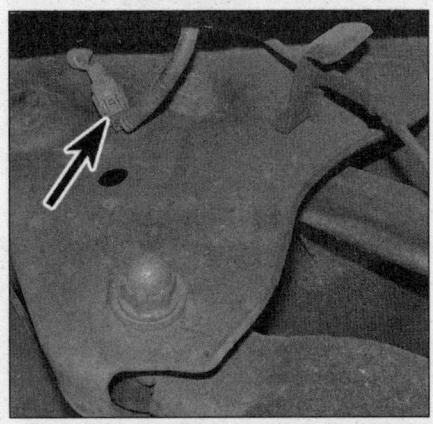

2.7c Disconnect the rear sensor wiring connector (arrowed) ...

2.7d ... and release the wiring from the support bracket

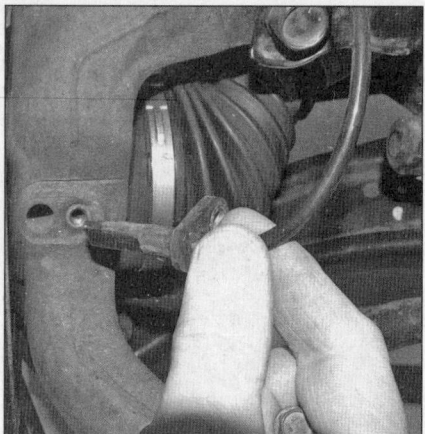

2.8a Remove the front wheel sensor

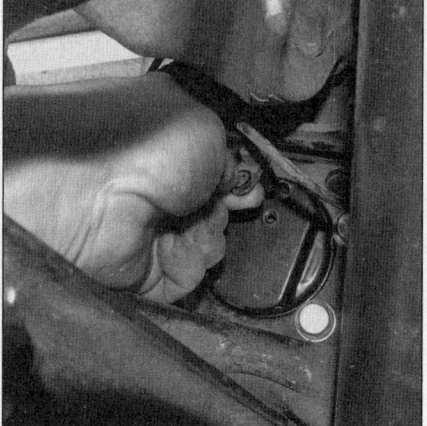

2.8b Remove the rear wheel sensor- 2WD models

2.8c Remove the rear wheel sensor- 4WD models

2.10 Location of ABS actuator

8 Undo the retaining bolt and pull the sensor from the hub carrier/stub axle assembly **(see illustrations)**. If the sensor is reluctant to move, apply releasing/penetrating fluid to the assembly, and leave it to soak for a few minutes before trying again. If the sensor still will not move, the hub carrier or rear brake disc must be removed, and the sensor driven from place.

9 Refitting is the reversal of removal, noting the following points:

a Ensure the mating faces of the hub carrier/stub axle assembly and sensor are clean and free from corrosion.

b Apply a thin smear of anti-seize compound to mounting surfaces of the sensor and hub carrier/stub axle assembly.

c Tighten the sensor retaining bolt to the specified torque.

Actuator (Modulator)

10 The actuator is located in the left-hand rear corner of the engine compartment **(see illustration)**. Disconnect the negative (-) battery terminal (see Chapter 5 Section 3).

11 Open two bleed screws in the system (one in each of the dual circuit), and gently pump the brake pedal to expel the fluid through a tube connected to the bleed screws. Alternatively, have some caps handy to plug the open ends of the brake pipes once they are disconnected from the actuator.

12 Remove the air cleaner assembly (see Chapter 4A Section 9 - petrol models or Chapter 4B Section 6 - diesel models).

13 Release the locking clip, and then disconnect the wiring plug from the side of the actuator **(see illustration)**.

14 Note their fitted locations, then undo the union nuts and disconnect the brake pipes from the ABS actuator **(see illustration)**. If the system has not been drained, be prepared for fluid spillage. Plug the end of the pipes to prevent dirt ingress.

15 Undo the actuator mounting nuts **(see illustration)**, and manoeuvre the actuator from the mounting bracket.

16 To refit the actuator, align the locating lug at the bottom of the unit with the corresponding hole in the mounting bracket, and then tighten the mounting nuts securely.

17 The remainder of refitting is a reversal of removal, bleeding the brake system (see Section 11).

3 Front brake pads – replacement

Warning: *Renew BOTH sets of front brake pads at the same time – NEVER renew the pads on only one wheel, as uneven braking may result.*

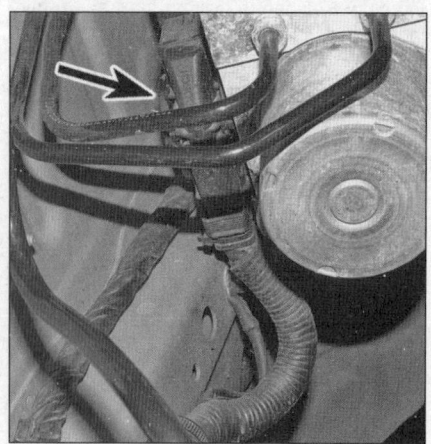

2.13 Release the wiring plug locking lever (arrowed)

2.14 Mark the location of the various brake pipes before disconnecting them from the actuator

2.15 Undo the actuator mounting nuts

Chapter 9 Brakes

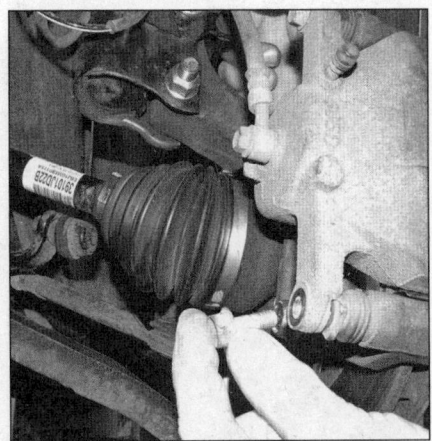

3.3 Remove the caliper lower guide pin bolt …

3.4a … then pivot the caliper upwards and away from the brake pads …

3.4b … and tie it to the suspension strut

3.6a Withdraw the inner …

3.6b … and outer brake pad from the caliper mounting bracket

3.6c Remove the lower …

Warning: *Note that the dust created by wear of the pads may contain asbestos, which is a health hazard. Never blow it out with compressed air, and don't inhale any of it. An approved filtering mask should be worn when working on the brakes. DO NOT use petrol or petroleum-based solvents to clean brake parts; use brake cleaner or methylated spirit only.*

1 Firmly apply the handbrake, loosen the front wheel nuts and then raise the front of the vehicle and support on jackstands (see Chapter 0 Section 7). Remove the front wheels.
2 Working on one side of the vehicle, push the caliper piston into its bore by pulling the caliper outwards.
3 Unscrew the caliper lower guide pin bolt (if necessary, use a slim open-ended spanner to counter-hold the head of the guide pin), then remove the bolt **(see illustration)**.
4 Pivot the caliper body upwards to expose the brake pads and secure the caliper in place **(see illustrations)**. Do not depress the brake pedal until the caliper is refitted. Take care not to strain the brake fluid hose.
5 Note the locations and orientation of the shims fitted to the rear of each pad, and the anti-rattle clips fitted to the top and bottom of the pads.
6 Lift out the brake pads and shims, followed by the anti-rattle clips **(see illustrations)**.
7 Separate the shims from the brake pads, noting that there are two shims fitted to the inboard pad **(see illustration)**.

3.6d … and upper anti-rattle shims, if required

8 First measure the thickness of each brake pad's friction material **(see illustration)**. If either pad is worn at any point to the specified minimum thickness or less, all four pads must be renewed. Also, the pads should be renewed if any are fouled with oil or grease; there is no satisfactory way of degreasing friction material, once contaminated. If any of the

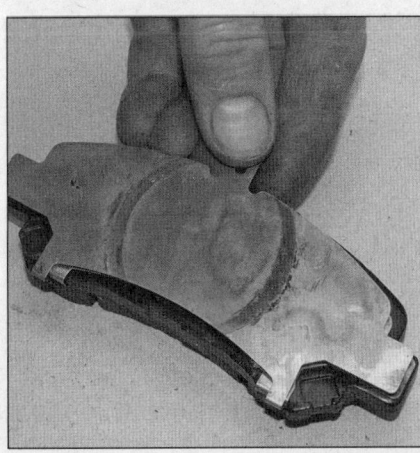

3.7 Remove the shim (where fitted) from the brake pad

3.8 Measure the thickness of the pads friction material

3.11a Check the condition of the guide pins …

3.11b … and the guide pin gaiters

3.13 Open the bleed screw and push the piston back (piston retraction tool shown)

9 If the brake pads are still serviceable, carefully clean them using a clean, fine wire brush or similar, paying particular attention to the sides and back of the metal backing. Where applicable, clean out the grooves in the friction material, and pick out any large embedded particles of dirt or debris.

10 Clean the anti-rattle clips, shims, and the brake pad locations in the caliper body/mounting bracket.

11 Prior to fitting the pads, check that the guide pins are free to slide easily in the caliper body/mounting bracket, and check that the rubber guide pin gaiters are undamaged (see illustrations).

12 Brush the dust and dirt from the caliper and piston, but do not inhale it, as it is a health hazard. Inspect the dust seal around the piston for damage, and the piston for evidence of fluid leaks, corrosion or damage. If attention to any of these components is necessary, refer to Section 1.

13 If new brake pads are to be fitted, the caliper piston must be pushed back into the cylinder, to make room for them. Either use a G-clamp or similar tool (see illustration), or use suitable pieces of wood as levers. Pro-

vided that the master cylinder reservoir has not been overfilled with hydraulic fluid, there should be no spillage, but keep a careful watch on the fluid level while retracting the piston. If the fluid level rises above the MAX level line at any time, the surplus fluid should be siphoned off or ejected via a plastic tube connected to the bleed screw.

Warning: *Do not syphon the fluid by mouth, as it is poisonous; use a syringe or an old antifreeze tester.*

14 Apply a little anti-squeal brake grease to the contact surfaces of the pad backing plates and the shims, but take great care not to allow any grease onto the pad friction linings (see illustrations). Similarly, apply brake grease to the contact surfaces of the anti-rattle clips – again take care not to apply excess grease, which may contaminate the pads.

15 Refit the anti-rattle clips to the caliper mounting bracket, and then refit the pads and shims in the positions noted before removal, ensuring that the pad friction material is against the disc (see illustrations).

16 Pivot the caliper back into position, over the pads and mounting bracket (see illustration).

brake pads are worn unevenly, or are fouled with oil or grease, trace and rectify the cause before reassembly. New brake pads and shim/clip kits are available from Nissan dealers. Do not be tempted to swap brake pads over to compensate for uneven wear.

3.14a Use the special grease to lubricate the rear of the brake pads …

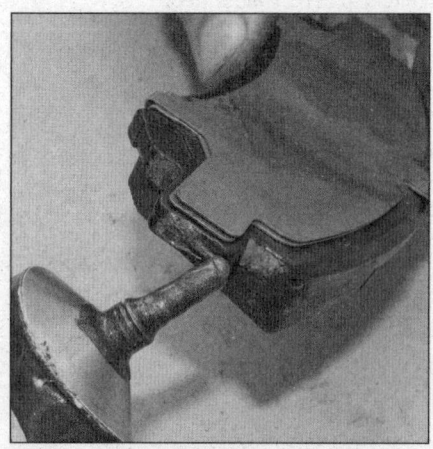

3.14b … and the ends that slide in the caliper

3.15a Ensure the shims at the top and bottom of the caliper mounting bracket are correctly fitted

Chapter 9 Brakes 9-7

3.15b Refit the inner …

3.15c … and outer brake pads

3.16 Pivot the caliper down and over the pads

4.2 Qashqai models have an electronic parking brake system - this is the inside of the rear caliper showing the wiring connector location (A) and the parking brake actuator (B). Do not attempt to replace rear brake pads on this vehicle without a scan tool capable of resetting the parking brake actuator

20 With both sets of front brake pads refitted, depress the brake pedal repeatedly until the pads are pressed into firm contact with the brake disc, and normal pedal pressure is restored.
21 Refit the road wheels, and lower the vehicle to the ground.
22 Finally, check the brake hydraulic fluid level (see Chapter 1 Section 4).
23 Note that new pads will not give full braking efficiency until they have bedded-in. Be prepared for this, and avoid hard braking as far as possible for the first hundred kilometres or so after pad renewal.

4 Rear brake pads – replacement

Warning: *Renew BOTH sets of rear brake pads at the same time – NEVER renew the pads on only one wheel, as uneven braking may result.*

Warning: *Before starting work, refer to the warning given at the beginning of Section 1, concerning the dangers of asbestos dust.*

Caution: *On models with an electronic handbrake you will need a scan tool to retract the brake pistons. Do not attempt to do this procedure unless you have a scan tool capable of performing this function.*

1 Chock the front wheels, loosen the rear wheel nuts and then raise the rear of the vehicle and support on jackstands (see Chapter 0 Section 7). Remove the rear wheels.
2 On models with an electronic parking brake, using a scan tool, go to the functions menu and select Start Brake Pad Replacement. Follow the on-screen prompts and continue with the procedure once instructed to do so by the scan tool.
3 Working on one side of the vehicle, push the caliper piston into its bore by pulling the caliper outwards.
4 Unscrew the caliper lower guide pin bolt (noting that it is also the guide pin), and then remove from the caliper **(see illustrations)**.
5 Pivot the caliper body upwards to expose the brake pads and secure the caliper in place **(see illustration)**. Do not depress the brake pedal until the caliper is refitted. Take care not to strain the brake fluid hose.
6 Note the locations and orientation of the shims fitted to the rear of each pad, and the anti-rattle clips fitted to the top and bottom of the pads.
7 Lift out the brake pads and shims, followed by the anti-rattle clips **(see illustrations)**.

17 Refit the caliper lower guide pin bolt, and then tighten it to the specified torque.
18 Check that the caliper body slides smoothly on the guide pins.
19 Repeat the procedure on the remaining front caliper.

4.3 Using a G-clamp to compress the piston into the caliper bore

4.4a Remove the caliper lower guide pin bolt (arrowed) …

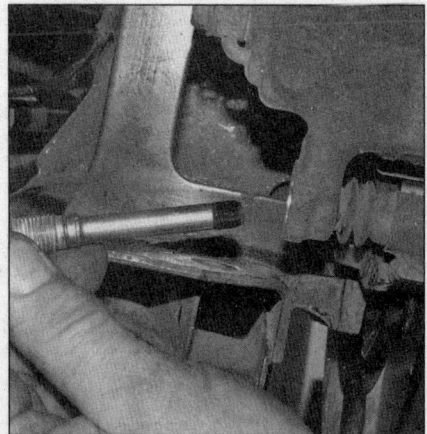

4.4b … noting that it is also the guide pin

4.5 Pivot the caliper upwards and tie it to the suspension

4.7a Withdraw the outer …

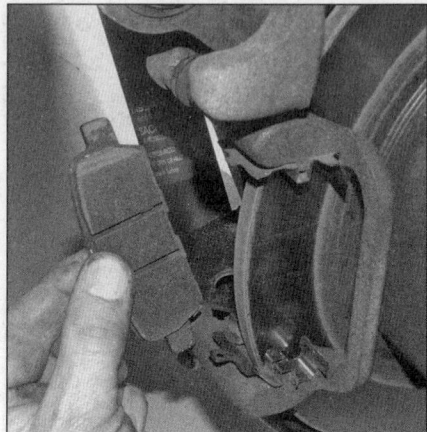

4.7b … and inner brake pad from the caliper mounting bracket

4.7c Remove the lower …

8 Separate the shims from the brake pads, noting their fitted position.
9 First measure the thickness of each brake pad's friction material **(see illustration 4.8)**. If either pad is worn at any point to the specified minimum thickness or less, all four pads must be renewed. Also, the pads should be renewed if any are fouled with oil or grease;

there is no satisfactory way of degreasing friction material, once contaminated. If any of the brake pads are worn unevenly, or are fouled with oil or grease, trace and rectify the cause before reassembly. New brake pads and shim/clip kits are available from Nissan dealers. Do not be tempted to swap brake pads over to compensate for uneven wear.
10 If the brake pads are still serviceable, carefully clean them using a clean, fine wire brush or similar, paying particular attention to the sides and back of the metal backing. Where applicable, clean out the grooves in the friction material, and pick out any large embedded particles of dirt or debris.
11 Clean the anti-rattle clips, shims, and the brake pad locations in the caliper body/mounting bracket.
12 Prior to fitting the pads, check that the rubber guide pin rubbers are undamaged **(see illustration)**.
13 Brush the dust and dirt from the caliper and piston, but do not inhale it, as it is a health hazard. Inspect the dust seal around the piston for damage, and the piston for evidence of fluid leaks, corrosion or damage (see Section 8).
14 If new brake pads are to be fitted, the caliper piston must be pushed back into the

cylinder, to make room for them. Either use a G-clamp or similar tool, on models with an electronic handbrake you must use a scan tool to retract the piston **(see illustration)**. Provided that the master cylinder reservoir has not been overfilled with hydraulic fluid, there should be no spillage, but keep a careful watch on the fluid level while retracting the piston. If the fluid level rises above the MAX level line at any time, the surplus should be siphoned off or ejected via a plastic tube connected to the bleed screw (see Section 11).
Warning: *Do not syphon the fluid by mouth, as it is poisonous; use a syringe or an old antifreeze tester.*
15 Apply a little anti-squeal brake grease to the contact surfaces of the pad backing plates and the shims, but take great care not to allow any grease onto the pad friction linings **(see illustrations 4.14a and 4.14b)**. Similarly, apply brake grease to the contact surfaces of the anti-rattle clips – again take care not to apply excess grease, which may contaminate the pads.
16 Refit the anti-rattle clips to the caliper mounting bracket, and then refit the pads and shims in the positions noted before removal, ensuring that the pad friction material is against the disc **(see illustration)**.

4.7d … and upper anti-rattle shims, if required

4.12 Check the condition of the guide pin rubbers

4.14 Open the bleed screw and push the piston back (piston retraction tool shown)

Chapter 9 Brakes

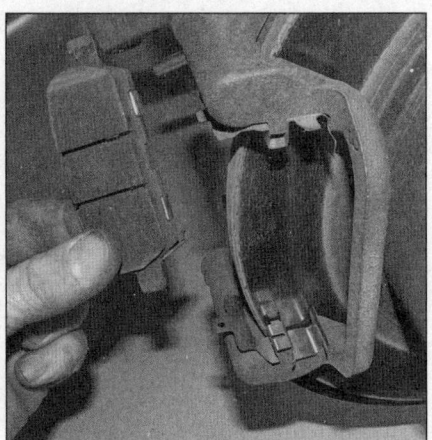

4.16 Refit the anti-rattle shims and the brake pads

4.17 Pivot the caliper down and over the pads

5.3 Checking the thickness of the brake disc with a micrometer

17   Pivot the caliper back into position, over the pads and mounting bracket (see illustration).
18   Refit the caliper lower guide pin bolt, and then tighten it to the specified torque (see Specifications).
19   Check that the caliper body slides smoothly on the guide pins.
20   Repeat the procedure on the remaining front caliper.
21   With both sets of front and rear brake pads refitted, depress the brake pedal repeatedly until the pads are pressed into firm contact with the brake disc, and normal pedal pressure is restored.
22   Refit the wheels, and lower the vehicle to the ground. Tighten the wheel nuts to the specified torque (see Chapter 1).
23   Finally, check the brake hydraulic fluid level (see Chapter 1 Section 4).

Note: *New pads will not give full braking efficiency until they have bedded-in. Be prepared for this, and avoid hard braking as far as possible for the first 30 to 40 kms or so after pad renewal.*

5 Front brake disc – inspection, removal and refitting

Warning: *Before starting work, refer to the warning at the beginning of Section 1 concerning the dangers of asbestos dust.*

Note: If *either disc requires renewal, BOTH should be renewed at the same time, to ensure even and consistent braking. New brake pads should also be fitted.*

Inspection

1   Firmly apply the handbrake, loosen the front wheel nuts and then raise the front of the vehicle and support on jackstands (see Chapter 0 Section 7). Remove the front wheels.
2   Slowly rotate the brake disc so that the full area of both sides can be checked; remove the brake pads (see Section 3), if better access is required to the inboard surface. Light scoring is normal in the area swept by the brake pads, but if heavy scoring or cracks are found, the disc must be renewed.
3   It is normal to find a lip of rust and brake dust around the disc's perimeter; this can be scraped off if required. If, however, a lip has formed due to excessive wear of the brake pad swept area, then the disc's thickness must be measured using a micrometer (see illustration). Take measurements at several places around the disc, at the inside and outside of the pad swept area; if the disc has worn at any point to the specified minimum thickness or less, the disc must be renewed.
4   If the disc is thought to be warped, it can be checked for run-out. Either use a dial gauge mounted on any convenient fixed point, while the disc is slowly rotated (see illustrations), or use feeler blades to measure (at several points all around the disc) the clearance between the disc and a fixed point, such as the caliper mounting bracket. If the measurements obtained are at the specified maximum or beyond, the disc is excessively warped, and must be renewed; however, it is worth checking first that the hub bearing is in good condition (see Chapter 10 Section 8). Also try the effect of removing the disc and turning it through 180°, to reposition it on the hub; if the run-out is still excessive, the disc must be renewed.
5   Check the disc for cracks, especially around the wheel stud holes, and any other wear or damage, and renew if necessary.

5.4a Secure the disc with washer and wheel nuts ...

5.4b ... then check the run out of the disc with a DTI gauge

5.7a Slacken the two caliper mounting bracket bolts (arrowed) ...

5.7b ... and withdraw the assembly from over the brake disc

5.8 Remove the brake disc from the hub

6.5a Slacken the two caliper mounting bracket bolts (arrowed) ...

Removal

6 If not already done, loosen the front wheel nuts and then raise the front of the vehicle and support on jackstands (see Chapter 0 Section 7). Remove the front wheels.

7 Unscrew the two bolts securing the caliper mounting bracket to the hub carrier (see illustrations). Withdraw the caliper assembly, and suspend it using wire or string. Take care not to strain the brake fluid hose – if necessary release the hose from the securing clip(s).

8 If the original disc is to be refitted, mark the relationship between the disc and the hub, then pull the disc from the road wheel studs (see illustration).

Refitting

9 Ensure that the mating faces of the disc and the hub are clean and flat. If necessary, wipe the mating surfaces clean.

10 If the original disc is being refitted, align the marks made on the disc and hub before removal, then refit the disc.

11 If a new disc has been fitted, use a suitable solvent to wipe any preservative coating from the disc.

12 Refit the caliper, ensuring that the pads locate correctly over the disc. Then tighten the caliper mounting bracket securing bolts to the specified torque. Where applicable, refit the brake fluid hose to the clip(s).

13 Depress the brake pedal repeatedly until the pads are pressed into firm contact with the brake disc, and normal pedal height is restored.

14 Repeat the above procedure on the remaining brake, if a new disc was fitted.

15 Refit the wheel, and lower the vehicle to the ground. Tighten the wheel nuts to the specified torque (see Chapter 1).

6 Rear brake disc – inspection, removal and refitting

Warning: *Before starting work, refer to the warning at the beginning of Section 1 concerning the dangers of asbestos dust.*

Note: *If either disc requires renewal, BOTH should be renewed at the same time, to ensure even and consistent braking. New brake pads should also be fitted.*

Inspection

1 Chock the front wheels, loosen the rear wheel nuts and then raise the rear of the vehicle and support on jackstands (see Chapter 0 Section 7). Remove the rear wheels.

2 Fully release the handbrake.

3 Inspect as described for the front disc in Section 5.

Removal

4 If not already done, chock the front wheels, loosen the rear wheel nuts and then raise the rear of the vehicle and support on jackstands (see Chapter 0 Section 7). Remove the rear wheels and release the handbrake.

5 Unscrew the two bolts securing the caliper mounting bracket to the hub carrier (see illustrations). Withdraw the caliper assembly, and suspend it using wire or string. Take care not to strain the brake fluid hose – if necessary release the hose from the securing clip(s).

6 If the original disc is to be refitted, mark the relationship between the disc and the hub, then pull the disc from the road wheel studs (see illustration).

7 If the disc cannot be withdrawn easily, it may be necessary to slacken the adjuster on the handbrake shoes inside the centre of the brake disc. Remove the grommet in the

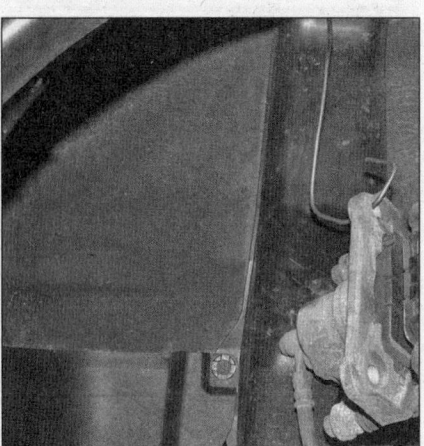

6.5b ... and support the caliper, so as not to strain the brake hose

6.6 Remove the brake disc from the hub

6.7a Remove the rubber grommet ...

Chapter 9 Brakes

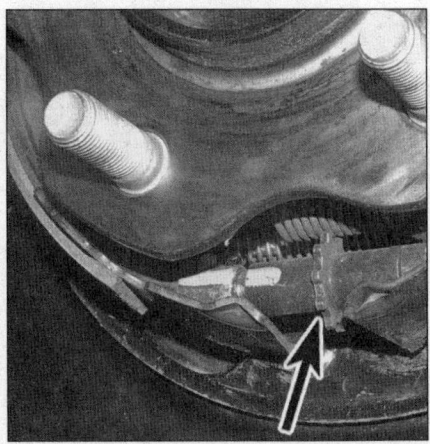

6.7b ... and slacken the adjuster wheel (arrowed)

7.2 Using a clamp to stop the flow of brake fluid from the master cylinder once the brake hose is uncoupled from the brake caliper - doing this limits the amount of air being drawn into the brake hydraulic system

7.3 Unscrew the brake hose union bolt (arrowed)

centre of the brake disc, and then slacken the handbrake shoe adjuster **(see illustrations)**. Remove brake disc from over the handbrake shoes.

Refitting

8 Ensure that the mating faces of the disc and the hub are clean and flat. If necessary, wipe the mating surfaces clean.
9 If the original disc is being refitted, align the marks made on the disc and hub before removal, then refit the disc.
10 If a new disc has been fitted, use a suitable solvent to wipe any preservative coating from the disc.
11 Refit the caliper, ensuring that the pads locate correctly over the disc. Then tighten the caliper mounting bracket securing bolts to the specified torque. Where applicable, refit the brake fluid hose to the clip(s).
12 Depress the brake pedal repeatedly until the pads are pressed into firm contact with the brake disc, and normal pedal height is restored.
13 Repeat the above procedure on the remaining brake, if a new disc was fitted.
14 Check and adjust the handbrake cable (see Section 13).

15 Refit the wheel, and lower the vehicle to the ground. Tighten the wheel nuts to the specified torque (see Chapter 1).

7 Front brake caliper – removal and refitting

Warning: *Before starting work, refer to the note concerning the dangers of hydraulic fluid, and to the warning concerning the dangers of asbestos dust at the start of Section 1.*

Note: *If caliper replacement is indicated (usually because of fluid leaks, a stuck piston or broken bleeder screw) explore your options. New and factory rebuilt calipers are available on an exchange basis.*

Removal

1 Firmly apply the handbrake, loosen the front wheel nuts and then raise the front of the vehicle and support on jackstands (see Chap-

ter 0 Section 7). Remove the front wheels.
2 To minimise fluid loss during the following operations, remove the master cylinder reservoir cap, then tighten it down onto a piece of polythene to obtain an airtight seal. Alternatively, use a brake hose clamp, a G-clamp or a similar tool to clamp the flexible hose running to the caliper **(see illustration)**.
3 Clean the area around the fluid hose union on the caliper, and then unscrew the hose union banjo bolt **(see illustration)**. Recover the two sealing washers noting that new washers will be required for refitting. Cover the open ends of the banjo and the caliper, to prevent dirt ingress.
4 Remove the brake pads (see Section 3).
5 Unscrew the caliper upper guide pin bolt. If necessary, use a slim open-ended spanner to counter hold the head of the guide pin.
6 Withdraw the caliper from the mounting bracket **(see illustration)**.
7 If desired, the caliper mounting bracket can be unbolted from the hub carrier **(see illustration)**.

Refitting

8 Where applicable, refit the caliper mounting bracket to the hub carrier, and tighten the mounting bolts to the specified torque.
9 Place the caliper in position, refit the upper guide pin bolt, and tighten it to the specified torque.
10 Refit the brake pads (see Section 3).
11 Check that the caliper slides smoothly on the mounting bracket.
12 Check that the hydraulic fluid hose is correctly routed, without being twisted, and then reconnect the union to the caliper, using two new sealing washers. Refit the union banjo bolt, and tighten to the specified torque.
13 Remove the polythene from the master cylinder reservoir cap, or remove the clamp from the fluid hose, as applicable.
14 Bleed the hydraulic fluid circuit (see Section 11). Note that if no other part of the system has been disturbed, it should only be necessary to bleed the relevant front circuit.

7.6 Undo the upper bolt and withdraw the brake caliper

7.7 Caliper mounting bracket bolts (arrowed)

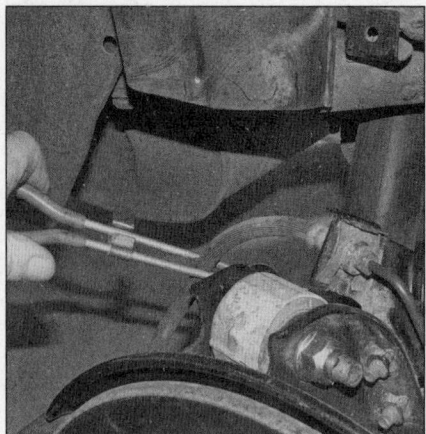

8.2 Using a clamp to stop the flow of brake fluid from the master cylinder once the brake hose is uncoupled from the brake caliper - doing this limits the amount of air being drawn into the brake hydraulic system

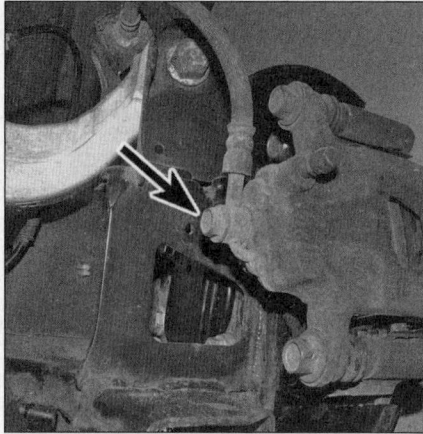

8.3 Unscrew the brake hose union bolt (arrowed)

8.5 Lift up the caliper and withdraw the upper guide bolt from the mounting bracket

15 Depress the brake pedal repeatedly to bring the pads into contact with the brake disc, and ensure that normal pedal pressure is restored.

16 Refit the wheel, and lower the vehicle to the ground. Tighten the wheel nuts to the specified torque (see Chapter 1).

8 Rear brake caliper – removal and refitting

Warning: *Before starting work, refer to the note concerning the dangers of hydraulic fluid, and to the warning concerning the dangers of asbestos dust at the start of Section 1.*

Note: *If caliper replacement is indicated (usually because of fluid leaks, a stuck piston or broken bleeder screw) explore your options. New and factory rebuilt calipers are available on an exchange basis. Models with electric handbrakes are also supplied as a sealed unit with no overhaul parts available.*

Caution: *On models with an electronic handbrake you will need a scan tool to retract the brake pistons. Do not attempt to do this procedure unless you have a scan tool capable of performing this function.*

Removal

1 Chock the front wheels, loosen the rear wheel nuts and then raise the rear of the vehicle and support on jackstands (see Chapter 0 Section 7). Remove the rear wheels.

2 To minimise fluid loss during the following operations, remove the master cylinder reservoir cap, then tighten it down onto a piece of polythene to obtain an airtight seal. Alternatively, use a brake hose clamp, a G-clamp or a similar tool to clamp the flexible hose running to the caliper **(see illustration)**.

3 Clean the area around the fluid hose union on the caliper, and then unscrew the hose union banjo bolt **(see illustration)**. Recover the two sealing washers noting that new washers will be required for refitting. Cover the open ends of the banjo and the caliper, to prevent dirt ingress.

4 Remove the brake pads (see Section 4).

5 Lift the caliper and then slide the upper guide pin bolt from the mounting bracket. If necessary unscrew the upper guide pin bolt from the caliper **(see illustration)**.

6 On models with an electronic handbrake you will need to disconnect the rear actuator plug on the caliper, withdraw the caliper from the mounting bracket.

7 If desired, the caliper mounting bracket can be unbolted from the hub carrier **(see illustrations)**.

Refitting

8 Where applicable, refit the caliper mounting bracket to the hub carrier, and tighten the mounting bolts to the.

9 Place the caliper in position, refit the caliper upper guide pin bolt and tighten it to the specified torque (see Specifications).

10 Refit the brake pads (see Section 4).

11 Check that the caliper slides smoothly on the mounting bracket.

12 Check that the brake fluid hose is correctly routed, without being twisted, and then reconnect the union to the caliper **(see illustration)**. Refit the union banjo bolt, using two new sealing washers, and then tighten to the specified torque (see Specifications).

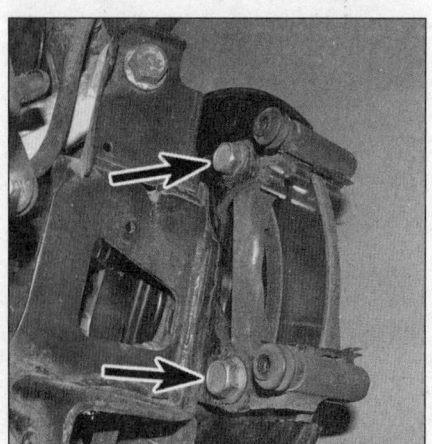

8.7a Undo the caliper mounting bracket bolts (arrowed) ...

8.7b ... and withdraw it from the brake disc

8.12 Make sure the brake hose is located correctly on the caliper

Chapter 9 Brakes

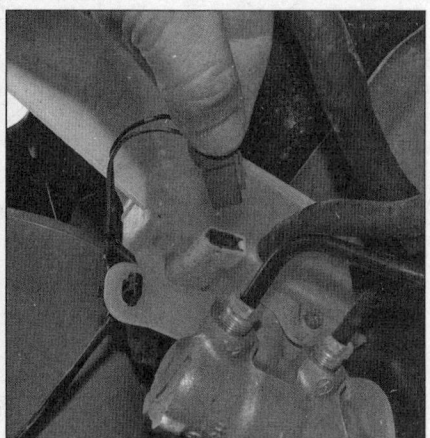

9.3 Disconnect the level sensor wiring plug

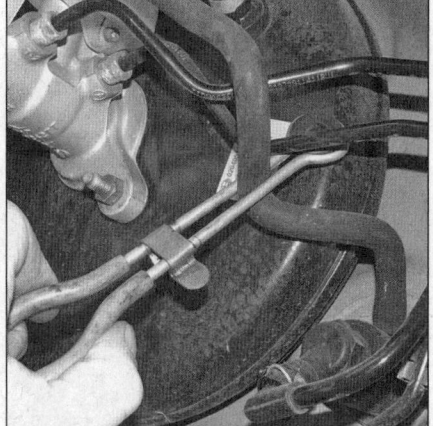

9.4a Fit a brake hose clamp to the clutch supply hose ...

9.4b ... and then disconnect the hose from the reservoir (arrowed)

13 Remove the polythene from the master cylinder reservoir cap, or remove the clamp from the fluid hose, as applicable.
14 Bleed the hydraulic fluid circuit. Note that if no other part of the system has been disturbed, it should only be necessary to bleed the relevant rear circuit (see Section 11).
15 Depress the brake pedal repeatedly to bring the pads into contact with the brake disc, and ensure that normal pedal pressure is restored.
16 Refit the wheel, and lower the vehicle to the ground. Tighten the wheel nuts to the specified torque (see Chapter 1).

9 Master cylinder – removal and refitting

Caution: *Make sure the ignition switch is in the OFF position before disconnecting any braking system hydraulic union and do not switch it on until after the hydraulic system has been bled. Failure to do this could lead to air entering the ABS modulator unit. If air enters the modulator pump, it will prove very difficult to bleed the unit.*

Note: *Before starting work, refer to the warnings concerning the dangers of hydraulic fluid at the start of Section 1.*

Removal

1 Disconnect the negative (-) battery terminal (see Chapter 5 Section 3).
2 Remove the master cylinder fluid reservoir cap, and syphon the hydraulic fluid from the reservoir. Alternatively, open two bleed screws in the system (one in each of the dual circuit), and gently pump the brake pedal to expel the fluid through a tube connected to the bleed screws

Warning: *Do not syphon the fluid by mouth, as it is poisonous; use a syringe or an old antifreeze tester.*

3 Disconnect the wiring connector from the brake fluid level sender unit on the side of the reservoir **(see illustration)**. Unclip the wiring loom retaining clip from the lower front part of the reservoir.
4 On models with manual transmission, use a brake hose clamp, a G-clamp or a similar tool, to clamp the supply hose to the clutch master cylinder, and then disconnect the hose from the reservoir **(see illustrations)**.
5 Wipe clean the area around the brake pipe unions on the side of the master cylinder, and place absorbent rags beneath the pipe unions to catch any surplus fluid. Make a note of the correct fitted positions of the unions, then unscrew the union nuts and carefully withdraw the pipes **(see illustration)**. Plug or tape over the pipe ends and master cylinder orifices, to minimise the loss of brake fluid, and to prevent the entry of dirt into the system. Wash off any spilt fluid immediately with cold water.
6 Slacken and remove the two nuts securing the master cylinder to the vacuum servo unit **(see illustration)**, and then withdraw the master cylinder complete with reservoir from the engine compartment.
7 If required, undo the retaining screw at the lower part of the reservoir **(see illustration)**, and then pull the reservoir upwards to release it from the master cylinder.

Refitting

8 Remove all traces of dirt from the master cylinder and servo unit mating surfaces.
9 If removed, refit the reservoir to the top of the master cylinder making sure the rubber seals are fitted correctly, and tighten the reservoir retaining screw.

9.5 Slacken the brake fluid pipes (arrowed)

9.6 Master cylinder securing nuts (arrowed)

9.7 Reservoir securing screw (arrowed)

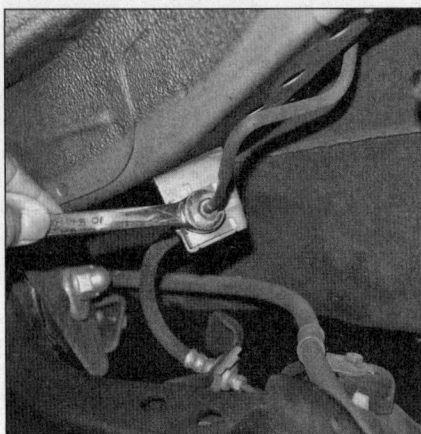

10.3a If you're removing a hose, loosen the threaded fitting on the brake line (use a pipe spanner to protect the corners of the nut)...

10.3b... then remove the u-clip

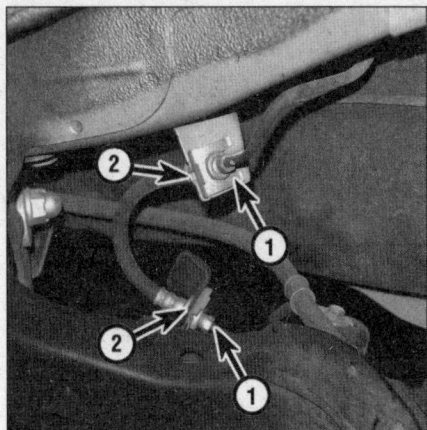

10.3c Rear brake hose details

1 Brake line fittings
2 U-clips

10 Fit the master cylinder to the servo unit, ensuring that the servo unit pushrod enters the master cylinder bore centrally. Refit the master cylinder mounting nuts, and tighten them to the specified torque.

11 Place absorbent rags around and beneath the master cylinder, and then fill the reservoir with fresh hydraulic fluid.

12 Have an assistant slowly depress the brake pedal fully, and then hold it in the fully depressed position. Cover the outlet ports on the master cylinder body with your fingers then have the assistant slowly release the brake pedal. Continue this procedure until the fluid emerging from the master cylinder is free from air bubbles. Take care to collect the expelled fluid in the rags and wash off any spilt fluid immediately with cold water.

13 When all air has been bled from the master cylinder, wipe clean the brake pipe unions, then refit them to the correct master cylinder ports, as noted before removal, and tighten the union nuts securely.

14 On manual transmission models, refit the clutch supply hose to the reservoir and remove the hose clamp. There should be no need to bleed the clutch system, but if required the clutch can be bled (see Chapter 8 Section 2).

15 Reconnect the wiring connector to the brake fluid level sender unit on the side of the reservoir, clip the wiring loom retaining clip back into position.

16 On completion, bleed the complete hydraulic system (see Section 11).

10 Brake hoses and lines - inspection and replacement

Inspection

1 About every six months, with the vehicle raised and supported securely on jackstands, the flexible hoses which connect the steel brake lines with the front and rear brake assemblies should be inspected for cracks, chafing of the outer cover, leaks, blisters and other damage. These are important and vulnerable parts of the brake system and inspection should be complete. A light and mirror will be helpful for a thorough check. If a hose exhibits any of the above conditions, replace it with a new one.

Replacement

Brake hoses

2 Loosen the wheel nuts, raise the vehicle and support it securely on jackstands. Remove the wheel.

Note: *If you're replacing a rear brake hose, it isn't necessary to remove the wheels.*

3 At the bracket, unscrew the brake line fitting from the hose **(see illustration)**. Use a pipe spanner to prevent rounding off the corners.

4 Remove the U-clip from the female fitting at the bracket with a pair of pliers, then pass the hose through the bracket.

5 At the caliper end of the hose, remove the banjo bolt **(see illustration 8.3)**, then separate the hose from the caliper. Note that there are two sealing washers on either side of the banjo fitting - they should be replaced with new ones during installation.

6 If you're replacing a front brake hose, remove the U-clip from the strut bracket, then detach the hose from the bracket.

7 To install the hose, pass the caliper fitting end through the strut bracket (front hose only), then connect the fitting to the caliper with the banjo bolt and new sealing washers.

8 Make sure the hose isn't twisted between the caliper and the strut bracket (or the chassis on rear brake hoses).

9 Route the hose into the frame bracket, again making sure it isn't twisted, then connect the brake line fitting, starting the threads by hand. Install the U-clip, then tighten the fitting securely.

10 Bleed the caliper (see Section 11).

11 Install the wheel and wheel nuts, lower the vehicle and tighten the wheel nuts to the specified torque (see Chapter 1).

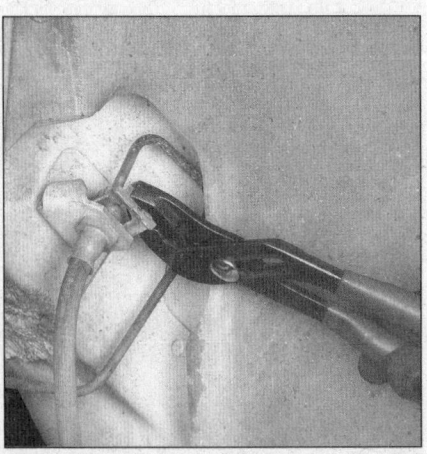

10.6a Using multi-grip pliers to remove the brake pipe fitting clip

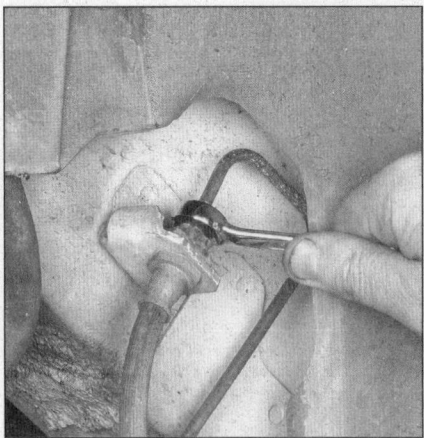

10.6b Using a pipe spanner to loosen the brake pipe fitting

Metal brake lines

12 When replacing brake lines, be sure to use the correct parts. Don't use copper tubing for any brake system components. Purchase steel brake lines from a dealer or auto parts store.
13 Prefabricated brake line, with the tube ends already flared and fittings installed, is available at auto parts stores and dealer parts departments.
14 When installing the new line, make sure it's securely supported in the brackets and has plenty of clearance between moving or hot components.
15 After installation, check the master cylinder fluid level and add fluid as necessary. Bleed the brake system and test the brakes carefully before driving the vehicle in traffic.

11 Brake hydraulic system – bleeding and replacing brake fluid

Warning: *Brake hydraulic fluid is poisonous; wash off immediately and thoroughly in the case of skin contact, and seek immediate medical advice if any fluid is swallowed, or gets into the eyes. Hydraulic fluid is flammable, and may ignite when allowed into contact with hot components. When servicing any hydraulic system, take precautions against the risk of fire. Hydraulic fluid is also an effective paint stripper, and will attack plastics; if any is spilt, it should be washed off immediately, using copious quantities of fresh water. Finally, it is hygroscopic (it absorbs moisture from the air) – old fluid may be contaminated and unfit for further use. When topping-up or renewing the fluid, always use the recommended type, and ensure that it comes from a freshly opened sealed container.*

General

1 The correct operation of any hydraulic system is only possible after removing all air from the components and circuit; and this is achieved by bleeding the system.
2 During the bleeding procedure, add only clean, unused brake hydraulic fluid of the recommended type; never re-use fluid that has already been bled from the system. Ensure that sufficient fluid is available before starting work.
3 If there is any possibility of incorrect fluid being already in the system, the brake components and circuit must be flushed completely with uncontaminated, correct fluid, and new seals should be fitted throughout the system.
4 If hydraulic fluid has been lost from the system, or air has entered because of a leak, ensure that the fault is cured before proceeding further.
5 Park the vehicle on level ground, switch off the engine and select first or reverse gear (or P), then chock the wheels and release the handbrake.

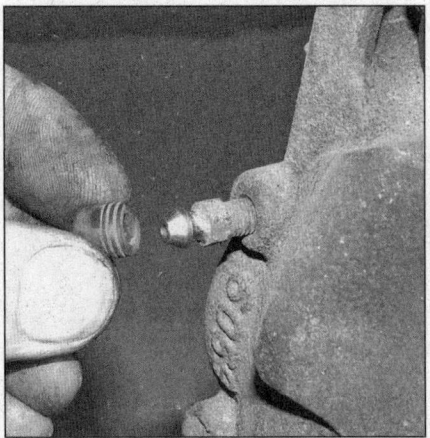

11.16a Remove the dust cap

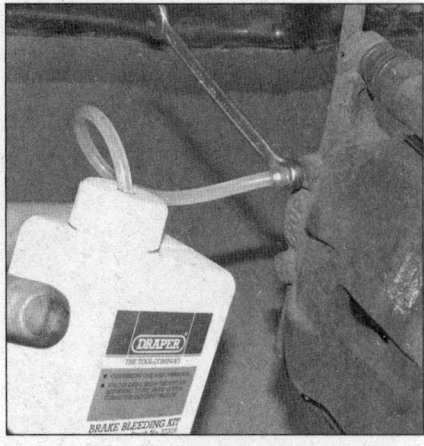

11.16b Connect the bleed kit to the bleed screw

6 Check that all pipes and hoses are secure, unions tight and bleed screws closed. Remove the dust caps (where applicable), and clean any dirt from around the bleed screws.
7 Unscrew the master cylinder reservoir cap, and top the master cylinder reservoir up to the MAX level line; refit the cap loosely. Remember to maintain the fluid level at least above the MIN level line throughout the procedure; otherwise there is a risk of further air entering the system.
8 There is a number of one-man, do-it-yourself brake bleeding kits currently available from motor accessory shops. It is recommended that one of these kits is used whenever possible, as they greatly simplify the bleeding operation, and also reduce the risk of expelled air and fluid being drawn back into the system. If such a kit is not available, the basic (two-man) method must be used, which is described in detail below.
9 If a kit is to be used, prepare the vehicle as described previously, and follow the kit manufacturer's instructions, as the procedure may vary slightly according to the type being used; generally, they are as outlined below in the relevant sub-section.
10 Whichever method is used, the same sequence must be followed (paragraphs 11 and 12) to ensure that the removal of all air from the system.

Bleeding sequence

11 If the system has been only partially disconnected, and suitable precautions were taken to minimise fluid loss, it should be necessary to bleed only that part of the system (i.e. the primary or secondary circuit).
12 If the complete system is to be bled, then it should be done working in the following sequence:
13 X-Trail T31 and Dualis
  a Left-hand rear wheel.
  b Right-hand rear wheel.
  c Left-hand front wheel.
  d Right-hand front wheel.

14 X-Trail T32 and Qashqai
  a Right-hand rear wheel.
  b Left-hand front wheel.
  c Left-hand rear wheel.
  d Right-hand front wheel.

Bleeding

Caution: *On models equipped with ABS, switch off the ignition and disconnect the battery negative terminal Chapter 5 Section 3, before carrying out the bleeding procedure.*

Basic (two-man) method

15 Collect a clean glass jar, a suitable length of plastic or rubber tubing which is a tight fit over the bleed screw, and a ring spanner to fit the screw. The help of an assistant will also be required.
16 Remove the dust cap from the first screw in the sequence. Fit a suitable spanner and tube to the screw, place the other end of the tube in the jar, and pour in sufficient fluid to cover the end of the tube **(see illustrations)**.
17 Ensure that the master cylinder reservoir fluid level is maintained at least above the MIN level line throughout the procedure.
18 Have the assistant fully depress the brake pedal several times to build-up pressure, and then maintain it on the final down stroke.
19 While pedal pressure is maintained, unscrew the bleed screw (approximately one turn) and allow the compressed fluid and air to flow into the jar. The assistant should maintain pedal pressure, following the pedal down to the floor if necessary, and should not release the pedal until instructed to do so. When the flow stops, tighten the bleed screw again, have the assistant release the pedal slowly, and recheck the reservoir fluid level.
20 Repeat the steps given in paragraphs 16 and 17 until the fluid emerging from the bleed screw is free from air bubbles. If the master cylinder has been drained and refilled, and air is being bled from the first screw in the sequence, allow approximately five seconds between cycles for the master cylinder passages to refill.

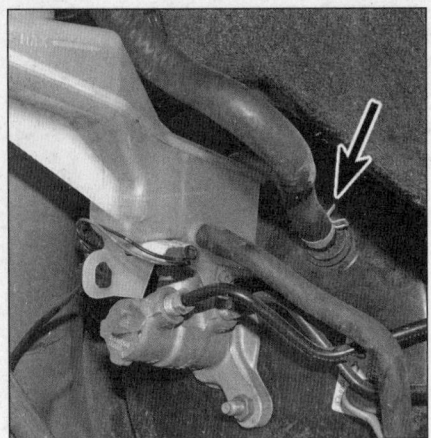

12.3 Disconnect the vacuum hose (arrowed) from the brake booster

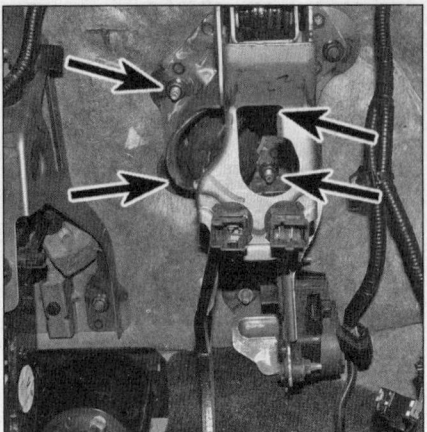

12.6 Undo the four brake booster mounting nuts (arrowed)

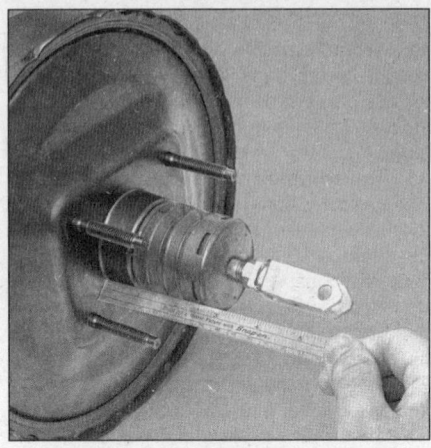

12.8a Measure the distance between the power brake booster and the hole in the clevis and compare your measurement to the dimension listed in the chapter's specifications; if necessary, adjust the clevis before installing the booster

21 When no more air bubbles appear, tighten the bleed screw securely, remove the tube and spanner, and refit the dust cap. Do not over tighten the bleed screw.
22 Repeat the procedure on the remaining screws in the sequence, until all air is removed from the system, and the brake pedal feels firm again.

Using a one-way valve kit

23 As their name implies, these kits consist of a length of tubing with a one-way valve fitted, to prevent expelled air and fluid being drawn back into the system; some kits include a translucent container, which can be positioned so that the air bubbles can be more easily seen flowing from the end of the tube.
24 The kit is connected to the bleed screw, which is then opened. The user returns to the driver's seat, depresses the brake pedal with a smooth, steady stroke, and slowly releases it; this is repeated until the expelled fluid is clear of air bubbles.
25 Note that these kits simplify work so much that it is easy to forget the master cylinder reservoir fluid level; ensure that this is maintained at least above the MIN level line at all times.

Using a pressure-bleeding kit

26 These kits are usually operated by the reservoir of pressurised air contained in the spare tyre. However, note that it will probably be necessary to reduce the pressure to a lower level than normal; refer to the instructions supplied with the kit.
27 By connecting a pressurised, fluid-filled container to the master cylinder reservoir, bleeding can be carried out simply by opening each screw in turn (in the specified sequence), and allowing the fluid to flow out until no more air bubbles can be seen in the expelled fluid.
28 This method has the advantage that the large reservoir of fluid provides an additional safeguard against air being drawn into the system during bleeding.
29 Pressure-bleeding is particularly effective when bleeding 'difficult' systems, or when bleeding the complete system at the time of routine fluid renewal.

All methods

30 When bleeding is complete, and firm pedal feel is restored, wash off any spilt fluid, tighten the bleed screws securely, and refit their dust caps.
31 Check the hydraulic fluid level in the master cylinder reservoir, and top up if necessary.
32 Discard any hydraulic fluid that has been bled from the system; it will not be fit for re-use.
33 Check the feel of the brake pedal. If it feels at all spongy, air must still be present in the system, and further bleeding is required. Failure to bleed satisfactorily after a reasonable repetition of the bleeding procedure may be due to worn master cylinder seals.

12 Brake booster - check, replacement and adjustment

Removal

1 Disconnect the negative (-) battery terminal (see Chapter 5 Section 3).
2 Remove the brake master cylinder (see Section 9).
3 Disconnect the vacuum hose from the brake booster **(see illustration)**.
4 Remove the driver's side lower dashboard trim panel (see Chapter 11 Section 21).
5 Working in the driver's footwell, remove the spring clip from the end of the brake booster pushrod clevis pin, and then withdraw the clevis pin **(see illustrations 12.2a, 12.2b and 12.2c)**.
6 Unscrew the four nuts securing the brake pedal mounting bracket to the brake booster studs **(see illustration)**.
7 Working in the engine compartment, withdraw the brake booster.

Installation

8 Installation is a reversal of removal, bearing in mind the following points:
   a Before installing the brake booster, check that the pushrod length is within Specifications (see Specifications), adjust if necessary by loosening the locknut and turning the pushrod **(see illustration)**.
   b Where applicable, tighten all fixings to the specified torque (see Specifications).
   c Refit the master cylinder (see Section 9).
   d On completion, check the brake pedal height (see Section 16).

13 Parking brake - check and adjustment

Check

1 The parking brake, when properly adjusted, should travel the specified number of clicks when a 20 kg force is applied (see Specifications).
2 If the parking brake travels less than the specified minimum number of clicks, it might not be releasing completely and the shoes could even be dragging against the drum. If it moves more than the specified maximum number of clicks, the parking brake may not hold adequately on an incline, allowing the car to roll.

Adjustment

3 If the number of clicks required to fully apply the park brake is not as specified, proceed as follows.
4 Working inside the vehicle, unclip the cup holder from the centre console (see Chapter 11 Section 22) or models with foot park brake remove the lower dash panel (see Chapter 11 Section 21).
5 The park brake adjuster nut is located

13.4 Unclip the cup holder from the centre console

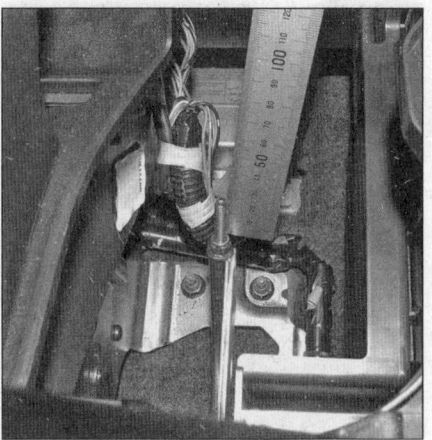

13.5 Measure the length of thread, before slackening the adjusting nut

13.7a Remove the rubber grommet ...

13.7b ... and turn the adjuster ...

under the cup holder on the threaded end of the front cable, on foot park brake it is just above the pedal (see Section 14). Measure the length of thread, protruding through the nut, as a guide for refitting **(see illustration)**. Slacken the adjuster nut until it is at the end of the threaded part of the cable.

6 If not already done, chock the front wheels, loosen the rear wheel nuts and then raise the rear of the vehicle and support on jackstands (see Chapter 0 Section 7). Remove the rear wheels.

7 Working on each side at a time, adjust the shoe positions as follows. Turn the rear disc until the access hole is positioned over the adjuster serrations. Using a screwdriver through the hole in the brake disc, tighten the adjuster until the brake disc cannot be rotated, then back the adjuster off, so that the brake disc is free to turn without any drag **(see illustrations)**. Repeat the adjustment on the other side of the vehicle, and then refit the plug to the access holes in the brake disc.

8 Working inside the vehicle, tighten the adjuster nut on the end of the front parking brake cable, until the handbrake operates correctly at approximately 7 to 8 clicks.

9 When tightening the adjuster nut on the end of the front cable, make sure the two rear cables are still located in the equalizer bar, under the rear end of the centre console **(see illustration)**.

10 Check that the parking brake 'on' warning light illuminates after the first click.

11 Refit the cup holder to the centre console or under dashboard trim panel and check the parking brake operation.

12 If this adjustment cannot be achieved, remove the handbrake shoes (see Section 15) and cables and check their condition (see Section 14).

13 On completion, refit the road wheels, and then lower the vehicle to the ground. Tighten the wheels to the specified torque (see Chapter 1).

Removal of parking brake assembly

14 Disconnect the negative (-) battery terminal (see Chapter 5 Section 3).

15 On models with foot parking brake, remove the drivers side lower dash panel (see Chapter 11 Section 21).

16 On all other models, remove the centre console (see Chapter 11 Section 22).

17 Chock the wheels, and fully release the parking brake.

18 Disconnect the wiring plug from the parking brake 'on' warning light switch **(see illustration)**.

19 Measure the number of exposed threads on the front cable adjuster (for reference when refitting), then unscrew the adjuster nut to the end of the threads **(see illustrations)**.

20 Disconnect the two rear parking brake cables from the equalizer bracket at the rear of the parking brake assembly **(see illustration)**.

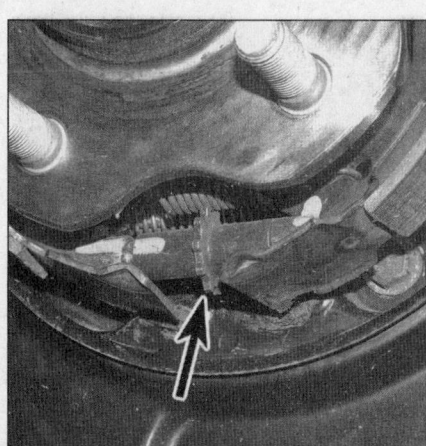

13.7c ... between the lower part of the brake shoes

13.9 Make sure the cables are still connected (arrowed)

13.18 Disconnect the switch wiring connector

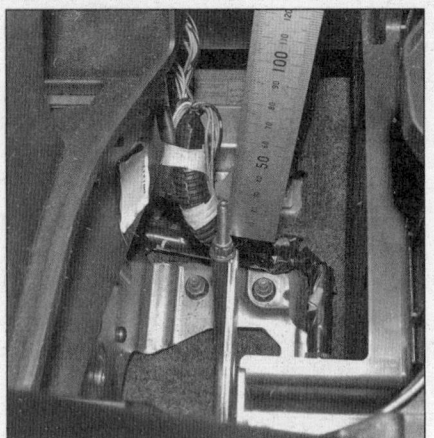

13.19a Measure the amount of threads ...

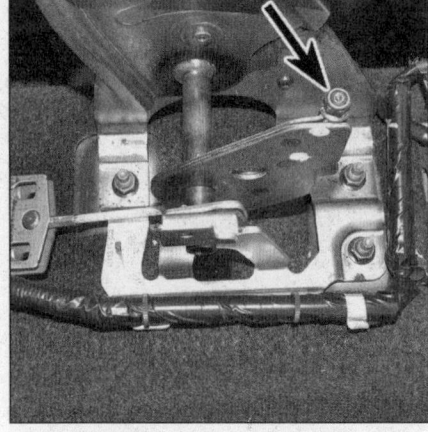

13.19b ... then slacken the adjuster nut to the end of the threads

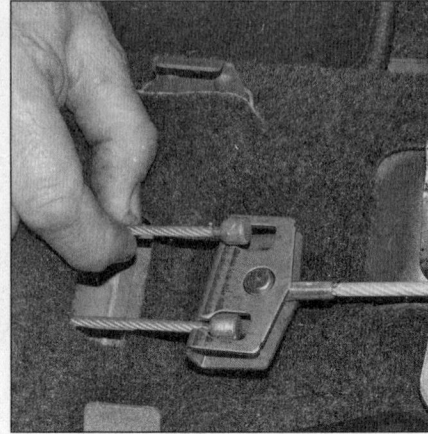

13.20 Disengage the cable end fittings from the equaliser plate

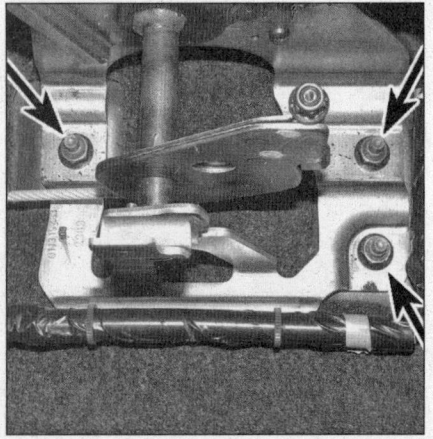

13.21 Undo the parking brake assembly mounting nuts

21 Remove the three securing nuts, and withdraw the parking brake assembly from the floor panel **(see illustration)**.

Installation

22 Installation is a reversal of removal, bearing in mind the following points:
23 Screw the adjuster nut onto the front cable to give the measurement noted before removal, then check the parking brake operation, and adjust if necessary.
24 Before refitting the centre console, check the operation of the parking brake 'on' warning light.

14 Parking brake cables – removal and Installation

Rear cables
Removal

1 There are two rear handbrake cables, one on each side of the vehicle. To renew either rear cable, proceed as follows.
2 Chock the front wheels, loosen the rear wheel nuts and then raise the rear of the vehicle and support on jackstands (see Chapter 0 Section 7). Remove the rear wheels.
3 Remove the parking brake shoes (see Section 15).
4 Unclip the parking brake cable spring, undo the retaining bolt and withdraw the parking brake cable from the brake back plate **(see illustrations)**.
5 Undo the retaining bolts and disconnect the parking brake cable securing clips from the top of the rear trailing arms and underbody of the vehicle **(see illustrations)**.
6 Working inside the vehicle, remove the cup holder/trim from the top of the centre console **(see illustrations)** on models with a foot parking brake you will have to remove the centre console (see Chapter 11 Section 22).

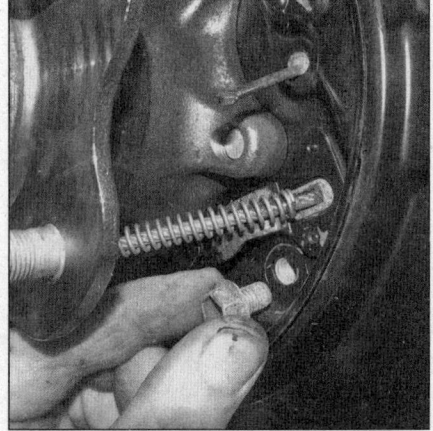

14.4a Undo the parking brake cable securing nut ...

14.4b ... and withdraw the cable from the back plate

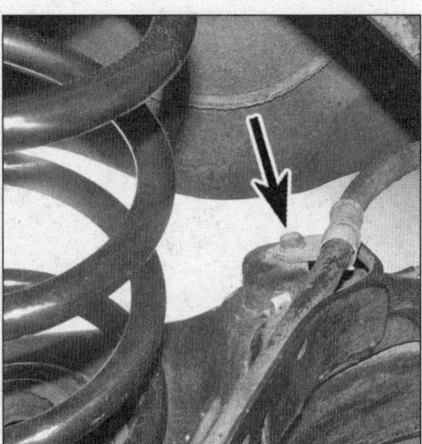

14.5a Undo the parking brake cable retaining clips (arrowed) ...

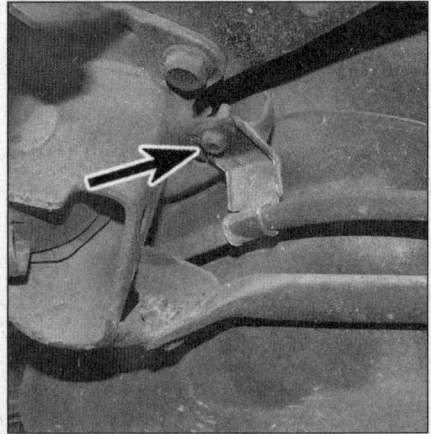

14.5b ... bolted to the underside of the vehicle

Chapter 9 Brakes

9-19

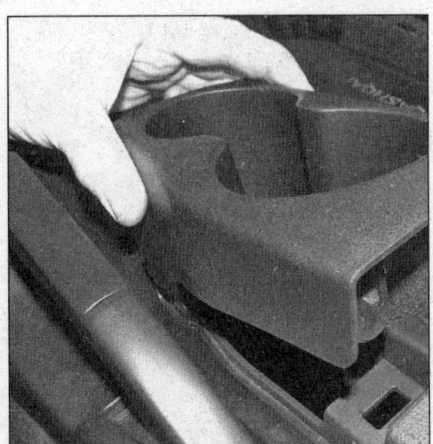

14.6a Unclip the cup holder from the centre console

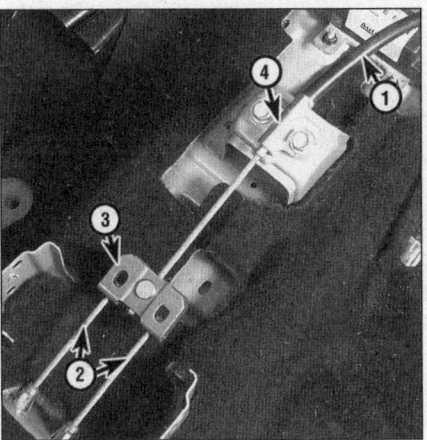

14.6b Parking brake cables; models with foot operated parking brake

1 Front brake cable
2 Rear brake cables
3 Equaliser
4 Front brake cable clamp

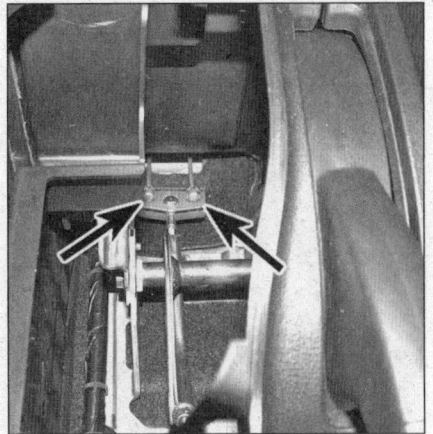

14.7 Disconnect the cables from the equalizer plate (arrowed)

7 Reaching inside the centre console, disconnect the two rear handbrake cables from the equaliser plate **(see illustration)**.

8 With the cables disconnected from the equalizer, from under the vehicle withdraw the cables from the floor panel **(see illustration)**. Note that on certain models it will be necessary to remove the exhaust heat shield for access to where the parking brake cables go through the floor panel.

Installation

9 Refitting is a reversal of removal, bearing in mind the following points:
 a Refit the parking brake shoes (see Section 15).
 b On completion, check the parking brake adjustment (see Section 13).

Front cable

Removal

Hand parking brake

10 Working inside the vehicle, remove the cup holder/trim from the top of the centre console **(see illustration 15.6)**.

11 Measure the number of exposed threads on the front cable adjuster (for reference when installing), then unscrew the adjuster nut from the end of the threads **(see illustration 14.9a)**.

12 Reaching inside the centre console, disconnect the two rear parking brake cables from the equaliser bracket **(see illustration 15.7)**.

13 Withdraw the front cable complete with equalizer plate out from inside the centre console.

Foot parking brake

14 Working in the driver compartment, remove the clips retaining the plastic cover beneath the steering column **(see illustration)**.

15 Working inside the vehicle, remove the centre console (see Chapter 11 Section 22).

16 Remove lower dashboard trim panel (see Chapter 11 Section 21).

17 Remove drivers side seat (see Chapter 11 Section 26).

18 Measure the number of exposed threads on the front cable adjuster (for reference when installing), then unscrew the adjuster nut from the end of the threads and remove both clips from plastic panel shown **(see illustration)**.

19 Disconnect the parking brake light switch connector and then remove the fasteners retaining the pedal bracket to the floor **(see illustration)**.

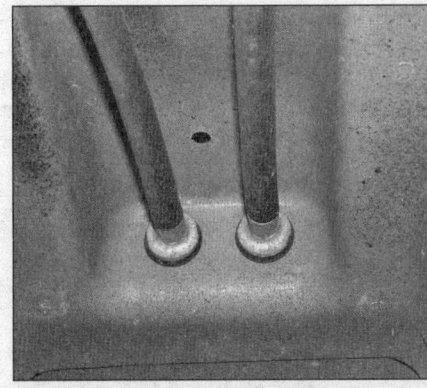

14.8 Withdraw the cables through the floor panel

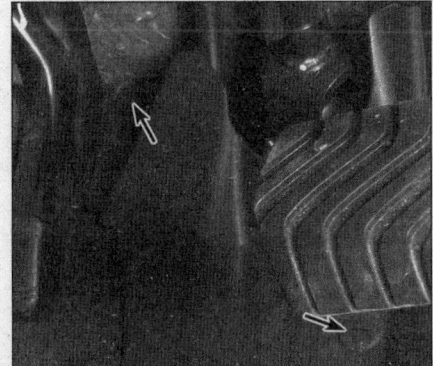

14.14 Remove the clips and manoeuvre the trim panel from beneath the steering column exposing the front end of the front cable

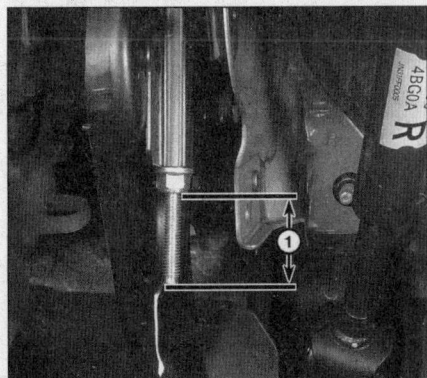

14.18 Measure the length of the thread (1) as a guide for assembly

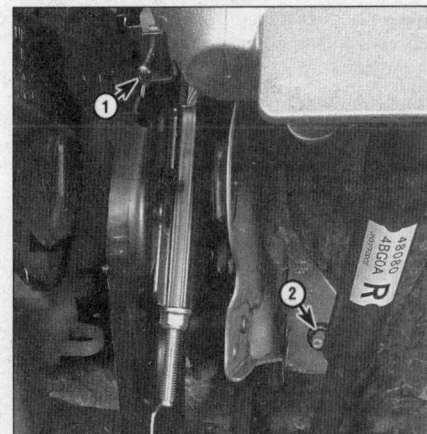

14.19 Foot parking brake components

1 Parking brake warning light switch
2 One of the four foot park brake assembly fasteners

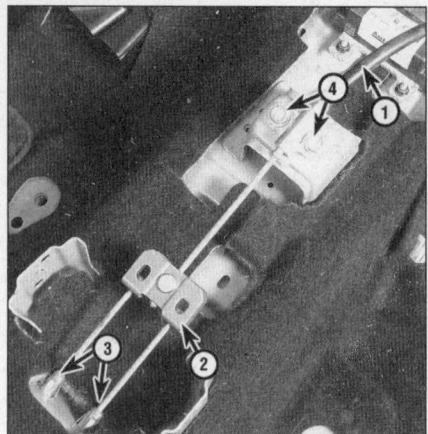

14.21 Console removed showing the parking brake cables on a T32 X-Trail with a foot operated parking brake

1 Front cable
2 Equaliser
3 Front of the rear cables
4 Front cable bracket bolts

15.4a If the disc can't be removed when the parking brake is fully released, you'll have to remove this rubber plug and use a screwdriver to turn the star wheel to retract the parking brake shoes

15.4b Wash the assembly with brake system cleaner; DO NOT blow off the brake dust with compressed air

15.4c Remove the lower spring...

15.4d... then take out the adjuster

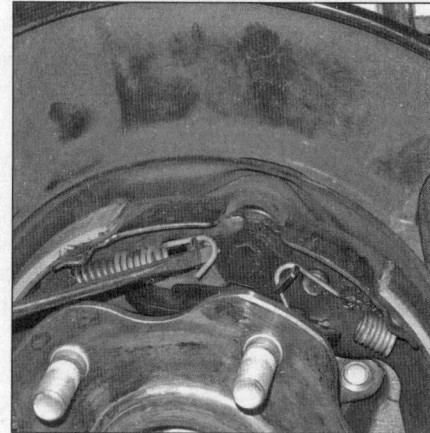

15.4e Use a screwdriver to remove the upper front retractor spring...

20 On automatic transaxle models, remove the shift lever assembly fasteners and position the shift lever assembly clear of the work area (see Chapter 7B Section 4).
21 Disconnect the two rear parking brake cables from the equaliser bracket **(see illustration)**.
22 Remove fasteners and remove cable.

Installation

23 Installation is a reversal of removal, bearing in mind the following points:
Screw the adjuster nut onto the front cable to give the measurement noted before removal. Check the park brake operation, and adjust if necessary (see Section 13).

15 Parking brake shoes - replacement

1 Chock the front wheels, loosen the rear wheel nuts and then raise the rear of the vehicle and support on jackstands (see Chapter 0 Section 7). Remove the rear wheels.
2 Release the parking brake. Remove the discs (see Section 6).

3 Inspect the surfaces of each disc for wear or damage. Replace the discs if necessary.

15.4f... then remove the upper rear retractor spring

15.4g Depress the spring and turn the shoe hold-down spring pin to release the spring...

Chapter 9 Brakes

9-21

15.4h . . . then lift the shoe off

15.4i Remove the brake strut

15.4j Separate the actuator lever pin from the rear shoe

15.4k Do the same to the remaining shoe

15.4l After cleaning the backing plates, apply brake grease to the raised contact surfaces around the perimeter

15.4m Install pin on the actuator lever (A) into the hole (B) in the new rear parking brake shoe. . .

4   Follow the accompanying photos **(see illustrations 16.4a through 16.4t)** for the actual parking brake shoe replacement procedure. Be sure to stay in order and read the caption under each illustration. Work on only one side at a time to avoid confusion.

5   Adjust the parking brake shoes (see Section 13).
6   When reinstalling the calipers, be sure to tighten the mounting bolts to the specified torque (see Specifications).

7   The remainder of installation is the reverse of removal.
8   The parking brake pedal may require adjustment in a few weeks after the parking brake shoes become seated.

15.4n . . . then slide the brake strut into place on the shoe. . .

15.4o . . . and secure the shoe with a hold-down spring and pin

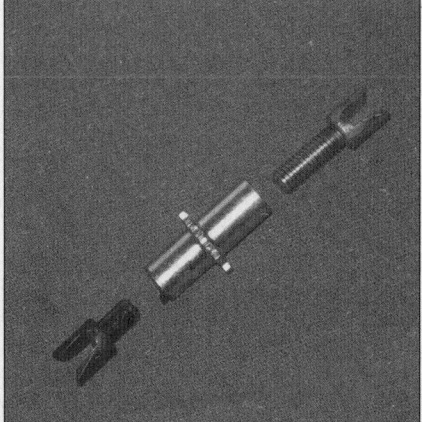
15.4p Disassemble the adjuster, clean it and lightly lubricate the threads with high-temperature brake grease

Chapter 9 Brakes

15.4q Install the front shoe, making sure the brake strut is seated correctly into the shoe, then secure the shoe with a hold-down spring

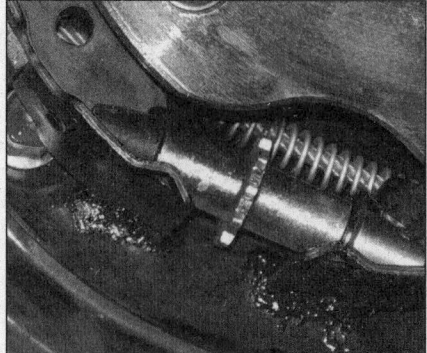

15.4r Place the adjuster between the shoes; the threaded end must face the rear of the vehicle

15.4s Install the lower spring, making sure the spring is hooked into the correct locations on the shoes and the coils rest on top of the star wheel

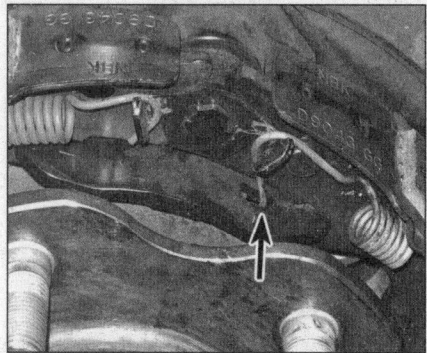

15.4t Attach the upper springs, making sure the end of the rear spring locks into the brake strut, then reinstall the disc

16.4 Power brake booster lock nut

16 Brake pedal - adjustment

1 With the brake pedal fully released, measure the distance from the top of the pad to the floor with the carpet and padding removed. Measure at a right angle to the floor.
2 If the height is not as listed, it must be adjusted.
3 Release the brake light and cruise control cancel switches by turning them counterclockwise 45 degrees.
4 Loosen the lock nut just in front of the power brake booster clevis (see illustration).

17.6 The clearance between the body of the switch and the pedal bracket must be as shown in the Specifications

5 Turn the booster input rod until the pedal height is correct.
6 Tighten the lock nut.
7 With the threaded portion of the brake light and cruise control cancel switches contacting the bracket, turn the switches 45 degrees clockwise to lock them in place.
8 Adjust the brake light and cruise control switches if necessary (see Section 17).

17 Brake light switch, cruise control cancel switch and brake pedal position sensor - adjustment and replacement

Adjustment

1 The brake light switch and cruise control cancel switch or brake pedal position sensor are located on a bracket near the top of the brake pedal. The switches activate the brake lights at the rear of the vehicle when the pedal is depressed and cancel the cruise control operation.
2 To check the brake light switch, simply note whether the brake lights come on when the pedal is depressed and go off when the pedal is released.
3 If the brake lights don't come on or the cruise control doesn't cancel when the brake pedal is depressed, make sure the brake pedal is correctly adjusted, then try adjusting the switch as follows (see Section 16).

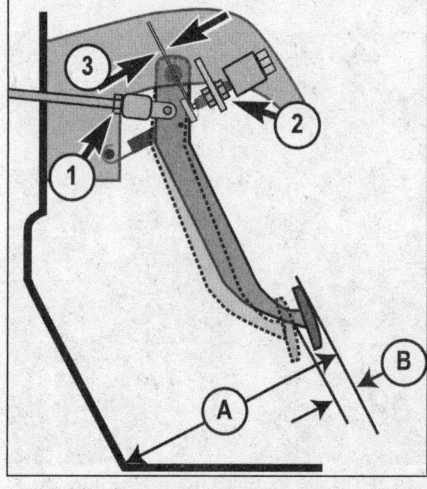

16.5 Brake pedal height and free play adjusting points

1 Power brake booster lock nut
2 Brake switch
3 Brake switch plunger clearance measuring point
A Brake pedal free height measuring point
B Brake pedal free play measuring point

4 Release the switch by turning it counterclockwise 45-degrees.
5 Pull the brake pedal back and hold it there, then push the switch into its bracket until the body of the switch (threaded portion) touches its stop.
6 Turn the switch 45-degrees clockwise to lock it in place. Measure the distance from the pedal and the body of the switch (see illustration).

Replacement

7 Disconnect the electrical connector from the switch.
8 Turn the switch 45-degrees counterclockwise, pull the switch to the rear and remove it.
9 Installation is the reverse of removal.
10 Adjust the brake pedal height, then adjust the switch (see Section 16).

Chapter 10
Suspension and steering systems

Contents

	Section		Section
Balljoints - replacement	6	Steering gear - removal and installation	17
Coil springs (rear) - removal and installation	10	Steering gear boots - replacement	16
Control arm - removal, inspection and installation	5	Steering knuckle - removal and installation	7
General information	1	Steering wheel - removal and installation	14
Hub and bearing assembly - removal and installation	8	Strut/coil spring assembly (front) - component replacement	3
Rear suspension arms and rear subframe - removal and installation	11	Strut/coil spring assembly (front) - removal, inspection and installation	2
Shock absorbers (rear) - removal and installation	9	Subframe (front) - removal and installation	18
Stabiliser bar (front) - removal and installation	4	Tie-rod ends - removal and installation	15
Stabiliser bar (rear) - removal and installation	12	Wheel alignment - general information	20
Steering column - removal and installation	13	Wheels and tyres - general information	19

Specifications

Torque specifications   Nm

Front suspension
Strut/coil spring assembly
  Strut upper mounting fasteners
    X-Trail 19
    Dualis and Qashqai 16
  Strut piston rod nut [1]
    T31 X-Trail 68
    T32 X-Trail 79
    Dualis and Qashqai 62
  Strut-to-steering knuckle [2]
    T31 X-Trail 142
    T32 X-Trail 90
    Dualis 168
    Qashqai .... Not specified
Stabiliser bar
  Stabiliser bushing clamp bolts
    T31 X-Trail 34
    Dualis and X-Trail T32 29
    Qashqai 60
  Stabiliser bar link nuts
    X-Trail 84
    Dualis and Qashqai 75
Control arm
  Control arm-to-subframe fasteners
    Rear bushing bolt/nut
      X-Trail 142
      Dualis 107
      Qashqai 98
    Front pivot shaft bolts
      X-Trail and Dualis 171
      Qashqai 138

Torque specifications (continued)

	Nm
Balljoint pinch bolt/nut [2]	
T31 X-Trail	63
Dualis and Qashqai	92
T32 X-Trail	103
Hub and bearing assembly bolts	88
Subframe	
Subframe stay mounting bolts	76
Subframe mounting bolts	
X-trail and Qashqai	94
Dualis	87
Wheel nuts	see Chapter 1

Rear suspension

	Nm
Shock absorber bolts/nuts [1]	
X-Trail	120
Dualis	110
Qashqai	90
Upper suspension arm [1]	
T31 X-Trail	
Suspension arm inner end-to-rear subframe bolt/nut	130
Suspension arm outer end-to-trailing arm bolt/nut	150
T32 X-Trail, Dualis, Qashqai	150
Lower suspension arm [2]	
X-Trail	
Suspension arm inner end-to-rear subframe bolt/nut	130
Suspension arm outer end-to-trailing arm bolt/nut	150
Dualis	150
Inner	83
Outer	150
Qashqai	
Inner	118
Outer	156
Trailing arm [1]	
Trailing arm-to-body bracket bolt/nut	
X-Trail	150
Dualis	83
Qashqai	113
Trailing arm body bracket-to-body bolts	
X-Trail	130
Dualis	83
Qashqai	115
Hub and bearing assembly bolts	80
Rear stabiliser bar	
Stabiliser bar bushing clamp nuts/bolts	35
Stabiliser bar link nuts	
X-Trail and Dualis	110
Qashqai	88
Rear subframe	
Subframe mounting bolts	
T31 X-Trail	100
Dualis	115
T32 X-Trail	130
Qashqai	108
Subframe support bracket bolts/nuts	
X-Trail	50
Dualis and Qashqai	38
Rubber bound bumper bolts	
X-Trail	25
Dualis and Qashqai	35

Steering

	Nm
Airbag module bolts	
T31 X-Trail and Dualis	9
Steering gear-to-subframe mounting bolts/nuts	147
Steering wheel nut/bolt	
T31 X-Trail and Dualis	34
T32 X-Trail and Qashqai	44

Chapter 10 Suspension and steering systems

Torque specifications (continued) — Nm

Steering intermediate shaft pinch bolts
  Upper bolt/nut
    T31 X-Trail, Dualis and Qashqai............................ 31
    T32 X-Trail... 26
  Lower bolt/nut [3]
    T31 X-Trail... 37
    T32 X-Trail... 45
    Dualis... 32
    Qashqai.. 50
Steering column mounting fasteners........................... 17
Tie-rod end-to-knuckle nuts... 34

[1] Fasteners must be replaced with new ones
[2] Nut must be replaced with new ones
[3] On X-Trail models replace fastener

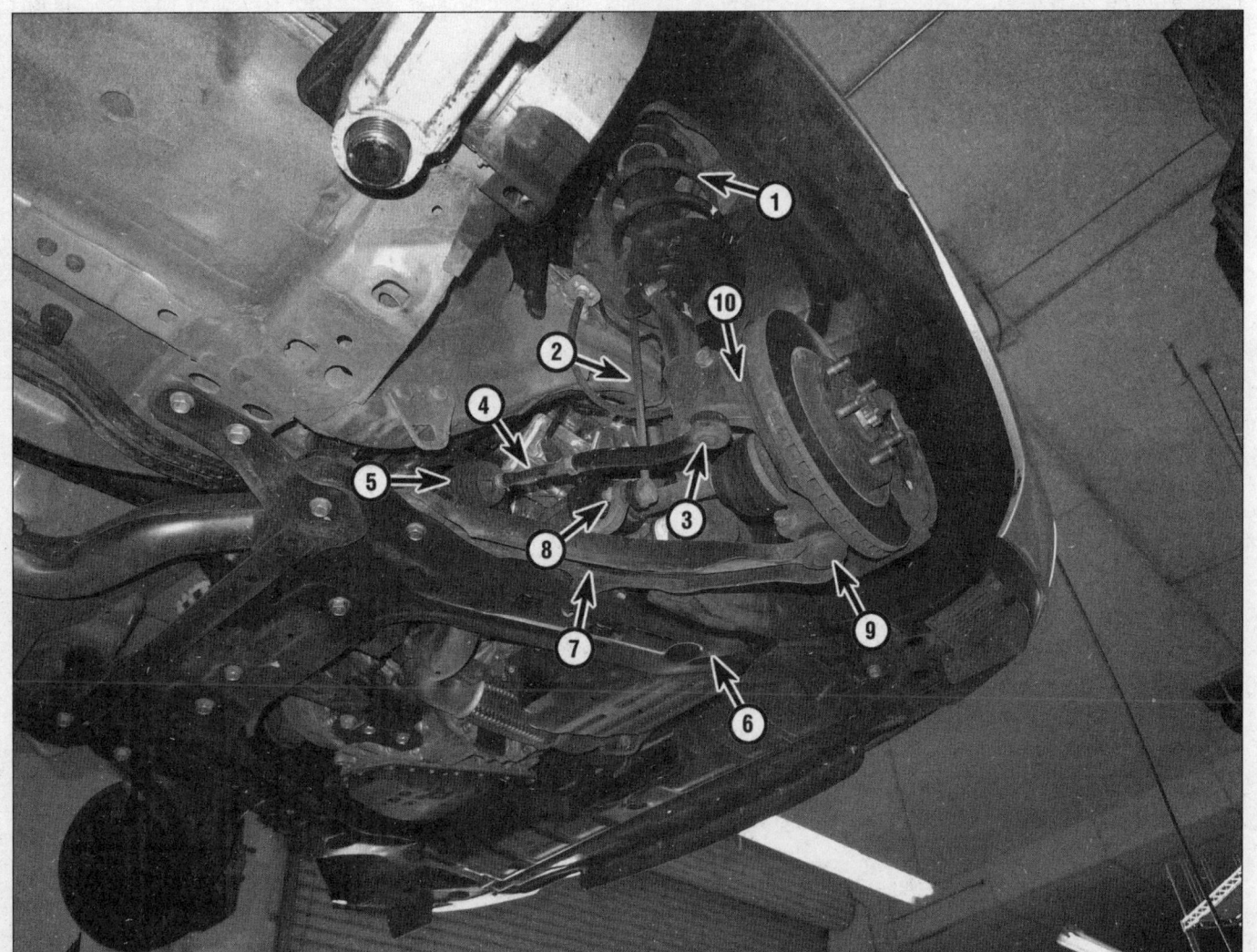

1.1 Front suspension components

1 Strut/coil spring assembly
2 Stabiliser bar link
3 Tie-rod end
4 Tie-rod
5 Steering gear boot
6 Subframe
7 Control arm
8 Stabiliser bar
9 Balljoint
10 Steering knuckle

Chapter 10 Suspension and steering systems

1 General information

The front suspension system is fully independent with **(see illustration)** a strut/coil spring design. The upper end of each strut is attached to the vehicle body. The lower end of the strut is connected to the upper end of the steering knuckle. The steering knuckle is attached to a balljoint mounted on the outer end of the control arm. The balljoint is an integral part of the control arm; if the balljoint is worn, the control arm must be replaced. A stabiliser bar is used on all models. The bar is attached to the subframe with a pair of clamps and to the struts with link rods.

The rear suspension is also fully independent **(see illustration)**. It consists of separate shock absorbers, trailing arms, upper and lower control arms, and a stabiliser bar. The upper end of each shock is attached to the body and the lower end is bolted to the trailing arm. The "knuckle" is incorporated into the trailing arm. The inner ends of the control arms are bolted to the subframe; the outer ends of the control arms are bolted to the trailing arm. The front ends of the trailing arms are bolted to the body. The stabiliser bar is attached to the subframe by a pair of clamps and is connected to the lower arms by links.

The rack-and-pinion steering gear is bolted to the subframe. The steering gear actuates the tie-rods, which are attached to the steering knuckles. The inner ends of the tie-rods are protected by rubber boots which should be inspected periodically for secure attachment, tears and leaking lubricant (which would indicate failed rack seals).

The power assist system consists of an electric motor mounted on the steering column.

The steering wheel operates the steering shaft, which actuates the steering gear through universal joints. Looseness in the steering can be caused by wear in the steering shaft universal joints, the steering gear, or the tie-rod ends, as well as loose retaining bolts.

Frequently, when working on the suspension or steering system components, you may come across fasteners which seem impossible to loosen. These fasteners on the underside of the vehicle are continually subjected to water, road grime, mud, etc., and can become rusted or frozen, making them extremely difficult to remove. In order to unscrew these stubborn fasteners without damaging them (or other components), be sure to use lots of penetrating oil and allow it to soak in for a while. Using a wire brush to clean exposed threads will also ease removal of the nut or bolt and prevent damage to the threads. Sometimes a sharp blow with a hammer and punch will break the bond between a nut and bolt threads, but care must be taken to prevent the punch from slipping off the fastener and ruining the threads. Heating the stuck fastener and surrounding area with a torch sometimes helps too, but isn't

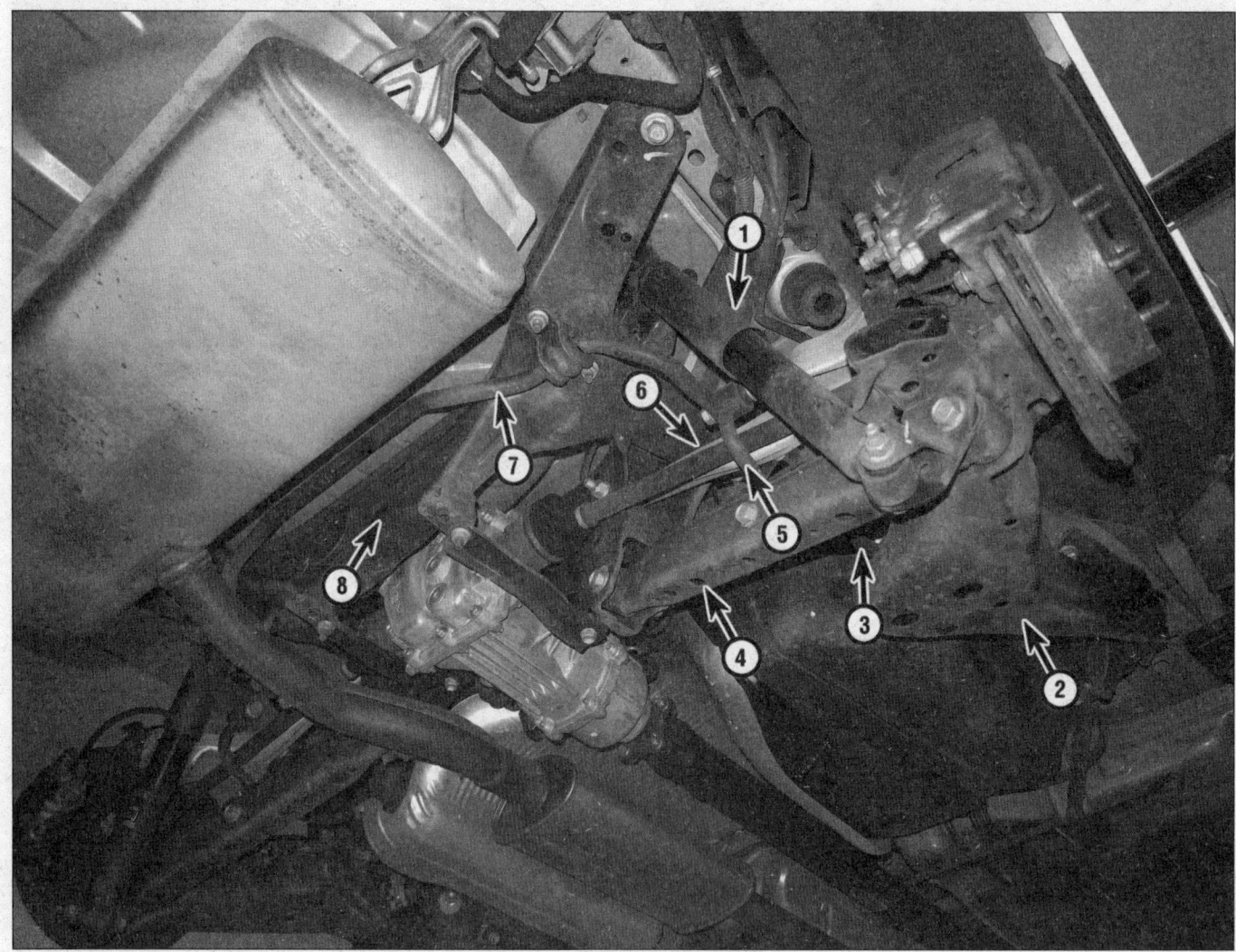

1.2 Rear suspension components

1 Shock absorber
2 Trailing arm
3 Coil spring
4 Lower control arm
5 Stabiliser link
6 Upper control arm
7 Stabiliser bar
8 Rear subframe

Chapter 10 Suspension and steering systems   10-5

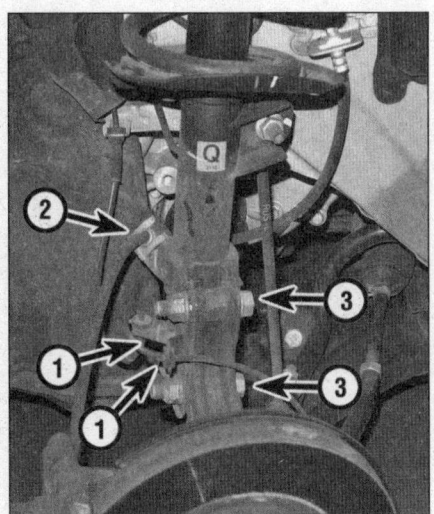

2.3a Strut lower mounting details - X-Trail T31 and Dualis

1 Wheel speed sensor harness bracket
2 Brake hose retaining clip
3 Strut-to-steering knuckle nuts/bolts

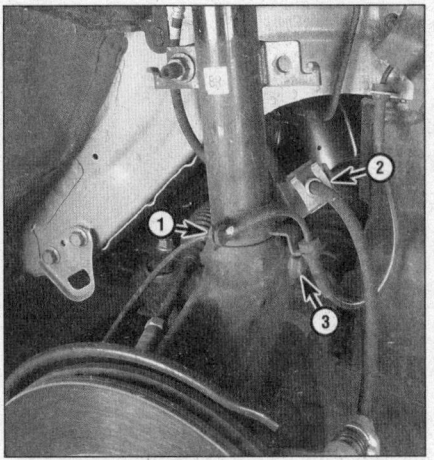

2.3b Strut lower mounting details - X-Trail T32 and Qashqai

1 Wheel speed sensor harness bracket
2 Brake hose retaining clip
3 Strut-to-steering knuckle nuts/bolts

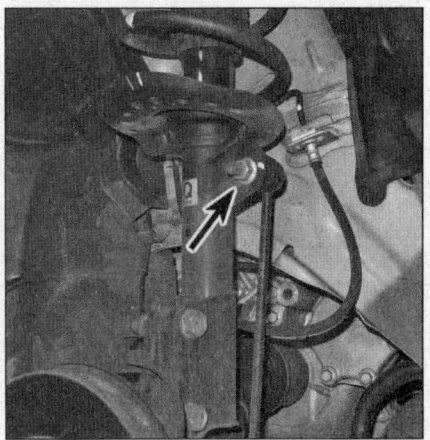

2.5 Stabiliser bar link-to-strut nut

recommended because of the obvious dangers associated with fire. Long breaker bars and extension, or cheater, pipes will increase leverage, but never use an extension pipe on a ratchet - the ratcheting mechanism could be damaged. Sometimes tightening the nut or bolt first will help to break it loose. Fasteners that require drastic measures to remove should always be replaced with new ones.

Since most of the procedures dealt with in this Chapter involve jacking up the vehicle and working underneath it, a good pair of jackstands will be needed. A hydraulic floor jack is the preferred type of jack to lift the vehicle, and it can also be used to support certain components during various operations.

Warning: *Never, under any circumstances, rely on a jack to support the vehicle while working on it. Whenever any of the suspension or steering fasteners are loosened or removed they must be inspected and, if necessary, replaced with new ones of the same part number or of original equipment quality and design. Torque specifications must be followed for proper reassembly and component retention. Never attempt to heat or straighten any suspension or steering components. Instead, replace any bent or damaged part with a new one.*

2 Strut/coil spring assembly (front) - removal, inspection and installation

Removal

1 Loosen the front wheel nuts, raise the front of the vehicle and support on jackstands (see Chapter 0 Section 7). Remove the wheels.

2 Remove the cowl cover (see Chapter 11 Section 25).

Note: *There is an access plug on each side of the cowl cover to access the rearmost strut upper mounting bolt, but in most cases it is easier to remove the cowl cover. If you decide to leave the cover in place, you'll need a magnet or magnetic socket insert, or for bolt installation, a piece of tape can be used to hold the bolt to the socket.*

3 Disconnect the wheel speed sensor wiring harness from the strut **(see illustration)**.
4 Remove the brake hose-to-strut retaining clip and detach the hose from the bracket.
5 Disconnect the stabiliser bar link from the strut **(see illustration)**.
6 On earlier models, remove the strut-to-knuckle nuts and knock the bolts out with a hammer and punch.
7 On later models, remove the strut-to-knuckle pinch bolt/nut **(see illustration)**.

2.7 Strut-to-knuckle pinch bolt/nut on later models

8 Separate the strut from the steering knuckle.
9 Support the strut and spring assembly with one hand and remove the three strut upper mounting bolts **(see illustration)**. Remove the assembly from the mudguard well.

Warning: *Don't unscrew the piston rod nut (the nut in the centre of the strut tower).*

Inspection

10 Check the strut body for leaking fluid, dents, cracks and other obvious damage which would warrant repair or replacement.
11 Check the coil spring for chips or cracks in the spring coating (this will cause premature spring failure due to corrosion). Inspect the spring seat for cuts, hardness and general deterioration.
12 If any undesirable conditions exist, proceed to the strut disassembly procedure (see Section 3).

Installation

13 Guide the strut assembly up into the mudguard well and install the upper mounting bolts, tightening them. This is most easily accomplished with the help of an assistant, as the strut is quite heavy and awkward.

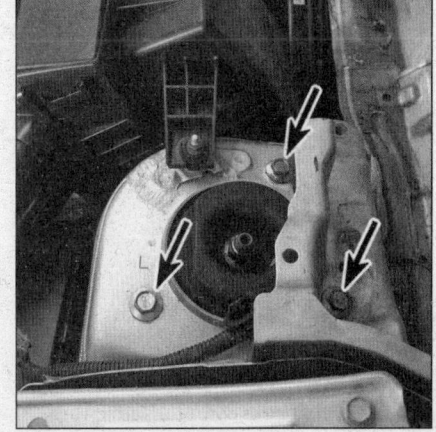

2.9 Strut upper mounting bolts

Chapter 10 Suspension and steering systems

3.2 Install the spring compressor according to the tool manufacturer's instructions and compress the spring until all pressure is relieved from the upper spring seat

3.3 Hold the piston rod with an Allen key, then unscrew the nut

3.4 Remove the upper suspension support mount and spring seat

14 Connect the steering knuckle to the strut and insert the bolt(s). Install the nut(s) and tighten to the specified torque.
15 The remainder of installation is the reverse of removal. Tighten the stabiliser bar link nut to the specified torque (see Specifications). Tighten the wheel nuts to the specified torque (see Chapter 1).
16 Have the front end alignment checked and, if necessary, adjusted.

3 Strut/coil spring assembly (front) - component replacement

Warning: *Always replace the struts or coil springs in pairs - never replace just one of them.*

Warning: *If the struts or coil springs exhibit the telltale signs of wear (leaking fluid, loss of damping capability, chipped, sagging or cracked coil springs) explore all options before beginning any work. The strut/shock absorber assemblies are not serviceable and* must be replaced if a problem develops. However, strut assemblies complete with springs may be available on an exchange basis, which eliminates much time and work. Whichever route you choose to take, check on the cost and availability of parts before disassembling your vehicle.
Warning: *Disassembling a strut is a potentially dangerous undertaking and utmost attention must be directed to the job, or serious injury may result. Use only a high-quality spring compressor and carefully follow the manufacturer's instructions furnished with the tool. After removing the coil spring from the strut assembly, set it aside in a safe, isolated area.*

Disassembly

1 Remove the strut and spring assembly (see Section 2). Mount the strut assembly in a vise. Line the vise jaws with wood or rags to prevent damage to the unit and don't tighten the vise excessively.
2 Following the tool manufacturer's instructions, install the spring compressor (which can be obtained at most auto parts stores or equipment yards on a daily rental basis) on the spring and compress it suffi- ciently to relieve all pressure from the upper spring seat **(see illustration)**. This can be verified by wiggling the spring.
3 Remove the piston rod nut **(see illustration)**.
4 Remove the upper suspension support **(see illustration)**. Inspect the bearing in the suspension support for smooth operation. If it does not turn smoothly, replace the suspension support. Check the rubber portion of the suspension support for cracking and general deterioration. If there is any separation of the rubber, replace it.
5 Lift the spring seat and upper insulator from the piston rod. Check the rubber spring seat for cracking and hardness, replacing it if necessary.
6 Carefully lift the compressed spring from the assembly **(see illustration)** and set it in a safe place.
Warning: *Carry the spring carefully and never place any part of your body near the end of the spring!*
7 Slide the dust boot off the piston rod.
8 Check the lower insulator (if equipped) for wear, cracking and hardness and replace it if necessary.

Reassembly

9 If the lower insulator is being replaced, set it into position with the dropped portion seated in the lowest part of the seat. Extend the damper rod to its full length and install the dust boot.
10 Place the coil spring onto the lower insulator, with the end of the spring resting in the lowest part of the insulator **(see illustration)**.
11 Install the upper insulator and the spring seat. Make sure the marks or arrow on the spring seat and mount insulator are facing out (away from the vehicle), in line with the strut-to-knuckle flange.
12 Install the dust seal and suspension support to the piston rod.
13 Install the nut and tighten to the specified torque (see Specifications).
14 Install the strut/shock absorber and coil spring assembly (see Section 2).

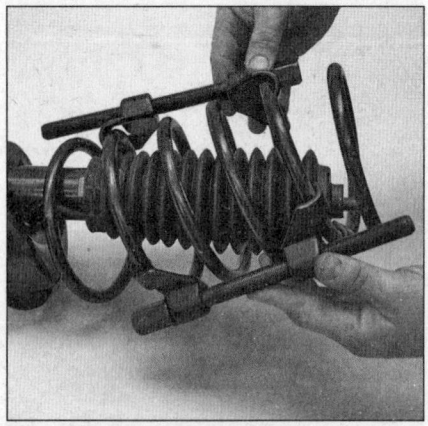

3.6 Remove the compressed spring assembly

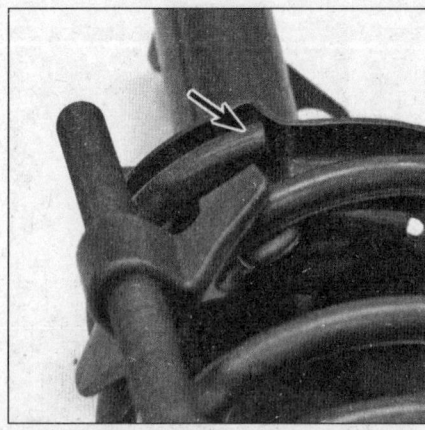

3.10 When installing the spring, make sure the end fits into the recessed portion of the lower seat

Chapter 10 Suspension and steering systems

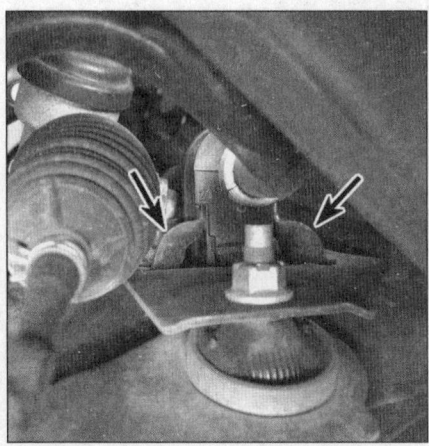

4.8 Stabiliser bar bushing clamp bolts

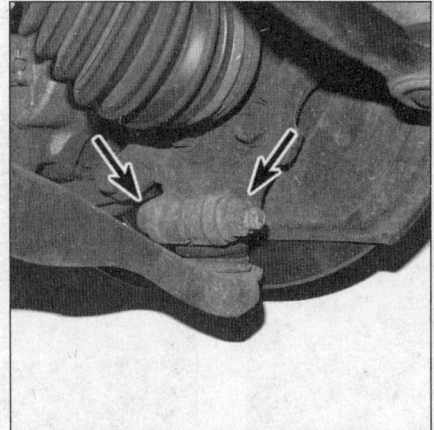

5.3a Remove the balljoint-to steering knuckle pinch bolt/nut

5.3b Pry the balljoint stud out of the steering knuckle, taking care not to damage the boot

4 Stabiliser bar (front) - removal and installation

1 Loosen the front wheel nuts, raise the front of the vehicle and support on jackstands (see Chapter 0 Section 7). Remove the wheels.
2 Separate the intermediate shaft from the steering gear shaft (see Section 17).
3 Detach the stabiliser bar links from the strut (see illustration 2.5).
4 Disconnect the tie-rod ends from the steering knuckles (see Section 7).
5 If you're working on a later model, remove front exhaust mount and the exhaust manifold/catalytic converter assembly (see Chapter 4A Section 11).
6 Remove the torque rod (see Chapter 2A Section 15 - 2.0 litre petrol models, Chapter 2B Section 17 - 2.5 litre petrol models or Chapter 2C Section 20 - diesel models).
7 Support the rear of the subframe with a floor jack. Remove the subframe stay bolts, remove the stay, loosen the subframe mounting bolts (see Section 18) and slowly lower the jack just enough to access the stabiliser bar bracket bolts towards the rear of the sub-frame.
8 Remove the stabiliser bar clamps and bushings (see illustration).
9 Remove the stabiliser bar.
10 Inspect the clamp bushings and the link bushings. If they're cracked or torn, replace them.

Note: *When installing new bushings, the slit in the bushing should face the front of the vehicle. Install the clamps in their original positions.*

11 Installation is the reverse of removal.
12 Tighten all suspension and steering fastener to the specified torque (see Specifications).
13 Tighten the wheel nuts to the specified torque (see Chapter 1).

5 Control arm - removal, inspection and installation

Removal

1 Loosen the front wheel nuts, raise the front of the vehicle, support it securely on jackstands and remove the wheel (see Chapter 0 Section 7).
2 Detach the stabiliser bar links from the stabiliser bar, then swing the ends of the stabiliser bar upward.
3 Separate the control arm balljoint from the steering knuckle (see illustrations).
4 Remove the control arm fasteners and remove the arm from the subframe (see illustration)

Inspection

5 Inspect the front and rear bushings for cracks and tears. If either bushing is damaged or worn, replace the control arm; the bushings are not replaceable.
6 Inspect the control arm for straightness. If it's bent, replace it. Do not attempt to straighten a bent control arm.

Installation

Note: *When installing the control arm, loosely tighten all the bolts, move the suspension to its normal ride-height angle and position (a floor jack can be used to do this), then fully tighten the bolts.*

7 Installation is the reverse of removal.
  a Tighten all of the fasteners to the specified torque.
  b Install the wheel and wheel nuts, lower the vehicle and tighten the wheel nuts to the specified torque (see Chapter 1).
  c It's a good idea to have the front wheel alignment checked and, if necessary, adjusted.

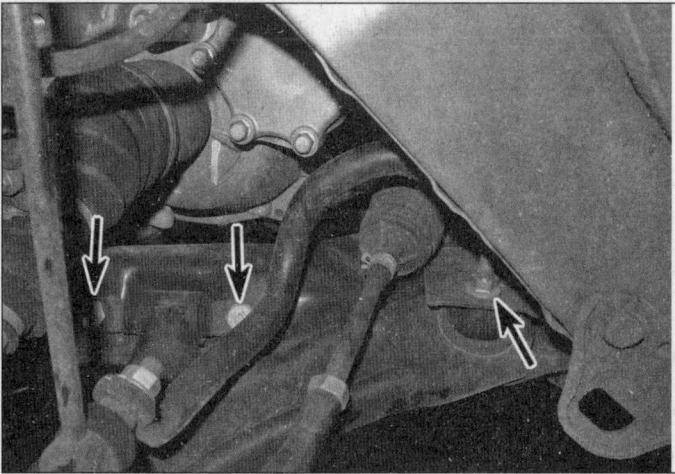

5.4 Control arm fastener locations

6 Balljoints - replacement

1 The balljoint is an integral part of the control arm. If it's worn or damaged, the control arm must be replaced (see Section 5).

8.7 Front hub and bearing mounting bolts

8.14 Rear hub and bearing mounting bolts

7 Steering knuckle - removal and installation

Warning: *Dust created by the brake system is harmful to your health. Never blow it out with compressed air and don't inhale any of it. Do not, under any circumstances, use petroleum-based solvents to clean brake parts. Use brake system cleaner only.*

Removal

1 Loosen the wheel nuts, raise the vehicle and support it securely on jackstands (see Chapter 0 Section 7). Remove the wheel.
2 Remove the driveshaft/hub nut (see Chapter 8 Section 7).
3 Remove the brake caliper and disc (see Chapter 9 Section 5).
4 Remove the ABS wheel speed sensor from the steering knuckle see (Chapter 9 Section 2).
5 Separate the tie-rod end from the steering knuckle (see Section 15).
6 On earlier models remove the strut-to-steering knuckle nuts, but don't remove the bolts yet. On later models, remove the strut-to-steering knuckle pinch bolt and nut.
7 Separate the control arm balljoint from the steering knuckle (see Section 5).
8 Separate the driveshaft from the steering knuckle (see Chapter 8 Section 7). Support the end of the driveshaft with a length of wire so the CV joints aren't overextended.
9 Remove the strut-to-knuckle bolts and separate the knuckle from the strut.

Installation

10 Lubricate the splines of the driveshaft with multi-purpose grease. Guide the knuckle and hub assembly into position, inserting the driveshaft into the hub.
11 On earlier models, push the knuckle into the strut flange and install the bolts and nuts, but don't tighten them yet.
12 On later models, insert the end of the strut into the top of the knuckle until the pinch bolt can be inserted, but don't tighten the bolt/nut yet.
13 Attach the control arm balljoint to the steering knuckle (see Section 5).
14 Attach the tie-rod end to the steering knuckle arm (see Section 7). Tighten the tie-rod end nut and the strut-to-knuckle nuts. On some later models, install a new cotter pin through the tie-rod end ballstud.
15 Place the brake disc on the hub, then install the caliper (see Chapter 9 Section 7).
16 Install the driveshaft/hub nut and tighten to the specified torque.
17 Install the wheel and nuts. Lower the vehicle and tighten the nuts to the specified torque (see Chapter 1).

8 Hub and bearing assembly - removal and installation

Front

1 Loosen the driveshaft/hub nut (see Chapter 8 Section 7).
2 Loosen the front wheel nuts, Raise the front of the vehicle and support on jackstands (see Chapter 0 Section 7). Remove the front wheels.
3 Remove the brake caliper and disc (see Chapter 9 Section 5).
4 Remove the driveshaft/hub nut.
5 Separate the control arm balljoint from the steering knuckle (see Section 5). Also detach the tie-rod end from the steering knuckle (see Section 7).
6 Pull the steering knuckle outward and detach the driveshaft from the hub. Once the driveshaft has been freed from the hub, support it with a length of wire to prevent overextension of the inner CV joint.
7 Remove the hub/bearing assembly mounting bolts from the rear of the steering knuckle **(see illustration)**.
8 Remove the hub/bearing assembly from the steering knuckle.

Note: *If the driveshaft splines stick in the hub, push the driveshaft out of the hub with a two-jaw puller.*

9 Installation is the reverse of removal. Tighten all fasteners to the specified torque.

Rear

10 Loosen the rear wheel nuts. Raise the rear of the vehicle and support on jackstands (see Jacking and Towing 0 Section 7). Remove the wheel.
11 Remove the wheel speed sensor (see Chapter 9 Section 2).
12 Remove the brake caliper and disc (see Chapter 9 Section 6).
13 On AWD models, loosen the rear driveshaft hub nut (see Chapter 8 Section 7).
14 Remove the hub and bearing assembly mounting bolts **(see illustration)**.
15 Remove the hub and bearing assembly. If you're working on an AWD model and the driveshaft splines stick in the hub, use a puller to push the driveshaft from the hub as the hub and bearing assembly is removed from the trailing arm.
16 Installation is the reverse of removal. Tighten all fasteners to the specified torque.

9 Shock absorbers (rear) - removal and installation

Warning: *Always replace the shock absorbers in pairs - never replace just one of them.*

1 Chock the front wheels, loosen the rear wheel nuts and then raise the rear of the vehicle and support on jackstands (see Chapter 0 Section 7). Remove the rear wheels.
2 Support the lower rear suspension arm with a floor jack placed under the coil spring pocket.

Warning: *The jack must remain in this position until the shock absorber is reinstalled.*

3 Remove the shock absorber upper mounting nut and bolt **(see illustration)**.
4 Remove the shock absorber lower mounting nut and bolt and remove the shock absorber **(see illustration)**.
5 Installation is the reverse of removal, noting the following points:
6 Raise the trailing arm with the jack to simulate normal ride height, then tighten the mounting fasteners to the specified torque (see Specifications).

Chapter 10 Suspension and steering systems

9.3 Shock absorber upper mounting bolt

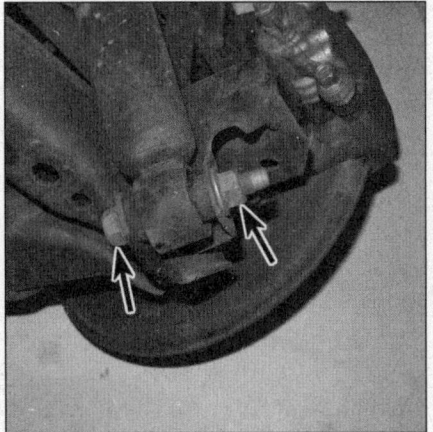

9.4 Shock absorber lower mounting bolt/nut

11.3 Mark the adjuster cam to the body bracket

7 Install the wheel and nuts. Lower the vehicle and tighten the nuts to the specified torque (see Chapter 1).

10 Coil springs (rear) - removal and installation

Warning: *Always replace the coil springs in pairs - never replace just one of them.*

1 Chock the front wheels, loosen the rear wheel nuts and then raise the rear of the vehicle and support on jackstands (see Chapter 0 Section 7). Remove the rear wheels.
2 Position a floor jack under the coil spring seat portion of the trailing arm, then raise the jack slightly.
3 Remove the brake caliper, caliper mounting bracket and brake disc (see Chapter 9 Section 8).
4 Remove the ABS wheel speed sensor (see Chapter 9 Section 2).
5 Unbolt the upper and lower suspension arms from the trailing arm (see Section 11).
6 Detach the stabiliser bar link from the lower control arm (see Section 12).
7 Separate the parking brake cable and brake pipe from the trailing arm. Also disconnect the height sensor, if equipped.
8 Remove both shock absorber lower mounting bolts (see Section 9).
9 On AWD models, remove the driveshaft (see Chapter 8 Section 7).
10 Carefully lower the suspension arm using the floor jack until the coil spring is fully extended.
11 Remove the coil spring, the rubber mount and the rubber seat.
12 Installation is the reverse of removal, noting the following points:
 a Raise the trailing arm with a floor jack until it is at normal ride height, then tighten the suspension component bolt/nuts to the specified torque.
 b Tighten the brake components to the specified torque (see Chapter 9 Section).
 c On AWD models, tighten the driveshaft/hub nut to the specified torque (see Chapter 8 Section 7).
 d Tighten the wheel nuts to the specified torque (see Chapter 1 Section).

Note: *It's possible that, when raising the trailing arm to connect the upper and lower control arms, the coil spring might force the trailing arm outwards. In the event that you have trouble aligning the upper and lower control arm bolt holes with the holes in the trailing arm, you can use a come-along connected to the trailing arm and the trailing arm on the other side. Tighten the come-along and use a long drift punch to align the bolt holes so the bolts can be inserted.*

11 Rear suspension arms and rear subframe - removal and installation

1 Chock the front wheels, loosen the rear wheel nuts and then raise the rear of the vehicle and support on jackstands (see Chapter 0 Section 7). Remove the rear wheels.

Trailing arm

2 Remove the coil spring (see Section 10).
3 Mark the position of the adjuster cams on the pivot bolt to the trailing arm bracket **(see illustration)**.
4 Remove the trailing arm-to-body bracket mounting bolt/nut **(see illustration)**.
5 Remove the trailing arm from the vehicle.

Note: *When the trailing arm is removed, the two rubber washers on either side of the pivot bushing will fall out. Be sure to reinstall them.*

6 Installation is the reverse of removal, noting the following points:
 a Replace the pivot bolt nut with a new one.
 b Align the previously made matchmarks on the adjuster cam and the body bracket.
 c Raise the trailing arm with a floor jack until it is at normal ride height, then tighten the trailing arm bolt/nuts to the specified torque (see Section).
 d Bleed the brake system (see Chapter 9 Section 11).
 e Tighten the wheel nuts to the specified torque (see Chapter 1).
 f Have the wheel alignment checked and, if necessary adjusted.

11.4 Trailing arm-to-bracket mounting bolt

11.8 Mark the adjuster cam to the subframe

10-10 Chapter 10 Suspension and steering systems

11.10 Remove the stabiliser link bolt (A) then the lower suspension arm fasteners (B)

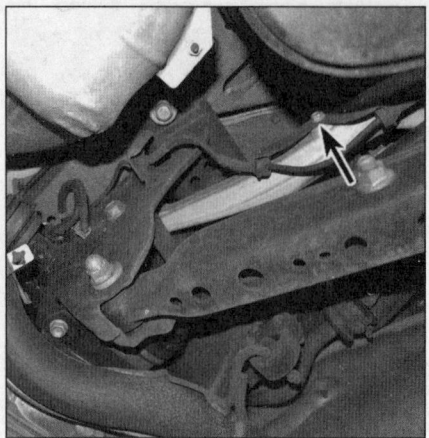

11.15 Undo the mounting bolt for abs wheel speed sensor harness

11.16 Remove the upper suspension arm fasteners from each end of the arm

Lower suspension arm

7 Remove the stabiliser bar link from the lower suspension arm (see Section 12).
8 Mark the position of the adjuster cams on the inner pivot bolt to the subframe (see illustration).
9 Support the trailing arm with a floor jack placed under the coil spring pocket.
Warning: *The jack must remain in this position until the arm is reinstalled.*
10 Remove the lower suspension arm-to-subframe and trailing arm pivot bolts/nuts (see illustration).
11 Remove the arm from the vehicle.
12 Installation is the reverse of removal, noting the following points:
  a Replace the pivot bolt nuts with a new ones.
  b Raise the trailing arm with a floor jack until it is at normal ride height, then tighten the suspension arm bolt/nuts to the specified torque (see Specifications). Be sure to align the marks on the adjusting cam and the subframe before tightening the bolt/nut.
  c Tighten the wheel nuts to the specified torque (see Chapter 1).
  d Have the wheel alignment checked and, if necessary adjusted.

Upper suspension arm

14 Support the trailing arm with a floor jack placed under the coil spring pocket.
Warning: *The jack must remain in this position until the arm is reinstalled.*
15 Remove the ABS wheel speed sensor harness mounting bolt (see illustration) from the arm and move the harness out of the way.
16 Remove the upper suspension arm-to-subframe and trailing arm pivot bolts/nuts (see illustration).
17 Remove the arm from the vehicle.
18 Installation is the reverse of removal, noting the following points:
  a Raise the trailing arm with a floor jack until it is at normal ride height, then tighten the suspension arm bolt/nuts to the specified torque.
  b Tighten the wheel nuts to the specified torque (see Specifications).

Rear subframe

19 Raise the vehicle and support it securely on jackstands.
20 Remove the coil springs (see Section 10).
21 Remove the rear Section of the exhaust system (see Chapter 4A Section 11 - petrol models or Chapter 4B Section 11 - diesel models).
22 On AWD models, remove the rear differential (see Chapter 8 Section 9).
23 Remove the shock absorbers (see Section 9).
24 Remove the upper and lower suspension arms as described earlier in this Section.
25 Remove the stabiliser bar (see Section 12).
26 Disconnect the wiring harness from the rear subframe.
27 Place two floor jacks under the rear subframe so it is securely supported.
28 Remove the subframe mounting bolts, then carefully lower the rear subframe a little at a time until it is clear of the body of the vehicle (see illustration).
29 Installation is the reverse of removal.
  a Tighten all subframe and suspension fasteners to the specified torque (see Specifications).
  b Tighten the wheel nuts to the specified torque (see Chapter 1).

Note: *Before tightening the suspension fasteners, raise the trailing arm with a floor jack until it is at normal ride height.*

12 Stabiliser bar (rear) - removal and installation

1 Chock the front wheels, loosen the rear wheel nuts and then raise the rear of the vehicle and support on jackstands (see Chapter 0 Section 7). Remove the rear wheels.
2 Detach the stabiliser bar link-to-lower suspension arm bolt/nut (see illustration).
3 Detach the stabiliser bar link-to-stabiliser bar bolt/nut.
4 Remove the stabiliser bar clamps and bushings.

Note: *On some models, it may be necessary to remove the muffler to access the stabiliser bar clamp bolts.*

5 Remove the stabiliser bar.
6 Inspect the clamp bushings and the link bushings. If they're cracked or torn, replace them.

11.28 Location of the rear subframe mounting points

Chapter 10 Suspension and steering systems

12.2 Stabiliser bar mounting details

1 Stabiliser link-to-lower suspension arm mounting bolt/nut
2 Stabiliser link-to-stabiliser bar mounting bolt/nut
3 Stabiliser bar clamp mounting bolt/nuts

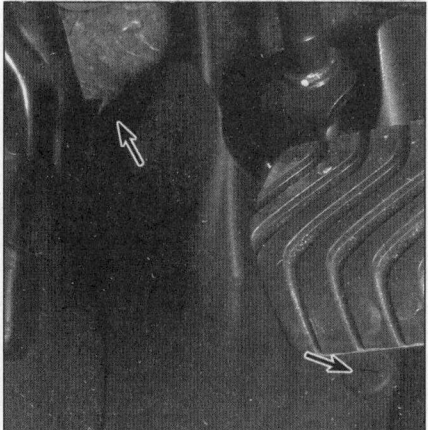

13.10a Remove the clips and manoeuvre the trim panel from beneath the steering column exposing…

13.10b … the intermediate shaft pinch bolt

Note: *When installing new bushings, the slit in the bushing should face the rear of the vehicle. Install the clamps in their original positions.*

7 Installation is the reverse of removal. Tighten the fasteners to the torque values listed in this Chapter's Specifications. Tighten the wheel nuts to the specified torque (see Chapter 1).

Note: *Before tightening the stabiliser bar link-to-lower arm fasteners, raise the trailing arm with a floor jack until it is at normal ride height.*

13 Steering column - removal and installation

Warning: *The models covered by this manual are equipped with Supplemental Restraint Systems (SRS), more commonly known as airbags. Always disarm the airbag system before working in the vicinity of any airbag system component to avoid the possibility of accidental deployment of the airbag, which could cause personal injury (see Chapter 12A Section 20). Do not use a memory saving device to preserve the PCM's memory when working on or near airbag system components.*

1 Disconnect the negative (-) battery terminal (see Chapter 5 Section 3).
2 Set the wheels in the straight ahead position.
3 Remove the steering wheel (see Section 14).
4 Remove the upper and lower steering column covers (see Chapter 11 Section 23).
5 Disconnect and remove the combination switch and the spiral cable (see Chapter 12A Section 4).
6 Remove the driver's lower dash panel (see Section).
7 Detach each of the switch connectors that are installed on the steering column.
8 Disconnect the steering column wiring harness.
9 On earlier models, remove the upper intermediate shaft bolt and detach the intermediate shaft from the column.

10 On later models, remove the clips retaining the plastic cover beneath the steering column **(see illustration)**. Remove the lower intermediate shaft bolt **(see illustration)** and separate the shaft from the steering gear.
11 Remove the steering column mounting fasteners and remove the steering column.
12 Installation is the reverse of removal, with attention to the following points:
13 Tighten all fasteners to the specified torque.
14 Reconnect the battery and perform the system initialisation procedure (see Chapter 5 Section 4).

14 Steering wheel - removal and installation

Warning: *The models covered by this manual are equipped with Supplemental Restraint Systems (SRS), more commonly known as airbags. Always disarm the airbag system before working in the vicinity of any airbag system component to avoid the possibility of accidental deployment of the airbag, which could cause personal injury Chapter 12A*

13.11 Steering column fasteners (1) and intermediate shaft (2) - T32 X-Trail shown

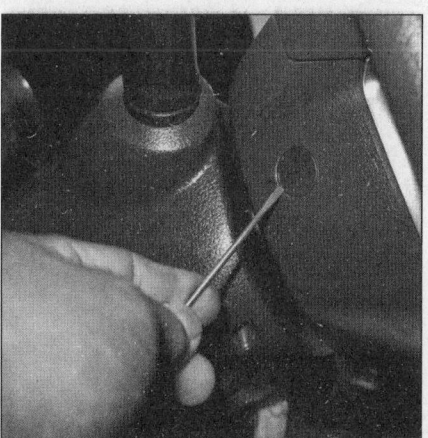

14.3a Pry off the covers to access the bolts

14.3b Remove the bolts on each side of he steering wheel

Chapter 10 Suspension and steering systems

14.3c You will need a security type Torx socket (this is one with a hole in the centre of the socket to go over the dimple in the centre of the screw) to unscrew the airbag retaining screws

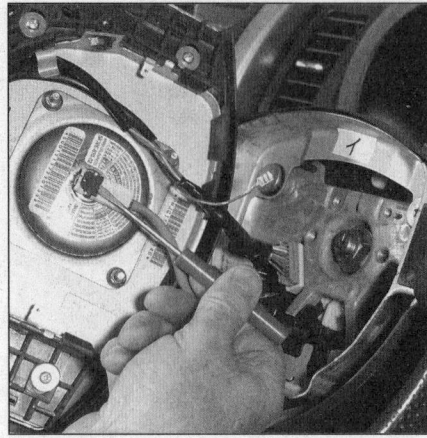

14.3d Pry up the locking tab on the airbag connector up, then unplug it

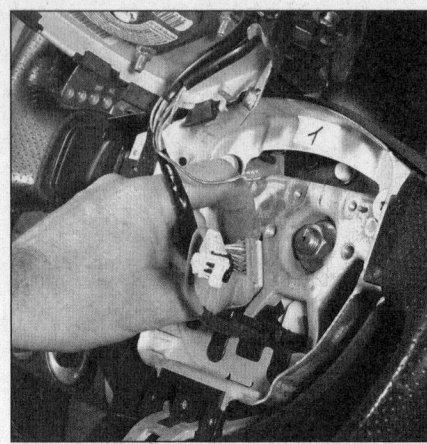

14.3e Disconnect the switch wiring before removing the airbag from the steering wheel

Section 20. Do not use a memory saving device to preserve the PCM's memory when working on or near airbag system components.

Driver airbag removal and installation

1   Disconnect the cable from the negative terminal of the battery Chapter 5 Section 3
2   Set the wheels in the straight ahead position.
3   The airbag removal differs from the earlier models to later models. The earlier models are bolted in and later models are clipped in **(see illustrations)**.

X-Trail T31 and Dualis

4   Installation is a reversal of the removal procedure, with attention to the following points:
  a Ensure the wiring is reconnected to the airbag and the locking tab is pushed into place.
  b Connect the wiring to the spiral cable for the steering wheel switches **(see illustration 14.3e)**.
  c Tighten the airbag Torx screws to the specified torque (see Specifications).

X-trail T32 and Qashqai

5   Disconnect the negative (-) battery terminal (see Chapter 5 Section 3).

Note: *The electric steering lock disengages once the battery is disconnected, allowing you to rotate the steering wheel.*

6   Using a round tool like a small Allen key or Torx key, probe through holes inline with wheel spokes (rotate steering wheel so hole is accessible with steering cover installed).
7   Lever the tool toward the steering column to release each upper clip **(see illustration)**.
8   Push the tab at the bottom (through the hole) up to release the bottom airbag clip **(see illustration)**.
9   Partially remove the airbag **(see illustration)** and disconnect the wiring connector **(see illustration)**.

14.7 Levering the Allen key (1) toward the steering column to release the clip (2) - viewed from the rear of the steering wheel for clarity

10   Installation is a reversal of the removal procedure, with attention to the following points:

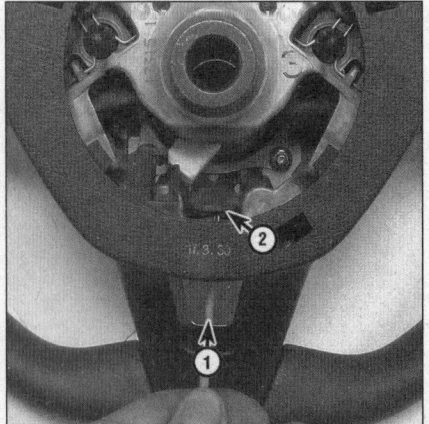

14.8 Push the Allen key (1) toward the steering column to release the clip (2) - viewed from the rear of the steering wheel for clarity

14.9a Removing the airbag from the steering wheel

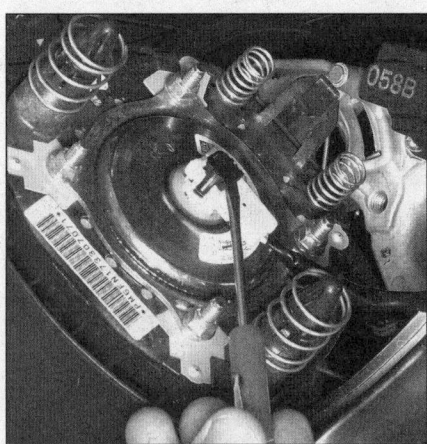

14.9b Pry up the locking tab on the airbag connector up, then unplug it

Chapter 10 Suspension and steering systems

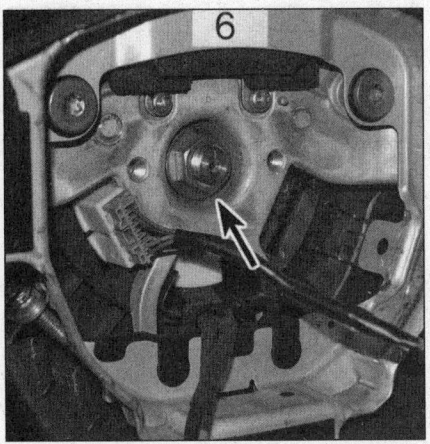

14.12a Remove the nut on earlier model

14.12b Remove Torx bolt on later models

14.12c Note the alignment marks on the wheel and shaft (if there are no marks, make your own)

a Ensure the wiring is reconnected to the airbag and the locking tab is pushed into place.

b Push the airbag onto the steering wheel, engaging the clips with the holes in the wheel. Push the airbag into the wheel until you feel the clips lock into place.

Steering wheel removal and installation

11 Remove the driver airbag as previously described.

12 Position the steering wheel in the straight ahead position and remove the nut or bolt, as applicable **(see illustrations)**.

13 On models with a nut retaining the wheel to the column, the steering wheel is on a splined shaft and will not just slide off the steering column. On these models, proceed as follows:

a If removed, install the steering wheel retaining nut approximately 3-turns back onto the steering column.

b Grasp the steering wheel with both hands placing them at opposite points around the circumference of the steering wheel. Rock the wheel back and forth while moving both hands around the steering wheel **(see illustration)**. After a short time, the steering wheel will come off the splines retaining it to the steering shaft. Remove the nut and lift the steering wheel from the shaft, guiding any wiring through the holes in the steering wheel.

Note: *If you can't remove the wheel using the previous method, use a commercially available steering wheel puller* **(see illustration)**.

Caution: *Do not hammer on the shaft or the puller in an attempt to loosen the wheel from the shaft. Also, don't allow the steering shaft to turn with the steering wheel removed. If the shaft turns, the airbag clock spring will no longer be centred, which may cause the wire inside to break when the vehicle is returned to service.*

14 On later models, remove the steering wheel from the shaft **(see illustration)**.

Caution: *Do not hammer on the steering wheel or shaft to break it loose.*

15 If it's necessary to remove the airbag spiral cable, remove the steering column covers (see Chapter 11 Section 23), remove the wiper/washer switch and the turn signal switch (see Chapter 12A Section 4), then remove the screws and release the tab at the top to remove the spiral cable **(see illustration)**.

Installation

16 Verify that the front wheels are pointing straight ahead. If the spiral cable for the airbag has been removed and/or its centre position lost, turn the spiral cable clockwise by hand until it becomes hard to turn (don't apply too much force), then rotate it about 2-1/2 turns counterclockwise until the marks align and the location pin is straight up at the 12 o'clock position **(see illustration)**.

17 Feed the airbag spiral cable harness through the hub in the steering wheel, then slip the wheel onto the shaft, making sure the marks are aligned. Make sure the spiral cable pin is properly engaged with the corresponding hole in the back of the steering wheel.

14.13a Rock the steering wheel back-and-forth to break the connection between the wheel and steering column

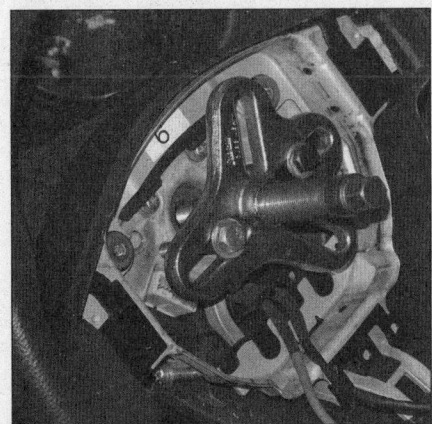

14.13b Use a steering wheel puller threaded into the holes in the steering wheel

14.15 Spiral cable details

1 Mounting screws
2 Retaining tab

Chapter 10 Suspension and steering systems

14.16 These two marks (A) on the surface of the spiral cable housing will be aligned when it's centred, and the locating pin (B) will be at the top (and must engage with the hole in the steering wheel).

18 Install the steering wheel retaining nut or bolt and tighten it to the specified torque.
19 Install the airbag module, tightening the bolts on earlier models to the specified torque. Install the covers.
20 Reconnect the battery (see Chapter 5 Section 3) and, with your body out of the path of the airbag, verify that the airbag circuit is operational by turning the ignition key to the On or Start position. The "AIR BAG" warning light should illuminate for a few seconds, then turn off.

15 Tie-rod ends - removal and installation

Removal

1 Loosen the front wheel nuts. Raise the front of the vehicle, support it securely on jackstands (see Chapter 0 Section 7), then remove the wheel.
2 Loosen the locknut enough to mark the position of the tie-rod end in relation to the threads **(see illustration)**.
3 Loosen, but don't remove, the nut on the tie-rod end balljoint **(see illustration)**.

15.4 Use a puller to detach the tie-rod end

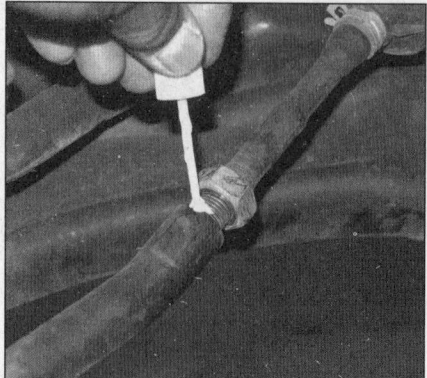

15.2 Loosen the locknut then mark the position of the tie-rod end on the threaded part of the tie-rod

4 Disconnect the tie-rod end from the steering knuckle arm with a puller **(see illustration)**.
5 Remove the nut and separate the tie-rod end from the steering knuckle.
6 Unscrew the tie-rod end from the tie-rod.

Installation

7 Thread the tie-rod end on to the marked position and insert the tie-rod stud into the steering knuckle arm. Tighten the locknut securely.
8 Install the nut on the balljoint and tighten it to the specified torque (see Specifications).
9 Install the wheel and wheel nuts. Lower the vehicle and tighten the wheel nuts to the specified torque (see Chapter 1).
10 Have the wheel alignment checked and, if necessary, adjusted.

16 Steering gear boots - replacement

1 Loosen the wheel nuts, raise the front of the vehicle and support on jackstands (see Chapter 0 Section 7). Remove the wheel.
2 Remove the tie-rod end and locknut (see Section 15).
3 Remove the outer steering gear boot clamp **(see illustration)** with a pair of pliers.

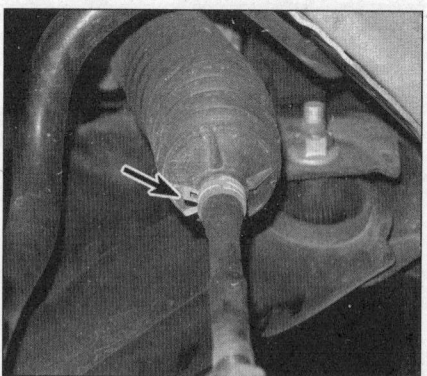

16.3a The outer end of the boot is secured by a spring clamp that can be slid off by pinching the ends together

15.3 Hold the ballstud from turning using a Torx bit while loosening the nut

Cut off the inner boot clamp **(see illustration)** with a pair of diagonal cutters. Slide the boot off.
4 Before installing the new boot, wrap the threads on the end of the steering rod with a layer of tape so the small end of the new boot isn't damaged.
5 Slide the new boot into position on the steering gear until it seats in the groove in the steering rod and install new clamps.
6 Remove the tape and install the tie-rod end (see Section 15).
7 Install the wheel and wheel nuts. Lower the vehicle and tighten the wheel nuts to the specified torque (see Chapter 1).
8 Have the wheel alignment checked and, if necessary, adjusted.

17 Steering gear - removal and installation

Warning: *The models covered by this manual are equipped with Supplemental Restraint Systems (SRS), more commonly known as airbags. Always disarm the airbag system before working in the vicinity of any airbag system component to avoid the possibility of accidental deployment of the airbag, which could cause personal injury (see Chapter 12A Section 20). Do not use a memory saving*

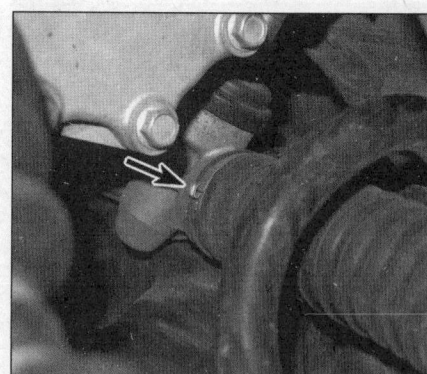

16.3b The inner end of the boot is retained by a clamp that must be cut off and discarded

Chapter 10 Suspension and steering systems

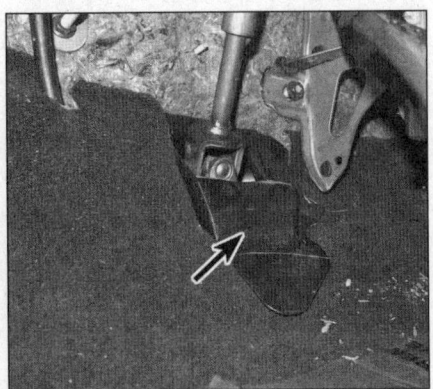

18.3a Pry the cover up to access the lower intermediate shaft bolt

18.3b Intermediate shaft pinch bolt

18.4a Disconnect the front ABS wheel speed sensor wiring connector

device to preserve the PCM's memory when working on or near airbag system components.

Removal

Warning: *Do not turn the steering wheel while the steering gear is removed. If the steering wheel is inadvertently turned, remove the steering wheel and centre the spiral cable (see Section 14). To prevent the steering wheel from turning, loop the seat belt through the steering wheel and fasten it into its latch.*

1 Set the wheels in the straight ahead position.
2 Remove the lower intermediate shaft joint cover **(see illustration 18.3a)**.
3 Remove the lower intermediate shaft bolt and remove the intermediate shaft from the steering gear **(see illustration 18.3b)**.
4 Loosen the front wheel nuts. Raise the front and rear of the vehicle and support it securely on jackstands (see Chapter 0 Section 7). Remove the front wheels.
5 Remove the subframe (see Section 18).
6 Remove the steering gear mounting nuts/bolts and remove the steering gear from the subframe.

Installation

Note: *Make sure the steering gear is centred from side to side before installing it. Ensure the mounting surface on the body side of the firewall seal is clean and free from damage.*

7 Place the gear on the subframe, install the bolts and tighten them to the specified torque
8 Install the subframe (see Section 18).
9 Install the wheels and wheel nuts, then lower the vehicle and tighten the wheel nuts to the specified torque (see Chapter 1).
10 Have the wheel alignment checked and, if necessary, adjusted.

18 Subframe (front) - removal and installation

1 Loosen the front wheel nuts. Raise the front and rear of the vehicle and support it securely on jackstands (see Chapter 0 Section 7). Remove the wheels.
2 Disconnect the negative (-) battery terminal (see Chapter 5 Section 3).
3 Separate the intermediate shaft from the steering gear pinion shaft.
4 Remove the ABS wheel speed sensors from the steering knuckles (see Chapter 9 Section 2).
5 Detach the stabiliser bar links from the stabiliser bar (see Section 4).
6 Detach the tie-rod ends from the steering knuckles (see Section 15).

7 Remove the torque rod (see Chapter 2A Section 15 - 2.0 litre petrol models, Chapter 2B Section 17 - 2.5 litre petrol models or Chapter 2C Section 20 - diesel models).
8 Remove the oxygen sensor bracket bolt from the subframe.
9 Separate the control arms from the steering knuckles (see Section 7).
10 Support the subframe with two floor jacks (one on each side).
11 Remove the subframe stay and the subframe mounting bolts **(see illustration)**. Slowly lower the jack, making sure nothing is still connected, until the subframe clears the rest of the vehicle, then remove it.
12 Installation is the reverse of removal, with attention to the following points:

  a *Tighten the subframe, suspension and steering fasteners to the specified torque (see Specifications).*
  b *Tighten the wheel nuts to the specified torque (see Chapter 1).*
  c *Reconnect the battery (see Chapter 5 Section 3)*
  d *Have the front wheel alignment checked, and, if necessary, adjusted.*

18.4b Unclip any wiring from the front suspension and then…

18.4c … remove the retaining bolt (arrow) and remove the ABS wheel speed sensor from the steering knuckle

18.8 Some models have a connector for the rear oxygen sensor mounted to the rear of the subframe - unclip this connector and position clear of the work area

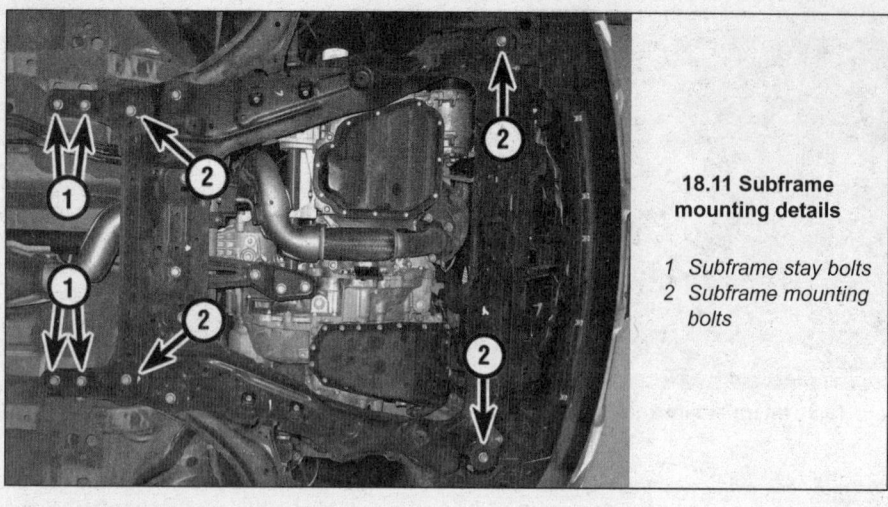

18.11 Subframe mounting details

1. Subframe stay bolts
2. Subframe mounting bolts

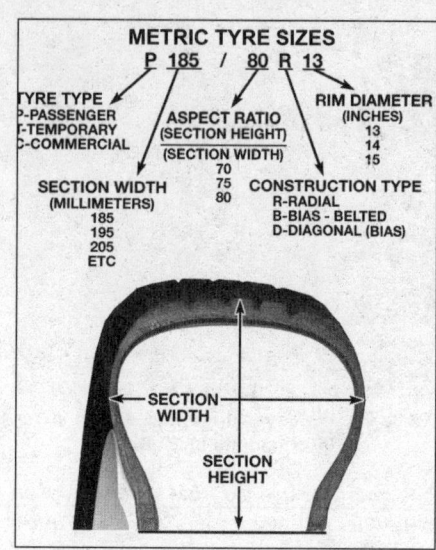

19.1 Metric tyre size code

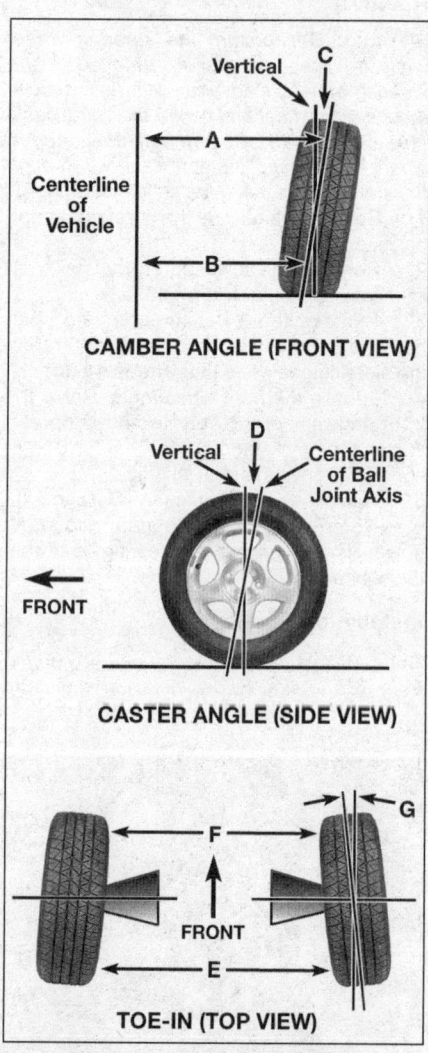

20.1 Camber, caster and toe-in angles

A minus B = C (degrees camber)
D = degrees caster
E minus F = toe-in (measured in mm)
G = toe-in (expressed in degrees)

19 Wheels and tyres - general information

1 All vehicles covered by this manual are equipped with metric-sized steel belted radial tyres (see illustration). Use of other size or type of tyres may affect the ride and handling of the vehicle. Don't mix different types of tyres, such as radials and bias belted, on the same vehicle as handling may be seriously affected. It's recommended that tyres be replaced in pairs on the same axle, but if only one tyre is being replaced, be sure it's the same size, structure and tread design as the other.

2 Because tyre pressure has a substantial effect on handling and wear, the pressure on all tyres should be checked at least once a month or before any extended trips (see Chapter 1 Section 7).

3 Wheels must be replaced if they are bent, dented, leak air, have elongated bolt holes, are heavily rusted, out of vertical symmetry or if the wheel nuts won't stay tight. Wheel repairs that use welding or peening are not recommended.

4 Tyre and wheel balance is important in the overall handling, braking and performance of the vehicle. Unbalanced wheels can adversely affect handling and ride characteristics as well as tyre life. Whenever a tyre is installed on a wheel, the tyre and wheel should be balanced by a shop with the proper equipment.

20 Wheel alignment - general information

1 A wheel alignment refers to the adjustments made to the wheels so they are in proper angular relationship to the suspension and the ground. Wheels that are out of proper alignment not only affect vehicle control, but also increase tyre wear. The front end angles normally measured are camber, caster and toe-in (see illustration). On the front end, camber and caster are preset at the factory; toe-in is the only adjustable angle (however, camber and caster are usually measured to check for bent or worn suspension parts). Toe-in and camber are both adjustable at the rear.

2 Getting the proper wheel alignment is an exacting process, one in which complicated and expensive machines are necessary to perform the job properly. Because of this, you should have a technician with the proper equipment perform these tasks. We will, however, use this space to give you a basic idea of what is involved with a wheel alignment so you can better understand the process and deal intelligently with the shop that does the work.

3 Toe-in is the turning in of the wheels. The purpose of a toe specification is to ensure parallel rolling of the wheels. In a vehicle with zero toe-in, the distance between the front edges of the wheels will be the same as the distance between the rear edges of the wheels. The actual amount of toe-in is normally only a few millimetres. Incorrect toe-in will cause the tyres to wear improperly by making them scrub against the road surface.

4 Camber is the tilting of the wheels from vertical when viewed from one end of the vehicle. When the wheels tilt out at the top, the camber is said to be positive (+). When the wheels tilt in at the top the camber is negative (-). The amount of tilt is measured in degrees from vertical and this measurement is called the camber angle. This angle affects the amount of tyre tread which contacts the road and compensates for changes in the suspension geometry when the vehicle is cornering or travelling over an undulating surface.

5 Caster is the tilting of the front steering axis from the vertical. A tilt toward the rear is positive caster and a tilt toward the front is negative caster.

Chapter 11
Body

Contents

Section		Section	
Airbag system – general information, precautions and system de-activation	See Chapter 12	Fastener and trim removal	6
Airbag system components – removal and refitting	See Chapter 12	Front bumper – removal and installation	18
		General information	1
Body repair - major damage	4	Hinges and locks - maintenance	7
Body repair - minor damage	3	Outside mirrors - removal and installation	20
Bonnet - removal, installation and adjustment	9	Radiator grille - removal and installation	11
Bonnet release latch and cable - removal and installation	10	Rear bumper – removal and installation	19
Centre console – removal and installation	22	Repairing minor paint scratches	2
Cowl panel - removal and installation	25	Seats - removal and installation	26
Dashboard - removal and installation	24	Steering column covers - removal and installation	23
Dashboard panels – removal and installation	21	Tailgate and trim panel - removal, installation and adjustment	12
Door - removal, installation and adjustment	16	Tailgate latch, opening switch and support struts - removal and installation	13
Door lock, cylinder and handles - removal and installation	17	Upholstery, carpets and vinyl trim - maintenance	5
Door trim panel – removal and refitting	14	Windshield and fixed glass - replacement	8
Door window glass and regulator – removal and refitting	15		

1 General information

Warning: *The models covered by this manual are equipped with Supplemental Restraint Systems (SRS), more commonly known as airbags. Always disable the airbag system before working in the vicinity of any airbag system components to avoid the possibility of accidental deployment of the airbags, which could cause personal injury (see Chapter 12A Section 20).*

Note: *The SRS module has an internal capacitor capable of supplying power to the system for about 2 minutes once power has been removed. This is to ensure that the airbags work if the vehicle is in an accident where the battery is destroyed.*

1 Certain body components are particularly vulnerable to accident damage and can be unbolted and repaired or replaced. Among these parts are the bonnet, doors, tailgate, bumpers and front mudguards.

2 Only general body maintenance practices and body panel repair procedures within the scope of the do-it-yourselfer are included in this Chapter.

2 Repairing minor paint scratches

No matter how hard you try to keep your vehicle looking like new, it will inevitably be scratched, chipped or dented at some point. If the metal is actually dented, seek the advice of a professional. But you can fix minor scratches and chips yourself. Buy a touch-up paint kit from a dealer service department or an auto parts store. To ensure that you get the right colour, you'll need to have the specific make, model and year of your vehicle and, ideally, the paint code, which is located on a special metal plate under the bonnet or in the door jamb.

Chapter 11 Body

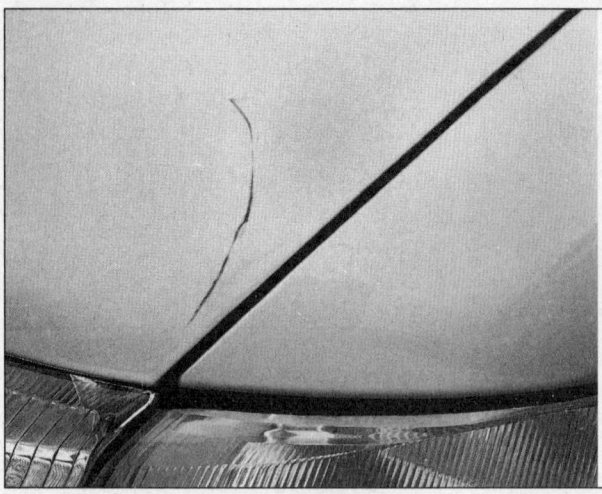

2.1a Make sure the damaged area is perfectly clean and rust free. If the touch-up kit has a wire brush, use it to clean the scratch or chip. Or use fine steel wool wrapped around the end of a pencil. Clean the scratched or chipped surface only, not the good paint surrounding it. Rinse the area with water and allow it to dry thoroughly

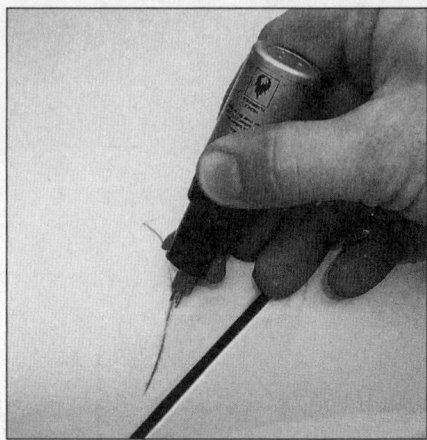

2.1b Thoroughly mix the paint, then apply a small amount with the touch-up kit brush or a very fine artist's brush. Brush in one direction as you fill the scratch area. Do not build up the paint higher than the surrounding paint

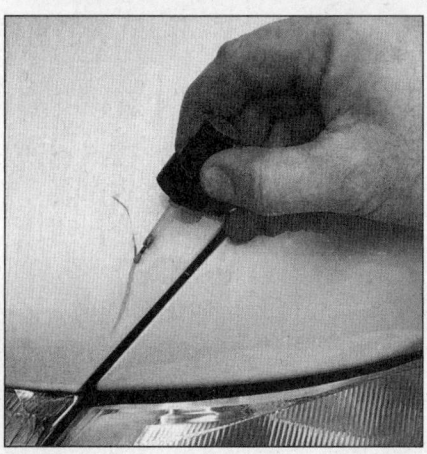

2.1c If the vehicle has a two-coat finish, apply the clear coat after the colour coat has dried

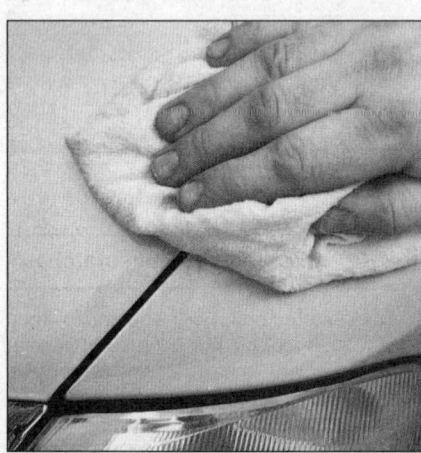

2.1d Wait a few days for the paint to dry thoroughly, then rub out the repainted area with a polishing compound to blend the new paint with the surrounding area. When you're happy with your work, wash and polish the area

3 Body repair - minor damage

Plastic body panels

1   The following repair procedures are for minor scratches and gouges. Repair of more serious damage should be left to a dealer service department or qualified auto body shop. Below is a list of the equipment and materials necessary to perform the following repair procedures on plastic body panels.

- Wax, grease and silicone removing solvent
- Cloth-backed body tape
- Sanding discs
- Drill motor with three-inch disc holder
- Hand sanding block
- Rubber squeegees
- Sandpaper
- Non-porous mixing palette
- Wood paddle or putty knife
- Curved-tooth body file
- Flexible parts repair material

Flexible panels (bumper trim)

2   Remove the damaged panel, if necessary or desirable. In most cases, repairs can be carried out with the panel installed.
3   Clean the area(s) to be repaired with a wax, grease and silicone removing solvent applied with a water-dampened cloth.
4   If the damage is structural, that is, if it extends through the panel, clean the backside of the panel area to be repaired as well. Wipe dry.
5   Sand the rear surface about 38 mm beyond the break.
6   Cut two pieces of fibreglass cloth large enough to overlap the break by about 38 mm. Cut only to the required length.
7   Mix the adhesive from the repair kit according to the instructions included with the kit, and apply a layer of the mixture approximately 3 mm thick on the backside of the panel. Overlap the break by at least 38 mm.
8   Apply one piece of fibreglass cloth to the adhesive and cover the cloth with additional adhesive. Apply a second piece of fibreglass cloth to the adhesive and immediately cover the cloth with additional adhesive in sufficient quantity to fill the weave.
9   Allow the repair to cure for 20 to 30 minutes at 15-degrees to 26-degrees C.
10 If necessary, trim the excess repair material at the edge.
11 Remove all of the paint film over and around the area(s) to be repaired. The repair material should not overlap the painted surface.
12 With a drill motor and a sanding disc (or a rotary file), cut a "V" along the break line approximately 10 mm wide. Remove all dust and loose particles from the repair area.
13 Mix and apply the repair material. Apply a light coat first over the damaged area; then continue applying material until it reaches a level slightly higher than the surrounding finish.
14 Cure the mixture for 20 to 30 minutes at 15-degrees to 26-degrees C.
15 Roughly establish the contour of the area being repaired with a body file. If low areas or pits remain, mix and apply additional adhesive.
16 Block sand the damaged area with sandpaper to establish the actual contour of the surrounding surface.
17 If desired, the repaired area can be temporarily protected with several light coats of primer. Because of the special paints and techniques required for flexible body panels, it is recommended that the vehicle be taken to a paint shop for completion of the body repair.

Steel body panels

Repairing simple dents

18 These photos illustrate a method of repairing simple dents. They are intended to supplement this Section and should not be used as the sole instructions for body repair on these vehicles.

These photos illustrate a method of repairing simple dents. They are intended to supplement *Body repair - minor damage* in this Chapter and should not be used as the sole instructions for body repair on these vehicles.

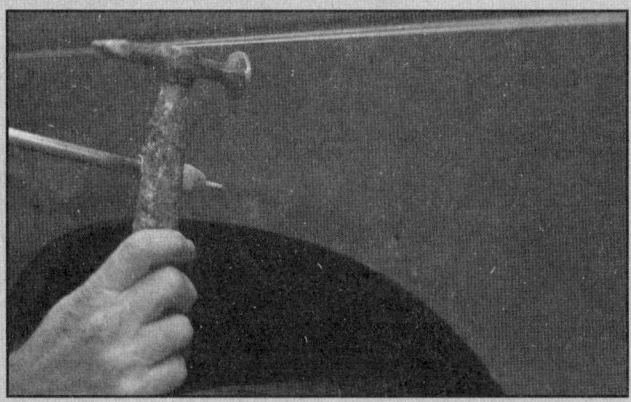

1 If you can't access the backside of the body panel to hammer out the dent, pull it out with a slide-hammer-type dent puller. Tap with a hammer near the edge of the dent to help 'pop' the metal back to its original shape, about 1/8-inch below the surface of the surrounding metal

2 Using coarse-grit sandpaper, remove the paint down to the bare metal. Clean the repair area with wax/silicone remover.

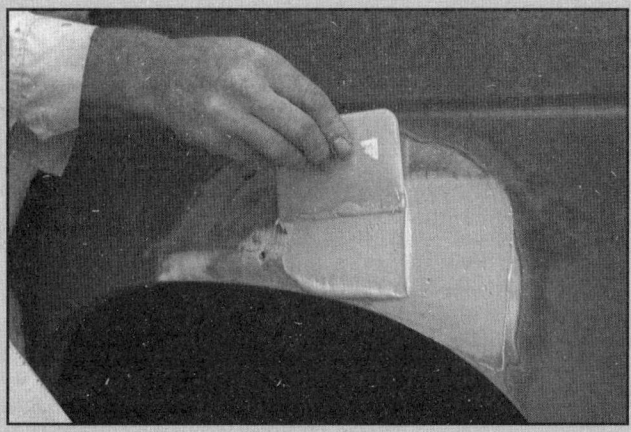

3 Following label instructions, mix up a batch of plastic filler and hardener, then quickly press it into the metal with a plastic applicator. Work the filler until it matches the original contour and is slightly above the surrounding metal

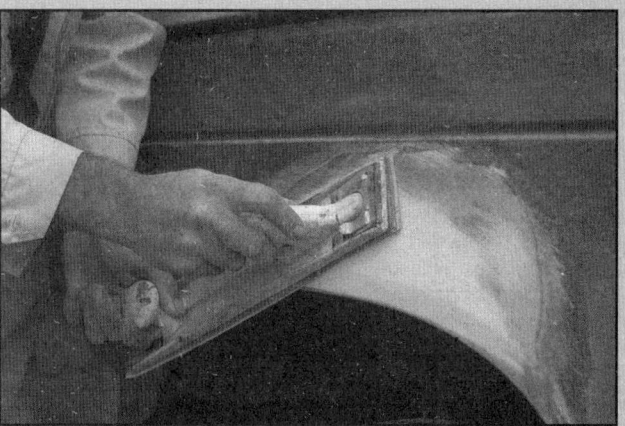

4 Let the filler harden until you can just dent it with your fingernail. File, then sand the filler down until it's smooth and even. Work down to finer grits of sandpaper - always using a board or block - ending up with 360 or 400 grit

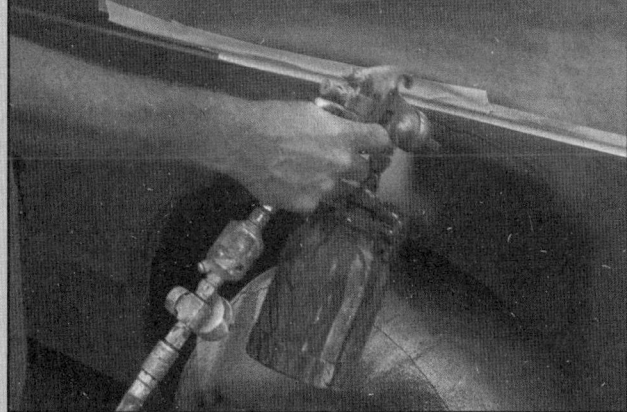

5 When the area is smooth to the touch, clean the area and mask around it. Apply several layers of primer to the area. A professional-type spray gun is being used here, but aerosol spray primer works fine

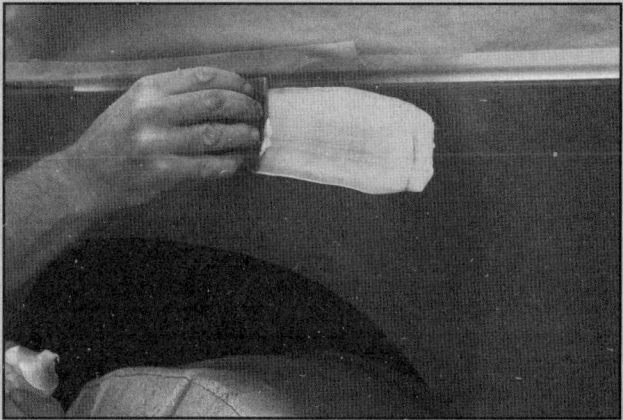

6 Fill imperfections or scratches with glazing compound. Sand with 360 or 400-grit and re-spray. Finish sand the primer with 600 grit, clean thoroughly, then apply the finish coat. Don't attempt to rub out or wax the repair area until the paint has dried completely (at least two weeks)

19 When repairing dents, the first job is to pull the dent out until the affected area is as close as possible to its original shape. There is no point in trying to restore the original shape completely as the metal in the damaged area will have stretched on impact and cannot be restored to its original contours. It is better to bring the level of the dent up to a point that is about 1/8-inch below the level of the surrounding metal. In cases where the dent is very shallow, it is not worth trying to pull it out at all.

20 If the backside of the dent is accessible, it can be hammered out gently from behind using a soft-face hammer. While doing this, hold a block of wood firmly against the opposite side of the metal to absorb the hammer blows and prevent the metal from being stretched.

21 If the dent is in a Section of the body which has double layers, or some other factor makes it inaccessible from behind, a different technique is required. Drill several small holes through the metal inside the damaged area, particularly in the deeper sections. Screw long, self-tapping screws into the holes just enough for them to get a good grip in the metal. Now pulling on the protruding heads of the screws with locking pliers can pull out the dent.

22 The next stage of repair is the removal of paint from the damaged area and from about 25 mm of the surrounding metal. This is easily done with a wire brush or sanding disk in a drill motor, although it can be done just as effectively by hand with sandpaper. To complete the preparation for filling, score the surface of the bare metal with a screwdriver or the tang of a file or drill small holes in the affected area. This will provide a good grip for the filler material. To complete the repair, see the Section on filling and painting.

Repair of rust holes or gashes

23 Remove all paint from the affected area and from about 25mm of the surrounding metal using a sanding disk or wire brush mounted in a drill motor. If these are not available, a few sheets of sandpaper will do the job just as effectively.

24 With the paint removed, you will be able to determine the severity of the corrosion and decide whether to replace the whole panel, if possible, or repair the affected area. New body panels are not as expensive as most people think and it is often quicker to install a new panel than to repair large areas of rust.

25 Remove all trim pieces from the affected area except those which will act as a guide to the original shape of the damaged body, such as headlight shells, etc. Using metal snips or a hacksaw blade, remove all loose metal and any other metal that is badly affected by rust. Hammer the edges of the hole in to create a slight depression for the filler material.

26 Wire-brush the affected area to remove the powdery rust from the surface of the metal. If the back of the rusted area is accessible, treat it with rust inhibiting paint.

27 Before filling is done, block the hole in some way. This can be done with sheet metal riveted or screwed into place, or by stuffing the hole with wire mesh.

28 Once the hole is blocked off, the affected area can be filled and painted. See the following subsection on filling and painting.

Filling and painting

29 Many types of body fillers are available, but generally speaking, body repair kits which contain filler paste and a tube of resin hardener are best for this type of repair work. A wide, flexible plastic or nylon applicator will be necessary for imparting a smooth and contoured finish to the surface of the filler material. Mix up a small amount of filler on a clean piece of wood or cardboard (use the hardener sparingly). Follow the manufacturer's instructions on the package, otherwise the filler will set incorrectly.

30 Using the applicator, apply the filler paste to the prepared area. Draw the applicator across the surface of the filler to achieve the desired contour and to level the filler surface. As soon as a contour that approximates the original one is achieved, stop working the paste. If you continue, the paste will begin to stick to the applicator. Continue to add thin layers of paste at 20-minute intervals until the level of the filler is just above the surrounding metal.

31 Once the filler has hardened, the excess can be removed with a body file. From then on, progressively finer grades of sandpaper should be used, starting with a 180-grit paper and finishing with 600-grit wet-or-dry paper. Always wrap the sandpaper around a flat rubber or wooden block, otherwise the surface of the filler will not be completely flat. During the sanding of the filler surface, the wet-or-dry paper should be periodically rinsed in water. This will ensure that a very smooth finish is produced in the final stage.

32 At this point, the repair area should be surrounded by a ring of bare metal, which in turn should be encircled by the finely feathered edge of good paint. Rinse the repair area with clean water until all of the dust produced by the sanding operation is gone.

33 Spray the entire area with a light coat of primer. This will reveal any imperfections in the surface of the filler. Repair the imperfections with fresh filler paste or glaze filler and once more smooth the surface with sandpaper. Repeat this spray-and-repair procedure until you are satisfied that the surface of the filler and the feathered edge of the paint are perfect. Rinse the area with clean water and allow it to dry completely.

34 The repair area is now ready for painting. Spray painting must be carried out in a warm, dry, windless and dust free atmosphere. These conditions can be created if you have access to a large indoor work area, but if you are forced to work in the open, you will have to pick the day very carefully. If you are working indoors, dousing the floor in the work area with water will help settle the dust that would otherwise be in the air. If the repair area is confined to one body panel, mask off the surrounding panels. This will help minimize the effects of a slight mismatch in paint colour. Trim pieces such as chrome strips, door handles, etc., will also need to be masked off or removed. Use masking tape and several thickness of newspaper for the masking operations.

35 Before spraying, shake the paint can thoroughly, then spray a test area until the spray painting technique is mastered. Cover the repair area with a thick coat of primer. The thickness should be built up using several thin layers of primer rather than one thick one. Using 600-grit wet-or-dry sandpaper, rub down the surface of the primer until it is very smooth. While doing this, the work area should be thoroughly rinsed with water and the wet-or-dry sandpaper periodically rinsed as well. Allow the primer to dry before spraying additional coats.

36 Spray on the top coat, again building up the thickness by using several thin layers of paint. Begin spraying in the centre of the repair area and then, using a circular motion, work out until the whole repair area and about 50 mm of the surrounding original paint is covered. Remove all masking material 10 to 15 minutes after spraying on the final coat of paint. Allow the new paint at least two weeks to harden, then use a very fine rubbing compound to blend the edges of the new paint into the existing paint. Finally, apply a coat of wax.

4 Body repair - major damage

1 Major damage must be repaired by an auto body shop specifically equipped to perform body and frame repairs. These shops have the specialized equipment required to do the job properly.

2 If the damage is extensive, the frame must be checked for proper alignment or the vehicle's handling characteristics may be adversely affected and other components may wear at an accelerated rate.

3 Due to the fact that all of the major body components (bonnet, mudguards, etc.) are separate and replaceable units, any seriously damaged components should be replaced rather than repaired. Sometimes the components can be found in a wrecking yard that specializes in used vehicle components, often at considerable savings over the cost of new parts.

5 Upholstery, carpets and vinyl trim - maintenance

Upholstery and carpets

1 Every three months remove the floormats and clean the interior of the vehicle (more frequently if necessary). Use a stiff whiskbroom to brush the carpeting and loosen dirt and dust, then vacuum the upholstery and carpets thoroughly, especially along seams and crevices.

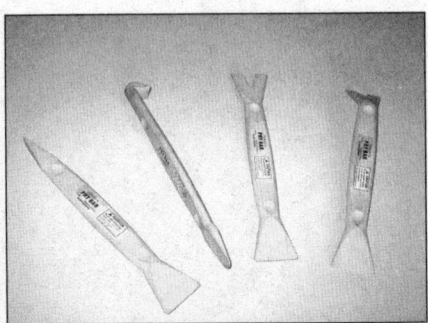

6.4 These small plastic pry tools are ideal for prying off trim panels

2 Dirt and stains can be removed from carpeting with basic household or automotive carpet shampoos available in spray cans. Follow the directions and vacuum again, then use a stiff brush to bring back the nap of the carpet.

3 Most interiors have cloth or vinyl upholstery, either of which can be cleaned and maintained with a number of material-specific cleaners or shampoos available in auto supply stores. Follow the directions on the product for usage, and always spot-test any upholstery cleaner on an inconspicuous area (bottom edge of a backseat cushion) to ensure that it doesn't cause a colour shift in the material.

4 After cleaning, vinyl upholstery should be treated with a protectant.

Note: *Make sure the protectant container indicates the product can be used on seats - some products may make a seat too slippery.*

Caution: *Do not use protectant on vinyl-covered steering wheels.*

5 Leather upholstery requires special care. It should be cleaned regularly with saddlesoap or leather cleaner. Never use alcohol, gasoline, nail polish remover or thinner to clean leather upholstery.

6 After cleaning, regularly treat leather upholstery with a leather conditioner, rubbed in with a soft cotton cloth. Never use car wax on leather upholstery.

7 In areas where the interior of the vehicle is subject to bright sunlight, cover leather seating areas of the seats with a sheet if the vehicle is to be left out for any length of time.

Vinyl trim

8 Don't clean vinyl trim with detergents, caustic soap or petroleum-based cleaners. Plain soap and water works just fine, with a soft brush to clean dirt that may be ingrained. Wash the vinyl as frequently as the rest of the vehicle.

9 After cleaning, application of a high-quality rubber and vinyl protectant will help prevent oxidation and cracks. The protectant can also be applied to weather-stripping, vacuum lines and rubber hoses, which often fail as a result of chemical degradation, and to the tyres.

6 Fastener and trim removal

1 There is a variety of plastic fasteners used to hold trim panels, splash shields and other parts in place in addition to typical screws, nuts and bolts. Once you are familiar with them, they can usually be removed without too much difficulty.

2 The proper tools and approach can prevent added time and expense to a project by minimizing the number of broken fasteners and/or parts.

3 The following illustration shows various types of fasteners that are typically used on most vehicles and how to remove and install them **(see illustration)**. Replacement fasteners are commonly found at most auto parts stores, if necessary.

Fasteners

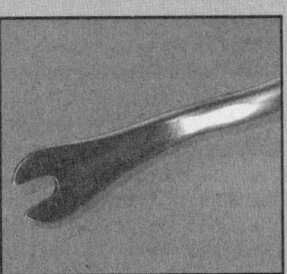

This tool is designed to remove special fasteners. A small pry tool used for removing nails will also work well in place of this tool

A Phillips head screwdriver can be used to release the center portion, but light pressure must be used because the plastic is easily damaged. Once the center is up, the fastener can easily be pried from its hole

Here is a view with the center portion fully released. Install the fastener as shown, then press the center in to set it

This fastener is used for exterior panels and shields. The center portion must be pried up to release the fastener. Install the fastener with the center up, then press the center in to set it

This type of fastener is used commonly for interior panels. Use a small blunt tool to press the small pin at the center in to release it . . .

. . . the pin will stay with the fastener in the released position

Reset the fastener for installation by moving the pin out. Install the fastener, then press the pin flush with the fastener to set it

This fastener is used for exterior and interior panels. It has no moving parts. Simply pry the fastener from its hole like the claw of a hammer removes a nail. Without a tool that can get under the top of the fastener, it can be very difficult to remove

Chapter 11 Body

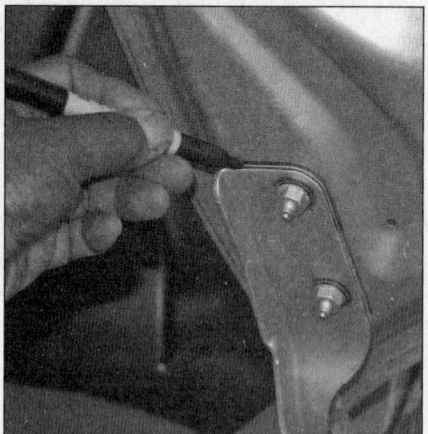

9.2 Before removing the bonnet, draw a mark around the hinge plate

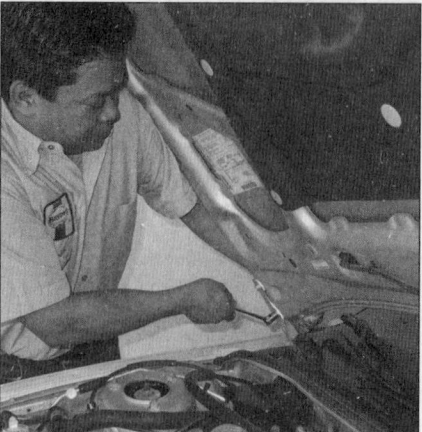

9.4 Support the bonnet with your shoulder while removing the bonnet nuts

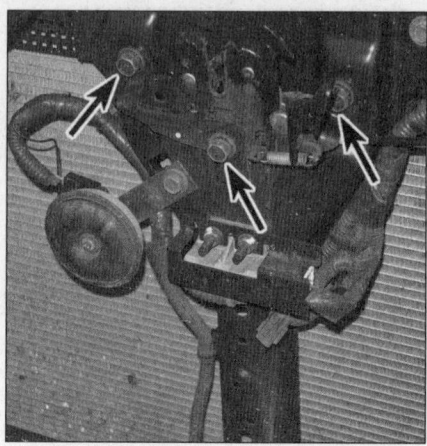

9.10 To adjust the bonnet latch, loosen the retaining bolts, move the latch and retighten the bolts, then close the bonnet to check the fit

4   Trim panels are typically made of plastic and their flexibility can help during removal. The key to their removal is to use a tool to pry the panel near its retainers to release it without damaging surrounding areas or breaking-off any retainers. The retainers will usually snap out of their designated slot or hole after force is applied to them. Stiff plastic tools designed for prying on trim panels are available at most auto parts stores (**see illustration**). Tools that are tapered and wrapped in protective tape, such as a screwdriver or small pry tool, are also very effective when used with care.

7   Hinges and locks - maintenance

1   Once every 20,000 km, or every 12 months, the hinges and latch assemblies on the doors, bonnet and luggage compartment should be given a few drops of light oil or lock lubricant. The door latch strikers should also be lubricated with a thin coat of grease to reduce wear and ensure free movement. Lubricate the door and luggage compartment locks with spray-on graphite lubricant.

8   Windshield and fixed glass - replacement

1   Replacement of the windshield and fixed glass requires the use of special fast-setting adhesive/caulk materials and some specialised tools. It is recommended that these operations be left to a dealer or a shop specialising in glass work.

9   Bonnet - removal, installation and adjustment

Note: *The bonnet is heavy and somewhat awkward to remove and install - at least two people should perform this procedure.*

Removal and installation

1   Use blankets or pads to cover the cowl area of the body and mudguards. This will protect the body and paint as the bonnet is lifted off.
2   Make marks or scribe a line around the bonnet hinge to ensure proper alignment during installation (**see illustration**).
3   Disconnect any cables or wires that will interfere with removal.
4   Have an assistant support one side of the bonnet while you support the other. Remove the hinge-to-bonnet nuts (**see illustration**).
5   Lift off the bonnet.
6   Installation is the reverse of removal.

Adjustment

7   Fore-and-aft and side-to-side adjustment of the bonnet is done by moving the hinge plate slot after loosening the bolts or nuts.
8   Scribe a line around the entire hinge plate so you can determine the amount of movement (**see illustration 9.2**).
9   Loosen the bolts or nuts and move the bonnet into correct alignment. Move it only a little at a time. Tighten the hinge bolts and carefully lower the bonnet to check the position.
10   If necessary after installation, the entire bonnet latch assembly can be adjusted up-and-down as well as from side-to-side on the radiator support so the bonnet closes securely

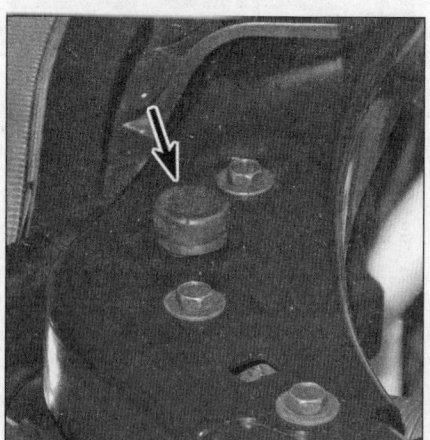

9.11 Adjust the bonnet closing height by turning the bonnet bumpers in or out

10.3 Pry out the cable retainer from the rear of the bonnet latch assembly, then disengage the cable end

10.7 The bonnet release cable is secured along its length with clips

Chapter 11 Body

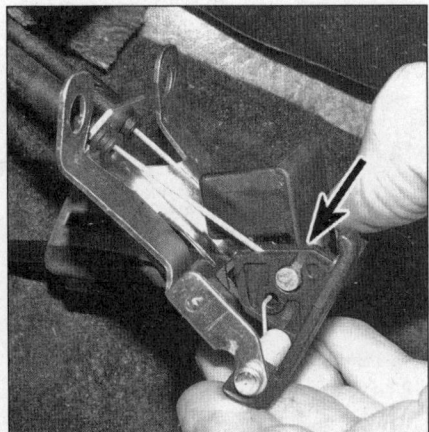

10.8 Release the end of the cable from the handle, then snap the cable housing from its retainer

11.2a Radiator grille upper fasteners - Dualis models

and flush with the mudguards. To make the adjustment, scribe a line or mark around the bonnet latch mounting bolts to provide a reference point, then loosen them and reposition the latch assembly, as necessary **(see illustration)**. Following adjustment, retighten the mounting bolts.

11 Finally, adjust the bonnet bumpers on the ends of the radiator support, so when closed, is flush with the mudguards **(see illustration)**.

12 The bonnet latch assembly, as well as the hinges, should be periodically lubricated with white, lithium-base grease to prevent binding and wear.

10 Bonnet release latch and cable - removal and installation

Warning: *The models covered by this manual are equipped with a Supplemental Restraint System (SRS), more commonly known as airbags. Always disarm the airbag system before working in the vicinity of any airbag system component to avoid the possibility of accidental deployment of the airbag, which could cause personal injury (see Chapter 12A Section 20). Do not use a memory saving device to preserve the PCM's memory when working on or near airbag system components.*

Latch

1 Remove the radiator grille (see Section 11).
2 Scribe a line around the latch to aid alignment when installing, then remove the latch retaining bolts **(see illustration 9.10)** and remove the latch.
3 Disconnect the bonnet release cable by disengaging the cable from the latch assembly **(see illustration)**.
4 Installation is the reverse of removal.

Note: *Adjust the latch so the bonnet engages securely when closed and the bonnet bumpers are slightly compressed.*

Cable

5 Disconnect the bonnet release cable from the latch assembly (see Step 3).
6 Remove the radiator grille (see Section 11) and the right inner mudguard liner.
7 Detach the cable from the clips along its length **(see illustration)**.
8 Detach the cable from the bonnet release handle **(see illustration)**.
9 Pull the cable grommet into the passenger compartment, then pull the cable through the hole.

Note: *Be careful not to kink the cable during handling.*

10 Installation is the reverse of the removal.

Note: *Push on the grommet with your fingers from the passenger compartment to seat the grommet in the firewall correctly; use sealant around the grommet.*

11 Radiator grille - removal and installation

Warning: *The models covered by this manual are equipped with a Supplemental Restraint System (SRS), more commonly known as airbags. Always disarm the airbag system before working in the vicinity of any airbag system component to avoid the possibility of accidental deployment of the airbag, which could cause personal injury (see Chapter 12A Section 20). Do not use a memory saving device to preserve the PCM's memory when working on or near airbag system components.*

1 Open the bonnet.
2 Remove the centre of the push-pin plastic fasteners at the top of the grille, then pull out the fasteners **(see illustrations)**.
3 On models with a front camera, reach behind the partially removed grille and disconnect the wiring from the rear of the camera.

11.2b Radiator grille upper fasteners - T31 X-trail models

11.2c Radiator grill upper fasteners - T32 X-Trail and Qashqai models

11.2d Using a trim clip removal tool to release one of the upper grille fasteners

11.4 Removing the grille from the front of the vehicle - T32 X-Trail shown, other models similar

12.3a Remove the retaining screw - Dualis models

12.3b Remove the retaining screw - Qashqai models

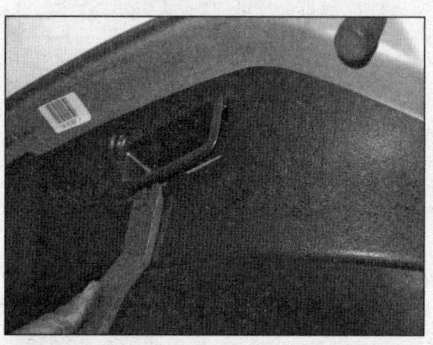

12.4 Using a trim removal tool to pry out the closing handle on X-Trail models

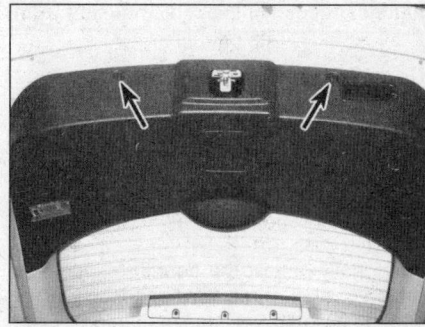

12.5 Release the two retaining clips from the lower edge

4   Pull the grille outward to release the lower clips from the bumper cover (see illustration).
5   Installation is the reverse of removal.

12 Tailgate and trim panel - removal, installation and adjustment

Note: The tailgate is heavy and somewhat awkward to remove and install - at least two people should perform this procedure.

Trim panel

Removal and installation

1   Open the tailgate all the way.
2   Disconnect the negative (-) battery terminal (see Chapter 5 Section 3).
3   Dualis and Qashqai models have a screw inside the door closing handle inside the trim panel that needs to be removed. Remove this screw (see illustration).
4   On X-Trail models, use a trim removal tool to pry out the closing handle from the bottom of the tailgate (see illustration).
5   Pull out the centre pins, and then release the two securing clips, from the lower edge of the tailgate trim (see illustration).
6   Carefully working your way around the trim panel, release the retaining clips and remove the panel from the tailgate (see illustration).
7   Unclip the trim panels from each side of the rear screen (see illustration).

Note: Dualis and Qashqai models have a screw on each trim panel that needs to be removed first.

8   Unclip the trim panel from the top inner edge of the rear screen (see illustration).
9   Refitting is a reversal of removal, but ensure that all clips are securely engaged.

Tailgate

Removal and installation

10   Remove the trim panel from the tailgate as previously described.
11   Disconnect all electrical connections,

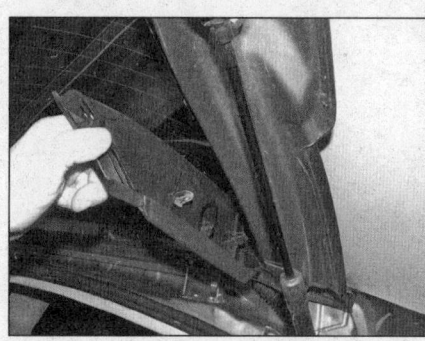

12.7 Removing one of the trim panels from the side of the rear screen

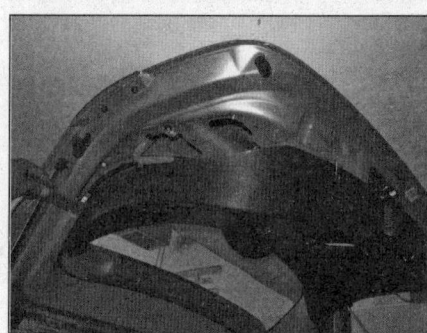

12.6 Using a trim removal tool, work around the circumference of the trim panel releasing each clip

ground wires and harness retaining clips from the tailgate.

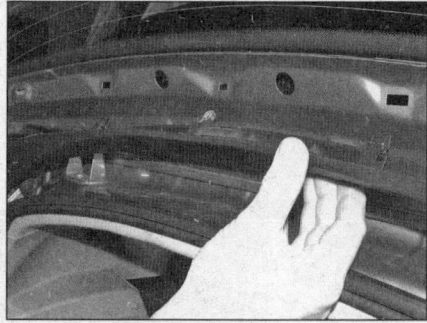

12.8 Removing the trim panel from the top of the rear screen

Chapter 11 Body

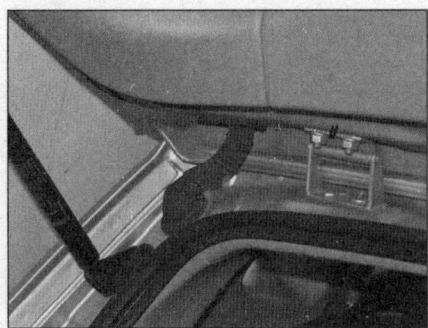

12.14 Mark around the tailgate hinges so it can be installed in the same position

13.3 Disconnect the electrical connector

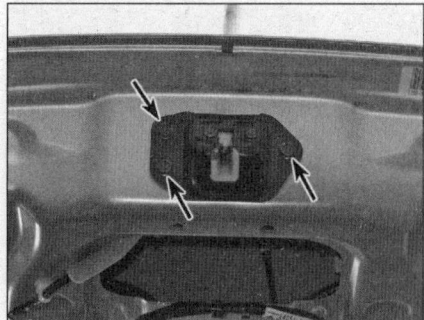

13.4 Tailgate latch fasteners

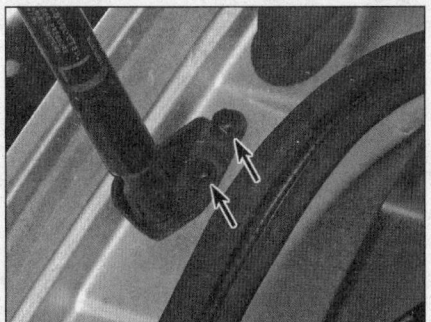

13.11a Remove the tailgate support strut-to-body bolts…

13.11b… or insert a small screwdriver under the locking clip and pry it up, then separate the ball socket connection

Note: *It is a good idea to label all connections to aid the reassembly process.*

12 Detach the rubber conduit between the body and the tailgate. Pull the wiring harness through the conduit hole and remove it from the tailgate.
13 Detach the tailgate support struts (see Section 13) and have an assistant hold the weight of the tailgate.
14 Mark around the tailgate hinges with a pen or a scribe to facilitate realignment during reassembly **(see illustration)**.
15 With the assistant still holding the tailgate, unscrew the hinge-to-tailgate nuts and remove the tailgate.
16 Installation is the reverse of removal.

Adjustment

17 Having proper tailgate-to-body alignment is a critical part of a well-functioning tailgate assembly. First check the tailgate hinge pins for excessive play. Fully open the tailgate and lift up and down on the tailgate without lifting the body. If a tailgate has 1.5-mm or more excessive play, the hinges should be replaced.
18 Tailgate-to-body alignment adjustments are made by loosening the hinge-to-body nuts or hinge-to-tailgate nuts and moving the tailgate. Proper body alignment is achieved when the top of the tailgate is parallel with the roof section, the sides of the tailgate are flush with the rear quarter panels, and the bottom of the tailgate is aligned with the lower tailgate sill. If these goals can't be reached by adjusting the hinge-to-body or hinge-to-tailgate nuts, body alignment shims may have to be purchased and inserted behind the hinges to achieve correct alignment.
19 To adjust the tailgate-closed position, scribe a line or mark around the striker plate to provide a reference point, then check that the tailgate latch is contacting the centre of the latch striker. If not, adjust the up and down position first.
20 Finally adjust the latch striker fore-and-aft position, so that the tailgate panel is flush with the rear quarter panel and provides positive engagement with the latch mechanism.

13 Tailgate latch, opening switch and support struts - removal and installation

Tailgate latch

1 Disconnect the negative (-) battery terminal (see Chapter 5 Section 3).
2 Open the tailgate and remove the trim panel (see Section 12).
3 Disconnect the electrical connector for the latch through the opening **(see illustration)**.
4 Remove the fasteners securing the latch to the tailgate **(see illustration)**. Remove the latch assembly.
5 Installation is the reverse of removal.

Opening switch

6 Open the tailgate and remove the trim panel (see Section 12).
7 Disconnect the electrical connector to the tailgate opening switch and rear view camera, if equipped.
8 Remove the tailgate opening switch trim panel mounting nuts and pull the trim panel off of the tailgate.
9 Remove the tailgate opening switch fasteners and separate the switch from the panel.
10 Installation is the reverse of removal.

Tailgate support struts or spindles

Note: *2014 and later models have an automatic open-and-close option for the tailgate. These models use powered spindles instead of support struts.*

11 On models without automatic open-and-close option, detach the tailgate support struts by either unbolting them at the top or using a small screwdriver to separate the ball socket connection **(see illustrations)**. Have an assistant hold the weight of the tailgate.
12 On models with automatic open-and-close option, disconnect the spindle electrical connectors, then unbolt the spindles from the tailgate and body. Have an assistant hold the weight of the tailgate while the spindles are being unbolted.
13 Installation is the reverse of removal.

14 Door trim panel – removal and refitting

Dualis

Front door trim panel

1 Disconnect the negative (-) battery terminal (see Chapter 5 Section 3).
2 Carefully unclip the switch panel from the top of the armrest and disconnect the wiring connectors **(see illustrations)**.
3 Unclip the trim finisher and remove it from the grab handle **(see illustrations)**.
4 Undo the two retaining screws and remove the grab handle and surround from the door trim panel **(see illustrations)**. Pull

11-10 Chapter 11 Body

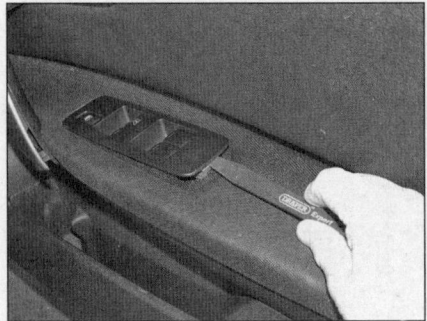

14.2a Unclip the switch panel ...

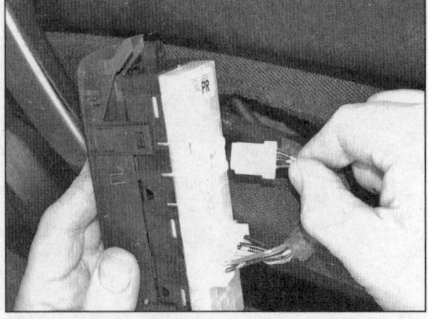

14.2b ... and disconnect the wiring connectors

14.3a Carefully lever the trim panel ...

14.3b ... to release the securing clips

14.4a Undo the two retaining screws ...

14.4b ... and remove the door handle trim

14.5 Lift and remove the trim panel from the door

14.8a Carefully lever the handle trim panel ...

a Make sure that the trim panel securing clips engage correctly with the door panel. Renew any broken clips.
b Check the upper weatherstrip engages correctly with the door trim panel as the panel is refitted.

Rear door trim panel (early models)

7 Disconnect the negative (-) battery terminal (see Chapter 5 Section 3).
8 Carefully prise the trim from around the door inner release lever **(see illustrations)**.
9 Carefully unclip the switch panel from the top of the armrest and disconnect the wiring connector **(see illustrations)**.
10 Working your way around the edge of the panel, release the retaining clips securing the trim panel to the door. Using a suitable forked tool, release the internal securing clips around the edge of the trim panel, then lift the panel upwards to release it from the door frame **(see illustration)**.

the door release lever outwards, as the trim is removed.
5 Working your way around the edge of the panel, release the retaining clips securing the trim panel to the door. Using a suitable forked tool, release the internal securing clips

around the edge of the trim panel, then lift the panel upwards to release it from the door frame **(see illustration)**.
6 Refitting is a reversal of removal, bearing in mind the following points:

14.8b ... to release the securing clips

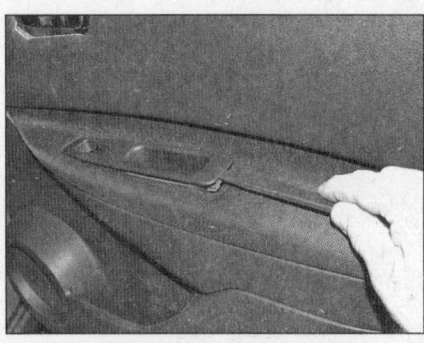

14.9a Unclip the switch panel ...

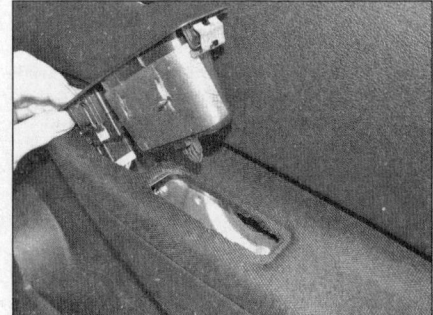

14.9b ... from the door trim panel

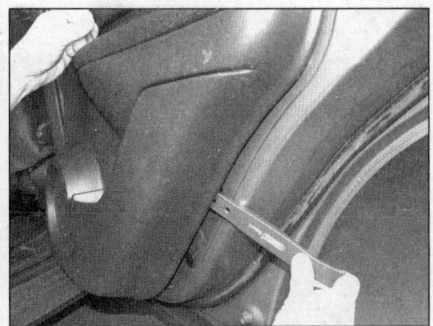

14.10 Using a forked tool, release the retaining clips around the door trim

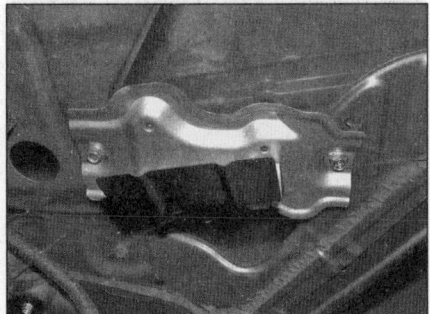

14.11a Undo the strengthener plate retaining bolts ...

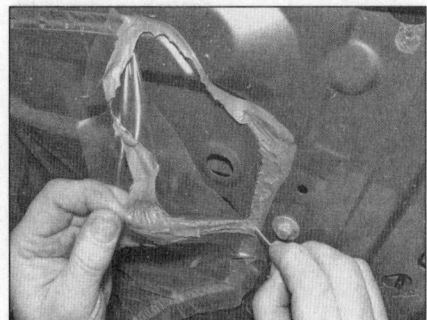

14.11b ... and use a knife to remove the sealing sheet

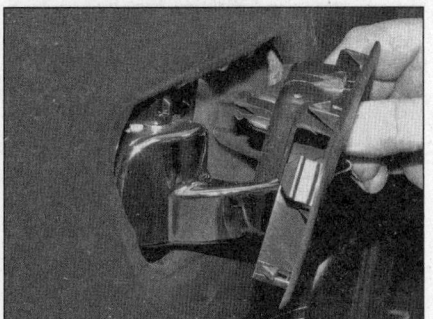

14.14 Carefully unclip the release lever trim panel

14.15a Unclip the switch panel ...

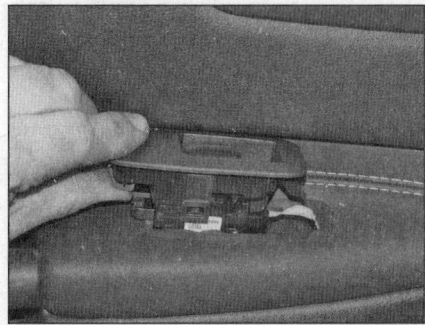

14.15b ... from the door trim panel

11 If work is to be carried out on the door internal components, it will be necessary to remove the plastic sealing sheet. Undo the retaining bolts and remove the strengthener plate from the door panel. Then using a sharp knife, carefully release the sealant bead and pull the plastic sealing sheet from the door **(see illustrations)**. Try to keep the sealant intact as far as possible, to ease refitting.

12 Refitting is a reversal of removal, bearing in mind the following points:

a *Ensure that the sealing sheet is correctly refitted, and sealed around its edge. It should be possible to use the original mastic sealant, but if necessary, new sealant can be obtained from a Nissan dealer.*

b *Make sure that the trim panel securing clips engage correctly with the door panel. Renew any broken clips.*

c *Check the upper weatherstrip engages correctly with the door trim panel as the panel is refitted.*

Rear door trim panel (later models)

13 Disconnect the negative (-) battery terminal (see Chapter 5 Section 3).

14 Carefully prise the trim from around the door inner release lever **(see illustration)**.

15 Carefully unclip the switch panel from the top of the armrest and disconnect the wiring connector **(see illustrations)**.

16 Unclip the trim finisher and undo the two retaining bolts for the grab handle **(see illustrations)**.

17 Working your way around the edge of the panel, release the retaining clips securing the trim panel to the door. Using a suitable forked tool, release the internal securing clips around the edge of the trim panel, then lift the panel upwards to release it from the door frame **(see illustration)**.

18 If work is to be carried out on the door internal components, it will be necessary to remove the plastic sealing sheet (where fitted). Using a sharp knife, carefully release the sealant bead and pull the plastic sealing sheet from the door **(see illustration 14.11a and 14.11b)**. Try to keep the sealant intact as far as possible, to ease refitting.

19 Refitting is a reversal of removal, bearing in mind the following points:

a *Ensure that the sealing sheet is correctly refitted, and sealed around its edge. It should be possible to use the original mastic sealant, but if necessary, new sealant can be obtained from a Nissan dealer.*

b *Make sure that the trim panel securing clips engage correctly with the door panel. Renew any broken clips.*

c *Check the upper weatherstrip engages correctly with the door trim panel as the panel is refitted.*

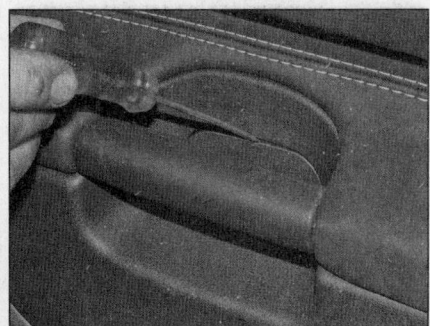

14.16a Unclip the plastic trim cover ...

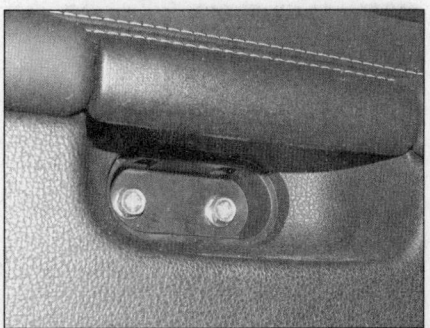

14.16b ... and undo the two retaining bolts

14.17 Using a forked tool, release the retaining clips around the door trim

Chapter 11 Body

14.21a Removing the cover to reveal…

14.21b … the screw in the door opening handle

14.22a Use a trim removal tool to pry up the power window switch assembly and then…

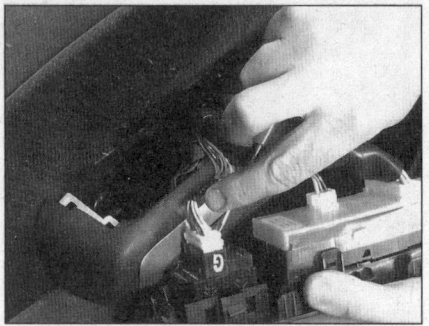

14.22b … disconnect the wiring from beneath the switch assembly

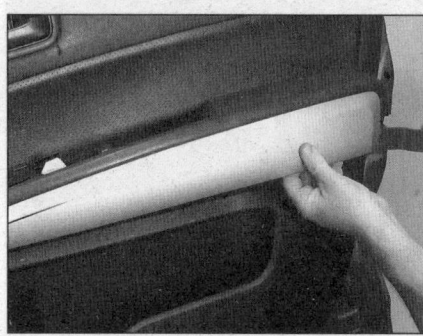

14.23a Prying out the trim panel from the outside of the armrest

14.23b Removing one of the screws from behind the trim panel, arrow indicates the second screw location

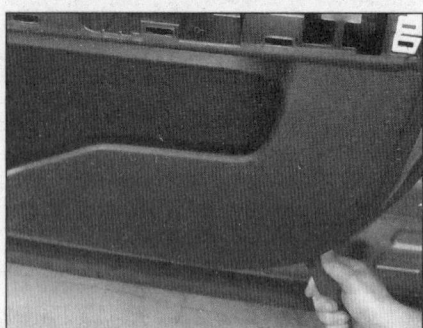

14.24 Use the trim removal tool to pry the door trim from door frame

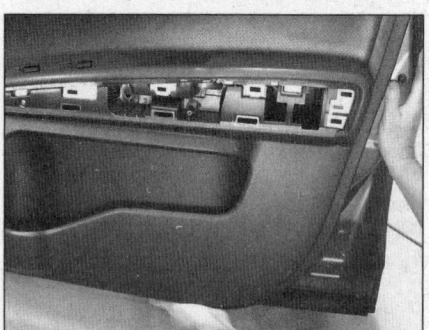

14.25 Removing the door trim

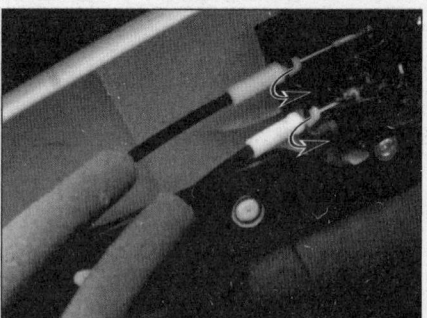

14.26 Disconnect the two cables from the rear of the opening handle on the door trim

T31 X-Trail

Front door trim

20 Disconnect the negative (-) battery terminal (see Chapter 5 Section 3).
21 Remove the screw cover from inside the door opening handle **(see illustration)**. Remove the bolt revealed with the cover removed **(see illustration)**.
22 Pry up the power window switch **(see illustration)** and disconnect the wiring from the underside of the switch assembly **(see illustration)**.
23 Using a trim removal tool, pry out the door trim panel from the outside of the armrest **(see illustration)**. Remove the screws revealed with the cover removed **(see illustration)**.

24 Using a trim removal tool, pry around the edge of the door trim releasing each retaining clip **(see illustration)**.
25 Lift the trim away from the top edge of the door and partially remove the door trim **(see illustration)**.
26 Reach in behind the door trim and disconnect the two cables from the door opening handle **(see illustration)**.
27 Remove the door trim from the vehicle.
28 Installation is a reversal of the removal procedure with attention to the following points:

a *Reconnect the cables to the rear of the door opening handle.*
b *Sit the top edge over the door frame and push the trim down until the clips align with the holes in the door frame.*
c *Check that the power window wiring is accessible out of the hole for the power window switch.*
d *Use the heel of your hand to snap the trim clips into the door frame.*
e *Install the retaining screws before installing the trim panels covering the screws.*

Rear door trim

29 Disconnect the negative (-) battery terminal (see Chapter 5 Section 3).
30 Remove the screw cover from inside the door opening handle **(see illustration)**. Remove the bolt revealed with the cover removed.
31 Using a trim removal tool, pry out the door trim panel from the outside of the armrest **(see illustration)**. Remove the screws

Chapter 11 Body

14.30 Removing the cover from the door opening handle to expose the screw

14.31a Pry the trim panel from the armrest to...

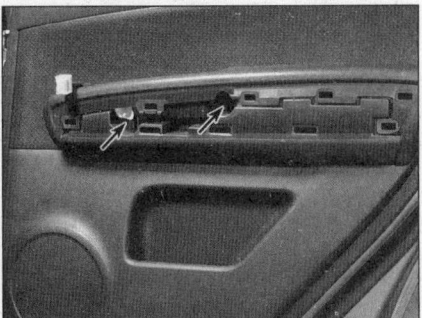

14.31b ... expose the door trim screws (arrows)

14.33a Lever the power window switch up with a trim removal tool and...

14.33b ... disconnect the wiring from beneath the power window switch

14.34a Levering the door trim panel from the rear door using a trim removal tool

14.34b Removing the door trim panel from the door frame

revealed with the cover removed **(see illustration)**.

2 Pry up the power window switch **(see illustration)** and disconnect the wiring from the underside of the switch assembly **(see illustration)**.

33 Using a trim removal tool, pry around the edge of the door trim releasing each retaining clip **(see illustration)**.

34 Lift the trim away from the top edge of the door and partially remove the door trim **(see illustrations)**.

35 Reach in behind the door trim and disconnect the two cables from the door opening handle **(see illustration 14.26)**.

36 Remove the door trim from the vehicle.

37 Installation is a reversal of the removal procedure with attention to the following points:

   a Reconnect the cables to the rear of the door opening handle.
   b Sit the top edge over the door frame and push the trim down until the clips align with the holes in the door frame.
   c Check that the power window wiring is accessible out of the hole for the power window switch.
   d Use the heel of your hand to snap the trim clips into the door frame.
   e Install the retaining screws before installing the trim panels covering the screws.

T32 X-Trail and Qashqai

Front door trim

38 Disconnect the negative (-) battery terminal (see Chapter 5 Section 3).

39 Use a trim remover tool to remove top door trim garnish **(see illustrations)**.

40 Unclip inner grab handle door trim and disconnect mirror switch connector **(see illustrations)**.

41 Remove the power window switch **(see illustration)** from the door trim panel using a trim removal tool.

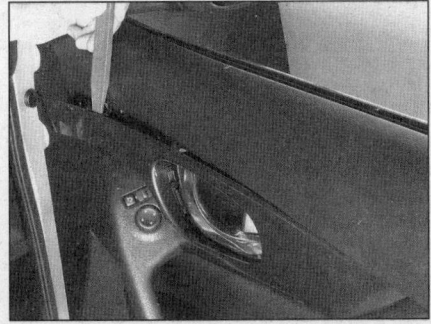

14.39a Using a trim removal tool to unclip the door trim garnish

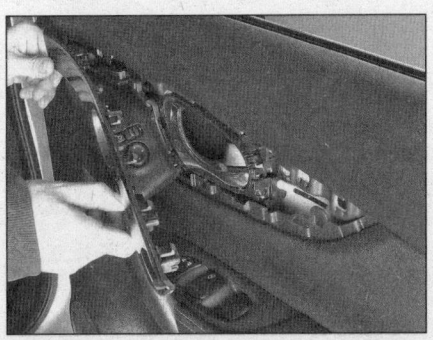

14.39b Removing the door trim garnish

14.40a Removing the inner grab handle trim

Chapter 11 Body

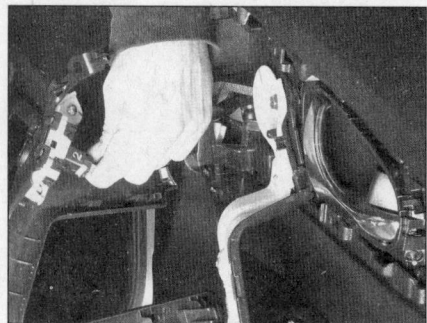

14.40b Disconnecting the power mirror switch wiring

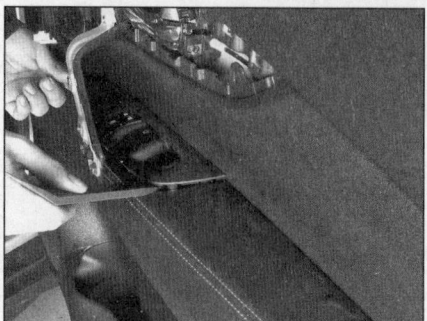

14.41 Unclipping the power window switch from the door trim panel using a trim removal tool

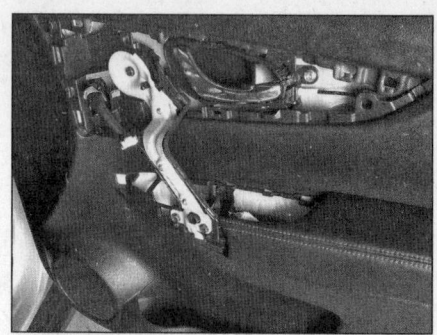

14.42 Undo the two retaining bolts

42 Remove two 10 mm bolts that were revealed after unclipping the outer grab handle trim **(see illustration)**.
43 Working your way around the edge of the panel, release the retaining clips securing the trim panel to the door. Using a suitable forked tool, release the internal securing clips around the edge of the trim panel, then lift the panel upwards to release it from the door frame **(see illustration)**
44 Installation is reverse of removal

Rear door trim

45 Disconnect the negative (-) battery terminal (see Chapter 5 Section 3).
46 Carefully use a trim remover tool to remove the top door trim garnish **(see illustration)**.
47 Remove the plug and the Torx screw from the bottom of the closing handle, then remove closing handle **(see illustration)**.

48 Removal the 10 mm bolt located beneath the closing handle **(see illustration)**.
49 Working your way around the edge of the trim panel, release the retaining clips securing the trim panel to the door. Using a suitable forked tool, release the internal securing clips around the edge of the trim panel, then lift the panel upwards to release it from the door frame **(see illustration)**.
50 Installation is reverse of removal.

15 Door window glass and regulator – removal and refitting

T31 X-Trail and Dualis models

Front window glass

1 Remove the door trim panel (see Section 14).

2 Peel back and remove the round sealing covers from the window regulator assembly **(see illustration)**.
3 Temporarily reconnect the electric window switch (and the negative battery terminal, if removed), and lower or raise the window until the two bolts securing the lower edge of the window glass to the regulator mechanism are accessible through the holes in the window regulator assembly **(see illustration)**. Support the glass, and then undo the two bolts **(see illustration)**.
4 Lift up the window glass, tilt it slightly and remove it from the door frame **(see illustration)**.
5 Installation is a reversal of the removal procedure, with attention to the following points:

a Take care not to dislodge the weather strips when fitting the glass.

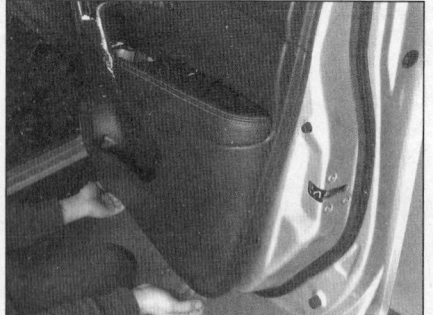

14.43a Unclipping bottom half of door trim

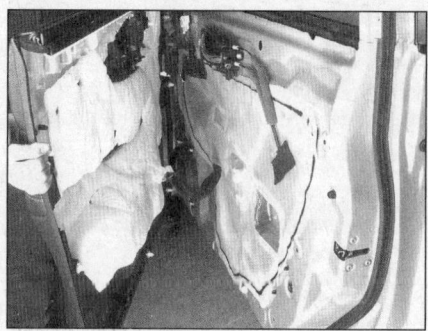

14.43b Removing door trim

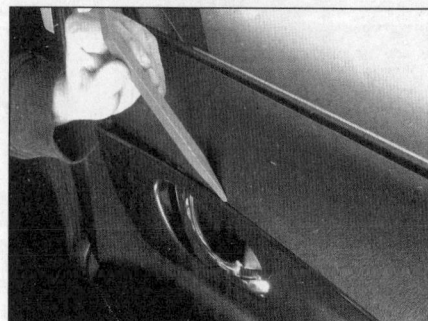

14.46 Removing upper door trim garnish with trim removal tool

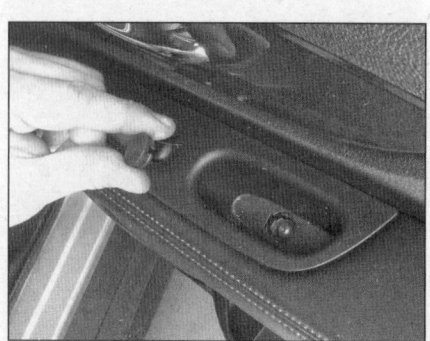

14.47 Use a small screw driver to remove the plug then remove the Torx screw

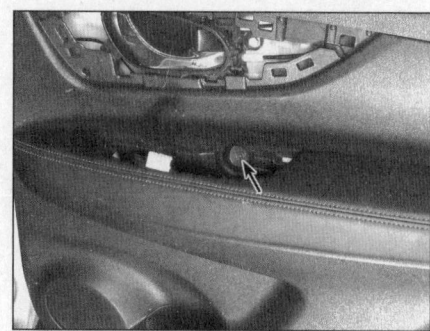

14.48 Remove the illustrated bolt

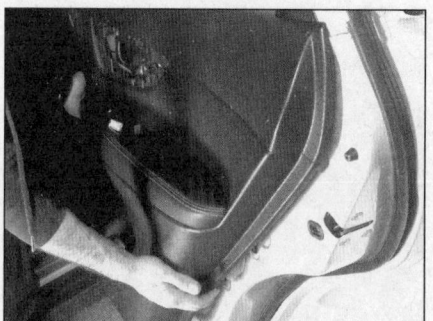

14.49 Removing the door trim from the door frame

Chapter 11 Body

15.2 Peel off the sealing covers to access the window glass bolts

15.3a Operate the power window switch until the window glass bolts (arrowed) become visible

15.3b Removing one of the two window glass securing bolts - T31 X-Trail models

15.3c The two window glass securing bolts on Dualis models

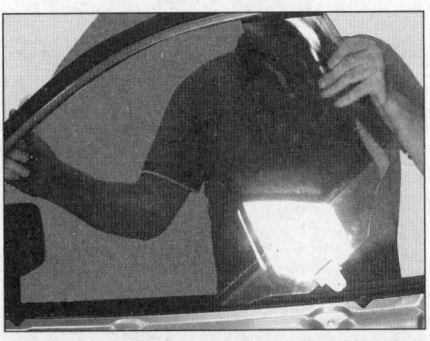

15.4 Manoeuvring the window glass from the door frame

15.7a Unclip the wiring loom retaining clip …

b Check the operation of the window mechanism before refitting the door inner trim panel.

c Refit the door trim panel (see Section 14).

Front window regulator

6 Remove the front window glass as previously described.

7 Unclip the wiring harness (see illustration), and then disconnect the wiring connector from the window regulator motor (see illustrations).

8 Undo the window regulator assembly securing bolts (see illustration), then manipulate the complete motor/regulator assembly out through the aperture in the door (see illustrations).

9 The motor and window tracks can be removed from the assembly as follows:

Note: *Check that separate parts are available before unnecessarily dismantling the window regulator/motor assembly.*

15.7b … and disconnect the motor wiring connector - Dualis models

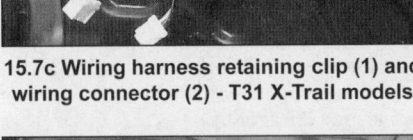

15.7c Wiring harness retaining clip (1) and wiring connector (2) - T31 X-Trail models

15.8a Only remove the circled bolts; the other four bolts retain the window tracks to the bracket assembly - T31 X-Trail shown, Dualis models similar

15.8b Removing the window motor/regulator assembly from the door - Dualis models

15.8c Removing the window motor/regulator assembly from the door - T31 X-Trail models

11-16 Chapter 11 Body

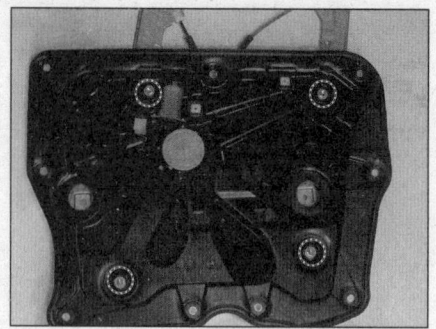

15.9a The circled bolts retain the window tracks to window regulator/motor assembly

15.9b The three screws retain the drive gear to the rear of the motor

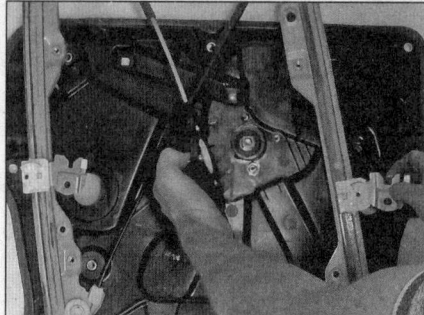

15.9c Removing the drive gear and window tracks from the rear of the window regulator/motor bracket

15.12a Disconnecting the rear speaker wiring

15.12b Peeling the plastic sealing sheet from the door frame

15.14a Removing the window guide on Dualis models

Remove the four bolts that retain the window tracks to the assembly **(see illustration)** and then turn the assembly over to access the inside of the window regulator/motor assembly.

Remove the three screws retaining the drive gear to the rear of the motor **(see illustration)**.

Lift the drive gear from the rear of the window regulator/motor assembly **(see illustration)**.

10 Installation is a reversal of the removal procedure, with attention to the following points:

  a Assemble the window regulator/motor assembly to the bracket and lubricate the window tracks with multipurpose grease.

  b Install the regulator assembly into the door frame and tighten the retaining bolts securely.
  c Tilt the window glass and slide it down the window tracks and position the tabs on the bottom of the glass with the brackets on the window tracks.
  d Check the operation of the window mechanism before refitting the door inner trim panel.

Rear window glass

11 Remove the door trim panel (see Section 14).

12 Disconnect the wiring from the rear speaker **(see illustration)** and then peel the plastic sealing sheet away from the door frame **(see illustration)**.

13 If not already done, temporarily reconnect the electric window switch (and the battery negative terminal, if removed), and raise the window glass to the top of the doorframe.

14 Undo the retaining bolt and remove the rear window guide from inside the door panel **(see illustration)**.

15 On Dualis models, proceed as follows: Unclip the plastic trim from the rear of the window frame **(see illustration)**. Lower the window glass, and then ease the inner sealing weather strip from the top of the door frame **(see illustration)**.

16 Working your way around the upper door frame, carefully remove the inner window channel/seal **(see illustration)**. Note this is one piece that is inserted all around the upper

15.14b Window guide bolt locations - T31 X-Trail models

15.14c Removing the window guide from the door frame - T31 X-Trail models

15.15a Unclip the plastic trim panel

Chapter 11 Body

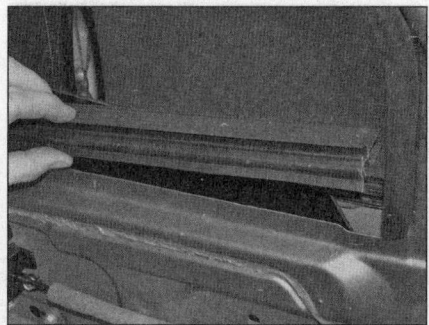

15.15b Carefully prise up the inner door seal

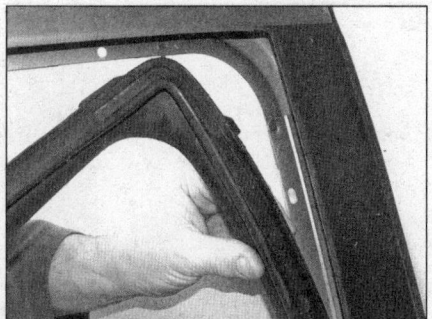

15.16 Carefully prise out the seal

15.17 Undo the two window glass securing bolts

15.18 Withdraw the window glass out from the door

15.19 Ensure the locating peg (arrowed) is located correctly in the door frame

15.23 Tape the window to the top of the frame

window frame; take care not to damage it, as it is removed.

17 Raise the window until the two bolts securing the lower edge of the window glass to the regulator mechanism are accessible through the holes in the doorframe. Support the glass, and then undo the two bolts (see illustration).

18 Disengage the window glass from the regulator, raise the glass at the rear, and then withdraw it from the outside of the door frame (see illustration).

19 Refitting is a reversal of removal, bearing in mind the following points:

a When fitting the rear window guide, make sure the upper part is located correctly in the door frame (see illustration).

b Take care not to dislodge the weather strips when fitting the glass.
c Check the operation of the window mechanism before refitting the door inner trim panel.
d Refit the door inner trim panel (see Section 14).

Rear window regulator

20 Remove the door trim panel (see Section 14).

21 Disconnect the wiring from the rear speaker (see illustration 15.12a) and then peel the plastic sealing sheet away from the door frame (see illustration 15.12b).

22 Temporarily reconnect the electric window switch (and the battery negative terminal, if removed), and lower or raise the window

until the two bolts securing the lower edge of the window glass to the regulator mechanism are accessible through the holes in the window regulator assembly. Support the glass, and then undo the two bolts.

23 Disengage the window glass from the regulator and slide it to the top of the window frame and tape it in position (see illustration).

24 Disconnect the wiring connector from the window regulator motor (see illustrations).

25 The bolt with the elongated hole does not have to be completely removed. Also the window regulator assembly has two locating pegs that hook onto the door frame to prevent it falling down inside the door panel when the bolts are removed (see illustrations).

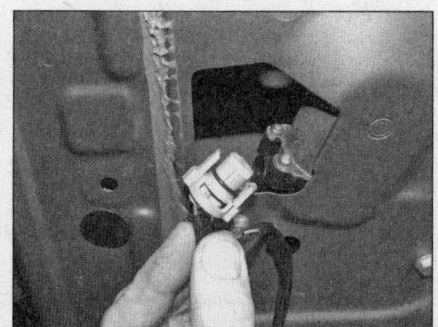

15.24a Disconnecting the motor wiring connector - Dualis models

15.24b Disconnecting the motor wiring connector - T31 X-Trail models

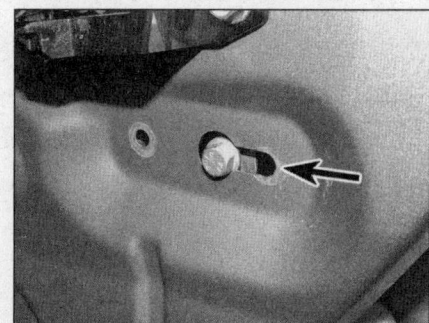

15.25a This bolt does not have to be completely removed on Dualis models

11-18 Chapter 11 Body

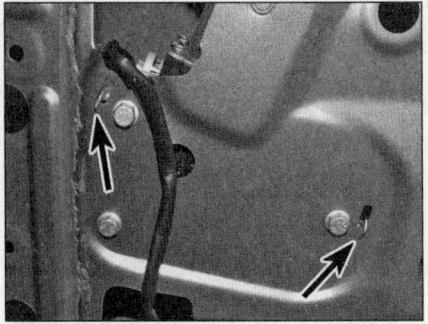

15.25b There are two hooks (arrowed) to support the motor on Dualis models

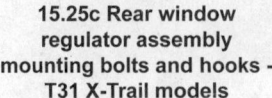

15.25c Rear window regulator assembly mounting bolts and hooks - T31 X-Trail models

1 Mounting bolts
2 Bolt with elongated hole; this bolt does not have to be completely removed
3 Locating hooks

15.26a Undo the window motor/regulator retaining bolts (arrowed)

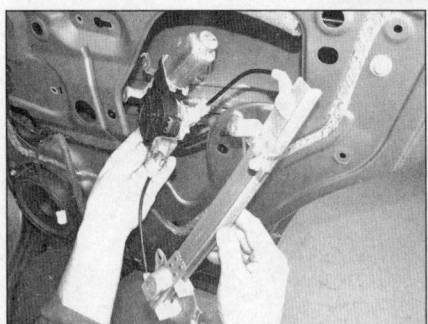

15.26b Remove the window motor/regulator from the door

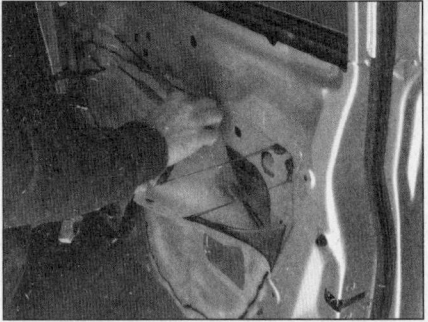

15.29 Peeling the plastic sealing sheet from the door frame

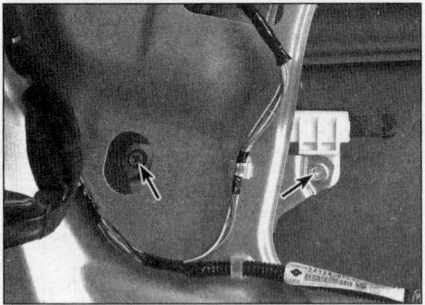

15.30 Operate the power window switch until the mounting bolts become visible in the door frame hole

26 Undo the window regulator and motor securing bolts, and then manipulate the complete motor/regulator assembly out through the aperture in the door **(see illustrations)**.
27 Refitting is a reversal of removal, bear-

15.31 Tilt the window glass forward and manoeuvre it from the door frame

ing in mind the following points;

a Refit the window glass and tighten the retaining bolts.
b Check the operation of the window mechanism before refitting the door inner trim panel.

c Refit the door inner panel (see Section 14).

X-Trail T32 and Qashqai
Front window glass

28 Remove the door trim (see Section 14).
29 Remove the plastic sealing sheet **(see illustration)**.
30 Reconnect the window switch then move the window up or down into position so you can remove the two window mounting bolts **(see illustration)**.
31 Disengage the window from the regulator and lift it to the top of door frame. Tilt the window glass forward and manoeuvre it from the door frame **(see illustration)**.
32 Installation is a reversal of the removal procedure, with attention to the following points:

a Take care not to dislodge the weather strips when fitting the glass.

15.33 Tape the window to the top of the frame

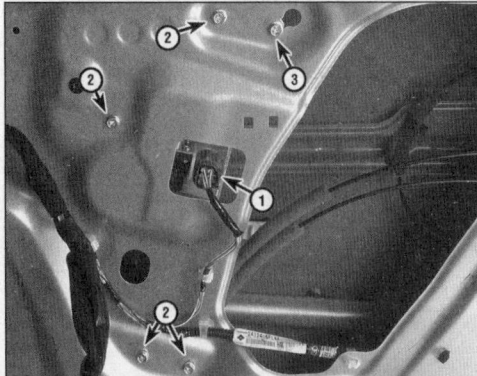

15.34 Front power window regulator components

1 Regulator motor wiring connector
2 Regulator mounting bolts
3 Loosen, but do not remove this bolt; it will support the regulator while the bolts are removed

Chapter 11 Body

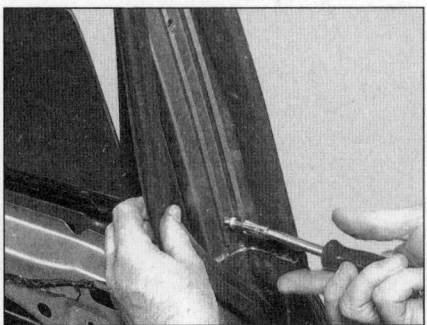

15.39a Removing one of the corner plate screws

15.39b Removing the cover plate from the door frame

15.40 Position the power window until the bolts are accessible through the door frame

   b Check the operation of the window mechanism before refitting the door inner trim panel.
   c Refit the door trim panel (see Section 14).

Front window regulator

33 Remove the window glass as previously described, or alternatively, tape the glass to the top of the door frame **(see illustration)**.
34 Disconnect the window regulator connector and remove the mounting bolts for the window regulator **(see illustration)**.
35 Manoeuvre the window regulator from the door frame by sliding out of opening.
36 Installation is a reversal of the removal procedure, with attention to the following points:
   a Install the regulator assembly into the door frame and tighten the retaining bolts securely.
   b Manoeuvre the window glass into position in the window guides and install the mounting bolts. Connect the wiring to the window regulator motor.
   c Check the operation of the power window before refitting the door inner trim panel.
   d Refit the door trim panel (see Section 14).

Rear window glass

37 Remove the door trim (see Section 14).
38 Remove the plastic sealing sheet **(see illustration 15.29)**.

39 Peel the door seal back exposing the corner plate screws **(see illustration)**. Disengage the corner plate and remove it from the door frame **(see illustration)**.
40 Reconnect the window switch then move the window up or down into position so you can remove the two window mounting bolts **(see illustration)**.
41 Disengage the window glass from the regulator, raise the glass at the rear, and then withdraw it from the outside of the door frame **(see illustration)**.
42 Installation is a reversal of the removal procedure, with attention to the following points:
   a Take care not to dislodge the weather strips when fitting the glass.
   b Check the operation of the window mechanism before refitting the door inner trim panel.
   c Refit the door trim panel (see Section 14).

Rear window regulator

43 Remove the door trim (see Section 14).
44 Remove the plastic sealing sheet **(see illustration 15.29)**.
45 Temporarily reconnect the electric window switch (and the battery negative terminal, if removed), and lower or raise the window until the two bolts securing the lower edge of the window glass to the regulator mechanism are accessible through the holes in the door frame. Support the glass, and then remove the two bolts **(see illustration 15.39)**.

46 Remove the window glass from the door frame as previously described. Alternatively, lift the window glass up the door frame and tape it in position **(see illustration 15.32)**.
47 Remove the window regulator retaining bolts **(see illustration)** and manoeuvre the window regulator assembly from the door frame.
48 Installation is a reversal of the removal procedure, with attention to the following points:
   a Install the regulator assembly into the door frame and tighten the retaining bolts securely.
   b Manoeuvre the window glass into position in the window guides and install the mounting bolts. Connect the wiring to the window regulator motor.
   c Check the operation of the power window before refitting the door inner trim panel.
   d Refit the door trim panel (see Section 14).

16 Door - removal, installation and adjustment

Note: *The door is heavy and somewhat awkward to remove and install - at least two people should perform this procedure.*

15.41 Removing the rear window glass from the door frame

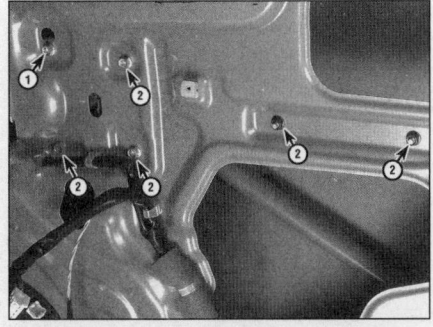

15.47 Rear power window regulator components

16.4 Door stop strut bolt

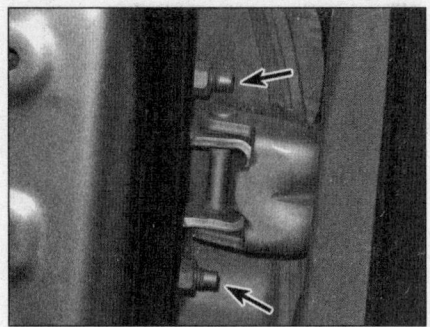

16.6 Unbolt the lower hinge first and allow the door to rest on its support while removing the upper nuts

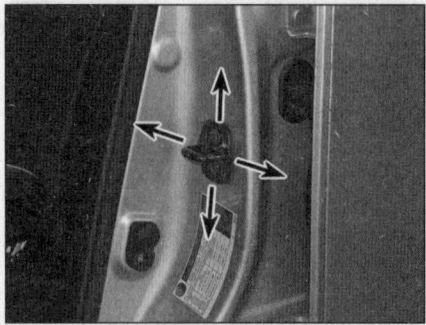

16.11 Adjust the door lock striker by loosening the mounting screws and gently tapping the striker in the desired direction

17.5 Pry out the grommet for access to the bolt underneath

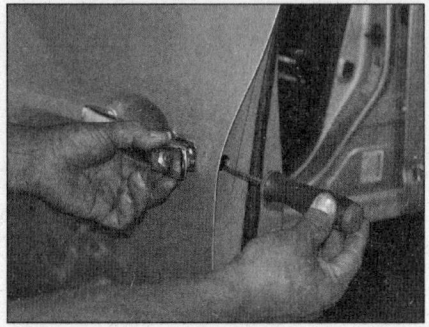

17.7a Pull the door lock cylinder away from the door

17.7b Use a small screwdriver to release the key rod clip and remove the key cylinder

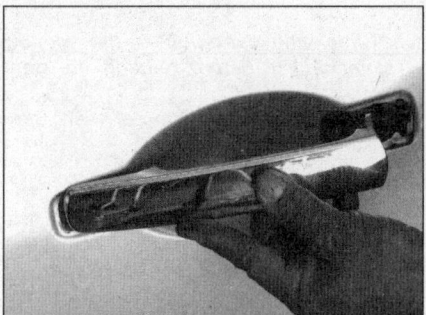

17.8a Slide the door handle toward the rear of the vehicle

Removal and installation

1   Lower the window completely in the door.
2   Open the door all the way and support it on jacks or blocks covered with rags to prevent damaging the paint.
3   Remove the kick panel underneath the instrument panel (if removing a front door) or the centre pillar trim panel (if removing a rear door), then unplug the door wiring harness electrical connectors. Push the rubber conduit out of the door pillar and pull the wiring harness through.
4   Unbolt the door stop strut **(see illustration)**.
5   Mark around the door hinges with a pen or a scribe to facilitate realignment during reassembly.

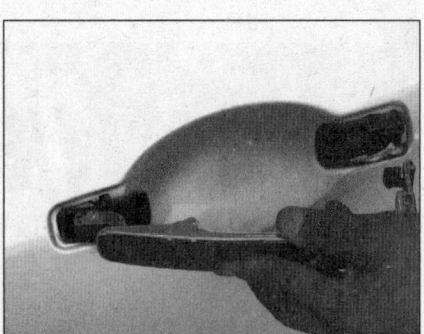

17.8b Pull the rear of the door handle away from the door

6   With an assistant holding the door, remove the upper and lower hinge-to-door nuts **(see illustrations)** and lift the door off.
7   Installation is the reverse of removal.

Adjustment

8   Having proper door-to-body alignment is a critical part of a well-functioning door assembly. First check the door hinge pins for excessive play. Fully open the door and lift up and down on the door without lifting the body. If a door has 1/16-inch or more excessive play, the hinges should be replaced.
9   Door-to-body alignment adjustments are made by loosening the hinge-to-body bolts or hinge-to-door bolts and moving the door. Proper body alignment is achieved when the top of the doors are parallel with the roof section, the front door is flush with the mudguard, the rear door is flush with the rear quarter panel and the bottom of the doors are aligned with the lower rocker panel. If these goals can't be reached by adjusting the hinge-to-body or hinge-to-door fasteners, body alignment shims may have to be purchased and inserted behind the hinges to achieve correct alignment.
10   To adjust the door closed position, scribe a line or mark around the striker plate to provide a reference point, then check that the door latch is contacting the centre of the latch striker. If not, adjust the up and down position first.
11   Finally, adjust the latch striker sideways position, so that the door panel is flush with the centre pillar or rear quarter panel and provides positive engagement with the latch mechanism **(see illustration)**.

17   Door lock, cylinder and handles - removal and installation

Note: *This Section applies to both front and rear doors.*

1   Remove the power window switch.
2   Remove the door trim panel and door plastic liner (see Section 14).
3   On Dualis and T31 X-Trail models, remove the door window regulator assembly (see Section 15).
4   On models equipped with "Intelligent Key system" disconnect the electrical connectors to the door antenna and door request switch, then remove the harness retaining clip from the door outside handle bracket.
5   Remove the door side grommet, and the door key cylinder trim panel bolt **(see illustration)**.
6   Disconnect the key lock rod from the lock cylinder from inside the door.
7   Remove the door lock cylinder and cover assembly while pulling the outside handle forward **(see illustration)**. If the key lock rod couldn't be disconnected from the inside, pull the door lock cylinder out enough to disconnect the key cylinder connection rod **(see illustration)** then remove the door lock cylinder.

Chapter 11 Body

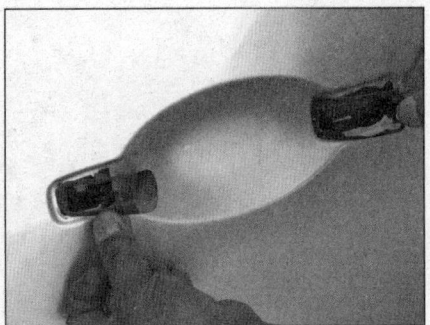

17.9 Carefully remove the front and rear gaskets

8 Pull out the outside door handle and slide it towards the rear of the vehicle to remove it **(see illustrations)**.
9 Remove the front and rear gaskets **(see illustration)**.
10 Remove the door lock assembly mounting bolts.
11 Slide the outside handle bracket towards the rear of the vehicle and remove the assembly.
12 If equipped, disconnect the door lock assembly electrical connector.
13 Separate the outside handle cable from the outside handle bracket.
14 Installation is the reverse of removal.

18.4a On some models there are screws retaining the wheel arch trims to the front bumper and to the guard; on these models, remove the fasteners retaining the trim to the front bumper and also…

18.4b … remove any retaining clips as well

18.3a Undo the lower securing clips (arrows) and screws (screws) - early models

18.3b Remove clips retaining the splashield (1) and remove the fasteners retaining the bumper to the inner guard liners (2)

18 Front bumper – removal and installation

Removal

1 Raise the front of the vehicle and support on jackstands (see Chapter 0 Section 7). To make access inside the wheel arch easier, remove the front wheels.
2 Working under the front of the vehicle, undo the retaining screws securing the engine undershield to the lower edge of the bumper.
3 Still working under the front of the vehicle, unscrew the lower securing screws at each end of the bumper and some models unclip the splash shield and remove **(see illustrations)**.
4 Carefully lever the wheel arch trim to release the retaining clips from the ends of the bumper and on later models there is a retaining bolt to be removed beneath the wheel arch trim **(see illustrations)**.

Note: *The wheel arch trims do not have to be completely removed from the front wing panels, they just need to be released from the ends of the bumper. Take care not to damage them as the bumper is removed.*

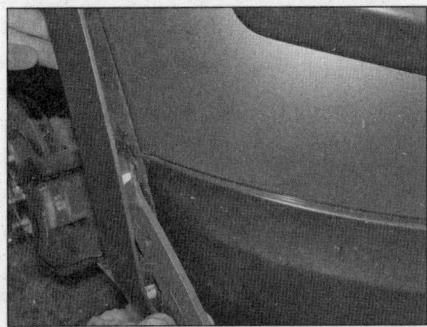

18.4c Unclip the wheel arch trim …

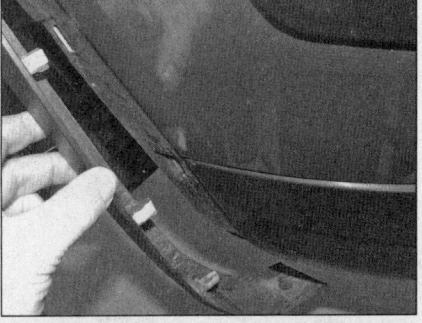

18.4d and remove it from the front bumper - early models shown

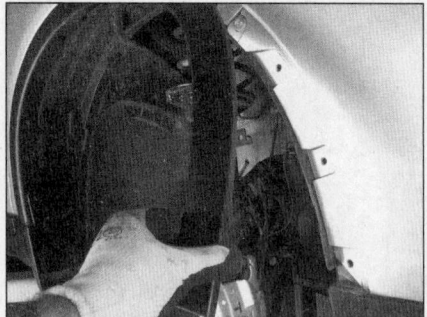

18.4e Removing the wheel arch trim on late models

18.5a Pull back the wheel arch liner …

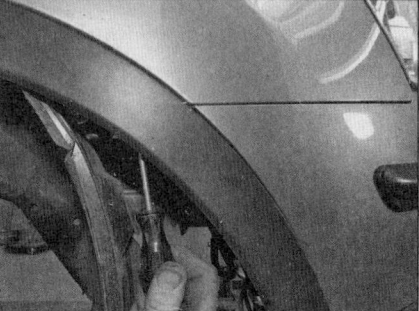

18.5b … and undo the bolt securing the upper part of the bumper

18.6a Release the retaining clips …

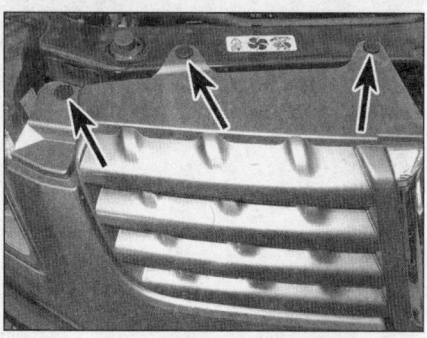

18.6b … along the top of the bumper trim (one side shown)

18.7 Disconnect the fog light wiring connector

5 Remove the securing clips from inside the wheel arch liner, then ease the liner away and undo the bolt securing the upper corner of the bumper to the front guard (see illustrations). Repeat the procedure on the other side of the vehicle.

6 Release the upper retaining clips from the top of the bumper and grille panel (see illustrations).

7 Reaching up behind the bumper, disconnect the fog light wiring connectors (see illustration).

8 Where fitted, disconnect the parking sensor wiring connector and headlight washer pipes.

9 Have an assistant support one end of the bumper, and then unclip the outer ends of the bumper from the front guards (see illustration). If not completely removed, take care not to damage the wheel arch trims, as the bumper is removed.

10 Check that there is nothing still connected to the bumper, and then with the aid of an assistant, draw the bumper forwards and remove it from the vehicle.

Installation

11 Refitting is a reversal of removal.

19 Rear bumper – removal and installation

Removal

1 Chock the front wheels and then raise the rear of the vehicle and support on jackstands (see Chapter 0 Section 7).

2 Working under the rear of the vehicle, release the retaining clips securing the lower edge of the bumper (see illustrations).

3 Working at the rear of the wheel arches, undo the two retaining screws, release the retaining clip and remove the lower plastic trim (see illustrations).

4 Still working under the rear of the vehicle, undo the lower securing screw and carefully lever the wheel arch trim to release the retaining clips from the ends of the bumper (see illustrations).

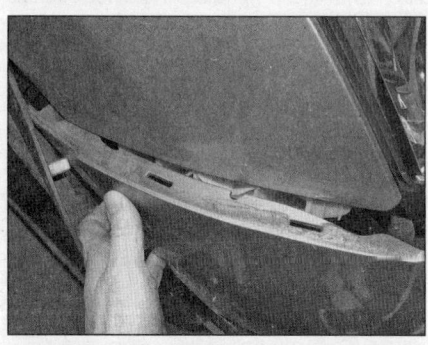

18.9 Release the bumper at each side, noting the locating slots

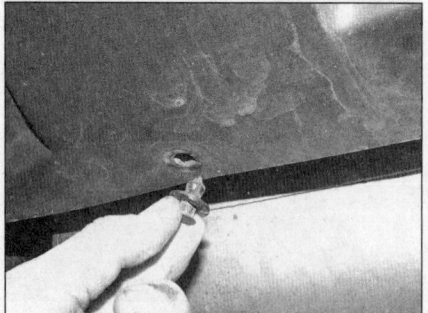

19.2a Release the retaining clips …

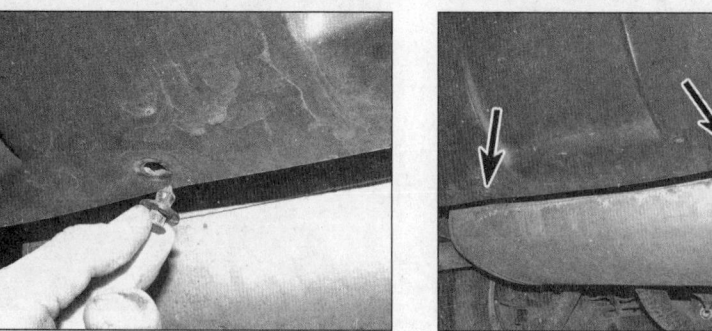

19.2b … along the lower edge of the bumper (arrowed)

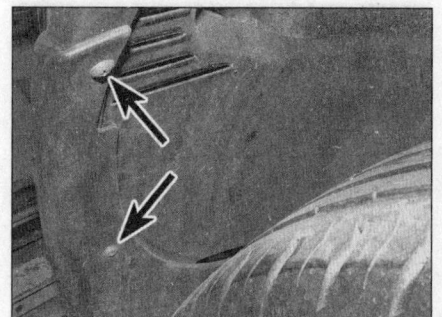

19.3a Undo the two retaining screws (arrowed) …

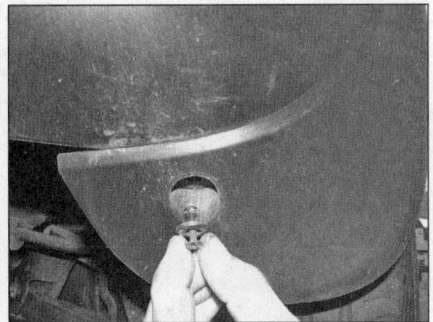
19.3b ... release the retaining clip ...

19.3c ... and remove the lower plastic trim

19.4a Undo the retaining bolt (arrowed) ...

19.4b ... and unclip the wheel arch trim

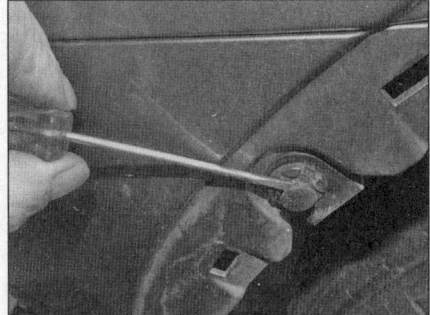
19.5a Release the retaining clips ...

19.5b ... from the inner wheel arch liner

Note: *The inner guard liners do not have to be completely removed from the rear inner guard, they just need to be released to access the ends of the bumper. Take care not to damage them as the bumper is removed.*

5   Release the retaining clips and on some models a retaining bolt, from the inner wheel arch liner to the ends of the bumper **(see illustrations)**.

6   Unscrew the two bolts (one each side) securing the upper corners of the bumper to the rear guard and body brackets **(see illustration)**.

7   On T32 X-Trail models, remove the rear tail light assemblies (see Chapter 12A Section 5).

8   Undo the upper bumper securing bolts (one each side) inside the tailgate aperture **(see illustration)**.

9   Peel back the rubber seal from the lower edge of the tailgate opening **(see illustration)**.

10 Have an assistant support one end of the bumper, and then unclip the outer ends of the bumper from the rear guard **(see illustrations)**.

11 On Dualis and Qashqai models, working between the bumper and the rear body panel lift the retaining clips to release the three bumper securing clips, and then withdraw the bumper from the rear of the vehicle **(see illustrations)**. If not completely removed, take

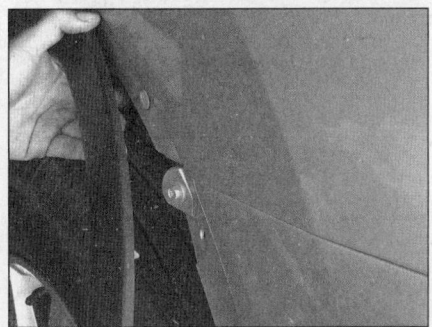
19.5c T-32 X-Trail and Qashqai have a bolt behind the wheel arch trim

19.6 Undo the bolt securing the upper part of the bumper

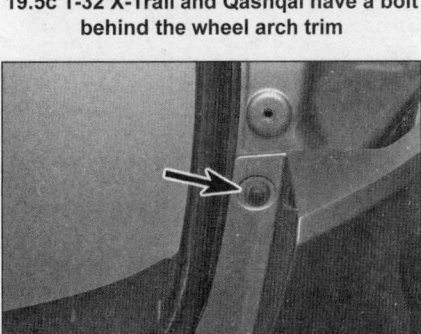
19.8 Undo the bumper upper securing bolt on X-Trail and Dualis models

19.9 Peel back the tailgate aperture seal

19.10a Release the bumper at each side of the rear guard ...

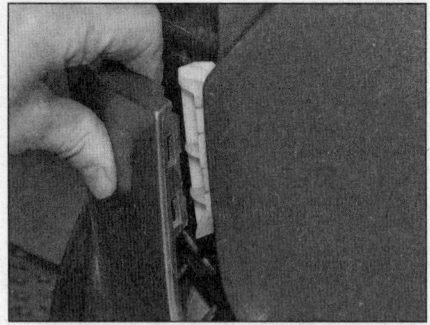

19.10b ... noting the locating slots

19.11a Lift up the centre clips ...

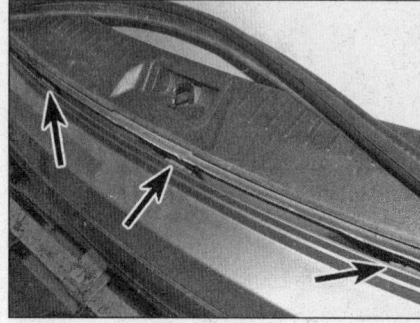

19.11b ... along the rear of the bumper ...

19.11c ... to release the retaining clips

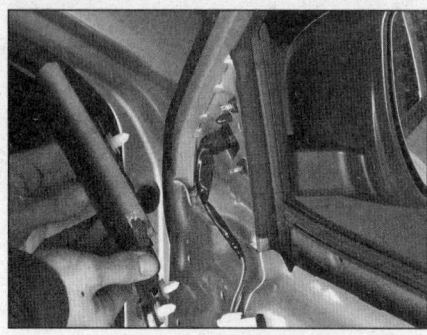

20.2 Removing the mirror trim panel from the door

20.3 Electrical connector

care not to damage the wheel arch trims, as the bumper is removed.

12 On models with rear parking sensors, disconnect the wiring connectors as the bumper is removed.

Refitting

13 Refitting is a reversal of removal.

20 Outside mirrors - removal and installation

1 Remove the door trim (see Section 14).
2 Remove the mirror trim panel (see illustration).
3 Disconnect the electrical connector from the mirror (see illustration).
4 Remove the mirror mounting fasteners, then remove the mirror assembly from the door (see illustration).
5 Installation is the reverse of removal.

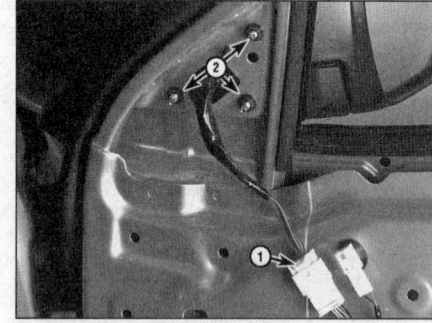

20.4 Mirror wiring connector (1) and mounting nuts (2)

Exterior mirror glass

6 Carefully press the mirror glass in at the top, and then working through the gap at the bottom edge of the mirror glass, use a lever to

20.6 Carefully lever the lower edge of the mirror glass

release the clips that secure the mirror glass to the mirror body (see illustration).
7 Withdraw the glass, and (where applicable) disconnect the heating element wiring connectors (see illustrations).

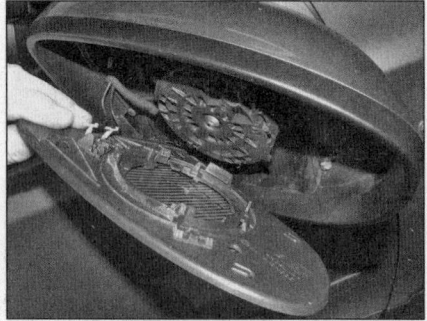

20.7a Unclip the mirror from the mirror base ...

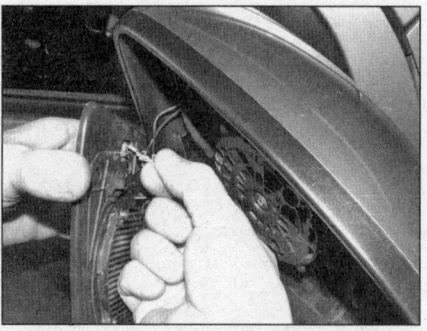

20.7b ... and disconnect the wiring connectors

20.8 Carefully push the mirror glass back into position

Chapter 11 Body

20.10a Release the retaining clips (arrowed) …

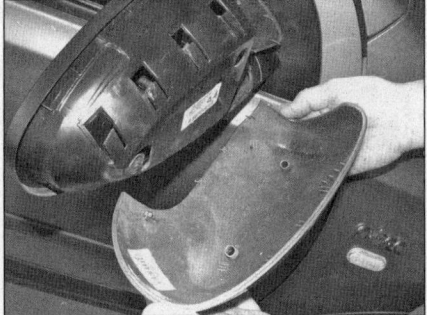

20.10b … and remove the mirror outer shell

20.14 Undo the three motor retaining screws (arrowed) …

20.15 … and disconnect the wiring connector

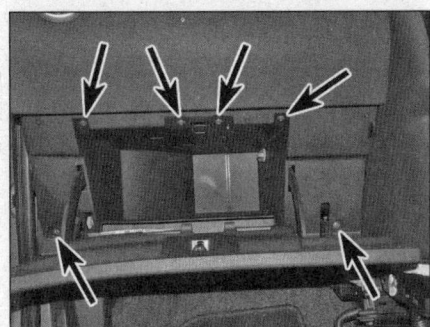

21.1a Glovebox retaining screws - Dualis models

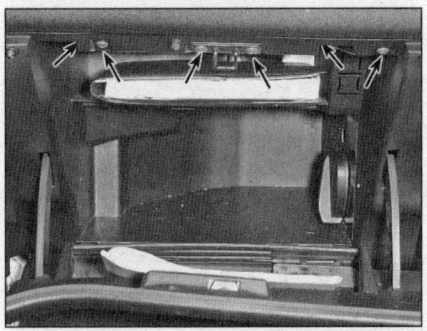

21.1b Upper glovebox surround screws - T31 X-Trail models

8 To refit, carefully push the mirror glass evenly until the securing clips lock into position on the mirror adjuster base (see illustration).
Warning: *It is advisable to wear gloves to protect your hands, even if the glass is not broken, due to the risk of glass breakage.*

Exterior mirror outer shell

9 Remove the mirror glass as described previously in this Section.
10 Working from inside the mirror housing, release the retaining clips, and then carefully remove the mirror shell from the mirror body (see illustrations).
11 To refit, carefully push the mirror shell onto the mirror body until the securing clips lock into position.
12 Refit the mirror glass as described previously in this Section.
13 Remove the mirror glass as described previously in this Section.

Exterior mirror electric motor

14 Working from inside the mirror housing, undo the three retaining screws and withdraw the motor from the mirror body (see illustration).
15 Disconnect the wiring connector as it is removed (see illustration).
16 Refitting is a reversal of removal, ensuring that the mirror glass is fitted securely as described previously in this Section.

21 Dashboard panels – removal and installation

Warning: *All models are equipped with an airbag system. The driver's airbag is mounted in the steering wheel centre pad and the passenger's airbag is mounted in the passenger's side of the dashboard. Make sure that the safety recommendations given in Chapter 12A Section 20 are followed, to prevent personal injury.*

Glovebox

T31 X-Trail and Dualis models

1 Open the glovebox door and remove the screws retaining the surround to the dashboard (see illustration).
2 On Dualis models, unclip the left-hand trim panel from the end of the facia (see illustration). Reach inside the end of the facia panel and unclip the glovebox illumination light bulb holder from the top of the glovebox (see illustration).
3 On X-Trail models, partially remove the glovebox and disconnect the wiring for the glovebox light.
4 Remove the glovebox from the dashboard (see illustration).

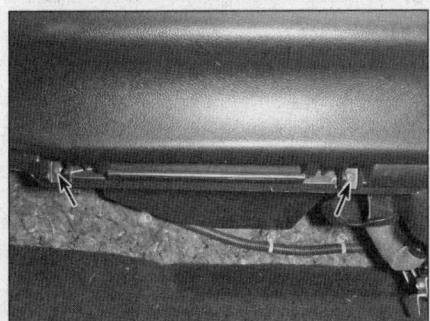

21.1c Lower glovebox surround screws - T31 X-Trail models

21.2a Unclip the facia end cover…

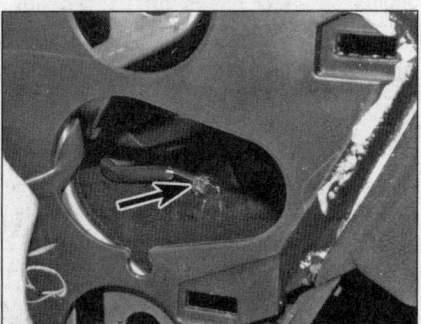

21.2b … reach inside the end cover opening and release the glovebox light from the top of the glovebox - Dualis models

21.3 Disconnecting the wiring from the rear of the glovebox surround - T31 X-Trail models

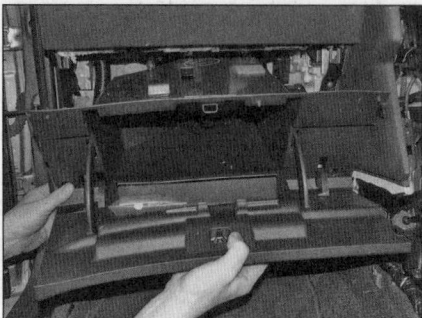

21.4 Withdraw the glovebox from the dashboard

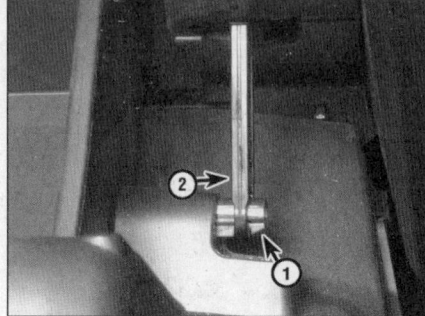

21.6 Compress the clip (1) and then slide the damper rod (2) off the glovebox door

21.7 Manoeuvring the glove box door out of the dashboard

5 Installation is a reversal of the removal procedure, ensuring the wiring for the glovebox lamp is reconnected.

T32 X-Trail and Qashqai models

6 Open the glovebox. Lower the glove box and disconnect the damper from the glovebox door **(see illustration)**.
7 Squeeze the sides of the glovebox door to allow the stops to pass out between the opening in the glovebox cover **(see illustration)**. Unclip the hinge from the bottom of the dashboard and remove the glovebox door.
8 Unclip the left-hand trim panel from the end of the facia **(see illustration)**.
9 Remove the screws retaining the glovebox cover **(see illustration)** and remove the cover from the dashboard **(see illustration)**.
10 Installation is a reversal of the removal procedure.

Driver's side lower dash panel

11 Undo the two retaining bolts and unclip the bonnet and fuel flap release levers, from the lower edge of the dash panel **(see illustrations)**.
12 Open the small flap that covers the fusebox, and release the diagnostic plug from the bottom dash panel, on later models remove the diagnostic plug cover **(see illustration)**.
13 Carefully pull the lower dash panel from the facia to release the retaining clips, and then as the panel is withdrawn, disconnect the wiring connector and air tubing from the left-hand side of the dash panel **(see illustrations)**.
14 Installation is a reversal of the removal procedure.

Centre panel

Note: *On T32 X-Trail and Qashqai models, the centre panel is part of the heater and air*

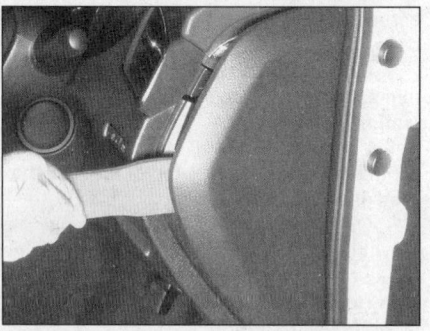

21.8 Method of removing the end trim panels from the dashboard using a trim removal tool

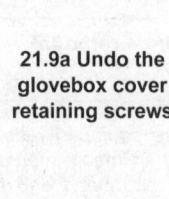

21.9a Undo the glovebox cover retaining screws

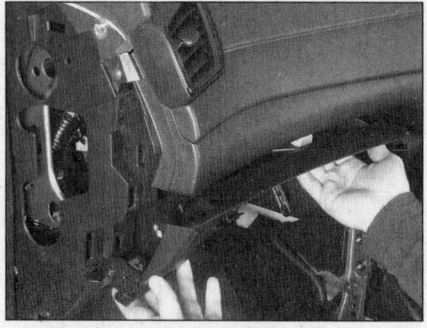

21.9b Removing the glovebox cover

21.11a Undo the two retaining bolts ...

21.11b ... and unclip the release levers from the facia

Chapter 11 Body

21.12a Release the diagnostic plug from the facia - Dualis models

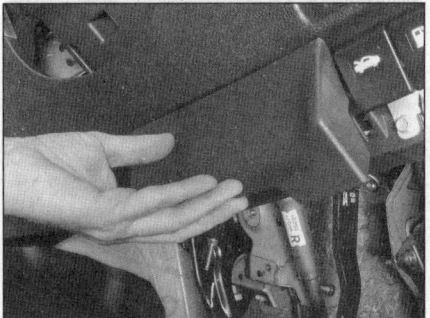

21.12b Removing the diagnostic plug cover - T32 X-Trail models

21.13a Unclip the lower dash panel ...

21.13b ... and disconnect the air vent pipe and wiring connector

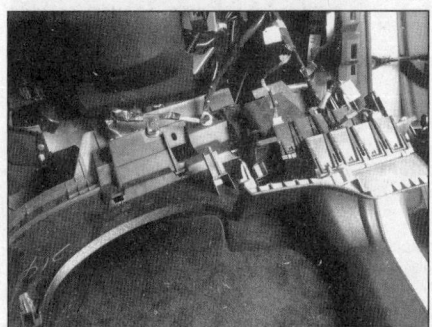

21.13c Removing the lower dash panel on a T32 X-Trail model

21.15 Unclip the trim panel from around the heater controls

Dualis models

15 Carefully unclip the heater control trim panel from the centre of the facia panel, and then disconnect the wiring connectors as it is removed **(see illustration)**.

16 Unclip the upper vent trim panel from the centre of the facia. Release the trim panel by carefully levering at each side of the trim, to release the securing clips **(see illustrations)**.

17 As the trim panel is withdrawn disconnect the wiring connectors from the rear of the panel **(see illustration)**.

18 Installation is a reversal of the removal procedure.

T31 X-Trail models

19 Use a plastic trim tool or a screwdriver wrapped with tape to carefully pry out the heating and air conditioning control panel or centre panel to access the control panel. Pull out the assembly and disconnect the electrical connectors **(see illustration)**.

21.16a Release the retaining clips ...

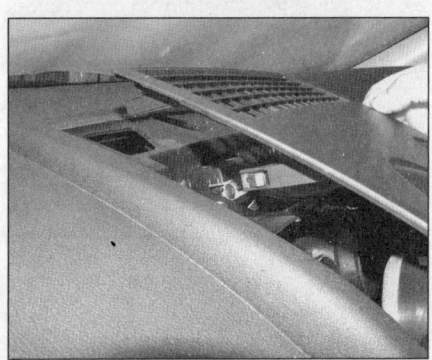

21.16b ... and unclip the upper trim panel from the facia

conditioning control assembly. A procedure to remove and install the heater and air conditioning control assembly is covered in the Cooling, Heating and Air Conditioning

Systems Chapter (see Chapter 3 Section 9). The centre vents can be removed as described later in this section.

21.17 Disconnect the wiring connectors

21.19 Using a trim tool to pry out the centre panel from around the audio centre - T31 X-Trail

21.20 Disconnecting the hazard lamp switch wiring from the rear of the trim panel

Chapter 11 Body

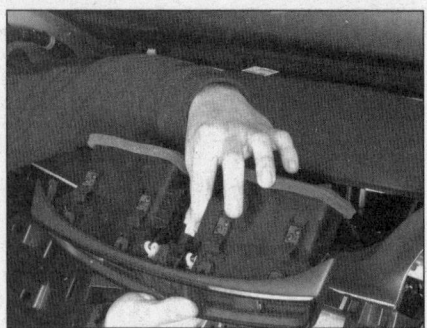

21.24 Disconnecting the hazard lamp switch wiring from the rear of the centre vent assembly

21.26 Using a lever to prise up the shroud ...

21.27 ... then release it from the facia

20 As the panel is withdrawn, disconnect the wiring from the rear of the hazard lamp switch (see illustration).
21 Withdraw the panel from the vehicle.
22 Installation is a reversal of the removal procedure.

T32 X-Trail and Qashqai

Centre vents

23 Use a plastic trim tool or a screwdriver wrapped with tape to carefully pry out the centre vent assembly.
24 Partially withdraw the vent panel and disconnect the wiring from the rear of the hazard lamp switch (see illustration).
25 Installation is a reversal of the removal procedure.

Instrument cluster surround panels

Dualis models

26 Using a lever, carefully prise the instrument panel upper shroud, to release the retaining clips (see illustration).
27 Ease the upper shroud away from the facia, disengaging the retaining clips and then remove it from the vehicle (see illustration).
28 Installation is a reversal of the removal procedure.

T31 X-Trail models

29 Remove the steering column covers (see Section 23).
30 Grasp the surround panel and pull away from the dashboard (see illustration).
31 Installation is a reversal of the removal procedure.

T32 X-Trail and Qashqai models

32 Pry the facia end trim panel away from the driver side of the dashboard.
33 Remove the steering column covers (see Section 23).
34 Remove the driver's side lower dash panel as previously described.
35 Pry out the RH vent from the dashboard (see illustration).
36 Using a trim removal tool, pry out the RH panel from around the instrument cluster (see illustration). With it partially removed, disconnect the wiring from the rear of the panel (see illustration).
37 Pry the LH panel from around the instrument cluster. With it partially removed, disconnect the wiring from the rear of the Start switch (see illustration).
38 Grasp the instrument cluster surround

21.30 Removing the instrument cluster surround panel from the dashboard

21.35 Removing the air vent from the RH side of the dashboard

21.36a Pry out the RH trim panel and...

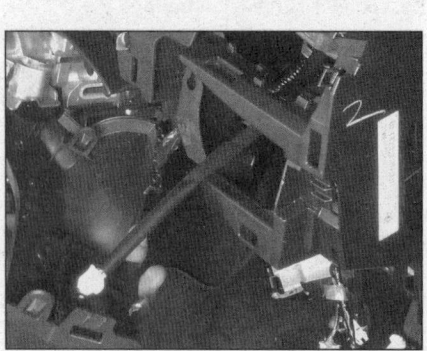

21.36b ... disconnect the wiring from the rear of the panel

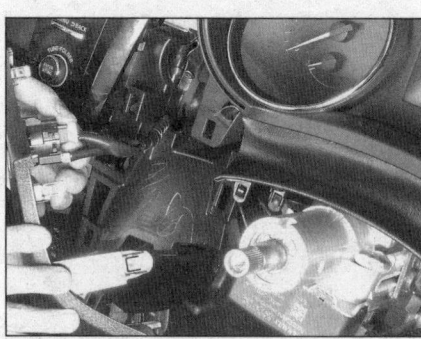

21.37 Disconnecting the wiring from the switches on the LH panel

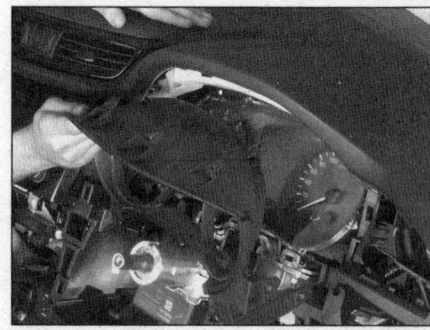

21.38 Removing the instrument cluster surround panel from the dashboard

Chapter 11 Body

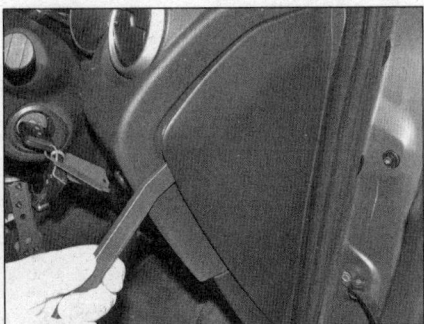

21.39a Using a lever to remove the facia side trim – Dualis models

21.39b Using a lever to remove the facia side trim – T32 X-Trail models

22.3 Unclip the shift lever trim and pass it back through the hole in the console so it won't interfere with the console removal

22.4a Using a screwdriver to pry the shift knob cover…

22.4b … and then remove the shift knob spring clip

22.4c Prying up the console top cover and…

panel on each side and pull it from the dashboard, disengaging the retaining clips (see illustration).

Facia end trim panels

39 Using a lever, carefully prise the trim panel from the end of the facia (see illustrations).
40 Installation is a reversal of the removal procedure.

22 Centre console – removal and installation

T31 X-Trail and Dualis models

Removal

1 Disconnect the negative (-) battery terminal (see Chapter 5 Section 3).
2 It is not necessary, but easier to remove the centre console with the front seats removed (see Section 26).
3 On manual transaxle models, pry up the shift lever boot surround panel and disconnect it from the top of the console (see illustration). Twist the surround panel slightly and pass it through and into the console.
4 On automatic transaxle models, proceed as follows:
  a Pry down the lower shift knob cover (see illustration) and remove the spring clip from the bottom of the shift knob (see illustration).
  b Pry up the console top cover, disconnecting it from the console (see illustration).
  c With it partially removed, disconnect the wiring from beneath the cover (see illustration).
5 Working at the front of the centre console, unclip the two front trim panels, from inside the front footwells (see illustration).
6 Release the lower securing clips and upper retaining screws on some models there is 2 screws, from the front end of the centre console (see illustrations).
7 Unclip the cup holder trim panel from the top of the centre console, on some models disconnect wring connectors underneath (see illustration).
8 On some models unclip the switch panel from the top of the centre console, and dis-

22.4d … disconnect the wiring from beneath the top cover

connect the wiring connectors as it is removed (see illustration).

22.5 Unclip the trim covers…

22.6a Release the retaining clips …

11-30 Chapter 11 Body

22.6b ... and screws from the front of the console

22.7 Unclip the cup holder from the console

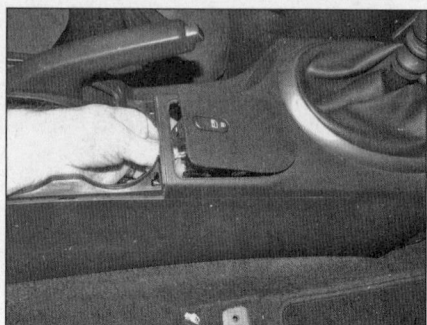

22.8 Unclip the switch panel

9 On Dualis models carefully unclip the heater control trim panel from the centre of the facia panel, and then disconnect the wiring connectors as it is removed **(see illustration)**.

10 Remove the screws revealed with the heater control trim panel removed, on Dualis models **(see illustration)**, or with the console top cover removed on T31 X-Trail models **(see illustration)**.

11 On Dualis models, pry the cover from the rear of the centre console and then disconnect the wiring **(see illustrations)**. Disconnect the wiring connector and release the wiring loom from the securing clip at the rear of the centre console **(see illustrations)**.

12 If fitted, slide the front seats forward and then undo the mounting screws from the rear of the centre console **(see illustration)**.

13 Lift the console up at the rear, manipulate it over the handbrake and gear lever, and

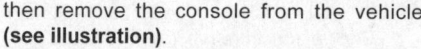

22.9 Disengaging the heater control trim panel from the centre of the facia panel

then remove the console from the vehicle **(see illustration)**.

Note: *If the console cannot be lifted over the handbrake lever, measure and note the length of thread on the handbrake adjustment rod*

22.10a Remove the illustrated screws on Dualis models

(see illustration) *and then slacken the adjustment nut until it reaches the end of the thread. This will allow for the handbrake lever to be pulled up further to allow for easier removal of the centre console.*

22.10b Remove the illustrated screws on T31 X-Trail models

22.11a Unclip the trim panel from the rear of the console

22.11b Disconnect the wiring connector

22.11c Release the wiring harness

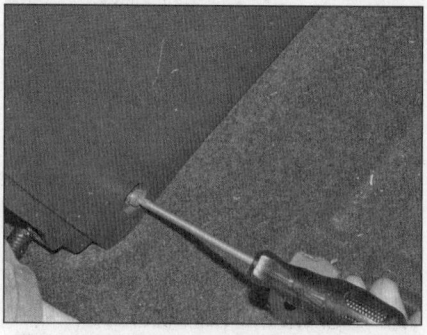

22.12 Undo the two screws at the rear of the console

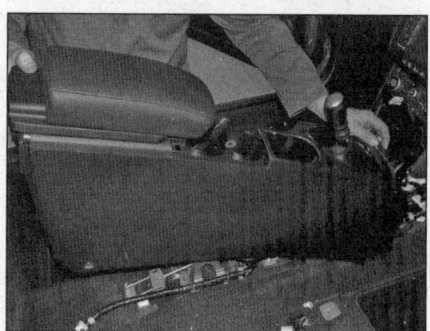

22.13a Removing the centre console

Chapter 11 Body   11-31

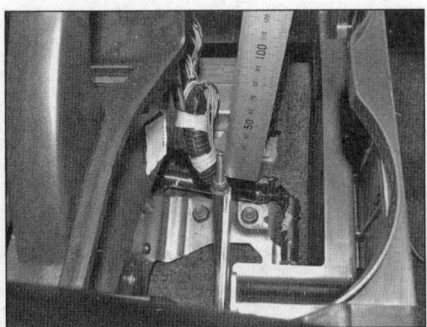

22.13b Measure the amount of threads on the handbrake adjuster

22.16a The Park lock override switch is beneath a cover forward of the selector lever – selector lever in Neutral for illustration

22.16b Depress the Park lock override switch and move the selector lever to the Neutral position

22.17 With the selector lever lifted up, cut the cable tie (arrow) retaining the boot to the bottom of the shift knob

22.18a Remove the screws and…

22.18b … lift the panel straight up to disengage the remaining clips holding the panel to the console

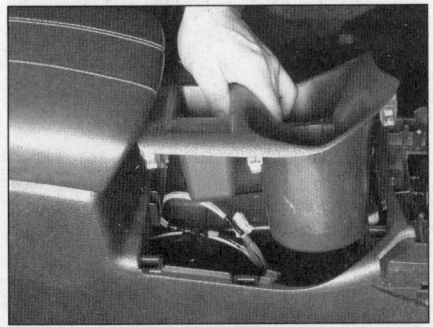

22.19 The cup holders are clipped into the console and are removed by pulling the assembly straight up

Installation

14 Installation is a reversal of removal, ensuring the handbrake adjustment nut is screwed back down the threads to the measurement noted before removal.

T32 X-Trail and Qashqai models
Removal

15 Disconnect the negative (-) battery terminal (see Chapter 5 Section 3).
16 On automatic transaxle models working inside the vehicle, remove the cover in front of the selector lever (see illustration) revealing the Park lock override switch. Pass a screwdriver into the hole and depress the override switch while moving the selector lever to the Neutral position (see illustration).
17 Pry up the selector lever panel and cut the cable tie (see illustration) securing the shift boot to the bottom of the shift knob. Lift the boot over the shift knob and disconnect any wiring from the selector lever panel and remove the panel from the console.

18 Remove the fasteners (see illustration) retaining the upper side trim panels and lift up the panels (see illustration) disengaging the retaining clips and remove from the vehicle.
19 Unclip the cup holder from the console by pulling it straight up (see illustration).
20 Reach inside the opening for the cup holders and disconnect the audio system/power supply wiring for the inside of the console box (see illustration). On some models, the wiring harness is clipped to the console and has to be disengaged.
21 Remove the two screws between the shift lever and the cup holder location (see illustration).
22 Working at the front of the centre console, unclip the two front trim panels, from inside the front footwells (see illustration). Remove the screws revealed once the covers are removed (see illustration).

22.20 Disconnecting the wiring going to the console box

22.21 Remove the two illustrated screws

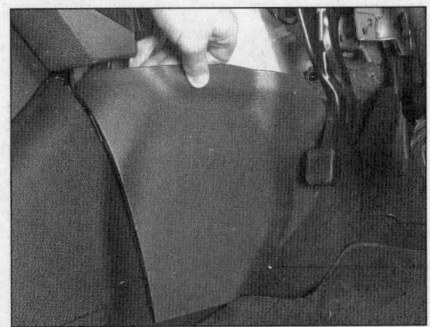

22.22a Unclip the trim covers…

Chapter 11 Body

22.22b ... and remove the screws

22.23 Remove the rear fasteners from each side of the console

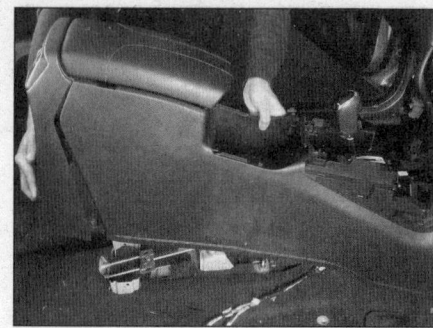

22.24 Removing the centre console

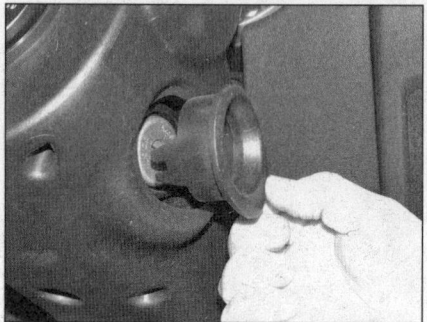

23.1 Unclip the trim from around the switch

23.3a Retaining screw locations (arrows) - Dualis models

23.3b Retaining screw locations (arrows) - T31 X-Trail models

23 If fitted, slide the front seats forward and then unclip the trim panel from the rear of the console to reveal the rear fasteners (see illustration). Remove the fasteners.
24 Lift the console up at the rear, manipulate it over the gear lever, and then remove the console from the vehicle (see illustration).

Installation

25 Installation is a reversal of the removal procedure, with attention to the following points:

  a When installing the console, check that you can move the wiring into position before installing any of the fasteners.
  b Connect the wiring to the connections for the console box.
  c Install the retaining fasteners and slide the rear cover back into position on the rear of the console.

  d Use a small cable tie to secure the boot to the bottom of the shift knob with the cable tie positioned in the groove in the knob.

23 Steering column covers - removal and installation

T31 X-Trail and Dualis models

Removal

1 Where fitted, unclip the plastic trim from around the ignition switch (see illustration).
2 Release the height adjustment lever and move the steering column downwards to its fully lowered position.
3 Working under the steering column lower shroud, undo the shroud securing screws. Release the clips securing the lower shroud to the upper shroud and then withdraw

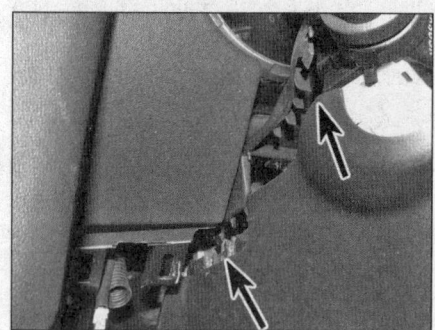

23.3c Release the clips at the front and sides ...

it from under the steering column (see illustrations).
4 Release the two retaining clips securing the upper part of the shroud to the lower part of the instrument panel, and then withdraw it from the top of the steering column (see illustrations).

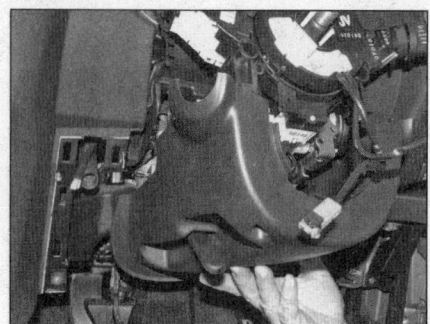

23.3d ... then remove the lower trim panel

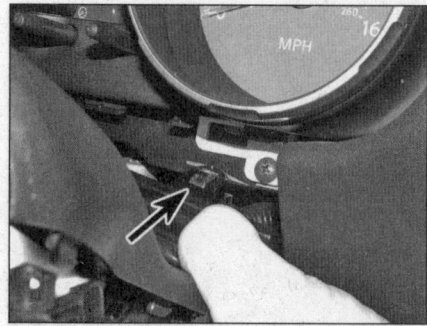

23.4a Unclip the upper trim panel ...

23.4b ... from the top of the steering column

Chapter 11 Body

23.7 Remove the illustrated screws

23.9 Release these two clips and separate the cover from the vinyl

T32 X-Trail and Qashqai models

Removal

6 Remove the steering wheel (see Chapter 10 Section 14).

7 Remove the screws from the rear of the lower steering column covers **(see illustration)**.

8 Prise the two halves of the covers apart and manoeuvre the lower cover from the vehicle.

9 Lift the upper cover up and unclip the vinyl piece from the front of the upper cover **(see illustration)**.

Installation

10 Installation is a reversal of the removal procedure.

24 Dashboard - removal and installation

Warning: *The models covered by this manual are equipped with a Supplemental Restraint System (SRS), more commonly known as airbags. Always disarm the airbag system before working in the vicinity of any airbag system component to avoid the possibility of accidental deployment of the airbag, which could cause personal injury (see Chapter 12A Section 20). Do not use a memory saving device to preserve the PCM's memory when working on or near airbag system components.*

Caution: *This is an involved procedure, and it is suggested that this complete Section is read through thoroughly before beginning the operation. It is advisable to make careful note of all wiring connections, and the routing of all wiring, to aid refitting.*

1 Disconnect the negative (-) battery terminal (see Chapter 5 Section 3).

2 Remove the centre console (see Section 22).

3 Remove the steering wheel (see Chapter 10 Section 14).

4 Remove the dashboard trim panels (see Section 21).

5 Remove the steering column covers (see Section 23).

6 Remove the door opening panel and kick panels **(see illustrations)**.

7 Remove the A-Pillar trim panels by prying them away from the pillars, disengaging the clips **(see illustration)**.

Caution: *On models with side impact airbags, use care if using a trim tool to pry the panels away as the airbags can be easily damaged.*

8 Where fitted, pry up the dash mounted speaker grilles, exposing a retaining bolt on each side of the dashboard **(see illustration)**.

9 Carefully pry the demister vent out of the instrument panel **(see illustration)**.

10 Remove the glove box assembly (see Section 21).

11 Unbolt the steering column from the instrument panel support brace (see Chapter 10 Section 13).

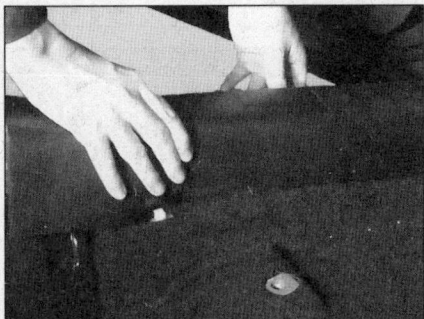

24.6a Remove the door opening trim panel

Installation

5 Installation is a reversal of the removal procedure, but ensure that the shroud halves engage correctly with each other.

24.6b Remove the kick panel mounting screw then remove kick panel

24.7b ... then disconnect the clip anchors

24.8 Some T31 X-Trail models have dash mounted speakers and some Dualis models have a trim panel on the outer edge of the dashboard; on these models, pry up the grille/panel to expose some bolts

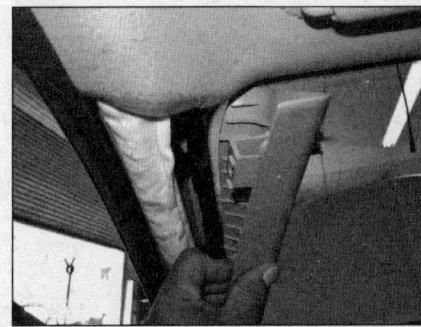

24.7a Pry the trim covers back...

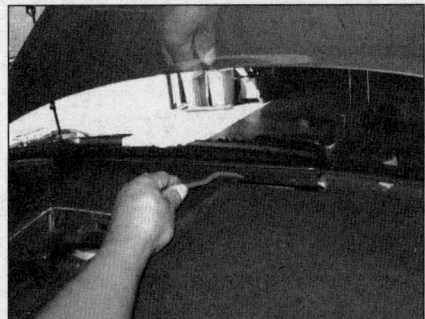

24.9a Carefully the pry out the demister vent - Dualis models shown

24.9b Removing the demister vent on a T32 X-Trail model

24.13 View through the glovebox opening showing the passenger airbag wiring connector location (1) and retaining fasteners (2)

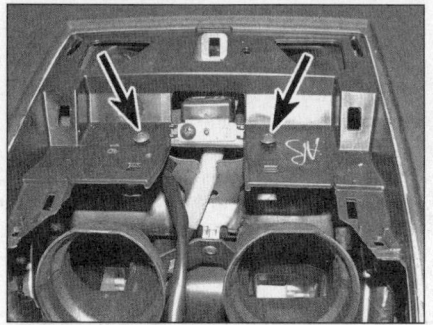

24.15a Remove the fasteners from behind the centre panel…

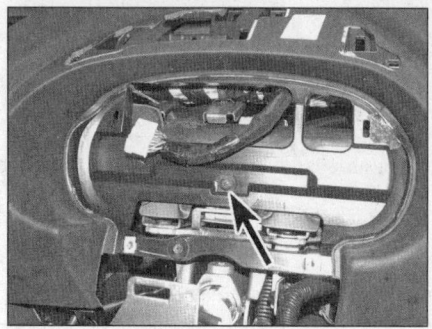

24.15b … behind the instrument cluster…

24.15c … each end of the dashboard…

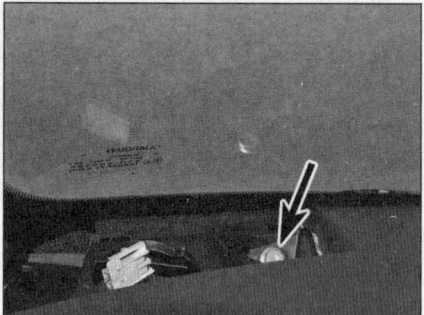

24.15d …. from the speaker grille openings…

12 Remove the instrument cluster (see Chapter 12A Section 9).
13 Remove the passenger's airbag module fasteners from the brace bar (see illustration).
14 Remove the fasteners retaining the heater and air conditioning controls and remove the assembly from the vehicle (see Chapter 3 Section 9).
15 Remove the instrument panel fasteners (see illustrations).
16 Disconnect the wiring from each side of the dashboard at the A-pillar locations and the kick panel locations.
17 Partially remove the dashboard and disconnect the radio aerial (see illustration).

18 Remove the support fasteners and lift out the instrument panel assembly.
19 Installation is the reverse of removal.

25 Cowl panel - removal and installation

1 Pry off the plastic trim cap on the windshield wiper arms, then detach the wiper arms retaining nuts and remove the wiper arms (see Chapter 12A Section 11).
2 Disconnect the windshield washer tube.
3 Disengage the cowl extension panels from each corner of the windshield (see illustration).

24.15e … and from the right side …

24.15f … and the left side of the dashboard - Early models

Chapter 11 Body
11-35

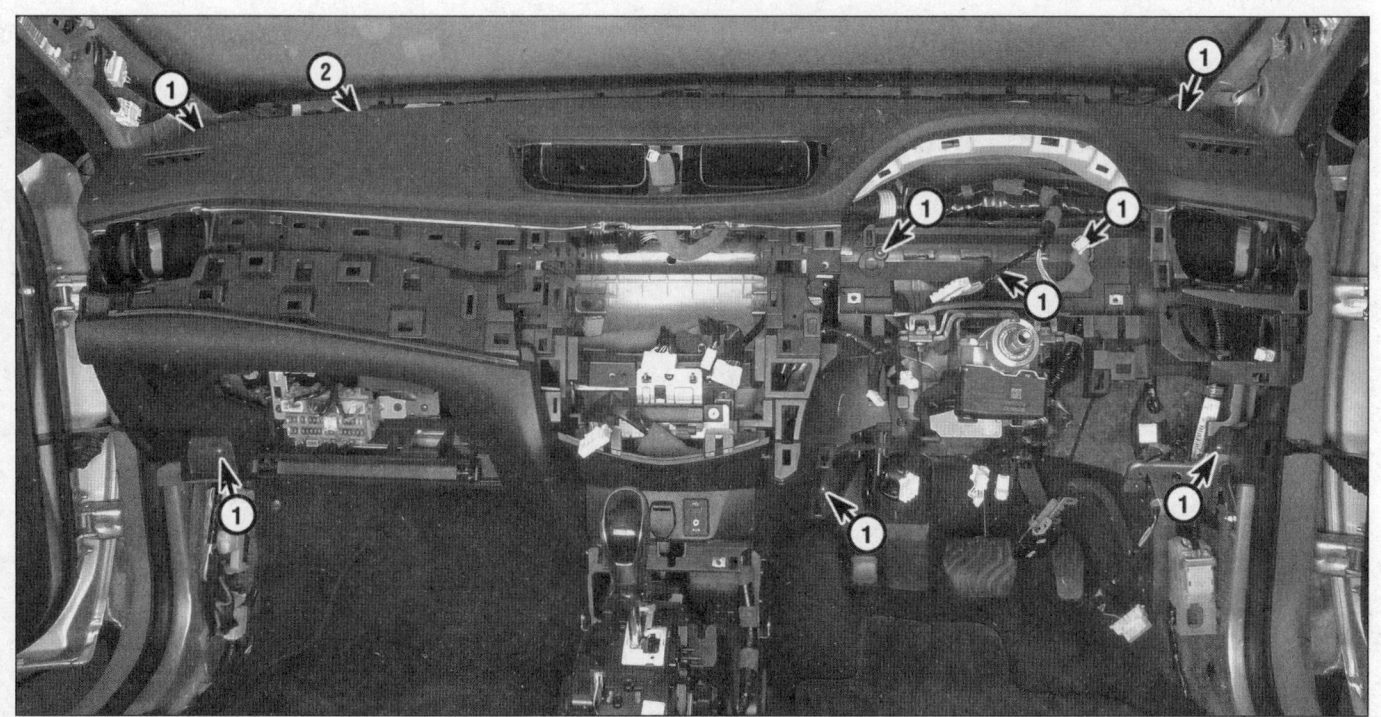

24.15g Dashboard retaining screws (1) and bolt (2) - Late models

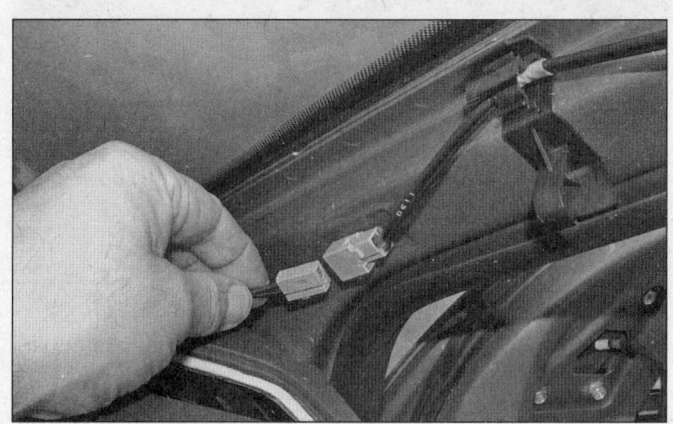

24.17 Disconnecting the aerial connector

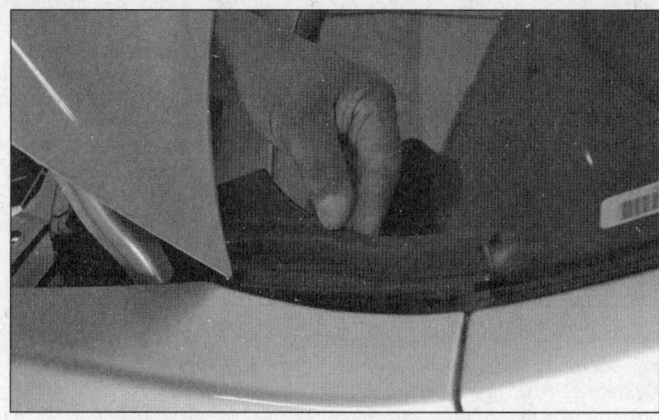

25.3 Disengage the cowl extension panels

4 Remove the cowl top cover fasteners **(see illustration)** then pull the panel forward and up to lift the panel out of the vehicle.
5 Disconnect and remove the front wiper motor and linkage assembly (see Chapter 12A Section 12).
6 Remove the bolts and remove the cowl extension panel **(see illustration)**.

7 Installation is the reverse of removal.

Note: *Always replace the sealant and double-faced adhesive tape when installing cowl top cover.*

25.4 Use a trim tool to pry out the cowl seal clips

25.6 Remove the cowl extension panel bolts.

26.4 With the seat moved forward, the rear Torx mounting bolt caps are exposed

26.5 Move the seat rearward to gain access to the mounting bolts

26.6a On Dualis models, the electrical connectors are at the rear of the seat on the outer side; disconnect them before removing the seat

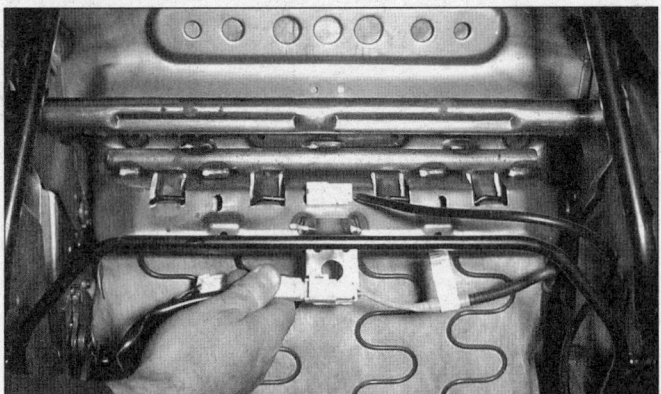

26.6b On all other models, the connectors can be accessed after removing seat fasteners and tilting the seat back. Disconnect the seat belt warning light switch and then...

26 Seats - removal and installation

Warning: *The models covered by this manual are equipped with a Supplemental Restraint System (SRS), more commonly known as airbags. Always disarm the airbag system before working in the vicinity of any airbag system component to avoid the possibility of accidental deployment of the airbag, which could cause personal injury Chapter 12A Section 20. Do not use a memory saving device to preserve the PCM's memory when working on or near airbag system components.*

Front seat

1 Disconnect the negative (-) battery terminal (see Chapter 5 Section 3).
2 Remove the headrest.
3 Disconnect the side airbag module connector.
4 Position the seat to the fully forward position and remove the two rear seat Torx bolt caps and bolts **(see illustration)**.
5 Position the seat to its fully backward position and remove the two front seat bolts **(see illustration)**.
6 Tilt the seat back and disconnect any wiring attached to the seat **(see illustration)**.
7 Installation is a reversal of the removal procedure.

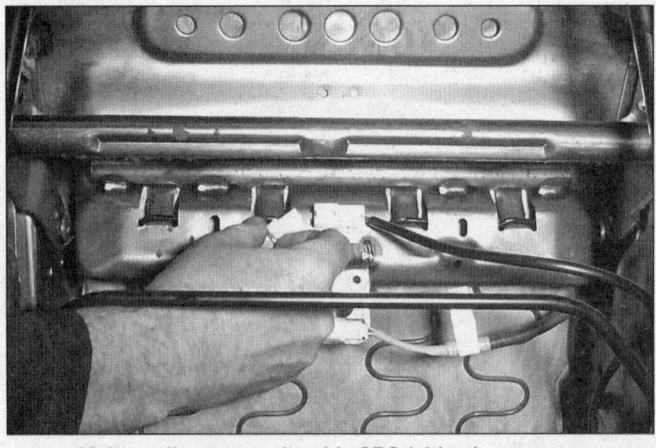

26.6c ... disconnect the side SRS (airbag) connector

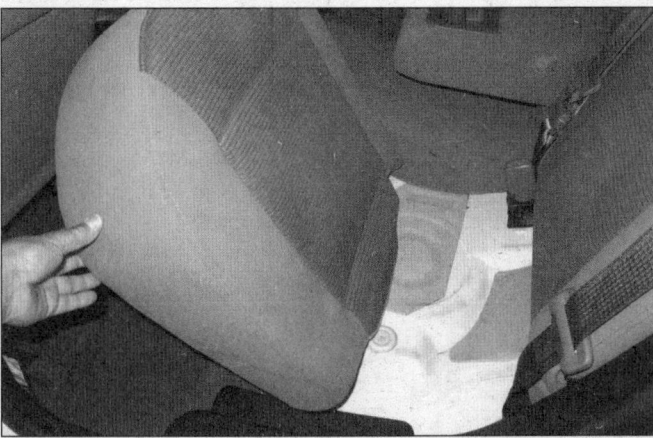

26.8 Rear seat cushion lifted up showing seat mounting hook and lock (left side shown)

Chapter 11 Body   11-37

26.9a Carefully remove seat back fastener trim covers…

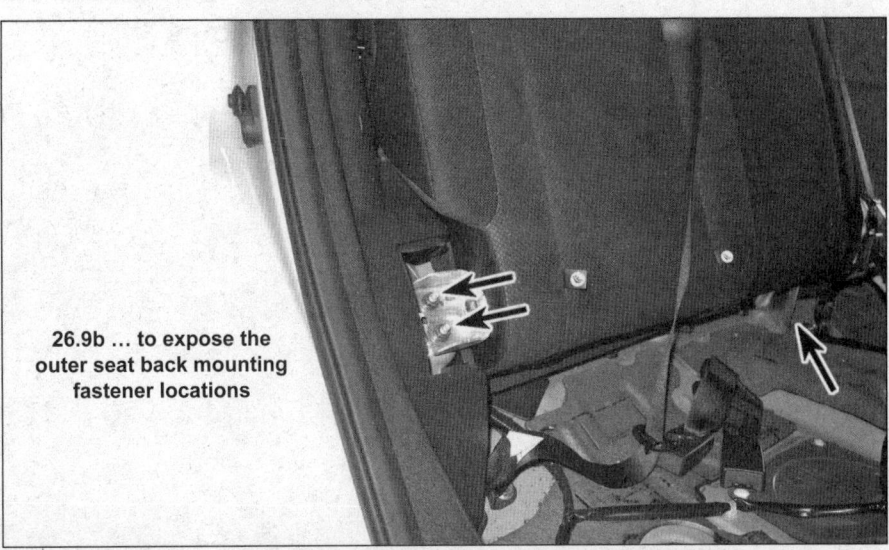

26.9b … to expose the outer seat back mounting fastener locations

26.9c Remove the RH seat back first and then remove the illustrated fasteners to remove the LH seat back

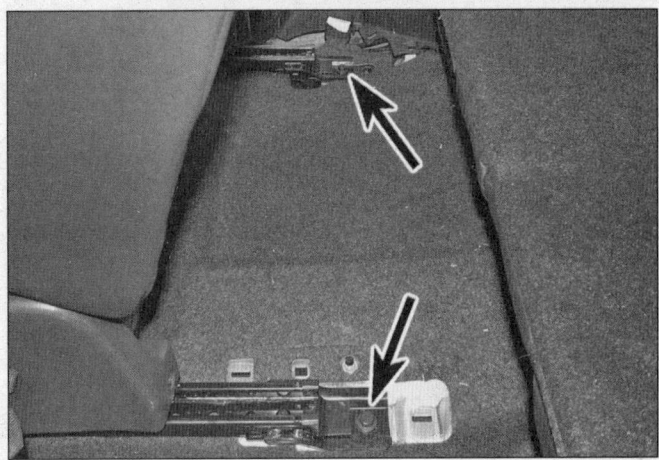

26.13 Seat retaining bolts at the rear of the sliding rails

Second row seats

Fixed type

8   Lift corners of the rear seat cushion up to disengage the fasteners (see illustration).
9   Remove the seat bolt trim covers then remove the seat fasteners and seats (see illustrations).

10 Remove the seat backs.
11 Installation is a reversal of the removal procedure.

Sliding type

12 Remove the headrest.
13 Position the seat to the fully forward position and remove the trim covers and two rear seat bolts (see illustration).

14 Position the seat to its fully backward position and remove the trim cover (see illustration) and two front seat bolts (see illustration).
15 Where fitted, disconnect any wiring from beneath the seat base (see illustration).
16 Remove the seat.
17 Installation is a reversal of the removal procedure.

26.14a Removing one of the front trim covers

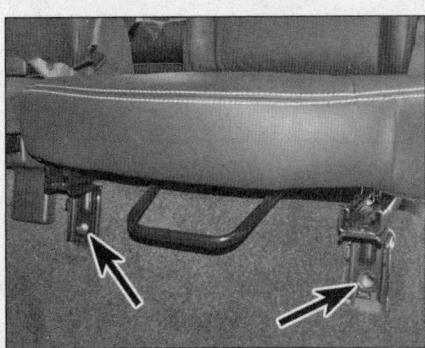

26.14b Seat retaining bolts at the front of the sliding rails

26.15 Depending on the model, there can be an SRS (airbag) fitted to the seat back and also a connection for the seat occupied sensor

Notes

Chapter 12
Chassis electrical systems

Contents

	Section		Section
Airbag system – general information, precautions and system de-activation	20	Instrument cluster – removal and refitting	9
Airbag system components – removal and refitting	21	Intelligent key system components – general information	19
Anti-theft system and engine immobiliser – general information	18	Radio aerial – removal and refitting	17
Bulbs (exterior lights) – renewal	5	Radio/CD player – removal and refitting	15
Bulbs (interior lights) – renewal	6	Speakers – removal and refitting	16
Electrical fault finding – general information	2	Switches – removal and refitting	4
Exterior lights – removal and refitting	7	Tailgate wiper motor – removal and refitting	13
Fuses and relays – general information	3	Windscreen wiper motor and linkage – removal and refitting	12
General information and precautions	1		
Headlight beam adjustment components – general information, removal and refitting	8	Windscreen/tailgate washer system components – removal and refitting	14
Horn – removal and refitting	10	Wiper arm – removal and refitting	11
		Wiring diagrams - general information	22

1 General information and precautions

General information

1 The electrical system is of 12-volt negative earth type. Power for the lights and all electrical accessories is supplied by a lead-acid type battery, which is charged by the alternator.

2 This Chapter covers repair and service procedures for the various electrical components not associated with the engine. Information on the battery, alternator and starter motor can be found in Chapter 5.

3 It should be noted that, prior to working on any component in the electrical system, the battery negative terminal should first be disconnected, to prevent the possibility of electrical short-circuits and/or fires. This is also done to prevent accidental deployment of any of the SRS (airbag) components while working in the vicinity of these components (see Chapter 5 Section 3).

Precautions

Warning: *Before carrying out any work on the electrical system, read through the precautions given in 'Safety first!' at the beginning of this manual. All models are equipped with an airbag system and pyrotechnic seat belt pretensioners. When working on the electrical system, refer to the precautions given in Section 20 to avoid the possibility of personal injury.*

2 Electrical fault finding – general information

Caution: *Refer to the precautions given in 'Safety first!' and in Section 20 of this Chapter before starting work. The following tests relate to testing of the main electrical circuits, and should not be used to test delicate electronic circuits (such as engine management systems or anti-lock braking systems), particularly where an electronic control unit is used.*

General

1 A typical electrical circuit consists of an electrical component; any switches, relays, motors, fuses, fusible links or circuit breakers related to that component, and the wiring and connectors which link the component to both the battery and the chassis. To help to pinpoint a problem in an electrical circuit, wiring diagrams are included at the end of this chapter.

2 Before attempting to diagnose an electrical fault, first study the appropriate wiring diagram, to obtain a more complete understanding of the components included in the particular circuit concerned. The possible sources of a fault can be narrowed down by noting whether other components related to the circuit are operating properly. If several components or circuits fail at one time, the problem is likely to be related to a shared fuse or earth connection.

3 Electrical problems usually stem from simple causes, such as loose or corroded connections, a faulty earth connection, a blown fuse, a melted fusible link, or a faulty

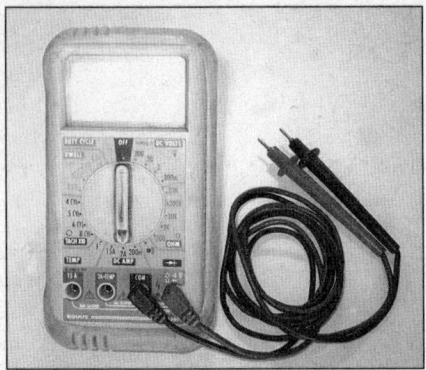

2.4a The most useful tool for electrical troubleshooting is a digital multimeter that can check volts, amps, and test continuity

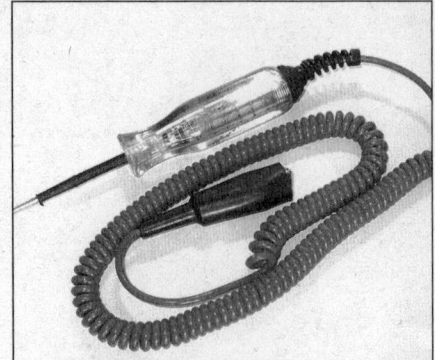

2.4b A simple test light is a very handy tool for checking voltage

relay (see Section 3). Visually inspect the condition of all fuses, wires and connections in a problem circuit before testing the components. Use the wiring diagrams to determine which terminal connections will need to be checked, in order to pinpoint the trouble spot.

4 The basic tools required for electrical fault finding include a circuit tester or voltmeter (a 12 volt bulb with a set of test leads can also be used for certain tests); a self-powered test light (sometimes known as a continuity tester); an ohmmeter (to measure resistance); a battery and set of test leads; and a jumper wire, preferably with a circuit breaker or fuse incorporated, which can be used to bypass suspect wires or electrical components. Before attempting to locate a problem with test instruments, use the wiring diagram to determine where to make the connections.

5 To find the source of an intermittent wiring fault (usually due to a poor or dirty connection, or damaged wiring insulation), a 'wiggle' test can be performed on the wiring. This involves wiggling the wiring by hand, to see if the fault occurs as the wiring is moved. It should be possible to narrow down the source of the fault to a particular Section of wiring. This method of testing can be used in conjunction with any of the tests described in the following sub-Sections.

6 Apart from problems due to poor connections, two basic types of fault can occur in an electrical circuit – open-circuit, or short-circuit.

7 Open-circuit faults are caused by a break somewhere in the circuit, which prevents current from flowing. An open-circuit fault will prevent a component from working, but will not cause the relevant circuit fuse to blow.

8 Short-circuit faults are normally caused by a breakdown in wiring insulation, which allows a feed wire to touch either another wire, or an earthed component such as the bodyshell. This allows the current flowing in the circuit to 'escape' along an alternative route, usually to earth. As the circuit does not now follow its original complete path, it is known as a 'short' circuit. A short-circuit fault will normally cause the relevant circuit fuse to blow.

Finding an open-circuit

9 To check for an open-circuit, connect one lead of a circuit tester or voltmeter to either the negative battery terminal or a known good earth.

10 Connect the other lead to a connector in the circuit being tested, preferably nearest to the battery or fuse.

11 Switch on the circuit, bearing in mind that some circuits are live only when the ignition switch is moved to a particular position.

12 If voltage is present (indicated either by the tester bulb lighting or a voltmeter reading, as applicable), this means that the Section of the circuit between the relevant connector and the battery is problem-free.

13 Continue to check the remainder of the circuit in the same fashion.

14 When a point is reached at which no voltage is present, the problem must lie between that point and the previous test point with voltage. Most problems can be traced to a broken, corroded or loose connection.

Finding a short-circuit

15 To check for a short circuit; first disconnect the load(s) from the circuit (loads are the components which draw current from a circuit, such as bulbs, motors, heating elements, etc).

16 Remove the relevant fuse from the circuit, and connect a circuit tester or voltmeter to the fuse connections.

17 Switch on the circuit, bearing in mind that some circuits are live only when the ignition switch is moved to a particular position.

18 If voltage is present (indicated either by the tester bulb lighting or a voltmeter reading, as applicable), this means that there is a short circuit.

19 If no voltage is present, but the fuse still blows with the load(s) connected, this indicates an internal fault in the load(s).

Finding an earth fault

20 The battery negative terminal is connected to 'earth' – the metal of the engine/transmission and the car body – and most systems are wired so that they only receive a positive feed, the current returning via the metal of the car body. This means that the component mounting and the body form part of that circuit. Loose or corroded mountings can therefore cause a range of electrical faults, ranging from total failure of a circuit, to a puzzling partial fault. In particular, lights may shine dimly (especially when another circuit sharing the same earth point is in operation), motors (e.g. wiper motors or the radiator cooling fan motor) may run slowly, and the operation of one circuit may have an apparently unrelated effect on another. Note that on many vehicles, earth straps are used between certain components, such as the engine/transmission and the body, usually where there is no metal-to-metal contact between components, due to flexible rubber mountings, etc.

21 To check whether a component is properly earthed, disconnect the battery, and connect one lead of an ohmmeter to a known good earth point. Connect the other lead to the wire or earth connection being tested. The resistance reading should be zero; if not, check the connection as follows.

22 If an earth connection is thought to be faulty, dismantle the connection, and clean back to bare metal both the bodyshell and the wire terminal or the component earth connection mating surface. Be careful to remove all traces of dirt and corrosion, and then use a knife to trim away any paint, so that a clean

2.10 In use, a basic test light's lead is clipped to a known good ground, then the pointed probe can test connectors, wires or electrical sockets - if the bulb lights, the part being tested has battery voltage

Electrical connectors

Most electrical connectors have a single release tab that you depress to release the connector

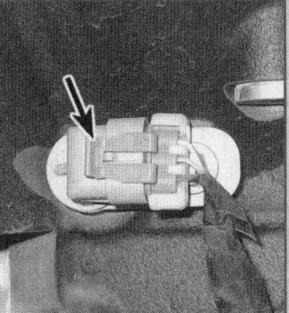

Some electrical connectors have a retaining tab which must be pried up to free the connector

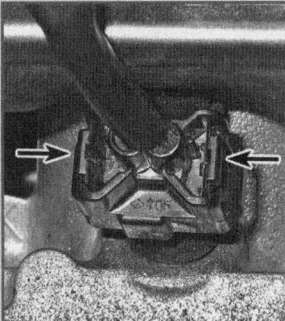

Some connectors have two release tabs that you must squeeze to release the connector

Some connectors use wire retainers that you squeeze to release the connector

Critical connectors often employ a sliding lock (1) that you must pull out before you can depress the release tab (2)

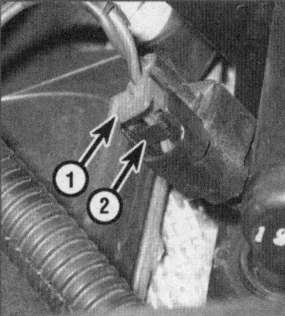

Here's another sliding-lock style connector, with the lock (1) and the release tab (2) on the side of the connector

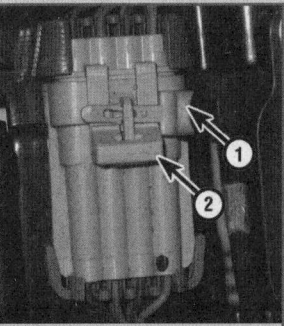

On some connectors the lock (1) must be pulled out to the side and removed before you can lift the release tab (2)

Some critical connectors, like the multi-pin connectors at the Powertrain Control Module employ pivoting locks that must be flipped open

metal-to-metal joint is made. On reassembly, tighten the joint fasteners securely; if a wire terminal is being refitted, use serrated washers between the terminal and the bodyshell, to ensure a clean and secure connection. When the connection is remade, prevent the onset of corrosion in the future by applying a coat of petroleum jelly or silicone-based grease, or by spraying on (at regular intervals) a proprietary ignition sealer.

Connectors

23 Most electrical connections on these vehicles are made with multi-wire plastic connectors. The mating halves of many connectors are secured with locking clips moulded into the plastic connector shells. The mating halves of large connectors, such as some of those under the dashboard, are held together by a bolt through the centre of the connector.
24 To separate a connector with locking clips, use a small screwdriver to pry the clips apart carefully, then separate the connector halves. Pull only on the shell, never pull on the wiring harness as you may damage the individual wires and terminals inside the connectors. Look at the connector closely before trying to separate the halves. Often the locking clips are engaged in a way that is not immediately clear. Additionally, many connectors have more than one set of clips.
25 Each pair of connector terminals has a male half and a female half. When you look at the end view of a connector in a diagram, be sure to understand whether the view shows the harness side or the component side of the connector. Connector halves are mirror images of each other, and a terminal shown on the right side end-view of one half will be on the left side end view of the other half.

3 Fuses and relays – general information

Fuses

1 Fuses are designed to break a circuit when a predetermined current is reached, in order to protect the components and wiring,

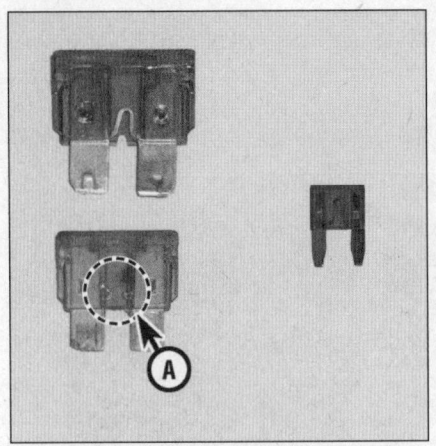

3.2 An example of the fuses used in these vehicles - (A) is an example of a blown fuse

3.3a Vehicle interior fuse and relay box - T31 X-Trail and Dualis models

3.4a Vehicle engine compartment fusebox - Dualis models

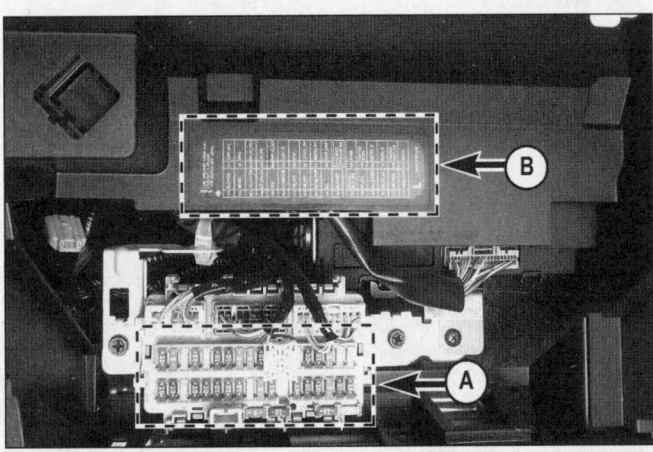

3.3b Vehicle interior fuse and relay box (A) on T32 X-Trail and Qashqai models is behind the glovebox; a label (B) shows the fuse identification

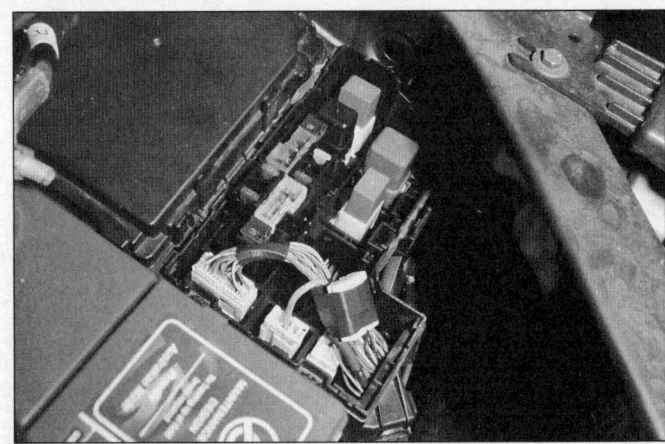

3.4b Engine compartment fuse and relay box - T31 X-Trail models

which could be damaged by excessive current flow. Any excessive current flow will be due to a fault in the circuit, usually a short-circuit (see Section 2).

2 The main fuses are located in the fusebox on the driver's side of the facia.

3 For access to the fuses, pull open the cover flap **(see illustration)**. On later models, remove the glovebox (see Chapter 11 Section 21).

4 Additional fuses and circuit-breakers are located in an auxiliary fusebox in the engine compartment, next to the battery **(see illustration)**.

3.4c Fuse box No.2 is next to the IPDM and fuse box No.3 is beneath the LH headlamp and is accessible after removing the LH headlamp - T32 X-Trail and Qashqai models

3.5a Vehicle IPDM also has fuses ...

Chapter 12 Chassis electrical systems

3.5b ... with fuse ratings and location on the side - Dualis models

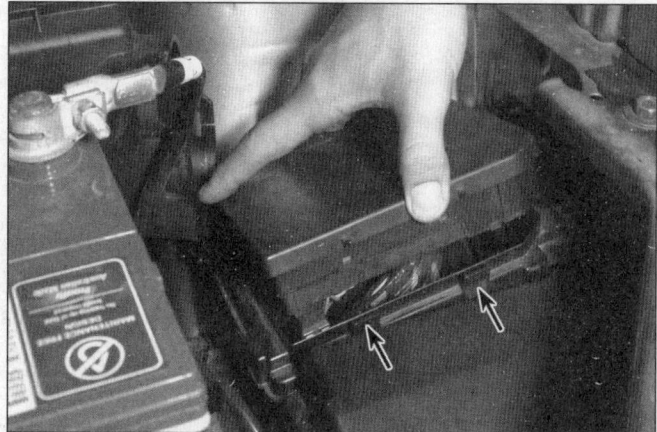

3.5c With the air intake duct removed, release the clips and lift the IDPM up and over to...

3.5d ... expose the fuses beneath on T31 X-Trail models, other models the same

5 The Intelligent Power Distribution Module (IPDM) is also located in the engine compartment, next to the fusebox **(see illustrations)**.
6 Depending on the model. It may be necessary to remove the air intake ducting, to access the engine compartment fuse and relay boxes **(see illustrations)**.

7 A blown fuse can be recognised from its melted or broken wire **(see illustration 3.2)**. Before removing a fuse, first ensure that the relevant circuit is switched off.
8 Using the plastic tool clipped inside the main fusebox, pull the fuse from its location **(see illustration)**.

9 Spare fuses are usually provided in the main fusebox.
10 Before renewing a blown fuse, trace and rectify the cause, and always use a fuse of the correct rating (fuse ratings are usually specified on the inside of the fusebox cover flap). Never substitute a fuse of a higher rating, or make temporary repairs using wire or metal foil; more serious damage, or even fire, could result.
11 Note that the fuses are colour-coded as follows.

Colour	Rating
Orange	5A
Red	10A
Blue	15A
Yellow	20A
Clear or White	25A
Green	30A

Relays

12 A relay is an electrically operated switch, which is used for the following reasons:

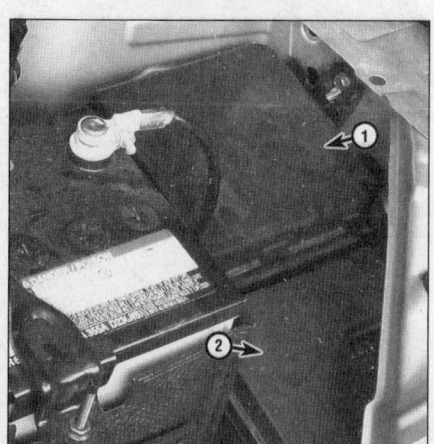

3.5e IDPM (1) and No.2 (2) fuse box viewed with the air intake duct removed - T32 X-Trail and Qashqai models

3.6a Release the retaining clips ...

3.6b ... and remove the air intake ducting

12-6 Chapter 12 Chassis electrical systems

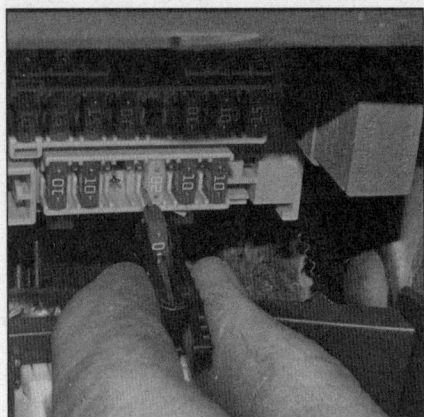

3.8 Pull the fuse from its position in the fusebox

14 If a circuit or system controlled by a relay develops a fault, and the relay is suspect, operate the system. If the relay is functioning, it should be possible to hear it 'click' as it is energised, If this is the case, the fault lies with the components or wiring of the system. If the relay is not being energised, then either the relay is not receiving a main supply or a switching voltage, or the relay itself is faulty. Testing is by the substitution of a known good unit, but be careful – while some relays are identical in appearance and in operation, others look similar but perform different functions.

15 To remove a relay, first ensure that the relevant circuit is switched off. The relay can then simply be pulled out from the socket, and pushed back into position.

4 Switches – removal and refitting

Note: *Disconnect the battery negative terminal (see Chapter 5 Section 3), before removing any switch, and reconnect the terminal after refitting the switch.*

Ignition switch/steering lock

Models with an ignition key

1 Remove the steering column covers (see Chapter 11 Section 23).

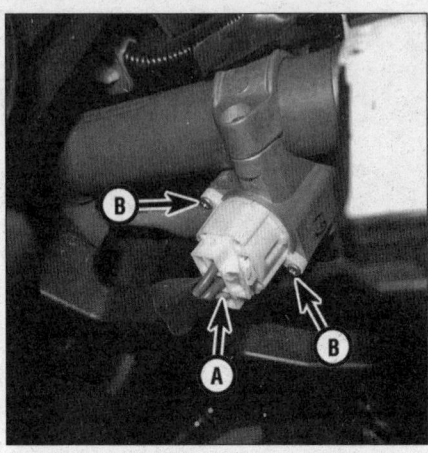

4.2 Disconnect the wiring connector (A) and remove the screws (B); slide the switch from the rear of the steering lock assembly

2 Disconnect the wiring from the rear of the switch **(see illustration)** and remove the switch screws. Slide the ignition switch from the rear of the steering lock assembly.

3 The steering lock assembly is retained to the steering column using shear bolts. When these bolts reach a predetermined torque, the head breaks off the bolt making it impossible to unscrew the bolt from the lock. The manufacturer uses this as a theft deterrent.

a A relay can switch a heavy current remotely from the circuit in which the current is flowing, therefore allowing the use of lighter-gauge wiring and switch contacts.
b A relay can receive more than one control input, unlike a mechanical switch.
c A relay can have a timer function – for example, the intermittent wiper relay.

13 Various relays are located throughout the vehicle **(see illustration 3.4a through 3.4c)**.

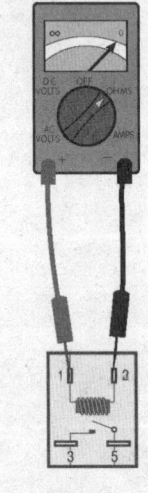

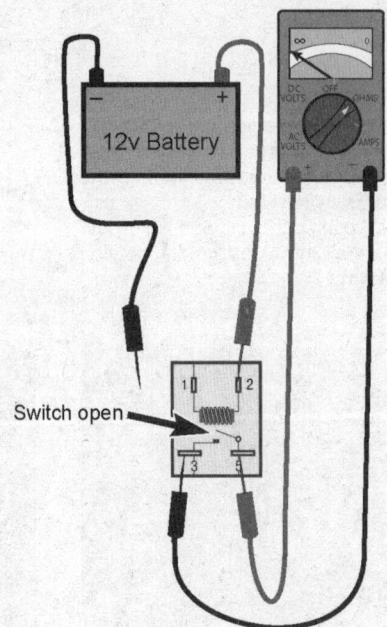

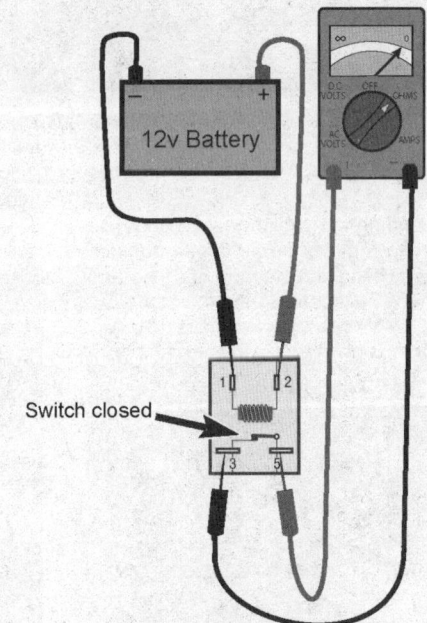

Check that continuity exists between the two terminals of the coil, indicating there is no open circuit in the coil

Check that continuity does not exist between the two switch terminals, indicating the switch is not stuck closed

Once battery power is applied to the coil terminals, the switch should close, allowing continuity between the two switch terminals

3.12 Method of testing relays used on this type of vehicle

Chapter 12 Chassis electrical systems 12-7

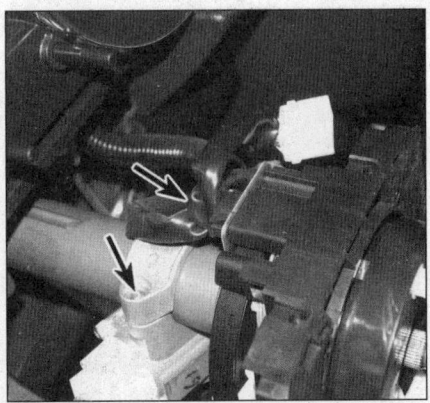

4.5a Shear bolt location on a Dualis model; X-Trail models are similar

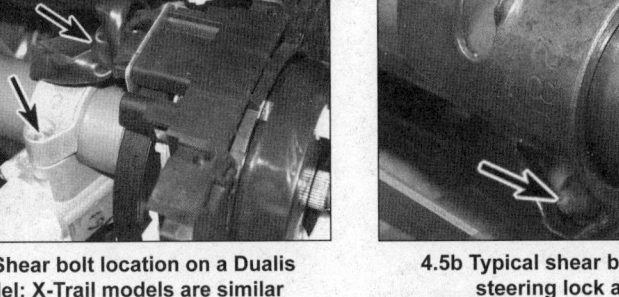

4.5b Typical shear bolt heads on a steering lock assembly

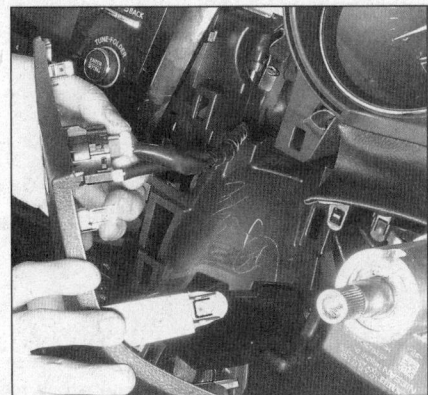

4.8 Disconnecting the wiring from the rear of the Start/Stop switch

4 To remove the steering lock, remove any necessary components to access the bolts on the steering lock clamp. The best method is to remove the steering column from the vehicle (see Chapter 10 Section 13).

5 Mount the steering column in a vice and centre punch the centre of the shear bolt head **(see illustration)**. Drill a hole into the bolt and use a screw extractor to remove the bolt from the lock assembly.

6 On assembly, use new shear bolts which can be purchased from the vehicle manufacturer.

Models with intelligent key

7 Remove the trim panel retaining the Start/Stop switch (see Chapter 11 Section 21).

8 Disconnect the wiring from the rear of the switch and unclip it from the trim panel **(see illustration)**.

Steering column switches

9 Remove the steering column covers (see Chapter 11 Section 23).

10 Disconnect the wiring from the top rear of the switch assembly and then slide the wiper stalk/switch out from the left-hand side of the combination switch housing **(see illustrations)**.

11 Release the retaining clips and slide the lighting stalk/switch out from the right-hand side of the combination switch housing **(see illustrations)**.

12 Refitting is a reversal of removal.

Heater/ventilation and demister switches

13 The heater/ventilation switches are integral with the heater control panel, remove the heater control panel, as described in the Cooling, Heating and Air Conditioning Systems chapter (see Chapter 3 Section 9).

Driver's side panel switches

14 These switches include the electric door mirror switch, the headlight height adjustment switch, electronic stability programme (ESP) switch, cruise control on/off switch and the headlight beam adjustment switch, according to model.

15 Carefully unclip the switch panel from the facia, and then disconnect the wiring connectors on removal **(see illustrations)**.

4.10a Disconnect the wiring connector...

4.10b ... then release the clips and withdraw the switch

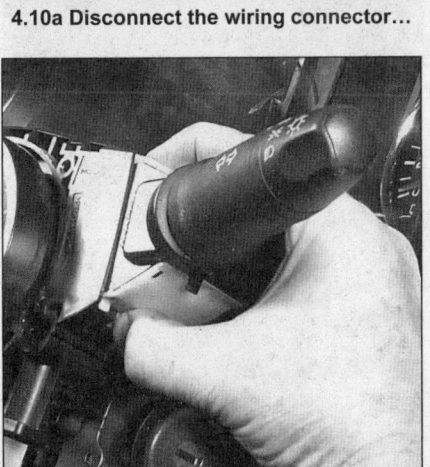

4.11 Release the securing clips and withdraw the switch

4.15a Unclip the switch panel from the facia ...

4.15b ... and disconnect the switch wiring connectors

4.16a Release the securing clips ...

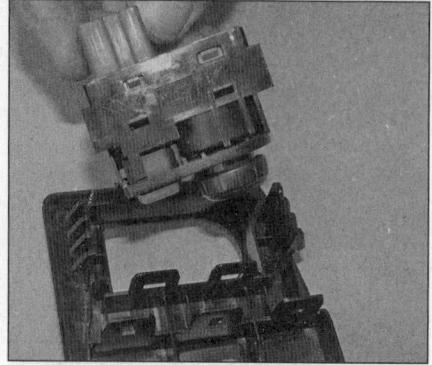
4.16b ... and release the switch from the trim panel

4.18 Unclip the trim panel from the door panel ...

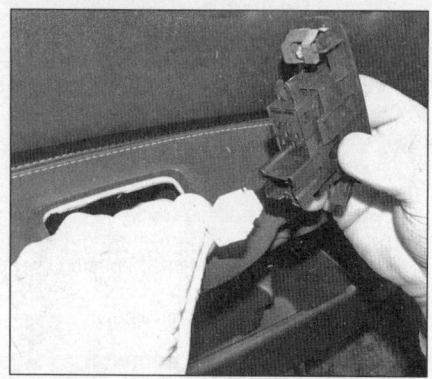
4.19 ... and disconnect the wiring connector

4.20a Release the securing clips and remove the switch

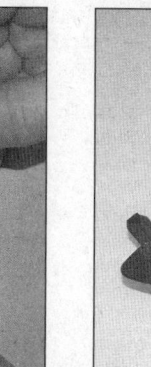
4.20b On the driver's door the switches are a complete assembly

16 To remove the relevant switch, turn the trim panel over, release the retaining clips and withdraw the switch from the trim panel (see illustrations).

17 Refit the relevant switch and trim panel, using a reversal of the removal procedure.

Power window switches

Dualis models

Front door switch

18 Unclip the door switch trim panel from the top of the armrest in the door trim panel (see illustration).

19 Disconnect the wiring connector from the switch panel as it is removed (see illustration).

20 To remove the relevant switch, release the retaining clips and withdraw the switch from the rear of the trim panel (see illustrations).

21 Refit the relevant switch and trim panel, using a reversal of the removal procedure.

T31 X-Trail models

Note: *The procedure to remove the front and rear door switches is similar.*

22 Using a trim removal tool, pry up the switch panel (see illustrations).

23 Disconnect the wiring from the rear of the switch assembly (see illustration).

24 If necessary, release the clips holding the switch assembly to the switch frame and remove the switch from the rear of the frame.

25 Installation is a reversal of the removal procedure, with attention to the following points:

a Install the switch into the frame ensuring it clips into place.
b Connect the wiring to the switch assembly before installing the assembly back into the door trim panel.

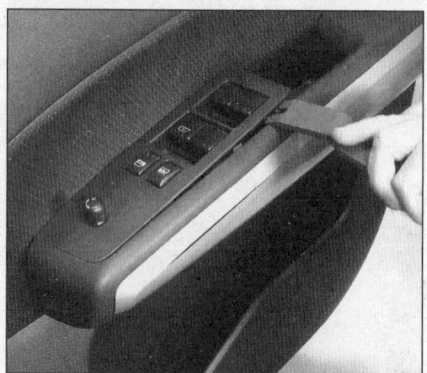
4.22a Using a trim removal tool to pry up the front power window switch assembly

4.22b Using a trim removal tool to pry up the rear power window switch assembly

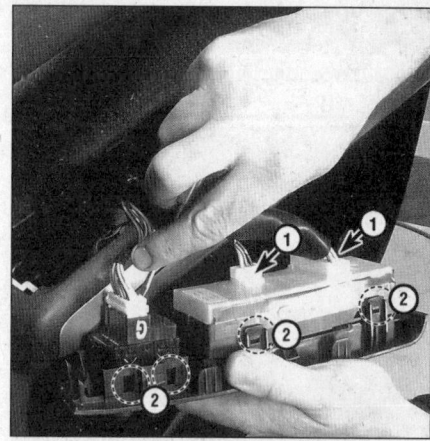
4.23 Disconnecting the wiring from the power mirror switch; (1) indicates the power window and power door lock switches wiring and (2) indicates the locations of the clips retaining the switches to the switch frame

Chapter 12 Chassis electrical systems

4.26a Using a trim removal tool to unclip the door trim garnish

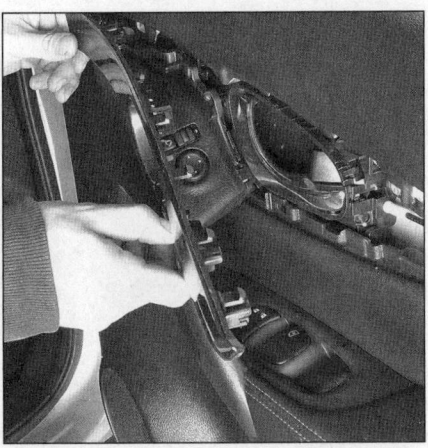

4.26b Removing the door trim garnish

4.27a Removing the inner grab handle trim

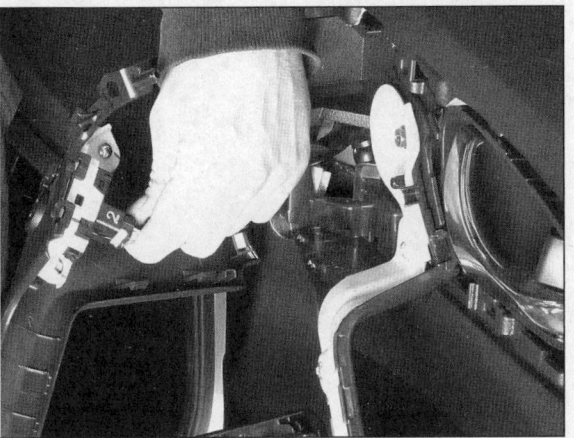

4.27b Disconnecting the power mirror switch wiring

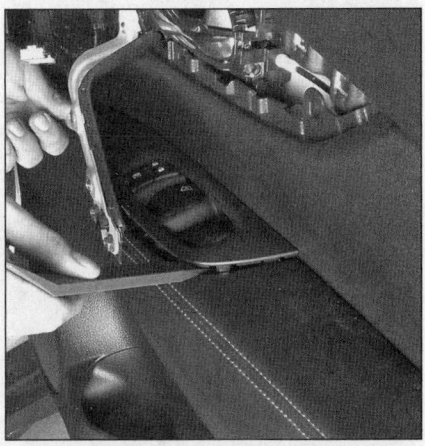

4.28 Unclipping the power window switch from the door trim panel using a trim removal tool

T32 X-Trail and Qashqai models

26 Use a trim remover tool to remove top door trim garnish **(see illustrations)**.

27 Unclip inner grab handle door trim and disconnect mirror switch connector **(see illustrations)**.

28 Remove the power window switch **(see illustration)** from the door trim panel using a trim removal tool.

Hazard warning light switch

29 The hazard warning switch is fitted to the centre trim panel, remove the trim panel (see Chapter 11 Section 21).

30 To remove the switch, release the retaining clips and withdraw the switch through the front of the trim panel **(see illustrations)**.

31 Refit the switch and trim panel, using a reversal of the removal procedure.

4.30a Release the securing clips …

4.30b … and release the switch from the front of the trim panel

4.30c Hazard warning light switch removed from the front of the centre vent panel - T32 X-Trail models

12-10 Chapter 12 Chassis electrical systems

4.33a Unclip the switch panel from the centre console ...

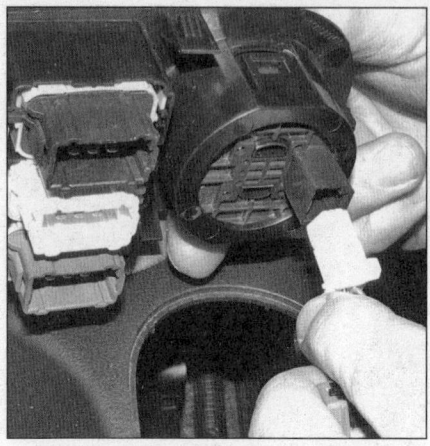

4.33b ... and disconnect the switch wiring connectors

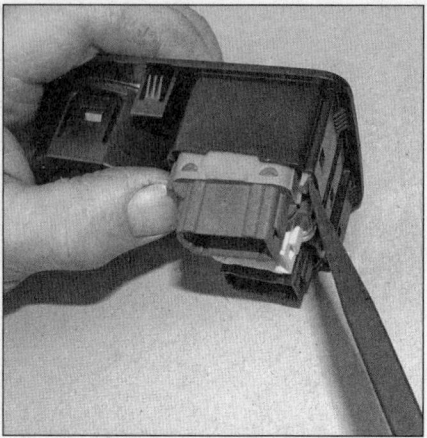

4.34a Release the securing clips ...

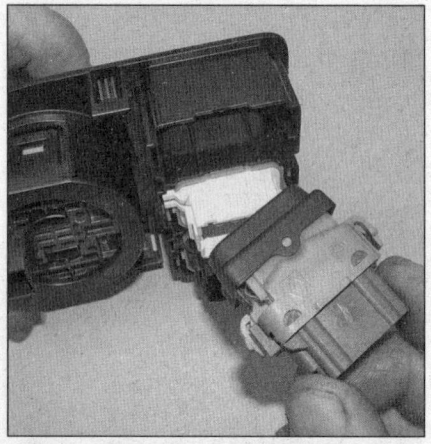

4.34b ... and remove the switches from the rear of the trim panel

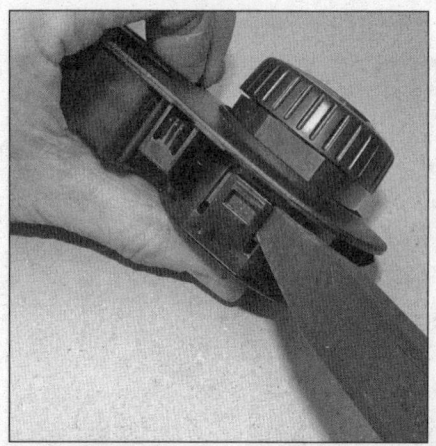

4.34c Release the securing clips ...

4.34d ... and remove the 4WD switch from the front of the trim panel

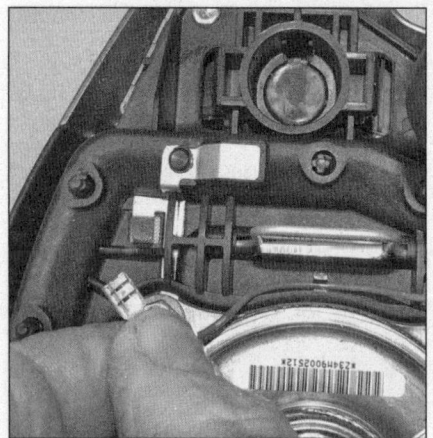

4.41 Disconnect the earth wire

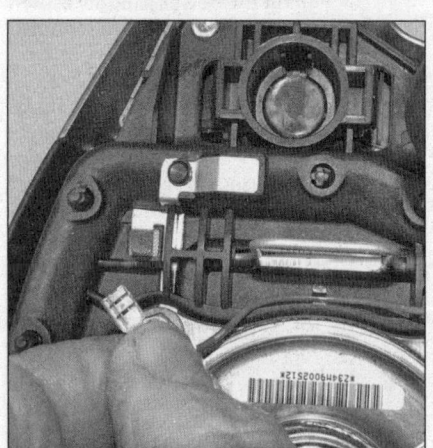

4.42a Undo the switch retaining screws (arrowed) ...

Centre console switches

32 These switches include the heated seat switches, central door-locking switch and 4WD/2WD/Automatic-setting switch, according to model.

33 Carefully unclip the switch panel from the top of the centre console, and then disconnect the wiring connectors on removal **(see illustrations)**.

34 To remove the relevant switch, turn the trim panel over, release the retaining clips and withdraw the switch from the trim panel **(see illustrations)**.

35 Refit the relevant switch and trim panel, using a reversal of the removal procedure.

Courtesy light/door warning switches

36 The door warning switches are part of the central locking system components (see Chapter 11 Section 17).

Luggage area light switch

37 The switch is integral with the boot lid/tailgate lock (see Chapter 11 Section 13).

Map reading/courtesy light switches

38 The switches are integral with the interior light assembly and cannot be renewed independently. See Section 6 for interior light bulb renewal.

Chapter 12 Chassis electrical systems

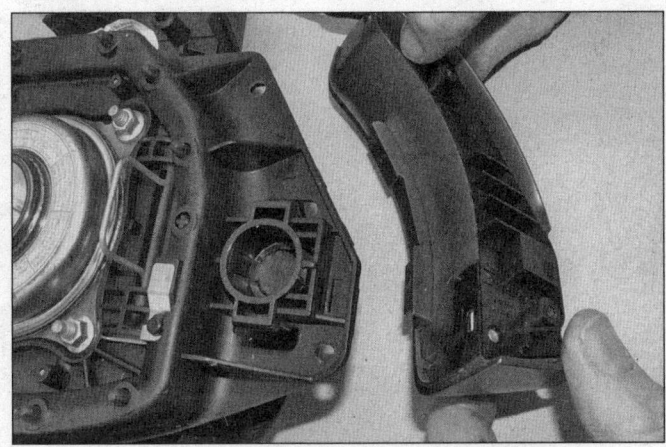

4.42b ... and remove the switch from the airbag

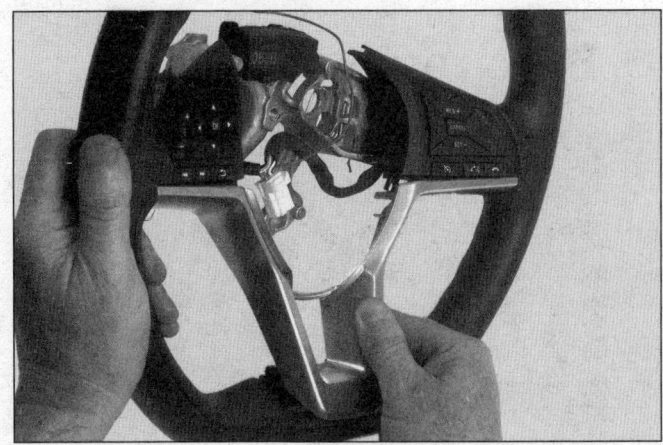

4.45 Removing the chrome garnish from the steering wheel

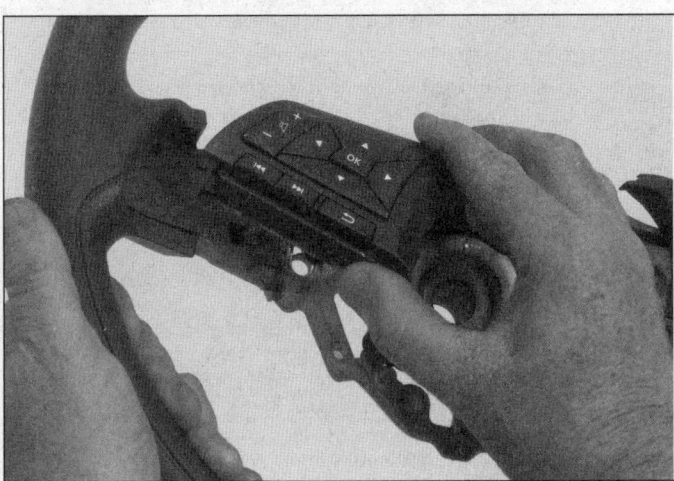

4.46 The switches are clipped into the steering wheel and can be pulled from the wheel

Steering wheel switches

39 These switches include the audio control switches to the left-hand side of the steering wheel, and cruise control system operation to the right-hand side of the steering wheel, according to model.

Warning: *When working on the airbag system, refer to the precautions given in Section 20 to avoid the possibility of personal injury.*

T31 X-Trail and Dualis models

40 Remove the airbag from the centre of the steering wheel, as described in Section 21.
41 Disconnect the earth wire connection from the rear of the airbag unit **(see illustration)**.
42 Undo the retaining screws, and disconnect the switch panel from the side of the airbag **(see illustrations)**.
43 Refit the switch and trim panel, using a reversal of the removal procedure. Refer to Section 21, when refitting the airbag.

T32 X-Trail and Qashqai models

44 Remove the steering wheel from the vehicle (see Chapter 10 Section 14).
45 Carefully pry the chrome trim panel from the bottom of the steering wheel **(see illustration)**.

46 Unclip each switch assembly from the steering wheel **(see illustration)**.
47 Installation is a reversal of the removal procedure.

5 Bulbs (exterior lights) – renewal

General

1 Whenever a bulb is renewed, note the following points:
 a *Disconnect the negative (-) battery terminal (see Chapter 5 Section 3).*
 b *Remember that, if the light has just been in use, the bulb may be extremely hot.*
 c *Always check the bulb contacts and holder, ensuring that there is clean metal-to-metal contact between the bulb and its live contact(s) and earth. Clean off any corrosion or dirt before fitting a new bulb.*
 d *Wherever bayonet-type bulbs are fitted, ensure that the live contact(s) bear firmly against the bulb contact.*
 e *Always ensure that the new bulb is of the correct rating (see Specifications), and that it is completely clean before fitting it; this applies particularly to headlight/fog light bulbs (see following paragraphs).*

Headlights

2 Open the bonnet and depending on model, to improve access to the left-hand headlight, remove the air inlet ducting **(see illustrations 3.6a & 3.6b)**.
3 When handling the new bulb, use a tissue or clean cloth to avoid touching the glass

5.4a Unclip the headlight bulb protective cover - Dualis models

5.4b On all other models, the cover is a hard plastic cover that is removed by rotating anticlockwise

Bulb removal

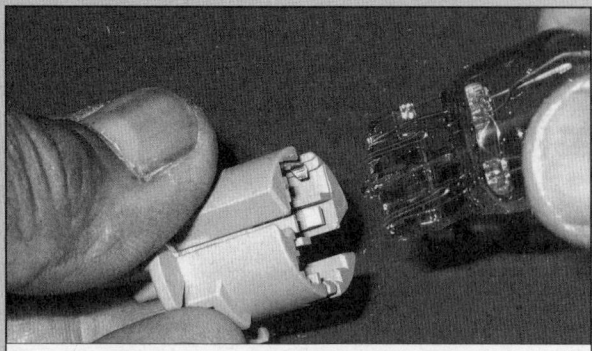
To remove a wedge type bulb from the holder, simply pull it straight out

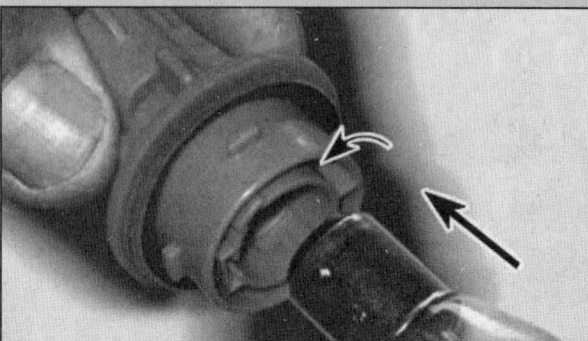
Bulbs with a cylindrical base are called bayonnet bulbs; the socket is spring loaded and a pair of small posits on the side of the base hold the bulb in place against spring pressure. To remove this type of bulb, push it into the holder, rotate it 1/4 turn anticlockwise, then pull it out

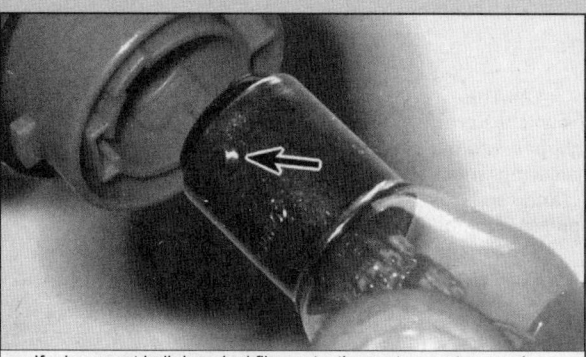
If a bayonnet bulb has dual filaments, the posts are staggered, so the bulb can only be installed one way

Some interior lights have a festoon type bulb; to remove these bulbs simply unclip them

with the fingers; moisture and grease from the skin can cause blackening and rapid failure of this type of bulb. If the glass is accidentally touched, wipe it clean using methylated spirit.

Halogen headlight

Low beam

4 Reach behind the headlamp, and unclip the low beam's protective cover and remove it **(see illustrations)**.

5 Twist the bulb holder anticlockwise and release it from the retaining clip in the headlight **(see illustration)**.

6 On Dualis models, pull the bulb to release it from the bulb holder **(see illustration)**.

5.5a Twist the bulb holder to release it - Dualis models

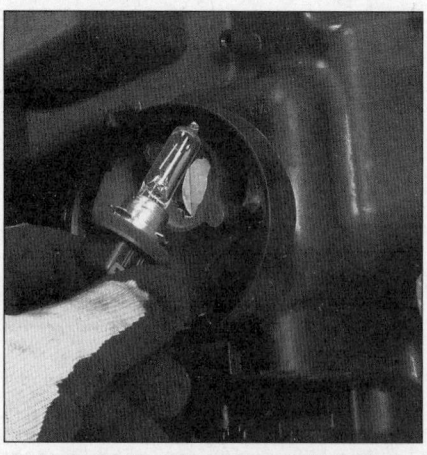
5.5b Removing the low beam bulb - late models

5.6 Remove the bulb from its holder

Chapter 12 Chassis electrical systems

5.7 Make sure the holder is located correctly in the headlight unit

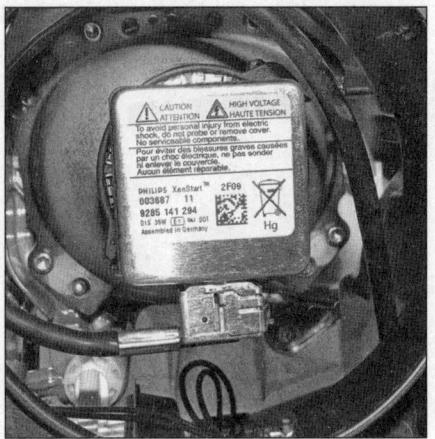

5.10 High voltage warnings on the rear of the bulb holder

5.11 Disconnect the wiring connector from the high voltage pack

7 Install the new bulb, ensuring that the bulb holder is located correctly in the headlight unit **(see illustration)**. When handling the new bulb, use a tissue or clean cloth to avoid touching the glass with the fingers; moisture and grease from the skin can cause blackening and rapid failure of this type of bulb. If the glass is accidentally touched, wipe it clean using methylated spirit.
8 Refit the protective cover.

Xenon headlight

Low beam

Warning: *Before carrying out any operations on xenon headlight units, it is recommended that protective gloves and safety glasses be worn. It is essential that the wiring connectors are disconnected from the rear of the headlight unit, and then wait until the module and bulbs have cooled down before removal. DO NOT switch the headlights on with the bulb removed, as it is harmful to the eyes.*

v 9 Make sure the battery negative terminal is disconnected (refer to 'Disconnecting the battery' in the Reference Chapter).
10 Reach behind the headlamp, and twist the plastic protective cover to remove it from the rear of the headlight. Take notice of the warnings on the high voltage unit on the rear of the headlight bulb **(see illustration)**. If in any doubt, go to your local Nissan dealer to have the bulb replaced.
11 Disconnect the wiring connector from the high voltage unit on the rear of the headlight bulb **(see illustration)**.
12 Twist the high voltage unit and bulb holder anticlockwise and release it from the retaining clip in the headlight **(see illustration)**.
13 Install the new bulb, ensuring that the bulb holder/high voltage unit is located correctly in the headlight unit. When handling the new bulb, use a tissue or clean cloth to avoid touching the glass with the fingers; moisture and grease from the skin can cause blackening and rapid failure of this type of bulb. If the glass is accidentally touched, wipe it clean using methylated spirit.
14 Refit the protective cover.

High beam

15 Reach behind the headlamp, and unclip the main beam's protective cover and remove it **(see illustration)**.
16 Twist the bulb holder anticlockwise and release it from the retaining clip in the headlight **(see illustration)**.
17 Pull the bulb to release it from the bulb holder **(see illustrations)**.
18 Install the new bulb, ensuring that the bulb holder is located correctly in the head-

5.12 Twist the high voltage unit to release it from the headlight

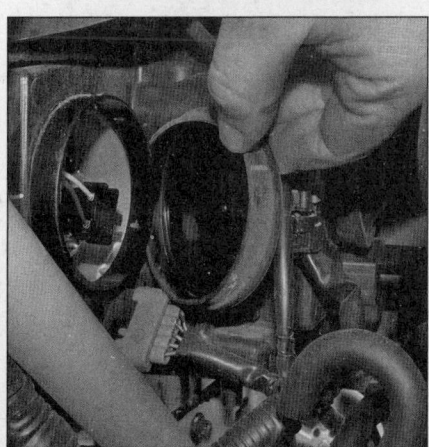

5.15 Unclip the headlight bulb protective cover, where fitted

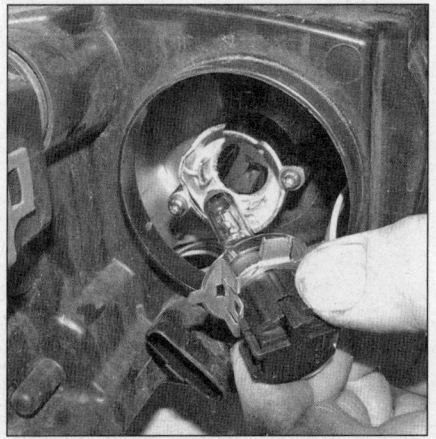

5.16 Twist the bulb holder to release it

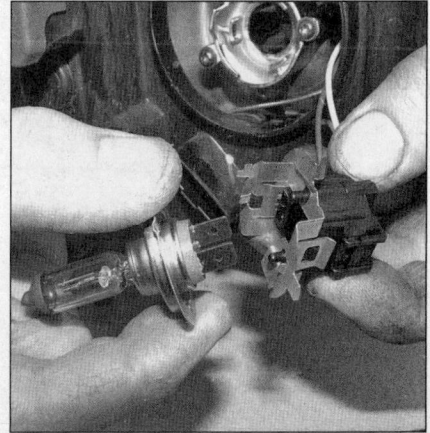

5.17a Remove the bulb from its holder

5.17b On later models, the bulb and bulb holder are renewed as an assembly, rotate the bulb holder anticlockwise and remove it from the rear of the headlight.

5.18 Make sure the holder is located correctly in the headlight unit

5.22 Rotate the bulbholder to remove ...

light unit **(see illustration)**. When handling the new bulb, use a tissue or clean cloth to avoid touching the glass with the fingers; moisture and grease from the skin can cause blackening and rapid failure of this type of bulb. If the glass is accidentally touched, wipe it clean using methylated spirit.

19 Refit the protective cover.

Sidelight

20 Open the bonnet and depending on model, to improve access to the left-hand headlight, remove the air inlet ducting **(see illustrations 3.6a & 3.6b)**.

21 Disconnect the wiring connector from the side light bulb holder at the top of the headlight unit.

22 Twist the bulb holder and withdraw the sidelight bulb and holder from the rear of the headlight unit **(see illustration)**.

23 The bulb is a wedge type. Pull the sidelight bulb to remove it from the bulb holder **(see illustration)**.

24 Fit the new bulb using a reversal of the removal procedure.

Front indicator

25 Open and support the bonnet.

26 Twist the bulbholder anticlockwise and withdraw it from the headlight light unit **(see illustrations)**.

27 The bulb is either a bayonet or wedge type, depending on model **(see illustration)**. Remove the bulb.

28 Fit the new bulb using a reversal of the removal procedure.

5.23 ... then pull the bulb from its holder

5.26a Rotate the bulbholder anticlockwise ...

5.26b ... and remove it from the headlight unit

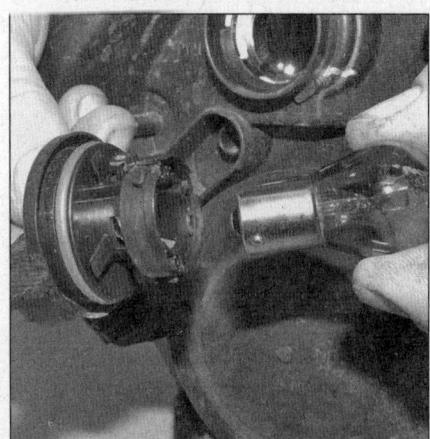

5.27a Press in the bulb and rotate it anticlockwise to remove it on early models, or...

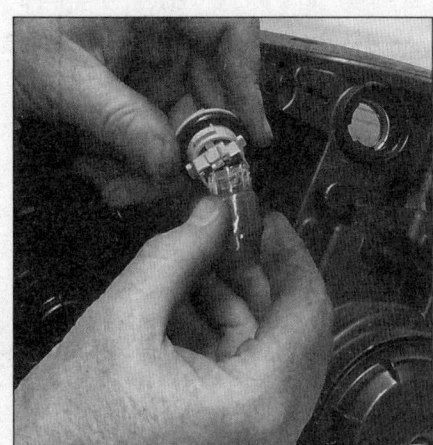

5.27b ... on later models, pull the wedge type bulb from the bulb holder

5.29 Carefully unclip the light unit

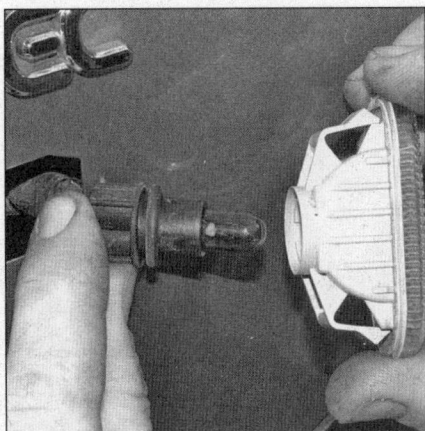

5.30 Remove the bulb holder …

5.31 … then pull the bulb from its holder

5.37 Pull back the inner wheel arch liner

Front indicator side repeater

29 Carefully unclip one end of the light unit and release it from the wing panel **(see illustration)**.
30 Withdraw the light unit, and then twist the bulbholder anticlockwise to release it from the light unit **(see illustration)**.

31 The bulb is a wedge type. Pull it from the the bulbholder **(see illustration)**.
32 Fit the new bulb using a reversal of the removal procedure.

Mirror mounted light

33 Remove the exterior mirror outer shell (see Chapter 11 Section 20).
34 Remove the screws retaining the lamp to the mirror assembly and partially remove the lamp assembly.
35 Rotate the bulb holder and remove the lamp from the mirror.
36 Installation is a reversal of the removal procedure.

Front fog light

37 Remove the inner wheel arch liner as described in Front Bumper section of the Body Chapter (see Chapter 11 Section 18) **(see illustration)**.
38 Reach behind the bumper and disconnect the wiring connector from the bulbholder **(see illustration)**.
39 Turn the bulbholder anticlockwise and withdraw it from the rear of the fog light **(see illustration)**.

40 The bulb can then be removed from the bulbholder, check new bulb before removing the bulb from its holder, as some new bulbs come with the bulb holder as part of the bulb. When handling the new bulb, use a tissue or clean cloth to avoid touching the glass with the fingers; moisture and grease from the skin can cause blackening and rapid failure of this type of bulb. If the glass is accidentally touched, wipe it clean using methylated spirit.
41 Fit the new bulb using a reversal of the removal procedure.

Rear lights (indicator/stop/tail lights)

42 Open the tailgate and remove the tail light assembly (see Section 7).

Dualis and T31 X-Trail models

Note: *On T31 X-Trail models, the turn signal lamp is in the rear pillar mounted tail light assembly. The bulb can be replaced. The stop/tail lights are LED and are part of the lamp assembly. The reverse lamps are in the rear bumper.*

43 Release the retaining clips and withdraw the bulbholder from the rear of the light unit **(see illustrations)**.

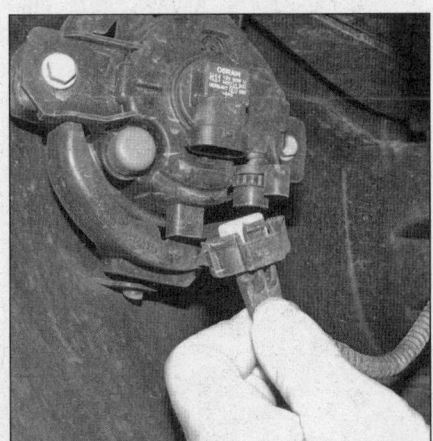

5.38 Disconnect the fog light wiring plug

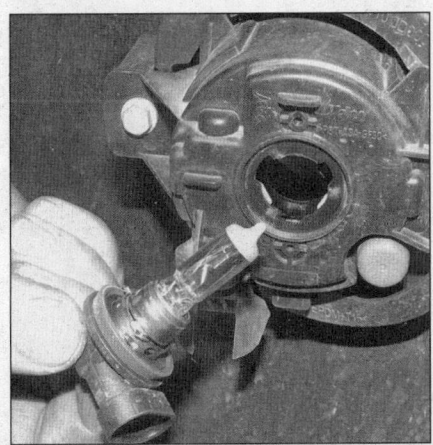

5.39 Rotate the bulbholder anticlockwise to remove

5.43a Unclip the bulb holder from the light unit…

5.43b ... then remove the bulb holder from the tail light on a Dualis models

5.43c On T31 X-Trail models, the indicator bulb is a wedge type bulb.

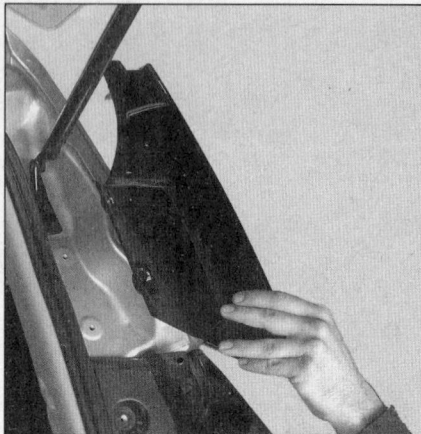

5.45 Removing the trim from above the tail light assembly - T32 X-Trail and Qashqai models

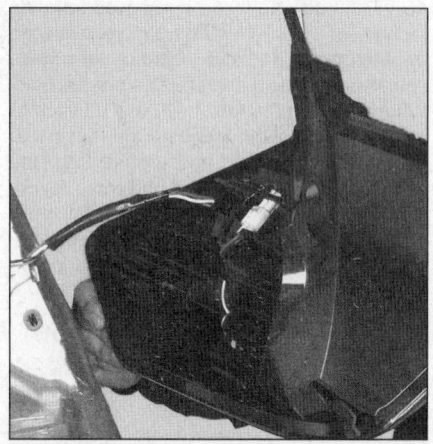

5.46 Removing the tail light from the vehicle

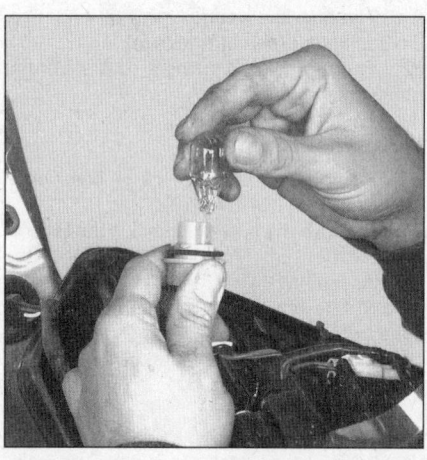

5.47 Removing one of the bulbs from the bulb holder

5.48a Carefully unclip the light unit ...

44 Fit the new bulb using a reversal of the removal procedure. Note that the stop/tail light bulb on Dualis models has offset pins, on the side of the end cap, to ensure correct installation.

T32 X-Trail and Qashqai models

45 Where fitted, remove the fasteners and remove the trim panel from above the tail light assembly (**see illustration**).

46 Remove the two fasteners and pull the tail light away from the back of the vehicle (**see illustration**).
47 Rotate the bulb holder anticlockwise and remove it from the rear of the light assembly. Pull the wedge type bulb from the holder (**see illustration**).

Rear fog light

48 Carefully prise the rear fog light from the rear bumper (**see illustrations**).
49 Turn the bulbholder anticlockwise and withdraw it from the rear of the fog light (**see illustration**).
50 The bulb is a bayonet fit in the bulbholder, push lightly and turn anticlockwise to remove the bulb (**see illustration**).

5.48b ... releasing the retaining clips

5.49 Rotate the bulbholder anticlockwise to remove

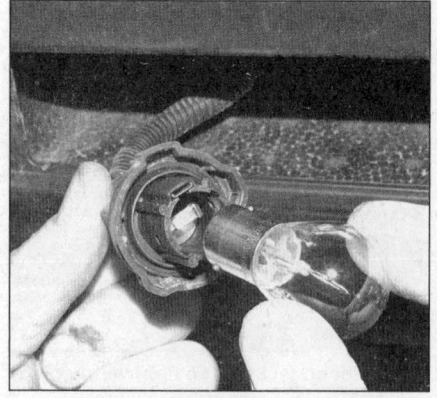

5.50 Press in the bulb and rotate it anticlockwise to remove it

5.54a Rotate the bulbholder anticlockwise to remove

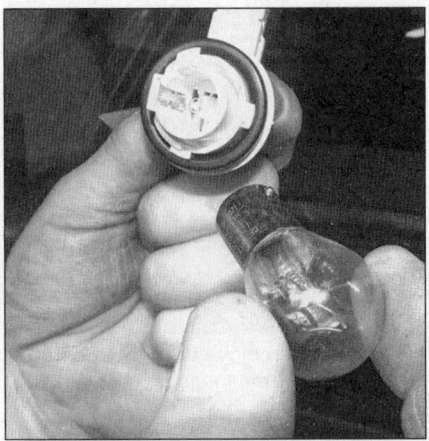

5.54b Press in the bulb and rotate it anticlockwise to remove it

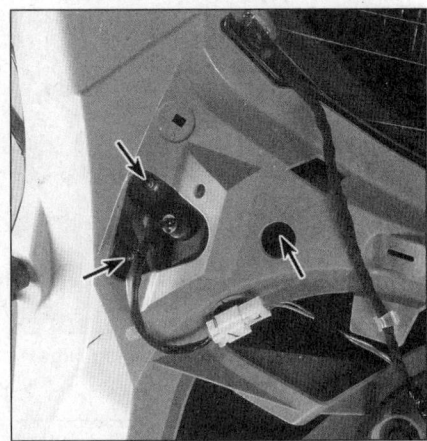

5.55 Tailgate mounted reverse lights fasteners on a T32 X-Trail

51 Fit the new bulb using a reversal of the removal procedure.

Reversing light

52 The reverse light and a second tail light is incorporated in the tailgate on all models except T31 X-Trail models. On these models, the reverse lights are in the rear bumper.
53 Remove the tailgate trim panel (see Chapter 11 Section 12).
54 On Dualis models, turn the bulbholder anticlockwise and withdraw it from the rear of the reversing light (see illustration). The bulb is a bayonet fit in the bulbholder, push lightly and turn anticlockwise to remove the bulb (see illustration).
55 On all other models, remove the fasteners (see illustration) retaining the tail light to the tailgate; pry the light assembly from the tailgate. Rotate the bulb holder and remove the bulb from the light assembly.
56 On T31 X-Trail models, to replace the reverse light bulb, reach up underneath the rear bumper and rotate the bulb holder anticlockwise (see illustration) and remove it from the rear of the light assembly. Pull the bulb from the bulb holder (see illustration).
57 Fit the new bulb using a reversal of the removal procedure.

Number plate light

58 Unclip the light unit from the tailgate trim (see illustrations).
59 Turn the bulbholder anticlockwise and withdraw it from the number plate light (see illustration).

5.56a One of the reverse light bulb holder locations

5.56b Removing the reverse light bulb from the bulb holder

5.58a Carefully unclip the light unit ...

5.58b ... and release it from the rear trim panel

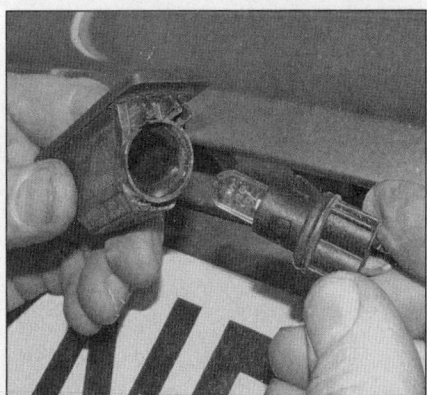

5.59 Twist the bulb holder to remove ...

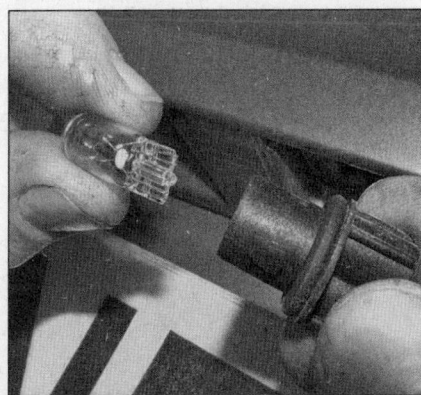

5.60 ... then pull the bulb from its holder

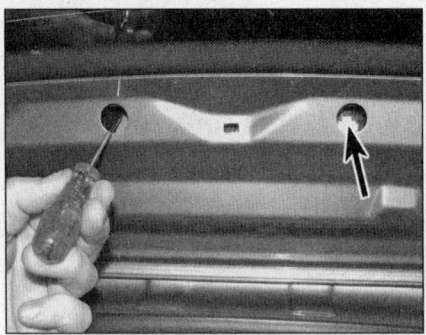

5.63a Release the two retaining clips (arrowed) ...

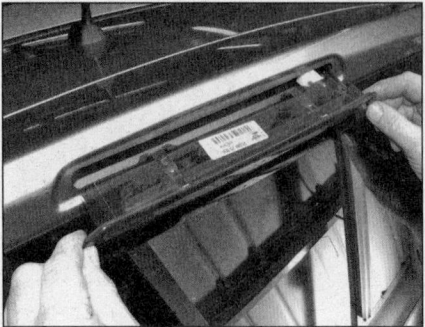

5.63b ... and remove the light unit from the tailgate

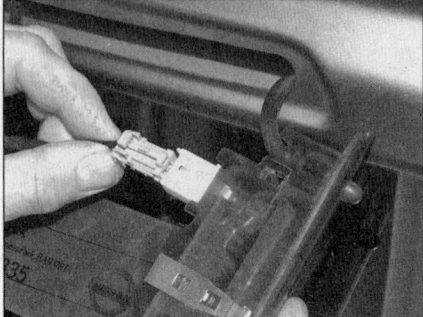

5.64a Disconnect the wiring connector ...

5.64b ... and washer fluid hose

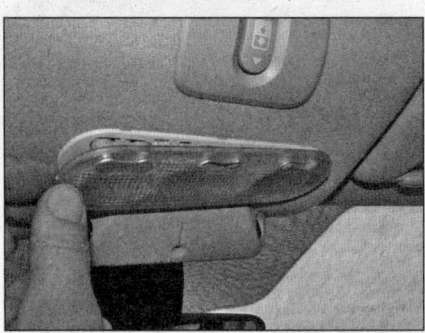

6.2 Carefully prise the light lens from place ...

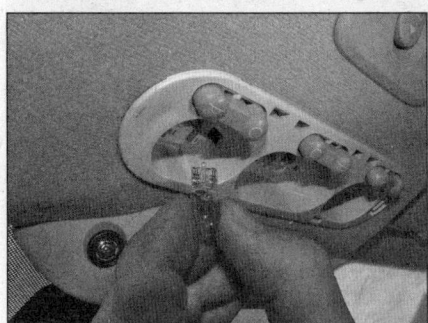

6.3 ... and pull the bulb(s) from the light unit

60 The bulb is a wedge type. Pull the bulb straight from the bulb holder (see illustration).
61 Fit the new bulb using a reversal of the removal procedure.

High-level stop-light

62 Open the tailgate and remove the upper tailgate trim panel (see Chapter 11 Section 12).
63 Working on the inside of the tailgate, release the two retaining clips and withdraw the high-level brake light from the top of the tailgate (see illustrations).
64 Disconnect the wiring connector and washer fluid hose, as it is removed (see illustrations).
65 The light unit has LED's (Light Emitting Diodes), and can only be renewed as a complete unit. Fit the new light unit using a reversal of the removal procedure.

6 Bulbs (interior lights) – renewal

General

1 A general bulb replacement description is covered in the Bulbs (Exterior Lights) – Renewal Section (see Section 5).

Map reading/courtesy light (front)

2 Carefully prise the lens from the light unit (if necessary, carefully use a flat-bladed screwdriver) (see illustration).
3 Pull the wedge type bulb from the interior light assembly (see illustration).
4 If required, release the securing clips to release the light unit from the headlining (see illustrations).
5 Fit the new bulb using a reversal of the removal procedure.

Courtesy light (rear)

6 Carefully prise the lens from the light unit (if necessary, carefully use a flat-bladed screwdriver) (see illustration).

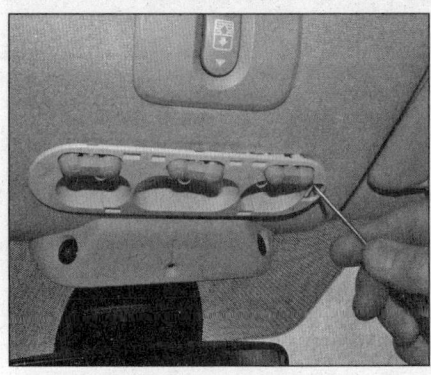

6.4a Using a thin screwdriver ...

6.4b ... to release the light unit from the roof panel

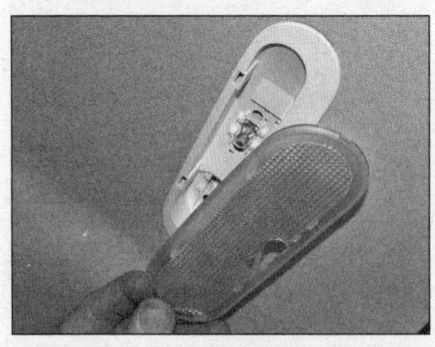

6.6 Carefully prise the light lens from the light unit

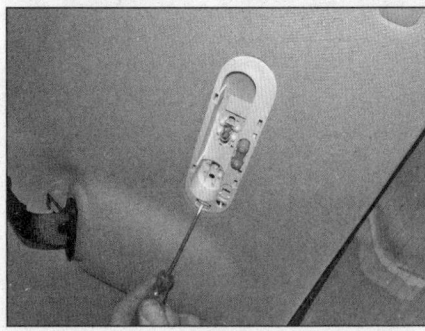

6.8 Release the light unit from the roof panel

Chapter 12 Chassis electrical systems

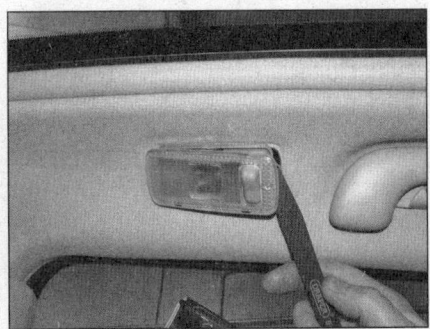

6.10 Carefully prise the light unit from the roof panel ...

6.11 ... and disconnect the wiring connector

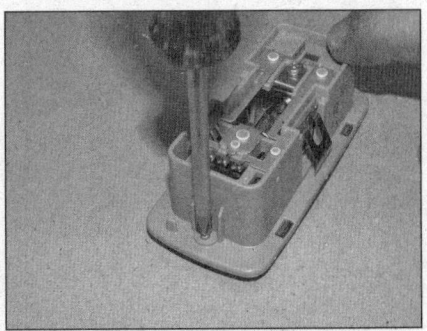

6.12a Undo the retaining screw ...

7 Pull the wedge type bulb from the courtesy light assembly (**see illustration 6.3**).
8 If required, release the securing clips to release the light unit from the headlining (**see illustration**).
9 Fit the new bulb using a reversal of the removal procedure.

Courtesy light (side)

10 Carefully prise the light unit from the side of the roof panel (**see illustration**).
11 Disconnect the wiring connector and remove the light unit (**see illustration**).
12 Undo the retaining screw and remove the lens from the front of the light unit (**see illustrations**).
13 Pull the bulb from the light unit; note that the bulb is a festoon type (**see illustration**).
14 Fit the new bulb using a reversal of the removal procedure.

Vanity mirror light

15 Carefully prise the lens from the light unit (if necessary, carefully use a small thin screwdriver) (**see illustration**).
16 Pull the bulb from the light unit; note that the bulb is a wedge type (**see illustration**).
17 Fit the new bulb using a reversal of the removal procedure.

Luggage area light

18 Open the tailgate.
19 Unclip the light unit from the trim panel.
20 Disconnect the wiring connector and remove the light unit, the bulb is a push-fit in the light assembly.
21 Fit the new bulb using a reversal of the removal procedure.

Instrument panel lights

22 The instrument panel is a complete unit and is lit by LEDs. If there is a fault on the illumination of the panel the complete unit will need to be renewed (see Section 9).

Heater control illumination

23 The heater control panel is a complete unit and is lit by LEDs. If there is a fault on the illumination of the panel the complete unit will need to be renewed.

Seat belt warning light illumination - Dualis models

24 The warning light panel is fitted to the lower edge of the centre ventilation trim panel, remove the ventilation trim panel (see Chapter 11 Section 21).
25 To remove the warning light panel, undo the two retaining screws, and withdraw the warining lights from the trim panel (**see illustrations**).

6.12b ... unclip the light lens ...

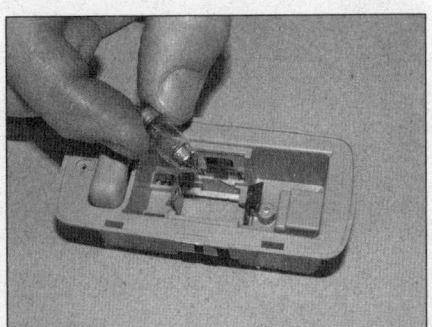

6.13 ... and remove the bulb from the light unit

6.15 Carefully prise the light lens from place ...

6.16 ... and pull the bulb from the light unit

6.25a Undo the two retaining screws ...

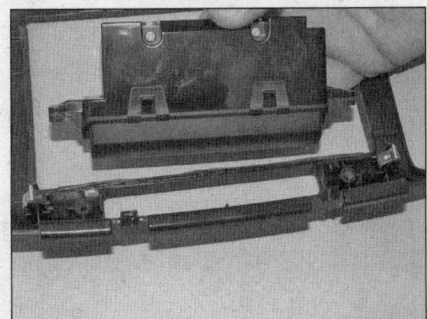

6.25b ... and remove the warning light assembly

12-20 Chapter 12 Chassis electrical systems

6.30a Turn the bulb holder ...

6.30b ... and remove it from the switch

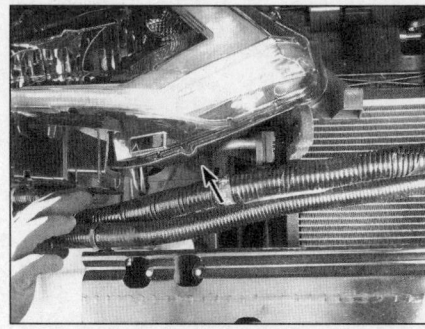

7.2b Lower inner headlight fastener on T32 X-Trail and Qashqai models

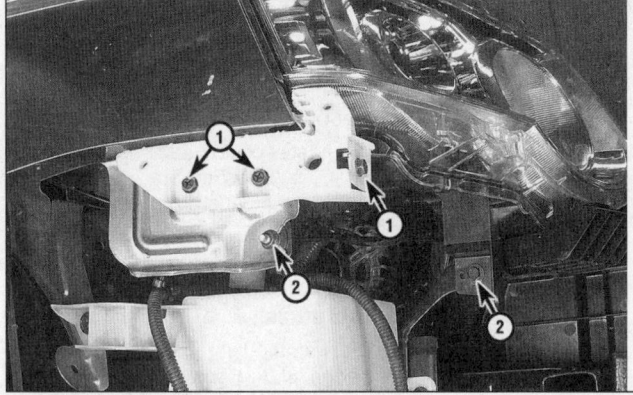

7.2a Headlight lower mounting fasteners - T31 X-Trail models

1 Fasteners retaining the bumper support bracket - remove this first
2 Lower headlight fasteners

7.2c Lower outer headlight fastener (1) and guide pin (2) on T32 X-Trail and Qashqai models

7.2d Lower inner headlight fastener on Dualis models

26 The warning light unit has LED's (Light Emitting Diodes), and can only be renewed as a complete unit.

27 Refit the warning light and trim panel, using a reversal of the removal procedure.

Switch illumination bulbs

28 All of the switches are fitted with illuminating bulbs, and some are also fitted with a bulb to show when the circuit concerned is operating.

29 In most cases, if a bulb blows, the complete switch must be renewed, but on certain models, some of the switch bulbs can be renewed. Check with a Nissan dealer for information on the availability of spare bulbs.

30 The electric mirror switch has a bulb fitted to the side of the switch. Remove the relevant switch (see Section 4), then using a small screwdriver, turn the bulbholder and remove the bulb and holder from the switch **(see illustrations)**. The bulbs are integral with the bulbholders.

31 Fit the new bulb using a reversal of the removal procedure.

7 Exterior lights – removal and refitting

Note: *Disconnect the negative (-) battery terminal (see Chapter 5 Section 3), before removing any light unit, and reconnect the terminal after refitting the light.*

Headlight

1 Remove the front bumper (see Chapter 11 Section 18).
2 Unscrew the headlight lower fasteners **(see illustrations)**.

7.3a Upper headlight retaining clip (1) and mounting bolts (2) - T31 X-Trail models

7.3b Upper headlight retaining clip (1) and mounting bolts (2) on T32 X-Trail and Qashqai models

Chapter 12 Chassis electrical systems

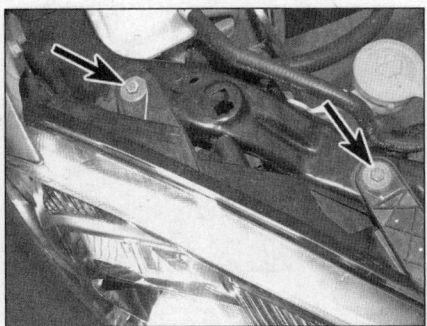

7.3c Upper headlight mounting bolts (arrows) - Dualis models

7.4 Disconnect the wiring connectors

7.9a Undo the fog light retaining bolts ...

7.9b ...and remove the light unit

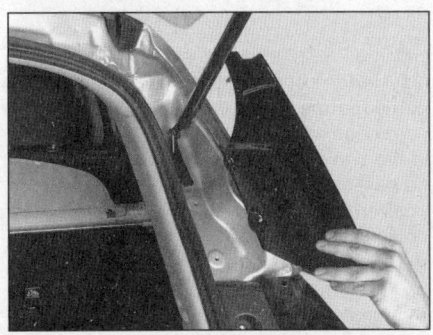

7.12 Removing the trim from above the tail light assembly - T32 X-Trail and Qashqai models

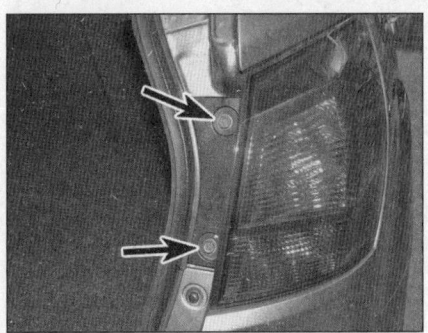

7.13 Undo the rear light retaining bolts

3 Unscrew the two headlight upper securing bolts (see illustration).
4 Remove the headlight unit, and disconnect the wiring connectors as the headlamp is withdrawn from the vehicle (see illustration).
5 Refitting is a reversal of removal. On completion, it is wise to have the headlight beam alignment checked (see Section 8).

Front indicator side repeater

6 The procedure is described as part of the bulb renewal procedure in Section 5.

Front fog light

7 Remove the inner wheel arch liner (see Chapter 11 Section 18) (see illustration 5.37).
8 Disconnect the wiring connector from the bulbholder (see illustration 5.38).
9 Undo the two securing bolts and remove the light unit from the rear of the bumper (see illustrations).

10 Refitting is a reversal of removal.

Rear light

11 Open the tailgate.
12 Where fitted, remove the fasteners and remove the trim panel from above the tail light assembly (see illustration).
13 Remove the tail light mounting bolts (see illustration).
14 Withdraw the light unit from the rear of the vehicle, disengaging the two locating pegs from the body (see illustration).
15 Disconnect the wiring connector at the rear of the light unit as it is removed (see illustration).
16 Installation is a reversal of the removal procedure.

Rear fog light

17 The procedure is described as part of the bulb renewal procedure in Section 5.

Reverse light

Except T31 X-Trail models

18 Open the tailgate and remove the inner tailgate trim (see Chapter 11 Section 12).

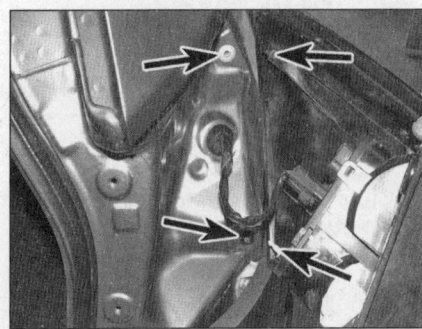

7.14a Pull the light unit to disengage the two locating pegs (arrowed) - Early models

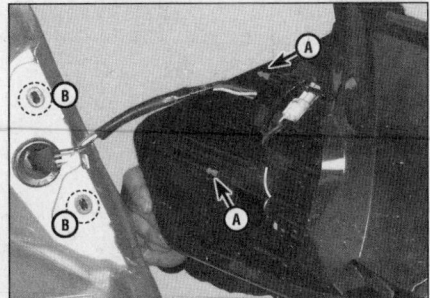

7.14b Pull the light unit to disengage the two locating pegs (a) from the sockets (B) in the body - late models

7.15 Disconnect the rear light wiring connector

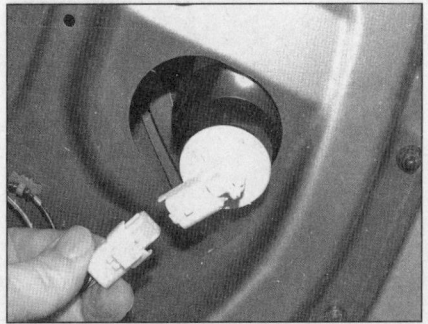

7.19 Disconnect the reversing light wiring connector

12-22 Chapter 12 Chassis electrical systems

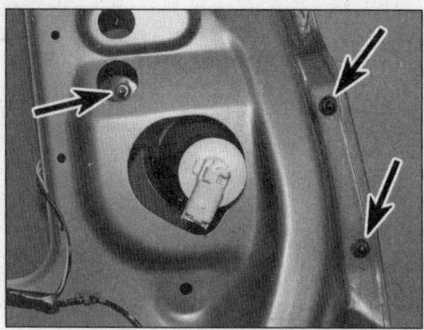

7.20a Undo the retaining nuts (arrowed) ...

7.20b ... and remove the reversing light unit

7.22 Disconnect the wiring connector (1); there are two holes in the bottom of the bumper to allow access to the reverse lamp retaining bolts (2) - T31 X-Trail models

19 Disconnect the wiring connector at the rear of the light unit as it is removed (see illustration).
20 Undo the three light unit securing nuts, and then remove the light unit from the tailgate (see illustrations).
21 Installation is a reversal of the removal procedure.

T31 X-Trail models

22 Working beneath the vehicle, disconnect the wiring connector from the bulb holder (see illustration).
23 Remove the two bolts and slide the reverse light housing from the bumper.
24 Installation is a reversal of the removal procedure.

Number plate light

25 The procedure is described as part of the bulb renewal procedure in Section 5.

High-level stop-light

26 The procedure is described as part of the bulb renewal procedure in Section 5.

8 Headlight beam adjustment components – general information, removal and refitting

General information

1 Models covered by this manual are equipped with a headlight beam adjustment system, controlled by a dial on the dashboard, which allows the aim of the headlights to be adjusted to compensate for the varying loads carried in the vehicle. The switch should be positioned according to the load being carried in the vehicle – e.g. position 0 for driver with no passengers or luggage, then increase the position to 1, 2, or 3 as the load is increased, or when towing.

Warning: *Before carrying out any operations on xenon headlight units, it is recommended that protective gloves and safety glasses be worn. It is essential that the wiring connectors are disconnected from the rear of the headlight unit, and then wait until the module and bulbs have cooled down before removal. DO NOT switch the headlights on with the bulb removed, as it is harmful to the eyes.*

2 Accurate adjustment of the headlight beam is only possible using optical beam-setting equipment, and this work should therefore be carried out by a Nissan dealer or suitably-equipped workshop. To make temporary adjustment of the headlights, position the vehicle on a level surface, 10 metres from a wall. The tyres must be all at the correct pressures, the fuel tank half full, and a person be sitting in the drivers seat. Turn on the ignition, and check that, where fitted, the manual adjustment inside the vehicle is set at 0. Measure the distance from the ground to the centre of the headlight, and then deduct 5.0 cm for models with halogen headlights, and 7.5 cm for models with xenon headlights. Draw a mark on the wall at this height, and then adjust the headlight beam centre point onto this mark by turning the adjustment screws on the rear of the headlight unit.

Headlight aiming motor

Note: *On X-Trail models, the headlight aiming motor is an integral part of the headlight assembly and if faulty, must be replaced as part of the headlight assembly. On Dualis and Qashqai models, the aiming motor can be removed from the headlight assembly.*

3 Open the bonnet and depending on model, to improve access to the left-hand headlight, remove the air inlet ducting (see illustrations 3.6a & 3.6b).
4 On models with electrical adjustable beam elevation, ensure the dial (see illustrations) is positioned at No.0 before disconnecting the wiring connector from the headlight adjuster unit on the rear of the headlight (see illustration).
5 Twist the adjuster anticlockwise, to disengage the adjuster from the headlight housing (see illustrations).
6 Remove the headlight bulb rear protective cover and pull the headlight bulbholder back, to aid removing and refitting the ball joint to the reflector (see illustration). Withdraw the adjuster, and then unclip the ball joint from the slot in the retaining clip on the inner reflector.
7 Refit the adjuster to the rear of the headlight unit using a reversal of the removal procedure.

Headlight adjuster switch

8 The procedure for removing the switch is described in Section 4.

8.4a Electrical adjustable beam elevation dial - Dualis models

8.4b Disconnect the headlight adjuster wiring connector (arrowed)

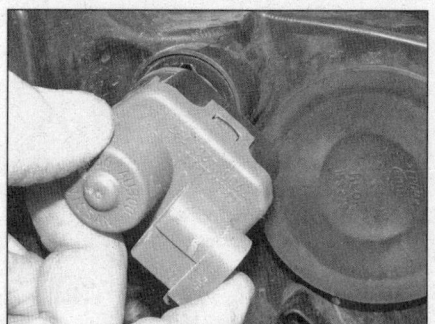

8.5a Rotate the headlight aiming motor anticlockwise ...

Chapter 12 Chassis electrical systems

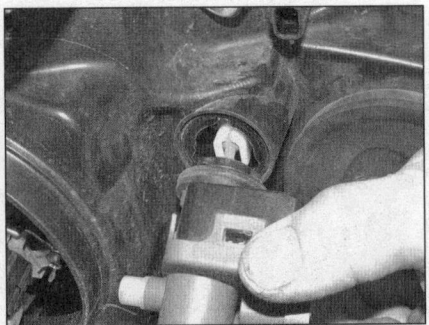

8.5b ... and remove it from the headlight unit

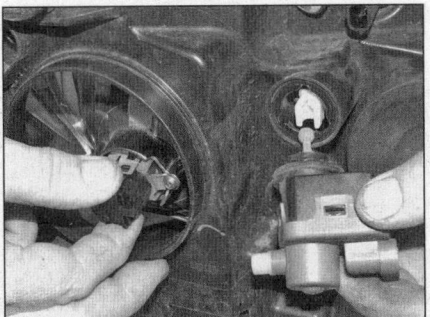

8.6 Hold the light unit reflector back to release the ball joint.

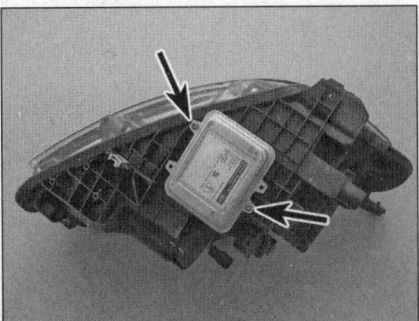

8.10 High voltage unit retaining screws (arrowed)

8.14a Disconnect the wiring connector (arrowed) ...

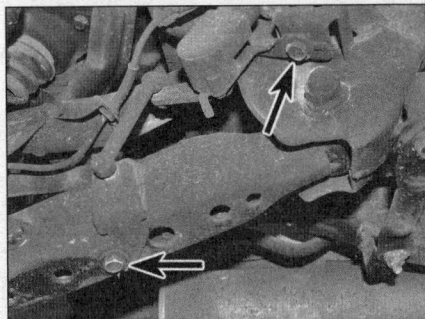

8.14b ... and undo the two retaining bolts (arrowed)

8.15a Headlight alignment manual adjustment horizontal (1) and vertical (2) screws - T31 X-Trail models

Xenon high voltage unit

Note: *Take note of the warnings at the beginning of this Section, when working on headlight units with Xenon bulbs.*

9 Remove the headlight unit, as described in Section 7.

10 Undo the two retaining screws and then withdraw the unit from the bottom of the headlight unit **(see illustration)**. Disconnect the wiring connector as it is removed.

11 Refit the high voltage unit using a reversal of the removal procedure.

Xenon headlight level sensor

12 A level sensor is fitted to the rear suspension. This forms an integral part of the headlight adjustment system for the Xenon headlights.

13 To remove the level sensor, raise the front of the vehicle and support on jackstands (see Chapter 0 Section 7).

14 Disconnect the wiring connector from the sensor, and then undo the two retaining bolts and remove it from the rear suspension **(see illustrations)**.

Headlight adjustment

Note: *The headlights must be aimed correctly. If adjusted incorrectly they could blind the driver of an oncoming vehicle and cause a serious accident or seriously reduce your ability to see the road. The headlights should be checked for proper aim every 12 months and any time a new headlight is installed or front-end bodywork is performed. It should be emphasised that the following procedure is only an interim step, which will provide temporary adjustment until the headlights can be adjusted by a properly equipped shop.*

15 The adjustment screws are located behind each headlight housing **(see illustrations)**.

8.15b Headlight alignment manual adjustment horizontal (1) and vertical (2) screws - T32 X-Trail models

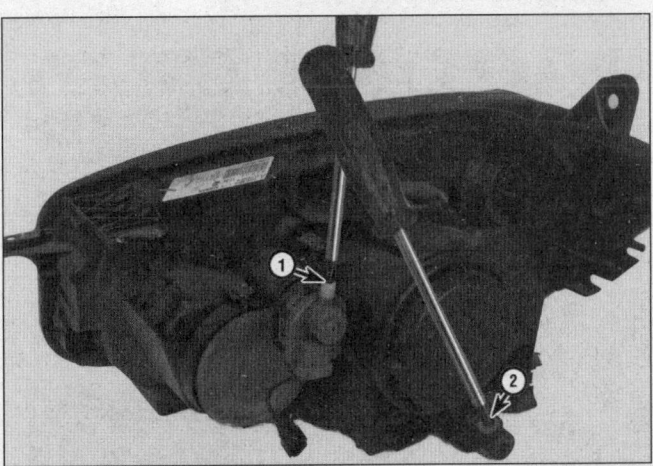

8.15c Headlight alignment manual adjustment horizontal (1) and vertical (2) screws - Dualis models

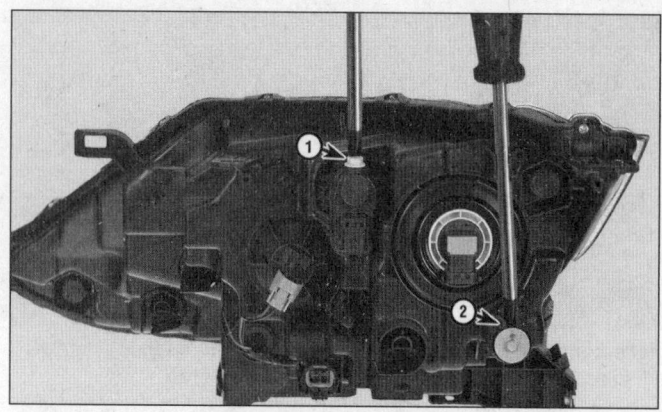

8.15d Headlight alignment manual adjustment horizontal (1) and vertical (2) screws - Qashqai models

9.4a Undo the two instrument cluster retaining screws (arrowed) - T31 X-Trail models

9.4b Undo the two instrument cluster retaining screws (arrowed) - T32 X-Trail models

9.4c Undo the two instrument cluster retaining screws (arrowed) - Dualis models

16 There are several methods for adjusting the headlights. The simplest method requires masking tape, a blank wall and a level floor.

17 Position masking tape vertically on the wall in reference to the vehicle centreline and the centrelines of both headlights (see illustration).

18 Position a horizontal tape line in reference to the centreline of all the headlights.

Note: *It might be easier to position the tape on the wall with the vehicle parked quite close to get an accurate centre line.*

19 Adjustment should be made with the vehicle parked 10 metres from the wall, sitting level, the fuel tank half-full and no heavy load in the vehicle.

20 Starting with the low beam adjustment, position the high intensity zone so it is 100 mm below the horizontal line. Adjustment is made by turning the horizontal adjusting screw.

21 Adjust the horizontal beam so that the high intensity area of the beam is 0 to 100 mm to the left of each headlight centre beam using the horizontal adjuster.

22 Have the headlights adjusted by a dealer service department or service station at the earliest opportunity.

9 Instrument cluster – removal and refitting

Removal

1 Disconnect the negative (-) battery terminal (see Chapter 5 Section 3).

2 Remove the steering column upper and lower covers (see Chapter 11 Section 23).

3 On X-Trail and Qashqai models, remove the instrument cluster surround panel (see Chapter 11 Section 21).

9.5a Withdraw the instrument cluster...

9.5b ... and disconnect the wiring connector

Chapter 12 Chassis electrical systems

10.3 Disconnect the wiring connector

10.4 Undo the horn mounting bracket retaining bolt

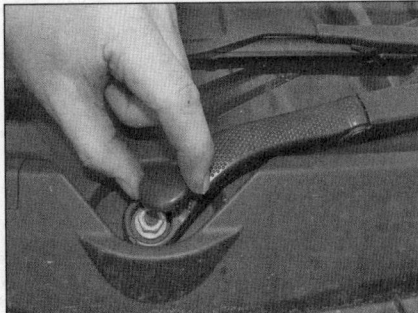

11.3a Unclip the plastic cap ...

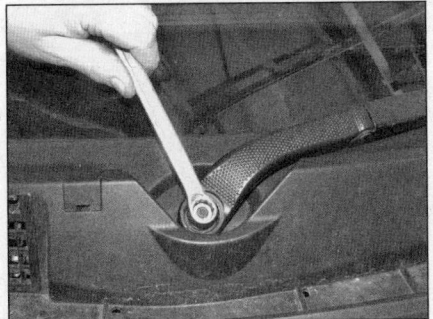

11.3b ... and undo the retaining nut

11.3c Rear wiper arm retaining nut

11.4 Remove the wiper arm ...

4   Remove the instrument panel two lower securing screws **(see illustration)**.
5   Pull the instrument cluster forwards, and disconnect the wiring connectors from the rear of the panel **(see illustrations)**. Withdraw the instrument cluster from the facia.

Refitting

6   Refitting is a reversal of removal.

10 Horn – removal and refitting

Removal

1   Disconnect the negative (-) battery terminal (see Chapter 5 Section 3).
2   Remove the front bumper (see Chapter 11 Section 18).
3   Disconnect the wiring connector from the horn **(see illustration)**.
4   Unscrew the securing bolt, and withdraw the horn complete with its mounting bracket **(see illustration)**

Refitting

5   Refitting is a reversal of removal.

11 Wiper arm – removal and refitting

Removal

1   Operate the wiper motor, and then switch it off so that the wiper arm returns to the at-rest/parked position.
2   If a windscreen or tailgate wiper is being removed, stick a piece of tape alongside the edge of the wiper blade, to use as an alignment aid on refitting. On some models there are marks on the screen to aid refitting.
3   Unclip the plastic cover from the wiper arm spindle nut, then slacken and remove the nut **(see illustrations)**.

4   Lift the blade off the glass, and pull the wiper arm off its spindle **(see illustration)**.
5   If necessary, the arm can be removed from the spindle, by using a suitable puller **(see illustration)**. If both windscreen wiper arms are removed, note their locations, as different arms are fitted to the driver and passenger's sides.

Refitting

6   Ensure that the wiper arm and spindle splines are clean and dry.
7   When refitting a windscreen or tailgate wiper arm, refit the arm to the spindle, aligning the wiper blade with the mark on the screen or tape fitted before removal.
8   If both front windscreen wiper arms have been removed, ensure that the arms are refitted to their correct positions as noted before removal.
9   Refit the spindle nut, tighten it securely and, clip the plastic nut cover back into position.

12 Windscreen wiper motor and linkage – removal and refitting

Removal

1   Disconnect the negative (-) battery terminal (see Chapter 5 Section 3).
2   Remove the windscreen cowl panels (see Chapter 11 Section 25).
3   Disconnect the wiring connector from the wiper motor **(see illustration)**.

11.5 ... if it is tight on the spindle, use a puller

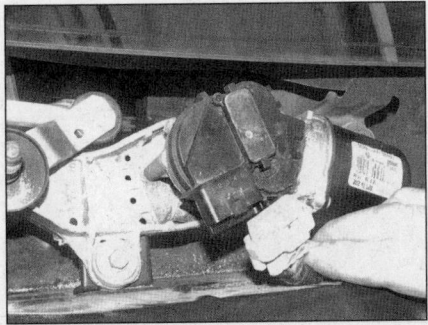

12.3 Disconnect the wiper motor wiring plug

12-26 Chapter 12 Chassis electrical systems

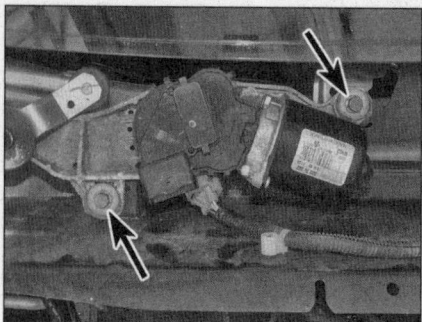

12.4a Undo the wiper linkage centre retaining bolts ...

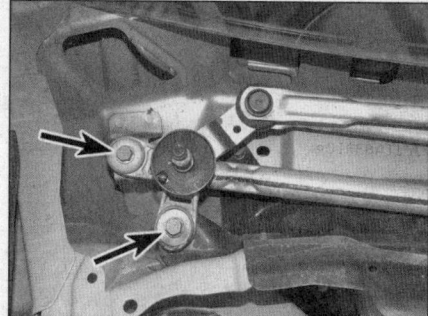

12.4b ... and right-hand retaining bolts ...

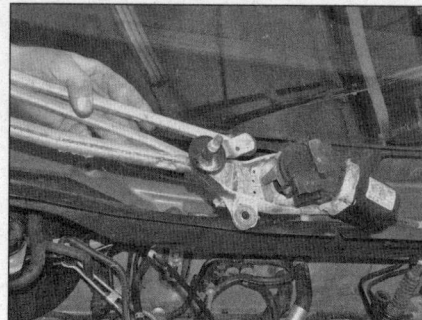

12.4c ... then remove the wiper motor assembly

Refitting

5 Refitting is a reversal of removal.

13 Tailgate wiper motor – removal and refitting

Removal

1 Disconnect the negative (-) battery terminal (see Chapter 5 Section 3).
2 Open the tailgate and remove the inner tailgate trim (see Chapter 11 Section 12).
3 Remove the rear wiper arm (see Section 11).
4 Disconnect the tailgate wiper motor wiring connector **(see illustration)**.
5 Unscrew the three bolts securing the wiper motor assembly to the tailgate and withdraw it from the tailgate **(see illustration)**.

Refitting

6 Refitting is a reversal of removal.

14 Windscreen/tailgate washer system components – removal and refitting

Washer fluid reservoir

Removal

1 Working in the engine compartment, release the retaining clip and then pull the filler neck upwards to remove it from the top of the reservoir **(see illustrations)**. Make sure the washer fluid level is low before removing the reservoir; be prepared for some spillage.
2 Disconnect the negative (-) battery terminal (see Chapter 5 Section 3).

13.4 Disconnect the wiper motor wiring plug

4 Unscrew the motor and linkage securing bolts, and withdraw it from the scuttle panel **(see illustrations)**.

13.5 Undo the rear wiper motor mounting bolts

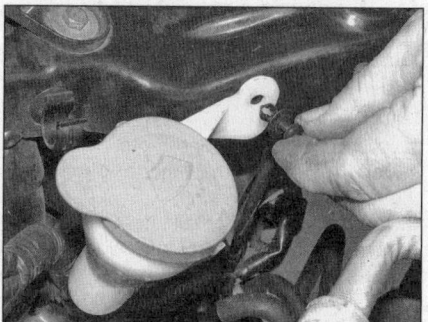

14.1a Release the securing clip ...

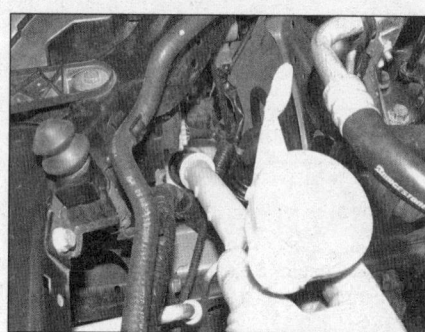

14.1b ... and withdraw the filler neck

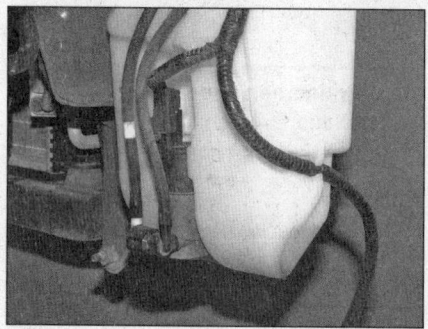

14.4 Unclip the wiring and the hoses from the reservoir

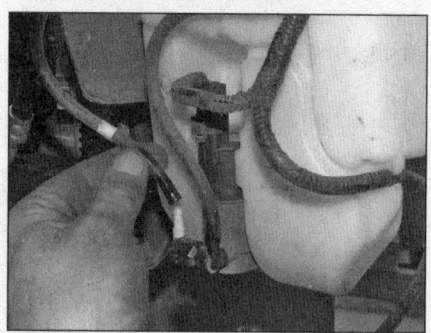

14.5 Disconnect the hoses from the washer pump

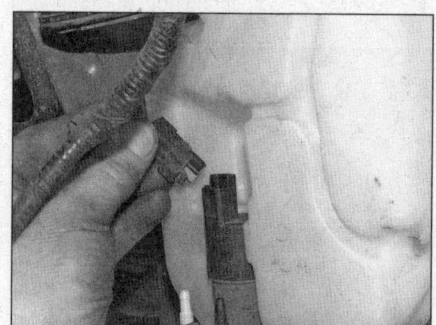

14.6 Disconnect the washer pump wiring plug connector

Chapter 12 Chassis electrical systems

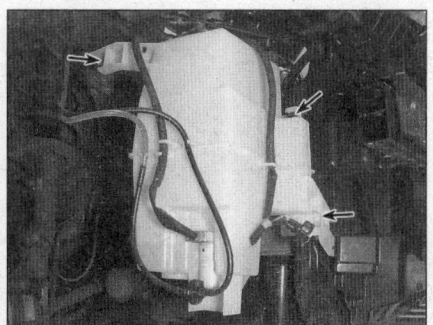

14.7a Washer reservoir retaining fasteners - T31 X-Trail models

14.7b Washer reservoir retaining fasteners - T32 X-Trail models

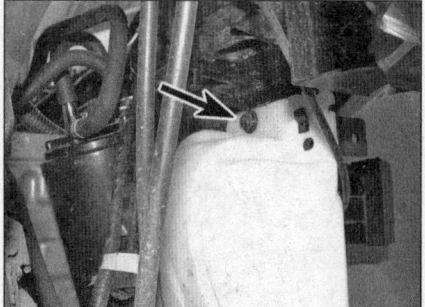

14.7c On Dualis models, undo the upper mounting bolt (arrowed) ...

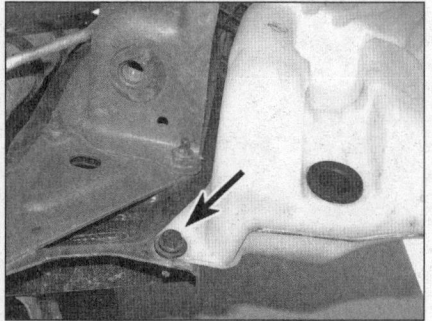

14.7d ... lower mounting bolt ...

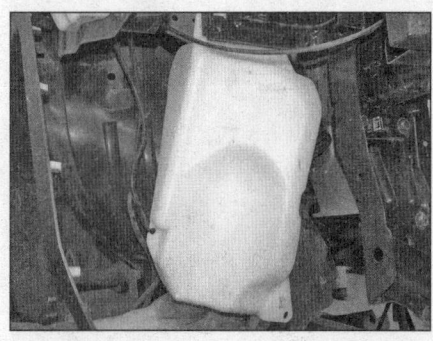

14.7e ... then remove the reservoir

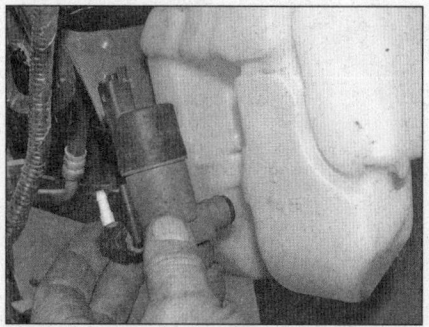

14.10 Ease the washer pump from the reservoir

3 Remove the front bumper (see Chapter 11 Section 18).

4 Release the wiring harness and fluid hoses from the retaining clips in the reservoir **(see illustration)**, and move the harness and hoses to one side to allow sufficient clearance to remove the reservoir.

5 Disconnect the fluid hose(s) from the washer pump **(see illustration)** – if the reservoir still contains fluid, be prepared for fluid spillage.

6 Disconnect the wiring connector(s) from the washer pump(s), and from the fluid level sensor, where applicable **(see illustration)**.

7 Remove the reservoir securing bolts, and then lower the reservoir from under the wheel arch **(see illustrations)**.

Refitting

8 Refitting is a reversal of removal.

Washer pump

Removal

9 Proceed as described in paragraphs 2 to 6.

10 Pull the washer pump from the reservoir and recover the grommet **(see illustration)**. If the reservoir still contains fluid, be prepared for fluid spillage.

Refitting

11 Refitting is a reversal of removal, making sure the grommet is fitted correctly in the reservoir before refitting the washer pump.

Windscreen washer nozzle

Removal

12 Open and support the bonnet, then unclip the small grille panel from the scuttle panel **(see illustration)**.

13 Reach inside the scuttle panel, and then release the windscreen washer nozzle from the scuttle panel. Disconnect the washer fluid hose and remove washer nozzle **(see illustration)**.

14 To adjust the position of the washer nozzle, unclip it from the scuttle panel. Then using a small screwdriver adjust the position of the washer nozzle **(see illustration)**.

14.12 Unclip the grille panel

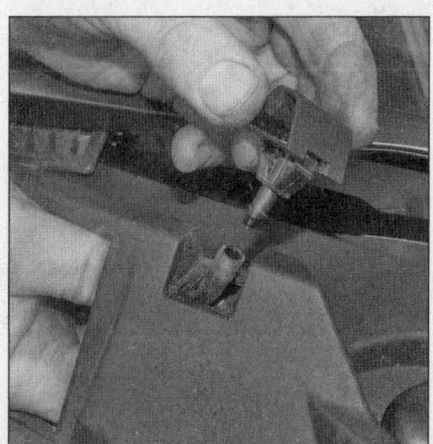

14.13 Unclip the washer nozzle from the scuttle panel

14.14 Turn the washer jet for adjustment position onto the windscreen

12-28 Chapter 12 Chassis electrical systems

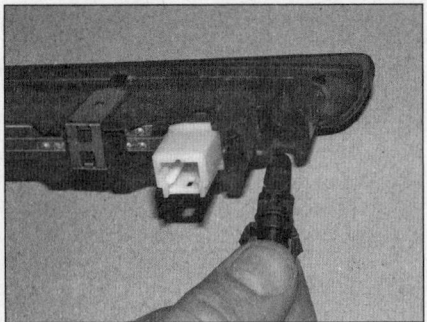

14.17 Unclip the rear washer jet from the light unit

15.3a Undo the four retaining screws (arrowed) - T31 X-Trail models

15.3b The four retaining screws (arrowed) - Dualis models

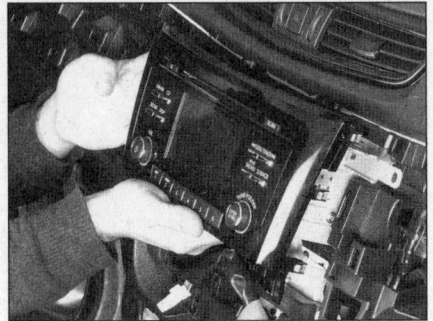

15.4a Withdrawing the audio unit from the dashboard…

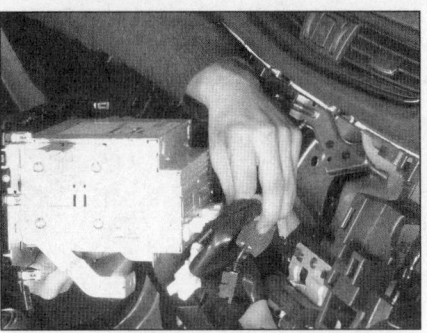

15.4b … and disconnecting the wiring connectors on T32 X-Trail models

15.4c Audio system partially removed showing the wiring connectors on Dualis models

Refitting

15 Refitting is a reversal of removal.

Tailgate washer nozzle

Removal

16 Remove the high-level brake light unit, as described in Section 5. The tailgate washer nozzle is located in the right-hand end of the high-level brake light unit.

17 Carefully unclip the washer nozzle from the end of the high-level brake light unit **(see illustration)**.

Refitting

18 Refitting is a reversal of removal.

15 Radio/CD player – removal and refitting

Removal

1 Disconnect the negative (-) battery terminal (see Chapter 5 Section 3).
2 Remove the dashboard centre trim panel (see Chapter 11 Section 21).
3 Remove the four now-exposed securing screws **(see illustration)**.
4 Pull the unit forwards from the facia, and then disconnect the wiring connectors and the aerial lead from the rear of the unit **(see illustrations)**.

Refitting

5 Refitting is a reversal of removal, ensuring that the wiring is freely routed behind the unit.

16 Speakers – removal and refitting

1 Disconnect the negative (-) battery terminal (see Chapter 5 Section 3).

Door-mounted speakers

2 Remove the door trim panel (see Chapter 11 Section 14).
3 Disconnect the wiring connector from the door speaker **(see illustration)**.
4 Undo the three securing screws, and then withdraw the speaker from the door panel **(see illustration)**.
5 Refitting is a reversal of removal, refit the inner door trim panel (see Chapter 11 Section 14).

Dashboard-mounted tweeters

6 Remove the A-pillar trim panel (see Chapter 11 Section 24).

16.3 Disconnect the speaker wiring connector

16.4 Undo the screws and remove the speaker

16.7 Unclip the grille panel …

Chapter 12 Chassis electrical systems

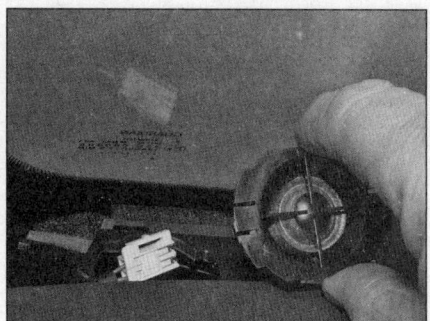

16.8 ... and remove the speaker

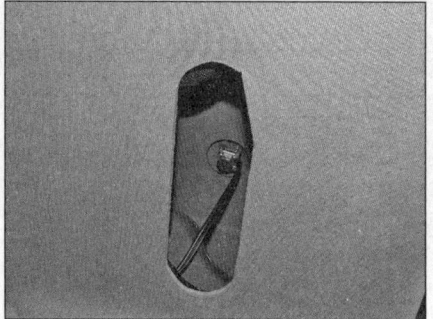

17.2 Roof aerial mounting nut

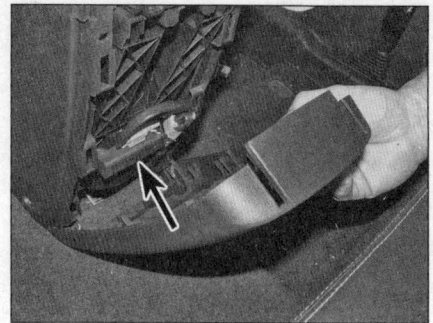

19.1a Antenna at rear of centre console

7 Working in the top corner of the facia panel, carefully unclip the speaker grille **(see illustration)**.
8 Release the loudspeaker from the top of the facia and disconnect the wiring connector **(see illustration)**.
9 Refitting is a reversal of removal.

17 Radio aerial – removal and refitting

Note: *An external aerial is not fitted to all models. Some late models have the aerial within the windscreen glass.*

Removal

1 Working inside the vehicle unclip the rear courtesy light from the rear of the headlining (see Section 6).

19.1b Antenna in luggage compartment

2 Undo the retaining nut and disconnect the aerial lead, remove the aerial from the roof **(see illustration)**.

Refitting

3 Refitting is a reversal of removal, but ensure that the aerial lead is securely connected.

18 Anti-theft system and engine immobiliser – general information

1 All models in the range are equipped as standard with a central locking system incorporating an electronic engine immobiliser function.
2 The electronic engine immobiliser is operated by a transponder fitted to the ignition key, in conjunction with an analogue module fitted around the ignition switch.
3 When the ignition key is inserted in the switch and turned to the ignition 'On' position, the control module sends a preprogrammed recognition code signal to the analogue module on the ignition switch. If the recognition code signal matches that of the transponder on the ignition key, an unlocking request signal is sent to the engine management ECU allowing the engine to be started. If the ignition key signal is not recognised, the engine management system remains immobilised.
4 When the ignition is switched off, a locking signal is sent to the ECU and the engine is immobilised until the unlocking request signal is again received.

19 Intelligent key system components – general information

1 The intelligent key system is a keyless entry system, which allows you to operate your vehicle without using an actual key. This can only be used when the Intelligent Key remote is within a specified operating distance (80 cm with new battery) from the antennas or ignition switch. The antennas are located in the following positions around the vehicle:

a *Rear of the centre console* **(see illustration)**.
b *In luggage compartment* **(see illustration)**.
c *Right-hand side of heater housing* **(see illustration)**.
d *Left-hand front door handle* **(see illustration)**.
e *Right-hand front door handle*
f *Behind rear bumper*

2 As the battery discharges over time, the operating distance becomes less, so a new battery will be required. Do not hold the Intelligent Key remote too close to the door, as this may also cause it to not function correctly. If a door is not closed securely, this will cause the Intelligent Key not to function properly. There is also a warning buzzer, which is positioned behind the front bumper **(see illustration)**.

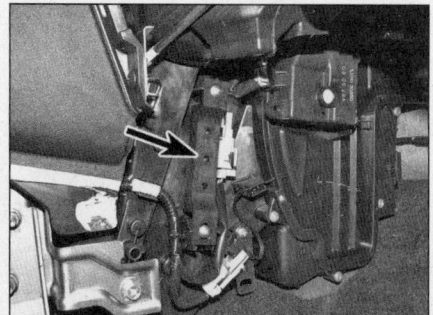

19.1c Antenna right-hand side of heater unit

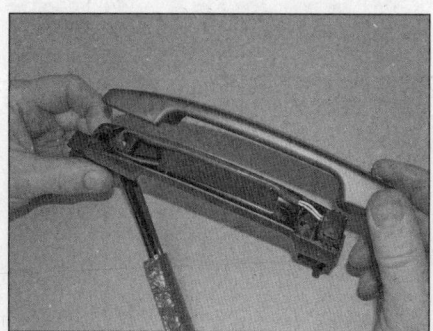

19.1d Antenna inside door handle

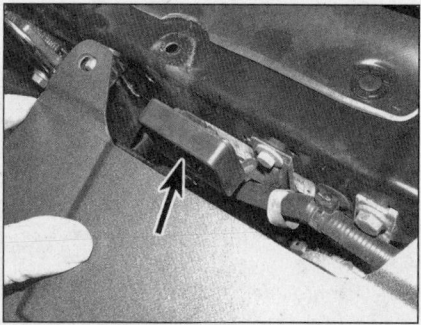

19.2 Warning buzzer behind front bumper

20 Airbag system – general information, precautions and system de-activation

General information

1 A driver's and passenger's airbag are fitted as standard on all models. The driver's airbag is located in the steering wheel centre pad and the passenger's airbag is located above the glovebox in the facia. Side airbags are also available on certain models and are located in the front seats. Curtain airbags are also fitted to some models and are located behind the headlining around the outer edge.

2 The system is armed only when the ignition is switched on; however, a reserve power source maintains a power supply to the system in the event of a break in the main electrical supply. The steering wheel and facia airbags are activated by a sensor (deceleration sensor), and controlled by an electronic control unit located under the centre console. The side and curtain airbags are activated by severe side impact and operate in conjunction with the main system.

3 The airbags are inflated by a gas generator, which forces the bag out from its location in the steering wheel, facia or seat back frame.

Precautions

Warning: *The following precautions must be observed when working on vehicles equipped with an airbag system, to prevent the possibility of personal injury.*

General precautions

a *Do not disconnect the battery with the engine running.*
b *Before carrying out any work in the vicinity of the airbag, removal of any of the airbag components, or any welding work on the vehicle, de-activate the system as described in the following sub-Section.*
c *Do not attempt to test any of the airbag system circuits using test meters or any other test equipment.*
d *If the airbag warning light comes on, or any fault in the system is suspected, consult a Nissan dealer without delay.*
e *Do not attempt to carry out fault diagnosis, or any dismantling of the components.*

Precautions when handling an airbag

a *Transport the airbag by itself, bag upward.*
b *Do not put your arms around the airbag.*
c *Carry the airbag close to the body, bag outward.*
d *Do not drop the airbag or expose it to impacts.*
e *Do not attempt to dismantle the airbag unit.*
f *Do not connect any form of electrical equipment to any part of the airbag circuit.*

21.2 Disconnect the wiring connectors

Precautions when storing an airbag

a *Store the unit in a cupboard with the airbag upward.*
b *Do not expose the airbag to temperatures above 80ºC.*
c *Do not expose the airbag to flames.*
d *Do not attempt to dispose of the airbag – consult a Nissan dealer.*
e *Never refit an airbag that is known to be faulty or damaged.*

De-activation of airbag system

4 The system must be de-activated before carrying out any work on the airbag components or surrounding area:

a *Switch on the ignition and check the operation of the airbag warning light on the instrument panel. The light should illuminate when the ignition is switched on, then extinguish.*
b *Switch off the ignition.*
c *Remove the ignition key.*
d *Switch off all electrical equipment.*
e *Disconnect the battery negative terminal (refer to 'Disconnecting the battery' in the Reference Chapter).*
f *Insulate the battery negative terminal and the end of the battery negative lead to prevent any possibility of contact.*
g *Wait for at least ten minutes before carrying out any further work.*

Activation of airbag system

5 To activate the system on completion of any work, proceed as follows:

a *Ensure that there are no occupants in the vehicle, and that there are no loose objects around the vicinity of the steering wheel. Close the vehicle doors and windows.*
b *Ensure that the ignition is switched off then reconnect the battery negative terminal.*
c *Open the driver's door and switch on the ignition, without reaching in front of the steering wheel. Check that the airbag warning light illuminates briefly then extinguishes.*
d *Switch off the ignition.*
e *If the airbag warning light does not operate as described in paragraph c), consult a Nissan dealer before driving the vehicle.*

21.3 Note the arrow must face forward when fitted

21 Airbag system components – removal and refitting

Warning: *Refer to the precautions given in Section 20 before attempting to carry out work on any of the airbag components. Any suspected faults with the airbag system should be referred to a Nissan dealer – under no circumstances attempt to carry out any work other than removal and refitting of the front airbag unit(s) and/or the rotary connector, as described in the following paragraphs.*

Note: *Disconnect the battery negative terminal (refer to Disconnecting the battery in the Reference Chapter), before the removal and refitting of components in the airbag system.*

Airbag electronic control units

1 The ECU is located under the centre console in front of the handbrake, and is accessible after removal of the centre console (see Chapter 11 Section 22).

2 Disconnect the wiring connectors from the control unit, then undo the retaining bolts and remove the control unit from the floor panel **(see illustration)**.

3 The arrow on the top of the unit must face forward when refitted **(see illustration)**.

Driver's airbag unit

4 Disable the airbag system (see Section 20).

5 The procedure to remove the driver airbag from the steering wheel is covered under the Steering Wheel - Removal and Installation heading (see Chapter 10 Section 14).

6 If the airbag unit is to be stored for any length of time, refer to the storage precautions given in Section 20.

Spiral cable

Removal

7 Remove the driver's airbag unit. Position the steering wheel in the straight-ahead position and then remove the steering wheel (see Chapter 10 Section 14).

8 Remove the steering column upper and lower shrouds (see Chapter 11 Section 23).

Chapter 12 Chassis electrical systems

21.10a Spiral cable alignment marks (1) and wiring connectors (2) - T31 X-Trail models

21.10b Secure the spiral cable in place using duct tape

21.11 Disconnecting the wiring from the spiral cable - Dualis models

21.12a Spiral cable retaining screws - T31 X-Trail models

21.12b Spiral cable retaining screws - T32 X-Trail and Qashqai models

21.12c Removing the spiral cable from steering column - T31 X-Trail models

21.12d Release the retaining clips …

21.12e … and withdraw the spiral cable assembly - Dualis models

21.12f Disconnecting the wiring from the rear of the spiral cable on T32 X-Trail models

9 Remove the steering column switches (see Section 4).
10 Align the alignment marks on the spiral cable (**see illustration**) and use some insulating tape to retain it in position (**see illustration**).
11 Disconnect the wiring connectors, below the steering column from the rear of the spiral cable (**see illustration**).
12 Remove the spiral cable retaining screws, release the clips from the top and remove it from the steering column (**see illustration**).
Note: On T32 X-Trail and Qashqai models, it is easier to remove the spiral cable first and then disconnect the wiring from the bottom of the spiral cable.

Refitting

13 Refitting is a reversal of removal, bearing in mind the following points:
a Make sure the spiral cable has not been turned and the insulating tape is still in position.
b Ensure that the roadwheels are in the straight–ahead position before refitting the rotary connector and steering wheel.
c If the spiral cable has been turned, ensure it is centred as follows before installing it to the steering column. Verify that the front wheels are pointing straight ahead. Turn the spiral cable housing anticlockwise by hand until it becomes hard to turn. Turn the spiral cable clockwise about 2-1/2 turns and align the marks made prior to removal (**see illustration 21.11a**).
d Before refitting the steering column shrouds, ensure that the rotary connector wiring harness is correctly routed as noted before removal.
e Refit the steering wheel (see Chapter 10 Section 14), and refit the airbag unit as described previously in this Section.

Passenger's airbag unit

Removal

14 The passenger's airbag is fitted to the upper part of the facia, above the glovebox.
15 Disable the airbag system (see Section 20).
16 Remove the glovebox (see Chapter 11 Section 21).
17 Disconnect the airbag wiring connectors (**see illustration**).
18 Undo the bolts securing the airbag

12-32 Chapter 12 Chassis electrical systems

21.17 Disconnect the airbag wiring connectors

21.18a Undo the airbag mounting bolts ...

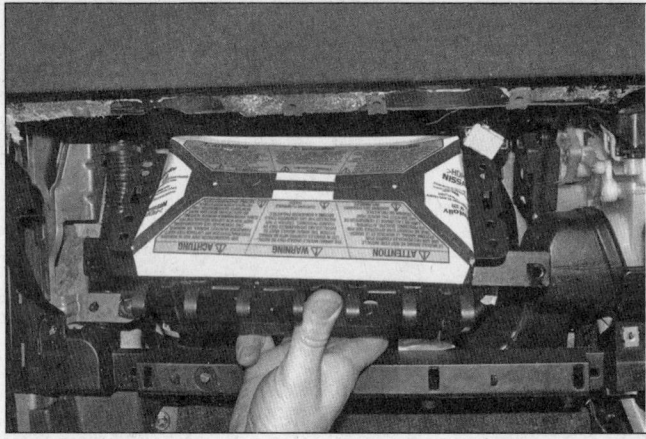

21.18b ... and remove it from under the facia

assembly to the facia support rail, and then carefully withdraw the airbag from the facia **(see illustrations)**.

19 If the airbag unit is to be stored for any length of time, refer to the storage precautions given in Section 20.

Refitting

20 Refitting is a reversal of removal, bearing in mind the following points:
  a *Use new bolts to secure the airbag unit and tighten the bolts to the specified torque.*
  b *Do not strike the airbag unit, or expose it to impacts during refitting.*
  c *On completion of refitting, activate the airbag system as described in Section 20.*

Side airbag units

21 The side airbags are located internally within the front seat back and no attempt should be made to remove them. Any suspected problems with the side airbag system should be referred to a Nissan dealer.

Curtain airbag units

22 The curtain airbags are located internally behind the headlining and no attempt should be made to remove them. Any suspected problems with the curtain airbag system should be referred to a Nissan dealer.

Chapter 12 Chassis electrical systems

22 Wiring diagrams - general information

Note: *At the time of publication, no wiring diagrams were available for the Dualis and Qashqai models.*

1 Prior to troubleshooting any circuits, check the fuse, fusible links and circuit breakers (if equipped) to make sure they're in good condition. Make sure the battery is properly charged, and check cable connections.
2 When checking a circuit, make sure that all connections are clean with no broken or loose terminals. When unplugging a connector, do not pull on the wires, pull only on the connector housing.

Wiring diagram symbols

The wiring diagrams used in this publication are designed to make tracing wiring, connections, power supplies and earth circuits quick and easy. Where possible, internals of the sensors, motors, solenoids and valves are shown to simplify understanding of how the circuit works. Terminal numbers within the components will coincide with terminal numbers shown on the connectors.

1 The earth location will be written beneath the earth symbol. This is useful when tracing a bad earth at a sensor or component.
2 Some circuits flow from one diagram to another. Where a circuit is continued on another diagram, a linking number contained in a shaded box will match to the identical number on an accompanying diagram. This allows the circuit to be easily traced.
3 Some components will have alternative circuits that are dependent on a differing body type. For example, the fuel pump earth may be in a different location on a sedan than it is on a station wagon. In this instance, a box surrounding the circuit will identify the locations for both a sedan and station wagon.
4 An alternative circuit can also be shown using a dotted line with an explanation of what this circuit is applicable to, or excluding next to it.
5 There are a variety of internal circuits shown within the powertrain, or engine control module. These are shown to help the user understand what the control module is doing with each particular circuit.

The 5 volt symbol shows where the control module is supplying 5 volts to one or more sensors, eg. throttle position sensor. The voltage will only be available with the ignition On.

5v

A driver is basically a switch that the control module uses to turn a circuit On or Off. Drivers may switch a circuit to earth, battery power or 5 volts. In this way, the control module can activate a component such as a transmission shift solenoid or a fuel injector. By switching the circuit to earth or power a number of times per second, the control module can create a pulse width or frequency to operate components such as an ISC valve or transmission pressure control solenoid.

The powered signal symbol is used where the control module supplies voltage to the sensor, and then notes the variation in voltage as the sensor resistance changes. The supply voltage can be either 5 volts or battery voltage. These circuits are commonly used on coolant temperature and air temperature sensor circuits.

S
5v

A signal symbol indicates an incoming signal from a particular sensor. Eg, oxygen sensor, knock sensor.

Sig

An earth symbol contained within the control module indicated that either the control module is connected to earth at that terminal, or supplies an earth to sensors or components.

A symbol with the letter "M" indicates a circuit that is monitored by the control module to check for incorrect system operation. The control module may monitor drivers, For example, when a driver is switched to earth, the voltage on the monitoring circuit should drop to zero. When the driver is switched open, the voltage on the monitoring circuit should go back to the original voltage. If the monitoring circuit reads voltages that are outside those it is programmed to read, it will assume there is a fault in this circuit.

M
B+

The monitored circuit can also be used on power inputs or power supplies to sensors or components.

M

The B+ symbol indicates constant battery power being supplied to the control module. These terminals are where power should be checked when instructed to check control module power supply and earth circuits.

B+

The IGN B+ symbol shows where the control module receives power with the ignition On. Like terminals with the B+ symbol, these terminals should be checked when instructed to check control module power supply and earth circuits.

IGN B+

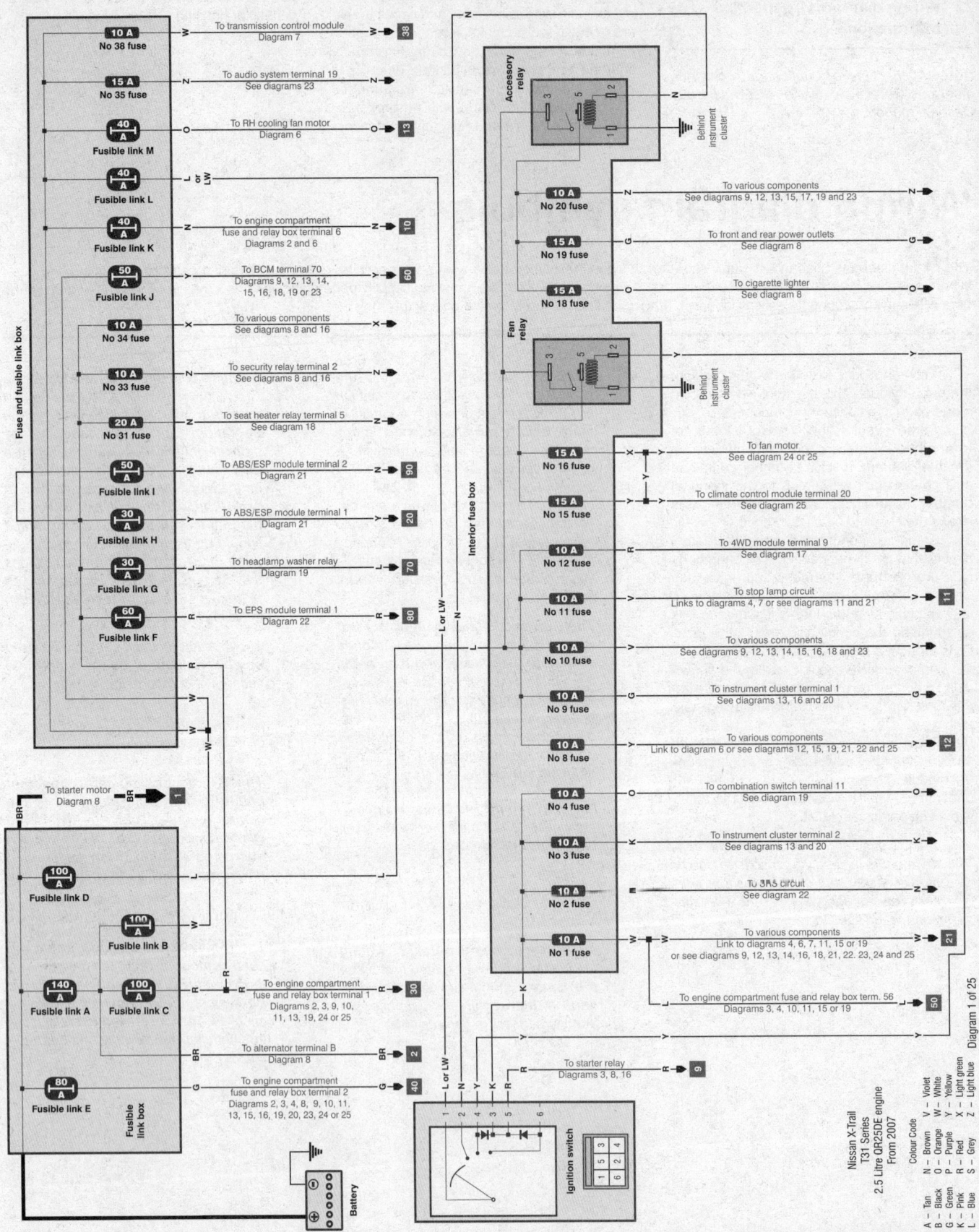

Diagram 1 - Power distribution. Fusible link box, fuse and fusible link box, interior fuse box, ignition switch – T31 X-Trail petrol models

Chapter 12 Chassis electrical system

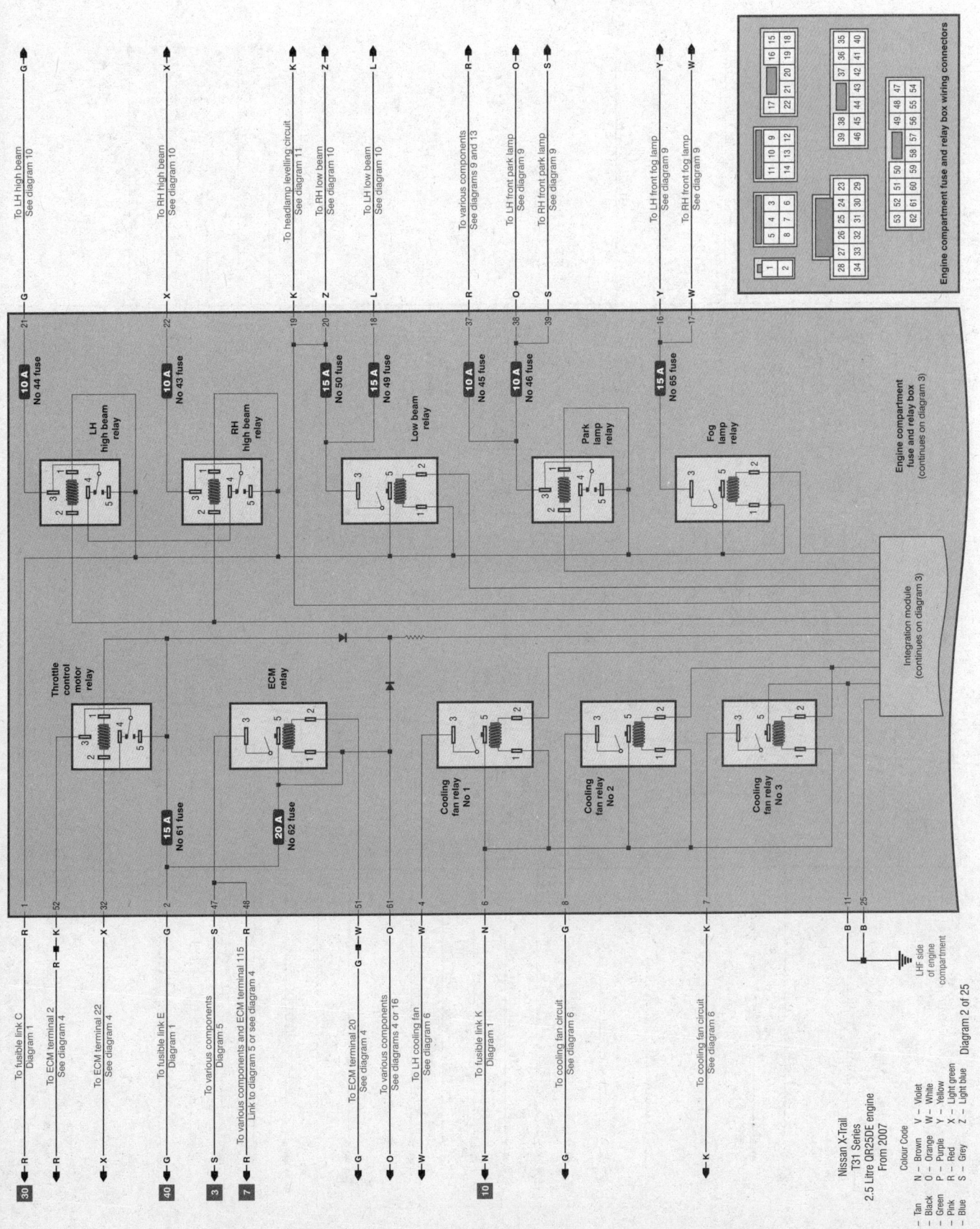

Diagram 2 - Power distribution. Engine compartment fuse and relay box – T31 X-Trail petrol models

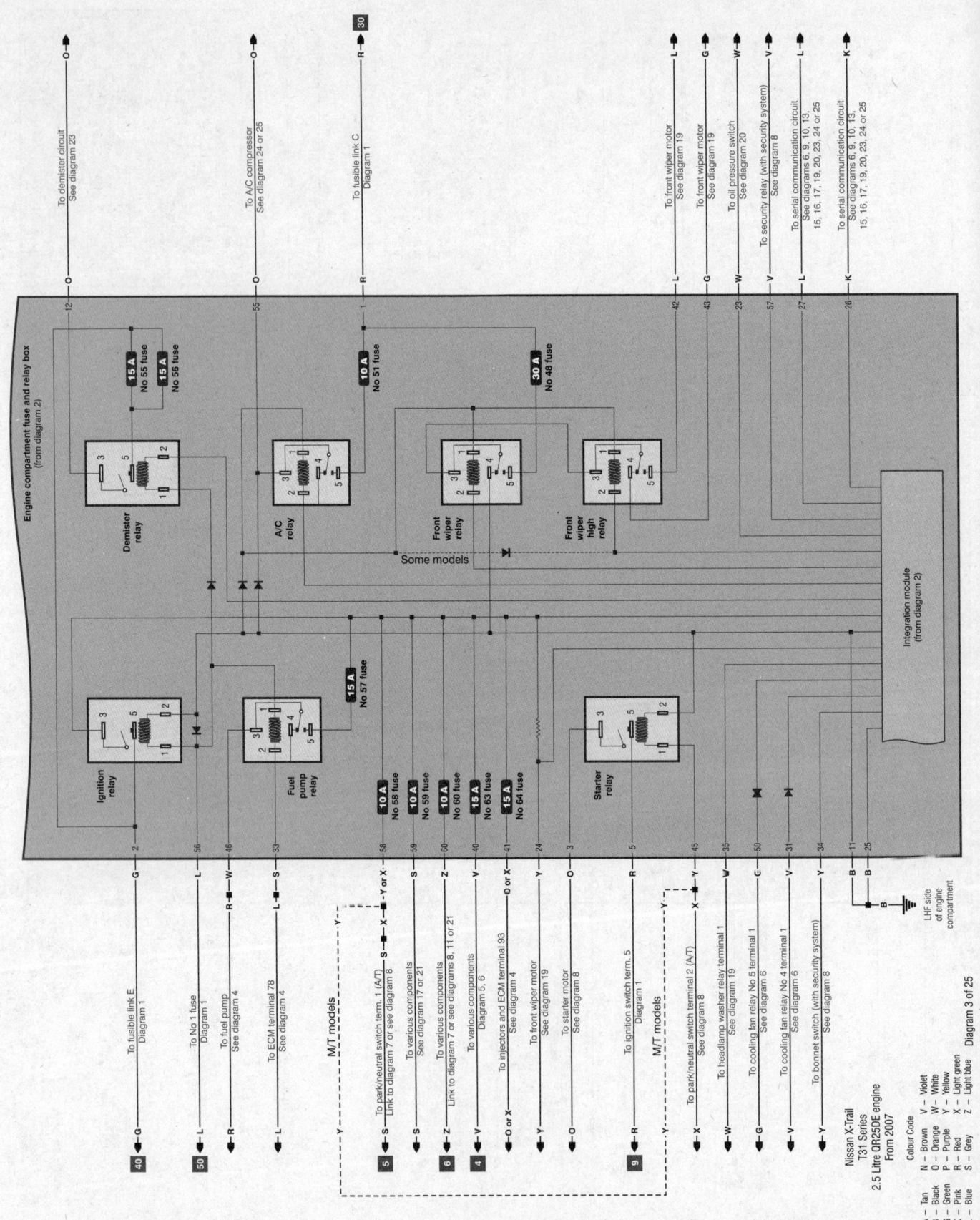

Diagram 3 - Power distribution. Engine compartment fuse and relay box – T31 X-Trail petrol models

Chapter 12 Chassis electrical system

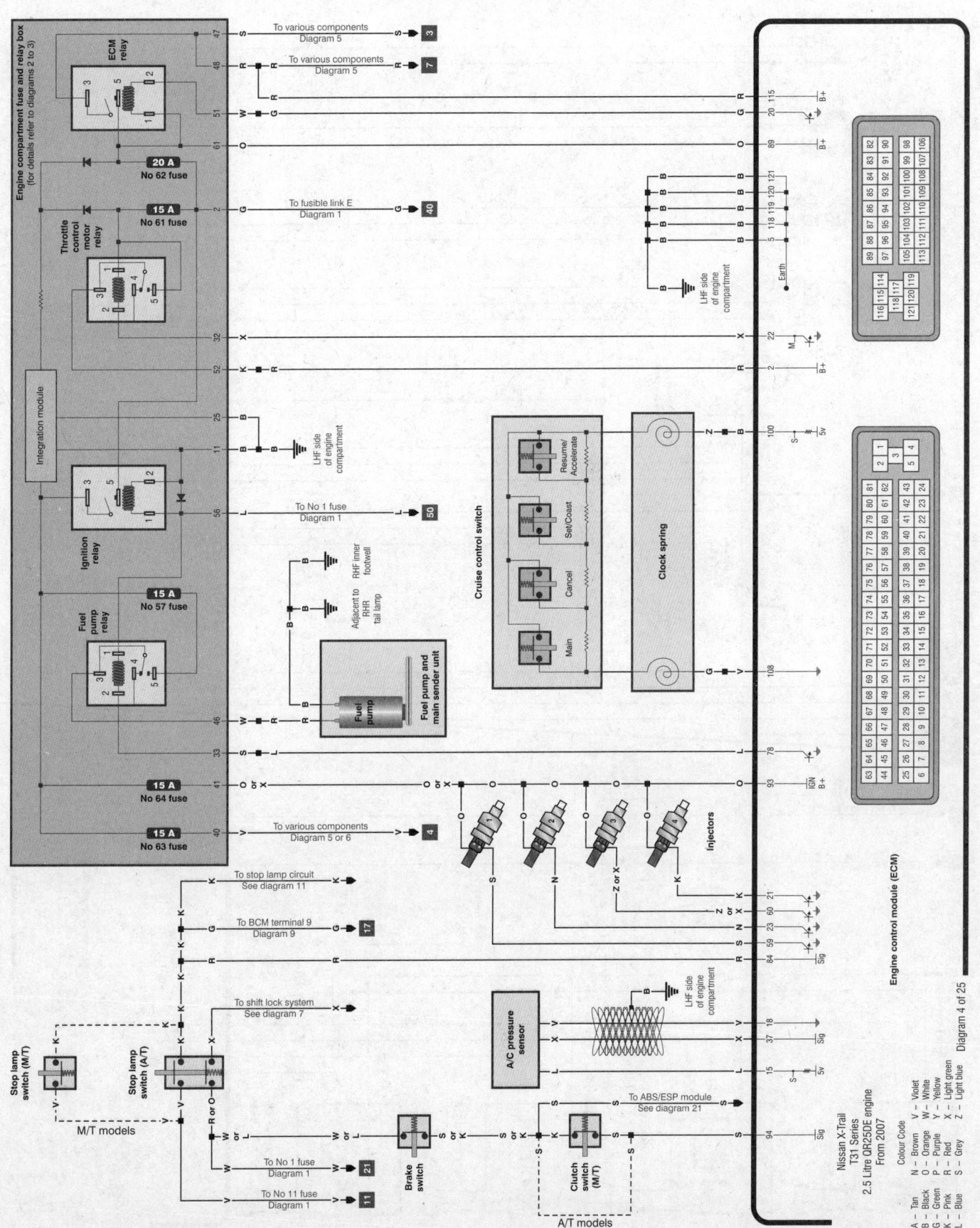

Diagram 4 - PCM power supply and earth circuits, fuel pump, injectors, cruise control – T31 X-Trail petrol models

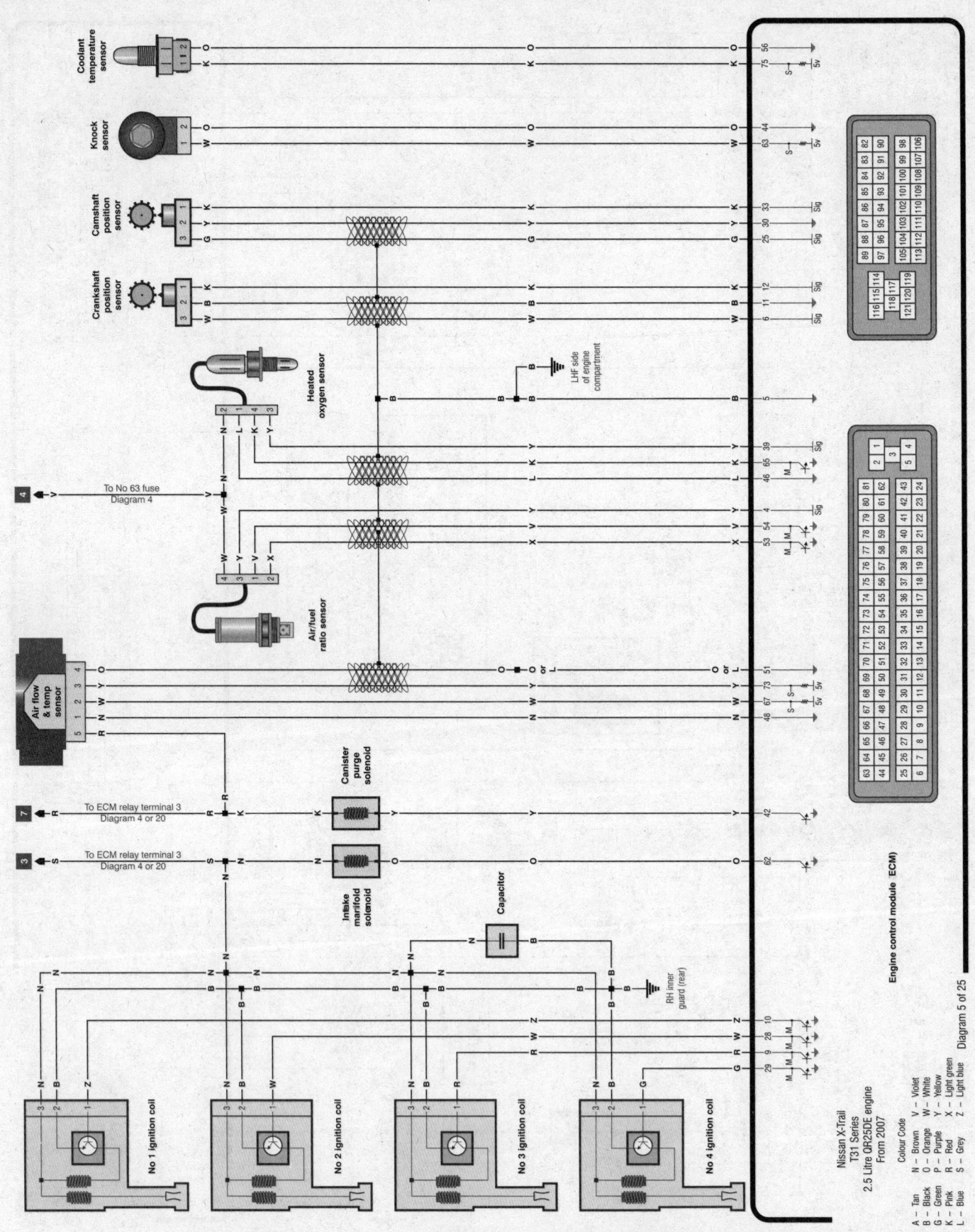

Diagram 5 - Ignition system, various sensors and solenoids – T31 X-Trail petrol models

Chapter 12 Chassis electrical system

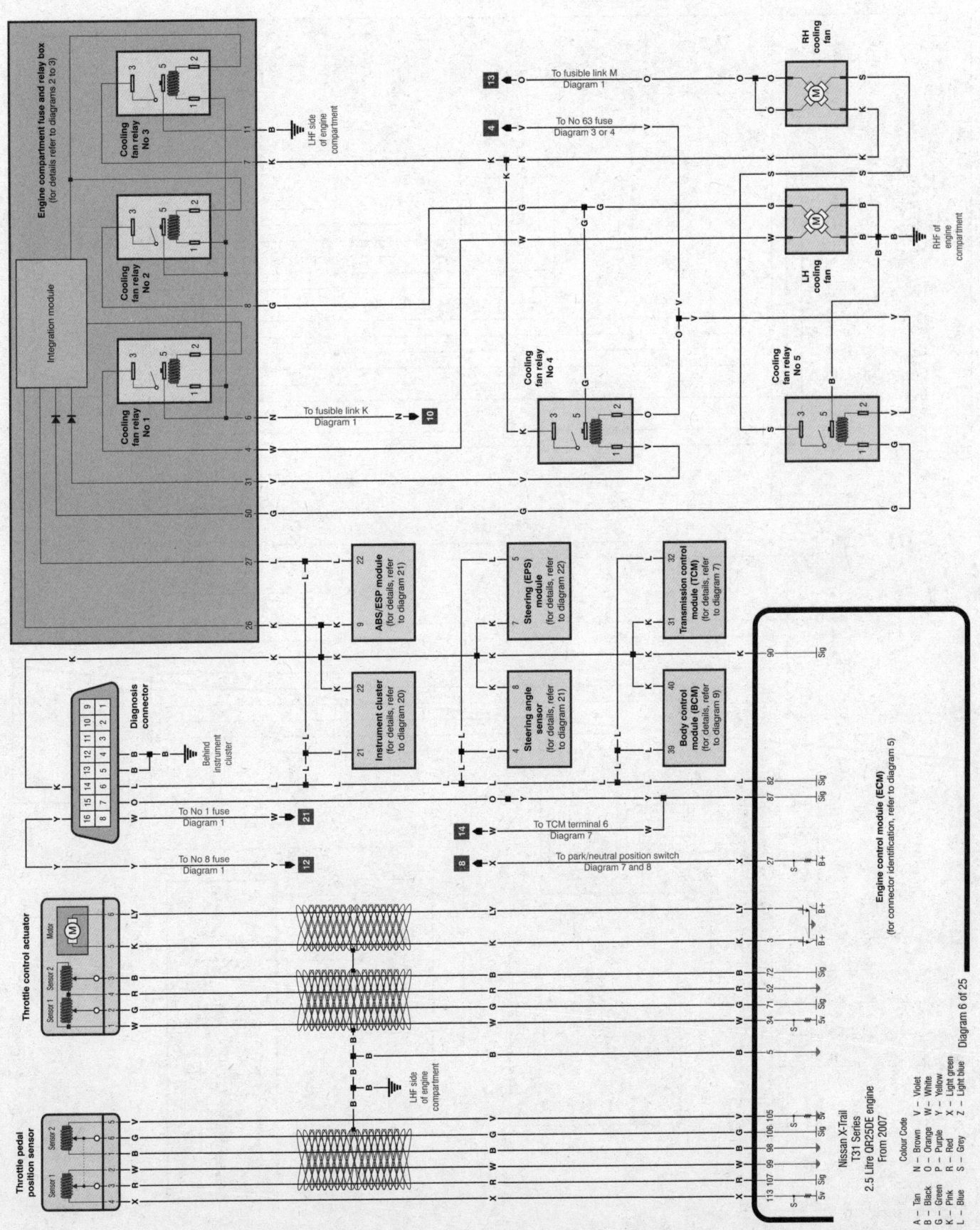

Diagram 6 - Throttle control system, diagnosis connector, serial data communication, cooling fans – T31 X-Trail petrol models

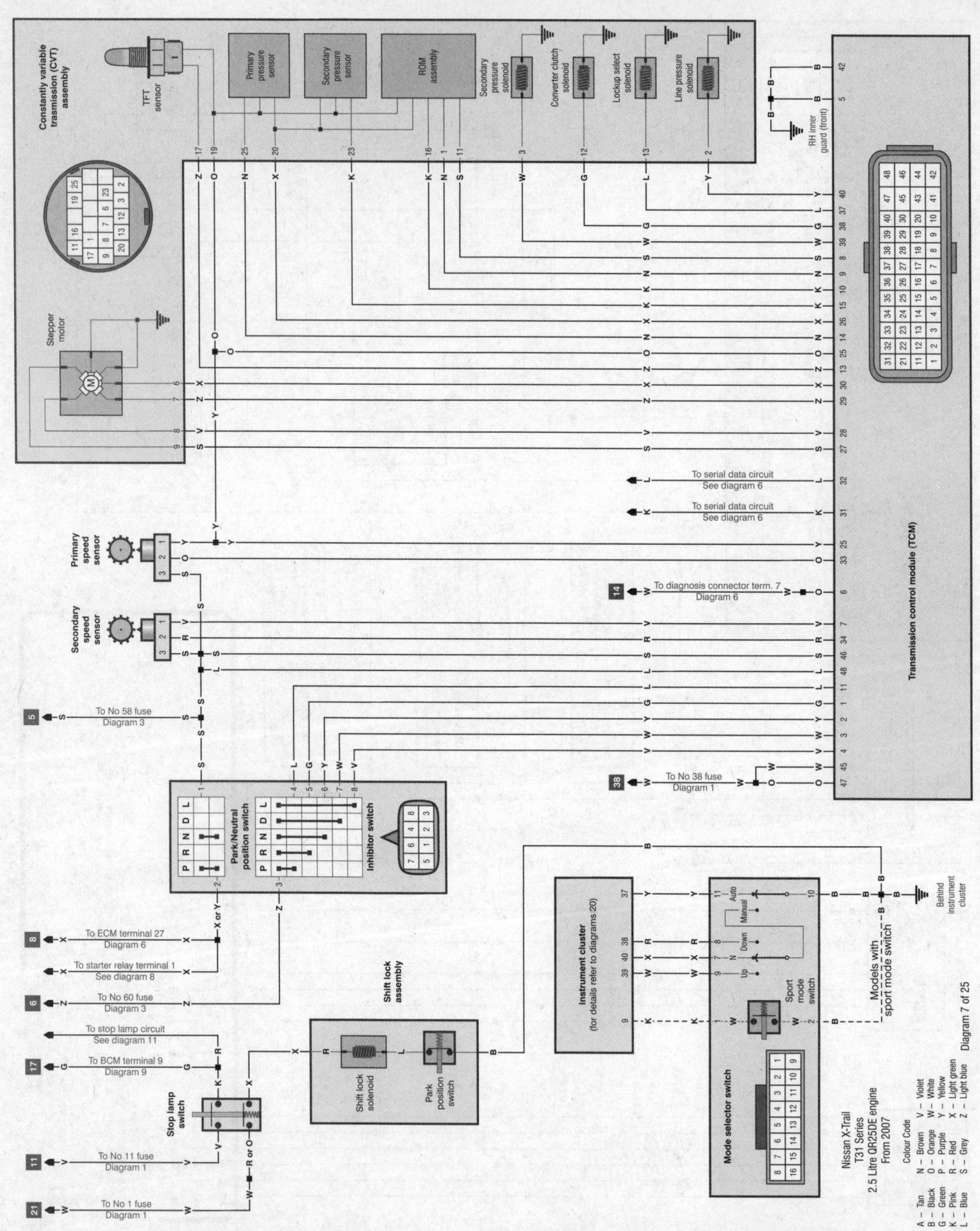

Diagram 7 - Automatic transmission, inhibitor switch, shift lock system – T31 X-Trail petrol models

Chapter 12 Chassis electrical system

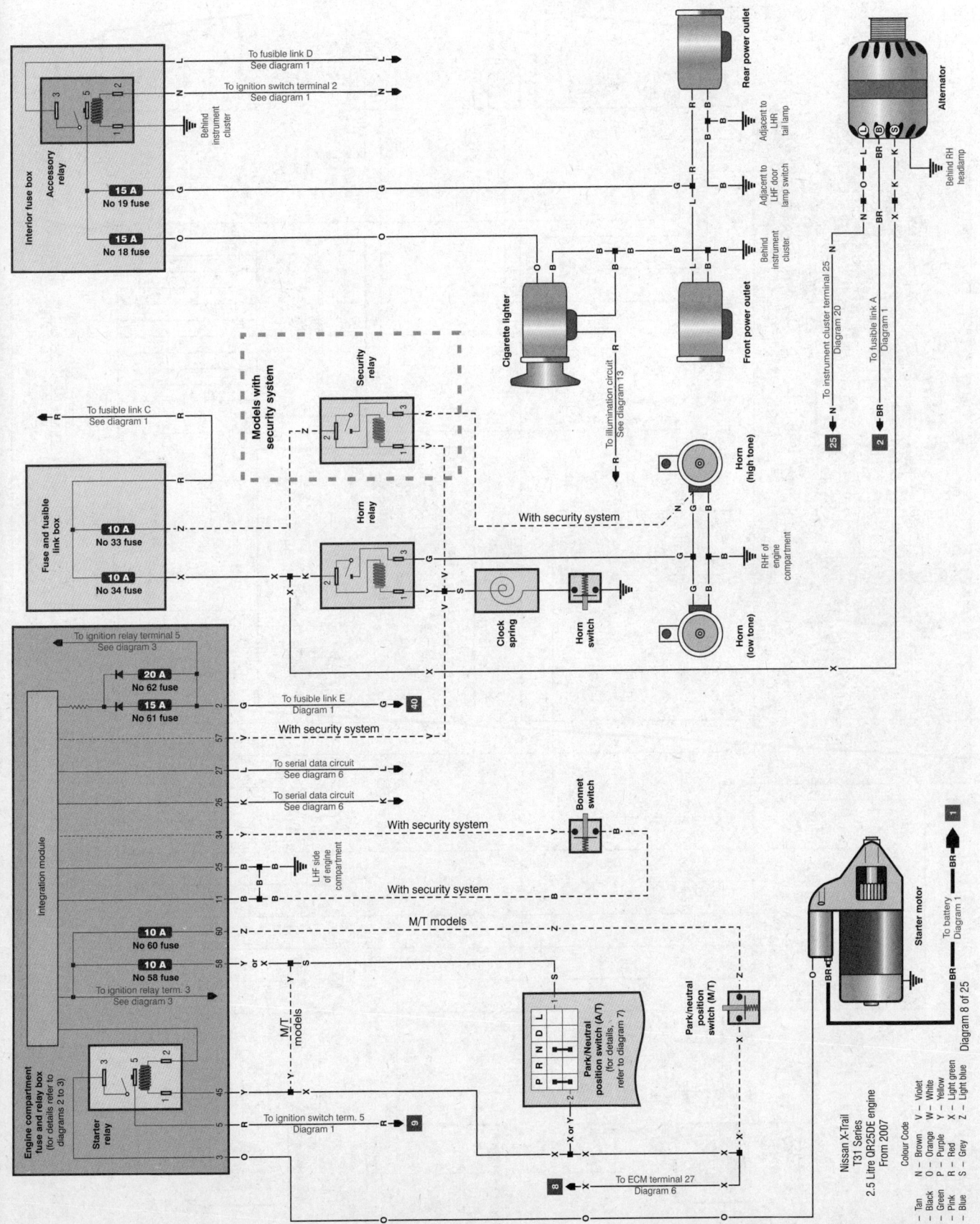

Diagram 8 - Starting system, charging system, cigarette lighter, power outlets, horn and security relay – T31 X-Trail petrol models

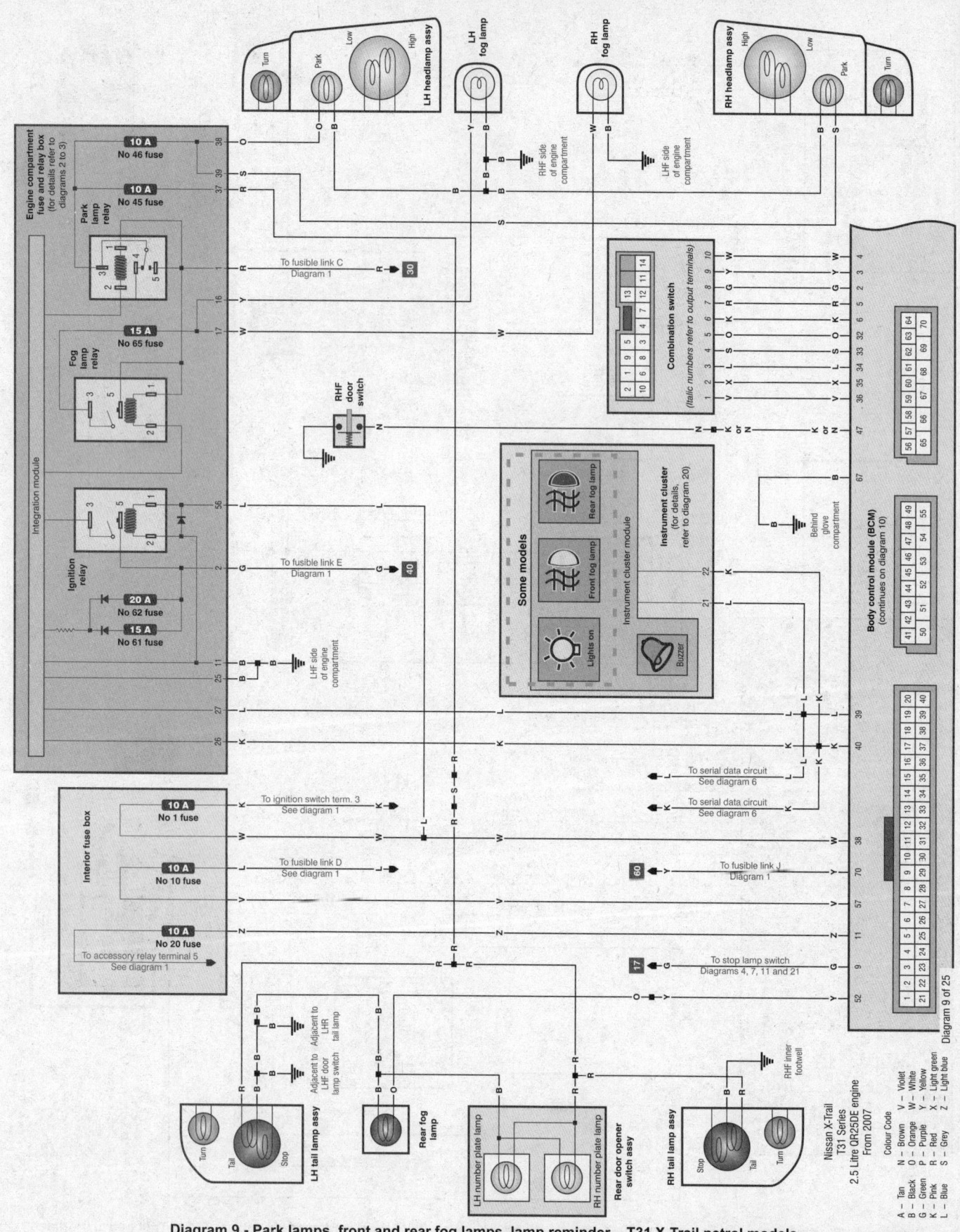

Diagram 9 - Park lamps, front and rear fog lamps, lamp reminder – T31 X-Trail petrol models

Chapter 12 Chassis electrical system

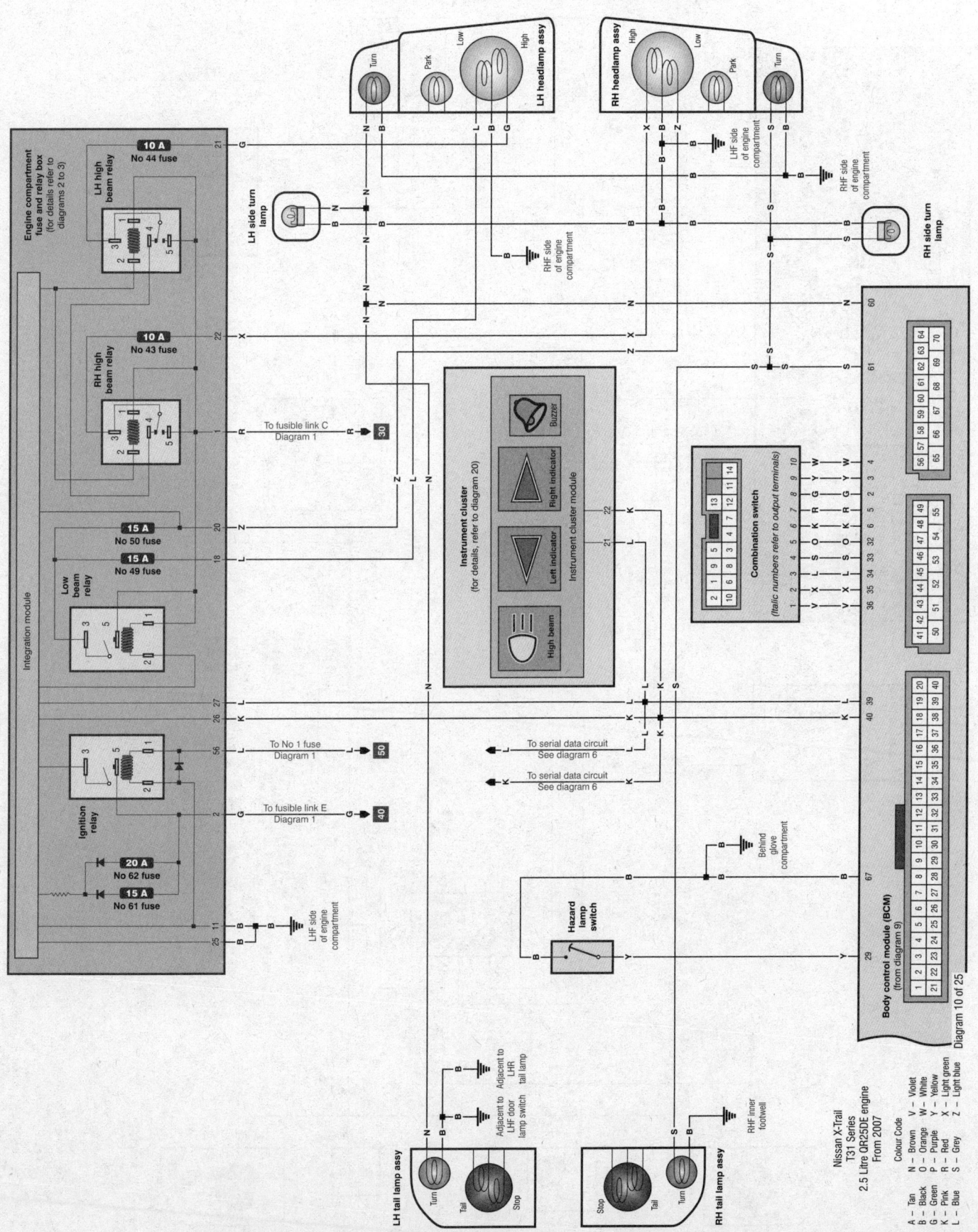

Diagram 10 - Headlamps, turn signal and hazard lamps – T31 X-Trail petrol models

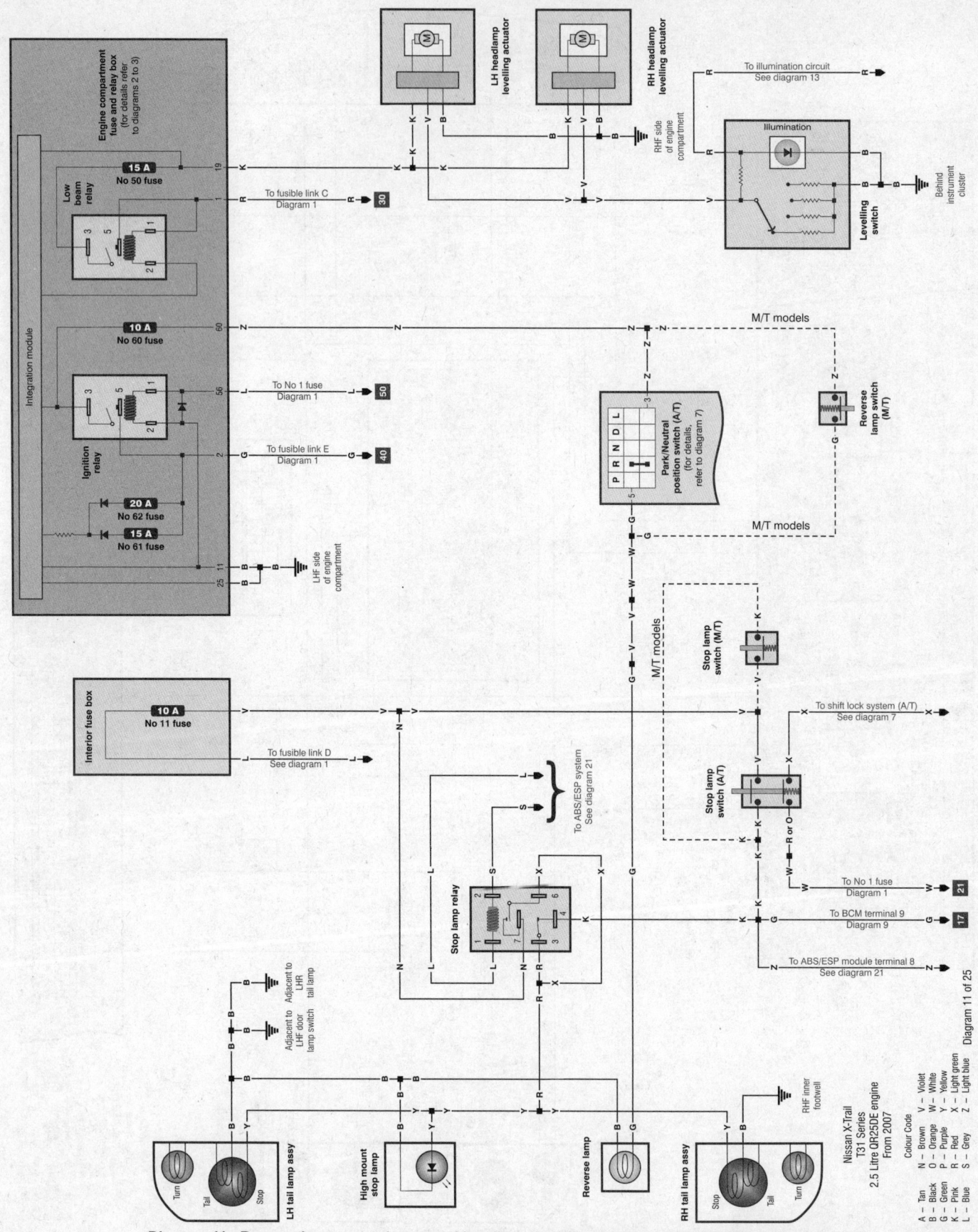

Chapter 12 Chassis electrical system

12-45

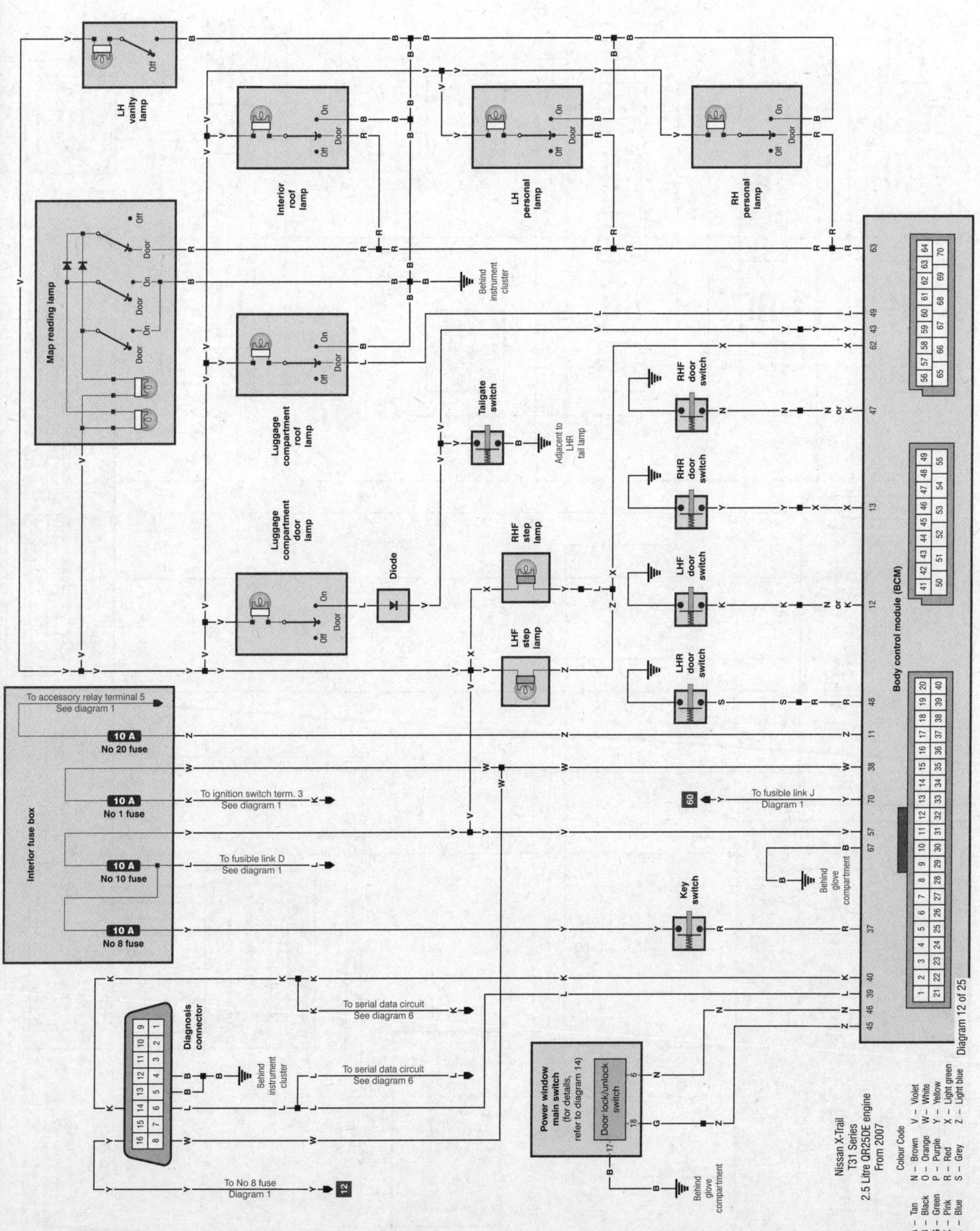

Diagram 12 - Interior lighting – T31 X-Trail petrol models

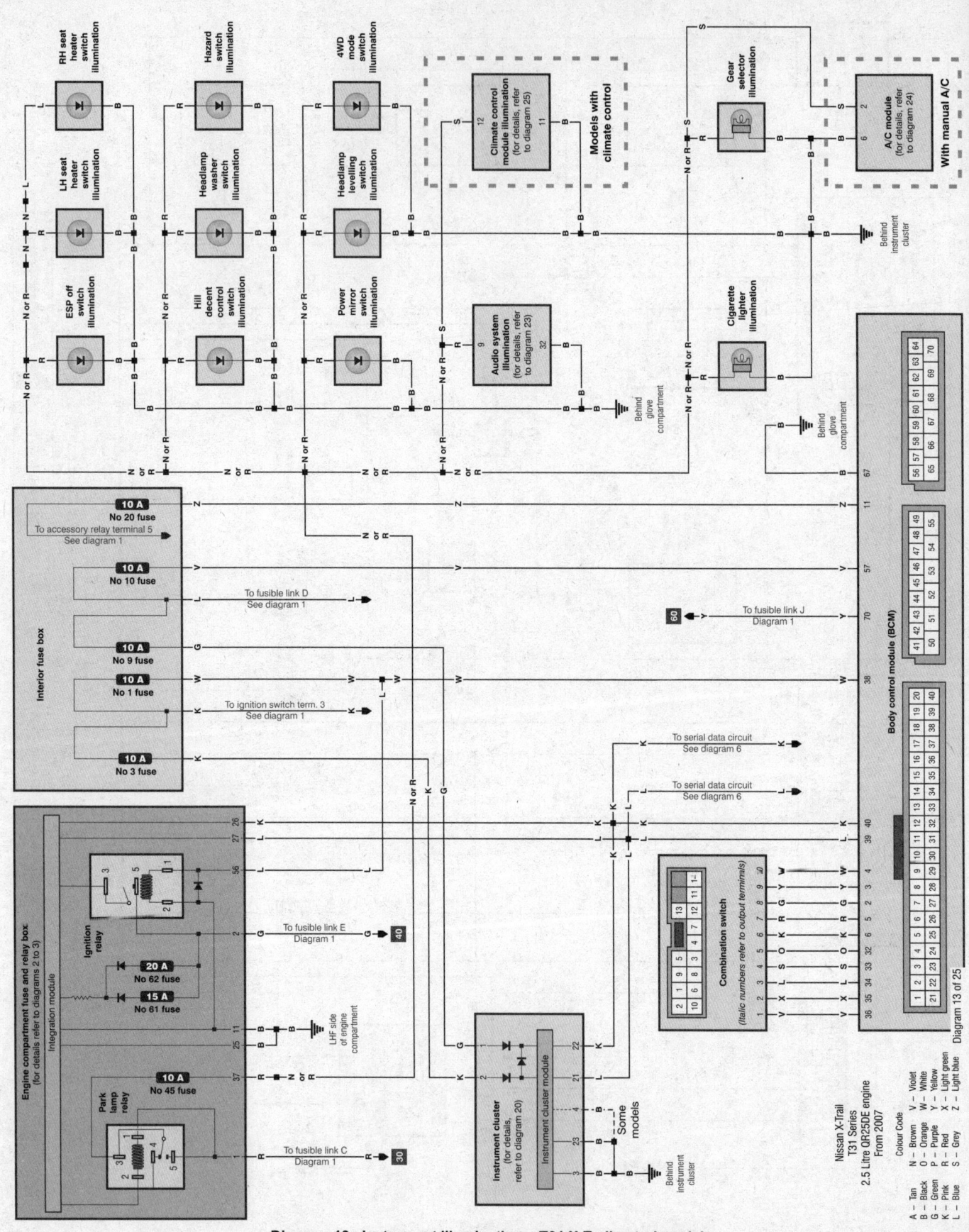

Diagram 13 - Instrument illumination – T31 X-Trail petrol models

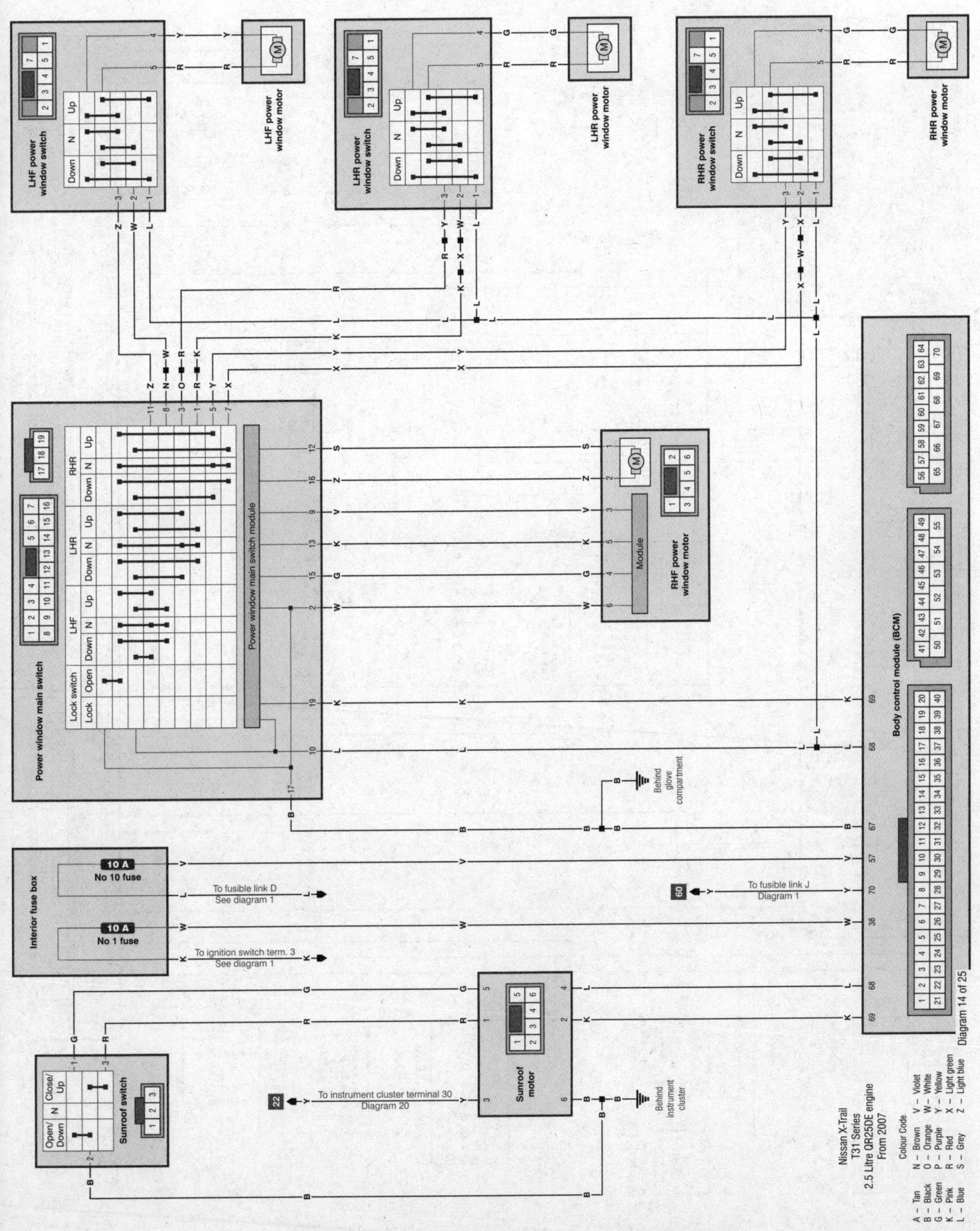

Diagram 14 - Power windows and sunroof – T31 X-Trail petrol models

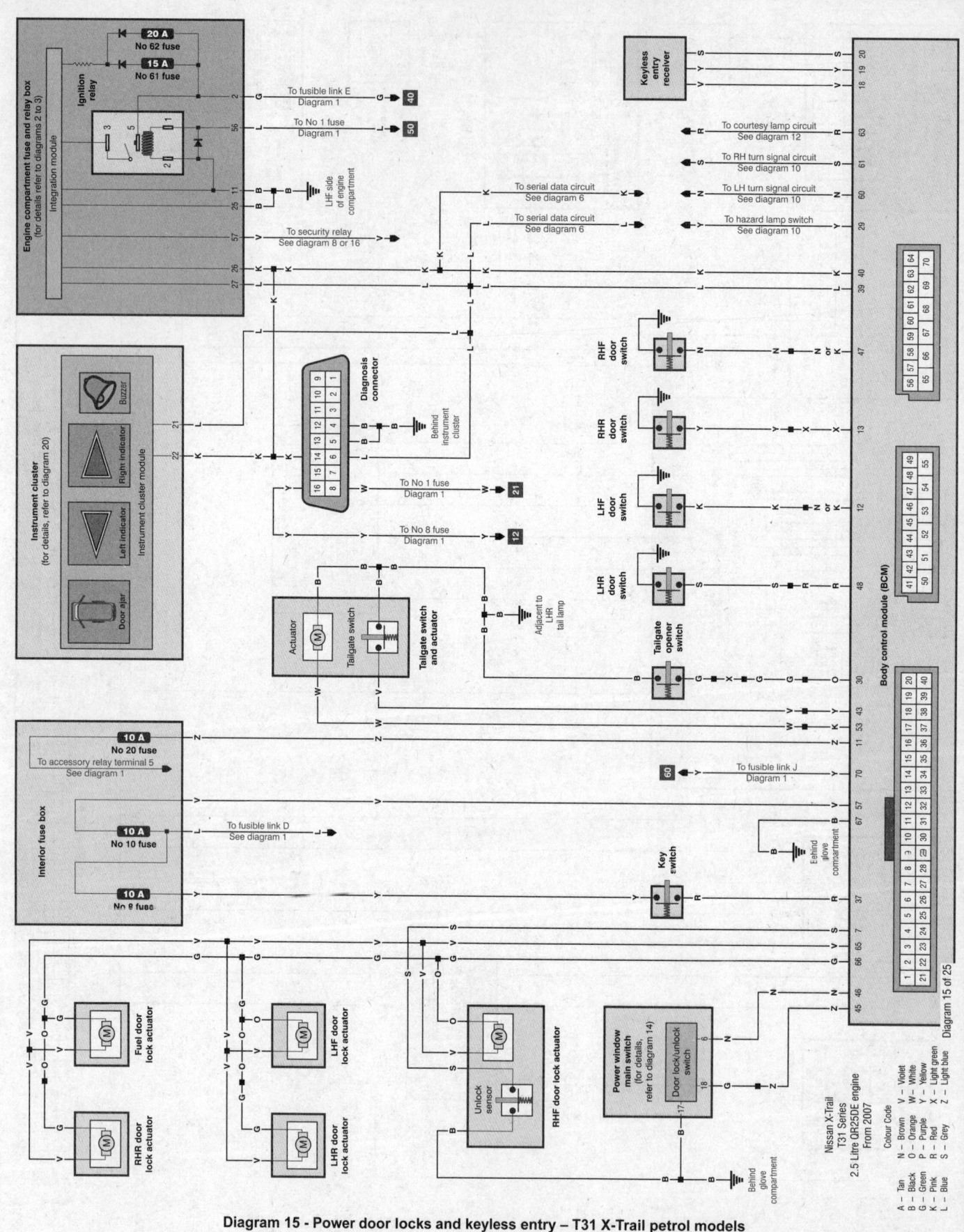

Diagram 15 - Power door locks and keyless entry – T31 X-Trail petrol models

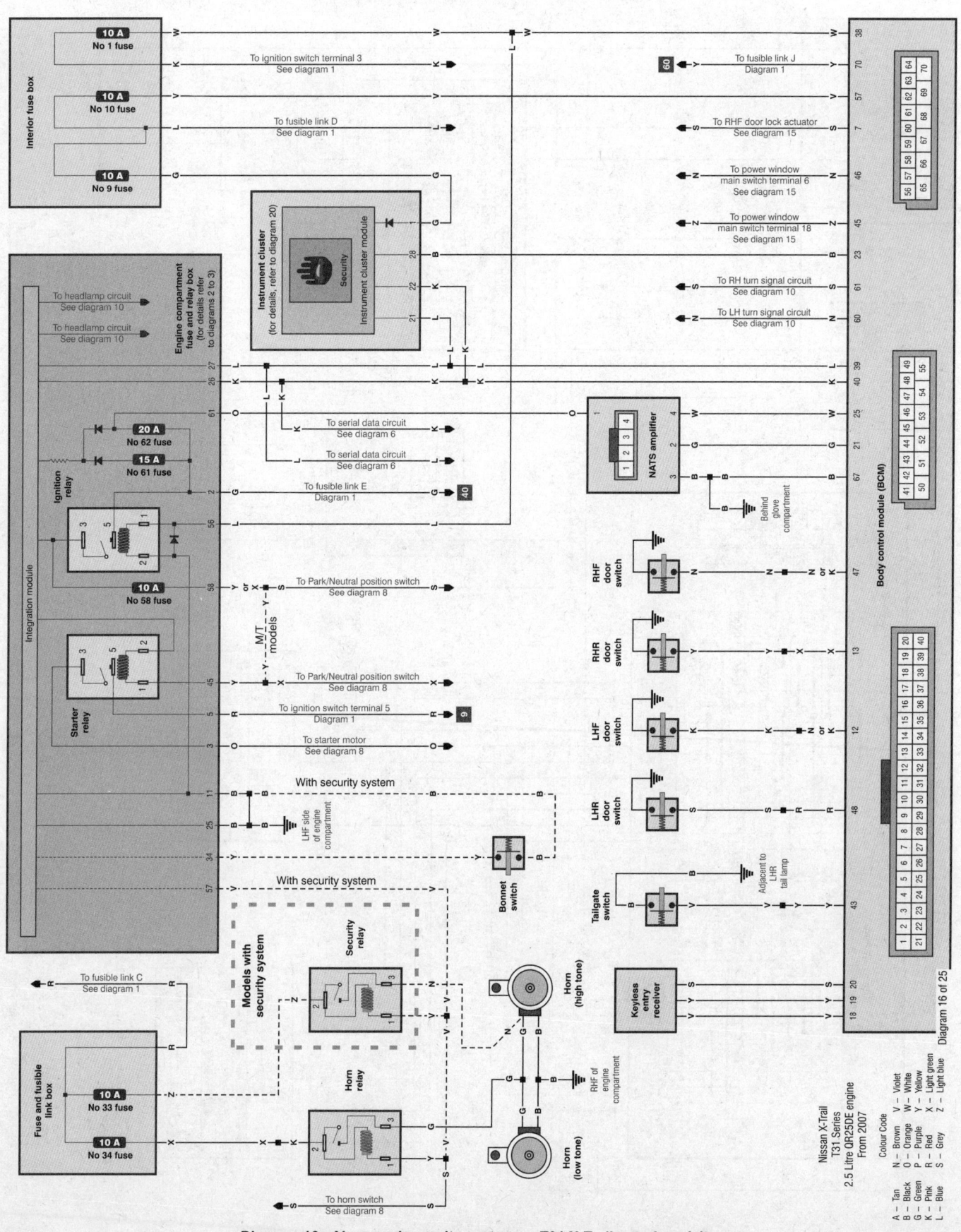

Diagram 16 - Alarm and security systems – T31 X-Trail petrol models

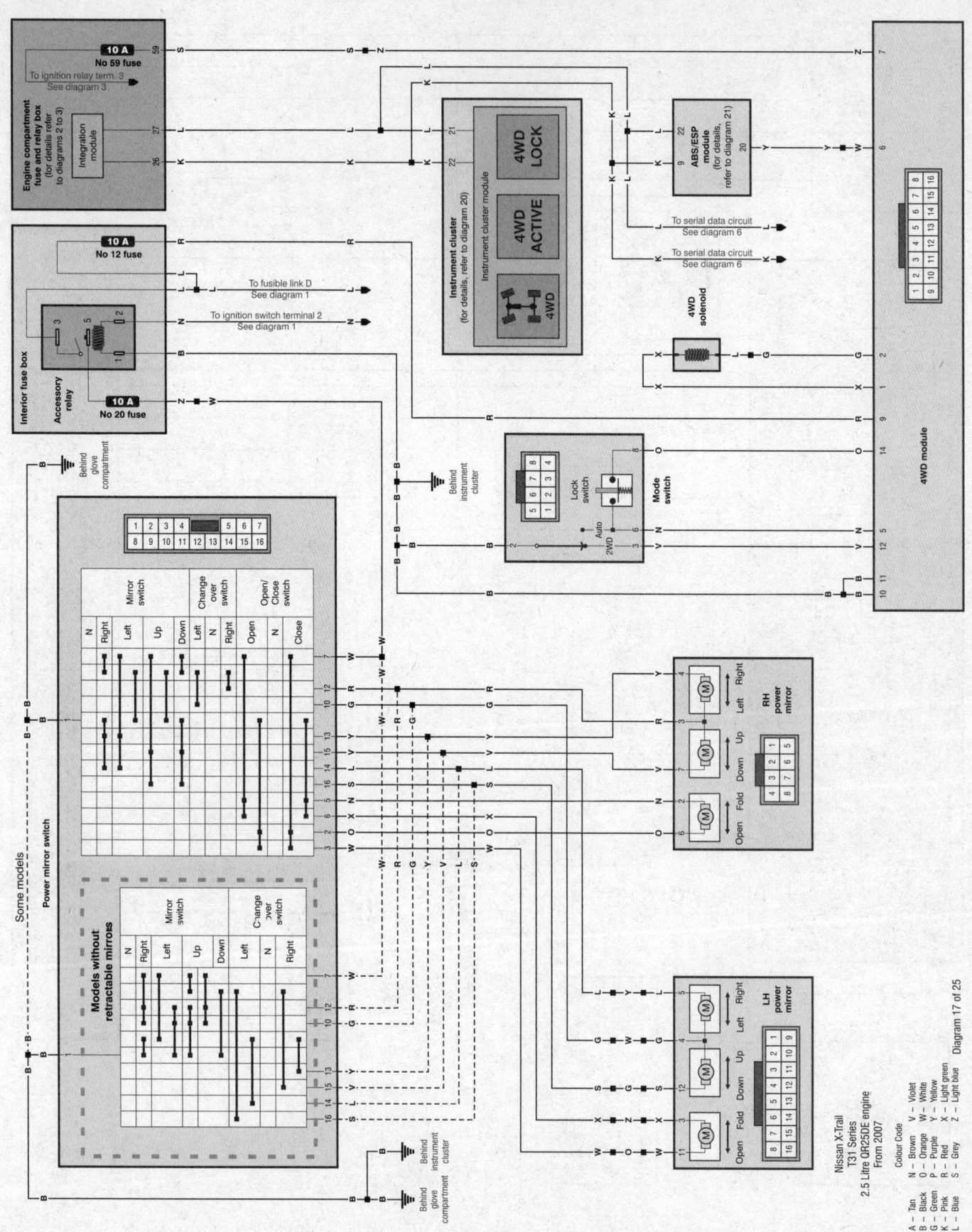

Diagram 17 - Power mirrors, 4WD system – T31 X-Trail petrol models

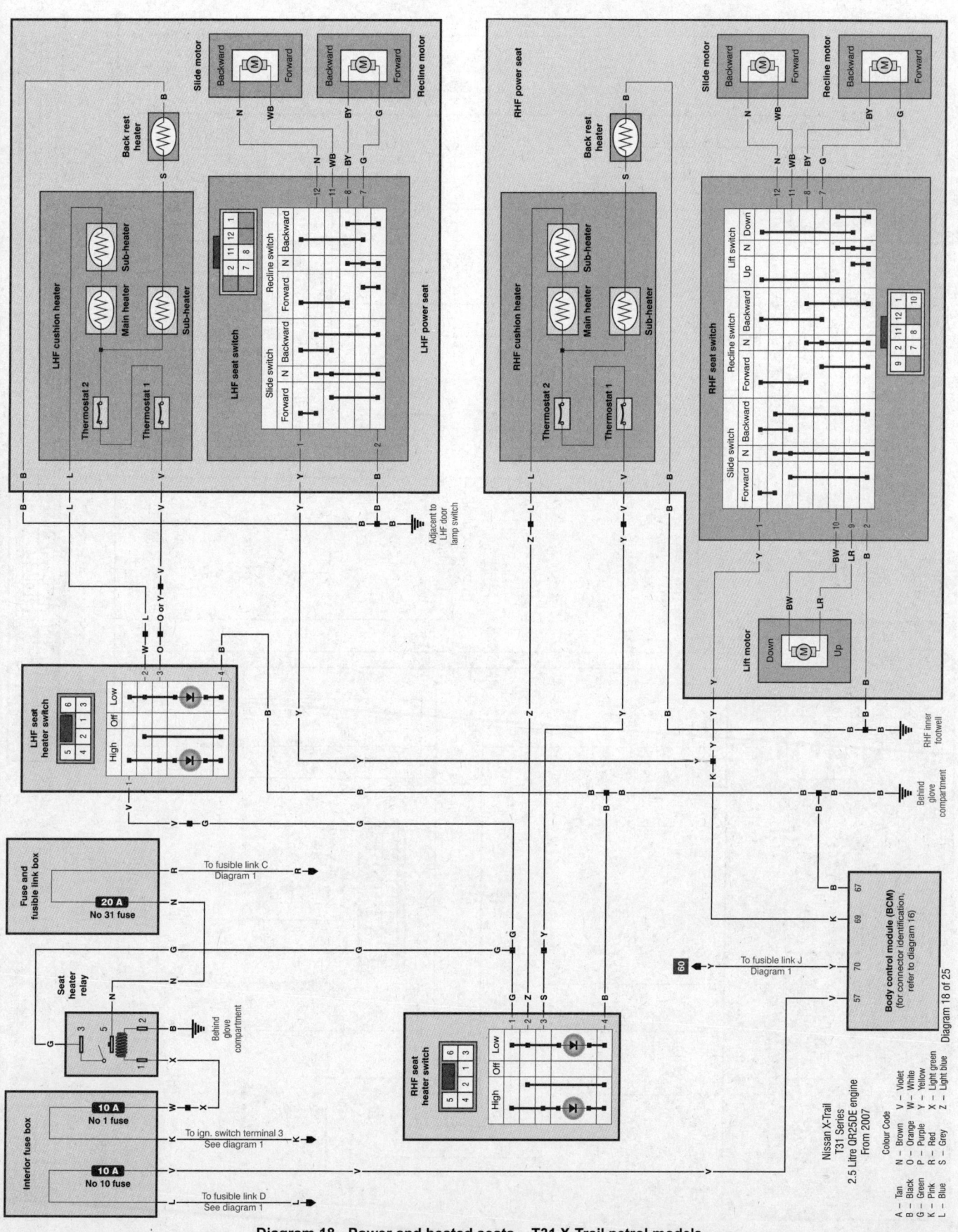

Diagram 18 - Power and heated seats – T31 X-Trail petrol models

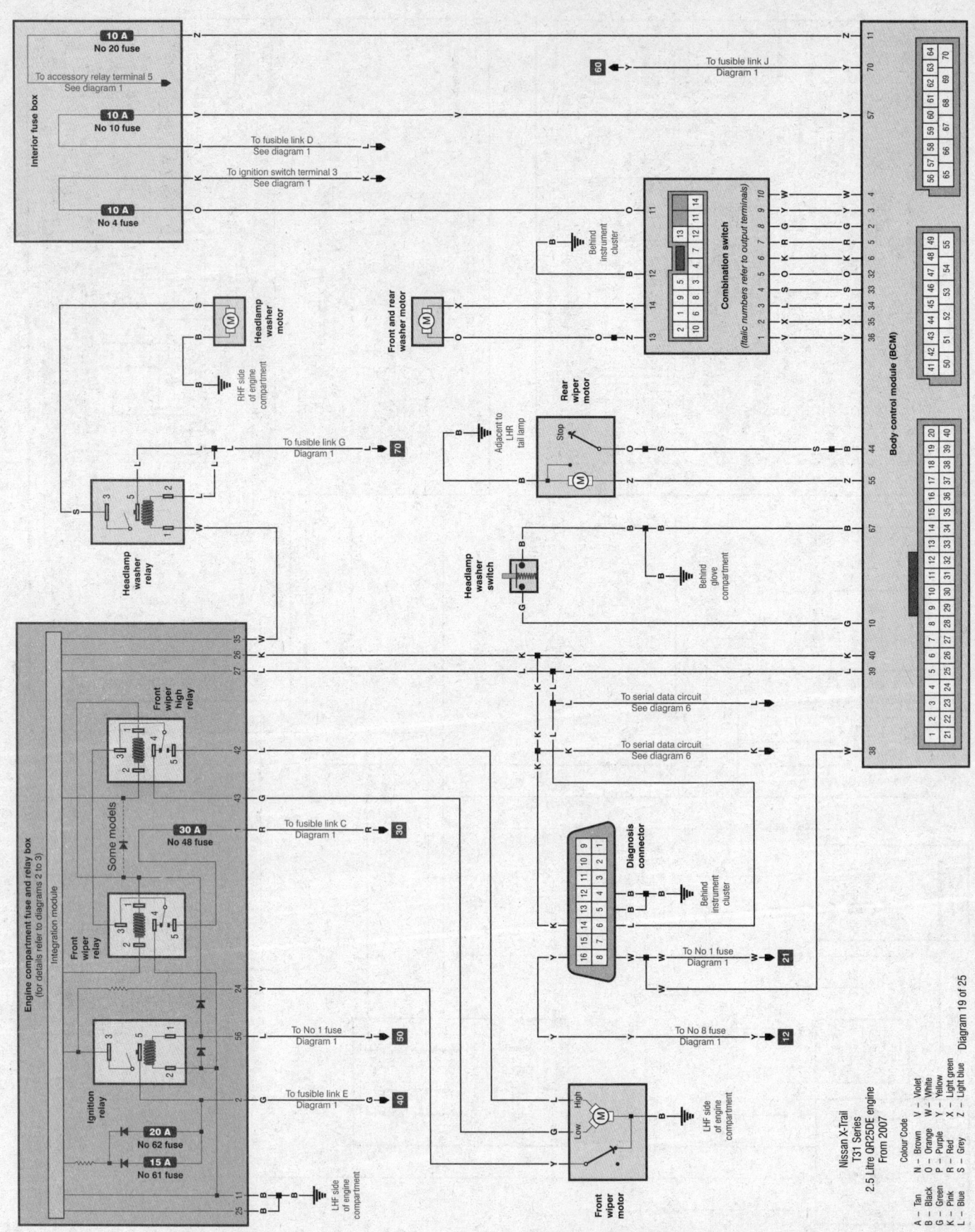

Diagram 19 - Front and rear wipers, washers and headlamp cleaner – T31 X-Trail petrol models

Chapter 12 Chassis electrical system

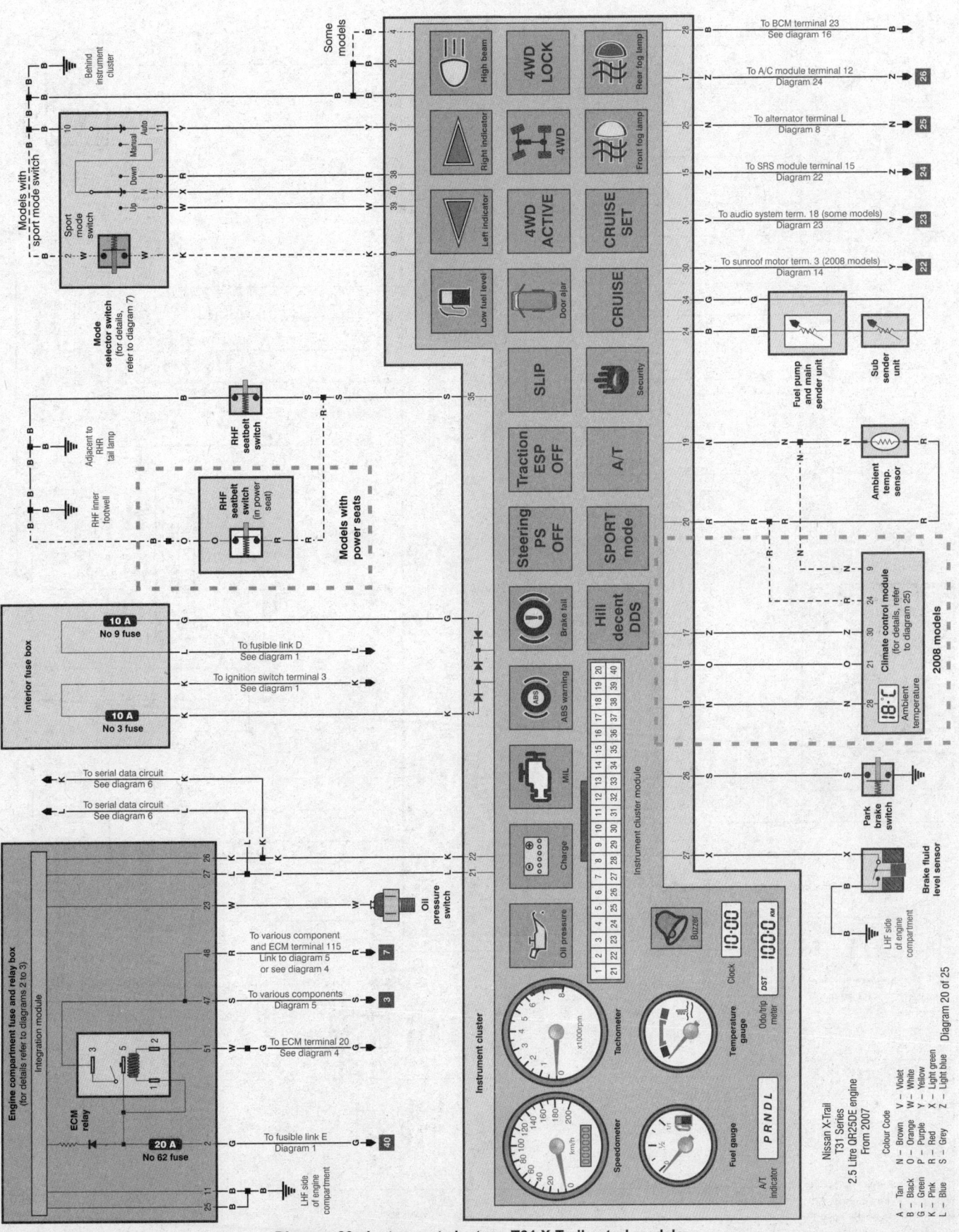

Diagram 20 - Instrument cluster – T31 X-Trail petrol models

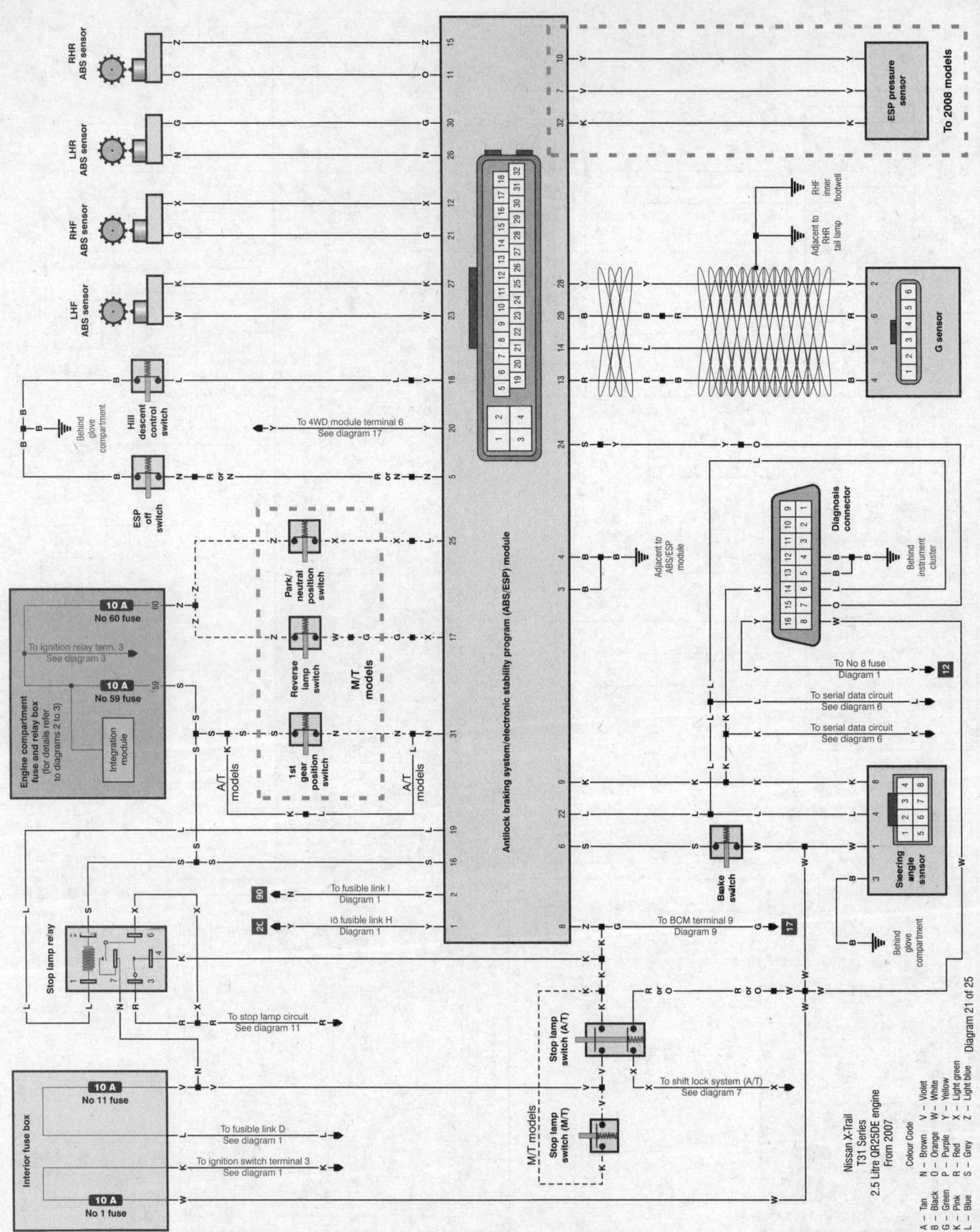

Diagram 21 - Antilock braking system/electronic stability program (ABS/EPS) system – T31 X-Trail petrol models

Chapter 12 Chassis electrical system

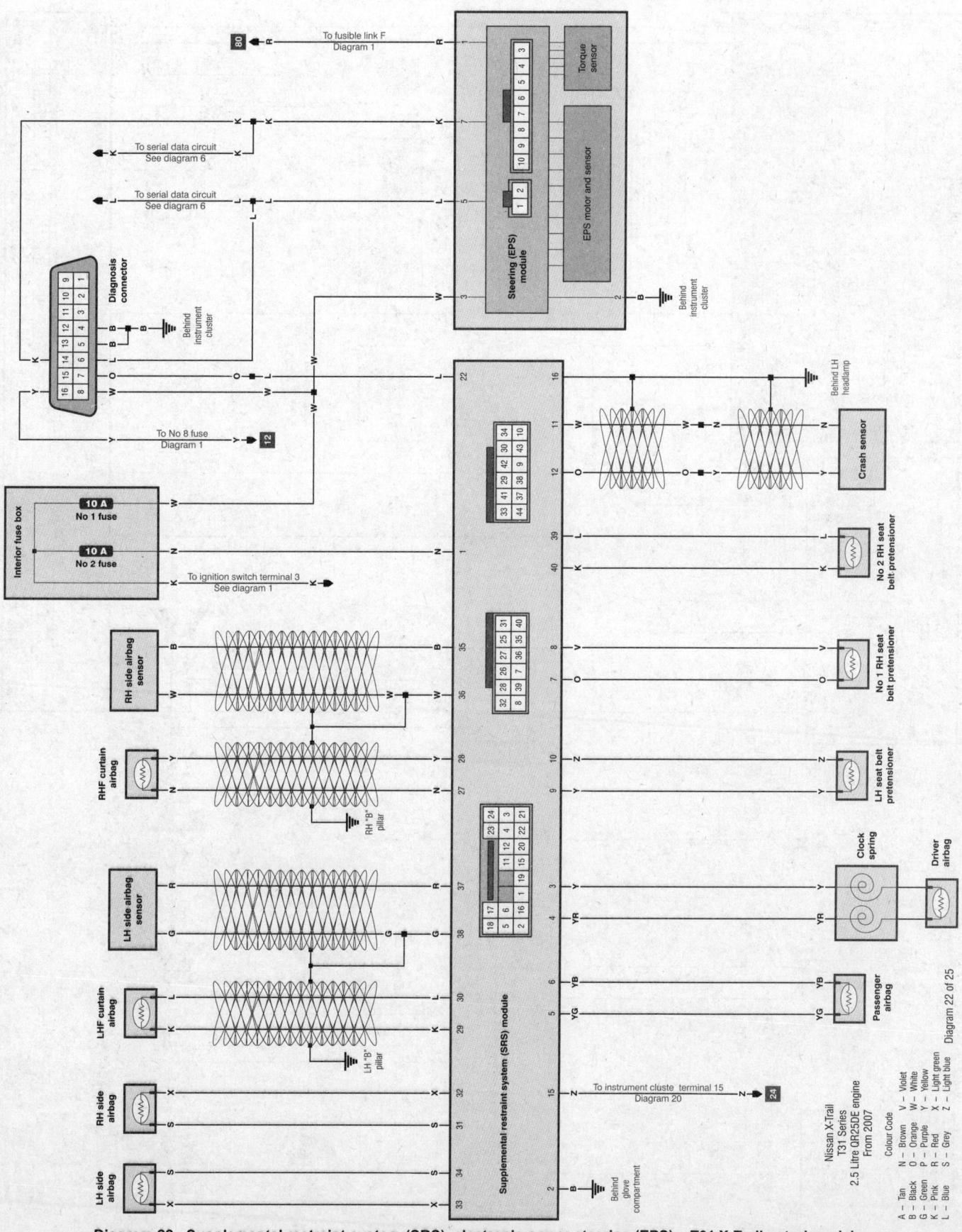

Diagram 22 - Supplemental restraint system (SRS), electronic power steering (EPS) – T31 X-Trail petrol models

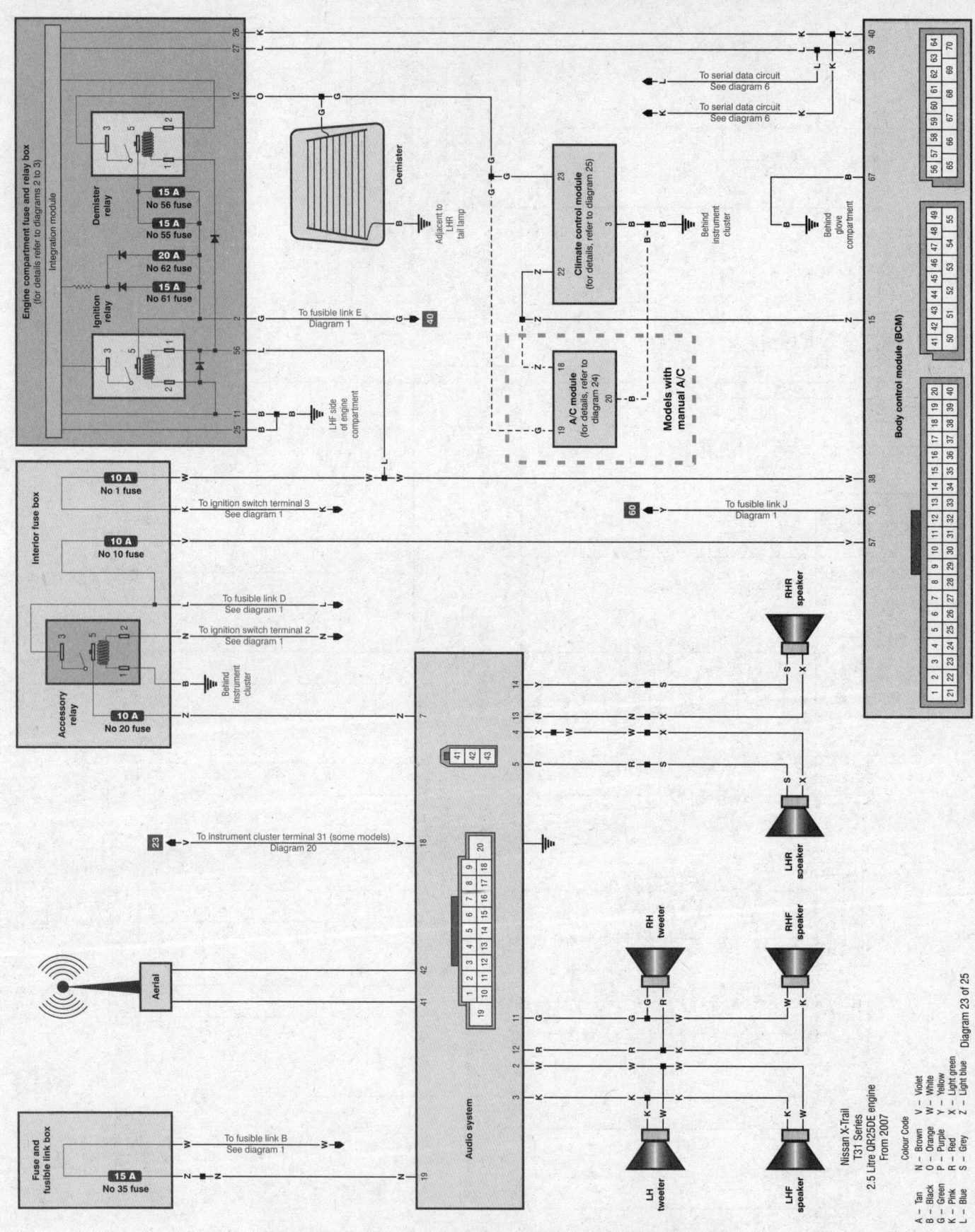

Diagram 23 - Audio system and demister – T31 X-Trail petrol models

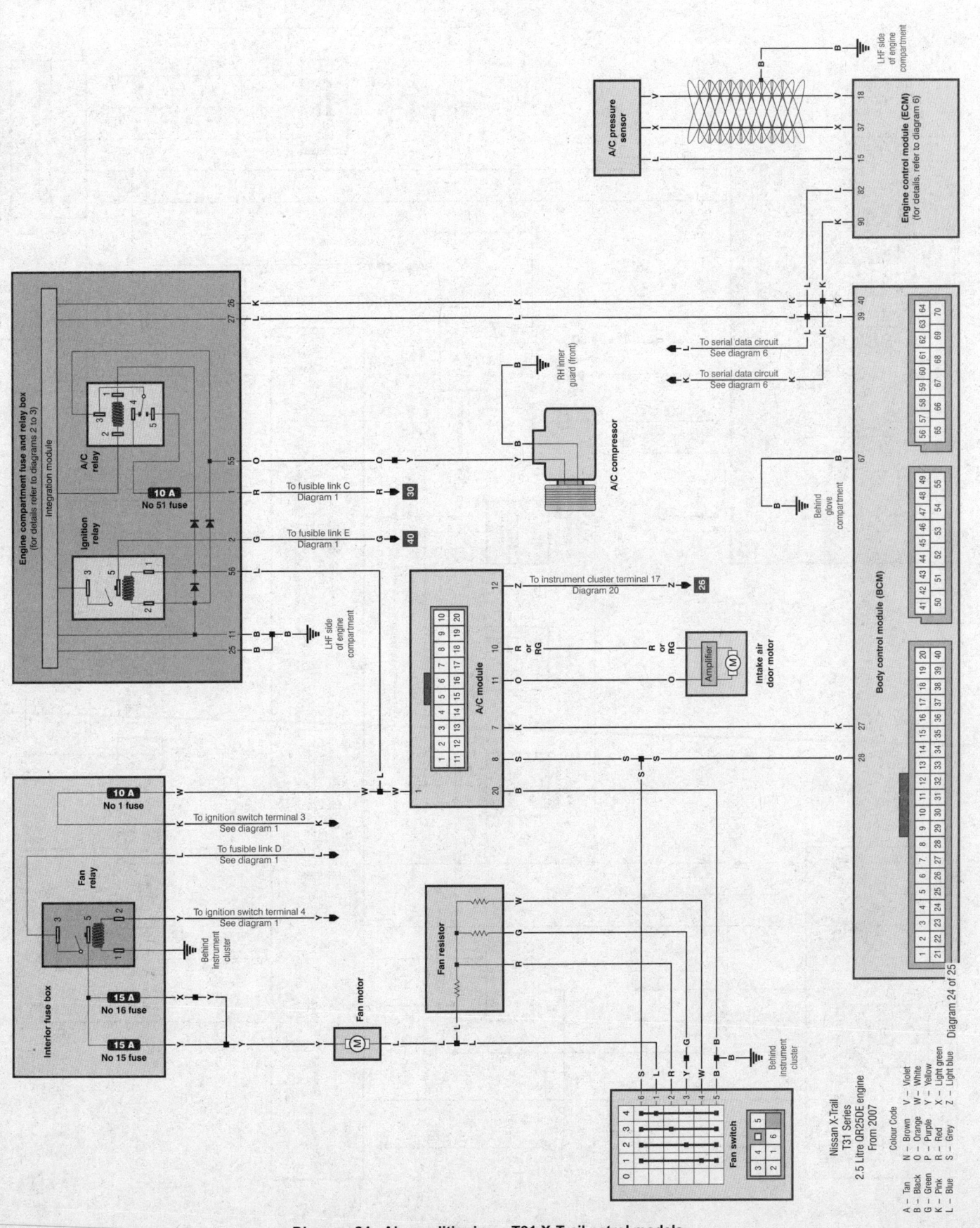

Diagram 24 - Air conditioning – T31 X-Trail petrol models

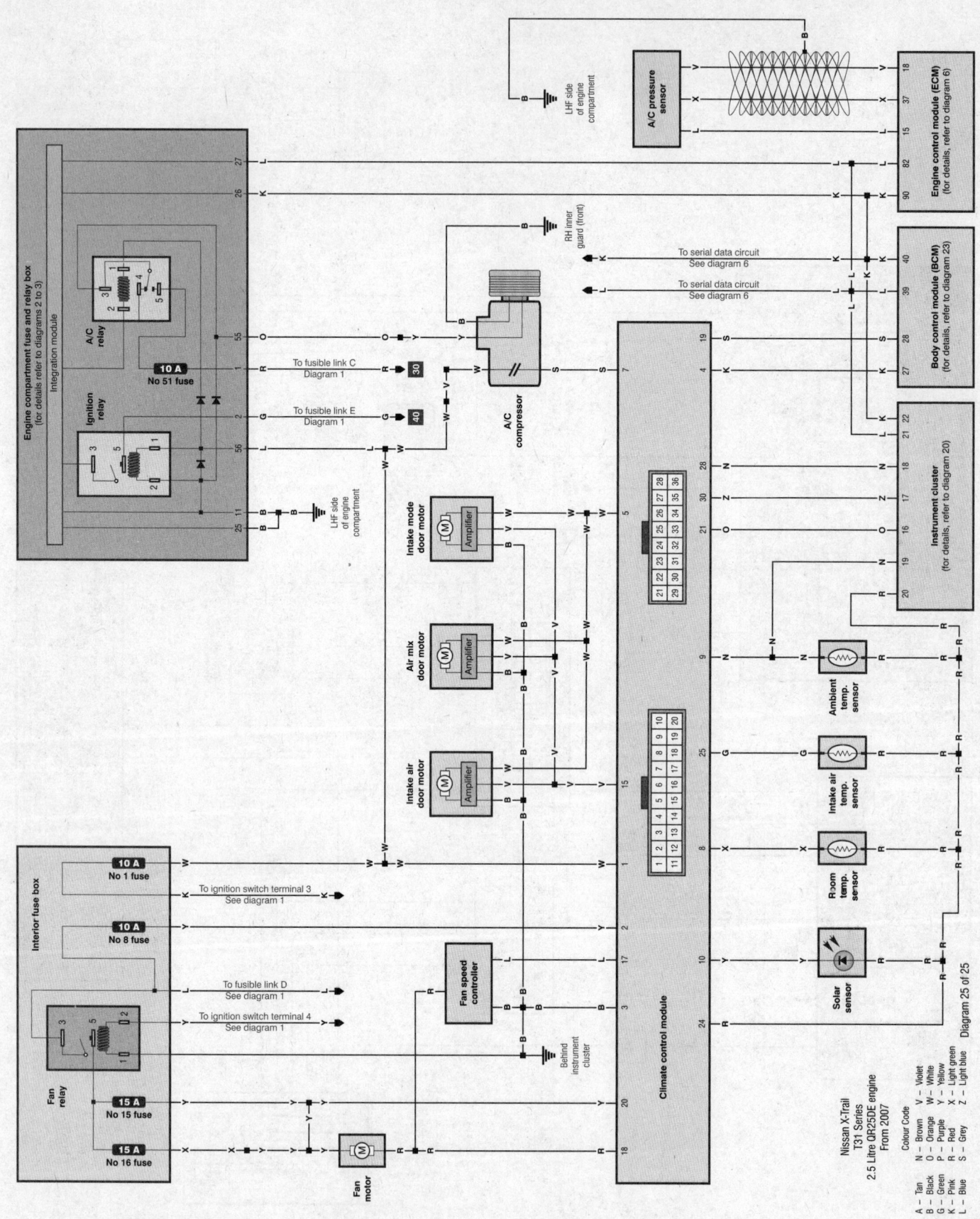

Diagram 25 - Climate control – T31 X-Trail petrol models

Chapter 12 Chassis electrical system

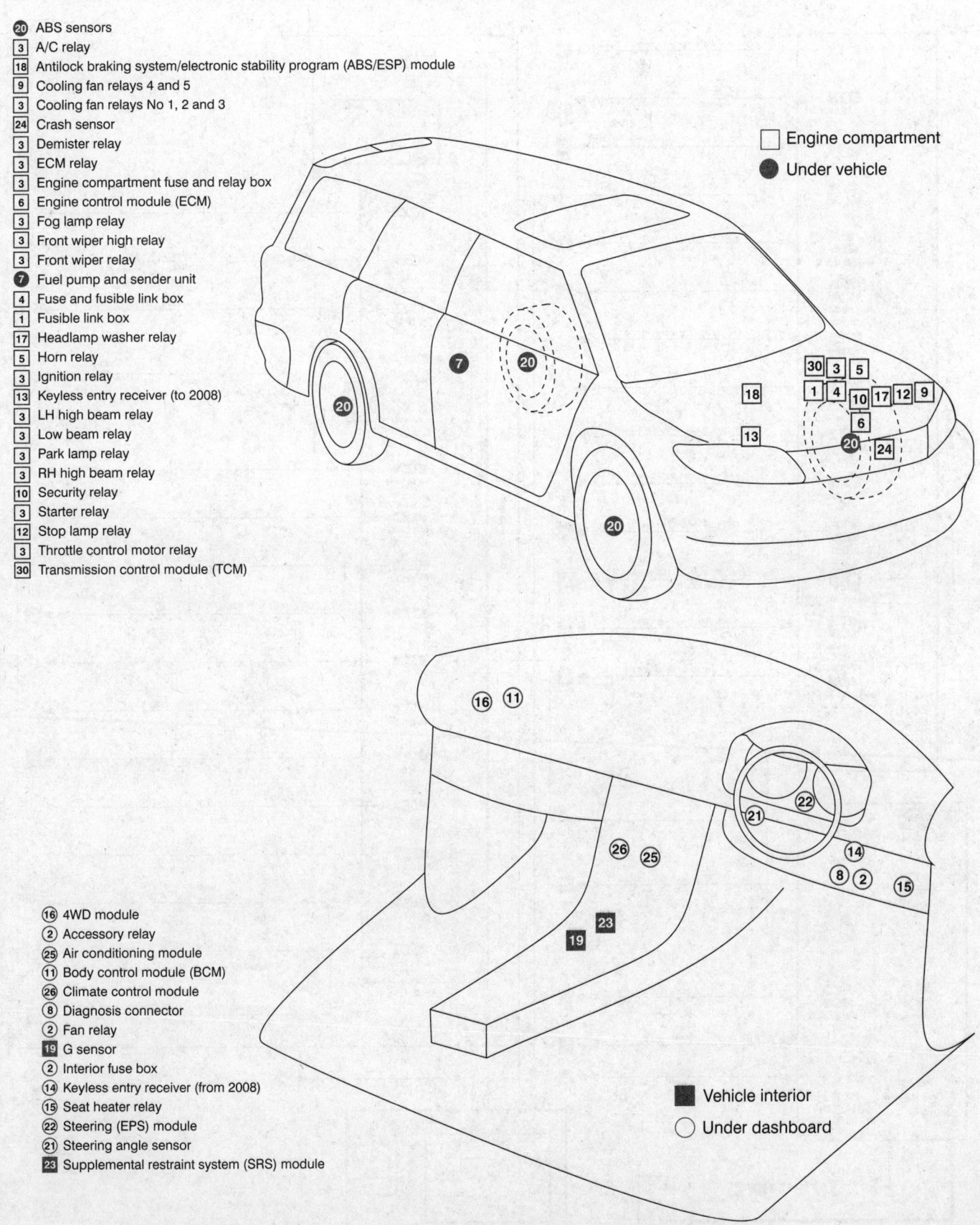

Diagram 26 - Component locations – T31 X-Trail petrol models

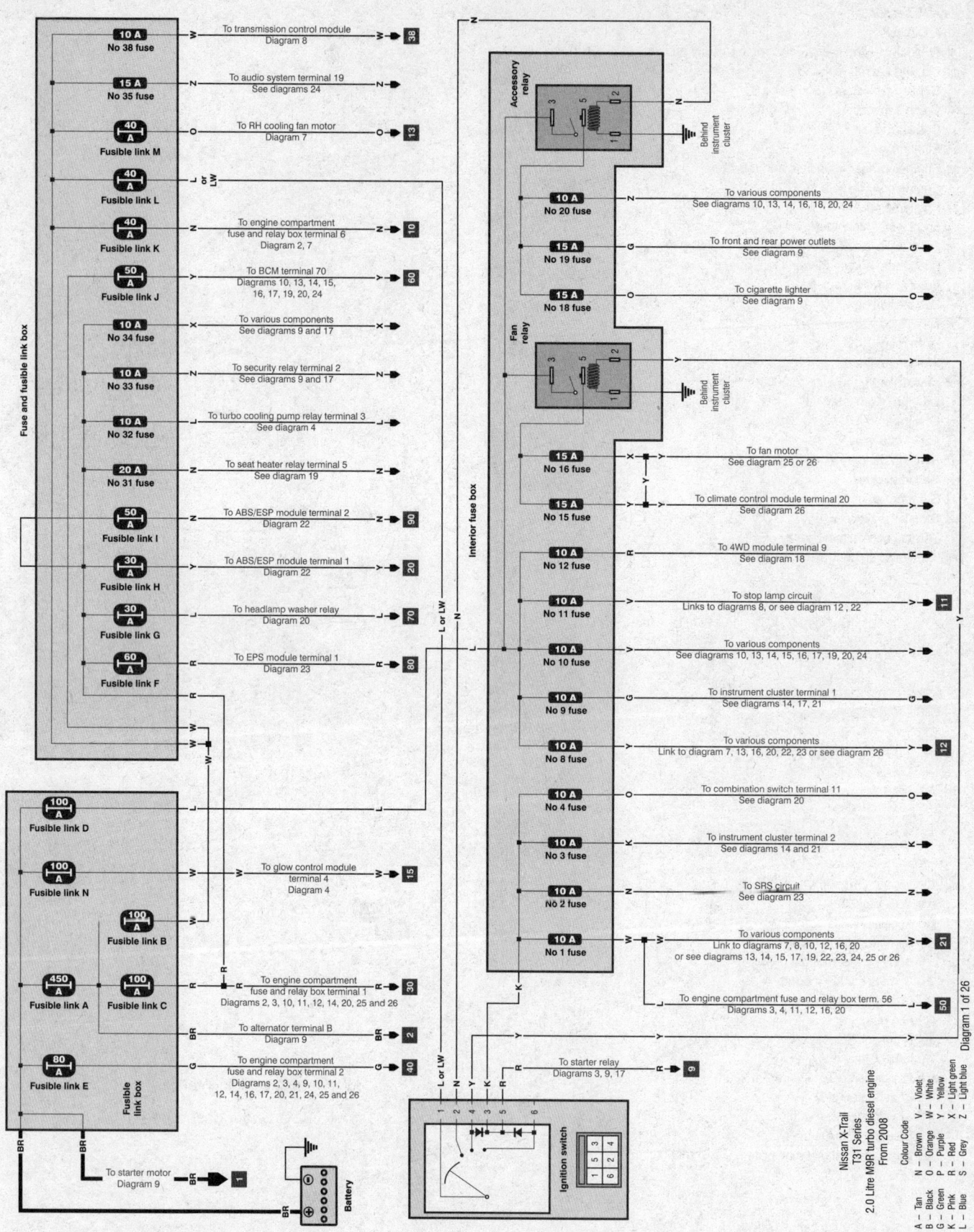

Diagram 1 - Power distribution - fusible link box, fuse and fusible link box, interior fuse box, ignition switch – T31 X-Trail diesel models

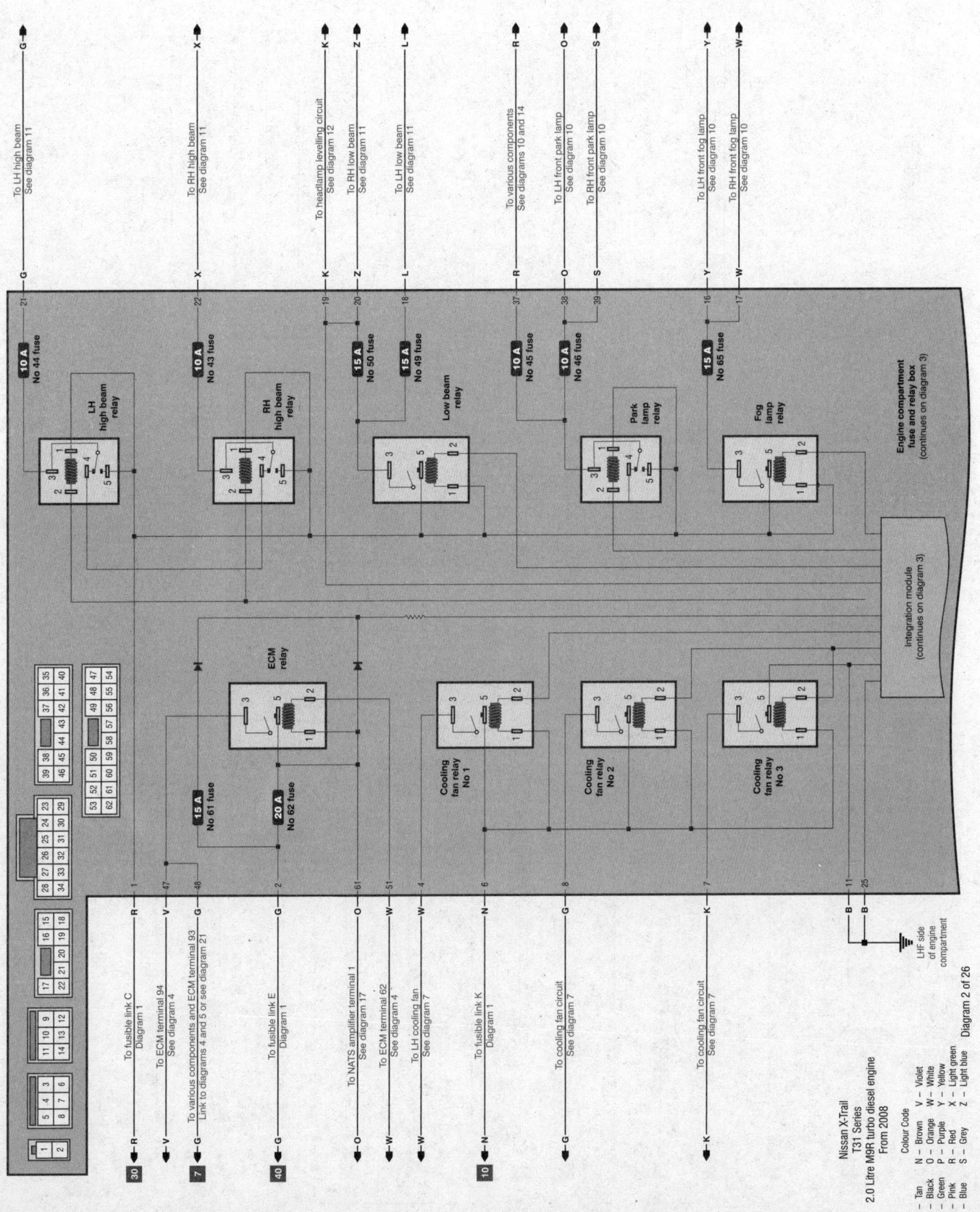

Diagram 2 - Power distribution - Engine compartment fuse and relay box – T31 X-Trail diesel models

12-62 Chapter 12 Chassis electrical system

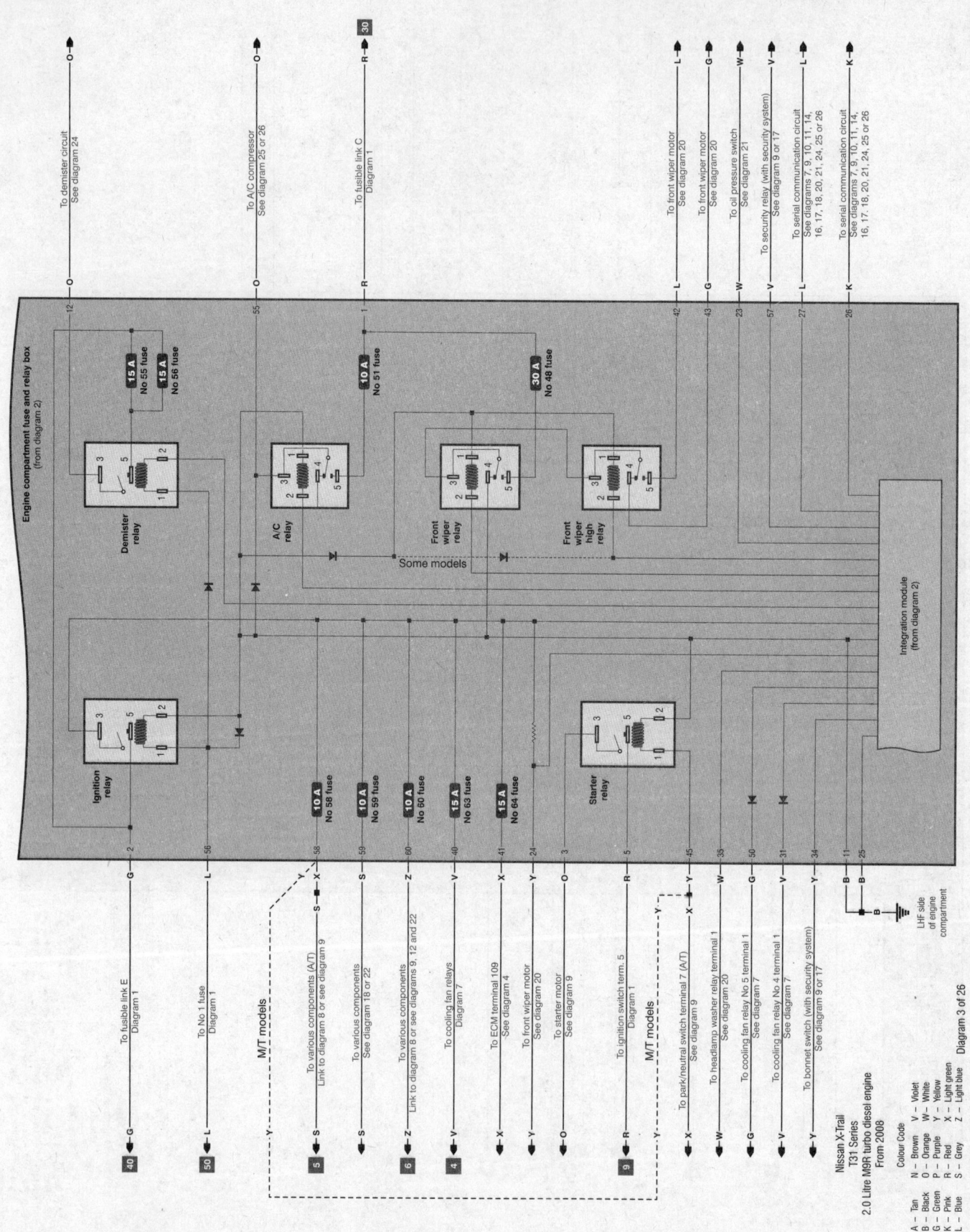

Diagram 3 - Power distribution - Engine compartment fuse and relay box – T31 X-Trail diesel models

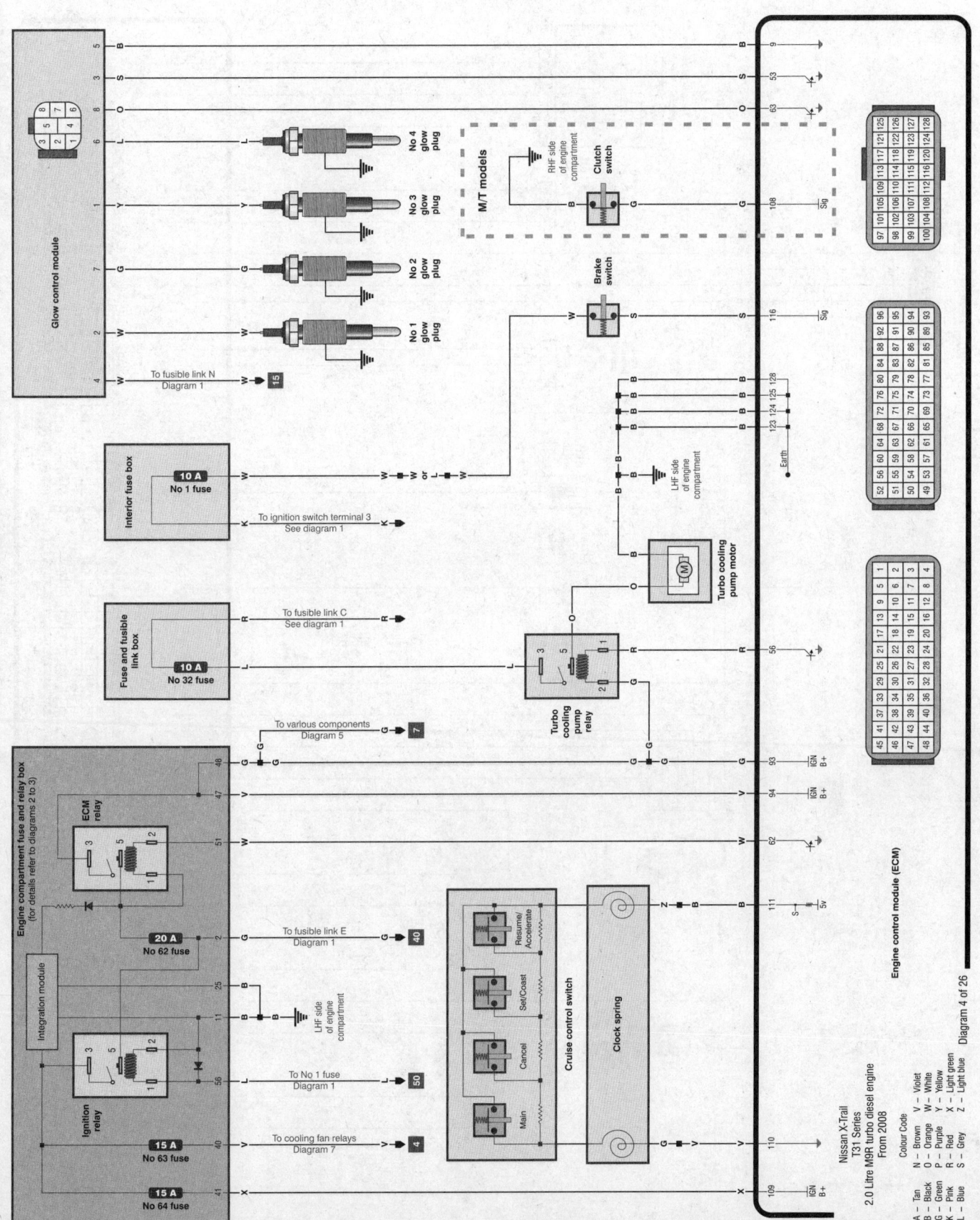

Diagram 4 - ECM power supply and earth circuits, glow plugs, turbo intercooler, cruise control – T31 X-Trail diesel models

12-64 Chapter 12 Chassis electrical system

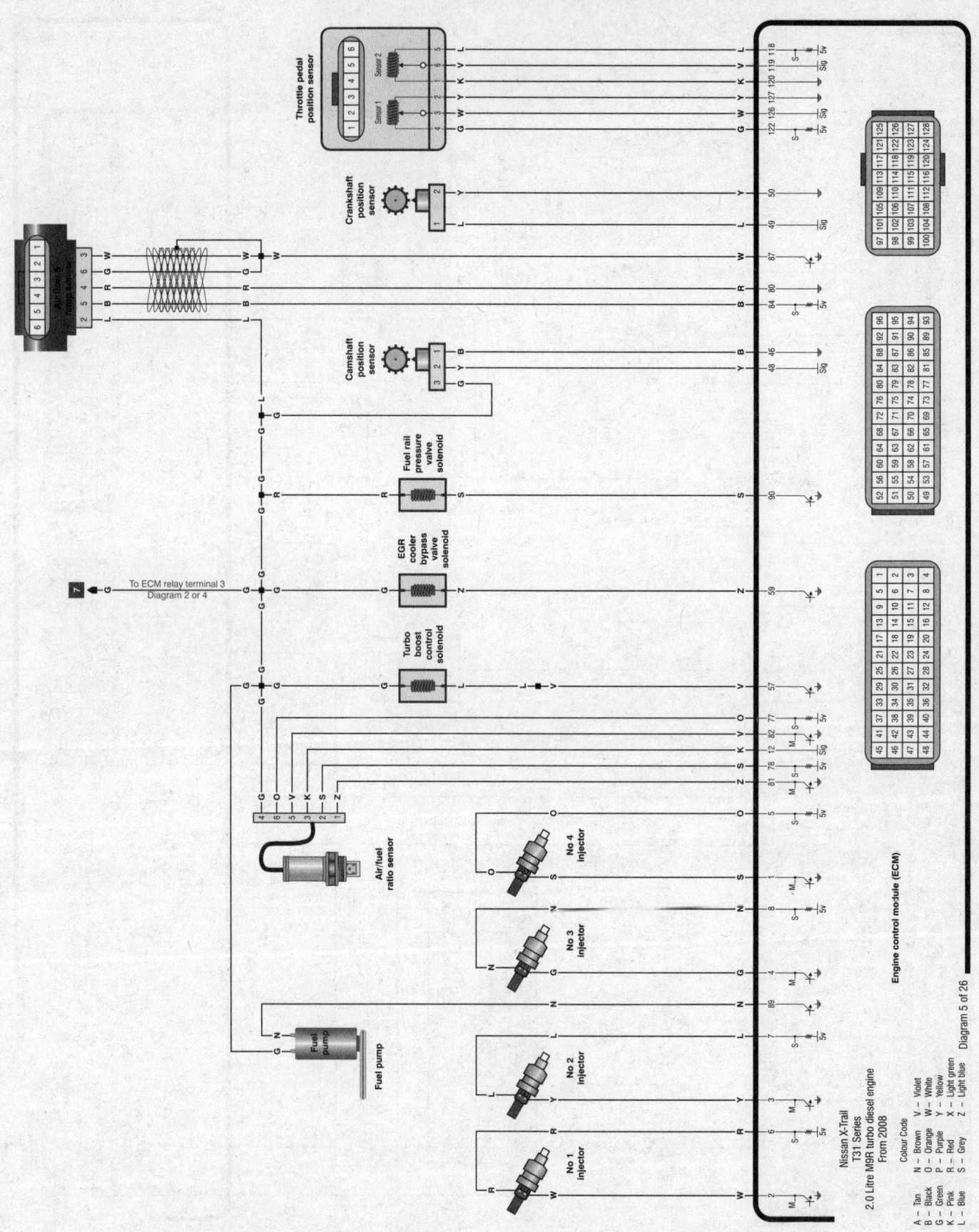

Diagram 5 - Fuel pump, fuel injectors, various sensors and solenoids – T31 X-Trail diesel models

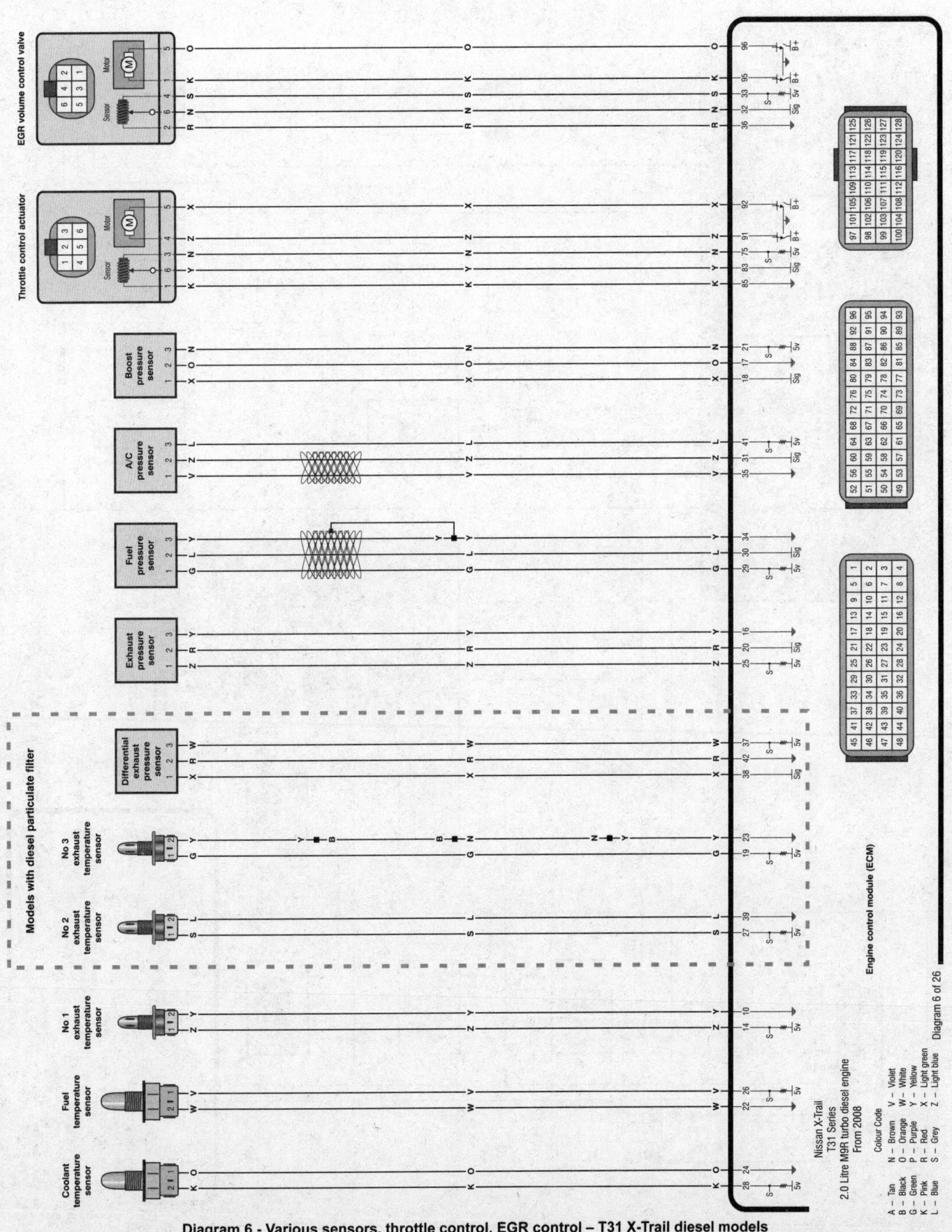

Diagram 6 - Various sensors, throttle control, EGR control – T31 X-Trail diesel models

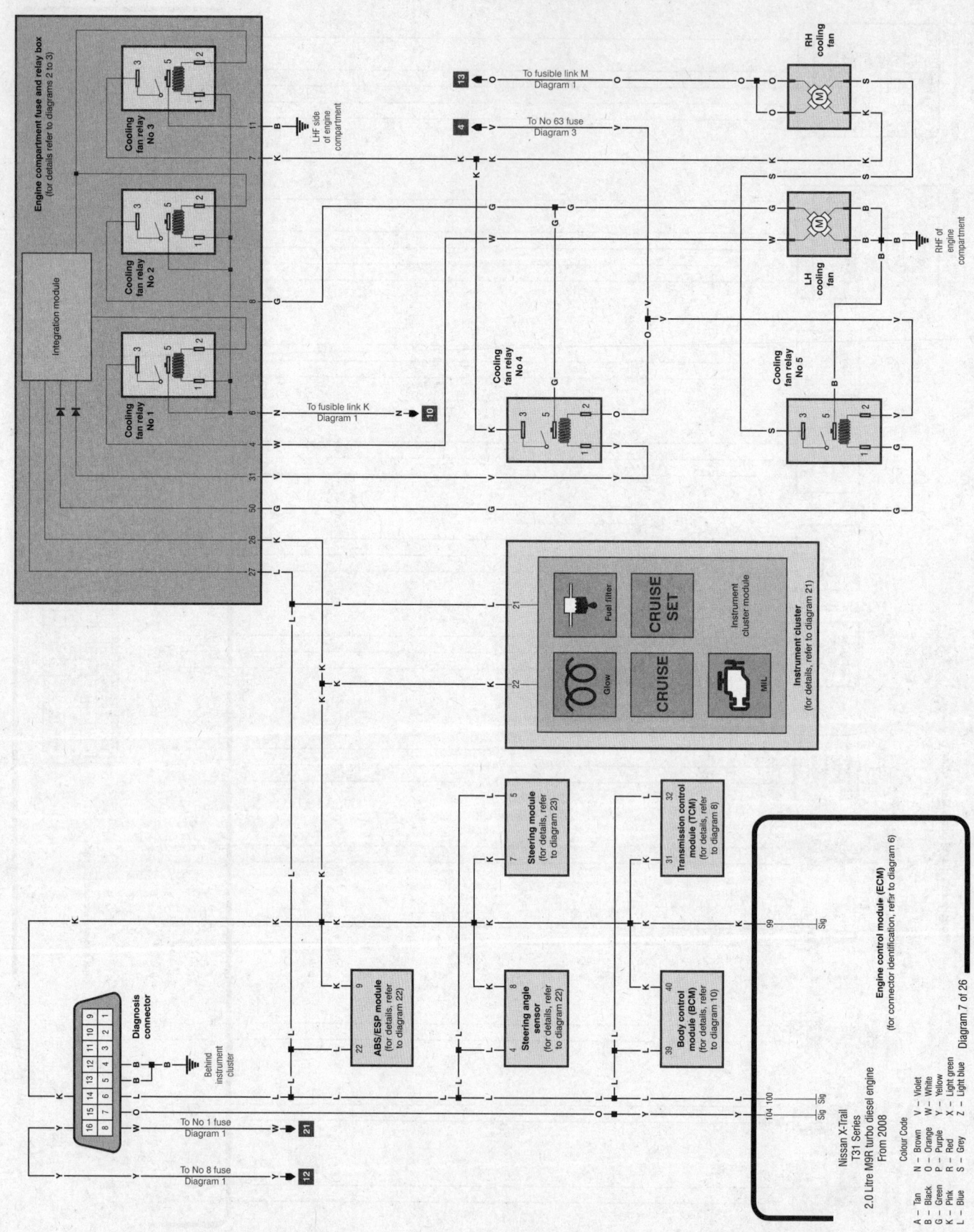

Diagram 7 - Diagnosis connector, serial data communication, cooling fans – T31 X-Trail diesel models

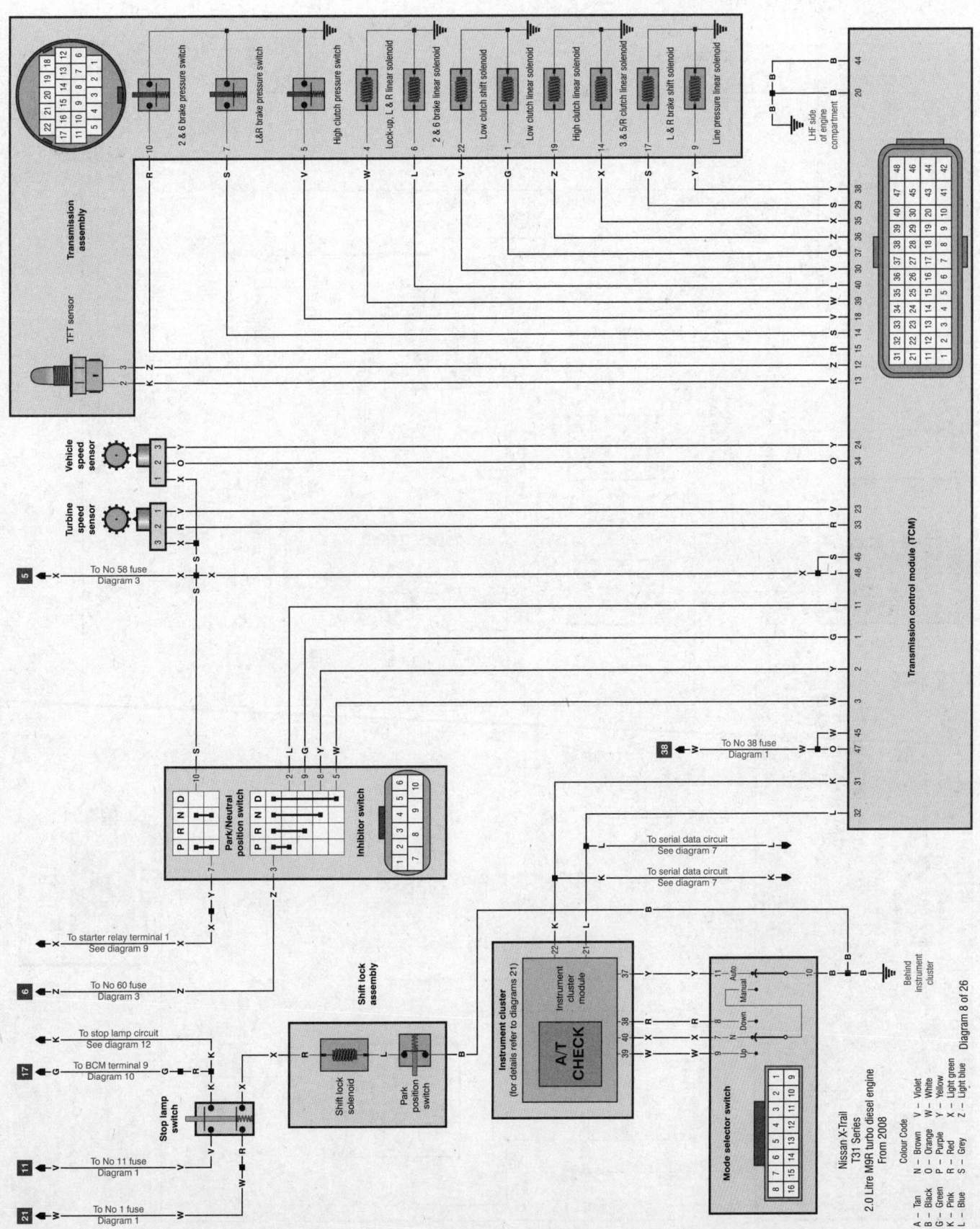

Diagram 8 - Automatic transmission, inhibitor switch, shift lock system – T31 X-Trail diesel models

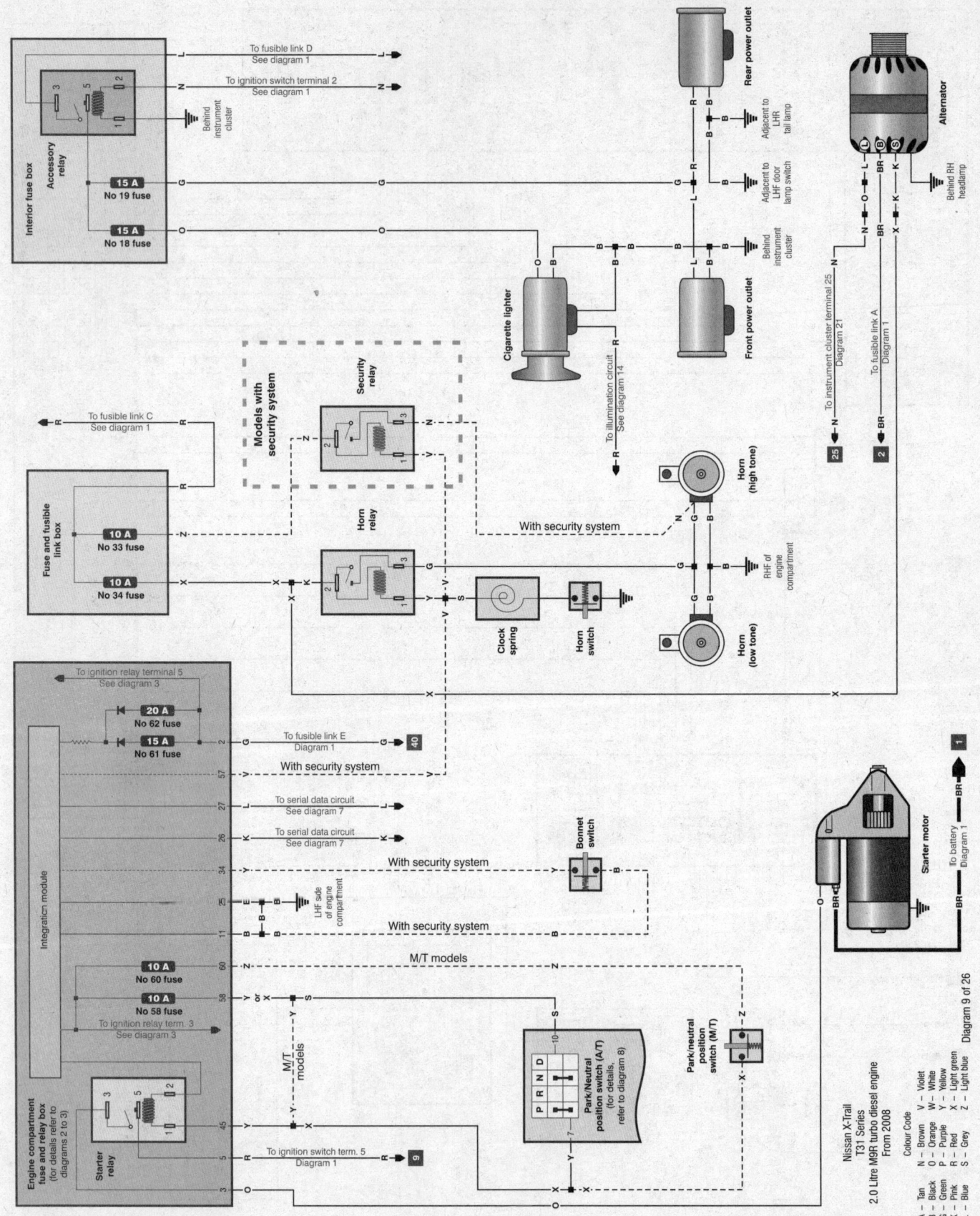

Diagram 9 - Starting system, charging system, cigarette lighter, power outlets, horn and security relay – T31 X-Trail diesel models

Chapter 12 Chassis electrical system

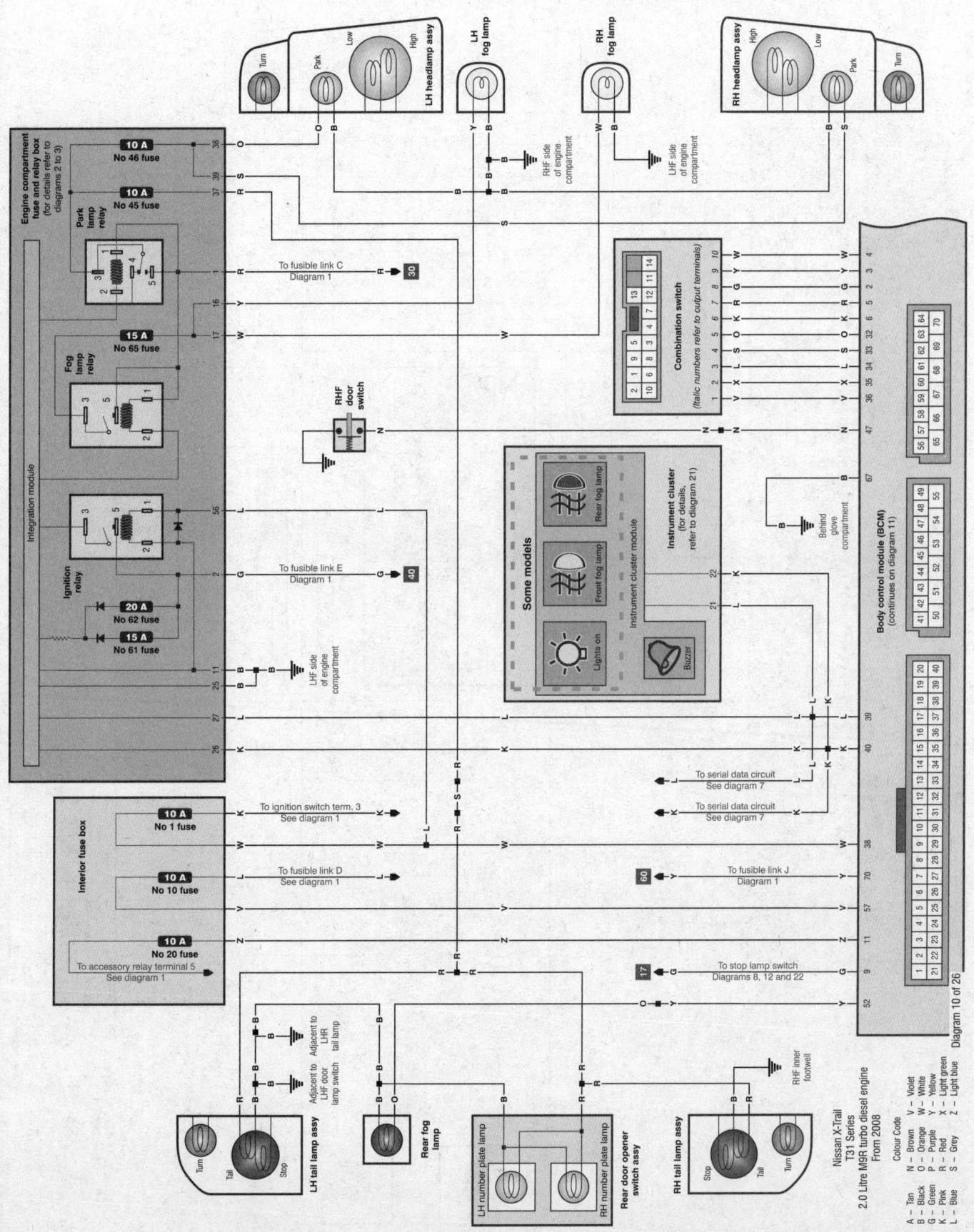

Diagram 10 - Park lamps, front and rear fog lamps, lamp reminder – T31 X-Trail diesel models

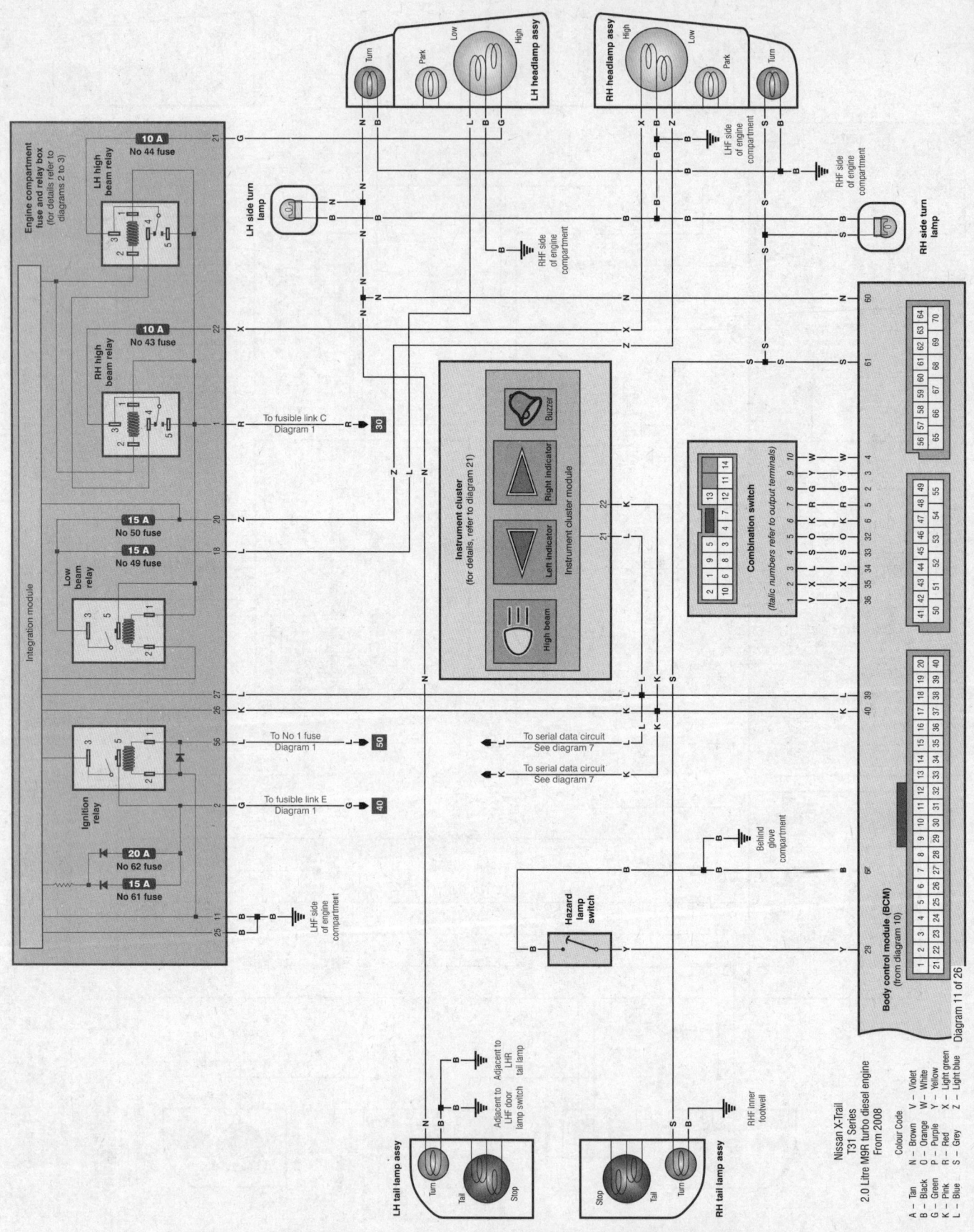

Diagram 11 - Headlamps, turn signal and hazard lamps – T31 X-Trail diesel models

Chapter 12 Chassis electrical system

12-71

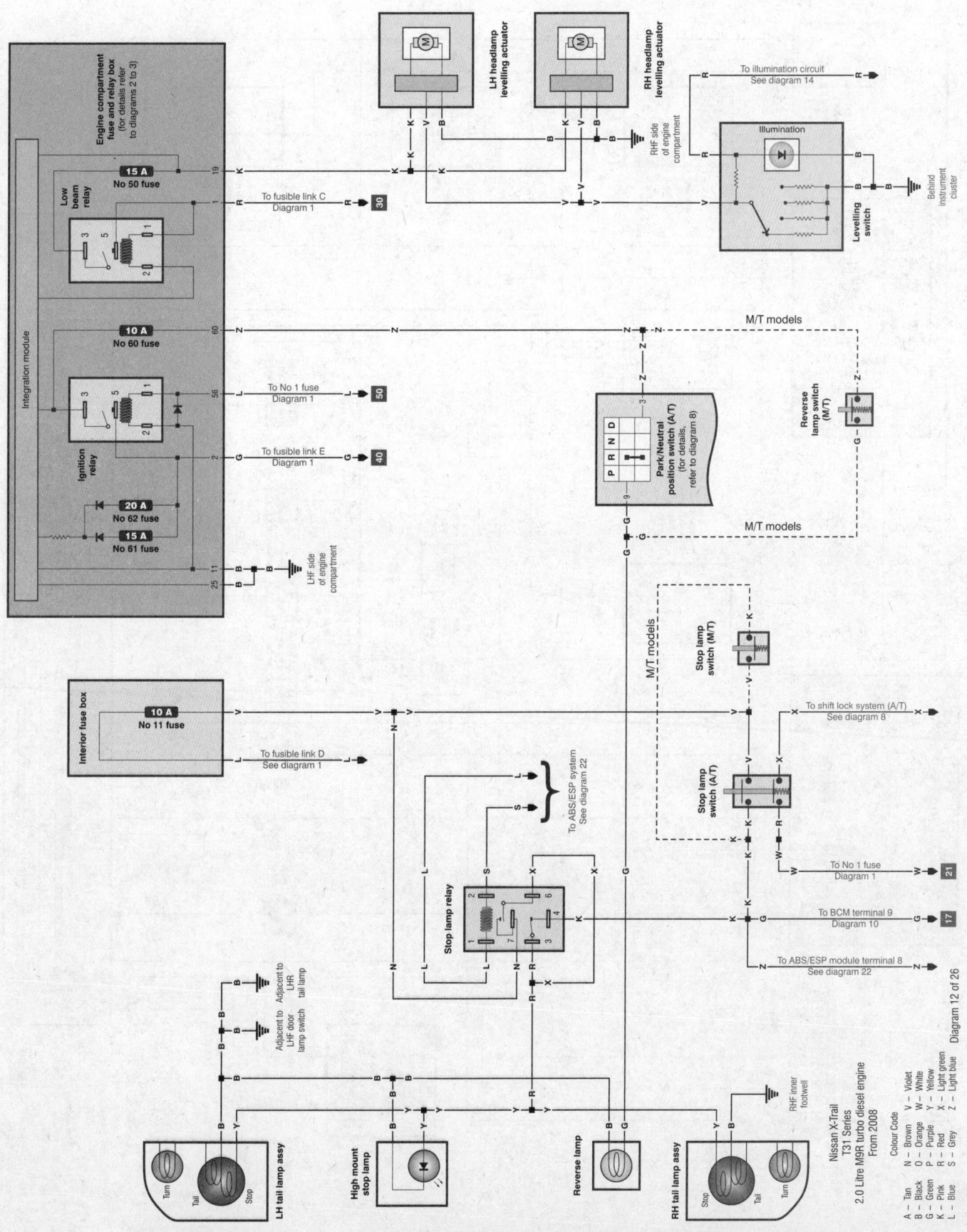

Diagram 12 - Reverse lamps, stop lamps and headlamp levelling system – T31 X-Trail diesel models

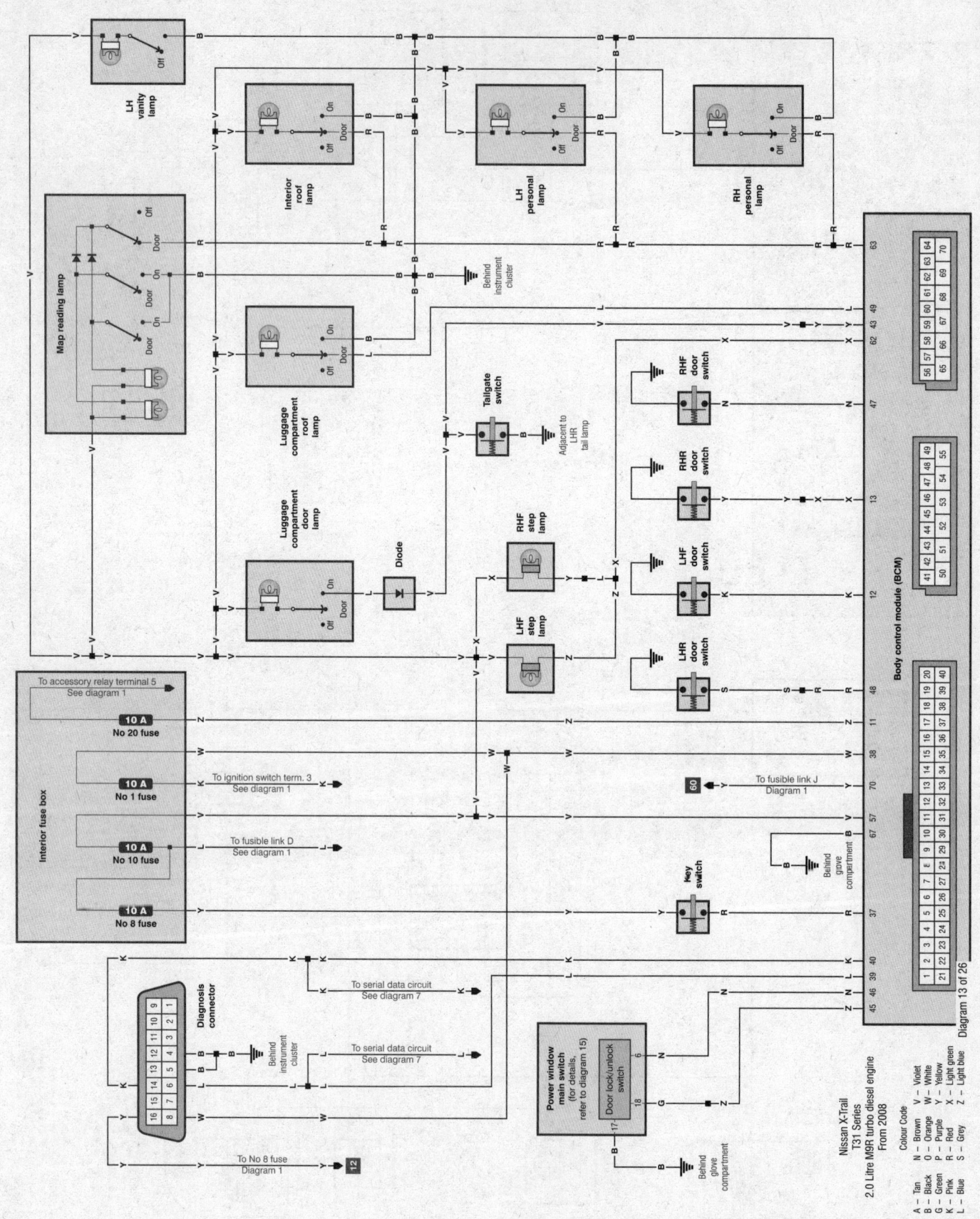

Diagram 13 - Interior lighting – T31 X-Trail diesel models

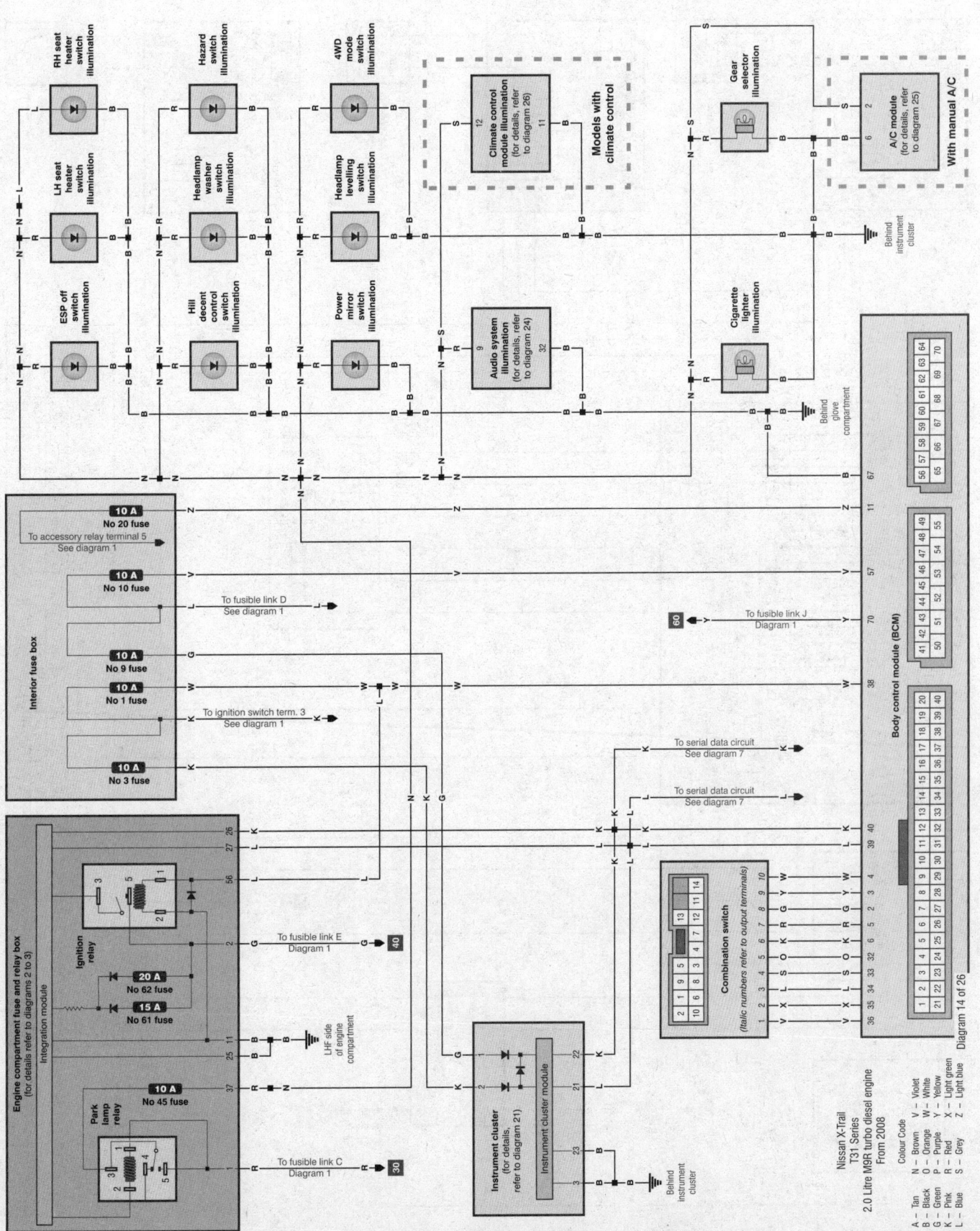

Diagram 14 - Instrument illumination – T31 X-Trail diesel models

12-74 Chapter 12 Chassis electrical system

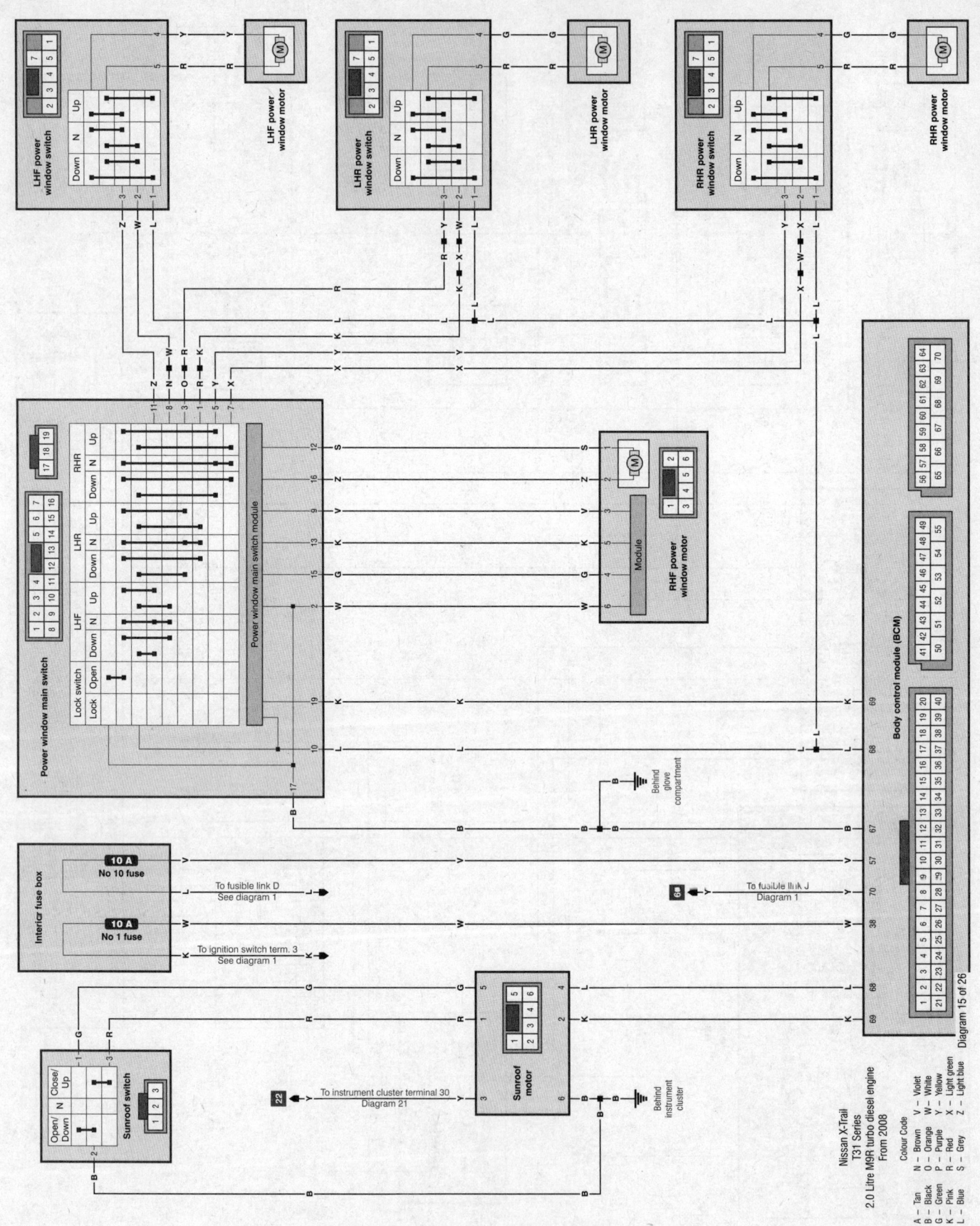

Diagram 15 - Power windows and sunroof – T31 X-Trail diesel models

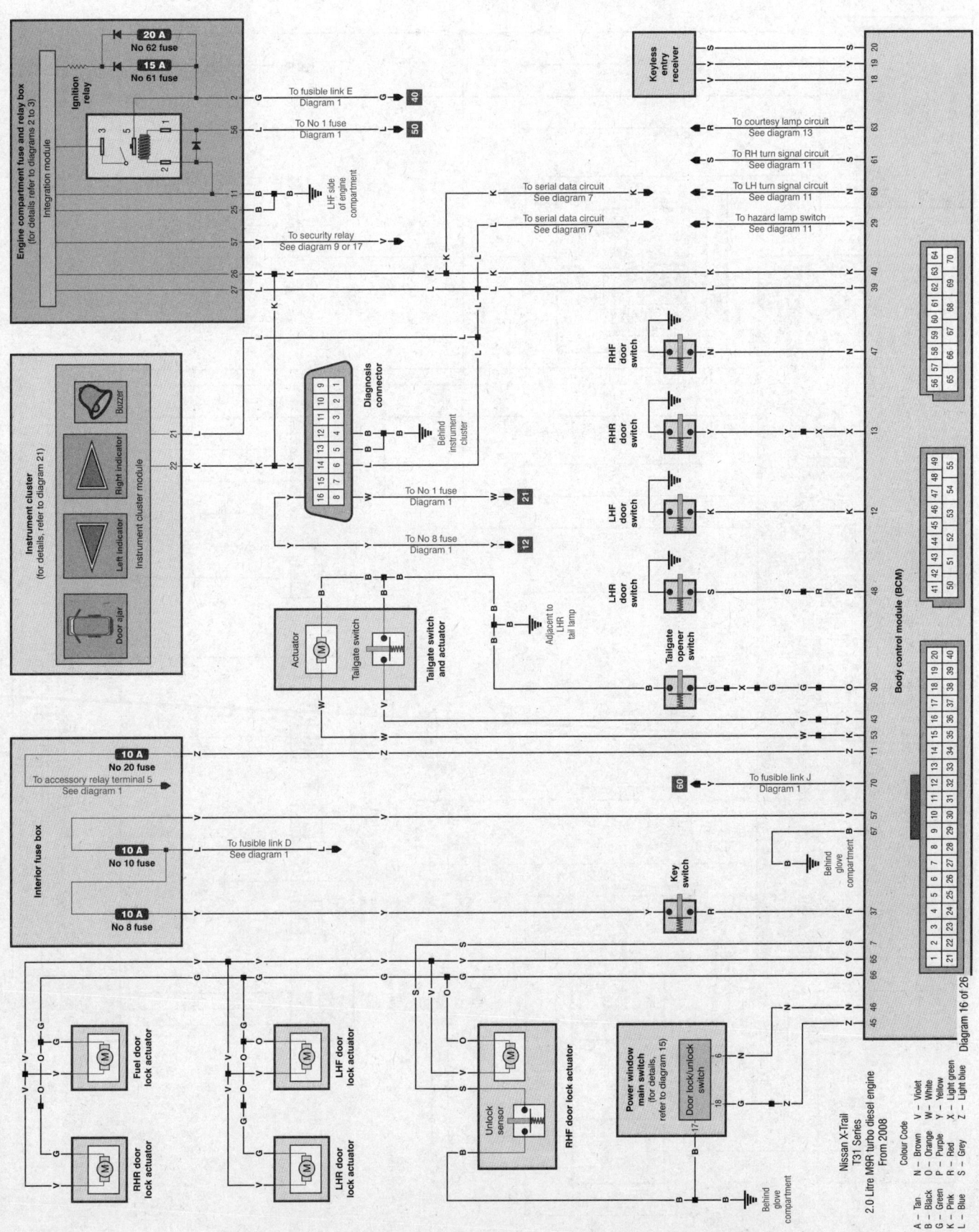

Diagram 16 - Power door locks and keyless entry – T31 X-Trail diesel models

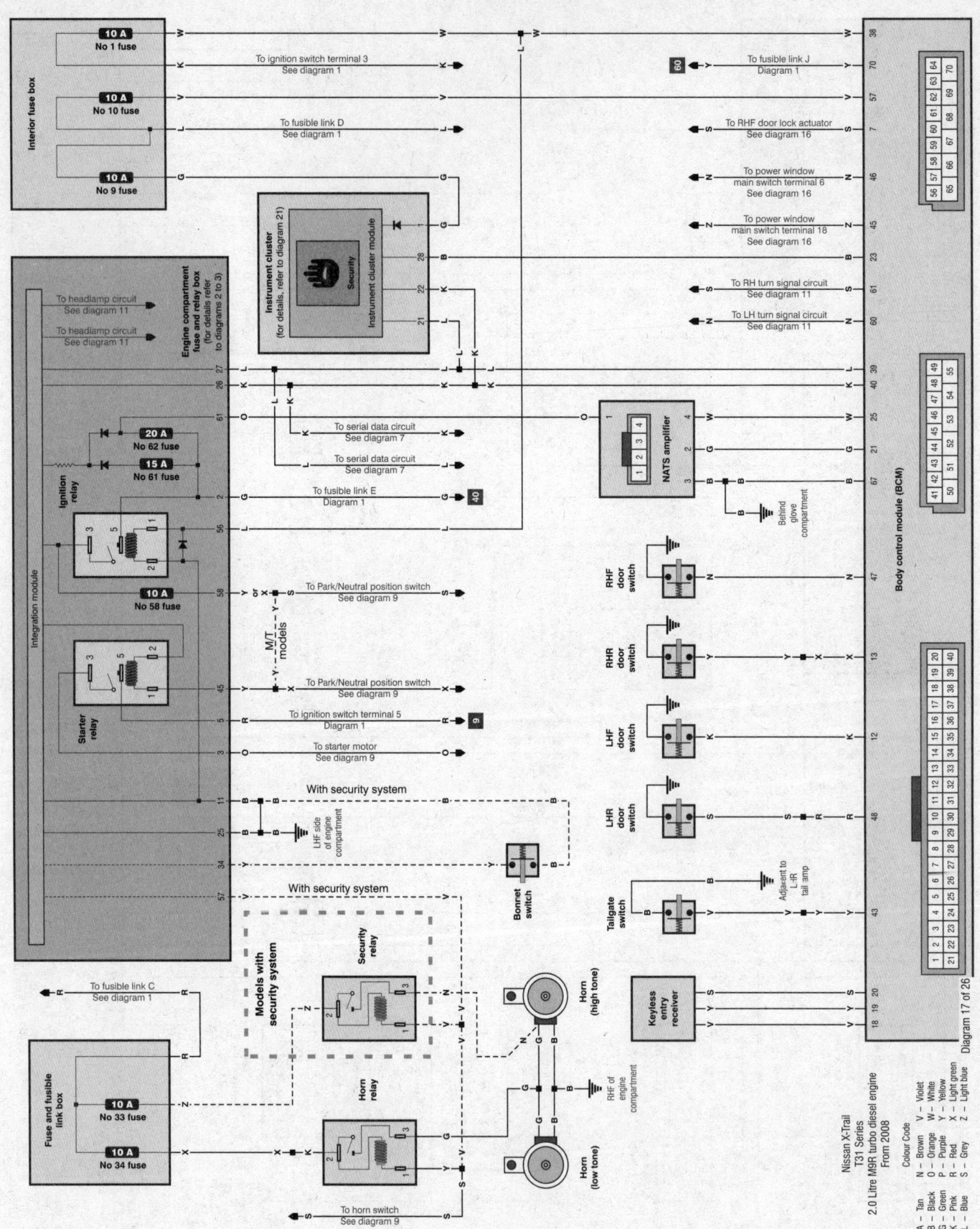

Diagram 17 - Alarm and security systems – T31 X-Trail diesel models

Chapter 12 Chassis electrical system

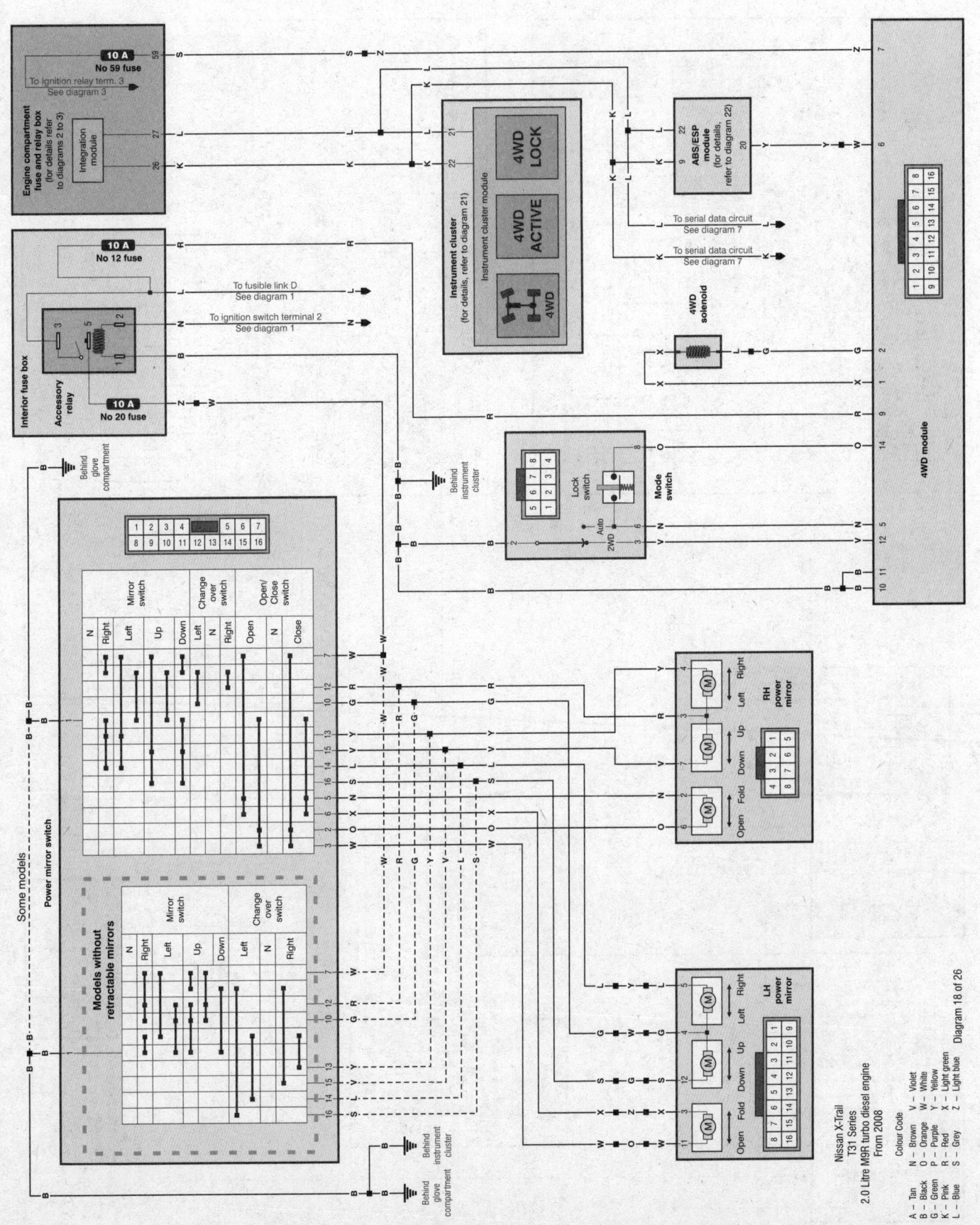

Diagram 18 - Power mirrors, 4WD system – T31 X-Trail diesel models

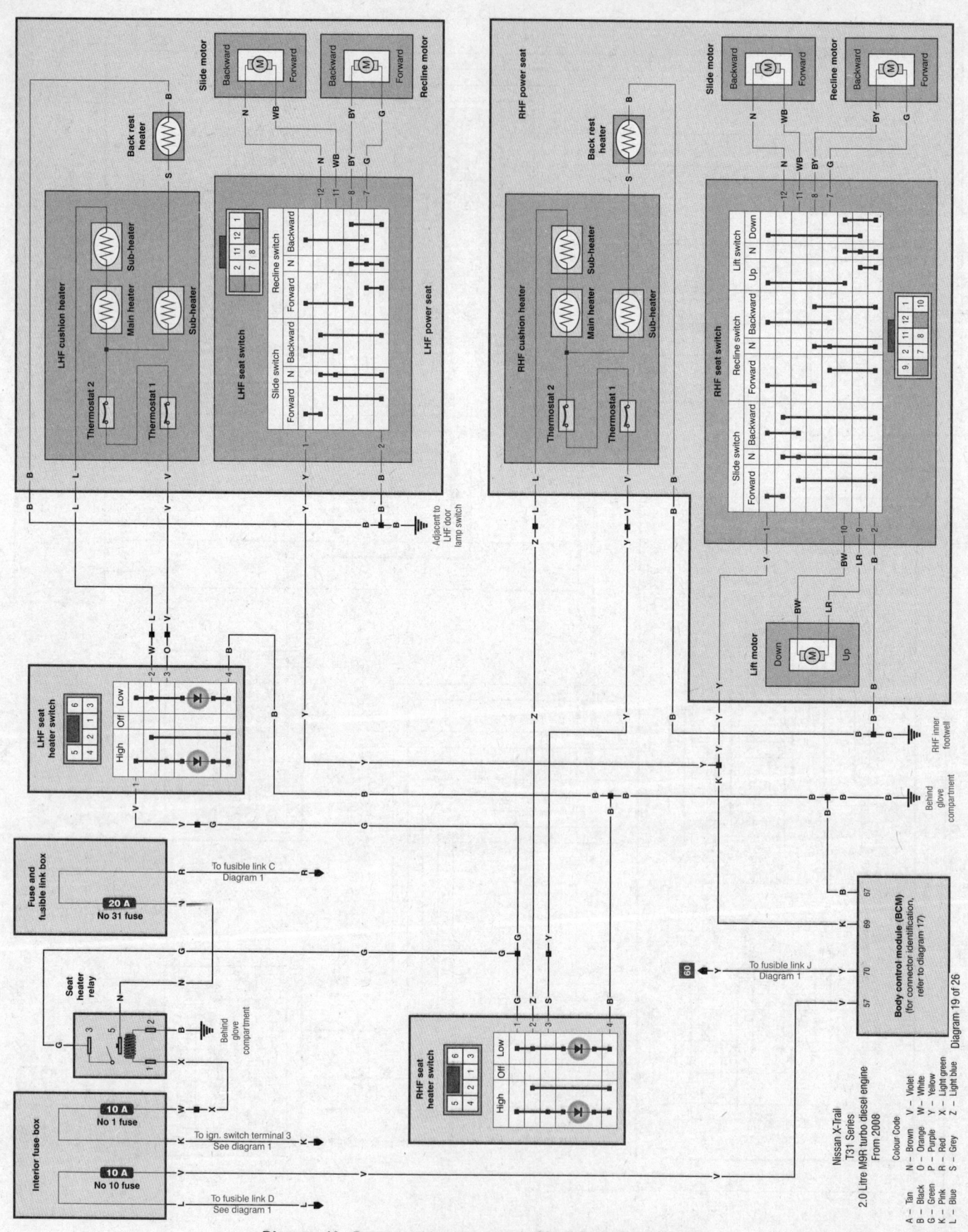

Diagram 19 - Power and heated seats – T31 X-Trail diesel models

Chapter 12 Chassis electrical system

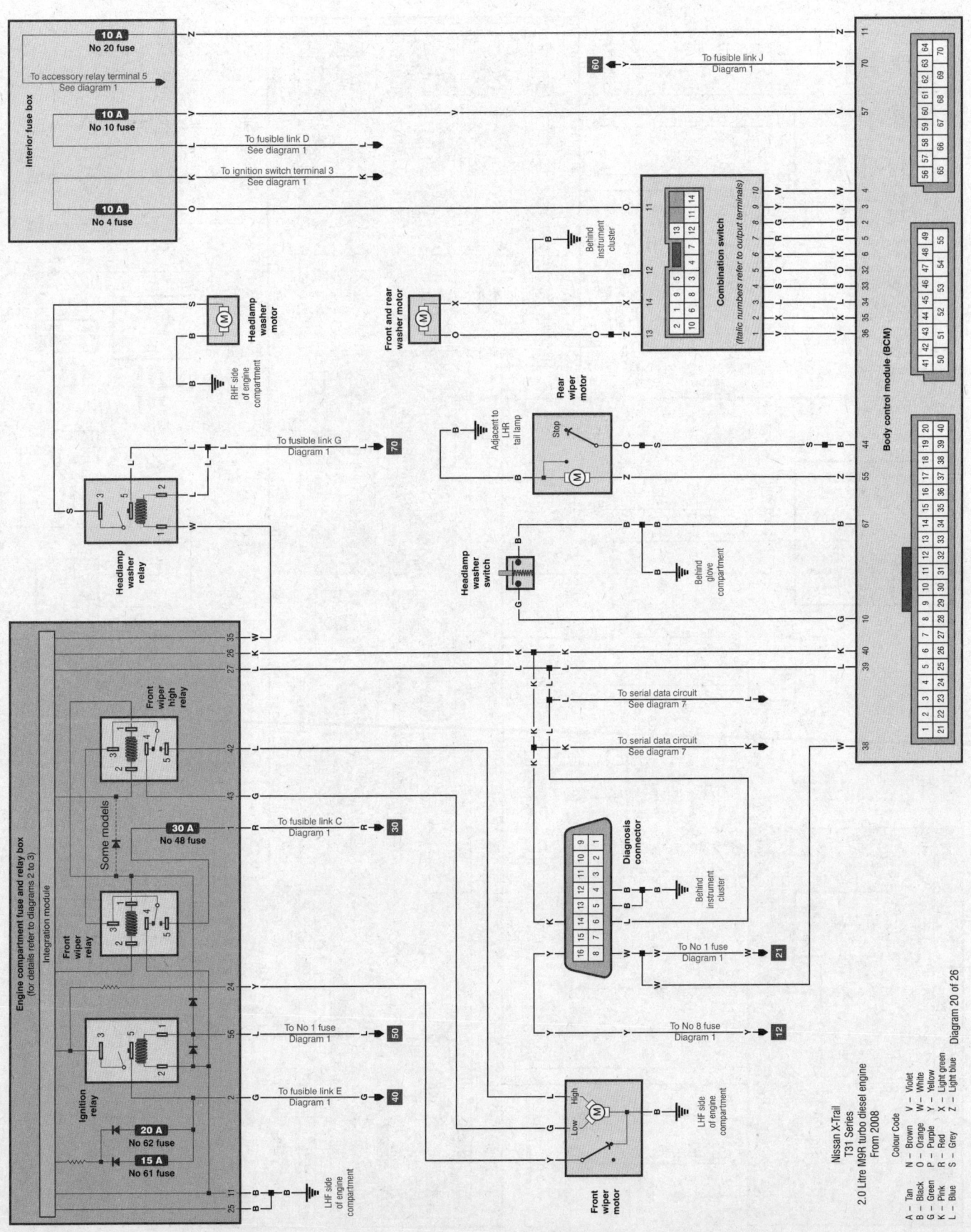

Diagram 20 - Front and rear wipers, washers and headlamp cleaner – T31 X-Trail diesel models

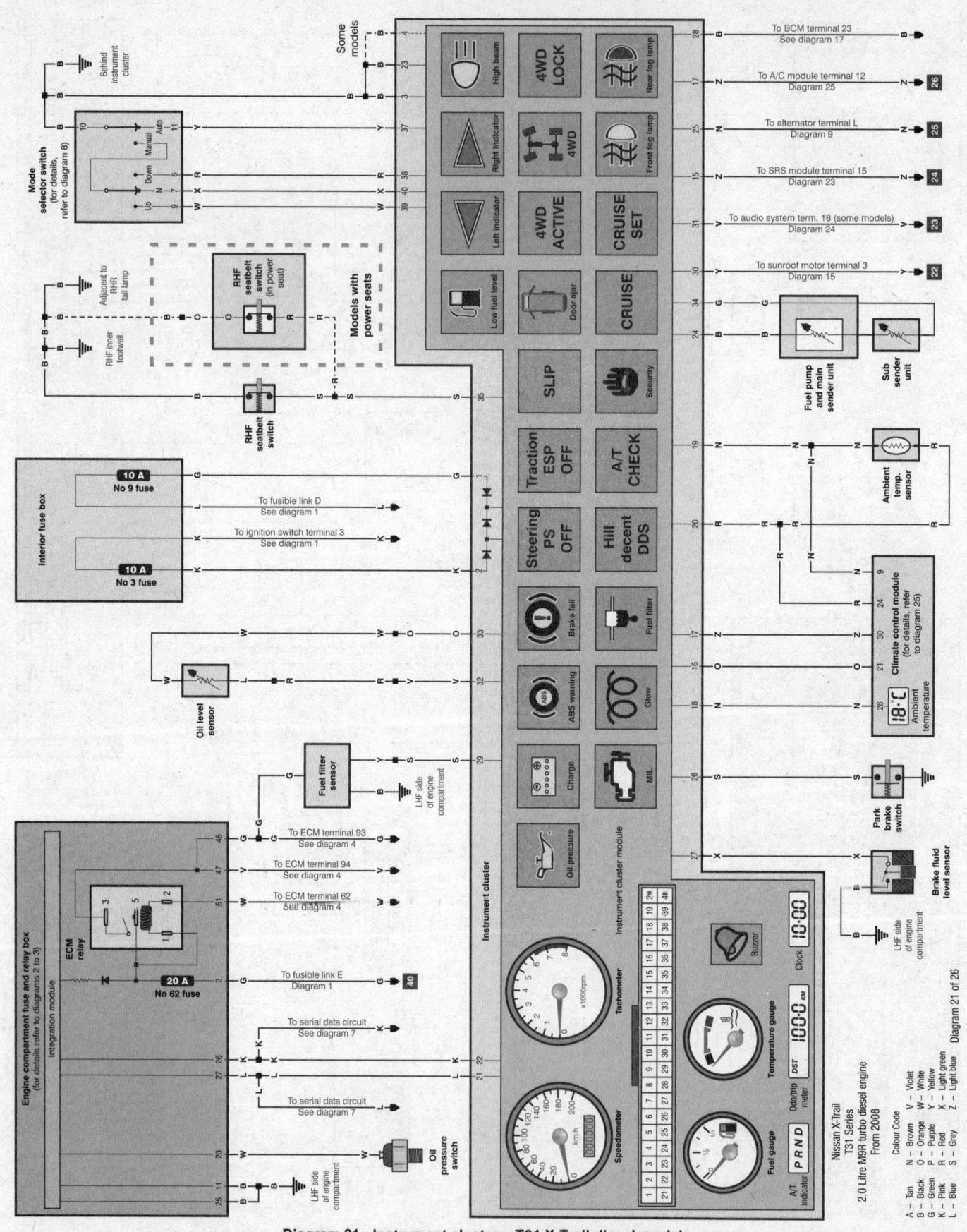

Diagram 21 - Instrument cluster – T31 X-Trail diesel models

Chapter 12 Chassis electrical system 12-81

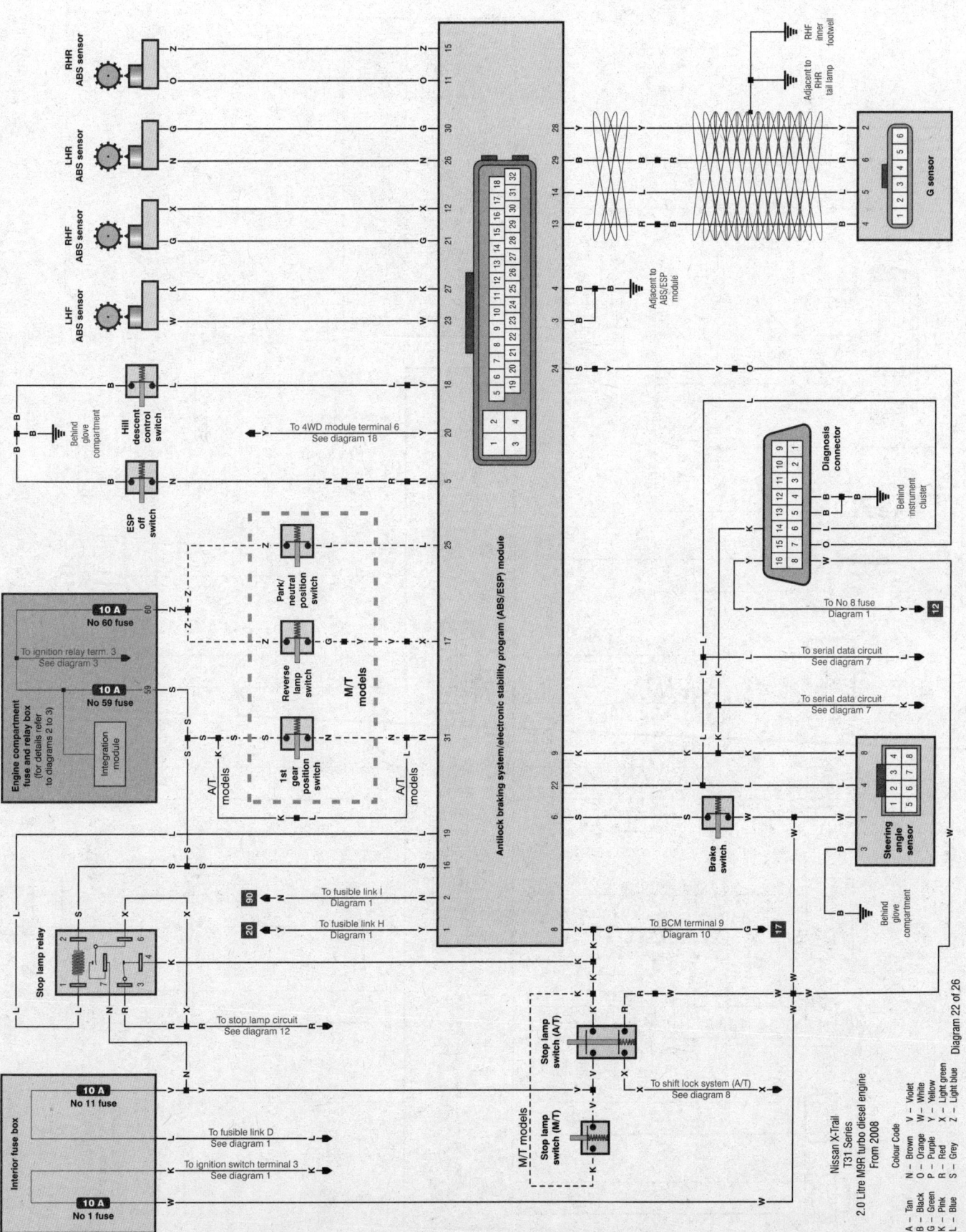

Diagram 22 - Antilock braking system/electronic stability program (ABS/EPS) system – T31 X-Trail diesel models

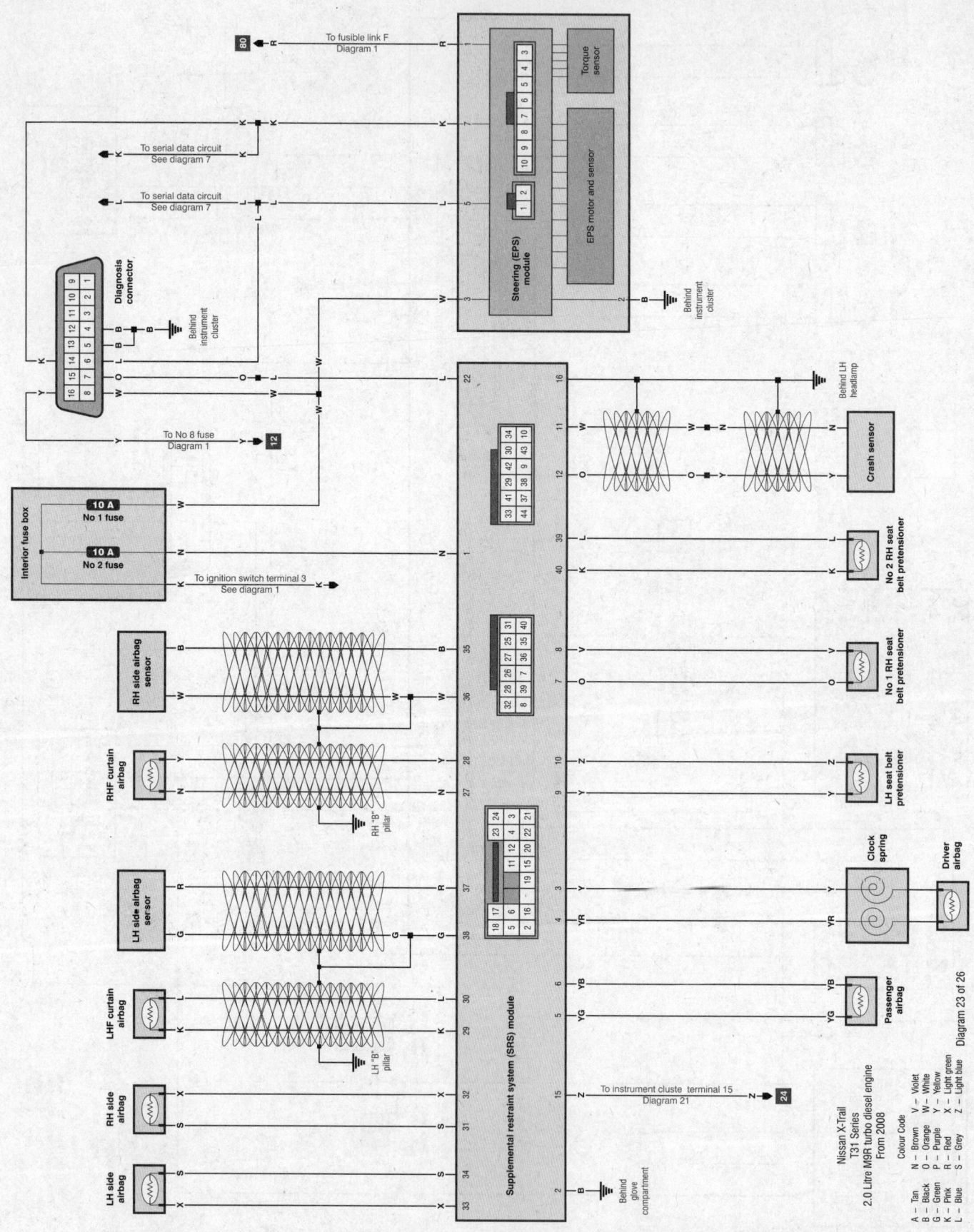

Diagram 23 – Supplemental restraint system (SRS), electronic power steering (EPS) – T31 X-Trail diesel models

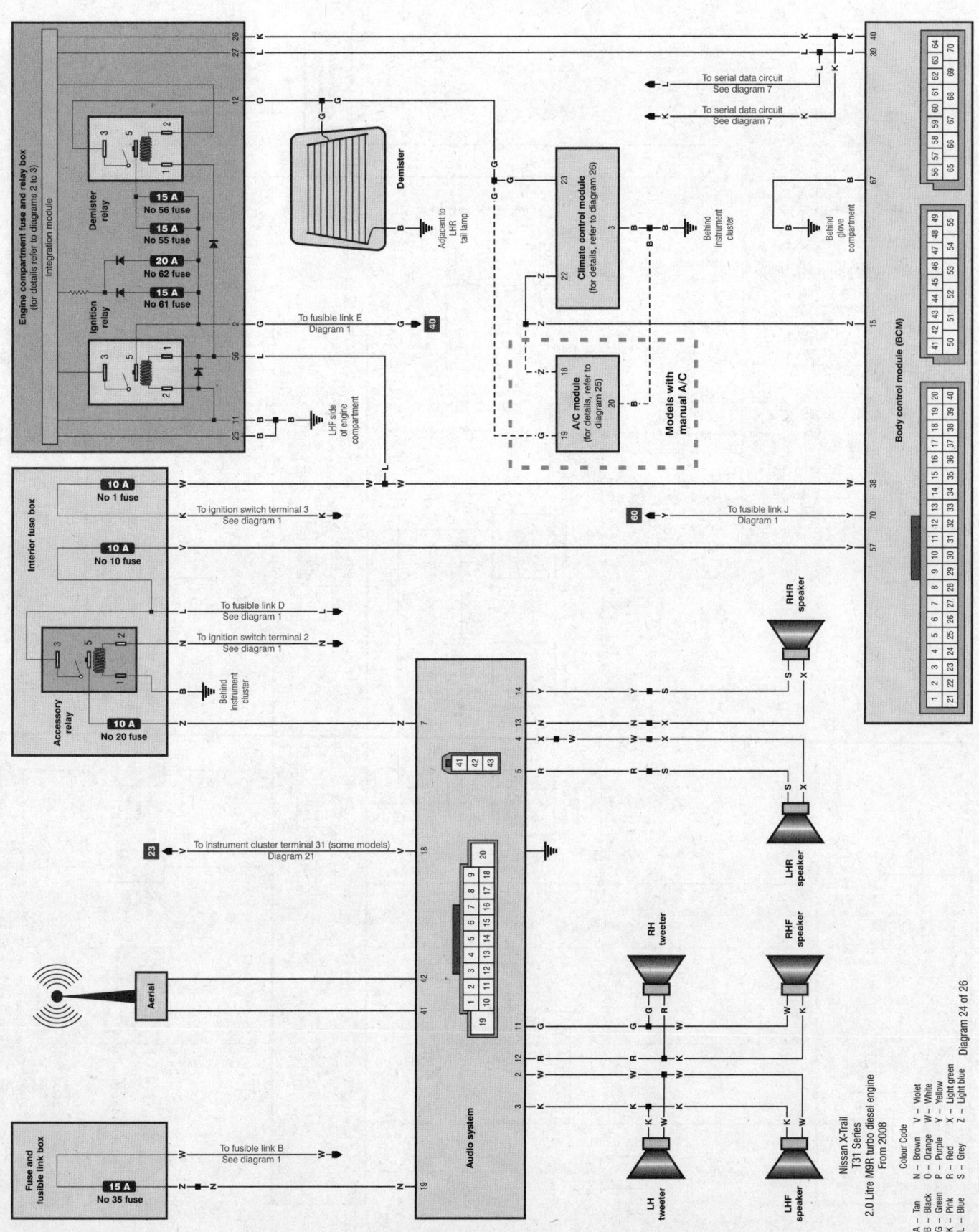

Diagram 24 - Audio system and demister – T31 X-Trail diesel models

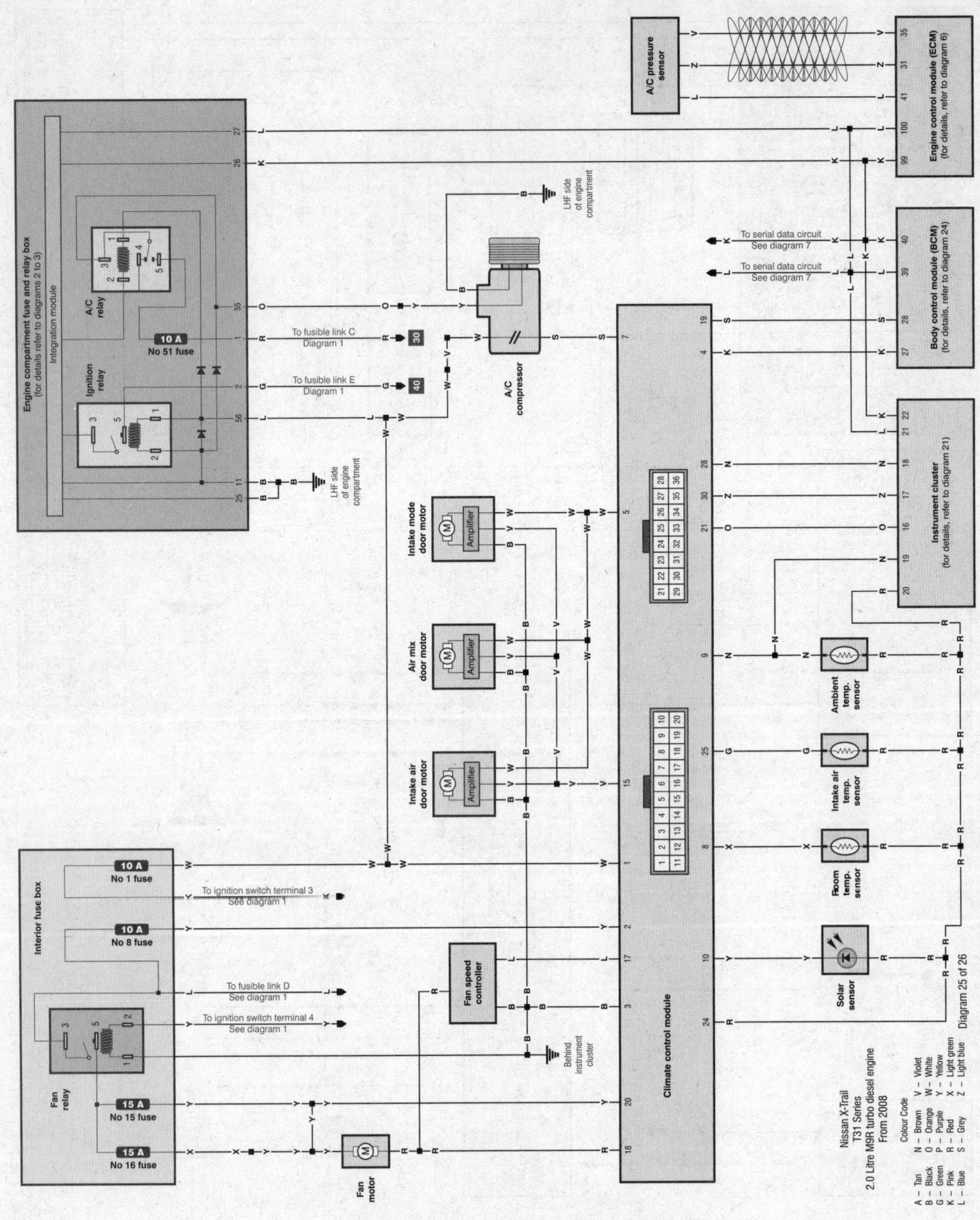

Diagram 25 - Air conditioning – T31 X-Trail diesel models

Chapter 12 Chassis electrical system

12•85

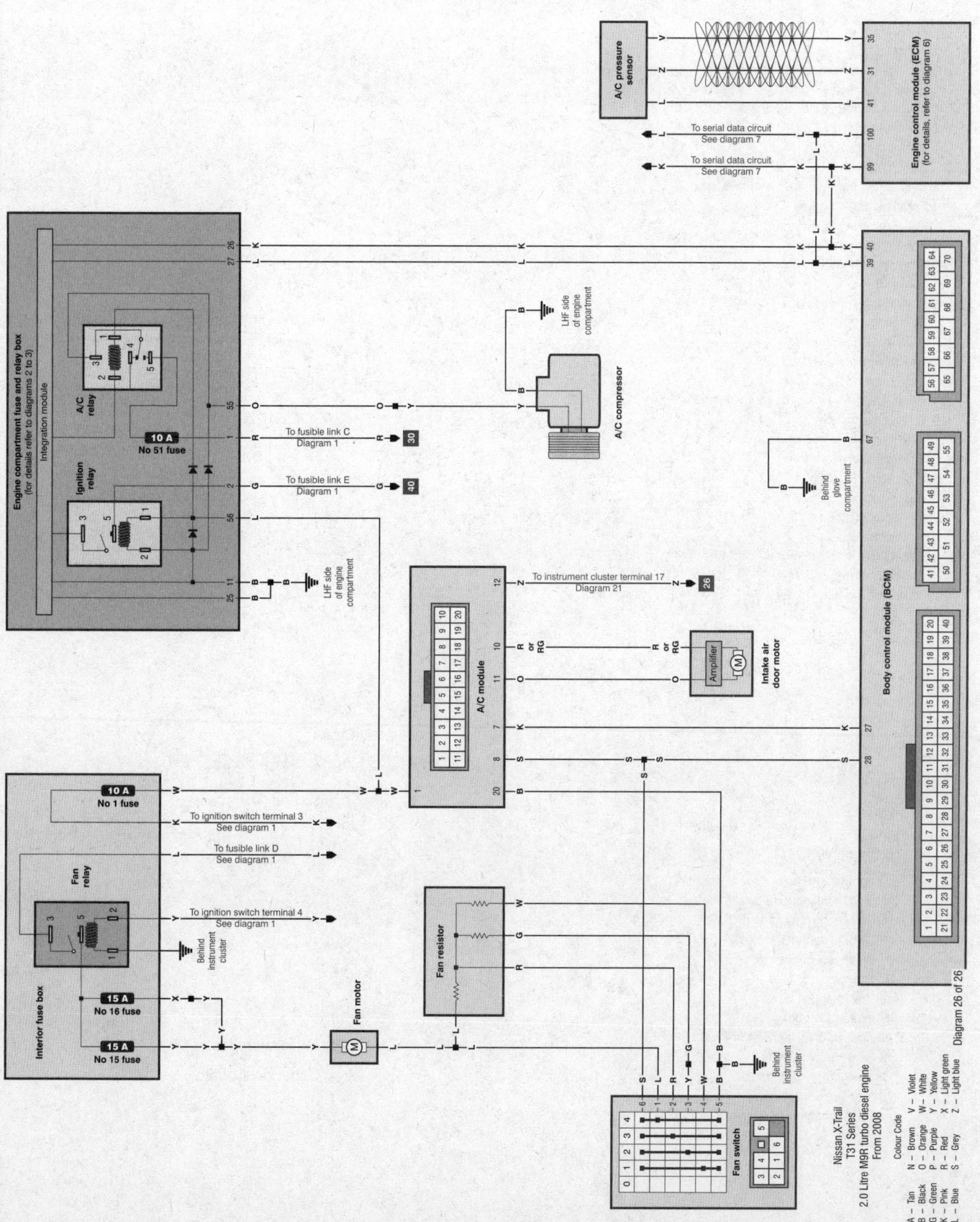

Diagram 26 - Climate control – T31 X-Trail diesel models

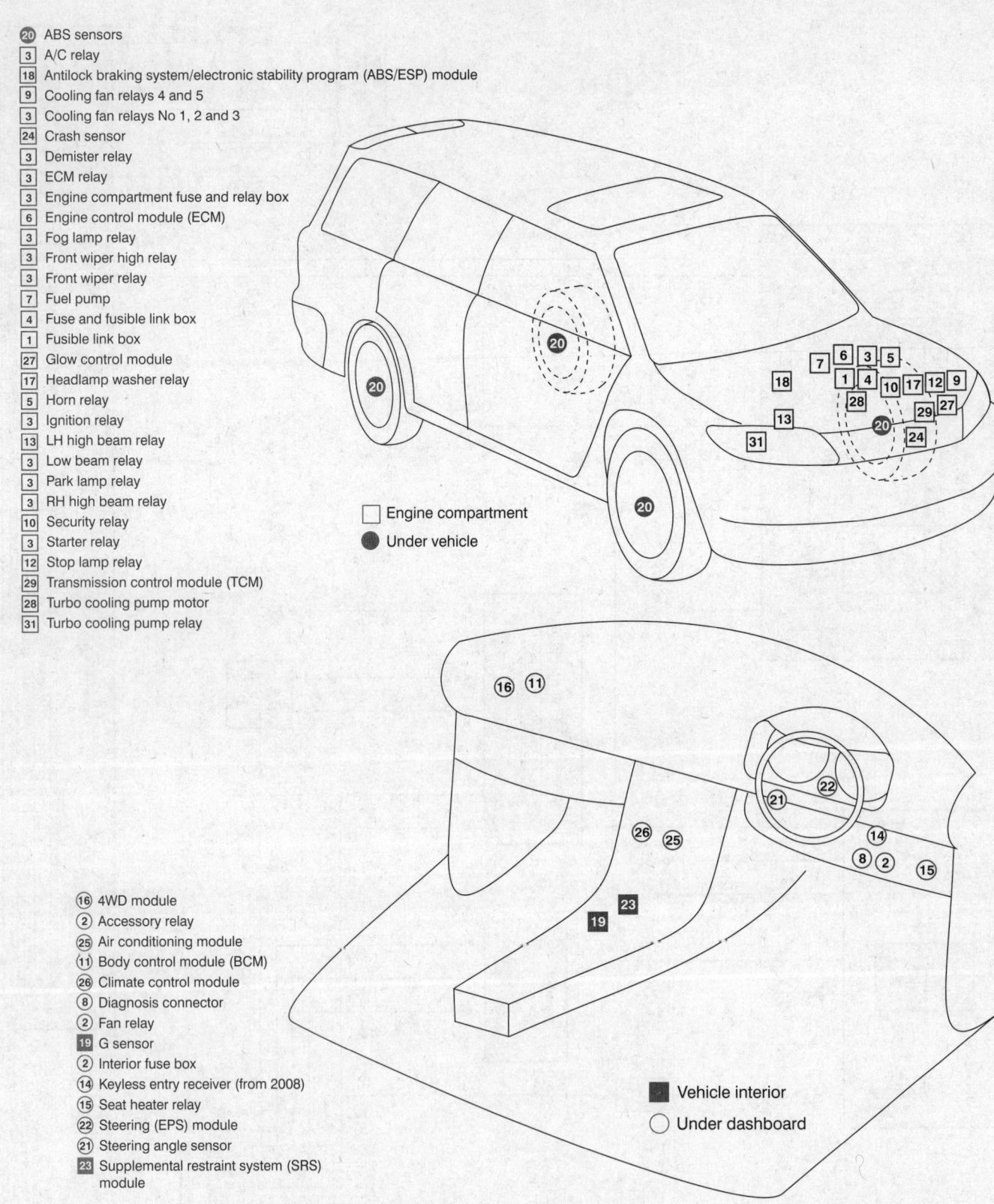

Diagram 27 - Component locations – T31 X-Trail diesel models

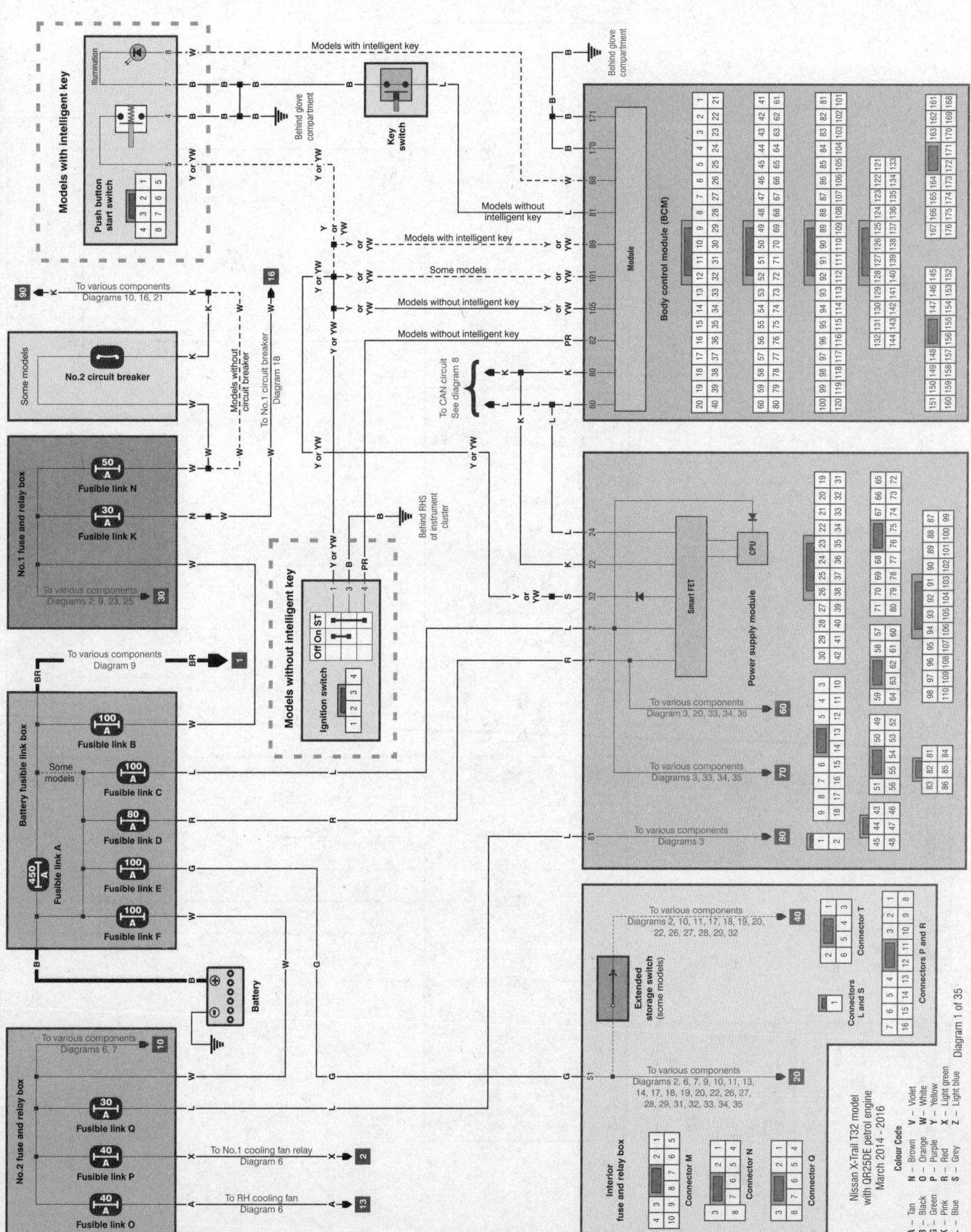

Diagram 1 - Power distribution, ignition and push button start switch, body control module (BCM) – T32 X-Trail petrol models

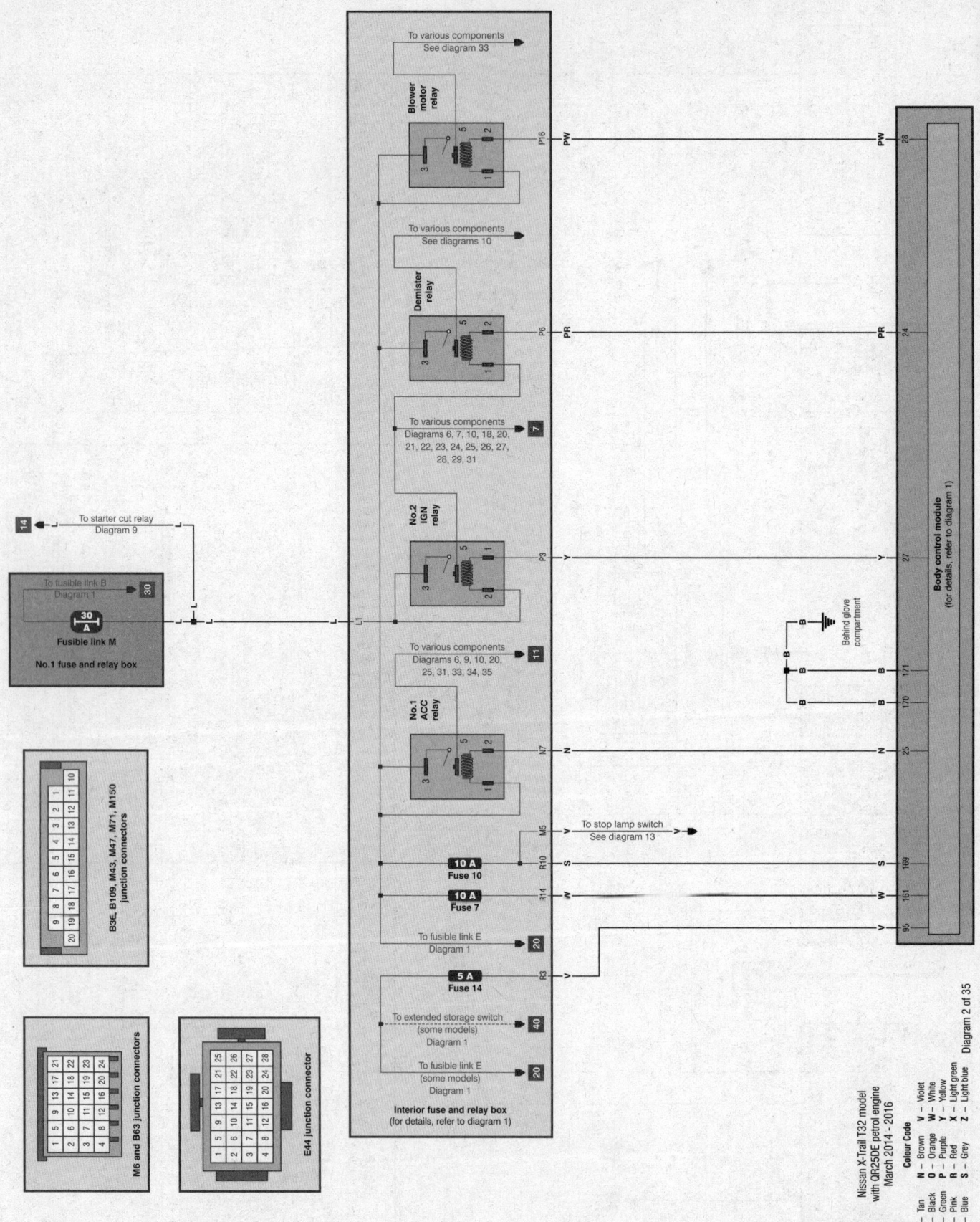

Diagram 2 - Power distribution, engine compartment fuse and relay box, junction box connectors – T32 X-Trail petrol models

Chapter 12 Chassis electrical system

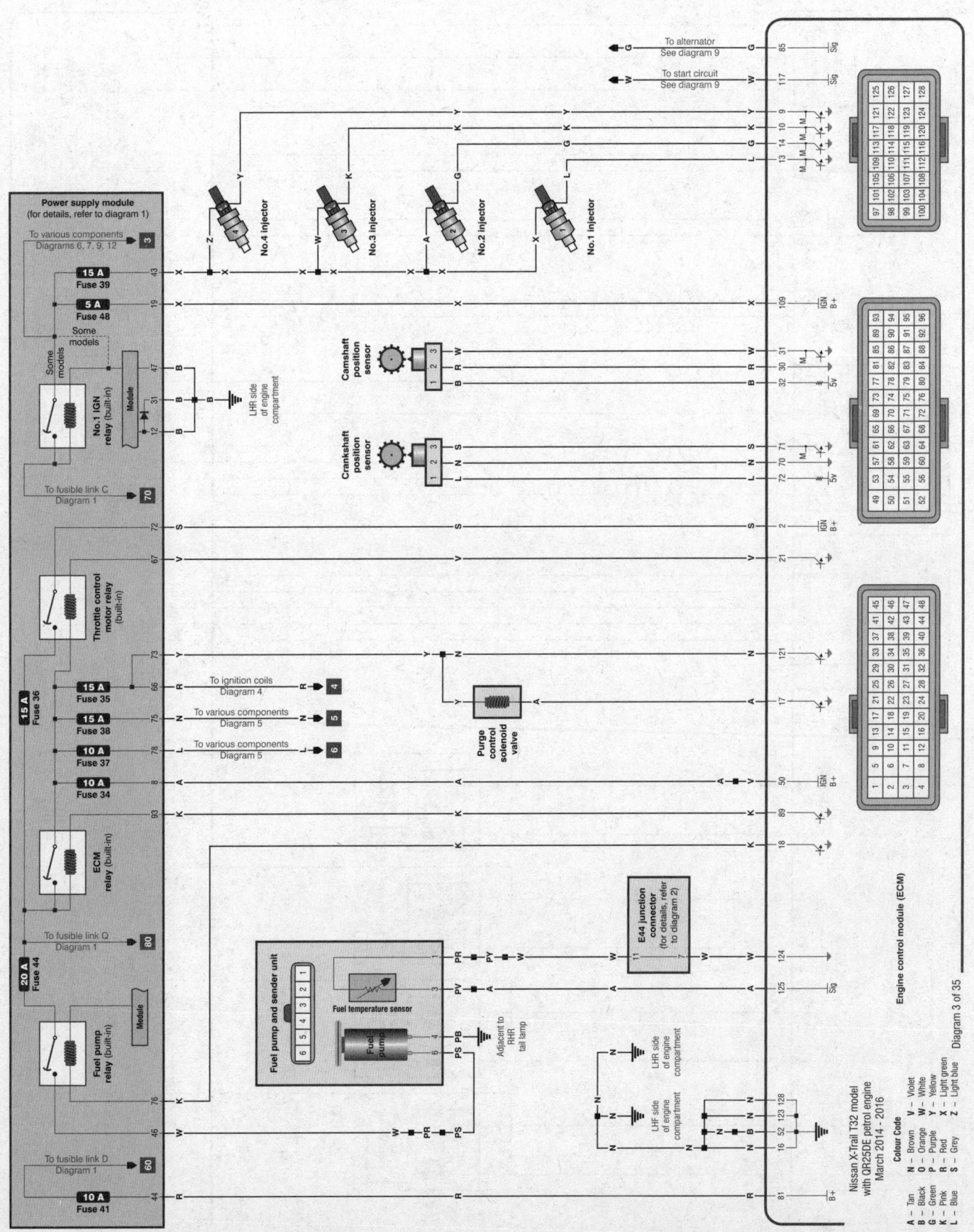

Diagram 3 - ECM power supply and earth circuits, fuel pump, injectors, various sensors – T32 X-Trail petrol models

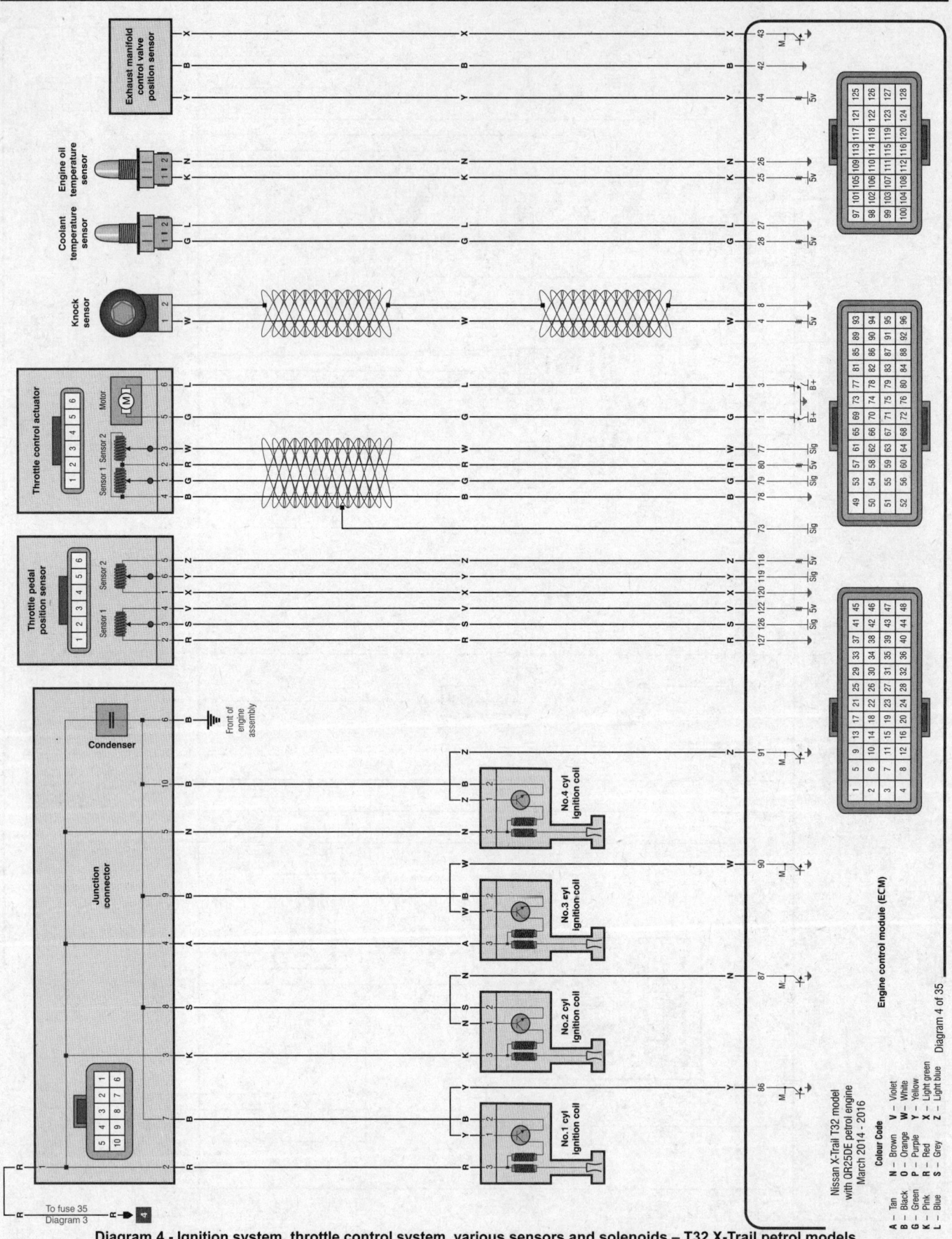

Diagram 4 - Ignition system, throttle control system, various sensors and solenoids – T32 X-Trail petrol models

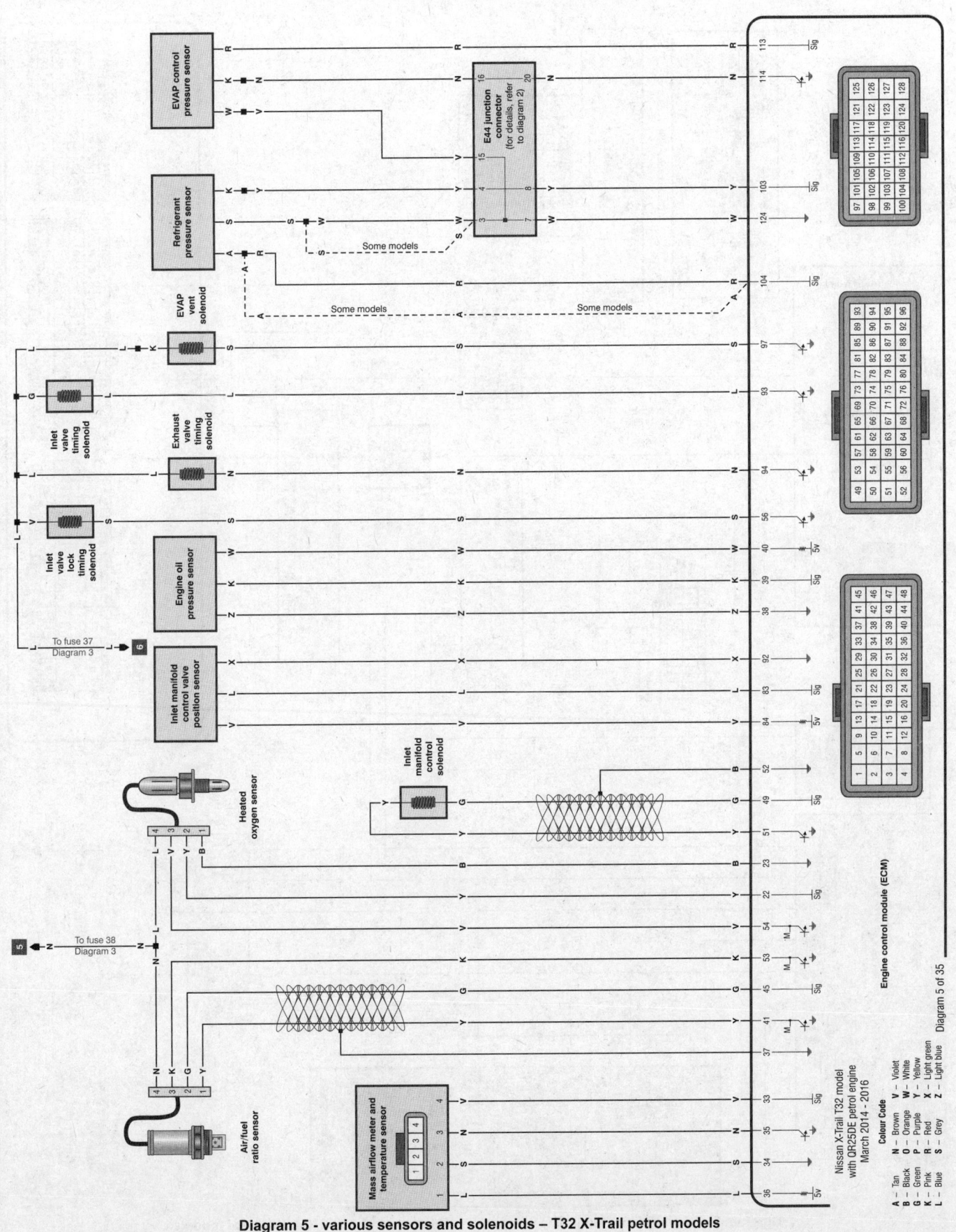

Diagram 5 - various sensors and solenoids – T32 X-Trail petrol models

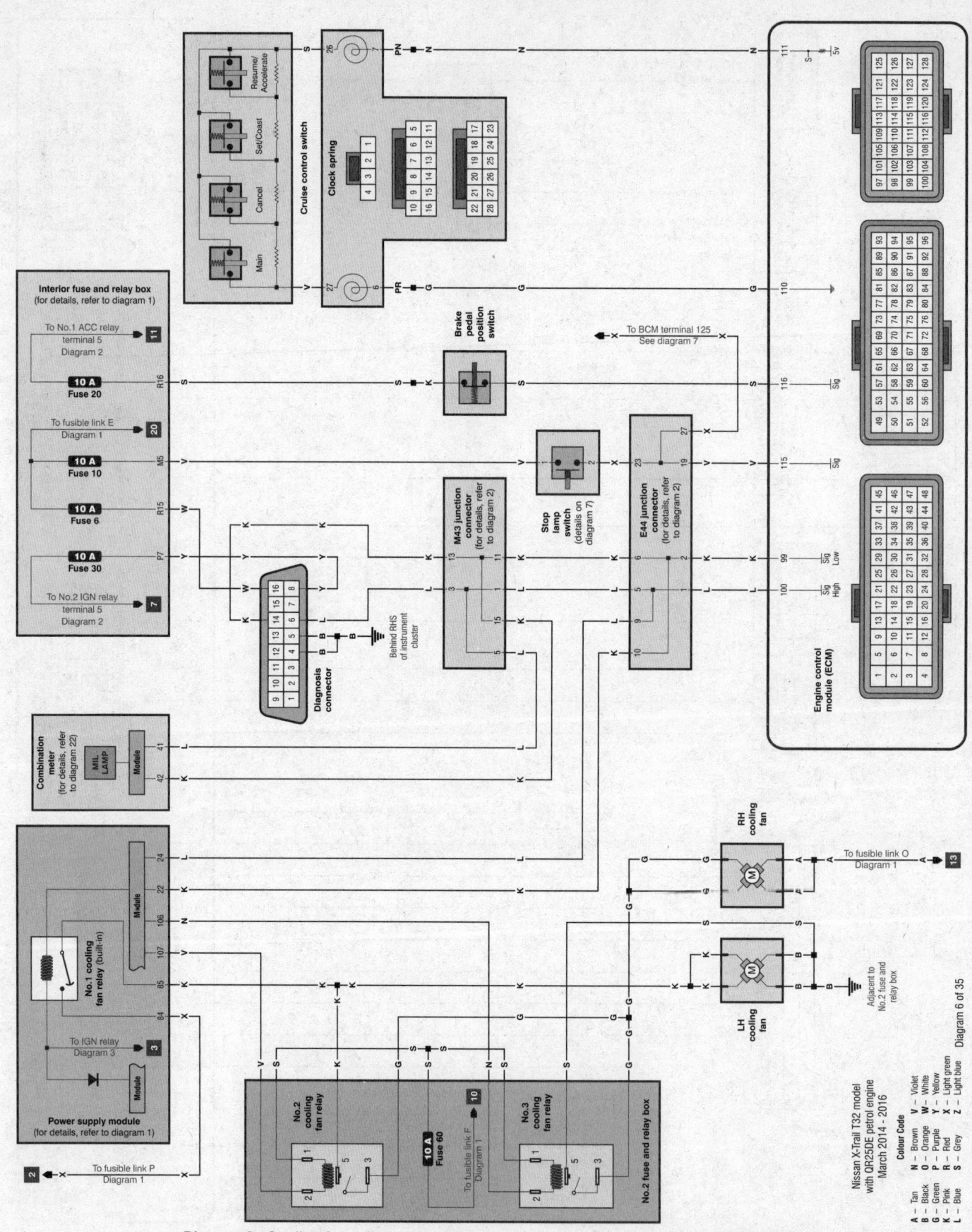

Diagram 6 - Cooling fans, diagnosis connector, cruise control – T32 X-Trail petrol models

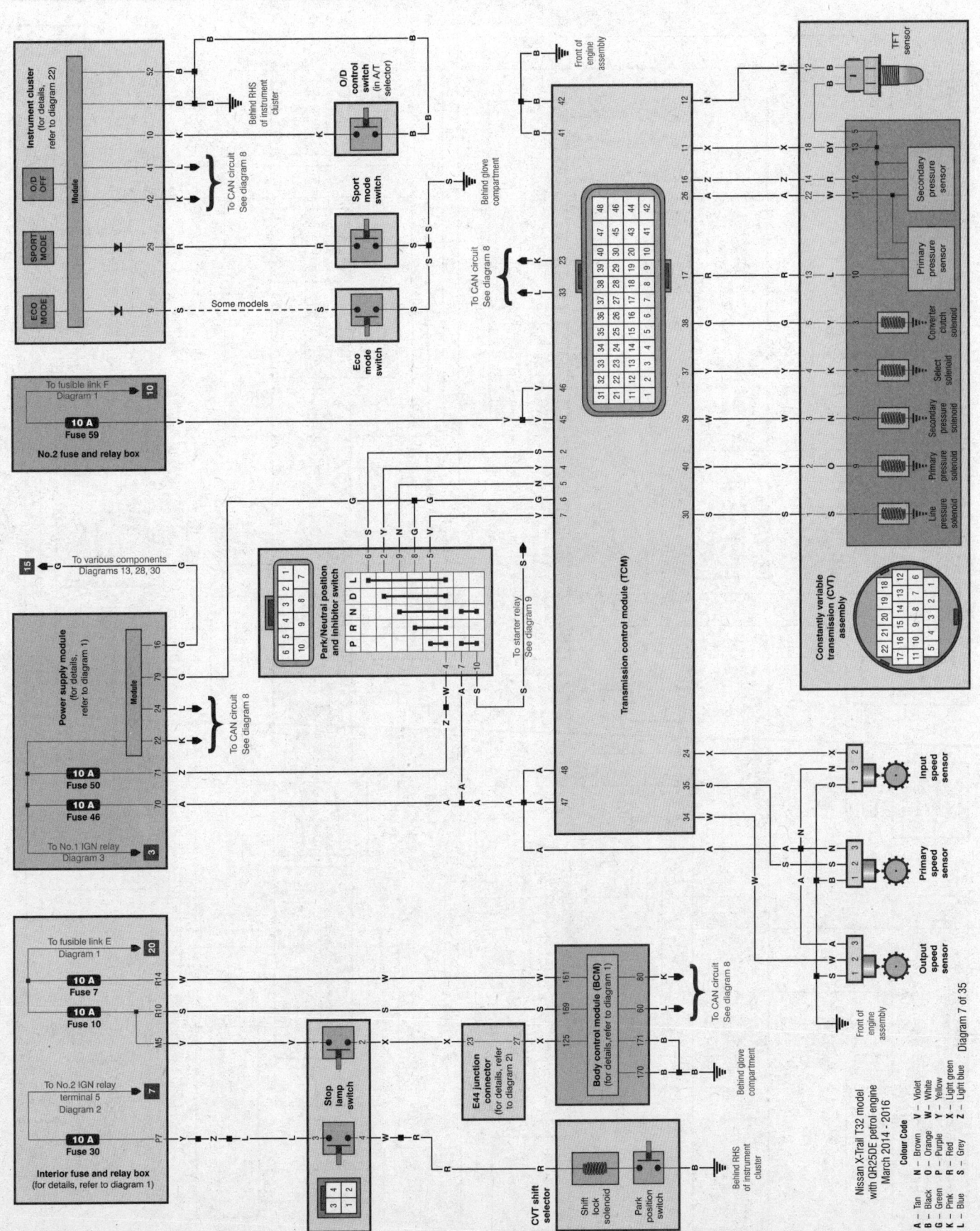

Diagram 7 - Automatic transmission, inhibitor switch, shift lock system, ECO and sport mode systems – T32 X-Trail petrol models

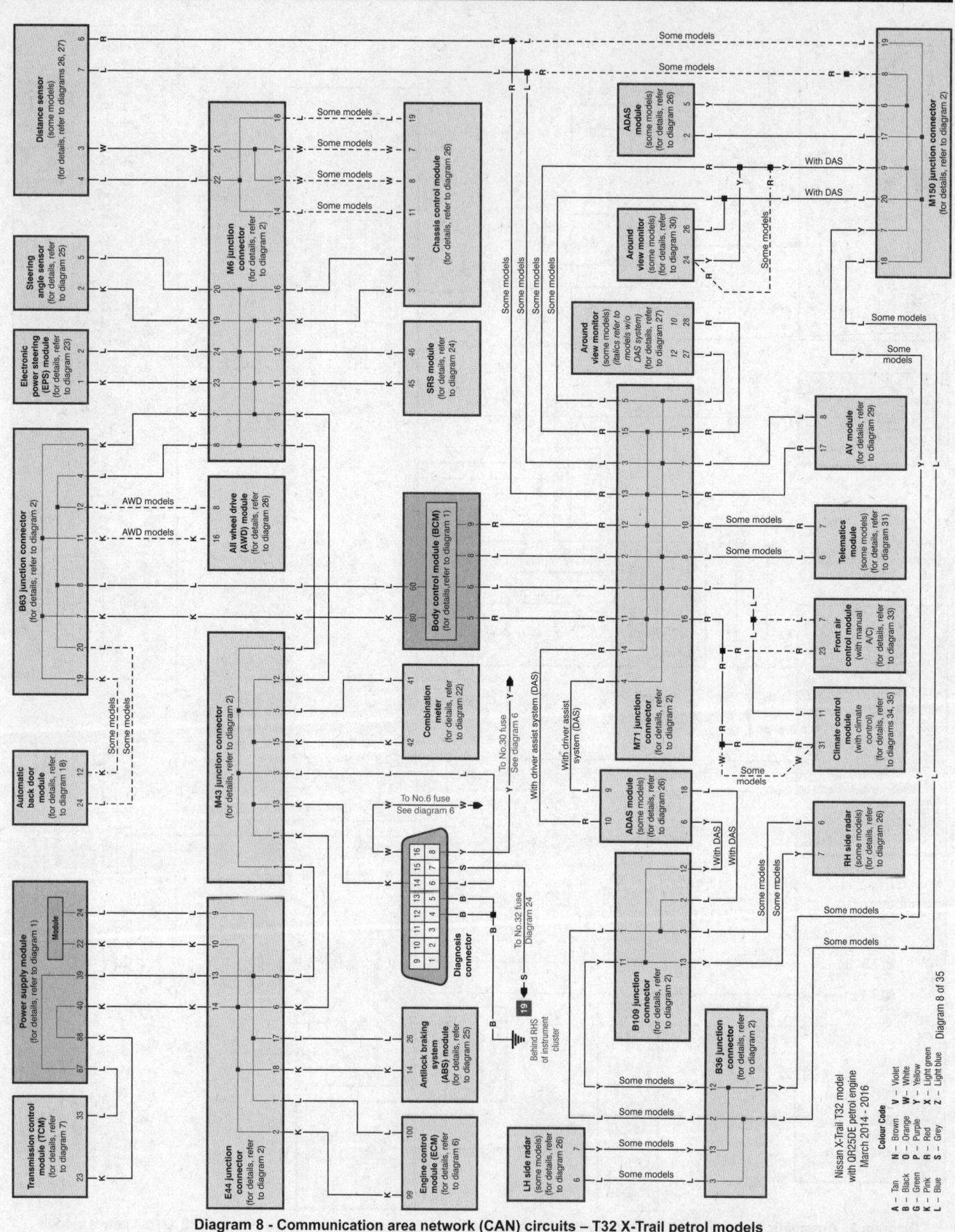

Diagram 8 - Communication area network (CAN) circuits – T32 X-Trail petrol models

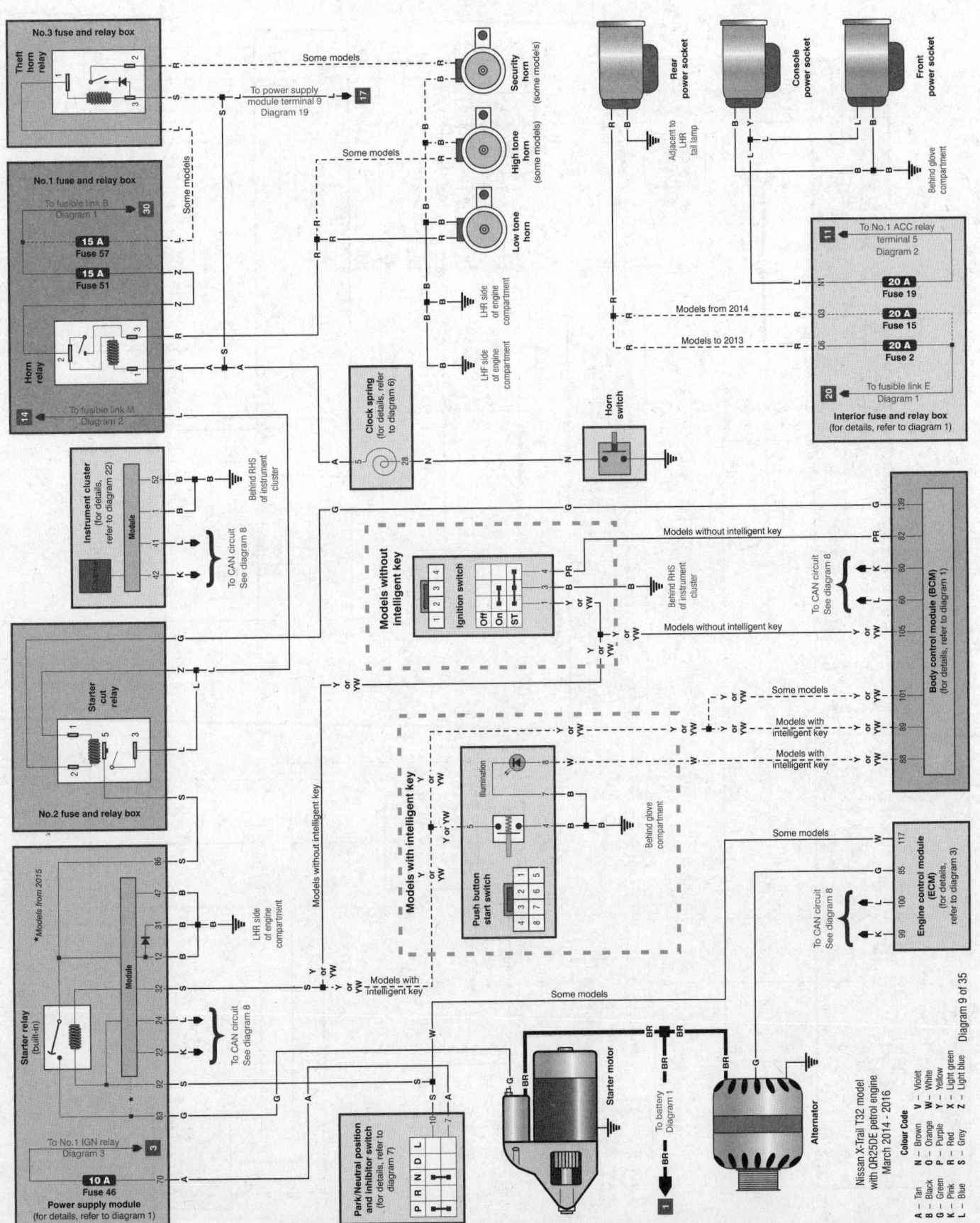

Diagram 9 - Starting system, charging system, power outlets, horn and theft horn relay – T32 X-Trail petrol models

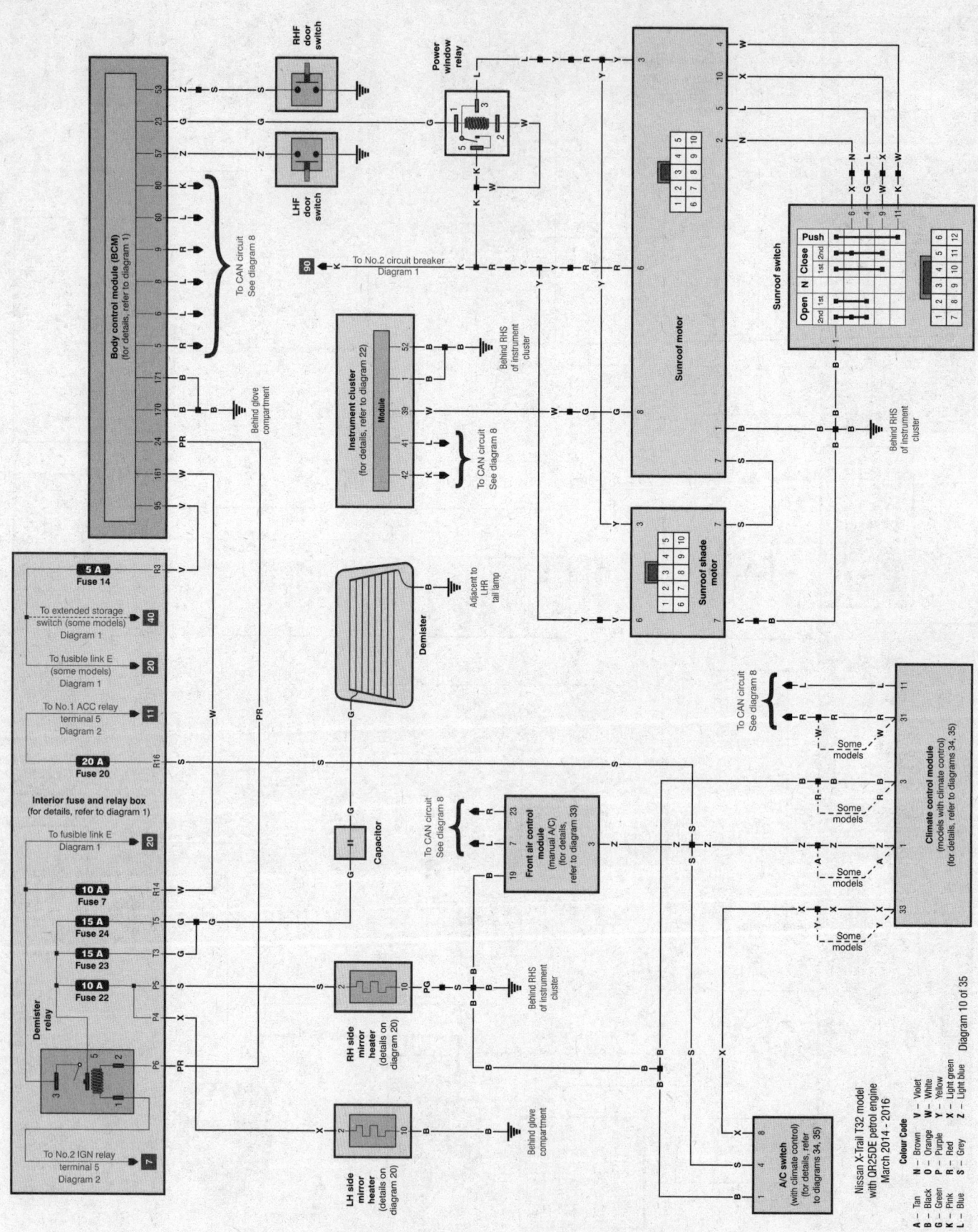

Diagram 10 - Demister and mirror heaters, sunroof – T32 X-Trail petrol models

Chapter 12 Chassis electrical system

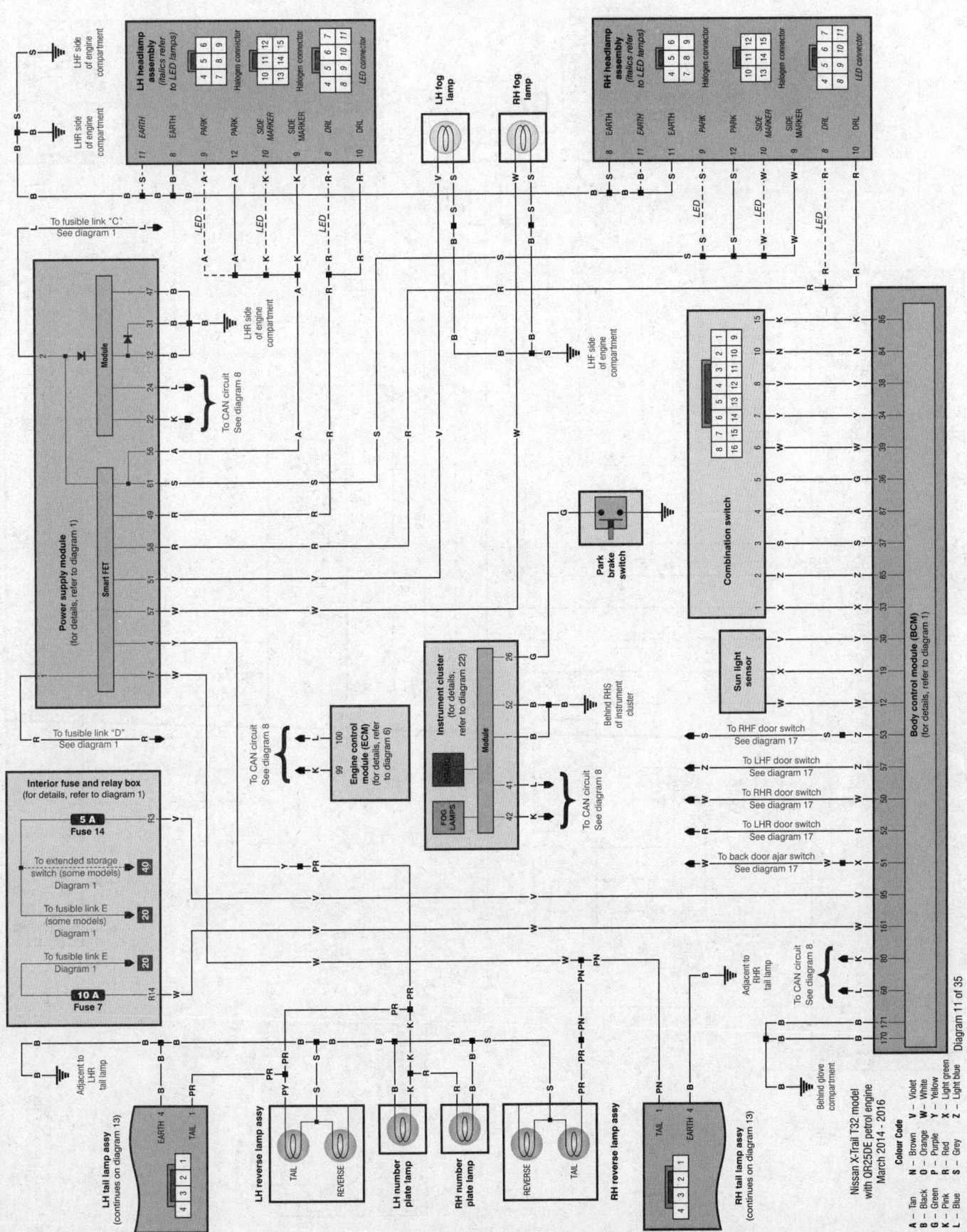

Diagram 11 - Park lamps, daytime running lights (DRL), fog lamps, automatic light control – T32 X-Trail petrol models

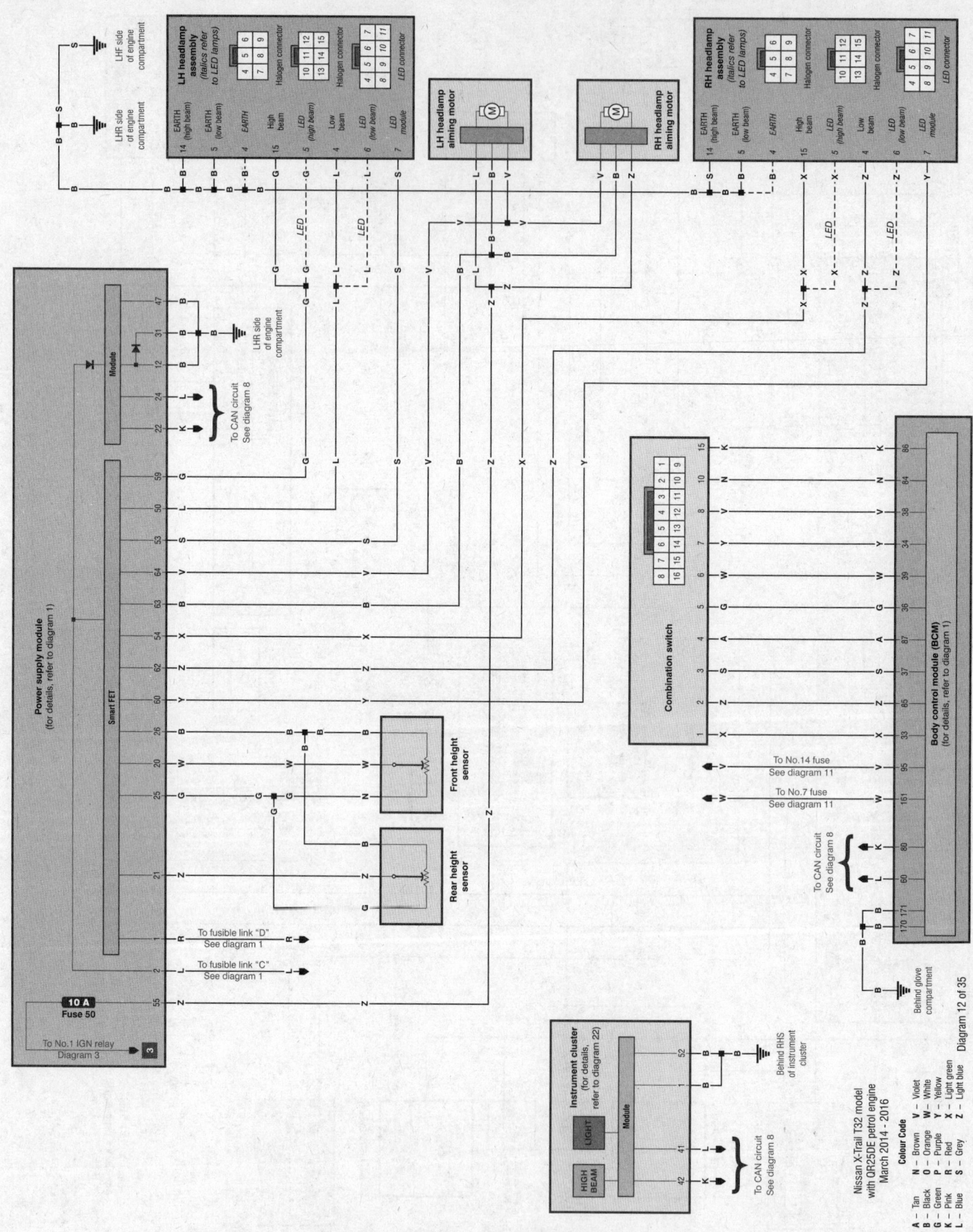

Diagram 12 - Headlamps and headlamp levelling system – T32 X-Trail petrol models

Chapter 12 Chassis electrical system

12-99

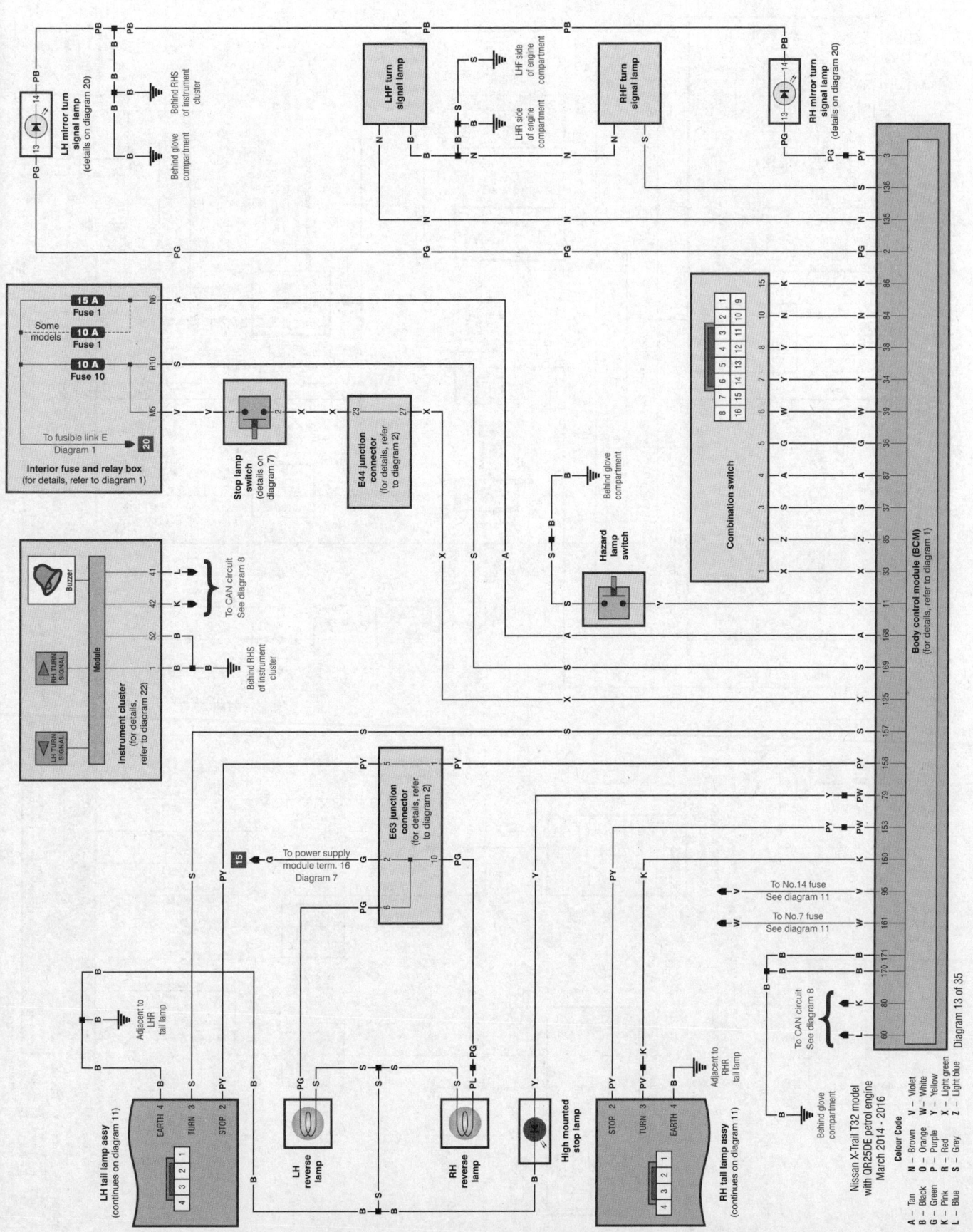

Diagram 13 - Reverse lamps, stop lamps, turn signal and hazard lamps – T32 X-Trail petrol models

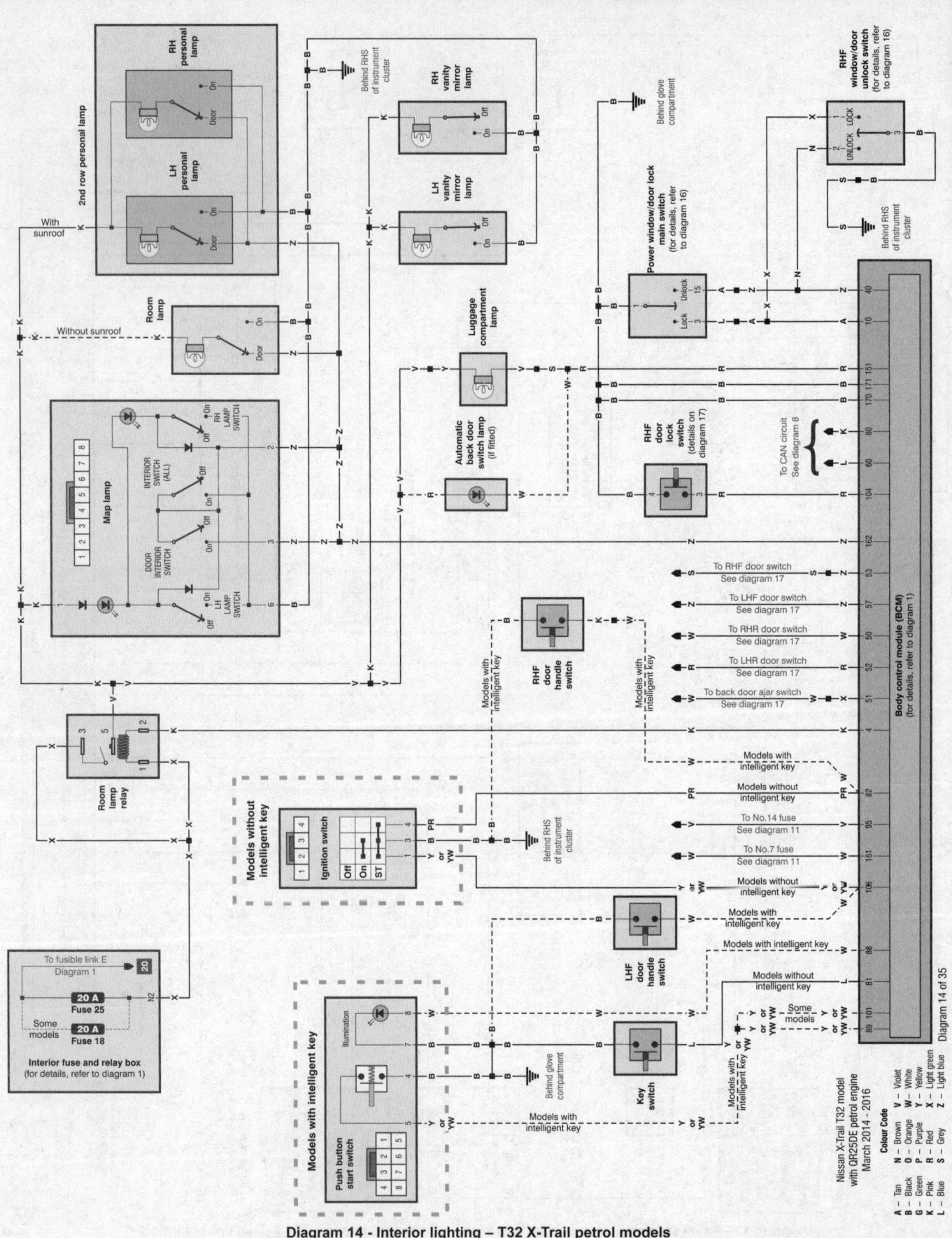

Diagram 14 - Interior lighting – T32 X-Trail petrol models

Chapter 12 Chassis electrical system

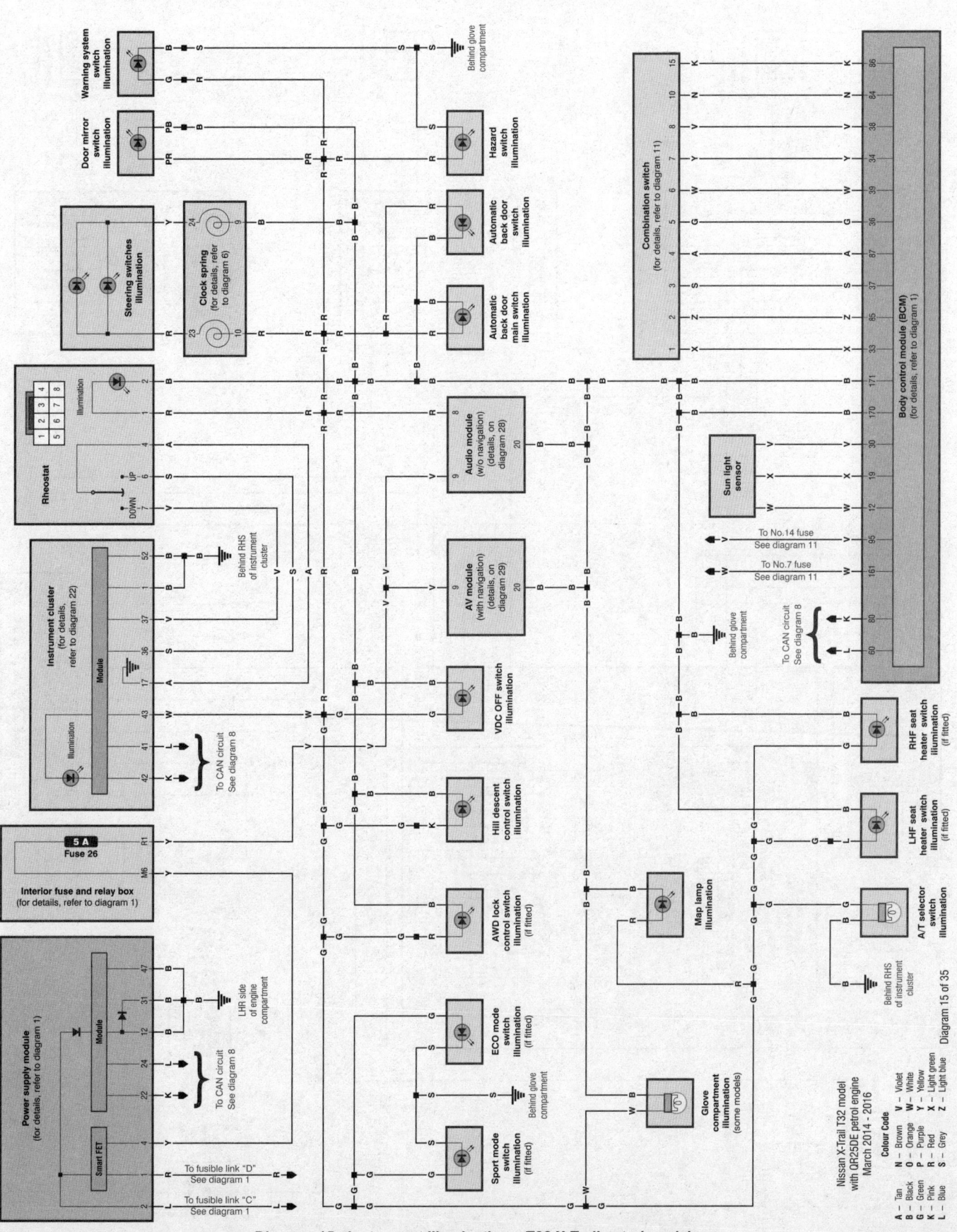

Diagram 15 - Instrument illumination – T32 X-Trail petrol models

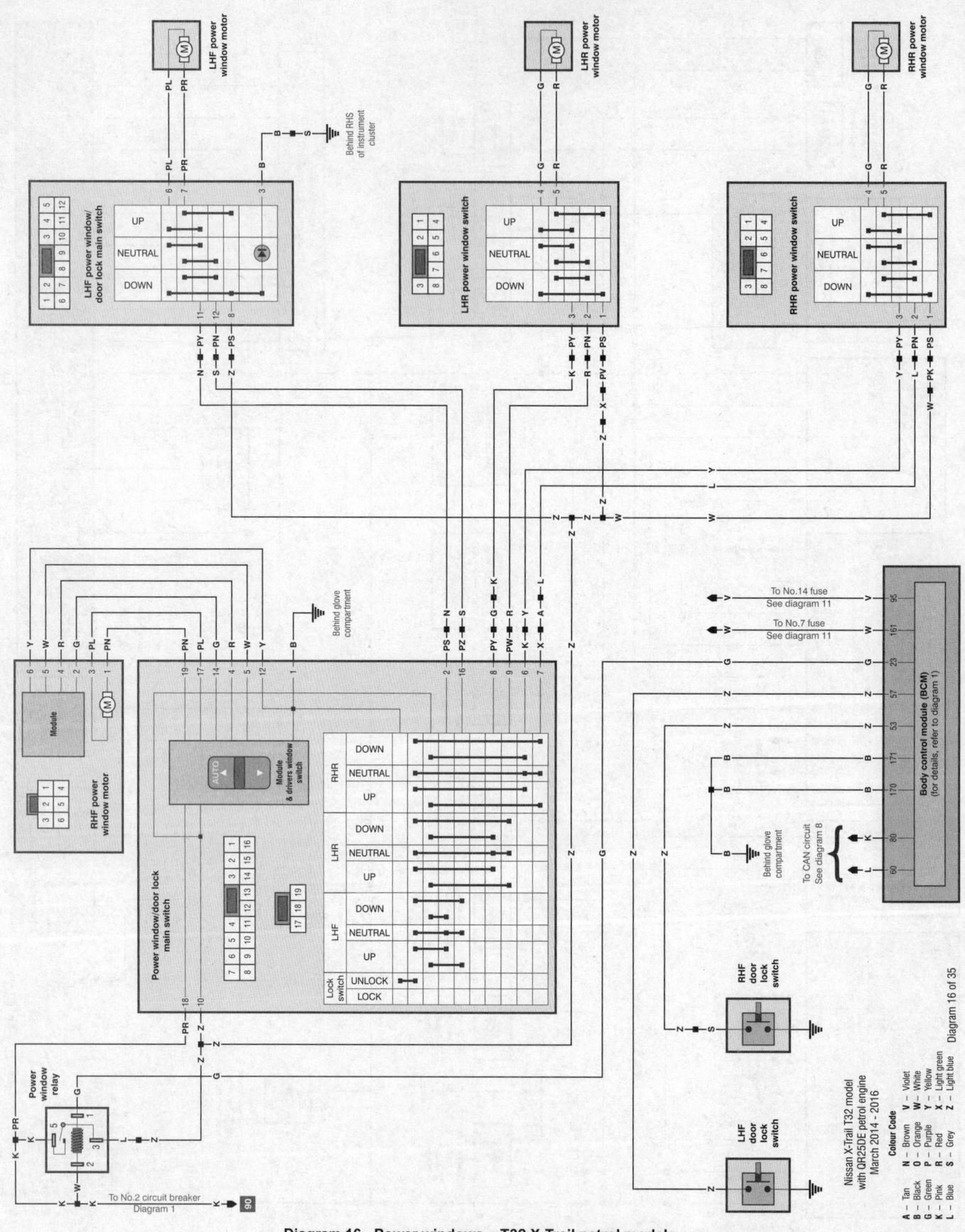

Diagram 16 - Power windows – T32 X-Trail petrol models

Chapter 12 Chassis electrical system

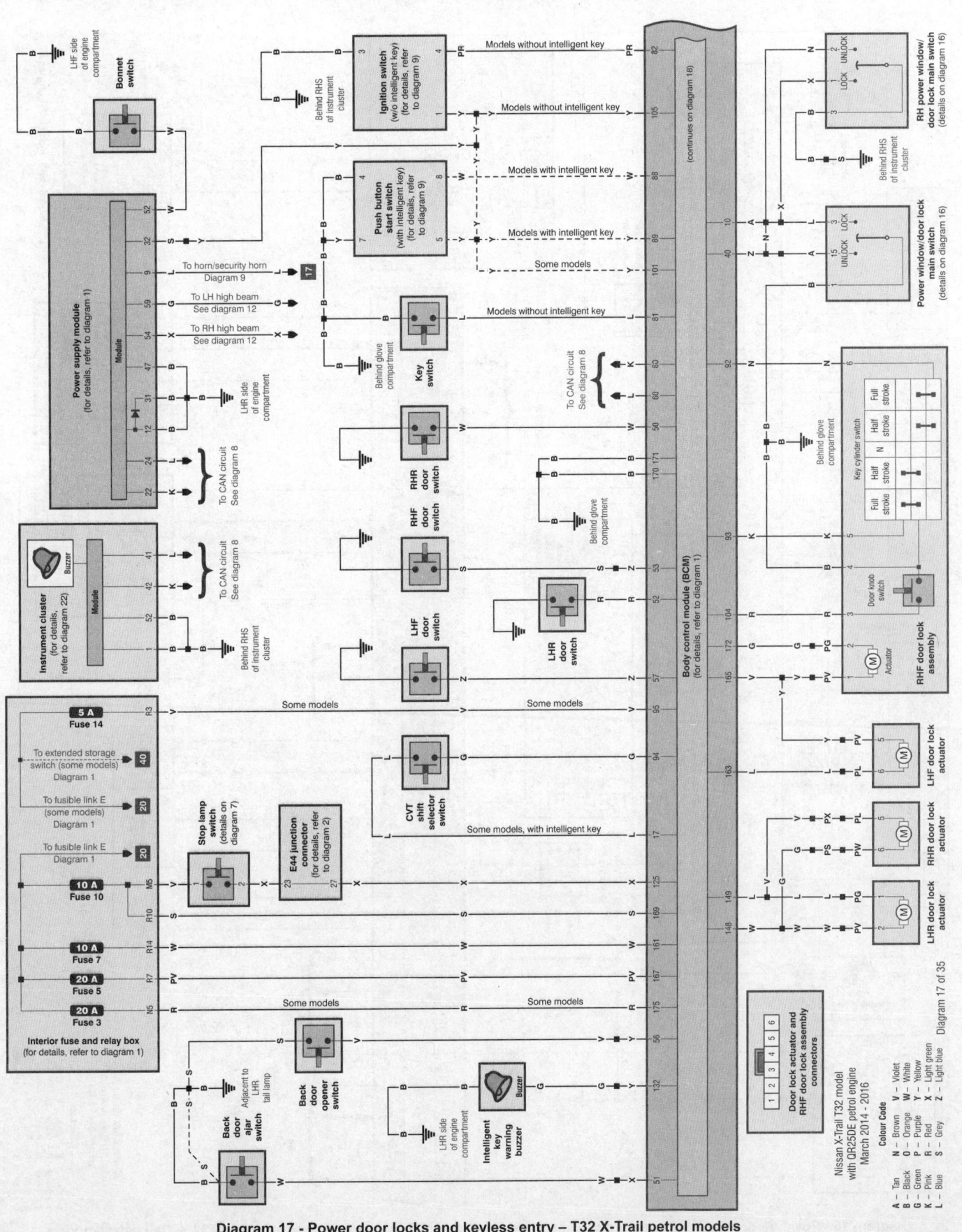

Diagram 17 - Power door locks and keyless entry – T32 X-Trail petrol models

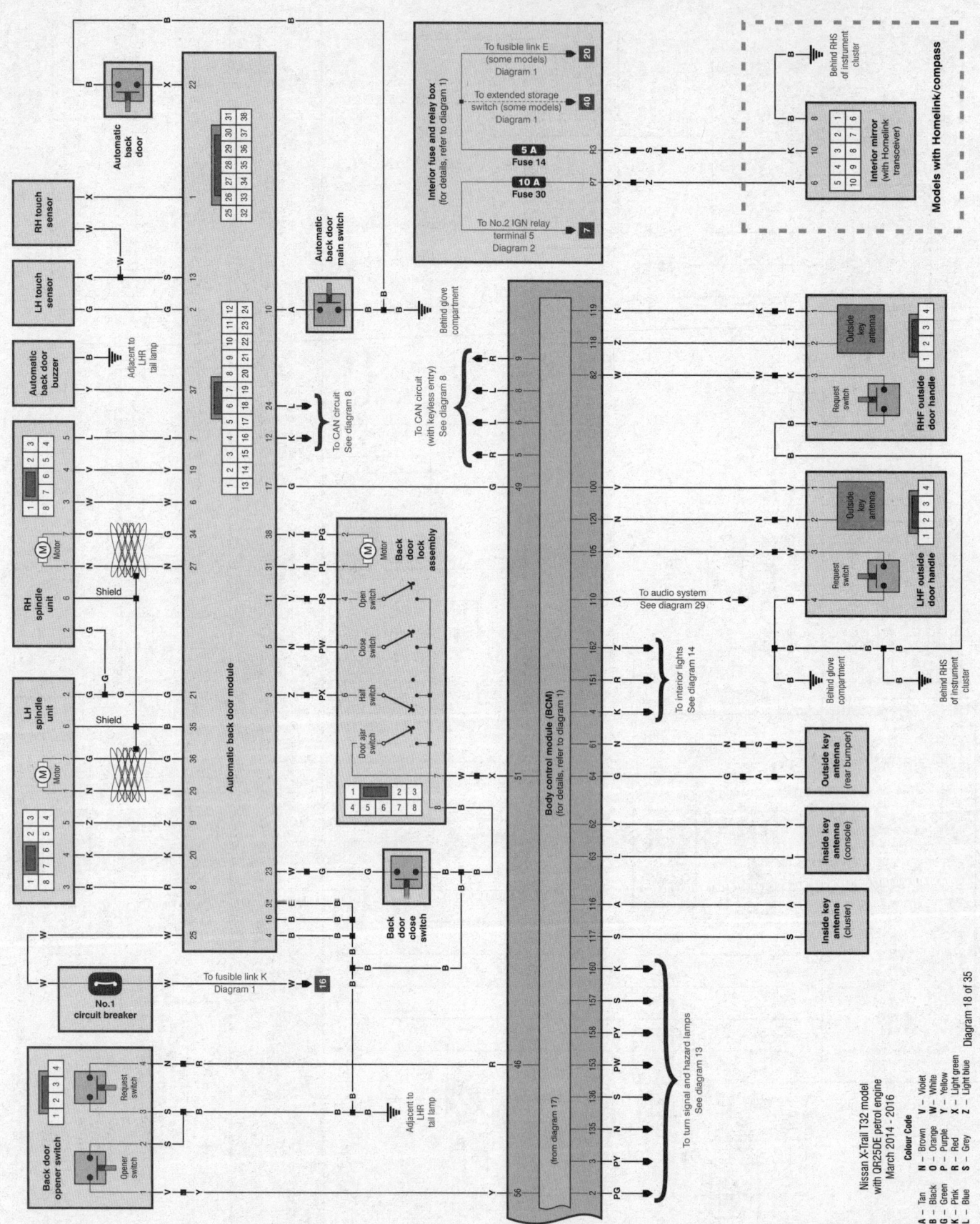

Diagram 18 - Power door locks and keyless entry, automatic back door, Homelink/compass system – T32 X-Trail petrol models

Chapter 12 Chassis electrical system

12-105

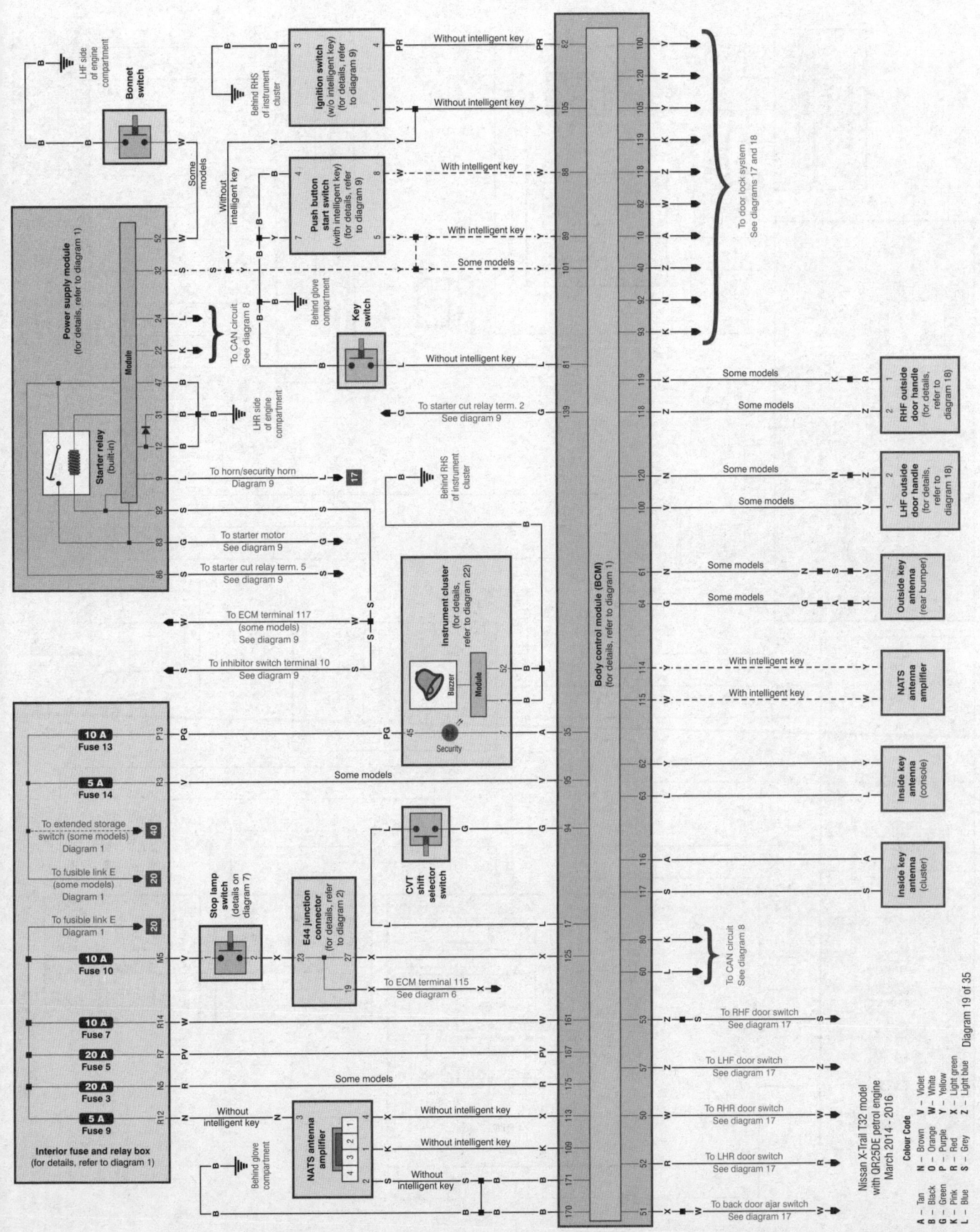

Diagram 19 - Alarm and security systems – T32 X-Trail petrol models

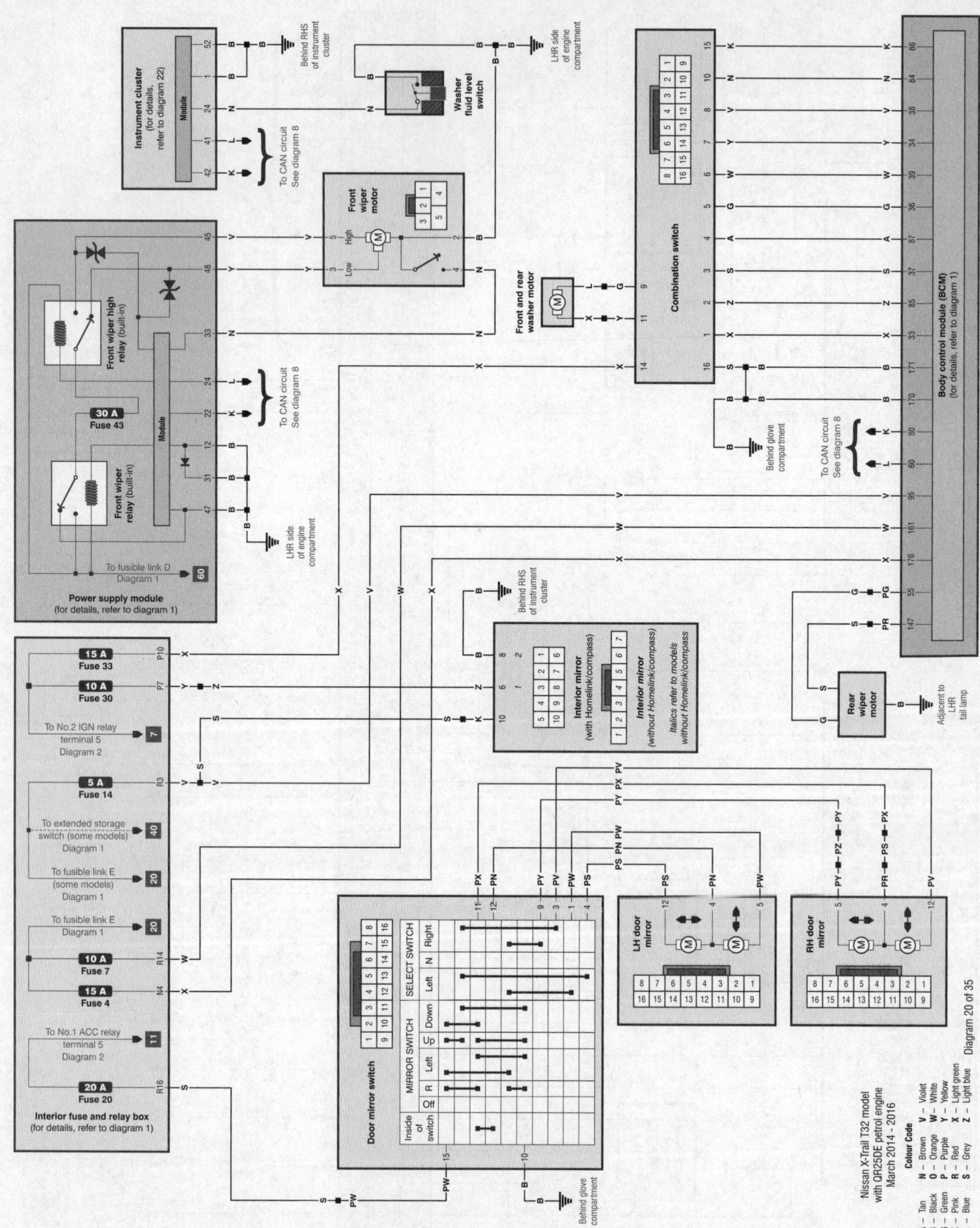

Diagram 20 - Front and rear wipers, washers, power mirrors, electrochromatic interior mirror – T32 X-Trail petrol models

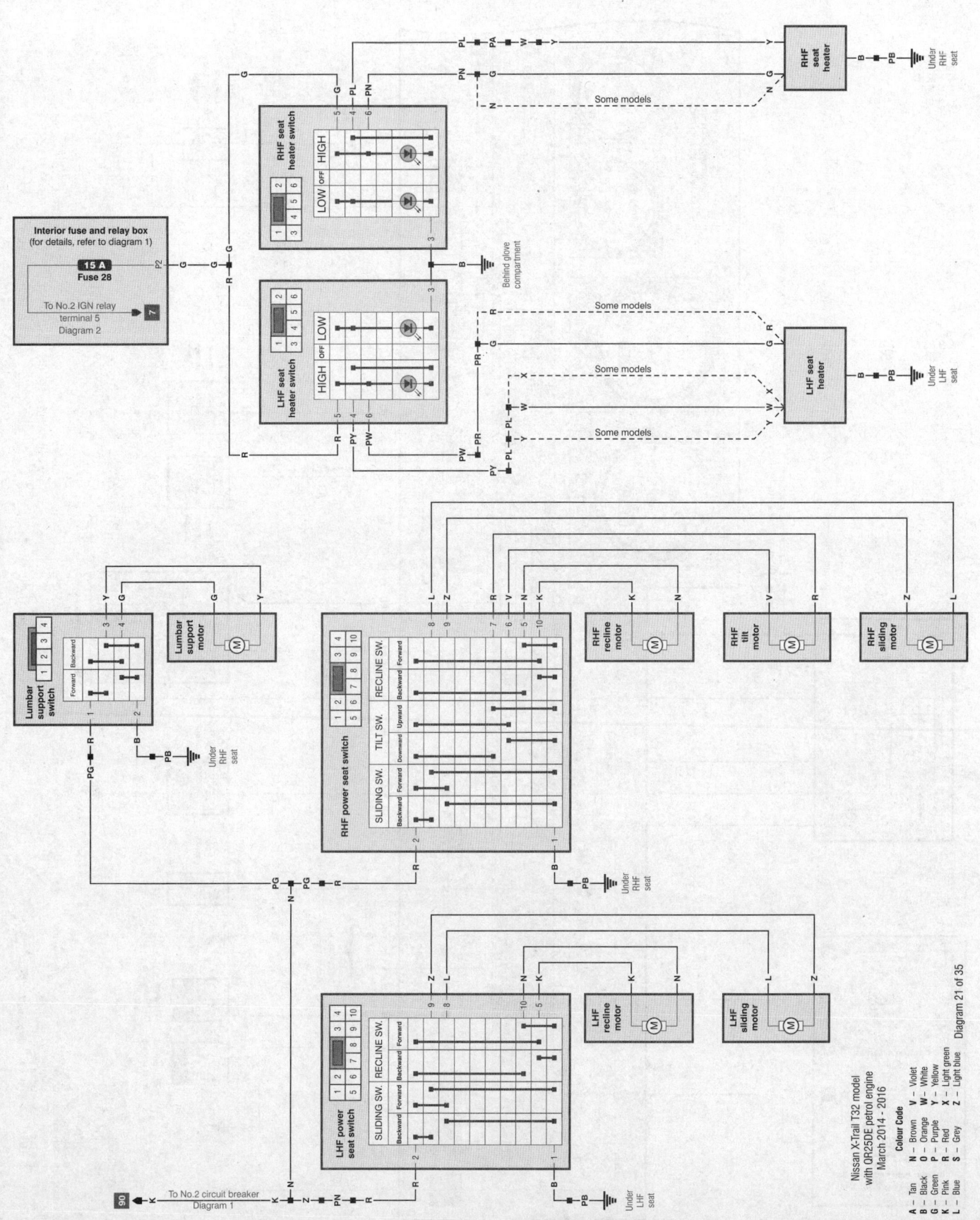

Diagram 21 - Power and heated seats – T32 X-Trail petrol models

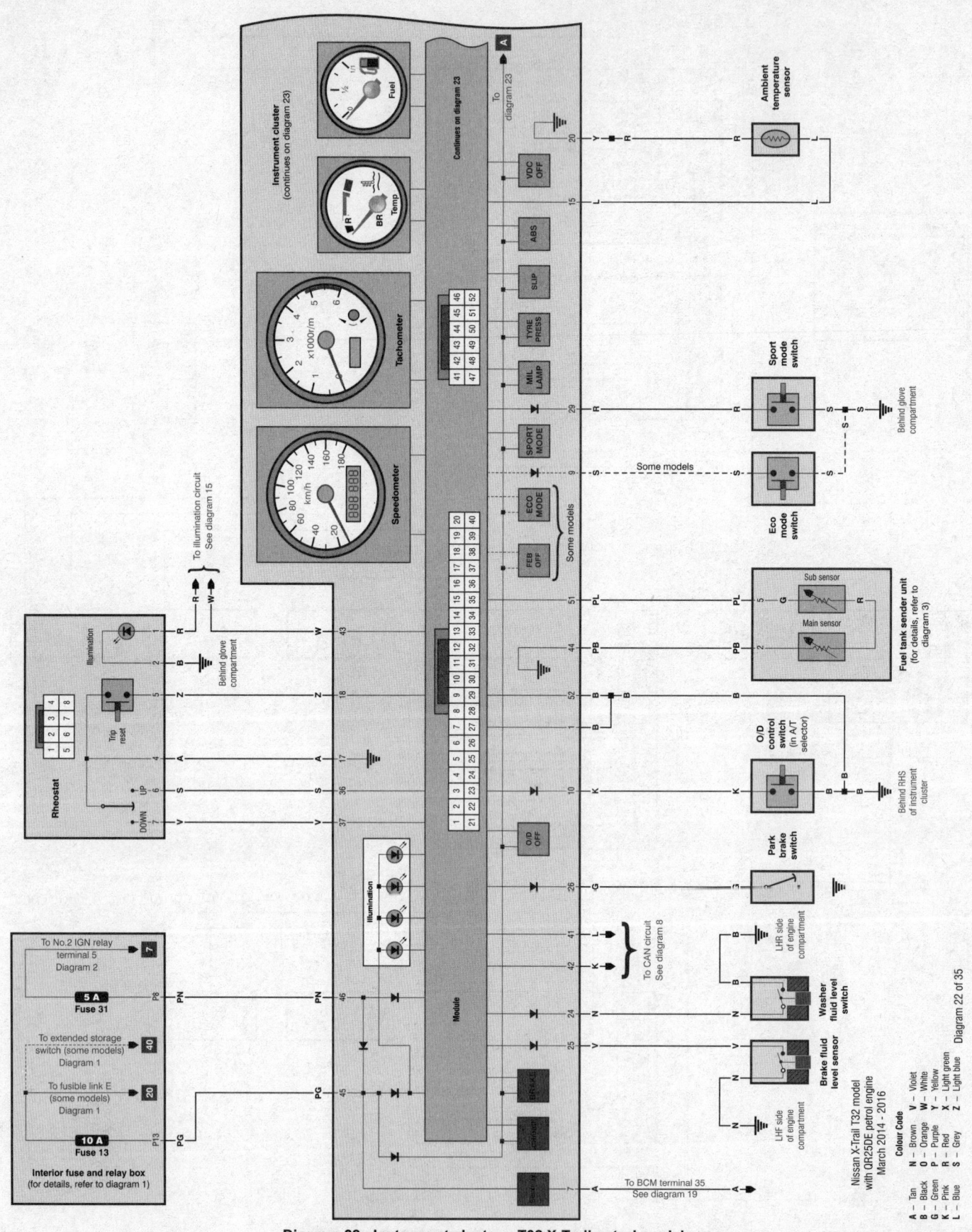

Diagram 22 - Instrument cluster – T32 X-Trail petrol models

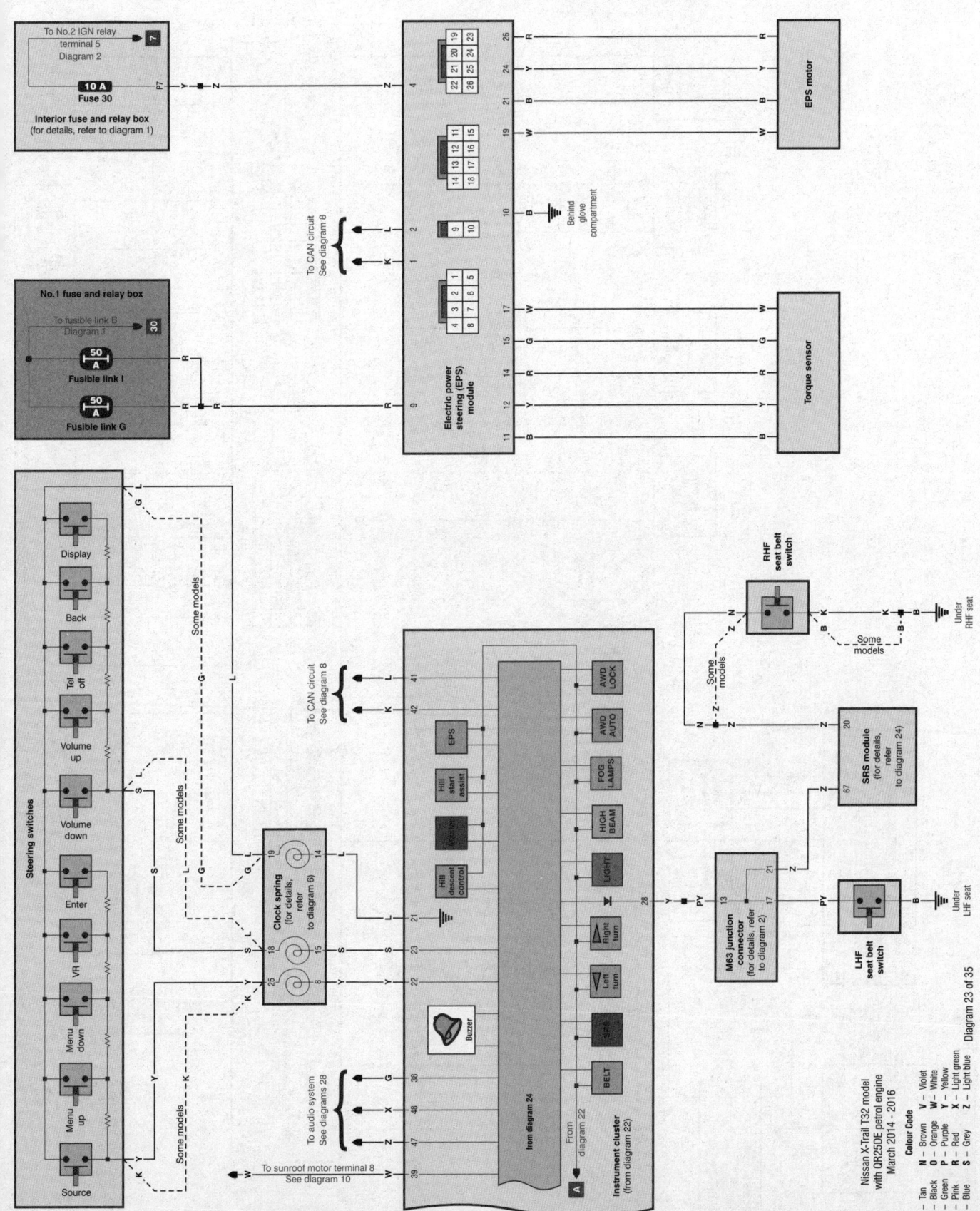

Diagram 23 - Instrument cluster, electric power steering (EPS) – T32 X-Trail petrol models

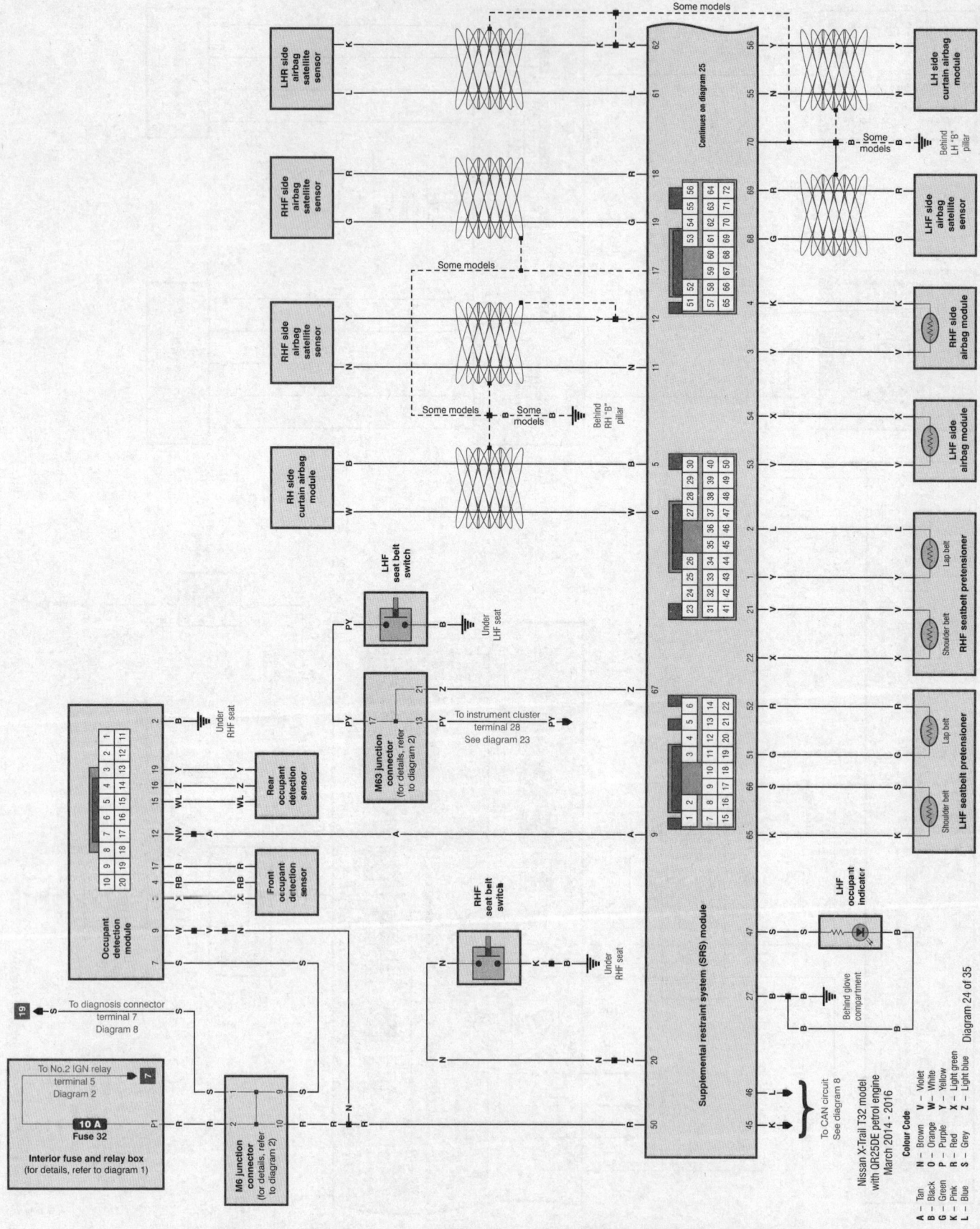

Diagram 24 - Supplemental restraint system (SRS) – T32 X-Trail petrol models

Chapter 12 Chassis electrical system

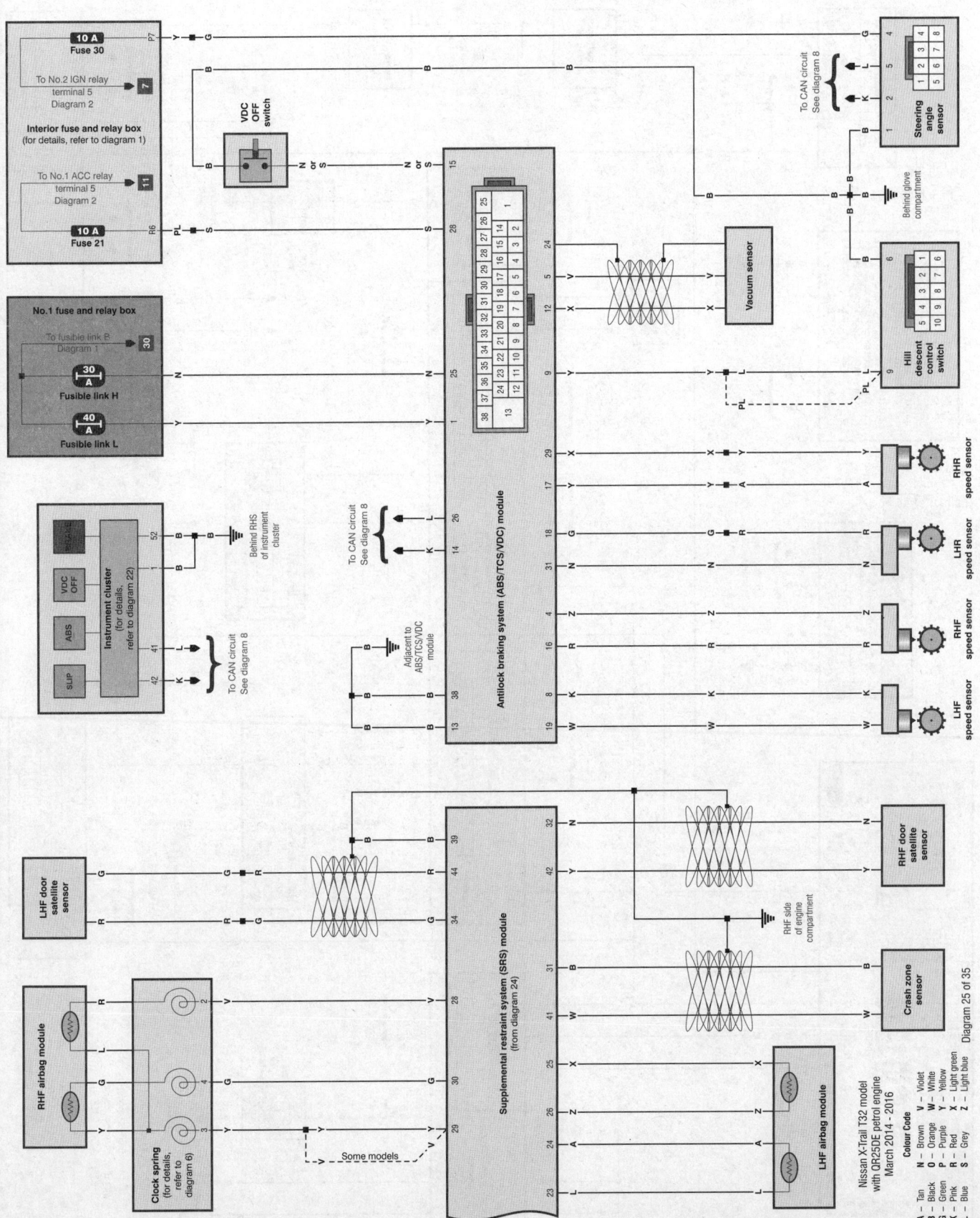

Diagram 25 - Supplemental restraint system (SRS), antilock braking/traction control/vehicle dynamic control (ABS/TCS/VDC) system – T32 X-Trail petrol models

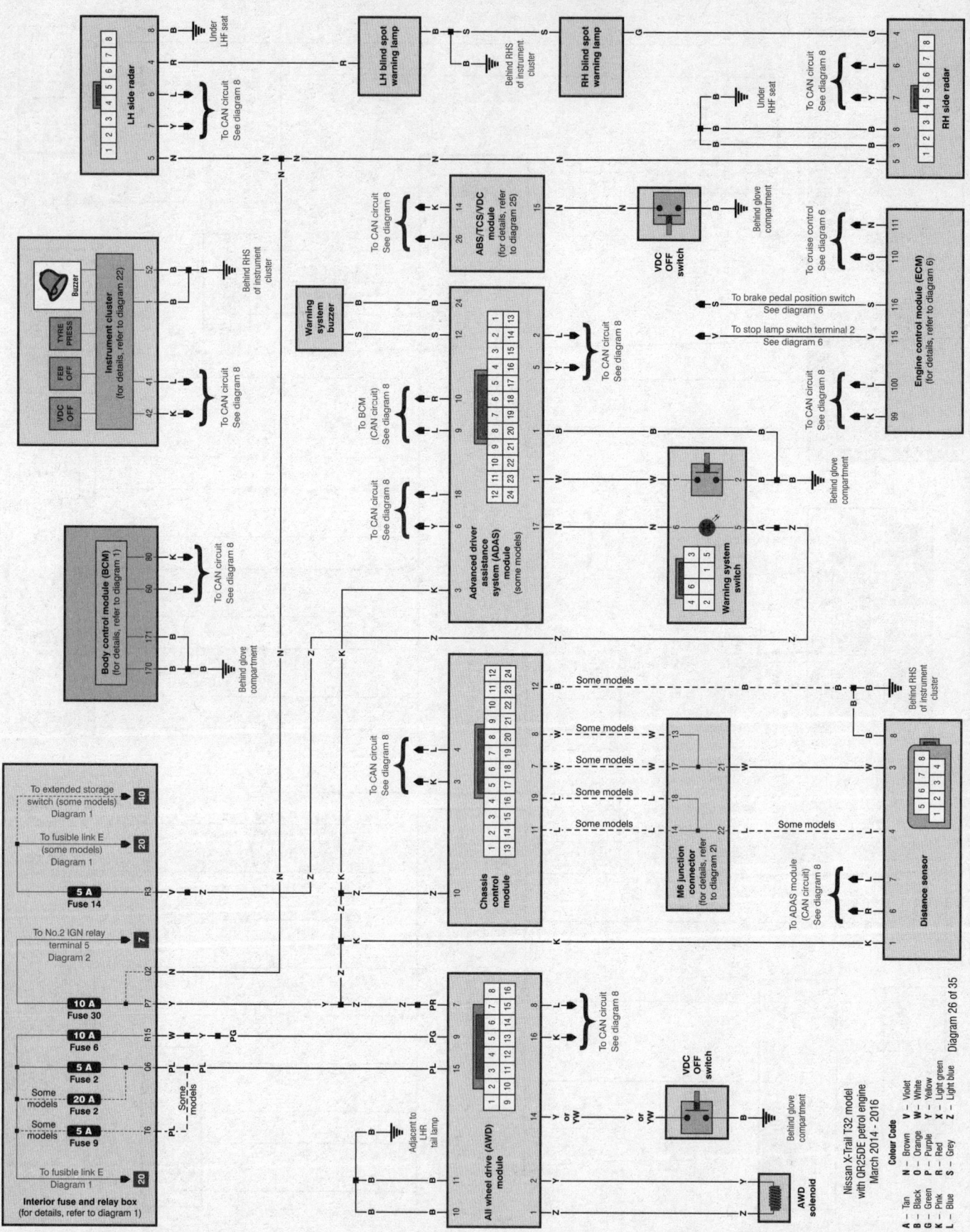

Diagram 26 - All wheel drive (AWD), chassis control, tyre pressure monitoring system, advanced driver assistance system (ADAS) – T32 X-Trail petrol models

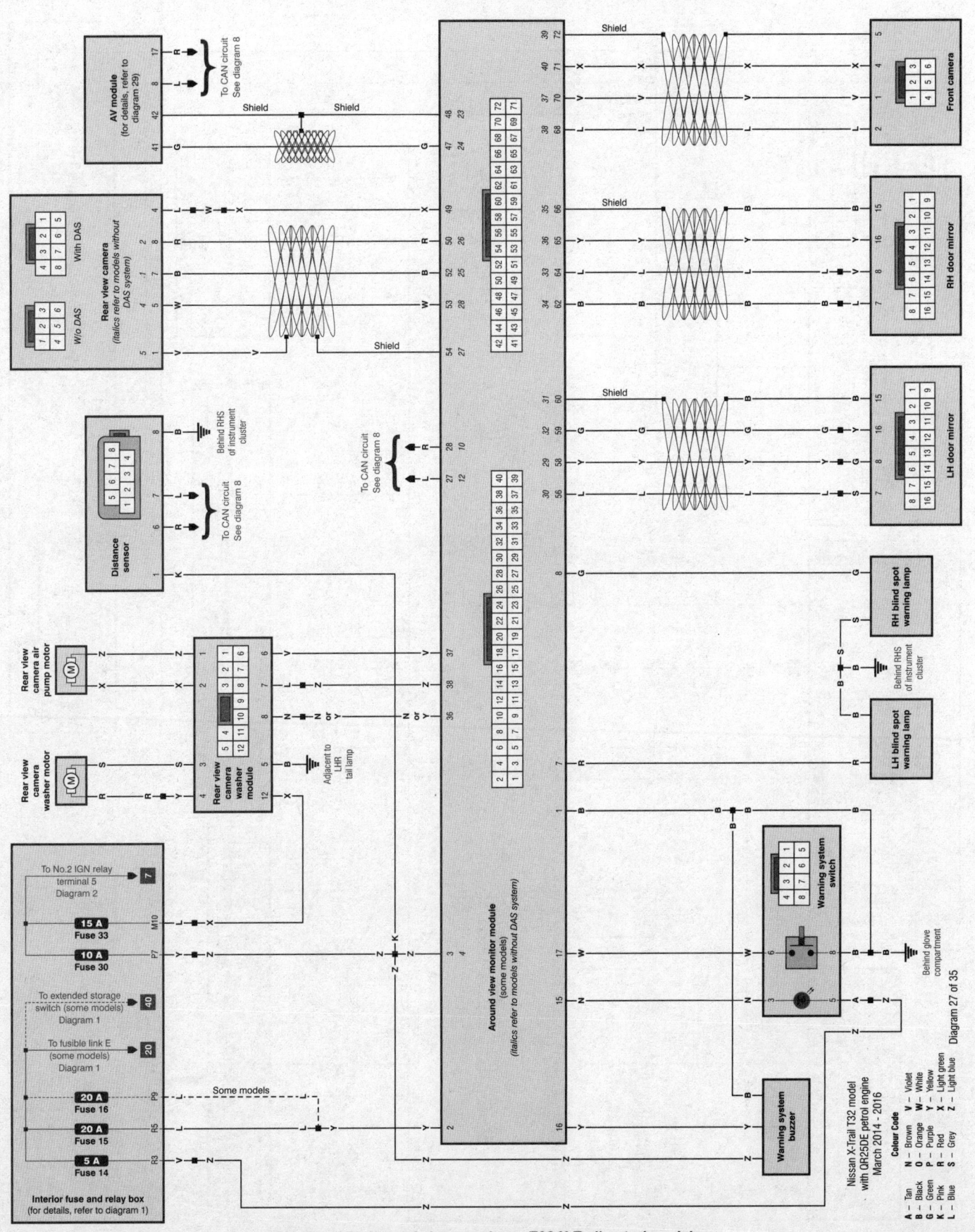

Diagram 27 - Around view monitor – T32 X-Trail petrol models

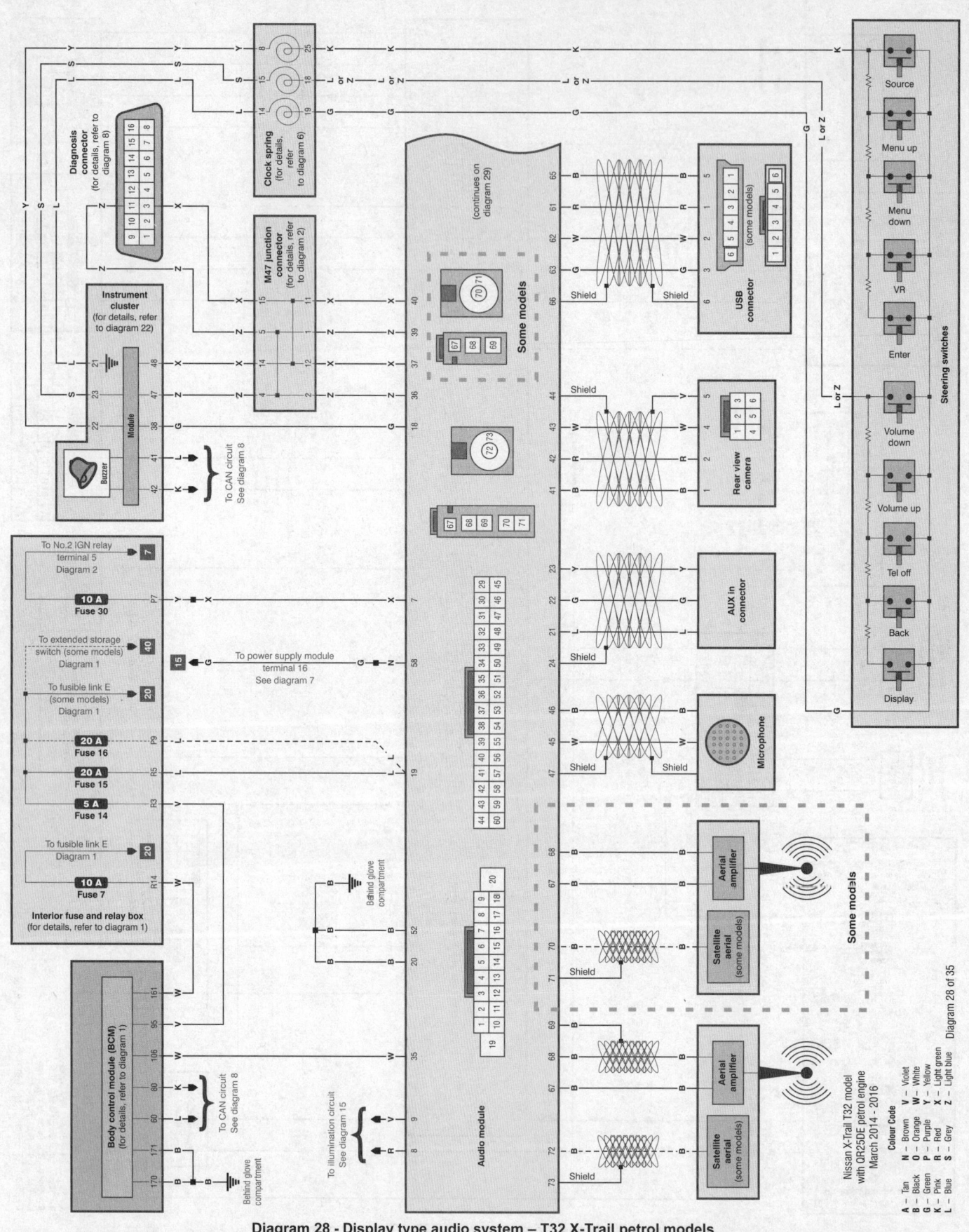

Diagram 28 - Display type audio system – T32 X-Trail petrol models

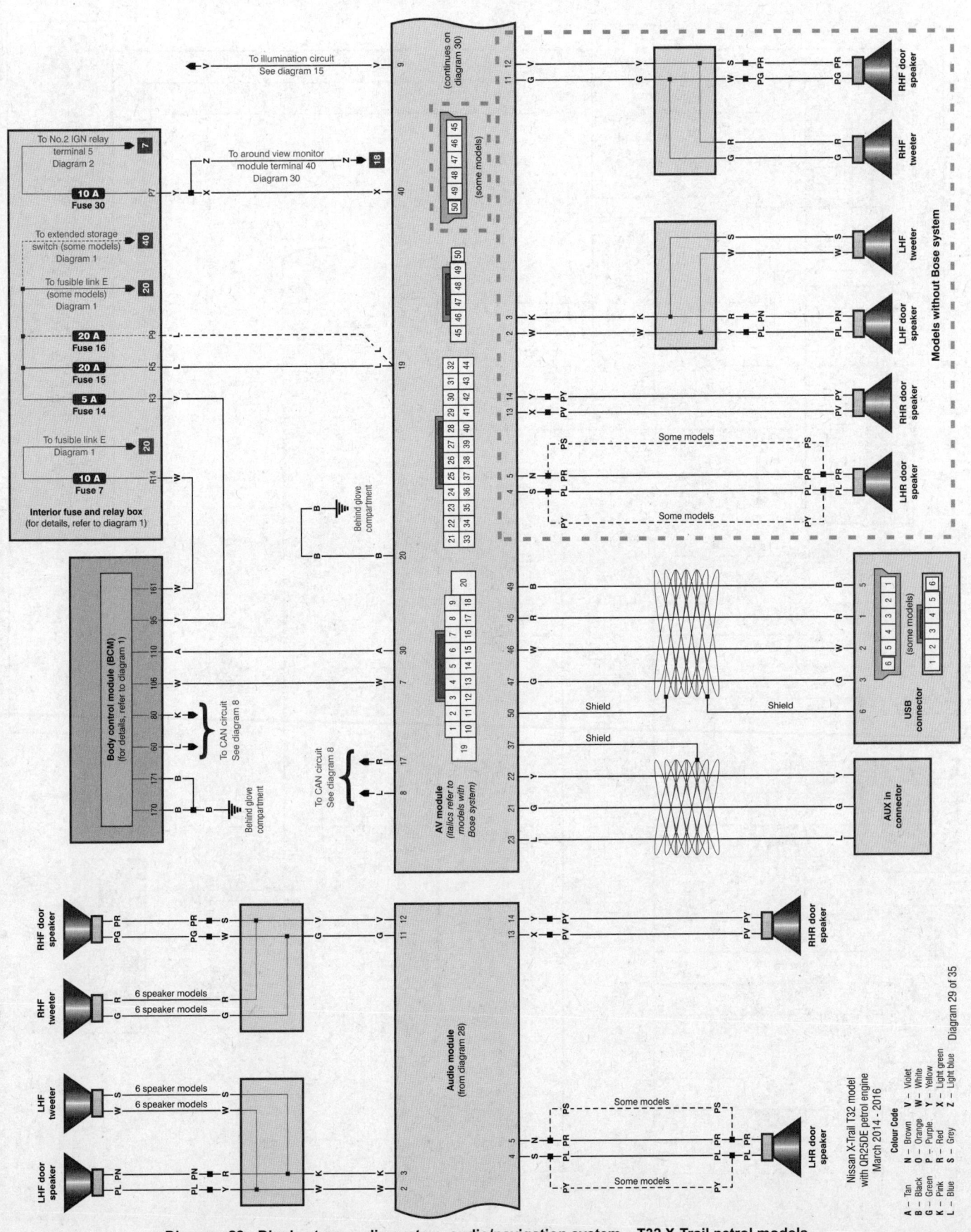

Diagram 29 - Display type audio system, audio/navigation system – T32 X-Trail petrol models

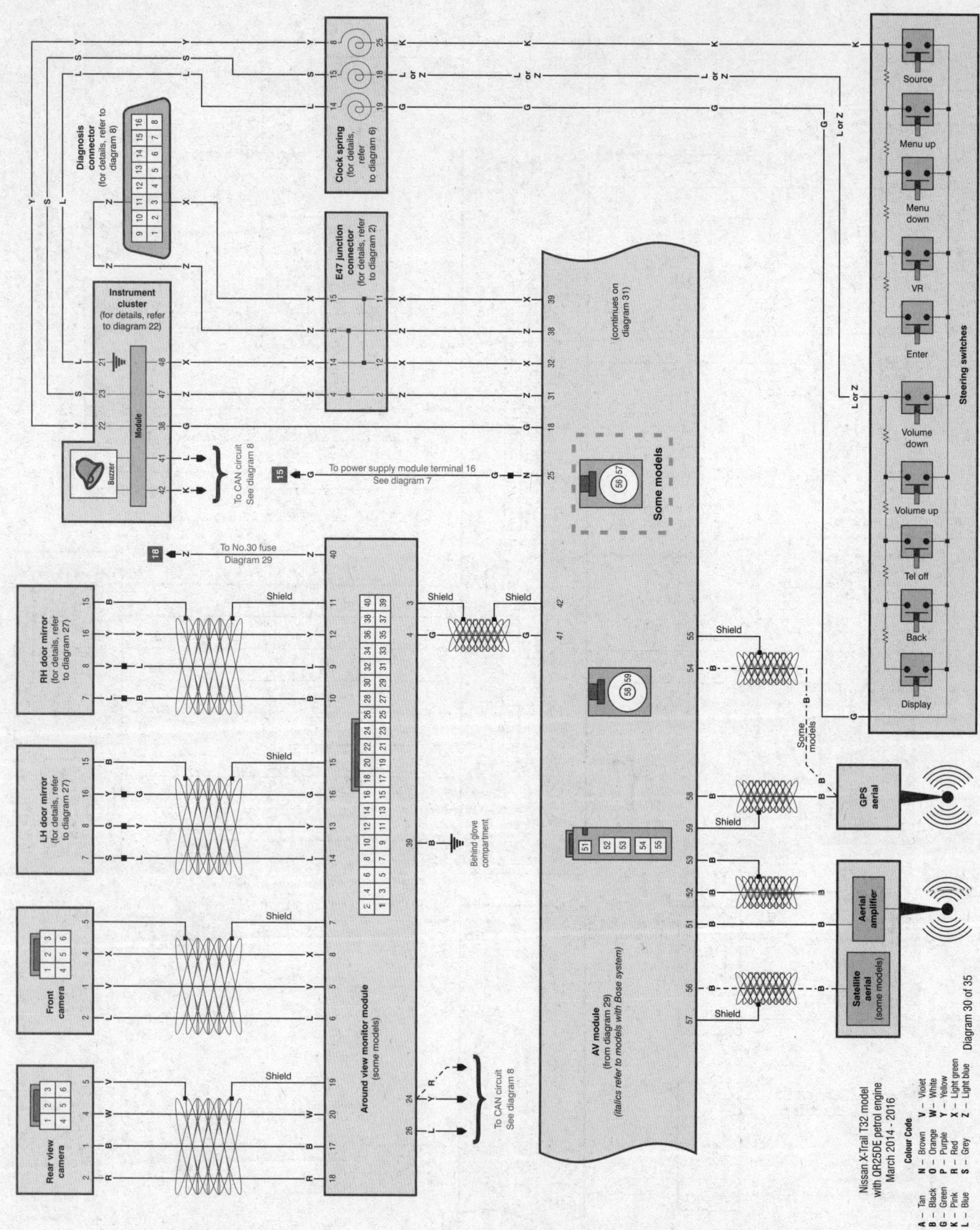

Diagram 30 - Audio/navigation system with around view monitor – T32 X-Trail petrol models

Chapter 12 Chassis electrical system

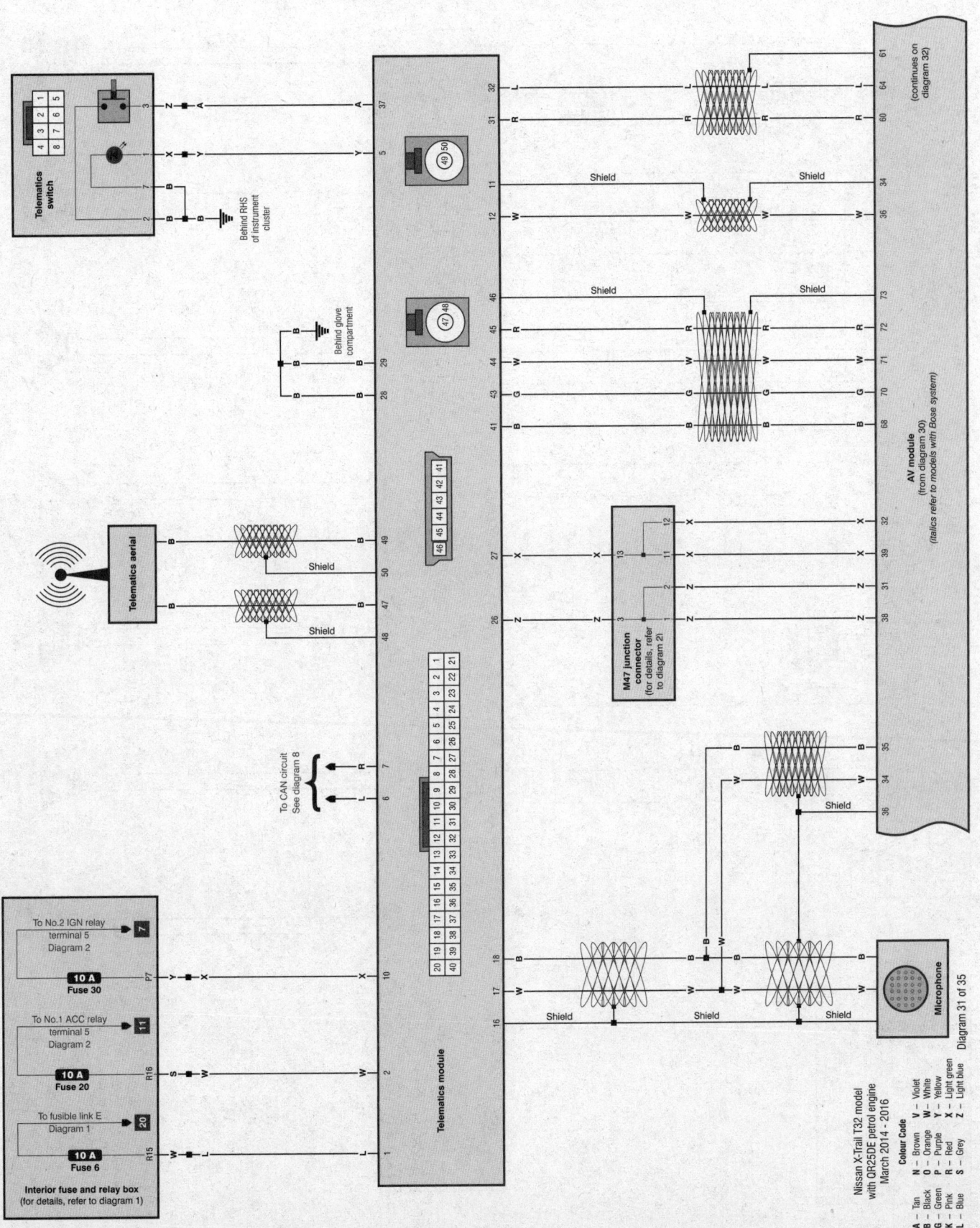

Diagram 31 - Audio/navigation system, telematics – T32 X-Trail petrol models

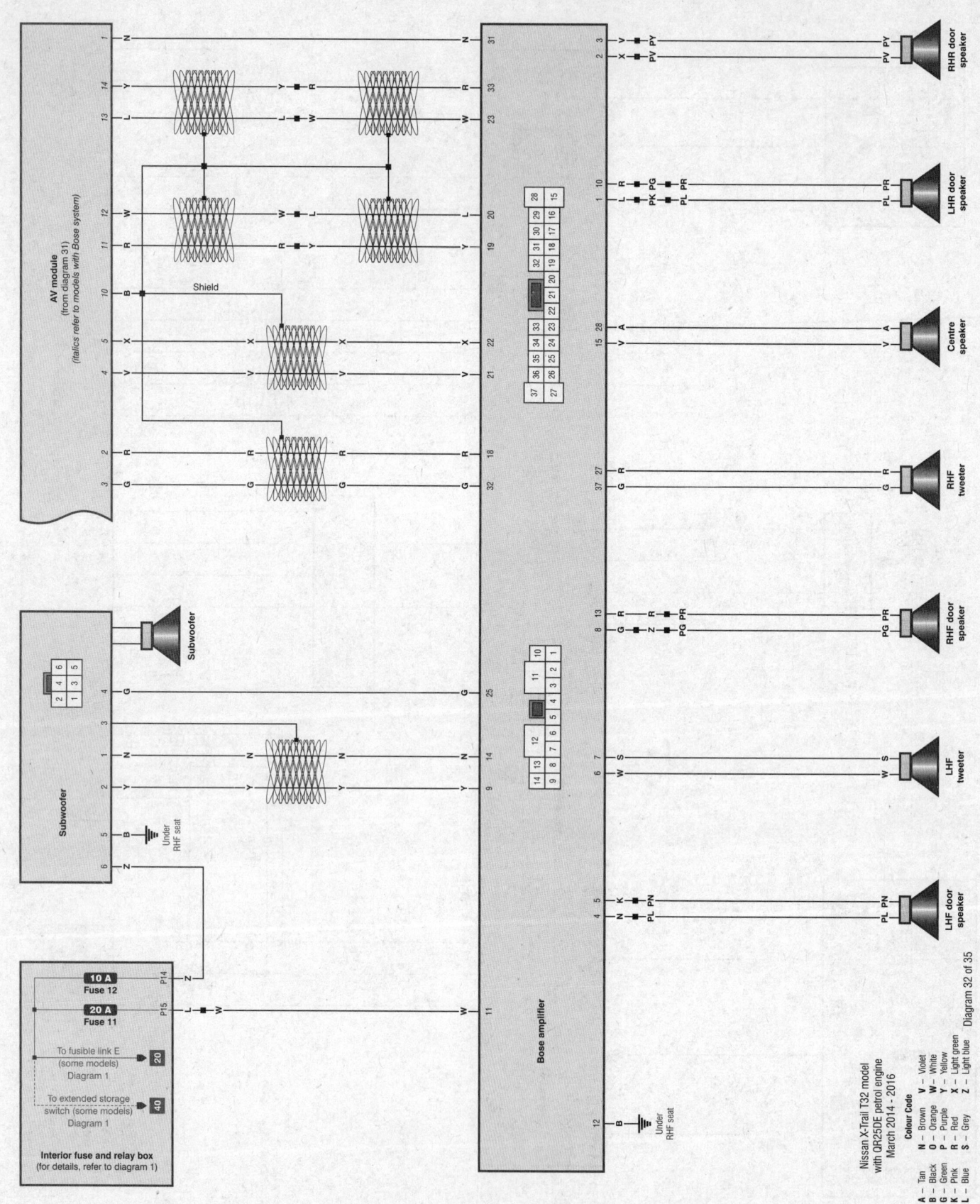

Diagram 32 - Audio system with Bose amplifier – T32 X-Trail petrol models

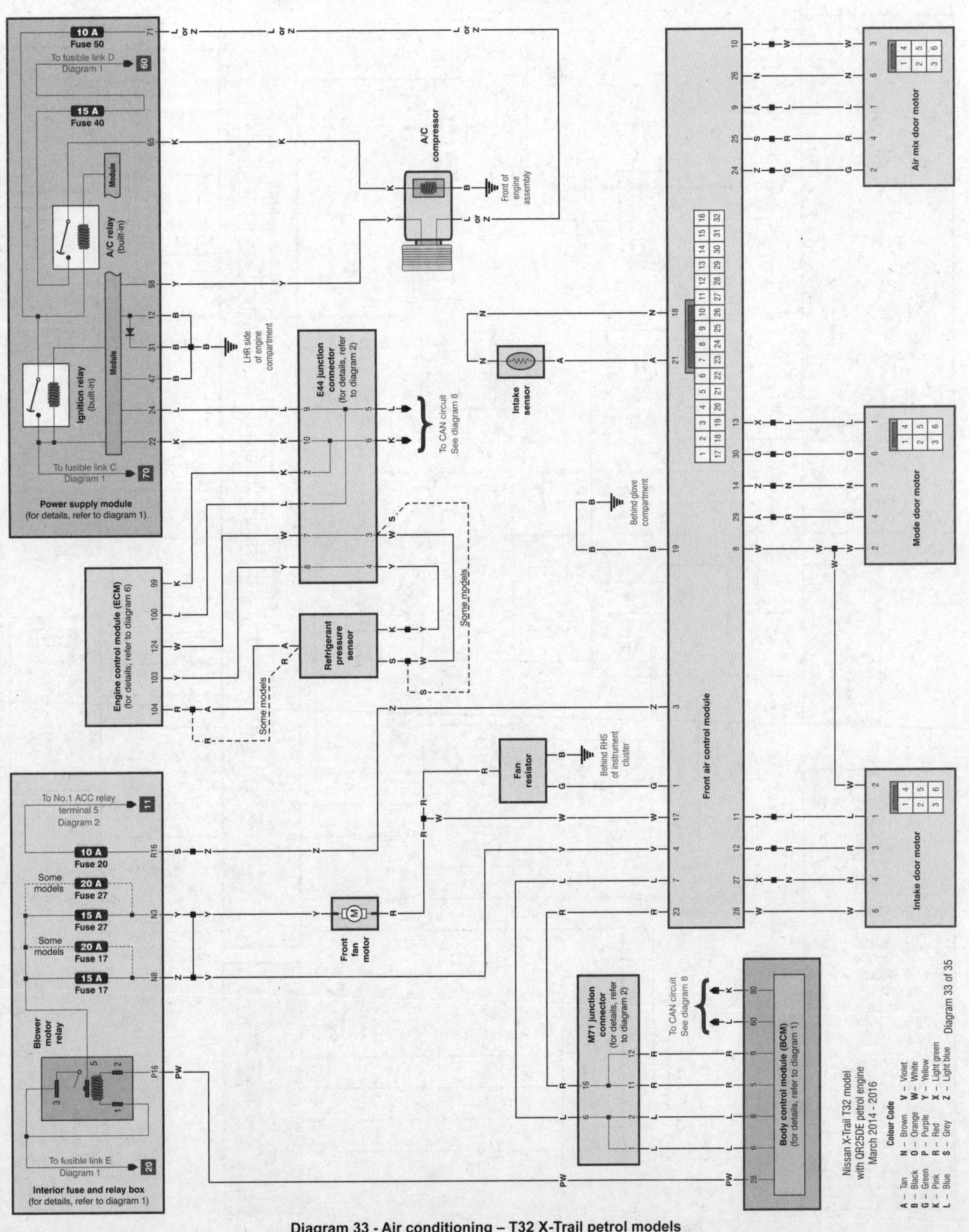

Diagram 33 - Air conditioning – T32 X-Trail petrol models

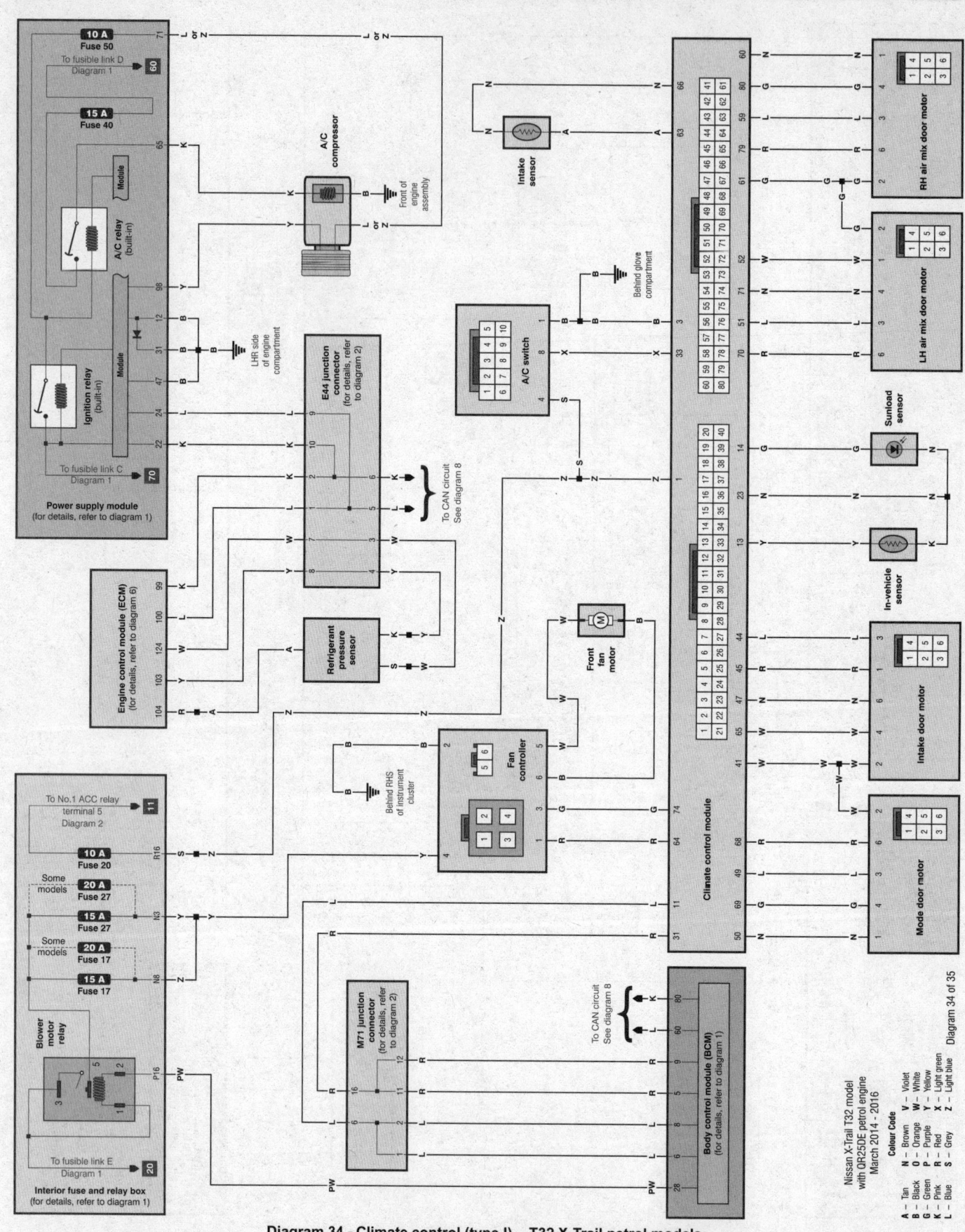

Diagram 34 - Climate control (type I) – T32 X-Trail petrol models

Chapter 12 Chassis electrical system

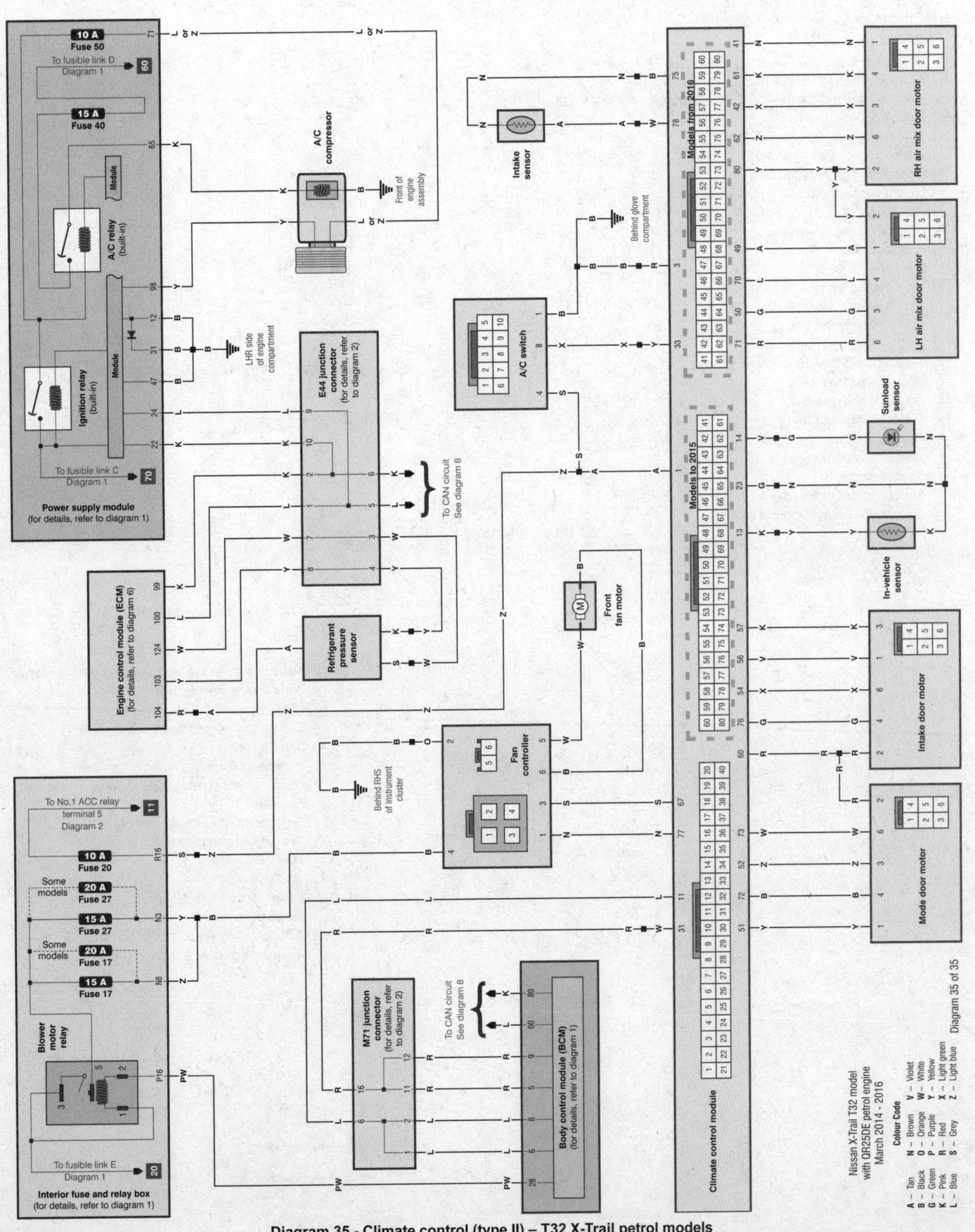

Diagram 35 - Climate control (type II) – T32 X-Trail petrol models

5 A/C relay (built-in)
23 ABS sensors
17 All wheel drive (AWD) module
16 Antilock braking system (ABS/TCS/VDC) module
12 Automatic back door module
5 ECM relay (built-in)
7 Engine control module (ECM)
5 Front wiper high relay (built-in)
5 Front wiper relay (built-in)
24 Fuel pump
5 Fuel pump relay (built-in)
6 Fusible link box
1 Horn relay
5 No.1 cooling fan relay (built-in)
1 No.1 fuse and relay box
5 No.1 IGN relay (built-in)
2 No.2 cooling fan relay
2 No.2 fuse and relay box
2 No.3 cooling fan relay
3 No.3 fuse and relay box
5 Power supply module
2 Starter cut relay
5 Starter relay (built-in)
3 Theft horn relay
5 Throttle control motor relay (built-in)
8 Transmission control module (TCM)

Vehicle interior
Engine compartment
Under vehicle

19 Advanced driver assistance system (ADAS) module
13 Body control module (BCM)
18 Chassis control module
22 Climate control module (automatic A/C)
4 Demister relay
9 Diagnosis connector
14 Electric power steering (EPS) module
4 Fan relay
21 Front air control module (manual A/C)
4 Interior fuse and relay box
4 No.1 ACC relay
4 No.2 IGN relay
10 Power window relay
11 Room lamp relay
15 2 Supplemental restraint system (SRS) 15
20 Telematics module

Vehicle interior
Under dashboard

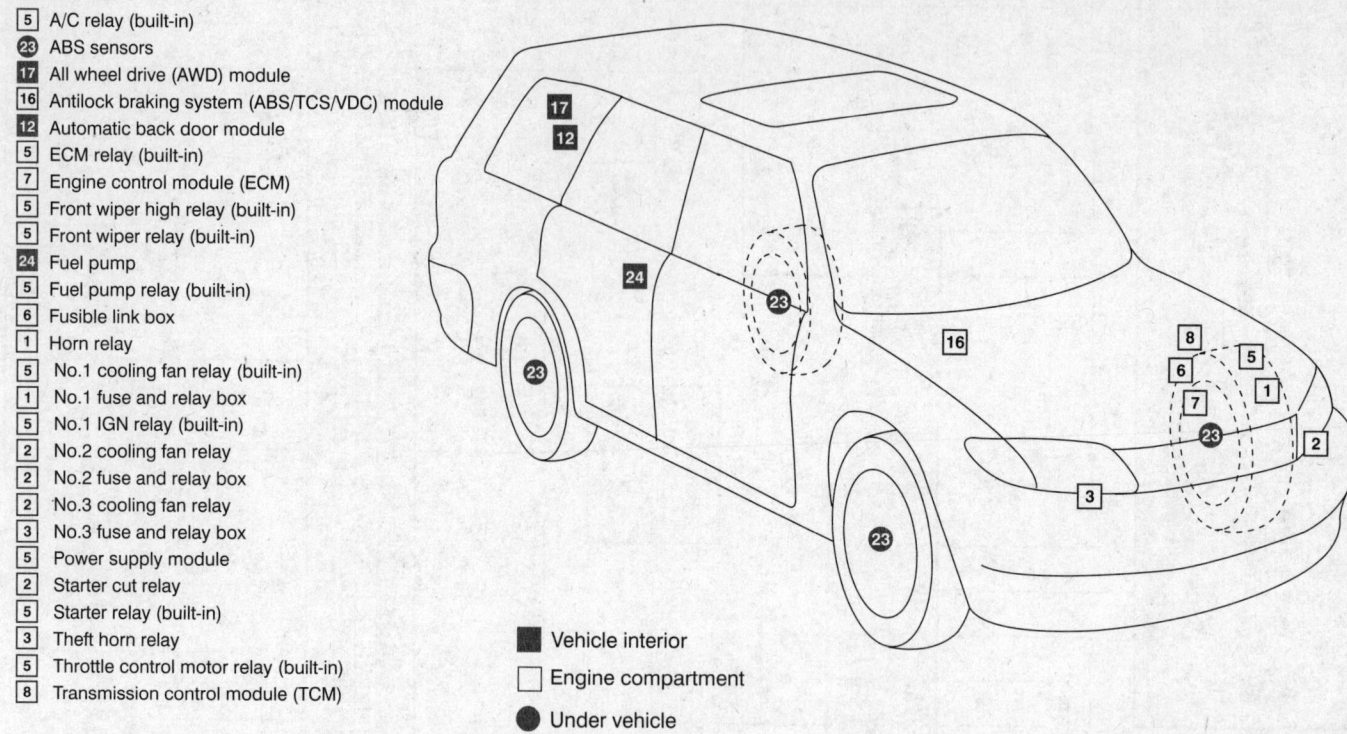

Component locations – T32 X-Trail petrol models

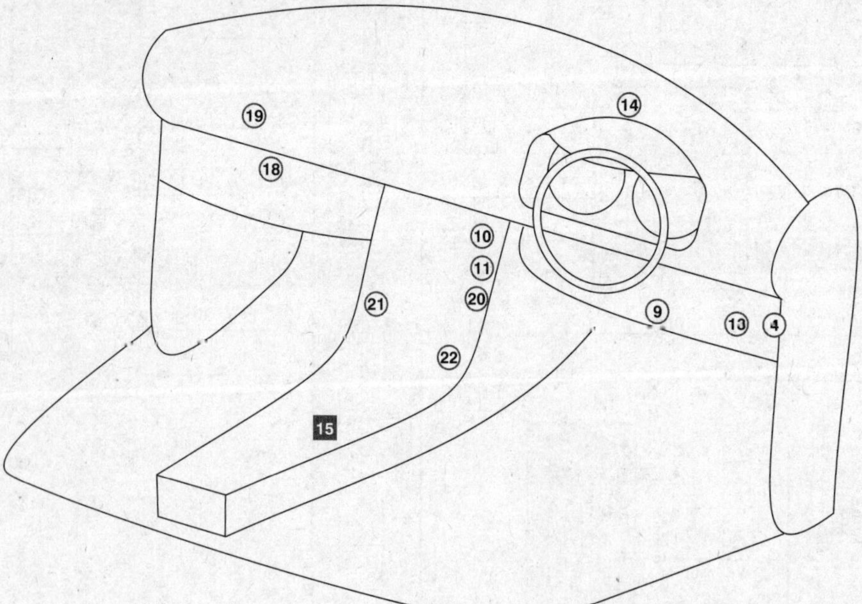

Service history

Date / Odometer \ Part No.	ENGINE OIL	ENGINE OIL FILTER	FAN BELTS	AIR FILTER	FUEL FILTER	RADIATOR HOSE	COOLANT	FRONT BRAKES	REAR BRAKES	BRAKE FLUID	WHEEL ALIGNMENT	WHEEL BALANCE										

Service history

Date / Odometer \ Part No.	ENGINE OIL	ENGINE OIL FILTER	FAN BELTS	AIR FILTER	FUEL FILTER	RADIATOR HOSE	COOLANT	FRONT BRAKES	REAR BRAKES	BRAKE FLUID	WHEEL ALIGNMENT	WHEEL BALANCE									

Index

A

Accelerator Pedal Position (APP) sensor - replacement, 6-6
Airbag system components – removal and refitting
  Activation of airbag system, 12-30
  Airbag electronic control units, 12-30
  Curtain airbag units, 12-32
  De-activation of airbag system, 12-30
  Driver's airbag unit, 12-30
  Driver airbag removal and installation, 10-12
    X-Trail T31 and Dualis
    X-trail T32 and Qashqai
  General information, precautions and system de-activation, 12-30
  Passenger's airbag unit
    Refitting, 12-32
    Removal, 12-31
  Side airbag units, 12-32
  Spiral cable
    Refitting, 12-31
    Removal, 12-30
  Precautions
    General precautions, 12-30
    Precautions when handling an airbag, 12-30
    Precautions when storing an airbag, 12-30
Air conditioning and heating system
  Compressor - removal and installation, 3-15
  Check and maintenance, 3-4
  Air conditioning system, 3-4
  Automatic heating and air conditioning systems, 3-5
  Eliminating air conditioning odours, 3-5
  Heating systems, 3-5
Air filter
  Check and replacement, 1-28
  Housing - removal and installation
    Petrol, 4A-10
    Diesel, 4B-3
  Resonator
    Lower resonator, 4A-11
    Upper resonator, 4A-10

Alternator – removal and installation
  Installation , 5-8
  Removal, 5-7
Anti-lock braking system (ABS) – general information and component renewal, 9-2
  Actuator (Modulator), 9-4
  General information, 9-2
  Wheel speed sensors, 9-3
Anti-theft system and engine immobiliser – general information, 12-29
Automatic and continuously variable transaxle (CVT)
  Diesel models with an automatic transaxle, 1-34
  Fluid change, 1-34
  Petrol models with CVT, 1-34
Automatic transaxle
  Fluid level check, 1-17
  Removal and installation, 7B-5
  Oil seal - replacement, 7B-5

B

Balance shaft, drive chain and sprockets – removal, inspection and refitting, 2B-24
  2.5 litre petrol engine, 2A-8
  2.0 litre petrol engine, 2B-24
  2.0 litre diesel engine, 2C-22
Balljoints - replacement, 10-7
Battery and battery tray - removal and installation, 5-5
  Battery, 5-5
  Battery tray, 5-5
Battery cables - replacement, 5-5
Battery check, maintenance and charging, 1-20
  Charging, 1-22
  Cleaning, 1-22
Battery - disconnection and reconnection, 5-4
  Disconnection, 5-4
Battery will not hold a charge, 0-20
Blower motor and resistor - removal and installation, 3-12
  Blower motor, 3-12
  Resistor, 3-12

Body

Front bumper – removal and installation
  Installation, 11-22
  Removal, 11-21
Outside mirrors - removal and installation
  Exterior mirror electric motor, 11-25
  Exterior mirror glass, 11-24
  Exterior mirror outer shell, 11-25
Rear bumper – removal and installation, 11-22
Repair - major damage, 11-4
Repair - minor damage, 11-2
  Plastic body panels, 11-2
  Steel body panels, 11-2
    Filling and painting, 11-4
    Repairing simple dents, 11-2
    Repair of rust holes or gashes, 11-4

Bonnet
Release latch and cable - removal and installation, 11-7
Removal, installation and adjustment, 11-6

Brake
Booster - check, replacement and adjustment, 9-16
Brake booster check, 1-26
Disc brakes, 1-26
Front brake caliper – removal and refitting, 9-11
Front brake disc – inspection, removal and refitting, 9-9
Front brake pads – replacement, 9-4
Parking brake, 1-27
Hoses and lines - inspection and replacement, 9-14
Hydraulic system – bleeding and replacing brake fluid , 9-15
Light switch, cruise control cancel switch and brake pedal position sensor - adjustment and replacement, 9-22
Parking brake
  Cables – removal and Installation, 9-18
  Check and adjustment, 9-16
Pedal - adjustment, 9-22
Rear brake
  Caliper – removal and refitting, 9-12
  Disc – inspection, removal and refitting, 9-10
  Pads – replacement, 9-7

Bulbs
Exterior lights – renewal
  Front foglight, 12-15
  Front indicator, 12-14
  Front indicator side repeater, 12-15
  General, 12-11
  Halogen headlight, 12-12
  Headlights, 12-11
  High-level stop-light, 12-18
  Mirror mounted light, 12-15
  Number plate light, 12-17
  Rear fog light, 12-16
  Rear lights (indicator/stop/tail lights)
    Dualis and T31 X-Trail models, 12-15
    T32 X-Trail and Qashqai models, 12-16
  Reversing light, 12-17
  Sidelight, 12-14
  Xenon headlight
    High beam, 12-13
    Low beam, 12-13
Interior lights – renewal
  Courtesy light (rear), 12-18
  Courtesy light (side), 12-19
  General, 12-18
  Heater control illumination, 12-19
  Instrument panel lights, 12-19
  Luggage area light, 12-19
  Map reading/courtesy light (front), 12-18
  Seat belt warning light illumination - Dualis models, 12-19
  Switch illumination bulbs, 12-20
  Vanity mirror light, 12-19

C

Cabin air filter replacement, 1-27
Camshaft Position (CMP) sensor - replacement
  Diesel models, 6-7
  Petrol models, 6-6
Camshafts – removal, inspection and refitting
  2.5 litre petrol engine, 2A-10
  2.0 litre petrol engine, 2B-15
  2.0 litre diesel engine, 2C-13
Catalytic converter - replacement, 6-12
Centre console – removal and installation
  T31 X-Trail and Dualis models, 11-29
  T32 X-Trail and Qashqai models, 11-31
Clutch
  Assembly – removal, inspection and installation, 8-6
  Hydraulic system – bleeding, 8-3
  Pedal – removal and installation, 8-4
  Release mechanism – removal, inspection and installation, 8-7
Coil springs (rear) - removal and installation, 10-9
Control arm - removal, inspection and installation, 10-7
Cooling system
  Check , 1-24
  Servicing (draining, flushing and refilling), 1-32
Cowl panel - removal and installation, 11-34
Crankshaft oil seals
  2.5 litre petrol engine, 2A-7
  2.0 litre petrol engine, 2B-22
  2.0 litre diesel engine, 2C-22
Crankshaft Position (CKP) sensor - replacement, 6-7
Crankshaft pulley – removal and refitting
  2.0 litre petrol engine, 2B-8
  2.0 litre diesel engine, 2C-4
Cylinder compression check, 2D-3
Cylinder head - removal and installation
  2.5 litre petrol engine, 2A-12
  2.0 litre petrol engine, 2B-18
  2.0 litre diesel engine, 2C-16

D

Dashboard panels – removal and installation
  Centre panel
    Dualis models, 11-27
    T31 X-Trail models, 11-27
    T32 X-Trail and Qashqai, 11-28
  Driver's side lower dash panel, 11-26
  Facia end trim panels, 11-29
  Glovebox
    T31 X-Trail and Dualis models, 11-25
    T32 X-Trail and Qashqai models, 11-26
  Instrument cluster surround panels, 11-28
Dashboard - removal and installation, 11-33
Differential electric controlled coupling – removal and installation, 8-11
Differential
  Lubricant change (AWD models), 1-35
  Lubricant level check (AWD models), 1-25
  Oil seals – renewal, 8-10
  Overhaul, 8-11
Door
  Lock, cylinder and handles - removal and installation, 11-20
  Removal, installation and adjustment, 11-19
  Trim panel – removal and refitting, 11-9
    Dualis, 11-9
    Front door trim panel , 11-9
    Rear door trim panel (early models), 11-10
    Rear door trim panel (later models), 11-11

Index

T31 X-Trail, 11-12
    Front door trim, 11-12
    Rear door trim, 11-12
T32 X-Trail and Qashqai, 11-13
    Front door trim, 11-13
    Rear door trim, 11-14
Window glass and regulator – removal and refitting
    T31 X-Trail and Dualis models
        Front window glass, 11-14
        Front window regulator, 11-15
        Rear window glass, 11-16
        Rear window regulator, 11-17
    X-Trail T32 and Qashqai
        Front window glass, 11-18
        Front window regulator, 11-19
        Rear window glass, 11-19
        Rear window regulator, 11-19
Drivebelt check and replacement
    Automatic tensioner replacement, 1-24
    Check, 1-22
    Drivebelt replacement, 1-22
Driveshaft boot check , 1-30
Driveshaft boots - replacement, 8-14
Driveshaft- removal and installation
    Front
        Installation, 8-9
        Removal, 8-8
        Oil seals, 7B-5
    Rear
        Installation, 8-9
        Removal, 8-9

E

Electrical fault finding – general information
    Connectors, 12-3
    Finding an earth fault, 12-2
    Finding an open-circuit, 12-2
    Finding a short-circuit, 12-2
    General, 12-1
Engine Coolant Temperature (ECT) sensor - replacement, 6-8
Engine cooling fans and resistor - removal and installation
    Cooling fan resistor, 3-8
    Dualis and Qashqai models, 3-8
    T31 X-Trail models, 3-6
    T32 X-Trail models, 3-7
Engine
    Mounts - check and replacement
        2.5 litre petrol engine, 2A-16
        2.0 litre petrol engine, 2B-26
        2.0 litre diesel engine, 2C-25
    Oil and oil filter change, 1-18
    Oil seal replacement
        Crankshaft front
            2.5 litre petrol engine, 2A-7
            2.0 litre petrol engine, 2B-22
            2.0 litre diesel engine, 2C-23
        Crankshaft rear
            2.5 litre petrol engine, 2A-16
            2.0 litre petrol engine, 2B-22
            2.0 litre diesel engine, 2C-24
    Oil Temperature Sensor - replacement, 6-9
    Overhaul - disassembly sequence, 2D-8
    Rebuilding alternatives, 2D-5
    Removal and installation
        Installation, 2D-7
        Methods and precautions, 2D-5
        Removal, 2D-6

Evaporative Emissions Control (EVAP) system - component replacement
    Check, 1-33
    Diesel engine emission control systems – testing and component renewal, 6-13
    Petrol engine emission control systems – testing and component renewal, 6-12
Exhaust
    Manifold - removal and installation
        2.5 litre petrol engine, 2A-6
        2.0 litre petrol engine, 2B-7
        2.0 litre diesel engine, 2C-5
    System check, 1-30
    System servicing
        Diesel models, 4B-9
        Petrol models, 4A-12
Exterior lights – removal and refitting
    Front fog light, 12-21
    Front indicator side repeater, 12-21
    Headlight, 12-20
    High-level stop-light, 12-22
    Number plate light, 12-22
    Rear fog light, 12-21
    Rear light, 12-21
    Reverse light, 12-21
        Except T31 X-Trail models, 12-21
        T31 X-Trail models, 12-22

F

Fastener and trim removal, 11-5
Final drive electric controlled coupling – removal and refitting, 7C-4
Fluid level checks
    Battery electrolyte, 1-13
    Brake fluid, 1-13
    Engine coolant, 1-12
    Engine oil, 1-11
    Windshield washer fluid, 1-13
Flywheel/driveplate – removal, inspection and refitting
    2.5 litre petrol engine, 2A-15
    2.0 litre petrol engine, 2B-23
    2.0 litre diesel engine, 2C-23
Four wheel drive (4WD) control unit – removal and installation, 7C-3
Fuel
    Filter replacement - diesel models, 1-14
    Filter water draining - diesel models, 1-14
    Injectors – testing, removal and refitting
        Refitting, 4B-7
        Removal, 4B-6
        Testing, 4B-6
    Lines and fittings - general information and disconnection, 4A-5
    Pressure - check, 4A-3
    Pressure relief procedure, 4A-3
    Pump and fuel gauge sender unit – removal and refitting, 4B-3
    Pump/fuel level sensor module - removal and installation, 4A-6
        Fuel pump/fuel level sensor module
            Installation, 4A-8
            Removal, 4A-7
        Sub fuel level sensor module
            Installation, 4A-9
            Removal, 4A-8
    Rail and injectors - removal and installation, 4A-5
    System check , 1-29
    System – priming and bleeding, 4B-2

Tank - removal and installation
   Petrol, 4A-9
   Diesel, 4B-3
Fuses and relays – general information
   Fuses, 12-3
   Relays, 12-5

G

Glow plugs – removal, inspection and installation, 5-6

H

Headlight beam adjustment components – general information, removal and refitting, 12-22
Heater and air conditioning control assembly - removal and installation, 3-13
Heater core - removal and installation, 3-14
High-pressure pump – removal and refitting
   Refitting, 4B-6
   Removal, 4B-5
Hinges and locks - maintenance, 11-6
Horn – removal and refitting, 12-25
Hub and bearing assembly - removal and installation, 10-8

I

Idle speed – general, 4B-2
Ignition coil(s) - replacement, 5-5
Initial start-up and break-in after overhaul, 2D-8
Injector rail (common rail) – removal and refitting, 4B-7
   Refitting, 4B-8
   Removal, 4B-7
Instrument cluster – removal and refitting, 12-24
Intake manifold - removal and installation
   2.5 litre petrol engine, 2A-5
   2.0 litre petrol engine, 2B-6
   2.0 litre diesel engine, 2C-5
Intake Valve Timing (IVT) and Exhaust Valve Timing (EVT) control solenoid(s) - replacement, 6-7
Intelligent key system components – general information, 12-29
Intercooler – removal and refitting, 2C-8

K

Knock sensor - replacement, 6-8

M

Maintenance schedule, 1-10
Manual transaxle
   Lubricant change, 1-33
   Lubricant level check, 1-25
   Overhaul – general information, 7A-8
   Removal and installation
      Refitting, 7A-7
      Removal, 7A-5
   Shift cable – removal and installation
      Adjustment, 7A-4
      Refitting, 7A-4
      Removal, 7A-2
         Gear change cables, 7A-2
         Shift lever assembly, 7A-2

Mass Air Flow/Intake Air Temperature (MAF/IAT) sensor - replacement, 6-8
Master cylinder – removal and installation
   Brake, 9-13
   Clutch, 8-5

O

Obtaining and clearing Diagnostic Trouble Codes (DTCs), 6-4
   Accessing the DTCs, 6-4
      Clearing the DTCs, 6-4
   Diagnostic Trouble Codes, 6-4
Oil cooler – removal and refitting, 2C-26
Oil level sensor – removal and refitting, 2C-28
Oil pans - removal and installation
   2.5 litre petrol engine, 2A-13
   2.0 litre petrol engine, 2B-21
   2.0 litre diesel engine, 2C-19
Oil pressure check, 2D-2
Oil pressure sensor – removal and refitting
   2.0 litre diesel engine, 2C-27
Oil pump, drive chain and sprocket – removal, inspection and refitting
   2.0 litre diesel engine, 2C-20
Oil pump – removal and refitting
   2.5 litre petrol engine, 2A-14
   2.0 litre petrol engine, 2B-22
On Board Diagnosis (OBD) system, 6-2
   Scan tool information, 6-2
Outside mirrors - removal and installation, 11-24
   Exterior mirror electric motor, 11-25
   Exterior mirror glass, 11-24
   Exterior mirror outer shell, 11-25
Oxygen sensors - replacement
   Downstream oxygen sensor, 6-8
   Upstream oxygen sensor, 6-8

P

Parking brake
   Cables – removal and Installation
      Front cable, 9-19
      Rear cables, 9-18
   Check and adjustment, 9-16
   Removal of parking brake assembly, 9-17
   Shoes - replacement, 9-20
Positive Crankcase Ventilation (PCV) valve check and replacement, 1-35, 6-11
Powertrain Control Module (PCM) - removal and installation, 6-11
Pre-heating system
   Control unit – removal and installation, 5-7
   Testing, 5-6
Propeller shaft (AWD models) - removal and installation, 8-11

R

Radiator and coolant reservoir - removal and installation, 3-9
Radiator grille - removal and installation, 11-7
Radio aerial – removal and refitting, 12-29
Radio/CD player – removal and refitting, 12-28
Rear differential
   Draining and refilling (AWD models), 8-9
   Removal and installation (AWD models), 8-9
Rear suspension arms and rear subframe - removal and installation, 10-9
Reversing light switch – testing, removal and installation, 7A-5

Index

S

Seats - removal and installation, 11-36
  Front seat, 11-36
  Second row seats
    Fixed type, 11-37
    Sliding type, 11-37
Shift cable – removal and installation
  Manual transaxle, 7A-2
  Automatic transaxle, 7B-4
Shifter assembly - removal and installation
  Automatic transaxle, 7B-3
Shift interlock cable - replacement and adjustment, 7B-5
Shift knob - removal and installation, 7B-2
Shock absorbers (rear) - removal and installation, 10-8
Spark plug check and replacement, 1-31
Speakers – removal and refitting
  Dashboard-mounted tweeters, 12-28
  Door-mounted speakers, 12-28
Stabiliser bar
  Front - removal and installation, 10-7
  Rear - removal and installation, 10-10
Starter motor – removal and installation, 5-8
Steering and suspension check, 1-29
Steering
  Column covers - removal and installation
    T31 X-Trail and Dualis models, 11-32
    T32 X-Trail and Qashqai models, 11-33
  Column - removal and installation, 10-11
  Gear boots - replacement, 10-14
  Gear - removal and installation
    Installation, 10-15
    Removal, 10-15
  Knuckle - removal and installation, 10-8
  Wheel - removal and installation, 10-11
Strut/coil spring assembly (front)
  Component replacement, 10-6
  Removal, inspection and installation, 10-5
Subframe (front) - removal and installation, 10-15
Switches – removal and refitting
  Centre console switches, 12-10
  Courtesy light/door warning switches, 12-10
  Hazard warning light switch, 12-9
  Driver's side panel switches, 12-7
  Heater/ventilation and demister switches, 12-7
  Ignition switch/steering lock
    Models with an ignition key, 12-6
    Models with intelligent key, 12-7
  Luggage area light switch, 12-10
  Map reading/courtesy light switches, 12-10
  Power window switches
    Dualis models, 12-8
    T31 X-Trail models, 12-8
    T32 X-Trail and Qashqai models, 12-9
  Steering column switches, 12-7
  Steering wheel switches
    T31 X-Trail and Dualis models, 12-11
    T32 X-Trail and Qashqai models, 12-11
System initialisation, 5-4

T

Tailgate and trim panel - removal, installation and adjustment, 11-8
  Tailgate
    Adjustment, 11-9
    Removal and installation, 11-8
  Trim panel - removal and installation, 11-8
Tailgate latch, opening switch and support struts - removal and installation
  Opening switch, 11-9
  Tailgate latch, 11-9
  Tailgate support struts or spindles, 11-9
Tailgate wiper motor – removal and refitting, 12-26
Thermostat and water control valve - replacement
  Coolant outlet housing and water control valve, 3-6
  Thermostat, 3-5
Throttle body - removal and installation
  Diesel models, 4B-4
  Petrol models, 4A-11
Throttle Position (TP) sensor - replacement, 6-11
Tie-rod ends - removal and installation, 10-14
Timing chain cover – removal and refitting
  2.0 litre petrol engine, 2B-10
Timing chain/oil pump drive chain or balance shaft chain and sprockets - removal, inspection and installation
  2.5 litre petrol engine, 2A-7
Timing chain, sprockets and guides – removal, inspection and refitting
  2.0 litre petrol engine, 2B-12
  2.0 litre diesel engine, 2C-8
Timing gears – removal, inspection and refitting
  2.0 litre diesel engine, 2C-12
Top Dead Centre (TDC) for No 1 piston – locating
  2.5 litre petrol engine, 2A-4
  2.0 litre petrol engine, 2B-4
  2.0 litre diesel engine, 2C-4
Transfer case
  Draining and refilling, 7C-2
  Lubricant change (AWD models), 1-35
  Lubricant level check (AWD models), 1-26
  Oil seals – renewal, 7C-3
  Overhaul, 7C-3
  Removal and installation, 7C-2
Transmission Control Module (TCM) - removal and installation, 7B-4
Transmission range switch - replacement and adjustment
  Adjustment, 6-10
  Replacement, 6-9
Transmission range switch - replacement and adjustment, 7B-4
Transmission speed sensors - replacement 6-10, 7B-4
Tune-up general information, 1-11
Turbocharger
  Description and precautions, 2C-6
  Removal and refitting, 2C-7
Tyre
  And tyre pressure checks, 1-16
  Rotation, 1-25

U

Underbonnet hose check and replacement, 1-24
Upholstery, carpets and vinyl trim - maintenance, 11-4

V

Vacuum gauge diagnostic checks, 2D-4
Vacuum pump – removal, refitting and testing, 2C-28
Valve clearance check and adjustment, 1-36
Valve cover - removal and installation
  2.5 litre petrol engine, 2A-4
  2.0 litre petrol engine, 2B-5

W

Water pump – removal, inspection and installation, 3-10
Welch plugs - replacement, 3-16
Wheel alignment - general information, 10-16
Wheels and tyres - general information, 10-16
Windscreen/tailgate washer system components – removal and refitting
  Tailgate washer nozzle
    Refitting, 12-28
    Removal, 12-28
  Washer fluid reservoir
    Refitting, 12-27
    Removal, 12-26
  Washer pump
    Refitting, 12-27
    Removal, 12-27
  Windscreen washer nozzle
    Refitting, 12-28
    Removal, 12-27

Windscreen wiper motor and linkage – removal and refitting, 12-25
Windshield and fixed glass - replacement, 11-6
Windshield wiper blade inspection and replacement, 1-20
Wiper arm – removal and refitting, 12-25
Wiring diagrams - general information, 12-33